OBJECT-ORIENTED PROGRAMMING WITH C++ AND SMALLTALK

CALEB DRAKE

College of Engineering
University of Illinois at Chicago

PRENTICE HALL
Upper Saddle River, New Jersey 07458

Library of Congress Cataloging-in-Publication Data

Drake, Caleb.
    Object-oriented programming with C++ and Smalltalk / Caleb Drake
      p.   cm.
    Includes bibliographical references and index.
    ISBN 0-13-103797-8
    1. Object-oriented programming (Computer science)   2. C++
(Computer program language)   3. Smalltalk (Computer program
language) I. Title.
QA76.64.D73   1998
005.13—DC21   97-18141
                                       CIP
                                       r97

Acquisitions editor: *LAURA STEELE*
Editor-in-chief: *MARCIA HORTON*
Managing editor: *BAYANI MENDOZA DE LEON*
Director of production and manufacturing: *DAVID W. RICCARDI*
Production editor: *KATHARITA LAMOZA*
Cover designer: *BRUCE KENSELAAR*
Manufacturing buyer: *DONNA SULLIVAN*
Editorial assistant: *KATE KAIBNI*

© 1998 by **PRENTICE HALL, Inc.**
Simon & Schuster/A Viacom Company
Upper Saddle River, NJ 07458

The author and publisher of this book have used their best efforts in preparing this book. These efforts include the development, research, and testing of the theories and programs to determine their effectiveness. The author and publisher make no warranty of any kind, expressed or implied, with regard to these programs or the documentation contained in this book. The author and publisher shall not be liable in any event for incidental or consequential damages in connection with, or arising out of, the furnishing, performance, or use of these programs.

The author gratefully acknowledges ParcPlace-Digitalk, Inc., for permission to use VisualWorks screen snapshots and source code excerpts in this text.

Printed in the United States of America

10 9 8 7 6 5 4 3 2 1

ISBN 0-13-103797-8

Prentice-Hall International (UK) Limited, London
Prentice-Hall of Australia Pty. Limited, Sydney
Prentice-Hall Canada Inc., Toronto
Prentice-Hall Hispanoamericana, S.A., Mexico
Prentice-Hall of India Private Limited, New Delhi
Prentice-Hall of Japan, Inc., Tokyo
Simon & Schuster Asia Pte. Ltd., Singapore
Editora Prentice-Hall do Brasil, Ltda., Rio de Janeiro

For
Marie,
Alex, and André

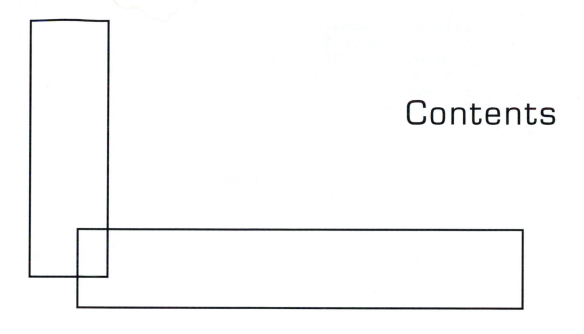

Contents

Preface   ix

Part I: General Principles   **1**

0. *Programming Language Semantics*   3
    0.1 Control Structure   5
    0.2 Name structure   24
    0.3 Data Structure   42
    0.4 Summary and review   81

1. *Software Architecture*   95
    1.1 Abstraction mechanisms   96
    1.2 Computing paradigms   136
    1.3 Object-oriented development   150
    1.4 Summary and review   168

2. *Classes, Messages and Methods*   182
    2.1 Class semantics   183
    2.2 Class definition   192
    2.3 Polymorphism   211
    2.4 Messages and method binding   214
    2.5 Summary and review   223

3. *Inheritance*   230
    3.1 Inheritance semantics   231
    3.2 Subclass definition   239
    3.3 Abstract classes   249
    3.4 Multiple inheritance   256
    3.5 Evaluation of inheritance   261
    3.6 Summary and review   265

4. *Object-oriented Programming Languages and Environments*   272
    4.1 Language selection criteria   274
    4.2 Object-oriented programming environments   281
    4.3 Precursors of object-oriented languages   286
    4.4 Pure object-oriented languages   290
    4.5 Hybrid object-oriented languages   304
    4.6 Summary and review   330

Part II: Smalltalk   **339**

5 . *Language and Environment*   341
    5.1 A quick introduction   342
    5.2 Lexical elements   350
    5.3 Message expressions   357
    5.4 Identifier and object semantics   366
    5.5 Flow of control   376
    5.6 The Smalltalk programming environment   395
    5.7 Summary and review   411

6. *Classes and Inheritance*   425
    6.1 Classes   426
    6.2 Inheritance   461
    6.3 Metaclasses   474
    6.4 Summary and review   479

7. *Foundation Classes*   490
    7.1 The class Object   491
    7.2 Classes for unique objects   507
    7.3 Classes for linearly ordered objects   509
    7.4 Numeric classes   516
    7.5 Basic graphics classes   532
    7.6 Summary and review   541

8. *The Collection Classes*   555
    8.1 The class Collection   556
    8.2 Unordered collections   564
    8.3 Ordered collections   572
    8.4 The stream classes   589
    8.5 Summary and review   601

Part III: C++   **615**

9.   *Enhancements to C*   617
     9.1 Basic language features   618
     9.2 Functions and overloading   640
     9.3 Basic input/output   656
     9.4 Summary and review   662

10. *Classes*   671
     10.1 The C++ class   672
     10.2 Creation, initialization and finalization of objects   691
     10.3 Class scope   716
     10.4 Summary and review   729

11. *Operators, Conversions and Iostreams*   743
     11.1 Operator overloading   744
     11.2 Programmer-defined type conversions   762
     11.3 The iostream class library   771
     11.4 Summary and review   803

12. *Inheritance and Dynamic Binding*   818
     12.1 Class derivation   819
     12.2 Inheritance and static typing   839
     12.3 Dynamic binding   858
     12.4 Multiple inheritance   880
     12.5 Summary and review   896

13. *Templates, Exceptions and Namespaces*   912
     13.1 Function templates   913
     13.2 Class templates   926
     13.3 Exceptions   954
     13.4 Namespaces   971
     13.5 Summary and review   980

Bibliography   997
Index   1003
Class Index   1009

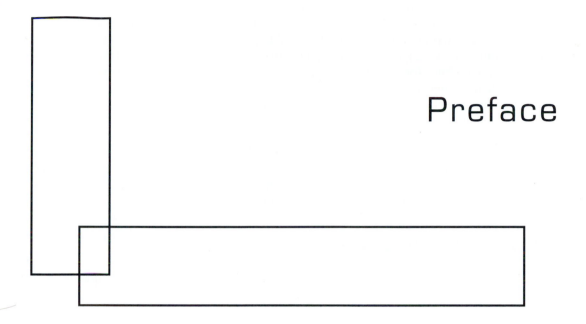

Preface

1. PURPOSE

There are now scores of books with titles applying the adjective "object-oriented" to almost every area of computer science. So why write another? I have been teaching course EECS 576, "Object-oriented Programming Languages and Systems," at the University of Illinois at Chicago, and I wanted a textbook that describes the design goals and language features of object-oriented languages, without applying the perspective of any particular language. I feel that a general understanding of the concepts of data abstraction, inheritance, polymorphism, and dynamic code binding gives you a conceptual framework for using a language well, and for learning any object-oriented language more rapidly and more comprehensively. In addition, a more general approach extends more readily to the analysis and design of software systems without the intrusion of language-specific details.

Upon surveying the texts available for my course, I discovered that they fall into three categories: (1) books of a general nature describing the expected benefits of the object-oriented approach for managers or users; (2) books presenting particular areas of computer science, such as software engineering or database technology, from an object-oriented perspective; and (3) texts that teach programming in a particular object-oriented language or for a particular platform's graphic user interface. The book I needed did not exist, so I began writing lecture notes for the course, which evolved into this book.

Of course, it is also necessary to present at least two representative languages in detail so that you can understand how these concepts are realized in languages and used in programming projects. Smalltalk and C++ take opposite approaches on almost every design goal and language feature. Together they illustrate the gamut of possibilities for object-oriented languages. Smalltalk is the prototypical object-oriented language that pioneered the object-oriented programming paradigm. It embodies the flexibility, extensibility, and programming environment that enable the style of exploratory programming and rapid prototyping typical of the object-oriented approach. C++ is a representative statically typed hybrid language that has high visibility due to its C heritage. Like many hybrid languages, C++ extends an existing procedural language with object-oriented features. It attempts to do this with the minimum run-time overhead, which affects the design and use of the language in ways of which the programmer must be aware.

2. AUDIENCE AND PREREQUISITES

This text addresses advanced undergraduates and beginning graduate students. Professional programmers looking for an exposition of this relatively new approach to their trade will also find the book useful.

The minimum prerequisite for this text is a course in data structures, preferably one that emphasizes data abstraction. I also assume that you know one modern programming language completely (either Pascal or C), and can read the other. It would be helpful if you have taken a course discussing programming language features, such as a programming language design or software design course. A previous course in software engineering would also help you understand the motivation for the object-oriented approach in terms of analysis, design, and system maintenance. For readers who do not have this background or might benefit from a review, Chapter 0 and Section 1.1 discuss the semantic features of higher-level languages and software design principles, respectively.

3. ORGANIZATION AND CONTENT

The text is divided into three parts. The first discusses the necessary background and object-oriented principles in a language-independent manner, with examples in traditional languages and an object-oriented pseudocode. The second part of the book covers Smalltalk, and the third examines C++. I feel that covering the material in this order is the most logical approach. In particular, it is better to discuss Smalltalk before C++ because the language is thoroughly object-oriented and much simpler, for a variety of reasons. In addition, Smalltalk includes a large robust class library that illustrates a number of important principles about inheritance and provides extensive opportunities for reuse. We then cover C++ from the perspective of "what does an object-oriented language look like if it is based on C?" The disadvantage of this order of topics in a course setting is that the material necessary to implement programming projects comes later in the course, especially if C++ is the only language available. For this reason, an instructor may wish to interleave topics from the second or third part with the corresponding sections in the first part.

Chapter 0, "Programming Language Semantics," reviews the concepts and terminology that will be used throughout the text. It covers control structures, subprograms, exceptions, declarations, scope and overloading, object allocation, and the purpose and definition of data types. Chapter 1, "Software Architecture," begins with the abstraction mechanisms that have been used to organize software, and the programming paradigms that provide models of computation. It describes the features of object-oriented languages as the natural outgrowth of programming language constructs that have been developed throughout the evolution of higher-level languages. We also look at the object-oriented model as an alternative way of describing the nature of both computation and programming systems, which is motivated by the requirements of modeling complex problem domains. We also briefly consider the application of object-oriented concepts to the development of large software projects, contrasting the object-oriented approach with the traditional structured method, and examining the manner in which the object model contributes to reuse of code units and facilitates extendability of existing code.

In the next two chapters, we cover object-oriented programming language features in detail. Chapter 2, "Classes, Messages, and Methods," discusses classes, their components, and polymorphism. It describes how classes are used in modeling a problem domain and designing a software system, and illustrates the elements of a class definition. It then introduces the concepts of generic message passing, polymorphism, and dynamic code binding, and describes how these result in looser coupling between the components of a software system. Chapter 3, "Inheritance," examines the purpose of inheritance, the problem domain semantics it mirrors, defining a subclass as an extension of its superclass, overriding superclass behavior, the use of abstract classes and multiple inheritance, and the benefits and costs of the use of inheritance. Chapter 4, "Object-oriented Programming Languages and Environments," gives a brief overview of representative object-oriented languages. The chapter begins with a discussion of criteria for the selection of a particular language in terms of both language features and external factors. It goes on to describe programming environments and their capabilities, since many object-oriented systems provide them. Next, it dicusses two precursors to object-oriented languages that support data abstraction, Simula and Ada83, followed by three pure object-oriented languages. It covers the motivation, design goals, and characteristics of Smalltalk, the language Eiffel, especially its innovative features for program verification, and Java, a language that has received attention recently due to its support for dynamic content in web pages and platform-independent user interaction components. Finally, we examine several hybrid object-oriented languages, including Object Pascal, Modula-3, Oberon, Delphi Pascal, Ada95, C++, Objective-C, and CLOS.

The subject of Part II is Smalltalk. Chapter 5, "Language and Environment," covers the syntax of message expressions, the semantics of identifiers and objects, how control structures are expressed in terms of message passing, and an overview of the facilities of the Smalltalk programming environment. Chapter 6, "Classes and

Inheritance," describes how we define classes and subclasses, as well as how a class is viewed as an object in its own right. Throughout the discussion, we see how the language supports and enforces the object paradigm. The next two chapters present the foundation and collection class in the Smalltalk class library, which provide functionality applicable to any programming project. Chapter 7, "Foundation Classes," discusses the class Object, which defines protocol available to all objects in the system, and classes for booleans, characters, dates and times, numeric objects, points and rectangles. Chapter 8, "Collection Classes," covers the subhierarchy of classes that represent groups of objects with various characteristics and implementations, such as sets, lists, and arrays.

Part III covers C++. Chapter 9, "Enahncements to C," discusses a number of procedural extensions to C such as symbolic constants, the reference type, the allocation and deallocation operators, strong typing, pass and return by reference, inline functions, and function overloading. Chapter 10, "Classes," describes the C++ class and its characteristics, definition of classes, access control for class components, object allocation, constructors and destructors for implicit object initialization and finalization, class scope, and static class members. Chapter 11, "Operators, Conversions, and Iostreams," presents programmer-defined operator overloading, type conversions, and the iostream class library for input/output. Chapter 12, "Inheritance and Dynamic Binding," covers how subclasses are defined, the interaction between inheritance and static typing, the definition and implementation of dynamically bound functions, and multiple inheritance and the language features necessary to support it. Chapter 13, "Templates, Exceptions, and Namespaces," presents these three relatively recent extensions to C++ designed for large-scale development.

4. ACKNOWLEDGMENTS

I want to acknowledge the assistance I received working on the book. First, I would like to thank the students who have taken the course at UIC for their remarks on the organization and presentation of the material, especially those who suffered through the early version of the course notes. Professors Ugo Buy, Robert Sloan, Dale Reed, and Patrick Troy also taught courses at UIC that used the book and made many helpful suggestions. The reviewers were indispensable to the development of the text. I thank one and all: Robert Sloan, Robin Rowe, Jay Zasa, Mark Guydial, Ray Ford, Bertrand Meyer, Christopher Jones, Joseph Wilson, Rhoda Baggs, and Randy Pollack. I also want to thank Frank Sperry, who was a graduate student at UIC during the first few years I taught the course. Our numerous discussions about programming languages and systems were very stimulating and helped me focus on what concepts are important. I would also like to thank my editors at Prentice Hall, Alan Apt and Laura Steele, especially for their patience while I was juggling writing this book, working three jobs, and being a father and husband. My production editor Katharita Lamoza has been very helpful in organizing the copy editing, catching those last few errors, and fine-tuning the presentation of the text. Of course, any errors that remain are my responsibility.

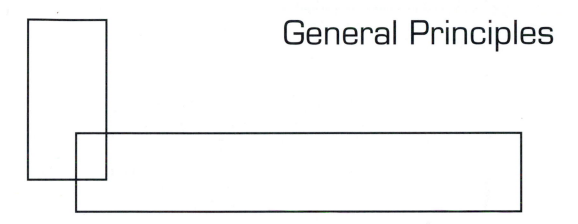

PART I

General Principles

In Part I of the text, we discuss programming language features, software design, and object-oriented programming in general terms. Chapter 0 presents a review of the semantics of programming language features, and introduces concepts and terminology that we will use throughout the text. Chapter 1 discusses the design of software and its organization into units. It presents the object model both as an extension of traditional programming language features, and as a new perspective on the nature of computation and the design of software systems. We also briefly contrast object-oriented development with traditional structured methods.

In Chapters 2 and 3, we examine the elements of the object model and the programming language features that support it. Our discussion is language-independent, although we generally use the terminology of Smalltalk, the prototypical object-oriented language. We also briefly describe how these features are expressed in various object-oriented languages. In this way, you will have a clear understanding of what features are necessary to support object-oriented programming, without dealing with the details of how they are manifested in a particular language. This will make it easier to understand whether a construct in a particular language is motivated by the object model or by other language design goals, and to learn new object-oriented languages. Chapter 4 presents a brief survey of object-oriented languages.

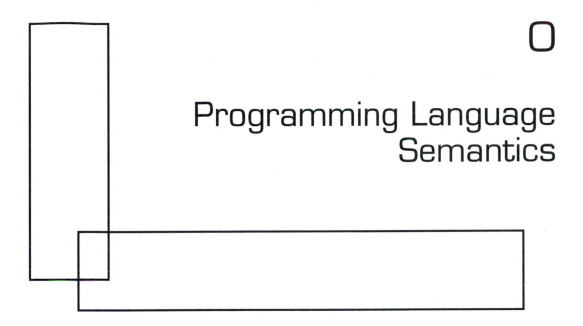

0

Programming Language Semantics

The *semantics* of a language construct or program describes its meaning. We can formulate this description in terms of a formal specification of a model of computation, or an informal model based on the operation of a typical computer. In this chapter, we will discuss programming language features from the latter point of view. We will not consider lexical elements, syntax, or the related issues of parsing and readability, but will concentrate on the semantics of and purpose of various constructs. In the process, you will encounter quite a large amount of terminology that will be used to describe languages throughout the text. This also sets the tone for the first part of the text, in which we consider each language feature for what it means and why we use it, rather than how it is manifested in a particular language. You are probably already familiar with much of this material, but we will discuss some features not present in better-known languages such as Pascal and C. While generally discussing the features of procedural languages such as Pascal and C, the text also mentions some different properties of functional languages such as LISP and ML so that you are aware of more than one way of organizing and coding programs. We will discuss the differences between these classes of languages in detail in section 1.2, and cover the unique features of functional languages in section 1.2.3. (This chapter will also cover some features that are not pursued further in the text for completeness.) More comprehensive coverage of these topics can be found in programming language design texts, such as [Pra96], [Fis93], and [Seb96].

A grasp of programming language semantics is essential for the correct use of a programming language. You can avoid programming errors or recognize them more quickly with this knowledge. For example, you must understand the distinction between issues within the name space of a program, and those that have to do with objects and their interactions during execution. Similarly, if you do not know how storage is allocated on the stack and the heap, you can make errors that the compiler does not catch, resulting in effects whose causes are difficult to determine (especially in C and C++). In addition, an understanding of data types, encapsulation, and first class support for instances of types is necessary to comprehend the object-oriented concept of a class. Concepts such as scope, binding time, static and dynamic typing, and their interaction with inheritance are intrinsic to the use of object-oriented languages.

We will divide our discussion of programming language features in this chapter into three sections: flow of control, the name space of a program, and the structure of data. The chapter covers the following topics:

- sequential control structures (0.1.1)
- subprograms and parameter passing (0.1.2)
- exception handling (0.1.3) and concurrency (0.1.4)
- identifiers (0.2.1), and declarations and definitions (0.2.2)
- static and dynamic scope, and the visibility of identifiers (0.2.3 and 0.2.4)
- programmer-defined visibility (0.2.5)
- overloading (0.2.6)
- data objects (0.3.1) and object allocation policies (0.3.2)
- the purpose and semantics of data types, and primitive types (0.3.3)
- defining types, and the type object (0.3.4)
- programmer-defined types, including pointers, enumerations, arrays, records, unions, abstract data types, and subprogram types (0.3.5)
- type checking, casts, conversions and coercions (0.3.6)

The text assumes that you are familiar with programming in a modern procedural programming language and understand the use of the features of such a language. Generally, we discuss these constructs with respect to Pascal and C since you will have experience with one or both of these languages. (I will assume that you can read both languages.) We will also refer to Ada several times because it includes some contemporary features not found in Pascal or C, and refines a number of features of these languages. The chapter also mentions the different properties of functional languages such as LISP and ML (which we will discuss in more detail in section 1.2.3). For the most part, we will discuss the properties of *compiled* languages such as Pascal, C, and Ada, in which programs are translated to platform-specific object code which is then executed, while occasionally pointing out some characteristics of *interpreted* languages such as BASIC and LISP, in which source code statements are translated and executed in one step.

0.1 CONTROL STRUCTURE

0.1.1 Sequential Control Structures

Sequence control within expressions and among statements

Generally, a program is not just a set of independent operations that can be performed in any order. A language must provide constructs for indicating the order in which actions are performed, or for specifying that the order is unimportant. In procedural languages such as Pascal and C, we indicate the order of execution by nesting of expressions and sequencing of statements. Some languages also provide mechanisms for specifying synchronization with concurrent processes.

A nested *expression* applies a function or operator to some arguments which, in turn, can be the results of other function or operator calls. For example,

```
/* a nested expression in C */
abs(cos(x + 3 * y) / z)
```

The order of nesting is affected by operator precedence, associativity, and parenthesization. For example, in the subexpression x + 3 * y in the previous example, the multiplication operation is nested within the addition, not vice versa. In traditional languages, the innermost function or operator invocations in an expression are evaluated first to provide the arguments to the function or operator call in which they are nested., e.g. cos() is executed before abs() in the preceding example. The subprogram that contains the expression is suspended, the inner function is invoked, and its return value is passed back to the caller, which uses that value as an argument to the next most nested function call in the expression, and so on.

The order of evaluation of the arguments of a particular function call might or might not be guaranteed by the language definition. It is not specified and is left to the language system in Pascal. In C, the &&, ||, and , (comma) operators always evaluate their left operand first, but the order is undefined for all other operators and for functions. The order is irrelevant if evaluating an argument expression does not cause a *side effect* that would affect evaluation of another argument expression, such as modifying a global used as an argument. A Pascal expression consisting entirely of operator applications performs no side effects, and can be executed in any order as long as each argument is evaluated before the call that uses it. For example, in the expression a * b + c mod d, it doesn't matter whether the multiplication or modulus operation is executed first. However, if a Pascal function func modifies its argument (i.e., the argument is passed by reference), then the result of the expression func(x) + x is indeterminate. The programmer must be particularly aware of this situation in C because many of its operators, such as *= and ++, cause side effects.

A *statement* is executed for its side effect, that is, to modify a program variable or perform input/output. Since statements do not return a value, we cannot use nesting to indicate the desired order of execution. In procedural languages, a program is a series of statements to be executed in sequence. The use of statement sequencing as the default flow of control reflects the fetch–execute cycle implemented in the hardware.

In contrast, functional languages such as LISP and ML do not include statements, and the entire program is written as a nested expression. In contemporary functional languages, no functions can cause side effects, so expressions can be evaluated from the outside in. An argument expression is evaluated only when its value is needed (often termed *pass by need*), and the resulting value is saved locally for further uses in the function. This is termed *lazy evaluation*, in contrast to the *strict evaluation* used in most procedural languages, which always evaluates every argument. In fact, a conditional in a traditional language is also evaluated lazily from the outside in, since either the then or the else clause will not be evaluated. Some procedural languages also use lazy evaluation for certain operations, such as "short circuit" logical operators, (the && and || operators in C, and the and then and or else operators in Ada).[1] This characteristic is useful for "guard conditions", for example,

```
/* using lazy evaluation for a "guard condition" in C */
while (index < size && arr[index] != key)
    index++;
```

The goto statement

The goto statement is the simplest control flow statement, and mirrors the unconditional branch instruction built into all computers. Early higher-level languages included this feature because programmers were familiar with using it to control flow of execution in assembly language, and because the concept of structured control constructs had not been developed. To support the goto statement, the language provides a way of labeling statements, and a goto statement transfers control to the specified statement directly. The programmer can use a conditional branch, (an if ... goto) to direct control flow, as in assembly language. Backward jumps are used to create loops, and forward jumps implement conditional execution.

The goto statement has a number of disadvantages. It has a negative effect on readability because the structure of the program is obscured by the way control flow is expressed. There is no syntactic indication of the type of control pattern used— whether an if ... goto is the beginning of a conditional or the end of a loop. The goto statement encourages the programmer to write code with tangled nonlocal flow of control, and such a program cannot be read from beginning to end to determine its behavior. Programs that use gotos often cannot be divided into independent units, and a program may have a large number of possible control paths to be analyzed. In

---

[1] Lazy evaluation could also be used in arithmetic expressions in certain cases; for example, consider evaluation of the expression a * (b + c + d) when a is 0.

particular, there may be several ways to reach a given point in the program, making it difficult to describe the state of the computation at that point. For these reasons, programs using gotos are much more difficult to understand, debug and maintain, and are difficult to test comprehensively or prove correct.

Dijkstra [Dij68] and others have strongly urged that programmers not use goto statements because their use results in code which is difficult to understand, debug, test, and maintain. A heated debate occurred during the 1960s as to whether a language should include a goto statement at all. Most programming languages continue to provide a goto statement, often for historical reasons (Modula-2 is an exception). We also use the statement to remedy deficiencies in the control structures a language supports—in Pascal, for example, we can use it to provide a loop exit at any point in the loop, multiple loop exits, or an exit from a nest of loops. There are usually restrictions on the target of a goto, (in Pascal we cannot transfer control into a control structure and labels are local to subprograms).

Control structures

A *control structure* is a language construct with a single entry point and a single exit point, which defines the order of execution of expressions, statements, or groups of statements, usually based on execution-time values of program variables. Control structures are typically statements in procedural languages, but can also be expressions. In a classic paper, Bohm and Jacopini [Boh66] showed that all single-entry single-exit control flow patterns can be expressed as nested applications of three basic control structures. These are

- the *sequence* structure (i.e., a series of operations)
- the *conditional* structure (e.g., an if ... then ... else statement)
- the *iterative* structure (e.g., a while loop)

This result showed that the goto statement is not essential in a programming language. A conditional branch is sufficient for constructing any pattern of control flow, as is done in assembly language. However, with gotos there is no restriction on the location of the target statement, so locality is not preserved. Each control structure, on the other hand, indicates the control flow pattern used, defines a delimited scope within the program, and has a single entry point and a single exit point. Languages that support control structures allow us to compose a program as a group of modular units that are sequenced or nested. In this way, the structure of the program reflects the dynamic flow of control. Such structured programs are easier to decompose and understand than programs that use arbitrary transfers of control with gotos.

A major contribution of Algol (inherited by all its descendants) is support for these control structures, and for nesting them to any depth. To support nesting a sequence of statements within a conditional or iterative control structure, Algol introduced the *compound statement*, which treats a group of statements enclosed within the delimiters begin and end as a single statement. This organization of the code gives Algol programs a hierarchical structure, rather than the linear structure of Fortran or Basic programs.

The conditional control structure

A *conditional control structure* includes a test expression and two statements or expressions, one of which will be executed, depending on the value of the test expression. With conditional branches, the target of the branch can be anywhere in the program. A structured conditional has exactly one exit point, so we can consider the conditional structure and the enclosed statements or expressions as a unit. The test expression is usually a boolean-valued expression. The exception is C, in which we can use any arithmetic or pointer expression, and a nonzero or non-NULL result is treated as "true".

The conditional construct can be either an expression or a statement. All procedural languages since Algol provide a conditional statement. For example, in Pascal,

```
{a conditional and a sequence nested within a conditional in Pascal}
if num < 0 then begin
   if num <> 0
      writeLn('number is negative')
   end
else begin
   total := total + num;
   count := count + 1
end
```

In this example, the begin and end in the then clause of the conditional are necessary so that the else clause is associated with the outer conditional, and the begin and end in the else clause allow nesting the sequence of statements within the conditional. For a conditional statement to be useful, the enclosed statements must cause side effects (i.e., assignments, data transfers or transfers of control), since the conditional itself returns no value.

In functional languages, there are no statements, and the conditional control structure is an expression that returns the result of evaluation of the selected subexpression. The simplest form is an if-then-else that evaluates either the then or else expression and returns that result as the value of the conditional. Two examples are the C ?: operator and the Algol if-then-else.

```
/* the if-else conditional expression in C and in Algol */
x = y + (x < 0 ? 0 : x);
x := y + (if x < 0 then 0 else x)
```

We can also regard "short circuit" logical operators (such as && and || in C and and and or in Modula-2), as conditional expressions because the right operand might or might not be evaluated. Since such a conditional is an expression, it can be embedded in another expression, and can communicate with other operations via its return value.

Many languages also support a conditional construct that contains an arbitrary number of conditions, each associated with an expression or statement to execute if that condition is true. Examples include the Lisp cond, and the Modula-2 and Ada if statement with elsifs, each of which evaluates the conditions in the order given. For example,

```
— the Ada if statement
if OverallAvg > 90 or ExamAvg > 85 then
    Grade := 'A';
elsif OverallAvg > 80 then
    Grade := 'B';
elsif OverallAvg > 70 then
    Grade := 'C';
elsif OverallAvg > 60 and ExamAvg > 50 then
    Grade := 'D';
else
    Grade := 'E';
end if;
```

In an Ada or Modula-2 if statement, any number of statements may appear after then or else without a begin because there is a closing delimiter for the group of statements in the statement syntax, namely elsif, else, or end if.

We sometimes need to use the value of a variable or expression to select one of a number of actions, each associated with a particular value. We can use a series of nested ifs or an if with elsifs, but this does not reflect the logic as clearly as an explicit switch on the value because it imposes an ordering on the tests and does not indicate that the values are mutually exclusive. Pascal introduced the single-entry single-exit case statement, which gives a discrete-valued expression and labels each action with the value(s) that specify its execution. In many languages, the programmer can associate an action with several values (e.g., separated by , in Pascal or | in Ada), or with a range of values (e.g., using .. in Modula-2 and Ada). A statement to execute when the expression value does not appear in any of the cases is essential for safety and convenience (i.e., so that the programmer does not have to give actions for every possible value). The lack of this feature is a major defect of the Pascal case statement, and is the cause of a number of incompatible extensions to the language (using else, otherwise, etc.). Ada improves on the safety of the Pascal case by providing the others clause, and by requiring that the case statement specify actions for all possible values of the switch expression if there is no others clause. The C switch is unusual and is less safe because each action "falls through" to the next, which is rarely desired, so the programmer must remember to place a break at the end of each action.

The iterative control structure

Instead of creating loops with gotos, modern programming languages provide a single-entry single-exit *iterative control structure*, which specifies repeated execution of a statement or group of statements, and whose beginning and end is delimited in the code. Even when an iterative control structure can specify more than one exit test within the loop body, each exit always transfers control to the statement directly after the control structure so that the entire control structure has a single exit. Most languages do not permit a transfer of control into an iterative control structure with a goto (C is an exception). The iterative control structure is translated to the same machine code as a backwards branch, but it is safer and easier to understand and maintain because it is more structured. Like all control structures, we can nest an iteration within a sequence or a conditional, and vice versa. Two kinds of iterative control structures are common, conditional iteration and counter-controlled iteration.

A *conditional iteration* control structure repeats execution of a statement or series of statements until a given condition is satisfied. A loop with a *preloop test* tests the loop exit condition before executing the loop body (like an if-goto at the top of the loop), and does not execute the body if the test is not satisfied initially. The Pascal and C while statements employ a preloop test. For example,

```
{ a Pascal while statement }
while num > 0 do begin
  num := num div 5;
  count := count + 1
end
```

With a *postloop test,* the condition is evaluated after execution of the body, and the loop is always executed once. Examples include the Pascal repeat statement and the C do while statement. The while loop is more common because we usually need to handle empty lists or files, or errors in accessing or setting up the data. The loop test may be satisfied when iteration is to continue (e.g., the Pascal while do) or when control is to exit (e.g., the Pascal repeat until). Clearly, the loop body must modify a variable used in the loop test so that the loop will terminate.

Restricting the loop test to the beginning or end of the loop as in Pascal can cause awkward code idioms, and is not necessary to maintaining the locality and structuredness of the program. For example, a read loop that exits upon reading a sentinel value or reaching the end of the input file cannot test for the exit condition until a read has been performed. Without a loop exit construct (or a goto), the programmer must unwind the loop such that part of the first iteration precedes the iteration control structure, or use an extra test within the loop. In addition, many loops have more than one logical exit. For example, an array search loop exits if it finds the key or encounters the end of the array. In some cases, the conditions can be combined with a logical and, but in others the validity of one test determines whether another should even be performed (i.e., lazy evaluation is called for). If this is the case, the Pascal programmer must set a boolean flag in the loop, and then test it in the loop condition. If several conditions must be tested, a number of boolean variables are necessary, and the logic of the code becomes obscured.

C provides the break statement, which exits the enclosing control structure. Ada supports a generalized loop construct enclosed in the keywords loop and end loop, in which an exit can appear at any point within the loop body. For example,

```
— an Ada loop with a loop exit
loop
  Put("Enter a number:");
  Get(Num);
  exit when Num = 0;
  Total := Total + Num;
  Count := Count + 1;
end loop
```

An Ada loop can also contain multiple exits, each of which transfers control to the statement after the loop.[2] We can also use an Ada exit to exit from several nested loop by specifying the loop label of the outermost loop to be terminated, which is useful for handling error conditions. In any case, exiting a loop still transfers control to the statement immediately following the loop. C also includes the continue statement, which transfers control directly to the loop test of the nearest enclosing loop.

Most languages provide a *counter-controlled iteration* control structure for the special case when a *loop variable* is initialized before the loop is executed, updated at the end of each execution of the loop body (usually incremented by a "step size"), and then tested against a limit value to determine whether to exit. The loop variable is usually an integer index used to automate processing sequential data structures such as arrays. In many languages, such as Pascal and Ada, the loop variable may be an instance of any discrete ordered type, for example, a character or an enumeration. Most machine architectures have an instruction that directly supports counting loops.

The details of the semantics of the counter-controlled iteration vary widely among languages. Usually, we cannot assign a new value to the loop variable within the loop. In some languages, such as Ada, the loop variable is local to the loop and cannot be used after the loop. Whether its value is defined after exiting the loop varies among languages (e.g., it is in Fortran 77, but is not in Pascal). Specifying a counted loop requires the initial value, the size (and sign) of the increment, and the terminating value or condition. In many languages, such as Fortran and Pascal, the number of iterations is determined at the beginning of the execution of the loop, and is fixed. If expressions are allowed in the update expression or the limit test, the language must specify whether they are evaluated once upon entering the loop, or on each iteration. When you learn a new language, these details must be clarified.

[2] In addition, the Ada loop statement allows prefixes that specify conditional iteration (while) or counted iteration (for).

Some languages provide a more general form of loop specification that we can use to express both conditional iteration and counter-controlled iteration. A *generalized iteration* gives initialization expressions, a loop test, and update expressions. The loop test is evaluated before the loop body, and the update expressions are executed after the loop body. This construct is provided by the C for statement, in which we can give more than one initialization or update expression separated by commas. For example,

```
/* the C generalized for loop */
/* reversing the order of a linked list */
for ( pNewlist = NULL, pCurr = pList;  pCurr != NULL;  pCurr = pSucc )
{
   pSucc = pCurr->next;
   pCurr->next = pNewlist;
   pNewlist = pCurr;
}
```

Each of the iteration expressions is optional, and an omitted loop test results in an infinite loop, requiring another way to exit (e.g., a conditional break or a return). The flexibility provided by this construct can be useful (e.g., with loops over linked lists such as the previous example) or confusing, because there are many ways to write a particular computation, some overly condensed.

Some languages support *implicit iteration* operations for objects representing collections of objects, which apply a given operation to each element of the collection. The operation is specified as a function argument to the iteration operation. This feature is common in functional languages that support function parameters, anonymous functions, and variable length lists. For example, we can "map" a function onto a list, which applies the function to each element of the list and returns a list of the resulting values. Similarly, a "selection" operation creates a new list consisting of the elements that return true for the given boolean-valued function. As we will see in Chapters 5 and 8, Smalltalk collection classes respond to several implicit iteration messages.

0.1.2 Subprograms

Purpose and definition

Subprograms were originally devised as a way of reducing the number of lines of code and the compilation time for a program by factoring out multiple occurrences of code segments. They permit us to package and parameterize a computation, code it once, and reuse it in other situations via an invocation. Since a subprogram definition essentially creates a new statement or operator, subprograms provide a mechanism for extending the language to reflect the structure of the problem domain or the design of the application, although there is execution time overhead. As we will discuss further in section 1.1.2, a subprogram is an abstraction that permits the programmer to view the structure of the program at a higher level.

The definition of a subprogram describes its inputs and outputs and the actions performed when it is called. A subprogram definition begins with a header that marks the beginning of that syntactic unit, gives a name for the subprogram, and specifies the names, types, and modes of the parameters. The *parameter mode* describes the parameter passing mechanism or whether the parameter is an input, an output, or both. The header is followed by a body that gives the series of statements executed when the subprogram is invoked. In most languages, a subprogram definition is identified by a keyword, for example, procedure or function in Pascal. This aids the parser and the reader of the program in identifying the construct, and facilitates searching for subprogram definitions with an editor. For example,

```
{ a Pascal procedure definition }
procedure swap(var left: integer; var right: integer);
var
  temp: integer;
begin
  temp := left;
  left := right;
  right := temp
end
```

In many languages, including Pascal and Ada, a distinction is made between *procedures*, which do not return a value, and *functions*, which do. A procedure call is a statement and a function call is an expression. To support functions, the language defines a statement or operation for indicating the return value that can be used in a function body.

Parameters, local variables, and scope

A subprogram can communicate with its caller either through parameters or nonlocal variables. Manipulating nonlocal variables tightly binds the subprogram to those variables, and prevents it from being an independent unit. Using parameters provides more flexibility because we can use the subprogram in a variety of contexts with different inputs and outputs. In this text, we refer to the "formal parameters" in the subprogram definition as *parameters*, and the corresponding "actual arguments" passed in an invocation as *arguments*.

In a statically typed language, the subprogram definition gives the type of each parameter. In a strongly typed language, the type of the argument must be the same as the type of the parameter, or must be convertible to it. If not, a compiler error results. Strong typing provides much more reliable code. For example, in the invocation sqrt(7) for which the parameter type of sqrt is real, a Fortran or pre-ANSI C compiler might not perform the necessary conversion, with unpredictable results. Pascal, Ada, ANSI C (almost), and Fortran 90 are strongly typed languages.

Some contemporary languages such as Ada and C++ allow the programmer to specify default values for the parameters of a subprogram. In this case, the subprogram can be called without providing arguments for those parameters, and the invocation will use the default values. The use of optional arguments allows an invocation to be more concise but less explicit. In a call with optional arguments, a language could allow the caller to use commas as placeholders, or may allow default values for the trailing parameters only. We will see in section 9.2.2 that C++ uses the latter technique. Using commas is error-prone because the symbol is easy to miss, and an invocation that specifies a small subset of the arguments may contain long strings of commas, which are difficult to count.

Subprograms can define *local variables* that maintain information needed only within an invocation of that subprogram. Their names are visible only within the subprogram code, and they must exist for the duration of an invocation of the subprogram. We will see in section 0.3.2 that local variables are statically allocated in Fortran and are automatically allocated in modern languages.

Each subprogram defines a scope in which a new set of names can be declared, and the subprogram's local variables and parameters are declared within that scope only. When those identifiers are used elsewhere in the program, they are bound to other program entities or are undeclared. This allows the programmer to choose local names for a subprogram freely. (We will discuss scope in detail in section 0.2.)

Subprogram call and return

A subprogram defines a parameterized sequence of operations that can be treated as an individual operation from the perspectives of syntax and program design. When a procedure is invoked, its code is executed and control returns to the statement after the invocation. For a function call, control returns to the point in the expression at which it is called, and its return value is used in continuing the evaluation of that expression. That is, subprogram invocation and return is also a single-entry single-exit control structure. If a subprogram proc1 contains an invocation of another subprogram proc2, then proc2 must complete execution before proc1 can continue. Similarly, if proc2 calls proc3, proc3 must complete execution before proc2 can continue, and so on in a sequence of invocations. Due to the possibility of nested invocations, subprogram invocation is sometimes referred to as a "hierarchical" control structure.

Unlike other control structures, a subprogram defines a lexical context, and an invocation can create objects —namely parameters and local variables—whose lifetimes are exactly the duration of that invocation. When one subprogram invokes another, the invoked subprogram must be completed before the calling subprogram can continue processing. Therefore, the state of the caller must be saved upon invocation, and restored upon return. In addition, the environment of the caller should not be accessible to the subprogram (except for arguments passed by reference). The structure that maintains the state of a subprogram is referred to as the *activation record* for that invocation. An activation record contains values for the subprogram's arguments and local variables (except in Fortran), and the *return address*, a program counter value indicating the point in its code at which execution will continue upon reactivation.[3] For implementation purposes, the activation record also includes the *dynamic link*, a pointer to the caller's activation record (since the sizes of activation records vary), and the contents of the processor registers, which are used for restoring the state of the calling subprogram. The activation record may also include temporary storage needed for expression evaluation. As we will see in section 0.2.4, activation records in a block-structured language also contain the *static link*, a pointer to the block's enclosing lexical scope, that is used to resolve references to nonlocal variables.

Since a subprogram can invoke another subprogram before its own completion, a sequence of these state structures may have to be retained at any one time. Since the subprograms must return in the opposite order from that in which they were called, a last-in-first-out stack is used to maintain this information. The *run-time stack* is a list of activation records, often called *stack frames*, that contain state information about subprograms that have been entered but not exited, that is, those that are awaiting completion. For example, if subprogram proc1 calls subprogram proc2, which calls subprogram proc3, we have the run-time stack structure illustrated in Figure 0.1 during proc3's execution.

If subprogram proc3 calls another subprogram, that subprogram's activation record is pushed on the stack above the record for proc3. When proc3's execution completes, its activation record is popped from the stack, and execution proceeds at the point given by the return address in proc3's stack frame. With this scheme, storage for a subprogram's local variables is only allocated during an activation of that subprogram. Similarly, since a subprogram can only access its own stack frame, it can only access its own variables and nonlocal variables accessed via the static link, but not those of the caller.

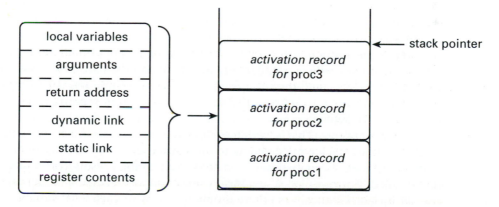

A typical stack frame   The stack after proc1 **calls** proc2 **and** proc2 **calls** proc3

Figure 0.1: The run-time stack.

_____

[3] The subprogram's code is also part of its state but is not stored on the stack.

Recursion

It is often necessary or convenient to define a function recursively, as in the following example:

$$fibonacci(n) = \begin{cases} 1 & \text{if } n = 0 \text{ or } n = 1 \\ fibonacci(n\text{-}1) + fibonacci(n\text{-}2) & \text{otherwise} \end{cases}$$

We refer to the nonrecursive case as the *base case* of the definition. Although the definition appears circular, it is not. The function's value is always well-defined (for the domain of natural numbers), since we do not define the value for a particular element in terms of the value for that same element. The function is defined in terms of its value for smaller elements of its domain, together with a definition of its value for the smallest elements.

The value of the function for any element can be computed by computing the value for all smaller elements back to the base case. The solution for *fibonacci(n)* involves setting up the subproblems of solving *fibonacci(n-1)* and *fibonacci(n-2)*, and then combining those solutions. The program directly mirrors the recursive definition of the function, which requires that the function call itself.[4]

```
/* A C function for computing fibonacci(n) */
long fibonacci(long n)
{
   if ( n == 0 || n == 1 )
     return 1;
   else
     return fibonacci(n-1) + fibonacci(n-2);
}
```

We define a recursive subprogram by first testing for the base case whose occurrence causes the recursive calls to stop. (We test the base case before the recursive calls to prevent "infinite recursion".) When that test is not satified, the subprogram calls itself, usually with a "smaller" argument. When the base case is satisfied, the recursive calls stop, and the succession of deferred computations is completed in reverse order. Each recursive call has its own activation record on the run-time stack, and each activation record contains a different value for the variable used to control the recursion. That is, with recursion, there can be several activation records on the run-time stack corresponding to invocations of the same subprogram. Each of these represents a computation "on hold" waiting for a result from a subprogram that it called. Fortran, Cobol, and Basic cannot support recursion because they allocate all variables statically, so there is only one copy of each local variable.

Recursive definitions of subprograms are often more succinct than the corresponding iterative code because no loop variable is necessary to control the repetition. There are many dynamic data structures such as trees and nested lists that

---

[4] You are probably aware that this is not an efficient way of performing this computation.

are defined recursively. For these structures, it is more natural to define subprograms that operate on them recursively, in the same manner as the definition of the data structure. Recursion is also appropriate for a "divide and conquer" problem that can be solved by reducing it to instances of the same problem for "smaller" inputs, such as *fibonacci(n)* or quicksort. Recursion is essential for problem solutions that require backtracking such as bin packing, graph search, or artificial intelligence problems.

Parameter passing

When we use *pass by value* for a parameter, it is a local variable initialized with the value of the argument expression. The argument expression is evaluated before the call, and the resulting value is copied into the subprogram's stack frame. Changes to the parameter within the subprogram only modify its local copy, so pass by value can only be used for input parameters. This is safer than other parameter modes because the subprogram cannot affect the environment of the caller. (However, if a pointer value is passed, the subprogram has access to its referent, and may modify that object.) Parameters are passed by value in Pascal by default, that is, when the var keyword is not given. All parameters in C are passed by value except for arrays, for which a pointer to the first element is passed. A disadvantage of pass by value occurs when the parameter type represents a large object such as an array or record. Copying the argument to the environment of the subprogram upon invocation is costly in both time and space.

The designers of Algol recognized that a subprogram often needs to pass information back to its caller or modify variables in the caller's environment, which we cannot do with pass by value (since Algol did not support pointers). A function can be used to return a single value, but sometimes the subprogram must return more than one value or modify the value of the argument itself, such as in a swap procedure. When an argument is *passed by name,* the argument expression is substituted for each occurrence of the parameter in the subprogram before execution. The argument expression is evaluated when flow of control reaches an occurrence of the parameter, and that value is used. If the parameter appears on the left side of an assignment, then the argument is assigned a new value.[5] Variable names in the argument expression refer to the object that they refer to in the environment of the caller. We will not discuss pass by name in detail because experience has shown that it is hard to understand and use, and is difficult and expensive to implement. It reduces to pass by reference when a single variable is used as the argument, and the latter provides the needed capability in a more straightforward way which is easier to implement. Pass by name has not been used since its introduction in Algol.

With *pass by reference*, the invoked subprogram receives a reference to the actual argument object. Essentially, the parameter is an "alias" for the argument variable. When the parameter is encountered upon executing the subprogram, that

---

[5] The argument must be an expression that can be used as an *l*-value (see section 0.3.1), namely a variable, an array subscription, a record component selection, or a dereferenced pointer. For example, it cannot be an arithmetic expression such as num + 1.

use refers to the location or value of the associated data object, depending on the context, e.g. on the left or right side of an assignment. For this reason, a subprogram can return an output by modifying a parameter passed by reference. (Usually, constants and expressions cannot appear as an argument corresponding to a parameter passed by reference.) We can also use pass by reference to avoid the overhead of copying an argument that is a large structure. This has the disadvantage that the subprogram cannot be prevented from modifying that object. C++ supports *pass by constant reference*, which passes the argument by reference but prevents the function from modifying the argument, and permits a constant argument. The compiler can implement pass by reference by allocating a pointer to the argument object in the subprogram's stack frame and automatically dereferencing the pointer in translating the subprogram code. Although this avoids copying the argument value, pass by reference has the additional cost of indirection each time the subprogram uses the parameter.

Fortran uses pass by reference for all parameters, and Pascal indicates pass by reference with the var reserved word. Pass by reference is more convenient than passing a pointer directly because the parameter need not be dereferenced in the subprogram. It also allows passing a local variable, array element, or record field as the argument (in Pascal, a pointer cannot refer to any of these). C does not support pass by reference, so to modify an argument or avoid copying a large object, we use a pointer parameter passed by value, and dereference the pointer within the function when referring to the object. (C allows the programmer to obtain a pointer to any object or component with the & operator.)

An alternate technique for providing an input/output parameter is *pass by value-result*. The argument object is initially copied to the subprogram's stack frame, and is then copied back to the caller's object upon exit. Modifications to the parameter during execution of the subprogram only affect the local copy, as opposed to pass by reference in which each change of the parameter affects the argument immediately. Pass by reference and pass by value-result have different semantics when the argument object is accessible in other ways during execution of the subprogram. This can occur when an object is passed as an argument for two parameters, when the argument is also available within the subprogram as a nonlocal variable, or with recursion or concurrent execution. Generally, pass by value-result is safer than pass by reference because effects are localized.

One difficulty with parameter passing in Pascal is that the only efficient mechanism for passing large objects is pass by reference, intended to return information by modifying a variable in the caller. That is, it merges a performance issue with a logical issue. In Ada, the programmer specifies the intended semantics by using the *parameter modes* in for an input parameter, out for an output parameter, and in out for an input/output parameter, and the translator selects the appropriate mechanism. For example, the compiler can implicitly use a pointer to the argument for an in parameter if it is a large object, and the compiler decides when an object is large enough to use indirection for efficiency. In this way, the appearance of the code better matches the intent of the programmer, and the implementation is left to the translator. The programmer cannot assign a new value to an in parameter since it is regarded as an input to the subprogram. Similarly, the subprogram cannot obtain the value of an out parameter.[6]

0.1.3 Exceptions

Execution-time errors

Attempting to perform an operation sometimes results in a state in which correct processing cannot proceed. This can occur because an argument has an invalid value for the operation, because required system resources are unavailable, or because of a hardware error. Execution-time errors include

- hardware-detected errors such as division by zero, arithmetic overflow, memory violations, and device errors
- system errors such as failure of a file operation or a full message queue
- logical errors such as an out of bounds array index or removing an element from an empty queue
- application-specific errors such as an invalid input format

In these cases, we say that an *exception* has occurred.

Exceptions occur infrequently during execution, but a robust system must be prepared to deal with them. The worst response is to simply continue execution with no notification that the results produced are invalid. The Pascal standard requires that a program terminate upon a subscript error, a subrange error, or an arithmetic error such as division by zero. However, immediate termination complicates implementation of the language, and is not a proper response for a production system that may need to deallocate system resources or restore the state of files. In addition, some indication of the nature of the error should be provided. In many cases, such as application-specific exceptions, it may be possible to limit the effect of the problem and proceed with execution. That is, the program can recover from the error and continue.

Error propagation

In many cases, the subprogram that detects an exception is not the one that has the information necessary to deal with it. For example, if a stack function signals stackUnderflow because the caller popped an empty stack, then it is more appropriate for the user of that object to specify the action to be taken than the designer of the stack module. Similarly, the module that detects an invalid input may not be the same module that communicates with the user. In addition, the subprogram that can detect the error condition might be called by many other subprograms in the system (like the stack pop function), and may have been written and compiled separately.

---

[6] Ada95 allows accessing an output parameter once a value has been assigned to it.

A direct transfer of control using a goto does not suffice because the subprogram that detects the error has no way of knowing where to transfer control (unless it is only called by one subprogram). In addition, most languages restrict the location of the target of a goto to the same scope or subprogram as the goto statement, so that the same static and dynamic context (i.e., activation record) can be maintained. A goto also cannot pass any information to the handler about the situation that occurred.

If the language supports error detection, the programmer can explicitly check for the error condition, and pass the error notification from one subprogram to another in a sequence of invocations. For example, C file operations and system calls return an error code upon failure. Each invocation of such an operation becomes a conditional statement that tests for a potential error condition, and specifies the action to be taken if an error occurs (see section 13.3.1 for an example). To propagate the error notification, each subprogram must pass that information back to its caller, and ultimately to the subprogram that can handle the error condition. However, this tightly binds those subprograms, and is inconvenient if subprograms must detect, propagate, or handle more than one exception. It also clutters the logic of all the intervening subprograms, especially since the error information and its propagation is irrelevant to the purpose of those subprograms. In addition, there is no guarantee that the caller of a function that may signal an error will check for the error condition.

Exception handling

Error handling is an essential part of programming so it is appropriate that it is reflected by a language construct. The designers of many contemporary programming languages such as ML, Ada, C++, and Java recognized that exceptions are semantically different from loop exits and other control structures, so they included a special mechanism for handling these situations in the language. Languages that support exception handling provide constructs for

- defining exceptions (or exception types)
- signaling the occurrence of an exception
- specifying handlers for different exceptions for a code unit

A subprogram or block can specify an *exception handler* that will be invoked when a particular error condition occurs in any subprograms it calls, or subprograms indirectly called. It can also specify different handlers for different types of exceptions. The translator must implement mechanisms for transferring control from a signaler to a handler. Unlike the use of error return codes, the programmer does not have to specify error handling separately for each operation, or for each subprogram in a sequence of invocations. In addition, if no subprogram in the sequence of invocations defines a handler for an exception that occurs, the program is terminated. The exception handler is intended to perform any clean-up of the program state necessary before proceeding or terminating the program. This feature allows the programmer to separate application logic from error handling code, making the operation of each clearer.

When an exception is raised, the rest of that block is skipped and any handler the block defines for that exception is invoked. If the subprogram that signaled the exception does not define an applicable handler, that of its caller is invoked. If the caller does not define a handler, the process of locating a handler for the exception continues back through the sequence of pending subprogram invocations on the run-time stack. That is, a block defines an exception handler for itself and for all the subprograms it calls, even those that are invoked indirectly.

We can think of the expression or statement that signals an exception as a non-local goto statement that transfers control to an exception handler, if one is defined. The transfer of control is safe because it returns to an existing environment. Signaling an exception is unlike a subprogram call because control does not return to the subprogram that signaled the exception, and is unlike a return statement because it might not transfer control to the subprogram's caller.

An exception handler must execute in the environment in which it is defined, not the environment of the signaling subprogram. Identifiers in the handler, refer to the objects and functions in the scope of the handler, not at the point of the error signal. Therefore, the environment of the subprogram that defines the handler must be restored as the active stack frame before executing the handler. When a subprogram does not define a handler for an exception it raises, its activation record is popped from the run-time stack and its caller is examined for an applicable handler. This process of "unwinding" the stack continues back through the sequence of invocations that lead up to the subprogram that signaled the exception. If no handler is found for the exception, the program terminates.

The language must also specify the behavior of a program if the handler does not terminate execution. Some languages, such as CLU, Ada, and C++, only support the *termination* model, in which execution always continues after the block whose handler was triggered by the exception. If it is necessary to retry the operation after an error has occurred, the programmer encloses that block in a loop that exits upon successful completion of the operation. Other languages, such as PL/I, support the *resumption* model, in which the handler may directly retry the operation that resulted in an exception after it performs some clean-up activity. This involves restoring the state of the program at that point (after having unwound the stack to the activation record for the handler). In Eiffel, the handler may only retry the operation or terminate execution, rather than continue without performing an operation in the program.

Some early programming languages such as COBOL and PL/I allowed the programmer to test for particular hardware exceptions and specify processing to perform when they occured. The program could then continue execution after the statement that caused the exception. However, these languages did not support defining or signaling new types of exceptions, for example, for logical or application-specific errors (just as they did not support defining new types). Standard Pascal does not support error detection, although many language systems provide functions for checking CPU status flags (e.g., to detect an arithmetic overflow). As stated previously, many C standard library functions return error codes upon failure. The C standard library also includes the setjmp() and longjmp() functions that can be used for error propagation, as described in section 13.3.1.

Exceptions in Ada

Ada supports an exception facility because it is intended for embedded and mission-critical applications that must behave reasonably under a variety of conditions. The name of a programmer-defined exception is declared as an Exception, and the language's standard packages define a number of hardware errors. An exception is signaled by a raise statement that gives the exception name, which typically occurs in a conditional that tests for the error condition.

Exception handlers can be defined for any block, and are demarcated from normal processing by the keyword Exception. The handler for each type of exception is coded as a when statement that specifies the processing to perform when that exception occurs. A block can specify a default handler for exceptions not explicitly handled with the clause when others => ... . The general format is as follows:

```
— format for exception handlers in Ada
begin
  — ... application code ...
Exception
  when exceptionName =>
    — ... handler for exceptionName ...
  when ...
  when others =>
    — ... default handler ...
end
```

The order of the when clauses is not significant. Error handling is not specified on an invocation-by-invocation basis, as it is with error return codes, and the logic of the application is not interrupted by error processing code. The name of the exception is the only information transmitted to the handler in Ada.

Upon detecting an exception, the rest of that block is skipped, and the appropriate handler is found and executed in the context in which it is defined. The stack is unwound as described in the previous subsection, and execution continues from the point after the block that handled the exception. If the programmer wishes to re-initiate the processing that lead to the exception, he or she can enclose the block in a loop. If no handler is found for the exception, the program terminates.

Exceptions in C++

C++ also provides a standard facility for programmer-defined exception handling. This mechanism is particularly important for an object-oriented language because vendor-supplied class libraries must have a way of signaling errors to users of the library. In C++, the exception itself is an object that the programmer can use to pass information from the signaler to the handler of the exception. We will discuss C++ support for exceptions in section 13.3.

0.1.4 Concurrency

Purpose

In some cases, a computation can be partitioned into subtasks that can be performed in parallel, or a system consists of a number of independent, cooperating programs that can execute concurrently. For example, a word processor may include a program that presents a user interface and permits editing, and a program that prints a document, and these tasks can be performed concurrently on a multi-processing system. Similarly, many windowing systems create a process for each application to respond to events in its window.

Some programming languages such as Simula67, Modula-2, and Ada support features that allow the programmer to specify a concurrent program as a collection of *tasks* (or *threads*), each of which is a sequential program, that is, a thread of control. A particular execution of one of these tasks is a *process* scheduled by the operating system on the platform's processor(s). These processes execute asynchronously in the sense that any possible interleaving of program steps can occur, as long as the steps in a particular process are performed in the given order. The processes may be executed concurrently on separate processors, or may be scheduled in an interleaved fashion on the same processor.

Language support

A programming language that supports concurrency must define mechanisms for

- defining processes and specifying the code that they execute
- starting processes, suspending an active process, re-activating a suspended process, and terminating processes
- synchronization among processes to prevent undesirable interleavings of program actions, for example, so that one process will wait until another performs some action or produces some result
- communication among processes

Some languages permit the programmer to give priority levels for processes, which are used to determine which process to activate when the active process terminates or suspends itself. Some languages also provide an operation that suspends a process for a particular amount of time and then re-activates it.

Programming languages have used two mechanisms for specifying process synchronization. A *semaphore* is an object visible to more than one process that a process can set to indicate that some condition of interest to other processes has occurred. This operation is usually called a *signal.* A process can indicate that it is waiting for the corresponding event by executing a *wait* operation on that semaphore. When a process performs a wait, it proceeds if the semaphore has received a signal, but is suspended if it has not. A process that is waiting for a semaphore to be signaled will be resumed when that signal occurs. Semaphores are often used to implement mutually exclusive use of shared resources. When the resource is created, a signal is sent to the associated semaphore to indicate that the resource is available. When a process wants to use the resource, it executes a wait on this semaphore. After obtaining the resource and using it, the process sends a signal to indicate that the resource is available to other processes.

Another mechanism for synchronization is to group program statements that access a shared variable into *critical regions*. Only one process at a time can execute a critical region associated with a particular shared variable. If a process is executing in a critical region, another process attempting to execute a critical region associated with the same variable must wait until the first process finishes its critical region. That is, executions of the critical regions associated with a variable are mutually exclusive. A similar construct is the monitor. A *monitor* defines a shared variable together with a set of operations for that object. The language system ensures that only one process can execute an operation for a particular monitor object at a time.

The subprograms in a single process can communicate through parameters and global variables, but asynchronous processes do not share an address space. Separate processes must communicate via mechanisms provided by the operating system that are available through language constructs or system calls. Two common techniques are *shared storage* and *message passing*. Processes that access shared storage must synchronize their accesses to prevent one process from reading a shared variable while another is updating it. With message passing, processes share *ports* or *mailboxes* provided by the operating system, which they access with primitives such as send and receive (e.g., an entry call and an accept statement in Ada). Message passing may be synchronous or asynchronous. With *synchronous* communication, a sender waits until the receiver accepts the message, and a receiver cannot proceed until it obtains a message. With *asynchronous* communication, a sender proceeds immediately after sending a message, and a receiver can proceed if no message is available. For example, a UNIX pipe is asynchronous for a writing process (unless it is full) because it proceeds after placing data in the pipe, but is synchronous for a reading process because it blocks if the pipe is empty.

A detailed discussion of issues in concurrent programming (race conditions, deadlock, etc.) and of programming language support for concurrency is beyond the scope of this text. We will discuss Smalltalk support for concurrency in section 5.5.6.

0.2 NAME STRUCTURE

0.2.1 Identifiers

Naming program entities

In writing a program, we manipulate various kinds of program entities such as objects, constants, subprograms, and types. In order to refer to an entity in a program, it must be given a name.[7] An *identifier* is a name in the source code used to refer to an object, constant, subprogram, parameter, or type in a program. We say that an identifier is *bound* to that program entity, and that the entity is the *referent of the identifier and is its meaning.* We use identifiers to refer both to execution-time entities such as objects and subprograms (i.e., code objects), and to compile-time entities such as data types and symbolic constants.

In contemporary functional languages, each name has a unique meaning and cannot be rebound. A name can be declared to stand for an expression, and a parameter name acquires a meaning, that is, the corresponding argument, during an invocation. The expression can always be substituted for the name and vice versa, without changing the meaning of the expression in which it occurs. However, in most programming languages the correspondence between identifiers and program entities is not one-to-one, and is different in different parts of the program. The same name can refer to several objects (the local variable of a recursive subprogram). An object can have no name, one name, or more than one name, for example, when it is passed by reference.

Identifiers have semantic value for the programmer (but not for the translator). Choosing identifier names is a common task, and is often one of the more difficult decisions in programming. To facilitate understanding and maintaining the program, an identifier name should always be suggestive of the meaning of the entity to which it refers. The rules for valid programmer-defined identifiers vary widely among languages. These include the permissible characters, the maximum length of a name, case sensitivity, and so on. For example, a Pascal identifier must begin with a letter, which can be followed by any number of letters and digits, and case is ignored. Allowing a non-alphabetic "word separator" character, such as - in Cobol or _ in C, is helpful for expressing multiple-word identifiers.

Reserved words

Each language defines a number of names that are part of the syntax of the language, such as control structure keywords, operators, and scope delimiters. In most modern languages, language-defined names are *reserved words* that the programmer may not use as identifiers. Many languages also define names for primitive types and for particular functions, constants, and objects that a language system must provide. The programmer usually cannot redefine these names.

Binding

The *binding* of an identifier gives the correspondence between the identifier and the program entity it refers to. A binding maps from the name space of the program to the set of entities manipulated by the program. In general, the process of binding may involve determining other attributes of an identifier as well, such as the

---

[7] Some objects such as objects on the heap and array or record components may only be named indirectly by expressions.

type or storage policy used for the referent object, or the correct subprogram definition with overloading. The *environment* of a statement or subprogram is the set of bindings in effect at that point, and it determines the referent for an identifier use. The environment provides the context in which names acquire meanings. As we will see in this section, the environment is modified by a declaration or by entry into a new level of scope.

The referent associated with an identifier and its attributes can be bound at various times during the translation and execution of a program. A binding is *static* if the association between an identifier and an entity or its attributes is made before execution, and cannot change during execution (the type of an identifier in a statically typed language). If a binding is determined at run time or can change during execution, it is *dynamic*. Examples include the location of a local variable, and the type of the referent of an identifier in a dynamically typed language.

For example, alocation to binding an object may occur at various times during the process of translating and executing a program. It is done at compile time for "absolute" addresses explicitly given in the code (e.g., with "memory mapped" device registers), and at load time for static variables (including all variables in Fortran, Basic, and Cobol). Binding of addresses for objects is done at execution time for both automatic variables allocated at block or subprogram entry, and for dynamically allocated objects that are assigned storage when the allocation operation is executed. With process swapping in a multiprocessing system, all location bindings may be recomputed during program execution.

0.2.2 Declarations

Purpose and definition

In Fortran, the programmer can use a variable name in an executable statement without declaring it beforehand. The type of the variable is determined by default according to the first letter of the identifier: names that begin with a letter between I and N are of type INTEGER and others are REAL. This was originally intended as a convenience, but it was found to be a major source of unreliability. If a programmer mistypes a variable name (at any time during development and maintenance), it creates a new uninitialized variable and the compiler does not catch the error. This situation can be very difficult to debug.

In modern languages, we must declare an identifier before using it so that the translator can associate properties with the name, identify misuses of the identifier, and catch typographic errors. A *declaration* is a nonexecutable statement that is an instruction to the language translator introducing a name into some scope in a program. We say that the name is *visible* in that scope. A declaration usually associates various attributes with the name, such as what kind of program entity its referent is (object, subprogram, type, etc.). In statically typed languages, an object declaration also gives a type for the referent of the identifier, and the compiler can verify that subsequent uses of that identifier are valid.

In most languages, all the declarations for a scope (i.e., a block or subprogram) must appear at the beginning of the scope, providing a dictionary that the programmer can examine to determine the meaning of an identifier. In C++, a declaration can appear at any point, so that the declaration of an entity can be placed nearer to its first use and an object need not be defined before the information necessary to initialize it is available.

Definitions

Most often, the language statement that declares an identifier also specifies that its referent is to be created and defines that object, subprogram, type, or constant. A *definition* is a declaration that also specifies that a program entity is to be created, and binds the name with that entity.[8] For example,

```
{ example object definitions in Pascal }
var
    count, limit: integer;
    total: real;
```

```
/* example object definitions in C */
int count, limit;
double total;
```

The entity created is a code object for a subprogram definition, or a compiler data structure for a constant or type definition.

Forward declarations

There are times when we need to introduce a name to the translator without specifying creation of its referent. Examples include

- when we call a subprogram before defining it
- when we use an object or subprogram in more than one compilation unit, since it must be defined exactly once
- when two definitions are mutually referential, for example, mutually recursive subprograms or two record types that contain pointers to instances of each other

A declaration that is not a definition is referred to as a *forward declaration* in Pascal or a *specification* in Ada. A forward declaration indicates that the programmer wants to use an identifier that is defined elsewhere in the program, either later in the source code or in another compilation unit. Uses of the identifier refer to the program entity specified in that definition. Forward declarations are necessary with information hiding because the interface (that is, the declaration) of a subprogram

---

[8] Our use of the terms "declaration" and "definition" is that of the C literature. Different terminology is sometimes used with other languages.

or type should be visible to users of the subprogram or type, but its implementation (its definition) should not be. They are also used with top-down functional decomposition in which a subprogram is written before those it calls.

In languages such as C and Ada that support separately compiled modules, the association between a declaration and the corresponding definition may be external to the compilation unit, so the linker must create it. An ANSI C function declaration (often called a "prototype") declares the name and argument types of the function to the compiler so that it can determine whether invocations in that module are syntactically correct. For example,

```
/* an ANSI C function declaration gives the function name and argument types */
/* min() is defined in another file to be linked with this one */
int min(int arrInt[], int size);
int main()

{
    const int NUM_SCORES = 5;
    int scores[] = { 70, 85, 75, 55, 90 };
    int worst;
    /* the compiler uses the function declaration to determine whether
       the invocation is syntactically correct */
    worst = min(scores, NUM_SCORES);
}
```

The declaration does not define the operation of the function, so the function definition (the body of the function) is expected to be given elsewhere, either later in the program or in a module linked to the resulting object code file. If a definition of that function name does not appear in the module or in a module linked to it, a linkage error results. The C programmer declares a variable name without defining it by using the extern reserved word, as follows:[9]

```
/* a declaration which is not a definition in C */
extern int arrSize;
```

Generally, a name may be declared more than once in the same scope (in the same way), but may not be redefined within a given scope (except when the language supports subprogram name overloading, as described in section 0.2.7).

The symbol table

The language translator maintains a data structure called the *symbol table*, which stores the attributes and bindings of the valid identifiers in the program. Initially, the symbol table contains entries for language-defined identifiers, such as the names of built-in types. A declaration enters the identifier into this table, together with information about the meaning of the referent. For example, the entry for an object name specifies its type and location, (say, a stack frame offset for a local vari-

---

[9] A function declaration in C is extern by default.

able). The form of this information depends on whether the referent is an object, subprogram, type, or constant.

In a compiled language, identifiers exist only during translation (except for symbols external to the compilation unit), and the symbol table is a compile-time structure (unless it is retained to provide symbolic debugging). In an interpreted language, it must be present at execution time.

Static and dynamic typing

In general, types may be associated with either identifiers or with the entities they are bound to. In *statically typed* languages, the declaration of each object, constant, or subprogram name gives a type, and this information is entered in the symbol table. The type of a subprogram is its *argument signature*, which consists of its parameter types and return type.[10] As we will see in section 0.3.6, the compiler for a strongly typed language can use this information to ensure that an object identifier only refers to objects of its type, and that the arguments of a subprogram invocation are of the correct type. Strong static typing provides safety and reliability because many typographical and logical errors are caught earlier in the process of coding, and the code is easier to understand. It also informs the compiler how much storage is required for the referent of an object identifier so that it can use static or automatic allocation. Fortran, Pascal, C, and Ada are statically typed languages.

In a *dynamically typed* language, identifier declarations (if any) do not specify a type. An identifier may refer to objects of different types during the execution of the program, and there are no invalid assignments. A variable cannot be said to "be" a real, but only to "refer to" a real at some point during execution, and the type of the object bound to an identifier can only be determined at run time. That is, we have *dynamic binding* of the type of an identifier, and identifiers are *polymorphic* because they can refer to objects of different types. In addition, binding of overloaded subprograms (see section 0.2.6) is also dynamic, which is essential for object-oriented languages. We will see that dynamically typed languages provide increased flexibility in programming, at the expense of efficiency. Lisp, APL, and Smalltalk are dynamically typed languages.

With dynamic typing, type information must be stored with each data object to determine whether an operation is meaningful, and to determine which operation to perform with overloading. In addition, it is not possible to associate a fixed size region of storage with an identifier because the size of its referent cannot be determined statically. In fact, the meaning of an assignment is quite different: an assignment binds the name on the left side to a different object (like an implicit pointer assignment), rather than copying the right side value into the storage bound to the identifier. Dynamically typed languages often provide built-in functions that the programmer can use to test the type of an object to ensure that the referent is an instance of the correct type, or to perform different operations for different types of

---

[10] The return type is not considered part of the argument signature in C++.

objects. For example, Lisp provides the "predicates" numberp, symbolp, atom, listp, and null. We will discuss dynamic typing in more detail in section 5.4.

Alias declarations

Many languages support *alias declarations* that introduce an alternate name for an existing entity. The Fortran EQUIVALENCE declaration and the Cobol REDE-FINES clause allow the programmer to use more than one name for the same region of storage, and were primarily provided to reuse storage because early machines had small memories. We can also obtain the effect of having two names that refer to the same storage by using a variant record in Pascal or a union in C. C++ includes the *reference type*, which declares an alternate name for an existing object. For example,

```
// A C++ reference
int num;
int& refNum = num;     // refNum is an alias for num
```

Any expressions that use the name refNum actually affect num. Such a declaration does not create an object or allocate storage, but enters the new name into the symbol table with the existing object as its referent. Many languages also allow the programmer to define aliases for types, for instance, the C typedef statement.

Generally the use of aliases for objects is questionable practice for several reasons. A hidden side effect can occur: A modification to the object through one identifier changes the referent of another name without mentioning it. Aliasing can break type safety when identifiers with different types alias the same storage, as occurs with Pascal variant records, C unions, and Fortran EQUIVALENCE specifications. In addition, aliasing can be confusing for the reader.

0.2.3 Scope

We often want to use the same name for different purposes in different parts of a program. For example, several subprograms may need a local variable called index. If all names are visible throughout the program (e.g., as in Basic or assembly language), then each subprogram could use a distinguishing prefix, such as avgIndex and sortIndex. However, this lengthens identifiers without adding any useful semantic information. Similarly, in a large system composed of code units written by several programmers, we would like each programmer to be able to choose his or her own variable names without being concerned with whether other programmers are using those names.

What we want is the ability to restrict the scope of a declaration so that there is no *name conflict* with other declarations of the same identifier. In a mathematics text, the author writes "let x be . . ." to declare an identifier to the reader, and the scope of the declaration is implied as the duration of a proof or an example. Unfortunately, compilers do not have the understanding of context necessary for such an approach, so programmers must specify scopes explicitly in the code.

A *scope* is a lexically delimited region of a program that specifies a name space in which a set of names is visible. The *scope of a declaration* is the portion of the source code in which occurrences of the declared identifier refer to the associated program entity. Scope allows us to use the same name to refer to different entities in different parts of a program, for example, in different subprograms. You must be aware of the rules by which identifiers are bound to data objects to write correct programs. An identifier has *global* scope if it is visible throughout the program. If the scope of an identifier declaration is restricted to some portion of the code, such as a local variable of a subprogram, we say that its scope is *local* to that section of the program.

0.2.4 Nested Scopes

Blocks and nested scopes

As we saw in section 0.1.1, Algol introduced the compound statement delimited by begin and end to permit nesting the sequence control structure within conditional and iterative structures. Any compound statement can also include declarations, in which case it is a *block*. Those declarations are visible throughout that block but not elsewhere, like the local variables of a subprogram. Like statements, blocks can be nested, which gives the name space of an Algol program a hierarchical structure.

A block introduces a new scope for its declarations, which is nested within the scope of the block in which it is defined. In a *block-structured language*, we can nest block scopes within other block scopes to an arbitrary level, and the names declared in enclosing blocks are visible in a block if the block does not redeclare them. That is, a block implicitly inherits access to the names declared in enclosing blocks. The body of a subprogram definition is also a statement in Algol, and can be a block that includes declarations, namely of parameter and local variable names. The name of the subprogram is declared in the enclosing scope.

Block structure allows us to organize the name space of the program, by restricting the declarations of a set of identifiers to the region of the code in which they are needed. For example, if several functions must access the same data structure, we can declare the structure in a block, and nest the subprograms that manipulate that data within that block. Nested name spaces also help reduce the amount of context the reader must remember. Nested subprogram definitions are supported in Algol and its descendants to support program design by *top-down functional decomposition*, also called *stepwise refinement*. A program is broken into main tasks, each of which is coded as a subprogram nested within the main program. If the task handled by a subprogram is large, it contains further subtasks and the corresponding subprograms are nested within it.

The symbol table must also reflect the hierarchical name structure of block-structured scope. Typically, the symbol table has a stack structure, in which the compiler pushes a subtable upon entering a block and pops it upon completing translation of the block. When the compiler searches for the binding of a name used in a statement, it examines the top subtable for the name, then the next sub-table, and so on.

All descendants of Algol, including Pascal, Modula-2, C, and Ada, are block-structured languages. However, the generality of Algol's block structure has been restricted in Pascal and C. In Pascal, declarations can only accompany a subprogram, but not an arbitrary compound statement. In C, function definitions cannot be nested, but any block within a function definition can contain local declarations (although C programmers rarely use this feature).

Identifier declarations and uses

The scope of an identifier declaration consists of the block or subprogram in which it is declared, and all contained blocks that do not include a redeclaration of that identifier. The declarations is not visible in enclosing scopes. An identifier declared in a block is *local* to that block, and is *relatively global* or *nonlocal* to all enclosed blocks that do not redeclare it. The declaration is *hidden* in those enclosed blocks that declare the name, that is, the entity it refers to is not accessible. All uses of a hidden name in an enclosed scope that redeclares the name (and all scopes nested within that scope that do not redefine the name) refer to the program entity corresponding to the enclosed scope declaration. Although the entity denoted by the outer scope declaration becomes inaccessible when the inner scope is entered, it continues to exist, and when the inner scope is exited, it becomes the referent of that identifier again. Two declarations of the same identifier always have disjoint scopes, and occurrences of that identifier in each scope refer to different entities. These rules apply to the parameter names and local variables of a subprogram as well.

A *use* of an identifier in an expression or statement (other than its declaration) must be within the scope of some declaration of that identifier. The process of *identifier resolution* determines which declaration of the identifier a use refers to. A use of an identifier is resolved to the declaration in the scope in which the use appears if there is one, or in the nearest enclosing scope that declares it. If no declaration of that name is encountered in any enclosing scope, the identifier use is an error. The declaration found by the search of enclosing scopes determines the entity denoted by that use of the identifier. In a statically typed language, it also specifies the referent's type, which the compiler uses to determine whether the use of the identifier is valid. The corresponding declaration is found first, and then the type is checked. The programmer cannot use the type demanded by the context in which the identifier occurs to indicate that the use refers to another, more global, declaration of that identifier.

To distinguish two different declarations of the same identifier or to access an identifier that is not visible, some languages name scopes and allow the programmer to use a *qualified name* that specifies both the scope name and the identifier name. A qualified name identifies the entity to which it is bound uniquely. In some languages, we can use a qualified name to refer to an identifier that is hidden by a declaration in an intervening scope, or to refer to a name declared in a scope that does not enclose the scope of the use. For example, qualified names take the form *scope.name* in Ada and *scope::name* in C++.

Lexical scope

A block that is not a subprogram definition can only be entered when control flows directly into it from the previous statement. When this occurs, its declarations become visible, and any declarations in the enclosing scope that are hidden in the block are no longer visible. Every time a statement is executed, the identifiers in it are bound statically according to the hierarchy of scopes defined in the source code.

For subprograms, the situation is more complex because the subprogram name is visible in any scope nested within its enclosing scope, and subprograms can be invoked by name. When a subprogram is called, nonlocal names in the subprogram could be bound either in the environment of the subprogram definition or in the environment of the invocation. We say that languages that use the former use or *static scope* also called *lexical scope* , because the structure of the source code determines the scope structure, and the bindings for nonlocal names are fixed for all invocations. Static scope is used in all block-structured languages. If identifiers are bound in the environment of the invocation, the language employs *dynamic scope*, which we will discuss later in this section.

The Pascal example in Figure 0.2 illustrates the rules of static scope (lines demarcate the scopes in the example). The interpretation of the diagram is that identifier resolution can see outward from a scope boundary, but not into a scope. Note that the scope boundaries cannot overlap, and two scopes are either disjoint or one encloses the other. Within the code for proc1, the identifiers i, c, x, proc2, and proc1 are visible. The first two are local to proc1, and the last three are relatively global to the block. Any use of i in proc1 refers to its parameter, not to the global variable, which is hidden. The procedure proc2 is defined in the same scope as proc1, but the compiler has not yet seen its definition when it is translating proc1's body. The forward declaration of proc2 allows proc1 to call proc2. (The parameter k in the forward declaration is a place holder and does not actually declare a name.) Within the code for proc2, the identifiers k, y, x, proc2a, i, proc1, and proc2 are visible. Any use of x in proc2 refers to its local variable, and an occurrence of i in proc2 refers to the global program variable. Within the code for proc2a, the same identifiers are visible but a use of k refers to proc2a's local variable, and a use of x refers to the local variable of proc2. Note that if proc2a uses the name x in a context in which a real is required, such as an assignment k := x, it is an error because the x in proc2 is boolean rather than a reference to the global x defined in nestedScopes. Within the code for nestedScopes, the identifiers x, i, proc1, and proc2 are visible, and that code cannot access any of the local variables or parameters nor invoke the procedure proc2a. The same scope rules illustrated here also apply to the identifiers in any const or type definitions in the program or its subprograms. Note that an invocation of proc1 within the body of proc2a

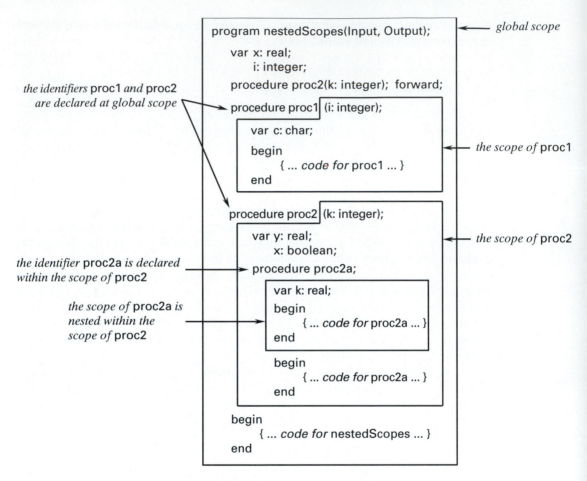

the identifiers proc1 and proc2
are declared at global scope

the identifier proc2a is declared
within the scope of proc2

the scope of proc2a is
nested within the
scope of proc2

Figure 0.2: Illustration of block-structured scope.

invokes a scope that does not enclose the scope of the call. With static scope, any occurrence of x in the code for proc1 is bound to the global declaration of x, not to the declaration in proc2a.

Implementation of block structure

Each variable local to a block only needs to exist for the duration of that block's execution. The compiler can implement block structure by using an activation record on the run-time stack for each block, and allocating the block's local variables in its activation record. When a block is entered, an activation record containing the objects defined in the block is pushed on the run-time stack, and that activation record is popped when the block is exited. The compiler translates a use of a local variable as an offset in the block's stack frame. This technique provides efficient use of storage since an object is only allocated for as long as necessary, which is especially useful for large objects. Memory is automatically shared among objects, rather than explicitly specified as with Fortran's EQUIVALENCE statement. In fact, objects that are stored in the same location can never be accessed in the same context with this implementation. Most machines now have hardware support for the stack manipulations necessary for block-structured allocation.

To provide access to variables defined in enclosing scopes, a block's stack frame includes a *static link* that points to the activation record of the block's enclosing scope. (Recall that the dynamic link points to the activation record of the caller.) The compiler can translate a use of a nonlocal variable as following a chain of static links to the correct activation record, and then using the variable's offset within that record. The number of static links traversed is the number of levels of nesting between the scope of the identifier use and the scope of the corresponding declaration, which is called the *static distance*. (For example, when the identifier i is used in procedure proc2a in Figure 0.2, two static links must be traversed to access the referent object in the activation record of nestedScopes.) The address of a variable with block-structured scope has two components, the static distance and the offset in the stack frame.

For a block that is not a subprogram, the static link always points to the stack frame directly below it on the stack (the top of the stack when the block is entered), and is the same as the dynamic link. However, a subprogram can be invoked in a scope nested within that in which its name is defined. For example, in the Pascal program in Figure 0.2, proc1 can be invoked in proc2 and proc2a, as well as in nestedScopes, the scope in which it is defined. When a subprogram is invoked in a scope other than the one that defines it, its static link does not point to the stack frame directly below its stack frame, and its static and dynamic links differ. Figure 0.3 illustrates the structure of the run-time stack when procedure proc1 is invoked within proc2 and within proc2a in the program in Figure 0.3.[11]

The remaining issue is what code the compiler should insert into the object module to set the static link when a subprogram is called. If proc1 is called within nestedScopes, i.e. in the same context that declares its name, the static link and the dynamic link of its activation record are the same. If proc1 is called within proc2, the static link for the activation record of proc1 can be found by following the static link of its caller. (The same would be true for an invocation of proc2 within proc1.) If proc1 is called within proc2a, the static link for proc1 can be found by following two static links beginning with that of the caller. In general, the static link can be correctly initialized by tracing n static links beginning with that of the caller, where n is the number of levels of scope between the definition of the subprogram name and the invocation, i.e. the static distance. Although the static distance is fixed at compile time, the traversal must be done at execution time. For example, there could have been several activation records between the calls of proc2 and proc1, or of proc2 and proc2a in Figure 0.3.

To see that we must use the static rather than dynamic links to access nonlocals, consider three procedures proc1, proc2, and proc3, each directly nested within

[11] We have shown the static and dynamic link at the bottom of the stack frame to make drawing the pointers easier. In fact, the links are typically at the top of the activation records so that they are located at a fixed offset into the record.

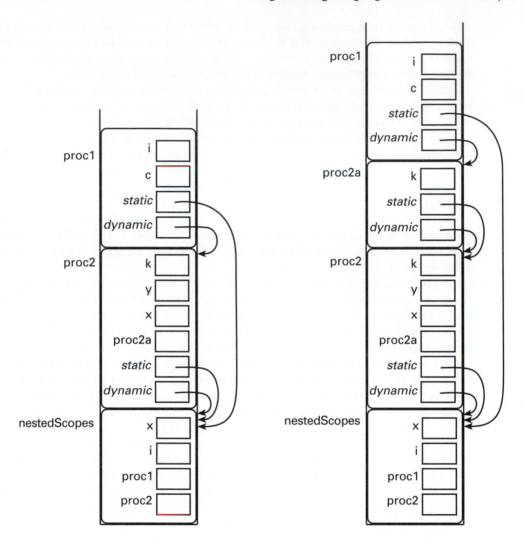

nestedScopes **calls** proc2 **which calls** proc1   nestedScopes **calls** proc2 **which calls** proc2a
which calls proc1

Figure 03: Implementation of block structure: static and dynamic links

a main program main. Suppose that main calls proc1 which calls proc2 which calls proc3. (Draw the stack if necessary.) The static and dynamic links for the activation record of proc1 are the same. The static link for proc2 is installed by following two links, one to the stack frame for proc1 and then its static link to main. The static link for proc3 is also installed by following two links, one to the stack frame for proc2 and then its static link to main, not its dynamic link to proc1. Note also that there must be an activation record on the stack for any enclosing scope of the new activation record. This will be true because a subprogram name is only visible in the scope in which it is defined, so that scope (and its enclosing scopes) will have been invoked.

Now consider the case in which the main program calls a recursive subprogram recProc, which then calls a subprogram proc whose definition is nested within it. When proc is called, there might be several stack frames containing bindings for recProc's local variables, but proc's static link can only point to one of them. In this case, the most recent bindings for any of recProc's variables occurring in proc should be used, so proc's static link should point to the most recent activation record of recProc. This is the behavior of the algorithm we have described.

Dynamic scope

With static scope, the referent of a nonlocal identifier depends on the nesting of scopes in the source code and is always the same. With *dynamic scope*, the scope of a subprogram is nested within the scope of the invocation, so the enclosing scope may differ among the activations of the subprogram. A use of a nonlocal identifier is resolved to the declaration of that identifier in the most recently invoked active subprogram or block containing a declaration of that identifier. That is, identifier resolution follows the dynamic links in the activation records (and the static links are no longer needed).

For example, if dynamic scope were used with the nestedScopes program in Figure 0.2, the scope of the procedure proc1 could be nested within the scopes of nestedScopes, proc2, or proc2a, depending on the location of the invocation. Static scope always chooses the scope of definition, nestedScopes. With dynamic scope, if proc1 is called from proc2 or proc2a as in the diagrams in Figure 0.3, uses of x in proc1's code refer to the definition of x in proc2, rather than that in nestedScopes. In this example, this would cause an error because the type of x in proc2 is different than that in nestedScopes, and Pascal is a statically typed language. Note that the offset used to access the referent of the nonlocal identifier within the activation record may also differ, depending on the sequence of invocations. For these reasons, the languages that have used dynamic scope are dynamically typed and are interpreted, so that the symbol table is available for determining the offset. (The alternative is to store variable names in the activation records.) Languages that use dynamic scope include Lisp, APL, and Snobol.

With dynamic scope, the referent of a nonlocal variable depends on the sequence of calls that lead to the invocation of the block in which the identifier occurs. The region of code in which a declaration applies depends on which subprograms are called by the subprogram in which it appears (and which subprograms they call, and so on). Since an invocation can appear in a conditional, the compiler cannot determine the scope of a declaration, nor can an examination of the source code. Similarly, a use of a nonlocal identifier can refer to different entities in different invocations of the subprogram. For example, an assignment statement may not always change the same variable, or an invocation may call different subprograms with the same name. These characteristics allow some flexibility because the programmer can use nonlocal variables like parameters, for example, to pass a comparison function to a sort subprogram implicitly.

However, dynamic scope has major problems, especially for program reliability. With static scope, a name always refers to the same entity, so the reader does not have to understand the dynamic behavior of the program to interpret the use of identifiers in the program. With dynamic scope, the result of modifying a nonlocal variable or calling a nonlocal subprogram is not predictable. The local names in a subprogram are not really local because they are visible to any subprogram it calls, and those they call, and so on. The programmer has no control over what a nonlocal refers to because it can be "intercepted" by another subprogram in the sequence of invocations that declares that name. Since compile-time type checking is not possible, many typographic errors are not caught. All subprograms in the system are tightly coupled because they can interact in ways that are not defined by their interfaces. For these reasons, no contemporary languages are dynamically scoped. In fact, although Lisp has always used dynamic scope, Common Lisp provides a function definition form that specifies static scope. As we described in section 0.1.3, dynamic scope does provide the correct semantics for locating exception handlers.

0.2.5 Programmer-Defined Visibility

Problems with use of nonlocal identifiers

With block-structured scope, a subprogram can access any identifier relatively global to it that is not hidden, for example, a subprogram can modify the value of a nonlocal variable. Any such interaction between the subprogram and its context that does not occur through its parameter list is called a *side effect*, because it is not visible in the subprogram call. Code with side effects is very difficult to understand. Side effects also present a problem for maintenance, such as when a programmer needs to determine all uses of the nonlocal variable. Side effects do not occur when the subprogram manipulates nonlocal variables that are passed as arguments.

Direct use of a nonlocal identifier within a subprogram prevents using the subprogram outside the context in which the subprogram was originally written, so it is not a self-contained unit. In some other context, a nonlocal identifier of that name might or might not exist, and might or might not have the same type and meaning as in the context in which the subprogram is defined. The subprogram is tightly coupled to the nonlocal identifier, and cannot be used independently of it. Of course, this is not an issue if the subprogram performs a subtask specific to the subprogram in which it is nested.

There are other problems associated with the direct use of nonlocal variables in subprograms. If a nonlocal variable accessed by a subprogram is also passed to it by reference, there are two names for the same object within the subprogram code. The object can be modified either directly or through the parameter, and changes through one name affect the referent of the other. When the programmer makes an identifier nonlocal to provide access by several subprograms, he or she cannot hide it from other subprograms at that level of nesting. If a nonlocal name is accessed in a deeply nested program, it is possible that reorganizing the program or introducing additional identifiers in intervening scopes will cause the use of the nonlocal to refer to a different entity than that intended. There is also a chance that a typing error will accidentally match a name defined in an enclosing scope. All of these situations are problems for reading, debugging, and testing the code.

Limitations of hierarchical scope

The hierarchical scope structure rules provide a mechanism for separating name spaces that should be disjoint and for sharing names. However, they are a hindrance when we need to control shared access to individual identifiers and their referents explicitly on a name-by-name or scope-by-scope basis. The only way to share access to an identifier is to declare it global to the scopes in which it must be visible. However, this causes it to be accessible within other scopes at the same level of nesting. For example, the subprograms that search for, insert, and delete elements in a table must be nested within the scope in which the table is declared so that they can access it. (Even if the table is passed as a parameter, both the table and the subprogram names must be visible in the scope of a caller.) However, the subprograms that use the table must be defined in the same scope so that they can call those subprograms, and therefore they can access the table data structure directly (which they might do for efficiency). These subprograms might not manipulate the structure consistently with its semantics, and even if they do, modifying the structure of the table might break them.

The problem is more severe in large programs that define several data structures, each intended to be accessible to a particular set of subprograms. For example, suppose table1 is used by subprograms proc1 and proc2, table2 is used by subprograms proc1, proc3, and proc4, and table3 is used by subprograms proc3, proc5, and proc6. To provide each subprogram with exactly the access it needs via static scope nesting, a nonhierarchical scope structure is necessary, as illustrated in Figure 0.4.

With hierarchical scope structure, it is not possible for scopes to overlap in this way. Two scopes either are disjoint or one wholly encloses the other. To implement the access necessary for this example in a block-structured language, we must declare table2 in a scope visible to both proc1 and proc3, table1 must be visible to proc1, and table3 must be visible to proc3, so all three tables will be visible to all six subprograms.

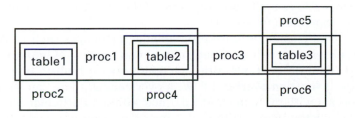

Figure 0.4: Three tables accessed by six subprograms

Exporting, importing, and hiding names

Instead of the implicit hierarchical sharing defined for block-structured scope, we would like a mechanism that allows the designer of a program unit to specify what names are visible within that unit. That unit will define some of these identifiers, and others will be defined in other units and only declared in the unit. The programmer should also be able to specify that some names are not visible outside the unit by dividing the name space into an *interface* visible to users of the unit, and an *implementation* which is private to the unit. This allows the designer to decouple the logical use of the unit from the physical implementation of that functionality.

The *module* construct supports division of a program unit into an interface and implementation. A module consists of a set of subprograms, objects, types, and constants with a single logical purpose. The designer of the module specifies which names the module *exports* to the rest of the program. A module may *import* identifiers exported by other modules with a forward declaration. In this way, all name visibility is explicit, and access to an entity through its name occurs only through mutual consent of both the designer exporting the name and the module importing the name. To support this feature, it must be possible to decouple the declaration of a name from the creation of the referent (i.e., to code a forward declaration), so that modules can import the name of an entity defined elsewhere.

This export/import relationship for name sharing involves disjoint scopes, rather than accessing names in a textually enclosing scope. An exported name can be made visible in exactly the modules necessary (rather than in all units at a given level of nesting), and a module can import the interfaces of more than one module (rather than importing access to all the names in a single enclosing scope). If all names are explicitly declared in this fashion, the problems that otherwise can occur when using nonlocal names—hidden side effects, unintended access, and name capture—cannot occur. We will discuss modules, their use in software design, and the associated programming language features in detail in section 1.1.3.

0.2.6 Overloading

In most languages, operators such as + and < are *overloaded* for built-in types, which means that the same operator symbol refers to different operations for different types of operands. For example, the + operator can mean either integer or floating point addition. (It can also denote set union in Pascal and string concatenation in Basic.) The compiler uses the types of the operands in an expression to determine which operation to perform.

Many contemporary programming languages such as Ada and C++ allow the programmer to overload subprogram names. (Operators are just a syntactic variant of functions, although operators for built-in types do not involve the same invocation overhead.) With overloading, there can be more than one subprogram with the same name defined within a particular scope. In this way, we do not have to use different names for the same conceptual operation, for example, insertLinkedList and insertHashTable (to say nothing of insertListOfIn-

tegers, insertListOfStrings, etc.). Ada and C++ also support operator overloading, which allows the programmer to use the standard expression syntax for
programmer-defined types. For example, we can code definitions for

- equality and inequality tests for any types
- arithmetic operators for complex numbers
- <, <=, > and >= for strings and dates
- [ ] (indexed access) for linked lists

Identifiers that refer to data objects cannot be overloaded.

Since more than one definition of the subprogram name or operator is visible
in the scope in which the overloadings are defined, there must be a way of determining which definition to invoke. Each overloading of a particular subprogram
name or operator must have a different argument signature. In translating an invocation of overloaded subprogram or operator name, the compiler chooses a subprogram to invoke by matching the argument signature of the call with those of the
subprogram definitions for that name. If there is no definition with the argument
signature of the invocation, it is an error. For example, in C++, we can define several print() functions, each for a different type of object:

```
/* example of function overloading in C++ */
/* each of the following functions are declared here and are defined elsewhere */
void print(Date);
void print(int arrInt[], int size);
void print(Employee);

int main()
{
    Date birthday;
    const int NUM_SCORES = 30;
    int scores[NUM_SCORES];
    Graph routes;
    /* ... other operations ... */
    /* the compiler determines which function to call by the argument type(s) */
    print(birthday);                      /* print(Date) invoked */
    print(scores, NUM_SCORES);            /* print(int[], int) invoked */
    print(routes);                        /* error: print(Graph) not declared */
}
```

Implicit conversions of arguments complicates resolution of overloaded subprogram invocations, and can result in ambiguity. For example, if we have two
overloadings func(long) and func(double) in C++, the invocation func('c') is ambiguous because a char can be converted to either a long or a double. That invocation,
not the existence of the two overloadings, causes a compiler error. The programmer can resolve the ambiguous call by explicitly converting the argument to the

desired parameter type, in this case func((long) 'c'). We will discuss this issue further in section 9.2.5.

Languages with dynamic typing can also support subprogram and operator overloading. The programmer specifies the parameter types for each definition, and the type information in the argument objects is used to select the subprogram to invoke at run time. That is, overloaded subprogram invocations are dynamically bound. We will see in Chapter 2 that this is an essential aspect of object-oriented programming languages.

0.3 DATA STRUCTURE

0.3.1 Data Objects

Purpose and definition

A *data object* maintains a package of information that the application must represent. Generally, we use an object to model an entity or relationship in the problem domain. Examples include the dimensions and weight of a package, the information associated with a transaction, and the description of a design component. We also use data objects to represent components of the computer system or the application itself, such as files, input/output devices, network connections, and user interaction components. The object is an abstraction that represents the relevant properties of an entity, but is not that entity.

We can also distinguish between the abstract "program object" and the "storage object" that implements it. The program object is a collection of values defined by the language, which is accessible via an identifier. The language also defines the valid operations for the program object. At the lowest physical level, an object consists of a region of storage and a collection of values encoded in that region. Typically, the storage allocated to an object is a contiguous collection of memory units (bits, bytes, words, etc.) defined by a starting location and a size. Storage objects can be adjacent in memory, so indexing beyond the region allocated to an object will access another object, while program objects are semantically independent (unless they are components of a composite object such as an array). Languages that support abstract data types provide facilities that allow the programmer to treat a data structure that consists of a discontinuous group of regions, such as a linked list, as a single program object.

It is also instructive to draw a distinction between "pure values" as used in mathematics, and the objects used in programming [Mac82]. A value such as the number 2 is a timeless abstraction that cannot be modified. Functional programming languages deal with expressions whose evaluation results in values, rather than commands that modify storage locations. In contrast, since an object is a data structure that represents a problem domain entity, it can be modified as a program execution that models the problem domain proceeds. That is, an object has a state that can change over time. Unlike values, objects can be created and destroyed, and can be shared so that changes to an object through one reference modify the object state accessible through another reference.

Each data object is an *instance* of a data type, which may be a built-in or programmer-defined type. The type of an object defines the valid values for that object and the encoding of those values, that is, the meaning of the stored data. The data type also specifies the set of operations that a program can perform on the object.

Variables

A *variable* is an association between a name and a data object that consists of a value stored at some location. (In fact, programmers use the term "variable" to refer to the object, its value, or its location items.) Figure 0.5 diagrams this relationship.

Usually, when we use a variable name as an operator operand or as the argument of a subprogram call, we are referring to its value. However, to modify an object (e.g., to assign a new value to a variable), we must have a reference to the object, which is the location for a storage object. Whether an identifier use refers to the object's location or its value depends implicitly on the context of its appearance. In an assignment, evaluation of the right-hand expression must result in a value, and identifiers within that expression refer to their values. The resulting value is copied into the location bound to the identifier on the left-hand side (i.e.,the identifier on the left-hand side refers to a location). We refer to the location and value of the data object to which an identifier is bound as the identifier's *l-value* and *r-value*, respectively (the *l* and *r* standing for "left" and "right", reflecting use of the identifier on the left or right side of an assignment).

There are other contexts in which an identifier or expression can refer to either a reference to an object or the object's value. When we invoke a subprogram, it receives the argument's *r*-value for parameters that are passed by value, and its *l*-value for parameters passed by reference. In addition, three kinds of expressions can be either *l*-values or *r*-values, namely

- an array subscription expression (e.g., array[index])
- a record component selection expression (e.g., record.field)
- a pointer dereference expression (e.g., pointer^ in Pascal or *pointer in C)

These expressions are *l*-values when we use them on the left side of an assignment or as arguments corresponding to reference parameters, or *r*-values elsewhere. The reader must take into account the context when considering an identifier or

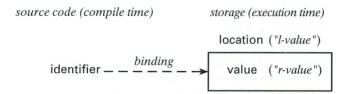

Figure 0.5: The components of a variable.

expression (in contrast to functional languages, in which an expression always denotes a value).

Constants

We often need to use a particular value in a program, for example, π or the number of months in the year. We can improve the readability of the program by using a symbolic name rather than the literal value— numMonths is more descriptive than 12. Named constants are also useful when we need to change the value of the constant during development. For example, a constant value that gives the size of several arrays might be used for the array declarations and for the limits of counter-controlled loops over the arrays. With a named constant, we only need to change the initialization in the constant declaration, rather than finding and changing each use of that value.

The programmer could assign the value to a variable, then use the variable in expressions and statements. However, a constant has different semantics than a variable, because a constant cannot be modified by an assignment or data transfer. If a language supports named constants, the programmer can use the symbolic name and the compiler will ensure that the identifier's *l*-value cannot be used.

To support named constants, Pascal includes *symbolic constants*, which declare a named constant with a value given by a literal. The type of a const definition type must be discrete (i.e., integer, enumeration, character, or boolean), for example,

```
{ Pascal symbolic constants }
const
   numScores = 20;
   fileDelimiter = '/';
```

The type of the literal value gives the type of the constant. The restriction that the value cannot be an expression is inconvenient when the value of one constant depends on that of another. In Fortran 77 and Modula-2, the value of a symbolic constant can be an expression using previously-defined constants. The compiler evaluates the expression and stores its value in the symbol table. The compiler can often avoid allocating storage for a symbolic constant by using an "immediate" or "direct" addressing mode for operations that use the identifier.

In pre-ANSI C, the programmer uses a *preprocessor macro* to specify a constant, for example,

```
/* specifying a constant with a preprocessor macro in C */
#define NUM_MONTHS 12
```

The preprocessor substitutes the text that is the "value" of the macro name directly for the constant name before compilation. When the macro value is an expression, this has three disadvantages: The expression must be fully parenthesized, it is evaluated each time the macro is used, and any names in the expression are bound in the environment of the use (see section 9.1.5). In addition, like Pascal symbolic constants, we cannot use a C macro for a constant array or structure object.

   Read-only variables provide somewhat different semantics for constants, and are supported by Ada and C++ (and have been incorporated into ANSI C). A variable of any type can be declared as a constant, which indicates that it cannot be modified after initialization. Clearly, the constant definition must also specify an initial value, which may be any expression of the correct type. For example (assuming that we have defined a structure Point with two members for the x and y coordinates, as in section 0.3.3),

```
/* read-only variables in ANSI C */
const int NUM_MONTHS = 12;
const struct Point origin = { 0, 0 };
```

A read-only variable can also be a local variable of a subprogram that is initialized differently each time the subprogram is called, for example, using argument values (see section 9.1.5). In this case, the value of the object is dynamically bound, and the compiler must allocate space for that object and evaluate the initialization expression for each call. If the compiler can determine that a particular read-only variable's value is static, it can use immediate addressing modes and avoid allocation, as described for symbolic constants.

   In C++ and ANSI C, we can also specify a function parameter as const, which indicates that the function does not modify that argument and the caller can pass a constant object. This is particularly useful with C++, which supports pass by reference. We can declare a parameter as a const reference to avoid copying the argument and to indicate that the function does not modify the argument, which allows the caller to pass a constant object.

The lifetime of an object

   We specify creation of a new object by a variable definition or by an explicit storage allocation operation, such as new in Pascal. Creation of an object *instantiates* the given data type, and causes unused storage for that object to be located and *allocated* to it. The object's type determines the amount of storage required, and allocation can be managed by the compiler, by a run-time system, or by both. (In the next section, we will discuss storage allocation policies for data objects.) An object is destroyed or *deallocated* when storage is no longer assigned to the object. It is a semantic error to access an object after it has been deallocated. The result of this error is unpredictable because that storage might already be allocated to another object.

   We refer to the duration of program execution during which an object exists as its *lifetime*. To use programming languages effectively, we must be clear on the distinction between the lifetime of an object at run time and the scope of an identifier in the source code. Clearly, an object must exist during execution of any code that includes an identifier bound to it. On the other hand, an object may exist when it is inaccessible to the subprogram executing. For example, a local variable name becomes invisible when that subprogram invokes another, or can be hidden when an enclosed scope is entered. With pass by reference, the period of time that the parameter name is associated with the argument object is shorter than the object's existence. Pass by reference also causes an object to be referred to by two different names with different scopes. Dynamic objects can outlive pointers that refer to them. Our discussion of static local variables (e.g., in C) in the next section, will also illustrate the distinction between scope and lifetime.

Initialization and assignment

Initialization of an object stores a meaningful value for its type in the region of storage allocated for the object immediately after it is created. Allocation of storage for an object and initialization of the value encoded in that region are separate operations, and are often specified by different language constructs. When storage is allocated for an object, that storage initially contains some arbitrary string of bits, often referred to as "garbage". Any operations performed using this undefined value will return invalid results, which is a frequent cause of programming errors that are difficult to debug. In general, the translator cannot detect this error.

Pascal does not support initialization. A var definition specifies the allocation of an object, but a value can only be placed in the object's storage by an assignment or input statement. Many languages, such as Fortran, C, Modula-2, and Ada, provide syntax for specifying an initial value for an object when defining it. For example,

```
/* an object definition with initialization in C */
int num = 1;
```

This statement declares an identifier num with type int, defines an object (since extern is not specified), and initializes that storage with the value 1. C also permits initializing static and automatic arrays and structures by enclosing a list of values in braces, as illustrated in section 0.3.5. In addition, all static variables in C are initialized to 0 by default. Support for initialization adds reliability to the language because there is less chance of forgetting the initialization, or of using the variable before it is initialized. It also makes it easier to find the initial value of the variable. In C++, all objects must be initialized when they are defined (except instances of C built-in types).

In procedural languages, we can use the same variable to store different values at various times during execution. An *assignment* replaces the current value of a variable by a new value, losing the old value.[12] The meaning of the variable has now changed, either because the entity it represents has changed, or because the variable represents a different entity. Assignment is a unique operation because it requires an *l*-value and modifies an existing object, and is a statement in most lan-

---

[12] We will see in section 1.1.5 that the distinction between initialization and assignment is important when defining the operations for abstract data types that are implemented by complex data structures.

guages.   In fact, we can view a program in a procedural language as a series of assignments and control statements that direct the flow of execution among them. Contemporary functional languages do not use assignments: When a value is computed, it is passed as an argument rather than stored in a variable.

In some languages such as C, assignment is an expression rather than a statement. This allows cascading assignments (e.g., i = j = k = 1 in C), and embedding assignments within other expressions. C also includes assignments such as the += and ++ operators that require both the *l*-value and the *r*-value of the target object.

0.3.2 Storage Allocation Policies

Memory management

Modern programming languages provide three storage allocation policies—static, automatic, and dynamic. Each policy has its own purpose, and each defines the lifetime of objects allocated using that policy. With static allocation, an object occupies the same location for the duration of program execution. With automatic and dynamic allocation, storage for the object is allocated and deallocated at execution time, so the language must provide *memory management.* The memory management process assigns storage to objects, attempting to be as efficient as possible, while ensuring that only objects with disjoint lifetimes use the same storage locations. The compiler can implement management of automatic objects, but allocation and deallocation of dynamic objects must be performed by a run-time system. As we will see, managing dynamic memory is a complex task.

The storage allocated to a program execution typically is addressed contiguously, and has a format similar to that diagrammed in Figure 0.6. Static storage is fixed in size for the duration of program execution. In the layout illustrated in Figure 0.6, the

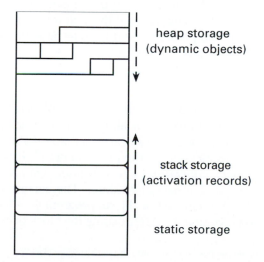

Figure 0.6: A typical storage layout

stack grows "upward" as functions are called and "downward" as they exit, and the heap grows "downward" as objects are allocated dynamically.

Static allocation

With *static allocation*, an object is allocated when the program is loaded and execution begins, and remains allocated until the program ceases execution. The lifetime of a static object is the entire execution of the program. The object is static in the sense that it always has the same address (or virtual address).

All objects in Fortran, Cobol, and Basic are statically allocated, and there are the same number of objects as identifiers. This simplifies compilation because there is a one-to-one correspondence between qualified names and objects, addresses are fixed, and no run-time allocation and deallocation overhead is necessary. However, it does not use storage efficiently because storage is allocated for objects whose lifetimes have ended (such as local variables of subprograms that are not active). As we stated in section 0.1.2, static allocation of local variables also does not permit recursion. Main program variables in Pascal and file scope variables in C are statically allocated. This is necessary because the lifetime of those objects is the entire execution of the program.

Some languages support local variables that maintain their values across executions of the subprogram or block, for example, static local variables in C or own variables in Algol. The compiler must allocate the referent of such a variable statically because it cannot know when the subprogram might be invoked. This construct provides an object whose lifetime (the entire execution of the program), differs from the visibility of the identifier bound to it (executions of the subprogram or block). For example, the C standard library function strtok() divides a string into tokens upon successive calls. The first argument to strtok() is a pointer to the string to tokenize, and if it is NULL, the function returns the next token in the string passed to it by the previous call. To do so, it keeps a static local pointer into that string which indicates the end of the last token it found, so that it can proceed from that point when the first argument is NULL. The name of this pointer is not visible elsewhere in the program. In Pascal, the pointer would have to be a global so that it continues to exist after the function exits.

Automatic stack allocation

As we discussed in sections 0.1.2 and 0.2.4, storage for the objects bound to the local variables and arguments of a subprogram is allocated in its stack frame. We refer to this as *automatic allocation* because the storage is allocated and deallocated automatically, without explicit specification by the programmer.[13] It is also sometimes referred to as *dynamic stack allocation* or *semidynamic allocation* because memory is allocated and deallocated at execution time. The corresponding data objects do not exist until the block is entered or the subprogram is called, and continue to exist until its execution is complete. After exiting the block or subprogram,

---

[13] This specification can be made explicit in C by using the auto storage class.

that physical storage may be used for other purposes. Automatic objects have nested lifetimes: An automatic object that is created after another automatic object is always destroyed before that object.

The compiler translates an access of a local variable as an offset into its stack frame. Accessing a nonlocal in a block-structured language follows a chain of static links, and then uses the variable's offset. Stack allocation of local variables is simple to implement (the compiler generates code that adds the total amount of automatic storage for the subprogram to the stack pointer upon entering the subprogram), and is usually supported by the processor hardware. It provides efficient use of the storage available because storage is only allocated for those data objects that need to exist at any point during execution. It also permits recursion because each invocation of a recursive subprogram has its own stack frame containing the values of the local variables for that invocation.

Dynamic heap allocation

Contemporary programming languages support *dynamic allocation* of objects under the direct control of the programmer. This is useful when the need for an object depends on execution-time conditions, or when an object must outlive the subprogram invocation that creates it. By dynamically allocating records that contain pointer fields, we can construct dynamically varying data structures such as linked lists, trees, and graphs.

A language that supports dynamic allocation includes an operation that allocates a new object and sets a pointer argument or return value to refer to it (e.g., the new procedure in Pascal). The type, and therefore the size, of the object is determined by the type of the pointer. The new object does not have a name of its own and can only be referenced through a pointer. The malloc() function in C takes the size of the object as an argument[14] and allocates the indicated amount of storage (rather than an object). It returns a pointer to the new region of storage, which can then be cast to the correct type and assigned to a pointer variable. Since the argument specifies only the size, the programmer can use malloc() to allocate an array dynamically by multiplying the sizeof a type by the number of objects desired. (In Pascal and Ada, we use a pointer to an array type for this purpose.) In Ada and C++, we can give an initialization for the object in the dynamic allocation operation. For example,

```
-- initializing a dynamically allocated object in Ada
type Integer_Ref is access Integer;      -- a type for pointers to dynamic integers
Int_Ptr: Integer_Ref := null;            -- a pointer definition and initialization
Int_Ptr := new Integer'(1);              -- create and initialize a dynamic integer
```

With this capability, the programmer can create an object at any time, not just at subprogram or block entry. The storage requirements of a subprogram cannot be determined at compile time because a data object created during an invocation

---

[14] The sizeof operator returns the size of a type or object.

can persist when that block of code is exited. For these reasons, dynamic allocation requires a storage management facility separate from the run-time stack. We refer to this storage as the *heap* or the *free store*, and it is administered by a run-time system included with the language system that cooperates with the operating system, which has the ultimate responsibility for storage allocation.

Initially, the heap is an empty region of storage and objects can be allocated contiguously. However, as objects are deallocated, the heap will contain empty regions of various sizes scattered throughout its area of storage, usable for other allocations. This situation is referred to as *fragmentation*. To provide efficient use of storage, the run-time memory management system must keep track of these free regions, coalesce adjacent free regions, and implement algorithms for choosing a free region for a new allocation (when possible). (Usually, it is not possible to relocate live objects because pointer variables in the program contain their addresses.) The efficiency of this system can have a large effect on the execution time and space requirements of programs that use such a language system.

Management of the free store is a complex task involving many tradeoffs because objects of any size can be allocated or deallocated at any time. Typically, the list of free regions is maintained as a doubly-linked list ordered by address to facilitate coalescing adjacent regions. There are three basic policies for selecting a region from which to allocate a new object. With *first fit*, the first free region that is large enough is selected, which requires less searching. Often, the system uses a "roving pointer" into the free list so that the "leftover" free regions are not concentrated in one part of the free store. *Best fit* selects the free region closest to the object's size, leaving the least extra space. With *worst fit*, the largest free region is selected, which leaves behind the largest possible free region, making it easier to use. Most systems have a minimum size allocation to reduce fragmentation (say, enough space for the two pointers and a size field). Another technique is to use separate free lists for each size of allocation necessary, or for commonly needed sizes. This is more efficient because the free regions can be treated equally, and all insertions and deletions in a particular free list can be done by pointer assignments at the front of the linked list with no search overhead.

Deallocation of dynamic storage

Deallocation of dynamically allocated objects when they are no longer needed can be handled either explicitly by the programmer or implicitly by the language's run-time storage management system. Many languages use *programmer-controlled deallocation* because the programmer is (presumably) in the best position to know when an object is no longer needed. This policy results in more efficient execution because it avoids the execution-time overhead necessary for the system to determine when an object can no longer be referenced. The language defines a deallocation operation that takes a pointer argument and returns the storage allocated to the object referenced by the pointer to the heap. Examples include dispose in Pascal and the free() function in C. Note that there will still be at least one pointer whose value refers to the deallocated region, namely the argument of the deallocation operation.

With explicit deallocation, the programmer must keep track of all dynamic objects and references to those objects. Three types of errors can occur with programmer-controlled deallocation, which are notoriously difficult to recognize and debug. A programmer may forget to release storage before reassigning or destroying the last pointer that refers to it, causing the region to be unusable. This situation is often referred to as a *memory leak* because some storage capacity has effectively "leaked away". If this occurs often enough (e.g., in an input loop), an allocation operation may fail because the free store is empty. Another error is to refer to previously released storage through a *dangling pointer* that still contains the address of the region, (e.g., the pointer used in the deallocation operation). This is especially an issue in an application in which there can be several pointers to the same object. At some point later in the program, another object may be allocated in that region, possibly of another type. An operation through the dangling pointer will be performed on the new object's representation using the implementation for the pointer's type. [15] A third error is to release the same storage more than once, that is, in different subprograms. This will corrupt the data structures that keep track of the free regions in the heap. In all three cases, the effects of the error occur some time after the actual error has happened. In addition, the symptoms exhibited by the program will not be directly related to the cause of the problem, and may not be repeatable.

To avoid these problems, many languages include a run-time facility that reclaims unreferenceable storage without programmer intervention. Languages that support *automatic storage reclamation* include Lisp, Ada, Smalltalk, and Java. [16] The storage management system can deallocate an object when there are no pointers referring to it. One simple technique is *reference counting*, in which each dynamic object contains a field hidden to the programmer that indicates the number of pointers that refer to it. These fields are updated whenever a pointer is initialized, assigned, or destroyed. When the reference count for an object is zero, it is returned to the free store. If the deallocated object also contains pointers, the reference counts for their referents are decremented, which may cause deallocation of those objects, and so on.

The disadvantages of reference counting are the additional overhead for pointer operations and the fact that it cannot detect when to deallocate a cyclically linked structure. A technique that can also handle cyclic structures is *garbage collection*. When very little free storage remains or when the application is inactive,

---

[15] In fact, the Pascal language definition states that all pointers that refer to an object should be set to nil when the object is deallocated with dispose to prevent dangling pointers. However, no language systems keep track of all pointers to each object so that they can do this.

[16] Ada does not actually require language systems to provide automatic storage reclamation, and some do not. If there is none, the programmer must use the "generic procedure" Unchecked_Deallocation to deallocate a dynamic object.

the application is suspended and the garbage collection process marks all dynamically allocated regions that the program can access. It does so by performing a search that traces all linked structures beginning with live pointers in the program, marking each region it encounters. It then examines the entire heap area and returns any unmarked regions to the free store. Finally, execution of the program proceeds. Since suspending the application at an arbitrary time is a problem for interactive or time-critical applications, system designers have developed techniques for "incremental" garbage collection that can be interrupted and restarted. For example, the garbage collection process starts up when the application is inactive (e.g., during data transfer operations or while the user is thinking), and is suspended when the application begins an activity.

0.3.3 Data Types

Purpose and definition

The properties of data objects are described by data types. Each data object is an instance of one data type, and its type defines the set of values that are valid for such objects.[17] Programmers often think of an object's type as specifying only the interpretation of an instance's value since this is all that is stored in the object. In addition, a type definition in Pascal or C only gives the structure of its instances. However, a value is not useful without operations that can be performed with it. For example, the operations for built-in types such as integers and booleans are defined by the language, even though they are not directly associated with instances of those types. To define a type completely, we must specify the valid operations for its instances, as well as the representation of the legal values. That is, the definition of a data type describes what its instances can "do", not just what they "are". For example, a phone number or a social security number might be more accurately modeled as a string than as an integer because a program never performs arithmetic on such objects.

As stated in section 0.3.1, a data object represents the relevant properties of an entity in the problem domain or a component of the system or application. A data type is a model that describes the common structure and operations of a category of such entities. That is, a data type is not just a set of values and operations, but is an abstraction that also has semantic intent. For example, the software for an automatic teller machine will have types that represent problem domain categories such as banks, customers, accounts, and transactions, as well as types for system devices such as the keypad, command buttons, and cash dispenser.

Early programming languages supplied a restricted set of types motivated by the hardware or a particular problem domain, and did not support programmer-defined types. However, if the types provided by the language do not mirror the structure and operations of the entities in the program's problem domain, the form

---

[17] We will see that in object-oriented languages, inheritance results in an object being regarded as an instance of more than one type.

of the code does not reflect the problem domain process, and the programmer must make mental associations between data objects and the corresponding entities. For example, Fortran does not support records, so programmers model a rectangle as an array of four numbers representing the x coordinate, the y coordinate, the width, and the height of an instance. Unfortunately, they must remember which subscripts correspond to which values when writing, reading, or maintaining that code.

In modern languages, we can define a new data type to represent a category of entities in the problem domain. The values and operations that we provide for the type should correspond clearly to states and behaviors of the corresponding problem domain entities. The better a data type mirrors the properties of the entities it represents, the easier it is to code, understand, and maintain programs using the type. Like subprograms, types provide a mechanism for extending the language to a dialect that reflects the structure of the problem domain and the application. As we will see in section 1.2.5, this concept of computation as simulation of a problem domain process is an essential part of the object-oriented paradigm.

There are a number of alternate views of what a data type is. For the compiler, types impose syntactic constraints on expressions, allow it to associate semantic features with expressions and statements, and indicate the amount of storage to allocate for an object. From an implementation point of view, a type specifies a mapping between a value for the type and an encoding of an instance in a region of storage, and vice versa. The type also defines how to manipulate those bit strings to implement the type's operations. Formally, a type can be considered a set consisting of the objects that are its instances, or a predicate which is true for those values. In this sense, a type defines a domain for the functions that operate on instances of the type. Similarly, types partition the set of possible values into classes with common attributes and operations. We can also think of a type as defining a finite state machine whose states are defined by the valid states of an instance, and whose transitions are defined by the type's operations.

Types and instances

It is important that you understand the difference between a type and a data object that is an instance of that type. In compiled procedural languages such as Pascal and C, a type is a compile-time construct that does not create an object, and instances of the type are created and manipulated during execution. In Pascal, there is a strict syntactic distinction between the definition of a subprogram's types and its variables. The former are introduced by the keyword type and the latter follow the keyword var. Type definitions must precede variable definitions so that the types are available for creating instances. For example,

```
{ a record type and three instances in Pascal }
type
  Point =
    record
      x: integer;
      y: integer
    end
```

```
var
  pt1, pt2, pt3: Point;
```

In C, the distinction is less clear in the structure of the code, because we can use the same statement to define an array, enumeration, structure, or union type, and also to create instances of that type. For example, the following statement creates a type struct Point, and allocates three instances pt1, pt2, and pt3:

```
/* a struct type and instances in C */
struct Point/* data type "struct Point" */
{
    int x;
    int y;
} pt1, pt2, pt3;    /* three instances */
```

In addition, C allows the programmer to define composite objects without explicitly defining and naming a type for them—for example, if the previous statement did not include the identifier Point.

Primitive and built-in types

Primitive types describe atomic values that have no accessible substructure, and often mirror types that are built into the instruction set of the hardware. Some typical examples include boolean, character, and various numeric types such as integer, fixed point, and floating point. Every language specifies a set of *built-in types* that every implementation must provide—primitive types or types motivated by the intended problem domain or type of application. For each built-in type, the language must provide constructs for creating instances, specifying values (e.g., by a literal notation), inputting and outputting values, and performing basic operations on such objects. Operations on these types are often indicated by infix operators such as > and +, or by reserved words such as and or mod. The programmer can define additional operations for a primitive type by using it as the type of a sub-program parameter.

The built-in types of Fortran are those necessary for numerical computation, and include INTEGER, REAL, DOUBLE PRECISION, and COMPLEX. Cobol does not have types per se, but the language provides constructs for describing files, records, and numeric and alphanumeric variables and fields. The built-in types of Pascal are integer, real, char, and boolean. Ada elaborates on these, especially in its treatment of numeric types. The primitive types for ANSI C are char, short, int, long, float, double, and long double, and any of the integral types (including char) may be specified as signed or unsigned. The C built-in type void indicates an unknown type of value, and is mainly used as the return type of a function that does not return a value (or as the parameter type for a function that does not take arguments in ANSI C).

Numeric types

Programming languages have used three kinds of numeric types: integers, floating point numbers, and binary coded decimal numbers.[18] Each is typically supported by the hardware. (On some machines, especially PCs, the processor does not implement floating-point numbers, so they must be emulated in software.) Beginning with Fortran, languages have overloaded arithmetic operators for all numeric types, and most languages have provided implicit conversions from less general types to more general types in mixed-mode expressions.

Typically, positive integers are encoded as binary integers, and negative integers are encoded using the two's complement representation because it permits using the same arithmetic operations for positive and negative values. The number of bytes the hardware uses to encode an integer affects the range of numbers that can be represented, so an integer type cannot model the corresponding mathematical abstraction exactly. The hardware signals an error if an operation causes an overflow, but most higher-level languages do not provide a construct for detecting and responding to this error. Many machines provide instructions that implement operations on more than one size of integers, perhaps on two, four, and eight-byte representations.

Fortran, Algol, and Pascal support a single integer type, which is mapped onto whatever representation the target platform implements. C provides the types short, int, and long, and a language system can assign them to different sizes if they are available on the target platform. C also allows the programmer to declare an integer variable as unsigned, which allows values with twice as much magnitude for a given storage size. Ada also includes the types Short_Integer, Integer, and Long_Integer. In Cobol, the programmer can specify the number of decimal digits required for a numeric value using a PICTURE clause, and the encoding of the value with a USING clause (i.e., as binary, binary coded decimal, or characters).

In C, an instance of any of the integral types char, short, int, and long can also be treated as a bit string. The language provides the bitwise logical operators &, |, ∧, and ~, and the shift operators >> and << for instances of these types. That is, the values of these types are not regarded as atomic. These operations provide additional flexibility necessary for system programming, but break the integrity of the integral types. Many Pascal dialects provide similar functionality because it is useful for these applications.

Computer designers have devised a number of ways of encoding real values in bit strings, each supporting a different range and precision. The IEEE has developed two standard formats for representation of reals as normalized "floating-point" values, which are used in most contemporary computers. The encoding uses bit fields for the sign, the mantissa (the leading 1 is not stored explicitly), and the exponent (offset by 127 or 1023). Two sizes of floating-point numbers are defined

---

[18] Binary coded decimal numbers were implemented by early business-oriented machines and languages, but are rarely supported directly by modern languages, so we will not discuss them.

(because many machines support two representations), and are referred to as single and double precision. To take advantage of multiple representations, Fortran includes the types REAL and DOUBLE PRECISION, C supports float and double, and ANSI C adds long double. Algol and Pascal only provide the type real since the designers of those languages considered the distinction between single and double precision to be a machine dependency.

The numeric types in programming languages are an approximation of the mathematical values that they represent. In practice, only a finite range of integer values can be represented, depending on the number of bytes used to represent an integer on the machine. Real numbers can only be represented to a finite precision, and real arithmetic is approximate. For these reasons, the specifics of the implementation of numeric values can affect the accuracy and even the correctness of the results obtained. These details are not accounted for in the definition of most programming languages because they depend on the hardware. This relieves the programmer from having to describe these characteristics, but does not permit specifying the size or precision of values to ensure consistent results when porting a program to another system.

Since robustness and portability are important design issues for Ada, the language provides a way of specifying the range and precision of a real value. For example, the following declaration defines a type with at least 10 decimal digits of accuracy, with the given range:

```
-- specifying the required range and precision of a floating point type in Ada
type Power is digits 10 range 1.0e-10 .. 1.0e10;
```

The compiler can choose whatever representation and operations would preserve these characteristics, and must do so. The language also supports the machine-dependent types Float, Long_Float, and Short_Float for convenience. The Ada programmer can also define fixed point numbers that represent non-integer values exactly (even in arithmetic operations).

```
-- specifying the required range and precision of a fixed point type in Ada
type Dollars is delta 0.01 range 0.00 .. 1_000_000.00;
```

The compiler usually implements such a type by using integers internally and scaling the values for reading and printing. An arithmetic operation involving an integer and a fixed-point value produces a fixed-point value with the same delta and range. The result of a multiplication or division involving two different fixed-point types is an instance of the type "universal fixed", and cannot be assigned to a variable of the same type as one of the operands.

Logical values

Due to its importance in reflecting the problem domain and program logic, most languages provide a built-in type for the logical values "true" and "false". For example, Algol and Pascal supply the type boolean, and Fortran 77 provides

LOGICAL.   Comparisons and other tests return instances of this type, and its values are used to control conditional evaluation and iteration. We can use the logical operations and, or, and not on its values. Only a bit is required to represent a logical value, but since most machines are not bit-addressable, a logical value is represented by the smallest addressable unit, typically a byte.

There is no Boolean type in C. C programmers use an int for logical values, with the value 0 denoting "false" and nonzero values denoting "true" in conditionals such as if or while statements.

Text data

Hardware vendors have used several different encodings of character data. Currently, most machines use the ASCII code, which defines the values 0 through 127 for printable characters and various "control codes". These include codes for controlling output devices such as TAB and FORMFEED and for byte-oriented communications protocols such as ACKnowledge. Most languages use the characters' ASCII values when comparing characters for ordering. For example, Pascal defines a built-in type char with the conversions ord, which returns the character's ASCII value, and chr, which creates a char with a given ASCII value. Characters can be tested for equality and for ASCII ordering. C permits implicit conversions between a character and an integer that gives its ASCII value.

Strings represent natural language text, and are different from primitive types because they are not atomic and are not supported by the hardware. They also differ from other composite types such as arrays and records because they are inherently of variable length, and operations can involve instances with different lengths. Most languages support fixed-length arrays of characters only, because of the storage management overhead necessary for variable-length strings. In Pascal, strings are represented by arrays of characters, and there are no predefined string operations, so they must be coded.   Strings of different lengths are instances of different types, so the programmer usually "pads" all string instances to the same size with blank characters so that there is one type for string variables and parameters. In Ada, the type String is predefined as an array of characters whose length is fixed when the object is created, as follows: [19]

```
-- the Ada String type, a fixed-size array with dynamically bound size
type String is array(Positive range <>) of Character;
```

Ada supports string literals enclosed in double quotes, initialization, assignment, comparison for equality or ordering, concatenation (using the infix & operator), and substring operations. For example, Str(3:6) denotes the string consisting of the third through sixth characters of Str.

To support the variable-length nature of strings implicitly in a built-in string type, a language must allocate and deallocate strings dynamically and implicitly,

---

[19] As we will see in section 0.3.5, the <> notation defines an "unconstrained array type" whose instances can be different sizes.

since the size of an instance cannot be known at compile time. Some languages such as Basic and Snobol handle allocation automatically using a "string pool" managed by a run-time system that employs reference counting or garbage collection. Support for variable-length strings provides convenience and writability for the programmer, at the expense of additional compiler complexity and the execution time cost of managing allocation. Two common representations for variable-length strings are the *counted string*, which gives the length in the first byte, and the *terminated string*, in which a delimiter character marks the end of the string. Both representations allow efficient processing loops, but use of a delimiter has poorer error behavior (i.e., when the delimiter is missing), and prohibits using the delimiter as a character.

C provides some support for variable-length strings. In C, strings are null-terminated character arrays, and the language supports string literals enclosed in double quotes. The programmer can allocate strings statically, automatically, or dynamically. Since arrays are passed to functions by passing a pointer to the first element, the programmer can use character pointer parameters to define functions that operate on strings, irrespective of their lengths. The standard library string.h defines numerous string functions. However, the programmer must explicitly manage allocation of dynamic strings, and must be aware of the size of static and automatic strings. This approach matches C's design goals of efficiency and flexibility rather than convenience and safety.

0.3.4 Defining Types

Development of the type construct

In first generation programming languages, aggregate objects such as arrays (Fortran) and records (Cobol) could be defined, but the concept of a structured type as a separate construct had not been developed. For example, a Fortran programmer can create an array object, but the language does not include a construct to define the type "array of 100 reals, indexed from 1 to 100". Similarly, a Cobol programmer can define a record variable, but each record object is specified separately and is not related to other objects with the same structure.

By the late 1960s, language designers recognized that a type is an abstraction independent of its instances, and that a language should include constructs for defining types and using them to create objects, specify parameters, and define further types. The designers of Algol 68 developed a comprehensive set of type constructors and selectors and clearly defined type compatibility rules. The programmer could define types based on both built-in types and programmer-defined types, e.g. to define a type for an array of records. Most of these constructs were incorporated into Pascal and clarified further in Ada. Ada also extended the notion of types to include generic packages in which a type can be a parameter to a type definition. Object-oriented programming languages extend the concept of type further by providing inheritance among type definitions, and programmer access to type objects and operations.

First-class objects

Throughout the development of programming languages, the kinds of objects that programs can refer to and process have increased. We say that a type is *first-class* in a language, and that its instances are *first-class* objects if the language provides complete support for manipulating that type of object. To illustrate this concept, let us consider the kinds of capabilities that are usually available for built-in types. We can perform initializations, assignments, and equality comparisons. We can use the type as a parameter or return type to provide additional operations for its instances, or as the base type of another type, for example, as the type of a record field. The language defines a literal notation for writing values of the type, and provides input and output operations, and ordering comparisons and infix arithmetic operators, if appropriate. As we discuss programmer-defined types in section 0.3.5, we will consider to what extent each kind of type is first-class in various languages. This will help us understand what is necessary to give a complete definition of a class in an object-oriented language.

Early programming languages do not provide the same status for arrays as for built-in types—they do not support array assignments, equality tests, and return values. In programming languages such as Pascal and C, support for treating aggregate objects such as arrays and records as objects in their own right is much better, but still not complete. In languages such as CLU and Ada that support abstract data types, we can manipulate complex data structures coherently in the same fashion as data objects. An important design goal of object-oriented languages is that programmer-defined types be first-class. Many languages provide some support for treating functions as objects (e.g., a function can be a parameter of another function or the referent of a variable). In functional languages, this support is complete, and function objects can be created during execution and manipulated. Some languages, such as Smalltalk, also support treating data types as first-class objects. A program can query the type of any object, and use the result as the value of a variable or an argument to a subprogram, and the language (actually, the class library) provides many operations for type objects.

Language support and type constructors

To support programmer-defined types, a language must provide constructs for naming and describing a new type, usually based on existing types. We can define the structure of a new type by

- listing its values (e.g., an enumeration type)
- restricting an existing type (e.g., a subrange type)
- describing the structure of composite objects in terms of the number and types of their components (e.g., an array or record type)

We can then use the type to create instances, declare parameters, and define other types. The language must also provide constructs for writing and initializing instances of the type, and for defining the type's operations, for example, selecting the components of a composite object.

Pascal was the first widely used language to include *type constructors* for defining new types. The type declaration statement describes the structure of a pointer, enumeration, subrange, array, record, or set type. Any of these may be based on existing programmer-defined types, so the programmer can create a type for an array of records that contains a set and an enumeration, and so on. However, these types are not first-class in Pascal. For example, we can only write instances of enumerations and subranges as literals, and functions cannot return arrays or records.

The Pascal programmer does not give the type's operations as part of the type definition, but defines them separately as subprograms that take a parameter of that type. Languages that support abstract data types, such as Ada, and object-oriented languages provide a construct for grouping a type's operations together with the definition of the structure of its instances.

Type definitions and the type object

A *type definition* gives the name of the type, the kind of type (e.g., array, record, etc.), and the structure of its instances. If the language supports abstract data types, the type definition also specifies the type's operations. Unlike an object definition, a type definition does not create any data objects or allocate storage during execution (in compiled languages). Instead, the translator creates a symbol table entry associated with the type name. This *type object* maintains information about the type such as[20]

- the type's name
- the kind of type
- the structure of the type's instances
- the size of an instance of the type
- the operations that are valid for the type

The symbol table initially contains such entries for the built-in types of the language. The compiler uses this information to allocate instances and check the validity of operations using instances of the type. The type object is usually not present at run time in compiled languages, but must exist at execution time in an interpreted language.

The information present in a type object depends on the kind of type it represents. It specifies

- the base type for a pointer type
- the constant names for an enumeration type
- the limits and base type for a subrange type

---

[20] In practice, the translator may store the information the type object represents in a number of different tables.

- the number of dimensions, index type or range, and element type for an array type
- the component names and types for a record or union type
- the argument signature for a subprogram type

In object-oriented languages, the information in the type object is more extensive (e.g., it includes the type's operations and class hierarchy relationships), and some of it must present at execution time to support dynamic binding of methods.

Type declarations

Like objects and subprograms, types can be declared without being defined. Such a declaration informs the compiler that the identifier is a type name, but does not define the structure of the type. (Of course, a type definition must be given elsewhere in the program.) For example, a forward type declaration is necessary in Pascal when two types contain pointers to instances of each other. We can use a type that is declared but not defined as the base type of a pointer (since all pointers are represented in the same way), or as the type of a reference parameter. However, we cannot define instances of the type since the compiler does not know how much space to allocate for that object.

Type operations

We sometimes want to code a general-purpose algorithm that varies only in the type of a parameter, for example, a subprogram that sorts the elements of an array of any orderable type. However, in a statically typed language, the subprogram that sorts an array of integers is different from the one that sorts an array of reals. If the language supports overloading, both functions can have the same name, but we must still code each separately, even though the code is the same except for the type name. Some languages provide a construct for defining a *generic subprogram*, which includes a type parameter that is bound according to the type of an argument in an invocation. The programmer can also define a *generic type*, perhaps to define a list type with a type parameter for the type of an element. This capability is provided by the Ada *generic package* and the C++ *template facility*. We will discuss generic types in section 1.1.4.

If a type can be a parameter, details of the code may depend on attributes of the actual type used. For example, a sort program needs the subscript bounds of the array type actually passed to the subprogram. It would be useful for the language to provide constructs for obtaining this information, that is, for making information in the type object available to the programmer. Similarly, a robust program may wish to check the range of values representable by a particular implementation for a built-in numeric type. If we think of the type as an object, these operations are *type operations* on the type object.

C defines just one type operation, sizeof, which returns the number of bytes required for an instance of the type. In addition, the standard library "header file" limits.h defines constants that give the lower and upper limits for an implementation's representation of the built-in numeric types. Pascal also defines constants such as maxint for this purpose. Ada provides access to a number of type attributes, which we refer to by the type name, a single quote, and the attribute name. Examples include

- the size in bits of an instance of the type (Point'Size)
- the smallest and largest values for a numeric or subrange type (Integer'Last)
- the number of elements of an array type (Scores'Length)
- the resolution of a fixed point type (Dollars'Delta)

Note that all these values are constants that the compiler can substitute for a use.

In object-oriented languages, a type is referred to as a *class*. In many languages, a class is an object that is present at execution time. For example, in Smalltalk, the type object maintains

- the operations of the class
- the "methods" that define the class's operations
- the superclass and subclasses of the class
- "class variables" that maintain information relevant to the class but not its instances
- a list of the class's instances

The interface of the class object includes operations to access this information. We can ask any object for its class at execution time, and can also use the resulting type object as the referent of a variable. That is, type objects are first-class and type operations are coded in the same manner as operations on data objects. Creating an instance of a type is performed by invoking an operation of the type object. In section 12.2, we will discuss the C++ run-time type information facility, which provides a more restricted set of operations dealing with type identity.

0.3.5 Programmer-Defined Types

Type aliases

In Pascal, we can define a *type alias* for a built-in or programmer-defined type to indicate semantic intent for instances of the type. The new type has the same representation and operations as the existing type. For example,

```
{ a type alias in Pascal }
type
  Length = real;
```

We can obtain the same effect in C with the typedef statement. However, these languages make no distinction between the existing type and the new type, and the types' operations can be performed on instances of the new type and the existing type together. For example, we can pass instances of real to subprograms that take a Length and vice versa, and can multiply a real and a Length or compare them for ordering.

Ada provides two mechanisms for creating a new type that uses the structure and operations of an existing type. A *subtype* of a base type is compatible with the base type in the sense that base type operations can be applied to its instances, and its instances can be assigned to a base type variable (like a Pascal type alias). We can also assign base type instances to a subtype variable, with a run-time check if the subtype uses a range constraint. For example,

```
-- an Ada subtype
subtype Variance is Float;
```

An Ada *derived type* defines a new type whose representation is the same as the base type, but is distinct from the base type. For example (note the reserved word new),[21]

```
-- Ada derived types
type Length is new Float;
type Area is new Float;
```

A derived type inherits all the operations, subprograms, and other attributes of the type from which it is derived, but they are considered separate operations (i.e., they are overloadings). This feature permits us to specify a new type that has the same structure and operations as an existing type, but is semantically a separate type. For example, an instance of Length cannot be added to an instance of Area or Float. Operations that are defined for the derived type cannot be performed on instances of the base type. For example, we can overload multiplication of Length objects so that the result is an Area, and can only be used as an instance of that type. An instance of a base type can be explicitly cast to the derived type, for example, Area(3.0).

Pointers

In most contemporary languages, we can declare a variable of type *pointer* or *reference* to a particular type of data object. (Ada uses the reserved word access.) Its value specifies a reference to another object elsewhere in storage (i.e., its value is an *l*-value). Its value is not the object itself, nor does the pointer contain the object. Defining a pointer variable does not create or initialize the object it refers to. The language supplies a special value to indicate that the pointer does not point to any object (nil in Pascal, NULL or 0 in C, and null in Ada). All pointers in Ada are initialized to null by default for safety. In most languages, pointers can only refer to dynamically allocated objects. (C is an exception.)

---

[21] Actually, we should give a range for these types, as illustrated in section 0.3.3, since instances cannot be negative.

The first higher-level language to support pointers was PL/I. However, a particular pointer could refer to any type of object, so it was not possible for the compiler to check the validity of operations using the referent of a pointer. In all succeeding statically typed languages, a pointer type specifies a *base type*, and instances of the pointer type can only refer objects of the base type. The type object for a pointer type includes the base type to ensure that uses of the pointer's referent are valid, and to indicate how much storage is needed when allocating a dynamic object. A pointer value is usually implemented as the address of its referent object. The storage required for a pointer object depends on the size of the address space, but not on the base type of the pointer type.

Several operations for pointers are typically supported. The *dereference* or *indirection* operation accesses the object the pointer refers to. It is denoted by the postfix ∧ operator in Pascal and the prefix * operator in C, and the type of that expression is the pointer's base type. [22] We can use the result of this operation, that is, ptr∧ in Pascal or *ptr in C, as an *r-value* to obtain the value of the indirectly referenced object, or as an *l-value* on the left side of an assignment that modifies that object. Attempting to dereference a null pointer is a run-time error that typically causes program termination. We may also consider the dynamic allocation and deallocation operations described in section 0.3.2 as pointer operations. A pointer variable can be assigned the value of another pointer variable of the same type, and pointers can be compared for equality, that is, to determine whether they point to the same object.

You must be clear on the difference between pointer assignment and object assignment. A pointer assignment causes both pointers to refer to the object referred to by the right-side pointer, while an object assignment involves copying the object referred to by the right-side pointer into the region referred to by the left-side pointer. For example, in C,

```
/* object and pointer assignment in C */
int main()
{
    int* pInt1;
    int* pInt2;
    /* ... other operations ... */
    /* object assignment: pInt1's referent is assigned the value of pInt2's referent */
    *pInt1 = *pInt2;
    /* ... other operations ... */
    /* pointer assignment: pInt1 now refers to pInt2's referent */
    pInt1 = pInt2;
}
```

Special care is necessary after a pointer assignment because both names now refer to the same object. If we change that object's value through one pointer, the value referred to by the other pointer changes, even though the assignment statement

---

[22] Pointer dereferencing is implicit in Ada, Fortran 90, and many object-oriented languages.

does not mention the latter. If we deallocate the object through one pointer, both pointers become dangling pointers. In addition, if the former referent of the reassigned pointer is no longer accessible, it should be deallocated before the assignment so that a memory leak does not occur. The same distinction occurs with respect to equality tests. An equality test between pointers (that is, pointer equivalence) tests whether they point to the same object. An equality test between dereferenced pointers tests whether they refer to equal objects, possibly stored in different regions.

C treats pointers as addresses in a linearly numbered storage unit, as in assembly language. In addition to referring to dynamic objects, a pointer may refer to an automatically allocated object, an element of an array, or a component of a structure. The prefix & operator returns the address of the object referred to by an *l*-value, which may then be assigned to a pointer variable.[23] Care is necessary when using a pointer to an automatic object because the pointer becomes a dangling pointer when the object's scope is exited.[24] The type void* is used to declare a "generic pointer". A void* pointer cannot be dereferenced directly, but it may be cast to any pointer type, and it is the return type of the malloc() allocation function.

C also supports arithmetic operations on pointers. An integer num may be added to or subtracted from a pointer that refers to an array element, and the result is a pointer to the element num positions after or before the element originally referenced. Pointer arithmetic is performed in units of the size of the array elements, whose type is the base type of the pointer. The programmer can also use the increment and decrement operators ++ and -- with pointers, and the pointer is incremented or decremented by the element size. Two pointers that point to the same array can be subtracted, and the result is the number of elements between their referents. The language also supports ordering comparisons for pointers that point to elements of the same array.

Unfortunately, C makes no distinction between a pointer to an object and a pointer to an array of objects. Therefore, pointer arithmetic can be used with any pointer (although it is meaningless for pointers to non-array objects), and the programmer cannot restrict a function parameter to being a pointer to an object or a pointer to an array only. In addition, no range checking is performed for any of the operations that modify pointer values. The use of pointer arithmetic in C is very unsafe, and errors are notoriously difficult to debug.

Enumerated types

We often need to represent an entity or attribute for which there is a fixed set of values, such as the days of the week or the colleges in a university. Similarly, many entities can be modeled by a state machine, in which case the corresponding

---

[23] The & operator is not used with the name of an array, and is optional when assigning a function to a pointer to function.

[24] For this reason, Pascal does not permit the programmer to obtain a pointer to a local variable. Algol 68 avoids this problem by requiring that the scope of the referent of a pointer be at least as large as the scope of the pointer variable.

object is in one of a fixed set of states. In Fortran or Algol, the programmer uses numeric constants for each value, and then uses an integer variable to model the object. For example,

```
C USING INTEGERS TO ENCODE A SET OF VALUES IN FORTRAN
C 5 MEANS FRIDAY
PAYDAY = 5
```

This technique is error-prone because the programmer must remember the codes, so a named variable might be used for each value. For example, the programmer could define FRIDAY = 5, and then use the assignment PAYDAY = FRIDAY. Unfortunately, the compiler cannot verify that a meaningful value is assigned to the variable, (to prevent assignments such as PAYDAY = –100 and PAYDAY = ENGINEERING). Integer operations are also permitted on the variable, which is meaningless. This technique does not retain the semantic intent of the type.

To avoid this lack of security, Pascal provides the enumerated type. An *enumerated type* allows the programmer to specify a set of mnemonic names for the values possible for an instance of the type. The use of an enumerated type is an improvement over the use of integer variables because it enhances the readability of the code, and allows type checking that prevents meaningless operations. In addition, the compiler can use a condensed representation whose size is determined by the number of values. We define an enumerated type by listing the value names, as in the following examples:

```
{ an enumerated type in Pascal }
type
   Day = ( Sunday, Monday, Tuesday, Wednesday, Thursday, Friday, Saturday );
```

```
/* an enumerated type in C */
enum Day { Sunday, Monday, Tuesday, Wednesday, Thursday, Friday, Saturday };
```

The value names are treated as symbolic constants, and must be unique within the scope in which the enumeration is defined (in Pascal and C). These names can be used as literal values for an instance of the type (e.g., in an assignment or equality comparison). The value names are typically mapped onto integers internally. The type object for an enumerated type specifies the size of an instance, the value names, and their encoding.

In Pascal, each enumerated type is a separate type that may be used for variable declarations and parameter types, and its instances are first-class objects. Assignments and equality tests are supported for instances of enumerated types. The constants are considered to be ordered according their order in the type definition, and the operations pred, succ, ord (conversion to integer), and the relational operators are supported for these values. We can use an enumerated type as the type of an array index, and can use an instance as the control variable in a for loop that iterates over the array. Input and output operations are not supported for enumerated types, and must be coded by the programmer.[25]

Ada extends the Pascal enumerated type by allowing two enumerated types in the same scope to use the same constant name—that is, enumeration values can be overloaded. For example,

```
-- overloaded enumeration values in Ada
type Screen_Color is (Red, Green, Blue);
type Traffic_Light is (Red, Yellow, Green);
```

If the value Red or Green is assigned to a variable, the type of the variable determines which value is used. If the usage is ambiguous (e.g., as an argument to a subprogram overloaded for both types), the type of the value must be specified by a cast, for example, Screen_Color'(Red).

In ANSI C, each enumeration is considered a distinct type that has integer values, the value identifiers are regarded as int constants, and integer values can be given for the constants. However, any integer value can be assigned to a variable of an enum type, and the enumeration constants can be used as integers in any context (e.g., they can be multiplied).

Constrained types

In many languages, the programmer can define a new data type as a *subrange* of an existing type to represent a kind of entity whose values are restricted to a subrange of the values of the existing type. The subrange type definition gives the name of the new type, the base type, and the limits for the values for an instance. In Pascal, the base type must be a discrete ordered type (i.e., integer, character, an enumerated type, or another subrange type). The following are example Pascal subrange type definitions (assuming that the enumerated type Day is defined as in the previous subsection):

```
{ subrange types in Pascal }
type
  Year = 0 .. 2200;
  Weekday = Monday .. Friday;
  Uppercase = 'A' .. 'Z';
```

The base type of the subrange type is implied by the type of the limits given in the type definition, which must be literals. The use of a subrange type permits the compiler to check whether a constant value being assigned to a variable of that type is within the valid range. The Pascal standard also requires execution-time checking of assignments. Subrange types provide safety and reliability because it is much easier to debug a subrange violation than the erroneous behavior that results some time

---

[25] To support input/output operations, the value names would have to be present at execution time.

later if that error is not caught. Since the subrange type has fewer valid values than the base type, the compiler can use a more compact representation to save space. The type object for a subrange type specifies the size, the base type, and the limits. Pascal programmers often use subrange types to specify the index type of an array.

A subrange type is compatible with its base type in the sense that a subrange instance can be assigned to a base type variable or passed as the argument corresponding to a base type parameter. The operations of the subrange type are those of the base type, and the base type's literal notation is used for specifying values. However, the base type is not compatible with the subrange type since the actual value of a base type object at execution time may be out of range (like integer, which is compatible with real, but not vice versa in Pascal).

The Ada *constraint* feature is a generalization of the Pascal subrange type. For example, we can create a new type by specifying a *range constraint*, for example, Character range 'a' .. 'z'. Both subtypes and derived types can be defined using constraints.

```
-- an Ada subtype defined by a constraint
subtype Weekday is Day range Monday .. Friday;
-- an Ada derived type defined by a constraint
type Percent is new Integer range 0 .. 100;
```

Ada also permits the limits to be expressions that cannot be evaluated at compile time, which implies execution-time range checking. For efficiency for production code, range checking can be suppressed with the compiler directive Pragma Suppress(Range_Check).

Ada supports a number of other kinds of constraints. As we saw in section 0.3.3, we can use *accuracy constraints* such as digits 10 or delta 0.01 to create a new type based on a numeric type. In the next subsection, we will see that an array type can be defined without specifying the subscript limits, which are provided by an *index constraint* when creating an instance or defining a subtype. With variant records, a new type whose instances are restricted to one of the possible substructures can be defined using a *discriminant constraint*. The tag that specifies the variant in an instance is checked upon an assignment from an instance of the variant record type to the new type. All these constraints can require run-time checking, and all can be disabled with compiler directives.

Arrays

The need to manage and process collections of like objects is common in programming. An *array* is a fixed-size, homogenous, indexable sequence of elements that is treated as an composite object. Almost every language permits definition of array objects or types. Formally, an array specifies a mapping from a contiguous range of integers (or of other types in Pascal or Ada) to a set of elements of the same type, called the *base type*. The definition of an array object or type gives the name, the base type, and the index type or the subscript limits (often called the subscript "bounds"). Informally, programmers usually consider an array to be a sequence of elements of the same type, which is the usual storage layout.

There are a number of characteristics of arrays that a language supporting arrays must address. In some languages, array indices must be integers, and the language may specify a fixed lower limit (e.g., 1 in Fortran or 0 in C). In other languages, such as Pascal and Ada, the index type may be any discrete, ordered, finite type. Fortran only permits statically allocated arrays, Algol allows automatic allocation, and C and Ada support dynamic allocation on the heap. With automatic allocation, the limit expressions may be evaluated at compile time (as in Pascal) or at execution time (as in Ada). The language must support accessing and modifying elements, and may provide syntax for initialization and for array literals. More recent languages provide better support for coherent operations such as assignment, equality tests, and mapped operations so array objects are first-class. The type object for an array type specifies the base type and the index type, or the upper and lower limits if the index type must be integer. It may also include the size of the array and the base type, for convenience.

The primary operation for arrays is *subscription*, which takes an array name and a subscript or index value as arguments, and returns the referenced element. We enclose the index in square brackets [ ] following the array name in Algol, Pascal, and C. (Fortran and Ada use parentheses.) The type of a subscription expression is the base type of the array. A subscription expression can be used as an *r*-value or as an *l*-value, and we use it on the left side of an assignment to store an element in the array. That is, subscription is a shorthand for the operations retrieve(Array, Index): Element and store(Array, Index, Element). Since each element is individually accessible, an array is a "random access" structure.

Subscription is undefined for an index argument outside the subscript bounds for that array object or type, and the language should address the result of this error. A subscript range error causes a run-time error in Pascal, but is undefined in C and usually accesses an unintended region of storage. These options reflect the trade-off between safety and efficiency. Ada requires execution time range checking, but it can be disabled with the directive Pragma Suppress(Index_Check);. This allows the programmer to include the range checking during development, and then remove it in the final version of the program, for efficiency.

The array is the only aggregate constructor in Fortran, and is supported because of the importance of vectors and matrices for scientific and engineering applications. Array objects of up to three dimensions can be declared using a DIMENSION statement. The index range begins with 1, and the declaration gives the upper limit for each dimension, which must be constants. For example,

```
C FORTRAN DEFINITION OF ARRAY OBJECTS
DIMENSION ARR1(50), ARR2(10, 10)
```

Subscription is indicated by parentheses. In Algol, the array construct is more general than that of Fortran, but still defines an array object, not a type. An array can have any lower limit and any number of dimensions, and arrays may be allocated automatically. The array bounds can be specified by expressions that contain variables, in which case the size of the array is determined at run time when the block is entered. This provides more efficient use of storage and additional flexibility because the array size needed may depend on input to the program or other runtime conditions. In Fortran, the programmer must use an array of the maximum size that might be necessary, and if there are more elements than that limit the program cannot execute. Algol uses the [ ] operator for subscription to distinguish subscription expressions from function calls.

Pascal supports an array type constructor that gives the base type and the index type, which may be any discrete, ordered, finite type, including char, boolean, subranges, and enumerations. (Programmers use a subrange for an array with integer indices.) The base type may be any type, including programmer-defined types such as records and arrays. For example (again, assuming that the enumerated type Day is defined as previously in this section),

```
{ array type definitions in Pascal }
type
   TotalPerDay = array[Day] of integer;
   GradeDistribution = array['A' .. 'E'] of integer;
```

All array types are one-dimensional, but multidimensional array types can be defined as arrays of arrays of reals, and so on.

In Pascal, the array bounds are considered to be part of the array type, and must be determinable at compile time. However, this prevents the dynamically sized arrays available in Algol, and implies that arrays with different bounds are instances of different types. Since Pascal is strongly typed, two arrays with different subscript ranges cannot be arguments of the same subprogram. To avoid rewriting each array subprogram for every array type, ISO Pascal introduced "conformant array parameters," which specify identifiers that can be used as the argument's subscript limits within the subprogram code. The limit identifiers are bound according to the limits of the index type of the type of the array actually passed to the subprogram. The type of the argument must have the same base type as that given for the parameter. For example,

```
{ an ISO Pascal conformant array parameter }
function sum(arr: array[low .. high: IndexType] of real): real;
   var
         total: real
         index: IndexType;
   begin
         total := 0.0;
         for index := low to high do
            total := total + arr[index];
         sum := total
   end
```

In Ada, we can define an "unconstrained" array type that gives the index and base type, but does not specify the actual array limits. We then give the limits for an array object when creating it with an *index constraint*. For example,

```
-- An Ada unconstrained array type, and two instances with different bounds
type Vector is array(Integer range < >) of Float;
Arr1: Vector(-100 .. 100);
Arr2: Vector(0 .. 50);
```

The limits in the definition of an array instance can be expressions including variables, so Ada supports dynamically sized arrays. Ada uses parentheses for subscription because an array is a mapping like a function. A subprogram can use an unconstrained array type as a parameter type, and can access the argument's limits within the subprogram using the type attributes 'First and 'Last. For example,

```
-- an Ada function with an array parameter
function Sum(Vec: Vector) return Float is
    Total: Float := 0.0;
begin
    for Index in Vec'First .. Vec'Last loop
        Total := Total + Vec(Index);
    end loop;
    return Total;
end Sum;
```

Both the objects Arr1 and Arr2 can be passed to the function Sum. Ada arrays also support the type attribute 'Range which gives the array's index range, so we can also write the loop as for Index in Vec'Range loop ... end loop;.

C does not define an array type, but we can create array objects statically, automatically, or dynamically. The index type is always int, and array indices always begin with 0. Arrays in C have a different interpretation than in most higher-level languages, mirroring the storage format. The array name is regarded as a pointer to the first element of the array, and succeeding elements can be accessed via pointer arithmetic and dereferencing.[26] An array can be passed as the argument of a function, but a pointer to the first element is actually passed, and an array argument can always be modified by a function. In addition, arrays cannot be assigned or compared, so there is essentially no array type in C. The programmer creates a two-dimensional array by defining an array of pointers, each of which points to an array, and higher-rank arrays are defined similarly. We can allocate an array of objects dynamically by calling malloc() with the product of the size of the element type and the number of elements as the argument. For example,

---

[26] In fact, the expression arr[index] is identical to *(arr + index) (as is index[arr]!), and may be used with any pointer, not just an array name. Using a pointer to access an array sequentially allows more efficient iteration over the elements of an array because the address of each element does not have to be calculated from the base address of the array and the index value for each access. However, most compilers for other languages can perform this optimization.

```
/* creating a dynamic array in C */
pArrDbl = (double*) malloc(sizeof(double) * ARR_SIZE);
```

Many languages provide a feature for initializing an array object. In C, we can give a list of values enclosed in braces, or use a string literal to initialize a char array. If the compiler can infer the number of elements from the initializer, it need not be given. For example,

```
/* initialization of arrays in C */
int arr[5] = { 1, 2, 4, 8, 16 };
char greeting[] = "hello";
```

Unfortunately, we cannot use the braces notation to specify an array literal in an assignment or as a function argument. As with other objects, Pascal does not provide initialization, so an array initially contains garbage, and its values are set by a series of assignments or input operations to individual elements. Ada supports specification of a list of initial values for an array enclosed in parentheses.

In addition to defining an array type, many languages allow us to treat the entire array as an object in its own right by supporting coherent operations on array objects. For example, the language may permit assignment or equality test operations for array objects. We can provide additional operations by defining subprograms with parameters of array type (e.g., isElement(Array, Element): boolean). Some languages, such as PL/I, Fortran 90 and APL, provide memberwise operations on array instances. Fortran 90, and APL also include predefined operations for matrix multiplication and transposition, and for vector dot products. Ada supports the infix concatenation operator & for arrays.

Records

The most important programmer-defined type for modeling problem domain categories is the record type. A *record* ("structure" in C) is a composite object made up of a collection of components or *fields* ("members" in C) of various types. The components store values for the attributes and relationships the application maintains for an instance of the category the type represents. Each component has a name and a type, and a record instance has a value for each component.

Cobol introduced the record variable to permit processing files of information about customers, inventory items, and so on. Algol 68, Pascal, and succeeding languages support a type constructor for records. We define a record type by listing the names and types of its components, which can be any previously defined types, including other record types. The type object for the record type maintains this information, and also contains the size of an instance and the field offsets for component selection operations. We saw examples of record type definitions in Pascal and C in section 0.3.3. Ada permits the programmer to specify default initial values for the fields of a record, as follows:

```
-- an Ada record type with default values for the fields
type Point is
   record
      X: Integer := 0;
      Y: Integer := 0;
   end record;
```

If the programmer creates an instance of the type Point without giving initial values for its fields, they are set to the default initial values.

The storage structure for a record type typically consists of a sequence of the storage structures for the individual fields' types. (The order of the fields in the storage structure of a record is not usually visible to the programmer.) If certain field types must be aligned on word or long word boundaries on the target hardware, "padding" within record objects may be necessary.

The basic selector operation for records is *component selection*, which takes a record instance name and a component name, and is usually denoted by an infix . (period). (Alternately, we can think of each component name as a selector function.) The type of a component selection expression is the type of the named field. Like an array subscription or pointer dereference expression, we can use a component selection expression as either an *l*-value or an *r*-value to set or obtain the value of a field in a record object.[27] For example (assuming that the record type Point is defined as in section 0.3.3),

```
{ component selection in Pascal }
var
    pt1, pt2: Point;
begin
    pt1.x := 1;
    pt2.y := pt1.x + 3
end
```

If a record contains a field of record type, selection operations can be composed to access fields of the nested record, e.g. employee.birthdate.year. Such an expression can appear in any context in which a simple variable of the last component's type can appear. The compiler translates a component selection expression as an offset into the record instance that is the sum of the sizes of the preceding components (plus any padding necessary for alignment).

Since we refer to the components of a record by names specific to the record type, a record type introduces a new level of scope, and the component names are declared within that scope. In this way, two record types may use the same name for a component, and a variable name can also be used as a component name without conflict. The component names (and their offsets) are stored in the type object for the record type, rather than directly in the symbol table. Pascal allows the programmer to specify a record scope and a particular record object via the with *record-*

---

[27] Languages that support records permit assignment of individual components, even though it may not be semantically meaningful for the problem domain entity represented.

Var do statement. This is less verbose and more efficient when several operations are performed on the components of a particular record, especially if that record is accessed as a record component or array element.

Many languages support treating a record instance as an individual object rather than as a group of related objects, and allow assignments or equality tests for records. We can also define subprogram parameters and return values of record type to define the operations required for instances. The language may also provide syntax for specifying each component value for an initialization or record literal. Support for such coherent operations on record instances is incomplete in the languages of the 1970s. Pascal allows record assignment, but not equality comparison, initialization, or record literals.[28] It also permits record parameters, but not record return values. Pre-ANSI C supports initialization for static structures and structure parameters, but not structure assignment or return values. ANSI C supports initialization and assignment of structures, but not equality tests. The definition of a C structure variable can include a list of initial values for the members in braces, for example,

```
/* structure initialization in C */
struct Point origin = { 0, 0 };
```

Initializers enclosed in braces can be nested to initialize a structure that contains a structure or array member. As with arrays, we cannot use the braces notation as a function argument or as the right side of an assignment. Records are first-class in Ada. The language supports record assignment, equality comparison, and initialization by a list of values enclosed in parentheses. We can use a record type name to construct an instance by giving values for each of the object's fields—for example, Point(1, 1)—which provides a literal notation for records. Ada also supports operator overloading for record types.

Clearly, two record variables that have different structures are not compatible with respect to coherent operations such as assignment. However, a program may define two record types with the same structure, that is, with the same number and order of component types. In most implementations of pre-ANSI C, these types are compatible because the language regards types as specifying the structure of objects, rather than semantic intent. This question was not resolved in the original definition of Pascal. After much discussion, ISO Pascal specified the use of type name equivalence rather than structure equivalence to determine compatibility, since the programmer most likely used separate types for the identifiers because they represent different categories of entities. In addition, name equivalence is easier to implement because the compiler does not need to examine the details of the type objects, and structure equivalence is vaguely defined (e.g., whether the component names are significant or only their types). Ada also uses name equivalence.

---

[28] To initialize a record instance as a unit, the programmer can define a "constructor" procedure that takes a record reference parameter and values for all the fields, and sets the fields in the object.

Unions

A *union* type allows an instance to represent different types of entities at various points during execution of the program.[29] Algol 68 introduced the *discriminated union*, which contains an indication of the type currently stored in the union object, and Pascal integrated this construct with the record type. A Pascal *variant record type* specifies a set of fields and a "variant part" introduced by the reserved word case that contains a *tag* component and a set of substructures. Only one substructure is present in a particular instance at any time, and its tag field indicates which it is. For example, we can define the following variant record type whose instances represent one of three different kinds of shapes:

```
{ a variant record in Pascal }
type
  ShapeType = (Circle, Rectangle, Spiral);
  Shape =
    record
      center: Point;    { Point defined in section 0.3.3 }
      case typeTag: ShapeType of
        Circle: (radius: integer);
        Rectangle: (height, width, tilt: integer);
        Spiral: (radius, spacing: integer)
    end
```

A particular Shape object can contain a Circle at some point in execution, and a Rectangle at another. The fields center and typeTag are present in all instances, and the typeTag indicates which of the other substructures is stored in an instance. We access the fields in a variant record using component selection, and usually process instances of the type using a case statement that tests the tag and specifies different operations for each variant. The type object for a variant record contains the size of an instance, the nonvariant field names and types, and a list of the type descriptions of the variant parts.

The variant record type avoids the storage inefficiency of including all possible fields in every instance. The storage structure includes the nonvariant fields and the amount of storage necessary for the largest of the variant substructures. In an instance of the Shape type, there is space for a Point, the tag field, and three integers. The height and width fields occupy the same storage as the radius and spacing fields in an object.

To ensure type-correct operation, you should always test the type tag of a variant record before manipulating the other fields in an instance. Unfortunately, Pascal defines no syntax for coherently assigning the type tag and the corresponding variant fields of an instance, so each component must be assigned independently. Since each assignment is a separate statement, the compiler cannot ensure that a complete set of assignments has been performed. The safety of a component access

---

[29] We will see that object-oriented languages support this capability in a safer, more controlled manner via inheritance.

cannot even be checked at execution time since the type tag and the contents of the variant part may not be consistent. For example, the programmer can define a record with integer and real variants, store an integer, change the tag field to the real indicator, and access the integer's representation as a real (even if the implementation provides run-time checking of tags). That is, a union defines aliases for the same storage that might not be the same type. Since a variant record can be used in semantically unsound ways, you should use the type with care.

The lack of type safety for variant records has been fixed in Ada. The language supports coherent assignment to a record object from a literal, disallows independent assignment of the tag field, and checks the validity of assignments to the variant parts at execution time. For example (assuming that we have defined a Shape variant record type as in the previous example),

```
-- type safety for variant records in Ada
Graphic: Shape;
Graphic := (Circle, (2, 2), 5);     -- a Circle literal specification
Graphic.Type := Spiral;             -- illegal, not a complete specification
Graphic.Height := 5;                -- illegal, Graphic is a Circle
Graphic.Radius := 3;                -- OK
```

In addition, we can define a subtype or derived type whose instances can only contain one of the possible variants with a discriminant constraint, for example, the type Shape(Circle).

An *undiscriminated union* does not explicitly store an indication of which substructure is present in an instance, and is inherently unsafe. For example, C supports the union construct that does not require a tag. The union in C is regarded as a structure that can store any one of a set of members in an instance. Each instance is allocated the maximum storage of the requirements of its members' types, and the offset for each member is zero. This construct allows using objects of different types in the same context. For example, we can define a union that can take any of three types of objects and two instances of the type, as follows:

```
/* an undiscriminated union in C */
union Data
{
    int in;
    char ch;
    double dbl;
} data1, data2;
```

We access the members of a union with component selection (e.g., data1.ch = '\n';). It is the programmer's responsibility to keep track of what type of object is stored in an instance. For example, the language does not prevent us from assigning an int to data1.in, and then retrieving a double from data1.dbl. For safety, the C programmer should nest a union within a struct that includes a member specifying the type of object currently stored in an instance.

Abstract data types

We can use a record type to group the information that the program stores about a category of entities, with the individual attributes and relationships of an entity stored as field values for the corresponding instance. We must also define the operations required for instances of the type. In languages that do not support abstract data types such as Pascal and C, the programmer accesses the fields within a record directly via component selection, and codes the operations for the record type as subprograms that take instances of the type as arguments. These languages provide no direct support for packaging the storage structure for instances of a type and the operations for the type as a unit, which can then be reused in other applications that deal with the same problem domain.

An *abstract data type* encapsulates the definition of the storage structure for a type (i.e., the components and their types) and the type's operations in a separate package, and allows the programmer to control access to the components of the type. These types are "abstract" in the sense that a programmer using the type need not know its internal structure, just as a programmer does not need to know how floating-point numbers are represented and how that storage structure is manipulated to provide arithmetic operations. Languages such as Ada and object-oriented languages that support abstract data types provide syntactic structures for this encapsulation, and for specifying which components of the abstract data type are visible externally. We will discuss abstract data types in detail in section 1.1.4.

Subprogram types

Many procedural languages allow a subprogram to take another subprogram as an argument. Such a subprogram encodes a higher-level algorithm that uses specific functionality supplied by the subprogram argument. Examples include a sort function that takes the function used to compare elements for ordering as an argument, and a "mapping" function that applies an arbitrary function to every element of an array or list. The use of subprogram parameters allows the general procedure to be coded once, then reused for particular subprograms as needed. For example, Pascal allows procedure and function parameters (but not return types, for reasons we will discuss in section 1.2.3). The following function returns the slope of the chord between the points $(x1, f(x1))$ and $(x2, f(x2))$ for a function f:

```
{ a function parameter in Pascal }
function slope(function f(x: real): real; x1, x2: real): real;
  begin
    if x1 = x2 then
        slope := 0
    else
        slope := (f(x2) - f(x1)) / (x2 - x1)
  end
```

The identifier x in the parameter declaration is just a place-holder. We invoke the function slope by using the name of a function with the correct argument signature as the first argument. For example,

```
{ passing a function object as an argument }
m := slope(sin, 3.0, 5.0);
```

C supplies the type *pointer to function*, which may be used for both function parameters and function variables.

It is also convenient for a language to support a variable whose value is a subprogram, for example, to assign an operation selected by a user interactively as its value. That is, we want to treat a subprogram as an object, and define parameters and variables of subprogram type. The basic operation on this type is invocation of the referent. Subprogram objects are not first-class in procedural languages such as Pascal and C. Pascal does not permit subprogram variables, and does not support writing anonymous subprograms or creating a new subprogram within a subprogram and returning it. In section 1.2.3, we will discuss functional programming languages in which function objects are first-class, examine how function objects are represented, and see why procedural languages do not support these features.

0.3.6 The Semantics of Types

Domains

In mathematics, the *domain* of a function is the set of objects for which the function is defined. As stated in section 0.3.3, a type specifies the structure of its instances and the operations that can be performed on those objects. That is, a type specifies a domain over which its operations apply. A subprogram with a parameter of that type depends on its argument being an object in that domain so that it can use the domain's selectors and other operations. These dependencies might or might not be enforced by the language.

Early programming languages specified a fixed set of domains that were built into the language. Languages designed since Algol 68 provide type constructors that we can use to introduce new domains. Domains represented by types can be independent, or can overlap in the sense that an instance of one type can be regarded as an instance of the other. Two overlapping domains can be intersecting or merged, or one can be a subset of another [Fis93]. The domains boolean and integer are regarded as independent in Pascal. The domains integer and real intersect (rather than there being a subset relationship) because some integers cannot be represented exactly as reals due to the limitation on the number of significant digits. We can create merged domains in Pascal by defining type aliases. A subrange definition creates a new domain that is a subset of the base type domain. In C, the domains logical value, character, and integer are merged since the translator makes no distinctions among them. This can be convenient in some circumstances, but it prevents the compiler from catching some errors. Merged domains can also be created in C using the typedef statement.

Type checking

In statically typed languages, the type of every identifier is known at compile time via its declaration. In a *strongly typed* language, the compiler enforces the domain identity of objects and the domain requirements of operators and subprograms for their arguments. It prevents the program from assigning values of one type to variables of another, and ensures that the type of an identifier in an expression is correct for the operation being performed on its referent. If the type of the object and the type expected do not match and the language defines a conversion that obtains the correct type, the compiler performs it implicitly. Type checking prevents programs from performing meaningless operations since such errors are usually typographic or logic errors. Ada is strongly typed, and Pascal is strongly typed except when variant records are used.

In a *weakly typed* language, type checking is incomplete or can be circumvented, and the resulting errors are not caught until incorrect results are obtained or the program aborts unexpectedly. Fortran is weakly typed due to the EQUIVALENCE and COMMON statements, and the use of "Hollerith" (string) constants stored in integer variables. In Fortran and pre-ANSI C, the types of the arguments of a function call are not checked, so these languages are weakly typed. For example, the C standard library function sqrt() expects a double argument. For the invocation sqrt(7), a pre-ANSI compiler might simply push the integer value 7 on the stack, rather than creating and pushing a double with that value. The function code will interpret that argument's bytes (and probably succeeding bytes!) directly as a double value, resulting in an incorrect return value.

Dynamically typed languages may employ either strong or weak typing. As stated in section 0.2.2, with strong typing, objects must contain a representation of their type, and type checking occurs when an operation is applied to the object, that is, at execution time rather than at compile time. If an object's type is inappropriate for the operation, an error occurs and execution is halted (if the programmer has not specified actions to be taken in that case). The language provides this checking for built-in operations. For programmer-defined subprograms, the built-in type checking is performed when an operation is applied to an argument or component, since parameter types are not specified. As stated in section 0.2.2, most dynamically typed languages provide type predicates so that a subprogram can perform type checking explicitly.

The process of type checking is complicated by overlapping domains, which indicate the compatibility or convertibility of some types. In Pascal, type aliases do not define new domains, so operations for one type can be applied to instances of the other. In Ada, the programmer can choose whether a new domain defined by mapping from an existing domain defines a new domain: A subtype is compatible with the base type, but a derived type is not. Instances of a constrained type can be passed to operations that require an instance of the base type, but not vice versa. For some subset or intersection relationships, the representation of equivalent objects is different for each domain (e.g., integer and real in Pascal), so the compiler must perform an implicit conversion. In some languages, domains that are represented in the same manner are considered compatible (e.g., enums and ints in C).

Type checking provides increased safety and reliability, but programmers occasionally need to break type safety. A system programmer may need to manipulate a region of storage irrespective of the type of object contained, or a programmer may wish to use the binary encoding of an object as the basis for a hash function. Some strongly typed languages provide mechanisms for evading type checking, or for interpreting the same region of storage as an instance of different types for these purposes. For example, in Pascal, the programmer can use a variant record with pointer and integer variants to provide address arithmetic. In C, the programmer can use a union, or access an object through pointers with different base types via a pointer cast. ANSI C's type checking can be circumvented because we can cast a pointer to any object to char*, and then access that object as a sequence of bytes. Ada specifically provides no loopholes in its type system so that programs are safe, readable, and portable.

Explicit casts and conversions

We will draw a distinction between "casts" and "conversions" because they are different operations.[30] A *type cast* is a change in the type label on an object that does not change the object's representation. Examples include interpreting an instance of a subrange as an instance of the base type in Pascal, and using an instance of unsigned int as an int in C. The purpose of a cast is to indicate to the compiler that it is meaningful to use the object in a context that is not normally valid for its defined type. The compiler generates no code for a cast, nor does it create a new object. A cast is inherently unsafe because it changes the semantics of an object, and should be used with good reason and care. In C, we may cast a pointer to a pointer of a different type (and in pre-ANSI C, this can occur implicitly).

In many cases, it is valid to convert a value for one type to a corresponding value for another type. A *type conversion* creates a new object whose value is equivalent to that of the converted object. The conversion creates a new object because instances of the types have a different size or encoding. Some numeric conversions preserve all the information in the object (e.g., converting an integer to a real, or a conversion from char to double in C). Such an operation is termed a "promotion" or a "widening" conversion because the size of the new object is larger than the original. Other conversions are "demotions" or "narrowing" conversions that lose information, such as a conversion from a double to an int in C. Each language defines a set of conversions among built-in types that can be invoked explicitly using function call syntax, for example, the Pascal functions trunc and round. (In C, we enclose the type name in parentheses preceding the object to be converted, e.g., (long double) num.) We can code conversions among programmer-defined types or between programmer-defined and built-in types as functions.

Implicit coercions

Casts and conversions can be invoked explicitly by the programmer or implicitly by the compiler. A cast or conversion that is performed implicitly is called a

---

[30] Both type casts and conversions are referred to as "casts" in the C literature.

coercion. The compiler can use coercions in an initialization, assignment, expression evaluation, or argument passing to obtain the type required for the operation. For example, when we add an integer and a real in most languages, the integer is automatically converted to a real, and real addition is performed. In C, when adding an int and a long int, the int is promoted to a long. In fact, either conversion could be done in these cases, but most languages perform the promotion so that no information is lost implicitly. Each language defines the coercions that the compiler can use. For example, reals can be coerced to integers in C, but not in Pascal. PL/I will even implicitly convert a string variable that contains a sequence of characters representing a numeric literal to a number in an arithmetic expression. For safety and portability, Ada does not support implicit coercions, but the programmer can overload operators and subprograms to provide any argument signatures necessary.

Some languages that support abstract data types, such as C++, allow the programmer to define conversions as part of the definition of the type, which can then be used implicitly by the compiler. We will discuss this in section 11.2.

0.4 SUMMARY AND REVIEW

0.4.1 Control structure

Sequential control structures

- Nested expressions are evaluated from the inside out (except in some functional languages), and operator precedence, associativity, and parenthesization determine the order of nesting.
- In early languages, programmers coded flow of control explicitly using goto statements and conditional branches, but programs using goto statements were found to be difficult to understand, debug, test comprehensively, and decompose into units.
- Modern languages include single-entry single-exit *control structure* statements that specify the order of execution of statements, which we can nest to compose a structured program. The sequence, conditional, and iterative control structures are sufficient to code any single-entry single-exit program.
- A *conditional control structure* selects one of a set of actions to execute, depending on the value of a test expression. It can be either a statement or an expression that returns a value. Examples include the if-else and case statements.
- An *iterative control structure* specifies repeated execution of a statement or group of statements.
- A *conditional iteration* repeats the enclosed statements until the test expression is true (or false for some forms). Examples include the Pascal while and repeat statements, which test the exit condition at the beginning or end of the loop body, respectively. The C break and Ada exit statements permit us to locate the loop test and exit at any point in the loop body, and code more than one exit test in a loop.

- A *counter-controlled iteration* initializes a loop variable at the beginning of execution of the construct, updates it at the end of the loop body, and then tests it against a limit value to determine whether to exit.

- A *generalized iteration* specifies a list of initializations, an exit test, a list of update expressions, and a loop body. The C for statement is an example.

- An *implicit iteration* applies an operation to each element of a collection.

Subprograms and parameter passing

- Subprograms provide an abstraction mechanism that extends the language to reflect the problem domain or application.

- A subprogram definition specifies the name of the subprogram, the parameters, the local variables, and the statements executed when the subprogram is invoked.

- Subprogram invocation is a control structure, and the state of the caller must persist during the execution of the called subprogram so that it can be restored. The *run-time stack* is a last-in first-out list of *activation records*, each representing the state of a subprogram invocation that has begun but is waiting for completion of a subprogram it called.

- An activation record contains the subprogram's arguments, local variables, return address, *dynamic link* to the caller's activation record, and *static link* to its enclosing scope, and the contents of the processor registers.

- With *pass by value*, the parameter is treated as a local variable that is initialized with the value of the argument expression. Pass by value can only be used for input parameters, and is inefficient when passing large objects.

- A parameter *passed by reference* is an alias for the argument, and operations the subprogram performs on the parameter are performed on the argument, including assignments. We use pass by reference for output parameters, or to avoid the overhead of copying a large argument.

- With *pass by value-result*, the argument is copied to the subprogram's stack frame and then copied back to the caller upon exit, so modifications to the parameter only affect the local copy until the subprogram exits.

- The Ada programmer indicates the meaning of a parameter directly by specifying its *parameter mode* as in, out, or in out, and the compiler chooses the implementation.

Exceptions

- An *exception* is a run-time error that results in an invalid computation state. Exceptions include hardware errors, system errors, logical errors, and application-specific errors. A robust system must detect exceptions and respond to them, rather than continuing with invalid results.

- We often need to propagate the occurrence of an exception from the subprogram that detects the error to the subprogram that can handle the exception. Since different activation records are involved, a goto will not work. We can use parameters or return values to propagate the exception through a series of invocations, but this tightly binds those subprograms and clutters the intervening subprograms with code irrelevant to their purposes. In addition, the caller of a subprogram that returns an error condition might not check for the exception.

- Languages that support exceptions, such as Ada and C++, allow us to define exceptions, signal the occurrence of an exception, and specify *exception handlers* for various types of exceptions for a block.

- When an exception occurs, the block's handler for that exception is executed. If it doesn't define one, its activation record is popped and its caller's handler is executed. If the caller defines none, the run-time stack is unwound until encountering a subprogram that defines a handler for that exception, and that handler is executed in the context in which it is defined. If no matching handler is found, the program terminates. If the handler does not terminate execution, control continues at the statement after the block that specified the handler which was executed.

Concurrency

- Some programming languages permit the programmer to define an application as a collection of concurrent *tasks* or *processes*, which can execute independently.

- Programming languages that support concurrency include features for defining processes and specifying the code that they execute, for starting, suspending, re-activating, and terminating processes, and for synchronization and communication among processes. These operations are usually implemented using the facilities of the operating system.

- Processes can synchronize their operations using *semaphores*. A process signals that an event has occurred, and another process can wait for that signal. If a process performs a wait for a signal that has not occurred, it is suspended until the signal is performed.

- Processes can synchronize their operations using *critical regions*: Only one process can execute a critical region associated with a particular shared variable at a time.

- Processes can communicate via *shared memory* or *message passing* provided by the operating system.

0.4.2 Name Structure

Identifiers and declarations

- An *identifier* is a name *bound* to an object, constant, subprogram, parameter, or type, which is its *referent*. An identifier can refer to different program entities in different parts of the program, and different identifiers can refer to the same entity.

- A *static binding* is fixed before execution (e.g., the location of a global variable), and a *dynamic binding* can change during execution (e.g., the location of a local variable).
- A *declaration* is a statement that introduces a name into a scope, and may associate attributes such as a type with that name. We must declare an identifier before using it so that the compiler can detect typographic errors and invalid uses of the identifier.
- A *definition* is a declaration that also creates the associated entity.
- A *forward declaration* introduces an identifier, but does not specify creation of its referent, so a definition of that entity must occur elsewhere in the program. Forward declarations permit calling a subprogram before defining it, using a program entity in more than one compilation unit, coding mutually referential definitions, and designing with information hiding and top-down functional decomposition.
- The *symbol table* contains the binding and attributes for each identifier. The symbol table is usually not present at execution time in a compiled language, but is needed during execution in an interpreted language.
- With *static typing*, a type is associated with every object, constant, and subprogram identifier. The type of a subprogram is its *argument signature*, which lists its parameter and return types. The compiler uses this information to catch type errors, perform implicit conversions, and allocate objects.
- With *dynamic typing*, types are not associated with identifiers, so identifiers are *polymorphic*. A variable can refer to any object, and the type of the referent of an identifier can only be determined at run time. The compiler cannot catch type errors, so objects must contain an indication of their types. Object allocation, type checking, and binding of overloaded subprograms must be performed at run time. Dynamic typing provides more flexibility, but reduces efficiency and safety.
- An *alias declaration* introduces a synonym for an existing entity, but does not create a new entity.

Scope

- A *scope* is a section of the program that defines a name space. We can use scope to structure a program and partition its name space, allowing an identifier to refer to different objects, subprograms, or types in different parts of a program without causing a *name conflict*.
- The *scope of a declaration* is the part of the program in which the declared identifier refers to that entity. A *global* declaration or identifier is visible throughout the program, and a *local* declaration or identifier is restricted to some scope in the program.

Nested scopes

- A compound statement (e.g., delimited by begin and end) that includes declarations is a *block*, and the scope of those declarations is the block. In a *block-structured language*, blocks can be nested within other blocks and the name space of a program has a hierarchical structure.

- A name declared in an enclosing block is visible in a block unless the block also declares it, which *hides* declaration in the enclosing scope within the block. The scope of a declaration is the block in which it occurs and all enclosed blocks that do not declare that name, and two declarations of the same identifier have disjoint scopes.

- The process of *identifier resolution* determines which declaration an identifier *use* refers to, and selects the declaration in the nearest enclosing scope. If there is no declaration of that name in any enclosing scope, the use is an error.

- Nonlocal identifiers in a subprogram can be bound in the environment of the subprogram definition or in the environment of the call. With *static scope*, nonlocals are resolved according to the environment of the subprogram. The scope of an identifier and the referent of an identifier use are determined by the nesting of scopes in the source code, and do not vary.

- Block-structured languages employ static scope. To implement block structure, the compiler creates an activation record for each subprogram or block, and allocate its local variables within that activation record. The compiler translates a local variable use as an offset in the activation record.

- The activation record also contains a *static link* that points to the activation record of the enclosing scope, and nonlocals are accessed by following a chain of static links. The number of links is given by the *static distance*, the number of levels of scope between the use and the declaration.

- When a subprogram is called in the scope in which it is defined, the static link points to the activation record of its caller. If a subprogram is called in a scope nested within the scope of its definition, its static link is set by following n static links beginning with that of the caller, where n is the static distance between the call and the subprogram definition.

- With *dynamic scope*, the scope of a subprogram is nested within the scope of the invocation, and the referent of an identifier use is resolved according to the sequence of invocations. The scope of a declaration depends on which subprograms call the subprogram in which it appears. Dynamic scope is rarely used because it compromises the readability and reliability of programs.

Programmer-defined visibility

- When a subprogram accesses a nonlocal identifier, a *side effect* that is not visible in an invocation occurs, and the subprogram is not an independent unit.

- Block-structured languages provide a hierarchical name space structure and implicit access to names in enclosing scopes so that names can be shared. However, they do not permit controlling visibility explicitly for each name or for an individual scope.

- Languages that support *modules* allow us to divide the set of names in a module into an *interface* visible outside that unit and an *implementation* private to the unit, and to explicitly import names declared in the interfaces of other modules. Name visibility relationships are explicit, and hidden side effects, unintended access, and name capture cannot occur.

Overloading

- Most languages *overload* operators for their built-in types so that programmers can use the same operator symbol for conceptually similar operations on different types. Many contemporary languages support this capability for subprogram names, and we can define more than one subprogram with the same name in the same scope if each has a distinct argument signature.
- The compiler resolves an invocation of an overloaded subprogram name by matching the argument signature of the invocation with those of the subprogram's definitions.
- Implicit conversions can cause an invocation to be ambiguous because there can be conversions from the argument signature of the call to the argument signatures of more than one subprogram definition.
- A dynamically typed language can support overloading, but the process of binding a subprogram definition to a call occurs at execution time.
- The ability to overload subprogram names is essential for object-oriented languages.

0.4.3 Data Structure

Data objects

- A *data object* consists of a region of storage in which a value is encoded, and represents a problem domain entity or a component of the system or application.
- Each data object is an *instance* of a data type, which defines the operations and storage structure of its instances.
- A *variable* is an association between a name and a data object consisting of a value stored at a location.
- A variable name use may refer to the object's value, or *r-value*, or its location, or *l-value*, depending on the context. An *l*-value is necessary to modify the object, that is, for the left side of an assignment or a reference parameter.
- Named constants improve a program's readability. A constant differs from a variable because it cannot be modified (i.e., the identifier's *l*-value is not available).
- A *symbolic constant* declares a named constant whose value can be computed by the compiler, and usually must be an instance of a built-in type with a literal notation. A *read-only variable* denotes a constant object of any type, whose initialization may have to be calculated at execution time.
- We create an object with a variable definition or a dynamic storage operation, which *instantiates* a type and *allocates* storage for it. The *lifetime* of an object

is the duration of execution from its creation to its destruction, when its storage is *deallocated*.

- The lifetime of an object at execution time and the scope of an identifier in the source code are different issues, and an object may exist when it is not accessible or have more than one name.

- Allocation of an object and *initialization* of that object, which places a valid value in that storage, are separate operations. No operations (besides assignment) are valid for an object that is not initialized. An *assignment* changes the value encoded in an existing object and requires an *l*-value.

Storage allocation policies

- The lifetime of a *statically allocated* object is the entire execution of the program. Some languages, such as C, support defining a static object whose name is local to a subprogram.

- An *automatically allocated* object exists for a particular execution of the subprogram or block in which it is declared. The compiler allocates it in the subprogram's activation record, and accesses it by its offset, possibly after following a chain of static links.

- A *dynamically allocated* object is created when indicated by the programmer, and deallocation of dynamic objects may be under programmer control or may be performed automatically, depending on the language.

- Dynamic objects are allocated separately from the stack in the *heap* or *free store* by a run-time system provided by the language system. Efficient management of heap storage is complex, and designers have developed several algorithms and data structures to manage it.

- With *programmer-controlled deallocation*, three errors that are difficult to debug can occur: omitting deallocation (a *memory leak*), using a *dangling pointer* to a deallocated object, or deallocating an object more than once.

- *Automatic storage reclamation* detects when an object can no longer be referenced by the program and reclaims its storage. Two common techniques are *reference counting*, which maintains a reference count stored with each object, and *garbage collection*, which marks all accessible objects and then reclaims the rest of storage. Automatic deallocation is more convenient and less error-prone for the programmer, but results in less efficient executable code.

Data types

- A data type models a category of entities in the problem domain or components of the system or application. The definition of a data type includes specification of both the valid values for instances, and the operations that may be performed on instances. These should mirror those of the category the type represents. The use of types extends the language so that the structure of the problem domain and application is reflected in the program.

- Every language specifies a set of *built-in types* such as the logical, character, and numeric types, which are usually types built into the hardware or motivated by the intended problem domain. The language provides constructs for creating instances, writing values, and performing basic operations and input/output on instances.

- Numeric types include integer and floating-point types, which are usually represented in two's complement and IEEE floating-point format, respectively. Some languages support more than one size for numeric types, and Ada allows the programmer to specify the range and precision of a real value.

- Most languages provide a logical type, for example, boolean, for the values "true" and "false". We can use the logical operations and, or, and not with booleans, comparisons and other tests return booleans, and boolean values control conditional evaluation and iteration.

- In most languages, character is a built-in type, and strings are treated as fixed-size arrays of characters. In Pascal, the size of a string object is fixed at compile time and different sizes are different types. In Ada and C, the size is fixed at creation time, we can allocate strings dynamically, and all string parameters are the same type.

Defining types

- Modern languages support defining types and using them to create objects, specify parameters, and define other types.

- The instances of a type are *first-class* objects if the language provides a complete set of features for using those objects (e.g., initialization, assignment, equality comparisons, input and output, and a literal notation for writing objects). The language must also support using of the type as a parameter or return type to provide its operations, or as the base type of another type.

- A *type constructor* is a language feature that defines a kind of type by listing its values, restricting an existing type, or describing the structure of composite objects.

- A *type definition* gives the name of the type, the kind of type, the structure of its instances, and the type's operations if the language supports abstract data types. The translator creates a *type object* that represents this information, which is a compile-time construct in compiled languages.

- Many languages provide *type operations* that return information about the type itself, rather than a particular instance, such as the size of its instances or the smallest and largest value of an ordered type.

Programmer-defined types

- A *type alias* gives an alternate name for an existing type, and is used to give a name that reflects the intended semantics for instances of the type. In Pascal and C, the new type name is a synonym for the existing type. In Ada, we can use a *subtype* to define a synonym, or a *derived type* to specify a distinct type with the same structure and operations as the base type.

- A *pointer type* specifies a base type, and the value of a pointer object is either a reference to an instance of the base type, or a special value that indicates that the pointer does not refer to an object. The type object includes the base type and its size for dynamic allocation.

- Pointer operations include *dereference*, which returns the referent and can be used as an *l*-value, allocation and deallocation of dynamic referents, assignment, and equality test.

- Pointer assignment causes both pointers to refer to the same object (rather than copying a referent), and pointer comparison tests whether the pointers refer to the same object (rather than comparing referents).

- A pointer object contains the address of its referent. C provides address arithmetic for pointers, which can be unsafe.

- An *enumerated type* models an entity or attribute for which there is a fixed set of values or states, and is defined by listing names for the values. The value names are symbolic constants declared in the scope in which the type definition appears (or in the enumeration scope in Ada), and provide a literal notation for instances. The type object specifies the size, the value names, and their encoding.

- The enumerated type is first-class in Pascal and Ada since they support initialization, assignment, equality tests, literals, enumeration parameters, and enumeration base types. Each enumeration in ANSI C is a separate type, but any integer can be assigned to an enumeration object, and enumeration values can be used as integers.

- A *subrange type* represents a category of entities with a restricted range of values, and its definition gives the type name and the value limits. The type object maintains the size, the base type, and the limits. The language ensures that a value assigned to a subrange instance is within the type's limits, possibly involving run-time checks. The subrange type provides safety and reliability, at the expense of execution-time efficiency.

- The operations and literal notation of the subrange type are those of its base type.

- In Pascal, subrange limits must be literals. In Ada, we can define a subrange type as either a subtype or a derived type using a range constraint, and can disable range checking with a compiler directive. Ada also includes several other kinds of constraints for defining new types.

- An *array* is a fixed-size, homogenous, indexable sequence of elements that is treated as a composite object. The definition of an array type gives the type name, the base type, and the index type (or the subscript limits), and the type object specifies the base and index types.

- *Subscription* is the selector operation for arrays, and returns a reference to an element that may be used as an *l*-value or a *r*-value. Subscription is indicated by square brackets in Pascal and C, or parentheses in Fortran and Ada.

- Fortran only provides static array objects with integer indices. Pascal introduced the array type with any discrete, ordered, finite type as the index type, but array limits are fixed at compile time, and arrays with different limits are different types. Ada introduced the unconstrained array type and array type attributes to facilitate defining dynamically sized arrays and subprograms that operate on arrays. C does not support an array type.

- Many languages support coherent operations such as assignment and equality comparison for arrays, and we can define additional operations by using an array parameter type.

- A *record* is a composite object consisting of a collection of components or *fields*, each with a name and a type. The components store values for the attributes and relationships of an instance of the category of entities the record type represents.

- A record type definition gives the type name and the names and types of its components. A record instance has a value for each component, and is typically stored as a sequence of the values for its fields. The type object includes the field names and types, the size, and the field offsets.

- The *component selection* operation accesses a field in a record object by the field name. The operation is usually indicated by *record.field*, and can be used as an *l*-value or a *r*-value.

- Support for coherent operations on records is incomplete in Pascal and C, while Ada supports record initialization, assignment, equality tests, literals, subprogram parameters, and operator overloading, so records are first-class.

- A *union type* specifies a set of alternate substructures of different types, and an instance can contain an object of one of these types. A Pascal *variant record type* specifies a set of fields and a variant part containing a tag component and a set of substructures, and only one of the substructures is stored in an instance at any time. We access variant record fields using component selection. The type object contains the size of an instance, the nonvariant field names and types, and the type descriptions of the variant parts.

- The variant record type is unsafe in Pascal because we cannot assign a tag and the associated variant part to an instance coherently, so the tag and the variant part in an object might not be consistent. Ada variant records are type-safe because the language supports coherent assignments and specifies that the type tag must be checked when a field is accessed. The C union does not indicate which substructure is present, and is inherently unsafe.

- *Abstract data types* allow us to explicitly associate a type's operations with the definition of its storage structure, and to hide that structure from users of the type.

- Some languages support subprogram parameters to permit coding higher-level algorithms as subprograms, and reusing them via an invocation with a particular subprogram as an argument. However, function objects are not first-class in procedural languages.

Type checking and conversions

- A type specifies a *domain* over which operations on instances of the type apply, and a subprogram with a parameter of that type depends on its argument being an object in that domain for correct operation.

- A *strongly typed* language enforces the domain requirements of assignments, operator operands, and subprogram arguments, which provides safety and reliability. Type checking can be done by the compiler in a statically typed language, but must be done at execution time for a dynamically typed language.

- In a *weakly typed* language, type checking is incomplete or can be circumvented.

- Overlapping domains complicate type checking: No distinction is made between merged domains, instances of a constrained type can be used as instances of the base type (but not vice versa), and some overlapping domains require implicit conversions because instances of the types are represented differently.

- A *type cast* changes the type of an object from the point of view of the compiler, but does not create a new object.

- A *type conversion* creates a new object whose value is equivalent to that of the converted object.

- Casts and conversions can be invoked explicitly by the programmer or implicitly by the compiler, and the latter are referred to as *coercions*.

0.5 EXERCISES

0.1 Give three reasons why programs that employ unrestricted use of goto statements are difficult to understand, debug and verify.

0.2 Discuss the issues for language designers in specifying the semantics of counter-controlled iteration. Give examples of how these issues are resolved in various languages.

0.3 **(a)** Construct an example program in the block-structured language of your choice that includes a function invocation that would return a different result depending on whether the language uses pass by value or pass by reference.

 (b) Construct an example program in the block-structured language of your choice that includes a function invocation that would return a different result depending on whether the language uses pass by value-result or pass by reference.

0.4 When does the behavior of pass by reference differ from that of pass by value-result for a given parameter? Explain how their behaviors differ.

0.5 List and describe the contents of an activation record for a block-structured language.

0.6 Suppose that proc1 calls proc2, which calls proc3, which calls proc4. Now suppose that proc4 can detect the occurrence of a particular error, but only proc1 can specify the processing necessary to recover from the error.

 (a) Give two ways of propagating an error indication from to proc4 to proc1 in a language that does not support exceptions.

 (b) What are the drawbacks of each method?

0.7 **(a)** What constructs are required for a language to support programmer-defined exception handling?

(b) Describe the flow of control when an exception is signaled in a language that supports exceptions.

0.8 **(a)** What is the meaning of a forward declaration?

(b) Give three situations in which a programmer would need a forward declaration.

0.9 **(a)** In a block-structured language, how is the referent of an identifier use determined?

(b) In a block-structured language, where is a declaration visible?

0.10 **(a)** Why are both static and dynamic links necessary in a block-structured language?

(b) How is each used? How is each initialized?

(c) When does an activation record in a block-structured language have static and dynamic links that point to different activation records?

0.11 Explain how nonlocal variables are accessed in a block-structured language.

0.12 Describe how the value of the static link is determined when a subprogram is called in a block-structured language.

0.13 Suppose we have a Pascal program main that contains a procedure proc2, which is nested within a recursive procedure proc1 nested within the program main. Suppose that main calls proc1, which calls proc2, which calls proc1, which calls itself—that is, we have the sequence of invocations main → proc1 → proc2 → proc1 → proc1.

(a) Draw a diagram of the run-time stack at that point showing the static and dynamic links (see Figure 0.3).

(b) Suppose that the last invocation of proc1 then calls proc2. Draw a diagram of the run-time stack at that point showing the static and dynamic links.

0.14 Construct an example program in the block-structured language of your choice that includes a function invocation that would return a different result depending on whether the language uses static or dynamic scope.

0.15 Describe the disadvantages of the use of hierarchical static scope for organizing the name space of a program.

0.16 **(a)** What is subprogram overloading and why is it useful?

(b) How does the compiler determine which subprogram definition to execute for an invocation of an overloaded subprogram? Are there cases in which an invocation cannot be disambiguated?

0.17 **(a)** Name three operators in C or Pascal whose result is an *l*-value.

(b) Name three C operators whose operand must be an *l*-value.

(c) Does the C unary & operator return an *l*-value?

0.18 **(a)** Why should a programming language provide a feature for named constants?

(b) What is the difference between a symbolic constant and a read-only variable?

0.19 Clearly distinguish between the lifetime and scope of a variable.

0.20 Clearly distinguish between instantiation and initialization.

0.21 Describe when and how an object is allocated and deallocated with each of the following storage allocation policies:

(a) static allocation

(b) automatic allocation

(c) dynamic allocation

0.22 In Fortran, all variables are allocated statically, including the local variables of subroutines. Give three disadvantages of this characteristic.

0.23 **(a)** What is a static local variable (e.g., in C)? Give an example for which a static local variable would be useful.

(b) Why can't a static local variable be allocated in the function's stack frame?

0.24 **(a)** The Pascal standard states that all pointers to a dynamic object should be set to nil when the object is deallocated. Give an advantage and two disadvantages of this design decision.

(b) A particular C compiler sets a pointer to NULL whenever the free() function is applied to it, although the language definition does not specify this behavior. Give an advantage and a disadvantage of this behavior.

0.25 Discuss the advantages and disadvantages of programmer-controlled and automatic deallocation of dynamically allocated objects.

0.26 **(a)** Describe three errors that can occur with programmer-controlled deallocation of dynamically allocated objects.

(b) Why are each of these errors difficult for the programmer to recognize?

(c) Explain why each of these problems cannot occur with automatic storage reclamation.

0.27 Describe three different views of the nature of a data type.

0.28 **(a)** What do we mean when we say that a type is first-class in a language?

(b) For each of the following types, describe the extent to which it is a first-class type or not in Pascal, C and Ada:

(i)   enumerations
(ii)   arrays
(iii) records/structures
(iv)   subprograms

0.29 **(a)** What is a type object, and how is it used?

(b) Describe the information contained in the type object for three kinds of types.

(c) Give an example type operation in C and in Ada.

0.30 Explain why the record type object is more complex than the array type object.

0.31 Discuss whether a type definition causes any storage to be allocated at execution time. Consider both C and Pascal.

0.32 What is the purpose of the Ada derived type construct?

0.33 Name two ways of creating a dangling pointer in C that are not possible in Pascal. Why are they present?

0.34 For each of the following types, give an example of a problem domain category that it would be used to represent (other than those in the text):

(a) enumeration
(b) subrange
(c) array
(d) record/structure
(e) union

0.35 List the operations for each of the following types in Pascal, C, or Ada:

(a) characters
(b) pointers
(c) arrays
(d) enumerations
(e) records/structures
(f) unions

0.36 Select five Pascal types and describe how Ada improves on each.

0.37 **(a)** Which Pascal programmer-defined types have literal representations, and which do not?

(b) Give a readable notation for those that do not.

0.38 An often-discussed point of programming language semantics is whether two arrays with the same base and index types but different subscript ranges are of the same type. Give arguments for each case.

0.39 How can strong typing be ensured for a dynamically typed language? (Consider both built-in operations and programmer-defined subprograms.)

0.40 **(a)** Carefully distinguish between a cast and a conversion.

(b) Give two examples of each (in any of the languages we have discussed).

1

Software Architecture

In Chapter 0, we discussed programming language features that support writing programs. In this chapter, we will examine issues that arise in the design of large software systems. We will survey the abstraction mechanisms that have been used to express programs and partition software systems, following the progression from abstraction of operation in early programming languages to contemporary abstractions that include both structure and operation. Next, we inspect four programming paradigms, each of which embodies a different perspective on the nature of computation and the constructs necessary to express a computation. We see that the object model is both a natural outgrowth of existing abstraction mechanisms, and a significantly different viewpoint on the nature of computation and the structure of software systems. Finally, we describe the impact that the object paradigm has on software engineering. Like structured programming before it, the object model affects the entire process of creating software systems, not just the activity of programming. In fact, the object model is likely to have a larger impact on analysis and design of software than on coding.

This chapter covers the following topics:

- sources of complexity in software systems, and human cognitive strategies for dealing with complexity (1.1.1)

- the purpose and meaning of abstraction in computing, encapsulation and information hiding, the interface and implementation of an abstraction, and subprograms as abstractions (1.1.2)
- procedural modules, the linker, the module interface and implementation, module scope, system design with modules, and language support for modules (1.1.3)
- abstract data types, representation independence, system design with abstract data types, modules and data abstraction, and generic abstract data types (1.1.4)
- an introduction to classes, object terminology, class variables and messages, inheritance, and dynamic binding (1.1.5)
- computing paradigms as models of computation (1.2.1)
- the imperative programming paradigm (1.2.2)
- the functional programming paradigm, and functions as first-class objects (1.2.3)
- the logic programming paradigm (1.2.4)
- the object-oriented programming paradigm, and computation as simulation (1.2.5)
- a brief review of software engineering and structured methods (1.3.1)
- the object model applied to analysis and design of contemporary applications, and its affect on system structure and development activities (1.3.2)
- the uniformity of object-oriented development, and software life-cycle models (1.3.3)
- reusability, and class libraries and frameworks (1.3.4)
- extendibility and incremental development (1.3.5)

1.1 ABSTRACTION MECHANISMS

1.1.1 Software Complexity

Problem domain complexity

Much of the complexity in a software system results from the characteristics of the real-world system that it models, and therefore is an essential property of the system. For example, the software that controls a manufacturing process must manage the properties and location of each component, the time dependencies among processes, quality control and error response, and so on. Similarly, a simulation of an astronomical system must represent the various types of stars, planets, nebulas, and other celestial bodies, and their structure, properties, and interactions.

Factors external to the system the software models make it difficult to specify the software system's requirements exactly and completely. For example, the software that controls a mobile robot must deal with objects and other robots in its environment. In addition, changes in the problem domain or in the requirements for the software's interaction with it frequently occur during the lifetime of the system. For example, changes in government regulations affect the information that a financial system stores and reports.

Programming system complexity

Early programs were written in assembly language, usually by a single programmer. As hardware capabilities increased, the tasks computers were applied to became more complex and varied. Higher-level languages provided facilities for larger, more structured programs, and the issue of dealing with complexity became crucial in software development. As the size of a software system increases, the total complexity increases faster than the number of components due to interdependencies among those components. For example, consider a system with ten modules. If another module is added to the system, the total complexity increases not only by the additional ten percent within that module, but also by the complexity of the new module's interactions with up to ten other modules.

For very large software systems consisting of millions of lines of code, it is impossible for one designer to understand the system in its entirety. Therefore, software engineers must also deal with the complexity of stating the system's requirements and describing its structure, and of communication among the members of the development team. For example, Brooks observed that n programmers working on a project do not complete it in $1/n$ the time necessary for one programmer [Bro75]. In addition, large systems often include the complexity associated with providing fault tolerance, concurrent access, usability, and maintainability. Complexity is also increased because software systems are frequently built from the smallest possible units, namely individual lines of code, rather than from larger components.

Managing complexity

We can see from this discussion that two central issues in software design are deciding how much of the problem domain complexity must be reflected in the software system, and determining how to structure the system to reduce its complexity (while maintaining its correspondence with the problem domain system). Human cognition uses a number of strategies for dealing with the complexity found in the environment, and these techniques are just as helpful in controlling software complexity. They allow us to handle more information, given the limits of human short-term memory, by structuring and grouping information, hiding complexity, and allowing us to understand the system at a higher, more abstract level. We will see in this chapter that these processes are also essential components of the object-oriented model of computation.

Decomposition is the process of dividing a complex system into loosely coupled components that can be considered individually. This partitioning reduces comprehension of the system to the smaller, independent problems of understanding each component and the interactions among components. We also use the inverse process, *composition*, when we recognize that a group of components makes up a higher-level component. For example, to understand the operation of a car, a mechanic divides it into the drive train, the electrical system, the suspension system, the braking system, and so on, and also decomposes each system into its components when necessary. We often find it useful decompose a system's components, and composite components are often components of other composites, so the structure of a system is described by a hierarchy of whole-part and aggregation relationships. Such composition hierarchies appear in all complex physical, biological, and social systems.

Software designers use decomposition and composition of both processing and objects in developing an application. For example, in a functional decomposition, a subprogram represents a particular subtask, and that subprogram is composed of individual statements. In sections 1.1.4 and 1.3.2, we will see that an object-oriented decomposition of an application organizes the system in terms of classes of objects and their behavior, rather than according to tasks and subtasks.

Classification is the process of recognizing commonalities and differences among individual entities to create categories or archetypes. Grouping entities into categories and then dealing with the categories controls complexity by reducing the number of concepts necessary to describe a situation. The resulting concepts can also be used to describe other systems with similar components. For example, we all have a concept of the category "chair" that helps us deal effectively with a wide range of such objects, including new kinds of chairs we have never encountered. We often find that categories have subcategories with additional or differing properties and behavior, resulting in a hierarchy of classifications. Like composition hierarchies, classification hierarchies appear in physical, biological, and social systems. For example, the taxonomy of plants and animals is a classification hierarchy. Software designers use classification when determining the subprograms and types necessary in an application. That is, a subprogram represents a category of tasks, and a type describes a class of objects.

Abstraction is the process of extracting the relevant information about a category, entity, or activity, and ignoring the inessential details. (We also use the term "abstraction" to refer to the constructs that result from this process.) By not paying attention to unimportant details, we simplify our view of the category or activity. For example, the driver of a car only deals with using the gas pedal to speed up and the brake pedal to slow down, rather than the complex chain of mechanics triggered by those devices. As we will see in this section, software designers use subprograms and modules to create abstractions of process, and types to define abstractions of structure.

There are many ways to determine the necessary categories and abstractions and use them to decompose a complex system. Doing so is not easy, and different people often create different representations for the same situation. The measure of whether one organization is better than another is its usability and predictive power for the task for which it was created. That is, we judge the quality of an abstraction according to whether it represents the appropriate properties from the perspective of using of the abstraction. For example, the classifications, decomposition, and abstractions that are effective for the driver of a car and for an auto mechanic are quite different. In human cognition, categories and abstractions are prototypes that are not fixed, but are developed as experience dictates.

1.1.2 Abstraction in Computing

Programming abstractions

Some basic abstractions were created early in the development of programming languages. Assembly languages used symbolic names for operations and locations to hide the details of the machine language encoding of instructions and the actual storage addresses of data. Fortran's algebraic expression syntax hid the use of temporary registers and individual machine operations to implement expression evaluation. Fortran also allowed the programmer to ignore the details of the encoding of real numbers and the manipulation of that representation. Algol hid the details of control flow and branching with the conditional and iterative control structures (rather than using gotos and statement labels as in assembly language). As we discussed in section 0.1.1, control structures also make it easier to decompose a program, and to do so hierarchically. Like all programming abstractions, each of these language features decreases the amount of detail we must deal with, and each represents a step away from the machine architecture and toward the problem domain.

Higher-level programming languages have implemented a progression of constructs for programmer-defined abstractions, beginning with abstractions of operation such as subprograms and procedural modules.[1] Later languages such as Pascal provided constructors for abstractions that structure information, such as enumeration and record types. Contemporary programming languages support abstract data types and classes that encapsulate both structure and processing, and provide information hiding. We will discuss each of these abstractions in more detail in this section.

Software designers use programming abstractions as components in the decomposition of the system, and these abstractions and their interactions provide the designer with a higher-level view of the structure and operation of the system. For example, in a functional decomposition, an application consists of a set of subprograms or procedural modules, and a diagram of the system structure is a graph with the subprograms as vertices and invocations (and argument passing) as edges. For the programmer, an abstraction such as a subprogram or type extends the language to reflect the problem domain or the design of the application. The use of abstractions simplifies programs, improves readability, and reduces the number of errors by revealing the logical structure of the program. A subprogram or abstract data type written by one programmer can be used by others, who do not need to understand its internal operation. In fact, a software development organization can

---

[1] Modules in Modula-2 and C were originally created to encapsulate a group of related subprograms. Although, as we will see in section 1.1.4, modules can be used to encapsulate the operations and structure of a type, we will use the term "module" in its original procedural meaning, and distinguish between "process-oriented" modules and "object-based" abstract data types.

maintain a library of abstractions to reuse in applications, thereby reducing coding effort and increasing programmer productivity.

Determining abstractions

Designers decide to use a particular kind of abstraction (e.g., a subprogram or type) by choosing either a top-down decomposition of the structure of the application, or a bottom-up composition of lower-level elements. Top-down design proceeds from the general to the specific, while bottom-up design leads from the specific to the general. These processes provide two complementary perspectives on the nature of the abstraction.

In *top-down* decomposition, we recognize that a computation or a data structure is a logical unit or that the application requires several instances of it (usually from analysis of the system requirements or problem domain). We determine the abstraction's external interface from those uses, and then design an appropriate internal implementation. For example, a program that provides user commands for managing a hierarchical file system (like the UNIX or DOS command shell) will have several commands whose argument is a path in the directory structure. The designer recognizes that the system needs a subprogram that takes a path and returns a reference to the specified file or directory, and that each subprogram that must evaluate a path will invoke this subprogram.

In *bottom-up* composition, we recognize that there are multiple occurrences of a series of operations or of a data structure. (We have all had the experience of writing some code, and thinking we have written those lines somewhere before.) We factor these out to create an abstraction, and replace each occurrence by a name and arguments (for an abstraction of processing), or by an instance of a type (for a data abstraction). As in classification, we notice that instances of similar processing or structure are present in the system, and create an abstraction that represents those instances.

Encapsulation and information hiding

The two processes of determining abstractions reflect the two essential characteristics of abstractions, encapsulation and information hiding. An abstraction is an *encapsulation* that groups a set of related lower-level units of processing and/or structure. From the bottom-up perspective, the process of designing an abstraction involves deciding which units make up the abstraction. For example,

- A subprogram encapsulates a series of operations.
- A module encapsulates a group of subprograms and objects.
- A record encapsulates its fields (but does not provide information hiding).
- An abstract data type encapsulates both its operations and storage structure.

Like classification, this packaging decreases the amount of information that must be retained to understand the structure of an application.

An abstraction provides *information hiding* because it hides inessential details from its users so that they can be ignored.[2] Information hiding reflects the top-down perspective that an abstraction is defined by its purpose and how the application uses it, rather than by how that processing or structure is implemented. An important aspect of designing a programming abstraction is the process of separating the logical use of a category of code or data objects from its physical algorithm or representation. The external appearance of an abstraction to its users is called its *interface*, and the internal structure not visible to users is its *implementation*. In particular, the code of a subprogram and the storage structure of an abstract data type are implementations that are not visible to their users. Information hiding implies that users of an abstraction do not need to know its implementation to use it, and also that users of an abstraction cannot access its implementation.

Information hiding provides a number of advantages for software design. It reduces the complexity that users of a subprogram or type must handle, and it allows the programmer to think about instances of the abstraction and their interactions with the rest of the application at a higher level. With information hiding, the components of a software system can interact only through their interfaces. This restriction simplifies the relationships among those components, reducing the opportunity for unintended or incorrect interactions and decreasing the number of coding errors. Since designers can implement program components independently, they can partition the development effort in a manner that reflects the structure of the system. Information hiding also allows the designer of an abstraction to change the abstraction's implementation without affecting other program units that employ it.

We refer to a program component that uses an abstraction through its interface as a *client* of that abstraction.[3] The clients of a subprogram are subprograms that call it. The clients of an abstract data type are subprograms that create and manipulate instances of the type, or types that use it as the type of components in their storage structure. The interface of an abstraction represents a contract between the designer of the abstraction and its clients that describes the capabilities and behavior that clients can expect from the abstraction.

Subprograms as abstractions

Subprograms were the first mechanism that programming languages supported for named, reusable, programmer-defined abstractions. As we saw in section 0.1.2, subprograms provide an abstraction that allows us to package a computation and reuse it via an invocation, and to view the structure of programs that call it at a higher level.

A subprogram is an encapsulation of operation whose interface consists of the subprogram name, the argument signature, and a description of its operation. The

---

[2] In fact, the enclosure around the components that an abstraction encapsulates may or may not be transparent [Ber93]. For example, a record encapsulates its fields but does not provide information hiding. However, many authors (e.g., [Boo94], [Gra94] and [Rum90]) use the term encapsulation to also imply hiding of the components of the abstraction.

[3] We will also occasionally refer to the programmers that use an abstraction as its clients.

description of a subprogram's operation can be either an informal explanation of its behavior, such as a comment or reference manual entry, or a formal specification of the pre-conditions and post-conditions of the subprogram's operation. The interface of a subprogram also specifies any error conditions that it can signal (or exceptions in a programming language that supports them).

The hidden implementation of a subprogram consists of its code (i.e., its algorithm) and its local variables. For example, the C programmer can use the standard library function sqrt() without being concerned with how it calculates the square root of its argument. (The interface of this function specifies that its return value is undefined if the argument is negative.) The designer of a subprogram can change its implementation, perhaps to improve its efficiency, without affecting its callers. As we saw in section 0.2.4, block-structured languages such as Pascal permit the programmer to nest auxiliary subprograms within a subprogram. In this case, the nested subprograms are also part of the implementation of the enclosing subprogram, and are not visible outside its scope.

As mentioned in section 0.2.4, subprograms are the basis for the design methodology of top-down functional decomposition. The designer decomposes the system according to the tasks that it must perform, then breaks those tasks into subtasks, and so on. Each task is coded as a subprogram that calls the subprograms that implement its subtasks. The interface for each subprogram is specified first according to the task it must perform and the information necessary to perform that task. After determining the necessary subprograms, the programmers design each subprogram's algorithm and local variables. (In fact, some subprograms may be temporarily coded as "stubs" that simply print a message so that their callers can be tested before they are implemented.) This partitioning of the system organizes its processing in levels of increasing detail, beginning with the main program, and allows subproblems at each level of granularity to be solved independently.

1.1.3 Modules

Separate compilation and linking

For a large application, keeping the entire source code in a single file quickly becomes unmanageable, especially when many programmers are involved. We would also like to avoid recompiling the entire source code of an application each time we modify a particular subprogram, and want to allow several programmers to work on different parts of the application simultaneously. These problems can be handled with the module construct. A *module* is a source code file that can be compiled individually to an object code file, even though it refers to objects, subprograms, and types defined in other modules.[4] A language that supports modules must provide syntax for partitioning a program into modules, and for declaring the subprograms, and objects used by a module that are defined in other modules. In

---

[4] Fortran supports separate compilation of individual subroutines. However, this is not the same as supporting modules because each compilation unit can contain only a single subroutine and no objects.

addition, some mechanism must implement cross-referencing and type checking of names that are used in more than one module. It is also helpful if the language provides a facility for determining which source code files in an application must be recompiled when a file is modified.

The *linker* combines the collection of object files corresponding to the modules in an application to create a complete executable program, and resolves references to identifiers that are used in one module but defined in another. It also links the object code for any standard library subprograms the application invokes. Figure 1.1 illustrates the action of the linker for an application with three modules containing five subprograms.

To support linking separately compiled modules, the compiler must include information about externally visible names with each object file. This consists of an

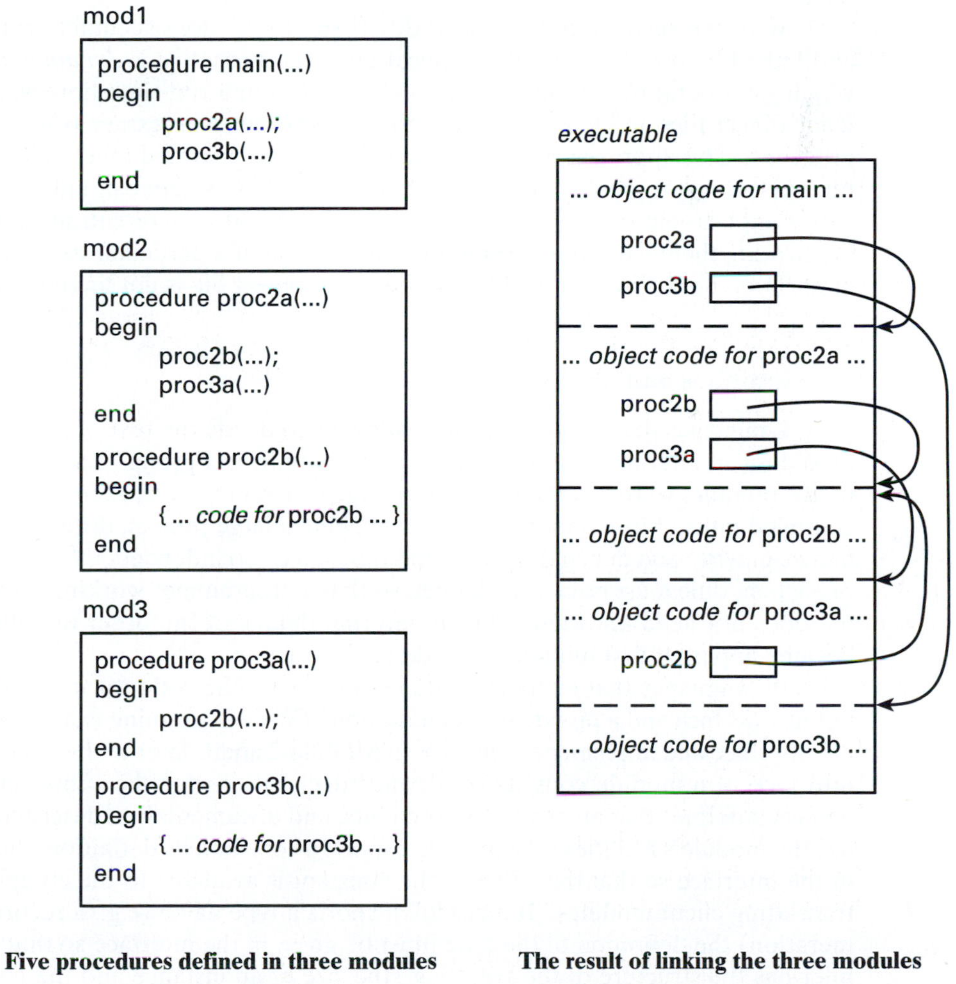

mod1

```
procedure main(...)
begin
      proc2a(...);
      proc3b(...)
end
```

mod2

```
procedure proc2a(...)
begin
      proc2b(...);
      proc3a(...)
end

procedure proc2b(...)
begin
      { ... code for proc2b ... }
end
```

mod3

```
procedure proc3a(...)
begin
      proc2b(...);
end

procedure proc3b(...)
begin
      { ... code for proc3b ... }
end
```

executable

```
... object code for main ...
            proc2a  [   ]
            proc3b  [   ]
- - - - - - - - - - - - - - - - -
... object code for proc2a ...
            proc2b  [   ]
            proc3a  [   ]
- - - - - - - - - - - - - - - - -
... object code for proc2b ...
- - - - - - - - - - - - - - - - -
... object code for proc3a ...
            proc2b  [   ]
- - - - - - - - - - - - - - - - -
... object code for proc3b ...
```

Five procedures defined in three modules   **The result of linking the three modules**

Figure 1.1   The linker resolves external references among modules.

external symbol table of the names exported by and imported into that module. The entry for an exported object or subprogram gives its location in the object code, and the entry for an imported object or subprogram gives a list of the locations of uses (or calls) of that entity. The linker uses these tables to substitute the location of the referenced object or subprogram (adjusted to its location in the entire executable) for each use, as illustrated in Figure 1.1.

The linker can be provided by the operating system or by the programming language system. If the programmer specifies the files necessary to build the executable (as in C), a linker supplied by the operating system (e.g., the UNIX linker) can link modules written in different languages. To relieve the programmer of this task, the language system can maintain the module library and deduce which modules are necessary for an executable from the import declarations in the modules (as in Ada).

With the *static linking* we have described, the entire executable is packaged and linked before executing the application. An alternative is *dynamic linking*, in which the operating system maintains object files in a run-time library, and then loads object files and links them with the application as necessary while execution proceeds. This approach is more efficient for system-provided functionality such as file operations or graphic interface components. The system can link several executing applications to the same library object files (if they are re-entrant) rather than duplicating them within each program. In addition, if a particular execution of the application never invokes the library code, that object file is not linked and loaded.

Interface and implementation

Languages that support modules allow us to divide the text of a program into modules (or, alternatively, to compose a program from a group of modules). Originally, modules were invented to allow a large program to be broken into separately compiled units. More importantly for managing a large project, different programmers can write and debug different modules. To do so independently, the interface of each module must be clearly defined so that a programmer working on one module does not need knowledge of the internal details of the other modules. So it became apparent that modules provide an abstraction.

In languages that support modules, we divide the code for a module into a public interface and a private implementation. (We will examine examples of module interface and implementation code in Modula-2 and C later in this section.) The interface of a module consists of forward declarations for the subprograms and objects it defines that are visible to its clients, and documentation describing how to use the module's facilities. If a module exports a constant, its definition must appear in the interface so that the value of the constant is available to the compiler when translating client modules. If a module exports a type name (e.g., a record or enumeration) the definition of the type must be given in the interface so that the compiler has the structure of the type (e.g., the size of an instance and the component names) when translating client modules.

The implementation of a module defines the subprograms and objects declared in its interface. In this way, each name is defined once in the entire application and each object or subprogram is allocated once in the application's executable (i.e., in the object code for its module). The implementation may also define subprograms, objects, constants, and types that are used only within the implementation of the module, and are not visible to clients. For example, the implementation may define auxiliary subprograms that are used by the module's subprograms, but are not intended to be invoked by clients.

The identifiers declared in a module's interface are *exported* to its clients. A language that supports modules must also provide syntax for *importing* module interfaces so that modules can use other modules' facilities. (The implementation of a module implicitly imports its interface.) A module cannot import another module's implementation. Depending on the language, an import declaration may specify an entire module interface (as in C and Ada), or a particular identifier in a module (as in Modula-2). Importing the declaration of an external object or subprogram permits the compiler to perform type checking of uses of that identifier in the client module. Note that an imported interface is located in a different code file than the client code, so the compiler must have a way of finding the interface file, given the module name. A name qualification or renaming feature is also helpful for resolving name conflicts among identifiers in the interfaces a module imports. Both the interface and the implementation of a module may contain import declarations for modules whose facilities they use, and the import declarations in a module interface are also visible in its implementation.

It is helpful if the language system allows the interface and implementation of a module to be written and compiled separately. This facilitates top-down programming because the interface can be specified and imported by other modules before the implementation has been designed and coded. Compiling a module implementation produces an object code file containing the code for its subprograms and allocations for any objects it defines. However, "compiling" an interface does not actually generate an object code unit in the traditional sense. It performs syntactic analysis of the declarations, and creates a symbol table that contains information allowing the compiler to perform type checking of uses of the exported identifiers in client modules. When compiling the corresponding implementation, that table is updated with references to the objects and subprograms in the implementation's object code. The compiler also ensures that the declarations in a module's interface match the definitions in its implementation.

Module scope

Information hiding is provided by the scope rules of the language.[5] An identifier declared at module scope (i.e., not as a local variable of a subprogram in the module) is visible from its point of declaration throughout the module, and is not

---

[5] We will see in section 12.1.3 that C++ makes a distinction between access control and scope (unlike any other language).

visible outside the module if it is not exported. That is, modules provide a level of scope structure that encloses the scopes of individual subprograms. Names declared in both the interface and the implementation of a module contribute to the name space of the module's scope, as do imported names. The scope of a declaration at module scope is that module, and if it is exported, any modules that import that name. Within the implementation of a module, block-structured scope is usually supported so that all the identifiers declared at module scope are implicitly visible within the code of the module's subprograms.

Objects declared at module scope are statically allocated, and exist during and between invocations of the module's subprograms. That is, each module has a state that persists even when no subprograms in the module are executing. The language must provide a mechanism for initializing these objects. Since the names of module scope objects might or might not be exported to clients of the module, using module scope objects rather than global variables allows the designer to control access to these objects.

Languages that support separate compilation have used two different approaches to defining the name space of exported names. C uses static scope with one global scope for the entire application in which all exported names are defined. The scope of each module is nested within this scope, and exported names are visible implicitly within all modules. Modula-2 and Ada support the import/export scope relationship we discussed in section 0.2.5, and permit us to qualify an imported name with its module name to resolve name conflicts. Recall that import/export scope provides programmer control over the visibility of names (rather than the implicit name sharing that occurs with block-structured scope), so that a name is visible exactly where necessary. The designer of the module has explicit control over names visible in a module, and a name can only be shared via an explicit contract between the designer and the client. We will discuss both approaches in detail in this section, since C++ uses both.

System structure

The code for a large system can consist of hundreds or even thousands of subprograms. Attempting to comprehend the structure of such a system by considering a list or invocation graph of these subprograms makes it difficult to "see the forest for the trees" because the representation is too fine-grained. An additional level of structure that groups related subprograms and the data objects they manipulate would facilitate understanding the structure of the system. Modules provide this higher-level abstraction.

Since each subprogram has its own scope, several programmers can use the same names for local variables without conflict. However, in a language without modules, such as standard Pascal, if more than one subprogram needs access to a data object, the object's name must be relatively global to those subprograms, and to all subprograms at that level of nesting. When subprograms communicate by manipulating global data structures, they are tightly coupled. An error or a modification to a data structure in one part of a program can have effects throughout the system, and coordination of the use of that data structure is complicated. Such systems are difficult to revise for the same reason.

Unlike the programming language features discussed in Chapter 0, the module construct was introduced specifically to support the demands of large-scale programming projects. In a functional decomposition of an application, the designers partition the code by using a module for each major task. Each module consists of a group of related subprograms and the data structures that they manipulate. A data structure that must be visible to several modules is imported in only those modules. With modules as the unit of system decomposition, the focus of design is on dividing the application into groups of related subprograms, and associating the necessary data with each module. Like all programming abstractions, modules reduce complexity by decreasing both the interdependency among code units, and the amount of communication and coordination necessary among the programmers working on a system.

The use of modules for structuring programming systems was championed by Parnas, who formulated "Parnas's rule" for information hiding [Par72]. This rule states that the designer of a module should provide a client with all the information necessary to use the module effectively and nothing more, and should provide the implementor with the information needed to code that module and nothing more. In this way, the client cannot write code that depends on the implementation. In addition, the implementor does not know what programs will use the module, and cannot write code that depends on characteristics of the module's clients. The clear distinction between the interface and implementation allows the modules that make up an application to be written, tested, and debugged independently.

Deciding on the right set of modules for the system is often a difficult problem, separate from determining the subprograms. However, it must be resolved because only very small systems can be contained in a single module. A good decomposition of the system's processing resulting from analysis of the requirements specification and the problem domain manages complexity by producing modules that we can design, understand, and code independently. It localizes the inevitable changes during the lifetime of the application to a small number of modules, so only those modules need to be considered and modified. The granularity of the modules is also an issue. If modules are too small, organization and documentation becomes intractable, programmers have a difficult time finding the subprograms they need, and changes to the system can involve reworking numerous modules. On the other hand, if modules are too large, they cannot be understood as a unit and more recompilation may be necessary when making modifications.

Once a set of modules has been developed, it provides a library of abstractions that can be used in other applications with similar requirements to reduce the coding effort. For example, we can write and debug a module containing statistical functions once, and then use it in many such applications. Similarly, the C standard library includes modules containing functions that perform input/output and file operations, mathematical operations, string and character operations, error handling, memory allocation, time and date functions, and various other tasks. No C programmer ever has to write these functions. The disadvantage of grouping library subprograms into modules is that the linker (usually) includes the object code for the entire module in the executable, even if the application only invokes a single subprogram in that module.

Coupling and cohesion

Various dependencies can exist among the modules in an application, and among the components of a module. *Coupling* describes the degree of interdependence between the modules in a system, and *cohesion* describes the degree of interconnectedness among the elements encapsulated within a module. Software engineers use these concepts as criteria for evaluating a system design. In particular, we attempt to minimize the coupling among modules, and to maximize the cohesion within each module.[6]

Coupling is reduced when modules communicate only through their interfaces, rather than by using global variables or accessing each other's data structures directly. Coupling is also reduced by decreasing the number of interactions between the modules in a system and the sizes of the modules' interfaces. When a module has a single clear purpose and implements a single well-defined task, it exhibits strong cohesion. This logical binding of the module's elements is expressed by the common sense saying that "things that belong together should be together", and things that do not should not. If a module has high cohesion, it should be possible to give a single sentence description of the purpose of the module. Cohesive modules furnish reusable components for applications that deal with the same problem domain or platform.

Modules in Modula-2 and Ada

Languages that support modules include constructs for forward declarations, for dividing a module into an interface and an implementation, and for importing interfaces. The compiler implements the import/export scope rules, and the language system must provide mechanisms for linking uses of imported names with the corresponding subprogram or object in another module, or use those of the operating system. Modula-2, Ada, and C (to a degree) provide these facilities. Most contemporary implementations of Pascal also support separately compiled units, although the language standard does not.

Modula-2 is a successor of Pascal that adds support for modules[7] (as well as providing concurrency, low-level facilities, procedure types, and improvements to control structures). The module interface and implementation are called the *definition module* and the *implementation module*, respectively. The following example illustrates Modula-2 definition and implementation modules:

---

[6] Constantine and Yourdan [Con79] present a list of various kinds of cohesion and coupling relationships, which is ordered by their desirability.

[7] In this section, we are discussing what Modula-2 refers to as "library modules". The language also supports "local modules" that define a name space with import/export scope within another module, but are not separately compiled.

```
(* a Modula-2 module interface and implementation *)
DEFINITION MODULE trigMath;
  CONST
    pi = 3.1415926535;
    radiansPerDegree = pi / 180.0;
  PROCEDURE sin(x: REAL): REAL;
  PROCEDURE cos(x: REAL): REAL;
  (* ... other trigonometric function declarations ... *)
END trigMath.


IMPLEMENTATION MODULE trigMath;
  PROCEDURE sin(x: REAL): REAL;
    (* ... code for sin ... *)
  END sin;
  PROCEDURE cos(x: REAL): REAL;
    (* ... code for cos ... *)
  END cos;
  (* ... other trigonometric function definitions ... *)
END trigMath.
```

A definition module may only contain declarations, not executable statements. Variables, procedures,[8] constants, and types declared in the definition module are visible throughout the implementation module (as if the corresponding definition module is implicitly imported), as well as in any modules that import them. The implementation module must define any procedures declared in the corresponding definition module, and it may also define variables, procedures, constants, and types that the module does not export. The implementation may also contain an unnamed block of code, which usually initializes variables declared at module scope in the definition and implementation parts. This code is executed before any of the module's procedures are invoked.

The declaration IMPORT *module*; imports all the identifiers in the definition module *module*, and the client must qualify those names with the module name, that is, as *module.identifier*. A client can also directly import individual names from a module's interface with the declaration FROM *module* IMPORT *identifier1, identifier2, ...*;, in which case he or she can use those names without qualification (but those names cannot already be declared in the module). The FROM declaration essentially declares a local alias for the entity whose name is imported.[9] If a module must import the same name from more than one module interface, it can include IMPORT declarations for each module and use qualified names so that there is no name conflict. Import declarations must appear at the beginning of the client module (after its header), and can be used in both interface and implementation modules. Identifiers imported into a definition module are visible in the corresponding

---

[8] Both procedures and functions that return a value are called procedures in Modula-2.

[9] We will see in section 14.4 that the C++ using namespace directive corresponds to the IMPORT declaration (although name qualification is not necessary if a name is not declared locally), and the C++ using declaration corresponds to the FROM declaration.

implementation module. There is no global scope visible throughout the program in Modula-2 (although predefined identifiers such as CHAR and TRUNC are visible in any module).

Ada supplies the same capabilities and semantics for modules as Modula-2, but the language uses different terminology and syntax. In Ada, modules are called *packages*. A module interface is called a *package specification*, and all names declared in the specification are exported, except for those in the private section. [10] A module implementation is called a *package body*, and it defines subprograms declared in the public part of the package specification, as well as private variables, subprograms, and so on. A client package imports the nonprivate names in a package specification with the with *package*; declaration, which makes those names visible as qualified names in the client. The use *package*; declaration declares local aliases for the identifiers in the specification of *package*, so that the client package can use them without qualification. If a name conflict occurs between names imported from two modules, we can resolve a use with a qualified name. We will see examples of Ada packages in the next section.

Both Ada and Modula-2 allow compiling the interface of a module separately from its implementation. The language system maintains a database of module interfaces and implementations so that the compiler can find imported interfaces and match corresponding interfaces and implementations. (The system might or might not use the facilities of the operating system file system.) The language system ensures that we do not compile a module unless we have created and compiled all the interfaces that it imports. However, we can compile a module (but not link and execute it) even if we have not coded the implementation of an interface it imports. Linking compiled object code units can be done statically or dynamically, but must be done by a language-specific linker that uses information in the module database.

The language system also manages *compilation dependencies* among modules. An implementation depends on the corresponding interface in the sense that the implementation must be recompiled when the interface is modified, but not vice versa. Similarly, a module that imports mod1's interface depends on that interface, but does not depend on mod1's implementation. To relieve the programmer of determining which modules must be compiled when modifying a module, the language system recompiles all modules that depend on an interface when it is edited and compiled. Use of top-down design minimizes the amount of recompiling necessary during development because the interfaces stabilize early in a project, with most modifications being made in the implementations. Note that if mod1 imports the interface of mod2, compiling the interface of mod2 should trigger recompiling mod1. However, there is no indication that the dependency exists in the code of mod2, so the module database must represent these dependencies explicitly (i.e., the compiler cannot deduce a module's dependents from its source code).

---

[10] We will see in the next section that having a private section in a package specification supports using packages to implement abstract data types.

Modules in C

C support for modules and separate compilation is somewhat implicit, and is provided partly by the language, partly by the preprocessor, and partly by the operating system environment. C does not support the import/export scope relationship provided by Modula-2 and Ada. Instead, each source code file defines a level of scope nested within the global scope of the entire program, and all exported names are declared in this global scope. A C program has three levels of scope: global scope, the scope of each file, and the function scopes nested within the file scopes. The usual static scope rules apply among these levels, including implicit access of names in enclosing scopes and hiding of names by declarations in an intervening scope.

Both global scope and the scope of each file are referred to as *file scope*, and only declarations are allowed at file scope. All file scope declarations are global by default, and the reserved word static indicates that a file scope declaration is only visible within that file.[11] That is, functions and objects that are private to a module are declared at file scope as static, and the compiler does not include those names in the module's external symbol table. The extern specifier indicates that a file scope declaration is not a definition, that is, that the referent is defined in another source code file to be linked with this file. Function declarations are extern by default.

Figure 1.2 illustrates C scope relationships in a program that consists of two modules containing three functions (dashed lines demarcate the text of the code files and solid lines indicate scope boundaries). The names file1.c and file2.c are not declared in the global name space, and are not even known to the compiler. file1.c defines two global names, num1 and func1a(), and defines the identifiers num2 and func1b() as local to itself. The scopes of the functions func1a() and func1b() are nested within the scope of the file (rather than the global scope): A static file scope identifier is implicitly visible in those function scopes if a local variable does not hide it, and static file scope identifiers hide global identifiers within the functions. (However, num2 is not visible in the code for func1a() because its declaration has not yet appeared at that point in the source code.) The extern declarations of num1 and func1a() in file2.c specify that those names are defined in another module, and permit the compiler to type-check uses of those names in file2.c. The two definitions of num2 in the two files do not clash because uses of that name in file1.c refer to its file scope variable, and similarly for uses in file2.c. The functions func1b() and func2() cannot be called outside their respective code files because their names are not entered into their modules' external symbol tables.

If we use an identifier in more than one code file, we define it in one file and declare in the global name space. Modules that import that name use an extern declaration. The convention in C is to place the forward declarations of objects and

---

[11] This is a completely different use of the term static than a static local variable. All file scope objects are statically allocated, whether they are globally visible or not.

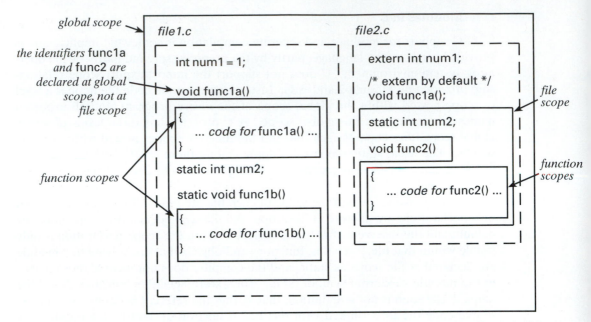

Figure 1.2   The three levels of scope in a C program. (Dashed lines demarcate the code files, and solid lines indicate scope boundaries).

functions used in more than one module in *header files*. Header files may also define constants, types, and preprocessor macros. A small program may use one header file for all its global declarations. For a large application with a modular design, we code each module as two files, a header file containing the module interface and a *code file* containing its implementation. By convention, we name the corresponding header and code file *module*.h and *module*.c. The following example illustrates a C header file:

```
/* a C header file, trigMath.h */
#define PI 3.1415926535
#define RADIANS_PER_DEGREE (PI / 180.0)
double sin(double);/* pre-ANSI C does not specify the parameter types */
double cos(double);
/* ... other trigonometric function declarations ... */
```

Note that there is no indication in the language that this group of declarations make up the interface for a particular module.

Rather than using a language-supported import declaration, client files textually include the module's header file with the preprocessor directive #include. This operation inserts the text of the header file directly into the client code file before compilation, making those declarations available. (We also include the header file in the module's code file to ensure that its declarations are consistent with the definitions in the code file.) This command uses the file name of the header file, as follows:

```
/* inclusion of interfaces coded in C header files */
#include <stdio.h>          /* a standard header file */
#include "trigMath.h"        /* a programmer-defined header file */
```

In this way, the language system avoids the complexity of dealing with compiled interfaces and the requirement of managing a module library. However, an interface is recompiled every time a client file or the implementation file is compiled, increasing the total compilation time. In addition, the compiler cannot ensure that every client of a module has included the same version of its header file.

The C compiler includes an external symbol table with each object file. The table does not include type information, which is why you should include a header file in the corresponding code file. The operating system linker uses the symbol tables to resolve each external declaration to the corresponding definition when creating the executable. If more than one module defines a particular identifier in the global name space, the linker (not the compiler) signals a "multiple definition" error. If an identifier declared as global is not defined in any of the files linked to it, the linker signals an "undefined symbol" error.

Although C's approach to separate compilation and module scope simplifies implementation of the language, the compiler has no information about modules and the name importing relationships in the program. Name qualification is not possible, so a module cannot import the same name from more than one module. In fact, since there is a single global name space for all exported names, uses of the same name in different interfaces in an application conflict, even if those names are not used in the same module. For example, in a Modula-2 program with four modules mod1, mod2, mod3, and mod4, mod2 can import the name proc from mod1 while mod4 imports proc from mod3 without conflict. If we attempt to use the same pattern of import relationships in a C program, the linker would flag the name proc as multiply defined because both mod1 and mod3 export that name to the global name space (and, therefore, proc is defined in the external symbol tables of both object files). Figure 1.3 illustrates these scope relationships.

Since C has no knowledge of modules, the language system cannot automatically manage compilation dependencies among source code files. When a source file is modified, either the programmer or a programming tool must determine which additional modules to recompile before linking the application. UNIX programmers use the make utility for this purpose, and pass it a "makefile" that specifies the dependencies among the various header, code, and object files that make up an application. The makefile associates an operating system command with each dependent file, usually to compile or link, that "makes" that file. When make executes, it checks the times of modification of the involved files, and executes the commands to make any files that depend on files with later timestamps (doing so

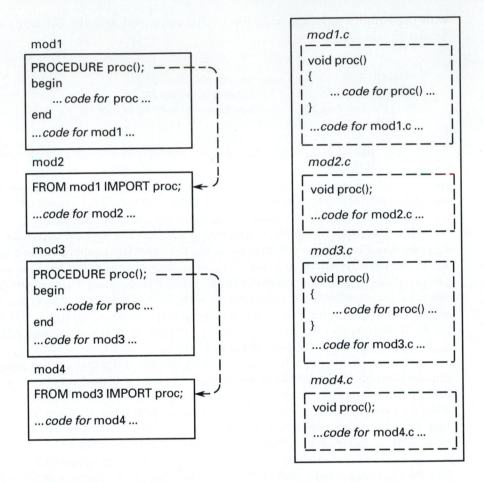

Figure 1.3 Exporting the same identifier twice in a program in Modula-2 and C.

recursively). However, it is the programmer's responsibility to encode the dependencies, and to maintain them as the application is developed. Many C programming environments include a "project" facility that handles these details automatically.

1.1.4 Abstract Data Types

Definition and purpose

As we mentioned in section 0.3.5, an *abstract data type* is a programmer-defined type that packages the structure of the type's instances and the operations

for those objects, and allows the designer to control access to those components. [12]
Typically, the structure of the type's instances is hidden from its clients (i.e., from
program units that create and use instances), and clients may manipulate instances
only with the operations defined for the type. That is, the definition of an abstract
data type consists of

- an interface presenting the behavior of its instances
- a hidden implementation describing how an instance is represented, and how
  that representation is manipulated to provide the type's operations.

The type is "abstract" in the sense that clients cannot see its concrete implementation (unlike a record type).

As we saw in section 0.3.3, types model categories of entities in the problem
domain, and the use of types improves readability and increases the correspondence
between the structure of the application and that of the problem domain system.
Abstract data types improve upon the type constructors of Pascal by encapsulating
the type's operations directly with the type to supply a more complete package. The
operations defined for a type should be motivated by the behavior of the real-world
category that the type represents. For example, the abstract data type Bank in an
ATM application includes operations for validating and executing transactions and
for creating accounts. Like modules, we can design and code abstract data types
separately, facilitating independent verification of the type's operations, isolation of
program errors, and localization of modifications. Like modules, abstract data types
can be stored as reusable components in a library.

Languages that support abstract data types provide constructs for

- packaging a type's operations with the definition of the type
- defining all the necessary operations so that the type is first-class
- specifying which components of the type are visible externally
- instantiating the type and using its operations on those objects.

We will see in this section that an Ada package can export a type's name and operations and hide its implementation, so packages support abstract data types. Object-
oriented languages also support abstract data types, and we will examine a small
C++ example in this section.

Interface and implementation

We describe the external appearance of an abstract data type by stating what
operations are valid for its instances and clearly describing the externally visible
effects of each. For example, the client of a set can add, delete, and search for elements, obtain the number of elements, check for equality and subset relationships,

---

[12] Some authors use the term "abstract data type" to mean only the interface of the type, exclud-
ing its implementation (because it is "abstract").

copy sets, obtain the intersection or union of sets, and so on. Each operation in an abstract data type's interface is specified by a subprogram declaration that gives its name and argument signature, any exceptions it can signal, and a logical description of the operation.

An important component of the interface of the type is an operation for initializing an instance of the type with a valid value. For example, an instance of the type Set begins with a logically empty data structure (e.g., an empty list, tree, or hash table), and the number of elements set to 0. For many types, initialization takes arguments that give values for the information stored in the object, and these values are necessary to create a valid object. For example, an instance of Book must be initialized with a particular title, author, publisher, date, and so on (rather than having garbage in those fields as a new Pascal record would). Initializing a Date object requires a year, month, and day, and the initialization operation must do range checks on the arguments. No operations should be performed on an object unless it has been properly initialized.

By prohibiting direct access to a type's data components, the designer of an abstract data type provides *representation independence*. Like all information hiding, representation independence

- relieves clients from understanding the details of the type's implementation
- prevents clients from manipulating that implementation in ways that are not consistent with the type's semantics, either accidentally or intentionally
- allows the designer to change the storage structure of the type without affecting clients.

These characteristics increase the reliability of programs that use the type. Representation independence is not a new concept in programming. For example, most languages provide floating-point types without supplying mechanisms for examining the actual bit string of an instance and the implementations of the arithmetic operations. However, application of representation independence to programmer-defined types is more recent.

Frequently, we can implement a particular logical entity in several different ways, each with its own storage structure and algorithms. For example, we can represent a set of elements as an array, a linked list, a binary search tree, or a hash table. We would implement the logical operations of searching for elements, adding and deleting elements, determining the number of elements, and so on, differently for each representation. With representation independence, clients of the type manipulate set objects via its public operations only, allowing us to use any representation or change the implementation. This contrasts with languages such as Pascal in which the structure of a type is visible throughout the program, and modifying the type's implementation can break other code units.

If the information maintained by a particular abstract data type should be accessible to clients, you should provide accessor functions, rather than declaring the data components as public, to achieve representation independence. For example, we can represent a point in either Cartesian or polar coordinates. By providing operations that access and set a point object's x, y, r, and θ coordinates, we can use either representation, or change representations during development, by defining each of these operations correctly for the chosen representation. (For example, the operation that sets a point's x coordinate performs a single assignment with the Cartesian representation, but calculates and sets both coordinates in the polar representation.) Client code will use the accessor operations, and will not be affected by changes to the structure of the type. Another advantage of defining operations that set an instance's components rather than permitting clients to assign values directly to those components is that the type's operations can perform validation such as range checking so that an instance does not have an invalid state.

The implementation of an abstract data type consists of declarations that describe the storage structure of an instance, and subprograms that define the type's operations in terms of that structure. A record may be sufficient for encoding the information maintained by an instance, or the designer may use a dynamic linked data structure. For example, the storage structure of a date can be a record containing two integers giving the day number and year number, whereas that of a set may be a linked list, a binary search tree, or a hash table. For each subprogram in the type's interface, the implementation gives a subprogram definition that describes how to examine and modify an instance's storage structure to achieve the result defined for that operation. As with modules, the type's implementation may also define private subprograms, constants, objects, and types (e.g., for the nodes in a linked structure) that aid in coding the type's operations and structure.

System structure

As designers developed larger systems, they often found that the complexity of the data objects in the application contributes significantly to the complexity of the system, and that most of the operations necessary were specifically relevant to certain types of data objects. In addition, designers noticed that once they had created a type for a category of objects or data structure, they could frequently use it directly in other applications dealing with the same problem domain, design characteristics, or user interface. These realizations caused a shift in the process of design from process-oriented functional decomposition to *object-based decomposition*.[13] With this design strategy, the focus is on determining the categories of entities that the system must represent and assigning operations to each, rather than on dividing the system structure according to the processing that it performs.

In the same way that subprograms and modules provide abstraction of operation, abstract data types provide abstraction of data. In moving from procedural modules to abstract data types as the basis for the structure of the application, there is a change of focus from a module and its data to a data object and its operations (i.e., from verbs to nouns). In object-based decomposition, the central task is determining the categories of entities that the system must represent, and their attributes

---

[13] We use the term "object-based decomposition" to distinguish from "object-oriented decomposition", which also takes advantage of the additional properties of inheritance, dynamic binding, and class information that are available for classes, but not for abstract data types.

and interactions. These interactions determine the interfaces necessary for each abstract data type. Rather than the system structure being a tree of tasks and the subtasks that they call, it is a graph of the interactions and relationships between abstract data types.

Parnas's rule and the principles of cohesion and coupling are as important for designing abstract data types as they are for designing modules. The interface of a type must include everything that a client needs to use instances of the type effectively, and the implementation should include exactly what is necessary to implement that interface. Clients should not be able to write code that depends on the representation of the type, and the designer should not make assumptions about code units that use instances of the type. The attributes and properties encapsulated within an abstract data type should be logically related, which will be true if each type is motivated by a distinct problem domain category. Instances of types should only communicate through their interfaces, rather than by using global variables or accessing each other's storage structure directly.

Modules and data abstraction

Although modules were originally designed as a technique for abstraction of operation, it became apparent that they could also be used for abstraction of data. To do so, we use a module to encapsulate a data structure and the subprograms that access and modify it, and then export the names of the subprograms, but not the names of the data objects. In this way, we package the subprograms that manipulate a particular data structure with it, and can modify the data structure without affecting clients. We can also use modules to implement shared access to data structures such as buffers and tables. For example, for the tables and accessing subprograms example illustrated in Figure 0.4, we can define each table in a separate module whose interface is imported in only the modules that contain subprograms that use it.

To illustrate using modules to hide the implementation of a data structure, let us define a C module that provides a fixed-size stack of characters.[14]

```
/* charStack1.h: interface for a fixed-size stack of characters in C */
void push(char ch);        /* insert ch on top of the stack */
char pop();                /* remove and return the top char on the stack */
int isEmpty();             /* return whether the stack is empty */
int isFull();              /* return whether the stack is full */
/* charStack1.c implementation for a fixed-size stack of characters in C */
#include "charStack1.h"    /* to ensure consistency among function declarations */
#define STACK_SIZE 32
#define EMPTY (-1)

static char elements[STACK_SIZE];
static int top = EMPTY;
```

[14] To simplify the code for the following examples, we leave it to the client to check whether a stack is empty before popping it, or whether a stack is full before pushing an element.

```
void push(char ch)
{
   elements[++top] = ch;
}

char pop()
{
   return elements[top--];
}

int isEmpty()
{
   return top == EMPTY;
}

int isFull()
{
   return top == STACK_SIZE - 1;
}
```

The objects elements and top in charStack1.c are not visible outside the code file because we have declared them as static, and clients can only access the stack with the functions push(), pop(), isEmpty(), and isFull().

Although we can use a module to package a data structure with its operations and protect the integrity of the data structure, this design does not support multiple instances of that data structure. Each stack module in an application must be named and compiled separately (and the operations for each must have different names in C since name qualification is not possible). To support instantiation, we can export both the definition of a data type that packages the data structure and the declarations of subprograms that take parameters of that type. Clients can then import this interface and create instances of the type as needed. We can redefine the C stack module in the previous example as an instantiable type, as follows:

```
/* CharStack2.h: an instantiable interface for a fixed-size stack of characters in C */
#define STACK_SIZE 32        /* visible to clients because it is needed in the type definition */

/* clients create and initialize an instance of this type */
typedef struct
{
   char elements[STACK_SIZE];
   int top;
} CharStack;

void initialize(CharStack*);          /* initialize the argument to an empty stack */
void push(CharStack*, char ch);       /* insert ch on top of the stack */
char pop(CharStack*);                 /* remove and return the top char on the stack */
int isEmpty(CharStack*);              /* return whether the stack is empty */
int isFull(CharStack*);               /* return whether the stack is full */
```

```
/* CharStack2.c implementation for a fixed-size stack of characters in C */
#include "CharStack2.h"
#define EMPTY (-1)

void initialize(CharStack* pStack)
{
    pStack->top = EMPTY;
}

void push(CharStack* pStack, char ch)
{
    pStack->elements[++top] = ch;
}

char pop(CharStack* pStack)
{
    return pStack->elements[top--];
}

int isEmpty(CharStack* pStack)
{
    return pStack->top == EMPTY;
}

int isFull(CharStack* pStack)
{
    return pStack->top == STACK_SIZE - 1;
}
```

Since each instance of the type CharStack must be initialized to an empty stack before using it, the module provides a function to do so. A client must pass the address of a CharStack object to the functions defined in the CharStack2 module because the stack operations modify the stack and C does not support pass by reference.

Exporting a type definition allows instantiation by clients, but gives clients direct access to the storage structure. For example, a client of the CharStack2 module can access or set the top and elements members of an instance of the type directly. That is, when we use C or Modula-2 modules to provide data abstraction, they cannot support both instantiation and information hiding. These languages can only achieve full data abstraction by defining the record type in the implementation and exporting only a pointer type whose base type is the record type. [15] Clients see the pointer type, but not the names of the record components. However, the compiler also only sees the pointer type when compiling client code, so it cannot allocate static and automatic instances of the record type. (That is, without the record type definition, it cannot determine how much storage to allocate.) Therefore, the initialize() function must create a new object dynamically. In addition, in a language

---

[15] This is referred to as exporting an "opaque type" in Modula-2.

such as C that uses programmer-controlled deallocation, the type also needs a function, say release(), that deallocates this object. The client must call this function explicitly, hopefully just before the client's CharStack pointer object is deallocated. We can redefine the C stack module from the previous example as an instantiable type with information hiding, as follows:[16]

```
/* CharStack3.h: an instantiable interface for a fixed-size stack of characters in C */
/* that provides information hiding */
/* Clients create and initialize an instance of this type */
typedef struct cStack* CharStack;

void initialize(CharStack*);        /* initialize the argument to an empty stack */
void release(CharStack);            /* deallocate the hidden stack object */
void push(CharStack, char ch);      /* insert ch on top of the stack */
char pop(CharStack);                /* remove and return the top char on the stack */
int isEmpty(CharStack);             /* return whether the stack is empty */
int isFull(CharStack);              /* return whether the stack is full */


/* CharStack3.c implementation for a fixed-size stack of characters in C */
#include "CharStack3.h"
#define STACK_SIZE 32
#define EMPTY (-1)

struct cStack
{
    char elements[STACK_SIZE];
    int top;
};

void initialize(CharStack* ppStack)
{
    *ppStack = (CharStack) malloc(sizeof struct cStack);
    (*ppStack)->top = EMPTY;
}

void release(CharStack pStack)
{
    free(pStack);
}

/* push(CharStack, char), char pop(CharStack), int isEmpty(CharStack), and
int isFull(CharStack) coded as in previous example */
```

Figure 1.4 illustrates the storage structures for the implementations defined by the modules CharStack2 and CharStack3 when a client creates a local variable of type CharStack in a function func().

---

[16] The typedef statement in the interface is legal because the declaration struct cStack within that statement declares the identifier cStack as a structure name.

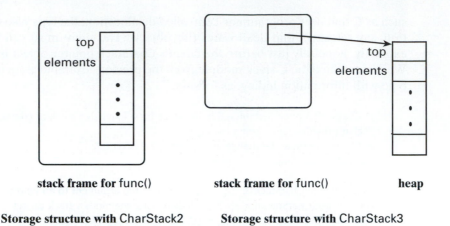

stack frame for func()   stack frame for func()   heap

Storage structure with CharStack2   **Storage structure with** CharStack3

Figure 1.4   Storage structures for instance of CharStark in C.

If a client function creates a CharStack object with CharStack2, the entire object is stored in the activation record of the function. With CharStack3, the function's activation record only contains a pointer and the stack object is allocated dynamically. [17] With the indirect design illustrated by CharStack3, changes in the representation of the type do not affect clients, and client code need not even be recompiled. Unfortunately, this design is rather inefficient due to the use of dynamic allocation for all instances of the type, especially if the type is used as a component of another type. It also allows clients to perform pointer operations such as assignments and equality tests with CharStack objects, but they will not have the expected effects. A more serious problem is that most programmers expect to initialize an object, but easily forget to call the release( ) function.

Abstract data types in Ada

To avoid the inefficiency of indirection and dynamic allocation, a language that supports using modules for abstract data types needs a construct for including information in the module interface for the compiler that is not visible to clients. For this reason, Ada allows a package specification to have a *private* section. Clients cannot use the identifiers in the private section, but that information is available to the compiler (and in the package body). We primarily use this capability to declare a type or constant in the public section of the package specification, and define it in the private section. In this way, the client cannot write code that depends on the structure of the type or the value of the constant. Ada refers to these as "private types" and "deferred constants", respectively.

---

[17] We will see in sections 2.4.3 and 5.3.1 that the representation CharStack3 implements is necessary for object-oriented languages to support inheritance and dynamic binding. In section 12.2.3, we will see that C++ supports both representations for objects.

We can code the specification of an Ada package that supplies the type Char_Stack with instantiation and information hiding as follows:[18]

```
-- an Ada package specification that provides an instantiatable type for a fixed-size
-- stack of characters with information hiding
package Char_Stack_Package is
  type Char_Stack is private;
  -- insert Ch on top of the stack
  procedure Push(Ch_Stk: in out Char_Stack; Ch: in Character);
  -- remove the top Character on the stack and set return_Char to it
  procedure Pop(Ch_Stk: in out Char_Stack; return_Char: out Character);
  -- return whether the stack is empty
  function Is_Empty(Ch_Stk: in Char_Stack) return Boolean;
  -- return whether the stack is full
  function Is_Full(Ch_Stk: in Char_Stack) return Boolean;

private
  Stack_Size: constant := 32;
  Empty: constant := 0;
  type Char_Vector is array(Integer range <>) of Character;
  type Char_Stack is
    record
      Top: Integer range Empty .. Stack_Size := Empty;
      Elements: Char_Vector(Empty + 1 .. Stack_Size);
    end record;

end Char_Stack_Package;
```

The type name Char_Stack is visible in client packages that import the type and its operations with the declaration with Char_Stack_Package, but its field names are not. When a client subprogram creates an instance of Char_Stack, the compiler can allocate that record directly in the subprogram's stack frame because it has the type's size and layout. The type Char_Stack does not need an initialization function because Ada permits specifying a default initial value for the Top field. The package body of Char_Stack_Package is introduced by the header package body Char_Stack_Package is, and gives the definitions of the stack subprograms.

Since the record type Char_Stack is available to the compiler, it can create static and automatic instances of the type in client packages. However, this means that those clients must be recompiled if the type's representation is changed, although they will not need to be recoded. (Recall that the Ada language system performs this recompilation automatically.) A client uses the Char_Stack_Package package and its type and subprograms as follows:

----

[18] The operation Pop must be a procedure because Ada functions cannot have in out parameters. The type Char_Vector is introduced because we cannot use an anonymous array type as the type of a record field. C programmers should note the use of ><, range constraints, and subrange specifications in defining the storage structure of the type.

```
-- creating an instance of the type Char_Stack and using its operations
with Char_Stack_Package;        -- import the interface of the package
procedure Main is
   use Char_Stack_Package;       -- use names from the package without qualification
   Ch_Stk: Char_Stack;
   Char: Character;
begin
   Push(Ch_Stk, '$');
   if not Is_Empty(Ch_Stk) then
       Pop(Ch_Stk, Char);
   end if;
   Ch_Stk.Top := 5;              -- error: Char_Stack is a private type
end Main;
```

Once a client has imported the package specification containing the type, that package can define further operations for the type by using it as a subprograms parameter type. There is nothing in the invocation syntax to distinguish these additional operations from the "primitive" operations of the abstract data type that are packaged with it: Both take a Char_Stack parameter. However, the language distinguishes the operations in a type's package because they are available for types derived from Char_Stack, while client subprograms are not.

Like all Ada types, Char_Stack supports equality tests. Unfortunately, a straightforward comparison of all the components of two Char_Stack objects is not correct, since the "unused" portions of the Elements arrays of two equal stacks can differ. Since Ada supports operator overloading, we can code the correct processing for this operation. If a type in a package specification is declared as limited private, then equality tests and assignments are not allowed for its instances.

Dynamic subobjects and abstract data types in C++

Since an abstract data type's implementation is hidden, the type can dynamically allocate substructures that are not visible to its clients. For example, we can define a list abstract data type implemented by a linked list. The type would be responsible for allocating and deallocating the list nodes, and must hide those details from clients. The distinction between instantiation and initialization is essential with such abstract data types. Instantiation creates an instance of the type, and initialization of that object creates and initializes the dynamic subobjects.

To avoid having a limit on the number of elements in a stack (since it is not logically part of the stack concept), our stack type can allocate the array of elements dynamically. If the stack is full upon a push, we will allocate a larger array, copy the elements to it, and deallocate the old array, before pushing the new element. We will code this version in C++ using a structure that contains three members: the current size of the array, the index of the top element, and a pointer to the dynamic array. Figure 1.5 illustrates the storage structure of an instance allocated as a local variable of a client function func().

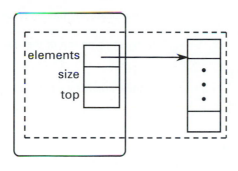

stack frame for func()   **heap**

Figure 1.5   Storage structure for the abstract data type CharStark.

The dashed line in the figure indicates that the three-member structure in the client function's stack frame and the dynamic array are logically a single object, although physically they are stored in different regions.

In C++, we define an abstract data type as a class, an expanded version of the C struct definition that includes

- *data members* that define the storage structure of the type
- *member functions* that provide the type's operations
- *access control* specifications, for example, public and private, that indicate whether members are visible to clients.

The syntactic unit that defines the type directly encapsulates the type's operations within the type itself, rather than grouping the type and its operations in a package as in Ada. A C++ class also does not define a separately compiled unit like an Ada package or a Modula-2 module. However, it does define a separate named scope, and the language supports name qualification with the scope operator :: and a class name.[19] We will discuss C++ class definitions and the use of header and code files with classes in detail in Chapter 10, but you should be able to read this example. We define the class CharStack as follows:

```
// a C++ class for a stack of characters
class CharStack
{
public:
   void initialize()          // initialize the object to an empty stack
   {
      size = INIT_SIZE;
      elements = new char[INIT_SIZE];
      top = EMPTY;
   }
```

[19] We will discuss C++ class scope in sections 10.3 and 12.1.3.

```
      void release()                     // deallocate the hidden stack object
      { delete [ ] elements; }
      void push(char ch)                 // insert ch on top of the stack
      {
         if ( top == size - 1 )
              grow();                     // the elements array is full
         elements[++top] = ch;
      }
      char pop()                         // remove and return the top char on the stack
      { return elements[top--]; }
      bool isEmpty()                     // return whether the stack is empty
      { return top == EMPTY; }
   private:
      char* elements;
      int top;
      int size;
      static const int INIT_SIZE;
      static const int EMPTY;
      void grow()
      {
         char* newElems = new char[size + INIT_SIZE];
         for ( int index = 0;  index < size;  index++ )
            newElems[index] = elements[index];
         delete [ ] elements;
         size += INIT_SIZE;
         elements = newElems;
      }
   };

   const int CharStack::INIT_SIZE = 8;
   const int CharStack::EMPTY = -1;
```

When a CharStack member function uses a data member name, it refers to that data
member in the stack object whose operation is being performed. As we will see in
section 9.1.5, C++ uses the new and delete operators for dynamic allocation and
deallocation, rather than the C malloc() and free() functions. Unlike C, C++ includes
a type bool for boolean values. The auxiliary member function CharStack::grow()
is private to the class and clients cannot invoke it. The "static data members"
CharStack::INIT_SIZE and CharStack::EMPTY are defined within the scope of the class
CharStack, but they are static objects that are not stored in each instance. To define
and initialize them, we use qualified names.

When a client creates an instance of CharStack as an automatic or dynamic
object, storage is allocated for its three data members elements, top, and size, but
they are not initialized. The member function initialize() provides these members
with initial values, and allocates the array referred to by elements on the heap. We
must define this function because the data members are private, and it relieves
clients from having to know how to initialize a CharStack object. A client must

invoke this function immediately after creating an instance of the type. If not, a run-time error or invalid result will eventually occur. With a data type such as CharStack that allocates substructures on the heap, we also need a function that deallocates those substructures when the object is no longer needed (since C++ uses program-mer-controlled allocation). The member function release() frees the dynamic array referred to by elements, and clients must call it just before deallocating a CharStack so that a memory leak does not result. In general, it is necessary to define initial-ization and finalization functions for any type whose instances use system resources so that clients of the type do not need to know what resources it uses. In fact, we will see in section 10.2 that C++ supports type-specific initialization and finalization functions—called "constructors" and "destructors" respectively—that the compiler invokes implicitly whenever an object is created or destroyed so that these errors do not occur.

For a type such as CharStack that defines a dynamic subobject, we must also distinguish between initialization of a new object and assignment to an existing object. For initialization, the target object is just raw storage whose values must be set. With assignment, the dynamic subobject of the target instance has already been allocated. For example, consider the assignment chStk2 = chStk1. A C structure assignment would assign the values of the corresponding data members of chStk1 to those of chStk2, which is incorrect. If chStk2.size >= chStk1.size, we can copy the contents of chStk1->elements into chStk2->elements and set chStk2.top. If chStk2.size < chStk1.size, we deallocate chStk2's subobject, allocate a new array of size chStk1->size (or larger), then copy the elements. As we will see in section 11.1.3, C++ allows the designer of a type to overload the assignment operation with the required behavior.

In C++ and object-oriented languages, the syntax for invoking a type's opera-tions distinguishes the type instance from the other argument of the call. We invoke a member function of an object using the component selection operator, like access-ing a public data member of the object, as follows:

```
// creating instances of the type CharStack and using their operations
#include "CharStack.h"          // import the interface
int main()
{
    CharStack chStk1, chStk2;
    chStk1.initialize();
    chStk2.initialize();
    chStk1.push('$');
    if ( !chStk1.isEmpty() )
        chStk2.push(chStk1.pop());
    chStk1.release();
    chStk2.release();
}
```

The C++ invocation syntax chStk1.push('$') makes it more apparent that the func-tion push() is directly associated with the chStk1 object than does the C call syntax push(chStk1, '$') because the C syntax makes no distinction between the arguments chStk1 and '$'. As we will see in sections 1.1.5 and 2.2.4, object-oriented languages refer to the expression chStk1.push('$') as sending the message push() to the object chStk1. We will see in Section 10.2 that if the member functions CharStack::initialize() and CharStack::release() are defined as a constructor and destructor, then the client would not have to call these functions explicity.

Generic abstract data types

A common use of abstract data types is to represent a collection with particular characteristics such as a stack, a set, or a sorted list. We can design, code, and verify the collection type, and then reuse it in numerous applications. In a statically typed language, all the elements of a collection must be of the same type, or are converted to that type. Whether the collection is implemented by a sequential or linked organization, all elements will be bound to an identifier of the same type, either that of the array elements or the "element" field of the records in the linked structure. An advantage of this characteristic is that the compiler can ensure that an element of the wrong type is not added to the collection. A problem that occurs with collection types is that the interface, storage structure, and subprogram definitions for a stack are the same, no matter what the type of the elements is. However, in a statically typed language, a stack of integers and a stack of characters are different types because their operations have different argument signatures and the types of their elements components are different.

We would like a language feature that allows us to code the interface and implementation for a particular type of collection once, without specifying the actual type of an element. The compiler would then use that specification to create a type for a collection with a particular element type when indicated by the programmer. We refer to the construct that the compiler uses to generate an actual abstract data type as a *generic* type definition. The generic type is not an actual type that can be instantiated, but a template from which the compiler can generate a compilable type definition. It is similar to the Pascal array of type constructor, which is not a type itself, but can be used to define a new array type by giving an index type and a base type.

The Ada *generic package* construct allows us to code a package template with a *type parameter*, from which the compiler can generate actual packages. The client gives an actual type when specifying creation of a package. The specification of a generic package is preceded by the reserved word generic and a list of parameters. These parameters may be objects (like subprogram parameters), types, or subprograms.[20] For example, the following code defines the specification of a generic package for generating stack packages that define a fixed-size stack type with a given element type and capacity:

---

[20] Ada uses the generic package mechanism rather than a subprogram type to support subprogram parameters.

```
-- an Ada generic package specification for a fixed-size stack type
generic
    Stack_Size: Positive;                   -- the capacity
    type Elem_Type is private;              -- the element type
package Stack_Types is
    type Stack is private;
    procedure Push(Stk: in out Stack; El: in Elem_Type);
    procedure Pop(Stk: in out Stack; out Elem_Type);
    function Is_Empty(Stk: in Stack) return Boolean;
    function Is_Full(Stk: in Stack) return Boolean;

    private
    Empty: constant := 0;
    type Elem_Vector is array(Integer range <>) of Elem_Type;
    type Stack is
        record
            Top: Integer range Empty .. Stack_Size := Empty;
            Elements: Elem_Vector(Empty + 1 .. Stack_Size);
        end record;

end Stack_Types;
```

This generic package does not actually define a package containing a stack type and
its operations. Instead, it supplies a template that the compiler uses to create a stack
package with particular bindings for the parameters when specified by the programmer. The following example instructs the compiler to generate a package that
defines a type for stacks of integers of capacity 100, and then creates an instance and
uses its functions:

```
-- generating a package from a generic package
with Stack_Types;
procedure Main is
    -- create the package for the type "stack of up to 100 integers"
    package Int_Stack is new Stack_Types(100, Integer);
    use Int_Stack;
    Stk: Stack;                      -- create an instance of Int_Stack.Stack
    Int: Integer := 0;
begin
    Push(Stk, 10);
    if not Is_Empty(Stk) then
        Pop(Stk, Int);
    end if;
end Main;
```

If a program uses stacks with different element types or sizes, it must generate a separate package for each stack type. Since each stack type is different, the subprogram names in the generic package are overloaded for each stack type used, and the
type of the stack argument determines which subprogram to call. However, since
type names cannot be overloaded, a program that uses more than one stack type

must qualify each use of a type name with the generated package name, for example, Int_Stack.Stack.

The generic package Stack_Types does not make demands on the actual type bound to the type parameter, other than that it can copy an instance to the Elements array (i.e., the type cannot be limited private). Other collection types may require the element type to provide certain operations. For example, a set type implemented as a binary search tree must compare instances of the element type (e.g., using the < operator). In Ada, these operations are passed as subprogram parameters to the generic package. Ada also provides many mechanisms for specifying constraints on the actual type bound to a type parameter, such as that it must be discrete.

The C++ template facility supports defining generic functions and types, and is discussed in detail in sections 13.1 and 13.2. In those sections, we will also discuss how generic constructs complicate scope, compilation, and linking.

1.1.5 Classes

Object terminology

In this section, we briefly describe how object-oriented languages extend the construct of the abstract data type to that of the class, the abstraction that characterizes object-oriented programming.[21] We will cover classes, polymorphism, and inheritance in detail in Chapters 2 and 3.

A *class* is an abstract data type that has the additional properties of

- class information and operations
- inheritance among classes
- dynamic binding of class operations, which implies that instances must maintain their type identity.

Like a data type, a class is an abstraction representing a category of entities in the problem domain, which is meaningful for the application, or a category of system components necessary in implementing the application. Each class is characterized by the activities that its instances are responsible for and the information that they must maintain. Like the features of all programming abstractions, class information and operations, inheritance, and dynamic binding are motivated by problem domain semantics and software engineering concerns, as we will discuss in sections 1.3, 2.1, and 3.1.

In the object model, an *object* is an encapsulation of state and behavior (i.e., it encompasses both "data" and "code") and represents a problem domain entity or a system component.[22] Each object is an *instance* of a class that defines its behav-

---

[21] In fact, [Mey88] suggests that object-oriented programming should be referred to as "class-oriented programming".

[22] Some authors use the term "object" to refer to classes as in the statement "all behavior is encapsulated in objects", or the Object Pascal definition type = object ... end. I will always use "class" to refer to a category and "object" to refer to an individual object.

ior and properties. Each class defines a *protocol* that lists the *messages* its instances can respond to, which gives the interface of the class. That is, the term "message" refers to an operation of the class.

Each class defines its instances' internal state as a set of *instance variables* that represents the attributes and properties of such objects. Each individual object has values for those variables that define its current state, and those values may change over time. The instance variables are not visible to clients, so classes support representation independence (although some object-oriented languages do not enforce it). For each message, the class defines a *method* that describes how its instances respond to that message, namely by accessing or modifying its state information or by sending messages to other objects. The instance variables and methods define the class's implementation, and are not visible externally. The terms "instance variable" and "method" correspond to the storage structure and operation definitions of an abstract data type.

Object-oriented programming makes extensive use of polymorphism. We say that an identifier, subprogram, or object is *polymorphic* if it can be of more than one type. For example, an identifier in a dynamically typed language is polymorphic because it can refer to different types of objects at different times. An overloaded subprogram is polymorphic because it can be invoked with arguments of different types. In section 3.1.5, we will see that inheritance results in polymorphic objects and identifiers.

A *pure* object-oriented language is one that is designed specifically to support object-oriented features of data abstraction, class information, inheritance, and dynamic binding, and to enforce the object-oriented paradigm. Smalltalk, Java, and Eiffel are pure object-oriented languages. A *hybrid* object-oriented language is created by extending an existing procedural or functional language with the object-oriented features, and permits both object-oriented and procedural programming. Hybrid object-oriented languages include Object Pascal, Modula-3, Objective-C, C++, and CLOS.

Message sending

We initiate an operation in an object-oriented system by *sending a message* to an object, the *receiver* of the message. The receiver is responsible for performing the requested activity according to a method defined in its class (or, as we will see, inherited from its superclass). This concept of sending a message to an object rather than directly calling a subprogram in order to perform an activity completes the change of focus from operations to objects. In the object model, the emphasis is on requesting services from an object, rather than on directly manipulating a data structure. In a pure object-oriented language, all interactions are coded as messages passed to objects, and there are no subprograms that are not encapsulated within a class. In fact, a method consists of message sends and control flow statements. (In section 5.5, we will see that even control flow expressions are message sends in Smalltalk.)

A message may be overloaded in the protocols of different classes. For example, both sets and sorted lists implement insertion and deletion of elements, returning the size of the collection, and so on. Message passing is characterized by loose coupling because the class of the receiver and the method it uses might not be known to the object sending the message (due to identifier polymorphism), and different objects may use different methods for a given message transparently. In addition, an object may only access data within another object by sending a message to that object. For example, we might obtain can obtain a collection of objects from another object without knowing whether the collection is a set or a sorted list (again, due to identifier polymorphism). We can insert and delete elements or obtain the collection's size by sending messages to the collection, but we do not know what code is executed and cannot access the collection's structure directly.

Class variables and messages

Some classes contain information that is conceptually associated with the class itself, rather than with any particular instance. Examples include

- class-wide constants, for example, the minimum balance and interest rate for a savings account class, or the default size for a window class
- information about a class's instances, for example, an index for accessing the instances of an employee class, given the employee number.

It is not appropriate for any particular instance of the class to be responsible for this information, nor should it be stored in each instance. In addition to defining the structure of its instances, a class may also define *class variables* that maintain class-wide information. In a traditional programming language, this information would be kept in global variables. Class variables allow us to encapsulate such information together with the class so that it is available wherever the class is imported, but not elsewhere, increasing cohesion and locality and decreasing coupling. Class variables are accessible to all instances of the class but are hidden from other objects, and are independent of the number or even the existence of instances of the class. We also use class variables for constants that are needed in the class's implementation, such as the values INIT_SIZE and EMPTY for the C++ CharStack example in the previous section. We will discuss the use of class variables for type information and method tables for dynamic binding in sections 3.2, 6.1.3, and 12.3.5. Different object-oriented languages use various constructs for defining class variables.

For example, consider a class Date that represents calendar dates. Information associated with this category of entities includes the number of months, the number of days in each month, the names of the months, and the number and names of the days of the week. We encapsulate this information within the Date class as class variables so that it can be made available to applications that use dates, and because it is required in some of the class's methods—such as if a date needs to print itself or respond with the date n days after itself. Instances of Date have direct access to this information.

Like instance variables, class variables are not directly visible to the clients of a class. We could define an instance method providing access to a class variable for other objects, but this would require sending the message to a particular instance of the class. Requesting the number of days in March from a particular date object is somewhat counterintuitive, to say the least. That information exists and should be accessible even if there are no instances of Date in existence. A *class message* provides client access to information stored in class variables or other class-specific operations. For example, the class UnionEmployee would define a class message to access the monthly contribution, which might be used by a Payroll class. Class messages can also provide class-wide computations, for example, the class Date might define a message that returns whether a particular year is a leap year. This is a class message rather than an instance message because that operation is not relevant to a particular date object, and the information necessary to compute the answer is relevant to dates as a whole. Class messages are passed to the class itself, rather than to a particular instance of the class. (We will discuss the syntax for doing so in sections 2.2.4, 6.1.3, and 10.3.2.) Type operations (recall section 0.3.4) such as querying the class's superclass or subclasses are also class messages. Each class message is implemented by a *class method* defined within the class.

Inheritance

In addition to supporting encapsulation and information hiding, the object model extends abstract data types by introducing *inheritance* among classes. Classes that represent problem domain categories that are related by generalization/specialization may share common protocol, instance variables, and methods, without duplicating the specifications of these items in the definitions of each class. The more general class is referred to as a *superclass* of the specific class, and the specific class is called its *subclass*. A subclass *inherits* the messages, methods, and instance variables of its superclass automatically. That is, instances of the subclass respond to superclass messages with superclass methods, and have values for superclass instance variables. The definition of a subclass does not repeat the specification of its superclass's components, and may add instance variables and protocol to those it inherits from the superclass. The subclass may also *override* methods inherited from the superclass for particular messages with methods that are appropriate for its instances. Object-oriented languages support these mechanisms by including syntax for specifying a superclass when defining a class, and the language provides both the superclass and subclass behavior and structure for subclass instances.

For example, a manager object is an employee object with additional information, such as the employees managed and the manager's level, and additional behavior associated with this information. We can represent this problem domain relationship directly in an object-oriented language by defining the class Manager as a subclass of Employee. We code the common behavior (i.e., messages and methods for handling those messages) and state information (i.e., instance variables) in the definition of the superclass Employee. When we define the class Manager, we specify it as a subclass of Employee, and only state the messages, instance variables, and methods specific to Manager. An instance of Manager responds to the messages defined in both classes, and has values for the instance variables defined in both classes. If Manager specifies a method for a message in the protocol of Employee, its instances respond to that message with the Manager method.

In an object-oriented design, a *class hierarchy* represents the generalization relationship among classes, in which a more specific class inherits behavior and structure from its superclass. The class hierarchy represents the type structure of the problem domain or application, and is usually diagrammed as a tree with a superclass as the parent of its subclasses. For example, Figure 1.6 illustrates a portion of the class hierarchy for a motor vehicle registration system. As in this example, the class hierarchy describes the taxonomy of the categories of entities in the problem domain. We also use class hierarchies to represent a set of system components or resources, for example, a class hierarchy of input/output streams and files. In general, the structure of the class hierarchy may be a tree, a forest, or an acyclic directed graph (with "multiple inheritance", in which a class can be a subclass of several superclasses).

When an object receives a message, it executes the method for that message defined by its class. If its class does not define a method, its superclass's protocol is searched for a method, and so on up its chain of ancestors in class hierarchy. We refer to the process of determining the method to invoke for a message as *method binding*. Object-oriented languages are strongly typed because the method binding process signals an error if it does not find a method for a message in the receiver's class or any of its ancestors.

Binding methods according to superclass relationships allows a superclass to define a "default method" for instances of subclasses that do not require more specific behavior. For example, the class MotorVehicle in Figure 1.6 can define a method tax that calculates the vehicle tax based on the general instance variables it defines (e.g., the value and age of the vehicle, its gas mileage, etc.). If a particular descendant such as SportsCar or Convertible needs to use a different method for calculating tax (e.g., with a "luxury car" surcharge), it is defined in that class. When the message tax is sent to an instance of a motor vehicle class that does not define a method for that message, it uses the method inherited from MotorVehicle. An instance of a class that does define a method uses its class's method, without encountering the conflicting behavior in the superclass.

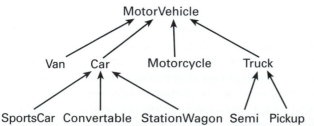

Figure 1.6   An example class hierarchy.

Inheritance provides a number of advantages for software engineering, which we will discuss further in section 1.3. It reduces the amount of code in the system because we only need to code the common interface and implementation of a superclass and its subclasses once, in the superclass. Inheritance reduces the amount of effort necessary to create a new class. In many cases, an existing class provides much of the behavior and structure necessary for the new class. The class designer can use this class as a superclass, write only the code necessary for the additional behavior and structure of the new class, and inherit the superclass's behavior and structure. We can also use a superclass to express commonalities among a set of subclasses. Defining new subclasses reuses the superclass code, and we can use inheritance to extend an application with new capabilities. With inheritance, the design better reflects the structure of the problem in which specialization relates categories of entities.

Dynamic method binding

Dynamic binding of methods for overloaded messages is an important characteristic of object-oriented languages. Determining which method to execute must be done at run time because the compiler might not know the class of the receiver of a message send, due to either dynamic typing or inheritance. For example, with inheritance, a variable of type MotorVehicle can refer to a motorcycle, a car, or a pickup truck because they are all motor vehicles. Since the referent of that variable may depend on run-time conditions (e.g., a user selection), selecting the method according to the class of the receiver must be done at execution time. In order for the method binding process to select the correct method, each object must contain an indication of its class. That is, in object-oriented languages, each object maintains its type identity explicitly.

Suppose that we have a class Owner that maintains a list of the motor vehicles owned by a particular person or organization, and we want to define a method that calculates the total tax due for that owner. The method for totalTax in Owner sends the message tax to each object on the list and keeps a running total to return. The actual method executed in response to the message tax depends on the type of the list element that receives it at execution time. Some objects will use their own class's method, and others will use the method defined in their ancestor MotorVehicle. The totalTax method does not need a case structure of tests, one for each of the different motor vehicle classes, to determine which subprogram to call (nor does any other method that sends an overridden message to a motor vehicle object). It also does not need to know which classes define a method for tax and which inherit the MotorVehicle method. That is, the responsibility for binding the code to the message send has been shifted from the sender to the receiver. A method that passes this message does not even need to know all the possible classes whose instances can receive that message. In addition, we might add new subclasses of MotorVehicle as we develop and maintain the application, for example, ElectricCar, which has an environments conscious tax method. We do not need to modify existing code in the system that uses the MotorVehicle interface, such as the totalTax method for Owner.

The disadvantage of the method binding process is its cost in terms of space and time. The run-time system that performs method binding requires tables that maintain the methods defined in each class, and a pointer in each object to its class's method table. Dynamic binding requires extra time for the method search when sending a message.

1.2 PROGRAMMING PARADIGMS

1.2.1 Definition and Purpose

"Whorf's hypothesis" is a well-known principle in psycholinguistics which states that the language a person uses to describe his or her environment is a lens through which he or she views that environment [Who56]. For example, the Inuit language has several words describing different kinds of "snow" among which a speaker can choose in describing a situation. An English speaker need not make this choice, but cannot describe the situation as concisely. This concept is relevant to computer science because each higher-level language manifests a particular model of computation that affects how a programmer structures a solution to a problem when using that language. It is especially important because most programmers work principally with one or two languages.

For example, consider the difference in outlook between a C programmer and a Pascal programmer with respect to types. A C programmer tends to think of a type as determining the storage format of its instances rather than as indicating semantic intent. The language permits characters, logical values, and enumeration values to be used as short integers, and integers to be used as bit strings because their representations are the same. In contrast, Pascal considers characters and integers to be two different types with different operations because they represent categories with different meanings. A Pascal programmer cannot assign a character to an integer variable or vice versa, and cannot perform arithmetic directly on characters, enumeration values, or logical values. The programmer must code an explicit conversion and then use that result in an arithmetic operation. Similarly, Fortran and Cobol programmers often have a difficult time understanding the concept of using types to represent semantic intent because those languages do not support programmer-defined types. However, as we will see in the next section, these four languages are all imperative languages that are based on the same general model of computation.

We refer to the various models of the nature of computation as *programming paradigms*. A paradigm is a set of theories, models, and techniques that provide a way of perceiving and organizing knowledge, that is, a world view [Kuh62]. Each programming paradigm is a model that describes the essence and structure of computation, and each model defines a different "virtual machine," which embodies the operations and information structuring that model provides. Programming languages that realize the same computing paradigm have similar semantics, although the way in which these semantics are expressed can vary widely. Experience shows that it is more difficult to learn a new programming paradigm than to learn a new programming language in a familiar paradigm.

In this section, we will see that object-oriented programming is not only an extension of standard programming techniques, contrary to the implication of language names such as C++ and Objective Pascal and the progression from abstract data types to classes. The object model is also an alternative way of viewing how information and processing are organized, how applications are structured, and what it means to compute. That is, it provides a different programming paradigm. To illustrate this point, we will survey four programming paradigms and discuss the perspective on computation exemplified by each. We will discuss four programming paradigms: the imperative, functional, logic, and object-oriented paradigms.

1.2.2 The Imperative Programming Paradigm

Computation as a series of storage modifications

In the traditional von Neumann model, a computer consists of a central processing unit and storage (registers and main memory), and performs a sequence of atomic instructions that access, operate on, and modify values stored in individually addressable storage locations. A computation is a series of arithmetic operations and side effects such as assignments or data transfers that modify the state of the storage unit, an input stream, or an output stream. We refer to this model as the *imperative* or *procedural paradigm* for computing. Clearly, this paradigm closely mirrors the actual architecture and operation of traditional computers.

In the imperative paradigm, the assignment is the basic operation from which all processing is built. A program consists of a series of statements that are either assignments or control statements, which route control among the assignments based on execution-time values in storage. A variable is seen as the name of one of the containers in the storage unit, rather than as the name of an object that represents an entity in the problem domain. A composite structure such as an array or record is seen as a collection of individually assignable variables. We emphasize the importance of assignments, statements, and variables as containers to the imperative paradigm because most programmers take these features for granted. In the next section, we will discuss the functional programming paradigm, which does not employ any of these three constructs.

Formally, the imperative paradigm views the computer as a finite state machine in which each state represents a possible state of the storage unit and input and output streams. Execution of an assignment or a data transfer represents a transition between states, and a program consists of a series of such transitions. To represent the dynamic behavior of a program (e.g., to discover whether the program computes the intended result), we must develop representations of both the program and the state of the store. We can then represent the state of a computation at any point by a "program counter" in the representation of the program and the state of the store. We can determine the result of an execution by examining the set of values stored.

Imperative programming languages

Traditional programming languages such as Fortran, Pascal, C, and Ada are based on the imperative paradigm. They provide a more abstract view of computation than machine language, but still treat computation in the same manner. Since imperative programming languages support the same model as the underlying machine, translation of these languages is relatively straightforward and the translator can produce efficient machine code.

Imperative languages provide variable declarations to name storage locations and assignments to modify them. They supply control structures to specify the order in which operations are performed dynamically, and support grouping of operations into units via subprograms. More recent imperative languages provide types to represent higher-level structuring of data (but instances are still regarded as containers). In the imperative paradigm, there is a clear separation between the program that specifies the actions to perform and the data objects encoded in storage that are affected by those actions.

1.2.3 The Functional Programming Paradigm

Computation as function application

In describing the functional paradigm, we must draw a clear distinction between what we mean by the terms "procedure" and "function". Since a procedure returns no value, it is executed for the purpose of modifying the state of data objects or creating and destroying data objects. In this section, we use the term "function" as it is used in mathematics to mean a function that maps values in a domain onto values in a range, rather than a function in Pascal or C that can also cause side effects such as modifying a nonlocal variable.[23]

The *functional* or *applicative paradigm* is based on the theory of recursive functions and the lambda calculus [Chu41], a formalism that supports treating functions as values. In fact, there is no distinction between functions and values at all in the lambda calculus because values such as "true" or "3" are represented as constant functions. The functional paradigm views computation as the evaluation of an expression that represents the application of a function to a list of argument values. The arguments may be function applications, which results in nesting of applications. Rather than consisting of a sequence of variable definitions and executable statements that modify storage, a program gives a number of function definitions and a nested expression involving applications of those functions that returns a value.

---

[23] However, we will continue to use the standard term "functional" decomposition to refer to the design technique of structuring a system according to tasks and subtasks, rather than, say, "procedure-oriented" decomposition.

Functional programming language features

In this section, we describe the semantics of "purely applicative" programming languages such as ML [Sta92] and Miranda [Tur86]. These languages have four features that differ significantly from imperative programming languages:

- There is no storage unit or destructive assignments.
- There are no statements or control structures.
- Functions are first-class objects.
- Variable-length lists are first-class objects.

We note that some primarily functional languages such as Common LISP and Scheme also have imperative features such as sequential and iterative control structures and assignments.

There is no concept of storage containers for values in functional languages, and no global variables defined outside all functions. Functional languages do not provide assignment statements or other side effects. The primary motivation for these characteristics is to facilitate reasoning about programs. Assignments cause the meaning of a name to depend on when it is used, the statements that have been executed, and their order. To know the meaning of a use of a name, we must understand the dynamic behavior of the program. In an applicative language, a value or the result of an expression can be given a name, but the binding of a name cannot be changed elsewhere in the program. Values are communicated to other functions via arguments and return values. Functional languages typically support nested scopes and local functions, and identifier resolution is still necessary because an expression can use the formal parameters of a function at a higher level of nesting in either lexical or evaluation order (depending on the language). A function can access an identifier defined in an enclosing scope (often called a "free variable" as in lambda calculus), but cannot cause a side effect by changing the binding of a non-local identifier.

In a functional language, we do not specify flow of control by listing the sequence of statements to be executed. Instead, we write a nested expression. Evaluating an expression that contains a function application as an argument may require evaluation of that subexpression to produce the argument needed. For example, evaluating the expression func1(x, func2(y)) in a traditional language requires evaluating func2(y) before invoking func1. However, no evaluation can produce a side effect in a functional language, so the translator can evaluate the arguments of an expression in any order without affecting the result of the computation. The argument expressions can even be evaluated concurrently, or on an "as needed" basis.[24] In fact, expressions can be evaluated from the outside in. In our example, the argument expression func2(y) need be evaluated only when an expression involving the second parameter of func1 is evaluated within func1's expression

---

[24] This is often termed *pass by need* or *lazy evaluation*, in contrast to the "strict" evaluation used by traditional imperative languages.

(if at all). In functional languages, we perform repeated execution of operations by recursion rather than by an iterative control structure statement. The language defines a primitive operation that performs conditional evaluation of expressions, which is also used to select the base case of a recursive function.

An identifier in a functional language can denote an atomic object such as a character or an integer, a list of objects, or a function. Unlike arrays, lists are not of fixed size, and the elements of a list can be lists, so representing hierarchically structured information is straightforward. The language defines a literal notation for lists, and primitive functions for constructing and decomposing lists and for testing whether an object is atomic or is a list. Although modern imperative languages allow definition of linked structures using records with pointer components, the program must explicitly describe the pointer operations and the allocations involved when manipulating lists. These details are not needed in the code in functional languages. The programmer can construct a list by simply listing its elements (e.g., enclosed in parentheses or brackets, depending on the language). The language also provides operations that implicitly iterate over the elements of a list, and programmers can define functions with this behavior using the list primitives.

Functions as first-class objects

An interesting and essential characteristic of functional languages is that functions are first-class objects that can be manipulated in the language. We can pass a function to another function as an argument, or can code a function that constructs and returns another function, which is later applied to arguments. We can bind an identifier to a function, store a function in a list, or construct an unnamed function, analogous to a literal for a built-in type in an imperative language. Like lambda calculus and unlike imperative languages, functional languages make no distinction between active programs and static data. We will discuss *function objects* in some detail because Smalltalk supports them and uses them in control flow and enumeration messages.

Functions that take function parameters, for example, the function slope defined in section 0.3.5, are more useful if the language supports a feature for specifying an unnamed argument function. Many functional languages use a notation based on the lambda calculus for this purpose. For example, we can use the following expression to denote the function $x^2 + 2.0$, and to specify that the argument x and the return values are reals:

```
{ using the λ-calculus to write function literals }
λx: real.(x*x + 2.0): real
```

The λ identifies the function's parameters, and distinguishes between the function object and the expression (x*x + 2.0). This notation provides a mechanism for writing anonymous function objects, that is, function literals, that we can use in a context that requires a function. For example, we can use this notation to construct an argument to pass to the function slope defined in section 0.3.5, as follows:

```
{ passing a function as an argument to a function }
m := slope(sin, 3.0, 5.0);
{ passing an anonymous function using the λ-notation }
m := slope(λx: real.(3.0*x*x + 5.0*x + 7.0): real, 2.0, 5.0);
```

The λ-expression specifies an unnamed function just as the literal 2.0 specifies an anonymous floating-point value. Imperative languages such as Pascal and C do not provide this capability, so we can only use named functions as arguments to a function such as slope. We can achieve the same effect in Pascal by defining a named function local to the scope of the call, but this is less convenient (like declaring a name for every value used in a program). However, we will see in the next subsection that Pascal cannot support defining a function that returns a function or function-valued variables.

Closure and representing function objects

Functional languages permit the programmer to create a new function (e.g., using the λ-notation), and assign it to a function-valued variable or return it as the value of a function. Let us consider how to represent the resulting function object. The expression that defines the function object can include both its parameters and any names that are visible in the scope in which that expression occurs. If the language employs static scope, the bindings for nonlocal identifiers in the expression must be determined at the point at which the expression occurs, no matter where the function is invoked after it is assigned to a variable or returned. For this reason, a function object is represented by a *closure* consisting of a pointer to the function code and a static link that refers to the activation record of the function invocation that created the function object.

We will write the examples in this section in an "extended Pascal" that uses the λ-notation for anonymous functions and borrows the Modula-3 syntax for defining a subprogram type. A procedure type appears like a procedure declaration without the procedure name (but we will use the reserved word function, rather than procedure). For example, the following statement defines a type IntFunc for functions that take and return an integer (the identifier num is a placeholder):

```
{ an "extended Pascal" type for function parameters and variables }
{ the referent must be a function that takes and returns an integer }
type
    IntFunc = function (num: integer): integer;
```

Given this type, consider the following program, in which a function creates an anonymous function and returns it:

```
{ the need for closures to represent function objects }
program returnFunction;
var
  num1: integer;
  func1, func2: IntFunc;                        { function-valued variables }
  function retFunc(arg: integer): IntFunc;      { a function that returns a function }
  var
    func: IntFunc;
    num2: integer;
```

```
    begin
        func := λn: integer.(n*n + arg*arg): integer;      { create a function object }
        num2 := func(3);       { OK, arg is bound here }
        retFunc := func        { the value of arg is needed wherever the function is called }
    end
begin
    num1 := 5;
    func1 := retFunc(num1 * 5);
    { the stack frame for retFunc(num1 * 5) is needed in the next call for arg }
    func1(gcd(num1, 12));
    func2 := retFunc(num1 * 2);
    { the stack frames for retFunc(num1 * 5) and retFunc(num1 * 2) are needed }
    num1 := func1(1) + func2(2)
end
```

In this example, we invoke the functions returned by the calls of retFunc in the context of the main program returnFunction, in which arg is not bound. When the code given in the λ-expression is executed, arg must be bound to the argument passed to the execution of retFunc that created that function object. For example, in the last statement in the program, the code of each function object must use a different arg object, namely the one in the activation record of retFunc in which it was created. In general, the λ-expression that defines a function object can refer to any variable visible in the scope in which it is defined (including variables in enclosing scopes), so the closure must contain a static link to access nonlocals.[25]

An activation record that a closure refers to must exist for the lifetime of that function object. If a function returns a function object, the activation record of that invocation must continue to exist after completing execution because the closure that represents the returned function contains a reference to that activation record. For example, the activation record of the call retFunc(num1 * 5) in the previous example must exist for as long as the variable func1 refers to the function object it returned. In particular, it must be maintained even while gcd, func1 and retFunc are called. For this reason, using a stack for allocation of activation records is inadequate when functions are first-class objects, so languages that provide first-class support for function objects must use a more flexible allocation process.[26] That is, stack frames have nested lifetimes, but a closure can have an arbitrary lifetime, like a dynamically allocated object. In general, an activation record referred to by a closure may contain a static link to another activation record that must also continue to exist for as long as the function object, and so on through a chain of static links.

---

[25] Actually, if the code in the function object (and in any other function objects that refer to that activation record) does not modify any nonlocal variable, the closure could contain copies of the nonlocal variables' values, rather than a static link. Functional languages that do not support destructive assignments can always use this optimization.

[26] In fact, Lisp originally used dynamic scope to avoid this problem. With dynamic scope, nonlocals in the function code are resolved in the environment of the call, so closures do not need a static link.

Even though Pascal supports subprogram parameters, a Pascal language system can use stack-based allocation of activation records. Subprogram parameters are represented by closures, but the static link of a closure always points to an activation record on the stack. Since the language does not support subprogram-valued variables or return values, a closure containing a reference to a stack frame cannot persist when the corresponding subprogram exits. In addition, the referents of nonlocal identifiers in a subprogram will exist on the stack whenever it is called. Even if the subprogram is passed as an argument to another subprogram, it cannot be used as an argument outside the context in which it is defined because its name is not visible. Once execution enters the context in which the subprogram is defined, activation records for all enclosing scopes are on the stack. To illustrate these points, suppose we define a function innerFunc nested within the function outerFunc, that accesses the variable num2 and num3 defined in outerFunc, as follows:

```
{ Pascal can use a stack for activation records }
program functionArgument;
var
   num1: Integer;
   function higherFunc(argFunc: IntFunc): integer;
   begin
     { ... function code that calls argFunc ... }
   end
   function outerFunc(arg: integer): integer;
   var
     num2, num3: integer;
     function innerFunc(arg: integer): integer;
     begin
       { ... function code that uses num2 and num3 ... }
     end
   begin
     num2 := higherFunc(innerFunc);       { OK in Pascal, num3 exists here }
   end
begin  { program }
   num1 := higherFunc(innerFunc);     { not valid in Pascal: innerFunc is not visible }
   num1 := higherFunc(outerFunc);     { OK in Pascal: outerFunc is visible }
end
```

The referents of num2 and num3 in innerFunc are always the most recently created objects, which are in the current activation record of outerFunc. Even when innerFunc is passed as an argument in a call within outerFunc, there is a current activation record of outerFunc active. innerFunc cannot be invoked outside the scope of outerFunc, that is, when there is no current activation record of outerFunc on the run-time stack.

Both elements of a closure (i.e., the code and the static link) are still necessary to implement a subprogram argument in Pascal. As we saw in section 0.2.4, access to nonlocal variables is implemented via the static link. When a function invokes a subprogram argument, a static link must be installed in the activation record for that call. The static link for the subprogram argument is computed before calling the function it is passed to according to the static distance between the scope of the sub-program definition and that of the invocation (recall section 0.2.4). Again, this computation must be done at execution time, although the static distance (and, therefore, the object code) is fixed at compile time. A closure containing a pointer to the subprogram code and the static link is then passed to the function.

Pascal does not support subprogram return values so that a reference to a sub-program cannot be passed outside the context in which is it defined. Similarly, Pascal does not support subprogram-valued variables because assigning a subprogram to a subprogram variable in an enclosing scope would have the same effect. A statically scoped language could support these features and still employ a stack for activation records if it enforces some weaker restrictions on their use. For example, Modula-2 supports subprogram variables, but only allows assigning a subprogram defined at module scope (i.e., at the highest level of scope) to such a variable. The static link for such a subprogram points to the static storage for the module's variables, which is always present. Alternatively, the language could restrict assignments to function variables to functions defined in the same scope as the variable (including functions defined in scopes that enclose the variable's scope).

C supports the type "pointer to function" for variables, parameters, and return values. We can assign a function to a pointer to function variable, and then invoke the function referent through the pointer. However, C functions can only be defined at file scope, so there are only two contexts for the names used in a function, its local scope and file scope. Static links are not needed, and the compiler can always determine the meaning of a nonlocal name. In addition, there is no notation for function literals that might refer to local variables of the function in which that expression appears.

Program verification

Many researchers have worked on issues such as proving whether a program is correct, whether two programs compute the same function, or whether a program will terminate given certain inputs. Applicative languages are attractive for this work because it is straightforward to use the mechanisms of the lambda calculus to reason formally about programs. To prove a program is correct, we state the pre-conditions required for a function and then show that the desired postconditions hold after its evaluation. Similarly, we can state and verify invariant conditions that describe relationships among the values of local and free variables at some point within a function definition. These assertions also provide commentary for readers of the program.

Such proofs are simpler in the functional paradigm than with an imperative model of computation for a number of reasons. Since there are no destructive assignments, it is not necessary to devise and maintain a representation for the state of the store. Without static or global variables, when a particular function is applied to a given argument in a given context, it always returns the same value. Like a function in mathematics, a function f can be treated as a set of ordered pairs $(x, f(x))$. Applicative programs have the property of *referential transparency*: A name cannot mean different things at different times, like "3" and "2 + 1" which always mean the same value. The definition of a name can be substituted for the name (and vice versa) at any time without affecting the meaning of the expression in which it occurs. Since an expression cannot modify the state of the computation in a manner that affects the results of other expressions, each function application can be treated individually.

Functional programming languages

The most well-known functional language is Lisp, which was designed for performing symbolic computations on list structures, especially for artificial intelligence applications. The ANSI standard Common Lisp [Ste90] does include variable binding, assignment, control structures, and other traditional programming constructs. Scheme [Spr89] is a variant of Lisp that uses lexical rather than dynamic scope to resolve free variable references, and specifies a much smaller set of predefined functions.

APL [Pol75] is an early functional language designed for operating on vectors and matrices. Logo [Pap80] is a functional language with a graphic component designed to teach problem solving to children. ML [Sta92] is a functional language that provides static typing, a type inference mechanism, higher-order functions, and data type constructors. Miranda [Tur86] is a contemporary function language that also includes guarded expression and "infinite" lists, specification of a list by its properties, and implicit list iteration operations. In Chapter 5, we will see that Smalltalk also includes functional capabilities such as anonymous functions and implicit iteration over collections.

1.2.4 The Logic Programming Paradigm

Computations as proof and declarative programming

In imperative programming, we specify the steps necessary to solve a problem or derive some result completely. In logic programming, a program is regarded as a collection of facts and inference rules written in a logic formalism. Computation consists of proving or satisfying an assertion based on those that are given. That is, we view a query as a theorem to be proved by the system, rather than as a program that specifies a series of operations. This approach is suited to applications such as expert systems and database systems for which it is more natural to specify constraints on a solution or properties of a solution than a detailed description of how to compute it. Most logic programming languages are based on the first-order predicate calculus, and as such have well-defined semantics.

Logic programming languages are a step toward the concept of *declarative programming* in which the programmer specifies "what" is to be done without specifying "how". They provide a higher-level description that abstracts out the actual operation of the proof procedure. For example, to sort an array in a declarative language, we give the property of the desired permutation—that for valid indices i and

j, i < j implies that arr[i] < arr[j]—and the language system determines how to find
that permutation. The system proves the statement that such a permutation exists
by exhibiting it.

Prolog

The most well-known logic programming language is Prolog [Bra90], which
was designed by Colmerauer and Roussel at the University of Marseilles in the early
1970s. Prolog is an interpreted system in which the programmer asserts "clauses",
that is, facts and inference rules, and presents queries for evaluation. Clauses are
expressed using the Horn clause form of first-order predicate calculus in which the
conclusion of an inference rule is a single term. Prolog also provides constructs for
integer arithmetic, list processing, and structured data objects. For example, we can
define a rule such as the following (Prolog variable names must be capitalized):

```
% a Prolog inference rule
grandfather(X, Y) :- male(X), parent(X, Z), parent(Z, Y).
```

We can read the notation :- as "is implied by", and , (comma) represents "and". The
rule states that for all X, Y and Z, if the facts on the right (the "body" of the rule) can
be proven, then the fact on the left (the "head" of the rule) is true. This rule states
that if X is male and is a parent of some Z such that Z is a parent of Y, then X is the
grandfather of Y. A program in which this rule appears might also contain facts such
as parent(chronos, zeus) and male(apollo). We can then present queries (also called
"goals") such as the following:

```
% queries to a Prolog interpreter
?- grandfather(zeus, apollo).
?- grandfather(X, apollo).
?- grandfather(chronos, X).
```

The first query asks whether the fact grandfather(zeus, apollo) is true. The next two
queries contain variables, so they ask whether bindings for those variables can be
found such that the fact presented is true. The first of these asks the system to find
an X such that X is apollo's grandfather, and the second asks for an X such that
chronos is X's grandfather. When presenting a query interactively, we can also ask
the system to successively give each variable binding that makes the fact true (e.g.,
for the last query).

In Prolog, the programmer frames a query without specifying how the system
will determine variable bindings that make the query true. That is, he or she adopts
a goal-oriented approach rather than an action-oriented approach to specifying a
solution. The programmer describes the logical properties required of the result of
a computation, and the Prolog interpreter searches for a result having those properties. Flow of control is implicit because the sequence of actions that occurs in
proving an assertion is not specified directly, but results as the interpreter attempts
to prove that assertion.

A rule such as the previous example has both declarative and procedural interpretations. It may be regarded either as a true statement (i.e., as an implication or definition of the relationship grandfather(X,Y)), or as a rule for deriving other facts (i.e., as a specification to be used procedurally by the proof mechanism implemented in the language system). As in applicative languages, there is no distinction between operational code and static data.

The proof procedure

Prolog uses pattern matching with a simplified form of unification to prove assertions. When a query is posed, the system attempts to match that query with facts or heads of rules in the database, with a variable in a query matching any formula. If a match with a fact is successful and the query contains variables, the system reports the bindings that make the queried fact true. If the head of a rule is matched, then values resulting from that match are substituted for the corresponding variables in the body, and the body becomes a set of subgoals to be matched. This illustrates the procedural interpretation of a rule: To prove the left side, the system must prove all the clauses on the right side.

If no match can be found at some point, the proof procedure backtracks by undoing the most recent variable binding and beginning again from that point in the database, searching for an alternative binding. For backtracking, the interpreter keeps a stack of the positions in the database corresponding to the various variable bindings that it has made. The system also uses this stack to give the user all possible bindings that make the query true. To do so, the proof procedure undoes each successive binding, and continues searching from that point to find further correct bindings.

For example, in solving the query ?- grandfather(zeus, apollo), the system finds the grandfather rule, binds zeus to X and apollo to Y, and then attempts to solve the three subgoals male(zeus), parent(zeus, Z), and parent(Z, apollo). Presumably, it finds the first subgoal to be true, and then finds a fact matching the second, say parent(zeus, artemis), which binds artemis to Z. Next the interpreter attempts to match the subgoal parent(artemis, apollo). If it cannot find such a fact or a matching rule head, it backtracks to its most recent binding, of artemis to Z in this case. It undoes that binding for Z, and proceeds from the fact that produced that binding. It then continues searching for another fact or rule head that will match parent(zeus, Z), and if it finds one, it binds Z and continues. The process continues until a match is found or a subgoal has been found to be unsuccessful. Note that for the query ?- grandfather(X, apollo), the same process is repeated for each X for which male(X) is in the database until a solution is found. Whenever the original query contains variables, the process of resolving the query will bind the variables and report those bindings.

Prolog is not completely declarative because the clauses in its database are ordered and are searched in order, and the clauses in the right side of a rule are matched from left to right. In addition, Prolog supports a mechanism for pruning the database search. The programmer can use the ordering of clauses to give some procedural meaning to a series of rules. For example, when defining a predicate recursively, the base case is placed before the recursive case in the database so that it is matched first. For example, the following two rules define the predicate ancestor:

```
% recursive definition of the predicate ancestor
ancestor(X, Y) :- parent(X, Y).
ancestor(X, Y) :- parent(X, Z), ancestor(Z, Y).
```

A strictly declarative interpretation of these clauses could repeat forever on the second rule. Prolog programmers often use the ordering of the database for efficiency, for example, to list a set of mutually exclusive tests with the most likely to be satisfied listed first. The order of the clauses in the right-hand side of the rules also affects efficiency. For example, the grandfather example rule will do less searching with the clause male(X) listed second if there are more males than parents in the database. Because the backtracking process can be very time-consuming, the programmer must be careful in ordering the clauses in the database and the facts in a rule body.

To aid in restricting the search for a match, Prolog defines the "cut" primitive, which allows the programmer to prevent examining certain branches of the search that he or she knows (or assumes) to be fruitless. Because the programmer is directing the search, use of the cut primitive attaches procedural meaning to clauses, and this meaning may differ from the declarative meaning of that clause (i.e., if a solution occurs in an eliminated branch of the search).

Expert systems

Expert systems attempt to model human reasoning about a problem domain as well as the problem domain itself. Their rules often deal with more complex structures that represent knowledge such as frames, rather than with simple Prolog predicates. Due to the uncertainty and vagueness of this information, most expert systems also augment inference rules with probabilities or fuzzy logic.

1.2.5 The Object-Oriented Programming Paradigm

Motivation

Currently, "object-oriented" is the most ubiquitous buzzword in computer science, and has been used to describe activities in almost every area in the field. There are object-oriented languages, programming environments, databases, software engineering methodologies, graphic user interfaces, expert systems, distributed file systems, VLSI architectures, and so forth. We expect that object-oriented techniques will increase programmer productivity and software reliability, especially by allowing more reuse of existing code, and by providing systems that are easier to extend and modify.

This goal is met by designing abstract objects that mirror the properties of problem domain entities. By doing so, we narrow the "semantic gap" between the program system and the activity or situation it models, allowing the designer to think about the representation in the same terms in which he or she views the problem domain. Inheritance is an important part of object-oriented programming because specialization is so common in problem domains, and is so essential in modeling them accurately.

The basic principle in the object-oriented approach is that classes are a more natural unit for understanding the problem domain and structuring the system than either state information or processing alone. An additional advantage is that these same abstractions may then be reused for other applications that model the same or similar real-world systems. Classes provide a library of standard high-level components for constructing new systems dealing with the same problem domain, similar to designing hardware or machinery, as opposed to building systems from "raw materials", that is, from individual lines of code [Cox86]. Inheritance provides structure for browsing and understanding this library.

Computation as simulation

Rather than viewing computation as a process of modifying stored values, evaluating functions, or proving theorems, the object-oriented model sees it as simulation of a problem domain system. Programming is seen as the process of developing a model rather than as writing instructions that operate on data. We structure this model as an interaction among various independent actors, each sending the other messages asking it to perform some activity. We create constructs that reflect the characteristics of the entities in the system being simulated (i.e., classes) and describes their interactions, rather than focusing on the processing that the application must perform. Object paradigm principles such as abstraction, classification, and inheritance are motivated by their usefulness in modeling.

This perspective corresponds more closely to our intuitive descriptions of activities in the real world, and experience has shown that nonprogrammers often understand the object-oriented approach more easily than computer professionals. In fact, a good estimate of the extent to which the system correctly mirrors the problem domain is how well a nonprogrammer familiar with the real-world system can understand the design.

Encapsulated objects and message passing

In a sense, there are two levels to the object-oriented paradigm. The higher-level description of the object paradigm is that it is concerned with simulation and modeling a problem domain system. The mechanism that embodies the difference between object-oriented programming and traditional procedural programming is the concept of expressing actions as message passing among encapsulated objects, with the receiver responsible for the operations performed. That is, the fundamental operation in object-oriented programming is the message send, and we use message passing to represent all interactions among the objects in the application that correspond to entities in the problem domain. In object-oriented programming, all behavior is encapsulated in the sense that each activity is the responsibility of the instances of a particular class, and can only be initiated by passing the appropriate message to an object of that class.

Comparison with other paradigms

Like the imperative paradigm, the object paradigm also draws a distinction between data objects and operations. However, it differs in that the focus of system design is on the objects to represent, rather than on the processing to perform. Processing is encapsulated within classes, in contrast with the imperative paradigm in which objects are encapsulated within subprograms (i.e., as local variables or parameters). By doing so, we expect that the units we design will be more amenable to reuse since they package all the relevant information for some category of entity. Although a paradigm shift from the procedural to object perspectives of computation is necessary at the system design level, it is not true that your skills in functional decomposition, stepwise refinement, and algorithm design are no longer relevant. Instead, these activities occur within the context of a class, rather than within procedural modules or at global scope.

The imperative, functional, and logic paradigms are based on the formal theories of Turing machines, lambda calculus, and first order predicate calculus, respectively, while the object-oriented paradigm is based on the metaphor of system simulation.[27] This permits a certain amount of latitude in deciding whether a particular language or system is object-oriented, but does not provide a method for verifying the correctness of object-oriented applications. The object-oriented paradigm, like the imperative paradigm, deals with the state and behavior of objects over time, as opposed to the functional and logical paradigms, which deal with timeless properties of mathematical or symbolic values, and relationships among them.

1.3 OBJECT-ORIENTED DEVELOPMENT

1.3.1 Structured Methods

Background

In this section, we briefly describe traditional structured methods so that we can contrast them with the object-oriented approach to software engineering. These methodologies are covered in detail in software engineering texts such as [Som96] and [Pre92]. [Bir85] gives a survey of many of the specific structured methodologies.

The advantages of structured programming and functional decomposition had become apparent by the 1960s. This resulted in the design and implementation of

---

[27] Work on extending denotational semantics to model type inheritance is in progress, for example, see [Dan88] and [Coo89].

languages such as Algol, Pascal, and PL/I that included features enforcing this approach to organizing code. Once these languages were available, attention shifted to incorporating those concepts of structure into system design, and then into problem analysis, culminating in the *structured method* for software engineering during the 1970s.

The designers of the various formulations of structured methods recognized that the size of modern software systems demands an organized way of partitioning the system and describing its structure so that it can be understood by mere mortals. They also developed these methodologies to provide structure to the software development process to make it more manageable. As Coad states [Coa91], a structured method is a set of standardized graphic notations and encodings of effective design practice that are cost-effective for large projects, rather than a formal, algorithmic procedure that guarantees a correct design.

Structured methods are strongly influenced by the procedural paradigm prevalent at the time when they were developed. Structured analysis is more oriented toward representing the transformations being applied to data values than toward the structure of those values. In structured design, the system architecture generally consists of a number of interacting subprograms or modules and a global data store.

The software life cycle

The classic approach to software engineering is described as the *software life cycle*, which consists of the following phases:

1. problem *requirements specification*
2. *analysis* of the problem domain and the system requirements
3. *design* of the software system itself
4. *implementation*, namely, coding, testing, and debugging
5. *maintenance* of the system after its delivery.

Analysis refers to activities involving understanding the system specification and the problem domain, while design refers to defining the architecture of the software system. Generally speaking, analysis deals with the problem and design deals with the solution. In terms of abstraction, analysis is concerned mainly with interfaces (i.e., of the subprograms and modules inspired by problem domain activities), while design implements those interfaces in terms of "lower-level" subprograms and data structures, so it involves both interface and implementation. Design also deals with defining aspects of the system not directly related to the problem domain, such as its user interaction, concurrency, and persistent data management components. We will often use the term "development" to refer to the entire process of creating an application, especially for object-oriented systems in which there is a closer correspondence between the structure of the levels, and therefore less distinction between them.

Originally, these phases were intended to be performed in sequence with each phase specified completely before work begins on the next, a procedure often referred to as the "waterfall" model because each phase flows down to the next. This paradigm provides a well-understood methodology that gives structure to the development process, as opposed to "hacking" an *ad hoc* solution. It also provides clear milestones and deliverables at each phase that the project manager can use to trace the progress of the project.

Graphic notations

Many other science and engineering disciplines use standardized graphic notations such as molecular diagrams or electronic circuit diagrams to represent the structure of the problem domain or the architecture of the system. A number of graphic notations for software engineering have been developed that represent the problem domain or the system architecture as a directed graph. Structured methods use nodes in the graph to represent entities such as processes, input sources, output sinks, and data stores, and arcs to represent data flow, invocation, or other dependencies between nodes. Different authors use different graphic symbols and labelings for different types of nodes or arcs.

Graphic representations of the model or the structure of the system are an integral part of most software engineering methods, and are useful because they exploit the special abilities of the human vision system for which "a picture is worth a thousand words". In particular, they provide a two-dimensional representation of a complex system design that allows simultaneous presentation of a web of interrelationships on one diagram. This allows the designer to apprehend individual relationships, chains of relationships, and clustering of relationships easily. Graphic notation also facilitates interaction among designers and communication with domain experts, managers, clients, and users.

Unfortunately, in practice, graphic diagrams are often not kept current because the physical size of the diagram for a large, complex system becomes unmanageable. The person-hours required for maintaining them as the system evolves would be taken away from other activities. In addition, there is the danger that the diagrams become an end in themselves for some developers, rather than a means of documenting a design.

Structured analysis

In structured analysis, *data flow diagrams* model the processing required by describing the transformations to perform on input data as it is processed into output data [Con79]. Processes are usually indicated by a circular graphic element, data stores (i.e., buffers, queues, databases, etc.) by double bold lines, and inputs and outputs to the system by rectangular boxes. The flow of data among processes, data stores, and input/output is represented by directed lines connecting these components. The data flow diagram must be acyclic, and no assumptions are made about timing of processes that are not connected by flow lines. The data flow approach emphasizes analysis of processing, and has weak data structuring facilities.

The designer can define a hierarchy of such charts to reflect the structure of the system's processing at various levels of granularity by describing a process at level *i* by a data flow diagram at level *i+1*. Extensions for indicating control flow and timing for event-driven and real-time systems have been developed (e.g., by using dashed lines and bubbles on the data flow diagram [War85] or by a separate control flow diagram [Hat87]).

The data flow diagrams are augmented with a *data dictionary* and a *process specification*. For each data item in the system, the data dictionary specifies its type, a text description of the item, its usage, and constraints on the data values permitted. The process specification describes the processing each process performs using pseudocode, a flowchart, or an abstract "program description language".

Structured design

The functional decomposition of the programming system is represented graphically by a *structure chart* [Con79]. The structure chart displays the hierarchy of invocations, with nodes representing each subprogram or module and edges representing invocations. Edges in the structure chart are typically labeled with the data or control information passed each direction between the modules denoted by the adjacent nodes. There are a number of design measures and heuristics that are used as criteria for the quality of the design (the branching factor of the hierarchy, for one).

The transition from system requirements (as specified by data flow diagrams with data dictionaries and process specifications) to the structure chart describing the software system is not algorithmic. Intuition and experience play a major role, and there is rarely an optimal solution for a large-scale system. For example, adjacent levels or siblings in one version of the subprogram hierarchy may be collapsed in another. Generally, the process proceeds as follows [Pre92]. First, the designer determines whether a section of the data flow diagram exhibits *transform* flow with incoming, transform, and outgoing flows, or *transaction* flow with a "reception" path, a "transaction center" (a bubble specifying selection of an action based on a transaction type), and "action paths" that indicate processing alternatives. Next he or she specifies "flow boundaries" between these portions of the diagram to indicate decomposition of the processing into subtasks. These subdiagrams of process bubbles are then mapped to program modules. For a transform flow subdiagram, a single module calls the modules that implement the incoming, transform, and outgoing flows. With transaction flow, a single module calls a reception path module and a dispatch module, which then calls modules for each of the action paths. The same technique is used at each level of data flow diagrams to factor process bubbles into modules, resulting in a hierarchy of tasks and subtasks.

CASE systems

Computer-aided software engineering or *CASE* systems are software environments that support the various activities at each phase in the software life cycle for a group of designers and programmers working together on a project. The purpose of such tools is to free the designer from the details of the process so that he or she can concentrate on the creative aspects of design. Each tool presents an abstraction that represents only the information necessary for that task. Individual CASE tools aid in tasks such as simulation and prototyping, planning and estimating costs, documentation preparation, version management, and the various types of programming support described in section 4.2. A number of vendors market CASE systems that support specific structured methodologies.

The power of CASE is best realized by an integrated development environment that includes a database and a group of tools that access it. The database stores information describing project plans, analysis and design results, system documentation, source code, and program information such as symbol tables, compilation dependencies, multiple versions, and test data. For each entity, the database stores its type, creator, dates of creation and modification, attributes and properties, relationships with other entities in the database, and so forth. An object-oriented database is more appropriate for this information since commercial relational systems are oriented more toward records consisting of uniform data items and frequent simple transactions. Each tool provides the operations relevant to its task, multiple views of graphic and text information, and context-sensitive help through a common user interface.

1.3.2 Applying the Object Model

Background and motivation

We stated at the beginning of the previous section that structured programming principles were eventually applied to the design and analysis levels of the software development process. A similar progression is occurring with the object model of system structure. By the mid-1980s, several object-oriented programming languages were implemented. As understanding of the object-oriented paradigm spread through use of these languages, researchers concentrated on applying the object model and its insights to system design, and then to problem domain analysis. That is, object-oriented analysis uses the concepts of objects, classes with encapsulated protocols, inheritance, and so on to represent the problem domain, while object-oriented design uses these concepts to describe the structure of the system. In this text, we concentrate on object-oriented programming, but it is worthwhile to discuss the impact that the object model has on the development process, since it is a major motivation for the paradigm and the associated language features.

Structured methods were originally developed for the batch-type, transaction-oriented business applications that characterized computing at that time (e.g., a payroll application). Typically, a program applied a fixed series of processing steps to a uniform stream of data to produce an updated data file and some reports. Contemporary systems tend to be much larger, more complex, and more volatile, and usually have the following characteristics:

- There are many kinds of data, and correct modeling of the structure of the data is a greater concern than the complexity of the processing.
- The operations required are naturally partitioned into units associated with particular classes of objects, rather than being globally defined.
- The specifications for the system frequently change while it is being designed and implemented, and different versions of the system are often needed (e.g., at different prices or for different platforms).
- The system has a long lifetime that includes a significant maintenance effort as features are added, bugs are fixed, and the capabilities of the hardware, operating system, and other applications that communicate with it change.
- Applications are frequently on-line systems that respond interactively to commands from a user to perform particular tasks (rather than performing a single, possibly complex, task), and an ergonomic user interface is expected.

For example, consider a desktop publishing system. It deals with characters, paragraphs, columns, graphic objects in various formats, style sheets, and so on. Some operations are relevant to characters and paragraphs (e.g., changing the text style or font) and others are relevant to style sheets (e.g., setting the number of columns or positioning a graphic element). The vendor sells the system for PCs, Macintoshes, and UNIX machines, and provides a less expensive edition for home users. The application goes through numerous major and minor revisions during its lifetime (look at the version numbers of commonly-used applications). There is no "top-level" task that describes the processing the application performs. In using the system, the user selects a particular object and then sends it a message in the protocol of its class to manipulate it, for example, via a menu selection.

The object model provides a framework that more naturally matches these characteristics. Classes are the focus of analysis and design, and processing is encapsulated within classes. The flexibility, uniformity, and extendibility of a system developed using object-oriented techniques facilitates accommodating changes in the problem specifications, producing multiple versions of the system, and adding functionality during maintenance. Object-oriented modeling is not based on decomposing a single task, but on representing a complex system of objects and their behaviors, properties, and interrelationships. Application frameworks provide reuse of interface components and graphic objects, which reduces the effort necessary to design and code an interactive application.

The larger a system is, the more apparent and more productive are the advantages an object-oriented approach provides for development. We prefer this paradigm for very large systems and more challenging problem domains because it results in systems that are

- easier to write, read, and maintain due to abstraction and the focus on simulation
- safer and more reliable due to encapsulation, information hiding, and strong typing
- easier to extend due to inheritance and dynamic binding.

The object model also provides more extensive reuse of design constructs and code units than the procedural model, increasing productivity and reliability and decreasing delivery time.

System decomposition

Clearly, determining the architecture of the system is a primary task in both analysis and design. The top-down functional decomposition used in structured methods is based on the algorithms necessary to perform a task—for example, on the verbs in the problem specification—and the system is organized in terms of modules, subprograms, and their interfaces. The designer recognizes the various subtasks from configurations of nodes and arcs in the data flow diagram, and stores shared state information in a global data area. Algorithms are encapsulated and shared data is globally available, resulting in tightly coupled modules. The diagram of system structure has a root, namely, the main task of the system. The nodes in the tree represent processes and data stores, and the arcs represent invocation and data flow.[28]

On the other hand, object-oriented decomposition is based on the objects and classes in the system, that is, the nouns, and their behavior. Processing is encapsulated within classes, and information and structure are localized in terms of classes, subclasses, and protocols rather than according to subprograms. When developing the system, we design the classes and protocols first and consider the algorithms later as implementations, rather than designing the algorithms first (i.e., in terms of their subtasks). In a diagram of the interactions between system components for an object-oriented system, the nodes represent objects or classes, and the arcs represent inheritance among classes and composition and associations among objects. Object-oriented architecture corresponds to the structure of the problem domain system, rather than to the processing the application must perform. This diagram usually does not have a distinguished root, as in top-down functional decomposition.

Object-oriented design provides increased cohesion and decreased coupling. Cohesion is increased because a class is a more natural unit than a module or subprogram since it is inspired by an existing problem domain category and includes both the relevant operations and information. Coupling among classes is looser due to information hiding, polymorphism, and dynamic binding.

As we stated in section 1.1.1, the model for a large system is too complex to apprehend in its entirety. In section 1.1.3, we stated that modules provide a level of structure above that of the system's thousands of subprograms. In object-oriented design, classes encapsulate methods and provide this level of organization. However, a very large system can have hundreds of classes, so many object-oriented design methodologies employ an additional level of structure between that of the entire-system and that of its classes. A "subsystem" (also called a "cluster") is a

---

[28] The diagram of a top-down functional decomposition might not be strictly a tree because more than one higher-level subprogram may call a particular lower-level subprogram.

group of classes and their interrelationships, which is designed to minimize interdependencies across subsystem boundaries. In a very large system, subsystems can be nested. Like all abstractions, subsystems provide an overview of the system by defining components that can be considered separately to avoid information overload. Like modules, they provide a hierarchical organization for the system, a structure for partitioning the development effort, and opportunities for reuse. In section 2.2.4, we will discuss how various object-oriented languages support grouping implementation-level classes into modules.

Analysis and design tasks

In object-oriented development, we use classes, encapsulated protocols, message passing, inheritance, and so on to structure our models in the analysis, design, and implementation phases. For example, object-oriented analysis uses objects and classes to model entities and categories in the problem domain. At each development phase, the designer must perform the following tasks:

- identify the objects and classes relevant to the application
- determine the activities and services required by the system, and assign them to classes, developing their protocols
- specify the attributes of a class's instances, and identify the state information in the system and assign it to classes
- determine the relationships among objects, for example, composition and functional associations
- represent specialization and commonalities among classes using inheritance.

Classes are the primary structural unit so we begin by recognizing some classes and objects. Since all information is encapsulated within classes, each activity or service provided is assigned to a class, and each piece of information is managed by a class or its instances. We delegate execution of an activity to the class whose instances are affected by that activity, rather than to the client requesting that service (which would involve the client manipulating the object directly). This mirrors the real-world system in which entities are responsible for performing activities, and decouples the client and provider of a service. Management of state information is delegated to the class that most logically maintains it, based on the problem domain category it describes and the services it provides. In capturing the structure of a model, we must also represent relationships among objects, such as composition and client–server (sender–receiver) relationships.

In practice, the activities necessary to develop a model are usually intermingled in an incremental, iterative process. Although we begin with classes, these tasks generally proceed in parallel and we often recognize further classes as we identify activities, state information, and relationships. For example, in assigning services to classes, the designer may recognize commonalities in behavior that causes him or her to reorganize elements of the inheritance hierarchy, or to add, delete, coalesce, or split classes. In this case, protocol, attributes, and relationships must also be reassigned. In addition, the desirability of reusing classes available from frameworks or other projects may affect the classes used in analysis or design.

Determining components of the model

In deciding what to model, the designer must include significant entities and behavior and exclude unimportant information, based on the goals and purpose of the system. For example, both computers and office furniture might be instances of the class Asset rather than separate classes in a home office management application. Throughout this process, components of the model may be redefined and reorganized as understanding of the system and its responsibilities grows.

The primary source of information for the model is the problem specifications. Some analysts begin by categorizing the words in the problem description [Abb83]. Nouns inspire objects and classes, active verbs describe services, stative verbs (e.g., "have") indicate relationships, adjectives provide attribute values, and "is a" phrases indicate inheritance. Compound nouns such as "deposit transaction" often indicate the existence of a superclass, Transaction in this case. Clearly, this technique is only a starting point due to the flexibility possible in natural language expression, and the ability and style of the writer of the specifications.

Another common technique is to analyze scenarios describing activities in the problem domain (for analysis) and scenarios of the behavior required of the system (for design, also called "use cases" [Jac92]) to determine what objects and services are necessary and which objects should be responsible for each service. As we identify each activity in a scenario, we assign the responsibility for performing it to a class and add that service to its protocol. This technique is neither top-down nor bottom-up, but is an empirical approach that proceeds from the known to the unknown. Perhaps a better description of object-oriented modeling is "outside-in" since we identify interfaces first, and then design implementations.

The designer also determines elements of the model from discussions with domain experts and users of the proposed system. For example, "knowledge acquisition" techniques developed for expert systems can be oriented toward encapsulation of behavior [Gra94b]. The semantics of the classes identified may suggest behavior they should provide and information they should maintain. In addition, much can be learned by analyzing similar systems and their designs.

Familiarity

The simulation orientation of the object paradigm facilitates interaction between the designers and domain experts, clients, managers, and users because mapping the problem domain as these individuals see it onto elements of the system is straightforward. For example, the classes, protocols, interobject relationships, and inheritance structure in a project management application will be familiar to managers, and the classes in a financial application will be familiar to accountants. This improves communication with members of each group, which is essential to successful delivery of the system. In contrast, the structure of data flow diagrams and functional decomposition charts reflects what the system must do to the information it receives, not what problem it solves, which is likely to be a less natural perspective for these individuals.

1.3.3 The Object-Oriented Development Process

Uniformity across development phases

In the structured method, designers use data flow diagrams and their associated process specifications and data dictionaries in analysis, but then use functional decomposition and structure charts to describe system structure in the design phase. The mapping between these two types of organization and their elements is not straightforward, especially the reverse correspondence between elements of the structure chart and the data flow diagram. This characteristic makes it difficult to trace design structures back to their origin in the problem specification, or to localize modifications demanded by changes in the problem domain or specifications.

In contrast, object-oriented development uses the same modeling techniques in the analysis, design, and implementation phases. In fact, the same classes, objects, and interrelationships discovered during analysis are also present at the design and implementation phases (together with finer-grained classes that implement them or represent system components). This similarity of concept and structure allows using the same vocabulary and graphic notation to describe both the structure of the problem domain and the system itself. More importantly, it simplifies defining successive phases in the process, and facilitates moving back and forth among phases as development proceeds. For these reasons, object-oriented development is often described as a "seamless" process. However, this does not mean that there is no distinction between activities at the analysis level that describe the problem and those at the design level that deal with the solution.

This close correspondence between the structure of the analysis and design phases has a number of advantages for development. With the structured method, the data flow diagrams must be complete before beginning the structure chart. With object-oriented development, the architecture of the design phase is an elaboration of the analysis model, so the developer can begin doing design when a portion of the analysis is complete (e.g., a subsystem). Similarly, implementation can begin before the entire design is complete. That is, since the same architecture and locality is present in the model at each phase, the phases can proceed in parallel to some degree.

The uniformity across development phases also facilitates working forward from the problem specification to trace the causes of bugs or to determine which units to modify during maintenance (since the client usually states modifications and enhancements in terms of the problem domain and requirement specification). In addition, a number of situations can cause developers to backtrack to previous phases in the life cycle. For example, analysis of the problem domain may affect the requirement specification, the client's requirements may change after some development has been done, or errors or inconsistencies in the analysis may be detected while producing the system design. Performing maintenance always involves revisiting analysis and design constructs.

Since the same concepts and techniques are used in each stage, the reuse and extendibility that characterize object-oriented programming constructs (which we will discuss in sections 1.3.4 and 1.3.5) apply to analysis results as well as to components developed at the design and implementation levels. For this reason, abstractions designed at all life-cycle phases can contribute to other systems that deal with the same problem domain.

Life-cycle models

The waterfall model of software development assumes that it is possible to state the requirements for the system completely when the project is initiated, so that successive phases can be based on that specification. The results of each phase are the input for the procedures that define the next phase, so each phase must be completed before working on the next. Design is performed in a top-down fashion, so the upper levels of the task hierarchy are fixed early in the process. It is difficult to trace a modification to the problem requirements or a change in the problem domain to the corresponding design and implementation level structures. For these reasons, modifying or extending a system developed using structured methods is burdensome, with the result that the software engineer often views change as a "wrench in the works".

The assumption that the problem specifications can be fixed *a priori* is often reasonable in some engineering domains, but experience with large software systems has shown that the requirements for complex applications continue to evolve as the system is designed, implemented, and used. These changes may result from the activities of clients, their competitors, users of the system, regulators, or management, as well as from changes in the problem domain itself. In many cases, the existence of the system alerts its users to other tasks it can help automate, expanding its requirements. In these circumstances, it would be advantageous to have a model oriented toward accommodating change since it is a fact of life, not simply the result of imprecise specification of system requirements by the client. In addition, the model a designer creates frequently changes as he or she gains more understanding of the situation. The expectation that the designer get it right the first time is a major drawback of the waterfall model.

The uniformity across development phases that characterizes object-oriented development is important because it is rarely possible to proceed from a complete specification to a complete analysis, to a complete design, and so forth. In fact, the development process is usually characterized by interleaved activity at all phases, although much analysis must precede design, and so on. Instead of the waterfall model in which developers complete each phase before beginning the next, a number of different metaphors have been proposed to describe object-oriented development. Henderson-Sellers [Hen90] suggests the "fountain" model in which development begins at the bottom with requirements analysis and proceeds upward through analysis, design, and so on, with the phases represented by overlapping circles. The process may flow back down to a previous phase as necessary, like a fountain spilling over. Boehm [Boe86] proposes the "spiral" life-cycle model in which development spirals out from the center, with a greater radius representing a more developed system and greater cost. The spiral is drawn across four quadrants, which represent identifying objects and constraints, evaluating alternatives, developing a prototype, and reviewing the prototype to plan the next iteration. Development iterates through these basic tasks in increasing detail. Berard [Ber93] suggests the "recursive/parallel process" in which the system is decomposed, and then for each component there is a process of analysis, followed by design, followed by implementation, followed by testing. Each of these sequences of activity proceeds in parallel.

Object-oriented analysis and design methodologies

Recently, several authors have developed methodologies that provide an object-oriented approach for the process of producing very large software systems.[29] These methodologies present techniques and recommendations for recognizing the relevant aspects of the problem domain, and for constructing an object-oriented model based on them. Some encompass the entire development life cycle and include procedures and guidelines for traditional software engineering concerns such as project management, deliverables, metrics, and unit testing.

Many of these methodologies use a graphic notation to capture the structure of the model—its classes, their protocols and attributes, the relationships among objects, and so forth—for the reasons given in section 1.3.1. Typically, the notation uses nodes to denote objects and classes, and various kinds of arcs to represent inheritance, composition, and other relationships among classes and objects. The class nodes will also include some notation for indicating the protocol and attributes of the class. Most methodologies are supported by CASE environments that provide functionality for drawing and verifying analysis diagrams, and for managing the development procedures and their results.

A detailed presentation of the object-oriented methodologies available is beyond the scope of this text. I will list some of the well-known ones here and provide references for further exploration (this list is not necessarily complete or ordered in any way).

- the Booch method [Boo94]
- the Rumbaugh Object Modeling Technique (OMT) [Rum90]
- Coad/Yourdan OOA, OOD, and OOP [Coa91] [Coa92] [Coa93]
- Jacobson's Objectory and the use case driven approach [Jac92]
- the Semantic Object Modeling Approach (SOMA) [Gra94a]
- Wirfs-Brock's Responsibility-Driven Design [Wir90a]
- CRC cards [Bec89]
- Martin/Odell OOAD [Mar95] [Mar96]

---

[29] Interestingly, many are former adherents of the various structured methodologies.

- Methodology for Object-oriented Software Engineering of Systems (MOSES) [Hen94]
- Shlaer/Mellor Object-Oriented Systems Analysis (OOSA) [Shl88] [Shl92]
- Wasserman's Object-Oriented Structured Design (OOSD) [Was90]

Many authors (e.g., [Boo94]) have pointed out that the various object-oriented development methodologies have more similarities than differences, and some convergence among them is likely over time.

1.3.4 Reusability and Class Libraries

Motivation

We would like to assemble software systems from reusable higher-level components, as is done in other engineering disciplines, rather than fabricating each application from scratch, that is, from individual lines of code. This would result in less effort in developing the system, and therefore increased productivity and shorter timespans in both building and maintaining systems. Systems constructed using thoroughly tested components would also be more reliable.

Although developers have been aware of the benefits of reusing software components since the 1960s [McI68], reuse has not been practiced widely for a number of reasons. Structured methods stress designing systems from scratch using the waterfall model, rather than seeking useful components from other projects. The program units that result from a top-down decomposition are influenced by that design and are specific to how they are used in that application, so they are not directly reusable. Due to the tight interconnectedness of software written using the structured design process and programming languages with monomorphic identifiers (see sections 2.4.1 and 2.5.3), it is often difficult to extract a portion of code to use for a similar purpose or a similar project. Using existing components involves bottom-up composition of the system (although not from the bottommost level), rather than the top-down design most developers are taught. In addition, programmers often prefer to create programs themselves due to the challenge involved, mistrust of the reliability of the work of others, or unsuccessful experiences with using another programmer's code. Many organizations measure productivity in terms of lines or functions written, so there is more incentive to code everything directly.

Successful reuse is difficult, and involves expenses that must be amortized over several projects. It requires an investment in creating components in a general fashion, in designing components that are complete and independent of their context, and in performing more stringent testing. More work must be done in the analysis and design phases to reduce the effort necessary in the implementation phase, and in developing other systems. For example, in developing an application that deals with dates, we should define a complete Date class, rather than just implementing the operations that the current application requires. Thus, orienting a software organization toward reuse requires managing for the long term, rather than for the immediate deadlines of the current project. Reuse also involves the overhead of managing the library of abstractions, and the learning curve of developers familiarizing themselves with the library. Facilities such as code databases or browsers are essential so that a developer can locate the appropriate component when needed.

The more specific a class is, the fewer opportunities for reuse it presents; on the other hand, the more general a class is, the fewer capabilities it provides upon reuse. For example, the class MortgageAccount has more behavior than the class Account, but can be used in fewer situations. Reusability is most effective when the class library contains classes defined at many levels of granularity.

As we stated in section 1.1.3, procedural languages have provided libraries of subprograms for reuse, such as Fortran numeric subroutine packages and the C standard library. However, we expect better reuse from classes than modules or subprograms because a class provides a more complete and coherent package that includes both behavior and state information, and is motivated by a distinct, well-defined problem domain category.

Mechanisms for reuse

Like abstract data types, classes allow reuse of code developed for similar systems through instantiation. (In fact, reuse is only possible because there are similarities among the applications we build.) For example, classes that represent transactions and accounts that were developed for one financial system can be used directly in another financial application. As with abstract data types, we can construct a new class by composition, that is, by using existing classes as the types of its components. In this way, the new class reflects the structure of the entities it represents and reuses the specifications of its components' classes. The new class is defined with instance variables that are instances of those classes, and its methods use their operations to implement its protocol. In section 1.1.4, we discussed generic abstract data types that allow reuse of optimally coded collection types. Many statically typed object-oriented languages support parameterized classes (e.g., templates in C++ and generic classes in Eiffel) that provide the same capability.

Inheritance supports further reuse of code because we can define new classes as subclasses of existing classes, which reuses the superclass code and refines it without the possibility of introducing bugs. That is, inheritance provides reuse of existing implementation, namely of the superclass's storage structure and method algorithms. Reuse also occurs as the class hierarchy is developed. The developer can perform design at the highest level possible in the hierarchy, allowing subclasses defined later to reuse those constructs. In effect, we can code classes and methods that solve a category of problems, rather than a particular problem. Note that we can use these inheritance techniques even when the original source code is not available, as long as the interfaces for existing classes are known. In addition, languages that support multiple inheritance permit the designer to combine functionality from existing unrelated classes in deriving a new class.

Dynamic method binding enables us to create classes that are more loosely coupled, which facilitates using them in other contexts. Message polymorphism and inheritance provide reuse of existing interfaces, namely those of superclasses. The designer can add new subclasses that interact with existing portions of the system in predefined ways, that is, according to the superclass interface, without affecting the senders of those messages. Inheritance and dynamic method binding also facilitate reuse of code when different versions of the system must be delivered. For example, the same problem domain class can be used with different view classes in applications for different platforms or different graphic user interfaces.

We have discussed the mechanisms the object model provides for reuse in terms of programming (i.e., the implementation phase). Due to the uniformity across development phases, object-oriented techniques provide opportunities for reuse of elements and interrelationships determined in the analysis and design phases of development as well. For example, an analysis-level class hierarchy developed for one collaborative work application can be used in another.

Class libraries and frameworks

A *class library* is a language-specific class hierarchy that provides a complete, tested, optimized collection of interrelated classes for instantiation, composition, and specialization. Class libraries can provide

- general-purpose classes, such as basic problem domain data types (e.g., strings, times, dates, and currency amounts) and mathematical objects (e.g., complex numbers, points, vectors, and matrices)
- implementation-level classes, such as collections (e.g., sets, lists, and arrays)
- design-level classes, such as file system components and user interface components
- analysis-level classes, such as those for three-dimensional graphics, simulations, manufacturing processes, or financial systems.

General purpose, implementation, and design classes can be used in any application, while analysis classes are specific to applications that deal with that problem domain. A class library differs from a code library in that its components are easily extended for a particular purpose without editing and recompiling the original modules. Many object-oriented languages such as Smalltalk [Gol84], Eiffel [Mey92], Java [Arn96], and Objective-C [Cox86] provide class libraries as part of the language's programming environment. C++ originally did not include a class library, but the new ANSI/ISO C++ Standard defines several classes [ANS97]. Many C++ programming environments include class libraries (e.g., [Cen93], [Spa95], [Bor96] and [Mic96]), and numerous commercial class libraries are available, as well as public domain libraries such as the NIH Class Library [Gor90] and the Free Software Foundation library.

A *framework* is an integrated class library designed for a particular problem domain or graphic user interface [Deu89]. A framework is more than a set of classes. It provides reuse of previous analysis and design effort by defining the skeletal structure of a system, and embodies a theory about the structure of that problem domain or that kind of application. The programmer creates a particular application by instantiating classes and extending classes with application-specific behavior for subclasses. Using a framework allows the designer to concentrate on the behavior and information specific to the application itself. The disadvantage is that there is often a steep learning curve before he or she can use the framework effectively.

The term "framework" is often used to describe two rather different kinds of class libraries. A *domain framework* is a set of classes that are specific to a particular problem domain, and provides reuse of previous analysis results. Frameworks in this category are available or under development for discrete-event simulations, financial systems, manufacturing processes, VLSI design, office automation system, operating systems, and many other problem domains [Wir90b]. Often these frameworks are proprietary, and are maintained in-house by an organization that produces applications for that problem domain.

An *application framework* is a set of classes that provides the foundation for an application for a particular platform or graphic user interface. Experience shows that if this functionality is coded using basic screen graphic primitives, more than half of the code in the application will be involved with managing the user interface. Using a standard framework reduces the amount of coding necessary to create an application, facilitates writing more portable code, and provides consistency of interface for users of that platform. The framework supplies user interface components such as push buttons, checkboxes, sliders, scrollable lists, text editing windows, menus, and dialogs that we can instantiate or subclass in creating the interface for an application. The library classes provide the standard behavior so the programmer does not have to be concerned with the details of displaying the component or its state, or of handling user interactions.

In addition to user interaction components, an application framework supplies abstraction of control. It defines a class for a "generic" application, which implements an event loop that dispatches methods based on user input events (i.e., user messages). The designer creates a particular application as a subclass of this class, containing instances of the component classes and overrides their event handling methods with application-specific processing. For example, the generic application superclass may open a main window with a title, components for moving and resizing the window, scrollbars for scrolling its contents, and a menu bar that provides pull-down menus. This instance responds correctly to mouse clicks and drags within these user interface components. The application subclass simply creates and maintains the contents of its window, and registers the menu items and messages to invoke when the user selects an item.

Many object-oriented language systems include extensive class libraries that include basic classes, collection classes, and a graphic interface framework. The first such framework was the Model-View-Controller user interface paradigm included with Smalltalk-80 [Kra88], which considers every application to be a specialization of a graphic interface front end. The current version is ParcPlace VisualWorks [Vis95], which includes hundreds of classes and thousands of methods. Many other frameworks for specific or general graphic interface design are available, including

- numerous products for MS-Windows for PCs, such as Borland's Object Windows Library [Bor96] and Microsoft's Microsoft Foundation Classes [Mic96]
- MacApp [Wil90], Symantec's THINK class library [Sym90], and PowerPlant [Met96] for Macintosh applications
- the InterViews [Lin89], OI [Ben92], and RogueWave [Rog96] toolkits for C++ and X windows
- NeWS [Gos89] for OpenLook on Sun workstations
- NeXTStep [Tho89] for Objective-C and the NeXT computer

Many of these systems also include browsing software to aid in finding the class needed for a particular use. There are also several commercial products that provide an application framework that can be compiled for different platforms, allowing the developer to write an application with a graphic interface once and make it available on several platforms. The language Java includes a library of platform-independent user interaction components among its standard packages [Gea97].

1.3.5 Extendibility and Prototyping

Motivation

As we stated in section 1.3.2, changing requirements are a fact of life for the software developer. In addition, experience has shown that very large systems have long lifetimes, and that up to 70 percent of the person-hours expended on a system occur after it is initially deployed, as bugs are corrected and new capabilities are added to the system. Part of the reason for this is that software systems are so malleable, compared to physical systems. (No client would consider asking an architect to add a new floor in the middle of a finished building!) In these circumstances, facilities that expedite augmenting the system without modifying any existing components are essential. The extendibility and flexibility in object-oriented systems facilitates all modifications to the system, including handling changing requirements, debugging, reorganizing the user interface, implementing enhancements during maintenance, and providing multiple versions of the application.

A common example of a maintenance enhancement is adding a new kind of entity, perhaps because of changes in the problem domain or the client adding a new service. For example, suppose we must add a new type of account in a financial system that was designed using the structured method and coded in a procedural language. Adding the new type will affect the subprograms that perform interest calculation, billing, reporting, and so on because those subprograms must select what processing to perform on the basis of the account type (whether the actual details are coded there or in separate subprograms). Each subprogram that works with accounts must be modified to test for the new type and then perform the appropriate action. With this style of coding, such a revision often has effects throughout the system, making it difficult to be certain that all the necessary modifications have been made, and made correctly.

In a sense, ease of extension and reuse are mirrors of each other because extending the system or a component reuses existing structure. The ease with which a system can be enhanced depends on how well the original designer planned for extendibility, by coding as generically as possible. For example, to allow dynamic binding of a message among instances of a group of classes, the message must have the same name (and argument signature in a statically typed language) in all of those classes. (We will see that, in a statically typed object-oriented language, those classes must also have a common ancestor in the class hierarchy.)

Mechanisms for extendibility

Abstraction contributes to extendibility because encapsulation localizes revisions and information hiding allows modifying components without affecting other units. The designer can also extend the system by using existing classes to compose new classes. Inheritance supports extending the system by creating new classes as subclasses of existing classes, reusing the superclasses' interfaces and implementations as much as appropriate.

The most important characteristic of object-oriented programming for extendibility is dynamic method binding. This feature allows us to add classes whose instances send and receive messages to and from existing objects, without changing the existing classes or their methods. Since the method executed is selected on the basis of the receiver's class, if an existing method sends a message and the receiver is an instance of a class added later, the new class's method is executed transparently. (In some languages, the existing code must be recompiled, although it need not be modified.) As stated in section 1.1.5, a method that sends a message does not need a case structure that selects which method to call on the basis of the receiver's type, so it is not necessary to update that case structure with the additional class. We will discuss dynamic binding and extendibility further in section 2.4.3.

Prototyping and incremental development

The extendibility and distributed structure of an object-oriented system allows performing the design process by evolving a system through *incremental development*. With this strategy, the designer builds a prototype system that includes the basic behavior necessary, and then add classes, objects, and methods as necessary. The system is initially constructed to satisfy fewer requirements, but is organized in a way that facilitates incorporating new capabilities. In this way, the development process is oriented toward accommodating change rather than resisting it.

For example [Cox86], the prototype of a form management system does not need to reflect all the possible forms that the final product will use. The designer can define the basic protocol for displaying and printing forms, entering information into forms, saving or transferring the information in a form, and so on, and then add a new type of form as a subclass of the superclass Form with its own specific behavior as the need arises. This contrasts with the "build one to throw away" approach to prototypes often used with programming languages that do not provide the dynamic flexibility of object-oriented languages. Of course, we must still perform analysis before building a prototype rather than using the technique as an excuse to begin "hacking".

Rapid prototyping allows the designer to test and evaluate alternative designs so that he or she can analyze design trade-offs and identify performance bottlenecks. The designer can determine if there is incorrect or missing information in the problem specifications at an earlier stage in development. Since he or she may begin implementation without waiting for specifications to be completely finalized, there can be more overlap between the development phases, resulting in faster project delivery.

A working prototype can also involve users of the system in aspects of the design that affect them at an earlier stage of development. It provides them with feedback about their concerns, allows them to make a smoother transition to the new system, and may indicate to the designer that portions of the design or interface are not effective. This is particularly true of graphic user interfaces with windows, pop-up menus, and so on that must be seen in action to be evaluated, as opposed to the static data entry screens that typified earlier systems. The client, managers, and implementors can see tangible results earlier, which improves communication and morale. The project is less likely to be discontinued if it falls behind schedule because there is something to demonstrate.

One disadvantage of the prototyping approach to system development is the issue of scale. Designs and techniques that are appropriate for small systems may not "scale up" to a system that is larger by orders of magnitude. For example, a linked list is acceptable for storing a list of a few dozen items, but searching becomes very time consuming when the number of items is very large.

1.4 SUMMARY AND REVIEW

1.4.1 Abstraction Mechanisms

Software complexity

- Software system complexity results from the characteristics of the problem domain system, from factors external to that system, and from changes in the problem domain or system requirements over time.

- Designing a software system involves determining how much problem domain complexity to represent, and how to reduce the inherent complexity of the system.

- With large systems, the total complexity increases faster than the number of components increases due to interdependencies among the components and communication among the design team.

- Like all humans, software designers use *classification*, *decomposition*, *composition*, and *abstraction* to manage complexity and structure information.

Abstraction in computing

- Early programming languages defined basic programming abstractions such as symbolic names, algebraic expression syntax, control structures, and subprograms.

- Higher-level languages have defined a progression of programming abstractions from abstraction of operation, to abstraction of structure, to abstractions that encapsulate both structure and operation.

- Abstractions provide a higher-level view of system structure, supply units for decomposing the system and organizing the development effort, allow independent design of individual components, and present opportunities for code reuse.

- Programming abstractions extend the language to mirror the problem domain, and therefore simplify programs, improve readability, and reduce errors.

- We can recognize abstractions either by *top-down* decomposition of the structure of the system, or by *bottom-up* recognition of multiple occurrences of processing or structure.

- A programming abstraction is an *encapsulation* that groups processing and/or structural units, and provides *information hiding* by separating its public *interface* from its *implementation*, which is not visible to *clients*.

- A subprogram is an abstraction whose interface consists of its name and argument signature, a description of the subprogram's operation, restrictions on argument values, and the errors it can signal. Its implementation is its algorithm and local variables. Subprograms support the design methodology of top-down functional decomposition.

Modules

- A *module* is a source code unit that can be compiled individually, even though it refers to program entities defined in other modules.

- The *linker* combines an application's object files into an executable program, and resolves references among identifiers that are used in one module but defined in another.

- The interface of a module is a set of forward declarations for the subprograms, objects, constants, and types *exported* by the module.

- The implementation of a module gives the definitions of the program entities whose names its exports, and possibly definitions of other auxiliary entities that are local to the module.

- An *import* declaration makes the interface of the named module visible in the module in which it appears. Implementations cannot be imported.

- A module defines a scope for the identifiers declared in the module. Module scope objects are statically allocated, but their names are hidden within the scope of the module (unless they are exported).

- Modules provide a level of structure between the level of the individual sub-program and that of the entire application, and allow the designer to group related subprograms and the data they manipulate as a unit.

- "Parnas's rule" states that the designer of a module should provide clients with exactly the information necessary to use the module, and should provide the implementor with exactly the information needed to code that module.

- *Coupling* describes the degree of interdependence between the modules in a system, and *cohesion* describes the degree of binding among the elements in a module. A good design minimizes the coupling among modules and maximizes the cohesion within each module, so that we can write and debug modules independently, and reuse them in similar applications.

- Modula-2 and Ada support module interfaces and implementations, import declarations, import/export scope rules for external names, and name qualification to resolve name conflicts among imported interfaces. A Modula-2 module is divided into a *definition module* giving its interface and an *implementation module*. In Ada, a module interface is called a *package specification*, and a module implementation is called a *package body*.

- Modula-2 and Ada support separate compilation of a module's interface and implementation. The language system maintains a module database to translate import declarations and manage compilation dependencies.

- C supports separate compilation, but not import/export scope. Each source code file defines a level of scope enclosing function scopes, which is nested within the global scope of the entire program, in which all exported names are declared. Names that are private to a module are declared static, and forward declarations are indicated by extern.

- We code a C module as a *header file* containing its interface, and a *code file* giving its implementation. A client includes the text of a header file with a pre-processor directive. The C compiler has no knowledge of module names, import relationships, or compilation dependencies, and cannot support name qualification.

Abstract data types

- An *abstract data type* encapsulates the operations and storage structure of a type, and allows the designer to control access to those components. Languages that provide first-class support for abstract data types allow defining a complete set of operations for a type.

- The interface of an abstract data type consists of subprogram declarations for its public operations. The type must provide initialization operations so that all objects have valid states, and no operations should be performed on uninitialized objects.

- To provide *representation independence*, the designer of the type hides its storage structure. This decouples the interface and the implementation of the type, and allows the designer to change the type's structure without affecting clients.

- The implementation of an abstract data type consists of declarations that describe its storage structure and subprograms that define the type's operations. It may also define private subprograms, constants, objects, and types that aid in coding the type.

- With *object-based decomposition*, we structure a system in terms of categories of problem domain entities or system components and their behavior, rather than according to the tasks it performs, and represent each as an abstract data type. Parnas's rule and the principles of cohesion and coupling are also important in designing abstract data types.

- We can use modules to encapsulate the operations and structure of an abstract data type, but C and Modula-2 modules cannot achieve both information hiding and multiple instantiation of the type.

- Ada packages support abstract data types because a package specification can contain a private section not visible to clients. This information is available to the compiler, and usually gives storage structure details necessary to translate instantiation of the type. Object-oriented languages also support abstract data types.

- Some abstract data types, e.g. for variable-sized collections, allocate dynamic subobjects and require initialization and release operations to hide that implementation from clients.

- The interface, storage structure, and subprogram definitions for a particular kind of collection are the same, irrespective of the element type. A *generic* abstract data type defines the interface and implementation of a collection type together with a *type parameter* for the element type. The compiler generates a collection type with an actual element type, e.g. a set of dates, when necessary. Ada generic packages and C++ template classes support generic abstract data types.

Classes

- A *class* is an abstract data type with three additional features: class information and operations, inheritance among classes, and dynamic binding of class operations.

- An *object* is an encapsulation of state and behavior that represents a problem domain entity or system component.

- Every object is an *instance* of a class that defines its operations and state information.

- A *message* is an operation that the instances of a class can perform.

- The *protocol* of a class lists the messages that make up its interface.

- The *instance variables* of a class describe the storage structure of its instances.

- A *method* is the code that implements a message.

- An identifier, subprogram or object is *polymorphic* if it can have more than one type, e.g. an identifier in a dynamically typed language or an overloaded subprogram.

- A *pure* object-oriented language supports object-oriented features and enforces the object-oriented paradigm. A *hybrid* object-oriented language extends an existing procedural or functional language with the object-oriented features, and permits both object-oriented and procedural programming.

- The fundamental operation in object-oriented programming is *sending a message* to another object, the *receiver*. The receiver responds by executing the method defined by its class or inherited from an ancestor.

- Message passing provides loose coupling because different objects may use different methods for a message, the sender may not know the receiver's exact class, and an object can only access another object's data by sending it a message.

- *Class variables* maintain information associated with the class as a whole, but not stored in each instance. This encapsulates that information within the class, rather than using global variables.

- *Class messages* provide client access to class variables (including type information) or other class-specific operations, and are implemented by *class methods*.

- *Inheritance* is the relationship between a *subclass* representing a problem domain category that is a specialization of the general category its *superclass* represents.

- A subclass *inherits* the protocol, instance variables, and methods of its superclass. The subclass may also introduce additional messages and instance variables, and *override* superclass methods with subclass-specific behavior.

- Inheritance defines a *class hierarchy* that represents the type structure of the problem domain, system resources, or application.

- Inheritance facilitates reuse of existing code and extendibility of the system, such as when a new subclass is defined.

- When an object receives a message, the *method binding* process searches for the method to execute beginning in its class's protocol, and continues up the class hierarchy if necessary.

- Since the compiler may not know type of the receiver of a message, object-oriented languages must employ *dynamic method binding*, in which the method to invoke is selected at execution time.

1.4.2 Programming Paradigms

Definition and purpose

- A *programming paradigm* is a model that describes the nature of computation and the programming language constructs necessary to describe a computation.

- Programming languages that realize the same paradigm have similar semantics. It is easier to learn a new language in a familiar paradigm than to learn a new programming paradigm.
- In addition to extending existing programming abstractions, object-oriented programming provides a different paradigm for describing the nature of computation and for organizing software.

The imperative programming paradigm

- With the *imperative programming paradigm*, a computation consists of a storage unit and a program, which is a sequence of operations that retrieve, compute, and store values in individual storage locations. The basic operation is the assignment, which replaces the contents of a storage cell.
- The imperative paradigm views a computation as a finite state machine in which a state of the computation is the set of stored values and a transition between states is an assignment.
- An imperative programming language supports variable declarations, assignments, control structures for specifying the order of operations, and subprograms for grouping operations. The imperative paradigm is the foundation for traditional programming languages such as Fortran, Pascal, and C.
- The imperative paradigm makes a clear distinction between the program that specifies the actions to perform and the data objects affected by those actions.

The functional programming paradigm

- The *functional programming paradigm* views a computation as the application of a function to a list of arguments, rather than as manipulation of stored values. This model is based on lambda calculus, a mathematical formalism that treats functions and values uniformly.
- Functional languages differ from imperative languages in that there are no stored values or control structure statements, and functions and variable-length lists are first-class objects. The nesting of an expression constrains the order in which its functions are called, but does not specify that order completely.
- Functional languages support function parameters and return types, function-valued variables, and creation of anonymous functions.
- A function object is represented by a *closure* consisting of a pointer to the function code and a static link through which nonlocal identifiers in the function code are accessed.
- If a function object is returned by a function or assigned to a nonlocal function variable, that function's code can be invoked in a different context than the one in which it is defined. In a functional language with static scope, the activation record for a function must be retained after the function exits if the static link in some function object refers to it. In this case, a stack is inadequate for maintaining activation records.

- The primary motivation for functional languages is that they facilitate formal reasoning about the operation of programs. Proofs are simpler than those for an imperative language because there are no destructive assignments that change the meaning of a name.

The logic programming paradigm

- The *logic programming paradigm* is based on the first-order predicate calculus. A program states facts and inference rules for deriving further facts that represent what is true in the problem domain, and the problem is framed as a theorem to prove.

- *Declarative programming* allows us to adopt a goal-oriented perspective in which we specify the logical properties of the solution, rather than an action-oriented approach in which we list the operations required to produce the solution.

- The primary logic programming language is Prolog, an interpreted system in which the programmer asserts facts and inference rules, and presents queries for evaluation.

- The Prolog language system implements a backtracking mechanism that derives the proof, given the facts and rules supplied by the programmer. Prolog is not completely declarative because the clauses in its database are searched in order, and it supports a mechanism for pruning the database search.

- Expert systems that attempt to model human reasoning about a problem domain also employ an elaboration of the logic paradigm.

The object-oriented programming paradigm

- The *object-oriented programming paradigm* is based on the concept that an application is a model of a problem domain system, that is, that computation is simulation. The programmer is concerned with creating abstractions that model categories of entities in the problem domain, rather than with specifying the processing the application must perform.

- Since classes include both behavior and state, they are more cohesive units that can be reused for other applications in the same problem domain.

- The model of the problem domain system is structured as an interaction among independent objects, each sending the other messages. The behavior and properties of these objects are represented by a set of encapsulated classes, which are related by inheritance when appropriate.

- The similarity of structure between the application and the problem domain allows the designer to comprehend the application in the same manner as the problem domain system.

1.4.3 Object-Oriented Development

Structured methods

- The *software life cycle* consists of five phases: problem *requirements specification*, *analysis* of the requirements and the problem domain, *design* of the system, *implementation* (coding, testing, and debugging), and *maintenance* after the system is delivered.

- *Structured methods* provide a procedural methodology for creating large-scale software systems, which encompasses every phase of the development process, with clearly define deliverables at each phase. They also define graphic notations to represent structures at each phase and procedures to derive them, and are supported by CASE systems.

- Structured methods focus on the structure of the processing performed by the application, but do not provide support for modeling complex data or encapsulated operations.

Applying the object model

- Like structured programming techniques, which eventually influenced the analysis and design phases of development, the object model is having a major impact on all phases of the software development life cycle.

- Current systems are typically interactive applications that deal with more complex objects such as those found in publishing or engineering design systems, and the processing performed is naturally associated with individual categories of objects. The specifications for the system frequently change as it is developed, and the system has a long lifetime that includes significant maintenance. The encapsulation, flexibility, uniformity, and extendibility of the object model assist considerably in handling these characteristics.

- An object-oriented decomposition is based on the classes that represent categories of entities in the problem domain and the relationships among them, rather than on the tasks the system performs. Some object-oriented methodologies divide the classes in the system into loosely coupled "subsystems" to aid in understanding the architecture of the system.

- At each life-cycle phase, we determine the classes and objects of interest, and assign each behavior or piece of information to the class that is most naturally responsible for it. We recognize attributes and relationships for instances of the classes, and use inheritance to represent specialization and commonalities among classes.

- We discover the activities and information to represent in the model from the problem specification, the characteristics of the problem domain, analysis of scenarios of behavior of the problem domain and the system, discussions with domain experts and users, and analysis of similar systems.

- The elements of an object model are motivated by entities, activities, and relationships in the problem domain, which improves communication between the designer and domain experts, clients, managers, and users.

The object-oriented development process

- The rigidity of structured methods is a hindrance when problem specifications are incomplete or change, or when analysis errors or inconsistencies are detected during design. This problem is compounded by the use of different structuring techniques at each phase.

- In object-oriented software engineering, the designer uses the same constructs in all phases of the development process. This uniformity across development phases facilitates interleaving activity at all phases, tracing requirements to the structures that represent them at each phase, tracing design and analysis constructs to the corresponding requirements, localizing modifications to the system during debugging and maintenance, and reusing and extending of analysis and design constructs.

- A number of life-cycle models and methodologies have been proposed for object-oriented development. Each methodology structures the overall process of analysis, design, and implementation, provides guidelines and procedures for recognizing classes, their components, and their interrelationships, and defines graphic notations for representing those results. Many are supported by CASE systems.

Reusability and class libraries

- The benefits of reusing existing software components are increased productivity, shorter development times, and more reliable systems.

- Reuse of existing components occurs infrequently because the structured method emphasizes creating new systems using top-down decomposition, and components created are tied to that structure. Programmers often prefer to write the code themselves, and productivity is often measured in terms of the amount of code produced. Reusable components require more general coding and more complete testing.

- It is easier to reuse classes than subprograms and modules because a class packages both state information and behavior, and is motivated by a problem domain category.

- The object model provides mechanisms that support reuse of both implementation and interface. These include instantiation of classes, composing new classes from existing classes, deriving new subclasses from existing classes, and dynamic method binding, which allows instances of new classes to interact transparently with existing system components.

- Since we use the same structuring techniques at the analysis and design levels, object-oriented development also facilitates reuse of constructs defined at those phases.

- A *class library* is a language-specific collection of implementation, design, or analysis level classes that developers can reuse and extend in creating applications. Many languages such as Smalltalk, Eiffel, Java, and Objective-C provide standard class libraries that include classes for basic problem domain types, collections, system facilities, and user interface components.

- A *framework* is an integrated class library designed for a particular problem domain, or for applications that employ a particular graphic user interface and platform.

- A *domain framework* captures the classification structure of that domain, and allows reuse of the results of that analysis effort.

- An *application framework* provides a skeletal structure for applications that use a particular graphic interface system, and classes for interface components such as buttons, scrollable lists, text entry areas, menus, and dialogs. An application is defined as a subclass of a generic application class, and its interface is composed from instances of the component classes.

Extendibility and prototyping

- The specifications for a large system usually continue to evolve as the system is designed, coded, and deployed. A flexible approach that facilitates incorporating additional capabilities in the system would ease development.

- Abstraction facilitates extendibility because encapsulation localizes revisions and information hiding allows modifying components independently. Composition of new classes from existing classes also contributes to extendibility.

- Inheritance and dynamic method binding permit extending an object-oriented system without modifying existing code. The existing methods in the system continue to send the same messages, and instances of the new classes respond using their own methods transparently.

- Dynamic binding enables the designer to perform enough analysis to understand the problem domain, and then design and implement a prototype system that can be extended incrementally until it fulfills the requirements for the system. This prototype also provides an early deliverable for managers and clients, and allows users to give the designer feedback on the functionality and interface of the system.

1.5 EXERCISES

1.1 Define information hiding and encapsulation, and describe why they are useful. Does one imply the other (consider both directions)?

1.2 Describe the responsibilities of the linker for languages that support separately compiled modules.

1.3 **(a)** Define coupling and cohesion, and discuss their importance in system design.
(b) How do coupling and cohesion relate to information hiding and encapsulation?

1.4 Suppose that a module contains a group of initialization functions that must be executed when the application starts. Evaluate this module with respect to coupling and cohesion.

1.5 Suppose that a module contains a group of statistical functions. Give an advantage and a disadvantage of this design.

1.6 Suppose that the function aux is used by the functions func1 and func2 but no others, and that func1 and func2 are called by other functions.
   (a) Using modules, how can we ensure that the name aux is visible only in func1 and func2 (and not to callers of func1 and func2)?
   (b) Can we make the name aux visible only in func1 and func2 (and not in their callers) with block-structured scope? Why or why not?

1.7 **(a)** If we could divide the implementation of a module into several files, different programmers could work on different subprograms in the module independently, and the size of the executable for an application that doesn't use all a module's subprograms would be reduced. What effect would this have on compiling and linking?
   (b) Suppose a logical module interface could be divided among several physical code files. What effect would this have on compiling and linking?

1.8 How does support for separate compilation in Modula-2 and in C differ?

1.9 **(a)** How is a name specified as being private to a module in C?
   (b) How is a name specified as being private to a module in Modula-2?

1.10 **(a)** In Ada and Modula-2, the same name can be imported from two different modules. What language feature makes this possible?
   (b) Why can't this be done in C?

1.11 **(a)** Why can't two modules in a C application export the same name, even if their header files are not included in the same code file?
   (b) How is this error reported?
   (c) Why is possible for two module interfaces in the same application to declare the same name in Modula-2 or Ada?

1.12 **(a)** Name and describe the two errors that can be signaled by the linker when building a C program.
   (b) Can these linker errors occur in Modula-2 or Ada?

1.13 **(a)** What is a compilation dependency?
   (b) Why can't the compiler handle compilation dependencies?
   (c) Can a language system handle compilation dependencies? How?

1.14 Describe the components of the definition of an abstract data type and give the purpose of each. Illustrate your discussion with an example abstract data type.

1.15 What is representation independence and why is it important?

1.16 **(a)** What capabilities do modules provide for system structure that are not available with subprograms alone?
   (b) What additional capability is provided by abstract data types that is not available with modules?

1.17 Name two characteristics that modules and abstract data types have in common. Name two ways in which they differ.

1.18 **(a)** Explain why a C module cannot be used to provide both information hiding and instantiation of an abstract data type.
   (b) What feature is necessary to support abstract data types, and why is it needed? How is this feature defined in Ada and in C++?

1.19 Recode the three C character stack module examples from section 1.1.4 in Modula-2.

1.20 Code the package body for the Ada Char_Stack_Package package in section 1.1.4.

1.21 In section 1.1.4, we coded a character stack in C++ with a dynamic subobject.
  (a) Give three other examples of abstract data types whose instances are variable size.
  (b) How does this storage structure affect object initialization, finalization, and assignment?

1.22 **(a)** What is the purpose for generic abstract data types?
  (b) Give five examples of abstract data types that should be defined as generic types.
  (c) Why is a generic type different from all other language constructs?

1.23 Write an Ada generic package specification and body for an unlimited-size stack with a dynamic subobject, as illustrated by the C++ example in section 1.1.4.

1.24 Suppose we define a List generic type, and write an application that uses lists of five different kinds of elements. A simple implementation is for the compiler to generate five complete list classes and their operations. Can you think of a way to avoid this duplication?

1.25 Describe the interface and implementation of each of the following abstractions:
  (a) subprograms
  (b) procedural modules
  (c) abstract data types
  (d) classes

1.26 Define the following terms, and give an example of each:
  (a) object
  (b) class
  (c) protocol
  (d) message
  (e) instance variable
  (f) method
  (g) polymorphic
  (h) receiver
  (i) class variable
  (j) class message
  (k) subclass
  (l) superclass
  (m) method overriding
  (n) class hierarchy
  (o) dynamic method binding

1.27 As a programming abstraction, classes have three features that abstract data types do not have. List them and describe the purpose and semantics of each.

1.28 Which of the following pieces of information should be represented as instance variables, and which should be represented as class variables? (Give the class that maintains the information as well.)
  (a) the number of bicycles in stock
  (b) the average outstanding balance of all current customer accounts
  (c) the number of departments in an organization
  (d) the default disk space allocation for users of a multi-user operating system

1.29 Suppose we want each instance of a class to have a unique numeric id. Explain how a class variable can be used to achieve this.

1.30 Describe the perspective on the nature of computation embodied in each of the following programming paradigms. For each, give an example of an application which is suited to that approach.
   (a) the imperative paradigm
   (b) the functional paradigm
   (c) the logic paradigm
   (d) the object-oriented paradigm

1.31 **(a)** List and describe the language features that distinguish functional programming languages.
   (b) Why do we say that functions are first-class in functional programming languages?

1.32 **(a)** Many contemporary architectures have more than one processor. What properties of functional languages allow them to make better use of this parallelism than imperative languages?
   (b) How can logic programming language make use of multiple processors?

1.33 **(a)** What is a closure?
   (b) Why isn't a closure necessary to represent the value of a C pointer to function?

1.34 Why does support for function objects in a block-structured language cause a fundamental change in the execution-time structures necessary to implement a program? Describe the changes necessary.

1.35 Why does Pascal support subprogram parameters but not subprogram return values?

1.36 Lisp uses dynamic scope to resolve occurrences of nonlocal variables. Why does this allow the language to use a stack-based implementation for activation records, even though functions can return functions and a function can be the referent of a variable?

1.37 Construct an example set of Prolog facts and rules that shows that the ordering of the clauses in a Prolog database can have a significant effect on the execution time of a query.

1.38 Suppose we need to write software to control a traffic light system at an intersection. One street is a two-lane street with a standard three-color light, and the other is a four-lane road whose signal also has a turn arrow. The system controls the lights based on information from both a timer and interrupt-driven sensors that may override it.
   (a) How would the structure of this application be viewed in the imperative paradigm? How would it be viewed in the object-oriented paradigm?
   (b) How would the system described be analyzed and designed using structured methods? How would it be developed and how would it be structured using object-oriented techniques?

1.39 **(a)** Distinguish between analysis and design in software development.
   (b) Distinguish between design and implementation in software development.

1.40 What are the advantages and disadvantages of using a graphic notation for describing a system's structure?

1.41 Examine some software engineering texts that describe structured methods (e.g., [Som96] and [Pre92]), and determine why data flow diagrams are used in analysis but structure charts are used in design.

1.42 Discuss the reasons why we expect object-oriented development to give good results with contemporary applications.

1.43 List the classes that you would expect to find in the model of each of the following systems:
   (a) a program for managing voice mail
   (b) a program for transferring files from one computer to another over a network
   (c) a program for creating and editing music scores

(d) a program for controlling a video cassette recorder

(e) a program for troubleshooting automobile problems

(f) a program that allows several users to play Monopoly

1.44 Discuss how the uniformity of object-oriented development affects the development process.

1.45 Discuss the following statement: "The programmer has to throw out all his or her familiar devices and habits in switching from the imperative to the object-oriented paradigm." Consider both the analysis and implementation phases.

1.46 Is object-oriented analysis and design useful without an object-oriented language for implementation?

1.47 Obtain descriptions of the graphic notations used by some of the object-oriented methodologies listed in section 1.3.3.

(a) Compare their graphic notations to determine what entities are represented by nodes and which by arcs. What information is represented in class nodes besides the class name? How many different kinds of arcs that connect class nodes does each notation use, and are there adornments on arcs for various purposes? For each notation, do you think all the distinctions it makes among the kinds of arcs are worth including in the graphic representation of the model? Are there any important distinctions missing?

(b) Does the methodology include procedures for determining the elements of the model? Do they seem complete?

(c) Does the model describe a model of the software life cycle? Does it include procedures for managing the entire process of development?

1.48 (a) Describe the factors that inhibit code reuse.

(b) Why do object-oriented languages provide more code reuse than imperative languages?

1.49 A common measure of programmer productivity is lines of code or subprograms written per time. Is this appropriate in an object-oriented environment? Can you suggest a better measure?

1.50 Obtain descriptions of several general-purpose class libraries for C++. (There are numerous publicly available libraries accessible via the Internet. Programming magazines contain many advertisements for commercial products, and you can obtain brochures or "white papers" from the vendor.) What classes do they have in common, and which classes are contained in one but not another? Are the inheritance hierarchies similar?

1.51 How is extendibility facilitated by inheritance? How is it facilitated by polymorphism and dynamic binding?

1.52 List three ways that object-oriented design facilitates maintenance of existing systems.

2

Classes, Messages, and Methods

In this chapter and the next, we will examine the elements of the object model and the programming language features that support it in language-independent terms. We will also code a few classes and methods in an object-oriented pseudocode, and briefly describe how these features are expressed in various object-oriented languages. (We will use Smalltalk and C++ to discuss them in detail in Parts II and III of the text.) This chapter presents the semantics of classes, the definition and use of classes in programming, identifier and message polymorphism, messages and methods, and method binding. Chapter 3 discusses inheritance.

This chapter covers the following topics:

- use of classes and objects to model problem domain and programming system abstractions (2.1.1 and 2.1.2)
- issues in designing classes and their components (2.1.3)
- definition of the interface and implementation of a programming language class (2.2.1 and 2.2.2)
- class, object, and message use in programming (2.2.3)
- example class definitions in an object-oriented pseudocode (2.2.4)
- the definition of polymorphism and identifier polymorphism (2.3.1 and 2.3.2)
- message polymorphism (2.3)
- the characteristics of message sending (2.4.1)

- static and dynamic method binding (2.4.2)
- how dynamic binding enables the extendibility and reusability characteristic of object-oriented systems (2.4.3)

2.1 CLASS SEMANTICS

2.1.1 Problem Domain Classes

The principle use of classes is to model categories of entities in the problem domain. Such classes represent abstractions useful in understanding that real-world system, structural units that carry through the entire development process. (Additional classes representing system components are introduced at the design stage.) Each class models the behavior of the corresponding kind of entity, and maintains the relevant properties, attributes, and relationships that describe it. As stated in section 1.3.2, the designer determines the classes necessary for the system by examining the requirements specification and the problem domain, by analyzing scenarios of behavior of the real-world system, and through discussions with domain experts and users. Recall from section 1.3.4 that an existing domain-specific framework can reduce this analysis effort.

We use classes to represent both concrete and conceptual problem domain categories. Example problem domain classes include

- physical objects or devices—for example, vehicles, roads, traffic lights, and sensors in a traffic control system
- abstract entities—for example, accounts, bonds, funds, etc. in a financial system
- events and interactions—for example, flights and transactions in an airline reservation system
- organizational units—for example, departments in a project management system, or wards in a hospital system
- roles played by people or other agents—for example, tellers in a banking system, or administrators and users of a computer network
- locations—for example, the bin number of an inventory item, or the position of materials in a manufacturing process
- other systems with which the system interacts—for example, the user of an ATM system

A simple example of a domain class is a database record, such as the information stored about an employee or an inventory item. The protocol for such classes provides *accessor* messages for the individual fields (e.g., to ask for an employee's name or office number). For some fields, the class may provide messages to change the value or referent (sometimes called "modifier" messages), for example, to assign an employee to a different department. The class also often defines messages that provide information computed from its instance variables. An example for an employee class is a request for an employee's age. The method that performs this computation from the stored date of birth and the current date is part of the employee object's responsibility, and is specified in the employee class. The computation is not the responsibility of the object or method that needs that information (nor is it a global subprogram).

Examples of classes with more complex operations and structure are the various types of objects in a three-dimensional graphics display system (e.g., for CAD or visualization applications). For example, objects are often represented as a "wire frame" consisting of a set of triangles in three dimensions. The application will also need classes that provide views of these objects, since displaying instances will not simply be a matter of listing the strings or numbers stored in their fields. Instances of both the model and view classes must perform computations for operations such as moving, rotating, resizing, and reshaping the object. The model instances often maintain intricate relationships with the other objects in the subsystem which they compose (e.g., among the components of an automobile design).

In addition to classes that maintain state information, we often need classes whose instances generate or accept messages to other objects, possibly including data for processing. These classes correspond to the various types of sensors and actuators in the physical system being modeled, and there often is an inheritance hierarchy of such classes. Example application domains in which these classes are common include manufacturing process control, environment control, mobile robots, and aircraft systems.

For many classes, it is useful to think of the class as defining a finite state machine. (In fact, many object-oriented software methodologies use state machines to model problem domain classes.) For example, an ATM machine is initially in the state "waiting for card", and upon receiving a card, it enters the state "waiting for PIN number". Each number entered changes the state to "n numbers accepted", and after the fourth number, it enters the state "verifying PIN number". Depending on the result from the database, it enters either "displaying invalid PIN number message" or "displaying main menu", and so on. The current state is maintained in an instance variable, and the class's messages define accessors or transitions between states.

2.1.2 Design and Implementation Classes

Domain-independent classes

Every application also requires classes that have to do with the design of the system, and with its implementation on the platform and operating system used. These classes are typically independent of the problem domain and its analysis, and include

- *foundation classes*, which are general-purpose classes such as numbers, characters, times, dates, and strings
- collection classes, such as sets, lists, and arrays

- classes for system services, such as file system components, input/output devices, and processes
- classes for windows and user interaction components
- graphics classes, such as points, rectangles, colors, shapes, and images

These classes are more general than problem domain classes in the sense that we can use them in all types of applications. As stated in section 1.3.4, many object-oriented programming environments and commercial class libraries provide a large hierarchy of such classes that the programmer can use in creating applications.

We sometimes need auxiliary classes that assist in the implementation of other classes. Examples include storage structure component classes such as a node class used in defining classes implemented by linked data structures, a buffer class used to implement file access, and a menu item class used in creating a class for pop-up menus. In some languages, such as C++, the designer can encapsulate these classes within the class that uses them.

Collection classes

Every application needs to maintain groups of objects, for example, the employees in a department or the elements of a drawing. We refer to classes that represent groups of objects as *collection classes*. These are classes such as arrays, lists, sorted lists, sets, stacks, queues, and indexed search tables. The various collection classes each have different characteristics. For example, arrays are fixed-length while sets and lists are not, sets are unordered and cannot contain duplicates, elements are inserted into and deleted from queues in first-in first-out order, and so on. Every class library includes such classes, and they are implemented using classic data structures such as linked lists and hash tables.

An important consideration for collection classes is the type (i.e., class) of the collection's elements. A dynamically typed language needs only one List class because any object can be bound to the "element" identifier. This characteristic also permits heterogeneous collections containing instances of various types. However, if a collection's elements must be restricted to a certain class or classes, the programmer is responsible for checking the type of the objects in the collection. As we saw in section 1.1.4, all the elements of a collection in a statically typed language must be of the same type, and we cannot use the same List class for a list of integers and a list of points, even though the implementation is exactly the same except for the type of the element.[1] For more extensive code reuse, a statically typed language needs a mechanism for generating classes such as StringList and PointList from a "generic" List class, like the Ada generic package construct. For this purpose, Eif-

---

[1] We will see in section 13.2.2 that we can define collections that can contain any object in a statically typed object-oriented language if there is a root class, say Object, that is an ancestor of all classes. For example, we can define a class for lists of instances of Object and use that class whenever lists are needed. However, the compiler only knows that the elements are instances of Object so an element of the collection must be cast to the expected type before using it.

fel supports generic classes, Modula-3 supports generic interfaces and modules, and C++ supports the template facility. We will cover the latter in sections 13.1 and 13.2.

In some cases, the implementation of a collection requires that the protocol of the class of the elements includes certain capabilities. For example, a collection class such as List that finds elements requires that the element class provide an equality operator or message (which is not necessary for elements of a Stack or Queue class). Similarly, a Set class implemented as a binary search tree requires that the element class implement an order comparison operator or message. The class designer must state these requirements as part of the documentation of the collection class.

Human interaction classes

In addition to a model of the problem domain, an interactive application needs mechanisms for communicating with the user, that is, for commands to the application and for presentation of information by the application. The input and display characteristics of an object are independent of its role in the model and their coding usually depends on the hardware, operating system, and graphic interface. Therefore, we factor out display behavior from the model class. Separating the problem domain protocol from the display behavior allows reusing the problem domain class for different platforms, and facilitates providing several views of an object to users. For example, many business and scientific systems support displaying different types of graph and charts for a given set of data, and VLSI design systems often present several logical and physical views of the design.

Most graphic user interface designs reflect the *Model-View-Controller* paradigm originally developed in the Smalltalk system class library. The application includes three kinds of classes.

- *model* classes that represent the problem domain
- *view* classes that display instances of the associated model class to the user
- *controller* classes that encapsulate user input from a mouse, keyboard, etc.

Model classes are analysis-level classes, and view and controller classes are design level. If a view object presents a representation that the user can manipulate, a controller is associated with the view so that it can receive user messages that affect the model. The corresponding instances of model and view classes contain references to each other in instance variables. In this way, when the user manipulates a controller object, the associated view object sends an update message to its model object specifying that manipulation in the model's terms. After updating itself, the model notifies all associated views of the change. For example, in a card game application, a model class maintains the state of a card—that is, its suit, rank, location (in a hand, a deck, etc.), and whether it is face-up or face-down. A view class has the responsibility of drawing the card, maintaining its screen location, and interacting with the controller for that view, which allows the user to select, move, or flip the card.

Separating the model and view behavior also permits us to use a particular view class with different model classes in different applications. For example, we can use a scrolling list, slider, or text entry view in the interface of many applications. As stated in section 1.3.4, there are application frameworks available that encapsulate the functionality for the windows, menus, dialogs, and other interface components for many languages, platforms, and interfaces. The designer creates the interface of the application by instantiating these view classes and associating them with model objects and messages, and can specialize the provided classes via inheritance to customize them. He or she also must define views for the display behavior of the objects in the application. We will discuss an overview of the Smalltalk application framework classes in section 6.1.1.

Many interactive applications also need a model of the user's activity or intentions. For example, a good interface design disables operations that are currently meaningless (e.g., the user cannot copy or cut an object until selecting an object), or may facilitate selecting the operation that the user is most likely to perform next, given a sequence of user activities. An example of an application that includes an analysis-level model of the user is a decision support system that gives advise on scenarios that the user may wish to examine.

2.1.3 Determining Class Components

Coupling and cohesion

The principles of increasing the cohesion within a class and reducing the coupling between classes are important in the design of both problem domain and design classes. The *Law of Demeter* [Lie89] is a rule of thumb that reduces the coupling between objects by limiting the number and kinds of connections among them. The rule states that a method can only depend on the structure of the class it is assigned to; it prohibits directly accessing instance variable values in an instance of another class. Further, the rule states that each method should send messages to instances of a small set of classes, to decrease the degree of interclass coupling in the system. As with modules, reduced coupling allows us to develop, code, understand, debug, test, and maintain each class independently. It also results in classes that are easier to reuse and extend because they are less dependent on their context.

Cohesion and locality are increased when each class has a specific logical purpose and contains only behavior and information directly related to that purpose. This is a natural result for a class that represents a well-defined category of entities in the problem domain. Evaluating a class's cohesion is more difficult than measuring the degree of coupling among classes because we can estimate the latter by counting interactions. An understanding of the problem domain is necessary to assess the cohesion of model classes, and experience with systems is necessary for judging design classes.

Protocol

The protocol of a class describes its instance's behavior, and represents a contract between the designer of the class and his or her clients who create and send messages to instances. Each message in the class's protocol describes a service that instances of that class are responsible for providing. The corresponding method may query or change the state of the receiver, calculate a result from its state information (and information obtained from the message arguments), send messages that affect the states of related objects, or monitor an external device or system. The protocol of a class also includes class messages that provide access to class-wide information. Each message in a class's protocol should have high cohesion in the sense that it performs a single logical activity. As with subprograms, the argument list of each message should be kept as short as possible to reduce coupling between a client and the receiver of the request, and to facilitate understanding of the purpose of the message.

The protocols of classes are developed through a process of iterative refinement. The behavior of the entities that the class represents will suggest messages to include. As we analyze scenarios of system activity, we may discover the need for additional services that must be assigned to classes. The primary criterion for deciding if a class should be responsible for an operation is whether the operation is conceptually relevant to the meaning of the class. Some additional concerns are whether the class maintains the information necessary to perform the operation, whether the message might be more appropriate in a subclass or superclass, and whether including the operation provides opportunities for reuse. In determining the granularity of the services a class provides, the designer must strike a balance between too much division of services into individual messages, which produces fragmentation of behavior, and too little, which results in unfocused messages with numerous options and arguments and large methods. In addition, a finer granularity often makes defining subclasses easier because the subclass's refinements can be more localized.

Protocol size

An issue that often arises in designing a class is how comprehensive its protocol should be. A minimal but sufficient interface allows clients to understand the purpose of the class and begin using it more quickly. It also facilitates verifying the correctness of the class's implementation and of uses of its instances. On the other hand, it is less convenient to use because clients often must write code to obtain information derived from the functionality provided. In many cases, this code would be more efficient if it were encapsulated as a method within the class so that it could make use of the details of the class's storage structure. Whether a class has a minimal or complete protocol, cohesion with the rest of the interface is an important issue in deciding whether to include a message.

To illustrate this design decision, consider a List class that represents an ordered, arbitrary size list of elements. An extremely minimal protocol might be the messages size (the number of elements), insertAt some position, delete a given element,[2] and elementAt, which returns the list element at the position given by its integer argument. If a client needs to know whether a list is empty, he or she must test whether the size is 0. To reorder a list, the client must insert and delete elements individually. If a client wants to know whether a given element is in a list, he or she can write a loop that checks each position in the list. To insert all the elements of a list into another list or determine whether one list is a sublist of another, the client must also code an iteration. With a linked implementation of List, these successive accesses of each element are very inefficient when compared with an encapsulated method that can access the storage structure directly.

We could include all of the above operations in the protocol of the class List as a convenience for its users. In addition, a list is ordered and the client may wish to make use of that ordering. For example, a user may want to order the list of files in a directory according to their importance (which may not correspond to sorting by name, date, etc.). For this purpose, we might provide messages such as insertAtFront, insertAfter a given element, move an element a distance forward or backward in the list, return the predecessor or successor of an element in the list, and so on. If the language supports function arguments, we might also want a message that returns the list that results from applying a function to each of the list's elements, or produces the sublist of elements for which evaluation of a boolean-valued function is true.

A list class that provides a very comprehensive protocol is the Smalltalk class OrderedCollection, discussed in section 8.4.2. It provides all the messages we described here and several variations on them. In fact, the Smalltalk system classes were designed to be as easy to use as possible and have what we might regard as maximal protocols. The system facilitates understanding these classes by grouping the messages that have similar purposes or characteristics into protocol categories.

In specifying the protocol of a class, we should also consider possible reuse of the class, that is, we should design classes for a category of problems rather than for a particular application. For example, the application for which we define the class List may only add and remove elements from lists. However, our knowledge of lists indicates that other applications might need to rearrange the elements of a list or ask whether one list is a sublist of another. We may choose to include these messages to increase the reusability of the class, although the current application does not use them.

Attributes and state information

In addition to delegating responsibilities for services, the designer specifies the attributes and state information for each class. The attributes of a class are the properties of its instances, for example, name, height, color, salary, etc. When describing a class's attributes, it is important to indicate the types of values, default

---

[2] I have seen a commercial List class that provides deleteFirst and deleteLast, but does not supply a message for deleting a given element. Consider what a client must do to implement that operation.

values, units of measure, mutability, and ranges or other constraints on the values possible for each attribute. Although both attributes and inter-object relationships are implemented by instance variables, most object-oriented development methodologies distinguish between scalar-valued attributes (e.g., the number of serial ports on a computer) and object-valued associations (e.g., the manager of a department).

We determine the attributes of a class by examining how such entities are described in the problem domain. The set of attributes defined for a class specifies an abstraction of those entities that includes only the properties relevant for the system. For example, a vehicle registration system may need to maintain the color, manufacturer, body style, engine size, and other characteristics for each vehicle, but not the condition or type of tires. Similarly, a class that represents companies that are vendors in an inventory application has different attributes than one that represents companies in an investment application.

The designer also must consider what information a class's instances need to perform their assigned services, and which class will manage each item of information. A piece of information (or an attribute) may be represented directly or may be calculated from other information stored in the object, and in either case, other objects must request it. The designer examines each activity to discover what data is involved in carrying out its task, and then determines whether that information should be managed by the receiver or by the client (in which case the information must be passed as an argument). If two objects both need a particular piece of information, it may be assigned to one or the other depending on its cohesion to the classes, a third class may be created to manage it, or the two classes may be collapsed.

The attributes of a class's instances are maintained in its instance variables, and state information is represented by instance or class variables, depending on whether it is specific to an instance. If this information is available to clients, the class provides accessor messages.

Relationships between objects

The relationship between a composite or aggregate object and its components is central to human knowledge structuring. We implement this relationship by the composite object containing instance variables that refer to its component objects. As in many relationships, the part objects may also need references to the whole if they are accessible separately. In some cases, the attributes of the composite apply to its parts (e.g., their location), but we do not represent this by inheritance because the parts do not share the protocol of the composite. (We will discuss the choice between using composition and inheritance in modeling in section 3.1.2.) Composition is indicated in object-oriented graphic notations by a distinguished arc connecting the nodes that represent the composite and component classes.

There are many other relationships besides composition possible among objects, such as

- interactions and associations meaningful to the problem domain, for example, the relationship between doctors and patients

- functional collaborations such as the interactions among the machines that make up a manufacturing process, or among the components of a digital camera

- client-server relationships, for example, a point-of-sales terminal using the services of a credit card database to authorize sales

- containment, for example, a library containing books, journals, and other media, and a course section containing students

- ownership, such as the accounts of a customer or the assets of a business

- update dependencies, for example, the formula cells in a spreadsheet requiring be recalculation when the contents of a cell in the formula changes

Object-oriented graphic notations represent these relationships as arcs between class nodes. Most also indicate the cardinality of a relationship (e.g., one-to-one, many-to-one, etc.), whether it is unidirectional or bidirectional, and the roles that the classes play in the relationship. As always, the designer should only represent the relevant relationships, and must eliminate duplicate or redundant associations.

If two objects are related, then one object must be able to send messages to the other to reflect that association, and often vice versa. In implementation, inter-object relationships are usually represented by an object explicitly maintaining a reference to another object in an instance variable. (Alternatively, an object may receive a reference to a related object as the argument of a message from another object, or the related objects may be visible to each other via an enclosing scope.) That is, in addition to modeling properties and components, instance variables are used to represent an association in which one object needs a reference to another to fulfill its responsibilities. For example, a shipment object might include an instance variable that refers to the purchase order object that corresponds to it (and vice versa), an employee object might have an instance variable whose referent is a list of the facilities to which that employee needs access, or a drug object might require references to the objects representing the conditions it alleviates.

We often must decide whether to represent a particular item of information as an attribute or as a relationship between objects. For example, the zipCode in an address object in a mailing list program might be represented by an integer attribute, but a more sophisticated direct mail system might associate other information with zip codes, such as the median income and common interests of people living in that area. In this case, ZipCode would be represented as a separate class, and the address object would contain a reference to the associated instance of ZipCode. We will discuss the issue of value versus object reference semantics for instance variables further in sections 2.2.3, 5.4.2, and 10.2.1.

In some cases, a relationship between objects has properties of its own. If those properties do not clearly belong to either of the participating classes, that relationship itself might be better modeled as a class. For example, we might have the relationship authorizedFor between users and databases, and that relationship might have attributes such as the user's access code, authorization level (e.g., access-only, record updates allowed, schema updates allowed), and a list of database views that he or she can use. If a user can access more than one database, this information cannot be stored as attributes of the user, so we design a separate Authorization class whose instance variables maintain this information and references to the related user and database objects. Representing a relationship as a class is often useful with such many-to-many relationships.

Refining the design

When creating a model of a complex system from several sources of information, developers often do not obtain the best design on the first pass, and much refinement is usually necessary. The model may include redundant classes (e.g., because both the classes User and Customer were extracted from the problem specifications) or unnecessary classes (e.g., that are part of the problem domain, but not this system's responsibilities). These classes must be pruned from the final model of the system. A class may need to be split according to semantically independent sets of responsibilities (e.g., a model class and the associated view class). Analyzing responsibilities and scenarios may indicate that a required class is missing. For example, if a CAD system allows the user to group drawable objects into "layers" that can be manipulated coherently, a separate class for that construct will make the system structure clearer, rather than having the objects themselves or the application maintain which objects are in which layer.

Each class should be sufficient in the sense that it embodies enough of the category that it represents to be useful, and complete in the sense that it includes all of the necessary protocol, attributes, and state information. Classes that are vague or unfocused must be reworked. Classes with too many responsibilities or a great deal of state information are difficult to understand and lack cohesion. On the other hand, if a class maintains a small amount of information and its only protocol accesses it, it might be more appropriate to use an attribute of the classes that refer to it. For example, a class Name that simply maintains the name of an object may not be worthwhile because classes whose instances are named can use an instance variable name with a string value. Classes with unused behavior can result from designing the class without considering scenarios, and indicate that the abstraction includes unnecessary information. A method that does not make use of its class's state information is probably assigned to the wrong class (i.e., it lacks cohesion and increases coupling). As we will discuss in the next chapter, behavior that is duplicated in two or more classes usually should be abstracted into a common superclass.

2.2 CLASS DEFINITION

2.2.1 Interface

Protocol

Now that we have discussed analysis and design issues in creating classes and their components, we will turn to defining classes in object-oriented programming languages. Like the interface of a subprogram in a procedural language, a class interface must provide the information necessary for a programmer to use the class and its instances effectively. The definition of a class's interface consists of a list of *messages* giving the message name and parameters, together with argument types in a statically typed language. (The receiver is not listed as one of the message's parameters, but is indicated in a message send by a special syntax, as we saw in section 1.1.4.) Since the method code is not part of the class's interface, the message specifications in a class interface are forward declarations, like the operations of an abstract data type. A class's message declarations are usually enclosed in the class definition, as shown for the C++ class CharStack in section 1.1.4 (Smalltalk is an exception, as we will see in section 6.1.2). Messages are also called member function declarations (C++), procedures (Modula-3 and Oberon), and features (Eiffel).

Many classes include attributes or information that clients can obtain or set, so their protocols include the corresponding accessor or modifier messages. In addition to protocol that provides the services assigned to the class, implementation classes need programming functionality so that the class's instances are first-class. This includes messages that

- initialize the receiver (recall our discussion in section 1.1.4)
- create a copy of the receiver
- test whether the receiver is equal to another instance of the class
- read, print, or store the receiver
- convert the receiver to an equivalent instance of another class (e.g., convert a string to a floating-point number or a circle to an ellipse).

Since objects must contain an indication of their class to support dynamic binding (recall section 1.1.5), most object-oriented languages also provide a feature for determining the class of an object. If the language or its standard class library defines a class that is an ancestor of all classes, it can provide default methods for these operations. For example, the classes Object in Smalltalk and Java and ANY in Eiffel serve this purpose. Most object-oriented languages support operator overloading, which also makes objects easier for clients to use.

The interface of a class also includes class messages that provide access to class variables or class-related operations. Class messages are often marked by a reserved word, for example, static in C++ and Java. In Smalltalk, the programmer selects an option in the programming environment to indicate whether a source code selection is a class or instance method (see section 5.6.3). Some languages, such as Modula-3 and Object Pascal, do not support class messages and variables. However, these two languages provide separate constructs for classes and modules so the class designer can get a similar effect by defining the class and a subprogram (i.e., the class message) together in a module. The same can be done with an object to emulate a class variable (which the module would not export). We will discuss sending class messages in section 2.2.3.

The class interface also lists the exceptions that each method can raise. For example, a Modula-3 procedure declaration gives a list of exceptions it can signal following the RAISES reserved word, and a C++ function can include an exception list following the throw reserved word (we will discuss the throw clause in section 13.3.2). In languages that do not support exceptions, a message can return an error, code, or a method may set an internal flag upon an error and the class can provide a message that returns whether the receiver is valid. We will see in section 11.3.4 that the C++ iostream library uses this technique.

Documentation

To completely specify the contract between the class designer and his or her clients, the interface of the class must also include the documentation necessary for a programmer to understand the logical purpose and operation of each message. This information may take the form of a manual, on-line help (e.g., for a commercial framework), or comments in the interface code, and is analogous to the data sheet for an electrical component. The documentation for an analysis class may include a list of related classes intrinsically involved in its use, and any other information necessary to complete the external description of the abstraction.

The contract between the designer and clients of a class must also describe the conditions under which that contract is valid. In particular, the documentation for a class may give constraints on the receiver and arguments of a message. For example, the message to draw a pixel on a pixmap object requires that the pixel's location is within the width and height of the pixmap. Similarly, a collection class that finds elements may require an equality test message for the class of the elements. In an object-oriented language that supports exception handling, the class designer can test whether such constraints are violated, and if so, signal an exception.

We can also specify the interface of a class with formal assertions about the behavior of the class's messages, namely preconditions and postconditions. A *precondition* states an expression describing the receiver and message arguments that must be true for an invocation of the message to return valid results. A *postcondition* states an expression that is guaranteed to be true after execution of the method if its preconditions held when it was invoked. For example, the message remove for a class Queue has the precondition that the receiver is not empty, and the class message new that creates a queue has the postcondition that the new queue is empty. Assertions and exceptions may be specified by a language construct, in the code database of a CASE tool or programming environment, or as comments in the code. In Eiffel, preconditions and postconditions for "routines" (methods) are part of the language, and an exception is signaled when an assertion is violated.

Access control

Among object-oriented languages, Smalltalk most closely follows the accessibility rules we have described: All messages are visible to clients of the class, and all class and instance variables are private to the class. Other object-oriented languages permit more flexible control of client access to the components of a class. This allows the class designer to define private messages for auxiliary methods that simplify implementation of an object's protocol, as well as providing the opportunity to violate the Law of Demeter by make storage structures visible. If the class variables or instance variables of a class are publicly accessible, they must also be regarded as part of the class's interface. (In Object Pascal, the fields of an object type cannot be hidden from clients.) Eiffel provides the most precise access control: The class designer can give a list of the classes that have access to each "feature" (component) of a class.

In section 10.1.3, we will see that C++ provides three levels of access control for the "members" of a class, as follows:

- *public* members are accessible to all objects
- *protected* members are accessible to instances of the class or its subclasses
- *private* members are accessible only to instances of the class

This permits the class designer to provide separate interfaces for clients of a class (the public members) and for subclasses of a class (the protected members). C++ also allows a class to declare *friend functions* that can access its nonpublic members. Java and Delphi Pascal use the same access control specifications as C++, but protected members of a class are also visible to all the classes in the same module.

Class names and protocols are visible globally in Smalltalk, or within modules in Object Pascal, Modula–3, and Java. C++ supports nesting an auxiliary class within the scope of another, and declaring it nonpublic.

Defining the interface and implementation

Most object-oriented languages allow the programmer to code the interface and implementation of a class separately (like those of a module in Modula-2). For example, we code the interface of a C++ class in a header file and the implementation in a code file. In this case, the interface unit may require private information for the compiler to use when translating client code (i.e., the class's instance variables), as discussed in section 1.1.4.

Some object-oriented languages do not support dividing the code for a class into an interface and implementation. In Smalltalk, each method is coded separately within the programming environment, and the environment provides a view of the class's protocol organized into message categories (see section 5.6.3). In Eiffel and Java, a class and its components are coded in one language construct. The Eiffel programming environment includes a command for producing the "short form" of a class that describes its interface, and the standard Java Development Kit provides a tool for creating the documentation of a class's public members from specially marked comments in the class code.

2.2.2 Implementation

Instance and class variables

The instance variables of a class represent an individual object's attributes, state information, components, and relationships to other objects. The class definition gives the names of the class's instance variables, together with their types in a statically typed language. Instance variable declarations usually appear like the declarations of record fields (recall the data members elements, top, and size in the C++ class CharStack in section 1.1.4). Individual objects each have different values for those variables and those values may change over time, but all instances of a given class have the same set of instance variables. The instance variable values in an instance of the class describe the state of that object at that point. Each object also has an implicit instance variable that identifies its class for dynamic binding, which usually refers to the class's method table (we will discuss this further in section 3.2.1).[3] Instance variables are also called data members (C++), fields (Object Pascal and Oberon), slots (CLOS), and attributes (Eiffel).[4]

As stated in section 1.1.5, a class can also define class variables that maintain information related to the class as a whole so that they are encapsulated with the class. Class variables are visible in both the class and instance methods of a class. In Smalltalk, class and instance variables names are given separately in the class definition message (see section 6.1.2), and in C++ and Java, class variables are designated static (see section 10.3.2). As discussed in the previous section, some languages do not support class variables.

In a traditional language, the programmer can define a record field as either a value directly embedded in the record instance or as a pointer to another object, and we might expect the same capability for the instance variables of a class. For example, we would represent an attribute whose value is an integer or a boolean by value, but would represent a relationship with another object as a pointer so that the referent maintains its unique identity for each object that refers to it. However, we will see in the next section that most object-oriented languages use reference semantics for all class type identifiers because they can be polymorphic. In this case, every instance or class variable of class type is implicitly a reference (i.e., a "hidden pointer"), rather than containing a copy of its referent.

Instance and class methods

Each instance method describes how the class's instances respond to the corresponding message. The method describes the messages sent to the receiver's instance variable values and the message arguments in performing the requested activity, and the value returned to the sender. The coding of methods depends on the language. Essentially, a method is a subprogram in which expressions represent

---

[3] We will see in section 12.3.5 that C++ avoids providing this information for instances of class that do not define any dynamically bound messages.

[4] I have seen every one of these synonyms in Java books.

message sends, and control structures determine which messages are sent, and in what order. In fact, methods in hybrid languages such as Object Pascal or C++ appear very similar to subprograms in the base language.

The class designer may also code "private" methods, that is, auxiliary subprograms local to the class, to simplify implementation of its protocol (e.g., the C++ method CharStack::grow() in section 1.1.4). Such methods perform operations used in several methods, or are dictated by a stepwise refinement of methods. They are not accessible to clients because they only realize some portion of the processing necessary to provide one of the class's services. Private methods may also rely on changes to the receiver performed by other methods, or might not leave the receiver in a consistent state because other operations are expected. In addition, the class designer should be able to reorganize the class's implementation (e.g., changing the purpose or argument signature of a private method) without affecting clients.

A class's instance methods can access the instance variable referents of the receiver directly, but must request those of other objects such as message arguments via an appropriate message. A method can also modify the receiver's instance variable referents. However, a class message does not have an instance of the class as a receiver, so class methods cannot directly refer to the class's instance variables. The class's class variables are accessible in both instance and class methods.

Object-oriented languages supply a special reserved word that refers to the receiver of the method so that a method can send messages to that object or use it as a message argument. This feature is provided by the identifier self in Smalltalk, Objective-C, and Object Pascal, the identifier Current in Eiffel, and the identifier this in C++ and Java. We will illustrate the use of this feature in section 2.2.4. We will see in section 3.2.4 that object-oriented languages also need a special feature for invoking an inherited method with the same name for method refinement.

Auxiliary classes

When implementing a class with a particular data structure, we sometimes need to define a type for substructures that should not be visible to clients (e.g., the nodes in a binary search tree). We will see in sections 10.3.3 and 10.3.4 that C++ allows the class designer to nest enumerations and classes within the scope of a class and declare these constructs as nonpublic to achieve this. Languages such as Object Pascal and Modula-3 that provide separate constructs for classes and modules allow the designer to get a similar effect by defining both classes in a module and not exporting the auxiliary class.

2.2.3 Programming Considerations

Classes, instances, and class objects

Classes are analogous to data types because they represent an abstraction of operation and structure, and are used exactly like types in programming to declare variables and parameters, create instances, compose other classes, and so on. However, many hybrid languages such as Object Pascal and C++ do not treat built-in types and classes exactly the same (see the discussion of instance variable semantics in the next subsection) because built-in types cannot be superclasses or subclasses, and do not use message sending or dynamic binding for their operations. Each object is an instance of a class, and instances correspond to data objects in conventional programming languages. All instances of a class respond to the set of messages given in the class's protocol and have the same internal structure, namely the instance variables defined for that class. Each instance has its own values for those variables, and that information may change over time.

In constructing applications, we sometimes need only one object of a particular kind. For example, a text editor will have one object that represents the text, such as a list of characters or strings with a cursor position. We should still define a class for that object so that other similar applications can make use of the effort of creating that abstraction. (In fact, we hope that the class already exists and can be used as is.) For this example, defining a class for the text also makes it easier to add support for multiple buffers to the application.

Like types in a compiled language, classes are (mostly) a compile-time construct, while instances are created, perform their methods, and are destroyed during execution. For applications that are not under development, the set of classes is fixed, but the set of objects in existence changes as the system is used. Of course, developers may define additional classes while maintaining the application.

We say that classes are "mostly" a compile-time construct because there is some class-related information that must be available at execution time, namely the method tables necessary to implement dynamic binding. In addition, some object-oriented languages and class libraries provide type operations such as obtaining the name of a class or a list of its subclasses. Smalltalk and CLOS go the furthest in this regard. In Smalltalk, the complete type object that represents a class exists during execution (because the language is interpreted), and is available to the programmer. That is, the class itself is considered to be an object with behavior and state, namely the class's class messages and variables, and a class object can be the referent of a variable or parameter.[5] We invoke a class message by sending the message to this class object. For example, a method that needs the number of days in March sends that message to the class object Date. In Smalltalk, the class object is also responsible for creating instances, that is, we send a class message such as new to the class object and it returns a reference to a new instance. (This is also true in Objective-C, which refers to class objects as "factory" objects.) We will discuss Smalltalk class objects further in section 6.1.3, and their extensive protocol in section 7.1.2.

Identifier semantics

In Pascal or C, we can define a local variable, parameter, or record field either as a value directly embedded in the activation record or record instance, or as a

---

[5] In fact, a Smalltalk or CLOS program can even create new classes during execution.

pointer to another object. However, in object-oriented languages, identifiers of class type can be polymorphic. For example, Smalltalk is dynamically typed so an identifier can refer to any object at all, of any size. Therefore, space for the referent of an instance variable cannot be allocated in the object, nor can space for local variables be allocated in a method's activation record. The value of a Smalltalk instance variable is a reference to another object, rather than containing a copy of that object. (We discuss this further in section 5.4.1.) In statically typed object-oriented languages, the referent of an instance variable can be an instance of any of the subclasses of the variable's class, which can also be of various sizes, so the same effect occurs for identifiers of superclass type.

For this reason, most object-oriented languages implicitly use *reference semantics* for identifiers of class type. In contrast, the value of an instance variable of built-in type is stored directly in the object, for efficiency, which we refer to as *value semantics*. That is, allocating a built-in type variable creates space for an object of that type, but allocating a variable of class type only creates space for a reference (in implementation, a pointer). Dereferencing a class type identifier is usually implicit (i.e., no ^or * is needed), and a special value such as nil indicates that an identifier does not refer to any object. We will discuss the implications of reference semantics for allocation, object identity, assignment, parameter passing, and equality tests in the context of Smalltalk in section 5.4.

Statically typed languages such as Modula-3, Object Pascal, Objective-C, and Java use reference semantics for class type identifiers and value semantics for built-in type identifiers. Unlike most languages, C++ allows the class designer to use either value or explicit reference (i.e., pointer) semantics for global, local, and instance variables of class type. We will discuss the reasons for this feature, the semantics of the alternatives, and the implications and design trade-offs that result from having the choice available in section 10.2.1 and 12.2. In Eiffel, the programmer can declare a variable as expanded so that its value is stored directly. Classes can also be declared as expanded so that their instances are stored by value (e.g., the classes for numbers, characters, and booleans are expanded).

Creating and initializing objects

Objects are created and destroyed as the entities they represent are created and destroyed or enter and exit the system. In C++, we can create new objects by the usual language mechanisms of static and automatic variable definition and dynamic allocation.[6] As stated in the previous paragraph, other object-oriented languages do not support static or automatic allocation of class instances, so all objects (except instances of built-in types) are created dynamically. The lifetime of an object ends when it is deallocated either explicitly or through garbage collection (or, in C++, when control leaves the scope of an automatic object definition). Presumably, the object is no longer relevant to the problem domain activity that the

---

[6] In C++, objects can also be created implicitly by a coercion or when an argument is passed or returned by value.

application models. Most object-oriented languages use automatic storage reclamation because managing programmer-controlled deallocation can be difficult with
reference identifier semantics (Object Pascal and C++ are exceptions).

Class variables must exist throughout program execution, whether there are
any instances of the class or not. In Smalltalk, the class variable references are
stored in the class object and exist for as long as that object is present. In C++, class
variables are statically allocated, and are instantiated and initialized before the function main() begins execution (see section 10.3.2).

Creating an object and initializing its state information are separate operations, although it is possible in many languages to code the methods such that both
are triggered by one message send. In Object Pascal, the programmer applies the
built-in procedure new to an object reference identifier to create an instance of its
class (like the use of new in Pascal), and then invoke a separate initialization function for the new object explicitly. Modula-3 also uses NEW to create objects, but the
procedure permits additional arguments that give initial values for the object's
instance variables.

C++ allows allocating objects statically, automatically, and dynamically (also
using the new operator), and the language supports class-specific "constructor"
and "destructor" member functions that the compiler invokes implicitly whenever
an instance of the class is created or destroyed. The constructor ensures each
object is properly initialized upon creation, and the destructor performs any finalization required when an object is destroyed, such as releasing its system resources
(e.g., recall the member functions CharStack::initialize () and CharStack::release ()
in section 1.1.4). This mechanism is much more powerful that just setting initial
values for the new object because the constructor can also allocate system
resources for the object, register the new object as a dependent, or do any other
processing necessary. We will discuss constructors and destructors in detail in section 10.2. Java also uses new for object creation and implicit constructor invocation, but does not include destructors because the language system uses garbage
collection.

In Smalltalk, classes are objects in their own right, which exist at run time, and
we create an object by sending a message to the class object requesting a new
instance. The class designer can define any number of class messages (and methods) for instance creation, with any names or numbers of arguments. For example,
the class Date has instantiation messages such as newDay:month:year: which takes
a day, month name, and year; readFromString:, which takes a string; and today,
which creates a new date object representing today's date. The class method creates the new object, then sends it an initialization message with arguments that specify the new object's state information. Like Smalltalk, Objective-C uses class
messages for instantiation. Eiffel also permits the class designer to define several
named creation messages for a class, but it uses a "creation instruction" beginning
with ‼ to invoke a creation message for an object reference. For example, if pt is a
reference to an instance of a class Point that defines a creation procedure make that
sets the new object's coordinates, then the statement ‼pt.make(3, 5) creates a point
object and initializes its x and y instance variables to 3 and 5, respectively.

Encapsulation of operation and application structure

In a pure object-oriented language, all operations are methods for which some class of objects is responsible, and there is no language mechanism for defining global, unencapsulated processing. In hybrid languages, we can also define free-standing subprograms that are invoked without reference to a receiver object, as in the base procedural language. Although this may be comfortable and familiar, using this feature compromises the object-oriented nature of the design, and complicates understanding the system. Similarly, hybrid languages support global variables, while pure languages do not.

This characteristic of object-oriented programming has a major impact on the structure of an application. In particular, there is no main program that creates a number of data objects and performs a series of statements and subprogram invocations, as in a traditional procedural language. Instead, due to the uniformity of the object-oriented perspective, we code the application itself as a class, and a particular execution of that application is an object that is an instance of the class. The code that we would usually give in the main program is encapsulated within an instance creation method for the class, for example, new or open. This activity typically consists of instantiating the model objects that represent the state of the application and a set of instances of window or view classes that implement its user interface. When that message is sent (e.g., Spreadsheet.open()), the class method performs instantiation and initialization of the application. We can use the instance messages of the application class for user commands, event handlers, and auxiliary methods. Representing applications as classes also allows us to use inheritance among applications (e.g., for a generic application class, as discussed in section 1.3.4). We can use the same design strategy in a hybrid language such as C++, and the main program simply creates an instance of the application class and sends it the start message.

Message sending syntax

The message sending syntax in most object-oriented languages appears like an access of a "subprogram field" within the receiver record (recall the C++ example in section 1.1.4). A message expression uses the component selection operator . (period) with the receiver as the left operand and the message name as the selected field, followed by the arguments enclosed in parentheses. The result of a message expression may be used as an argument to another message (if it returns a value), and message expressions associate from left to right (like component selection). In our examples in this section and the next, we will use an empty pair of parentheses to denote an empty argument list, to distinguish a message send from accessing a public instance variable, as is done in C++.[7] This syntax is illustrated by the following examples:

---

[7] Eiffel and many languages that use Pascal syntax do not include these parentheses for zero-argument messages.

```
{ message expression syntax used in most object-oriented languages }
table.insert(key, value);
pen.moveTo(square.center());
dist := square.center().distanceFrom(point);
```

We will use this syntax for the remainder of this chapter, since it is likely to be more familiar to you. C++ also uses the -> operator to send a message through a pointer to an object (like selecting a structure member through a pointer in C). In CLOS, messages are not encapsulated within classes, so a message send appears the same as a function call, with the "receiver" as one of the arguments. Message expression syntax in Smalltalk is quite different, and is described in section 5.3.2.

In most languages, class messages are invoked in the same fashion, with the class name as the left operand of the selection expression (e.g., Date.getMonth-Name(3)). We will see in section 10.3.2 that C++ uses the scope operator :: rather than the . (period) for this purpose.

Object-oriented languages also support the familiar infix syntax for operators such as arithmetic and comparison operators, and most allow the programmer to overload them with methods for class objects. Usually, the left operand is considered the receiver of such a message. For example, the expression x + y sends the message "what is the result of adding y to yourself" to x. If the language permits overloading the square brackets operator [] or the parenthesis operator (), the compiler will be aware that the argument is enclosed within the operator symbols in an invocation.

Organization of classes into modules

As we stated in section 1.3.2, a very large system can have hundreds of classes, so many object-oriented design methodologies partition the system's classes into subsystems or clusters. In many object-oriented languages such as Eiffel, classes are the top-level abstraction.[8] Other languages provide separate features for classes and modules (i.e., each module is a separate namespace with an interface and implementation, and import declarations are provided), and developers can organize classes into modules, for example, by subsystem, application, or class library. This additional level of structure also helps manage class name conflicts when using several class libraries on a project. For example, most class libraries define foundation classes such as strings, dates, and rectangles.

The focus in creating modules in an object-oriented system is on classes that belong together, rather than on subtasks that belong together. Cohesion and coupling issues are important is this decision: Arbitrary modularization is worse than none at all. We group related classes, and the interface of the module includes only those elements needed in other modules. For example, if class A uses the services of class B and vice versa, they should be in the same module. Similarly, the coupling between a class and its subclasses is fairly tight: Data and operations in the super-

---

[8] Meyer feels that clusters do not require language support, but can be reflected by a development methodology, or by the organization of classes in the file system [Mey92].

class are accessible implicitly in the subclass, so the overall complexity is reduced if this coupling occurs within a module.

Smalltalk provides no facilities for separate code modules because it is incrementally compiled, and the entire application and the system classes are contained in a single "system image". Classes are organized into categories to facilitate finding classes, but the categories are not part of the language and do not define scopes. C++ follows the C convention of using header files for interfaces and code files for implementations. Standard practice is to use one header and code file for each class, but the language does not enforce this, so a programmer could place several classes in the same header and code file. However, there is still one global name space, as in C. The recent "namespace" extension to C++ supports defining separate scopes for groups of classes, functions, and objects, and provides import declarations for namespaces and their elements (this is covered in section 13.4). Modules are supported by Modula-3, Object Pascal, and Oberon (in which they are called "units"), and Java and CLOS (in which modules are called packages, as in Ada). In Java, classes are the unit of compilation (not packages), but any number of class may be enclosed within the same package scope and class files can import either complete packages or individual classes.

2.2.4 Example Classes

Object pseudocode

For the examples in this section and the next chapter, we will use a statically typed Pascal-like object-oriented pseudocode, so that we can avoid many of the details of the syntax and semantics of particular object-oriented languages.[9] We define the interface and implementation of a class separately, and introduce components with reserved words, that is, class protocol, instance protocol, instance variables, etc. (Note that object-oriented languages vary widely on how they specify class components.) We will also use "bracketed" end statements for clarity (as in Ada). In listing the messages in a class's protocol, we use the reserved word return to indicate the return type (as in Ada), and we use an operator symbol as the message name to indicate operator overloading. We do not list the receiver as an argument of the message, as we would in a procedural language. Instead, it appears as the left operand in the message send expression, as in the examples in the previous section.

Instead of giving access specifications for a class's components, only the components declared in the class interface (which will never include instance variables)

---

[9] We base our pseudocode on Pascal because it is the basis for numerous object-oriented languages such as Eiffel, Object Pascal, Modula-3, Ada95, and Oberon, and is intentionally very readable. We do not use C++ in this section because it introduces a number of other complexities due to its concern for efficiency, and it does not directly reflect the object model. For example, in C++, header files include both interface and implementation information, messages requiring dynamic binding must be identified, objects are represented differently depending on whether they require dynamic binding, class variables are marked as static, and instance variables may be specified as public.

are visible to clients. We treat identifiers and parameters of class and array type as if they have reference semantics (for the reasons given in section 2.2.3), and assume that the language uses automatic deallocation. Both these characteristics are features of most object-oriented languages. We code methods in the same fashion as Pascal subprograms with message expressions rather than subprogram calls. The object pseudocode is case-sensitive, and we follow the convention introduced in Smalltalk of capitalizing class names and using a lowercase initial letter for message names, instance variables, and local variables.

Character strings

Most programs need to represent text, so they require a class for variable-length character strings. We would like to design this class so that programmers can use strings in the same way as built-in types (i.e., its instances should be first-class). In particular, clients should not have to worry about storage allocation and the details of changing the referent of a string variable or the size of a string. Instance operations that we might define for this class include comparison for equality or alphabetic order, copying a string, requesting the length or the nth character of a string, determining if one string is a substring of another, searching a string for a character or a matching substring, concatenating and splitting strings, and so on.[10]

The class method new takes initialization information as its argument and creates a new instance. It is overloaded so that clients can initialize a string object from an array of characters, a single character, or another string. (In most languages, coding these methods involves defining a private initialization method, as we will see in section 6.1.2.) Since our language uses automatic storage reclamation, we do not need to define a "release" function that clients must call when finished with an object, as we did for the C++ class CharStack in section 1.1.4. The class String has the following protocol:[11]

```
{ a class for variable length character strings }
class String interface

    { forward declarations that specify the class messages }
    class protocol
        { the new object contains the characters in the argument }
        new(argChars: CharArray) return String;
```

---

[10] In many class libraries (e.g., those of Smalltalk and Java), string objects are fixed-size, like arrays. To avoid creating numerous temporary string objects when working with strings, both libraries define classes for composing strings, namely WriteStream in Smalltalk (see section 8.4.3) and StringBuffer in Java. In contrast, instances of the Eiffel class STRING are resizable.

[11] Using implicit reference semantics and operator overloading complicates the semantics of equality tests. If we overload comparison operators for strings, we expect the expression str1 < str2 to compare the strings, not the references. However, the equality test str1 = str2 could mean testing either whether the operands are equal strings or whether they are the same string object. For example, in Java, the equality test has the latter meaning and the String message equals() tests string equality. In our pseudocode, we assume that an equality test compares the objects.

```
      { the new object is a one-character string }
      new(argChar: char) return String;
      { the new object is a copy of the argument }
      new(argStr: String) return String;
   end class protocol

   { forward declarations that specify the instance messages }
   instance protocol
      { is the receiver equal to the argument? }
      =(argStr: String) return boolean;
      { is the receiver before the argument in ASCII order? }
      <(argStr: String) return boolean;
      { ... other comparison operators ... }
      { is the argument a substring of the receiver? }
      isSubstring(argStr: String) return boolean;
      { return the number of characters in the receiver }
      length() return integer;
      { return the index^th character in the receiver }
      [ ](index: integer) return char;
      { return the index of first occurrence of the argument in the receiver, or 0 if not found }
      indexOf(elemChar: char) return integer;
      { add the argument to the end of the receiver }
      append(argStr: String);
      { return the concatenation of the argument and the receiver }
      concat(argStr: String) return String;
      { ... other messages ... }
   end instance protocol

end class String interface
```

Programmers can then use String as the type of instance variables and the parameters and local variables of methods, and manipulate them by sending them the messages in its protocol. For example,

```
   { instance method for class Example illustrating use of instances of the class String }
   class Example implementation

      instance method message(argStr: String);
      var
         tempStr: String;
         test: boolean;
         ch: char;
      begin
         tempStr := String.new("quux");
         if argStr.length() > 1 then
             ch := argStr[2];
         test := (argStr.isSubstring(tempStr)) or (argStr < tempStr);
         tempStr.append(String.new(" help"));
      end

      { ... other Example methods and variables ... }

   end class Example implementation
```

Many storage structures are possible for character strings. We can use an array of characters for each object with either an additional instance variable giving the length or a delimiter character that marks the end of the string, as in C. To facilitate inserting and removing characters, we could use a linked structure. A more sophisticated facility might save space by managing a string pool that stores each string in use once with a reference count, and having all String identifiers with the same value refer to the same stored string. Clearly, the methods that implement the String messages will be different depending on which storage structure the class uses. Since no other methods are allowed to access the storage structure directly, the class designer may change from one storage format to another without affecting any other code, as long as the new methods implement the class's operations correctly.

Rational numbers

Some applications need a class for rational numbers that provides an exact representation for these values. We would represent an instance with two instance variables, numerator and denominator. To avoid the possibility of overflow for the instance variables, we could define an arbitrary precision integer class and use it as their type. This class is implemented in the Smalltalk class library as the class Fraction.

For this class, we would overload the standard arithmetic and comparison operators with methods that perform the appropriate actions so that clients can use the class's instances with the same expression syntax as the standard numeric objects. Additional instance messages might include accessing the receiver's numerator or denominator, returning the reciprocal or absolute value of the receiver, converting the receiver to an integer (either rounded or truncated) or a floating-point number, and printing the receiver.

Instantiation would be performed by a class message new that takes one or two integer arguments as the numerator and denominator (and the denominator is 1 for the single-argument overloading). The corresponding initialization method divides the arguments by their greatest common divisor, normalizes their signs so that the denominator is always positive, and creates an instance with those results as the instance variables. It raises an exception if a client attempts to initialize an object with a 0 denominator.

Display squares

Let us create a class for rotatable squares that are displayed in a drawing program. We will assume that classes for Point, Angle, and Color, have been defined appropriately, so that we can use those classes as the types of message parameters and instance variables (i.e., the class Square is a client of those classes). For example, Point might be represented by x and y coordinates, Angle as a number modulo 360 or 2π, and Color as red, green, and blue intensity values. We will also assume that there is a class Canvas that represents objects that we can draw on (e.g., it might have the subclasses Pixmap and Window).

We overload the class message new to take values for all the new object's attributes, to provide a default value of 0 for the new object's tilt, and to permit initialization of all the instance variables from an existing Square object. We define accessor messages for an instance's attributes, including a message corners returning an array of the points at which the four corners of the receiver are located. No message is provided to modify individual corners of the object directly because the result might not be a square. The message draw draws the receiver on the argument canvas, and erase erases the receiver from its canvas. The modifier messages moveTo, rotate, resize, and setColor erase the receiver, set the appropriate attribute, and then redraw the receiver.

The class Square has the following protocol:

```
{ a class for rotatable squares }
class Square interface

   class protocol
      { the arguments give the new object's attributes }
      new(center: Point, tilt: Angle, size: integer, color: Color) return Square;
      { the new object's tilt is 0 }
      new(center: Point, size: integer, color: Color) return Square;
      { the new object is a copy of the argument }
      new(argSq: Square) return Square;
   end class protocol

   instance protocol
      { return the center of the receiver }
      center() return Point;
      { return the tilt of the receiver }
      tilt() return Angle;
      { return the size of the receiver's sides }
      size() return integer;
      { return the color of the receiver }
      color() return Color;
      { return an array containing the receiver's four corners }
      corners() return Array of Point;
      { draw the receiver on the argument canvas }
      draw(canvas: Canvas);
      { erase the receiver }
      erase();
      { set the receiver's color to the argument and redraw the receiver }
      setColor(newColor: Color);
      { move the receiver so that its center is the argument and redraw the receiver }
      moveTo(newCenter: Point);
      { rotate the receiver by the argument angle and redraw the receiver }
      rotate(amount: Angle);
      { set the size of the receiver's sides to the argument and redraw the receiver }
      resize(newSize: integer);
   end instance protocol

end class Square interface
```

We define the instance variables and accessor methods of the class as follows: [12]

```
class Square implementation

    { "fields" in a Square instance }
    instance variables
        center: Point;           { the center of the receiver }
        tilt: Angle;             { the tilt of the receiver }
        size: integer;           { the size of the receiver's sides }
        color: Color;            { the color of the receiver }
        where: Canvas;           { the canvas the receiver is currently drawn on }
        visible: boolean;        { whether the receiver is currently drawn on any canvas }
    end instance variables

    { return the center of the receiver }
    instance method center() return Point;
    begin
        return center
    end

    { ... other Square methods ... }

end class Square implementation
```

The instance variable where must be a reference to a Canvas object, rather than a copy of that object embedded within an instance of Square, because each object on that canvas must refer to exactly the same canvas object. That is, the canvas has a unique identity that must be maintained. In addition, Canvas might have subclasses such as Pixmap and Window that have different methods for drawing, so we require polymorphism for where and dynamic binding for messages to its referent. On the other hand, the values of the other five instance variables could be stored directly within an instance of Square because they are treated as attributes of the object, rather than unique objects with which the square object has a relationship. It is also unlikely that their classes will have subclasses or that dynamic binding will be necessary for their messages. We will discuss the instance variable visible later in this section. From the point of view of a client of the class, it is irrelevant whether the class stores an instance's corners and computes the center, size, and tilt, or vice versa. However, in languages such as C++, the compiler needs the storage structure while compiling client code, so the class interface file must contain a private section containing the instance variable declarations (as discussed in section 1.1.4). The identifier center in the return statement in method center refers to that instance variables in the receiver of the message.

---

[12] In our object pseudocode, a message and an instance variable in the same class can have the same name. This is true is some object-oriented languages, but not in others.

Classes for objects that we can draw on such as pixmaps and windows typically include protocol for drawing points, lines, rectangles, elliptical arcs, and so on. In the method for draw, the receiver must obtain its corners so that it can ask the canvas to draw the four lines that make up the square. As stated in section 2.2.2, object-oriented languages include a reserved word that allows a method to send messages to the receiver of the original message or use it as a message argument. Like Smalltalk, Objective-C, and Object Pascal, we use the identifier self for this purpose. We implement the methods for draw as follows (we assume that Canvas implements a message drawLine that takes the line's endpoints and color as arguments):

```
{ instance method for class Square, illustrating the use of self }

class Square implementation

    { draw the receiver on the argument canvas }
    instance method draw(canvas: Canvas);
    var
        corners: Array of Point; { the receiver's corners }
    begin
        where := canvas;
        corners := self.corners();
        where.drawLine(corners[1], corners[2], color);
        where.drawLine(corners[2], corners[3], color);
        where.drawLine(corners[3], corners[4], color);
        where.drawLine(corners[4], corners[1], color);
        visible := true
    end

    { ... other Square methods and variables ... }

end class Square implementation
```

Again, the identifiers where, color, and visible refer to those instance variables in the receiver. We can imagine that there is an implicit reference to the receiver provided by the compiler that is available within a method. The programmer can refer to this reference explicitly with self, and the compiler also uses that reference to access the receiver's instance variables.

The return value of the method corners illustrates some important points about identifier semantics and the allocation and deallocation of objects. When a subprogram in a traditional language returns a value, there is a local variable in the subprogram's stack frame that maintains that value, which is then copied into the stack frame of the caller. However, this *return by value* is inefficient with a large object such as an array of points. We have stated that in our pseudocode, identifiers are references and that all objects are allocated dynamically. In this case, the language (like most object-oriented languages) uses *return by reference* in which a reference to the new point array object is returned and assigned to the

local variable corners in the draw method. In languages that use programmer-
controlled deallocation, a serious problem occurs with return by reference, namely
that the client becomes responsible for deallocating the object returned. Of
course, this is a memory leak waiting to happen, especially if the returned object
is passed immediately to another message rather than being assigned to an identifier. With automatic deallocation, we do not have to be concerned with which
method is responsible for deallocating temporary objects created during the
course of performing some activity.

To erase an object from a canvas, we can set the receiver's color to the canvas's background color and then redraw the square.[13] At this point, we must
decide whether a square object can exist independently of whether it is displayed.
For example, in a CAD program, the square could be a component of a "layer"
that might or might not be visible at any point, depending on messages from the
user. Suppose that we choose to maintain objects that are not visible. The boolean
instance variable visible indicates whether the square is displayed, and is set by the
draw and erase methods. We can code the method for erase as follows (we assume
that a canvas maintains a background color that can be obtained with the message
backgroundColor):

```
{ instance method in class Square }
class Square implementation

  instance method erase();
  var
    tempColor: Color;
  begin
    tempColor := color;        { the color of the receiver }
    color := where.backgroundColor();
    self.draw(where);
    color := tempColor;
    visible := false
  end

  { ... other Square methods and variables ... }

end class Square implementation
```

The messages moveTo, rotate, and resize erase the receiver, set an instance
variable, and then redraw the receiver. The first and third operations are accomplished by sending messages to self, for example:

---

[13] For the purposes of this discussion, we ignore the possibility of damage to overlapping visible
objects upon erasing an object. This would be the responsibility of a "picture" or "layer" object, and the
necessary code (e.g., obtaining the erased object's bounding rectangle, determining whether other objects
in the picture have intersecting bounding rectangles, redrawing them, checking whether this damages
other objects, and so on) would obscure the point of this example.

```
{ instance method in class Square }
class Square implementation

  instance method moveTo(newCenter: Point);
  begin
    self.erase();
    center := newCenter;
    self.draw(where)
  end

  { ... other Square methods and variables ... }

end class Square implementation
```

The methods for rotate and resize would be coded in a similar fashion, and the set-Color method would not have to erase the receiver first. Note that all the above methods are accomplished by sending messages to instance variables, method arguments, and local objects created within the method.

2.3 POLYMORPHISM

2.3.1 Definition

Polymorphism is a central concept in object-oriented programming, and in the semantics of object-oriented programming languages. The word *polymorphic* literally means "having many forms". With respect to programming languages,

- an identifier is polymorphic if it can refer to more than one type of object
- a subprogram (or message) is polymorphic if an invocation can operate on arguments (or receivers) of more than one type.
- an object is polymorphic if it has more than one type.

Traditional statically typed programming languages such as Pascal and C are *monomorphic* because each identifier, subprogram, or value is always of exactly one type.

In fact, there are some limited kinds of polymorphism in these languages due to conversions and merged and overlapping domains (recall section 0.3.6). There are cases in which we can assign an object of one type to an identifier of another (e.g., an integer to a real variable or a subrange instance to a variable whose type is the subrange's base type). However, identifiers are still monomorphic because a conversion or a cast takes place and the referent of the identifier is always the same type as the identifier. (The same is true for parameter passing and initialization.) Traditional languages support operator overloading for built-in types, which provides subprogram polymorphism for those types and operations. However, since identifiers are monomorphic, the actual operation to execute is known at compile time. We really have two operations—integer addition and real addition, for example—that have the same name, rather than the same function operating on more than one type of argument. (We discuss this further in section 2.3.3.) Constrained types and type aliases result in object that are polymorphic, although the storage representations of the types are the same. For example, the character 'C' in Pascal is an instance of both the built-in type char and the subrange type UpperCase we defined in section 0.3.5.

In object-oriented languages, identifiers, messages, and objects can be polymorphic. In this chapter and the next, we will see that polymorphism gives object-oriented languages much of their power and flexibility, although it may run counter to concepts you have acquired in using traditional monomorphic languages.

2.3.2 Identifier Polymorphism

Identifier polymorphism can result from either dynamic typing or static typing and inheritance. In a dynamically typed language such as Lisp or Smalltalk, every identifier is polymorphic because it can refer to objects of various types during its lifetime. In addition, the type of the referent at any point during execution can only be determined at run time. As we will discuss in section 3.1.5, inheritance results in object polymorphism because a subclass object is also an instance of its class's superclass, to mirror the semantics of the specialization relationship. That is, the object is an instance of more than one type. For example, a stationwagon object is an instance of the classes StationWagon, Car, and MotorVehicle. In languages with static typing and inheritance, an object identifier can refer to an instance of the identifier's class or of any of its subclasses, since those objects are also instances of the identifier's class. For example, a Car identifier can refer to instances of Sedan, StationWagon, SportsCar, and so on. That is, an identifier of superclass type is polymorphic. Identifiers whose type is a built-in type or a class without subclasses are monomorphic. Subprogram overloading also results in identifier polymorphism because an overloaded subprogram name has referents with different types, that is, with different argument signatures.

Polymorphism for object identifiers has a number of implications that we will discuss throughout the text. We already mentioned in section 2.2.3 that it results in reference semantics for those identifiers and requires dynamic allocation for their referents. Identifier polymorphism also affects collection classes. As discussed in section 2.1.2, with monomorphic static typing, all the elements of a collection class must be of the same type, but with dynamic typing, heterogeneous collections containing members of various types can be created. With static typing and inheritance, we can define a collection of elements of a superclass type and insert instances of any of its subclasses, providing a limited form of heterogeneity. Identifier polymorphism also implies that operations on the identifier's referent must be dynamically bound, and that type checking of those operations must be done at execution time. Identifier polymorphism and dynamic binding of overloaded messages enable the loose coupling and extendibility of systems coded in an object-oriented language.

2.3.3 Message Polymorphism

Overloading

Traditional languages support some subprogram polymorphism for built-in types, such as the arithmetic and comparison operators and the printf() function in C.[14] As we saw in section 0.2.7, languages such as Ada that support subprogram overloading provide the same capabilities for programmer-defined subprograms and types. For example, they permit the programmer to invoke various objects' printing behavior in a uniform manner.

Overloading is an essential aspect of object-oriented languages. A message name is overloaded if two or more classes define methods for it with the same number of arguments. For example, the message draw might be overloaded by the classes Square, Spiral, Line, etc. Overloading also occurs when a method is overridden by a subclass. In a statically typed language, we can also overload a message with different argument signatures within the protocol of a particular class, as illustrated by the class message new in the classes String and Square in section 2.2.4. Binding the correct method for a particular message send can be performed either at compile time or at execution time, as we will discuss in section 2.4.2.

Usually, the methods associated with an overloaded message are implementations of the same conceptual operation tailored to instances of that particular class. However, the methods for an overloaded message are sometimes semantically dissimilar due to ambiguity in how that message name is used in practice (e.g., opening a file or opening a window).

Categories of function polymorphism

Researchers in functional programming and denotational semantics describe two broad classifications of function polymorphism [Str67] [Car85]. In *ad hoc* polymorphism, the same function name may be applied to different types of arguments, and different operations are specified for each argument signature, as occurs with function overloading. In such cases, the function name, rather than the function itself (i.e., the code), is polymorphic. Polymorphism that occurs due to implicit coercions is also considered to be *ad hoc*, since the function body is not applied to arguments of different types.

In *universal* polymorphism, one function body may be applied to a range of argument types.[15] For example, the function that returns the minimum of two values merely performs a comparison and returns one value or the other, so we can

---

[14] Although it can take arguments of various types, write in Pascal is a statement rather than a procedure because the language is strongly typed and each procedure must have a unique argument signature.

[15] The distinction between ad hoc and universal polymorphism (also called "pure" polymorphism) is important for the purpose of theoretical analysis. With *ad hoc* polymorphism, the various overloadings of a function name can be treated as logically separate functions. On the other hand, universal polymor-

pass two instances of any type that provides an ordering comparison. This is an example of *parametric* polymorphism, in which there is an implicit "type parameter" to the function that is bound to the type of an argument in a function invocation. In section 13.1, we will discuss C++ function templates, which support parametric polymorphism. Universal polymorphism also occurs through *inclusion* polymorphism, in which there are overlapping domains, as occurs with inheritance. In particular, a method that has a parameter of superclass type can be passed an instance of the superclass or of any of its subclasses. For example, if the class Canvas described in section 2.2.4 has the subclasses Window and Pixmap, we can pass an instance of either class as the argument of the Square message draw.

In object-oriented terms, we can think of *ad hoc* polymorphism as "message polymorphism", because several classes respond to the same message name, possibly using different methods. We would consider universal polymorphism to be "method polymorphism" since the same method operates on arguments that are instances of various classes. The distinction between message and method polymorphism is a matter of perspective for programmers (as opposed to for formal analysts) in the sense that method polymorphism often occurs because the messages sent by the method are polymorphic. For example, the method for draw in the class Square in section 2.2.4 is polymorphic because the message drawLine is polymorphic, since both the classes Window and Pixmap implement it.

2.4 MESSAGES AND METHOD BINDING

2.4.1 Characteristics of Message Sending

Comparison to subprogram invocation

When an object receives a message, it may change state, respond with some information, or both, similar to when a subprogram is applied to a data structure. Like subprograms, messages provide two-way communication between objects since arguments are passed to the receiver and the method can return a value to the sender.

In most object-oriented languages, a message send is synchronous like a subprogram call because the sender waits until execution of the receiver's method is completed and control is returned before proceeding. Control is sequential and the execution environment can use a list of activation records to keep track of pending method executions (i.e., a stack if there are no function objects passed out of nested scopes). A concurrent asynchronous implementation in which the sender does not wait is also possible, and is supported in some languages. In fact, many problem domains exhibit concurrency, and concurrent control is more in keeping with the concept of the model consisting of a group of objects sending each other messages.

phism requires the semantic formalism to support the additional capability of representing type parameters and inferences concerning them. Some authors reserve the term polymorphism for universal polymorphism.

For example, Smalltalk includes the message fork that creates a new independent process with the receiver "block" (function object) as its code, whose sender does not wait for the return value before continuing execution (see section 5.5.6). The class library also provides classes for synchronization of process activities and communication among processes. Java and Modula-3 support concurrency by defining a standard library class Thread that represents an asynchronous thread of control with protocol for creating, starting, suspending, interrupting, and terminating threads. Both languages also support specifying that executions of a method or statement must be mutually exclusive (like the critical regions we discussed in section 0.1.4). Researchers have designed and implemented a number of other concurrent object-oriented languages such as Concurrent Smalltalk [Yok86], Dragoon [Atk91], and languages based on the actor model [Agh86] such as ABCL/1 [Yon86b].

The message/object paradigm for system activity differs conceptually from the subprogram/data or operator/operand paradigm in three major ways:

- All operations are encapsulated within some class.
- Methods do not have direct access to the components of their arguments.
- Since the sender has less information about the receiver and the method executed, they are more loosely coupled.

Encapsulation of operation

A message is always sent to a receiver object that knows how to perform the operation requested. For example, in the object-oriented encoding of the operation insert(table, key, value), we send the message insert(key, value) to the object table. Each activity is the responsibility of the appropriate class, and can only be initiated by requesting it from that type of object. If the information returned by that process is derived in some way, the responsibility for performing the computation is delegated to the receiver of the message, not to the code the caller applies to the object, as in a procedural programming language. For example, the code and local variables for the message corners in section 2.2.4 is localized within the definition of the class Square, rather than being embedded in other functions that need that information. This increases the modularity of the system because operations and objects that belong together are packaged together. Message sending focuses on the object that includes the necessary actions as part of its behavior, rather than on applying an operation to a value or data structure.

Information hiding

The connotation with the subprogram/data paradigm is that an active subprogram is manipulating a passive data structure directly. However, in object-oriented programming, an object's storage structure is considered to be private, and accesses, modifications, or computations must be requested in accordance with its interface. For example, it is not necessary for a subprogram to access the state of an instance of Square (its center, size, and tilt) and perform the calculations for corners directly. For many classes, it might not even be possible to obtain the state of an instance (i.e., if the class defines no accessor messages). That is, we consider an object to be an active entity that performs its own state manipulation in response to a request. As Ingalls states [Ing81], "instead of a bit-grinding processor raping and plundering data structures, we have a universe of well-behaved objects that courteously ask each other to carry out their various desires".

Loose coupling between sender and receiver

A message send is generic in the sense that it describes what to do, but not how to do it. In addition to not knowing what operations are performed, the sender may not even know what type of object the receiver is, due to identifier polymorphism. For example, we can send the message corners to an instance of any class that defines it (e.g., Polygon, Star, etc.). Since a receiver identifier can refer to any of these classes (due either to dynamic typing or a common superclass), the sender (and, as we will see in the next section, the compiler) does not know what method is invoked, but can count on that method returning an array of the receiver's corners. In fact, that message send can rely on obtaining an array of points from the receiver even if that object is an instance of a class that is added to the application later.

The distinction between the invoking code being in control of the processing performed and the receiver being in control of that activity may appear subtle or even contrived at first. However, this concept provides abstraction and information hiding, and the resulting looser coupling between program units facilitates developing and understanding them independently. This reduction of interdependency among classes has major benefits in terms of modularity, reuse of program components, and extendibility of the system. In addition, this perspective has an effect on how the designer organizes the system. The unit of modularity is the class rather than the subprogram, and the structure of the system reflects relationships between classes rather than between subprogram modules.

2.4.2 Method Binding

Strong typing

Object-oriented languages are strongly typed because an error will result if an object receives a message that is not in the protocol of its class. In dynamically typed languages such as Smalltalk and CLOS, this error is detected and signaled at execution time when the language's run-time system is examining the method tables for the receiver of a message.

In statically typed languages, the compiler rejects message expressions that use a message not in the class of the receiver identifier. However, this means that the compiler will also prohibit some messages that might be valid. For example, suppose that the class Employee is a subclass of the class Person, and that Employee defines a message weeklyPay and Person does not. The compiler must disallow the message aPerson.weeklyPay() even though aPerson might refer to an employee object, because it might also refer to an instance of Person or of one of its subclasses that does not define this message.

Static binding

As we discussed in section 0.2.7, contemporary languages such as Ada support subprogram overloading, and the compiler selects the subprogram definition to execute according to the argument signature of the invocation. In a statically typed object-oriented language, the argument signature of a message definition or a message send also includes the class of the receiver, and each method for a message name must have a unique signature. If the receiver identifier in a message send is monomorphic, the compiler can determine which method to execute by examining its argument signature.[16] For example, if the class Square does not have subclasses, then the compiler can translate the invocation aSquare.draw(aPixmap) as a standard subprogram call of the Square method for draw, and the overhead for dynamic binding does not occur. The compiler can deduce the method to invoke even if it is inherited because each class definition lists its superclass, and the superclass and its protocol must have been defined. If there is no matching argument signature among the definitions of that message name or more than one definition can apply due to coercions, then the invocation is in error. Operations on built-in types are also statically bound.

Although static binding of message sends is more efficient, there are drawbacks to using it. The major problem is losing the extendibility characteristic of message sending because the operation to execute is hard-wired in the object code produced by the compiler. Suppose we create a subclass of Square, say FilledSquare, that defines a draw method. If the identifier aSquare refers to an instance of that class, the wrong draw method will be executed for the expression aSquare.draw(aPixmap). In addition, for the compiler to deduce whether an identifier is monomorphic, it must examine the entire application's source code (and, perhaps, that of a class library) to find out whether its class has subclasses, since this information is not given in the class definition. These hierarchy relationships may be managed by a programming environment (like the application-wide compilation dependencies we discussed in section 1.1.3), or the programmer can indicate whether dynamic binding is necessary for each class or message. For example, the C++ programmer must mark methods that require dynamic binding as virtual, and the Java programmer designates methods that can be statically bound as final. As we will see in section 12.3.2, statically bound messages should not be overridden.

---

[16] Object-oriented languages do not perform dynamic binding on the basis of an argument type, except for CLOS, as discussed later in this section.

Dynamic binding

In a dynamically typed language, the method to execute for an overloaded message can only be determined at execution time when the type of the receiver is known. [17] For example, suppose that instances of the classes Stack, Set, and List respond to the message isEmpty with class-specific behavior that depends on their storage structures. The method to execute for the message send collection.isEmpty() depends on whether collection refers to an instance of Stack, Set, or List at the moment of invocation, and can only be determined at that time. To allow dynamic method binding, each object must maintain its class identity so that the method binding process can use it to select a method. As we will see in section 3.2.1, this information is usually represented by a reference to a "class object" that maintains the class's methods. (Monomorphic objects in a statically typed language do not need this information.) All method binding in Smalltalk and CLOS is dynamic.

As we saw in section 2.3.3, identifier polymorphism also occurs with static typing and inheritance. A message in the protocol of a superclass may be defined differently in its various subclasses. When we send a message to a variable of the superclass type, the method executed depends on the class of the instance bound to the identifier at the time of invocation. For example, suppose the classes Stack, Set, and List are subclasses of the class Collection, and each defines a method for the message isEmpty. If a method sends the message isEmpty to an identifier of type Collection, the method executed depends on whether the identifier refers to a stack, a set, or a list, which may depend on run-time conditions. (Presumably, the programmer used a Collection identifier because it might refer to more than one kind of collection.) As we stated previously, statically typed object-oriented languages support both static and dynamic binding of methods.

Multiple polymorphism

For the operation insert(table, key, value), it is obvious which of the three participants should be responsible for providing the service: the object table maintains the collection and is the object affected by the activity. In addition, different kinds of tables (i.e., with different implementations) perform different methods for this message. However, in some cases, none of the objects that participate in providing a service clearly has the primary responsibility. For example, an application may need to print different types of documents (e.g., text, bitmaps, Postscript graphics, etc.) on different types of printers (e.g., dot matrix, ink jet, laser, etc.) with different resolutions. The actual operations performed depend on the classes of both the document and the device, so it is not clear which object should receive the message. Similarly, for an arithmetic operation, different methods must be executed depending on the types of the operands, and the types of both operands equally determine which method to execute. In these cases, we need dynamic binding of the method based on the types of both operands, which is referred to as *multiple polymorphism*

---

[17] A compiler may be able to deduce the class of some identifiers by analyzing the program's control flow, but there will always be identifiers whose referents can only be determined at run time.

(as opposed to the "single polymorphism" provided by most object-oriented languages). In section 7.4.6, we will describe a technique called double dispatching that you can use to factor out multiple polymorphism.

Multiple polymorphism is the basis for method dispatching in CLOS, an object-oriented extension of LISP. CLOS does not associate messages with a particular receiver. Instead, a set of methods for the same message name constitutes a *generic function*, and each method is an overloading of that name with a different argument signature. That is, operations are not encapsulated within classes, but are organized into generic functions. Determining the method to execute for a generic function invocation is based on the classes of all its arguments equally. The method that matches the most specific set of classes compatible with the argument list via conversion or inheritance is selected. However, this general rule is complicated by precedence ties among applicable methods, a facility for combining the applicable methods, and support for multiple inheritance, and is discussed further in section 4.5.4.

2.4.3 Implications of Dynamic Binding

Overhead of dynamic binding

The disadvantage of dynamic method binding is that it requires an execution-time mechanism to select the method to execute every time an object receives a message. This involves both the time overhead of choosing a method, and the space overhead of the data structures necessary. (Of course, this is also true of using dynamic rather than automatic allocation of objects, which provides flexibility at the expense of a run-time system.) Since reference semantics are necessary for dynamic binding, there is also the expense of allocating objects dynamically and accessing them indirectly.

Statically typed languages have less of this overhead because they can use static binding for some messages and for operations on built-in types. In addition, the implementation of dynamic method binding can be quite efficient if the compiler always knows which messages require dynamic binding and has the definitions of all of a class's ancestors when compiling the class. (We will describe the technique C++ uses in section 12.3.5.) Language implementors have developed techniques for reducing the run-time cost of method binding for dynamically typed languages, for example, caching methods to avoid the hierarchy search when that message is sent again.

Receiver responsibility

To illustrate the advantages that dynamic binding provides for design and coding, let us consider a situation in which different processing is required for different types of objects. Suppose that we have a CAD system that allows the user to draw and position graphic objects, and to group graphic objects together into a "layer" that he or she can treat as an object in its own right. There will be program variables that have to be able to refer to any kind of object (e.g., the selected object), so in a monomorphic statically typed language such as Pascal, each object must be of the same type, say DisplayObject. The DisplayObject type would be implemented as a variant record with a type field whose type is an enumeration of the kinds of graphic objects, fields for the information common to all graphic objects, and variant parts representing the information associated with each type of object, as follows:

```
{ a Pascal type for graphic objects in a CAD system }
type
   DisplayObjectType = (Ellipse, Line, Text, { ... other display object types ... } );
   DisplayObject =
      record
         { ... common information for display objects, e.g. color ... }
         case typeTag: DisplayObjectType of
            Ellipse: (width, height, tilt: integer);
            Line: (startPoint, endPoint: Point);
            Text: (font: Font;  string: CharArray);
            { ... variant parts for other object types ...}
      end
```

In C, we would use a struct containing a type member and a union of struct members. A layer is represented by a list of the objects that make up that object, say of type DisplayObjectList. (If layers can contain layers, we also need a variant part for that purpose in DisplayObject.) A subprogram that draws a layer must explicitly decide which subprogram to call with a case structure, as in the following Pascal procedure (we assume that a DisplayObjectList is represented as a linked list):

```
{ a Pascal procedure for drawing the components of a layer }
procedure drawLayer(var layer: DisplayObjectList;  var canvas: Canvas);
var
   pDispObjList: DisplayObjectList;
   dispObj: DisplayObject;
begin
   pDispObjList := layer;
   while ( pDispObjList <> nil ) do begin
      dispObj := pDispObjList^.elem;
      case (dispObj.type) of
         Ellipse: drawEllipse(dispObj, canvas);
         Line: drawLine(dispObj, canvas);
         Text: drawText(dispObj, canvas);
         { ... cases for other kinds of display objects ... }
         end
      pDispObjList := pDispObjList^.next
   end
end
```

Overloading would not help avoid the case because the arguments to the subprograms drawEllipse, drawLine, and so on are the same types in each subprogram. (Alternatively, the case could appear in a subprogram drawDisplayObject, but the problems we are discussing remain.)

Now consider an implementation in an object-oriented language. We would define a superclass DisplayObject that maintains common instance variables such as the color, bounding rectangle, canvas, and whether the object is visible. The class Layer would add an instance variable components, which is an instance of the class DisplayObjectList. With static typing and inheritance, we can insert instances of any subclass of DisplayObject in that list. To draw a layer, the method for draw in the class Layer sends draw to each element of the list components, and each object on the list responds with its own draw method. We code the method for draw in Layer as follows in our object pseudocode (we assume that DisplayObjectList provides the message size and overloads the [] operator to return the nth element):

```
{ implementation of a class Layer for groups of display objects }
class Layer implementation

    instance variables
        components: DisplayObjectList;   { the elements of the receiver }
    end instance variables

    { draw the receiver's components }
    method draw(canvas: Canvas);
    var
        index: integer;
    begin
        for index := 1 to components.size() do
            components[index].draw(canvas);
    end

    { ... other Layer methods ... }

end class Layer implementation
```

The code for the draw method in Layer does not need to know the type of each object, nor how they draw themselves. The method executed is selected by dynamic binding on the basis of the receiver.

Extendibility

In a traditional monomorphic language, the decision about how the draw operation is implemented is made in the environment of the caller, so part of the responsibility for drawing an object has been delegated to the subprogram that enumerates the objects in the list. As stated in section 1.3.5, the programmer must find, modify (correctly), and recompile all subprograms that make this distinction whenever adding a new type of object to the system.[18] In fact, the procedure drawLayer explicitly states that it handles certain types and is only usable for these. That is, monomorphic identifiers and static binding inhibit "generic" programming, in which we describe a solution for an open-ended category of problems, because it restricts us to constructs that can be type-checked statically.

Identifier polymorphism and dynamic binding transfer the task of method binding from the programmer to the run-time system. (In fact, there is late binding of methods in the Pascal version, but it is implemented explicitly by the programmer, and must be extended explicitly.) We can assign the responsibility for managing the code to be executed to the individual display object classes, resulting in better locality and cohesion. This design also provides looser coupling among the components of a software system because the sender of a message needs less information about the receiver and the operations that are performed.

The major advantage of dynamic binding is that we can add a new type of DisplayObject to the system without changing or even recompiling the draw method in the class Layer, or any other methods that need to draw display objects. For example, a financial system can introduce a new type of account during maintenance without affecting any existing methods, as long as that class specifies its own behaviors for messages that those methods use. As we saw in section 1.3.5, this extendibility affects the entire development process because it enables incremental development and supports the flexibility necessary when errors are discovered or the system's requirements change. In effect, dynamic binding trades execution time, for development time which is often justifiable because hardware performance is still increasing rapidly and development time is widely regarded as being out of control.

Reuse of higher-level algorithms

Traditional structured design results in a hierarchy of subprograms, with more general code at higher levels and increasingly more specific code at each successive level in the functional decomposition. With traditional programming languages and structured methods, we often find that lower-level routines are reused in other projects, but higher-level routines cannot be, because of their explicit ties to particular lower-level routines and data structures (e.g., the calls to the subprograms drawEllipse and so on in drawLayer).

Identifier and message polymorphism allow reuse of existing code in the system because that code can be used directly with new types as they are designed. In particular, higher-level algorithms can be reused with various types of objects supplying the object-specific operations the algorithm uses. For example, a sort method in a list class can be used with elements of any class that defines the message <. Similarly, we can implement a search table as a binary search tree without regard for the type of elements it contains, as long as the keys can respond to <. The appro-

---

[18] If a single procedure draw(DisplayObject, Canvas) were coded, the case would not be eliminated but would appear within that procedure rather than in each client invocation. This would reduce the number of changes to be made, but would not eliminate the fundamental problem.

priate "lower-level" code is dynamically linked from among a set of methods for an overloaded message used in that algorithm. That is, dynamic binding enables generic programming in which we describe a solution for a category of problems, including for classes that may not have been anticipated. We will see further examples of this type of reuse in section 3.3.3, in which we define other DisplayObject methods in terms of draw. In fact, this is another instance of loose coupling, in this case between the higher-level and lower-level code.

2.5 SUMMARY AND REVIEW

2.5.1 Class Semantics

Problem domain classes

- Classes model categories of concrete or abstract entities in the problem domain relevant for the application. Each class is an abstraction that reflects the behavior, components, attributes, and relationships of the type of entity it represents.
- We recognize problem domain classes during analysis activities in system development.

Design and implementation classes

- Classes also represent categories of system components used in the design and implementation of the application. These domain-independent classes include *foundation classes* such as dates and strings, *collection classes* that represent groups of objects such as lists, sets, and queues, and classes for system services such as files, user interaction components, and graphics.
- Contemporary applications typically require a graphic user interface. In the *Model-View-Controller* paradigm pioneered by Smalltalk, *model* classes represent problem domain entities, *view* classes present graphic representations of model objects, and *controller* classes accept user input.
- Separating model and view classes allows using model classes with different view classes (e.g., for different platforms), and permits using view classes for different applications on a particular platform.

Determining class components

- The principles of decreasing coupling and increasing cohesion are as important for the design of classes as they are for modules. We strive for loosely coupled classes so that they can be understood and developed individually, and reused more easily.
- We decrease coupling by reducing the amount of information classes have about each other (e.g., by only accessing objects through their interfaces) and by reducing the number of classes with which a class interacts.

- A class should have high cohesion in the sense that all of its protocol and components are logically related to the purpose of the class.
- To design a class, we must determine its protocol, attributes, components, state information, and relationships with other classes.
- First, we specify the class's protocol, which lists the operations its instances are responsible for and represents a contract between the class and its clients. The protocol should provide all the operations necessary to use instances of the class effectively, and each operation should be logically related to the class.
- A large protocol facilitates using and reusing a class, but makes it more difficult to understand the class completely and to choose a message for a particular purpose.
- We determine the attributes and components of instances and the state information that they maintain by recognizing the properties of the entity that are relevant to the application, and the information they need to perform the class's operations.
- Our model must also represent the relationships in which the instances of a class participate with other objects.

2.5.2 Class definition

Interface

- The interface of a class declares the messages that the class and its instances respond to, each of which specifies the message name, parameters (and their types in a statically typed language), and a logical description of that operation.
- Implementation classes need messages for initializing an instance, copying an instance, testing whether two instances are equal, and reading, printing, and storing an instance.
- The interface may also include preconditions and postconditions for messages, and exceptions that the class's methods may generate.
- Many object-oriented languages allow the class designer to specify which class components are visible to clients. This permits defining private methods and public instance variables, but the latter violate representation independence. C++ and Java provide separate interfaces for the clients of a class and the subclasses of a class.

Implementation

- The implementation of a class specifies its instance and class variables, and instance and class methods.
- The instance variables represent the attributes, state information, components, and relationships for that type of object, and describe the storage structure for instances of the class. The values of an object's instance variables give its current state.

- An instance variable may contain a value or refer to another object. A reference is necessary if the variable is polymorphic or its messages require dynamic binding.

- Each instance method implements the operation of the corresponding message in terms of the receiver's storage structure and messages to its arguments. Essentially, a method is a subprogram in which expressions denote message sends. Instance methods can access the instance variables of the receiver and the class's class variables.

- Class methods can access the class's class variables, but cannot access instance variables directly because there is no instance that is the receiver of the message.

Programming considerations

- In programming, classes are analogous to data types and objects are instances of classes.

- In Smalltalk, the class itself is an object that exists during execution. Its behavior and state are the class's class messages and variables, and instantiation is a class message.

- In most object-oriented languages, all class instances are created dynamically and are deallocated automatically. C++ supports creating objects statically, automatically, or dynamically, and uses programmer-controlled deallocation for dynamic objects.

- Class variables must exist throughout execution. They are statically allocated in C++, and maintained by the class object in Smalltalk.

- Instantiation and initialization of the new object are separate operations. C++ supports programmer-coded "constructors" for initialization that are invoked automatically whenever an object is created. In Smalltalk and Eiffel, the programmer can define creation messages whose methods invoke an initialization message for the new object.

- In a pure object-oriented language, all operations are encapsulated in classes, while many hybrid object-oriented languages allow definition of global subprograms, as in the base language. The application itself is a class rather than a main program, and the user creates an instance to use by sending it a class message.

- In most object-oriented languages, message sending syntax uses the component selection operator with the receiver as the left operand and the message name followed by an argument list as the right operand. A class message uses the class name as the left operand. Operators can be overloaded for class objects, and most languages consider an operator expression to be a message to its left operand.

- A method sometimes needs to send a message to the receiver of that method,

or use it as a message argument. Object-oriented languages define a special
reserved word to provide this capability (e.g., self in Smalltalk or this in C++).

- In Smalltalk and Eiffel, classes are the top-level language construct. Some languages such as Modula-3 and Java support modules that define import/export
scope separately from classes, and allow organizing classes into modules. The
recent namespace extension provides this capability for C++.

2.5.3 Polymorphism

- A programming language construct is *polymorphic* if it can be associated with
more than one type. Polymorphism is an essential property of object-oriented
programming languages, which gives them their characteristic genericity and
flexibility. Traditional statically typed programming languages are *monomorphic* because each identifier, subprogram, or value is always of exactly one
type.
- *Identifier polymorphism* occurs when an identifier can refer to objects of more
than one type, and results from either dynamic typing or static typing with
inheritance.
- *Message polymorphism* occurs when a message can operate on arguments of
more than one type, for example, with overloading. It also occurs when the
same method can operate on arguments of various types, either due to the
genericity of its code that invokes polymorphic messages, or due to inheritance, because the method can operate on instances of subclasses of the types
in its argument signature.

2.5.4 Messages and Method Binding

Characteristics of message sending

- Message sending is the fundamental operation in object-oriented languages.
Like a subprogram invocation, message sending provides two-way communication and is a sequential, hierarchical control structure.
- Message sending has different characteristics than subprogram invocation that
result from the data abstraction inherent in the object model. All processing
is encapsulated within classes, and the internal states of the arguments are not
directly accessible to a method. In addition, the type of the receiver and the
method it uses may not be known to the sender of the message. These properties provide looser coupling between the components of a system coded in
an object-oriented language.

Method binding

- Object-oriented languages are strongly typed because an error will result if an
object receives a message that is not in its class's protocol. This error is

detected at execution time in a dynamically typed language, or at compiler time in a statically typed language.

- In a statically typed object-oriented language, the compiler can determine which method to invoke for a message to a monomorphic receiver, as in languages with subprogram overloading.

- Static binding prevents extendibility because the operation to execute is hardwired in the object code. In addition, the compiler must know whether an identifier's class has subclasses to determine whether it is monomorphic.

- To support loose coupling, object-oriented languages support polymorphic identifiers, so selecting the method for a message send must be delayed until execution time.

- In most object-oriented languages, dynamic binding is performed only on the basis of the message's receiver. In CLOS, methods are organized into generic functions, rather than being encapsulated in classes, and the language supports *multiple polymorphism* in which the method invoked depends dynamically on the classes of all the arguments equally.

Implications of dynamic binding

- Dynamic binding requires run-time support, which results in the time and space overhead necessary to determine which method to invoke. This overhead is less in statically typed languages that use static binding for many operations, and can use information about classes and their protocols to reduce the method search time.

- Without identifier polymorphism and dynamic binding, a method that sends a message must know the types of the objects that can receive that message, and must include a `case` structure to select which method to call. The sender is responsible for performing method binding, and is more tightly coupled with those classes. With dynamic binding, the receiver determines the method invoked at execution time, even if the receiver's class did not exist when the code sending the message was written.

- The genericity provided by dynamic binding allows us to design a solution for a class of problems, and provides reuse of that code for each new problem. Dynamic binding also facilitates enhancing a system with new capabilities and supports incremental development.

2.6 EXERCISES

2.1 Examine a real-world domain that you are familiar with (e.g., a retail store, an office, a kitchen, a repair shop, etc.), and find some classes and determine their protocols.

2.2 List the classes necessary to simulate the operation of a water heater, and give the protocol of each.

2.3 Give the protocols of the classes you listed for each part in exercise 1.43.

2.4 Suppose we have the four collection classes Set for an unordered set of elements, List for an unordered list of elements, SortedList for a sorted list of elements, and Array for a fixed-size ordered list of elements. Which of the following messages should each class include in its protocol?

(a) add an element to the end of the collection

(b) return the number of elements in the collection

(c) return the predecessor of an element in the collection

(d) remove an element from the collection

(e) test whether another collection is equal to the collection (is the meaning of this operation the same for all the classes?)

2.5 Consider the binary search tree data structure. If we were to use it as a collection class, what would its interface be? What would you call this class? (Remember that the fact that an instance is stored as a tree is used should not be visible to a client.)

2.6 Why is it useful to define the model aspects of a problem domain category separately from its display characteristics in the application?

2.7 Consider a class for a user interface component PushButton as found in Motif, the Macintosh interface, MS-Windows, etc. What is the protocol for this class (from the point of view of the programmer, not the user of the object)?

2.8 Explain how the principles of coupling and cohesion relate to the design of classes.

2.9 **(a)** Suppose we want to define a class for calendar dates. Give a minimal interface for this class.

(b) Define some additional messages that would increase the usability of the class.

2.10 Problem 1.50 asks you to obtain documentation on several general-purpose C++ class libraries. Compare the protocols of the classes they have in common, such as String, Date, and Point. For messages that are in one library's class, but not the other, can you see how the client can obtain that effect with the remaining messages? For each, would you expect an implementation of that operation internal to the class to be more efficient? What aspects of each library's protocols do you like, and what do you dislike?

2.11 Describe the elements of the definition of the interface and implementation of a class.

2.12 What are the advantages and disadvantages of an object-oriented language providing access control for the components of a class?

2.13 Frames [Min75] are an information structure proposed for representing problem domain knowledge, quite similar to objects in many ways. Frames are composed of "slots" that we may think of as instance variables. Explain how we can implement the following properties of frames within the definition of a class.

(a) A frame can have "active" slots for which a given procedure is executed each time that slot is accessed.

(b) A frame can define a default value for a slot, for example, 4 for the numberOfLegs slot in a Chair frame. A class can change the default value at execution time, and this change is reflected in each instance whose value for that slot is the default.

2.14 Why are class variables accessible in both class and instance methods, but instance variables are accessible only in instance methods?

2.15 In most object-oriented languages, all variables of class type are references rather than values.

(a) Why is this true?

(b) How does this affect allocation of class instances?

(c) How does this affect the representation and efficiency of composite objects that have instance variables of class type?

2.16 Even in compiled object-oriented languages, defining a class causes storage to be allocated at execution time. Why is this so?

2.17 Code the interface, instance variables, and instance methods for the class Rational described in section 2.2.4 in the object pseudocode used in this chapter.

2.18 Code the remainder of the instance methods for the class Square described in section 2.2.4 in the object pseudocode used in this chapter.

2.19 **(a)** What is identifier polymorphism?
 (b) Why is identifier polymorphism necessary for object-oriented languages?
 (c) How is identifier polymorphism achieved for statically typed languages?
 (d) How does identifier polymorphism affect the semantics of collection classes?

2.20 Describe three differences between messages sending and procedure invocation.

2.21 In what cases can a message send be statically bound? What are the disadvantages of doing so?

2.22 List three operations for which multiple polymorphism would be useful (besides those mentioned in section 2.4.2).

2.23 Discuss the advantages and disadvantages of dynamic binding.

2.24 We have discussed how in a traditional programming language such as C, the code that selects and runs events must use a "case" structure such as the following to determine which function to execute to handle the event:

```
switch (eventPtr->type)
{
    case KBD:
      handleKbd(eventPtr);
      break;
    case MOUSE:
      handleMouse(eventPtr);
      break;
    /* ... other cases ... */
}
```

 (a) How would the various types of events be declared in C?
 (b) Why is the switch unnecessary in an object-oriented language?
 (c) What is the disadvantage of this code with respect to program maintenance? Suppose one encapsulated the switch in a function, for example, handleEvent(). Does this solve the problem?

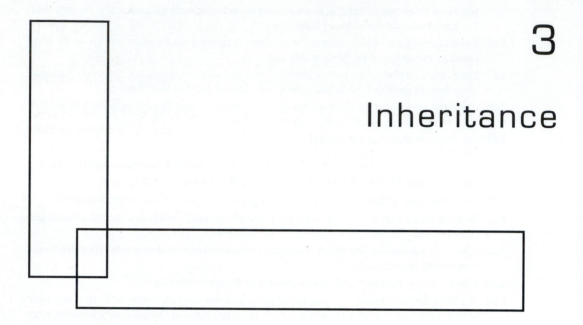

3

Inheritance

In this chapter, we will cover inheritance in detail. We discuss the semantics of inheritance among problem domain categories and design abstractions, describe defining a subclass by extending the superclass and overriding superclass methods, introduce abstract classes that encapsulate the interface for a subhierarchy but do not define a complete implementation, examine multiple inheritance, and consider the advantages and disadvantages of inheritance.

This chapter covers the following topics:

- the relationships modeled by inheritance, and the distinction between inheritance and composition (3.1.1 and 3.1.2)
- the class hierarchy (3.1.3), and the process of developing that structure (3.1.4)
- object and inclusion polymorphism, and identifier polymorphism for statically typed languages (3.1.5)
- the meaning of a subclass definition (3.2.1)
- definition of the interface of a subclass (3.2.2)
- definition of the implementation of a subclass, and the storage structure of objects (3.2.3)
- the method binding process, method overriding, and refining superclass methods (3.2.4)
- the motivation for abstract classes (3.3.1)

- abstract classes, abstract messages, and deferred methods (3.3.2)
- encapsulation of higher-level algorithms that send abstract messages in abstract classes (3.3.3)
- multiple inheritance, and the resulting class hierarchy structure (3.4.1)
- name ambiguity with multiple inheritance (3.4.2) and repeated inheritance (3.4.3)
- the advantages provided by inheritance, namely better problem domain modeling, reusability, extendibility, code library structure, and polymorphism (3.5.1)
- the drawbacks of increased execution time and compromised encapsulation and information hiding that result from inheritance (3.5.2)

3.1 INHERITANCE SEMANTICS

3.1.1 Specialization

Purpose for inheritance

In our discussion of a class system in the previous chapter, each object is an instance of a single class, and each class is an independent encapsulation of behavior and state. However, in most problem domains, we find entities that are described by a number of overlapping categories at varying levels of generality. For example, a particular chair is a member of the class Chair, as well as of the more general class Furniture. Similarly, a DC-10 is a jet, which is an airplane, which is a transportation vehicle. These relationships mirror an essential property of real-world systems and of human perception of them, namely that categories frequently have subcategories with more specialized behavior and attributes. The feature of inheritance among types was introduced by the language Simula67 [Dah67] specifically to allow programmer-defined types to mirror this *specialization* relationship. Due to its importance in understanding a problem domain, this subcategorization relationship also plays a central role in many artificial intelligence knowledge representation formalisms, such as semantic networks [Qui67] and frames [Min75].

As stated in section 1.1.5, we say that the more specialized class Jet is a *subclass* of the more general class Airplane, and that Airplane is a *superclass* of Jet. The class Jet *inherits* the behavior and state information of the class Airplane because every instance of Jet is also an instance of Airplane. Therefore, each jet has the same behavior and state as that defined in the class Airplane, but since a jet is a special kind of airplane, it also includes properties that are specific only to jets. Inheritance is transitive since Jet also inherits the behavior and state of the superclass of Airplane, of its superclass, and so on.

The most common and straightforward use of inheritance occurs when one category of objects is a specialization of another. For example, a claw hammer is a special kind of hammer that has the additional ability to remove nails. Similarly, a touch-tone telephone is a special type of telephone that also allows performing financial transactions and using telephone menus, and a touch-tone telephone with memory adds the ability to redial and store shortcuts for frequently called numbers. We can also view a subclass as an extension of its superclass since it extends the capabilities of the superclass with additional behavior and state information.

The inheritance relationship is also important in describing the properties of classes that represent design abstractions. For example, the category input/output device has subcategories such as terminal, file, printer, and network connection. File has subcategories such as directory, text file, and executable file, and printer has subcategories for Postscript printer, ink jet printer, dot matrix printer, and so on. The class Queue might have a subclass SynchronizedQueue that adds a semaphore instance variable and enforces mutual exclusion of accesses to the queue by concurrent processes. The class String might have a subclass Text that also specifies fonts for its characters.

Comparison with other relationships

Note that each item in the sequence DC-10, jet, airplane, transportation vehicle, etc. denotes a class, not an individual object. The "instance of" relationship between a particular airplane and the class DC-10 is not the same as the "is a kind of" relationship (also called "is a") between the class DC-10 and the class Jet. If we think of a class as the set of its instances, the "instance of" corresponds to set membership, while the "is a kind of" relationship corresponds to the subset relationship. You should also be careful not to confuse specialization with the composition relationship that holds between an object and its components. For example, a jet "has a" engine, but engines do not have the same behavior as jets, nor is the set of engines a subset of the set of jets.

Clearly, there are many important relationships among instances of classes. We described several, such as composition, functional collaborations, client–server relationships, associations, containment, and dependencies in section 2.1.3. All of these are relationships between individual objects, whereas inheritance is a relationship between classes. In addition, these interactions do not provide the same opportunities for reuse and extendibility as inheritance. They are modeled using the other mechanisms of an object-oriented language, rather than being reflected in the structure of the language itself. For example, we use instance variables to represent composition or containment, and message passing to represent functional interactions.

Specialization versus composition

As described in section 3.1.1, the "is a kind of" and "has a" relationships are not the same. For example, a Rectangle has two Points as components (i.e., to represent the upper left and lower right corners), but is not a special subcategory of Point. Similarly, a SalesTour has a number of instances of City as components, but it certainly does not respond to messages asking for its population or mayor. On the other hand, a graphic interface library can define the class Window as a subclass of the class Rectangle because windows should be able to respond to Rectangle protocol such as origin, height, width, containsPoint, and intersection (with another rectangle or window).

Often, the distinction between specialization and composition is not obvious, especially if you are accustomed to the perspective of what a data type "is" (i.e., its storage structure), rather than what it "does". Frequently, when creating a new class, we find that there is an existing class that has protocol or storage structure similar to the new class. In deciding whether to represent a new category as a subclass, the primary consideration is whether the new class should inherit functionality from the proposed superclass, not whether its storage structure includes that of the proposed superclass. That is, the designer must decide whether the new class is conceptually a specialization of the existing class that extends its behavior, or whether it has a component whose type is the existing class.

For example, we can represent a stack as an array together with an indication of the top of the stack, so we might consider defining the class Stack as a subclass of Array. This technique is sometimes referred to as inheritance of implementation, and some programmers consider it a reuse of code, specifically of the specification of the instance variables and methods. However, Stack should not inherit behavior such as random access of elements from the class Array, so it should not be defined as a subclass of Array. To define the class Stack as composed of an array rather than as a subclass of Array, we define Stack with an instance of Array and a top index as its instance variables. In this case, none of the Array class protocol is available to clients of Stack. If a composite class requires any of the component class's protocol, those messages must be coded in the composite class, that is, by methods that pass them to that instance variable. In using composition, we are still reusing the Array storage structure and methods to define the class Stack.

As a less obvious example, suppose we have a class List that represents ordered variable-size lists of objects, and we need a class Set that represents finite sets, which are unordered collections of elements with no duplicates. The protocol of such a List class appears in section 3.2.2. If we define Set as a subclass of List, Set can inherit the List methods for size, isElement, and delete directly without recoding them. Since sets do not permit duplicates, Set must refine the method for insert to check whether the argument is already present in the list, and do nothing if so. However, Set must disallow any messages that refer to the ordering of the elements, such as successor and insertAfter (e.g., by overriding them with methods that produce error messages or signal exceptions). Alternatively, if we implement the class Set with a List instance variable, then when an instance of Set is created, its initialization method creates an instance of List. We must write methods for size, delete, and the other List messages that Set also needs, and those methods simply pass the message to the instance variable and return its return value. We code the other Set methods in terms of messages to the instance variable, but we do not need to disallow any inherited messages. For example,

```
{ using composition to define the class Set with a List instance variable }
class Set implementation

    instance variables
        elements: List;
    end instance variables

    { return the number of elements in the receiver }
    instance method size() return integer;
    begin
        return elements.size()
    end

    { delete the argument from the receiver }
    instance method delete(elem: ElemType);
    begin
        elements.delete(elem)
    end

    { insert the argument in the receiver }
    instance method insert(newElem: ElemType);
    begin
        if not elements.isElement(newElem)
            elements.insertAtFront(newElem)
    end

    { ... other Set methods ... }

end class Set implementation
```

Whether we use inheritance or composition, we must write methods for Set-specific operations such as union(Set).

In general, subclassing can inherit useful behavior, and therefore often requires less coding. On the other hand, composition is appropriate when the class used for implementation contains behavior that should not be present in the new class's protocol. Composition also hides the implementation of the Set as a List, so we can change the implementation without affecting clients. For example, defining the Set class with a list as an instance variable permits the designer of Set to maintain a sorted list, for example, to provide more efficient methods for the messages isElement, union, and intersection. For these reasons, we prefer using composition rather than inheritance to define the class Set based on the class List.

3.1.2 Restriction

In some cases, we regard a class as a specialization of another class conceptually, with some superclass message absent from its protocol. For example, we usually think of a square as a special type of rectangle that must have equal sides, rather than considering a rectangle a special kind of square that can also have unequal width and height. Similarly, most programmers would regard a queue as a special kind of list restricted to insertions at one end and deletions at the other, rather than considering a list to be a queue with the additional capability of searching for an element, inserting or deleting an element at any position, moving elements, and so on. We say that such a subclass is a *restriction* of its superclass.

We encode restrictive inheritance by overriding the disallowed superclass methods to produce error messages or signal exceptions in the subclass. You might think that in a language such as C++ that provides access control for class components, we could simply redefine those messages as private in the subclass. However, remember that a superclass identifier can also refer to an instance of the subclass without the compiler's knowledge, and the compiler enforces access control. If the disallowed message is sent to this identifier, the compiler allows the message and the subclass method will be selected by the dynamic binding process. Therefore, the disallowed messages must be overridden to signal an error.

Subclassing for restriction runs counter to the semantics and intention of inheritance because an instance of a subclass is an instance of the superclass, and should be able to behave like one. However, if an instance of a restrictive subclass is substituted for a superclass instance in a method that sends it a disallowed message, an error will occur that the client does not expect. (This is also a problem for inheritance of implementation.) For example, suppose Queue is defined as a subclass of List. It is invalid to send the message isElement to a List identifier that refers to an instance of the subclass Queue. Due to the inconsistency between the subclass and the superclass, subclassing for restriction often results in programs that are difficult to understand and maintain, particularly when the technique is used in a large class inheritance structure with classes below and above those involved. However, subclassing for restriction may be necessary when using an existing class hierarchy that cannot be modified.

We sometimes find that two classes have some functionality in common, but neither is a subclass of the other because each also has class-specific behavior. That is, their protocols intersect, but neither wholly includes the other. The designer might consider putting the common behavior in one class together with its own specific behavior, and then defining the other class as a restrictive subclass of the first. The subclass would override the superclass-specific messages to signal an error, and add its own specific behavior. We prefer using an abstract superclass containing the shared functionality for such a case, as described in section 3.3.2.

3.1.3 Class Hierarchy Structure

For the moment, we will assume that each class has at most one superclass, which is termed *single inheritance*. It is conventional to diagram the inheritance relationship among a set of classes as a tree or a forest with superclasses as parents of subclasses. This inheritance graph is called the *class hierarchy*, and it reflects the overall structure of the classes for a problem domain, system, or application. We use the terms "ancestors", "descendants", and "siblings" of a class in the hierarchy with the usual meanings for trees. We will often need to distinguish between a "direct" superclass of a class in the hierarchy and an arbitrary ancestor, so we will reserve the term "superclass" for the superclass given in a class's definition (and similarly for "subclass" and "descendant"). (Many authors use the term "superclass" to refer to any ancestor of a class.) We will use the term "subhierarchy" to refer to the portion of the class hierarchy rooted at a class (like the term "subtree"). For example, Figure 3.1 gives a portion of the inheritance hierarchy for a small business. The arcs that represent the inheritance relationship lead from the subclass to the superclass because a subclass must be aware of its superclass, since it inherits behavior and state from it. On the other hand, the superclass is unaffected by the existence of subclasses.[1] In addition, there is no direct relationship between classes that have a common ancestor. Clearly, there cannot be cycles in the class hierarchy graph.

   In some languages, especially those with a standard class library such as Smalltalk, Eiffel, and Java, there is a root class that specifies functionality provided for every object (Object for Smalltalk and Java, and ANY for Eiffel). In this case, the entire class hierarchy is a tree. Any class that the programmer creates must be defined as a subclass of an existing class, the root class if no other applies. In other languages, such as C++, we can define a class without specifying a superclass, so the class hierarchy is a forest.

   In languages that support *multiple inheritance*, a class may have more than one superclass, in which case it inherits behavior and state from all of those classes. This structure frequently mirrors the category relationships in problem domains (e.g., a bomber has the characteristics of both jets and military equipment). With multiple inheritance, the class hierarchy has the structure of a directed acyclic graph. Some special considerations occur with multiple inheritance, which we will discuss in sections 3.4 and 12.4.

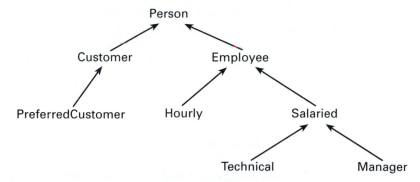

Figure 3.1   An example class hierarchy.

---

[1] We will see in section 12.2 that C++ programmers usually represent instances of classes that do not have subclasses differently from those that do.

3.1.4 Developing the Class Hierarchy

The identification of classes and the class hierarchy structure for an application is often the most difficult task in object-oriented development. The result of this process defines a model of the classification taxonomy of the problem domain or the structure of the software system. A very large application can have hundreds of classes, and there is rarely an obvious or perfectly correct class hierarchy for such a large system.

The designer will have determined portions of the domain class hierarchy during the analysis activities that discover the relevant classes, protocols, and attributes. The process of developing the class hierarchy may proceed in a top-down fashion, in which higher-level abstractions are designed first and then specializations of those classes are created. Alternatively, the class hierarchy may be derived in a bottom-up fashion as commonalities of behavior and state between existing classes are recognized and encapsulated as superclasses. In practice, both techniques usually enter into the design process. Experience shows that we develop the class hierarchy through an incremental and iterative process, which often continues into the maintenance stage after the application is delivered. If an appropriate domain or application framework is available, it may provide much of the structure necessary, and the designer can define additional classes as subclasses of those classes.

Throughout the process of development, the designer may coalesce or split existing classes, derive new classes, or reorganize the class hierarchy as understanding of the problem domain and system requirements grows. For example, if a message is not applicable for some of the objects in a class, the designer can create a subclass that represents those objects for which it is appropriate. A group of classes that have similar responsibilities or interact with other parts of the system in the same way (i.e., that have a common interface) presents a candidate for a superclass of those classes. This reduces coupling by centralizing references to that group of classes, reducing the number of interactions between those classes and other parts of the system. To aid in recognizing this situation, the designer should use the same name for messages that perform conceptually similar services. In general, we attempt to position protocol and state information at the highest appropriate level in the hierarchy. As scenarios are considered and the hierarchy is developed, the designer adds new methods or overrides methods in superclasses. He or she rarely removes a behavior from a class, except to relocate it elsewhere in the class hierarchy.

Sometimes an existing class contains most of the behavior required, and we must choose between creating a new subclass and modifying the existing class. The latter is not possible when other programs use that class, although they may benefit from some changes, such as a more efficient implementation. On the other hand, if several programmers working on a system each create new classes whenever additional behavior is required, documenting and maintaining the class hierarchy can become complicated.

When programmers first begin using an object-oriented language, they often tend to overuse inheritance. For example, we may have a class for a PushButton user interface component, and need several buttons in the application, say "load", "save," and "quit". In this case, it is not necessary to define three subclasses for the three buttons. We may use a single class with three instances, each of which has different values for the instance variables that maintain the label on the button, its location in the interface, and the action invoked when the user activates the button. In addition, you should not use subclasses to represent dynamic states or conditions of an object because the class of an object does not change. For example, in a library application, we should use an attribute location for the class Book, rather than subclasses such as BookOnShelf and BookCheckedOut.

3.1.5 Polymorphism

Object polymorphism

With inheritance, an instance of a subclass is also an instance of its superclass. Such an object is polymorphic, that is, it has more than one type, because it is an instance of the class of which it is defined, and is also an instance of each of that class's ancestors in the class hierarchy. For example, an instance of the class Manager in Figure 3.1 is also an instance of the classes Salaried, Employee, and Person, and, therefore, can be bound to an identifier whose type is any of those four classes. This property reflects the semantics of inheritance in which a subclass is a specialization of its superclass, responding to the protocol of its ancestors and containing the state information of its ancestors. Object polymorphism occurs in any language that supports inheritance, whether it is statically or dynamically typed.

Inclusion polymorphism

Object polymorphism implies that we should be able to use an object in any context in which an instance of any of its class's ancestors can occur. That is, inheritance results in inclusion polymorphism for methods whose receiver or arguments are of types that have subclasses. These methods can function correctly using receivers or arguments that are instances of either the superclass or one of its descendants since descendant instances can respond to the superclass messages sent by the method. For example, we can pass an instance of either Hourly or Salaried to a method that has a parameter of type Employee. This characteristic supports generic programming in which the programmer deals with higher-level abstractions, and permits more extensive reuse of that code.

Identifier polymorphism for statically typed languages

As stated in section 2.3.2, inheritance provides identifier polymorphism for object-oriented languages that employ static typing. Since an object is also an instance of its class and that class's ancestors, an identifier is permitted to refer to an instance of the identifier's class or any of that class's descendants. For example, a Person identifier can refer to an instance of Customer, Employee, etc. In this case, the class declared for an identifier can differ from the class of its actual referent, which must be a descendant of the identifier's class. This has a number of implications in languages with inheritance and static typing, such as the validity of assignments or conversions from an ancestor class identifier to a descendant class identifier, and whether the programmer can determine the actual class of the referent of an ancestor class identifier. We will examine these issues in detail in the context of C++ in section 12.2.

Since inheritance provides identifier polymorphism for statically typed languages, it enables dynamic binding, with the implications we described in section 2.4.3. A message may be redefined differently in various descendants of a class. With dynamic binding, when a message is passed to a variable of that type, the method executed depends on the class of the instance bound to the identifier at the time of invocation.[2]

Static typing and inheritance also provides a limited form of heterogeneity for collection classes. We can create a collection of elements of a given type, and insert instances of any of that type's descendants since the element identifier can refer to them. For example, a list of customers can contain instance of both Customer and PreferredCustomer. Dynamic binding of messages passed to the elements produces the correct class-specific behavior.

3.2 SUBCLASS DEFINITION

3.2.1 Purpose and Meaning

The definition of a subclass gives

- an interface consisting of the subclass name, the name of the superclass from which it inherits, and additional instance and class messages
- an implementation consisting of additional instance and class variables, methods for the additional instance and class messages, and overridings of inherited instance and class methods.

We often say that the subclass is *derived* from its superclass. A subclass definition specifies that the subclass's instances are the same as those of its superclass, except in ways that it explicitly states. In particular, the subclass inherits the messages, instance variables, and methods of its superclass, and also those of its ancestors. By this, we mean that its instances respond to superclass messages and contain the superclass instance variables, without repeating them in the subclass definition. For example, the class Person in Figure 3.1 might include a message age whose method calculates the difference between the receiver's dateOfBirth instance variable value and the current date. This method is automatically available in all seven classes in

---

[2] We will see that static binding is also provided in some such languages.

that subhierarchy (and any further classes derived from them) because those classes are defined as descendants of Person.

Since a subclass definition may add class components to provide subclass-specific semantics, the set of behaviors and data associated with a subclass is equal to or larger than that of its superclass (which may cause some confusion with the terms "subclass" and "superclass"). However, there are fewer instances of the subclass than of the superclass because every subclass object is also an instance of the superclass, that is, the subclass instances are a subset of the superclass instances.

3.2.2 Interface

A subclass frequently adds protocol specific to the abstraction that it models. The interface of the subclass specifies these messages (which are not in the protocol of the superclass), and the superclass. As a result, instances of the subclass will respond to messages not understood by instances of the superclass. For example, an instance of the class Employee will respond to a message asking which department that entity works in. Instances of Person and its other descendants do not respond to that message, but instances of all descendants of Employee do. A subclass also inherits the class messages of its superclass in the sense that these messages can be sent to the subclass. A subclass may also define additional class messages.

For example, consider a class List that represents an ordered (but not necessarily sorted) variable-length list of elements. The class has the following protocol (we use ElemType as the type of list elements):

```
{ A class for lists of elements of type ElemType }
class List interface

    class protocol
        { the new object is initially empty }
        new() return List;
    end class protocol

    instance protocol
        { return the number of elements in the receiver }
        size() return integer;
        { is the argument an element of the receiver? }
        isElement(argElem: ElemType) return boolean;
        { return the indexth element of the receiver }
        [ ](index: integer) return ElemType;
        { insert the argument as first element of the receiver }
        insertAtFront(argElem: ElemType);
        { insert the first argument after the second in the receiver }
        insertAfter(newElem, oldElem: ElemType);
        { delete the first occurrence of the argument from the receiver }
        delete(argElem: ElemType);
        { return the successor of the argument in the receiver }
        successor(argElem: ElemType) return ElemType;
```

```
            { Is the argument equal to the receiver? }
            =(argList: List) return boolean;
            { Is the argument a sublist of the receiver? }
            isSublist(argList: List) return boolean;
            { append the argument list at the end of the receiver }
            append(argList: List);
            { ... other List messages ... }
        end instance protocol

    end class List interface
```

Now, let us define a subclass of List called PositionableList that also maintains a reference to a particular element, and provides protocol for moving the position reference in the list and accessing elements relative to it. In defining its interface, we give List as its superclass and only describe the additional information necessary for the subclass. We define the subclass's interface as follows:

```
    { A class for positionable lists of elements of type ElemType }
    class PositionableList interface
        superclass List;

        class protocol
            { the new object is initially empty, with its position "at end" }
            new() return PositionableList;
        end class protocol

        { additional protocol besides that inherited from the superclass List}
        instance protocol
            { set the position reference to first element }
            reset();
            { move the position reference forward }
            advance();
            {is the position reference invalid, i.e. beyond the last element?}
            atEnd() return boolean;
            { return the element at the position reference }
            current() return ElemType;
            { insert the element after the position reference }
            insertAfter(newElem: ElemType);
        end instance protocol

    end class PositionableList interface
```

The declaration of the superclass in a class interface (superclass List, in the example) is similar to an import declaration in a language that supports modules. It makes the superclass interface available in the subclass interface. However, it also makes the superclass implementation available in the subclass implementation. The definition of PositionableList does not restate the protocol of List, but those messages are available to its instances because PositionableList declares List as its superclass. We overload the message insertAfter in the sub-class with a one-argument version that inserts the new element after the position reference.[3]

To define the implementation of PositionableList, we specify

- the instance variable that maintains the position reference, for example, an index for an array implementation or a pointer for a linked list
- the methods for the new messages, including the overloading of insertAfter
- the refinement of the List method for delete that deals with the position reference if it refers to the deleted element (we will code this method in section 3.2.4)

The implementation of PositionableList need not restate specification of the list storage structure and the methods inherited from List.

3.2.3 Implementation

Additional instance and class variables

A subclass definition may augment the structure of its superclass by defining state information relevant to the specialization that it represents. The subclass definition only specifies the additional instance variables, and the subclass inherits the instance variables of its superclass (and ancestors) implicitly. The instance variables are defined in the same manner as for class definitions, with types for a statically typed language (and access specifications in C++ and Java). Instances of the subclass have values for the instance variables defined in all its ancestors as well as the subclass-specific instance variables, so they are larger than instances of the superclass. The types and access specifications given in the ancestor apply to the inherited instance variables in subclass instances.

For example, suppose the classes in Figure 3.1 define the following instance variables:[4]

- Person defines name, address, dateOfBirth, socSecNo
- Employee adds employeeID, department, vacationDays
- Customer adds orders, creditLimit and balanceDue
- Hourly adds payRate and overtime
- Salaried adds payRate (which is interpreted as a monthly salary)
- Manager adds subordinates, level and perquisites

Because inheritance is transitive, instances of Manager have values for all the instance variables of Person, Employee, Salaried, and Manager, although the definition of the class Manager only specifies the last of these.

---

[3] In some languages, the subclass must also redeclare the superclass argument signature.

[4] We will ignore the types of the instance variables since they are not important to the point of this example.

Now consider how we would define the structure of these classes in a traditional language such as Pascal or C. To permit a variable to refer to any Person object (e.g., for a list of people), we would define a Person record that includes a variant part for each of the possible substructures that could occur (and type tags for identifying the variant parts).[5] To allow an Employee variable, we would define an Employee variant record that would be used as a variant in the Person record, and so on. This scheme would be complex and error-prone to code, especially for a hierarchy with several levels. Many subprograms that use instances of the types would require case structures as illustrated in section 2.4.3, which would be nested as deep as the number of levels in the hierarchy. In addition, each instance of any of the types in the "hierarchy" of variant record types would be allocated storage for the largest possible variant at that level. Even worse, if we discover a new variant during analysis or require a new variant for enhancement of the system, we must rewrite all the type definitions and all the subprograms that include case structures.

Subclass methods can access class variables defined in the superclass, but they are not inherited in the sense of the subclass having its own values for those variables. There is exactly one instance of each class variable, so if a subclass method changes the value of a class variable defined in its superclass, that variable's value is changed for the superclass and all its descendants and their instances. If some classwide information requires a subclass-specific value, then each subclass must have its own class variable that maintains that class's value. Clients access the information with a class message, which each class overrides with a method that returns its value. A subclass may define additional class variables, and those class variables are accessible within its class and instance methods.

Instance and class methods

The subclass must define methods for its additional protocol, and subclass methods are coded in the same manner as any methods. The method can access an inherited instance variable directly without component selection (except for private inherited instance variables in C++ and Java), and that identifier refers to that variable in the receiver, just like accessing an instance variable defined by the subclass.

A subclass definition may also *override* inherited methods with subclass-specific behavior by defining a subclass-specific method for that message. In this case, subclass instances respond to such a message with behavior that differs from that of superclass instances. With method overriding, the behavior of the subclass is not strictly a superset of the behavior of the superclass (although its protocol is). Method overriding results in polymorphism because such a message has several meanings, depending on the class of the receiver. To override a superclass method,

---

[5] As mentioned in section 2.4.4, we would use a struct containing a union of structs as a member in C. The process of creating a hierarchy of type described here would involve unions with unions as members but would be essentially the same.

a subclass can either replace it with subclass-specific behavior, or "refine" it by defining a method that also includes the behavior of the superclass. We will discuss method binding and method overriding in the next section.

Storage structure

To illustrate the structures that are stored in memory at execution time, we will diagram the representation of an object as a sequence of the representations of its instance variables, together with a class reference to a structure that represents the class.[6] Conceptually, this class structure (i.e., the type object for the class) maintains the class variables and the instance methods for the class, and possibly information such as instance variable names and types. It also contains a pointer to the structure representing its superclass, which is used by the method binding process, as described in the next section. In practice, the compiler for a statically typed language can avoid representing some of this information explicitly (see section 12.3.5). Figure 3.2 diagrams the state of instances of some of the classes in the hierarchy in Figure 3.1 and the corresponding class structures. As Figure 3.2 illustrates, an object contains all the state information defined by its class and its class's ancestors. In fact, it is often useful to think of an object as having an anonymous instance of each ancestor embedded within it. This embedded ancestor object provides the receiver necessary for performing inherited methods. Note that there is no direct relationship between instances of classes that are related hierarchically.

3.2.4 Method Overriding

Method binding with inheritance

We can think of the method binding process that implements inheritance of behavior as performing the following procedure: When a message is sent, the receiver's class object is found via its class pointer (see Figure 3.2), and its protocol is searched for a matching message. If none is found, the superclass object is accessed via the superclass pointer in the receiver's class object and its protocol is searched, and so on up the class hierarchy until that message is found. When the message is found, the associated method is executed. If at some point the message is not found in a class that has no superclass, an error is signaled because the receiver has no method for that message.

This mechanism allows us to code and debug an operation once, then use it in many other classes (i.e., in the descendants of the class containing the method). This sharing of functionality takes advantage of the redundancy in the problem domain, and reduces the amount of code necessary to create an application. This method binding process also allows a subclass's response to a particular message to differ from its superclass's without conflict. If a class's method for a particular message

---

[6] We will see in section 12.3.5 that C++ does not include this class pointer in objects whose classes have no messages that require dynamic binding.

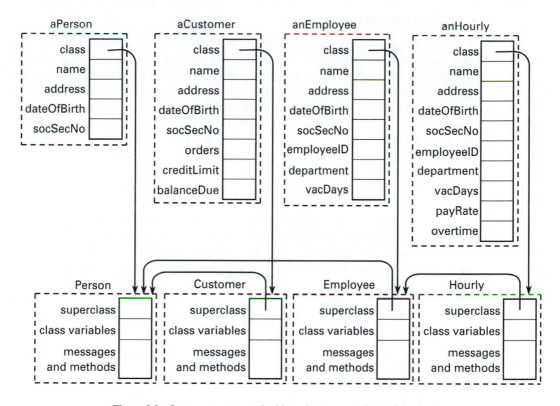

Figure 3.2   Storage structure of sublcass instances and class information.

overrides that of its superclass, the method binding process will encounter the class's method first when one of its instances receives that message. The concept is similar to identifier scope in block structured languages in the sense that the subclass method hides the superclass method.

For example, the class Hourly in Figure 3.1 can define a method for weeklyPay that calculates the pay amount from the payRate and the number of hours worked. This provides a default method for any descendants that do not need special processing. Now suppose that we need to define a new subclass UnionHourly, with the union dues for its instances deducted directly from the pay amount. We would define this method in the class UnionHourly. When a union hourly object receives the message weeklyPay, it uses the new method, but instances of Hourly or its other descendants will use the method in Hourly.

The disadvantage of the method binding process is its cost in terms of space and time. We will see in section 12.3.5 that the compiler in a statically typed language can use the class hierarchy relationships, the class of the identifier, and the methods present in the hierarchy to reduce the amount of information stored, avoid performing a search of the class object and the ancestors of receiver's class, and recognize invalid messages.

Method replacement

A subclass can completely redefine the behavior of its superclass for a particular message by specifying a method for that message. With this form of method overriding, we say that the method in the subclass *replaces* the method in the superclass. Replacing a superclass method generally occurs because the subclass can define a more efficient method that takes advantage of its storage structure, or because a restrictive subclass must disallow the message. In a statically typed language, the method must have the same argument signature as the superclass message. Some languages require an indication of method replacement in the subclass definition. For example, Object Pascal and early versions of C++ use the reserved word override in the subclass definition, and Eiffel specifies a method replacement with the redefine clause.

Method replacement is useful for modeling the behavior of exceptions to the rule (e.g., ostriches are birds that don't fly). For example, in Smalltalk the system class Number is the superclass of all the numeric classes such as Integer, Fraction, and Float. The class Number defines a method for the message sqrt (the receiver's square root) that sends the receiver the conversion message asFloat and then sends sqrt to the Float object that results, which is inherited by each numeric subclass. The exception is the class Float, which overrides this general behavior with a method that performs the square root computation directly.

Method refinement

More frequently, the semantics of a subclass demand that the subclass respond to a message by a method that includes the behavior of its superclass, but extends it in some way. In this case, we say that the subclass method *refines* the superclass method. For example, a print method can invoke the superclass method to print the inherited instance variables, and then perform additional output for the subclass-specific instance variables. Method refinement is more common than method replacement because it provides semantics consistent with specialization.

We could refine methods by copying the relevant superclass method statements into the subclass method. However, we would like the language to provide a mechanism that supports automatic sharing of the superclass method code, so that reuse of that code is error-free and improvements to that code are propagated to descendants. Note that in method refinement, both the subclass and superclass messages have the same name. In addition, we must send the message that invokes the superclass method to the original receiver whose method is being coded (that is, the processing must be performed by the subclass instance using its own instance variables). However, if the message is sent to self in the subclass method, the translator will interpret that invocation as a recursive call of the subclass method, as follows:

```
{ An unsuccessful attempt to refine the Person method for print }
class Employee implementation
```

```
instance method print()
begin
   { we want to invoke the Person print method for the receiver }
   self.print();        { appears to the compiler like a recursive call }
   { ... print Employee-specific information ... }
end

   { ... other Employee methods and variables ... }

end class Employee implementation
```

Because of these considerations, object-oriented languages need a special syntactic construct to specify invocation of the superclass method with the receiver of the method in which it occurs as the receiver. Such an invocation is meaningful because the subclass receiver does contain values for all the superclass instance variables (the method provides inclusion polymorphism). However, this operation should not be available to clients because it only performs part of the processing necessary for the subclass instance to respond correctly to the message.

In Smalltalk, the programmer uses the pseudo-variable super as the receiver of a message send to designate method refinement. This feature specifies that the method to invoke is that defined for the superclass of the class in which the method is defined (i.e., the search for a matching method begins in the superclass and continues up the class hierarchy if necessary). The actual receiver of the message is the original receiver (not some other superclass object), and its instance variables are used in the operations the method performs. Such semantics allow refinement of any method in the superclass's protocol, even those that are inherited. The keyword inherited in Object Pascal operates in the same fashion.

For example, recall the class PositionableList described in section 3.2.2. Suppose we decide that if the element at the position reference is deleted, the method should set the position to the deleted element's successor, so that the position reference is still valid. Suppose that List defines a private method internalFind that returns the position of the argument in the receiver (i.e., a pointer for a linked implementation or an index for a sequential implementation). We can then code the method for delete in PositionableList as follows:

```
{ instance method in class PositionableList that refines the method in the superclass List }
class PositionableList implementation

   instance method delete(elem: ElemType);
   begin
      if self.internalFind(elem) = position then
         self.advance();
      super.delete(elem);
   end
```

{ ... *other PositionableList methods and variables* ... }

end class PositionableList implementation

That is, if the element to be deleted is at the position reference, then advance the position to its successor and delete the element using the method defined in the superclass. The notation super.*message* indicates that the method to execute is the one in effect for the superclass (i.e., that it is not a recursive invocation), but that self is the receiver.

Other object-oriented languages use a variety of syntactic constructs to indicate method refinement. In C++, the programmer uses the scope operator :: and names the ancestor whose method is invoked explicitly, as in the expression List::delete(elem). Using an ancestor class name is necessary with multiple inheritance. In Eiffel, superclass messages may be renamed for use within a subclass. For example, the definition of PositionableList might contain the clause inherit List rename delete as listDelete, which gives the class's superclass and renames one of that superclass's messages. PositionableList's method for delete would then use the message Current.listDelete to invoke the superclass method with the receiver as its receiver. In Simula67, all overriding is refinement and the subclass-specific code is inserted in the superclass code at the point at which an inner statement appears in the superclass code. The CLOS programmer can give the subclass-specific processing as a :before or :after method for the generic function (i.e., this example is a :before method), or can define the subclass method as an :around method that invokes the superclass method with call-next-method.

Semantic consistency

When overriding a method, you should be careful not to alter the intention of the message in the superclass, because this would violate the specialization relationship between the two classes. That is, any method that expects an instance of the superclass should be able to work correctly if an instance of the subclass is passed to it, and should not need to know that the object is actually a subclass object. (As we saw in section 3.1.2, this principle does not hold with restrictive subclassing.) Unfortunately, in practice, programmers are not always so meticulous.

Semantic consistency between subclasses and superclasses is an issue both for understanding the class and its use, and for program verification. Clearly, it is more complicated to use a class and to comprehend code that uses it if clients have to be aware of differences in behavior among its subclasses. Semantic consistency is necessary for program specification and verification so that reasoning about contexts in which superclass instances can occur is still valid if a subclass instance is substituted. This is the minimum condition for maintaining the integrity of the superclass type and the specialization relationship. Strictly speaking, the subclass method should affect the embedded superclass part of the receiver in the same manner as the superclass method.

Few programming languages enforce semantic consistency for subclass methods, so it is the programmer's responsibility to be aware of this issue. The language Eiffel includes facilities for specifying preconditions and postconditions for a message, which must also be satisfied when that message is overridden in a subclass. The language system allows the programmer to set a translator option so that the compiler includes code in the executable that checks these assertions and signals an exception if they are violated.

3.3 ABSTRACT CLASSES

3.3.1 Encapsulation of Interface

As we discussed in section 2.4.3, dynamic binding allows us to write generic code because a method can send a message to an object without knowing its class. Inheritance facilitates this process because a superclass encapsulates a common interface for a set of classes. The designer can deal with the abstraction that the superclass represents and ignore the details of its descendants by writing code that interfaces with instances of the descendants through the common protocol defined in the superclass. This allows him or her to think of the behavior of the system at a higher level of abstraction than that of the individual classes.

For example, we described a class DisplayObject in section 2.4.3 that is the superclass for a set of classes representing objects that can be drawn on a canvas, such as Line, Rectangle, Circle, Star, and Text. In addition to the message draw, this class would include protocol such as erase, moveTo, rotate, and resize. We can view the class DisplayObject as a port through which the rest of the system can communicate with various displayable objects, as illustrated in Figure 3.3. This use of superclasses also facilitates development and maintenance because we can add descendants with the same interface (e.g., Polygon or Spiral) without affecting the existing system. The manner in which the new class interacts with the rest of the application is already specified by the DisplayObject protocol, and neither the superclass nor the code that sends messages to instances of its descendants requires mod-

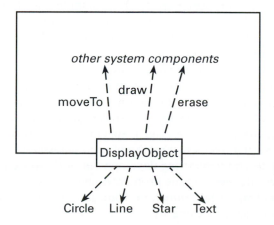

Figure 3.3 The interface of DisplayObject as a port to its subclasses. (Arrow indicate message passing).

ification. This characteristic supports extendibility, incremental development, and design by prototyping.

3.3.2 Definition and Purpose

Although the class DisplayObject is a useful construct as an encapsulation of an interface, it is rather peculiar as a type, because it is not clear what it would mean for an object to be an instance of that class, but not one of its descendants. In particular, we do not know how to represent such an object or how to draw it. As we will see in the next section, this class defines other parts of its protocol in terms of the draw message, but does not define that message or give a complete specification for the state of an instance.

A class that provides a common protocol for a set of descendants, but whose implementation is incomplete, is called an *abstract class*. It is abstract in the sense that it cannot be instantiated because its behavior and state are not completely defined. For this reason, an abstract class is not a type in the usual sense. Its purpose is to be used as a superclass from which we derive *concrete*, that is, instantiatable, descendants. Such a descendant is a realization of the partial specification given by the definition of the abstract class, rather than a specialization that extends a complete class definition.

An abstract class defines a protocol and implements some portion of that interface, but leaves other operations to be specified by its descendants. That is, the interface of the class includes *abstract messages* such as draw for DisplayObject for which it cannot define a method, and which are intended to be overridden by methods in concrete descendants. Abstract messages are also referred to as "deferred methods" in Eiffel because implementation of the method is deferred to concrete descendants. In addition, an abstract class often does not provide a complete definition of the state information of the category of objects it represents, again leaving the details to be completed by descendant class definitions.

You can also think of an abstract class as describing a set of objects such that its descendants form a partition of those objects. For example, the class Employee introduced in section 3.1.3 is likely to be an abstract class because each employee must be an instance of either Hourly or Salaried. Even though it has no direct instances, the class Employee is still a useful abstraction because it represents an important category in the problem domain, and centralizes definition of the behavior and state relevant for all employees. It includes instance variables for an instance's employeeID and department, and defines messages for accessing that information. Its protocol includes the message weeklyPay, although it cannot define a method for this operation itself. This message is specified as abstract, which indicates that its descendants must implement a method for that message, including any new descendants that are determined during development of the system. Abstract classes provide a more accurate model of the problem domain because we often find general categories such as Employee, Animal, or Transaction whose instances are always an instance of a more specific category.

An abstract class can also have descendants that are abstract. For example, we might have an abstract class IODevice that encapsulates behavior and state for input/output devices. It might have concrete subclasses such as Screen and Keyboard, and abstract subclasses such as Printer and File. Printer would have concrete subclasses for different kinds of printers, and File would have concrete subclasses such as Directory, TextFile, and ExecutableFile. In this case, the abstract descendant only specifies methods for some of the abstract messages, and its concrete descendants complete the specification for their instance's behavior.

The abstract class feature is important for statically typed object-oriented languages. It supplies a type clients can use to declare an identifier that can be bound to an instance of any of the concrete descendants. For example, we can declare a variable, parameter, or instance variable of type DisplayObject or Employee. The abstract class type indicates to the compiler that the identifier's referent can accept the messages in the common protocol, even though no method is defined in the abstract class. The appropriate behavior of the actual receiver of the message is invoked via dynamic method binding.

Abstract classes are also useful when two or more classes share behavior, but are not directly related as specializations of one another. We create an abstract class that describes the shared behavior only, and then define each of the other classes as a subclass that implements its own class-specific behavior. The shared behavior is then centrally defined, any changes or improvements are shared automatically, and that behavior is available for other subclasses if necessary.

To support abstract classes, an object-oriented language must have a syntactic feature for specifying that a message is in a class's protocol, but has a deferred method. This is necessary so that the compiler can distinguish an abstract message from a situation in which the programmer has forgotten to define a method. Note that deferring a method is not the same as defining a method that does nothing. For a class with abstract messages, the compiler can ensure that the class is not instantiated, and that descendants do define behavior for the abstract messages, unless they are also intended to be abstract. An abstract message is indicated in C++ by the "pure virtual function" initializer (see section 12.3.1), and in Eiffel as a deferred feature. In Smalltalk, we code the method for an abstract message as sending the receiver subclassResponsibility, whose method signals an error when an instance of the class that was intended to be abstract receives that message (see section 6.2.3).

3.3.3 Example Abstract Classes

The class Orderable

As a simple example of an abstract class, consider a class Orderable that represents objects for which a linear ordering is meaningful.[7] The protocol of this class includes

---

[7] This class is included in the Smalltalk class library as the class Magnitude.

- comparison operator messages =, ≠, <, <=, >, and >=
- min and max, which return the minimum and maximum of the receiver and argument, respectively
- between, which returns true if the receiver is between its two arguments in the ordering.

We can implement the methods for each of these messages in terms of the messages < and = in Orderable. However, the messages < and = are abstract because their definitions are specific to the meaning of the ordering in the concrete subclass. In this way, we can define a class for which an ordering is appropriate as a subclass of Orderable, provide methods for the two abstract messages, and then inherit the methods for the other messages. In the examples in this section, we use the keyword abstract in the declaration of a message to indicate an abstract message (and also in the class declaration as a reminder). Clearly, the existence of abstract messages is part of the interface of a class. We can define the class Orderable as follows:

```
{ an abstract class for linearly orderable objects }
abstract class Orderable interface

    class protocol
        { Orderable cannot be instantiated }
        new() return Orderable; abstract;
    end class protocol

    instance protocol
        { is the receiver equal to the argument? }
        =(arg: Orderable) return boolean; abstract;
        { is the receiver less than the argument? }
        <(arg: Orderable) return boolean; abstract;
        { is the receiver unequal to the argument? }
        ≠(arg: Orderable) return boolean;
        { is the receiver less than or equal to the argument? }
        <=(arg: Orderable) return boolean;
        { is the receiver greater than the argument? }
        >(arg: Orderable) return boolean;
        { is the receiver greater than or equal to the argument? }
        >=(arg: Orderable) return boolean;
        { return the minimum of the receiver and argument }
        min(arg: Orderable) return Orderable;
        { return the maximum of the receiver and argument }
        max(arg: Orderable) return Orderable;
        { is the receiver between the arguments, inclusive? }
        between(low: Orderable, high: Orderable) return boolean;
    end instance protocol

end class Orderable interface
```

For example, we define the methods for the messages between and min as follows:

```
{ instance methods for class Orderable that send abstract messages }
class Orderable implementation

    { return the minimum of the receiver and argument }
    instance method min(arg: Orderable) return Orderable;
    begin
       if arg < self then
           return arg
       else
           return self
    end

    { is the receiver between the arguments, inclusive? }
    instance method between(low: Orderable, high: Orderable) return Boolean;
    begin
       if low <= self and self <= high then
          return true
       else
          return false
    end

    { ... other Orderable methods ... }

end class Orderable implementation
```

The other Orderable methods would be defined in a similar fashion.

A somewhat surprising characteristic of this class is that it defines no instance variables. Each concrete subclass would provide these, and would use them in defining its methods for < and =. For example, a subclass String might define a list of characters as an instance variable and use ASCII ordering for <, or a subclass Employee might order instances according to employee IDs or social security numbers.

The class DisplayObject

Consider again the abstract class DisplayObject, with subclasses such as Line, Rectangle, Circle, Star, and Text. The class DisplayObject defines the methods and instance variables that are common to all the subclasses. This includes methods for center, color, setColor, erase, and moveTo, and the instance variables center, color, where, and visible (like the class Square in section 2.2.4). We cannot define a method for draw in DisplayObject because it is specific to each subclass, but we specify that message in DisplayObject's protocol. Each subclass adds its own instance variables—such as radius and numPoints for Star, height and width for Rectangle, and string and font for Text—and codes methods for the abstract messages in terms of them. We code the interface of DisplayObject as follows:

```
{ an abstract class for displayable objects }
abstract class DisplayObject interface
```

```
class protocol of DisplayObject
   { DisplayObject cannot be instantiated }
   new() return DisplayObject; abstract;
end class protocol

instance protocol
   { draw the receiver on the argument canvas }
   draw(canvas: Canvas); abstract;
   { erase the receiver }
   erase();
   { return the center of the receiver }
   center() return Point;
   { return the color of the receiver }
   color() return Color;
   { set the receiver's color to the argument and redraw the receiver }
   setColor(newColor: Color);
   { move the receiver so that its center is the argument and redraw the receiver }
   moveTo(newCenter: Point);
   { rotate the receiver by the argument angle and redraw the receiver }
   rotate(amount: Angle); abstract;
   { resize the receiver by the argument scale factor and redraw the receiver }
   resize(amount: real); abstract;
end instance protocol

end class DisplayObject interface
```

We have declared the messages **rotate** and **resize** as abstract because their implementations depend on how the receiver is represented. We code the instance variables and accessor methods of DisplayObject as follows:

```
class DisplayObject implementation

   instance variables
      center: Point;          { the center of the receiver }
      color: Color;           { the color of the receiver }
      where: Canvas;          { the canvas the receiver is currently drawn on }
      visible: boolean;       { whether the receiver is currently drawn on any canvas }
   end instance variables

   { return the center of the receiver }
   instance method center() return Point;
   begin
      return center
   end

   { ... other DisplayObject methods ... }

end class DisplayObject implementation
```

Three kinds of methods are typically present in an abstract class. Some methods, such as draw, are deferred because they deal with behavior and information that can only be specified by descendants. Some methods, such as center and color, can be defined completely because they refer to information given in the abstract class, and need not be refined by descendants. In languages such as C++ and Java in which the class designer differentiates between messages that require dynamic binding and those that do not, these messages can be statically bound. Finally, some abstract class methods encode higher-level, generic algorithms that include details to be filled in by methods in the receiver's class that are invoked via messages sent to self. For example, we code the methods for erase and moveTo as follows: [8]

```
{ the methods erase and moveTo invoke the descendant method for draw }
class DisplayObject implementation

    { erase the receiver }
    instance method erase();
    var
        tempColor: Color;
    begin
        tempColor := color;
        color := where.backgroundColor();
        self.draw(where);
        color := tempColor;
        visible := false
    end

    { move the receiver so that its center is the argument and redraw the receiver }
    instance method moveTo(newCenter: Point);
    begin
        self.erase();
        center := newCenter;
        self.draw(where)
    end

    { ... other DisplayObject methods ... }

end class DisplayObject implementation
```

We implement the methods for erase and moveTo in terms of abstract messages passed to self, the actual receiver of the message at the time of invocation. Since method resolution begins in the class of the receiver for messages to self, these messages will invoke the draw method for the relevant descendant. moveTo also invokes the method for erase, which will be found in the ancestor of the receiver by the method binding process, and which invokes the receiver's draw method. For

---

[8] As in section 2.2.4, we ignore damage to other objects upon erasing or moving an object.

example, if we send the message moveTo to a rectangle, the following trace gives the methods executed with that object as the receiver:

the DisplayObject method for moveTo
   the DisplayObject method for erase (after searching in Rectangle)
      set the rectangle's color
       the Rectangle method for draw (since the search begins in Rectangle)
      set the rectangle's color and visible
   set the rectangle's center
   the Rectangle method for draw

To define a new class of display objects, we specify the class's instance variables and the deferred methods, but do not need to code erase and moveTo. The rest of DisplayObject's protocol and its interaction with the rest of the system will be available to the new class automatically. We will see several examples of this kind of reuse in the Smalltalk class library in Chapters 7 and 8.

   We can see from this example that the DisplayObject method for moveTo relies on the subclass method for draw to set visible back to true. Certainly, any draw method should do so because the object is now visible. The designer of an abstract class must clearly document the requirements for descendant methods for abstract messages. It would also be useful if the language allowed the programmer to define a default method for an abstract message that descendant methods must refine. In this case, that method for draw in DisplayObject would set visible to true.

3.4 MULTIPLE INHERITANCE

3.4.1 Basic Concepts

Purpose

   In describing the problem domain, we sometimes find that a class conceptually includes behavior from several unrelated classes—for example, a deer is a mammal, is a terrestrial animal, and is a herbivore. We can view these as a set of orthogonal classifications, each of which provides behavior that the class inherits. In other cases, a class blends functionality and state from more than one class. For example, the class HybridObjectOrientedLanguage inherits characteristics from both ObjectOrientedLanguage and ProceduralLanguage. A programming example is the class String, whose instances contain both behavior associated with lists (of characters in this case) and ordering behavior (e.g., an ASCII ordering).

   Languages such as C++, Eiffel, and CLOS that support *multiple inheritance* provide features and mechanisms for modeling such relationships. We can define a class with a set of superclasses, and the translator implements inheritance of the behavior and state of the superclasses in the subclass. Support for multiple inheritance is sometimes considered controversial because it complicates language features, compilation, and message resolution, and can be confusing and difficult to use correctly. However, it clearly adds expressive power to the language, and frequently matches the semantics of relationships in the problem domain.

Multiple inheritance allows the programmer to blend functionality from several superclasses to create a class. This encourages a programming style in which the designer defines a number of small abstract classes (often called "mixins") such as the class Orderable in the previous section, and then mixes them to create concrete classes with various capabilities. Another example mixin is a class Linkable that provides an instance variable that refers to another instance of that class, and protocol to access and set the link. This approach was a major motivation for the language Flavors [Moo86] (and for its name), a variant of Lisp that greatly influenced CLOS.

Example mixin classes include

- Orderable, which provides ordering messages
- Linkable, which provides an instance variable referring to another instance of its class, and protocol to access and set the link
- Storable, which defines protocol for savings instances to files and retreving them.

Inheriting behavior and state

In a language that supports multiple inheritance, a subclass definition may specify more than one superclass, and its instances inherit all the behavior and state of each superclass and its ancestors. The inherited protocol is the union of the protocols of the superclasses, and the subclass may add messages and override inherited methods. The method binding process is more complex because several chains of ancestors in the hierarchy must be searched to find the method for a message. Note that each individual object is still a direct instance of one particular class.

An instance of the subclass contains values for all the instance variables of all of its superclasses, so we can regard it as containing instances of each superclass and their ancestors embedded within it. As expected, the subclass may also add instance variables. In the storage layout illustrated in Figure 3.2, a particular instance variable has the same offset within instances of the class or any of its descendants. This relationship no longer holds with multiple inheritance because there may be other embedded superclass objects preceding the one that contains that variable within a descendant instance's representation.

Class hierarchy structure

Since a class can have more than one superclass with multiple inheritance, the inheritance hierarchy has the structure of a directed acyclic graph rather than a tree or forest. In this case, ambiguous or conflicting inheritance can occur. The two issues that must be dealt with are

- name conflicts between instance variables and messages inherited along different ancestor paths in the hierarchy
- situations in which one class is an ancestor of another class along more than one path in the inheritance hierarchy.

We will briefly describe these problems in the next two sections, and examine them in detail in the context of C++ in section 12.4.

Mimicking multiple inheritance

It is possible to code a problem domain analysis involving multiple inheritance in a language such as Smalltalk, Objective-C, or Object Pascal that only supports single inheritance. First, we must decide which superclass is the most "natural" one for a class with more than one superclass in the problem domain, and then use it as the class's superclass. A brute force technique would be to copy the code that defines the instance variables and methods from the other superclasses to the new class. However, this does not allow the new class to profit from modifications to those classes during debugging and maintenance.

A better approach is to define instance variables, each of which refers to an instance of the other "superclasses". That is, we use composition to simulate the other inheritance paths. The referent of such an instance variable does not exist conceptually as a separate entity in its own right, but is merely an implementation device that allows the subclass to represent that superclass's state information and use its behavior. It stores values for the instance variables that would have been inherited, and the subclass's methods use those values to implement that superclass's protocol. The subclass must include the superclasses' messages explicitly in its own protocol, and the corresponding methods pass those messages to the instance variable, possibly with other processing in the case of refinements. When the subclass is instantiated, its initialization must create the instance variable referents. Clearly, we must document this technique well so that the proper changes can be made if one of the superclasses is modified.

Unfortunately, when we use composition to simulate inheritance, the compiler in a statically typed language will not permit instances of the new class to appear in contexts that require an instance of one of the "simulated" superclasses. In some languages, such as C++, we can define conversions from the subclass to those classes that the compiler can use in these cases.

3.4.2 Name Ambiguity

With multiple inheritance, two or more ancestors of a class might have messages with the same name and argument signature, or instance variables with the same name and type. A language that supports multiple inheritance needs a construct for disambiguating an invocation of such a message or a use of such an instance variable within the class's methods. Note that with message names, this ambiguity extends to clients of the class.

As described in section 3.2.4 with respect to method refinement, the language Eiffel allows renaming superclass instance variables and messages within a subclass, so the class designer can rename conflicting inherited names uniquely within the subclass. In C++, if two ancestors along different paths in the hierarchy define the same message or instance variable name, a use of that name in the subclass is ambiguous. As we will see in section 12.4.2, subclass methods and clients must use a qualified name with the scope operator and the name of the desired ancestor to specify the intended instance variable or message.

3.4.3 Repeated Inheritance

Cases occur in which a class inherits from two superclasses that share a common ancestor, a relationship we refer to as *repeated inheritance*. For example, suppose that classes B1 and B2 are subclasses of A, and class C has superclasses B1 and B2, as illustrated in Figure 3.4. As we have described, the storage structure for instances of C contains the instance variables of both B1 and B2, as well as C-specific instance variables. In class C, it appears that there would be two copies of the instance variables of A, one in the embedded B1 object, and one in the embedded B2 object. That is, the object structure behaves as if A is repeated above both B1 and B2 in the inheritance hierarchy, rather than there being a single ancestor. If a method in class C refers to an instance variable in the receiver defined in class A, that use is ambiguous because the compiler cannot determine which embedded ancestor object is intended. In addition, an invocation of a message defined in A with a C receiver (either by a client or in a C method) is ambiguous even though there is one such message (and method), because it is not clear which embedded A object is the intended receiver.

In some cases, it is appropriate to have multiple instances of a repeated ancestor class object within a subclass object. For example, suppose we derive both the classes Customer and Employee from an abstract class Linkable so that we can maintain lists of each kind of object. Now, suppose that we derive a class CustomerEmployee representing an employee who is also a customer from those two classes. An instance of this class would need to include both types of links since it can be on both kinds of lists, as illustrated in Figure 3.5.

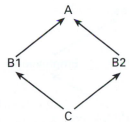

Figure 3.4   Repeated inheritance.

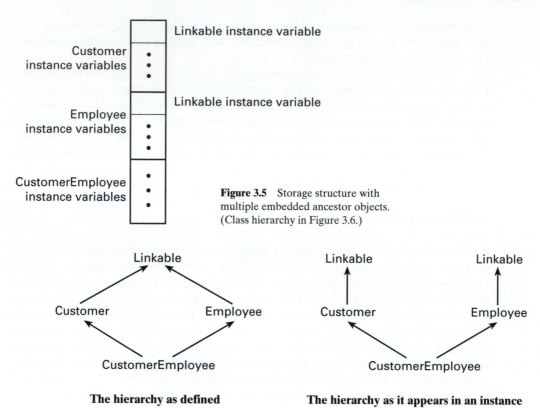

Figure 3.5 Storage structure with multiple embedded ancestor objects. (Class hierarchy in Figure 3.6.)

The hierarchy as defined   **The hierarchy as it appears in an instance**

Figure 3.6 The class hierarchy with repeated ancestors.

That is, the class definitions imply the hierarchy structure on the left side of Figure 3.6, but the structure of an instance appears as if the hierarchy were that on the right, because it contains two Linkable objects, one in the embedded Customer object and one in the embedded Employee object. For an instance of such a class, we would use the language's name disambiguation mechanism (i.e., renaming in Eiffel or the scope operator in C++) to indicate which link we are referring to in dealing with an instance of CustomerEmployee. In other cases, this instance structure is semantically incorrect. Recall that we derived both the classes Customer and Employee from the class Person in Figure 3.1. Clearly, an instance of CustomerEmployee represents one instance of the repeated ancestor Person, as illustrated in Figure 3.7.

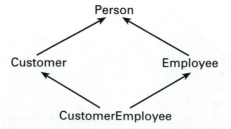

Figure 3.7 The hierarchy as it should appear in an instance.

We can resolve the ambiguity of referring to a message or instance variable inherited from Person within CustomerEmployee with the scope operator in C++ or renaming in Eiffel. However, the redundancy of including two Person subobjects causes other problems, namely wasted space and the possibility of inconsistency. Instead, we would like an instance of CustomerEmployee to contain one copy of the Person instance variables so that references to that information or to Person messages in CustomerEmployee are not ambiguous.

Ideally, we would like a language that supports multiple inheritance to accommodate both duplication and sharing of components inherited from repeated ancestors. As we will discuss in section 12.4.3, C++ includes the "virtual base class" construct for specifying a shared ancestor such as Person for CustomerEmployee. Specifying a superclass as virtual indicates to the compiler that if the class appears multiple times as an ancestor of a subclass of the class in which that reserved word appears, only one copy of its instance variables should be included in subclass objects. (We will see why virtual appears in the intermediate superclass rather than the descendant in section 12.4.3.) In this case, references to messages or instance variables inherited from the repeated ancestor are not ambiguous. If the derivation is not virtual, multiple embedded objects result, as required for Linkable. Eiffel supports making this distinction for each multiply inherited message or instance variable. If the message or instance variable is renamed to the same name in the inherit clauses of each superclass, then only one occurrence of it exists within the subclass. If it is renamed with different names in the inherit clauses of different direct superclasses, then it is duplicated within a subclass instance.

3.5 EVALUATION OF INHERITANCE

3.5.1 Advantages of Inheritance

Modeling the problem domain

The primary advantage of support for inheritance is that the structure of the type system in the application more accurately reflects the categorization relationships present in the problem domain. Narrowing the semantic gap between the problem domain and the system facilitates mapping behaviors, structures, and modifications in the problem domain to the corresponding components in the software system.

Reuse and extendibility

Languages that support abstract data types provide reuse of these constructs through instantiation and composition. Inheritance enables more extensive reuse of both interface and implementation. Interface is reused when the designer defines new classes as subclasses because existing portions of the system will interact with the new class in the same manner in which they relate to the superclass. When a subclass is added, neither the existing system components nor the superclass need to be modified. This reuse of interface is a major motivation for abstract classes. Inheritance also promotes consistency of interface, as the interfaces for related objects are similar. Implementation structure is reused when we define new subclasses because they include existing instance variables and methods. This inheritance of functionality results in the benefits of code reduction and code sharing. In addition, the subclasses automatically benefit from any improvement to the implementation of the superclass. Reusability and extendibility provide increased reliability and code readability, and facilitate development, debugging, and maintenance.

Another aspect of reusability is that inheritance supports extension and enhancement of the system without modification of existing program components. In fact, due to the loose coupling provided by dynamic binding, we do not even need to recompile existing code units when we define a new subclass with which they interact. This property enables designers to develop an application using the techniques of prototyping and incremental development. It also permits a software vendor to offer a class library without supplying its source code. Clients can extend the functionality of those classes by deriving subclasses without considering the details of their implementations.

Class hierarchy structure

Inheritance provides an organizational structure for a library of encapsulations that facilitates understanding them and navigating among them. Object-oriented programming environments usually include "browsing" tools that take advantage of this structure to present the classes available (i.e., as a tree or directed acyclic graph). This organization makes it easier for the designer to determine whether a class with the required properties is already available, or to find the appropriate class to use as a superclass when defining a new class.

Polymorphism

Inheritance provides object polymorphism because an object is an instance of each of its ancestors in the class hierarchy, like the problem domain entity that it represents. Object polymorphism also results in inclusion polymorphism because we can pass a descendant object to a method that takes an ancestor parameter, which supports generic programming and reuse of polymorphic code.

Inheritance provides identifier polymorphism for statically typed languages. This permits dynamic binding of methods and the resulting flexibility of loose coupling together with the safety of compile-time type checking. It also allows the programmer to define heterogeneous collection classes such that the compiler can restrict a collection's elements to instances of the desired subhierarchy.

3.5.2 Disadvantages of Inheritance

Efficiency considerations

Inheritance implies identifier polymorphism, and, therefore, dynamic binding, which has a higher cost than subprogram invocation. In addition, using message

passing to access an instance variable involves more overhead than direct component selection if it is implemented as a subprogram invocation. C++ addresses these
issues directly by requiring the programmer to indicate when dynamic binding is
necessary for each message, and by providing the inline declaration for very small
functions such as the instance variable accessors required by encapsulation. The
additional cost for a dynamically typed language like Smalltalk is greater.

Using software libraries can increase the size of a program's executable, especially with a built-in class library that includes classes and methods the program does
not use. Most Smalltalk systems have a "code stripper" tool that eliminates unused
classes and methods from the executable because the class library is so extensive.
With compiled languages, this factor will depend on the sophistication of the linker
the language system uses. For example, if the linker deals with code modules as
atomic units, programmers may need to place each method in a separate module to
obtain a minimal executable (which is not possible in some languages). Clearly, this
would complicate code management during development.

Execution time and space usage is often greater for general-purpose structures
and algorithms (e.g., inherited generic methods) than for programs tailored to a specific kind of data object. For example, a List class might be implemented as a linked
list, which would be inefficient in terms of space when the elements are characters.
Similarly, suppose that we have a class Collection, which is the ancestor of all collection classes. A Collection method that returns the number of elements by counting the elements works for all collections (e.g., for a linked list), but is inefficient for
collections such as hash tables that store the number of elements explicitly. Clearly,
the latter classes should override that method.

Encapsulation and locality

Inheritance compromises the locality of function and structure that a class represents. This problem is compounded by the fact that a class can inherit behavior
and components from an ancestor many levels above it due to the transitivity of
inheritance. This distribution of a class's components among several program units
also means that a subclass has weaker cohesion because some logically related components are packaged elsewhere. For this reason, the use (and especially the mis-
use) of inheritance can have a negative impact on code readability and maintenance.
Inheritance is a powerful tool that programmers can use for semantics other than
those for which it was intended.

To determine the complete protocol or internal structure of a class, we must
examine the class and its ancestors. We obtain its protocol and instance variables
by merging those of the class's ancestors. Determining a class's methods is more
complex due to overriding. For each message, we must find the method closest to
the class in the hierarchy. A programming tool can manage this task since all of this
information is statically defined. For example, many object-oriented programming
environments provide a "class flattener" that coalesces this information into a single description of the class's protocol and implementation.

In examining the operation of a class's methods, we often need to consider
methods defined in an ancestor class, because the class either inherits or refines

them. However, these methods might be implemented via messages sent to self that invoke methods from actual receiver's class (like the methods for erase and moveTo in section 3.3.3), these methods are defined in descendants of the class whose method we are examining. In attempting to understand a particular method, we may need to traverse up and down the class hierarchy, examining methods from several related classes due to self and super references. For this reason, the learning curve for understanding a class library can be steep.

Information hiding and coupling

There is a certain amount of conflict between the features of inheritance and information hiding because inheritance compromises the boundary around a class. (Of course, a subclass and its superclass are inherently more tightly coupled than two arbitrary classes because the specialization is also true of the problem domain categories they represent.) The methods of a class's descendants can depend on the details of its nonpublic components. That is, a class provides two interfaces, one for "outsiders" (i.e., client programmers who may only use an instance by passing it messages) and one for "insiders" (i.e., designers of subclasses who must have knowledge of the class's instance variables and methods). C++ and Java provide separate interfaces for a class's components for each of these groups with the public and protected access specifiers, and allows hiding class components from both groups with the private access specifier. In most other languages, subclasses always have access to a class's implementation, while clients never do.

In addition to complicating information hiding, inheritance results in tighter coupling between a class and its ancestors due to the direct access provided.[9] A programmer attempting to improve the behavior or efficiency of a class might affect the operation of its descendants in unforeseen ways. The three levels of access control supported by C++ help manage this problem. The implementation of a class can be divided into a protected interface for descendants and a private implementation. To achieve this in other languages, the programmer can define messages for accessing an object's state information, and follow the convention of using these messages rather than inherited instance variables when defining subclass methods.

Static typing

The interaction between the polymorphism that results from inheritance and static typing complicates a number of features in statically typed programming languages, especially our expectations about compile-time type checking.   For example, the validity of an assignment a := b in which the classes of a and b are related hierarchically depends on the classes of the objects they refer to at that point. Conversions from a descendant reference or object to an ancestor reference or object are valid. However, we sometimes need to convert an ancestor reference to a descendant reference because we know the actual type of the referent and the com-

[9] There is no direct access between individual instances of the classes.

piler does not. In addition, the fact that there are different-sized objects that are type compatible causes some unexpected effects, especially with static and automatic object allocation and type conversions. We will examine the details of these issues in the context of C++ in section 12.2.

Program verification

Inheritance can also complicate program specification and verification. Since an instance of a subclass is an instance of the superclass, it should be possible to substitute it in any context in which a superclass object may appear. However, a subclass method can override the operation of the superclass method in an arbitrary way, so it may have very different behavior from that called for in the specifications or postulated in the proof. If this is done, the verification process must take account of these special cases. To provide consistency, all method overriding should be refinement so that the superclass behavior for a message holds for subclass instances.

3.6 SUMMARY AND REVIEW

3.6.1 Inheritance Semantics

Specialization

- Analysis of the problem domain often indicates that there are categories at varying levels of generality, and that more specific categories are specializations of more general categories. This "is a kind of" relationship is represented in the object model by *inheritance*, in which a *subclass* inherits the behavior and structure of its *superclass*. Inheritance is also useful in characterizing classes that represent software system components.

- A subclass inherits the behavior and state information of its superclass, and can also define additional behavior and state information relevant to the abstraction it models. That is, the subclass is a specialization or extension of its superclass.

- Inheritance is not the same as the composition (or "has a") relationship, which we model by the composite class containing an instance variable whose referent is an instance of the component class.

- When choosing between defining a new class as a subclass of an existing class (i.e., specialization), and using that class as a component of the new class (i.e., composition), you should decide on the basis of the semantics and protocols of the classes, rather than on the basis of similarities among their storage structures.

Restriction

- In some cases, a specialization of a class has a more restricted protocol than the more general class, so the subclass must disallow superclass messages, usually by overriding them with methods that produce error messages or exceptions.

- You should use restrictive inheritance with caution because it results in subclass objects that cannot function correctly as superclass objects.

Class hierarchy structure

- The *class hierarchy* is a graph that represents the inheritance relationships among the classes in a problem domain, system, or application.

- With *single inheritance*, in which a class has at most one superclass, we diagram the class hierarchy as a tree or a forest in which the parent of a class is its superclass.

- With *multiple inheritance*, the class hierarchy has the structure of a directed acyclic graph.

Developing the class hierarchy

- The class hierarchy for a large system can be complex, and we develop it by recognizing the relevant categories and subcategories. We may create classes by top-down analysis beginning with more general categories, or by bottom-up recognition of commonalities among classes.

- As we analyze the problem domain and assign responsibilities to classes, we may coalesce classes, split a class into siblings or a superclass and subclass, recognize new superclasses for classes with protocol in common, or relocate protocol or attributes in the hierarchy. Generally, we place behavior and state information as high in the class hierarchy as appropriate.

Polymorphism

- With inheritance, a subclass object is polymorphic because it is an instance of each of its class's ancestors, and should be able to be used as an instance of those classes. This provides the semantics of specialization and of the problem domain category the class represents.

- Object polymorphism results in inclusion polymorphism because a method with a receiver or argument of superclass type can operate correctly using an instance of any of that class's descendants. This allows generic programming and reuse of such methods.

- Inheritance also provides identifier polymorphism for statically typed languages because the referent of an identifier can be an instance of any of the descendants of the identifier's type. This permits dynamic binding for these languages, with the benefits of receiver responsibility, loose coupling, and extendibility, and supports heterogeneous collections.

3.6.2 Subclass Definition

Purpose and meaning

- A subclass definition describes the manner in which its instances differ from those of its superclass. It may specify additional messages, methods, and instance variables for subclass instances, and may define methods that override those of the superclass. Superclass messages, instance variables, and methods that are not overridden are present in subclass instances automatically.

Interface

- The interface of a subclass gives its superclass and the additional instance and class messages it defines. It does not repeat elements of the superclass's interface.

Implementation

- The implementation of a subclass gives additional instance and class variables, methods for the additional messages, and overridings of inherited methods.
- The class variables of the superclass are available in the subclass methods, but the subclass does not have its own values for these. The subclass may define additional class messages, methods, and variables for the subclass object, and override superclass class methods.
- Since a subclass instance has values for the instance variables of each of its ancestors in the class hierarchy, we can regard it as containing an embedded instance of each ancestor. These objects provide the information necessary for performing inherited methods.
- Each object also contains a pointer to the type object for its class, which provides a starting point for method binding.

Method overriding

- When an object receives a message, the method binding process searches that object's class object for a method. If there is none, it examines the superclass object, and so on up the chain of ancestors. It selects the method defined closest to the receiver's class along its chain of ancestors in the class hierarchy.
- A subclass can *replace* a superclass method if the abstraction it represents requires different behavior, or can *refine* the superclass method by defining a method that invokes the superclass method as well as performing subclass-specific processing.
- To support refinement of superclass methods, an object-oriented language must include a special construct to distinguish method refinement from a

recursive invocation, because the message names are the same and the receiver is the original receiver of the message.

- Method replacement is usually used for efficiency or for disallowing a message. Method refinement is more common because it reflects the semantics of specialization and extension.

- In overriding a method, you should ensure that the subclass method is consistent with the semantics of the superclass method. In this way, client code that operates correctly with superclass objects will function properly with subclass instances, and statements made about that code are valid for all cases.

3.6.3 Abstract Classes

Encapsulation of interface

- A superclass encapsulates the common interface for its descendants in the class hierarchy. That protocol supplies a port through which other system components can interact with its descendants without having to be aware of the details of those classes.

- Encapsulation of interface provides the benefits of looser coupling between components, code genericity, and higher-level abstraction. We can extend the system by adding subclasses with that interface without affecting other system components with which the class interacts.

Definition and purpose

- An *abstract class* defines a protocol and a partial implementation, which the definitions of its *concrete* descendants complete. It provides a higher-level abstraction than that of the individual descendants for other parts of the system.

- An abstract class declares *abstract messages* whose methods are deferred because subclass-specific information is required to code them. Object-oriented languages must include features to identify abstract classes and messages.

- An abstract class exists only to define a protocol, and to use for deriving descendants. We cannot instantiate an abstract class directly because its implementation is incomplete.

- In a statically typed language, an abstract class provides a type for identifiers that can refer to instances of any of its concrete descendants. The compiler ensures that only messages in the abstract class's protocol are sent to the referent of the identifier, and that the abstract class itself is not instantiated.

- In addition to specifying abstract messages, an abstract class can define state information necessary in all descendants and methods that access that information. An abstract class may also provide methods that implement higher-level algorithms whose details are filled in by the class of the receiver via dynamic binding. It does so by defining methods that send abstract messages to the receiver.

3.6.4 Multiple Inheritance

Basic concepts

- Problem domain analysis often indicates that a category specializes two or more categories, and inherits behavior and state from each. Object-oriented languages that support *multiple inheritance* allow the designer to give a set of superclasses for a class to reflect this.
- With multiple inheritance, the protocol of a class is the union of the protocols of its superclasses, and its instances have values for all the instance variables its ancestors define.
- With multiple inheritance, the structure of the class hierarchy is a directed acyclic graph.

Name ambiguity

- With multiple inheritance, ancestors of a class along different inheritance paths in the class hierarchy may define a message or instance variable with the same name and type. Languages that support multiple inheritance must include a feature for disambiguating use of such a name by a subclass client or within a subclass method.

Repeated inheritance

- In *repeated inheritance*, a class is an ancestor of another along more than one superclass path in the class hierarchy graph. Depending on the semantics of the categories represented, instances of the subclass might or might not be required to contain duplicate embedded instances of the repeated ancestor. Languages that support multiple inheritance must include a feature for distinguishing these cases.

3.6.5 Evaluation of Inheritance

Advantages of inheritance

- Subcategorization is an essential part of any problem domain and of our view of it, and inheritance allows the structure of the type system to reflect those relationships.
- Inheritance supports reuse of both interface and implementation when we define subclasses of existing classes. Reuse of interface facilitates extendibility of object-oriented systems because we can add new subclasses, and their interaction with the rest of the system are already defined.
- Inheritance provides structure for a library of classes that facilitates understanding the classes and selecting a class for instantiation or derivation.
- Inheritance results in object and inclusion polymorphism, which permit code genericity and allow identifier polymorphism for statically typed languages.

Disadvantages of inheritance

- Inheritance can reduce efficiency. The method binding process increases the execution time for message passing compared to that for subprogram invocation., using software libraries can increase the size of executables, and general-purpose structures and algorithms are less efficient for some cases.
- Inheritance compromises encapsulation, locality, and cohesion because a class's components may be defined in any of its ancestors. Understanding the operation of a class's methods may involve traversing up and down the class hierarchy examining methods in various ancestors and their interactions, due to uses of self and super.
- Inheritance affects information hiding and coupling because a class's implementation is accessible to its subclasses.
- To decouple a class and its descendants so that we can develop them independently, some languages such as C++ and Java provide three access levels for a class's components, namely the client interface, the subclass interface, and the private implementation.
- Inheritance complicates static typing due to object, inclusion, and identifier polymorphism.
- Inheritance complicates program specification and verification because few languages enforce constraints on how descendants redefine methods.

3.7 EXERCISES

3.1 **(a)** Examine a real-world domain with which you are familiar (e.g., a retail store, an office, a kitchen, a repair shop, etc.) and determine some specialization relationships among the categories of entities in that domain.
   (b) Draw a diagram of the class hierarchy you have designed.
   (c) Which subclasses in your class hierarchy have behavior and attributes that their superclass does not have? Which subclasses in your class hierarchy perform operations that their superclass performs in a different manner?
3.2 Consider the problem of writing the software to control an automatic teller machine. Define the classes and their protocols that would model this application. (There are a number of opportunities for subclassing.) Compare your design with those of [Bud91] and [Wir90a].
3.3 Suppose we have a class String representing character strings with the protocol described in section 2.2.5, and want to use it to define a class Name for names of people. Assume that each name consists of strings for first, middle, and last name. Briefly describe the methods that we would write for each of the following alternatives. Indicate which you would prefer and describe why you think it is better.
   (1) Define the class Name as a subclass of String.
   (2) Define the class Name with three instance variables that are instances of String.
3.4 In terms of the class hierarchy, what should the relationship between the classes List and SortedList be? What should the relationship between the classes FIFOQueue and PriorityQueue be?

3.5 Examine a real-world domain with which you are familiar and find examples of specializations that are restrictions of the general category.

3.6 In what circumstances would it be useful to define the classes MalePerson and FemalePerson as subclasses of Person? When would it be unnecessary, and how would we represent this information in this case?

3.7 **(a)** Explain how inheritance results in object, inclusion, and identifier polymorphism.
   (b) Explain how inheritance allows heterogeneous collections in statically typed languages.

3.8 How can we provide object polymorphism in C or Pascal?

3.9 What do we mean by the statement that a subclass inherits the state and behavior of its superclass?

3.10 **(a)** Why does each object require a pointer to the type object for its class?
   (b) What does that structure include?

3.11 Describe the method binding process and how it implements overriding of methods.

3.12 **(a)** In discussing method refinement, we pointed out that a special syntactic construct not found in traditional procedural or functional languages is required to support this capability. Why is this true?
   (b) Describe some of the constructs that various object-oriented languages use for this purpose.

3.13 What is an abstract class? Give three reasons for the use of this construct.

3.14 What is an abstract message, and what is the purpose of this construct?

3.15 Describe the three kinds of methods that the definition of an abstract class may include.

3.16 Redefine the class Square in section 2.2.4 as a subclass of the class DisplayObject in section 3.3.3. Give the complete definition of the interface and implementation of the class (except for the creation methods).

3.17 We defined the abstract classes Orderable and DisplayObject in section 3.3.3 in a top-down fashion in the sense that we designed these classes before specifying their concrete descendants. Consider a situation in which we discover the usefulness of an abstract superclass by recognizing that some existing classes share a common protocol, for example, if the classes Circle and Rectangle have been designed independently. Describe the process of creating an abstract superclass for such a set of concrete classes.

3.18 Examine a real-world domain with which you are familiar and find examples for which multiple inheritance would be appropriate.

3.19 How can we represent a model that contains multiple inheritance in a programming language that only supports single inheritance?

3.20 **(a)** What is repeated inheritance?
   (b) Why is a special language construct necessary when repeated inheritance can occur?

3.21 Describe four advantages of support for inheritance in a programming language.

3.22 How does inheritance negatively impact each of the following?
   (a) execution time efficiency
   (b) encapsulation
   (c) information hiding
   (d) coupling among classes
   (e) program specification and verification

3.23 How does inheritance affect the validity of assignments and other operations in a statically typed language?

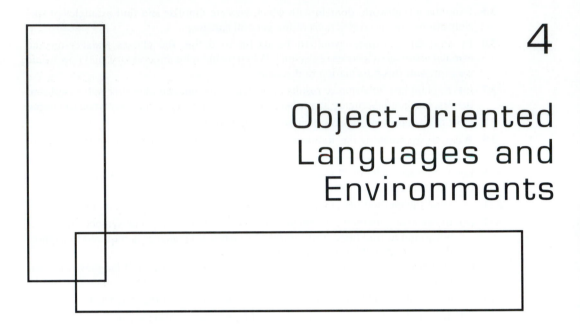

4

Object-Oriented Languages and Environments

In this chapter, we will survey a number of object-oriented languages. First, we examine their design goals and features, and other criteria for selecting a language. Next, we briefly discuss software engineering and programming environments, because many object-oriented languages include a class library and programming tools. Finally, we cover three pure object-oriented languages, Smalltalk, Eiffel, and Java, and several hybrid languages based on Pascal, C, and Lisp.

This chapter covers the following topics:

- programming language features (4.1.1) and other criteria (4.1.2) for evaluating an object-oriented language and its suitability for a project
- CASE tools (4.2.1) and programming environments (4.2.2)
- predecessors of object-oriented languages, including Simula 67 (4.3.1) and languages that support data abstraction, such as Ada83 (4.3.2)
- three pure object-oriented languages: Smalltalk (4.4.1), Eiffel (4.4.2), and Java (4.4.3)
- the characteristics of hybrid object-oriented languages (4.5.1)
- hybrid languages based on Pascal (4.5.2), C (4.5.3), and Lisp (4.5.4)

We will illustrate each language with a short example class definition to give you an idea of the "look and feel" of each, and so you are aware of the range of possible ways of expressing object-oriented features. We will define the class

Square discussed in section 2.2.4 as a subclass of the abstract class DisplayObject coded in section 3.3.3. Because Square is now a subclass of DisplayObject, its definition does not need to include the instance variables for its center, color, display canvas, and visibility, or the corresponding accessor messages. We also do not need to list the messages draw, erase, setColor, moveTo, rotate, and resize in the protocol of Square because they are declared in the protocol of its superclass. (In some languages, the overridden messages draw, rotate, and resize must be redeclared.) In the examples in this chapter, we will not comment each class component as we normally would, both for conciseness and because you know their meanings. As a reminder, the following is the definition of the class Square and its draw method in our object pseudocode (note that the draw method can access the inherited instance variables where, color and visible):

```
{ a class for rotatable squares, subclass of the class DisplayObject in section 3.3.3 }
class Square interface
    superclass DisplayObject

    class protocol
        new(center: Point, tilt: Angle, size: integer, color: Color) return Square;
    end class protocol

    instance protocol
        tilt() return Angle;
        size() return integer;
        corners() return PointArray;
    end instance protocol

end class Square interface

class Square implementation

    instance variables
        tilt: Angle;
        size: integer;
    end instance variables

    instance method draw(canvas: Canvas);
    var
        corners: PointArray;
    begin
        where := canvas;
        corners := self.corners();
        where.drawLine(corners[1], corners[2], color);
        where.drawLine(corners[2], corners[3], color);
        where.drawLine(corners[3], corners[4], color);
        where.drawLine(corners[4], corners[1], color);
        visible := true
    end

    { ... other Square methods ... }

end class Square implementation
```

4.1 LANGUAGE SELECTION CRITERIA

4.1.1 Language Features

Pure vs. hybrid languages

As stated in section 1.1.5, a *pure* object-oriented language includes the object-oriented features of data abstraction, class information, inheritance, and dynamic binding, and enforces the object-oriented paradigm. In a pure object-oriented language,

- every type is a class,
- all operations and information are encapsulated within classes,
- every operation is a message send.

That is, there are no distinctions between built-in types and classes, nor between their instances. Even numeric, character, and boolean types are classes with protocol and a superclass, able to have subclasses. For example, in Smalltalk, the numeric classes are descendants of the abstract class Number that defines common protocol for numeric objects and several default methods. In addition, the language does not support global functions or variables that are not encapsulated in a class or invoked without a receiver. As stated in section 2.3.3, the application itself is a class, rather than a main program.

A *hybrid* object-oriented language is created by extending an existing procedural or functional language, which we call its *base* language, with object-oriented features. Hybrid object-oriented languages have the advantages of

- backward compatibility with existing code and libraries in the base language
- familiarity for programmers who know the base language

Hybrid languages permit both object-oriented and procedural design and programming. They allow programmers to incrementally migrate to use of the object-oriented features, and to choose the coding style appropriate for the problem. Generally, they treat classes as data types, rather than as objects that have their own behavior and state, and there are usually distinctions between classes and built-in or base language types (besides the lack of inheritance for the latter). For example, built-in type or record type identifiers are represented by value, but class type identifiers are represented by reference. Like its base language, a hybrid language allows defining global variables and unencapsulated subprograms that are invoked without a receiver. That is, hybrid languages support both subprogram invocation and message sending.

The major difficulty with a hybrid object-oriented language is that programmers familiar with functional decomposition often do not fully re-orient themselves to the object paradigm, and end up with a hybrid design that contains both procedural and object-oriented components. This mix usually results in a design that is difficult to understand and modify. The lack of uniformity in hybrid object-oriented languages also means that programmers must choose among using objects and messages, base language types and subprogram calls, or a mixture of both, in coding the application. The multi-paradigm model can also cause confusion in reading and writing the code.

Smalltalk, Eiffel, and Java are pure object-oriented languages. Hybrid object-oriented languages include Object Pascal, Modula-3, Oberon, Ada95, C++, Objective-C, and CLOS (and even Object COBOL, eventually). Generally, pure object-oriented languages emphasize exploratory programming, flexibility, and rapid prototyping, while hybrid languages stress execution-time efficiency. (However, CLOS is an exception to both these generalizations.) In fact, some systems have been built using Smalltalk during the development stages, and then recoded in C++ to deliver an efficient product to the client.

Static and dynamic typing

The choice between static and dynamic typing involves a trade-off, as follows:

- static typing provides the convenience and security of compile-time type checking, and the resulting efficiency of allocation and method binding,
- dynamic typing supports more flexibility and extendibility in design and programming, but requires execution-time type checking and binding for all messages.

Statically typed object-oriented languages provide some of the characteristics of dynamic typing for some objects and identifiers, such as polymorphism, reference semantics, dynamic method binding, and run-time type identity. As we will discuss in section 12.2, the interaction between static typing and inheritance complicates some language features such as object allocation, assignment, and type conversions.

Not all pure object-oriented languages are dynamically typed, and vice versa. Smalltalk is a dynamically typed pure object-oriented language, while Eiffel is a statically typed pure language. Most hybrid languages support static typing, except for CLOS, which is dynamically typed like its base language, Lisp.

Language translation

A compiler translates programs to platform-specific object code, which is then linked and executed. In an interpreted language, source code statements are translated and executed in one step. Interpreters are simpler to use because there is no compile step between coding and execution, and they facilitate debugging and testing a program. The program can be stopped at any point to examine variable values, statements can be edited and then interpreted, code segments can be tested immediately, a source level trace can be obtained, and so on. (We discuss this further in the context of Smalltalk in sections 5.1.1 and 5.6.1.) However, interpreted code executes much more slowly than compiled code because the translation occurs at execution time. In addition, the source code and the translator must be present during execution in an interpreted language. All statically typed object-oriented languages except Java are compiled, and most language systems include a "project manager" that handles compilation dependencies automatically.

Most interpreted languages, such as Smalltalk and CLOS, are actually "incrementally compiled". The translator analyzes the code for a program unit (e.g., a method) and generates "intermediate" code, often called "bytecodes", for a virtual machine. The *virtual machine* is an abstraction of a typical computer and operating system, and the intermediate code is its "machine language". For example, bytecodes include basic operations such as arithmetic operations and numeric comparisons, as well as file system, process scheduling, and bitmapped display operations. The virtual machine is then implemented for each platform that the language runs on. Execution is faster than with interpretation (but not as fast as compiled code) because source statements are not parsed, etc. at execution time, and the bytecodes do not have to be recompiled for each platform. In some language systems, the intermediate code for a unit can be saved in a file, and then loaded and linked when necessary. For example, Java makes use of incremental compilation to provide portability without having to deliver source code. Each platform implements the Java virtual machine that interprets the bytecodes delivered by the vendor or transmitted over a network.

Deallocation of dynamic objects

Traditional languages such as Pascal and C support programmer-controlled deallocation of dynamically created objects to avoid the run-time cost of automatic storage reclamation (and because the programmer should know when an object is no longer needed). As we saw in section 0.3.2, a number of errors can occur with explicit deallocation that are only detected when they cause incorrect behavior not obviously related to the cause of the error. On the other hand, automatic deallocation is more convenient and reliable, especially with reference semantics. In particular, when calling a method that creates and returns a new object, the caller does not become responsible for deallocating that object. The disadvantage of automatic deallocation is that it requires a run-time system to perform reference counting or garbage collection, so applications usually require more time and memory. We sometimes hear that garbage collection is a problem for systems with time constraints because the process might be invoked at a time-critical moment, but this is less of a problem with concurrency and incremental garbage collection techniques.

Like their base languages, C++, Objective-C, and Object Pascal use programmer-controlled deallocation. Smalltalk, Modula-3, Ada95, Java, and CLOS support automatic storage reclamation. Delphi Pascal uses programmer-controlled deallocation for record instances and automatic allocation for class instances.

Multiple inheritance

In describing the problem domain during the analysis stage of system development, we sometimes find that a class conceptually includes behavior from several unrelated classes. As we saw in section 3.4.1, multiple inheritance allows the programmer to blend functionality from several superclasses to create a new class.

However, multiple inheritance can result in semantic questions (e.g., with repeated inheritance), and it adds to the complexity of the language, the translator, and the process of dynamic binding. Recall from section 3.4.1 that it is possible to emulate multiple inheritance with composition if necessary.

Eiffel, C++, and CLOS support multiple inheritance, while Smalltalk, Objective-C, Object Pascal, and Modula-3 do not. Java provides partial support for multiple inheritance. The language includes *interfaces*, which are "completely abstract" classes that contain only abstract messages and define no instance variables. A class can only inherit instance variables and methods from one class, but it can extend any number of interfaces by defining methods (and instance variables, if necessary) that implement the protocol of each. This allows the designer to inform the compiler that the class's instances can receive any of the messages in the interfaces that the class implements, but avoids the problems of name conflicts among inherited class components and the meaning of repeated inheritance.

Other language features

Object-oriented languages also differ with respect to their support for other programming language features. In Smalltalk, Eiffel, and Java, the class hierarchy has a root class and every class has a superclass, which is not true in other languages. Some object-oriented languages support defining separate modules or namespaces that contain classes, but in others, the class is the top-level design unit. Some languages do not support class messages and variables, but if the language supports modules, the class designer can define a class, subprograms (i.e., its class messages), and objects (i.e., its class variables) together in a module. Some languages allow operator overloading so that class instances can be used with the standard infix expression syntax (e.g., for equality tests), but others do not. Some statically typed languages support generic classes with type parameters, and others do not. In some object-oriented languages, the class definition is the only type constructor, while others support enumerations, subranges, and so on. Object-oriented languages also differ in the details of control structure syntax, parameter passing semantics, support for exception handling, and other language features.

Figure 4.1 summarizes the major features of the object-oriented languages we discuss in this chapter.

Object-oriented languages also vary somewhat in the terminology that they use for class components. Figure 4.2 shows the correspondence between the terminology of Smalltalk, which we have been using, and that of other object-oriented languages.

4.1.2 Other Factors

Familiarity and ubiquity

For hybrid object-oriented languages, familiarity with the base language often reduces the learning curve for a new programmer. On the other hand, that knowledge and the presence of familiar features make it easy to avoid

language	type	typing	dynamic deallocation	multiple inheritance	class information	modules	operator overloading	generics	concurrency
Smalltalk	pure	dynamic	automatic	no	yes	no	yes	N/A	yes
Eiffel	pure	static	automatic	yes	no	no	yes	yes	yes
Simula67	hybrid	static	automatic	no	no	no	no	no	yes
C++	hybrid	static	programmer	yes	yes	namespaces	yes	yes	no
Objective-C	hybrid	both	both	no	yes	no	no	no	no
Java	pure	static	automatic	no*	yes	packages	no	no	yes
Object Pascal	hybrid	static	programmer	no	no**	units	no	no	no
Modula-3	hybrid	static	automatic	no	no**	modules	no	yes	yes
Delphi Pascal	hybrid	static	both	no	no**	units	no	no	no
Oberon	hybrid	static	automatic	no	no**	modules	no	no	no
Ada95	hybrid	static	automatic	no	no**	packages	yes	yes	yes

* Java supports "interfaces" that provide some of the features of multiple inheritance.
** Languages that support modules can include the class and class-wide constructs in a module.

Figure 4.1

Smalltalk	Eiffel	C++	Pascal-based	CLOS
superclass	superclass	base class	superclass	superclass
subclass	subclass	derived class	subclass	subclass
instance variable	attribute	data member	field	slot
message	feature	member function	procedure	function
method	routine	member function	procedure	method
class variable	constant attribute	static data member	N/A	class slot
class method	N/A	static member function	N/A	method
self	Current	this	self	N/A

Figure 4.2

adopting the object paradigm. Familiarity with most object-oriented languages is somewhat low at this point but is certain to increase, especially for C++ and Java.

    A popular language such as C++ will also have a larger base of texts, tutorials, programming tools, class libraries, and so forth available. Existing code is important both for learning the language and its idioms and for reuse. Numerous magazines and trade journals include advertisements for commercially available programming systems, programming tools, and class libraries, particularly for C++ and Java.

Performance

As we discussed in section 2.2.3, identifier polymorphism requires indirection and dynamic allocation of objects. Most object-oriented languages use automatic deallocation which also requires run-time overhead, and dynamic binding is more costly than static binding. All of these factors negatively affect the performance of applications written using object-oriented techniques.

Dynamically typed languages such as Smalltalk and CLOS have the greatest overhead because all messages are dynamically bound and may require a search of the hierarchy. Statically typed languages have less of this overhead because many messages (and unencapsulated subprograms in hybrid languages) are statically bound, and no hierarchy search is necessary at run-time for those that arc dynamically bound (see section 12.3.5). In addition, statically typed languages employ value semantics for built-in types (and base language types in hybrid languages), and C++, Oberon, and Ada95 permit value semantics for class instances. For interactive application, this is less of an issue because human activity is so much slower than that of the CPU. For system programs, C++ is the best choice because it uses static binding and value semantics whenever possible, and does not employ automatic deallocation. However, we will see that these characteristics also inhibit extendibility.

Class libraries

Most modern languages also specify a standard library of subprograms or composite types to reduce the programming effort and increase code portability and reusability. All object-oriented languages include standard class libraries, some more extensive than others. As discussed in section 1.3.4, these libraries provide foundation classes, mathematical classes (e.g., for complex numbers, vectors, and matrices), collection classes, and classes for input/output streams and files. They also often define classes that support features of the language such as a root class, type information classes, and exception classes. More extensive libraries support graphic display operations, user interaction components and an application framework, concurrency, network operations, and so on.

A robust class library for the operating system and platform can reduce the coding effort considerably. This is especially true for applications that require a graphic user interface because the amount of code necessary to develop one using basic screen manipulation primitives can be prohibitive. However, it is often difficult to get classes in libraries from different vendors to function together properly because of name clashes and differences in protocols and storage structures. The language's standard library reduces this problem because all class libraries will use its classes for foundation classes, collections, and other common components.

Smalltalk includes an extensive class library and application framework that has been refined over many years of use. Section 6.1.1 surveys the major class categories, and chapters 7 and 8 cover the foundation and collection classes, respectively. Eiffel, Objective-C, Java, Object Pascal, and Oberon also include class libraries with the language system. C++ did not originally include a standard class library, but the current ANSI/ISO C++ Standard defines a number of classes for language support, internationalization, input/output, complex numbers, vectors, strings, and collections. Many commercial and public domain class libraries are available for all of these languages, especially for C++.

Programming environment

As we will discuss in section 5.6, a Smalltalk system includes a comprehensive programming environment for application development. It includes tools that

- present hierarchical views of the class library and programmer-defined classes
- list all senders or implementors of a message
- display the structure of an object at run-time
- trace the sequence of message sends executed.

Debugging and exploratory programming are easier because the language is interpreted and every message send is dynamically bound. The programmer can suspend execution, modify a method, resume execution, and that program will use the new method. The programming tools in the environment are coded as Smalltalk classes, so the programmer can extend them or modify their interfaces as desired.

Eiffel, Delphi Pascal, and Objective-C also include standard programming environments that provide these capabilities. A number of programming environments are available for C++ and other compiled languages. These often provide other development tools such as a source-level debugger, incremental compilation, a cross-referencer, a profiler, and a source code version control system (see section 4.2.2 for more detail on these tools). Unfortunately, sophisticated programming environments are usually very expensive, especially for workstations. On the other hand, the Free Software Foundation provides a free C++ compiler (g++), programmable editor with formatting options (emacs), and debugger (gdb).

Organizational constraints

Many organizations have standards with respect to analysis and design methodologies, programming languages, development environments, and coding style that might not be compatible with a particular language, or even with the object-oriented approach in general. Inertia on the part of management and programmers may also have an effect on the choice of language.

Platforms

Most languages are portable, but some are associated with a particular platform or operating system for historical reasons or because of vendor preferences. For example, developers usually use C++ with UNIX systems, Object Pascal with the Macintosh, Objective-C with NeXTStep, and Java for worldwide web applications. Delphi is only available for PC compatibles, and Ada is required for Department of Defense systems. Object-oriented programming has made little impact on mainframe systems on which much existing Cobol code is in use. However, the CODASYL standards committee is working on designing Object Cobol.

4.2 OBJECT-ORIENTED PROGRAMMING ENVIRONMENTS

4.2.1 Analysis-Level Tools

CASE tools

As we mentioned in section 1.3.1, many vendors have created CASE (computer-aided software engineering) systems that support and maintain the graphic notations in use in structured methods, such as data flow diagrams, structure charts, state diagrams, and timing charts. (These are also called "front-end" development tools because they support the early stages in the software life cycle.) These systems provide the designer with diagram editing operations that

- create and position notation elements in a diagram
- scroll through diagrams, and zoom in and out to show more or less detail
- cut, copy, and paste selected elements or subdiagrams.

For example, if the designer moves an element that represents a function in a structure chart, the associated invocation arcs are moved and redrawn automatically. Many CASE systems perform additional functions such as

- validating the integrity and consistency of a design, for example, to prevent dangling links or ensure that input arrows go to inputs
- enforcing design guidelines, for example, a maximum on the number of submodules
- automating generation of source code from the diagrams.

The system also manages the textual information associated with the model, such as data dictionaries, process specifications, and documentation of system components, and supplies forms for entering and editing this information and a search process for accessing it. Systems that are intended for a development team also manage multiple versions of diagrams and other constructs, and provide controls for authorization and concurrent access. Some CASE environments also help automate management functions such as assigning tasks and facilities to members of the development team and estimating costs.

Of course, the tool only has "knowledge" about the diagramming formalisms, and cannot contribute to understanding the problem domain or partitioning the system into modules. It is important to recognize that quality designs come from good designers, not from good tools.

Object-oriented CASE tools

Several object-oriented analysis environments with similar capabilities are now available for use with the various object-oriented methodologies described in section 1.3.3. Like those for structured methods, they support creating, editing and accessing the graphic notations and textual documentation that describe the model, and provide version management, concurrency controls, and so on.

For example, selecting a class icon in a diagram of system structure might bring up a dialog form for describing its superclasses, messages, attributes, associations, and other documentation. The environment can also automate consistency checks. For example, it can check whether a message connection to a class that reflects an association is part of the receiver's protocol, whether there is unused state or behavior in a class, or whether there are cycles in the inheritance hierarchy. If the graphic notation supports a hierarchy of design levels, the tool can allow the designer to create a diagram for a subsystem that can be collapsed to show its relationships with other subsystems, or expanded to show its internal structure as a group of interacting classes.

In the next section, we discuss "class browsers" and code databases that facilitate finding classes for reuse. An object-oriented analysis environment can implement similar capabilities to facilitate reuse of analysis and design results.

4.2.2 Programming Tools

Programming tools and environments

The tools available to a programmer for creating and understanding the structure of the application and for managing the programming process have a large effect on his or her productivity. These include tools for inspecting both the application's static structure (e.g., for editing code and browsing system components) and its dynamic structure (i.e., for testing and debugging). The most basic programming environment consists of an editor, a compiler, a linker, a loader, and an operating system that provides a file system and system calls for input/output. The operating system also provides a command interpreter or shell that the programmer can use to execute tools and programs and to access the file system.

Programming environments that provide a number of implementation-oriented "back-end" tools were the first integrated development environments, and are usually specific to a particular programming language. For example, most environments include a language-sensitive editor with formatting options (e.g., "pretty printing" to reflect nesting of constructs), and macros for language constructs and standard header comments. An essential tool is an interactive source-language debugger, one that uses information produced by the compiler to give a symbolic view of objects and a statement-by-statement view of the sequence of execution. The debugger typically provides break points, incremental execution, and run-time inspection and modification of data objects and activation records.

Other facilities that programming environments often provide include

- incremental compilation and linking to facilitate making small modifications to a large system
- a cross-reference tool for finding the definition and uses of an identifier in the source code units that make up an application
- a tool that provides a graphic display of the subprogram call structure
- application delivery optimizers for producing efficient executables
- a code profiler that indicates what proportion of execution time is spent in each unit (module, subprogram, or control structure)
- test data generators that exercise the program's control paths
- graphic user interface builders for designing the user interface of the system and generating the corresponding code
- version control systems for keeping track of multiple versions of program units
- configuration management tools for keeping track of components of configurations of the application for different platforms or customers
- documentation management systems
- target machine simulators.

Integrated development environments are often organized around a database containing source code, symbol tables, linkage and version information, compilation dependencies, documentation, and so forth.

Each of these capabilities can be adapted to object-oriented programming, although tracing the control paths possible in a program can be more complex due to inheritance and polymorphism. For example,

- the editor can contain class and method definition templates
- the debugger can allow tracing message sends at several granularities of execution, setting breakpoints in methods, and examining the state of an object
- the cross-reference tool can display all classes whose methods send a message, or all methods that implement a message
- the call graphic tool can display a representation of message sending structure
- the profiler can indicate the number of sends of a message, or the cost of evaluation of a method
- version control can keep track of multiple versions of classes as prototypes are created.

Class hierarchy browsers

A *class hierarchy browser* is a navigation aid that provides a view of the structure and components of a class library or framework. A browser facilitates selecting a class for instantiation, composition, or derivation from a framework, understanding the relationships among classes, and positioning messages and instance variables in the hierarchy. Typically, the browser includes commands for following interclass relationships, examining the components and clients of a class, and for organizing the views it provides. The browser is usually integrated with an editor so that the programmer can select a class to open an editable window containing its interface or implementation.

The Smalltalk system browser was the first class hierarchy browser, and it presents information in four scrolled lists and a text editor subwindow, rather than graphically. Classes are organized into categories by class hierarchy relationships, functionality, or subsystem. For example, there are categories for collections, streams, graphics, system services, kernel classes, and interface components. Messages are also organized into categories such as accessing, testing, printing, and enumerating messages. The four scrolled lists display the class categories, the classes in the selected category, the message categories of the selected class, and the messages in that category, and the text editor displays the selected method (see Figure 5.15). Each list also has a popup menu that provides commands to add or find an item, or print, store, browse, remove, or rename the selected item. The menus also provide commands to reorganize categories, or open a "method browser" on the senders or implementors of a message, the methods that use a particular instance or class variable, or methods in other classes that refer to the class. The method browser displays a scrolled list of the method names and a text editor that displays the selected method, and contains a menu of browsing and editing commands (see Figure 5.17). While browsing, the programmer uses the mouse to select items and commands. We will describe the Smalltalk system browser in more detail in section 5.6.3.

Many browsers display a graph of the inheritance hierarchy with classes as nodes and inheritance relationships as arcs, like figures 1.6 and 3.1 (or from left to right). Like the diagram editing tools we discussed in the previous section, the programmer can scroll the diagram, zoom in and out, and reposition nodes, and the tool will redraw the arcs. The tool's menus might include commands for highlighting the classes in the hierarchy diagram that instantiate a class, that send or implement a message, or that a method uses. The browser might also include a hypertext-enabled editor that can interact with the hierarchy display. For example, selecting a class in the hierarchy displays its definition in the editor, selecting a message in the editor highlights the classes that implement it in the hierarchy display, or defining a new class in the editor updates the display. The system might also display other graphs with the classes as nodes, for example, with labeled arcs that represent instance variable references or message sends (rather than inheritance).

As applications and class libraries become larger, visually browsing a hierarchy graph becomes less effective, and a code database may prove more useful [Gib90]. The database provides a query language, and maintains indices of interclass relationships, classes by messages, and keywords associated with classes. For example, we might ask for the classes that define some set of messages, the clients of a class, the classes that have similar functionality to a class, or the graphics classes, wherever they may appear in the hierarchy. An object-oriented database system also provides features necessary for large projects such as concurrency controls and transaction locking for multi-user access, security controls, recovery from system failure, and versioning capabilities.

With inheritance, the definition of a class's interface and implementation can be distributed among its ancestors in the hierarchy. A useful tool is a *class flattener*, which provides a complete description of a class by merging information in the definitions of its ancestors. It also lists the ancestor from which the class inherits each method or instance variable. The tool must detect overriding to correctly display the class's methods, and might also display ancestor methods invoked by the class's methods due to refinement.

Interface builders

Applications with a graphic user interface often have a major portion of their code dedicated to handling graphic interface functionality, and graphic interface "toolkits" typically define dozens of types (or classes) and hundreds of subprograms (or messages). An *interface builder* allows the programmer to design the graphic user interface of an application by using the mouse and drawing tools, thereby avoiding much of this complexity. Some interface builders are platform-specific and others can generate code for several different graphic interface systems.

As in a drawing program, we select interface components such as pushbuttons, checkboxes and scrollable lists from a palette (rather than selecting rectangles, lines, and arcs), and place them in the application's windows and dialogs. We can then position and size the components to achieve the desired layout (usually, by dragging handles at the corner of a selected component), and cut, copy, and paste components. The tool will also provide commands for aligning the edges or centers of components, aligning components to a grid, sizing components equally, or distributing components with equal spacing. An important aspect of this design is specifying how the components will be distributed and sized in the window if the user changes its size. Typically, some components or subwindows remain the same size (e.g., a row of pushbuttons) and others grow or shrink (e.g., scrolled lists or canvases). Unfortunately, interface toolkits vary widely in how these constraints are expressed.

We then specify the properties of each interface object by entering information in dialog boxes, rather than by writing code. This includes general properties of the component such as its size, position, and colors, as well as type-specific properties. For example, for a pushbutton, we can set the label and font, the message sent when the user clicks, and that message's receiver. For a text editor subwindow, we specify a string instance variable in the application that it models so that updates to the text change the variable's value, and vice versa.

The tool then generates the code that implements our interface design, together with "hooks" for the application-specific code. Usually, this takes the form of a class for the application which is a subclass of the abstract application class that has instance variables for the interaction components and model objects specified when designing the components, and messages specified for the components. Each component is an instance of a class provided by the associated library, with instance variable values defined by the drawing process. The application class also refines its superclass's initialization method to create the components and model objects, set the properties and arrangement of the components, and register dependencies among components and models. The code generated by the builder interacts with our application-specific code by sending it the messages we specified during the interface design process. We are only responsible for coding those methods and the representation of the model. That code may also send messages to components, for example, to change the label or a button or disable a menu item in certain circumstances.

4.3 PRECURSORS OF OBJECT-ORIENTED LANGUAGES

4.3.1 Simula 67

Background

Like many simulation languages developed during the 1960's, Simula 67 [Dah67] was designed for directly emulating the behavior of real-world systems. Its features encouraged writing programs that mirror the vocabulary and structure of the problem domain, and performing design by analyzing scenarios of behavior of the real-world system. Simula 67 was the first language to introduce the terminology "class" and "object" and the concept of inheritance of properties among type definitions.

In the United States, Simula 67 was viewed as an extension of Algol (which was little used) oriented specifically toward simulation, not general-purpose programming. Little attention was paid to the language until the development of Smalltalk and C++, which it influenced in many ways. This lack of interest was also due to the large demands that dynamic deallocation and concurrency placed on the computer, given the capabilities of hardware and operating systems at that time.

Objects and classes

Simula 67 begins with Algol and extends the concept of the block by allowing generation of coroutine blocks called *objects* from *class* definitions. A class definition specifies the code that the new object executes upon instantiation, and the object's *attributes*, which can be either data values or local procedures (like instance variables and methods in a contemporary object-oriented language). Each individual object has its own value for the data attributes defined by its class, and those values are set by the object's code as it executes. An object is created by invoking the primitive operation new with the class name, and that operation can also specify arguments for the object's code.

In contrast with the contemporary object-oriented perspective, Simula 67 views an object as a coroutine that executes concurrently, rather than as a package of information with its associated operations. Like processes in a multiprocessing environment, objects can be in the "active" or "suspended" state. Synchronization among objects is supported by the control primitives resume (transfer control to another object) and detach (return control to the object that resumed the executing object).   When an object is created, it executes the code defined by its class up to a detach statement, at which point the instantiating routine is reactivated at the statement including the new operation.   When control reaches the final end statement of an object's code (e.g., upon instantiation, if the class definition has no detach statement), the object is in the "terminated" state, and becomes a structure that maintains its data attribute values.   A terminated object is deallocated automatically via garbage collection when there are no longer any references to it.

A ref variable definition names a class and represents a reference to an object obtained by invoking new with that class name (and arguments).   An object that maintains a reference to another object can resume that object, or access its attributes with the component selection operator (referred to as "remote access"), even if that object has terminated.   That is, the data components of an object can be accessed directly by any object that contains a reference to that object.   The procedural view of objects and the lack of information hiding reflected the point of view prevalent at that time, which focused on procedural rather than data abstraction. Contemporary versions of Simula now support data abstraction as well as inheritance and dynamic binding [Kir89].

As in any language with coroutines, an object's activation record must be retained when it performs a detach or resumes another object so that it can resume. The data attributes of an object also must remain accessible if any other object maintains references to it.   An automatic stack implementation of execution contexts is insufficient for this situation, so activation records are deallocated automatically (as in functional languages).

Inheritance

Simula 67 includes inheritance specifically to model specialization hierarchies in the problem domain.   The language supports this concept by providing *subclass* definitions that add attributes and code to an existing class definition.   Objects generated from the subclass have the attributes of both the subclass and its superclass. The subclass code is inserted into the superclass code via an inner statement, which can appear at any point in the superclass code (i.e., subclass code always refines superclass code).   For example, a superclass declaration might consist of common initialization code, followed by an inner statement for subclass-specific code, followed by common finalization code.   Simula 67 supports single inheritance and a class definition does not require a superclass, so the class hierarchy is a forest.

As we discussed in sections 1.1.5 and 3.1.5, inheritance results in object and identifier polymorphism.   A ref variable can refer to objects generated from its class or one of that class's descendants (but not from its ancestors), and the referent's class may not be known to the compiler.   Simula 67 was the first language with inheritance and static typing, and many of the complexities that do not occur with monomorphic typing were originally discovered, understood, and implemented in Simula 67.   This includes the semantics of assignments and conversions among ancestors and descendants, dynamic binding of resumptions and procedure attribute invocations, and determining the actual class of the referent of a superclass identifier.

The designers of Simula 67 knew that if the classes StationWagon and Sports-Car define an attribute tax, then accessing that attribute through a StationWagon or SportsCar reference should execute that class's procedure. They could also see that accessing that attribute through a Car identifier should be valid only if Car also defines that attribute, and must be dynamically bound to execute the correct procedure. Simula 67 introduced the implementation of dynamic binding we described in section 3.2.3, which uses class pointers in objects and per-class method tables. To allow type checking and reduce the overhead of dynamic binding, the programmer declares procedure attributes that require dynamic binding as virtual (as in C++).[1] To provide an "abstract message," he or she defines an empty virtual procedure. Simula 67 also allows invoking a superclass procedure attribute for refinement with the reserved word this.[2]

The boolean primitive is tests whether an object is an instance of a given class (by checking its class pointer), and the primitive in tests whether the object is an instance of any subclass of a particular class. Simula 67 also provides the inspect statement, which operates like a case selection based on the class of the referent of an identifier (again, due to its procedural perspective).

Built-in class libraries

Simula 67 includes system class libraries containing classes that programmers frequently need in applications. The BASICIO classes support input/output and data transfer operations. SIMSET classes provide list processing and sequencing facilities. SIMULATION classes support scenario and process descriptions, scheduling and synchronization constructs, and the time flow mechanisms necessary for simulation. For example, the latter library includes classes for a system clock, and for generation, manipulation, and cancellation of event notices. The simulation library also includes classes that generate booleans, integers, or reals according to various distributions (uniform, normal, Poisson, etc.) to provide input events for simulations.

4.3.2 Object-Based Languages

Languages with abstract data types

Many languages that support data abstraction were developed during the 1970s and early 1980s, such as CLU [Lis77], Mesa, and Ada83. These languages are often referred to as *object-based* languages (as opposed to object-*oriented* languages [Car85]), because they provide the data abstraction feature of the object model, but not inheritance, polymorphism, and dynamic binding. That is, they allow the programmer to associate operations with types and hide the storage structure of the

---

[1] In fact, the efficient implementation of dynamic binding in C++ that we discuss in section 12.3.5 was first used in Simula 67.

[2] That is, this in Simula 67 corresponds to super in Smalltalk, while this in C++ corresponds to self in Smalltalk.

type's instances from its clients. Because they allow the designer to view the problem space in terms of objects, types and their behavior, it is possible to use them with object-oriented analysis and design techniques. However, identifiers are monomorphic and these languages do not support inheritance and dynamic binding, so there are fewer opportunities for reuse and extendibility. When a category has subcategories, the programmer must use unions to represent objects and case statements to implement type-specific processing.

Ada

The most widely used of these languages is Ada, which was commissioned by the U.S. Department of Defense, the largest consumer of software in the world. Ada was designed to deal with the problems of cost overruns in software projects and the proliferation of languages that were in use at the time (more than 450 languages were in use for Department projects by 1974), especially for embedded systems. The use of numerous languages prevented reusing existing code and designing uniform programming tools. The Department sponsored a three-stage competitive design process whose results were evaluated by hundreds of organizations worldwide. At first, there were few Ada translators due to the size of the language, and because the Department chose to prohibit implementation of subsets of the language to ensure consistency among language systems.

As befits a language designed ten years after Pascal and C, Ada includes a number of features not present in those languages, and refines a number of features that it inherits from Pascal. It also focuses more on the special needs of large software systems than earlier languages, a characteristic of most object-oriented languages as well. The major design goals for the language were improved reliability and maintainability, so its designers employed a readable syntax based on that of Pascal. In addition to the features of Pascal, Ada supports

- packages and import declarations to provide abstraction and modularity, and allow writing, using, and reusing libraries
- generic packages (recall section 1.1.4) to support reuse of well-defined, tested data structures and algorithms with new types
- exception handling to facilitate design of fault-tolerant embedded systems
- concurrent processes ("tasks" in Ada) that can synchronize and communicate, to support concurrent activities in embedded systems

As we discussed in Chapter 0, Ada also makes several improvements to Pascal's control structures, parameter passing, and type constructors, and supports subprogram and operator overloading. We saw several Ada code examples in Chapter 0 and section 1.1.4.

We saw in sections 1.1.3 and 1.1.4 that we can use Ada packages to define both modules and abstract data types. The process of designing an Ada program is a matter of specifying packages, and their interfaces and implementations.

4.4 PURE OBJECT-ORIENTED LANGUAGES

4.4.1 Smalltalk

Background

Beginning in 1971, a group of researchers led by Alan Kay at Xerox PARC began to develop a new computing environment based on the idea that computing hardware would eventually become inexpensive enough that nonprogrammers would have access to machines. Kay conceived of the "Dynabook," a notebook-sized computer with a touch-sensitive bit-mapped screen that would be as revolutionary for society as the widespread availability of books during the Industrial Revolution. To make computers accessible and enjoyable to the nonspecialist, he wanted an interactive graphic environment, and an interpreted extensible programming language oriented toward simulation and based on a small number of intuitive concepts. As Goldberg [Gol89] states, the Smalltalk system is intended to be more than a language or a programming environment: It is a vision of human-computer interaction.

Smalltalk, its environment, and the object model generated a great deal of interest but few programmers had access to a Smalltalk system. This was partly because the computers available at that time could not easily handle the demands of dynamic typing, automatic storage management, the graphic environment, concurrency, and so forth. In addition, many programmers found it difficult to adjust to the new design style of the object paradigm. Smalltalk has demonstrated its utility and flexibility for applications in simulations, graphics, office automation, computer-assisted instruction, artificial intelligence, games, and even system programming, namely the Smalltalk system itself.

Uniformity of concept

In the Smalltalk language and environment, every application and every application component (whether a model or view object) is an object that is an instance of a class, and all operations are performed by passing messages among objects. The system class library includes classes for applications, programming tools, and operating systems services such as file operations and process management that are available to users and to programs, as well as foundation classes, collection classes, and so on. The user starts an application by sending its class an instance creation message whose method creates the objects for that application (including its interface components) and displays its interface. The user can then send that instance messages to perform some task.

There are no built-in types that are treated differently from programmer-defined classes. The class library includes classes for numbers, characters, and booleans, and their operations are messages in those class's protocols. For example, the message expression (num + 1) abs sends the message "what is the result of adding one to yourself?" to the object bound to num, and then passes the message "what is your absolute value?" to the resulting object. That is, integers are regarded as objects that respond to messages such as + and abs rather than being a special type with built-in operations. In fact, the method for the second message might be inherited from Number, the superclass of the receiver's class.

Rather than indicating flow of control with control structure statements as in traditional languages, the protocols of certain classes control the order of message invocation. For example, a "block" object represents a function object that a client can evaluate or pass argument to (like the λ-expressions in section 1.2.3), and is written as a series of message expressions enclosed in square brackets. If [...] is a block,

- boolean objects respond to the messages ifTrue: [...] by evaluating the block if the receiver is true
- integers respond to the message timesRepeat: [...] by evaluating the block the number of times represented by the receiver
- all collections respond to the message do: [...] by evaluating the block for each element of the collection.[3]

Exception handling and concurrency are also expressed as message passing involving blocks (see sections 5.5.6 and 5.5.7). In Smalltalk, we pass messages to graphic objects interactively to draw graphics or display text on an output window object, rather than the language including special input/output statements as do Pascal and Fortran.

This uniformity of concept simplifies the language considerably. There are no reserved words for identifying built-in types or delimiting control structures, or special operations for built-in types that are part of the language syntax. Messages are also used for copying and comparing objects, for data transfer, and for type operations. As we stated in section 2.2.3, object allocation is a message to the class object, and we will see in section 6.1.2 that even defining a new class is performed via a message send (to its superclass object), so the language does not require special constructs for these operations either.

The environment

The developers of Smalltalk created a computing environment that pioneered many features that we now take for granted as the most natural way of interacting with a computer. Implementing their concepts required new hardware: the bit-mapped screen allowed graphic presentation of information, and a pointing device (usually a mouse) permitted interacting with the system without typing or memorizing commands. The Smalltalk environment introduced the concept of the computer screen as a "desktop" that displays windows for tasks in progress, and allowed the user to interactively switch among activities and select commands from popup menus. The user can resize and move windows, bring a window to the top in the

---

[3] In this case, the block has a parameter that is bound to each element of the collection in turn. We will discuss several other such "enumerating" messages for collections in sections 5.5.5, 8.2.1, and, 8.4.1.

stacking order, iconify or de-iconify windows, and so on, to arrange his or her workspace as desired. The user can also scroll the contents of a window or subwindow if that information does not fit in the space allotted for the window.

The Smalltalk language and environment are completely integrated and uniform, and there is no distinction between applications, programming tools, and operating system services. All these components are treated as objects in the system. The user can open a text window for commands to the system, which are expressed as Smalltalk messages, and text windows provide a popup menu with text editing commands. Since the language is interpreted and everything in the system is an object, the user can evaluate Smalltalk expressions to start applications or programming tools, issue file system commands, examine the classes in the class hierarchy, and test the behavior of program fragments. He or she can write and store Smalltalk expressions or code fragments that perform frequently needed operations in a text window for editing and evaluation. The environment also includes a number of programming tools such as the class hierarchy browser and the debugger. We will discuss the Smalltalk programming environment and the process of programming in Smalltalk in sections 5.1.1, 5.6, and 6.1.2.

The language

A series of experimental languages culminating in Smalltalk-80[4] were developed based on

- the data abstraction of CLU
- the type inheritance mechanism and simulation orientation of Simula-67
- the dynamic typing, automatic storage reclamation, extendibility, and functional semantics of LISP
- bit-mapped graphic operations, and the drawing protocol of LOGO.

The intended paradigm for use of the language was simulation of a problem domain system by abstracting behavior and state information from objects in the real-world system. The concepts of objects, classes, message passing, and inheritance became what is now known as the object-oriented paradigm. In addition to object-oriented features, Smalltalk supports concurrency and operator overloading, and most dialects provide exception handling. Smalltalk does not support multiple inheritance or organizing classes in modules, and has no need for generics as it is dynamically typed.

To maximize flexibility and simplicity, Smalltalk uses dynamic typing. Identifiers do not have types and have reference semantics, including instance and class variables, and the parameters and local variables of methods. All objects are created dynamically and deallocated automatically, and all method binding and type

---

[4] Smalltalk-72 supported classes, messages, and dynamic binding, defined the virtual machine and storage management, and introduced bit-mapped graphics operations. Smalltalk-76 defined the current syntax and added inheritance and class variables and messages. Smalltalk-80 introduced metaclasses and clarified the definition of the language and the virtual machine for vendors outside Xerox PARC.

checking is dynamic. An object's behavior is determined by its class and ancestors, and that behavior is initiated by passing the object a message. Programmer-defined classes have the same status as system classes, and we can add methods to system classes (or, in fact, change them in any way!). That is, the language, class library, and environment are completely extensible.

The syntax and specification of Smalltalk are much simpler than those of traditional languages, more like a "scripting" language than a programming language. As we stated previously in this section, Smalltalk needs no reserved words or constructs for built-in types or their operations, or for control structures, object allocation, or class definition. We program in Smalltalk by entering individual class and method definitions in subwindows of the "class browser" (see section 5.6.3), so the language needs no delimiters for classes, class interfaces and implementations, or method code. In addition, all messages are public and all variables are private, so access control specifiers are not needed.

As we stated in section 2.2.3, Smalltalk classes themselves are objects that perform class messages and contain the class variables and methods, and these objects are accessible to the programmer. The protocol of a class object includes messages that access class-specific information, messages that create instances and subclasses of the class, and messages that access the class's type information. Having the class's type information such as its name, superclass, subclasses, and selectors available facilitates creating programming tools and using Smalltalk queries to help understand a class, its hierarchy relationships, and methods.

We will cover the basic structure of Smalltalk and message expressions in Chapter 5, and defining classes and methods in Chapter 6.

The system classes

The Smalltalk system contains a large class hierarchy of several hundred classes that provide reusable, extendible components for use in applications, and a complete environment for interaction with the computer system and for application development. The library includes

- the class Object, the root of the hierarchy that provides protocol and default methods for all objects
- foundation classes such as numbers, characters, booleans, blocks (function objects), exceptions, times, and dates
- a subhierarchy of collection classes such as sets, dictionaries, arrays, strings, and unsorted and sorted lists
- classes for system services such as processes and interprocess communication, files and directories, input/output devices, memory management, and parsing and compiling
- application framework classes including classes for windows, dialogs, menus, and layout of components; classes for user interface components such as push-buttons, text entry fields, scrolled lists, and so on; classes for controllers to provide event handling; and an abstract application superclass

- classes for two-dimensional raster graphics, for example, points and rectangles, pixmaps and images, pens (or graphics contexts) for drawing, graphic objects, texts with fonts, colors and palettes
- classes for applications and programming tools, such as text editors, class browsers, file browsers, object inspectors, and debuggers.

The system classes significantly reduce the amount of coding necessary to develop an application, especially interactive, graphic applications. The graphics and inter-action classes are also helpful because a user or programmer can see the results of programming immediately. All this code is available to the programmer, which helps in learning the language, the library, and Smalltalk programming techniques. We will survey the Smalltalk class library in section 6.1.1, and cover its foundation and collection classes in detail in Chapters 7 and 8, respectively.

An example

To define a class in Smalltalk, we send a message to its superclass giving the names of the new class, its instance and class variables, and its "class category" ("pool dictionaries" are rarely used). For example, the class Square is defined as follows:

```
"definition of the class Square in Smalltalk"
DisplayObject subclass: #Square
    instanceVariableNames: 'tilt size'
    classVariableNames: ' '
    poolDictionaries: ' '
    category: 'Graphics-DisplayObjects'
```

Note that no types are given for the instance variables. Smalltalk does not include a language construct that gives the interface of a class. (In section 5.6.3, we will see that class interfaces are presented by the system browser.) The following code fragment gives the Square method for draw in Smalltalk:

```
draw: aCanvas
    "Draw the receiver on the argument canvas."

    | corners |
    where := aCanvas.
    corners := self corners.
    where drawLineFrom: (corners at: 1) to: (corners at: 2) with: color.
    where drawLineFrom: (corners at: 2) to: (corners at: 3) with: color.
    where drawLineFrom: (corners at: 3) to: (corners at: 4) with: color.
    where drawLineFrom: (corners at: 4) to: (corners at: 1) with: color.
    visible := true
```

The "message pattern" draw: aCanvas gives the message and parameter names, and local variable names are enclosed in vertical bars (and, again, no types are given for parameters and local variables). There are no delimiters (e.g., **begin** and **end**) surrounding a method's code because each method is entered separately in a text window, usually in the system browser. Smalltalk uses := for assignment, which binds the object resulting from the right side message expression to the variable on the left side. In a message expression, the receiver precedes the message name and arguments (e.g., self corners sends the message corners to the receiver of the draw method). We will discuss the unusual syntax for sending the message drawLineFrom:to:with: in section 5.3.2. The names where, color, and visible refer to the inherited instance variables in the receiver, and corners is the name of both a message in the receiver's class and a local variable of the draw method.

4.4.2 Eiffel

Background

The language Eiffel [Mey92] is an object-oriented language designed by Bertrand Meyer and others at Interactive Software Engineering with a syntax similar to that of Ada. Like Smalltalk, Eiffel is a pure object-oriented language in the sense that all operation and state is encapsulated and there are no global variables or subprograms. Unlike Smalltalk, Eiffel is statically typed and its control structure statements are like those in traditional Algol-like languages (i.e., they are not message expressions). Like Smalltalk, Eiffel is a complete programming environment that includes programming tools and an extensive class library. However Eiffel language systems are not commonly available. To provide portability, some Eiffel compilers produce C code.

Eiffel adds the design goal of reliability to the object-oriented goals of reusability and extendibility. Its major innovation in this regard is a set of constructs designed to facilitate "programming in the large" and program verification. These include documentation options, exception handling, and assertions.

Language features

Eiffel employs a different terminology than other object-oriented languages. A class definition declares "features" (messages), which may be implemented as "routines" (methods) or as stored "attributes" (instance variables). The language makes no distinction between computed or stored features outside a class, so how a class implements a feature is not visible to clients. Eiffel supports abstract classes and messages, multiple inheritance, operator overloading, and exception handling, but not class variables and messages. To avoid some of the restrictiveness of static typing, the language supports generic classes with type parameters.

Classes are the top-level structural unit, and Eiffel does not support organizing classes into modules. Eiffel defines the interface and implementation of a class in a single syntactic unit, but the environment provides a tool that extracts the class interface from its definition and formats it. An Eiffel class definition gives the class's superclasses and features. Every Eiffel class has at least one superclass, the system class ANY (the root of the class hierarchy) if no others. The class also defines "creation procedures" that initialize a new instance. The designer of a class has complete control over which features are visible outside a class, and can specify which classes can access each feature, including inherited features. Inherited features can be renamed to provide method refinement, and to disambiguate name clashes and repeated inheritance with multiple inheritance. Abstract messages are declared as deferred.

Methods in Eiffel are coded similarly to procedures in Pascal-based languages with message expressions. (The details of the control structures, e.g., the reserved words, are somewhat different from Pascal and Ada.) The identifier Current refers to the receiver of the method, but is optional when sending messages to that object.

Eiffel does not support class messages and variables. If a class defines an attribute feature by giving a literal value, that attribute has the same value for all instances and is not stored in each instance. This is like a class variable that cannot be modified, which is adequate for some purposes. Unfortunately, only types with literal notations (numbers, characters, booleans and strings) can be used in this way.

Eiffel uses reference semantics for identifiers and supports automatic deallocation of objects. The programmer can declare a variable or attribute as containing a class instance directly by specifying it as expanded. A class can also be declared as expanded (examples include classes for numbers, characters, and booleans), which indicates that all variables of that type have value semantics.

Software engineering features

To aid in designing and maintaining large systems, a class definition may include an indexing clause that specifies documentation used by programming tools such as browsers and version management software. Versions of methods that are no longer current but are included for backward compatibility can be marked obsolete. To aid reliability, Eiffel includes an exception facility. An exception triggers unwinding the stack to find a routine that defines a rescue block, which can retry the operation (i.e., Eiffel supports the resumption model). The library defines an Exceptions class that specifies a number of exception codes.

An important language component introduced to support software reliability is the assertion facility, which is motivated by research in program specification and verification. An *assertion* is a boolean expression that specifies a "contract" between a feature and clients of the class, and violation of an assertion raises an exception. Each feature can have a require clause that states preconditions that the client must satisfy, and an ensure clause that states postconditions that must be satisfied by the feature. The latter may refer to an attribute's old value, or may specify that an attribute cannot change value. A routine that overrides an inherited routine must satisfy a weaker or equal precondition than the superclass routine, and ensure a stronger or equal postcondition than the superclass routine. The invariant reserved word identifies assertions that the instances of the class must satisfy. Invariants of superclasses hold for instances of subclasses, and a class may not inherit from superclasses with conflicting invariants. Invariants may also be specified for loops in routines. The require, ensure and invariant conditions are checked by the compiler when subclasses are defined, and while the program is executing. The programmer can set a compiler option to disable these checks to build an efficient executable for delivery.

An example

An Eiffel class definition consists of an optional indexing clause, a class header, inheritance declarations, creation declarations, feature declarations, and an optional invariant assertion. For example, the class Square is defined as follows:

```
-- definition of the class Square in Eiffel
class SQUARE
    inherit DISPLAY_OBJECT
        redefine
            draw, rotate, resize
        end

    creation
        make

    feature {ANY}
        tilt: ANGLE;

        size: INTEGER;

        corners: ARRAY[POINT] is
            -- code for corners method

        draw(canvas: CANVAS) is
            local
                tempCorners: ARRAY[POINT]
            do
                where := canvas;
                tempCorners := Current.corners;
                where.drawLine(tempCorners.item(1), tempCorners.item(2), color);
                where.drawLine(tempCorners.item(2), tempCorners.item(3), color);
                where.drawLine(tempCorners.item(3), tempCorners.item(4), color);
                where.drawLine(tempCorners.item(4), tempCorners.item(1), color);
                visible := true
            end       -- draw

        make(center: Point; tilt: Angle; size: integer; color: Color) is
            -- code for initialization method

        -- ... other SQUARE features ...

    end       -- class SQUARE
```

The programmer does not need to explicitly list the classes that a class is a client of (i.e., DISPLAY_OBJECT, ANGLE, ARRAY, POINT and CANVAS for SQUARE) because the compiler deduces them and the language system handles compilation dependencies. The inherit clause names the superclasses and for each, specifies which inherited features are renamed or overridden. It can also give new client lists for inherited features. The creation clause lists the names of messages that can be used in a creation instruction. A feature clause introduces a set of features, and gives a list of the classes that can access those features enclosed in braces. In this example, the features are visible to all classes because every Eiffel class is a descendant of the class ANY. The client list {NONE} indicates the features are private to the class. A class definition can contain any number of feature clauses, which introduce features with the same clients list. The features tilt and size are attributes, and the features corners, draw and make are routines. The features size and corners are accessed in the same way by clients, for example, as square.corners, so there is no distinction to clients whether an object stores or computes a piece of information it manages. The class ARRAY[POINT] is generated from the generic class ARRAY with the class POINT as the type parameter binding, i.e. as the element type. As you can see within the routine for draw, array elements are accessed with the feature item.

4.4.3 Java

Background and motivation

Java was created at Sun Microsystems in the mid-1990's, originally for embedded applications in networked consumer devices. It was designed to be platform-independent, and to allow receiving software components from other locations and executing them safely. It has achieved quite a bit of notoriety in a short time because world wide web browsers such as Netscape, HotJava, and Explorer support defining "applets" (mini-applications) in Java. By using the Java class library, a programmer can design web pages with user interaction components and dynamic content.

To achieve portability, Java programs are translated to a platform-independent abstract machine language called *bytecodes*, which are then interpreted by a Java *virtual machine* on the host computer.[5] For example, the web browser implements the virtual machine, so a web page can transmit Java bytecodes to a client to be executed there, rather than the server performing all processing and interaction with the user. In addition, the Java language definition specifies the size and range of numeric types so that programs using them are portable (unlike most languages).

The designers of Java used the syntax of C and C++ because those languages are the most widely available and the most commonly used. For example, Java uses the lexical conventions, identifier and literal formats, operators, control structures, definition syntax, and built-in type names of C and C++. However, they wanted a language that is less complex, easier to learn, and safer than C++, and one that

---

[5] We will see in sections 5.3.2 and 5.6.1 that Smalltalk also uses this approach to translation.

enforces the object model (unlike C++). Although Java and C++ code appear similar, C++ code is not valid Java code, and vice versa. C code is also not valid Java, although the language supports "native methods" which are usually coded in C to allow using existing C code with a Java program.

Language features

Unlike other pure object-oriented languages, Java was created by removing several features from a hybrid object-oriented language, namely C++. These include

- the preprocessor
- pointers and pointer arithmetic, and pointers to functions
- file scope functions and global variables
- const parameters (read-only variables are designated as final)
- enumerations, structures and unions
- value variables of class type, and explicit reference parameters and variables
- separate definition of a class and its methods
- operator and conversion overloading
- multiple inheritance
- templates

Pointers and pointer arithmetic are disallowed because they are notoriously unsafe and error-prone, and because they present opportunities for a software component received from another system to access memory outside its address space. File scope functions and global variables are not supported to enforce the object model. To simplify the language, the class is the only type constructor, the entire class is defined in a single construct, and the language does not support forward declarations, operator overloading, multiple inheritance, or generics (templates in C++). Class type identifiers have reference semantics to provide polymorphism, but built-in type identifiers employ value semantics (recall section 2.2.3).

A Java program consists of a set of classes, one of which defines a class message main(), which is the first method executed. Typically, this class represents the application itself. A class definition gives the class's name, superclass, variables and methods, and class variables and methods are designated as static. As in C++, a class can define constructors for initializing instances whose names are the name of the class. Unlike C++, Java does not include destructors for automatically finalizing a class's instances because the language system uses garbage collection. Rather than marking messages that require dynamic binding as virtual as in C++, the Java programmer specifies those that cannot be overridden as final. Abstract classes and messages are designated with the reserved word abstract. Like C++, Java uses the access control specifiers public for class components accessible to clients, protected for components accessible to subclasses but not clients, and private for components that are accessible only within the class. Classes are organized into *packages*, each of which defines a named scope for the enclosed class definitions, and the import statement makes the named package's classes and their public members visible in a class. Protected class members are visible to other classes in the same package.

All Java classes have a superclass (specified following the reserved word extends in the class definition), except for the system class Object. If a class definition does not indicate a superclass, the class is a subclass of Object. As stated in section 4.1.1, the language provides partial support for multiple inheritance with *interfaces*, and allows a class to extend any number of interfaces by defining methods for their messages. The Java class library defines several interfaces that a class can implement, like using mixins (recall section 3.4.1). Java does not currently support generic classes ("templates" in C++). Since all classes are descendants of the class Object, the Java collection classes are coded as having elements of type Object, but the programmer must cast a collection element to its correct type after obtaining it. Such casts are checked by the run-time system, which signals an exception if the object is not an instance of the indicated class.

Java methods are coded like C functions with message passing, and the method can refer to the receiver's components directly. As in C++, the identifier this in a method refers to the receiver of the message (and it is optional when sending a message to the receiver). Like Smalltalk, method refinement uses a message with the reserved word super as the receiver.

Like Pascal-based object-oriented languages but unlike C++, Java uses implicit reference semantics for class type identifiers and supports automatic storage deallocation. (The language's surface resemblance to C is likely to confuse some programmers, since the semantics of assignment, parameter passing, and other features are so different from that of C, due to reference semantics.) All class instances are allocated dynamically with the reserved word new, the class name, and an initializer, which must match the argument signature of one of the class's constructors. A constructor is always invoked implicitly whenever an object is created.

Java also does not include a goto statement, but allows labeling a loop so that a break can exit several nested loop or switch statements (the loop label is given after the reserved word break). Like C++, Java supports exception handling, which the system library classes use for all error signaling. All methods must specify the exceptions that they can signal. Unlike the try statement of C++ (see section 13.3.4), the Java try statement also includes a finally block that is executed whenever a function is exited, even if the function execution is terminated due to propagation of an exception. Unlike C++, Java supports concurrency. The class library provides a class Thread for independent threads of control, and a method or statement can be marked as synchronized to indicate that only one thread can execute it at a time.

The class library

Java includes a standard class library that provides

- language support classes, such as type information classes and "wrapper classes" for primitive types

- classes for concurrent threads, thread synchronization, and communication among threads
- foundation and collection classes, such as String, Date, Vector, and HashTable
- classes for input/output streams, files, and network access
- platform-independent user interaction components, graphics, and image manipulation classes, including "applets" for web pages

The library classes are divided into eight packages. The package java.lang includes language support classes. It defines the root class Object, the class Class, an instance of which contains type information for each class, and the classes Process, System, Runtime, and SecurityManager, which encapsulate communication with the host system (e.g., to start a process or obtain the current date). The class String represents immutable strings, and StringBuffer is used to compose strings. The abstract class Number and its subclasses Integer, Long, Float, and Double, as well as the classes Boolean and Character provide wrapper classes so that instances of built-in types can be treated as objects (e.g., as collection elements). The class Math provides class messages for several mathematical operations (e.g., cos(), floor(), sqrt(), and PI). The class Thread and the interface Runnable support concurrency. The package java.lang also defines numerous classes that represent unrecoverable errors and exceptions that a program can handle.

The package java.util defines various utility classes. It includes the collection classes Vector, Stack, HashTable, and BitSet, the interface Enumeration that provides messages for enumerating the elements of a collection, and the exceptions EmptyStackException and NoSuchElementException. (Arrays are a built-in class in Java.) The class Date represents dates, the class StringTokenizer is used to parse a string into a sequence of tokens, and the class Random provides messages for obtaining a sequence of pseudo-random numbers. An instance of the class Observable notifies its dependents whenever its value changes, and the dependents implement the interface Observer.

The package java.io provides classes for input/output streams and files. The abstract classes InputStream and OutputStream provide basic messages for reading and writing data, respectively, and have concrete subclasses such as FileInputStream, ByteArrayInputStream, DataInputStream (for translating binary data to built-in type values), and PipedInputStream (for communication among threads). The class File represents files on the host system and provides messages for accessing a file's attributes, deleting and renaming files, and creating and listing directories. The java.io package also defines the class IOException and subclasses such as EOFException and FileNotFoundException. The package java.net defines classes for writing network applications, especially for use on the internet. These include the class InetAddress for representing an internet host and its name and IP address, and classes such as URL (a "uniform resource locator" that gives a protocol, a host name, an optional port number, and a file name), URLConnection, URLStreamHandler, Socket, DatagramPacket, and various exceptions.

The package java.awt ("abstract window toolkit") defines a set of classes that support platform-independent user interaction components and graphic operations. The fact that these classes are included in the standard class library provides much of the appeal of Java. In particular, we can write an application with a graphic user interface once, and then execute that application on any platform for which there is an implementation of the virtual machine, rather than rewriting the application for each platform's GUI API.

The package java.awt includes numerous classes. The abstract class Component has subclasses for interaction components such as Button, Checkbox, List, TextField, and Canvas. Its abstract subclass Container is the superclass of classes that can contain components such as Frame (a top-level window), Dialog, and Panel (a sub-window). The package java.applet defines the class Applet, a subclass of Panel, that can be embedded in a web browser. Each container has a "layout manager" (an instance of a class such as BorderLayout, CardLayout or GridLayout) that determines how it places and sizes the components it contains. The package also defines the abstract class MenuComponent, and its subclasses MenuBar, Menu, and MenuItem. User activity is represented by instances of the class Event, and each of the components defines methods for responding to events. Each component has an instance of the class Graphics that provides messages for drawing lines, rectangles, arcs, and strings, and for copying images (although programs usually only draw on a canvas). The library also defines classes such as Color, Font, FontMetrics, and Image to represent the corresponding kinds of objects. The package java.awt.image defines classes for creating images, loading them from producers asynchronously, and filtering images.

An example

Java does not permit the programmer to separate the definition of a class into an interface and an implementation. Usually, each class is defined in a separate file called *Class*.java, and the class file must explicitly import any classes it uses. We define the class Square in the package examples in Java as follows:

```
// definition of the class Square in Java

package examples;

import examples.DisplayObject;
import java.awt.Point;
import examples.Angle;
import java.awt.Color;
import java.awt.Image; [6]
```

---

[6] We use the Java class java.awt.Image, which is used for off-screen images, as the target of draw operations in this example. This class java.awt.Canvas defines an interaction component that we can draw on, but Image and Canvas do not have a common superclass.

```
class Square extends DisplayObject
{
  // constructor to initialize an instance
  public Square(Point center, Angle tilt, int size, Color color)
  {
    super(center, color);
    this.tilt = tilt;
    this.size = size;
  }

  public final Angle getTilt()
  {
    return tilt;
  }

  public final int getSize()
  {
    return size;
  }

  public final Point[] getCorners()
  {
    // code for getCorners() method
  }

  public void draw(Image canvas)
  {
    Point[] corners = this.getCorners();
    where = canvas;
    Graphics gr = where.getGraphics();
    gr.setColor(color);
    gr.drawLine(corners[0].x, corners[0].y, corners[1].x, corners[1].y);
    gr.drawLine(corners[1].x, corners[1].y, corners[2].x, corners[2].y);
    gr.drawLine(corners[2].x, corners[2].y, corners[3].x, corners[3].y);
    gr.drawLine(corners[3].x, corners[3].y, corners[0].x, corners[0].y);
    visible = true;
  }

  // ... other Square methods ...

  // instance variables
  protected Angle tilt;
  protected int size;
}
```

The package statement indicates which name space includes this class, and the import statements give the names of classes of which this class is a client, qualified by their package names. Unlike C++, the class definition gives an access specifier for each component individually. As in C++, the constructor has the same name as the class. The constructor for Square invokes the superclass constructor to initialize the inherited instance variables, and then assigns values to the Square instance variables. We follow the Java convention of naming accessor messages as get...(), and mark these messages as final because they will not be overridden. The type Point[] indicates a reference to an array of points, and arrays are allocated dynamically like class instances. Note that all class type identifiers are references; for example, the assignment to where does not make a copy of the referent of canvas (as it would in C). The Java class library uses an instance of the class Graphics to perform drawing protocol.

4.5 HYBRID OBJECT-ORIENTED LANGUAGES

4.5.1 Basic Concepts

Purpose

Language designers have defined or proposed object-oriented extensions for numerous existing languages including Pascal, C, Lisp Ada, Prolog, Logo, Forth, and even Cobol. Such a language adds features for encapsulation, information hiding, inheritance, polymorphism, and dynamic binding to the base language. Many hybrid languages also add contemporary language features such as modules, exception handling, operator overloading, and generics to the base language.

As stated in section 4.1.1, hybrid languages provide backward compatibility with base language code libraries, and familiarity for programmers who know the base language. Extending an existing language often results in a more efficient implementation that for a pure language because the compiler can translate basic types and their operations (e.g., integers) using machine operations directly, and can use static binding for subprograms, as in the original language. The disadvantage is that familiarity with base language techniques may keep programmers from making the conceptual shift to the object paradigm, resulting in a design that contains both procedural and object-oriented components.

Coding

Hybrid languages typically implement class definitions as an elaboration of the record type (or the struct type in C) that gives a superclass, instance variables as fields, and methods as subprograms associated with the class (recall the C++ class CharStack in section 1.1.4). Most languages also provide a mechanism for indicating the interface and implementation of a class, i.e. which fields and subprograms are externally visible, and for defining the implementation separately from the interface. Hybrid languages often distinguish between the operations and features of programmer-defined classes and the built-in types of the base language, and usually support unencapsulated subprograms and global variables, as in the base language.

As we described in section 2.2.3, message passing syntax appears like a subprogram call in which the message is indicated by component selection of the method within the receiver object. Methods are coded in the same manner as subprograms in the base language, which may be procedural or functional.

4.5.2 Extensions to Pascal

Object Pascal

Object Pascal is an extension to Pascal defined by Larry Tesler, Niklaus Wirth, and others at Apple Computers for use with the Apple Lisa and then the Apple Macintosh [Tes85]. Object Pascal adds the object-oriented features of encapsulation, inheritance, polymorphism, and dynamic binding to Apple Pascal, an earlier extension to Pascal that added modules (called units) and other features to standard Pascal.[7] The language does not support class variables and messages, multiple inheritance, generics, operator overloading, exception handling, or concurrency. The language system includes a large class library that provides foundation and collection classes, as well as classes for primitive graphic operations and Macintosh user interface components.

As in languages that support modules, a program consists of a set of units containing classes, procedures, and functions, and each unit is divided into an interface and an implementation. A class definition is introduced by the reserved word object (rather than record), and may include a superclass, fields for the instance variables, and procedure and function declarations for the class's messages. Unfortunately, a class's instance variables and messages cannot be hidden from clients (like the fields of a Pascal record). Programmers can obtain the effect of defining a private method by defining a procedure or function in the implementation part of the unit and not listing its declaration in the unit's interface. If a class overrides an inherited message, the message's declaration must include the reserved word override. As stated in section 4.1.1, the programmer can achieve the effect of class variables and messages by encapsulating objects and receiverless procedures in the class's module.

Method definitions are coded separately from the class definition in the implementation part of the unit, and are defined using the method name qualified by the class name. Methods are coded like Pascal procedures or functions with message expressions. A method can refer to the receiver with the reserved word self, but this is rarely necessary because the body of a method is enclosed in an implicit with statement, so the method can refer to the receiver's components directly. The reserved word inherited is used to invoke a superclass method for refinement.

All variables of class type are references, and dereferencing is implicit in the same manner as for var parameters in Pascal (i.e., no ∧ is needed). All objects are allocated on the heap, and are created with the built-in procedure new, which takes a class type identifier or pointer argument, as in Pascal. The object must

---

[7] These additional features include variable initializations, an OTHERWISE clause for the CASE statement, the LEAVE statement for loop exits, constant parameters, record return types for functions, a string type, multiple sizes of numeric types, procedure and function variables, untyped pointers (like void* in C), pointer arithmetic, and pointer casts.

then be given a valid state by passing it an initialization message. Deallocation is controlled by the programmer, and objects are deallocated with the built-in procedure dispose. The programmer can use a class name as an explicit type conversion, and can set a compiler option to include code to validate such conversions at run-time. The built-in function member returns whether an object is an instance of a particular class.

A unit is coded in a single code file that includes its interface and implementation. We define the class Square and the method for draw in Object Pascal in the unit SquareClass as follows:

```
{ definition of the class Square in Object Pascal }
unit SquareClass;

interface

uses DisplayObjectClass, PointClass, AngleClass, ColorClass, CanvasClass;

type
   PtrPointArray = ^ array [1 .. 4] of Point;
   Square = object(DisplayObject)
      { instance variables }
      tilt: Angle;
      size: integer;
      { instance messages }
      {we do not define accessor functions for tilt and size because they are public }
      procedure init(center: Point; tilt: Angle; size: integer; color: Color);
      function corners: PtrPointArray;
      procedure draw(canvas: Canvas);  override;
      procedure rotate(amount: Angle);  override;
      procedure resize(newSize: integer);  override;
   end


implementation

{ draw the receiver on the argument canvas }
procedure Square.draw(canvas: Canvas);
var
     tempCorners: PtrPointArray;
begin
   where := canvas;
   tempCorners := self.corners;
   where.drawLine(tempCorners^[1], tempCorners^[2], color);
   where.drawLine(tempCorners^[2], tempCorners^[3], color);
   where.drawLine(tempCorners^[3], tempCorners^[4], color);
   where.drawLine(tempCorners^[4], tempCorners^[1], color);
   visible := true;
   dispose(tempCorners)
```

```
end

{ ... other Square methods ... }

end      { unit SquareClass }
```

The uses statement imports the interfaces of the listed units. Like any type in Pascal, a class is defined in a type declaration, and its superclass name is enclosed in parentheses after the reserved word object. In this example, we do not define accessor functions for the instance variables tilt and size because they are directly visible to clients. Unlike Smalltalk, Eiffel and Java, Object Pascal does not provide automatic deallocation so the method for draw must deallocate the referent of temp-Corners (a new object created by the corners method in Square) before returning.

Modula-3

Modula-3 was designed at Digital Equipment Corporation and Olivetti in the late 1980's [Har92]. The language is a descendant of Modula-2 that incorporates encapsulation, inheritance, polymorphism, and dynamic method binding. Modula-3 also defines constructs for generic modules (i.e., with type parameters), concurrency, and exception handling, but does not support class variables and messages, multiple inheritance, or operator overloading.

A Modula-3 program consists of a set of interfaces and modules (which correspond to definition modules and implementation modules in Modula-2), which can be compiled separately. An interface declares classes, types, procedures, exceptions, and objects that can be used by clients that import it. Interfaces are implemented in modules, and a module can implement more than one interface and vice versa. Both interfaces and modules can import interfaces, and importing an interface does not import the interfaces it imports. As in Object Pascal, a class definition uses the reserved word OBJECT and may include a superclass, fields for the instance variables, and procedure declarations for the class's messages. The field declarations may include a default initialization which will be done each time an instance of the class is created. To provide information hiding, Modula-3 supports "opaque types". The class designer defines a class that contains the public components of the class and an opaque subtype of it in an interface, and then "reveals" the implementation of the opaque subtype in a module. (Record types can also defined as opaque types in Modula-3.) The details of this process are illustrated in the code example later in this subsection.

A class's messages are implemented by procedures that take an additional first argument, the receiver (which is usually called self, but need not be), and the class definition initializes each message name with the corresponding procedure name. When a class overrides an inherited method, the class definition initializes that message with a different procedure name after the reserved word OVERRIDES. To specify that a message is abstract, the programmer initializes it with NIL, in which case, concrete descendants must define a procedure for that message. The procedures that implement messages are coded like Modula-2 procedures. Although methods are coded as procedures that take the receiver as an argument, a message expression appears like selection of that message in the receiver (as described in section 2.2.3). To invoke the superclass method for refinement, the procedure casts self to the superclass type (with the NARROW function discussed in the next paragraph), and then sends the message to the result.

Variables of class type are references and dereferencing is implicit. (The reserved word REF is used to declare references to built-in types, enumerations, arrays, records, and sets.) Dynamic objects are created with the built-in function NEW. Its first "argument" is the name of the type, and succeeding arguments give initial values for the object's fields. This initialization can also initialize the object's messages to different procedures than those in its class definition (of course, they must be type compatible), which essentially creates an anonymous subclass containing that object. (The method references cannot be changed after the object is initialized.) An opaque class must define an initialization message for clients (usually called init) since the class's instance variables are not accessible. Unlike Modula-2, Modula-3 uses automatic deallocation for dynamic objects and class instances. The built-in function ISTYPE tests whether a reference identifier refers to an instance of a class, and the built-in function NARROW can be used to convert an object reference to that of a related class, with a run-time check for conversions to descendants.

It is the convention in Modula-3 to define a class in an interface named by the class name that exports a type named T. For example, to define the class Square, we define the following interface:

```
(* definition of the interface of the class Square in Modula-3 *)
INTERFACE Square;

IMPORT DisplayObject, Point, Angle, Color;

TYPE
  T <: Public;
  Public = DisplayObject.T OBJECT
  METHODS
    (* public instance messages *)
    init(center: Point.T; tilt: Angle.T; size: INTEGER; color: Color.T): Public;
    tilt(): Angle.T;
    size(): INTEGER;
    corners(): REF ARRAY OF Point.T;
  END

END Square.
```

The statement T <: Public declares T as an opaque subtype of the type Public. Clients that import this interface use the type name Square.T as the type of references to squares, but can only use the messages defined in its ancestors Square.Public and DisplayObject.T. The message corners returns a reference to an array of points. The module Square "reveals" the opaque type by defining its instance variables and messages, and the procedures that implement its messages, and is coded as follows:

```
(* definition of the implementation of the class Square in Modula-3 *)
MODULE Square;

IMPORT DisplayObject, Point, Angle, Color, Canvas;

REVEAL
  T = Public BRANDED OBJECT
    (* instance variables *)
    tilt: Angle.T;
    size: INTEGER;
  METHODS
    init(center: Point.T; tilt: Angle.T; size: INTEGER; color: Color.T): Public := Init;
    tilt(): Angle := Tilt;
    size(): INTEGER := Size;
    corners(): REF ARRAY OF Point.T := Corners;
  OVERRIDES
    draw := DrawSquare;
    resize := ResizeSquare;
    rotate := RotateSquare;
  END;

(* draw the receiver on the argument canvas *)
PROCEDURE DrawSquare(self: T; canvas: Canvas);
VAR
  tempCorners: REF ARRAY OF Point.T;
BEGIN
  self.where := canvas;
  tempCorners := self.corners();
  self.where.drawLine(tempCorners[0], tempCorners[1], color);
  self.where.drawLine(tempCorners[1], tempCorners[2], color);
  self.where.drawLine(tempCorners[2], tempCorners[3], color);
  self.where.drawLine(tempCorners[3], tempCorners[0], color);
  self.visible := true;
END

(* code for the procedures Init, Tilt, Size, Corners, ResizeSquare, and RotateSquare *)

BEGIN
END Square.
```

The declaration that T is a BRANDED type indicates that the compiler should use name equivalence rather than structural equivalence in determining type compatibility for its instances. The initializations in the METHODS and OVERRIDES clauses of the class definition give the names of the procedures that implement those messages. The procedures that implement the class's messages access the receiver's components via the additional first argument, self in the procedure DrawSquare. A module also has a block of initialization code that is executed when the program begins, which is empty in this example.

Oberon

Oberon is based on Pascal and Modula-2 and was designed by Niklaus Wirth and others at the Institute for Computer Systems, ETH Zürich in 1986. Two years later, the language was extended with encapsulation, inheritance (which it refers to as "type extension" of record types), polymorphism, and dynamic method binding (and is sometimes called Oberon-2). Oberon also simplifies several features of Pascal and Modula-2 and enhances others. The language does not support class variables and messages, multiple inheritance, generic modules, operator overloading, concurrency, or exception handling. Like Smalltalk, Oberon provides a complete operating environment for a computer user including an operating system and graphic user interface, as well as programming tools and a module library.

As in all the Pascal-based hybrid languages, an Oberon program consists of a set of modules that define types, procedures, variables, and constants. A module is not divided into an interface and implementation. Instead, the identifiers that a module exports are marked with trailing asterisks. (The environment includes a tool that extracts and displays the interface of a module.) A class is defined by defining a record type, which may give a "base type" that the record type extends, together with fields for the class's instance variables and dynamically bound messages. Messages that are statically bound (e.g., accessors), are defined as procedures in the module that defines the class, but are not encapsulated within the record type. The class's dynamically bound messages are defined as procedure-valued fields in the record type. The initialization message that creates a new instance assigns the procedures that implement the class's messages to that object's procedure fields. (If the class uses inherited methods, then the superclass procedure is assigned using a qualified name.) However, these procedure fields are instance-specific rather than class-specific, so the value for a particular object's message can be assigned a different procedure than that defined in the class's initialization message. That is, different instances of a class may have different methods for a particular message. The class designer can define an abstract message by omitting initialization of that procedure field (which effectively makes the record type abstract).

Methods in Oberon are defined like any procedure. The receiver is passed as an argument, and programmers usually nest the body of a method procedure within a WITH statement that names the receiver so that the code can access its fields directly. Statically bound messages use traditional subprogram call syntax with the subprogram name qualified by the module name and the receiver as one of the arguments (e.g., Squares.corners(sqr)). Dynamically bound messages appear like selections and invocations of the procedure field in the receiver, but the receiver is still passed as an argument of the invocation (e.g., sqr.draw(sqr, canvas)). To refine a superclass method, the subclass procedure uses a qualified name to invoke the procedure with that name in the module that defines the superclass.

Unlike other object-oriented languages, identifiers of class type are not automatically references. (In fact, there is no class type separate from the record type in Oberon.) By convention, the class designer exports a pointer type and an instantiation procedure that creates and returns a new dynamic instance, but this is not enforced. (As we will see in section 12.2, a pointer is necessary for polymorphism and dynamic binding.) The instantiation procedure creates the object with the built-in function NEW and then initializes its fields (see the following code example). Oberon uses automatic storage deallocation for all dynamic objects. A pointer can refer to instances of its own type or of any of that type's descendants, and a pointer can be cast to a descendant type with a "type guard" consisting of the desired class name enclosed in parentheses following the pointer name (e.g., pDisplayObject(Square)). However, the type guard is not checked at run time, so the programmer must first test the referent's type with the IS operator, which returns true if the left operand is an instance of the right operand type, or false otherwise.

It is the convention in Oberon to define a class in a module that exports a type whose name is the class name, with the plural of the class name as the module name. For example, to define the class Square, we define the module Squares, as follows:

```
(* definition of the class Square in Oberon *)
MODULE Squares;

IMPORT DisplayObjects, Points, Angles, Colors, Canvases;

TYPE
  PtrPointArray* = POINTER TO ARRAY 4 OF Point;
  Square* = POINTER TO SquareDesc;
  SquareDesc* = RECORD (DisplayObjects.DisplayObject)
     (* instance variables *)
     tilt*: Angles.Angle;
     size*: INTEGER
  END;

(* create, initialize and return a new instance *)
PROCEDURE New*(cntr: Point; tlt: Angle; sz: integer; clr: Color)
   : DisplayObjects.DisplayObject;
VAR
   newSquare: Square;
BEGIN
  NEW(newSquare);
  newSquare.center := cntr;
  newSquare.tilt := tlt;
  newSquare.size := sz;
```

```
    newSquare.color := clr;
    newSquare.draw := Draw;
    newSquare.resize := Resize;
    newSquare.rotate := Rotate
  END New;

  (* draw the receiver on the argument canvas *)
  PROCEDURE Draw*(self: DisplayObjects.DisplayObject; VAR canvas:
  Canvases.Canvas);
  VAR
    tempCorners: PtrPointArray;
  BEGIN
    WITH self: Square DO
      where := canvas;
      tempCorners := corners(self);
      Canvases.drawLine(where, tempCorners^[0], tempCorners^[1], color);
      Canvases.drawLine(where, tempCorners^[1], tempCorners^[2], color);
      Canvases.drawLine(where, tempCorners^[2], tempCorners^[3], color);
      Canvases.drawLine(where, tempCorners^[3], tempCorners^[0], color);
      visible := true
    END
  END Draw;

  (* code for the procedures corners, Resize, and Rotate *)

END Squares.
```

An asterisk after an identifier marks it as visible to clients that import the module. The module Squares exports the types Square and SquareDesc, the fields tilt and size, and the procedures New, corners, Draw, Resize, and Rotate. The intention is that clients will use the type Square, but the type SquareDesc and the procedures Draw, Resize, and Rotate are exported for use by subclasses. A client declares a Square identifier as sq: Square, and then initializes it with sq := Squares.New(...). The fields draw, resize, and rotate are defined as procedure fields in the superclass DisplayObject. For example, draw is defined as draw: PROCEDURE (self: DisplayObjects.DisplayObject; VAR canvas: Canvases.Canvas);. The procedure New creates a new square object and sets its fields, including the procedure fields that represent its dynamically bound messages. Its return type is DisplayObjects.DisplayObject so that the result can be assigned to a DisplayObject variable. The first parameter of the procedure Draw is a DisplayObjects.DisplayObject for type compatibility with other Draw methods. The method uses a "regional type guard" consisting of a WITH statement that casts the argument to a Square so that the fields where, color, and visible can be accessed directly. We do not check the validity of this cast because Squares.Draw will only be installed in instances of Squares.Square.

Delphi Pascal

Borland International's Turbo Pascal for PC compatibles [Bor96] has gradually expanded Pascal by adding modules and other features.[8] Beginning with version 6.0, the language supports classes, inheritance, and dynamic binding. The most recent version is part of a programming system called Delphi which contains an extensive class library and application framework for developing MS-Windows applications, and a programming environment that includes an interface builder. Borland now refers to the language as Object Pascal rather than Turbo Pascal, but we will call it Delphi Pascal to distinguish it from the earlier language with that name designed at Apple. Delphi Pascal provides exception handling, but does not support multiple inheritance, generics, or operator overloading.

Like Object Pascal, Delphi Pascal uses modules called units, and the interface and implementation of a unit are coded in a single code file. The programmer can use name qualification with unit names to resolve conflicts among imported names. As in Object Pascal, a class definition appears like a record type (introduced by the reserved word class) with embedded procedure and function declarations for its messages. All classes have a superclass, the predefined class TObject if none is specified in the class definition. (By convention, class names begin with T.) The language supports class messages (indicated by the reserved word class), but not class variables. Delphi Pascal also includes a number of features inspired by C++ (perhaps because Borland also markets a C++ programming environment). These include the access specifiers public, protected, and private for class components, class constructors and destructors for initialization and finalization, programmer-specified dynamic binding with the reserved word virtual, and inline functions. However, there are some differences from C++: a class's protected and private components are accessible to classes in the same unit, public is the default access level, and constructors and destructors are not invoked implicitly. Method overridings are declared with the reserved word override, and abstract messages are designated with virtual abstract. Delphi Pascal also includes features that are specific to MS-Windows. For example, a class message can be specified as an MS-Windows message handler, and the access specifier automated is used for class components accessible via Microsoft's OLE inter-application interface.

Delphi Pascal includes a feature not found in other statically typed object-oriented languages. An identifier whose type is a "class-reference type" refers to a class, and can be used to invoke class messages, create instances with a class constructor, or check the class of an object. Since the variable can refer to different classes at different times, this provides dynamic binding of these operations. For example, a variable WindowClass declared of type class of TWindow can refer to any descendant of the class TWindow. If we invoke a constructor, for example, Win-

---

[8] Turbo Pascal supports an else clause for the case statement, constant parameters, record and array return types, a string type, multiple sizes of numeric and character types, bitwise logical operators and shifts for integers (as in C), record and array literals and constants, procedure and function variables, untyped pointers, pointer arithmetic, and pointer casts.

dowClass.Create(rectangle) with the argument giving the size and location, the method invoked is that of the class WindowClass refers to at the point, and the object created is an instance of that class. In all other statically typed languages, the class of the object created must be specified directly in the source code because there are no class-valued variables.

Methods are defined using a qualified name, and are coded like Pascal procedures or functions with message expressions. As in Object Pascal, the body of a method is enclosed in an implicit with statement so the receiver's fields and messages can be accessed directly. A method can refer to the receiver as Self, and can invoke a superclass method for refinement with the reserved word inherited.

Variables of class type have reference semantics and dereferencing is implicit. Objects are created dynamically by sending a constructor message to the desired class, for example, TSquare.Create(. . .), which also initializes the new object. Deallocation is automatic, but if the instances of a class require finalization, the client must send the message Free to such an object when finished using it to invoke its destructor.[9] The actual class of an object can be obtained with the message ClassType, which returns a class-reference to the object's class. The built-in operator is returns whether its left operand is an instance of a descendant of the class represented by the right operand class name or class-reference. The built-in operator as converts its left operand to the class represented by the right operand class name or class-reference if it is an instance of a descendant of that class, or returns nil if it is not.

We define the class TSquare and the method for draw in Delphi Pascal in the unit Square as follows:

```
{ definition of the class Square in Delphi Pascal }
unit Square;

interface

uses DisplayObject, Point, Angle, Color, Canvas;

type
   PPointArray = ^ array [1 .. 4] of Point;
   TSquare = class(TDisplayObject)
      { instance messages }
      constructor Create(Center: TPoint; Tilt: TAngle; Size: integer; Color: TColor);
      function GetTilt: TAngle;
      function GetSize: integer;
      function GetCorners: PPointArray;
      procedure Draw(canvas: TCanvas);  override;
      procedure Rotate(amount: TAngle);  override;
      procedure Resize(newSize: integer);  override;
```

---

[9] Earlier versions of Turbo Pascal used the reserved word object in class definitions and employed programmer-controlled deallocation for their instances. The current language system provides automatic deallocation for instances of classes created with the reserved word class.

```
protected
    { instance variables }
    Tilt: TAngle;
    Size: integer;
end;


implementation

{ draw the receiver on the argument canvas }
procedure TSquare.Draw(var Canvas: TCanvas);
var
    TempCorners: PPointArray;
begin
    Where := Canvas;
    TempCorners := Self.Corners;
    Where.DrawLine(TempCorners^[1], TempCorners^[2], Color);
    Where.DrawLine(TempCorners^[2], TempCorners^[3], Color);
    Where.DrawLine(TempCorners^[3], TempCorners^[4], Color);
    Where.DrawLine(TempCorners^[4], TempCorners^[1], Color);
    Visible := true;
end;

{ ... other Square methods ... }

end.
```

The messages are all public, but the instance variables are not accessible to clients. The constructor message Create creates an instance of the class if sent to the class TSquare, or re-initializes the receiver if sent to an instance. The messages Draw, Rotate, and Resize were declared virtual in the superclass TDisplayObject (the reserved word appears in the same position as override).

Ada95

Although Ada is much safer and more expressive than previous languages, it is basically a static, monomorphic language. A new version of the language called Ada95 incorporates features for object-oriented programming as well as enhancements to Ada's support for generics, package libraries, and concurrency. (The earlier version of the language described in section 4.3.2 is now known as Ada83.) Ada95 does not support class variables and messages, or multiple inheritance.

As in Ada83, a program consists of a set of packages, and a package is divided into a package specification and a package body. Like Oberon, Ada95 supports inheritance by providing extension of record types. For a record type to have subclasses, it must be designated as tagged. This reserved word indicates that the type's instances maintain a tag giving their type identity that the run-time system can check to implement dynamic binding. As in Oberon, the class's operations are not encapsulated within the record type, but are defined as procedures or functions that take an instance of the record type. In Ada, subprograms defined in the same package specification as a type that use it as the type of a parameter or return value are the type's *primitive operations*. Other subprograms with that type as a parameter type are not primitive operations, so they are not inherited and are not dynamically bound. Abstract classes and abstract messages are specified as abstract.

Methods are coded like any Ada subprogram and a message expression appears like a subprogram call with the receiver as an argument. The subprograms that implement a class's methods use that class rather than a superclass as the type of the "receiver" parameter. For example, the first parameter of the subprogram Draw in the package Squares is Square, while its first parameter in Circles is Circle. A method can invoke a superclass method for refinement by casting the "receiver" parameter to the superclass type and invoking the subprogram.

To support polymorphic identifiers, Ada95 provides "class wide types". For example, if a subprogram has a parameter of type Display_Object'Class, the caller can pass an instance of any descendant of Display_Object. The class wide types are regarded as "indefinite" types (like the unconstrained array type), so they cannot be the type of a value variable because the compiler cannot determine how much storage to allocate. To define a variable that can refer to an instance of any descendant, we define a pointer of the class wide type (using the reserved word access). If that identifier is used as the argument of a subprogram that is a primitive operation of the corresponding parameter type, the subprogram to execute is selected by the type tag of the referent of the argument. For example, if Display_Object_Ptr is of type access all Display_Object'Class, then the subprogram executed for the invocation Draw(Display_Object, Canvas) is determined by the type tag of the object that Display_Object_Ptr refers to.

Objects are treated as record instances in Ada, so they can be created as value variables or allocated dynamically. If the record type's fields are not private, the programmer can initialize them when creating an object. If they are, the type must supply an initialization procedure. Ada95 uses automatic deallocation for dynamic objects. An object or type's tag attribute is available via the Tag attribute, and tags can be compared for equality. The in operator returns whether its left operand object is an instance of its right operand class, or is an instance of a descendant of its right operand class wide type. A class wide type pointer can be converted to the type of a descendant, and the language system raises an exception if the conversion is not valid.

We define the package specification that exports the class Square and its primitive operations in Ada95 as follows:

```
-- definition of the class Square in Ada95
package Squares is

    with Display_Objects, Points, Angles, Colors, Canvases;
    use Display_Objects, Points, Angles, Colors, Canvases;

    type Ref_Point_Array is access array (1 .. 4) of Point;
```

```
type Square is new Display_Object with private;

-- "primitive operations" for the class's messages
procedure Init(Self: in out Square;
   Center: in Point; Tilt: in Angle; Size: in Positive; Clr: in Color);
function Tilt(Self: in Square) return Angle;
function Size(Self: in Square) return Positive;
function Corners(Self: in Square): Ref_Point_Array;
procedure Draw(Self: in Square; Cnvs: in out Canvas);
procedure Rotate(Self: in Square; Amount: in Angle);
procedure Resize(Self: in Square; NewSize: in Positive);

private
   type Square is new Display_Object with
      record
         -- instance variables
         Tilt: Angle;
         Size: Positive;
      end record;

end Squares;
```

The fact that Square is an extension of Display_Object is visible to clients, but its fields are not. We can tell that Square is a tagged type by the syntax new Display_Object with. (The superclass Display_Object is declared as tagged.) Although the first parameter of the procedure Draw is of type Square (it is defined in Display_Object as an abstract message whose first parameter is a Display_Object), Draw can be called with an argument whose type is a class wide type that is an ancestor of Square. If that identifier refers to a square object, this procedure is invoked. The method for draw is defined in the package body of Squares as follows:

```
package body Squares is

with Display_Objects, Points, Angles, Colors, Canvases;
use Display_Objects, Points, Angles, Colors, Canvases;

-- draw the receiver on the argument canvas
procedure Draw(Self: Square; Cnvs: in out Canvas);
   Temp_Corners: Ref_Point_Array;
begin
   Self.Where := Cnvs;
   Temp_Corners := Corners(Self);
   Draw_Line(Where, Temp_Corners(1), Temp_Corners(2), Color);
   Draw_Line(Where, Temp_Corners(2), Temp_Corners(3), Color);
   Draw_Line(Where, Temp_Corners(3), Temp_Corners(4), Color);
   Draw_Line(Where, Temp_Corners(4), Temp_Corners(1), Color);
```

```
    Self.Visible := true
end Draw;

-- ... other Square methods ...

end Squares;
```

The private fields Where and Visible in the square Self are accessible in the procedure Squares. Draw because that procedure is defined in the implementation of the
package that defines them as private. In Ada, parentheses are used for array subscription.

4.5.3 Extensions to C

C++

C++ was designed by Bjarne Stroustrup and others at AT&T's Bell Labora-
tories during the middle and late 1980's [Str91]. Stroustrup had programmed some
event-driven simulations in Simula67 but found the executable to be too inefficient,
so he began work on "C with classes", which eventually become C++. C++ retains
ANSI C as a subset so that existing C libraries would be available. In this way, the
language would have C's capability of dealing directly with the storage representation and hardware, as well as the abstraction capabilities of an object-oriented language. A major design emphasis was enabling the compiler to produce efficient
executables, even if it made the language and its use more complex. In particular,
the designers felt that the language should not impose overhead for a feature on
programs that do not use it. For example, dynamic binding is not used for all message sends so that the overhead of run-time type information and method resolution are not present for programs that do not need them. Similarly, value class type
variables are supported because they are more efficient, although this complicates
use of the language (see section 12.2). C++ supports class variables and messages,
abstract classes and messages, multiple inheritance, generics, and operator overloading. Recent extensions to the language provide exception handling and "namespaces" with import/export scope. Due to its C heritage and compatibility, C++ is
currently the most popular object-oriented language.

The terminology used with C++ is somewhat different and owes much to C
(see figure 4.2). We define a class with a class definition, an expanded version of
the struct definition that includes the class's

- *base classes* (superclasses)
- *member functions* (instance messages and methods), including its *constructors*
  for initialization and *destructors* for finalization
- *data members* (instance variables)
- *static member functions* (class messages and methods)
- *static data members* (class variables)

- *access specifications* for members and *friend function* declarations.

A superclass is not required in C++, and the class hierarchy does not have a root class (as do those of Smalltalk, Eiffel, Java, and Delphi Pascal). As stated in section 2.2.1, public members are accessible to clients, protected members are accessible to descendants, and private members are only accessible in the class's methods. Friend functions are functions that are not members of the class but have access to its non-public components. Class messages and variables are marked with the reserved word static. C++ supports both static and dynamic binding for member functions, and the class designer identifies member functions that require execution-time method resolution with the reserved word virtual. C++ programmers often refer to dynamically bound messages as *virtual functions*. Abstract messages are referred to as *pure virtual functions*, and are declared with the marker =0. A class that defines or inherits pure virtual functions is an abstract class that cannot be instantiated. Generic classes and functions are defined as *templates* with type parameters.

Methods in C++ are written like C functions, with the addition of message passing expressions. The method can refer to the receiver's members directly, i.e. messages to the receiver do not require a receiver syntactically. If necessary, a method can refer to the receiver with the reserved word this (which is a pointer), for example, to use the receiver as an argument or an operator operand. A method can invoke an inherited method for refinement by using the message name qualified with the name of the desired base class.

Unlike most object-oriented languages, C++ supports static, automatic, and dynamic allocation of class instances. Constructor and destructor member functions provide automatic programmer-controlled initialization and finalization of objects. The compiler always ensured that a constructor is invoked when an object is created and the class's destructor (if any) is invoked when an object is destroyed. The class designer can overload the constructor to provide several initialization options. Unlike most object-oriented languages, C++ employs programmer-controlled deallocation because it is more efficient. The operators new and delete replace the C functions malloc() and free() for dynamic allocation, and they implicitly invoke the object's constructor and destructor. In this way, all objects are properly initialized upon creation and the environment is "cleaned up" at the end of an object's lifetime. Originally, C++ did not support querying the type identity of the referent of a polymorphic identifier. The recent "run-time type information" extension (discussed in section 12.2.5) provides the dynamic_cast operator for casting an ancestor pointer to a descendant pointer, and the typeid operator for querying the class of an object.

Some of the constructs introduced in C++ are procedural improvements on pre-ANSI C. These include features that have become part of the ANSI C standard such as function declarations with parameter types and type checking and coercions (including across code files), the void type, and the const specifier. Like Ada, C++ supports a number of contemporary features for functions such as default function arguments, call and return by reference, and overloading of functions and operators. Small functions that provide information hiding or give a descriptive name to a sequence of operations can be declared inline, which indicates to the compiler that it can substitute the function's code for an invocation to avoid the overhead of calling and returning from the function. C++ also supports exception handling. A function raises an exception with a throw expression, and can define handlers for exceptions that might occur in functions it calls with a try statement. Exceptions are defined like any class, and the exception object can be used to pass information from the signaler of an exception to the handler. We will discuss C++ exception handling in detail in section 13.3.

The definition of a C++ class is usually given in a header file, Square.h in this case. A class's header file also contains preprocessor directives that include the header files of its base class and the classes of its data members.[10] We define the header file Square.h in C++ as follows:

```
// Square.h: definition of the class Square in C++
#include "DisplayObject.h"
#include "Point.h"
#include "Angle.h"
#include "Color.h"[11]
#include "Canvas.h"
#include "Array.h"                 // a "class template" for array classes

class Square : public DisplayObject
{
    public:
        // messages ("member functions")
        // the class constructor, which is always used to initialize an instance
        Square(const Point&, const Angle&, int, const Color&);
        Angle tilt();
        int size();
        // Array<Point> is the class for arrays of points
        Array<Point> corners();
        virtual void draw(Canvas& canvas);
        virtual void rotate(const Angle&);
        virtual void resize(int);
    protected:
        // instance variables ("data members")
        Angle tilt_;
        int size_;
};
```

A constructor is coded as a member function with the same name as the class, Square() in this example, and takes arguments that it uses to initialize the new object.

[10] As we will see in section 10.1.3, the class header file also includes declarations of file scope functions associated with the class, definitions of inline member functions, and a preprocessor directive to prevent multiple definition errors from the compiler in code files that include the class header file more than once.

[11] As we will see in section 10.1.3, the header file Square.h can simply declare the classes Color and Canvas rather than including their entire definitions since those classes are only used as the type of a reference.

The parameter specification const Point& indicates that the argument is passed by reference (the "&"), and is not modified by the member function (the "const"). The name Array<Point> specifies the class generated from the class template Array with the class Point as the type parameter binding for the element type. The member functions Square::draw(), Square::rotate(), and Square::resize() are declared virtual because invocations must be dynamically bound. As we discussed with respect to Ada packages in section 1.1.4, the header file contains a private section not available to clients so that the compiler can allocate Square objects in client code. We have given the data members names with a trailing underscore because a member function and a data member in the same class cannot have the same name.

The method Square::draw() would be defined in a code file Square.cc, as follows:

```
// the code file for the class Square in C++
#include "Square.h"

// draw the receiver on the argument canvas
void Square::draw(Canvas& canvas)
{
    Array<Point> corners = this->corners();
    // we assume that the data member where is defined as a pointer in the base class
    where = &canvas;
    where->drawLine(corners[0], corners[1], color);
    where->drawLine(corners[1], corners[2], color);
    where->drawLine(corners[2], corners[3], color);
    where->drawLine(corners[3], corners[0], color);
    visible = true;
}

// ... other Square methods ...
```

To indicate to the compiler which class's method we are defining, we use the qualified name Square::draw() with the "scope operator" :: and the class name. The name Array<Point> is a type name like any other, and is used in this method as the type of the local variable corners. That object is initialized with the result of sending the message corners() to the receiver, which we assume returns the new object by value. We do not deallocate that object before exiting the function because the object is automatically allocated in the activation record of Square::draw(). We use the -> operator to send the message corners() because the C++ receiver identifier this is a pointer.[12] C++ supports both reference and pointer variables, but a reference variable cannot be re-assigned to refer to a different object, so we assume that the inherited data member where is defined as a pointer to an instance of Canvas or a descendant. Therefore, we assign the address of the argument canvas to it, and use the -> operator to send it mes-

---

[12] We will see in section 10.1.4 that the this-> is optional in C++ for messages to the receiver of the method.

sages. C++ supports operator overloading, and the previous method assumes that the class template Array overloads the [ ] operator to access the elements of the array.

Objective-C

Objective-C was designed by Brad Cox [Cox86], and is marketed by the Stepstone Corporation for a variety of platforms. It is also the primary language used with NeXT systems. The language is a superset of C, and is designed to provide the readability and flexibility of Smalltalk as well as the efficiency of C. Objective-C does not support multiple inheritance or operator overloading, and does not provide generic classes because it uses dynamic typing for identifiers that refer to objects. Objective-C includes a class library based on that of Smalltalk (called ICpaks™ in the Stepstone implementation), and a programming environment with programming tools such as a browser, debugger and project manager. The NeXT system also includes an application framework and an interface builder.

To support object-oriented design and programming, Objective-C adds class definitions with inheritance, and dynamically typed identifiers and dynamically bound messages to C. A class definition is divided into an interface file and an implementation file, and always gives a superclass, the library class Object if no other applies. The class interface file lists the messages available to clients, and can define both instance and class messages. The message declarations use the same syntax as message patterns in Smalltalk. The interface file also includes the instance variables for the compiler (like a C++ header file), but they are not accessible to clients (unless the compiler directive @public is used). The implementation file defines the class's methods, and can also define methods that are not available to clients (which are not listed in the interface file). The language also includes a feature for adding messages and methods to existing classes so that a programmer can add messages to system classes or divide the implementation of a class into several code files. Objective-C does not directly support class variables, but the class designer can define a static variable outside the methods in a class's implementation file and provide class methods that access or manipulate that information.

Method headers use the same syntax as Smalltalk message patterns. The body of a method is coded like a C function using C declarations and control structure statements, with message expressions written using Smalltalk syntax enclosed in square brackets. As in Smalltalk, the receiver's instance variables are accessible directly, the identifier self refers to the receiver of the method, and the identifier super is used as the receiver for method refinement.

Identifiers that refer to class instances are declared of type id, an implicit reference that can refer to any object (like a Smalltalk variable). Every class instance is created dynamically using a "factory method" defined by the object's class. That is, Objective-C uses dynamic typing and reference semantics for objects, but uses static typing and value semantics for data values defined as in C (including structures). In addition, messages sent via id variables are dynamically bound with dynamic type checking, while C functions applied to instances of C types are statically bound. To obtain compile-time type checking of messages to a variable that refers to objects, the programmer can use a C pointer whose type is its class—for example, Square*, rather than an id variable. All objects respond to the message class by returning a reference to their class, and Objective-C does not require conversions for objects since it uses dynamic typing for class instances.

We define the interface file Square.h in Objective-C as follows:

```
// Square.h: definition of the class Square in Objective-C
#import "DisplayObject.h"
#import "Angle.h"

@interface Square : DisplayObject
{
    // instance variables
    Angle tilt;
    int size;
}

// a "factory message" used to create and initialize an instance
+ newCenter: aPoint tilt: anAngle size: (int) anInt color: aColor;

// instance messages
- tilt;
- (int) size;
- corners;

@end
```

The directive #import imports an interface file without causing multiple inclusions of that interface file (unlike C's #include). The class interface is enclosed by the reserved words @interface and @end, and consists of the class name, a colon, the superclass name, instance variables declarations enclosed in braces, and a list of message declarations. Class messages are preceded by a + and instance messages preceded by a -. Message parameters and return values whose type is a C built-in type use a cast-like notation to specify their types. This allows the compiler to perform static type checking when an expression sending that message is embedded in a C expression. All other parameters and return values are of type id. Messages cannot be overloaded, so each class that defines a particular message must use the same parameter and return types. For example, a parameter of a particular message cannot be a id in one class and a built-in type in another. As in Smalltalk, an instance variable and an instance method can have the same name.

The implementation of the class Square is defined as follows:

```
// the implementation of the class Square in Objective-C
#import "Square.h"

// draw the receiver on the argument canvas
- draw: canvas
{
    // the Square method for corners returns an instance of the system class IdArray,
    // an array of dynamically typed references
    id corners = [ self corners ];
    where = canvas;
    [ where drawLineFrom: [ corners at: 1 ] to: [ corners at: 2 ] with: color ];
    [ where drawLineFrom: [ corners at: 2 ] to: [ corners at: 3 ] with: color ];
    [ where drawLineFrom: [ corners at: 3 ] to: [ corners at: 4 ] with: color ];
    [ where drawLineFrom: [ corners at: 4 ] to: [ corners at: 1 ] with: color ];
    visible = true;
    [ corners free ];
}

// ... other Square methods ...
```

We will discuss the Smalltalk syntax illustrated by the message to where in section 5.3.2. Like Object Pascal, Objective-C does not provide automatic deallocation so the draw: method deallocates the referent of corners before returning. A class can override the method for free inherited from Object if it is necessary to perform any finalization before releasing the object's storage (similar to the destructor in C++).

4.5.4 CLOS

Background

Lisp was specifically designed to be extendible, and has several characteristics in common with Smalltalk that facilitate extendibility (actually, Smalltalk adopted these features from Lisp):

- Lisp is completely uniform: Every operation is a function (or macro) call, including control structures, instantiation, and type definitions.
- Lisp has a very small core language, and the rest of the language is defined in Lisp as extensions to the core. The language makes no distinction between built-in functions and programmer-defined functions.
- Lisp uses a very simple syntax that mirrors the nested list structure of data. Since programs and data have the same structure, it is common to write functions that compose and execute other functions.
- Lisp is interpreted, so the symbol table and type information are available at execution time. Programs can define new functions and types dynamically.

The Lisp culture is based on experimentation and customization, and programmers have extended the language with several sub-languages for various applications. As interest in the object paradigm grew in the early 1980's, several groups designed and implemented object-oriented extensions to Lisp, the most well-known being Flavors [Moo86] and LOOPS [Ste86]. Flavors was designed by David Moon and others at MIT and the Symbolics Corporation to implement the operating system and graphic user interface of the Symbolics Lisp workstation. LOOPS (Lisp Object-Oriented Programming System) was designed by Daniel Bobrow and Mark Stefik at Xerox PARC, originally for an integrated circuit design system. The Common Lisp Object System, or CLOS, [Kee89] incorporates features of these languages, and is now part of the ANSI standard for Common Lisp [Ste90].

CLOS supports classes with class and instance variables, and multiple inheritance. As we discussed in section 2.4.2, methods are organized according to generic functions, rather than being encapsulated within classes. Therefore, CLOS does not support abstract messages or abstract classes. Like Lisp, CLOS is dynamically typed and uses automatic deallocation. Lisp packages (name spaces with import/export scope) can be used to provide information hiding. CLOS has no need for generics because it is dynamically typed. Common Lisp supports exception handling, but not concurrency. Most Lisp systems provide an extensive programming environment and a package library.

An important difference between CLOS and other object-oriented languages is the flexibility that it provides the programmer to customize virtually every aspect of the language. For example, the method combination procedure that implements refinement is written in CLOS and the programmer can redefine it if desired. CLOS classes can also be redefined by adding and deleting instance variables or superclasses at execution time, and the run-time system automatically updates all the objects and definitions affected. CLOS also provides the function change-class which changes the class of an existing object.

Classes and inheritance

Common Lisp provides the macro defstruct for defining a structure type (like a record type) and its initialization and accessor functions. CLOS adds the macro defclass, which lists the class's superclasses and *slots* (instance variables), and can provide a number of options with each slot. However, a class definition does not declare the class's messages. The class standard-object is the superclass of classes that do not list superclasses in their definitions. Since every class is a descendant of the class standard-object, programmers and CLOS systems can define behavior for all objects by defining methods for this class. For example, there is a generic function print-object that has a default method defined for a standard-class argument. The general format of a class definition appears as follows (identifiers preceded by colons are keywords that identify options):

```
; defining a class in CLOS
(defclass class (superclass₁ superclass₂ ...)
    ( (slot₁ :accessor access-fn₁ :initform expr₁ :initarg :init-symbol₁ ... other options ...)
      (slot₂ ... options ...)
      ... other slots ...)
    ... class options ...)
```

There are two class options: The :documentation option provides information for programming tools, and the :metaclass option provides the class with a different metaclass than standard-class (see section 6.3 for a discussion of metaclasses). There are eight slot options. The :accessor option names two generic functions that provide read and write access to a slot value, respectively. The defclass macro generates these functions. (That function accesses the object's slots with the function slot-value, and can be redefined by the class or refined in descendants.) The programmer can use :reader or :writer instead to generate only a function that reads from or writes to the slot, respectively. If none of these are given, the slot is not accessible to clients. The expression associated with :init-form is evaluated to provide an initial value for the slot when an instance of *Class* is created (if no value is given for the slot). The programmer can use the symbol associated with :initarg as a keyword parameter to give a value for the slot when creating an instance with the function make-instance. Usually, this symbol is the slot name. The :allocation option specifies whether the slot is an instance or class variable with the values :instance or :class, and :instance is the default.[13] The programmer can indicate the type expected for each slot with the option :type, but like Lisp, the language definition does not require the translator to perform type checking. The class definition can also give a :documentation option for each slot.

Classes can be defined in any order in CLOS, and a class can be defined before its ancestors. The system updates all the related type information when a new class is defined. However, a class cannot be instantiated until all its ancestors are defined. A class inherits all of the slots of its superclasses, and can give options for inherited slots that augment or override those declared in the super-class. However, if two of a class's superclasses declare the same slot name, then its instances have only one slot with that name. Due to the method binding process, a class also inherits the methods defined for its superclasses and may refine or replace them.

Each class has a *precedence list* consisting of itself and its ancestors that is used in method binding. The precedence list is ordered from the most specific ancestor to the least specific. For example, with single inheritance, the precedence list consists of the class, its superclass, its superclass's superclass, and so on to standard-object. With multiple inheritance, the precedence list is a depth-first traversal of the class's ancestors, with the superclasses of each class ordered according to the superclass list in class's definition. That is, a class always has precedence over its superclasses, and a class's superclass list is ordered from left to right. The first element is the class, followed by the class's first superclass, followed by that class's precedence list, followed by its second superclass, and so on. Repeated ancestors appear in the list the first time they are encountered by the search of ancestors.

---

[13] Instance and class variables are often referred to as "local slots" and "shared slots", respectively, in CLOS.

The macro make-instance creates an instance of *Class*, and gives initial values for its slots:

```
; creating an object in CLOS
(make-instance 'class :init-symbol₁ value₁ :init-symbol₂ value₂ ... )
```

The first argument is the class name, and each succeeding *:initarg* symbol specifies the slot for the associated value (as in a keyword parameter format). If no initial value is given for a slot, its :initform expression is evaluated to supply a value. Alternatively, the programmer can define a constructor function (usually called make-*class*) that takes initialization arguments, calls make-instance, performs any other setup necessary for the new object, and returns it. In this way, the class designer can ensure that clients provide the necessary information to completely specify the new object.

As in Lisp, the function type-of returns the class of the argument, the function typep returns whether an object is an instance of a given class (or a descendant), and the function subtypep returns whether its first argument class is a descendant of its second. Like Smalltalk, Lisp is interpreted so type information must be maintained at execution time. As in Smalltalk, each class is represented by a class object bound to the class name symbol, and defclass returns this object. The function find-class returns the class object with a given name, and the accessor class-name returns or sets the name of a class.

Generic functions and multiple polymorphism

The collection of methods with the same name (i.e., a set of overloadings), constitute a *generic function*, and all such methods must have the same number of parameters.[14] A message passing expression appears like a generic function application, i.e. (*message arg₁ arg₂* ...), and no argument is distinguished as the receiver. The macro defmethod defines a method in CLOS, as follows:

```
; defining a method in CLOS
(defmethod message ((param₁ class-name₁) (param₂ class-name₂ ) ... )   body )
```

The body of a method is coded like a Lisp function. Unlike Smalltalk and other object-oriented languages, a method can be associated with a list of classes, i.e. the types of the method's parameters, which specify whether this method can apply for an invocation using that function name.[15] The programmer can use the macro defgeneric to give options for a generic function, such as documentation, the number of parameters, and the argument precedence order and method combination rule it

---

[14] Strictly speaking, the methods for a generic function must be "congruent"; they must have the same number of required parameters, the same number of optional parameters, and either all or none must use the feature &rest, which is used for functions that take a variable number of parameters.

[15] In fact, the programmer can define a method for particular objects by using (eql 'obj-name) rather than a class name in the parameter list of defmethod.

uses. If it is not used, defmethod generates a generic function with the given number of parameters, no documentation, and default behavior for the other options when a method with that name is defined.

As stated in section 3.2.4, CLOS supports two mechanisms for method overriding, "before" and "after" methods, and "around" methods. A method that is not a before, after, or around method is the *primary* method for the generic function for that class and its descendants. Descendants can define a refinement of this method as a "before" method or an "after" method by using the keyword :before or :after after the function name in defmethod. When a generic function is invoked with an argument of a given class, the before methods of the class's ancestors are invoked in the order of the precedence list (i.e., most specific first), followed by the most specific primary method, followed by the after methods in reverse order of the precedence list (i.e., most specific last). The return value is the return value of the primary method (i.e., before and after methods are used to perform side effects). If the class of the argument defines an around method with the keyword :around, then it is invoked. The around method can call the inherited methods with call-next-method, and can test whether there is a next method with next-method-p. The return value is the return value of the around method.

This "standard method combination rule" can be altered for a particular generic function with an option in defgeneric. For example, if we want the descendant method to return a value that is the sum of the return values of its ancestors' methods, we can use (defgeneric func (arg) (:method-combination +)). Several other method combination rules are supplied and the language provides a facility for defining new rules.

When a generic function is invoked, the interpreter must determine the *effective method* to evaluate from those corresponding to that function name. If the classes of the arguments in an invocation match exactly the parameter classes of one of the methods, the interpreter invokes that method. In general, when each argument in a function invocation is an instance of a descendant of the corresponding method parameter for some method, that method is *applicable* to the message. In this case, method binding involves selecting one method from the set of methods applicable to the message, or possibly combining methods if some methods are defined as refinements. Among the applicable methods for a generic function application, a method that matches a more specific set of classes compatible with the argument list (i.e., closer to those classes in the hierarchy) takes precedence.

This is similar to resolving overloadings in the presence of conversions, namely from a class to any of its ancestors. For example, suppose sub is a subclass of super1 and super2, and we have the methods (defmethod foo ((s1 super1) (s2 super2)) ...) and (defmethod foo ((s2 super2) (s1 super1)) ...). If sub-obj is an instance of sub, it appears that the call (foo sub-obj sub-obj) is ambiguous. However, if an invocation of a overloaded function in C++ is ambiguous due to coercions, the compiler can signal an error. In CLOS, this process is performed at run time, so some method must be called. For this reason, classes have a precedence list and the parameters of a generic function have a precedence ordering. If more than one method is applicable for a generic function invocation, the interpreter uses a left-to-right comparison of specificity of the argument types. (The programmer can change this ordering for a generic function with the :argument-precedence-order option of defgeneric.) When considering the methods for a given parameter, the argument's class precedence list is used to select a method. In the previous example, the first parameter is examined, and if super1 precedes super2 on the precedence list of sub, then the method with super1 as the first parameter type is invoked. That is, a class is considered a better match for its leftmost superclass, and so on left to right in the list of superclasses. Once the argument signature of the method to execute has been determined, the generic function's method combination rule is used to select the group of methods to invoke and their order of execution.

An example

The class square is defined in CLOS as follows:

```
; definition of the class square in CLOS
(defclass square (display-object)
    ((tilt :allocation :instance :accessor tilt :initform 0 :initarg :tilt :type angle)
     (size :allocation :instance :accessor size :initarg :size :type integer))
    :documentation "A class for rotatable squares.")
```

The method draw that applies to squares is defined by the following expression:

```
; draw the receiver on the argument canvas
(defmethod draw ((sq square) (cnvs canvas))
    (let ((corners (corners sq)))
        (setf (where sq) cnvs)
        (drawLine (where sq) (svref corners 0) (svref corners 1) (color sq))
        (drawLine (where sq) (svref corners 1) (svref corners 2) (color sq))
        (drawLine (where sq) (svref corners 2) (svref corners 3) (color sq))
        (drawLine (where sq) (svref corners 3) (svref corners 4) (color sq))
        (setf (visible sq) true)))
```

We assume that the superclass display-object has defined the accessors where, color, and visible for those slots. The function setf assigns the value of its second argument to its first argument, which must be "settable" (analogous to an *l*-value).[16] The function let declares and initializes local variables for a series of expression, corners in this method. Array elements are accessed with the function svref (sv stands for "simple vector").

---

[16] Strictly speaking, the name of the writer function is the list (setf where), termed a "function specifier".

4.6 SUMMARY AND REVIEW

4.6.1 Language Selection Criteria

Language features

- In a *pure* object-oriented language, every type is a class, all operations and information are encapsulated within classes, and every operation is a message send. Smalltalk, Eiffel, and Java are pure object-oriented languages.

- A *hybrid* object-oriented language adds data abstraction, class information, inheritance, and dynamic binding to an existing procedural or functional language. Hybrid object-oriented languages include Object Pascal, Modula-3, Oberon, Ada95, C++, Objective-C, and CLOS.

- Pure object-oriented languages enforce the object model, while hybrid languages stress efficiency, backward compatibility, and familiarity. Using a hybrid language often results in a mix of procedural and object-oriented design elements and code.

- Dynamically typed languages such as Smalltalk and CLOS provide flexibility at the expense of run-time overhead, while statically typed languages such as Eiffel, Java, and hybrid languages based on Pascal and C provide compile-time type checking and run-time efficiency.

- Incrementally compiled languages such as Smalltalk, CLOS, and Java are translated to code for a virtual machine that is implemented on each platform. This facilitates incremental development and debugging, but results in less efficient execution than compiled code.

- Automatic deallocation of dynamic storage is more convenient and reliable, but requires run-time support. Programmer-controlled deallocation avoids this overhead, but can result in memory leaks and dangling pointers, and it complicates reference semantics. C++ and Object Pascal use programmer-controlled deallocation like their base languages, and all other object-oriented languages use automatic deallocation.

- Multiple inheritance adds to the expressive power of the language, but complicates the language, its translation, and dynamic binding. Eiffel, C++, and CLOS support multiple inheritance, while Smalltalk, Objective-C, and Pascal-based hybrid languages do not. Java provides *interfaces*, which are "completely abstract" classes that contain only abstract messages and define no instance variables, and a class can extend any number of interfaces (but can only have one superclass from which it inherits instance variables and methods).

- Object-oriented languages also differ in terms of other language features such as support for modules, class messages and variables, operator overloading, generic classes (for statically typed languages), and exception handling.

Other factors

- Familiarity with the base language of a hybrid language facilitates learning the language and permits reuse of base language code. A popular language will have more texts, programming tools, and class libraries.
- Most object-oriented languages include a class library that reduces the coding effort by providing classes for instantiation, composition, and inheritance. Smalltalk, Java, Object Pascal, Delphi Pascal, and Objective-C also provide classes that support an application framework and graphics.
- Many language systems provide a programming environment that provides tools to browse the class library and inspect the execution of a program.
- Some languages are not implemented on all platforms, and some platforms have a preferred language.

4.6.2 Object-Oriented Programming Environments

Analysis-level tools

- CASE tools that aid in managing the entire software development process have been available for structured methods for some time. These tools support a particular methodology's graphic notation, manage a database of analysis and design results, and sometimes generate code from design diagrams. Similar systems are now available for several object-oriented methodologies.

Programming tools

- Programming environments are language-specific, and provide an integrated interface to editors, translators, debuggers, cross-referencers, code browsers, optimizers, profilers, version control systems, and other tools. Each of these also are useful with object-oriented programming.
- A *class hierarchy browser* provides a view of the structure of a class library or framework. It facilitates selecting a class from a framework, understanding the relationships among classes, and positioning class components in the hierarchy. Many browsers display a graph of the inheritance hierarchy.
- A browser allows the programmer to view individual classes and methods and edit that code, and examine the clients of a class, the classes it uses, and the senders or implementors of a message.
- A *class flattener* merges information in the definitions of a class and its ancestors to provides a single description of the class.
- An *interface builder* allows the programmer to create the graphic user interface of an application by positioning interface components in its windows and dialogs with drawing tools. He or she then specifies the visual attributes of the components, and their interactions with the application, for example, the message invoked by a pushbutton or the instance variable connected to a list or

slider. The tool then generates an application class with those components, messages, and instance variables, and an initialization method that implements the interface.

4.6.3 Precursors of Object-Oriented Languages

Simula 67

- Simula 67 was designed for writing programs that directly reflect the behavior and structure of a problem domain system. It introduced the concepts of objects, classes, and inheritance among classes that represent categories and subcategories in the problem domain.

- Objects are generated from class definitions that give the object's attributes and code. An object is a concurrent coroutine whose code is executed once (although it may be suspended and resumed), rather than as a package of information with its associated operations. The attributes of an object cannot be hidden.

- A subclass contains all the attributes of its superclass, and its code consists of the superclass code with the subclass code appended or inserted at an inner statement in the superclass code. The programmer identifies procedure attributes that require dynamic binding with the reserved word virtual.

- A ref variable declaration gives a class, and it can refer only to objects generated from that class or one of its descendants, i.e. it is polymorphic. The programmer can use the primitives is and in to determine the actual class of the referent.

- Simula 67 also defines a class library that includes classes for data transfer, collections, and simulation components.

Object-based languages

- *Object-based* languages provide data abstraction, but not inheritance and dynamic binding. They allow the designer to use object-based decomposition, but the programmer must code unions and case statements to implement subcategorization.

- The most well-known object-based language is Ada83 (whose support for data abstraction we discussed in section 1.1.4), which also supports packages, generics, exceptions, and concurrency, and improves on Pascal's control structures and type constructors.

4.6.4 Pure Object-Oriented Languages

Smalltalk

- The Smalltalk system is intended to be more than a language or an environment, but provides a paradigm for human-computer interaction.

- The Smalltalk language and environment are uniformly based on the object model. Every system or application component is an object whose behavior and state is defined by its class. All operations are performed by passing messages among objects, including arithmetic operations, input/output, control flow specification, object allocation, and class definition.

- The Smalltalk environment introduced the "desktop" metaphor for user interaction that presents windows, dialogs, popup menus, and other interaction components, and uses a pointing device for user interaction. It includes numerous programming tools such as editors, browsers, object inspectors, and debuggers.

- The Smalltalk language is based on data abstraction, the type inheritance and simulation orientation of Simula 67, the dynamic typing, automatic deallocation, extendibility, and functional semantics of Lisp, and an interactive graphic environment. It introduced the concepts of objects, classes, message passing, and inheritance that compose the object model. The language is designed to be very simple and uniform.

- Smalltalk is dynamically typed, so method binding and type checking are performed at execution time. Identifiers have reference semantics, and all objects are allocated dynamically and deallocated automatically.

- The Smalltalk system includes an extensive class library including classes for numbers, dates, collections, system services, graphics, user interaction components and controllers, and programming tools.

Eiffel

- Eiffel is a statically typed pure object-oriented language with a syntax similar to Ada. Eiffel supports multiple inheritance, generics, automatic deallocation, and operator overloading, but not modules or class messages and variables.

- Like Smalltalk, Eiffel includes a programming environment and a comprehensive class library.

- Eiffel provides special features for program verification, such as exceptions and assertions that are checked at execution time.

Java

- Java is a pure object-oriented language, which is primarily known as a language that supports designing platform-independent world wide web pages with user interaction components and dynamic content.

- Java is based on C++, but is simpler and safer. It does not support several C++ features, including the preprocessor, pointers, file scope functions, global variables, enumerations, unions, value variables of class type, operator overloading, multiple inheritance, and templates. The language provides automatic deallocation, packages, concurrency, and partial support for multiple inheritance via interfaces.

- Java includes a standard class library that provides classes for language support, strings, dates, collections, input/output, files, network access, user interaction components, graphics, and concurrency.
- The classes in the package java.awt support writing platform-independent interactive applications with graphic user interfaces.

4.6.5 Hybrid Object-Oriented Languages

Basic concepts

- Hybrid object-oriented languages provide backward compatibility with existing base language code and familiarity for programmers, but often results in hybrid designs and code.
- A class definition is a variation on the record type that gives a superclass, instance variables and messages, and indicates which components are visible to clients. There are often distinctions between programmer-defined classes and the built-in types of the base language.
- Methods are coded like subprograms in the base language, and message passing is indicated by component selection.

Extensions to Pascal

- Object Pascal is a statically typed extension to Pascal designed for programming the Apple Macintosh. The language provides modules, but does not support information hiding, automatic deallocation, class variables and messages, multiple inheritance, generics, or operator overloading. It also provides a class library that includes graphics and user interaction classes.
- Modula-3 incorporates data abstraction, inheritance, and dynamic binding into Modula-2. It also provides automatic deallocation, generic modules, concurrency, and exceptions, but does not support class variables and messages, multiple inheritance, or operator overloading.
- Oberon supports inheritance by providing extension of record types, but does not encapsulate a type's operations within the type. Oberon supports modules and automatic deallocation, but does not provide class variables and messages, multiple inheritance, generics, or operator overloading. Like Smalltalk, the Oberon system is a complete operating environment, together with programming tools and a class library.
- Delphi Pascal for PC compatibles is an object-oriented extension of Pascal that evolved from Turbo Pascal. The language provides modules, class variables and messages, class-reference types, and exception handling, but does not support multiple inheritance, generics, or operator overloading. It includes a number of features inspired by C++, such as constructors and destructors, and separate interfaces for clients and subclasses. The system includes a programming environment and class library.

- Like Oberon, Ada95 supports inheritance by providing extension of "tagged" record types, and does not encapsulate a type's operations. "Class wide types" provide polymorphism. Like Ada, Ada95 provides packages, generics, operator overloading, exception handling, and concurrency. It does not support class variables and messages, or multiple inheritance.

Extensions to C

- C++ adds data abstraction, inheritance, polymorphism, and dynamic binding (and other contemporary features) to ANSI C. Its major design goals (besides support for simulation and the object model) are efficiency and safety. C++ supports abstract classes, class variables and methods, multiple inheritance, template functions and classes (generics), exceptions, and namespaces (with import/export scope).

- A C++ class definition is an expanded version of the struct definition that includes the class's base classes, data members, member functions, and access specifications for members.

- C++ supports static, automatic and dynamic allocation of class objects. Constructor and destructor member functions provide automatic programmer-controlled initialization and finalization of objects.

- Objective-C adds classes, inheritance, polymorphism, and dynamic binding to C, and uses Smalltalk syntax for messages. It does not support multiple inheritance, generic classes, or operator overloading. The language uses dynamic typing and reference semantics for class instances and static typing and value semantics for instances of C types. Like Smalltalk, it includes a programming environment and class library.

CLOS

- CLOS is an object-oriented extension to Lisp that supports classes with instance and class variables, and multiple inheritance. Like Lisp, it uses dynamic typing and automatic deallocation. In fact, the facilities of CLOS are defined in Lisp and can be customized.

- CLOS provides the macro defclass for defining a class's superclasses, variables, accessor and initialization functions, and documentation. Each class has a *precedence list* of ancestors ordered from the most specific ancestor to the least specific, which is used in method binding.

- CLOS does not associate methods with classes. Instead, the methods with the same name and number of parameters compose a *generic function*. The interpreter performs dynamic binding on the basis of the classes of all the arguments to a generic function invocation, rather than only on the basis of a particular receiver.

4.7 EXERCISES

4.1 Give two advantages and two disadvantages of the use of a hybrid object-oriented language extension rather than a pure object-oriented language.

4.2 **(a)** Which object-oriented languages support exception handling?
    (b) Why is exception handling important for an object-oriented language?

4.3 Discuss the factors that enter into choosing an object-oriented language for a particular project.

4.4 **(a)** What is the purpose of an interface builder? Describe the process of using such a tool.
    (b) Using any interface builder you have available, design the interface for an appointment calendar program. How much code does this process generate, and how much code must still be written to implement the application?

4.5 **(a)** What two major concepts did Simula 67 contribute to the object-oriented programming paradigm?
    (b) How does the Simula 67 conception of an object differ from that in contemporary object-oriented languages? How is it similar?

4.6 In pure object-oriented languages, the class definition is the only type constructor. Describe how to use a class definition to define each of the following:
    (a) a type alias
    (b) a subrange type
    (c) an enumeration type
    (d) a subprogram type

4.7 **(a)** Which of the languages discussed in this chapter have a root class that is an ancestor of all classes?
    (b) Give an advantage and a disadvantage of this characteristic.

4.8 **(a)** Which of the languages discussed in this chapter support multiple inheritance?
    (b) How does each deal with the issues we described in section 3.4?

4.9 Describe how each of the languages discussed in this chapter provides method refinement.

4.10 **(a)** Which of the languages discussed in this chapter support abstract messages and classes?
    (b) For those that do, how does the class designer specify a message as abstract?

4.11 For each of the languages discussed in this chapter, describe how to determine the class of the referent of a polymorphic identifier.

4.12 **(a)** Which of the languages discussed in this chapter support organizing classes into modules? Give an advantage and a disadvantage of this characteristic.
    (b) Some of the languages discussed in this chapter do not support class variables and messages. Explain how to simulate the effect of class variables and messages if the language supports modules.

4.13 **(a)** Which of the languages discussed in this chapter allow separating the definition of a class into an interface and an implementation?
    (b) Give an advantage and a disadvantage of defining a class in a single construct.

4.14 Describe the intentions and goals of the designers of Smalltalk.

4.15 What features does Eiffel provide to support program specification and verification?

4.16 Although Java code looks very much like C code, we do not classify Java as a hybrid language. Why not?

4.17 Which C++ features are not supported by Java? For each, explain why it is not present.

4.18 **(a)** We stated in section 4.1.1 that Java includes interfaces, which are classes that contain only abstract messages and define no instance variables. A class can only inherit instance variables and methods from one class, but it can extend any number of interfaces. Clearly explain why this feature avoids the problems of name conflicts among inherited class components and the meaning of repeated inheritance.

(b) Why are interfaces useful in a statically typed language?

4.19 **(a)** How are classes and methods usually coded in a hybrid language?

(b) Compare and contrast class definitions in the Pascal-based hybrid languages.

4.20 In most hybrid object-oriented languages, base language type identifiers are values while class type identifiers are references. Give an advantage and a disadvantage of this situation.

4.21 Describe how the Delphi Pascal class reference type helps avoid coding a case statement when reading a file containing instances of various classes.

4.22 Describe the design goals of Smalltalk and C++ in terms of both their similarities and their differences.

4.23 List and describe six differences between Smalltalk and C++ in terms of language features.

4.24 Why is it true that Oberon and Ada95 must support automatic allocation of class instances?

4.25 **(a)** Describe the various kinds of method refinement in CLOS.

(b) Give an example for which each kind of refinement would be appropriate.

(c) Describe how method combination works in CLOS.

4.26 CLOS gives the programmer a number of ways to control the details of the method binding process, such as ordering the superclass lists of each class and setting the combination rule for each generic function, and these can be modified while a program is executing. Discuss the advantages and disadvantages of this flexibility. (Consider both programming and software engineering issues.)

PART II

Smalltalk

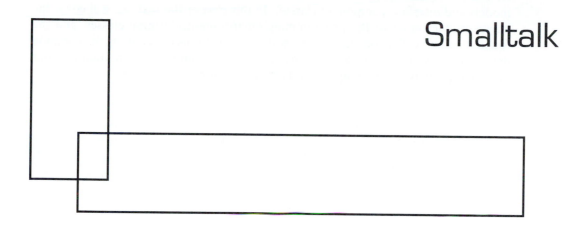

In Part II of the text, we discuss Smalltalk, the archetypical object-oriented language. Smalltalk is an excellent pedagogical tool for a number of reasons. With its simplicity and uniformity of concept, Smalltalk is easy to learn and use. The structure of the language consistently enforces the object paradigm. Its language features and large class library enable easy expression of an interactive application in object-oriented terms. Since almost all of the system is written in Smalltalk and the language is interpreted, the system is very malleable. Because of this, and because the system classes support graphic operations and graphic user interface components, Smalltalk is the ideal language for prototyping and incremental development.

A Smalltalk system is a comprehensive environment for object-oriented programming, which provides the services of traditional operating systems, language translators, and program development tools. In contrast, Smalltalk is a rather small language. Its syntax is much less complicated than most languages due to the uniform application of the object and message paradigm, and the use of programming tools for defining classes and methods. Constructs denoting control structures, built-in operations, object allocation, type constructors and selectors, and access control are unnecessary, and no syntactic structures that delimit class definitions, class components, and method definitions are needed.

Unfortunately, the Smalltalk language and class library are not standardized, although an ANSI standardization committee is now active. Several dialects have evolved since the introduction of Smalltalk-80 in the classic Goldberg and Robson text [Gol89]. ([Man94] gives a list of Smalltalk vendors, development systems, users groups and conferences.) There is very little variation among implementations with respect to the language itself. However, the foundation and collection classes differ somewhat among implementations, and different vendors use different graphics models and interface component classes. In this part of the text, we will cover the language, the basics of the programming environment, defining classes, and the foundation and collection classes. We will describe differences among the common dialects as they arise. You should consult the browser and documentation for your system, especially for the graphics and interface component classes.

5

The Language
and Environment

In this chapter, we will cover the basic structure of Smalltalk code, the meaning of a Smalltalk variable, control flow messages, and the use of the Smalltalk programming environment. The next chapter discusses defining classes, and the following two chapters describe the foundation and collection classes, respectively.

This chapter covers the following topics:

- the basics of programming in the Smalltalk environment (5.1.1), and an example Smalltalk program (5.1.2)
- the language's lexical structure, including the formats of comments, literals, and identifiers (5.2.1 and 5.2.2)
- *private variables*, *shared variables*, and *pseudo-variables* (5.2.3)
- the meaning of a *message expression* (5.3.1)
- message expression syntax, including *unary*, *keyword*, and *binary* message selectors, and precedence and associativity (5.3.2)
- message overloading and dynamic binding (5.3.3)
- dynamic typing's effect on the semantics of identifiers, objects, and strong typing (5.4.1)
- *value semantics* versus *reference semantics* for identifiers, and *unique* objects (5.4.2)

- the meaning of assignments, parameters and return values, comparisons, and copying (5.4.2)
- implementation of control structures in terms of message passing (5.5.1)
- the classes Boolean (5.5.2) and BlockClosure (5.5.3)
- conditional messages (5.5.4), and iteration messages and iteration over collections (5.5.5)
- concurrency (5.5.6) and exception handling (5.5.7)
- user interaction, the process of coding in Smalltalk, and the design concept of applications as classes (5.6.1)
- programming tools, including text editors (5.6.2), browsers (5.6.3), and the debugger (5.6.4)

5.1 A QUICK INTRODUCTION

5.1.1 The Smalltalk Experience

Using the Smalltalk system

Before we get into the details of the syntax and semantics of Smalltalk, we will cover the basic use of the Smalltalk environment for programming. Hopefully, you have a Smalltalk system available to you, not only because you must use a language to learn it, but also because the nature of interacting with a Smalltalk system is so different from using a compiled language such as C or Pascal. By understanding how to enter and execute code as soon as possible, you can

- try the examples in the text
- store and evaluate code fragments, and edit code and reevaluate it
- test your knowledge of the syntax and semantics of the language
- examine the behavior of the system classes and the structure of the class hierarchy
- issue commands to the system, for example, to run applications or perform file operations

We will see that it is much easier to perform these tasks in Smalltalk because the language is interpreted and the system provides scrollable windows for text editing. As we discussed in section 4.4.1, Smalltalk originated graphic interfaces that present windows, menus, and so on, and interaction with a pointing device, usually a mouse. In this section, we will describe entering text and evaluating code using the system interface. We will cover the Smalltalk programming environment in detail in section 5.6.

Interacting with an interpreted language

You may have only programmed in compiled languages, so let us consider how we use an interpreted language such as Smalltalk. If you have programmed in Lisp,

Basic, or APL, you have used an interpreted language. Shell scripting languages such as Perl, Bourne shell for Unix, and DOS batch scripts are also interpreted. Rather than using the two-step process of compiling code and then executing the resulting object code, the translator for an interpreted language translates a program or code fragment directly to the machine language of the hardware and executes it. For a language system with a command line interface, the translator prompts the programmer, reads a code selection, evaluates it, prints the result, and prompts the programmer again, which is called the *read-evaluate-print loop*. For example, we can use the language system as a calculator, as follows (we assume that the system provides some mathematical functions and uses >> for its prompt):

```
>> 3 + 4 * 13
55

>> sin(5.0) * exp(5.0)
-142.316981

>>
```

The run-time system for an interpreted language also maintains an environment that persists across code executions. This symbol table maintains global variables, function definitions, and type definitions for the code selections the programmer evaluates. The initial environment declares built-in functions and types (such as sin and exp in the previous example). When a code selection includes a declaration, that name and the object, function, or type object it refers to are stored in the environment. (The language usually also allows object declarations that are local to the code selection being evaluated.) This allows us to define a new function or type to use in successive executions, or to define a global variable and use it to test functions that act on its type. We can do this without the extra effort of defining a main program with input and output statements. For example, suppose we have an interpreter for C with the additional reserved word global that indicates a global object declaration (and function declarations are global by default).[1] A programmer might use the system as follows:[2]

```
>> int sum(int arr[], int size)
{
   int total = arr[0];
   for ( int index = 1;  index <= size;  ++index )
     total += arr[index];
   return total;
}
function int sum(int[], int) defined
```

---

[1] I am using C syntax for this interpreted system because you can read C. I will ignore some differences from C, for example, that we can't define and call a function in the same scope in C.

[2] I assume that the system provides a way of entering multi-line code fragments, such as a special "end of statements" delimiter.

```
>> global int array[] = { 1, 2, 3, 4, 5 };
{ 1, 2, 3, 4, 5 }

>> sum(array, 5);
-32045

>> int sum(int arr[], int size)
{
    int total = arr[0];
    for ( int index = 1;  index < size;  ++index )
        total += arr[index];
    return total;
}
function int sum(int[], int) defined

>> sum(array, 5);
15


>>
```

In this example interaction, the programmer types a function definition (the system responds by indicating that it has defined the function), then creates a global object to use in testing the function. Because the value returned by the first evaluation of the expression sum(array, 5) is incorrect, the programmer examines the original function definition, corrects it, and tests the function again. With immediate response and persistent symbolic environment, interpreted languages simplify learning the language, testing code, and understanding the behavior of types and subprograms provided by the system.

Evaluating code in Smalltalk

When you start your Smalltalk system (e.g., by executing a command or double-clicking on the system's icon), the system displays one or more windows on the screen. At least one of these will be a scrollable *text window* labeled as a "workspace" or "transcript". If you have used a word processor or window-based text editor, you already know how to use this object. You enter text at the position of the cursor by typing, and move the cursor with the arrow keys or by clicking the mouse button at the new cursor location. You select text by dragging across it with the mouse button depressed, or by clicking at one end of a selection and shift-clicking at the other. The text window highlights the selected text by displaying it in reverse colors. The window presents a menu of editing commands such as

- deleting the selection
- cutting or copying the selection to the "buffer"
- pasting the contents of the buffer at the cursor
- undoing the last command

- searching for a string
- replacing each occurrence of a string with another

On some systems, this menu pops up when the user presses a special mouse button, and on others, the user pulls it down from a menu bar.

To evaluate a code fragment, we first type the code in a text window and select it. In addition to editing commands, the menu for a Smalltalk text window includes three commands, called do it, print it, and inspect, for executing the selected text. If you select print it, the text window evaluates the selected expressions and prints the result of the last expression. (The result is also selected so that you can delete, cut, or copy it easily.) The command do it evaluates the selection without printing the result, and is useful for expressions that mainly perform a side effect such as adding an element to a collection. The command inspect opens an "inspector" on the object that results from the evaluation, as described in section 5.6.4.

We will cover a few examples of this process in this section so that you can begin using the system, but will not yet explain all the details of the expressions involved. A Smalltalk *message expression* consists of a receiver, the message name (the "selector"), and possibly an argument. For example, suppose we notice that the class String defines an instance message asUppercase, and we wonder about its effect on non-alphabetic characters in the receiver. We decide to examine the result of sending that message to the string '123hello!!' (string literals in Smalltalk are enclosed in single quotes). Figure 5.1 shows a text window in which that expression is selected, with the window's menu posted and print it selected (comments in

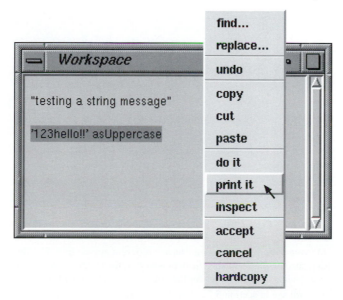

Figure 5.1 Evaluating an expression in a text window.

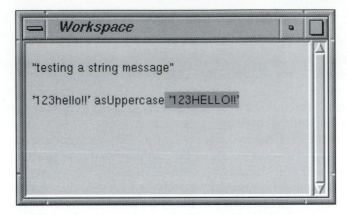

Figure 5.2   The result of evaluating an expression in a text window.

Smalltalk are enclosed in double quotes).[3] When the user releases the mouse button, print it is executed, resulting in the window in Figure 5.2.

We can also evaluate a series of expressions separated by periods, and declare temporary variables by enclosing them in vertical bars. For example, the expressions in Figure 5.3 declare a temporary variable aSet, assign a new set to aSet, add some elements, and then create a new set by selecting elements of aSet. The expression Set new is a message to the class Set that creates a new empty set, which is then assigned to aSet (Smalltalk uses := for assignment, like many languages). The next line adds the elements 1, 3, 5, …, 25 to the set.[4] (We could verify this by evaluating the first three lines of the code fragment.) The loop vari-

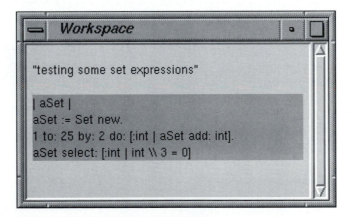

Figure 5.3   Evaluating a series of expressions in a text window.

[3] On your system, windows may have a different appearance than the figures in this section, especially with respect to platform-specific details such as the window title bar and scrollbars. Most Smalltalk systems use the host's conventions for the appearance of window frames and interaction components.

[4] We will see in section 5.5.5 that the message to:by:do: performs counted iteration, similar to a for loop in Pascal.

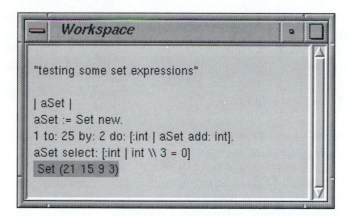

Figure 5.4   The result of evaluating a series of expressions in a text window.

able int is local to the "block" enclosed in square brackets. The third line creates a new set by selecting the elements of aSet that are divisible by 3. The "enumerating" message select: executes its block argument with each element of the receiver bound to the block's local variable (int in this case), and creates a collection containing the elements for which the expression in the block returns true. (Smalltalk uses the \\ operator for the modulus function, and = for equality test.) When print it is executed, the text window in Figure 5.4 results. As you can see, a collection is printed by printing the name of its class, followed by a list of its elements enclosed in parentheses. Sets are not ordered, so the elements are printed in an arbitrary order, not the order in which they were inserted. (The result is printed on a separate line in Figure 5.4 because we selected the newline after the last message expression in Figure 5.3.)

In the previous subsection, we examined an example in which the programmer used a C interpreter to define and test the function sum(). Because Smalltalk uses text windows rather than a command line, when you discover an error in a code fragment, you can edit the code in place rather than typing it again. For example, after testing the message select: in Figures 5.3 and 5.4, we could use the same instantiation and initialization of aSet with another message by replacing the last line in the series of expressions. In general, the programmer can store any number of expressions and code fragments in text windows to edit and evaluate. The contents of a text window can also be saved to a file, and text files can be inserted into text windows.

As we will see in section 6.1.1, many operations that are traditionally provided by the operating system (such as file manipulations) are encapsulated in system classes, and we perform these actions by sending messages to instances of these classes. Therefore, we can use a text window to issue system commands in the same manner as a command line interface to an operating system. For example, if we evaluate the expression (Filename named: 'CalendarApp.st') fileSize, the system prints the size of the file CalendarApp.st. Interpreted languages must maintain type objects for the programmer's types, and Smalltalk provides extensive protocol for obtaining information from type objects (discussed in sections 6.1.3 and 7.1.3). This protocol allows us to use text windows to query aspects of the system classes or of our own classes. For example, the message expression Collection allSubclasses returns a list of the descendants of the system class Collection.

5.1.2 An Example Program

In the next four sections of this chapter, we will cover the syntax and semantics of Smalltalk, beginning with literals and variables and working our way up to expressions and control structures. Before we get into all these details, let's examine a small program to get a sense of the way the language looks. Normally, Smalltalk programmers write classes rather than programs, and all the processing necessary for an application is encapsulated in methods. However, we can also declare variables and evaluate a series of expressions in a text window, which is essentially the same as writing and executing a "main program".

Our example program queries the user for the name of a file, counts the number of occurrences of each word longer than three characters in the file, and then prints each word and its count. The first program in most programming texts uses terminal input and output (e.g., stdin and stdout in C). But with Smalltalk programs relying on a graphic user interface, we use a dialog rather than a prompt to obtain information from the user, and write the program's output to the "transcript", a text window that is always open. The program appears as follows (explanations of its expressions follow the program):

```
"Count the number of occurrences of each word longer than 3 characters in a file
chosen by the user.  Print the results in the transcript window."

"declare temporary variables"
| wordBag filename inStream word wordStream char |
"initialize the collection of words"
wordBag := Bag new.
"get the file name from the user"
filename := Dialog requestFileName: 'Which file''s words do you want to count?'.
(filename ~= '') ifTrue: [
    "create a read stream over the file, and a write stream for composing words"
    inStream :=  (Filename named: filename) readStream.
    wordStream := WriteStream on: (String new: 16).
    "read characters from the file until the end of the file"
    [inStream atEnd not]
        whileTrue: [
            char := inStream next.
            char isSeparator
                ifTrue: [
                    word := wordStream contents.
                    (word size > 3) ifTrue: [wordBag add: word].
                    wordStream reset]
                ifFalse: [wordStream nextPut: char].].
```

```
"print the words and counts to the transcript"
wordBag asSet do: [:wrd |
    Transcript show: wrd.
    Transcript tab.
    Transcript show: (wordBag occurrencesOf: wrd) printString.
    Transcript cr]. ]
```

Let's go through the example from the beginning. Smalltalk is dynamically typed, so variable declarations do not give a type. A "bag" is an unordered collection of objects, strings in the case of wordBag.[5] When we send the message request-FileName: to the class Dialog, its method creates and posts a dialog with the string argument as the message, a text entry field for the user to enter a file name, and OK and Cancel push buttons, as illustrated in Figure 5.5 (in the figure, the user has already entered a file name). The message requestFileName: returns the string entered by the user, or an empty string if the user cancels the dialog without entering a file name. (The ~= operator tests for inequality.) The program waits until the user responds to the dialog before continuing execution (like calling scanf() in C).

Most object-oriented languages use "streams" for input and output (we discuss the Smalltalk stream classes in detail in section 8.5). A "read stream" obtains a sequence of objects (characters in this example) from a source, the file chosen by the user in this case. To obtain a read stream over a file, we create a Filename object with the message named:, and send it the message readStream.[6] In Smalltalk, string objects are fixed size, so we use a "write stream" over a string to compose words from the characters read from the file. (The sink for this write stream is an array of characters in memory, rather than a file or the terminal screen.) The read stream message next obtains the next object in the receiver stream, and the write stream message nextPut: appends the argument to the stream receiver. The message atEnd returns whether the entire stream has been read, contents returns the entire contents of the stream (the string in this example), and reset repositions the point at which the stream inserts objects back to the beginning of the sink.

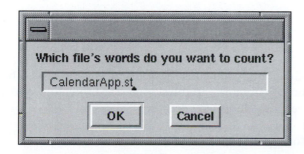

Figure 5.5   A Smalltalk file dialog created with Dialog requestFileName:.

---

[5] Smalltalk programmers often use the intended type of a variable in its name because declarations do not give the type.

[6] If the file does not exist, an error dialog will be posted.

Control structures in Smalltalk appear rather strange to programmers accustomed to C or Pascal (we discuss them in detail in section 5.5). To perform a conditional selection, we send the message ifTrue: to a boolean-valued expression, (filename ~ = ") in this example. The "block" argument enclosed in square brackets is evaluated if the expression returns true. The loop that extracts characters from the file illustrates conditional iteration. The logical message not is postfix in Smalltalk, so the condition inStream atEnd not is true when inStream is not at the end. We send the message whileTrue: to a block containing a boolean-valued expression with a block argument containing the loop body expressions. The whileTrue: method evaluates the block argument and the receiver repeatedly until the receiver returns true. The character message isSeparator returns true if the receiver is a space, tab, newline, or carriage return. We use the expression char isSeparator as the receiver of the message ifTrue:ifFalse:, which evaluates the ifTrue: block (the "if" block in a traditional conditional control structure) if the receiver is true, and the ifFalse: block (the "else" block) otherwise. The expression word size returns the length of the string.

Finally, to report the results to the user, we use the transcript message show:, which prints its string argument in the transcript at its cursor. Since we want to print one line for each word and the bag wordBag can contain many copies of a particular word, we first convert the bag to a set (an unordered collection that does not contain duplicates) with the message asSet. The resulting set contains exactly one copy of each word in the file. The enumerating message do: executes its block argument with each element of the receiver (the set in this case) bound to the block's local variable (wrd in this case). The message occurrencesOf: returns the number of occurrences of the argument in the receiver, and we send printString to the resulting number to convert it to a string.

5.2 LEXICAL ELEMENTS

5.2.1 Code Structure

Code layout

Like all languages, Smalltalk code consists of a series of tokens. The valid tokens are literals, identifiers that name variables or message selectors, and special language symbols. The special symbols include

- parentheses (and) for nested expressions
- the expression separator . (period)
- the assignment operation :=

- the return indicator ∧
- the block delimiters [and]

All other non-alphabetic characters are treated as binary operators (the Smalltalk class designer can define new operators). Tokens are separated by "white space" characters (i.e., space, tab, and newline) and the white space is optional between an identifier and an operator symbol. As in all modern languages, the programmer can format code in whatever manner makes its structure and intent clear.

Like functional languages, Smalltalk has no statements, only expressions. We will see that even control structures, object creation, and class and method definitions are coded as message expressions.

Comments

Comments in Smalltalk are enclosed in double quotes, as follows:

```
"this is a comment in Smalltalk"
```

With the same delimiter marking the beginning and end of a comment, it is not possible to "comment out" a section of code that contains comments.

5.2.2 Language Tokens

Literals

There are seven kinds of literals in Smalltalk:

- integers
- floating-point numbers
- characters
- strings
- symbols
- arrays
- byte arrays

When we use a literal in an expression, an instance of the indicated class is created. We can assign that object to an identifier, or use it as the receiver or an argument in a message expression.

The following examples demonstrate the syntax of numeric and character literals:

```
"examples of numeric literals"
-123   16rFF   1234567890   -30.5   6.02e23

"examples of character literals"
$A  $7  $@  $$
```

The first two numeric literals are instances of the system class SmallInteger. An r in an integer constant indicates that the digits preceding it give a radix in which the remaining digits are to be interpreted. The radix may be any number less than or equal to 36 (and is written in decimal), and we use alphabetic characters (of either case) for digits greater than 9, as is commonly done in writing hexadecimal numbers. The third numeric literal is an instance of the class LargePositiveInteger (on most systems). Smalltalk supports integers of arbitrary size, and whether a particular value is represented as a small or large integer is handled automatically by the methods of the integer classes.[7] Some implementations also permit the use of scientific notation for integer literals (e.g., 3e10). The last two numeric literals are instances of the class Float. A float literal must have digits on both sides of the decimal point (so .3 and 7. are not valid literals). The range of floating-point numbers supported depends on the implementation.[8] The object corresponding to a printable character is written as that character preceded by a $ symbol. The programmer can obtain a reference to a nonprintable character by passing a class message to the system class Character, as illustrated in the next section.

The following examples illustrate string and symbol literals:

```
"examples of string literals"
'hello, world'   'What''s up?'
```

```
"examples of symbols"
#name   #at:put:
```

Character string literals are enclosed in single quotes, and are instances of the system class String. There is no limit on the size of a string literal, and a string literal may include any character. To include the single-quote character within a string literal, we write it twice, as in the second example. Each time the programmer writes a particular literal string, that use refers to a different string object. A *symbol* denotes an object that is a fixed array of characters whose identity is guaranteed to be unique, and is written as a sequence of characters preceded by a # character.[9] Unlike strings, each use of a particular symbol always refers to the same object, which is an instance of the system class Symbol.[10]

The following examples demonstrate the syntax of array and byte array literals:

---

[7] The cutoff between small and large integer values is implementation-dependent. Generally, it is not a concern, but we will see in section 5.4.2 that the semantics of small and large integers differ in some ways.

[8] VisualWorks also defines a class Double for double precision floating-point numbers, and provides the literal notation 6.02d23 for instances of this class.

[9] Actually, the string that gives a symbol must be a valid variable or message name. It must consist of either a string of letters and digits that does not begin with a digit, or one or two special characters.

[10] If you are familiar with Lisp, the # in a symbol literal is similar to the quote function in Lisp in the sense that the name that follows is not evaluated as an identifier to obtain its referent object. In fact, we will see that much of the semantics of Smalltalk is reminiscent of Lisp due to its dynamic typing, support for function objects, and lack of statements.

"examples of array literals"
#(1 2 3) #($2 'two' 2 ('due' 'dos'))

"an example byte array literal"
#[1 77 16rCC]

An array literal is written by enclosing a list of literals within parentheses after a #
character, which creates an instance of the system class Array. Since Smalltalk is
dynamically typed, an array may contain instances of various classes, as illustrated
by the second array literal in the previous example. That literal also shows that an
array element that is also an array need not be preceded by the # character. Similarly, if an identifier appears within an array literal, it is taken to be a symbol rather
than a variable name (i.e., a leading # is assumed). A *byte array* is an array whose
elements are positive integers less than or equal to 255, and is an instance of the system class ByteArray. A byte array literal is written by enclosing a list of such values
in square brackets preceded by a # character.[11]

There are also three special identifiers that we can regard as literals in the
sense that each always refers to the same object (although syntactically they are
identifiers, not literals). These are the object nil, which is the referent of an uninitialized variable, and the boolean objects true and false.

Identifiers

Lexically, an identifier is a sequence of letters and digits that begins with a letter. There is no limit on the length of an identifier, and identifier names are case-
sensitive. The convention in Smalltalk programming is to use lowercase letters for
identifiers, and to capitalize each word in a multiple-word identifier name, such as
myListOfObjects. Smalltalk programmers also typically use complete words in identifiers rather than abbreviations. As we will see in the next two sections, "private"
variables and message selectors must begin with a lowercase letter, and "shared"
variables such as class names must begin with a capital letter. We will also see that
an identifier naming a message that takes arguments ends with a colon.

The Smalltalk language does not define any reserved words per se. As we will
see, the language does not include any control structure statements or built-in types or
operations, and no syntactic delimiters are needed for class or method definitions. We
can regard the pseudo-variable names nil, true, false, self, and super as reserved words
in the sense that we cannot use them as the names of classes, messages, or variables.

5.2.3 Variables

Characteristics

Smalltalk is dynamically typed so types are not associated with identifiers. For
this reason, the use of descriptive variable names is essential. A variable name may

---

[11] Smalltalk-80 does not support a literal notation for byte arrays.

either indicate the function of the associated object (e.g., the origin of a rectangle or the balance of an account) or the type of referent expected. For example, Smalltalk programmers often use names such as aSet or aNumber to indicate that the referent is intended to be a set or a numeric object. Semantic names such as balance are more descriptive than typed names such as aFloat, and are more flexible because they do not indicate how the object is implemented (e.g., the class used may change during development). Generally, Smalltalk programmers use typed names for method parameters and semantic names for all other variables.

A variable name must be declared before it is used in message expressions, and the way in which a variable name is declared depends on the kind of variable. Every variable is initialized to refer to the object nil when it is created.[12] When an error occurs, we can always determine whether a variable is uninitialized or has been assigned an incorrect value. Once a variable is created, the programmer can assign another object as the referent of the variable. There are two categories of variables in Smalltalk, private variables and shared variables, which differ in their visibility and lifetime.

Private variables

Private variables are only accessible to one object, and must begin with a lowercase letter. Private variables include an object's instance variables, and the local variables and parameters of a method or code fragment.[13] Local variables are often referred to as "temporary" variables in Smalltalk [Gol89].

The instance variables of an object exist for the lifetime of that object, and are visible only within its methods. The names of a class's instance variables are specified in the message that defines the class, as illustrated in section 6.1.2.

The parameters and local variables of a block or method are visible only within that block or method, and exist only for the duration of an execution of that block or method.[14] (Blocks and method definitions are discussed in sections 5.5.2 and 6.1.2, respectively.) A method's parameters are declared in the "message pattern" that introduces the method definition. We declare local variables by enclosing them in vertical bars, as follows:

```
"declares two local variables"
| count sum |
```

A list of local variables can be declared in a block or a method, or in a selection in a text window (as we saw in section 5.1.1). A variable declaration must appear at

---

[12] There is one exception to this rule: the elements of a byte array are initialized to 0.

[13] Code fragments executed in a text window are considered to have nil as their receiver.

[14] As we will see in section 5.4.2, an exception to this occurs when a block is assigned as the referent of a variable that persists beyond execution of the method containing the block. If the block refers to the method's local variables, the method's activation record must continue to exist after its execution completes.

the beginning of the block, method, or workspace text. We will see in section 5.4.1 that the preceding declaration allocates storage for two named references to objects, count and sum, but does not create any objects (unlike variable definitions in C or Pascal).

Shared variables

Shared variables are accessible to more than one object, and must begin with an uppercase letter. Shared variables include global variables, class variables, and pool variables.

The global variables in the system are accessible to all objects, and usually only consist of class names and certain system resources. Class names are visible throughout the system and must begin with a capital letter. Examples of global variables that are not class names include

- the Processor object that schedules processes
- the Transcript that logs system messages
- the Display on which the user interface is presented
- Smalltalk, the dictionary of global variables (i.e., the environment)

The system class Dictionary represents a set of key-value pairs in which the values are accessed via the keys. In the system dictionary Smalltalk, globally visible identifiers are the keys and their referents (objects or classes) are the values. For example, when we define a class, the method creates the class object, and enters the class name into the dictionary Smalltalk with the class object as its value. The names of shared system resources are entered into that dictionary when the system is initialized. The lifetime of a global variable extends from the time at which it is created until that entry is removed from the dictionary Smalltalk.

The use of global variables by applications is strongly discouraged (but not prevented) in Smalltalk, because global variables are visible throughout the system. However, it is sometimes useful when testing a class's methods to bind an instance of the class to a global variable so that we can test successive messages to that object. For example, suppose we want to experiment with drawing operations. We can create and open a window, and define a global variable DrawWindow that refers to it, as follows (the Dictionary message at:put: is discussed in section 5.3.3):[15]

```
"define a global variable DrawWindow for testing drawing operations"
Smalltalk at: #DrawWindow put: (ScheduledWindow new label: 'test')
```

We can then open the window with the message DrawWindow open, and send messages to draw lines, circles, etc. to that window (or to its "graphics context" in VisualWorks). The effect of each drawing operation will be visible immediately in the

---

[15] The keys in the dictionary Smalltalk must be symbols, not strings.

window. We remove a global variable from the system dictionary by sending
Smalltalk the message removeKey: (see section 8.2.3).

```
"remove the global variable DrawWindow from the system dictionary"
Smalltalk removeKey: #DrawWindow
```

On most Smalltalk systems, if you use a capitalized name in a text selection to be
evaluated, the text window queries whether to enter it as a global variable.

As we discussed in section 1.1.5, the class variables of a class are only visible to the class, its subclasses, and their instances. Class variables are created
when the class is defined and exist until the class is removed from the system.
A class can also define a *pool dictionary*, which is a set of shared variables
called *pool variables* that allows sharing of information among classes not
related by inheritance. Pool variables are usually named constants. For example, there are several classes that deal with text, which share access to a pool
named TextConstants. This dictionary includes variables for nonprintable characters such as Tab and CR, format codes such as Underlined and Subscripted,
and constants such as DefaultTabsArray and DefaultTextStyle, so that these are
available to the methods of these classes. Variables are inserted into or
removed from pool dictionaries using the protocol of the class Dictionary, with
the identifier symbol as the key and the referent object as the value (as in the
previous examples). Like the instance variable names of a class, the names of
a class's class variables and pool dictionaries are given in the message that creates the class.

Pseudo-variable names

A *pseudo-variable* is an identifier that cannot appear on the left side of an
assignment. There are five predefined pseudo-variables in Smalltalk.

- nil, the undefined object
- true and false, the boolean objects
- self, which refers to the receiver of the method
- super, which refers to the receiver of the method, and is used in refining inherited methods (see in section 6.2.2)

The identifiers nil, true, and false each refers to a specific object. The two pseudo-
variables self and super can appear only in a method (not in a text window selection). The parameters of a method or block are also pseudo-variables, so they
cannot be assigned to refer to different objects than those to which they are bound
when the block or method begins execution. In addition, we should regard the identifier Smalltalk, which refers to the dictionary of global variables, as a pseudo-variable, since assigning it another value causes the system to lose track of all classes
and objects.

5.3 MESSAGE EXPRESSIONS

5.3.1 Purpose and Semantics

In Smalltalk, all processing is encapsulated within classes. An operation can only be performed by sending the corresponding message to an instance of a class responsible for that operation. The language does not include syntax for defining subprograms that are not methods of some class, nor for invoking a subprogram without reference to a receiver. Global accessibility and applicability for a message can be provided by adding it to the protocol of the system class Object, since it is an ancestor of every class in the system. However, the programmer must still choose one of the participants in the activity whose class is responsible for performing the processing, and the operation can only be invoked by passing the message to an instance of that class.

Smalltalk defines no built-in operations that are part of the language itself: Every operation is a message send. All of the functionality that traditional languages provide with built-in operations or library subprograms is encapsulated within the appropriate system class. For example, the class Float (not a built-in type) defines arithmetic and comparison operators, and messages such as sin, abs, and log. In this chapter and the next, we will see that even object allocation, control flow specification, and definition of classes and methods are performed by message passing.

A *message expression* represents a request to the receiver to perform the indicated operation. The receiver responds by executing the method defined for its class (which may be inherited from an ancestor class). For example, messages to numbers represent arithmetic operations such as +, <, sin, rounded, asFloat, and gcd:. Messages to collections represent accessing, inserting, or deleting elements, or requests for information about the collection. Example collection messages include first, indexOf:, add:, removeLast, size, and isEmpty. Messages to graphic objects represent graphic calculations (e.g., the system class Rectangle responds to center, containsPoint:, and intersect:). Messages in the protocol of a problem domain class represent requests for services that its instances provide.

Message expressions can appear in methods or in a code fragment directly presented to the Smalltalk interpreter from a text window. In either case, the variable names that can appear in an expression depend on the context in which it occurs, and must have been declared.

5.3.2 Syntax

General format

A message expression consists of a *receiver* object, a *selector* that names the operation to be performed, and possibly *arguments*. The receiver appears first, followed by selector–argument pairs, and the same syntax is used for sending both instance and class messages. Figure 5.6 illustrates the components of a message expression. This syntax is intended to suggest an active English sentence in which the receiver is the subject performing the activity, the selectors are verbs or prepositions naming the activity, and the arguments are objects used in the activity or affected by the activity. For example, the expression in Figure 5.6 states that the object aSet is adding the string 'hello' to itself. The receiver and arguments in an expression may be literals, variables, or the results of other message expressions. The selector for a message is defined by the receiver's class (or inherited from an ancestor), and should be a descriptive name for the operation. By convention, selectors include only letters (except for "operator" selectors such as + and <=), and begin with a lowercase character.

Execution of a method always returns a value to the sender (i.e., a message send is an expression, not a statement, and expressions can be nested). Messages that modify the state of the receiver return either the receiver in its new state or an argument. The receiver or an argument in an expression can be a message expression, in which case the result of the nested expression is used as the receiver or an argument of the enclosing expression. Parentheses may be used to indicate the order of evaluation within nested expressions. We will discuss the details of precedence and associativity in this section.

There are three syntactic formats for message expressions, depending on the kind of selector. These are unary messages, keyword messages, and binary messages.

Unary messages

A *unary message* is a message with no arguments, and consists of a receiver followed by a selector. A unary message appears like a sentence with an intransitive verb (e.g., aWindow open), and the receiver may be a variable, a literal, or an expression. The following are some example unary message expressions and their meanings:[16]

```
"example unary message expressions"
7.0 sin               "returns the sine of 7.0"
aChar asUppercase     "returns the upper case character corresponding to the receiver"
aDate weekday         "returns the day of the week of the receiver"
aSet isEmpty          "returns true if the receiver set is empty, and false otherwise"
#(1 $1 'one') size    "returns the number of elements in the receiver array"
aRectangle center     "returns the point at the center of aRectangle"
aList removeLast      "removes the last element from aList and returns it"
Character tab         "a message to the class Character that returns the tab character"
Set new               "returns a new empty instance of the system class Set"
```

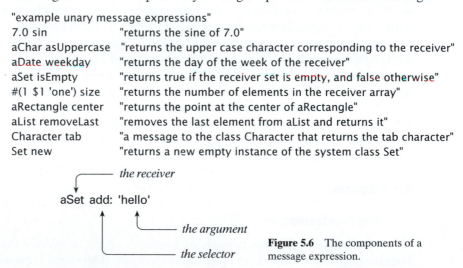

Figure 5.6   The components of a message expression.

---

[16] In this section, I will not declare and initialize the variables I use in the examples, but will rely on the descriptive value of the variable and selector names to indicate the operation of each message.

Unary messages correspond to single-parameter functions in a procedural language in which the receiver is the argument, for example, sin(7.0), asUppercase(aChar), isEmpty(aSet), or center(aRectangle). In a language with abstract data types or a hybrid object-oriented language, these expressions would be written as aSet.isEmpty() or aRectangle.center().[17] The last two examples illustrate expressions that pass messages to class objects. The first asks the class Character for the tab character (for which there is no literal notation), and the second asks the class Set for a new empty instance of that class. As we will see in sections 5.4.1 and 6.1.3, a class message is the only way to create an object in Smalltalk.

In Smalltalk, there is no syntax for directly accessing another object's instance variables, like the component selection operator provided by languages that support records. The information stored in an object is only available to other objects if its class defines a unary accessor message. For example, the programmer uses the message aPoint x to obtain the x coordinate of aPoint, rather than the expression aPoint.x.

A sequence of unary message sends is evaluated from left to right. The result of the first message is the receiver of the second, and so on. For example,

```
"sends sqrt to 77.5 first, and then sends rounded to the resulting object"
77.5 sqrt rounded
```

Keyword messages

A *keyword message* is a named message that takes arguments. After the receiver of the expression, each argument is prefixed by a selector keyword that ends with a colon. Some example single-argument keyword message expressions are

```
"example single-argument keyword message expressions"
1.2 raisedTo: 3        "returns 1.2 * 1.2 * 1.2"
aDate addDays: 14      "returns the date 14 days after aDate"
aPoint x: 5            "sets the x coordinate of aPoint to 5"
aRect1 merge: aRect2   "returns the rectangle enclosing the receiver and the argument"
aSet remove: 'hello'   "removes that string from aSet and returns it"
Array new: 20          "returns a new array of 20 references to elements"
```

In a procedural language, these operations would be multiple-parameter function invocations such as raisedTo(1.2, 3) or remove(aSet, 'this'), or assignments such as aPoint.x := 5. Note the difference between the message x (which has no parameter) and the message x: (which does). Such pairs of messages are frequently used for retrieving and setting an instance variable, x in this case. The last example is a message to the class object Array that creates a new array in which each

---

[17] I did not give expressions corresponding to 7.0 sin and aChar asUppercase because instances of built-in types are usually not treated as receivers in hybrid languages.

element reference is initialized to nil (i.e., it does not create an array of 20 objects).

The syntax for keyword messages that take more than one argument is rather unusual (to a programmer). The message selector consists of a keyword for each argument, and each argument is preceded by the corresponding keyword in a message expression. For example,

```
"example multiple-argument keyword message expressions"
"returns true if aValue is between 3 and theMax inclusive, and false otherwise"
aValue between: 3 and: theMax
"inserts newObject into aList just after predObject"
aList add: newObject after: predObject
"returns a new array which is a copy of the third through seventh elements of anArray"
anArray copyFrom: 3 to: 7
"returns a new rectangle with the given edge coordinates"
Rectangle left: 3 right: 10 top: 5 bottom: 8
```

The selectors in a multiple-argument keyword message are usually verbs and prepositions, again to make the expression read like an English sentence (e.g., consider the first three expressions in the previous example). The arguments in a multiple-argument message are evaluated from left to right. The keyword identification of arguments does not allow us to use an arbitrary order of keywords and associated arguments in a message expression (as we can do with Ada's position-independent parameters). That is, between:and: and and:between: are two different messages.

We refer to a keyword message by its selector (e.g., raisedTo: or addDays:). For multiple-argument messages, the selector is the concatenation of the keywords, for example, between:and: or copyFrom:to:. Some Smalltalk programmers read between:and: as "between and", and others say "between colon and colon". For single-argument keyword messages, stating the colon explicitly is necessary in some cases (e.g., to distinguish between the messages new and new:).

In Smalltalk, we access the elements of an array object using messages in the protocol of the system class Array, rather than with the [ ] operator as in Pascal or C. The message at: returns the element whose index is its argument, and the message at:put: stores its second argument at the index given by its first argument. The elements of an array are numbered from 1 to the size of the object, which is fixed (there are other collections that are of variable size). For example,

```
"accessing and modifying the elements of an array"
anArray at: 7                 "returns the 7th element of anArray"
anArray at: index put: $k    "replaces the indexth element of the array with $k"
```

The methods for these messages signal an error if the subscript argument is smaller than 1 or larger than the size of the receiver, or is not an integer. The messages at: and at:put: can also be used to access the characters in a string since String is a subclass of Array. The same messages are also overloaded in the system class Dictionary to access a value by its key, or to insert a value for a given key into a dictionary. For example,

```
"budget is an instance of the system class Dictionary"
budget at: #food          "what is the budget amount for food?"
"replace the value associated with 'entertainment' or if there is none, add a key-value pair
to the dictionary"
budget at: #entertainment put: 200
```

Binary messages

To provide the familiar infix arithmetic operators and expression syntax, Smalltalk supports binary message selectors. A *binary message* is a single-argument message indicated by a selector consisting of one or two special characters (with no trailing colon). These expressions have the same form as the corresponding expression in a traditional language, but are regarded as messages to the left operand with the object on the right as the argument. Figure 5.7 lists the binary selectors defined by the system classes. The following examples illustrate binary message expressions:

```
"example binary message expressions"
aNumber + 4        "returns the sum of the receiver and 4"
total <= max       "returns true if total is less than or equal to max, and false otherwise"
'hello' , aString  "returns a new string, the concatenation of the receiver and the argument"
7 / 4              "returns a new instance of the system class Fraction"
7 // 4             "returns 1, the result of the integer division"
x @ y              "returns a new instance of the system class Point"
```

operator	operations
+ - *	arithmetic operators
/	returns a new fraction or integer if the receiver and the argument are fractions or integers, returns a float if either the receiver or argument is a float
//	integer division
\\	modulus
< <=> =>	ordering comparisons
& |	logical operators, AND and OR
== ~~	identity and non-identity tests (see section 5.4.2)
= ~=	equality and inequality tests (see section 5.4.2.)
@	creates a new point with the receiver as the x coordinate and the argument as the y coordinate
,	creates a new collection which is the concatenation of the receiver and argument; valid for strings, lists, and arrays
->	creates an instance of the class Association (a key-value pair) with the receiver as the key and the argument as the value

Figure 5.7 Binary message selectors.

There are no unary or ternary "operator" selectors in Smalltalk. In particular, there is no unary − operator: the additive inverse of a number is obtained with the unary (postfix) message negated.

In most programming languages, arithmetic operators have higher precedence than comparisons, which have higher precedence than logical operators, and the language defines a precedence ordering for the operations within each category (e.g., between * and +). However, in Smalltalk, a sequence of binary messages is evaluated from left to right with all the selectors at the same level of precedence. That is, the leftmost message is sent first, followed by sending the second message to its result, and so on. For example, consider the following message expressions:

```
"a sequence of binary messages is evaluated from left to right"
3 + 4 * 7 - 5          "results in 44"
3 < 4 + 5              "error: a boolean does not know how to + 5"
```

The first example sends the message + 4 to 3, then sends * 7 to the resulting object, and finally sends - 5 to that object. The second example is an error because 3 returns the boolean object true upon receiving < 4, and boolean objects cannot respond to the message + 5. We can specify the order of evaluation and the intended receiver and argument of each message in a nested expression with parentheses. For example,

```
"parentheses can be used to indicate the order in which messages are sent"
3 + (4 * 7) - 5        "results in 26"
3 < (4 + 5)   "results in true"
```

The class designer can introduce new binary selectors if desired, although the meaning of an expression in which they are used should be apparent to the reader. Since all operators have the same arity (number of operands), precedence, and associativity, it is not necessary to specify this information when defining a method for a binary message.

Precedence in nested expressions

Message expression precedence in Smalltalk is defined among the syntactic categories of messages, rather than among individual operators as in most languages. The order of evaluation within a nested expression is

1. parenthesized subexpressions
2. all unary messages from left to right
3. all binary messages from left to right
4. keyword messages

The following examples illustrate message precedence:

```
"message precedence is unary, then binary, then keyword messages"
aNumber1 + aNumber2 abs          "abs is sent first"
aNumber max: aSet size           "size is sent first"
aPoint1 x: aPoint2 x             "x is sent first, then x: is sent"
'hello' at: index + 1            "+ is sent first"
(aNumber1 + aNumber2) abs        "+ is sent first"
(anInteger gcd: 48) + max        "gcd: is sent first"
```

Of course, the same associativity and precedence ordering among selector types holds within a parenthesized subexpression.

Note that keyword message expressions cannot be nested without enclosing the nested expression within parentheses. That is, if we use the result of a keyword message expression as the receiver or an argument of another keyword expression, that expression must be parenthesized. For example, consider these three expressions:

```
"keyword messages cannot be nested without parentheses"
obj1 a: obj2 b: obj3 c: obj4     "one message send of a:b:c:"
obj1 a: obj2 b: (obj3 c: obj4)   "the result of obj3 c: obj4 is the second argument of a:b:"
(obj1 a: obj2) b: obj3 c: obj4   "the result of obj1 a: obj2 receives the message b:c:"
```

The first example sends the message a:b:c: to obj1. The second sends c: to obj3, and then uses that result as the second argument in sending a:b: to obj1. The third example sends a: to obj1, and then sends b:c: to the result of that expression. Consider the following examples:

```
"parentheses are necessary since we do not want to send at:put:at: to anArray"
anArray at: index + 1 put: (anArray at: index)
budget at: #entertainment put: (budget at: #entertainment) + 100
```

In the first expression, the parentheses are necessary because arrays do not respond to at:put:at:, but parentheses are not needed around the subexpression index + 1 since binary messages have higher precedence then keyword messages. Similarly, parentheses are necessary in the second example, and the close parenthesis must precede the message + 100 rather than follow it.

Cascaded messages

Several messages can be sent to the same object by separating each group of selectors and arguments with semicolons. These are referred to as *cascaded* messages. For example,

```
"cascaded expressions that send several messages to the same receiver"
aSet add: 1; add: 2; add: 3; add: 4
aPen go: 20; up; go: 30; down; turn: 90; go: 20
anArray at: 1 put: $a; at: 2 put: 2@2; at: 3 put: 3; yourself
```

The first example adds four elements to aSet. The second example is shorthand for the sequence of expressions aPen go: 20. aPen up. aPen go: 30., and so on. The result returned by the entire cascaded expression is the result of the last message sent. The original receiver rather than the result of the last message can be returned by including the unary message yourself as the last message in the sequence, as in the third example (the return value of the at:put: message is the argument). This syntax is only useful with messages that cause some side effect such as changing the state of the receiver, because the return value of each message in the series except the last is lost.

Coding errors

Although Smalltalk is interpreted, the system does not translate source code directly to the platform's machine language. Instead, code is parsed and compiled into an intermediate language referred to as *bytecodes*, which is essentially a platform-independent machine language.[18] The bytecodes are then interpreted by the system's "virtual machine" which runs on the host platform. The parser detects and signals syntax errors such as unmatched parentheses, unmatched block delimiters, and undeclared identifiers before the code is executed. When a syntax error occurs, the parser inserts an error message at that point in the text selection, and that message is selected so that the programmer can delete it easily and proceed. For example, a special character or a name that ends in a colon is a selector that must be followed by an argument, which cannot be a binary selector or an identifier that ends in a colon. Figure 5.8 shows the error message we receive when such errors occur. The parser will reject a declaration of an identifier that begins with a digit or contains a special character, and detects errors in literals such as a symbol name that begins with a digit, or a string within a byte array literal. It also signals an error when an expression uses a selector that is not defined in any class at all.

The Smalltalk compiler cannot detect type mismatch errors that the compiler for a statically typed language catches, because it does not know what class of object will be bound to an identifier when the expression is executed. However, if an identifier receives a message and the protocol of its referent's class does not include that message, the interpreter signals an error at that point. It does so by posting a "notifier" dialog that indicates that the receiver "does not understand" the message. (Notifiers are discussed in section 5.6.4.) This can occur if the programmer mistypes a selector or misunderstands or forgets the expression evaluation rules. For example, evaluation of the expression value < max + 1 results in the error message that a boolean object cannot perform the message +. Similarly, evaluation of anArray at: 3 = $c causes the error message that the argument of at: must be an integer (it is a boolean due to message precedence). It takes a bit of practice to become accustomed to deciphering the cause of such errors.

Some mistakes that would be syntax errors caught at compile time in a traditional language are run-time errors reported as an incorrect protocol errors in Smalltalk. For example, there is no syntactic distinction between the names of variables and unary messages. Consider the difference in interpretation of the

---

[18] This language is similar to Forth and the stack-based intermediate languages often used internally by compilers (see [Gol89] for details).

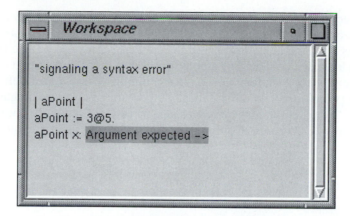

Figure 5.8   Signalling a syntax error in a text window.

identifier abs in the expressions aPoint x abs and aPoint x: abs. In the first expression, abs is a unary message to the referent of x, but in the second case, it is the argument of x:. If you omit the trailing colon for a keyword selector that takes an argument, the selector will be taken as a unary message and the argument will be taken as a message to the result of that operation (unless it is a literal). We saw in section 5.1.1 that the message expressions in a code fragment are separated by periods. If a period is missing between two expressions and the receiver of the second is an identifier, that name will be interpreted as a unary message to the result or the last argument of the first expression. In addition, if the programmer accidentally types a letter in an integer literal such as 345y7, a run-time error is reported stating that 345 cannot respond to the message y7. Of course, the problem of error messages that are not clearly related to the cause of the error is not unique to Smalltalk.

5.3.3 Message Overloading and Dynamic Binding

Many message selectors are defined in the protocols of more than one class. For example, the binary selectors <, >, and so on are defined for numeric classes and the system classes Character, Date, Time, and String, and are usually overloaded for any application class for which a linear ordering of some kind is appropriate. Arithmetic messages are overloaded in each numeric class to perform class-specific operations. Much of the protocol of the collection classes such as remove:, includes:, and isEmpty is implemented differently in each class, depending on the class's semantics and storage structure. The messages readFrom:, printOn:, and storeOn: are used for input and output, and are also typically defined in every class. Because parameters are not typed, the same selector cannot be overloaded within a class.

Identifiers are not typed either, so an identifier can refer to an instance of any class. When an expression is evaluated, the method to be invoked can only be determined at execution time according to the class of the receiver object. As described in section 3.2.4, the interpreter searches the method dictionary in the receiver's class object for the message selector, and if it is not present, the class object of its superclass is examined, and so on up the class hierarchy. Note also that in Smalltalk, we can have dynamic binding among any classes in the system that define the same message selector, whether they have a common ancestor that defines that message or not (which is not true for statically typed object-oriented languages).

For example, the system classes Array and Dictionary both define methods for the message at:put:. Consider the following message expression:

```
"an overloaded message is bound dynamically"
aCollection at: 7 put: 'seven'
```

If aCollection is bound to an instance of the class Array, the string 'seven' is stored in that object's seventh "indexed" instance variable (see section 6.1.2). However, if that identifier is bound to a dictionary, and that object contains a key–value "association" with the key 7, that association's value is replaced with 'seven'. If the dictionary object does not contain that key–value pair, its at:put: method creates a new instance of the class Association with the key 7 and the value 'seven' and adds it to the table. If aCollection is bound to an instance of the class Set, an error results because sets are unordered and do not support the message at:put:.

5.4 IDENTIFIER AND OBJECT SEMANTICS

5.4.1 Implications of Dynamic Typing

Storage allocation

In a monomorphic statically typed language such as Pascal or C, every object that can be bound to a particular variable or record field is of the same type, and therefore is the same size. The compiler can reserve a fixed amount of storage for each local variable or field, depending on its declared type. It allocates the storage for a subprogram's local variables in its activation record, and allocates the storage for the fields of a record instance within the record's storage. The representation of the value of a variable or field is directly embedded within the stack frame or record.

In Smalltalk, identifiers are not typed, so a variable can refer to an instance of any class. For this reason, it is not possible to determine statically how much space is necessary for the referent of an identifier. Suppose that some fixed amount of storage is allocated for a local variable in an activation record. If a different object is assigned to that variable, whose storage requirement is greater than that allocated to the target identifier, its representation cannot be copied into that space. Because such an assignment should be valid, Smalltalk cannot allocate objects within the activation record of a method. Similarly, storage for the referents of the instance variables of an object cannot be directly within the object. (As we will discuss further in sections 10.2.1 and 12.2, this is true for polymorphic identifiers in any language.)

Automatic stack allocation of objects not being feasible, all objects are allocated dynamically in Smalltalk. Every object is created by passing an instantiation request such as new or readFrom: to the desired class, which returns a reference to the newly created object.[19] That is, declaring a variable does not allocate a "garbage" object into which we must copy a valid value. Instead, a declaration allocates space for a reference to an object, as discussed in the next subsection. Note also that there is no separate language construct for dynamically allocating an object. Like the use of message passing for control structures (as described in section 5.5), expressing object allocation as message passing simplifies the language, and makes its use more uniform.

Management of dynamic memory is more transparent to the programmer in Smalltalk than in traditional languages such as C and Pascal. The Smalltalk runtime system provides automatic storage deallocation, so the programmer does not have to keep track of when an object is no longer accessible.[20] For example, when we perform an assignment, we do not have to decide whether to deallocate the former referent of the left-side identifier. If a nested message expression creates a temporary object that is the result of one expression and the receiver or argument of another, the programmer does not need to be concerned with deallocating that object. For example, in evaluating the expression 7.7 squared log rounded, two temporary float objects are created, and automatically deallocated.

Memory management is also more transparent because the object reference returned by an instantiation message is not a pointer in the sense of containing the specific (virtual memory) address at which the object's representation is located. The virtual machine's object memory system may relocate objects during execution, for example, to compact the free space available. Because all access to an object is through its system-supplied object identifier, executing programs are not affected by this activity. This storage model allows the programmer to concentrate on the objects rather than on their manifestations in memory or on memory management issues. In this way, a program reflects the problem domain model, rather than the details of its implementation.

Reference semantics for identifiers

In C and Pascal, when we define a variable or structure member, the object it refers to is directly embedded in the subprogram's stack frame or in a record instance. We refer to this as a *value representation* for that identifier because the

---

[19] We will see in the next section that unique objects are exceptions to this rule. Instances of the classes SmallInteger, Boolean, Character, and UndefinedObject (i.e., nil) are regarded as having been created during initialization of the Smalltalk system.

[20] [Ing81] states that "to be truly object-oriented, a computer system must provide automatic storage management". He compares programmer-controlled deallocation to requiring a speaker to inform listeners each time he or she is finished with a topic so that it can be forgotten, and points out how this would impede communication.

storage for the identifier contains its value directly, and we say that the identifier has *value semantics*. Local variables and instance variables in Smalltalk have *reference semantics* so that they can be bound to any object. Semantically, a variable is a name that can refer to various objects, rather than a container into which a copy of an object can be placed. For example, several identifiers can refer to the same object, rather than each containing an independent copy. As we will see in the next section, reference semantics for identifiers affects the meaning of assignments, parameter passing, and comparisons. Reference semantics also holds for the elements of collection classes. When we insert an object into a set or an array, the collection contains a reference to the original object, not its own copy of that object. For example, the same object can be an element of several collections. We will discuss choosing between value and reference semantics in section 10.2.1, as C++ supports both representations.

Internally, each local variable or parameter is represented by a system-supplied *object identifier*[21] in an activation record for that method, and each instance variable is represented by an object identifier in an instance of the class.[22] We will draw these object identifiers as pointers in the storage structure diagrams that illustrate object layouts in this part of the text, but keep in mind that they are actually more abstract than actual address values. For example, the class Rectangle contains two instance variables origin and corner, which represent an instance's upper left and lower right corners, respectively. These are intended to refer to instances of the class Point, and Point defines two instance variables for its x and y coordinates. Suppose we create an instance of the class Rectangle with the class message Rectangle left: 3.1 right: 10.5 top: 5.2 bottom: 8.3 and assign it to the variable aRectangle. Figure 5.9 illustrates how that object is represented in storage.[23]

Although all Smalltalk variables are references, dereferencing is implicit, in contrast to Pascal and C, which use a dereference operator and support both pointer and object operations for identifiers.

Strong typing

Although the compiler cannot perform type checking, Smalltalk enforces type safety and the language is strongly typed. Every object is an instance of a class and includes a reference to its class object, as illustrated in Figures 3.2 and 5.9. The interpreter can determine the type of any object to ensure that an operation is valid. As we discussed in section 3.2.4, the method binding process uses the receiver's class

---

[21] [Gol89] and others refer to these identifiers as "object pointers", but we will not use this terminology to stress that an object identifier is not actually an address. You should regard an object identifier as a "handle" that the virtual machine's memory management system uses to access the object.

[22] For performance reasons, instances of the classes SmallInteger, Boolean, Character, and UndefinedObject are embedded within the object identifier in the activation record or object, and are flagged as such.

[23] We have simplified the diagram by not showing the structure of the float objects. An instance of Float represents its value as a four-element byte array containing the host machine's encoding of a floating-point value.

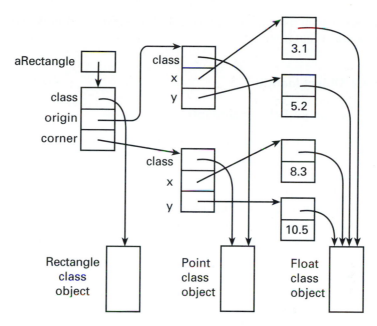

Figure 5.9   Representation of an instance of class Rectangle.

pointer to locate its class object, which contains a dictionary of methods. If the message is not in that dictionary, the superclass class object's dictionary is searched, and so on through the chain of ancestors in the hierarchy. When an object receives a message that is not defined in the protocol of its class or of any ancestor, execution is suspended rather than continuing with invalid results. That is, type checking is performed when each message is sent.

This error is detected and reported as part of the method resolution process. When a message is not defined in the chain of ancestors of the receiver's class, the interpreter sends the message doesNotUnderstand: to the receiver with the message selector as the argument. The class Object defines a method for doesNotUnderstand: that opens a "notifier" dialog (see section 5.6.4.), which states that the receiver cannot perform the operation, and gives the receiver's class and the undefined selector. This method is inherited by all classes since Object is the root of the Smalltalk class hierarchy.

In many cases, a type error is detected some time after execution of the incorrect operation that actually caused the error, although it is always caught eventually. For example, the class Rectangle defines a class method origin:corner: that allows the programmer to create a new instance by passing the points that are to be its upper left and lower right corners. If we send this message with an argument that is not a point, the creation of the rectangle and the initialization of its instance variables are not flagged as errors. However, when a Rectangle method passes a Point message such as x to that object, that message send fails and the error notifier appears at that point.

5.4.2 Object Identity

Value and object semantics

In traditional languages such as Pascal and C, a variable is considered a container that stores a value of a given type. That value is not regarded as having an identity of its own in the sense that if several variables contain the same value, there is no relationship among those values. When a value is assigned to a variable, the variable receives its own independent copy of that value. That is, values (including record instances) are treated as attributes rather than as objects.

In contrast, consider an instance of the class Employee that represents a particular employee. This object should be a unique object that directly represents a particular problem domain entity. All objects or methods that refer to that employee object should contain a reference to the same object in an instance variable or local variable, not an independent copy. In this way, the employee object maintains its unique identity. For example, if an object that maintains a reference to the employee object sends it a message that changes the employee's address or pay rate, that change should be made in exactly one place so that it is visible to all other objects that refer to the employee object. To obtain this semantics in Pascal or C, we must explicitly define a variable or field as a pointer and use pointer operations. Normally, we do not expect this meaning for values such as integers and characters because we regard them as attributes, rather than as objects that have a unique identity and a state that can change over time.

In Smalltalk, each object that exists is created individually and all access to an object occurs through its object identifier. Generally, the system classes are organized around the concept that each object has a unique identity, which is reinforced by the reference semantics of variables. For example, each time the literal notation for a floating-point number or string is used, it denotes a different, distinguishable object. Messages typically return a new object rather than modifying the receiver. For example, the Date message addDays: returns a new date object rather than "adding" the argument to the receiver. That is, its method creates a new date object rather than modifying a date container. In fact, the class Date defines no messages that modify the receiver so each date object always represents the same date.[24] Similarly, when an object is inserted into a collection such as an array or a set, the collection keeps a reference to the original object rather than a copy. In addition, unlike values in traditional languages, each object contains a class pointer indicating its type (including floating-point numbers and strings).

In section 10.2.1, we will see that C++ supports both value and reference

---

[24] Some classes, such as Point and Rectangle, include messages that modify components of the receiver, so their instances can be used as containers.

semantics for instances of classes. As in C, a variable or member must be defined as a pointer (or reference) to obtain object semantics for its referent.

Unique objects

In Smalltalk, instances of the classes SmallInteger, Character, Symbol, UndefinedObject (i.e., nil), and Boolean (i.e., true and false) are treated as *unique objects*.[25] Conceptually there is exactly one object 14, and all references to that integer refer to this same object. In contrast, there can be several Point objects with x coordinate 3 and y coordinate 5, each with a different object identifier. For integers, characters, and symbols, the object referred to by a particular literal constant is always the same object in every expression in which it appears. However, this is not true for floating-point, string, array, and byte array literals. The objects nil, true, and false, and the small integers and characters are regarded as having been created when the system was initialized, and their classes do not provide instantiation messages. The programmer can create symbols as necessary.

In the underlying implementation of objects, the nest of object references used to represent information must stop at some "atomic values" that are encoded directly. The object memory system does not actually create an instance of each character or small integer and place a reference to that object in each local variable or instance variable that refers to it. Instead, a few of the bits in the object identifiers that represent variable values are used as flags to indicate whether the referent of that variable is a standard object reference, a small integer, nil, a boolean, or a character. If the referent is a small integer or a character, its value is encoded in the remaining bits. The interpreter is aware of this representation and maintains references to the necessary class objects to use in the method binding process. We will use this representation in our storage structure diagrams for the rest of this part of the text.

Assignment semantics

As stated previously, a variable declaration allocates space for an object reference, which is initialized to refer to the object nil. The binding for a variable is modified by an assignment, which is indicated by := as in Pascal (or by the more descriptive ← in earlier versions of Smalltalk). The left side of an assignment must be a single variable name. The language is dynamically typed, so any assignment is valid. If the new referent of the left-side identifier is an instance of a different class than the former referent, then the protocol that is valid for that identifier changes.

Evaluation of an assignment causes the identifier on its left side to refer to the object returned by the expression on its right side, which can be an existing object or a newly created object. That is, the expression obj1 := obj2 means "bind obj1 to the same object that obj2 refers to" rather than "copy the contents of obj2 into the

---

[25] [Gol89] and others refer to these objects as "immutable" objects, but we will use the terminology "unique" objects because there are other classes such as Float and Date that do not provide modifier messages and whose instances have identity.

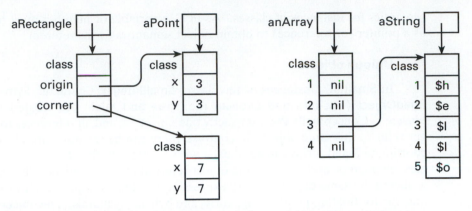

Figure 5.10 Reference semantics for assignments (class objects not shown).

storage allocated for obj1". As a result, both obj1 and obj2 refer to the same object (as in a pointer assignment), and a message to the object through one identifier that changes its state will modify the referent of the other identifier. Because Smalltalk provides automatic deallocation, the programmer does not need to be concerned with deallocating the former referent of obj1 if there are no more references to it. Note that an assignment never modifies an object: The state of an object can only be modified if its class defines messages that do so.

The assignment operation is part of the language. The symbol := does not denote a message send, and is not a selector defined in some class. An assignment returns the object that results from evaluation of the message expression on its right side, so assignments may be cascaded as in the expression count := total := 0. A parenthesized assignment may also be nested within a message expression (as if the assignment "operator" has lower precedence than all selectors). For example, the expression aSet add: (aPoint := 3@3) creates the point (3, 3), assigns it to aPoint, and adds the same object to aSet.

Reference semantics also apply to instance variables and collection elements. For example, Figure 5.10 illustrates the results of the following assignments:

```
"reference semantics for instance variables and collection elements: see figure 5.10"
| aPoint aRectangle aString anArray |
aPoint := 3@3.
"aPoint and the origin instance variable of aRectangle refer to the same point object"
aRectangle := Rectangle origin: aPoint corner: 7@7.
aString := 'hello'.
anArray := Array new: 4.
"aString and anArray at: 3 both refer to the same string object"
anArray  at: 3  put: aString
```

In Figure 5.10, aPoint refers to the same point object as the origin instance variable of aRectangle. This occurs via an assignment to the receiver's instance variable in the method that initializes the new rectangle object. (That assignment would have copied the argument point in a traditional language, losing its identity.) For example, the message aPoint x: 2 modifies aRectangle, but the assignment aPoint := 2@2 does not. Note the difference between the modifier message x: that changes an object in all its uses and the assignment that changes the binding for a name, but does not affect any objects. Similarly, the third element of anArray refers to the same object as the identifier aString. If another object is assigned to the variable aRectangle, then the object memory system deallocates the rectangle object and the anonymous point 7@7, but does not deallocate the referent of aPoint.

Parameter semantics

As with assignments, any object can be passed as a method argument because parameters are not typed. However, if the argument object cannot perform the operations requested by the method, an error is signaled at that point. Passing arguments to methods uses the same semantics as assignments: The parameter name in the method refers to the same argument object, that is, the object is passed by reference. Messages that the method sends to the parameter are sent to the argument object, and affect it immediately. However, there are some differences from pass by reference as supported by var parameters in Pascal. In Smalltalk, the argument can be an anonymous "temporary" object created by evaluating an argument expression (in Pascal, it must be a variable). In addition, it is not possible to change the binding of an argument identifier because method parameters are pseudo-variables, and cannot appear on the left side of an assignment. (An assignment to a var parameter in Pascal copies the right-side value into the argument.) The object bound to a parameter can only be modified by passing a message that does so to that identifier.

The return value of a method is also passed by reference. When a method completes execution, the sender receives the object identifier of the object named in the method's return expression (return expressions are discussed in section 6.1.2). This object may be an existing object such as the referent of an instance variable or parameter, or an anonymous object created by a message expression in the method's return expression. Note that if the returned object is a new object, neither the sender nor the method that created the object is responsible for deallocating that object, due to automatic storage reclamation.

Comparisons

Comparisons also reflect the distinction between references to the same object and references to copies of the same object. The protocol of the class Object contains the binary messages == ("identical to") and ~~ ("not identical to") for determining whether the receiver and the argument are the same object. These messages test whether the two object identifiers are equal. The class Object also defines the messages = ("equal to") and ~= ("not equal to") that test whether the receiver and the argument are equal copies (i.e., whether they represent objects with equal attributes).[26] Two variables can refer to objects that are equal but not identical, but not vice versa. For example,

```
"identity and equality comparisons"
| string1 string2 string3 test |
string1 := 'hello'.
string2 := 'hello'.
string3 := string1.
test := string1 = string2.      "true, the referents are equal according to = in class String"
test := string1 == string2.     "false, the referents are not the same object"
test := string1 == string3      "true, the referents are the same object"
```

The same results would occur for instances of Float, LargePositiveInteger, Array, Point, and so on.

For unique objects, the identity and equality test messages always return the same result. For example,

```
"identity and equality comparisons for unique objects"
| boolean test symbol1 symbol2 |
boolean := false.
test := boolean = (3 >= 5).     "true, both the receiver and the expression evaluate to false"
test := boolean == (3 >= 5).    "true, since false is a unique object"
symbol1 := #hello.
symbol2 := #hello.
test := symbol1 = symbol2.      "true, the referents are equal according to = in class Symbol"
test := symbol1 == symbol2.     "true, since symbols are unique objects"

test := 2.0 == 2.0.             "false, two different float objects"
test := 2 == 2                  "true, since small integers are unique objects"
```

Because we cannot distinguish between two "different" but equal unique objects on the basis of their identities, these objects behave more like attributes than objects, although they do maintain their class identities.

An equality test is class-specific: The method for determining whether two strings are equal is not the same as the method for determining whether two points are equal. The default implementation of the equality test message = defined in Object is to use == since there is no information available about the receiver other than its identity. The message = should be reimplemented by the designer of a class in a manner consistent with the semantics and usage of that class.[27] Typically, the = method checks whether corresponding instance variable values are equal (although some instance variables may not be relevant). Because Smalltalk is dynamically typed, there is no guarantee that the argument is an

---

[26] If you know Lisp, == corresponds to Lisp's eq, and = is like equal.

[27] In addition, any class that defines = should also reimplement the message hash such that instances that are = have the same hash value. This message is used in the implementation of the collection classes Set and Dictionary.

instance of the same class as the receiver. If it is not, the test should return false rather than resulting in an error, so a method for = must first check the class of the argument.

Copying objects

Of course, there are situations in which it is necessary to create a new object that is a duplicate of an existing object. The protocol for the system class Object, which is the root of the inheritance hierarchy, includes three copying operations—shallowCopy, deepCopy, and copy—inherited by all classes. The message shallowCopy returns a new copy of the receiver object that shares its instance variable referents (i.e., their object identifiers are copied but the objects are not). The message deepCopy returns a copy of the receiver whose instance variables are complete copies of the receiver's instance variable referents.[28] If a unique object receives a message asking for a copy of itself, it returns a reference to itself.

For example, Figure 5.11 illustrates the result of the following three assignments:

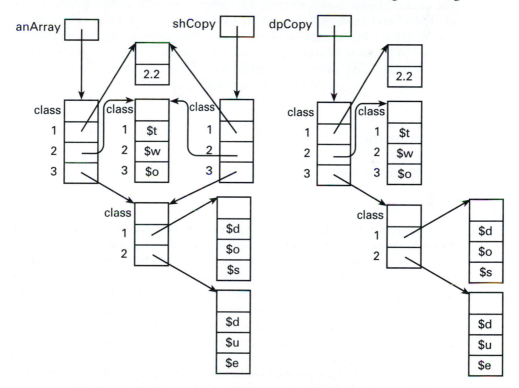

Figure 5.11   The shallowCopy and deepCopy messages (class objects not shown).

---

[28] VisualWorks Smalltalk no longer includes the message deepCopy. Instead, the method for copy in Object sends the receiver shallowCopy followed by postCopy, whose method in Object does nothing. A class whose copy method does more than a shallowCopy should override postCopy with whatever behavior is necessary.

```
"shallowCopy and deepCopy: see figure 5.11"
| anArray shCopy dpCopy test |
anArray := #(2.2 'two' ('dos' 'due')).
shCopy := anArray shallowCopy.
dpCopy := anArray deepCopy.

test := anArray at: 2 == shCopy at: 2.    "true, they are the same object"
test := anArray at: 2 == dpCopy at: 2    "false, they are different objects"
```

The method for deepCopy calls itself recursively, so dpCopy's third element is a complete copy of the array that is the third element of anArray. The recursion for deepCopy stops at unique objects such as characters because they return themselves in response to copying messages without causing further copying. Clearly, deep-Copy can be an expensive operation, and applying it to a circular structure results in infinite recursion.

The message copy is intended to provide class-specific duplication of objects. The class designer should override this message with some appropriate combination of shared and unshared instance variable referents, default values, and so on, depending on the semantics of the class. The default implementation of copy defined in the class Object is to invoke shallowCopy, which is also used by collections such as arrays and sets. Clients should always use the message copy for copying to maintain the intentions of the class designer.

5.5 FLOW OF CONTROL

5.5.1 Basic Concepts

Message sequencing

In section 5.3.2, we described how precedence among message categories and parenthesization controls the order of execution within a nested message expression. When sending a series of messages to various objects in the sequence control structure, we list the message expressions separated by periods. Like the Smalltalk message expression syntax, this delimiter makes each message send appear like an English sentence. The period is an expression separator like the semicolon in Pascal, rather than an expression terminator like the semicolon in C, so a period is not necessary after the last expression in a sequence. For example,

```
"a series of message expressions to be executed sequentially are separated by periods"
| string index char digit |
string := 'hello'.
index := 3.
char := string at: index.
digit := char asDigit + 1.
string at: index put: digit asCharacter
```

Control flow as message passing

Unlike traditional languages, there are no conditional or iterative control structure statements in Smalltalk. Instead, conditional execution and iteration are provided in terms of objects and message passing, like all operations. The primary objects involved in control flow messages are boolean objects and blocks, which receive conditional evaluation messages. A *block* is an object containing a sequence of message expressions, which are evaluated upon receiving a request to do so (i.e., a function object). Blocks are also used as the arguments of control flow messages. In addition, numeric objects provide protocol for definite iteration (i.e., for for loops), and collection classes define a number of messages for iterating over their elements. With control structures implemented using the same mechanism as all other activity, the language is simpler and more uniform. It is also possible for a programmer to create custom control messages.

5.5.2 The Class Boolean

In most programming languages, logical values are represented by a built-in type boolean whose operations are defined by the language. Comparison and testing operations return boolean values, logical operations take and return boolean values, and boolean-valued expressions are used in conditional control structures. Comparisons and tests on built-in types and logical operations are defined by the language itself, as are conditional control structures.

In Smalltalk, Boolean is a system class that has exactly two unique instances, true and false, and this behavior is encapsulated within that class. Comparison and testing messages return an instance of Boolean, and the selector is usually a stative verb or verb phrase (e.g., includes: anElement, or isEmpty). For example,

```
"expressions that return instances of the system class Boolean"
anObject = key
aDate < today
anInteger odd
aSet includes: 'hello'
aRectangle containsPoint: selectedPoint
('yikes' at: 3) isVowel
```

Logical operations are implemented as messages in the protocol of the class Boolean. Consider the following expression:

```
"a message expression using the protocol of class Boolean"
test := (aNumber >= 0) & (aNumber <= max)
```

Each condition is evaluated by passing the testing messages to aNumber, and then the message & (logical "and") is sent to the boolean object returned by (aNumber >= 0) with the boolean object returned by (aNumber <= max) as its argument. The

selector	operations
&	and
|	or
not	not
eqv:	equivalence
xor:	exclusive-or

Figure 5.12 Logical message selectors.

resulting boolean is then assigned to test, which can now be sent any message in the protocol of Boolean.

Figure5.12 lists the selectors for the logical messages. Note that like any unary message, the usage of the message not is postfix.

5.5.3 Blocks

Function objects and the class BlockClosure

Syntactically, a *block* consists of a sequence of message expressions separated by periods, enclosed in square brackets. For example,

```
"the message expressions for a block object are enclosed in square brackets"
[aSet add: 'this'; add: 'that'. anArray at: 1 put: aSet size]
```

The square brackets are not merely a syntactic marker like the reserved words begin and end in Pascal or the braces { and } in C. In those languages, the block delimiters group a series of statements so that they are treated as a single statement syntactically. When control enters the block, the statements are evaluated. In Smalltalk, the square brackets specify that the interpreter should create an instance of the system class BlockClosure[29] containing those expressions, but should not evaluate the expressions. A block object is essentially an unnamed function object, that is, an object that can be executed, and the square brackets are a literal notation for creating such function objects.

As we discussed in section 1.2.3, functional programming languages provide a notation for defining anonymous function objects (e.g., the lambda form in Lisp). For example, the programmer can create such an object and assign it to a variable, then apply it to a list of arguments at some later point. There is no analogous construct in procedural languages such as Pascal and C, in which a subprogram must be named, and can only be executed by an invocation using that name in a scope in which the name is visible. Functions are first-class objects in Smalltalk, as in functional languages. Like any object, a block can be assigned to a variable, stored in an array, passed as a message argument, or constructed and returned by a method. The block's messages are sent when that variable, array element, or argument receives the message value. For example, the system class SortedCollection main-

[29] This class is called BlockContext in Smalltalk-80 and Block in IBM Smalltalk.

tains a sorted list of objects, and each sorted collection object can have a different sort function (e.g., in ascending or descending order). We can pass a block that performs a comparison on its two arguments as the comparison function when creating an instance. For example (we will discuss the notation for the block parameters pt1 and pt2 in the next subsection),

```
"Create a sorted collection of points in order of increasing x coordinate."
| pointList |
pointList := SortedCollection sortBlock: [:pt1 :pt2 | pt1 x < pt2 x]
```

The sorted collection pointList will store a reference to that block object in an instance variable, and use it when placing a new element in the list.

Like any object, a block can receive messages. In particular, a block object evaluates its message expressions upon receiving the unary message value. The evaluation returns the value of the last expression in the block to the sender of value. The expression [ ] value (i.e., evaluate an empty block) returns nil. In addition to providing support for function objects, the protocol of BlockClosure includes messages that implement control structures, concurrency, and exception handling.[30] We will discuss these messages in the next three sections.

Parameters and local variables

Like a subprogram, a block can define parameters and local variables that are local to the block scope and exist only during its execution. The parameter names are listed at the beginning of the block, each preceded by a colon (which is not part of the parameter name). The parameters are separated from the block's message expressions by a vertical bar, as in the previous example. As discussed in section 5.4.2, parameters are passed by reference and may not appear on the left side of an assignment within the block's expressions.

We send the message value: to evaluate a single-parameter block and pass it an argument. BlockClosure defines the messages value:value:, value:value:value:, and value:value:value:value: for evaluating two-, three-, and four-parameter blocks, respectively. Blocks also respond to the message valueWithArguments: whose argument is an array containing the correct number of arguments. Each parameter is initialized with the corresponding argument before the block's expressions are evaluated. For example,

```
"creating and evaluating a block with two parameters"
| testBlock test |
testBlock := [:obj1 :obj2 | obj1 < obj2].
"test is set to true"
test := testBlock value: 'abc' value: 'xyz'.
"test is set to false"
test := testBlock value: Date today value: (Date readFromString: '5/18/82')
```

---

[30] In fact, few Smalltalk programmers use its functional capabilities. Most only use blocks in control structure messages as discussed in sections 5.5.4 and 5.5.5.

If the wrong number of arguments is passed to a block, the system displays an error dialog.

Blocks can also define local variables, although this is rarely done. As in methods and code fragments, you enclose a list of identifiers in vertical bars following the block parameters (and the corresponding vertical bar), but preceding the expressions, as follows:

```
"syntax for a block with both parameters and local variables"
[:param1 :param2 ... | | local1 local2 ... | ... msgExprs ... ]
```

Scope

Because a block may declare parameters and local variables, it defines a new level of scope that contains those declarations. Uses of those names appearing elsewhere have a different meaning. Identifiers that are not local to the block can also occur in the expressions within the block, for example, the local variables of the method or code fragment in which the block appears. The nesting of a block's scope is determined statically, so the bindings for its nonlocal variables are sought in the environment in which the block occurs. That is, when a block is compiled, the search for the declaration of a nonlocal identifier begins in the method or block in which the block is defined. For example,

```
"evaluation of a block that accesses nonlocal variables"
| aNumber aBlock |
aNumber := 1.
aBlock := [:num | num + aNumber].        "aNumber is 1 at this point"
aNumber := 5.
aNumber := aBlock value: 3.               "returns 8 since aNumber was 5"
aNumber := aBlock value: 3                "returns 11 since aNumber was 8"
```

During execution, the block object accesses its nonlocal variables via a static link (maintained by an instance variable of BlockClosure), as we discussed for subprograms in section 0.2.4 and function objects in section 1.2.3.[31]

The nonlocal private variables that appear in a block may be the local variables or parameters of the enclosing method or block, or the instance variables of the receiver of that method. A shared variable in a block may be a global variable, or a class or pool variable of the class of the enclosing method. Blocks can be nested, and the usual static scope rules apply in determining the referent of a nonlocal private variable. Because Smalltalk uses static scope resolution, the compiler can signal an error when it encounters a name for which a declaration cannot be found, before the interpreter evaluates the method or code fragment or creates the block.

---

[31] We will see in the next section that the system actually translates most blocks "in line" rather than creating an instance of BlockClosure.

Closure

A block can be returned by a method, or can be bound to a variable that persists after the method containing the block exits (e.g., if it is passed to an argument that keeps a reference to it). In these cases, the lexical environment in which the block receives the message value differs from the environment in which it is defined, and the compiler cannot know what that environment of invocation will be when compiling the block. For example, suppose we have a class ExampleClass with an instance variable instVar and a class method var: that creates a new object and sets its variable's value to the argument. Suppose that the class defines the following method, which returns a block (as we will see in section 6.1.2, the symbol ∧ identifies the return value of a method):

```
"a method that returns a block containing nonlocal identifiers"
"the class defines an instance variable instVar"
modifierBlock                        "the method name"
   | localVar |                      "a local variable of the method"
   localVar := 2 * instVar.
   ∧[instVar := instVar + localVar.  localVar := instVar]
```

If an instance of ExampleClass receives the message modifier, it returns a block object to which the client can send value to evaluate its expressions. For example,

```
"using a block returned by a method"
| aBlock |
exObject := ExampleClass var: 5.        "exObject's instVar is set to 5"
aBlock := exObject modifierBlock.        "localVar := 10"
"values for instVar and localVar are necessary to evaluate the block"
aBlock value.                            "instVar := 15.  localVar := 15"
aBlock value.                            "instVar := 30.  localVar := 30"
```

When aBlock is evaluated, the identifier instVar must refer to the receiver of that modifierBlock message (i.e., exObject), and the identifier localVar must refer to the variable in the activation record of the invocation exObject modifierBlock.

Like the function objects discussed in section 1.2.3, a block must be represented by a closure that includes both its message expressions and a reference to its environment of definition (i.e., a static link), which determines the bindings for the block's nonlocal variables.[32] This information is represented by the instance variables method and outerContext of the class BlockClosure. In Smalltalk, the static link outerContext is a reference to an instance of the system classes MethodContext or BlockContext. This object represents an activation of the enclosing method or

---

[32] In fact, a block object only needs a reference to the enclosing context if it assigns new values to the local variables in that activation record. If not, the block object contains an array of references to the receiver, parameters, and local variables in the instance variable copiedValues, rather than a static link in the instance variable outerContext.

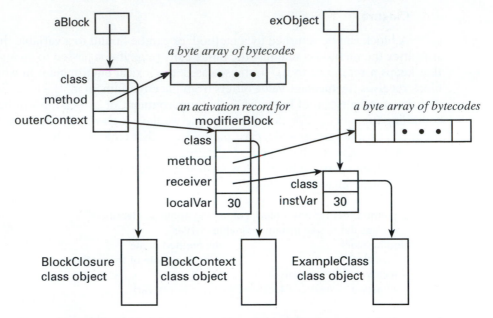

Figure 5.13   A block is represented by a closure that refers to an activation record (class objects not shown).

block, and contains references to the receiver and its arguments and local variables. Figure 5.13 illustrates these objects for the previous example.

Because a block that refers to nonlocal identifiers can be passed outside the context in which it is defined, the activation record of a method invocation may have to exist after that invocation has completed execution. For example, the activation record of exObject modifierBlock in the previous example must exist for as long as aBlock (or any other object that contains a reference to the returned block object). Like functional languages, Smalltalk cannot allocate activation records automatically using a stack. The interpreter creates an instance of MethodContext when a message is sent, and the object memory system deallocates it automatically when there are no more references to it. That is, activation records are allocated dynamically and garbage collected, like all other objects in the system.

A block can also contain a return expression, which gives the return value of the enclosing method and specifies that control should exit the method, like the return statement in C. (Return expressions are discussed in section 6.1.2.) However, it is the execution of the enclosing method that terminates with the given value, not that of the block. Clearly, storing or passing a block containing a return expression outside the context of the method in which it is defined should not be done, because an error will occur when the program attempts to exit that method invocation a second time.

5.5.4 Conditional Execution

To perform conditional execution, we pass a message to the boolean object that results from evaluating the condition expression. The "then" and "else" parts of a conditional statement in a traditional language are represented by block arguments of the message, one of which is evaluated depending on which boolean object is the receiver. (Recall the expression char isSeparator ifTrue: [...] ifFalse: [...] in the code example in section 5.1.2.) To support conditional expressions, the protocol of the system class Boolean includes the four messages ifTrue:, ifFalse:, ifTrue:ifFalse:, and ifFalse:ifTrue:. The argument(s) of these messages are block(s), and the boolean receiver responds by sending the message value to the appropriate block argument.[33] For example,

```
"conditional message expressions: the boolean receiver's method sends the message value
to the ifTrue: block argument if the receiver is true, otherwise it sends value to the ifFalse:
block argument"

aNumber < 0 ifTrue: [aNumber := aNumber negated]

aString first isUppercase
    ifFalse: [aString at: 1 put: aString first asUppercase]

aNumber < 0
    ifTrue: [
        aNumber := aNumber negated.
        negativeCount := negativeCount +1]
    ifFalse: [positiveCount := positiveCount + 1]
```

If the message expression used as the condition is a unary or binary message, then it need not be enclosed in parentheses since the conditional execution messages are keyword messages. To code a nested conditional, we place a conditional expression within the block argument of another conditioned expression.

Like all modern languages, Smalltalk code can be formatted in whatever way makes its intent clear. However, Smalltalk code layout is not entirely standardized. Frequently, programmers give a short ifTrue: or ifFalse: expression on a single line, as in the first expression in the previous examples. For an ifTrue:ifFalse: expression, each keyword and argument block is placed on a separate line indented below the expression defining the boolean receiver, as in the second and third examples. If the argument block contains several expressions, they are typically placed on separate lines below the keyword and indented. For the third example, some programmers would put the [delimiter or the delimiter and the first expression in the ifTrue:

---

[33] In VisualWorks, the message value is implemented in Object to return the receiver, so any object can be used as the argument of a conditional message. This is useful for nesting a conditional expression within another message expression, like C's ?: operator.

block on the same line as the ifTrue: selector. Smalltalk programmers usually do not place the [and] delimiters on separate lines as Pascal and C programmers often do with block delimiters.

Like all message expressions, a conditional expression returns a value. This value is the value of the block that was evaluated (or nil when ifTrue: is sent to false or ifFalse: is sent to true). Thus, we can nest a conditional expression within another message expression as an argument or a receiver, or use it as the right side of an assignment expression. For example,

```
"using the return value of an ifTrue:ifFalse: message"
aNumber := aNumber < 0 ifTrue: [aNumber negated] ifFalse: [aNumber]
```

That is, the conditional messages are expressions like the conditional in a functional language, rather than statements like the Pascal and C if statements.

Many languages include "short circuit" logical operations that only evaluate their second argument if necessary (e.g., C's && and || operators). This behavior is supported by the selectors and: and or: in the protocol of Boolean. Like ifTrue:ifFalse:, these messages take blocks rather than boolean objects as arguments because the argument might or might not be evaluated. If the message and: is sent to false, it responds with false and the block argument is not evaluated. If and: is sent to true, the message value is sent to the block argument and the value of its last expression (which is typically a boolean object) is returned. The selector or: operates analogously. For example,

```
"the block argument is only evaluated if aNumber is positive"
test := 0 < aNumber and: [aNumber < theMax]
```

Smalltalk does not provide a message that corresponds to the case statement found in most imperative languages. Selecting an operation on the basis of an object's type is performed via dynamic binding of methods. Selecting an operation on the basis of an object's value is done with a series of conditional messages.

It would be very inefficient if the system actually created and then deallocated instances of BlockClosure for every conditional expression. Instead, the compiler recognizes when a block is only used in a control flow expression, rather than as a function object assigned to a variable or passed as an argument. In this case, it translates the conditional expression "in line" using the branch instructions of the virtual machine's bytecode language, rather than creating a block object. In fact, almost all the blocks Smalltalk programmers write are translated in line.

5.5.5 Iteration

Conditional iteration

For a conditional execution message, the receiver is an expression that is evaluated once to obtain a boolean object. However, with conditional iteration (e.g., a while loop), the "loop test" expression must be evaluated before each pass through the loop. This expression might be evaluated many times, so the receiver of a conditional iteration message is a block, not a boolean. We perform conditional iteration by passing either of the messages whileTrue: or whileFalse: to a block that returns a boolean object. For example,

```
"set every element of anArray to 0"
| index |
index := 1.
[index <= anArray size] whileTrue: [anArray at: index put: 0.  index := index + 1]
```

The receiver block of the whileTrue: message corresponds to the "loop test" in a traditional language, and the argument block corresponds to the "loop body". When a block receives the whileTrue: message, it sends itself the message value. If the response is true, the message value is sent to the argument block and then the original whileTrue: message is sent again.[34] The method for whileFalse: evaluates the argument block while the receiver returns false. If evaluation of the receiver block returns false, evaluation of the whileTrue: message is complete and nil is returned. Blocks also respond to the unary messages whileTrue and whileFalse, which are equivalent to the messages whileTrue: and whileFalse: with empty argument blocks.

The code layout for whileTrue: messages varies widely among Smalltalk programmers and systems. The following are some common alternatives:

```
"code formats for whileTrue: messages"

[index <= anArray size]
    whileTrue: [anArray at: index put: 0.  index := index + 1]

[index <= anArray size] whileTrue:
    [anArray at: index put: 0.
    index := index + 1]

[index <= anArray size]
    whileTrue: [
        anArray at: index put: 0.
        index := index + 1]

[index <= anArray size]
    whileTrue:
        [anArray at: index put: 0.
        index := index + 1]
```

Perhaps the best advice is to choose a format that seems natural and use it consistently.

---

[34] The BlockClosure method for whileTrue: can be coded recursively in Smalltalk as described here. In fact, the compiler translates a whileTrue: expression using the branch instructions of the virtual machine language.

Smalltalk does not include a construct such as break in C or exit in Ada that can be used to exit from a loop in the middle of the loop body. As in Pascal, we enclose the code following the mid-loop exit test in a conditional, and repeat the mid-loop test in the loop test. For example,

```
"set found to true if key is in anArray or false otherwise"
| index found |
found := false.
index := 1.
[found not and: [index <= anArray size] ]
    whileTrue: [
      (anArray at: index) = key
         ifTrue: [found := true]
            ifFalse: [index := index + 1] ]
```

If the block argument of a whileTrue: expression within a method includes a return expression, the method exits immediately when it is executed (terminating execution of the loop). Therefore, if a mid-loop exit test returns from the enclosing method, the test need not be repeated in the loop test.

The protocol of BlockClosure also includes the message repeat, which provides an "infinite loop". When a block receives this message, it continually sends itself the message value. Clearly, the block must provide some way of terminating the loop, such as a return expression.

Definite iteration

In addition to performing arithmetic operations, integer objects respond to the iteration message timesRepeat:. The receiver sends the message value to the argument block the number of times represented by its value. For example,

```
"draw a regular polygon with numSides sides of length length"
numSides timesRepeat: [aPen go: length; turn: 360 // numSides]
```

To supply the behavior of a for loop in a traditional language, the protocol of the abstract class Number (the ancestor of numeric classes such as SmallInteger and Float) includes the messages to:do: and to:by:do:. The receiver is the initial value of the loop variable, the argument corresponding to to: gives the limit, that corresponding to by: gives the step size (which is 1 for to:do:), and the argument corresponding to do: is a single-parameter block evaluated for each successive value of the loop variable. For example, the following expression increments every third element of anArray:

```
"increment every third element of anArray"
3 to: anArray size by: 3
    do: [:index | anArray at: index put: (anArray at: index) + 1]
```

Instances of Number's concrete subclasses respond to the messages to:do: and to:by:do: by sending the appropriate sequence of value: messages to the block argument corresponding to the do: keyword. In the previous example, the receiver 3 sends the messages value: 3, value: 6, and so on to the block argument.

Iteration over collections

In most languages, we can perform some operation for each element of an array with an iteration such as a for loop. Many functional languages provide operations that support iteration over the elements of a list. For example, the Lisp mapcar function takes a list and a one-parameter function, and returns a list consisting of the results of applying the function to each element of the argument list. Smalltalk provides the same capabilities (and more) for all collection classes with *enumerating* messages. The protocol of the abstract class Collection (the ancestor of the collection classes) includes a number of enumerating messages that take a single-parameter block argument. When a collection object receives such a message, it supplies its elements in turn to the argument block via the message value:, and some enumerating messages also return a result based on those evaluations. The enumerating messages are defined in each concrete collection class in a manner appropriate for its implementation.

The fundamental enumerating message is do:, whose method evaluates the argument block for each element in the receiver collection. When a collection object receives this message, it sends the message value: to the argument block repeatedly with each of its elements as the argument of that message. For example,

```
"move each point in aSetOfPoints ten pixels to the right"
aSetOfPoints do: [:point | point x: (point x + 10) ]

"add each element of the array to aSet"
#(1 3 5 7 9) do: [:int | aSet add: int]

"compute the number of vowels in aString"
| numVowels |
numVowels := 0.
aString do: [:char | char isVowel ifTrue: [numVowels := numVowels + 1] ]
```

The value returned by do: is the value resulting from the last block evaluation. As with whileTrue: messages, Smalltalk programmers use a number of code layouts for do: messages, as follows:

```
"code formats for do: messages"

aSetOfNumbers do:
    [:number |
    sum := sum + number.
    product := product * number]
```

```
aSetOfNumbers do: [:number |
  sum := sum + number.
  product := product * number]

aSetOfNumbers
  do: [:number |
    sum := sum + number.
    product := product * number]
```

With the message do:, the effect of the successive block evaluations must occur due to expressions in the block that use each element as a receiver or argument, or must be reflected by a variable external to the block. There are also several other enumerating messages that return a value based on the block evaluations. Like do:, the message collect: evaluates its argument block for each element of the receiver, but it returns a collection containing the objects produced by successive evaluations of the block. (It "maps" the block onto the collection, like the Lisp mapcar function.) collect: returns a collection of the same type as the receiver.[35] For example,

```
"collect: creates a collection of the results of the block evaluations, and returns it"
'hello' collect: [:char | char asUpperCase]       "returns 'HELLO'"

| oddCheck |
oddCheck := [:number | number odd].        "using a block-valued variable"
#(3 6 9 12) collect: oddCheck               "returns #(true false true false)"
```

The enumerating message select: filters the elements of the receiver collection according to a test block that returns a boolean object. Its method evaluates the argument block for each element of the receiver, and returns a new collection containing references to the elements for which the evaluation resulted in true. (That is, the elements are not copied into the resulting collection.) The message reject: returns a collection consisting of the elements for which evaluation of the argument block resulted in false. Like collect:, both messages return a collection of the same type as the receiver. For example,

```
"clippedSet contains the points in aSetOfPoints that are within aRectangle"
clippedSet := aSetOfPoints select: [:point | aRectangle containsPoint: point]

"compute the number of vowels in aString"
numVowels := (aString  select: [:char | char isVowel]) size
```

The string object created by the select: message in the second example is deallocated automatically, as no references to it are maintained.

When a dictionary receives an enumerating message, only its values are passed to the block. There are a few other enumerating messages defined for collections, and several others for ordered collections. We will discuss these in sections 8.2.1 and 8.4.1.

---

[35] We will see a few exceptions to this statement in Chapter 8.

5.5.6 Concurrency

Process scheduling

The Smalltalk virtual machine supports a model of concurrency in which a single processor is shared among multiple, asynchronous, nonpreemptive processes. At any time, one process is executing and the others are either ready to execute or blocked waiting for some other activity to occur. The system contains processes that monitor the mouse and keyboard, the free storage size, and the system clock, and each window on the display is controlled by a process. Applications or users can create processes with BlockClosure messages described in this section, such as to perform a task in the background.

The processor manager is the only instance of the system class Processor-Scheduler, and is referred to by the global variable Processor. This object is responsible for coordinating activation and deactivation of processes, and for supplying the process priority levels when requested. It contains two instance variables, active-Process, a reference to the currently executing process, and quiescentProcessLists, a set of lists of the ready processes, one for each priority level. The standard priority levels are maintained as class variables, and are available via class messages (which we discuss later in this section).

Process creation

Processes are instances of the system class Process, which defines scheduling and process state protocol, and each process has a priority level. A process represents an execution of a series of expressions that can be suspended and restarted. We create a new process by passing either the message fork or new-Process to a block that contains the new process's message expressions. When a block receives the message fork, it creates a new process that will execute its expressions (actually, its bytecodes) when activated, and schedules the process with the processor. The new process will begin execution when the processor activates it (e.g., when the sender terminates or becomes blocked). Control then returns to the sender of fork without waiting for evaluation of the block's expressions. The fork method returns a reference to the process object, rather than the return value of the block, because execution of the new process may not have completed (or even begun). For example, the following code fragment creates a process that prints the integers from 1 to 10 in the transcript at five-second intervals (we discuss the class Delay and the message wait later in this section):

```
"creating a new independent process"
[ | index |                        "index is a local variable, not a parameter"
index := 1.
10 timesRepeat: [
    (Delay forSeconds: 5) wait.
    Transcript show: index printString;  cr.
    index := index + 1.] ] fork
```

In fact, the new process may not print its messages at exactly five-second intervals if there are higher-priority processes active.

When a block receives the message newProcess, it creates a suspended (i.e., not scheduled) process that will execute its expressions, and returns a reference to that object. The creator of the new process (or another method that obtains a reference to that object) can then send the message resume to the process object so that it schedules itself. (The BlockClosure method for fork creates a new process with self newProcess, sends it resume, and returns a reference to the process.) When the processor chooses a process to be the active process, the expressions in its block are evaluated. If the block that defines the activity for a new process has parameters, the sender uses the message newProcessWithArguments: to pass an array of arguments to the new suspended process.

The process state

We can describe the state of a Smalltalk process using a state transition diagram, as illustrated in Figure 5.14 (the ovals represent process states, the solid lines represent state transitions, and the dashed lines represent process creation). Each state transition in Figure 5.14 is labeled with the process message or other activity that triggers that transition. When a suspended process receives the message resume, it passes itself to the Processor, which places it on the ready list for the process's priority level. When the active process receives suspend or terminate, the processor suspends or terminates that process, and resumes execution of the next process on the highest-priority non-empty ready list (*schedule* in Figure 5.14). A process can send itself suspend or terminate if necessary, or it can receive those messages from a process with which it is communicating. (suspend and terminate can also be sent to processes in a ready queue.) When a process is suspended, it continues at the next message send when it receives resume. Processes can also be suspended or resumed by the Semaphore messages wait and signal, as discussed later in this section. If the active process receives the message error: (e.g., this message is sent by the method for doesNotUnderstand:), it is suspended and a notifier is displayed and made active. The running process can send the processor the message yield if it wishes to relinquish control but remain in the ready state, and the processor places that process in the ready queue and schedules another ready process.

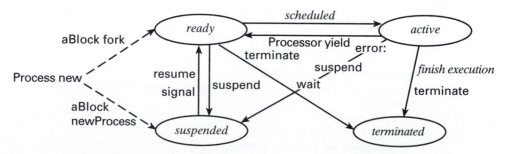

Figure 5.14   State transition diagram for instances of the Smalltalk class Process.

Process priority

The system defines seven priority levels, which are obtained by passing a message to the Processor object, for example, Processor userSchedulingPriority. From highest to lowest priority, these messages are

- timingPriority for real-time processes
- highIOPriority (e.g., for network input)
- lowIOPriority (e.g., for printer output)
- userInterruptPriority
- userSchedulingPriority for normal user interaction
- userBackgroundPriority
- systemBackgroundPriority (e.g., for garbage collection)

A process's priority level can be obtained or set with the messages priority and priority:, respectively. With fork and newProcess, the new process's priority is that of the process that spawned it. The message forkAt: takes an argument that gives a priority for the new process. For example, we can create and schedule a background process as follows:

```
"creating a background process"
["... background operations ..."] forkAt: Processor userBackgroundPriority
```

Process synchronization and communication

The protocol of the system class Semaphore supports synchronization and mutual exclusion among asynchronous processes without "busy waiting". Its instances behave like the semaphores provided by traditional multiprocessing operating systems. Synchronization is controlled by the messages signal and wait, and each semaphore object maintains a queue of processes that are waiting for a signal to be sent to the semaphore. A process sends the message signal to a semaphore object to indicate that some activity of interest to other processes has occurred. A process sends the message wait to a semaphore to indicate that it cannot continue unless some process has sent signal to that semaphore. If a semaphore has not received a signal when it receives a wait, it suspends and queues the process so that it can send the process resume when it receives signal from another process. When a semaphore object receives a signal message, it resumes the process of the highest priority that first began waiting for it. If a semaphore receives several signal messages without any intervening waits, it maintains the number of signals received in an instance variable excessSignals, and lets that many processes proceed when they send it wait messages.

We create a new semaphore with the class message Semaphore new. The new semaphore object has not received a signal, so if the first message it receives is a wait, it will queue the sender. The Semaphore class message forMutualExclusion creates a semaphore that behaves as if it has already received a signal. The first process that sends it wait will continue, and succeeding processes that send wait will be suspended. When the executing process is finished with its mutually exclusive operations, it sends signal to the semaphore so that another (possibly waiting) process can proceed with its mutually exclusive operations.

Asynchronous processes often need to pass information to each other. Transfer of information to a shared buffer must be controlled to prevent race conditions that can corrupt its contents due to simultaneous reads and writes. The system class SharedQueue provides transfer of objects between processes, with mutual exclusion controlled by semaphores within the shared queue object. Objects in the queue can be obtained or examined with the messages next and peek, and nextPut: inserts an object into the queue.

The Smalltalk system class Delay provides a mechanism for delaying execution of a process for a specific amount of time, or for synchronizing with a real-time clock. The class message forSeconds: creates a delay object that will suspend the active process for the number of seconds given by its argument when it receives the message wait. For example, the expression (Delay forSeconds: 10) wait suspends the process for ten seconds. The system will send the signal that reactivates the process when the system clock reaches the appropriate value. The class message forMilliseconds: allows the client to give the new object's delay time in milliseconds. The class message untilMilliseconds: creates a delay object that will suspend the active process until the system clock reaches the value given by the argument when it receives the message wait. The class message millisecondClockValue in both the classes Delay and Time returns the current value of the system clock. The Delay instance message resumptionTime gives the value of the system clock at which the process suspended by the receiver will resume.

5.5.7 Exception Handling

Error propagation

When an object receives a message it cannot respond to or an argument that it cannot handle because it is the wrong type or an invalid value, it sends itself the message error:. The argument of that message is a string that indicates the nature of the problem. The method for error: displays a notifier dialog labeled by the argument string that allows the user to enter debugging mode and correct the error (as discussed in section 5.6.4).

Clearly, this behavior is not appropriate for an application being run by an end user. For example, if the application asks the user to enter some information and the string he or she enters has an invalid format for its use in the application, the application should indicate what is wrong with the input and request the information again. However, the method that determines that the format is invalid might be one in a system class or a model class, not the method that requests information from the user. For example, an application can create a date object from a string with the Date class message readFromString:, but only that class method can determine whether a string entered by the user is a valid date. In such a case, the application needs a mechanism for propagating the error condition from the Date class method to the method that interacts with the user.

The original definition of Smalltalk-80 in [Gol89] did not support exception handling. Several contemporary Smalltalk systems such as VisualWorks [Vis95] and VisualAge [Smi95] include a set of system classes and methods that support exception propagation and handling. We will briefly describe the mechanisms provided by VisualWorks in this section.

The class Signal and raising exceptions

In VisualWorks, the two classes Signal and Exception are used for exception handling. A signal represents a type of error condition, and an exception object represents a particular occurrence of an exception. Many system classes define signals for the errors that can occur in their methods as class variables, and provide access to these signals via class messages. Some examples include

- ArithmeticValue (the ancestor of all numeric classes) defines divisionByZeroSignal, overflowSignal, underflowSignal, domainErrorSignal, and rangeErrorSignal
- Collection defines notFoundSignal, which is raised when a client refers to an element that is not in the collection (e.g., to remove it)[36]
- Dictionary defines keyNotFoundSignal
- Object defines subscriptOutOfBoundsSignal and nonIntegerIndexSignal for objects such as arrays that contain indexed instance variables (see section 6.1.2)

You can use the class hierarchy browser (see section 5.6.3) to examine the definition, initialization, and use of signals in the system classes to see how to define signals for errors that can occur in your classes.

Visualworks uses signal objects for both raising and handling exceptions. When a signal receives the message raise, its method creates an exception object and sends it a message that triggers the search for a handler. The signaler of the exception can also use the exception object to transmit information to the method that handles it. The signal message raiseWith: sets the exception object's "parameter" (an instance variable) to its argument and raises the exception. The handler can access the parameter object by sending parameter to the exception object that it receives as an argument (see the next subsection). The signaler can also pass an error message with the messages raiseErrorString: or raiseWith:errorString:.[37]

---

[36] Actually, this signal is defined in Object, but it logically belongs in Collection.

[37] In IBM Smalltalk, instances of the class ExceptionalEvent identify the error type and provide default error handling (as opposed to signals in VisualWorks), and an instance of the class Signal is passed to the exception handler. An exception is signaled by sending the message signal to an exceptional event. The message signalWith: is used to supply an argument for the exception handler.

Handling exceptions

To handle an exception, we first create an instance of that type of signal. For example, the expression (ArithmeticValue domainErrorSignal) newSignal creates a signal that we can use to specify a handler for the case when an arithmetic operation has an invalid receiver or argument. (For example, the method for arcSin raises this signal if the receiver is not between −1 and 1.) To specify an exception handler for an error condition, we send the message handle:do: to a signal of that type. The first argument is a single-parameter block that gives the exception handler, and the second block argument is the application code. The general format is as follows:

```
"specifying an exception handler for aSignal in VisualWorks"
aSignal
    handle: [:exception | "... error handling ..."]
    do: ["... normal application operations ..."]
```

If aSignal is raised in any method executed as a result of the expressions in the do: block, then the handle: block is executed (unless another handler for that signal is defined in an intervening context). The exception object created when the signal was raised is bound to the parameter of the handle: block argument.[38]

Each signal object has a "parent" object (not a superclass), and the programmer can specify a handler for a group of signals by giving a common ancestor as the receiver of the handle:do: message. The class variable ErrorSignal in the class Object is the root of this object hierarchy, so a handler for the signal (Object errorSignal) newSignal handles any signal. To handle a particular set of signals, the programmer creates an instance of the class SignalCollection, inserts the desired signals, and sends that object the message handle:do:.

As described in section 0.1.3, when a signal is raised, the interpreter examines the sender of that message to determine whether the signal occurred in the do: block of a handle:do: message sent to that signal. If so, it executes the corresponding handle: block. If not, the caller of that method is examined, and so on back through the sequence of message sends leading up to the occurrence of the exception. If no handler for that exception is encountered, a notifier dialog with the message 'Unhandled exception' is displayed.[39]

The class Exception provides protocol that an exception handler can use to specify control flow in response to an exception. The messages that the handler can send to the exception are

---

[38] In IBM Smalltalk, an exception handler is specified by sending the messag when:do: to the block that performs the normal processing. The first argument is the exceptional event, and the second is the block that gives the error handling.

[39] This behavior is appropriate during program development, but not for end-user applications. The VisualWorks programmer can change this behavior by modifying the method for the class message emergency:from: in the class Exception (e.g., to give a technical support telephone number!).

- return, which exits the method in which it occurs
- restart, which retries the handle:do: block
- reject, which raises the exception again, continuing the search for a matching handler back through the sequence of method activations
- proceed, which returns control to the point at which the signal was raised

If the handler block does not send any of these messages, control continues with the message expression following the handle:do: expression.

In some cases, the programmer needs to specify different handlers for different signals that can be triggered by operations in the same block of code. This effect can be achieved by nesting handle:do: messages, but the resulting expression is difficult to read. The class HandlerCollection is provided for such circumstances, and is used as follows:

```
"using a HandlerCollection to handle several signals in the same code"
HandlerCollection new
    on: signal1 handle: [:exception | "... handler for signal1 ..."];
    on: signal2 handle: [:exception | "... handler for signal2 ..."];
    on: signal3 handle: [:exception | "... handler for signal3 ..."];
    handleDo: ["... normal application operations ..."]
```

5.6 THE SMALLTALK PROGRAMMING ENVIRONMENT

5.6.1 Programming in Smalltalk

User interaction

Before we examine defining classes and the system classes in the next three chapters, we will cover the process of programming using the Smalltalk system. Since the details of individual implementations vary somewhat, we will discuss the programming environment in general terms. The intention of this section is to give you an idea of the capabilities of a typical Smalltalk system and of the quality of interacting with it to develop applications, rather than to present a reference manual for any one system.[40] I will assume that you are familiar with graphic user interfaces consisting of windows, menus, dialogs, and so on, in which you use a pointing device to select text or graphics and manipulate interaction components such as scrollbars, pushbuttons, and popup menus.

The Smalltalk user interface is designed to be used with a three-button mouse. (On systems such as PCs or Macintoshes that have fewer mouse buttons, the user presses a modifier key such as the control key when clicking to simulate pressing the other mouse buttons.) Typically, the left button is the <Select> button, and is used to select text or graphic items by double clicking on them, dragging across

---

[40] For a more complete discussion of the use of the programming environment, see [Gol84] or [LaL90] on Smalltalk-80, or the documentation for your Smalltalk system.

them, or clicking at one end of a selection and shift-clicking at the other end. The middle mouse button is the <Operate> button, and the right button is the <Window> button. [41]

The Smalltalk system uses popup menus that appear when the middle or right mouse button is pressed, rather than pulldown menus that are activated by pressing on a menu header button. [42] The <Window> button pops up a menu with commands for performing window management operations such as moving, resizing, iconifying, or closing the window containing the pointer. Each *view* (i.e., each particular rectangular subwindow) has a popup menu specific to that type of view, which is activated when the <Operate> button is pressed in that view. For example, text views (instances of the system class TextCollectorView) have an <Operate> menu that includes the text editing and evaluating commands we discussed in section 5.1.1 (see Figure 5.1).

Any Smalltalk system will provide a way of performing commonly needed operations such as invoking particular programming tools or applications, opening text windows, saving or loading the image (see the next paragraph), or exiting to the platform's operating system. The original Smalltalk-80 system supplied these commands via an <Operate> menu for the background of the display screen. Many systems provide a platform pulldown menu or a window with icons for selecting these operations.

The image

As we have stated, everything in a Smalltalk system is an object. For example, an executing application is an object, as are the elements of its interface such as windows, scrollbars, pushbuttons, and so on. Each object is stored in object memory and maintains its current state in instance variables (which are also stored in object memory). In fact, the Smalltalk system itself is defined as a collection of objects. The complete state of the system is the set of objects that exist at that point, and is referred to as an *image*. Each time an operation is performed, it modifies the state of the image.

The image includes all the classes and methods defined either by the vendor's initial system image or by the programmer, as well as the state of object memory. The image includes

- the system class library: foundation and collection classes, and classes for user interaction and graphics
- classes that provide system capabilities (e.g., manipulation of files and processes)

---

[41] Originally, the left, middle, and right mouse buttons were called the red, yellow, and blue buttons. Some controller message names still reflect this terminology.

[42] Smalltalk systems for PCs and Macintoshes sometimes use menus that pull down from a menu bar, like all applications on those platforms.

- classes that define programming tools and applications (e.g., browsers and debuggers)
- all executing applications and programming tools and their states (e.g., the positions and sizes of interaction components), and any objects they have created
- the dictionaries of global variables and pool variables

The Smalltalk system allows the programmer to save the current image. This operation essentially takes a snapshot of the current state of the working environment and stores it in a file. The information stored includes all code, all windows presented on the interface, the state of any executing applications, and so on. When that image file is loaded, the system returns to exactly that state. You can save several different image files if you like.

Filing code

Image files are quite large, several megabytes on most systems. The Smalltalk system also allows the programmer to *file out* the code for an individual class category, class, message category, or method by selecting a command in the <Operate> menus in various views in the system browser, or by evaluating the corresponding message in a text window. This operation saves the definition of the class or method in an ASCII text file.[43] We can *file in* class or method definitions by using a menu selection in the file browser, or by sending the corresponding message. Filing code out and in is also useful for transferring code between different systems or among several developers.

The programming process

In a traditional compiled programming language, the programmer creates a set of source code files with an editor, compiles and links them, and then executes, tests, and debugs the result. Each of these activities is performed using a different programming tool, and each tool is separate from the others. The only relationships among the tools are that the output file produced by one is the input to another, and that programmers use them in developing applications. In this way, the same editor and linker can be used with different programming languages. However, this has the effect that the development process becomes a series of discrete steps, and the programmer must always be aware of which task he or she is performing, and which tool is being used. This is particularly true in command line systems in which the programmer must return to the operating system to execute a different tool.

In Smalltalk, the various class and method definitions that make up an application are each entered interactively using the facilities of the programming envi-

---

[43] The file format uses the exclamation point ! as a delimiter, so you should not use it in comments in your code.

ronment. Any programming tool is available at any time, and the programmer can switch from one tool to another at the click of a mouse button. The tools are integrated in the sense that they all refer to the same code base (i.e., the set of class definitions in the system), and can be invoked from each other using menu commands. The interface to the programming tools is uniform across the tools, for example, each text editing window in the various tools has the same popup <Operate> menu with the same commands. If the programmer gets stuck (or even goes home for the day!), he or she can save the system image, and when that image is restarted, every application and tool will be in the same state as when the image was saved.

As we mentioned in section 5.3.2, Smalltalk code is *incrementally compiled*. When a new method definition is entered and accepted, the compiler translates its source code to the machine language for the virtual machine, and adds that array of bytecodes to the class's method dictionary. That code is invoked when an instance of the class receives the corresponding message, even within an application that is already executing. Unlike in a compiled language such as C, the programmer does not need to recompile and relink other parts of the application when modifying a method, because each message send is bound according to the current method dictionary in the receiver's class. Dynamic binding provides the flexibility to change any method, even while the application is running, at the expense of run-time selection of every message.

In Smalltalk, we can execute an application, trace its behavior, stop it and examine or modify objects or methods, and then continue the same execution. This approach is often referred to as "modeless" programming because the programmer does not have to switch between the various activities and their corresponding tools when creating and testing an application. The uniformity of the programming environment, the ability to examine an executing application, and the extensive class library permit us to create an application incrementally in Smalltalk. We can design and debug the necessary classes and methods individually, and can gradually build and test the program interactively. In fact, each application is essentially an extension of the base system, which is created by composition and inheritance using existing classes.

Application structure

In traditional procedural languages, an application is a main program that creates a number of objects and then performs a series of statements and subprogram invocations. (The subprograms and types it uses might be coded in separate modules.) However, in Smalltalk, all processing is encapsulated as the responsibility of some class. A Smalltalk application is defined as a set of classes, one of which represents the application itself. The processing that would typically be coded in the main program in a procedural language is encapsulated within an instance creation method for the application class, usually open. The instance variables of the application class maintain the "data" usually found in the main program, namely the representation of the model, the components of the application's interface, and the state of the use of the application (e.g., whether a file has been saved). The open method instantiates the application, initializes its instance variables, presents its interface to the user, and sets up an event loop or event dispatching mechanism to respond to user input. The application class defines instance methods that provide its functionality (that send messages to model objects), which are triggered by messages from the user via controller objects.

To perform some activity, a Smalltalk user instantiates an application class, rather than executing a program. When he or she sends the instance creation class message, the corresponding method creates and initializes the application. For example, if we type and evaluate the expression TextCollectorView open in a text window, an instance of that class is created, which presents a text window on the display. The user can instantiate instances of several applications and use them simultaneously, if desired.

In many Smalltalk systems, the programmer defines an application class as a subclass of a system-provided generic application class, as described in section 2.2.4.[44] This class defines a class message that creates and displays a main window and registers the application object with the system event-dispatching mechanism. The application class refines this method so that these operations are performed, and instantiates and initializes its model objects and a set of instances of subclasses of the Window and View system classes that implement the interface of the application and permit the user to interact with it. The application class also defines instance methods for the messages sent when the user manipulates interaction components.

Designing applications as classes also allows developers to use inheritance among applications, which facilitates reuse and extendibility in application design. For example, we can design, implement, and debug a basic drawing program, and later define a subclass that provides additional capabilities.

5.6.2 Text Windows

The workspace

A *workspace* is a window that displays a text collector view (see figures 5.1 through 5.4). As we saw in section 5.1.1, we use workspace windows to edit, store, and evaluate Smalltalk code. We can type and evaluate expressions to help understand the behavior of the system classes, or to test classes and methods that are under development. A series of useful expressions can be kept in a workspace and evaluated when necessary, or used as templates for editing. We can also create an instance of an application or programming tool by sending an instantiation message from the workspace. For example, we can create a new workspace by evaluating the expression TextCollectorView open. We can give the new workspace a label (usually, in its title bar) with the following expression:

```
"creating and displaying a labeled workspace"
TextCollectorView open: TextCollector new label: 'my text window'
```

---

[44] This class is called ApplicationModel in VisualWorks, and it also defines protocol for interacting with code generated by that system's interface builder.

The first argument of this expression is the model for the text collector view and the second is the window label. As stated in section 5.1.1, we also use a workspace to issue commands to the system, like a command line interface to an operating system. More than one workspace window can be open at once, and we can copy text from one to another.

Like all text collector views, the workspace <Operate> menu includes the items undo, cut, copy, and paste (see Figure 5.1). The commands find... and replace... open dialogs asking for the string to search for, and the dialog for replace... also requests the replacement string.[45] As we saw in section 5.1.1, the text collector view <Operate> menu contains the operations do it, print it, and inspect, which evaluate the selected Smalltalk expressions. The compiler also uses the workspace window to report syntax errors in code entered in the workspace, as we discussed in section 5.3.2 (see Figure 5.8). The menu command cancel clears a workspace text view, or returns the text view contents to its initial state in the browser or debugger. The command accept is used in programming tools to accept class and method definitions, but does nothing in the workspace. The command hardcopy prints the contents of the text view.

The transcript

The *system transcript* is a special text window that is always open, generally used for informational messages from the system. For example, when an image is loaded or saved or code is filed in or out, a message to that effect including the file name, date, and time is displayed in the transcript. Error messages are not reported on the transcript, but are reported by dialogs as described in sections 5.4.1 and 5.6.4. In some systems, the transcript also provides icons or menu selections for launching commonly used programming tools and applications.

The transcript is the referent of the global variable Transcript. An application or a text selection can use the transcript for output by sending the message Transcript show: aString. Smalltalk programmers often use this facility for trace output during debugging. For convenience in formatting output to the transcript, the transcript (like all text streams) also responds to the messages space, cr, and tab, which print a space, newline, and tab, respectively.

5.6.3 Browsers

The system browser

The primary programming tool for the Smalltalk developer is the *system browser*, an instance of the system class Browser. This application provides mechanisms for navigating among the classes and methods in the system, so that the programmer can examine the characteristics and behavior of classes and the interrelationships among

---

[45] Some Smalltalk systems use the command again for search and replace operations. It searches for and then selects the next occurrence of the contents of the "paste buffer" (which is updated by a cut or copy command). If the text copied to the paste buffer was replaced by editing, the occurrence found is also replaced.

classes. The system browser is used both for finding existing classes for instantiation, composition, and derivation, and for defining new classes and methods (as we will discuss in section 6.1.2). We can display several instances of the system browser, each viewing different classes, or can define a specialized browser with different display behavior as a subclass of Browser. Figure 5.15 illustrates the system browser.[46]

The top part of the browser window contains four scrollable list views and two "radio buttons" (i.e., exactly one of them is always selected) that provide a search path for classes and their methods, with more specific information to the right. We use these list views to select a class or method definition for viewing in the text view in the lower part of the browser. In Figure 5.15, the programmer has selected the class category Graphics-Geometry and the class Rectangle within that category. The instance radio button is selected, so the third scrollable list displays Rectangle's instance message categories. The programmer has selected the message category accessing and the message center within that category, so the text view displays that method. Each of the five views has an <Operate> menu associated with it that provides operations relevant to that view.

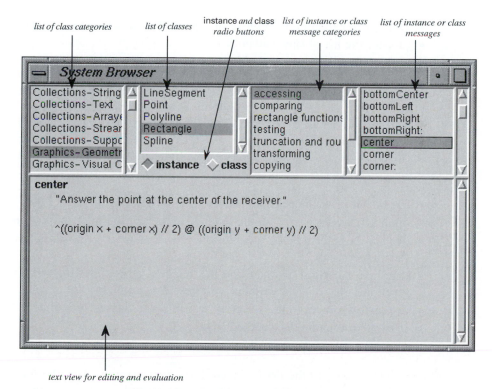

Figure 5.15   Layout of the Smalltalk system browser.

[46] Figure 5.15 illustrates the browser in Smalltalk-80 and VisualWorks. The IBM Smalltalk browser does not use class and message categories, and contains an additional list view that displays a list of the applications or subsystems in which the class is used.

The leftmost list view gives the categories of classes in the system. We use class categories to access classes because a typical Smalltalk system contains several hundred classes. The categories are not part of the language, but simply provide a search path for accessing classes. By convention, the class category names are capitalized and the categories are grouped into areas. For example, there are collection categories such as Collections-Abstract, Collections-Unordered, and Collections-Streams, and graphics categories such as Graphics-Geometry, Graphics-Images, and Graphics-Fonts. Some system class categories are organized according to the class hierarchy, others are grouped by their functionality (e.g., Interface-Dialogs), or by the subsystem that they support (e.g., Kernel-Processes). Programmer-defined classes are usually organized into categories according to the application for which they were created. The <Operate> menu in the class category list view provides commands that allow the programmer to

- file out or print the selected class category
- open a "category browser" on the selected class category (see the next sub-section)
- add a class category, or remove or rename the selected class category
- reorder the list of class categories
- find a particular class.

When a class category is selected (and no class is selected in the second list), the text view displays a class definition template (as discussed in section 6.1.2).

The second list view from the left displays the names of the classes in the category selected in the first list view. Below it are two radio buttons for selecting either instance or class messages for viewing. The class list view's <Operate> menu provides commands to

- file out or print the selected class
- open a "class browser" on the selected class (see the next subsection)
- display the selected class's definition, class comment, or position in the inheritance hierarchy
- display a "method browser" on the selected class's methods that refer to a given instance or class variable (see the subsection after the next)
- display references to the selected class in other classes' methods
- remove or rename the selected class
- move the selected class to a different category.

When a class name in the list is selected, the text view displays the message that defines the class (if the instance radio button is selected). This message presents the names of the class's superclass, instance variables, class variables, pool dictionaries, and class category. It is discussed further in section 6.1.2.

The third list view presents the instance or class message categories for the selected class, depending on which radio button is selected below the class list view.

Messages are grouped into categories to facilitate viewing related messages and methods, and because many system classes have extensive protocols. Like class categories, message categories are not part of the language. Message category names are not capitalized and are often gerunds (e.g., accessing, testing, enumerating, etc.). By convention, the message category private identifies methods that are not intended to be part of the class's interface. The <Operate> menu in the message category list view contains commands to

- file out or print the selected message category
- open a "method browser" on the selected message category
- add a message category, or remove or rename the selected message category
- reorder the list of message categories
- find a particular method.

When a message category is selected (and no message is selected in the fourth list), the text view displays a method definition template (as discussed in section 6.1.2).

The fourth list view displays the message selectors in the selected message category. This list gives only the messages defined in the selected class, not those inherited from its ancestors. The <Operate> menu for the message list view presents commands to

- file out or print the selected method
- open a "method browser" on the senders or implementors of the selected message
- open a "method browser" on the implementors of any message in the selected method
- remove the selected message, or move it to a different message category.

When a message selector in the list is selected, the text of its method is displayed in the text view.

The browser text view presents the selected class or method definition. It has the same <Operate> menu described in sections 5.1.1 and 5.6.2 for text collector views such as the workspace, and these operations can be used to edit the method or evaluate expressions. The text view <Operate> menu also contains the command accept, which causes the code in the text view to be compiled as the new definition of that class or method. In section 6.2.1, we will discuss the use of the browser text view to enter new class and method definitions.

Category and hierarchy browsers

The Smalltalk programming environment includes several other types of browsers that we can use to examine classes, methods, objects, and files. A *category browser* presents the classes in a given category. It is similar to the system browser, except that it has no class category list. Its views contain the same <Operate> menus as those found in the system browser.

A *hierarchy browser* is an instance of the system class HierarchyBrowser that allows the programmer to examine the methods of a given class and its ancestors and descendants. The class browser presents an indented list of the class's ancestors and descendants, instance and class buttons, a list of message categories, a list of messages in the selected category, and a text view containing the code for the selected method. For example, if we request a class hierarchy browser on the class ArrayedCollection, the browser in Figure 5.16 is displayed. We can see that Arrayed-Collection is a subclass of SequenceableCollection, and so on. The programmer has selected the message category testing and the message includes:. Class hierarchy browsers are helpful because they allow us to examine all the methods for a class, whether they are defined in that class or inherited. They are useful when trying to understand a method that refines an inherited method because both methods are available directly. The HierarchyBrowser class message newOnClass: with a class name argument creates a hierarchy browser on that class.

Smalltalk programmers have also created "flattening" browsers that present all the instance variables and methods of a class, including those that are inherited from ancestors. The browser specifies which ancestor defines an instance variable or method. It may contain operations to list the instance variables and methods of a particular ancestor, or list all ancestor definitions of a particular message to aid in understanding method refinements, and so on. Such a tool may or may not be available for your system.

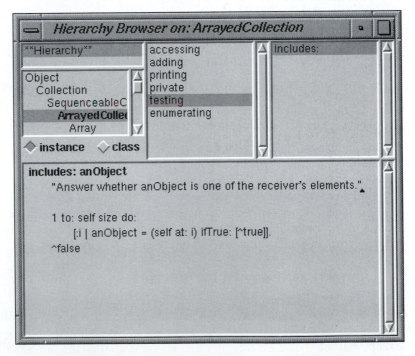

Figure 5.16   A class hierarchy browser on ArrayedCollection.

Method browsers

A *method browser* is an instance of the system class MethodListBrowser that presents a list of method names above a text view displaying the selected method. An instance of this browser is displayed when the programmer selects a menu command in a browser or debugger to view the senders or implementors of a particular message, or the methods that use a particular instance or class variable. For example, if we browse the implementors of the message includes:, the method list browser in Figure 5.17 is displayed.

The method browser list view <Operate> menu contains commands to

- file out or print the selected method
- browse the senders or implementors of the selected message
- browse the senders or implementors of a selected message in the method
- remove the selected message, or move it to a different message category.

The text view contains the standard text view <Operate> menu, which allows the programmer to edit and accept the selected method.

File browsers

A *file browser* is an instance of the system class FileBrowser that interfaces with the operating system file system and presents three views in a column. The top view is a text field containing a file system path, in which you can use an asterisk as a wild-card character (e.g., /home/caleb/Smalltalk/*.st on a Unix system). The class message defaultPattern: can be used to set the initial pattern that a new file browser presents. The middle view is a list of the files and directories that match the pattern

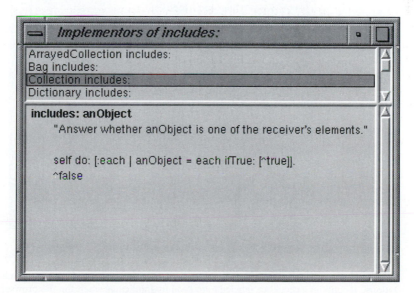

Figure 5.17   A method browser on includes.

given in the text field. The bottom view is a text view that displays the contents of the entry selected in the middle view. If that entry is a directory, the text view displays its contents. If it is a text file, the file browser queries the user whether to display the text of the file or its attributes (size, creation date, etc.). Figure 5.18 illustrates a file browser.[47] The text field is a one-line text collector view in which you can type, select text, and move the cursor with the left and right arrow keys. Its <Operate> menu provides editing operations and a command, volumes..., that displays a list of mounted volumes from which you can choose a new path pattern. The middle list view <Operate> menu contains commands to

- file in the selected file
- remove, rename, or copy the selected file or directory
- make the selected directory the path pattern in the text field.

The text view contains the standard text view <Operate> menu, which allows the user to edit the selected file. It contains the commands save and save as... for saving the edited file (rather than the command accept).

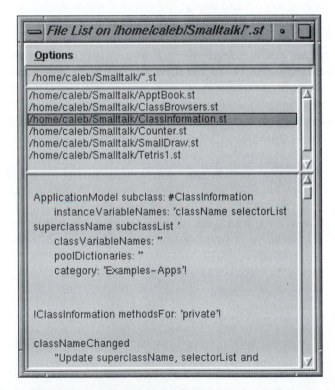

Figure 5.18   A file browser on /home/caleb/Smalltalk/*.st .

[47] Figure 5.18 is a snapshot of the Visualworks file browser, which also has a pulldown menu titled Options. It contains a checkbox labeled Auto Read that indicates when the file browser will be updated automatically whenever the user chooses a new path in the text field.

5.6.4 Debugging

Inspectors

An *inspector* is an instance of the system class Inspector that allows the programmer to examine and modify an object's instance variable referents. We can create an inspector by sending the message inspect to any object. We can also inspect the result of an expression in a text view by selecting the expression and then selecting inspect from the view's <Operate> menu.

An inspector presents a list view containing self and the object's instance variable names on the left and a text view on the right, and shows the name of the object's class in the title bar. If self is selected in the list view, the text view displays the value of the object, and if an instance variable name is selected, the text view displays the value of that variable. (In fact, the text view displays the result of sending the message printString to the instance variable referent, for example, it displays a literal representation if the object's class defines one.[48]) Figure 5.19 illustrates the result of evaluating the expression (Rectangle corner: 2@3 origin 4@10) inspect.

If the referent of the selected instance variable name is a composite object, the list view <Operate> menu contains a command inspect to open another inspector on that object. For example, if we select inspect from the list's <Operate> menu in Figure 5.19, we get an inspector on the point 2@3. The inspector text view that displays the referent's print behavior has the usual text view <Operate> menu. We can assign a different referent to an instance variable of the inspected object by typing an expression that creates a new object in the text view and selecting accept. This expression may include literals, instance variable names, and the pseudo-variable self, which refers to the inspected object.

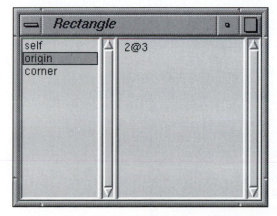

Figure 5.19   An inspector on Rectangle origin: 2 @ 3 corner: 4 @ 10.

---

[48] The default behavior for printString defined in class Object is to print a or an followed by the class name, but most classes define a method that returns a string describing the object more specifically.

The notifier

When an error occurs—for example, when the message doesNotUnderstand: is sent—the process is suspended and a *notifier* dialog is displayed (an instance of the system class NotifierView). The notifier gives the error message, and displays a list of the last five active message sends leading up to the point at which the error occurred (i.e., a "stack trace" of the pending activation records). Each entry in the list gives the class of the receiver and the name of the message, usually in the format Set>>add:. If the method actually executed is defined in an ancestor of the receiver's class, the ancestor name is also given. For example, if an invalid message is sent to a float object, the first entry in the stack trace will be Float(Object)>>doesNotUnderstand:. Figure 5.20 illustrates a notifier (we discuss the pushbuttons in the next paragraph). Often, the list of messages sent is enough information to determine the cause of the problem (e.g., if a selector was mistyped). If so, you can close the notifier window to terminate execution, then correct the error and begin again.

The notifier's <Operate> menu provides commands to instantiate a debugger, proceed with execution, or terminate. (These commands are pushbuttons in Figure 5.20. The command correct it. . . attempts to correct the erroneous expression.) Proceeding may be appropriate if the error is not serious, or if the notifier was created as a result of a breakpoint (as described in the next subsection) or the user pressing the interrupt key (usually control-c). Usually, however, the programmer will want to open a debugger to examine the nature of the problem. Selecting the debug command on the notifier's <Operate> menu replaces the notifier with a debugger.

The debugger

A *debugger* is an instance of the system class Debugger that presents a detailed view of the state of a process. The debugger permits the programmer to examine and modify the state of each pending message send on the execution stack, includ-

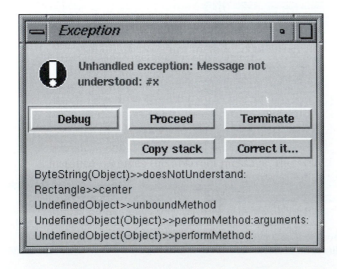

Figure 5.20   A notifier that the receiver does not understand the message x.

ing the code of the method executed and the states of the receiver, arguments, and local variables. It also provides operations for proceeding incrementally from any point in the stack trace.

The layout of the debugger window varies considerably among Smalltalk implementations. The window always includes a scrollable list view, a text view, and two inspectors (each of which consists of a list view and a text view), and some versions include pushbuttons for incremental execution operations (as in Figure 5.21). Suppose we evaluate the expression (Rectangle origin: 2@3 corner: 'oops') center in the workspace. The method that creates the new rectangle does not check the types of the objects given as its origin and corner, which should be points. In this case, the error occurs when the Rectangle method for center (see Figure 5.15) sends x to the corner, which is the string 'oops'. This produces the notifier in Figure 5.20, and after selecting Debug, we get the debugger illustrated in Figure 5.21.

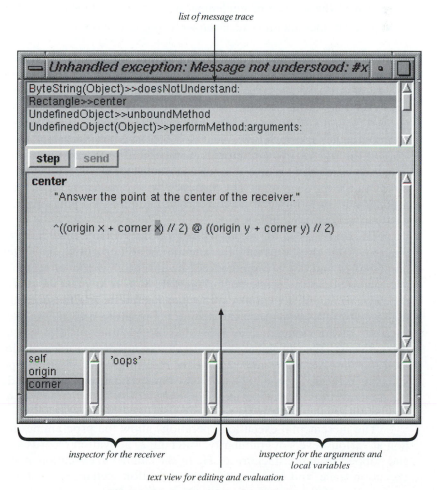

Figure 5.21   Layout of the Smalltalk debugger.

The list view presents the message send trace in the format described previously for the notifier. (The notifier and debugger use the name unboundMethod for a code fragment evaluated in a text view.) When the programmer selects a message send in the trace list, the text view displays the corresponding method with the active message send highlighted. For example, in Figure 5.21, the method center was sending the message x to the instance variable corner when the error occurred. The left inspector displays the instance variables of the receiver of the displayed method, and the right inspector displays the state of its method context, that is, the arguments and local variables of that invocation (there are none in this example).

The list view <Operate> menu contains commands to

- proceed or restart execution
- browse the senders or implementors of the selected message
- browse the senders or implementors of a selected message in the method
- perform incremental execution with step and send.

The command step executes the method for the selected message send completely and then updates the debugger window (without "stepping into" that method). This operation never adds a stack frame to the stack trace in the list view. (If the message executed is the last one in a method or is a return expression, an entry is popped from the stack trace.) The command send sends a single message and then updates the debugger window. That is, it performs a "single step" of execution, and stops at the first expression in the method bound to the message. In most cases, a new entry is pushed on the stack trace in the list view corresponding to the method bound to the message sent. The names of these commands vary among implementations, and many implementations provide them as pushbuttons in the debugger window, as illustrated in Figure 5.21.

The text view in the debugger has the same <Operate> menu described previously. If the displayed method is modified and accepted, the system is updated immediately and the new method will be executed whenever that message is sent. We can also type an expression and evaluate it, as in any text view. This expression can refer to any of the variables whose names are visible in the method, including the receiver self, the instance variables of the receiver, and the parameters and local variables of the method. This allows the programmer to send messages to any of these objects. We can assign new values to the instance variables or local variables, then continue execution and examine the resulting state. We can inspect any of the live objects or browse their classes at any time. The inspectors in the debugger have the standard inspector <Operate> menus that allow the programmer to inspect subobjects and evaluate expressions.

The incremental execution operations allow the programmer to trace execution at various levels of granularity, watching as activation records are pushed onto and popped from the stack trace. He or she can begin execution at any point in the execution trace, and examine different execution scenarios. Each time a message send in the stack trace is selected, the method text view and the inspectors are updated, and sender and implementor browsers are available at each step. The programmer can also modify a method or the state of a variable and then continue execution incrementally. As we discussed previously, the development process is modeless because the programmer can examine the details of the execution trace and modify class and method definitions without leaving the debugger.

The message halt

We can suspend a process and display a notifier at any time by sending the message halt to any object. (The method that performs this behavior is defined in the class Object.) From the notifier, we can open a debugger. In particular, Smalltalk programmers use the expression self halt to set a breakpoint in a method during debugging, making all the facilities of the debugger available when execution reaches that point. We can use the message halt: to give the message string that will be displayed as the label of the notifier and debugger, so that we can identify a particular breakpoint.

We can also use the message halt to examine the sequence of message sends triggered by a message send (e.g., to understand the implementation of a particular message in a system class). To do so, we type self halt. followed by the message expression in a workspace, then select and evaluate those expressions. When the notifier appears, we open a debugger, and send the next message (i.e., the one following self halt). We can then trace execution at the desired level of detail.

5.7 SUMMARY AND REVIEW

5.7.1 A Quick Introduction

The Smalltalk experience

- An interpreted language evaluates code and executes it immediately, and maintains a symbol table of objects, functions, and types that persists across code evaluations. These characteristics simplify learning the language, testing code, and understanding the behavior of types and functions provided by the system.

- Smalltalk systems present scrollable text windows that you can use to edit and store text and evaluate expressions. These operate like a word processor or window-based text editor.

- You can evaluate code in text windows to test your knowledge of the language, examine the behavior of the system classes and the structure of the class hierarchy, and issue commands to the system.

5.7.2 Lexical Elements

Code structure

- Smalltalk code consists of a series of tokens, and the programmer can use any code layout desired.

- Comments are enclosed in double quotes.

Language tokens

- Integer and floating-point literals follow the usual formats. You can give the radix for an integer literal by preceding it with the radix value and an r.

- Character literals are preceded by $, string literals are enclosed in single quotes, and symbols are preceded by #.

- An array literal is a sequence of literals enclosed in parentheses preceded by a #. A byte array literal is a sequence of positive integers less than 255 enclosed in square brackets preceded by a #.

- Each use of a large integer, floating-point, string, or array literal refers to a distinct object.

- A valid identifier is a sequence of letters and digits of unlimited length beginning with a letter, and identifier names are case-sensitive.

Variables

- Because Smalltalk is dynamically typed, identifiers are not typed, so you must use descriptive identifier names.

- A variable name must be declared before it is used. Local variables in methods or code segments are declared by enclosing them in vertical bars, method parameters are declared in the message pattern, and instance and class variables are declared in the class definition.

- *Private variables* are only accessible to one object, and must begin with a lowercase letter. Private variables include an object's instance variables, and the local variables and parameters of a method or code fragment.

- *Shared variables* include global variables (e.g., class names) that are visible to all objects, and the class and pool variables accessible to instances of a class. Shared variable names must be capitalized.

- *Pseudo-variables* cannot be assigned a different value. They include the objects nil, true, and false, the identifiers self and super (which refer to the receiver of a method), and method parameters.

5.7.3 Message Expressions

Purpose and semantics

- A message send is the only kind of expression in Smalltalk, and all operations occur in response to sending a message to an object. In fact, arithmetic operations, control structures, object instantiations, and class and method definitions are all performed by sending messages.

- Smalltalk does not support subprograms that are not encapsulated within a class and are not invoked through a receiver.

Syntax

- A *message expression* consists of a *receiver*, a *selector* identifying the message, and possibly *arguments*. It represents a request that the receiver object perform a given operation, and the receiver responds by executing the method for its class. The receiver and arguments may be variables, literals, or nested expressions.
- A message send always returns a value, and is an expression, not a statement.
- A *unary message* has no arguments and consists of a receiver followed by a selector. A series of unary message sends is evaluated from left to right.
- In a *keyword message*, the receiver is followed by one or more selector–argument pairs, and each selector ends in a colon. Associativity is not defined for keyword messages since we cannot nest them without parenthesization.
- The selector for a *binary message* is one or two special characters, and indicates a message to the left operand with the right operand as the argument. Binary selectors provide the familiar infix expression syntax for arithmetic and logical operations and comparisons. Binary messages are left-associative, and there is no precedence ordering among binary messages.
- Unary messages have higher precedence than binary messages, which have higher precedence than keyword messages. We can use parentheses to indicate the order of evaluation in a nested expression.
- A *cascaded* message expression sends a sequence of messages to the same object, and consists of a receiver and a series of selectors with arguments, separated by semicolons.

Overloading and dynamic binding

- Many message selectors are defined in the protocols of several classes. Since an identifier can refer to an instance of any class, all message sends are dynamically bound in Smalltalk and the compiler cannot detect type errors (although they are caught eventually).

5.7.4 Identifier and Object Semantics

Implications of dynamic typing

- Because identifiers are not typed, a variable can refer to an instance of any class and can be any size, so the compiler cannot determine the amount of storage necessary for a variable. Storage for the local variables and parameters of a method cannot be allocated in its stack frame, nor can storage for an object's instance variables be allocated within the object.
- All objects are allocated dynamically, and are created by passing an instantiation message to a class object.
- Smalltalk employs automatic storage reclamation so the programmer does not need to keep track of when an object is no longer needed.

- Smalltalk variables have *reference semantics*: A variable behaves as a name that can refer to various objects, rather than as a container into which values can be copied.

- An object is accessed via a system-supplied *object identifier* returned by the instance creation message, which is an opaque reference, rather than an actual address.

- Although the compiler cannot do type checking, Smalltalk is strongly typed. If the receiver's class (or any ancestor) does not define a method for a message, the interpreter halts execution and displays an error dialog.

Object identity

- Smalltalk objects are generally treated as objects that have a unique identity, rather than as values or attributes. For example, several variables can refer to the same object, rather than each containing a copy.

- The *unique* objects—namely, instances of SmallInteger, Character, Symbol, UndefinedObject, and Boolean—are treated as attributes. Conceptually, there is one instance of each of these objects. In fact, these values are encoded directly in the object identifier that represents a variable.

- An assignment is indicated by :=, and causes a variable to refer to a different object, rather than modifying the object that the left-side variable refers to. This is true for assignments to instance variables and collection elements as well.

- Parameters and return values also have reference semantics. A method parameter refers to the argument object (not a copy), and the return value of a method is a reference to a new or existing object.

- The identity comparison messages == and ~~ test whether the receiver and argument are the same object, and are defined in the class Object for all objects.

- The equality test messages = and ~= determine whether the receiver and argument are equal objects, and are class-specific. Equality tests return the same value as identity tests for unique objects.

- Assignments and parameter passing do not copy objects, but a duplicate of an object can be created by sending it the message copy.

5.7.5 Flow of Control

Control flow as message passing

- The message expressions in a method or a code fragment are separated by periods, and are evaluated in the order given.

- Smalltalk does not include control structure statements. Instead, conditional evaluation is specified using messages to instances of the system classes Boolean or BlockClosure, with instances of BlockClosure as arguments. Collections also provide messages that iterate over their elements and take block arguments.

The class Boolean

- The class Boolean represents logical values and has two unique instances, true and false. Tests and comparisons return boolean objects.
- Boolean defines the logical messages & (and), | (or), not, eqv: (equivalence) and xor: (exclusive-or).

Blocks

- A *block* object is written as a series of message expressions separated by periods and enclosed in square brackets. The interpreter does not evaluate those expressions, but creates an instance of the class BlockClosure, which represents function objects.
- The programmer can create a block at any time, and can assign a block to a variable, pass a block to a method, or return a block from a method. Function objects are first-class in Smalltalk.
- Blocks can also define parameters, each preceded by a colon. The parameter list is followed by a vertical bar. A block can contain local variables enclosed in vertical bars.
- A block evaluates its expressions when it receives one of the messages value, value:, value:value:, etc. (up to four value:'s), depending on how many parameters it defines.
- A block defines a scope for its parameter and local variable names, which is nested within the scope of the method or block in which it appears.
- Because a block can be returned by a method or can be assigned to a variable that persists after the method in which it appears exits, a block must be represented by a closure that includes the code for the block's expressions and a reference to the enclosing method's activation record.

Conditional execution

- We code conditional selection of message expressions by passing a control flow message to a boolean object with block arguments. The boolean is the condition and the blocks are the code alternatives. The method for ifTrue:ifFalse: sends value to its first block argument if the receiver is true, or to the second if it is false. The messages ifTrue:, ifFalse:, and ifFalse:ifTrue: are also provided for convenience.
- The boolean messages and: and or: evaluate their block argument if necessary, like && and || in C.
- The compiler translates control messages using the branch instructions in the virtual machine language, rather than creating and destroying closures for each.

Conditional iteration

- The test condition of a conditional iteration might be evaluated repeatedly, so conditional iteration is a message to a block containing the test expression, rather than to a boolean, with the loop body as the argument block.

- The method for whileTrue: sends the receiver value, and if the result is true, sends value to the argument block and then sends the original whileTrue: message again. When the receiver evaluates to false, the method exits. The other conditional iteration messages are whileFalse:, whileTrue, and whileFalse. Smalltalk does not include a loop exit construct.

- Counter-controlled iteration is provided by the messages to:do: and to:by:do: in the class Number. The receiver is the initial value of the loop variable, the to: argument gives the limit, the by: argument gives the step size, and the do: argument is a one-parameter block that is evaluated for each value of the loop variable.

- The Smalltalk collection classes define several *enumerating* messages, such as do:, which evaluate the single-parameter block argument for each element of the collection. The message collect: returns a collection of the results of the successive evaluations, and select: returns the collection of elements for which the evaluation returned true.

Concurrency

- The Smalltalk virtual machine supports multiple processes, each scheduled on a single processor. The global variable Processor refers to an instance of ProcessorScheduler that controls use of the processor, keeps track of the processes in the system, and maintains the process priority levels.

- A process is an instance of the system class Process, representing an execution of a series of expressions that can be suspended and restarted.

- We create a new process by sending either fork (for a ready process) or newProcess (for an initially suspended process) to a block containing the process's message expressions.

- A process may be active (running), ready, suspended, or terminated. The Process message resume makes a suspended process ready, and the messages suspend or terminate suspend or terminate the receiver, respectively. The Processor selects a ready process to activate when the active process yields the processor, suspends itself, or terminates.

- Processes have priority levels that the Processor uses to choose the next active process. A process's priority level can be obtained or set with the messages priority and priority:, respectively. Process priority levels are obtained by passing a message to the Processor object.

- The class Semaphore provides synchronization of processes via the messages wait and signal. A process sends a semaphore object wait to wait for an occurrence of an event, and signal to indicate the occurrence of an event. When a semaphore receives a wait for which there has been no signal, it suspends that process until it receives a signal. Each semaphore maintains the number of signals it has received without corresponding waits and a queue of waiting processes.

- The class SharedQueue supports safe transfer of objects among asynchronous processes with the messages next and nextPut:.

Exception handling

- Smalltalk-80 did not support exception propagation and handling, but many current Smalltalk systems provide this feature.

- VisualWorks defines the class Signal, whose instances represent the various types of error conditions, and the class Exception that represents an occurrence of an exception and the object passed from the signaler to the handler of an exception.

- We raise an exception by sending the message raise to a signal, and handle an exception by sending a signal the message handle:do:. The first argument is a single-parameter block that gives the exception handler , and the second block argument is the application code. The exception object will be bound to the handle: block parameter when the exception occurs.

- A block can define a handler for a set of signals by defining a handler for their ancestor in the signal object hierarchy, or specify different handlers for different sets of signals with a HandlerCollection.

- The Exception class provides messages that a handler can use to exit the enclosing method, retry the handle:do: expression, raise the signal again so that it can be handled by another handler in the sequence of method activations, or continue after the signaling expression. If the handler does none of these, execution continues after the handle:do: expression.

5.7.6 The Programming Environment

Programming in Smalltalk

- The Smalltalk system presents a graphic user interface consisting of windows, menus, dialogs, and other interaction components that we manipulate with a pointing device, usually a three-button mouse.

- The left mouse button is used for selecting text or graphics, the middle button triggers a component-specific popup menu, and the right button triggers a popup menu containing window management commands.

- The *image* is a snapshot of the complete state of the system, and includes all classes and methods, the global and pool dictionaries, and executing applications and their states (i.e., their model objects and the states of their interfaces). An image can be saved to a file, and restored to reinstate that configuration of the system.

- We can *file out* class and method definitions to ASCII files, and then later *file them in.*

- The Smalltalk system contains an integrated suite of tools for application development, which access and manipulate the same set of class and method definitions. The programmer can instantiate several tools, each examining different code or application activations, and switch among them as desired. Methods are incrementally compiled and changes to methods take effect immediately, even for executing applications. The programmer can execute an application, trace its behavior, stop it and modify objects or methods, and then continue execution.

- In Smalltalk, all processing is encapsulated and an application is defined as a class, rather than as a main program. The code that creates and initializes the application's model and interface objects and responds to user input is written as an instantiation method for the application class. A user sends the corresponding class message to start an instance of the application.

- Defining applications as classes permits the programmer to use inheritance in application design (e.g., to derive an application from a generic application class that provides functionality needed by all applications) or to create several versions of an application.

Text windows

- A *workspace* is a window used to store and edit text and evaluate Smalltalk code. Its <Operate> menu provides editing and evaluation messages.

- The user can evaluate expressions in a workspace to start applications, print text, and manipulate files. The programmer can create objects and send them messages to examine and test classes and methods.

- The *transcript* is a text window that displays informational messages from the system. For example, it logs saving and loading images and filing code in and out. Programmers also often use it for debugging output.

Browsers

- The *system browser* is a programming tool used to view the classes and methods in the system, and supports coding, editing, and compiling class and method definitions. Classes are organized into categories according to hierarchy relationships, functionality, or application. The browser window contains four list views, two radio buttons, and a text view.

- The leftmost list view in the system browser presents a list of the class categories, and its <Operate> menu provides commands for manipulating class categories and finding a class.

- The second list view in the system browser displays the classes in the selected category. Its <Operate> menu includes options for filing out, printing, renaming, removing, and displaying various information about the selected class.

When a class name is selected, the text view displays the class definition message that gives the class's superclass, instance and class variables, and category.

- The third list view in the system browser contains the selected class's instance or class message categories, depending on whether the class or instance radio button is selected. Its <Operate> menu provides commands for working with message categories and finding a method.

- The rightmost list view in the system browser displays the messages in the selected message category. Its <Operate> menu presents commands for filing out, printing, and removing the selected method, and for browsing the senders and implementors of the selected message. When a message is selected, the text view displays the corresponding method.

- The text view in the system browser presents the selected class definition or method. The text view's <Operate> menu supports editing and compiling class and method definitions.

- A *hierarchy browser* is used to examine a class and its ancestors and descendants.

- A *method browser* displays a list of methods, for example, the senders or implementors of a message, or the methods that use an instance or class variable. Its interface consists of a list of method names and a text view that displays the selected method.

- A *file browser* is used to manipulate files and directories, and to view and edit text files. Its interface presents a text field containing a file system path, a list of the files which match that path, and a text view. If the entry selected in the list is a directory, its contents are displayed in the text view; if it is a text file, the text view displays the file or its attributes.

Debugging

- An *inspector* is used to examine and modify an object. We create an inspector by sending the message inspect to an object, or by selecting an expression in a text view and then selecting inspect from the <Operate> menu. Its interface includes a list of the receiver's instance variables and a text view displaying the referent of the selected variable. We can modify the referent or assign a new referent by accepting an expression in the text view.

- A *notifier* dialog is displayed when an error occurs. It lists the active message sends (i.e., a "stack trace"), and its <Operate> menu presents operations for proceeding, aborting, and opening a debugger. These operations are sometimes available as pushbuttons.

- A *debugger* is used to examine the state of an executing process. The programmer can examine and modify each message activation (including the method code and the receiver, arguments, and local variables), and updates to these methods or objects take effect immediately. The programmer can also continue incrementally from any point, tracing execution either one message send or one expression at a time.

- The debugger's interface consists of a list view giving a stack trace, a text view displaying the method executed for the selected message send, and inspectors for the method's receiver, arguments, and local variables. The list view <Operate> menu includes commands for proceeding, for restarting execution, for browsing the senders and implementors of a message, for browsing implementors of a message invoked in the selected method, and for incremental execution. The command **step** executes the selected method and then updates the debugger window, and **send** sends a single message and then updates the debugger window.

- When an object receives the message halt, the system displays a notifier, which allows the user to create a debugger. Programmers use this message to set breakpoints or to examine the behavior triggered by a message send.

5.8 EXERCISES

5.1 Describe the meaning of each of the following Smalltalk tokens:
  (a) 'hello'
  (b) "hello"
  (c) 13r3A5
  (d) $$
  (e) foo:
  (f) #sharp
  (g) ~~
  (h) Dictionary
  (i) Smalltalk

5.2 **(a)** What are private variables? What are the three kinds of private variables and how is each declared?
  (b) What are shared variables? What are the three kinds of shared variables and what objects can access each kind?
  (c) What are pseudo-variables? Which identifiers name pseudo-variables, and what does each refer to?

5.3 Name four operations typically specified by the definition of a language that are provided by message passing in Smalltalk. What objects are the receivers of these messages?

5.4 For each of the following message expressions, indicate whether there is a syntax error and what the error is. For the expressions that are not erroneous, fully parenthesize the expression to indicate which messages are sent to which receivers.
  (a) a b c: d e: f g
  (b) a b c d: e: f g
  (c) a b: c d e: f g
  (d) a b: * c + d e
  (e) a b * c + d e
  (f) a b: c = d e f: g

5.5 Why can't keyword messages be nested without the use of parentheses?

5.6 Translate the following C expressions into Smalltalk:
  (a) sqrt(x) + sqrt(y) != z
  (b) sqrt(x + y) < x * z

      (c) arr[i] = gcd(3, k)

      (d) k = arr[i] + abs(pt.x)

      (e) pt.x++

5.7 Which of the following expressions result in errors? Are they compile-time or execution-time errors? For those that are erroneous, correct them. Assume that aString is a string, anArray is an array of numbers, and aPoint is a point.

      (a) aString at: 3 asUppercase

      (b) 3 < anArray at: 3

      (c) (anArray at: 3) between: 0 and: anArray at: anArray size

      (d) x @ y ~= (4 @ 7)

      (e) aPoint x := 3

5.8 Why do instance variables and local variables in Smalltalk have reference semantics? Give an advantage and a disadvantage of this characteristic.

5.9 Why are all Smalltalk objects allocated dynamically?

5.10 **(a)** How is type checking performed in Smalltalk?

      (b) Suppose a method does not check the type of its parameter explicitly, and it is passed an argument of the wrong type. Explain why the error that is reported may not be clearly related to the actual cause. (Illustrate your discussion with an example.)

5.11 **(a)** Why do we say that instances of certain classes are treated as unique objects in Smalltalk?

      (b) How does this affect the semantics of comparisons and copying?

      (c) How are nil, booleans, characters, and small integers represented in storage?

5.12 How do reference semantics and automatic deallocation contribute to object identity in Smalltalk?

5.13 **(a)** How does the meaning of assignment differ in Smalltalk from that in C or Pascal?

      (b) How does the meaning of a return value differ in Smalltalk from that in C or Pascal?

5.14 Suppose that in defining a method for the binary message =, the class designer omits testing the class of the argument. What happens if the argument of an = message is not of the same class as the receiver? (For concreteness, suppose the method for = in class Point does not perform this test, and the argument is not a point.)

5.15 What is the result of evaluating the following series of message expressions?
```
| anArray1 anArray2 |
anArray1 := #('first' 'second' 'third').
anArray2 := anArray1 copy.
anArray1 at: 1 put: 'hello'.
(anArray1 at: 3) at: 3 put: $o.
anArray2 yourself
```

5.16 What is the result of evaluating the following series of message expressions? [Smi95]
```
| anArray aPoint |
aPoint := Point new.
anArray := Array new: 5.
1 to: anArray size do: [ :index | anArray at: index put: (aPoint x: index y: index)]
anArray at:1
```

5.17 **(a)** List and describe four semantic features of Smalltalk that it has in common with Lisp.

      (b) Which of the features in part (a) are supported by Pascal and C?

5.18 For each of the following messages, give the classes of the receiver and the arguments. For each, explain your answer and describe the action of the message.

      (a) xor:

      (b) value:

(c) ifTrue:ifFalse:

(d) and:

(e) whileTrue:

(f) to:do:

(g) select:

5.19 Why can we say that functions are first-class objects in Smalltalk? How are each of the necessary capabilities provided?

5.20 Translate the following Pascal code fragment into Smalltalk:
```
if (min <= num) and (num <= max) then
    if (num < 0) then
        num := -num
    else begin
        sqSum := sqSum + num * num;
        posCount := posCount + 1
        end
else
    badCount := badCount + 1;
```

5.21 Translate the following C code fragment into Smalltalk:
```
if ( overallAvg >= 90 || examAvg >= 90 )
    grade = 'A';
else if ( overallAvg >= 80 )
    grade = 'B';
else if ( overallAvg >= 70 )
    grade = 'C';
else if ( overallAvg >= 60 && examAvg >= 40 )
    grade = 'D';
else
    grade = 'E';
```

5.22 Translate the following C code fragment into Smalltalk. For prompting the user and obtaining his or her response, use the message Dialog request: '*promptString*'. It returns the user's response, which is a string that you can convert to a number with the message asNumber.
```
for ( posTotal = 0, posCount = 0; ; )
{
    printf("Enter a number:");
    scanf(&num);
    if ( num == 0 )
        break;
    if ( num > 0 )
    {
        posTotal += num;
        posCount++;
    }
}
```

5.23 Translate the following Pascal code fragment into Smalltalk:
```
for index := low to high do begin
    if index mod 2 = 0 then
        evenProduct := evenProduct * index;
    sum := sum + index;
    end
```

5.24 Translate the following C code fragment into Smalltalk:
```
for ( num = 2;  num <= limit;  num++ )
{
    isPrime = true;
```

```
    for ( divisor = 2;  isPrime && divisor * divisor < num;   divisor++ )
        if ( num % divisor == 0 )
            isPrime = false;
    if ( isPrime )
    printf("%d is prime.\n", &num);
}
```

5.25 Write a Smalltalk code fragment that sets index to the index of the num[th] occurrence of the character $= in the string aString.

5.26 Suppose windows is a set of rectangles. Write a code fragment that returns each of the following (use your browser or section 7.5.2 to find the necessary Rectangle messages):
  (a) the number of elements of windows that do not contain the point aPoint
  (b) the set of elements of windows that are completely within the x coordinate bounds lowX and highX
  (c) the set of rectangles whose elements are obtained by rotating each element of windows 180° about its origin (its upper left corner). If rotating an element of windows would result in a negative coordinate for the new rectangle's origin, then that result is not included in the set returned.

5.27 Write a Smalltalk expression that creates and schedules a new process, which prints 'hello' on the system transcript every 3 seconds for 30 seconds. Test the expression on your system.

5.28 **(a)** Write a Smalltalk code fragment that prints a table showing the number of processes at each priority level. (Browse the class ProcessorScheduler on your Smalltalk system to find the necessary messages.) Test the expression on your system.
  (b) Run several instances of the process you wrote for exercise 5.27 at different priority levels using forkAt:, and then execute the code fragment in part (a).

5.29 Describe the contents of a Smalltalk system image.

5.30 **(a)** A Smalltalk programmer can save an image or file out code to save his or her work. Describe the operation of each technique. For each, give an example situation in which you would prefer its use over the other.
  (b) Perform both operations on your Smalltalk system and compare the sizes of the files produced.

5.31 How does dynamic binding of every message send facilitate developing and debugging an application?

5.32 **(a)** How does the structure of a Smalltalk application differ from that of a Pascal or C application?
  (b) How are the objects and function calls in the main program of a Pascal or C program coded in Smalltalk?

5.33 Give the purpose of each of the following programming tools. For each, describe some of the commands on its <Operate> menus.
  (a) a workspace
  (b) a system browser
  (c) a hierarchy browser
  (d) a method browser
  (e) a file browser
  (f) an inspector
  (g) a debugger

5.34 For each of the following expressions, use the debugger on your Smalltalk system to trace the messages sent and the classes in which the methods are found. As you do, save a list of the messages and classes in a text window. Save each list to a file.

(a) 36 / 96

(b) 3 + 3.0

(c) (1 to: 50 by: 3) size

(d) 2 @ 3 extent: 4@7

6

Classes and Inheritance

In this chapter, we will discuss classes, inheritance, and metaclasses. This chapter covers the following topics:

- an overview of Smalltalk system classes, including foundation and collection classes, system classes, user interaction and application framework classes, and graphics classes (6.1.1)

- definition of classes and methods, and the pseudo-variable self (6.1.2)

- class objects, and how they support class variables and messages, instantiation, and execution-time access to type information (6.1.3)

- definition of subclasses (6.2.1)

- method refinement and the pseudo-variable super (6.2.2)

- two messages for expressing restriction and abstract messages, and some examples of abstract classes among the system classes (6.2.3)

- the metaclass, a special class of which a class object is an instance, and the relationships among class instances, class objects, and metaclasses (6.3).

6.1 CLASSES

6.1.1 The Smalltalk System Classes

Purpose

As we saw in sections 0.3.3 and 2.1, a type (or class) is an abstraction used to model a category of problem domain entities or system components. The Smalltalk system includes a comprehensive, well-developed class hierarchy that supplies a complete set of services for application development and interaction with the computer system. These system classes provide reusable, extendible components that facilitate higher-level domain-oriented design and programming. For example, no Smalltalk programmer ever needs to design and implement types for dates, dictionaries, or scrolled list interaction components, just as no C programmer ever needs to write a sqrt() function. The developer can concentrate on representing the problem domain and designing the application and its interface.

Most programming languages define a set of built-in types and operations, which are usually motivated by the types directly supported by the hardware, or by the kinds of basic data items in the intended problem domain. The type and operation names are reserved words, or the operations are indicated by special operator symbols that are part of the language syntax. Strictly speaking, the Smalltalk language does not include any built-in types. (Classes that have a literal format such as Float, String, and BlockClosure are part of the language syntax.) In a sense, the system classes are the built-in types of Smalltalk because every implementation provides them, but technically they are a standard library. However, the classes provided by the Smalltalk system have no special status. Everything that we can do with a system class or an instance of a system class we can do with our own classes or objects, and vice versa. In fact, we can add messages to system classes or redefine any system class or method.

All classes are defined ultimately in terms of the primitive methods that perform the operations implemented by the Smalltalk virtual machine. These operations are the only predefined, fixed components of a Smalltalk system.

Foundation and collection classes

The class Object is the root of the Smalltalk class hierarchy. It defines protocol available for all objects in the system, and default methods for many messages, which particular classes can override as necessary. Its instance protocol includes

- identity and equality comparisons, and tests such as isNil and isInteger
- copying messages
- class membership tests
- error handling messages
- printing and storing messages
- protocol for handling dependencies among objects.

Object's class protocol includes the basic instantiation messages new and readFrom:, and a number of messages for accessing information about the receiver class, such as its class hierarchy relationships and its variable and selector names.[1] This class information protocol is useful for understanding a class, for debugging, and for creating programming tools, but is generally not used in application code. Object is an abstract class that defines no instance variables. We will discuss the class Object in detail in section 7.1.

In section 5.5, we discussed the class Boolean that provides logical values and operations, and the class BlockClosure that represents function objects. As we saw, these classes also define messages that are used to specify control flow, and the protocol of BlockClosure supports concurrent processes and exception handling. We will discuss the class Boolean and the class UndefinedObject (the class of nil) further in section 7.2.

The Smalltalk system classes include a number of basic classes such as Character, Time, Date, and the abstract class Number and its subclasses SmallInteger, LargePositiveInteger, LargeNegativeInteger, Float, and Fraction. The protocols for these classes are quite extensive and include accessing, comparison, conversion, and arithmetic messages, as well as special messages that support implicit conversions among numeric objects in arithmetic and comparison expressions. All of these classes are descendants of the abstract class Magnitude, which defines ordering messages, and are discussed in sections 7.3 and 7.4.

The abstract class Collection is the root of the subhierarchy of collection classes. It defines protocol for accessing, adding, removing, and enumerating elements, and for testing, comparing, printing, storing, copying, and converting collection objects. Collection does not define a storage structure and some of its methods are deferred, but it defines many methods in terms of these abstract messages. Its concrete descendants represent collections with different characteristics, and each defines a storage structure, implements the deferred methods, and overrides some inherited methods for efficiency. The collection classes include sets, dictionaries, arrays, strings, and unsorted and sorted lists. They are discussed in Chapter 8. We will also discuss classes that allow a client to view a collection as a stream of objects in that chapter.

System classes

The Smalltalk class library also provides a uniform platform-independent interface to services that are traditionally supported by the operating system rather than the programming language. This includes both user-level commands and system calls for programming. In section 5.5.6, we discussed the classes Process and ProcessorScheduler, which provide concurrent processes and scheduling, and the classes Semaphore and SharedQueue, which implement interprocess synchronization and communication. Memory management is performed by an instance of the

---

[1] As we will see in sections 6.3.3 and 7.1.3, this behavior is actually supplied by the system classes Behavior, ClassDescription, and Class.

class MemoryPolicy, which manipulates an instance of ObjectMemory. A memory policy defines the actions to be taken in the idle state when no expressions are being evaluated or when the available memory space is low.[2]

The class Filename defines an extensive interface for working with files and directories. It provides the instantiation message named: whose argument is a string giving the name (or path) of the file or directory (recall the example in section 5.1.2). Its protocol includes messages to

- check for the existence of files and directories
- delete, rename, copy, and move files and directories
- access the components of the path to a file or directory (e.g., its directory or volume)
- obtain the contents of a file or directory
- obtain a file or directory's attributes such as its size, creation and modification dates, access permissions, whether it is writable, and whether it is a directory
- file in a text file so that its expressions are evaluated, or print a text file
- create a stream attached to the file, allowing the client to read objects from the file and write objects to the file using stream protocol.[3]

Filename also includes class variables that maintain the current directory, a list of volumes, the system line delimiter, the system path delimiter, and other global file system information, and provides class messages to access this information.

The system classes also define classes and messages that encapsulate the primitive methods supporting communication with hardware devices. For example, the virtual machine defines numerous primitive methods for bitmap graphics operations such as displaying images, lines, and arcs. These methods are invoked by methods in the class DisplayScreen in Smalltalk-80, GraphicsContext in VisualWorks, or Drawable in IBM Smalltalk (graphics support varies considerably among Smalltalk dialects). Input events from the keyboard and pointing device are represented by the class InputState, and are available from the instance of WindowSensor associated with a window. The window sensor also queues window resizing, exposing and closing events.

The user view of operating system services is also object-oriented. Recall our discussion in section 5.6 of the Smalltalk user interface and programming environment, in which we described using the classes TextCollectorView, Browser, MethodListBrowser, FileBrowser, Inspector, NotifierView, and Debugger. Both user facilities (like text editors and file system browsers) and programming tools (like debuggers)

---

[2] Memory management on most Smalltalk systems is quite cor..plex, and typically involves dividing object memory into several regions for "permanent" and new objects, and for different size objects. Each of these regions may have its own size and storage reclamation policy. The programmer can redefine these policies by modifying methods in the class MemoryPolicy, or by defining a subclass and installing an instance as the current memory policy.

[3] We saw an example of streaming over a file in section 5.1.2, and will discuss this further in section 8.6.5.

are classes written in Smalltalk. Because we can evaluate code in a text window, we can use the Smalltalk language as a command line interface to the system. We can run applications, perform file operations, set timers, store and evaluate scripts, or, in fact, send any message to any object. For example,

```
"using Smalltalk as a 'command line' to perform 'operating system' functionality"

"start an application (select 'do it' from the <Operate> menu)"
HierarchyBrowser newOnClass: 'Filename'

"can I write to this file? (select 'print it' from the <Operate> menu)"
(Filename named: '/etc/passwd') isWritable

"returns an array of strings giving the names of files in the receiver directory that
match the pattern '*.st' (select 'print it' from the <Operate> menu)"
(Filename named: '/home/caleb/Smalltalk') filesMatching: '*.st'

"create a new directory (select 'do it' from the <Operate> menu)"
(Filename named: '/home/caleb/Smalltalk/examples') makeDirectory

"move a file (select 'do it' from the <Operate> menu)"
| stDir |
stDir := '/home/caleb/Smalltalk/'.
"the , (comma) operator concatenates strings"
(Filename named: stDir , 'ClassInformation') moveTo: stDir , 'examples/ClassInformation'
```

We can write conditions and loops, and use all the facilities of the language in these scripts. Recall also that when we evaluate a code fragment with print it, the result appears selected in the text window (see Figure 5.2). We can then cut it and paste it in another text window to save it or use it in further commands. Alternatively, we could write code fragments, such as those above, that write the result to the transcript with show:. The system's browsers provide on-line help for the command language.

The implementation of the language is also defined using classes in Smalltalk. Instances of the class Scanner perform lexical analysis of source code. For example, this class includes instance messages to obtain the next token from a string, and to create an array of tokens from a string. The class Parser is a subclass of Scanner whose instances build a parse tree from a string (using classes such as ProgramNodeBuilder, StatementNode, and LiteralNode). The class Compiler includes messages for parsing code to a parse tree and generating the bytecodes,[4] and for compiling and then executing code. Accepting a method definition sends the former message, which adds the resulting instance of CompiledMethod to the class's instance of MethodDictionary with the message selector as its key. (When a code fragment is evaluated using do it, the bytecodes are discarded after execution.) The

---

[4] In practice, some implementations compile methods directly to the native machine code of the platform.

run-time environment is also implemented in Smalltalk. As illustrated in Figure 5.13, the classes BlockContext and MethodContext represent activation records of blocks and methods.

User interface and application framework classes

As we discussed in section 2.1.2, Smalltalk applications are organized according to the Model-View-Controller paradigm in which an application is divided into two parts, the model and the user interface. A number of classes and messages in the system class hierarchy support this design strategy. Unfortunately, the names and organization of these classes vary considerably among Smalltalk dialects. In this section, we will give an overview of the application framework classes in Visualworks, which are an elaboration of the original Smalltalk-80 view and controller classes. A complete discussion of this framework is beyond the scope of this text, and you should refer to the documentation for your Smalltalk system for the details of using it in developing applications.

The class Window and its subclass ScheduledWindow represent windows on the display. Applications typically use scheduled windows because they include instance variables that maintain a model, a controller, and a "visual component" displayed whenever the window is made visible. The abstract class VisualComponent has concrete subclasses for

- passive components such as labels and images
- active "views" that respond to user interaction or changes in the model
- "composite parts" that present a group of visual components.[5]

A composite part can contain other composite parts that contain components and so on, and the structure of a window is a hierarchical composition of visual component objects.

A *view* is a rectangular portion of a window, displaying a visual representation of an object. It allows the user to interact with it via a controller. The view presented can change to reflect changes to its model. The abstract class View is the root of a subhierarchy that provides many different kinds of views.[6] Its concrete descendants include the familiar interaction components such as

- ActionButton for pushbuttons that can be labeled with either a string or an image
- LabeledBooleanView for check boxes and radio buttons
- ScrollBar for scrollbars
- MenuView and MenuItemView for menus and menu items
- SelectionInListView for scrollable lists in which the user can select an item

---

[5] For readers who are familiar with the Xt or OSF/Motif widget sets, composite parts correspond to composite or manager widgets, which contain a number of widgets and control their layout.

[6] In IBM Smalltalk, the view classes are patterned after the OSF/Motif widget classes [You94].

- TextCollectorView for scrollable text editing views
- TableView for scrollable two-dimensional tables of cells in which the user can select a cell, a row, or a column
- Dialog for popup dialogs.

There are also view classes that are used in particular programming tools such as NotifierView, HierarchicalClassListView, and BitView (a bitmap editor). We instantiate the view classes and combine those objects as components of composite parts to create the interface for an application. The view classes encapsulate displaying the component, interacting with the user, and redisplaying the component when its window is resized or hidden and then exposed, so programmers do not have to deal with these issues. We can also create specialized views for a particular object or application by subclassing from the abstract class View or from one of its concrete subclasses.

The class Dialog illustrates the convenience provided by standard view classes. It defines a number of class messages that create commonly needed dialogs and return the choice made by the user. We use these in interactive graphic applications in the same manner as printing a prompt and reading the response in a command line application. For example,

"class messages in the class Dialog for querying the user"

"presents a dialog containing the argument string and pushbuttons labeled 'Yes' and 'No', and returns true or false, depending on the user's selection"
exitTest := Dialog confirm: 'Are you sure want to quit?'

"presents a dialog containing the request: argument string, a text entry field initialized with the initialAnswer: argument string, and push buttons labeled 'OK' and 'Cancel', and returns the text typed by the user, or an empty string if the user selects cancel"
name := Dialog request: 'What is your name?' initialAnswer: userName

Recall also the example in section 5.1.2 that used the Dialog class message requestFileName: (see Figure 5.5). The programmer does not need to be concerned with the details of creating the view containing the string and push buttons, displaying it, reading the key presses or the mouse click location, highlighting the selected button, and so on.

A *controller* object is associated with each window and view object that handles user input via the mouse and keyboard. A controller maintains references to its view and model in instance variables. The window controller provides the <Window> popup menu. A view controller is responsible for providing an <Operate> menu, notifying the model of user selections and key strokes, and displaying a cursor. Each view class has a default controller, which the view class instantiates when it creates an instance. For example, the default controller for TextCollectorView is ParagraphEditor. This controller permits the user to insert text at the insertion point via the keyboard, position the insertion point with the <Select> button, and select text by dragging across it while pressing the <Select> button. It also provides the <Operate> menu described in sections 5.1.1 and 5.6.2 for text editing and code evaluation. The programmer can also provide a different controller than the default for a view object with the message controller:.

As with views, the system classes include an abstract class Controller (which is the root of a subhierarchy of controller classes), and its subclass ControllerWithMenu (which is the superclass for controllers that provide a popup menu).[7] Example concrete descendants of Controller include

- StandardSystemController, which supplies the standard <Window> menu
- DialogController, which retains control until the user responds to the dialog (and does not provide a <Window> menu)
- MenuController, which receives input for a menu view (e.g., it highlights items as the user drags, and selects an item and/or removes the menu when the mouse button is released)
- ScrollbarController, which handles input to a scrollbar (e.g., clicking on the arrow buttons and dragging the slider)
- ParagraphEditor, which provides text selecting and the text editing <Operate> menu
- SelectionInListController for use with a SelectionInListView (e.g., allowing the user to select and deselect list items).

We can extend a controller—for example, to provide keyboard shortcuts for ParagraphEditor—by modifying the controller class's event handling method. We can also create a specialized controller by defining a subclass of a system controller class whose methods use the protocol of WindowSensor to obtain input events, and can create an instance of PopupMenu to associate with the controller.

The global variable ScheduledControllers is an instance of the class ControlManager that maintains the collection of active window controllers, and routes control to a particular window controller, depending on the cursor's location when the input event occurs. The window controller may then propagate that event to the controller for a particular view (e.g., if the user presses a key or the <Select> or <Operate> mouse button while the cursor is within that view).

View and controller objects contain references to each other and to their model object in instance variables. A model object must also maintain references to any views that depend on it so that it can inform those view objects when its state changes. As any object can be a model, this behavior is implemented in the class Object. An object (usually a view) can be registered as a *dependent* of another object. When that object changes state, it sends itself the message changed, and that method notifies its dependents via the message update:. (The dependent must

---

[7] In IBM Smalltalk, event handling is patterned after event handling in the Xt widget classes [You94].

implement update:.) The view message model: assigns the argument to the view's model instance variable, and also registers the view as a dependent of the argument. We will discuss this protocol further in section 7.1.2.

In section 5.6.1, we saw that Smalltalk applications are defined as classes that the user instantiates to perform some activity. Many Smalltalk systems supply an abstract class that implements much of the basic behavior necessary for all applications (such as registering its controllers with the control manager), from which we derive application classes. For example, VisualWorks includes the class ApplicationModel for this purpose. We define each application class as a subclass that maintains the application's model and view objects, as well as any state information having to do with the use of the application, such as whether the user has modified the model but not saved it.

The VisualWorks system also contains a user interface builder that the programmer can use to design an application's interface by placing and sizing interaction components, as in a drawing program. The interface builder presents dialogs that allow the programmer to specify the message sent when the user selects a pushbutton, or the model object associated with a list view, text view, or slider. It also includes a command that automatically defines a subclass of ApplicationModel containing the information specified with the interface builder. It creates a class with the name given by the programmer, the models as instance variables (and their views as dependents), message stubs for pushbutton and menu messages, and a class method windowSpec that creates the views and their layout. The programmer only needs to code the model logic of the application.

Graphics classes

In addition to supporting user interaction, the system class library provides classes and messages for two-dimensional raster graphics. A complete discussion of concepts, structures, and algorithms for graphics programming is beyond the scope of this book (for example, see [Fol94]). In this section, I will give a brief overview of the Smalltalk graphics classes, and will introduce graphics terminology as needed.

An object on which drawing operations take place is referred to as a *canvas*, and a canvas can be either a window on the screen or an object in memory that stores an image constructed using graphic operations. A canvas is treated as a rectangular two-dimensional array of picture elements or *pixels*, each of which has a color. We refer to the storage representation of an image as a *pixmap* (or a *bitmap* if there are only two color values). In Smalltalk, the origin of a canvas is at the upper left corner, with x coordinate values increasing to the right and y coordinate values increasing downward (i.e., the coordinate values are always non-negative integers).

The basic classes for positional values in the Smalltalk graphics system are Point and Rectangle, which represent locations and areas, respectively. The class Point represents a position, for example, a pixel in a window or pixmap. It defines two instance variables x and y for the point's coordinates, which are either small integers or floats. Point objects also are used to encapsulate the x and y values for a translation factor or a scale factor or the width and height of a rectangular extent.

The class Point defines extensive initialization, accessing, comparing, and geometric protocol, and includes arithmetic messages to facilitate coding graphic methods. For example, the selectors + and - perform translation, the selectors * and / perform scaling, and the selector @ provides a literal notation for creating points. We will cover the class Point in detail in section 7.5.1.

The class Rectangle represents a particular rectangle at a given offset from the origin of the canvas or view. Instances are used to specify the location and size of a window or view, the bounding box of an ellipse, and the clipping rectangle for a graphic operation. Rectangle defines two instance variables origin and extent, which are points that give the instance's upper left and lower right corners. The class provides a number of instance creation messages, and extensive instance protocol for accessing, testing, comparing, translating, scaling, intersecting, merging, aligning, copying, printing, converting, and displaying rectangles. We will discuss the class Rectangle in more detail in section 7.5.2.

The original Smalltalk-80 system only supported monochrome graphics, in which each pixel in a canvas is represented by a bit. Current systems support color, and each pixel is represented by n bits, so a total of 2^n colors can be represented. n is often called the *depth* of the canvas, and is usually a multiple of 8 for efficiency. In most color display systems, the pixmap itself does not specify the actual colors of its elements. Instead, a pixmap is a two-dimensional array of integers that are indices into a *palette*, an array of color values representing actual colors. A particular color is represented by values for its red, green, and blue components. The number of bits, and therefore the granularity, of the red, green, and blue components of a color value is usually fixed by the hardware.

As with views, the details of the graphics classes vary among Smalltalk implementations. In this section, we will briefly describe the classes in the original Smalltalk-80 system, and in VisualWorks, which supports color. Figure 6.1 illustrates the graphics classes in the Smalltalk-80 system class hierarchy that we will discuss. The abstract class DisplayObject represents displayable objects, and has three subclasses, DisplayMedium, DisplayText, and Path. The class DisplayMedium is an

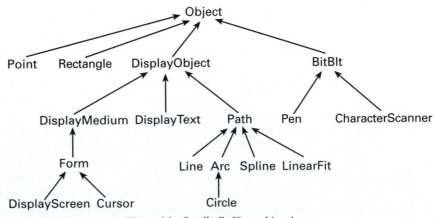

Figure 6.1 Smalltalk-80 graphics classes.

abstract class that represents canvases.   Form is a concrete subclass of DisplayMedium, which defines instance variables for a bitmap (an instance of ByteArray), and a height and a width.   Forms are used extensively both to store and construct images, and as "brushes" used to paint on display mediums.   The class DisplayScreen is a subclass of Form, which represents the display screen, an instance of which is the referent of the global variable Display.   An instance of Cursor is a form used as the visual representation of the pointing device, which tracks its movements. The class adds an instance variable for the "hot spot" in the form that specifies the point at which a click occurs.   Cursor also defines class messages that return a number of standard system cursors, which it stores in class variables.

An instance of DisplayText contains a Text object and a TextStyle that maps the text's emphasis codes (italic, etc.) onto fonts.   The abstract class Path represents graphic objects that are represented mathematically, rather than as pixmaps. It defines instance variables for a list of points and a form used as the brush to paint the path.   It provides protocol for displaying the path on a display medium, and for adding, removing, and enumerating its points.   Path has the concrete subclasses Line, Arc, Circle, LinearFit (for a polyline), and Spline, each of which defines a different way of drawing the path represented by the object's list of points.

For flexibility, the process of copying a form onto a medium uses numerous parameters.   Smalltalk-80 defines the form copying operation as a separate class, rather than as a DisplayMedium or Form message, to encapsulate the attributes for a drawing operation or a series of similar drawing operations.   This class is named BitBlt after the "bit block transfer" instruction available on most processors, which copies an array of bytes in memory.   The parameters of a "bit-blit" operation are maintained as the object's instance variables, and consist of

- the height and width of the area transferred
- the source and destination forms
- the origins in the source and destination forms for the operation
- the clipping rectangle
- a "halftone mask" used as a stencil in the operation
- a logical "combination rule" that determines how to combine source and destination pixel values (e.g., the exclusive-or of the source and destination bits).

BitBlt provides protocol for accessing and setting the various drawing parameters, the message copyBits (which performs the copy operation by calling a primitive method), and the message drawFrom:to: (which uses the source form to paint a line between the argument points on the destination form).

BitBlt has two system subclasses, Pen and CharacterScanner.   The class Pen defines protocol for using the source form as a brush to paint on the destination form, which is usually a window.   It adds instance variables for a location (a point) and a direction (an integer giving the number of degrees) to those it inherits from BitBlt.   The class provides accessing messages and drawing messages based on Logo "turtle graphics" [Pap80], such as

- up and down, which determine whether the pen draws as it moves
- go: a distance in the current direction, goto: a point, and home, which places the pen in the center of the destination form
- turn: to a new direction, the accessors direction and direction:, and north, which points the pen toward the top of the screen
- changeNib:, black, darkGray, gray, lightGray and white, which change the source form.

In the class CharacterScanner, the source form contains a font as an array of bitmaps for each character, and the class defines an additional instance variable containing a text object that it can display using that font.

Figure 6.2 illustrates what we will discuss regarding the graphics classes in the VisualWorks system class hierarchy. The abstract class DisplaySurface represents canvases, and has two subclasses Window and UnmappableSurface. If an application draws on a window, the result is visible on the screen if the window is visible. However, a window does not maintain a representation of its visual contents, so they are lost if the window is resized or covered and then exposed. UnmappableSurface is an abstract class for display surfaces that are stored in memory, not displayed directly by the host system window manager. It has two subclasses, Pixmap and Mask. Instances of Pixmap are used to assemble and store images that will be copied to a window to be displayed. A pixmap is an array of indices into an instance of Palette, a collection of ColorValue objects. The class ColorValue maintains three small integer instance variables for the red, green, and blue components of a color object. It defines class messages to create color values that correspond to three different ways of specifying a color, namely red:green:blue:, cyan:magenta:yellow:, and hue:saturation:brightness:. ColorValue also defines numerous class messages for accessing specific color values such as orange, brown, etc. An instance of Mask is a bitmap used as a stencil in a drawing operation. The model for drawing in VisualWorks mirrors the design of graphic operations in the X Window System [Sch92]. To reduce the complexity of drawing messages, a *graphics context* maintains a number of parameters that control the details of a drawing operation (i.e., it serves the

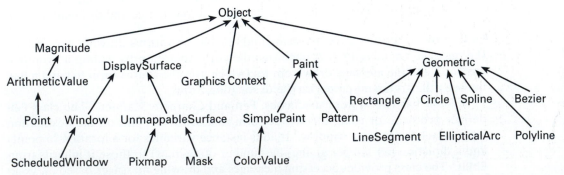

Figure 6.2 VisualWorks graphics classes.

same function that BitBlt serves for Smalltalk-80.) The class GraphicsContext maintains parameters for

- the display surface
- the clipping rectangle
- the default paint, which may be an instance of ColorValue or Pattern
- the line width
- the line cap style (for the ends of wide lines) and the line join style (e.g., with rounded or pointed outer corners)
- the translation point (offset)
- the default font for text.

The class GraphicsContext defines instance variables and protocol for accessing and
setting this information, and for performing drawing operations on the associated
display surface. These include messages for copying images, and for displaying lines,
polylines, polygons, rectangles, arcs, wedges, ellipses, circles, and strings. The methods for drawing messages invoke primitive methods because many current machines
implement these operations in hardware. To draw on a window or pixmap, we
obtain a graphics context from that object and send it the drawing message, as follows:

```
"drawing a triangle with 3-pixel-wide blue lines and rounded corners on aPixmap"
"Each time we send 'graphicsContext', the canvas creates a new graphics context object
for drawing parameters, so we must send all the messages to the same object."
aPixmap graphicsContext
    lineWidth: 3;
    paint: ColorValue blue;
    joinStyle: GraphicsContext joinRound;
    displayPolyLine: (Array with: 5@5 with: 105@5 with: 55@55 with: 5@5)
```

The abstract class Geometric represents geometric objects that are
described mathematically, rather than as images. Its protocol includes four
abstract messages that a concrete subclass must define. The messages display-
FilledOn: and displayStrokedOn: take a graphics context argument whose medium
and drawing parameters are used. The first draws a filled shape, and the second
draws the shape's outline. The messages scaledBy: and translatedBy: take a point
argument. The system subclasses of Geometric include LineSegment, Polyline,
Rectangle, Circle, EllipticalArc, Bezier, and Spline. Pixmaps, masks, strings, and
text objects (that include font and emphasis information) also implement the
message displayOn:.

6.1.2 Class and Method Definition

Programmer-defined classes

Modern programming languages provide type constructors, but there are usually capabilities for built-in types that are not available for programmer-defined types, and programmer-defined types are not first-class. For example, in most languages, input and output operations cannot be extended to programmer-defined types, and there is no literal notation for programmer-defined types. In Smalltalk, all operations are message sends, so we can always define a complete set of operations for a new class, including instantiation, copying, equality test, and data transfer operations. As stated in the previous section, Smalltalk makes no distinction between system classes and programmer-defined classes.

When a new class is defined, its name becomes a globally shared variable whose referent is the object representing that class. The method for the class creation message described in this section creates the class object, and adds the key–value pair consisting of the class name and the class object to the global dictionary Smalltalk. (We will discuss class objects in section 6.1.3.) All class names are visible at global scope and the language does not support nesting of class definitions (as does C++). Like all shared variables, a class name must begin with an uppercase character.

Defining classes and methods with the browser

A class is defined by specifying both its operations and the structure of its instances. We normally add new classes to the system image by using the facilities of the system browser. After selecting or creating a category for the new class, you type and accept the definition of the class in the browser text view. Next, you create class and instance message categories for the class in the message category list. Finally, you code the individual methods in the text view and accept them.

As we saw in section 5.6.3, the contents of the system browser text view depend on the selections made in the list views. When a class name is selected in the class list view, the text view displays the class's superclass name, and selectors identifying the subclass: (the class name), classVariableNames:, instanceVariable-Names:, poolDictionaries:,[8] and the class category:. For example, when we select Magnitude-General in the class category list view, and then Date in the class list view, the text view displays the following text:

```
"contents of the browser text view when Date is selected in the class list view"

Magnitude subclass: #Date
    instanceVariableNames: 'day year'
    classVariableNames:
        'DaysInMonth FirstDayOfMonth MonthNames SecondsInDay WeekDayNames'
    poolDictionaries: ''
    category: 'Magnitude-General'
```

---

[8] Pool dictionaries are rarely used, and were described briefly in section 5.2.3.

This expression indicates that the class Date is a subclass of Magnitude with the instance variables day and year and the five class variables listed. From the format of this expression, we can see that a class definition consists of a message to the superclass object asking it to create a subclass with the information given as arguments. We define a class with a message send, so the language does not need a special type constructor construct. As we have seen several times, message passing is used for all operations, which contributes to the uniformity of the language. In fact, an executing application can create new classes by sending this message.

When a class category is selected but no class is selected in the class list view, the text view displays the following template:

```
"template in the browser text view for defining a new class"

NameOfSuperclass subclass: #NameOfClass
    instanceVariableNames: 'instVarName1 instVarName2'
    classVariableNames: 'ClassVarName1 ClassVarName2'
    poolDictionaries: ''
    category: 'the selected class category'
```

We then edit this template to create the definition of a new class. We replace the placeholders in the template (e.g., NameOfClass) with the superclass name, the class name, the instance variable names, and so on. When editing is complete, we add the new class to the system by selecting accept in the text view's <Operate> menu. Existing class definitions can be modified at any time by the same process. The browser maintains documentation about each class, so we should also give a comment describing the purpose and use of the new class. To do so, we select comment in the class list <Operate> menu, type the comment text in the text view, and accept it.

When a message name is selected in the message list view, the browser text view displays the code for the corresponding method. A method consists of a "message pattern" giving the selector and parameter names, a comment, local variable declarations, and a series of expressions. (We will examine several examples later in this section.) When a message category is selected but no message selector is selected in the message list view, the text view displays the following template:

```
"template in the browser text view for defining a new method"

message selector and argument names
    "comment stating purpose of the message"

    | temporary variable names |
    statements
```

As with classes, when we finish coding the new method, we select accept to add it to the class's method dictionary (and add the message to the selected message category). We also use the browser text view to modify and accept existing methods as we develop classes and applications.

Because methods are displayed in a text view, Smalltalk class designers often include sample message expressions that you can evaluate in the comments for a method to illustrate the behavior of a class. For example, the method for the Dialog class message confirm: appears as follows:

```
"the Dialog class message confirm: includes a sample expression to evaluate"
confirm: messageString
    "Ask the user a question with a true/false answer. Return the response."

    "Dialog confirm: 'Delete all horrible memories?' "

    ^self confirm: messageString for: nil
```

Many system classes also define a class messages category examples that includes example messages.

Protocol description

The client view of a message is described by a *message pattern*, which corresponds to a function declaration in Pascal or C, and a comment.[9] The comment describes the action of the method and the object it returns, using the parameter names in the message pattern. For example,

```
"an example message pattern and comment"
between: min and: max
    "Answer whether the receiver is between min and max inclusive."
```

Smalltalk does not include a construct that gives a separate description of the interface of a class (i.e., a list of message patterns and associated comments), like the interface of a module. However, we can define a programming tool that obtains this information from the class object and displays it.[10] A protocol listing would be organized according to browser message categories, but the categories have no significance in the language itself.

---

[9] It is the convention in Smalltalk to place the comment after the message pattern in a method, unlike Pascal and C, in which the comment typically precedes the entire subprogram.

[10] Like the system browser, this tool would use the protocol described in sections 6.1.3 and 7.1.3 to obtain the class's messages and methods.

Instance variables

The instance variables of a class represent the state of an instance of the class, and correspond to the fields in a record in a traditional language. Each instance of the class has its own set of referents for those variables. There are two kinds of instance variables in Smalltalk: named and indexed.

A class's *named instance variables* are listed in its class definition message as the string argument corresponding to the selector instanceVariableNames:. Each must begin with a lowercase letter. As discussed in section 5.2.2, the use of mnemonic names is essential because types are not associated with identifiers.

Instance variable names are local to the scope of the class, and can be used in other classes or methods without conflicting. They are visible only in the methods of the class and its subclasses, and the name always refers to that variable in the receiver of the method. Smalltalk does not provide a component selection construct for accessing the referents of an object's named instance variables (like . in Pascal or C), even those of an instance of the same class. The referents of an object's instance variables are only accessible to clients if the class's protocol includes accessing messages. That is, the unit of information hiding in Smalltalk is the individual object, not the class. [11]

When an instance variable name occurs in a method, it denotes the referent of that variable in the receiver of the message. If an expression uses the name as a receiver or argument, that object is the receiver or argument. If an instance variable name appears on the left side of an assignment, that variable in the receiver is bound to the object resulting from evaluation of the right side of the assignment. Like all variables, an object's instance variables are set to nil when the object is created. In the next section, we will describe how to define a class's instance creation method such that it triggers initialization of the new object.

For some classes, it is necessary to allow instances with different sizes. Examples include LargePositiveInteger (which can be an arbitrary size), and collection classes such as String and Array (which can contain an arbitrary number of element references). This capability is supported by *indexed instance variables*, which are essentially an array of instance variables embedded within the object. Each variable is referred to by an integer index rather than by a name. (Recall Figures 5.10 and 5.11, which number the indexed instance variables in the array objects.) We use the following class message to define a class whose instances contain indexed instance variables (note the first keyword): [12]

```
"class definition message for a class with indexed instance variables"
NameOfSuperclass variableSubclass: #NameOfClass
    instanceVariableNames: 'instVarName1 instVarName2'
```

---

[11] We will see in section 10.1.3 that C++ allows instances of a class to access each other's instance variables.

[12] The message variableByteSubclass:... is used to define a class whose instances contain an embedded byte array. Some systems also provide variableWordSubclass:... and variableLongSubclass:....

```
classVariableNames: 'ClassVarName1 ClassVarName2'
poolDictionaries: ''
category: 'class category'
```

The class message new: creates an instance of a class with indexed instance variables, and its argument gives the number of indexed variables. Each instance of the class may have a different number of indexed instance variables (and, therefore, a different size), but that number is fixed for each object at its creation. For example, the expression anArray := Array new: 4 creates an array object with 4 indexed instance variables, and then the message anArray size returns 4. If a class defines both named and indexed instance variables, each instance has the same set of named instance variables, and may have a different number of indexed instance variables.

We saw in section 5.3.2 that we access and modify indexed instance variables with the selectors at: and at:put:, respectively. Index values begin with 1 and continue to the size of the receiver. If an invalid index argument is used in an at: or at:put: message, execution of the process stops and a notifier is displayed with the title Subscript out of bounds. The following examples illustrate these messages:

```
"accessing indexed instance variables"
| anArray squareRoot |
anArray := Array new: 4.
anArray at: 3 put: 5.              "anArray[2] = 5; in C"
squareRoot := (anArray at: 3) sqrt.   "squareRoot = sqrt(anArray[2]); in C"
anArray at: 5 put: 3               "error, notifier displayed"
```

Because these same selectors are used both by clients of the class and within the class's methods, indexed variables cannot be hidden (unless the class overrides these selectors).

Instance methods

A method definition consists of

- a message pattern that gives the selector names and descriptive parameter names
- a comment that describes the purpose, operation, and return value of the message
- a list of local variables enclosed in vertical bars
- a series of message expressions separated by periods, that are sent when the method is invoked.

By convention, the method comment follows the message pattern, but precedes the local variable declarations and message expressions. Parameters are not typed, so overloading selectors within a class is not meaningful.[13] However, a message may have the same name as an instance variable of the class, and this is common practice for accessor methods (e.g., x in class Point and numerator in class Fraction).

---

[13] Recall that the selectors center and center: are regarded as two different message names.

A *return expression* begins with an up arrow ↑, or ^ on most keyboards, and gives an expression that returns the object the method returns. If a method does not contain a return expression, it returns the receiver itself after its last expression is evaluated. Evaluation of a return expression terminates execution of the method, like the return statement in C, Modula-2, and Ada. For example, the following method for the class Fraction returns the reciprocal of the receiver:

```
"instance method for class Fraction"
reciprocal
    "Answer 1 divided by the receiver.  The result is a new Fraction or Integer."

    numerator = 1 ifTrue: [^denominator].
    numerator = -1 ifTrue: [^denominator negated].
    ^Fraction numerator: denominator denominator: numerator
```

The parameter names in the message pattern are pseudo-variables, and are initialized to refer to the argument objects given in the message invocation. Like all pseudo-variables, parameter names cannot appear on the left side of an assignment within the method. As discussed in section 5.2.2, we declare local variables by enclosing their names in vertical bars at the beginning of the method. (We cannot define indexed local variables, but we can define a local variable that is an instance of Array.) Local variables are initialized to nil when the method is invoked. The object identifiers that maintain a method's parameter and local variable referents exist for the duration of a method invocation (and longer if a block that refers to them is passed out of the method, as discussed in section 5.5.2). For example, we could define the following method for the class Point, which returns the distance between the receiver and the argument point:[14]

```
"a possible instance method for class Point"
distanceFrom: aPoint
    "Answer the distance between aPoint and the receiver."

    | dx dy |
    dx := x - aPoint x.
    dy := y - aPoint y.
    ^(dy * dy + (dx * dx)) sqrt
```

Because a method may define parameters and local variables, it specifies a scope. The names of a method's parameters and local variables are visible only within the method, and do not conflict with other uses of those names elsewhere. Those names must be unique within a method. Because a class's instance variable names are visible in its methods, the method scope is nested within the scope of its class. If a parameter or local variable name is the same as the name of an instance variable defined by the class, that variable is hidden and cannot be accessed in the

---

[14] In most dialects, this message has the selector dist:, and its method is coded using Point messages.

method. (Clearly, this is poor coding practice.) An identifier in a method is either a parameter, a local variable, an instance variable of the class or one of its ancestors, or a class, global, or pool variable. The compiler can always determine the corresponding declaration statically.

Smalltalk class designers place messages in the message category private to indicate that they are intended for use only within the methods of their class. However, this convention is not enforced by the language, and clients can access any method in a class's protocol. This has the unfortunate consequence that it is not possible to prevent a client from re-initializing an object, as the class needs some method that initializes an instance's state. In addition, private methods often access an instance's representation in ways that violate information hiding, and may not leave the receiver in a consistent state since they are intended to be used within the class's methods.

Because all activity is message passing and messages are defined by methods that merely send more messages, there must be some built-in *primitive methods* that invoke machine operations. The Smalltalk virtual machine specifies several hundred primitive methods that an implementation must provide, and all methods are ultimately defined in terms of these operations.[15] Primitive methods include both operations usually performed by the hardware and "operating system" services. Some examples are

- arithmetic operations on small integers and floats
- conversions between small integers and floats
- the identity test
- allocation and access of objects, and accessing an object's class
- procurement of the current time and date
- process scheduling and semaphore operations
- file operations, for example, creation and deletion of files, data transfer, and file locking
- allocation of system resources, such as windows, fonts, and colormaps
- bit-mapped display operations (e.g., bit block transfer; drawing lines, arcs and text; and accessing the dimensions and depth of the screen).

All other methods are written in Smalltalk in terms of existing methods, and the programmer can modify them if necessary.

A method invokes a primitive method with the expression <primitive: *num*>, where *num* is the primitive method's number. Invocation of a primitive method terminates execution of the method unless the primitive fails, in which case control continues after that expression. For example, the method for + in class SmallInteger is coded as follows (the message sumFromInteger: supports mixed-class arithmetic and is discussed in section 7.4.6):

---

[15] Many Smalltalk systems also provide the capability of writing and registering additional primitive methods, for example, in C.

```
"instance method in class SmallInteger that invokes a primitive method"
+ aNumber
    "Answer the result of adding the receiver to the argument.
    The primitive method fails if the argument or the result is not a SmallInteger."

    <primitive: 1>
    ^aNumber sumFromInteger: self
```

Application programmers should not call primitive methods directly. Instead, they should use the Smalltalk message that triggers that operation.

The pseudo-variable self

As we discussed in section 2.2.5, we use the pseudo-variable self within a method to refer to the receiver of the corresponding message. Instance variable names in the method refer to those variables in the object to which self refers. The pseudo-variable self may be used as the receiver or an argument in an expression, or as the method's return value, but it cannot appear on the left side of an assignment. Using self as the receiver is necessary when implementing a message involves the result of another message in the receiver's protocol. In addition, if the receiver has indexed instance variables, its method must send the messages size, at: and at:put: to self to access the receiver's size and indexed instance variables. For example, in some Smalltalk systems, the class String (which keeps its characters in indexed instance variables) defines the following method that converts the receiver to an integer:[16]

```
"instance method for class String"
asInteger
    "Answer the integer conversion of the receiver. The receiver is expected to be
    a sequence of digits with an optional leading minus sign."

    | answer char |
    answer := 0.
    self size = 0 ifTrue: [^answer].
    (self at: 1) = $-
        ifTrue: [^(self copyFrom: 2 to: self size) asInteger negated].
    1 to: self size do: [:index |
        char := self at: index.
        char isDigit ifFalse: [^answer].
        answer := answer * 10 + char digitValue].
    ^answer
```

This method also sends the message copyFrom:to: to its receiver to make a copy of part of the receiver. We also use the pseudo-variable self to code recursive meth-

---

[16] The message copyFrom:to: creates an instance of the receiver's class by copying the indicated range of indexed instance variables. The meaning of the other messages in this method should be clear.

ods. For example, the method factorial for the class Integer could be coded as follows (of course, an iterative method would be more efficient):

```
"recursive coding of an instance method for class Integer"
factorial
    "Answer the factorial of the receiver."

  self = 1
     ifTrue: [^1]
     ifFalse: [^self * (self - 1) factorial]
```

The classes Queue and Node

Let us define a class for first-in first-out queues of elements. The protocol of this class consists of insertion of an element (at the rear of the queue only), deletion of an element (the front element only), and a test of whether the queue is empty. In a dynamically typed language like Smalltalk, any type of object can be added to any queue. We only need to define one Queue class, rather than having a class for queues of integers, another class for queues of strings, and so on. However, if a particular queue should only contain a certain class of object, it is the client's responsibility to ensure this. If he or she inserts an object of the wrong type into the queue, the error will occur when it is removed and sent a message that is not in its class's protocol.

We will define the class Queue using a linked list of references to elements. To do so, we must first define an auxiliary class Node for the nodes in the linked list. These objects have two instance variables, the queue element and a reference next to the next node on the list. An instance of the class Queue contains the data members front and back that point to the first and last nodes in the linked list. Figure 6.3 diagrams the structure of a Queue object into which the client has inserted elements 'this', 'that', 'these', and 'those'.

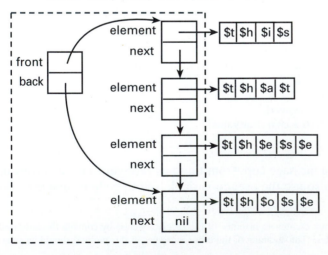

Figure 6.3 An instance of class Queue (class pointers and class objects not shown).

To define the class Node, we first create a class category, say Examples. Next, we select the category and edit the class definition message template to indicate the class name and instance variables, as follows:[17]

```
"creating the class Node"
Object subclass: #Node
    instanceVariableNames: 'element next'
    classVariableNames: ''
    poolDictionaries: ''
    category: 'Examples'
```

Every class must have a superclass, so we define Node as a subclass of Object. After accepting this code, we enter the following methods for the class:[18]

```
"class method for class Node"

new: newElement
    "Answer a new Node with newElement as the element.  The instance variable next
    is set to nil by the superclass method."

    ^super new element: newElement

"instance methods for class Node"

element
    "Answer the element the receiver contains."

    ^element

element: newElement
    "Set the element the receiver contains."

    element := newElement

next
    "Answer the receiver's successor."

    ^next

next: newNext
    "Set the receiver's successor."

    next := newNext
```

[17] The system class Link provides the behavior of maintaining and manipulating a successor. We would actually define Node as a subclass of this class that adds the element instance variable and its accessors.

[18] We will ignore the message categories for our example classes.

The class method new: creates a new node containing a reference to the argument object. The new object's next instance variable is set to nil by the Object class method for new.[19] (We will cover instantiation and initialization messages in the next section, and the use of the pseudo-variable super in section 6.2.2.) The instance messages of Node provide access to the receiver's instance variables. We can define these methods in any order, even if they call other methods that are not defined yet (e.g., we can define the class method new: before the instance method element:). The compiler warns us if a particular selector is not defined, but allows us to proceed.

The class Node is intended to be an auxiliary class used to aid in the implementation of the class Queue. However, it is not possible in Smalltalk to restrict access to the nodes to Queue methods, because all methods are accessible throughout the system. Nor can we encapsulate the class Node within class Queue, because all class names are global variables and have the same visibility.

We code the class definition message and the instance methods for the class Queue as follows:

```
"a class Queue for queues of elements (linked list implementation)"
Object subclass: #Queue
    instanceVariableNames: 'front back'
    classVariableNames: ''
    poolDictionaries: ''
    category: 'Examples'

"no class methods are necessary for class Queue"

"instance methods for class Queue"

isEmpty
    "Answer whether the queue has no elements."

    ^front == nil

add: newElement
    "Add the new element at the back of the queue."

    self isEmpty
        ifTrue: [front := back := Node new: newElement]
        ifFalse: [
            back next: (Node new: newElement).
            back := back next]
```

---

[19] We will see in section 6.2.2 that the expression super new invokes the class method for new in the superclass Object. This method creates an object of the correct size with a class pointer referring to the Node class object and both instance variables set to nil.

remove
    "Answer and remove the element at the front of the queue."

    | returnElement |
    self isEmpty
        ifTrue: [^self error: 'attempt to remove from an empty queue'].
    returnElement := front element.
    front := front next.
    ^returnElement

Generally, every class defines at least one class method that creates and initializes a new instance of the class. However, because all instance variables are set to nil when an object is created, the method for new inherited from the superclass Object correctly initializes the new object to an empty queue.[20] Therefore, we do not need to define an instantiation message for the class Queue, and we can create an empty queue object with the message Queue new. To determine whether the receiver is empty, the methods for add: and remove send the message self isEmpty. The method for the message error: is defined in Object, and displays a notifier window with its argument as the title. In the method for remove, we do not need to deallocate the node containing the reference to the removed element because Smalltalk uses automatic storage reclamation.

Once we have defined the class and its methods, we can test them by typing a code fragment in the workspace that creates an instance and sends it messages, and evaluating it. For example,

    "testing the class Queue"
    | aQueue anInteger |
    aQueue := Queue new.
    aQueue add: 4; add: 2.
    aQueue isEmpty
        ifFalse: [aQueue add: 5; add: 7].
    anInteger := aQueue remove.   "anInteger is 4 "
    aQueue remove.
    anInteger := aQueue remove   "anInteger is 5 "

The messages add:, remove, and isEmpty provide the complete protocol for a first-in first-out queue. However, there are other messages inherited from the class Object for which we may want to provide class-specific methods. In particular, a client might expect to be able to test queue objects for equality, and to copy and print queues. We must either provide methods for these messages, or disallow them (using the technique presented in section 6.2.3). In the Smalltalk collection classes, the message copy returns a copy of the receiver, containing references to the same elements referred to by the receiver. That is, it copies the object identifiers for the

---

[20] We will see how the inherited method for new determines how many instance variables are needed for the new object in section 6.2.2.

elements into the new collection, but the element objects themselves are not copied. We will use the same semantics for the copy method for the class Queue, which we code as follows:[21]

```
"instance method for class Queue"
copy
    "Answer a copy of the receiver containing the same object identifiers for the elements."

    | returnQueue currentNode |
    returnQueue := Queue new.
    currentNode := front.
    [currentNode ~~ nil]
        whileTrue: [
            returnQueue add: currentNode element.
            currentNode := currentNode next].
    ^returnQueue
```

In coding the Queue method for =, we discover a problem, namely that the method does not have access to the elements or nodes in the argument queue. In Smalltalk, the receiver is a client of the argument object, and has no special access just because it is an instance of the same class. Therefore, to provide an equality test method for Queue, we must first define the following private message:[22]

```
"private instance method for use in class Queue's = method only"
front
    ^front
```

Given this private method, the following method performs the queue equality test:[23]

```
"instance method for class Queue"
= aQueue
    "Answer whether aQueue and the receiver have equal elements in the same order."

    | myNode argNode |
    (aQueue class) = Queue ifFalse: [^false].
    myNode := front.
    argNode := aQueue front.
    [myNode ~~ nil and: [argNode ~~ nil]]
        whileTrue: [
            myNode element = argNode element ifFalse: [^false].
            myNode := myNode next.
            argNode := argNode next].
```

---

[21] We will change the Queue methods for copy, =, and printOn: slightly in section 6.2.2 to accommodate subclasses.

[22] It is common practice to omit the comment in a private method.

[23] As we will discuss in section 8.2.1, any class that implements = should also implement the message hash such that two objects that are equal have the same hash value.

```
(myNode == nil and: [argNode == nil])
    ifTrue: [^true]
    ifFalse: [^false]
```

The message printOn: appends a readable representation of an object to the argument stream, and is also invoked indirectly by an inspector to display an object. For queue objects, the method inherited from Object appends the string 'a Queue' to the stream. Instead, we would like to print a string that describes the elements in the queue. We will follow the format the Smalltalk collection classes use, in which the class name is followed by a parenthesized list of the elements' print strings (e.g., see Figure 5.4). We code the printOn: method as follows:

```
"instance method for class Queue"
printOn: aStream
    "Append a sequence of characters representing the receiver to the argument aStream."

    | currentNode |
    aStream nextPutAll: 'Queue ('.
    currentNode := front.
    [currentNode ~~ nil]
        whileTrue: [
            currentNode element printOn: aStream.
            aStream space.
            currentNode := currentNode next].
    aStream nextPut: $)
```

The message nextPut: appends its argument to the stream receiver, and nextPutAll: appends each element in the argument collection (a string, in this case) to the stream.[24] This method assumes that the class of the queue's elements implements the message printOn:, as it must since it cannot know how to print the elements. We note that if the class Queue provided a message do: that enumerates its elements as in the collection classes, then we could have used it to code the copy and printOn: methods without referring to a local Node variable. This message would be private for the class.

The class FinancialHistory

The presence of a large class library that includes foundation and collection classes facilitates creating problem domain classes. For example, [Gol89] defines a class FinancialHistory that summarizes a series of financial transactions. It keeps track of the total balance, the total amount received from each of a number of sources, and the total amount spent for various reasons. We create an instance with either the class message initialBalance:, for which the argument is the initial balance, or new, for which the initial balance is zero. We use the messages receive:from: and spend:for: to record financial transactions. The first argument

---

[24] We will cover streams and stream protocol in detail in section 8.5.

to these messages is a string naming the source or reason (although any type of object could be used), and the second is a number giving the amount. We access an instance's state information with the messages cashOnHand, totalReceived-From: and totalSpentFor:.

The class defines three instances variables: cashOnHand, incomes, and expenditures. cashOnHand (the total balance) is a number initialized upon instantiation of a FinancialHistory object, and can only be modified via the messages spend:for: and receive:from:. The instance variables incomes and expenditures are dictionaries that keep track of the total income or expenditure for each of the sources or reasons given in the receive:from: and spend:for: messages. The class FinancialHistory and its methods are defined as follows:

```
"a class FinancialHistory which tracks income sources and expenditure reasons"
Object subclass: #FinancialHistory
   instanceVariableNames: 'cashOnHand incomes expenditures'
   classVariableNames: ''
   poolDictionaries: ''
   category: 'Examples'

"class methods for class FinancialHistory"

initialBalance: amount
   "Answer a new instance with cashOnHand set to amount."

   "setInitialBalance: is a private instance message"
   ^super new setInitialBalance: amount

new
   "Answer a new instance with cashOnHand set to 0."

   ^super new setInitialBalance: 0

"instance methods for class FinancialHistory"

receive: amount from: source
   "Add amount to the value associated with source in incomes, and update cashOnHand."

   incomes at: source put: (self totalReceivedFrom: source) + amount.
   cashOnHand := cashOnHand + amount

spend: amount for: reason
   "Add amount to the value associated with reason in expenditures,
   and update cashOnHand."

   expenditures at: reason put: (self totalSpentFor: reason) + amount.
   cashOnHand := cashOnHand - amount
```

```
cashOnHand
   "Answer the cash on hand."

   ^cashOnHand

totalReceivedFrom: source
   "Answer the total received from source, or 0 if none."

   (incomes includesKey: source)
      ifTrue: [^incomes at: source]
      ifFalse: [^0]

totalSpentFor: reason
   "Answer the total spent for reason, or 0 if none."

   (expenditures includesKey: reason)
      ifTrue: [^expenditures at: reason]
      ifFalse: [^0]

"private initialization method: should not be called by clients"
setInitialBalance: amount
   cashOnHand := amount.
   incomes := Dictionary new.
   expenditures := Dictionary new
```

The class methods initialBalance: and new create an instance with super new, then
send the new object the private message setInitialBalance:, which initializes it by creating its instance variable referents. Clearly, a client should never use the message
setInitialBalance:. We will discuss instantiation and initialization methods further in
the next section. The methods for receive:from: and spend:for: use messages to self
to obtain the current total for that source or reason. They call totalReceivedFrom:
and totalSpentFor:, rather than accessing the dictionaries directly with at:, because it
is an error to access the value at a nonexistent key. Those methods check whether the
source or reason is present with the message includesKey:, and return 0 if there were
no transactions for that source or reason. Because incomes and expenditures are dictionaries, the first time the client uses a source or reason, the dictionary method for
at:put: creates a new association with that source or reason as the key. Subsequent
at:put: messages update the value component of that association.

6.1.3 The Class Object

Classes as objects

Most programmers have experience with compiled, statically typed languages
such as Pascal and C. In those languages, a data type is a language construct used
in declaring identifiers, creating pointer and composite types, defining objects, and

allocating dynamic objects. As we discussed in section 0.3.4, the compiler maintains a type object representing each built-in or programmer-defined type that allows it to perform type checking and determine the size of an instance for allocations. Some languages also provide type operations that allow the programmer to query attributes of the type and its instances (e.g., sizeof in C and 'LAST in Ada). Variables are monomorphic, so the compiler can always compute the results of these operations from the type object, and little or no information about types is retained at run-time. In contrast, type objects must exist at run-time in an interpreted language for it to do type checking. However, this type information is usually not available to the programmer.

In Smalltalk, classes are objects with state and behavior that exist at execution time. When a class's superclass receives the class definition message, that method creates a *class object* representing the class, and binds it to the shared variable named by the class name (e.g., String or FinancialHistory). The class definition message subclass:... lists the class object's variables as the argument corresponding to the selector classVariableNames:. (It also inherits variables that maintain its type information.) The class object's messages and methods are defined in the browser by first selecting the class radio button.

Class objects are available to methods via their names. In addition, when one of a class's instances receives the message class, it returns the class object. We can assign a class object as the referent of a variable, use one as the receiver or an argument in a message expression, or examine a class object with an inspector. That is, classes themselves are first-class objects in Smalltalk. This feature is unusual because very few languages support direct manipulation of data types. Because all objects respond to class, it is possible to determine the class of any object during execution and test whether two objects are instances of the same class.

Like any object, a class object has a protocol, namely the class's class messages.[25] The protocol of a class object includes messages that

- access the class information of the problem domain category it represents
- create instances of the class
- create a new class object representing a subclass
- access type information such as the class's name, superclass, and selectors.

The last three functions distinguish class objects from "non-class" objects. To create an instance, we send a class message such as new to the class object (not to any of its instances). In Pascal and C++, new is a language-supplied operation. To create a subclass object, we send the class definition message subclass:.... In both cases, the form of the operation is in keeping with the language design principles that all activity is performed by message passing, and that each operation must be the responsibility of some object. We will discuss a class object's type information later in this section, and in section 7.1.3.

---

[25] Like any object, a class object's protocol is specified by the class of which it is an instance. We will discuss this "metaclass" and the representation of class variables and messages in section 6.3.

Note also that a class object and an instance of that class respond to different sets of messages. For example,

```
"instance and class messages for class Array"
| anArray aClass |
anArray := Array new: 5.        "a class message to the class object named Array"
anArray at: 5 put: 'five'.      "an instance message to an instance of Array"
Array at: 5 put: 'five'.        "error: at:put: is not in the class object's protocol"
aClass := anArray class.        "aClass refers to the class object Array"
aClass := aClass superclass     "aClass now refers to the ArrayedCollection class object"
```

Class variables

As we discussed in section 1.1.5, we often find that there is information associated with a problem domain category as a whole, which is not specific to an individual entity. This information need not be stored in each instance, but it should be encapsulated within the class, rather than being represented by global variables. Furthermore, it must be accessible to all instances of the class, but not directly available to clients. In Smalltalk, this information is maintained in *class variables*, which are stored in the class object. The class object also stores class variables that maintain class constants and type information associated with the class.

Several system classes define class variables. The class Date contains the class variables MonthNames, WeekDayNames, DaysInMonth, and FirstDayOfMonth (the day of the year that is the first day of each month). This information can be requested from the class object, and is available within Date's class and instance methods. For example, the variable MonthNames is used in the methods for the class messages nameOfMonth: (which takes an integer index) and indexOfMonth: (which takes a month name), and in the methods for the instance messages month-Name (of the receiver) and printOn:. Other examples of class variables in the system classes include

- Float defines two constants, Pi and RadiansPerDegree
- ProcessorScheduler defines class variables for the process priority levels
- Filename defines class variables that maintain the current directory, a list of volumes, the system line delimiter, and the system path delimiter
- ColorValue (in VisualWorks) specifies class variables that give color values for Brown, Orange, and so on
- many VisualWorks classes define error signals that their methods can raise as class variables.

The names of a class's class variables are given in the class definition message subclass:... as the argument corresponding to the classVariableNames: selector. (Indexed class variables are not supported, but a class variable can refer to an array.) A class variable is shared among the class object and its instances, so its name must begin with a capital letter. We can think of the class variables as the instance variables of the class object. However, in practice, the class variables are stored as a dictionary referred to by the class object's instance variable classPool (for example, inspect Date on your system). In this way, we can add and remove class variables while the class object exists. When a class is created, the class variable names are entered as keys in the dictionary with the value nil. Once initialized by a class method, the class variables exist for as long as the class exists. As described in section 5.6.3, when the class name is selected in the browser, the text view displays the class variables and allows editing them. Accepting the new set of class variables updates the classPool dictionary.

Class variable names may be used directly within the class and instance methods of the class. They are declared in the scope of the class, and hide uses of those names in pool dictionaries or as globals.[26] Although they are shared among the class and its instances, class variables are not directly accessible to other objects in the system.[27] Clients can request the information represented by class variables from either the class object or one of its instances if the class provides accessing messages.

Class messages and methods

As we discussed in section 1.1.5, we define messages that access or modify class information as *class messages* in the protocol of the class object, rather than as instance messages. For example, the class Date includes class messages such as nameOfMonth:, indexOfMonth:, nameOfDay:, and dayOfWeek: that access its class variables. It also defines several other class messages that provide information about dates. Examples include leapYear:, which returns whether the argument is a leap year, and daysInMonth:year:, which returns the number of days in the month indicated by the arguments. (Several more Date class messages are listed in section 7.3.3.) Class messages also support creation of instances and subclasses of the class. In addition, all class objects respond to messages such as allSubclasses, instanceCount, classVarNames, and addSelector:withMethod: that access the type information about the class. We will discuss instantiation and initialization in the next subsection, and type information in the following subsection.

Like all variables, class variables are initialized to nil when the class object is created, so they must be given values by a class message. By convention, the class message that initializes class variable values is called initialize, and is listed in the class message category class initialization. For example, the class variables Month-Names, WeekDayNames, and so on in class Date are initialized by the Date class method initialize (check your system browser). The class definition method cannot send the message initialize because its method must be coded and accepted *after* the

---

[26] The compiler searches for shared variables first in the class's classPool dictionary for class variable names, then in its sharedPools dictionary for pool variable names, and finally in the dictionary Smalltalk for global names.

[27] Actually, access cannot be prevented because classes provide a message that the compiler and programming tools use to access the dictionary of class variables. We can access a class variable outside its class by an expression such as Date classPool at: #MonthNames.

class definition message has been accepted. We must explicitly initialize the variables in the class object by sending initialize to the class object after defining the initialize method (e.g., from a workspace). Clearly, we should send this message before creating any instances of the class. When a class is filed out, the last expression in the resulting text file sends initialize to the class object so that the class is ready to use when it is filed in.

We code and accept class methods in the same manner as instance methods. (Recall the examples in the previous section.) Class methods may define parameters and local variables, and can access class variables. The receiver of the class message is the class object. When self appears in a class method, it refers to the class object, and the message must be in the class object's protocol. A class method cannot use the class's instance variable names because the class object does not have variables with those names. (If it used an instance variable name, there would be no indication of which object's variables the use refers to.)

Instantiation and initialization

The class Object defines a method for the class message new that allocates a new object with the correct number of instance variable references, initializes those instance variables to nil, and sets the new object's class pointer. Object also includes the class message new: for classes with indexed instance variables, for which the argument is the size. These methods provide default initialization procedures because all classes are subclasses of Object. In addition, Object defines the class messages copy and readFrom:, which create objects. The message readFrom: creates a new object from the contents of the stream argument, which contains an expression whose evaluation creates the new object. This text was usually written by the instance method for storeOn: defined by the object's class. (storeOn: and readFrom: are covered in sections 7.1.2 and 7.1.3, respectively.)

Because instantiation and initialization are performed via message passing, a class can provide its own descriptive instantiation messages, and can have several such messages. These messages can also allow a client to provide initialization information for instance variables as arguments, as we did for the FinancialHistory message initialBalance: in section 6.1.2. In this way, all instances will have valid instance variable referents. The following expressions illustrate some example system class messages that return a new instance of the class:

```
"instance creation expressions using mnemonic selectors"
"each returns an initialized instance of the receiver class"
Point x: 50 y: 50.                         "the x and y coordinates"
Fraction numerator: 5 denominator: 3.      "the numerator and denominator"
Rectangle origin: 3@3 corner: 10@10.       "the upper left and lower right corners"
Rectangle origin: 3@3 extent: 7@7.         "the upper left corner and the size"
Time now.                                  "the time when the message is received"
Time fromSeconds: 1234.                    "the time 1234 seconds after midnight"
Date today.                                the date when the message is received"
Date readFromString: '5/18/82'.            "the date given by the argument"
```

Date newDay: 18 month: 'May' year: 1982. "the date given by the arguments"
Set with: 1 with: 2 with: 3.   "the initial elements are given by the arguments"

The class method that creates an instance can also be invoked by a instance method in another class. Conversion messages also entail creating new objects. For example,

```
"instance messages that call a class message for another class to create an instance"

"a message to an integer that creates an instance of Fraction"
5 / 3.
"a message to an integer that creates an instance of Point"
5 @ 3.
"a message to a point that creates an instance of Rectangle"
5 @ 3 corner: 10@10.
"a message to an integer that creates an instance of Interval consisting of 2, 5, 8 and 11"
2 to: 11 by: 3.
"a message to a block that creates an instance of Process with aBlock as its code
and schedules it"
aBlock fork.
"a message to a string that creates an instance of SmallInteger"
'345' asNumber.
"a message to a string that creates an instance of ReadStream"
'hello' readStream.
"a message to a set that creates an instance of Array containing the same elements"
aSet asArray
```

Typically, the method for such an instance message passes the receiver as an argument to the class message that creates the resulting object, as in the following examples:

```
"example instance methods which send a class message to create an instance"

"instance methods for class Number"
@ y
    "Answer a new point with the receiver as the x coordinate and the argument as
    the y coordinate."

    ^Point x: self y: y

to: stop by: step
    "Answer a new interval from the receiver to the argument with increment step."

    ^Interval from: self to: stop by: step
```

Because instantiation is a class message rather than a built-in operation, the class designer can refine the message new to trigger default initialization of the new object (e.g., instantiation of instance variables referents or any other set-up necessary). For example, we refined new for the class FinancialHistory in section 6.1.2 to send setInitialBlance: 0 to the new object, to create the incomes and expenditures dictionaries, and to set cashOnHand to zero (as well as creating the new object). Descriptive instantiation messages such as fromSeconds: in Time and initialBalance: in FinancialHistory also initialize the new object. However, we cannot code the operations that initialize the new object's instance variables directly in the class method that creates that object because the class object is the receiver of the instantiation message. In addition, the class object is a client of the newly-created instance and does not have access to its variables. The class must define a separate instance message to perform initialization, which the instantiation method sends to the new object before returning it. For the class Node, the instantiation message new: calls the instance message element: to set that instance variable. For FinancialHistory, setInitialBalance: is the initialization message sent by the instantiation methods initialBalance: and new.

Let us clarify this point with an example. To create an instance of FinancialHistory, we send either the message initialBalance: or new to the class object. Each class method sends the expression super new, which invokes the class method new of its superclass Object to create a new instance. (The class object FinancialHistory is still the receiver of this message.) Next, the class method sends the instance message setInitialBalance: to the new object to initialize cashOnHand and create the dictionaries referred to by the instance variables incomes and expenditures (Dictionary new initializes each as an empty dictionary). The assignments to cashOnHand, incomes, and expenditures that appear in the setInitialBalance: method would be invalid in the class method initialBalance: because its receiver, the class object FinancialHistory, does not have variables with those names.

In most cases, we do not want the initialization message that the instantiation method uses to be available to clients, either because the class must control setting instance variable values or because its instances are treated as immutable objects, rather than as containers. For example, no object should ever send setInitialBalance: to an existing FinancialHistory object and re-initialize it with a different cashOnHand value and empty dictionaries. Similarly, the class Date defines no messages that modify the receiver, and messages such as addDays: create a new date object. However, the Date instantiation methods need the initialization message day:year:, and Smalltalk does not prevent clients from using it to modify an existing date object, even though it is in the category private.

Another implication of first-class class objects and instantiation as message passing is that a method can dynamically select the class of a new object it creates. In statically typed languages, the source code always gives the type of an object. For static and automatic objects, the type is given by the declaration, and for dynamically allocated objects, it is given by the pointer type (or the type name with new in C++). In Smalltalk, the message aClass new creates a new instance of whatever class object is bound to aClass when the expression is evaluated. For example, an application can create a file containing objects of various types (e.g., subclasses of a problem domain class such as Transaction), each of which is preceded by its class name. A method can read the string giving the class name, obtain a reference to the corresponding class object from the global dictionary Smalltalk, and then send that object the class message readFrom: to create a new instance using the succeeding information in the file.

Type information

In a dynamically typed or interpreted language that performs type checking, type information such as a type's operations and the names of its components must exist at execution time. In Smalltalk, the type information for a class is stored in the class object for use by the compiler, the method binding process, and the various programming tools. The class Object defines class variables that maintain this type information, and includes extensive class protocol for accessing it, which is available for all class objects.[28]

Each class object includes class variables for

- its name
- its superclass
- its set of subclasses
- its instance variable names
- its dictionary of methods, keyed by selectors
- the organization of its messages into browser categories.

The type information protocol that class objects inherit from Object includes messages that

- access, test, add, remove, and enumerate the class's superclass, subclasses, ancestors, and descendants
- manipulate the class's method dictionary to access, test for, add, remove, and enumerate the class's selectors and source and compiled methods
- access information in the class definition, such as the class name, the number and names of named instance variables, whether there are indexed variables, and the names of class and pool variables
- access browser information, such as the class category and comment, and the class's class and instance message categories
- add and remove class and instance variables
- access and enumerate the class's instances.

We will cover this protocol in detail in section 7.1.3.

Applications rarely use this protocol because explicit type dependencies make a program less extendible. The system provides it so that programming tools can be constructed in Smalltalk, including both those supplied with the system and new

---

[28] As we will see in section 6.3.2, the class variables and methods described in this section are actually defined in the classes Behavior, ClassDescription, and Class.

tools that programmers design. These messages are also helpful because we can use them as a query language when attempting to understand a class and its methods. For example, suppose we want to know the instance messages for the class Date that are defined by Date or its superclass Magnitude, but are not inherited from the class Object. The following expression returns a set containing the symbols for those selectors:

```
"returns the set of symbols for Date messages that are not inherited from Object"
Date allSelectors reject: [:selector | Object selectors includes: selector]
```

6.2 INHERITANCE

6.2.1 Subclass Definition

The superclass

In section 6.1.2, we saw that the message that defines a class is a message to the superclass class object asking it to create and return a new class object. A class definition in Smalltalk always specifies a superclass (Object if no other superclass applies), and therefore every class definition is a subclass definition, except that for Object. The definitions of a class and its methods describe how the state and behavior of its instances differ from those of superclass instances.

Because all classes except Object are subclasses and Smalltalk does not support multiple inheritance, the class inheritance hierarchy has the structure of a tree, with Object as the root class. Object's methods provide functionality that is available to every class in the system. Dialects of Smalltalk that support multiple inheritance have been implemented.

Instance variables

A class inherits the instance variables of its superclass, and, therefore, those of all of its ancestors. The class's instances contain references for each of those instance variables. The class's instance methods can access the referent of an inherited variable in the receiver by using the name defined by the ancestor from which the variable is inherited. If the superclass defines or inherits indexed instance variables, the class's instances also have them. A class also inherits access to its ancestors' class and pool variables, and can refer to them in its class and instance methods.

A class definition can add named or indexed instance variables, in which case its instances are larger than instances of its superclass. As we saw in section 6.1.2, we give the names of the additional named instance variables as the argument corresponding to the selector instanceVariableNames: in the class definition message. A new class may add indexed instance variables by using the class definition message variableSubclass:... only if no ancestors have indexed instance variables. A class definition cannot define a named instance variable with the same name as an ancestor instance variable, as there is no way to distinguish between them.[29]

Instance messages and methods

A class inherits the messages of its superclass and ancestors, due to the method binding procedure discussed in section 3.2.4. When an instance of the class receives an inherited message, it performs the method defined in the nearest ancestor in the class hierarchy. This is valid because the object must have referents for the instance variables that the method can use.

The class designer can define additional messages for a class that are not in the protocol of its superclass, and instances of the class will respond to both sets of messages. The designer can also replace or refine inherited methods by defining methods for selectors in the superclass's protocol. (No indication that the method overrides an inherited method is necessary.) As discussed in section 6.1.2, we code new methods and modifications to methods using the system browser. We will cover method refinement in the next section.

Class variables and methods

A class inherits the class and pool variables defined by its ancestors in the sense that they are accessible within the class's methods. However, there is exactly one instance of each class variable, so a class cannot have a different referent for an inherited class variable than that of the ancestor that defined it. If a method in the class changes the referent of an inherited class variable, that variable's referent is changed for the ancestor and all its descendants, and for their instances. If a class adds class or pool variables, they are accessible to the class and its instances, but not to its ancestors or their instances.

A class also inherits the class messages of its superclass and ancestors. When the class object receives those messages, it responds with the inherited method (if it has not defined its own method). For example, when we send the message Queue new, the class method for the superclass object is executed because Queue does not define a method for that class message.

If each class in a set of classes must maintain its own value for some class information, then each class must have its own class variable containing that value. Each class should define a class message that returns its value so that clients can obtain that information, and the message send will return the correct value via dynamic binding.

The class DeductibleHistory

[Gol89] defines the class DeductibleHistory, which is a subclass of Financial-History that also keeps track of the subtotal of the client's expenditures that are tax

---

[29] If the name of an instance variable matches the name of an inherited variable, the class definition method creates a notifier dialog stating that an instance variable name conflicts with an existing name.

deductible. The class defines an additional instance variable deductibleExpenditures for this value, and inherits the three instance variables cashOnHand, incomes, and expenditures.

DeductibleHistory inherits its superclass's methods for six instance messages (including the private message setInitialBalance:). It also defines four additional public instance messages and methods. These are the accessor totalDeductions, the testing message isItemizable, and the spending messages spend:for:deducting:, and spendDeductible:for:. For spend:for: deducting:, the third argument gives the amount of the expenditure that is deductible, and spendDeductible:for: is used when the entire expenditure is deductible. DeductibleHistory refines the instantiation message initialBalance: with a method that invokes the superclass method, then sends the private instance message initializeDeductions to the new object.[30]

DeductibleHistory also defines a class variable MinimumDeductions that records the minimum amount of deductions necessary to itemize deductions on a tax report. Instances of the class need this information to respond correctly to the instance message isItemizable, but do not each need their own copy of this value. As discussed in section 6.1.3, MinimumDeductions is initialized by the class message initialize, which we must send before using the class.

The class DeductibleHistory and its methods are defined as follows:

```
"a subclass DeductibleHistory for financial histories that also track deductible expenses"
FinancialHistory subclass: #DeductibleHistory
    instanceVariableNames: 'deductibleExpenditures'
    classVariableNames: 'MinimumDeductions'
    poolDictionaries: ''
    category: 'Examples'

"class methods for class DeductibleHistory"

initialBalance: amount
    "Answer a new instance with cashOnHand set to amount and
    deductibleExpenditures set to 0."

    ^(super initialBalance: amount) initializeDeductions

new
    "Answer a new instance with cashOnHand and deductibleExpenditures set to 0."

    ^(super initialBalance: 0) initializeDeductions

initialize
    "Initialize the class variable MinimumDeductions."

    MinimumDeductions := 2300
```

[30] We will discuss the pseudo-variable super further in the next section, and trace the execution of this method in section 6.3.2.

"instance methods for class DeductibleHistory"

spend: amount for: reason deducting: deductibleAmount
  "Do spend:for:, and add deductibleAmount to deductibleExpenditures."

    self spend: amount for: reason.
    deductibleExpenditures := deductibleExpenditures + deductibleAmount

spendDeductible: amount for: reason
  "Do spend:for:, and add amount to deductibleExpenditures."

    self spend: amount for: reason.
    deductibleExpenditures := deductibleExpenditures + amount

isItemizable
  "Answer whether the receiver's deductions can be itemized."

    ∧deductibleExpenditures >= MinimumDeductions

totalDeductions
  "Answer the receiver's total deductions."

    ∧deductibleExpenditures

"private initialization method: should not be called by clients"
initializeDeductions
    deductibleExpenditures := 0

6.2.2 The Pseudo-Variables self and super

self and inheritance

When we send a message to the pseudo-variable self, the method search begins in the class of the receiver, and continues up its chain of ancestors. For example, when an instance of DeductibleHistory receives the message spend:for:deducting:, it sends the message spend:for: to self. The method dictionary in the receiver's class object (i.e., DeductibleHistory) does not include that selector, so the method dictionary of FinancialHistory is searched, and the method is found and executed. The method search for a message to self begins in the receiver's class even if the expression occurs in an inherited ancestor method. For example, when an instance of DeductibleHistory receives the message spend:for:, it executes the superclass method, which sends the message totalSpentFor: to self. If DeductibleHistory had defined its own method for totalSpentFor:, that method would have been invoked.

Because a message to self is bound according to the class of the receiver, we can use a message to self to invoke the class-specific behavior of the actual receiver. We can code the general strategy for a method once in the ancestor of the relevant subhierarchy, and each descendant can then use it, providing reuse of the higher-level algorithm. (Recall the methods for DisplayObject.erase and DisplayObject.moveTo in section 3.3.3.) For example, the class method for new for the class Object determines how many instance variable references to allocate for the new object by sending the message self instSize, which returns the number of named instance variables for the receiver class. This is the only class-specific information the method needs to create an object (besides the receiver class, which is the referent of the new object's class reference).

Using self is also helpful when a class that has descendants defines a method that refers to the receiver's class, for example, to create an instance. Such expressions should use self class rather than the name of the class. That message is dynamically bound, so in an instance of a descendant using the method (either directly or for refinement), the expression will refer to its own class object, rather than that of the ancestor.

Refining methods and super

As we discussed in section 3.2.4, a method that refines an inherited method must send that same message to the receiver, together with an indication that the ancestor method should be executed, so that the expression does not appear to be a recursive invocation of the same method. In Smalltalk, we use the pseudo-variable super as the receiver to invoke the superclass method from a method of the same name. Like the pseudo-variable self, super refers to the receiver of the message whose method is being executed. Uses of instance variables in the ancestor method selected by the method search access that object's instance variable referents. (These names are valid because the method selected is defined in an ancestor of the receiver's class, so the receiver has those variables.) If the superclass of the method's class does not define a method for a message to super, the method search continues up the class hierarchy. That is, we use super to refine any message in the superclass's protocol, even those whose methods it inherits, and the class designer does not need to know which ancestor defines the method being refined. super may only be used as the receiver of a message, and cannot appear as an argument or on the left side of an assignment.

Although the pseudo-variables self and super both refer to the receiver of the message, they differ in how the method search determines its starting point. super indicates that the method search begins in the superclass of the class that defines the method containing the message to super, not in the superclass of the receiver. The class of the method and the class of the receiver differ when super occurs while evaluating an inherited method. In this case, the method search begins in the superclass of the class of the method (which will be an ancestor of the receiver's class), not the superclass of the receiver. Remember that the same object is the receiver (an instance of the ancestor whose method is invoked may not even exist). For a message to super, the class at which the method search begins is defined statically according to the class that defines the method including the expression. This class is the same, no matter what the actual class of the receiver is. For a message to self, the class at which the method search begins is defined dynamically in terms of the actual receiver. In a sense, super is a syntactic device that is a message to the method resolution process.

To illustrate the meaning of self and super, we will use the following classes, instance methods, instances, and message expressions:

```
"example classes and objects illustrating the meaning of expressions involving self
and super"
Object subclass: #A
    instanceVariableNames: ''
    classVariableNames: ''
    poolDictionaries: ''
    category: 'Examples'
"instance methods for class A"
who
    ^$A
whom
    ^self who

A subclass: #B
    instanceVariableNames: ''
    classVariableNames: ''
    poolDictionaries: ''
    category: 'Examples'
"instance methods for class B"
who
    ^$B
what
    ^super who
where
    ^super whom

B subclass: #C
    instanceVariableNames: ''
    classVariableNames: ''
    poolDictionaries: ''
    category: 'Examples'
"instance methods for class C"
who
    ^$C
why
    ^super whom

| instB instC |
instB := B new.
instC := C new.
instB whom.        "finds A's whom, calls B's who, and answers $B"
instC whom.        "finds A's whom, calls C's who, and answers $C"
instB what.        "calls A's who, and answers $A"
instC what.        "finds B's what, calls A's who, and answers $A"
instB where.       "calls A's whom, calls B's who, and answers $B"
```

```
instC where.          "finds B's where, calls A's whom, calls C's who, and answers $C"
nstC why              "finds A's whom, calls C's who, and answers $C"
```

In the first two messages that send whom, the method search begins in the class of the receiver, and proceeds to class A where whom is defined. In each case, the message who is then sent to the receiver, which responds with the method defined in its own class. For the message instB what, the method for who defined in its superclass A is invoked. For instC what, the method search begins in class C, proceeds to B, and encounters the same method with the same result. Note that the use of super in the method for what refers to the superclass of the class B that defines the method, not the superclass of C, the class of the receiver. The message instB where invokes the method for whom in class A, which sends who to the receiver, resulting in $B. When where is sent to instC, the method search finds the definition of where in its superclass, class B. However, since the receiver is instC, when that method sends it whom and then who, the result is $C. Finally, when instC why is sent, the search for the method for whom begins in class B and continues to class A, where it is found and evaluated with instC as the receiver.

The class PriorityQueue

To illustrate method refinement, let us define a class that represents priority queues. When an instance receives the message remove, it removes and returns the "least" element in the queue according to a comparison function that is specific to that instance, rather than the element that was inserted earliest, as in the class Queue. We will derive the class PriorityQueue from the class Queue defined in section 6.1.2. The subclass inherits the storage structure of class Queue,[31] and its methods for remove and isEmpty. When an element is inserted into a priority queue, we position it in the queue's linked list in sorted order according to the comparison function.

PriorityQueue adds an instance variable compareBlock that maintains the block an instance uses to order elements upon insertion, and an instance creation message compareBlock: that takes this block as an argument. The default comparison block is [:left :right | left <= right], that is, ascending order. It is good practice to define class variables for such constants rather than hard-coding them (in this case, in the method for new that uses the default block), so we define a class variable DefaultCompareBlock and a class method initialize that sets its value.

We define the class PriorityQueue as follows:

```
"a subclass PriorityQueue for queues in which the order is controlled by a compare block"
Queue subclass: #PriorityQueue
    instanceVariableNames: 'compareBlock'
    classVariableNames: 'DefaultCompareBlock'
    poolDictionaries: ''
    category: 'Examples'
```

---

[31] Of course, this is not the most efficient storage structure for a priority queue.

```
"class methods for class PriorityQueue"

new
    "Answer a new empty priority queue with the default compare block."

    ^super new initializeCompareBlock: DefaultCompareBlock

compareBlock: aBlock
    "Answer a new empty priority queue with the compare block aBlock."

    ^super new initializeCompareBlock: aBlock

initialize
    "initialize the class variable"

    DefaultCompareBlock := [:left :right | left <= right]

"instance methods for class PriorityQueue"

add: newElement
    "Add the new element at correct place in order in the queue."

    | currentNode predNode |
    "use the superclass method if the receiver is empty or the new element goes at the back"
    (self isEmpty or: [compareBlock value: back element value: newElement])
        ifTrue: [^super add: newElement].

    "check if the new element goes at the front"
    (compareBlock value: newElement value: front element)
        ifTrue: [
            front := (Node new: newElement) next: front.
            ^self].

    "otherwise, find the position of the new element in the linked list and insert it"
    predNode := front.
    currentNode := front next.
    [compareBlock value: currentNode element value:  newElement]
        whileTrue: [
            predNode := currentNode.
            currentNode := currentNode next].
    predNode next: ((Node new: newElement) next: currentNode)

    "private initialization method: should not be called by clients"
    initializeCompareBlock: aBlock
        compareBlock := aBlock
```

The class methods new and compareBlock: invoke the corresponding superclass
methods to create the new object and initialize its inherited instance variables. They

then send the new object initializeCompareBlock: to set its compareBlock. Clearly, initializeCompareBlock: should not be sent to an existing queue object because the order of the elements in its linked list might not be consistent with the new compare block. The add: method uses the superclass method via a message to super if the receiver is empty or if the new element follows the last element in order. Otherwise, it inserts a new node containing the element in order in the linked list.

Now let us implement the messages copy, =, and printOn: for PriorityQueue. First, consider printOn:. Instances of BlockClosure do not maintain their source code, so we cannot print a priority queue's compare block. We could refine the printOn: message inherited from Queue so that it prints 'PriorityQueue' followed by its elements, but the following small change to the Queue method for printOn: allows it to be used with any subclass of Queue:

```
"revised instance method for class Queue"
printOn: aStream
    "Append a sequence of characters representing the receiver to the argument aStream."

    | currentNode |
    aStream nextPutAll: self class name , ' ('.
    currentNode := front.
    [currentNode ~~ nil]
       whileTrue: [
          currentNode element printOn: aStream.
          aStream space.
          currentNode := currentNode next].
    aStream nextPut: $)
```

As we discussed earlier in this section, the expression self class returns the receiver's class object (no matter what descendant of Queue it is). The type information message name returns the class's name, a string. Recall that the , (comma) binary selector performs concatenation. By using the expression self class rather than the class name Queue, we have made Queue's printOn: method more general. We should also recode Queue's methods for = and copy in the same way to facilitate refining them, as follows:

```
"recoding the = and copy instance methods for class Queue to make them more general"
= aQueue
    "Answer whether aQueue and the receiver have equal elements in the same order."

    | myNode argNode |
    aQueue class = self class ifFalse: [^false].        "'self class' rather than 'Queue'"
    "... as coded in section 6.1.2 ..."


copy
    "Answer a copy of the receiver containing the same object identifiers for the elements."

    | returnQueue currentNode |
```

```
returnQueue := self class new.      "create an instance of the receiver's class"
              "... as coded in section 6.1.2 ..."
```

Because we often do not know whether a class will be used for derivation at some later point, you should always use self class rather than the class name in methods.

Next, we need to refine the methods for copy and = to copy or compare the referent of the additional instance variable. In coding the method for =, we have the same problem that we encountered with Queue's = method, namely that the method does not have access to the argument's instance variables. We must first code a private accessor message so that the PriorityQueue method for = can obtain the argument's compare block.

```
"private instance method for use in class PriorityQueue's = method only"
compareBlock
    ^compareBlock
```

Given this private method, we code the PriorityQueue method for = as follows:

```
= aPriorityQueue
    "Answer whether aPriorityQueue and the receiver have equal elements in the
    same order, and equal compare blocks."
    ^super = aPriorityQueue and: [compareBlock = aPriorityQueue compareBlock]
```

super can appear as the left "operand" of a binary selector (but not an assignment), because it is the receiver. It cannot appear as the right operand. BlockClosure does implement =, and the names of a block's parameters and local variables are not relevant to the test. Note also that if the argument is an instance of Queue, then it does not have a compare block. If so, the superclass equality test will fail because it compares the classes of the receiver and argument, and the compare block test will not be done. If the receiver of = is a queue and the argument is a priority queue, the super class equality test also fails.

We would like to define the PriorityQueue method for copy analogously using super (assuming that the Queue copy method creates an instance using self class new rather than Queue new). As a refinement, we would expect to code the PriorityQueue method for copy as follows:

```
"incorrect instance method for class PriorityQueue"
copy
    "Answer a copy of the receiver containing the same elements and compare block."

    ^super copy initializeCompareBlock: compareBlock.
```

The expression super copy will invoke Queue's new class method to create the copy. However, that method sends the message self class new, which will give the new object the default compare block, then insert the elements in that order. This behavior is incorrect for priority queues that do not use the default compare block. Somehow, we need to install the compare block before the element copying loop in Queue's copy method. We can only do this by coding an entirely new copy method for PriorityQueue, as follows:

```
"instance method for class PriorityQueue"
copy
   "Answer a copy of the receiver containing the same elements and compare block."

   | returnPriorityQueue currentNode |
   returnPriorityQueue := self class compareBlock: compareBlock.
   currentNode := front.
   [currentNode ~~ nil]
      whileTrue: [
         returnPriorityQueue add: currentNode element.
         currentNode := currentNode next].
   ^returnPriorityQueue
```

6.2.3 Subclass Semantics

Restriction

When a method detects an error, it sends the message self error:, which opens a notifier with the argument string as the title. The class Object also defines two special error messages to express the semantics of particular inheritance relationships, shouldNotImplement and subclassResponsibility.

As we discussed in section 3.1.3, the class designer sometimes finds that a class is a restriction of its superclass in the sense that it cannot respond to a message in the inherited protocol. However, due to dynamic typing, the language cannot prevent an instance of the subclass from receiving such a message, and that object will perform the inherited method if its class does not define one. The class Object defines the message shouldNotImplement for this purpose, as follows:

```
"instance method for class Object"
shouldNotImplement
   "Announce that the receiver should not implement this message, even though
   it is inherited."

   ^self  error: 'This message is not appropriate for this object'
```

The class designer overrides the disallowed message with the method ^self shouldNotImplement (and a comment explaining why the message is not appropriate), so that the cause of the error is clear if the subclass object receives the invalid message.

For example, the system class Array is a descendant of the class Collection because arrays are collections, and Array can inherit many useful generic methods from Collection. However, elements in arrays are replaced rather than inserted and deleted, so the Collection messages add: and remove: are disallowed for arrays. For example, add: is defined as follows in ArrayedCollection, the superclass of fixed-size collections:[32]

```
"disallowing the message add: for fixed size collections"
add: newObject
    "ArrayedCollections cannot implement add:."

    ^self shouldNotImplement
```

We can also use the message shouldNotImplement to disallow messages that are inherited from Object, if necessary. For example, suppose we have a class such that each instance has a particular identity corresponding to a problem domain entity, and instances should only be created by the class's instantiation messages. By disallowing the messages shallowCopy and copy, we can prevent methods from creating an instance by copying an existing instance. Similarly, if there is no appropriate default initialization for a class, the designer can disallow the message new.

It might occur that a class disallows a message, and an ancestor method that the class uses (i.e., one the class does not reimplement) sends the disallowed message to self. If this occurs, when an instance of the class receives the message, it executes the inherited method and sends itself the disallowed message, resulting in a shouldNotImplement notifier. The solution is to copy the ancestor method to the class and change self to super in those message expressions so that those expressions are permitted. Clearly, use of this technique should be commented in case the ancestor method is changed during development.

Abstract classes

As we discussed in section 3.3, the protocol of an abstract class includes abstract messages that must be implemented by concrete subclasses. Smalltalk provides the message subclassResponsibility for indicating that a method is deferred, which is implemented in Object as follows:

```
"instance method for class Object"
subclassResponsibility
    "Announce that the receiver should have implemented this inherited message."

    ^self error: 'My subclass should have overridden one of my messages'
```

If a new subclass is created that does not define a deferred method, when an instance receives the abstract message, the system displays a notifier and the nature of the error is apparent. However, the language does not completely support the concept of abstract classes because a method can create an instance of the class, unless its designer explicitly disallows all instantiation messages.

---

[32] We will see in section 8.3 that remove: is disallowed in SequenceableCollection, the superclass of ArrayedCollection.

The Smalltalk system classes include many abstract classes. For example, the class Magnitude is an abstract class that specifies an interface for objects that can be ordered linearly. Its protocol consists of the messages <, >, <=, >=, between:and:, max: (of the receiver and the argument), and min:. The methods for the binary selectors < and = are deferred, and the other messages are implemented by methods that invoke those selectors directly or indirectly. For example, the Magnitude methods for <, >=, and between:and: are coded as follows:

```
"instance methods for class Magnitude"

< aMagnitude
   "Answer whether the receiver is less than the argument."

   ^self subclassResponsibility

>= aMagnitude
   "Answer whether the receiver is less than or equal to the argument."

   ^(self < aMagnitude) not

between: min and: max
   "Answer whether the receiver is less than or equal to the argument max,
   and greater than or equal to the argument min."

   ^min <= self and: [self <= max]
```

The method for between:and: invokes the method for <=, which invokes the method for >, which invokes the receiver's method for <. The binary comparison messages are defined in each of the concrete numeric classes, and call primitive methods in Float and SmallInteger. The methods in Magnitude's subclasses Character, Date, and Time convert the receiver and the argument to integers, then compare them. We can define a class for which an ordering is applicable as a subclass of Magnitude with methods for < and =, and its instances will also respond to the other comparison messages.

Another abstract system class is Number, the ancestor for the numeric classes. Several messages, such as +, -, *, /, //, negated, asFloat, and printOn:, are deferred to its subclasses. The arithmetic operations are primitive methods for the classes SmallInteger and Float, and are defined in terms of the numerator and denominator in class Fraction. Number can define methods for much of the protocol of the numeric classes using the abstract messages, or messages that are implemented using them. For example,

```
"instance methods for class Number"
abs
    "Answer aNumber that is the absolute value of the receiver."
    self negative
```

```
        ifTrue: [^self negated]
        ifFalse: [^self]

cos
    "Answer the angle in radians."

    ^self asFloat cos
```

Each concrete numeric class defines the messages negative and negated in a manner appropriate for its representation. All numeric classes define the conversion message asFloat, and the class Float defines methods for mathematical functions such as cos.

A third example of an abstract class is the system class Collection, the root of the collection class subhierarchy. In Collection, the three messages add:, remove:ifAbsent: and do: are coded as ^self subclassResponsibility, and the class defines much of the behavior for groups of objects using methods that send these three messages. Each concrete collection class implements the deferred messages for its storage structure and characteristics. We will discuss the collection classes and their protocols in detail in chapter 8.

6.3 METACLASSES

6.3.1 The Class/Instance Relationship

Classes as instances of metaclasses

Like all objects, a class object is an instance of a class that defines its protocol, state, and methods, just as it defines the structure and behavior for its instances (either directly, or via an ancestor). The class of which a class object is an instance is called a *metaclass*. Conceptually, the metaclass maintains the messages, methods, and class variable names for the class object, in the same manner that the class maintains the messages, methods, and instance variable names for its instances.[33] Each class object has a class reference to its metaclass. Note that metaclasses are also classes because they have instances.

If all class objects were instances of the same metaclass, then all class objects would have the same protocol.[34] To allow class-specific instantiation messages and class messages, each class is an instance of its own metaclass. Each metaclass has a single instance, namely the corresponding class. Because of this one-to-one correspondence between classes and metaclasses, a separate definition of a class's metaclass is unnecessary. Like the instance variables, the class variables are specified when accepting the class definition message. The class messages and methods are defined in the browser text pane with the class button selected. All of the infor-

---

[33] This is not strictly true because the class variable names are stored as keys in the class object's classPool dictionary. The metaclass does maintain the method dictionary for class methods.

[34] This was true in early versions of the Smalltalk system.

mation describing the variables, protocol, and methods for a class and its instances constitutes the definition of a new class of objects and the associated metaclass. The class definition method creates both the class object and the metaclass object.

Unlike class objects, metaclass objects are not named as global variables. We obtain a reference to a metaclass object by passing the message class to its instance, the class object, just like accessing the class of any object. For example, we refer to the metaclass of the class Queue by the expression Queue class. Like any object, a metaclass object can be assigned to a variable, passed to a method, or inspected.

Object, class and metaclass structure

As illustrated in Figures 3.2 and 5.9, an object contains references to its instance variables and a class reference to its class object. As we saw in section 6.1.3, instance messages and methods are stored in the class object's method dictionary with the message selectors as keys and compiled methods as values. In this way, each instance of the class can access them for method binding via its class reference. The class object also encodes the specification of instance variables, that is, their names in Smalltalk (and their types in a statically typed language). A metaclass defines the variables and protocol for its instance, which is a class object, so the class variables are stored in the class object (recall our discussion of the classPool class object variable in section 6.1.3), and the dictionary of class methods resides in the metaclass object. The metaclass object also contains an instance variable this-Class that refers to the corresponding class object. These relationships are diagrammed in Figure 6.4.[35]

All objects follow their class reference to begin a method search, or to access class variables. When a method is invoked, its activation record includes a reference to the receiver. A class method receives a reference to the class object, but it has no reference to any instances of the class. This is why the class method that performs instantiation cannot initialize the newly created object's instance variables directly. The class method is contained in a different object than the instance methods, namely the metaclass object, and its receiver is the class object. The class method has direct access to the class variables through its receiver reference, but it cannot access any instance variables.

6.3.2 Inheritance Among Metaclasses

Metaclass inheritance structure

A metaclass is a class, so it has a superclass from which it inherits state and behavior. When a class message is sent, if a method is not found in the method dictionary in the class's metaclass, the method dictionary in the superclass of that metaclass is searched (just like the method search for instance messages). Since a class inherits the class messages of its superclass, the superclass of a class's meta-

---

[35] We have not shown all the objects that the instance variables refer to. The reason that the superclass references point "up" in the figure will be apparent in the next two figures

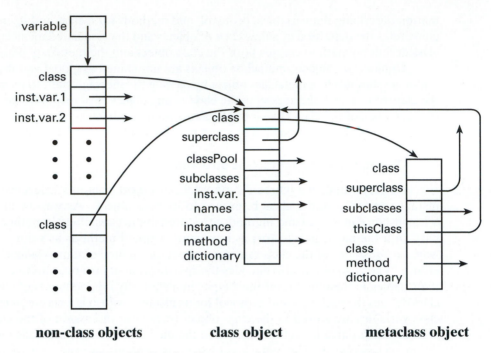

non-class objects   **class object**   **metaclass object**

Figure 6.4 Relationships among objects, classes, and metaclasses.

class must be the metaclass of the class's superclass. For example, Integer super-class is Number, and therefore Integer class superclass is Number class. Consider also uses of super in methods. When an instance method uses super, the starting point for the method search is found by following the superclass reference in the class object of the class that defines the method. A reference to super in a class method must refer to the superclass of that class's metaclass, so that a class method is invoked. That is, to allow inheritance and refinement of class methods by subclasses, the superclass of a metaclass must be the metaclass that corresponds to the superclass of the class.

These considerations imply that the inheritance hierarchy among metaclasses must mirror that among their instances (i.e., among the classes), as illustrated in Figure 6.5.[36] In Figures 6.4 and 6.5, the horizontal axis indicates the class/instance relationship, and the vertical axis in the second and third columns indicates the inheritance relationship. We can imagine that there is an inheritance hierarchy in a vertical plane through the column labeled "class objects", and another that mirrors it exactly through the column labeled "metaclass objects".

For example, in defining DeductibleHistory in section 6.2.1, we refined the class message initialBalance: by sending that message to super. Let us now trace in detail the methods executed in response to the instantiation message Deductible-

---

[36] We will discuss the class reference of the metaclass objects in the next section.

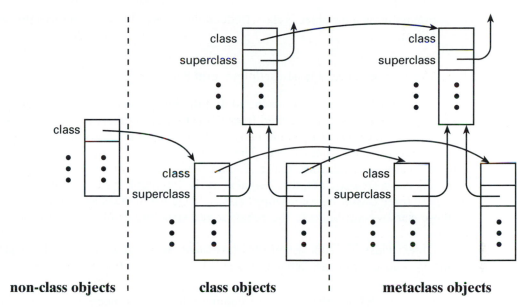

Figure 6.5 Inheritance relationships among classes and metaclasses (subclasses and other variables not shown).

History initialBalance: 500, and the classes in which they are found. We use indentation to indicate that nesting of method invocations.

(1) The class method in the metaclass DeductibleHistory class sends super initial-Balance:, which invokes the initialBalance: class method in its superclass FinancialHistory class.

    (1.1) That method sends super new, which invokes the new method in its superclass Object class.[37] The receiver for the message new is the class object DeductibleHistory, so the method creates an instance of that class and initializes its instance variables to nil.

    (1.2) Next, the initialBalance: method in FinancialHistory sends setInitialBalance: to the new object. The method search begins in the method dictionary of DeductibleHistory (the new object's class), but continues to its superclass FinancialHistory.

        (1.2.1) The method for setInitialBalance: is found, and it initial izes the three inherited instance variables, completing the evaluation of the expression super initialBalance: in the DeductibleHistory method.

(2) The class method then sends the new object initializeDeductions (because it cannot directly access the instance variable), which is found in the method dic-

---

[37] We will see in the next paragraph that Object class inherits the primitive method for new from its ancestor Behavior.

tionary in the new object's class, DeductibleHistory. Finally, it returns the new object.

The classes Class, ClassDescription, **and** Behavior

The metaclass Object class is the root of the hierarchy of metaclasses, and the hierarchy of metaclasses descended from Object class parallels that of the classes descended from Object. Object has no superclass, but Object class does because all classes must descend from Object. Therefore, the hierarchy of metaclasses must ultimately also descend from Object. Rather than implement all of the behavior of class objects in Object class, the designers of the Smalltalk system classes chose to interpose three classes between Object class and Object in the class hierarchy. Each of these classes contributes to the behavior and structure of objects that represent classes.

Object class is a subclass of the class Class, which is a subclass of ClassDescription, whose superclass Behavior is a subclass of Object (see Figure 6.7).

- Behavior defines the state and behavior for class objects that maintain a method dictionary, and can create instances and subclasses.
- ClassDescription adds instance variables for the class's instance variable names and its browser information, and accessors for this information.
- Class adds instance variables for the class name, the classPool of class variables, and the sharedPools of pool variables, and provides the class definition messages.

The protocol of these three classes is specified as a set of instance messages, but those messages are passed to class objects because all of their concrete subclasses are metaclasses. Class is an abstract superclass for all of the metaclasses (i.e., all metaclasses are subclasses, but not instances, of Class). As such, Class and its ancestors ClassDescription, and Behavior define the general protocol and structure of class objects, and each metaclass adds the behavior particular to its instance. We will discuss the classes Class, ClassDescription, and Behavior in detail in section 7.1.3.

6.3.3 The Class Metaclass

As objects, metaclasses are also instances of a class, and that class is also a metaclass since the metaclasses are class objects. However, unlike classes, all metaclasses share the same protocol, namely the message that creates their single instance. Therefore, the metaclass objects are all instances of the same class, namely the system class Metaclass. For any class C, the expression C class class returns Metaclass. Metaclass defines a single instance variable, thisClass, which refers to the metaclass's instance.

Now consider Metaclass class, which is the metaclass of Metaclass. Every metaclass is an instance of Metaclass, so Metaclass class is an instance as well. Because Metaclass is the instance of Metaclass class, this is the point of circularity in the system with respect to class (i.e., "instance of") references. The class/instance relationships among objects, classes, metaclasses, Metaclass and Metaclass class, are illustrated in Figure 6.6.[38]

Metaclass is a subclass of ClassDescription so that the protocol of Behavior and ClassDescription are available for it, but is not a subclass of Class because it has no name or class variables. These considerations result in the class hierarchy diagrammed in Figure 6.7.

To summarize, every object is an instance of a class, and every class is a descendant of Object. Every class object is the single instance of a metaclass (of which there is a single instance), and all metaclasses are subclasses of Class. Every metaclass is an instance of Metaclass, including Metaclass class. The methods of Object support the behavior common to all objects. The methods of Class and its ancestors Behavior and ClassDescription describe the behavior common to those objects that are classes, and the methods of instances of Metaclass add the behavior specific to particular classes.

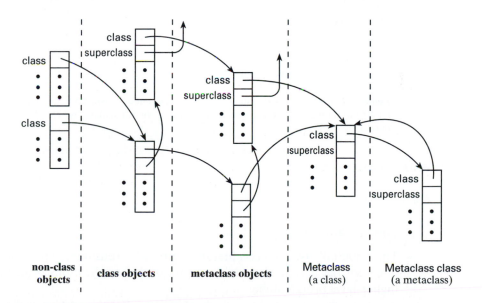

Figure 6.6   Class/instance relatioships with the class Metaclass.

---

[38] Strictly speaking, Metaclass should be in the second column with the "class objects", and Metaclass class should be in the third column with the "metaclass objects".

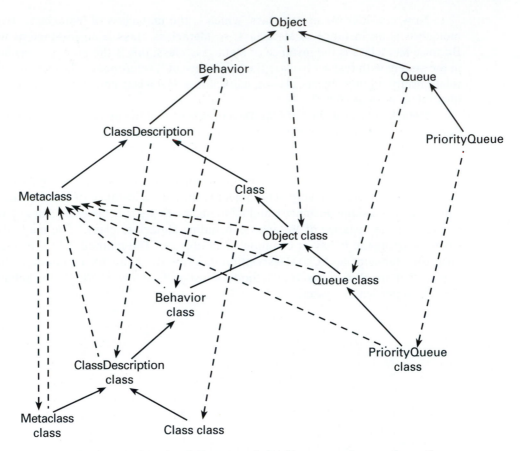

Figure 6.7 Hierarchy and instance relationships among classes and metaclasses (solid lines indicate superclass references and dashed lines indicate class references).

6.4 SUMMARY AND REVIEW

6.4.1 Classes

The system classes

- The Smalltalk system class hierarchy provides reusable, extendible components for the design of models, interfaces, and applications, which facilitate higher-level programming.
- A Smalltalk system has hundreds of "built-in" types, although they are not actually part of the language itself. These include foundation classes, collection classes, classes that provide operating system services, graphic display classes, and application framework classes such as views, controllers, and interaction components.

- The class Object is the root of the class hierarchy, and specifies both class and instance protocol for all objects. It defines default methods for many messages.

- The system classes include a subhierarchy of numeric classes, and classes for booleans, characters, times, and dates, and all have extensive protocols.

- The subhierarchy of collection classes include sets, dictionaries, arrays, strings, and unsorted and sorted lists. The stream classes provide sequential access to collections.

- Several classes support services usually provided by the operating system. These include classes for concurrent processes, process scheduling, inter-process synchronization and communication, memory management, file operations, and communication with hardware devices.

- The class Filename provides extensive instance protocol for manipulating files and directories, and for accessing files via streams. It also defines class variables that maintain global file system information.

- The user can start applications and programming tools, perform file operations, set timers, store and evaluate scripts, and so on by evaluating message expressions in a text window.

- The implementation of the language is also defined in terms of classes, such as those for parsers, compilers, compiled methods, and activation records.

- The system class library includes many classes that support the model-view-controller paradigm for interactive application design. An instance of ScheduledWindow includes references to its model, its controller, and a hierarchy of instances of visual component classes that make up that portion of the application's interface.

- Visual components can be images, views that respond to user input and changes in the model, or composite components that contain other components. Example view classes include pushbuttons, text fields, scrollable lists, scrollable text editors, menus, and dialogs. We instantiate, compose, and subclass these classes to create an application's interface.

- Controller classes handle user input events and provide popup menus, and a controller is associated with each interactive view. The application designer can extend system controllers by modifying their methods, or by creating subclasses.

- Any object can be the model for a view, so support for the connection between a model and its views is provided by the class Object. A view can be registered as a dependent of a model object so that the view is informed automatically whenever the model changes state.

- Many Smalltalk systems provide an abstract class that represents a generic application, from which we derive application classes. This class maintains an application's model objects, state information, and references to its views.

- The system class library defines classes for two-dimensional raster graphic objects and operations, but the details of the graphics classes vary among implementations. There are classes for canvases on which we can draw, including both windows and pixmaps in memory. Points and rectangles are represented by classes with extensive protocols for graphic computations.

- Smalltalk-80 defines the class Form for images, the class Bitblt for drawing operations and their parameters, classes such as Line and Arc for graphic objects, and the class Pen for painting on one form with another.

- VisualWorks defines classes for display surfaces, pixmaps, and masks, and encapsulates drawing attributes and operations in a graphics context object. VisualWorks also supports color and includes classes for color values, palettes, and patterns, and defines a subhierarchy for geometric objects.

Class and method definition

- As all operations are message sends, the class designer can provide a complete set of services for a class, and class instances are first-class.

- Class definition is performed by a message send, so the language does not need a type constructor construct. Defining a new class creates a class object that represents the class, and adds the class name to the set of global variables. Class names are visible throughout the system, and must be capitalized.

- We define new classes and methods and modify existing classes and methods using the system browser. To do so, select the class's category, edit and accept the class definition message, create class and instance message categories, and code the methods.

- The interface of a class is described by a set of *message patterns*, each of which gives a message's selector and parameter names, and is organized by message categories.

- *Named instance variables* are listed in the class definition message, and must begin with a lowercase letter. They are accessible in the methods of the class and its subclasses, and are only accessible to clients if its class defines accessor messages. An instance variable name refers to that variable in the receiver of the method.

- *Indexed instance variables* are an array of instance variables embedded within an object, and the message variableSubclass:... defines a class with indexed instance variables. Each instance of the class can have a different number of variables, but the number is fixed when the object is created with the class message new:. Indexed instance variables are numbered beginning with 1, and are accessed with the messages at: and at:put:.

- A method definition consists of a message pattern, a comment, a list of local variables enclosed in vertical bars, and a series of message expressions.

- A *return expression* is indicated by or ∧, and gives the object the method returns. Evaluation of a return expression terminates execution of the method.

- A method's parameters and local variables exist for a method invocation, and their names are local to the method. Parameters cannot appear on the left side of an assignment.

- We use the message category private for messages that should only be invoked within the methods of the class. The language does not enforce this.

- The Smalltalk virtual machine defines several hundred *primitive methods*, and all methods are ultimately defined in terms of these operations.

- The pseudo-variable self refers to the receiver of the method, and can appear as a receiver or argument of a message expression, but not on the left side of an assignment.

The class object

- In traditional languages, the type object is a structure the compiler uses for performing type checking and determining type attributes. In Smalltalk, the *class object* that represents a class is an object with state and behavior that exists at execution time, and is the referent of the global variable whose name is the class name. Its protocol consists of the class's class messages, and its instance variables are the class's class variables.

- Class objects are first-class: a class object can be the referent of a variable or the receiver or argument of a message expression, and we create a class object like any other object, by a message expression. Class objects are distinguished from non-class objects by their ability to create instances and subclasses.

- Each object responds to the message class by returning a reference to its class object.

- *Class variables* maintain information related to the class as a whole, and type information for the class. The class variable names are given as the classVariableNames: argument in the class definition message, and must begin with a capital letter. Class variables are accessible in the class and instance methods of the class and its descendants, but not elsewhere.

- *Class messages* provide access to information stored in class variables, and are sent to the class object, not to its instances. By convention, class variables are initialized by the class message initialize, which we must define and send to the class object before using the class. Class methods do not have access to the class's instance variables because the class object is the receiver.

- We instantiate a class by sending the class object an instance creation message. The class Object defines the messages new and new:, which initialize the new object's instance variables to nil. A class can override these messages, and can define descriptive instance creation messages that take arguments providing initialization for the new object. Objects can also be created by an instance message whose method invokes a class message.

- We cannot code initialization of a new object's instance variables in the instance creation method because it is a class message and the class object is the receiver. We define an instance message that performs the initialization (which is usually private), and the class method sends this message to the new object.

- The class object also maintains type information for the class, such as its super-class and subclasses, its method dictionary, and the information in the class definition. The class Object defines numerous class messages for accessing, testing, adding, removing, and enumerating this information. The compiler, the method binding process, and programming tools use this protocol, and we can use it to examine classes. To avoid hard-coded type dependencies, applications rarely use these messages.

6.4.2 Inheritance

Subclass definition

- Every class except Object has a single superclass, and the class hierarchy is a tree with Object as the root.
- A class definition specifies how the state and behavior of its instances differ from those of its superclass's instances. A class inherits the instance and class protocol of its superclass, and can add messages and refine methods. It inherits the instance variables of its ancestors and inherits access to its ancestor's class and pool variables, and can add instance and class variables.

The pseudo-variables self and super

- The method search for a message to self begins in the class of the receiver, even if the expression occurs in an inherited ancestor method. An ancestor method can use a message to self to invoke the class-specific behavior of the actual receiver.
- A method should use the expression self class rather than its class name, so that the receiver's class is used if the class has descendants whose instances use that method.
- To invoke a superclass method for refinement, we use the pseudo-variable super as the receiver of the message. Like self, super refers to the receiver of the method. The method search begins in the superclass of the class of the method, which may not be the superclass of the actual receiver's class, and continues up the chain of superclasses.
- We cannot use super as an argument or on the left side of an assignment.

Subclass semantics

- We use the method ^self shouldNotImplement to override an inherited method that is not appropriate for the class, that is, for restriction.
- We use the method ^self subclassResponsibility for deferred methods in abstract classes. Smalltalk does not prevent instantiation of abstract classes. However, if an object receives an abstract message that its class does not

define (either because its class is abstract or the designer forgot to implement the message), the subclassResponsibility method displays an error notifier.

- There are several abstract classes among the system classes (such as Magnitude, Number, and Collection) that use the message subclassResponsibility.

6.4.3 Metaclasses

The class/instance relationship

- Each class object is an instance of a *metaclass* that defines its state and behavior, and the class reference of a class object points to its metaclass object.
- Each class is an instance of its own metaclass so that each class object can have its own protocol, and each metaclass has a single instance. The class definition method creates both the class object and the metaclass.
- Metaclasses are unnamed, but we can obtain a reference to one by passing the message class to the corresponding class object.

Inheritance among metaclasses

- Like all classes, a metaclass has a superclass. To obtain the correct behavior for the method search for class messages and refinement of class methods, the superclass of a metaclass is the metaclass of the class's superclass.
- The metaclass Object class is the root of the hierarchy of metaclasses, and is a subclass of Class, which is a subclass of ClassDescription, which is a subclass of Behavior, a subclass of Object. The abstract classes Class, ClassDescription, and Behavior define state and behavior for all class objects. Each metaclass adds the behavior specific to the corresponding class.

The class Metaclass

- All metaclasses are instances of the system class Metaclass, which is a subclass of ClassDescription. This includes Metaclass class since Metaclass is a class object.

6.5 EXERCISES

6.1 **(a)** What characteristics do the Smalltalk system classes have in common with built-in types in a traditional language?

(b) In what ways do the Smalltalk system classes differ from built-in types in a traditional language?

6.2 Browse the class Filename on your Smalltalk system to determine how to write expressions that perform each of the following operations:

(a) return the directory containing a file

(b) list the files in a directory

(c) list the size and creation and modification dates for a file

(d) rename a file

(e) return the total number of files in all the subdirectories of a directory

6.3 Define a global variable that refers to a scheduled window. (You may have to define a subclass of ScheduledWindow because its instance creation messages do not return a reference to the new window.) Use it to experiment with the drawing protocol on your system.

6.4 Why do we say that instances of programmer-defined classes are first-class in Smalltalk?

6.5 Describe the process of defining a class in Smalltalk. How does it differ from writing a program in C?

6.6 Define a *protocol browser* programming tool using the facilities of your Smalltalk system. Its interface contains two toggle buttons, a list view, and a text view (choose your own layout). The toggle buttons permit choice of class or instance messages, and the list view displays the message categories for that choice. When a category name is selected in the list view, the text view displays the message patterns and comments for that category. Provide an operation for saving the class interface to a text file. To compose the string for the text view, use a stream with the messages nextPut: and nextPutAll: as illustrated in the Queue method for printOn:, then use the stream message contents to obtain the resulting string. You may assume that all methods begin with a one-line message pattern followed by a comment. Use the system browser to find the other classes and methods you need.

6.7 The messages for all methods in Smalltalk are publicly visible. Give two examples of situations in which the inability to hide a method is undesirable.

6.8 Using your system browser, make a list of the primitive methods invoked by instance methods in the class Object.

6.9 Why are the methods for =, printOn:, and copy that the class Queue in section 6.1.2 inherits from Object inadequate?

6.10 **(a)** Define the private message do: for the class Queue in section 6.1.2, and recode its copy and printOn: methods using this message.

(b) Why doesn't the message do: help in coding the Queue method for =? Can you see how a stream on a queue would solve the problem?

6.11 Define a class List that has the same linked list storage structure and auxiliary class Node as the class Queue in section 6.1.2.

(a) Define the accessing messages size, first, last, at:, and indexOf:.

(b) Define the testing and comparing messages includes:, isEmpty, isSublist:, and =.

(c) Define the adding and removing messages addFirst:, addLast:, addAllFirst:, addAllLast:, add:after:, add:before:, remove:, removeFirst, removeLast, removeAt:, removeAll, and at:put:. You may wish to define private methods to aid in coding these methods.

(d) Define the copying messages copy, copyReverse, and copyFrom:to:.

(e) Define the enumerating messages do:, collect:, and select:.

6.12 **(a)** Define the copy and printOn: methods for the class FinancialHistory in section 6.1.2.

(b) If we want to define an = method for FinancialHistory, what assumption must we make about a system class? Use your system browser to determine whether this assumption is true.

6.13 **(a)** Why do we say that class objects are first-class in Smalltalk?

(b) Give two operations that are possible due to this feature that are not possible without it.

6.14 List the four different kinds of messages to class objects.

6.15 Explain why we must code instantiation and initialization of a new object separately in Smalltalk.

6.16 **(a)** Write a Smalltalk expression that returns a list of the descendants of the class Magnitude that do not define the message =.

(b) Write a Smalltalk expression that returns a list of the descendants of the class Magnitude that define indexed instance variables.

6.17 **(a)** In what sense does a subclass inherit its ancestors' instance variables?

(b) In what sense does a subclass inherit its ancestors' class variables?

6.18 What happens on your Smalltalk system when you attempt to define a class with a class variable whose name is the same as a class variable defined in an ancestor?

6.19 Define the copy and printOn: methods for the class DeductibleHistory in section 6.2.1.

6.20 Why does the use of self permit us to code more generic methods?

6.21 **(a)** Explain why the super construct is necessary in Smalltalk.

(b) Precisely describe the actions taken by the Smalltalk interpreter when it encounters the expression super *aMessage* in evaluating a method.

6.22 Can the expressions self message and super message within the same method ever invoke the same method?

6.23 Suppose that the pseudo-variable super referred to the superclass of the receiver.

(a) Could a meaningless messaging situation result?

(b) Explain why this results in incorrect semantics for refinement.

6.24 In a method with a local variable var, which of the following assignments are valid? Explain your answer for each.

(a) var := self

(b) self := var

(c) var := super

6.25 Consider the following Smalltalk classes:

classname: Grandma	classname: Mom	classname: Me
superclass: Object	superclass: Grandma	superclass: Mom
instance methods:	instance methods:	instance methods:
who ∧'grandma'	who ∧'mom'	who ∧'me'
whom ∧self who	why ∧'why me'	why ∧self whom
	where ∧self why	how ∧super whom
	what ∧super who	

Indicate which messages are sent and what value is returned for each of the following message expressions:

(a) Me new why

(b) Me new where

(c) Me new what

(d) Me new how

6.26 Define a Smalltalk class MonitoredArray as a subclass of Array that keeps track of how many times each element of the monitored array is accessed. Its protocol consists of the instance message countAt:, as well as the Array class message new: and instance messages at: and at:put:. When an element is replaced, its counter is reset.

6.27 The system class Time represents immutable time values. That is, when an instance receives addTime: or subtractTime:, it creates a new object rather than modifying itself. The protocol of Time also includes the instance creation messages fromSeconds: and now, the accessors hours, minutes, and seconds, the comparing messages < and =, and the printing message printOn:. We wish to define a class Clock that represents a timer that might be used to keep track of the elapsed time in a simulation. It is set to 0 by the message reset, its value is incremented modulo 86400 by the message tick, and addTime: and subtractTime: affect the receiver rather than creating a new object. Instances of Clock respond to all other messages with the behavior defined in Time.

(a) Define the class Clock as a subclass of Time.

(b) Define the class Clock with a Time instance variable.

(c) Which of these definitions of Clock do you prefer, and why?

6.28 Define a subclass of the class Clock defined in exercise 6.27 called AlarmClock, which also maintains a set of alarms. Each alarm is represented by a Time object indicating the time at which the alarm should occur and a block to be evaluated when the Alarm-Clock reaches that time (e.g., due to receiving a tick message). Like a Time or Clock object, an instance is created with the class messages fromSeconds: and now, and a new object has an empty alarm list. We add and delete alarms with the messages addAlarm: aBlock: at: aTime and removeAlarmAt: aTime. If the alarm clock's timer value is changed with reset, addTime:, or subtractTime:, only the alarm at the resulting time is executed (if any). (Hint: You may use either a dictionary or two priority queues for the alarms.)

6.29 Define a Smalltalk class BudgetHistory, which keeps track of a budget giving the maximum that should be spent for each reason, as a subclass of the class FinancialHistory defined in section 6.1.2. The class BudgetHistory has the same instance creation messages as its superclass. We set the budget entry for some reason with the instance message budget: amount for: reason, and access it with budgetFor: reason. The message totalBudget returns the total budget. If a particular spend:for: message causes the total amount spent for that reason to exceed the stated budget, notify the user and ask whether to proceed with that transaction. (If there is no budget entry for that reason, the user is also queried.) To query the user, use the message Dialog confirm: aString, which displays a dialog box containing the string argument and buttons for "yes" and "no", and returns true or false depending on the user's choice.

6.30 Define a class FilledRectangle as a subclass of Rectangle that also maintains an instance variable paint whose value is a color or pattern used to fill the rectangle when it is drawn. Recall that Rectangle defines an instance creation message origin:corner: that takes two points and sets its origin and corner instance variables to the arguments.

(a) Define the class FilledRectangle, its instance creation message origin:corner:paint:, and accessor messages for the paint instance variable.

(b) Some Rectangle messages return a new rectangle, and we would like instances of FilledRectangle to return a new filled rectangle with the same paint as the receiver for those messages. For example, code the FilledRectangle method for intersect:, which returns the intersection of the receiver and the argument rectangle. What assumption must we make about the Rectangle method for intersect:?

6.31 Suppose we want to allow a client of PriorityQueue to change the comparison block of an existing priority queue (and, of course, reorder the elements in the queue). Code the method for the message compareBlock:.

6.32 How can we factor out the common code in the Queue and PriorityQueue methods for copy, rather than repeating it in both methods?

6.33 Using your Smalltalk system, browse the senders of shouldNotImplement. For as many of those classes as possible, explain why that class is a subclass of its superclass.

6.34 How can we tell if a Smalltalk class is abstract? (Think carefully.)

6.35 The class Queue in section 6.1.2 and the class List in exercise 6.11 have the same storage structure and similar protocols.

(a) Should one of these classes be a subclass of the other? (Consider both possibilities.)

(b) Should we define an abstract class of which they are both subclasses?

6.36 **(a)** What is a metaclass?

(b) How do we refer to a metaclass?

(c) Why does the inheritance hierarchy among metaclasses mirror that among classes?

(d) Why are all metaclasses instances of a single class?

7

Foundation Classes

In this chapter and the next, we will cover the foundation and collection classes in the Smalltalk class library in detail. These classes represent objects with which you are familiar, and are general-purpose classes useful in any application. They also illustrate a number of important points about the structure of the system, and the use of object paradigm concepts such as composition, inheritance, abstract classes, and dynamic binding. We have already discussed the class BlockClosure, and the classes that support concurrency (Process, Semaphore, ProcessorScheduler, and so on) in section 5.5. We described the functionality of the programming tool classes such as TextCollectorView, Browser, Notifier, Inspector, and Debugger in section 5.6. In section 6.1.1, we surveyed the classes for operating system services, the language and system implementation, the application framework, user interface components, and graphics (but as they vary among dialects of Smalltalk, we do not have space to examine them in detail). In Chapter 8, we will discuss the collection and stream classes.

In presenting each system class, we will describe both its interface and implementation, and will group the messages in its protocol according to browser categories. The best way to learn about the system classes and their implementation is to browse through them and experiment with them on a Smalltalk system. Unfortunately, the details of even these basic classes vary among implementations. You may find additional dialect-specific messages, instance variables, and classes on your system.

This chapter covers the following topics:

- the instance protocol of the class Object, the root of the class hierarchy (7.1.1 and 7.1.2)
- the classes that define the common protocol of class objects, Behavior, Class-Description, and Class (7.1.3)
- the classes UndefinedObject (7.2.1) and Boolean (7.2.2)
- the abstract class Magnitude that defines ordering protocol (7.3.1)
- the classes Character (7.3.2), Date (7.3.3), and Time (7.3.4)
- the characteristics of numeric objects (7.4.1), and the abstract class Number (7.4.2)
- the integer classes (7.4.3), the class Fraction (7.4.4), and the class Float (7.4.5)
- two techniques for implementing mixed-class arithmetic (7.4.6)
- the VisualWorks numeric classes, including ArithmeticValue, Double, Complex, and FixedPoint (7.4.7)
- the class Point (7.5.1)
- the class Rectangle (7.5.2).

7.1 THE CLASS Object

7.1.1 Definition

The class Object is the only class that does not have a superclass. It is defined as a subclass of nil since that object represents a null reference.

```
"definition of the class Object"
nil subclass: #Object
    instanceVariableNames: ''
    classVariableNames: 'Dependents'
    poolDictionaries: ''
    category: 'Kernel-Objects'
```

Object is an abstract class because it defines no instance variables. We will discuss the class variable Dependents in the next section.

7.1.2 Instance Protocol

Purpose

Because all classes are descendants of the system class Object, all objects respond to its protocol. Although it is an abstract class, Object defines many methods that provide the default behavior for the corresponding messages. In each class,

Object's method may be inherited, replaced, or refined, as we discussed with respect to the class Queue in section 6.1.2.

Copying, comparing, and testing protocols

In section 5.4.2, we discussed Object's *copying* protocol, which consists of the messages copy, shallowCopy, and deepCopy. The method for shallowCopy uses the system primitive messages discussed at the end of this section. It creates a new instance of the receiver's class using self class basicNew:, then copies the receiver's instance variable references to the new object using basicAt: and basicAt:put:.[1] copy is implemented as shallowCopy in Object, and should be redefined in classes for which this behavior is not appropriate. Classes whose instances must not be copied override copy to produce an error message. deepCopy can be implemented recursively, and must be designed as a graph search to avoid infinite recursion and duplicating shared subobjects.[2]

Section 5.4.2 also covered the *comparing* protocol of Object, which includes the identity tests == and ~~, and the equality tests = and ~=. The message == should never be overridden, and each class should redefine = to reflect what it means for its instances to have equal values. Object's method for == invokes a primitive method, and the default method for = in Object uses ==. The Object methods for ~~ and ~= are coded in terms of == and =.

The comparing protocol of Object also includes the message hash, which is used in the methods of the classes Set and Dictionary that implement search structures using hashing. All objects respond to hash with a small integer, and two objects that are equal according to = must return the same hash value. A class that overrides = must also define hash such that this property holds. hash is implemented by a primitive method in Object. Object also defines a message identity-Hash, which returns a hash code unique to the object itself for "identity sets" and "identity dictionaries" that use identity tests rather than equality tests to find elements (see sections 8.2.1 and 8.2.3). identityHash calls the same primitive method as hash, and should not be overridden.

The *testing* protocol of Object includes the messages isNil and notNil, whose methods in Object return false and true, respectively. isNil and notNil are overridden in the class UndefinedObject (the class of nil) to return true and false, respectively. Object also defines the testing messages isInteger, isString, isSymbol, and isBehavior (which returns true if the receiver is a class object), each of which returns false in Object. Each message is then overridden to return true in the appropriate class, and the method search selects the correct response.

---

[1] Some Smalltalk systems define a primitive method for shallowCopy for efficiency.

[2] VisualWorks no longer supports the message deepCopy. Instead, copy is implemented as ^self shallowCopy postCopy, and classes for which shallowCopy is inadequate refine the message postCopy. postCopy is defined as ^self in Object.

Class membership protocol

We saw in section 6.1.3 that every object responds to the message class by returning a reference to its class object. This message is implemented as a primitive method invocation in Object. The *class membership* protocol of Object also includes the message isMemberOf:, which returns true if the argument is the receiver's class object, or false if it is not. The message isKindOf: returns true if the argument is the receiver's class object or one of its ancestors. For example, 3.0 isKindOf: Number returns true, but 3.0 isMemberOf: Number returns false. The message respondsTo: returns true if the symbol argument is a message selector in the receiver's protocol, whether defined in its class or an ancestor. For example, anObject respondsTo: #class is always true. The methods for these three messages send type information messages to self class (see the next section).

Error handling protocol

The methods for Object's *error handling* protocol report errors to the user with notifiers, as described in section 5.6.4. We discussed the general message error:, whose argument is a string displayed as the title of a notifier window, in section 6.2.3. Numerous methods in the system classes indicate an invalid argument value or type or other error conditions by sending the message self error: with a string argument describing the problem. The programmer can also use this message to report run-time errors.

The error handling protocol includes several messages we have already discussed, including

- doesNotUnderstand: for a message not in the receiver's protocol (section 5.4.1)

- shouldNotImplement for restrictive inheritance (section 6.2.3)

- subclassResponsibility for deferred methods (section 6.2.3)

- nonIntegerIndexError: and subscriptBoundsError:, whose argument was an invalid index for an at: or at:put: message (section 6.1.2).

The error handling protocol also includes notFoundError, which indicates that an element was not found in the receiver collection, and primitiveFailed, which opens a notifier if a primitive method cannot be executed and the method that called it supplies no code for such a case. Like error:, these messages are usually sent to self. The methods for these messages send the message self error: with a string argument describing the error.

Object also defines error handling protocol for use with the programming environment, especially for debugging. In section 5.6.4, we discussed the messages

- inspect, which creates an inspector window for examining the receiver's instance variable referents[3]
- halt and halt:, which suspend the process and open a notifier (permitting creation of a debugger)
- browse, which opens a browser on the receiver's class.

Object also defines the message notify:, which opens a notifier displaying the argument string. Like the error handling messages, the messages halt, halt:, and notify: are usually sent to self.

Systems such as VisualWorks and IBM Smalltalk that support exceptions use the exception handling mechanism for error notification. For example, in Visual-Works, the class Object defines signals such as ErrorSignal, HaltSignal, and IndexNot-FoundSignal as class variables. The methods for messages such as error:, halt, and at: raise those signals if they detect an error. If the resulting exception is not handled within the application, then a notifier is displayed.

Accessing protocol for indexed instance variables

The protocol of Object includes the *accessing* messages for indexed instance variables and their number discussed in section 6.1.2, namely at:, at:put:, and size. Object defines these messages because there is no single ancestor for classes that contain indexed instance variables, which could define them.[4]

The accessing protocol also contains the system messages basicAt:, basicAt:put:, and basicSize. Smalltalk supports both sets of messages so that we can implement a class using indexed instance variables, but override the behavior of at:, at:put:, and size (e.g., to disallow them by defining them as ^self shouldNotImplement). Similarly, all collection classes override size to return the number of elements. The class's methods can then use the messages basicAt:, basicAt:put:, and basicSize to access the receiver's variables or physical size. The methods for the six accessing messages call primitive methods (e.g., at: and basicAt: call the same primitive method), and send error handling messages if the primitive operation fails due to an invalid index argument.

As we saw in section 5.3.2, the accessing message yourself answers the receiver.

Printing protocol

Messages in the *printing* protocol of Object return a sequence of characters that represents the receiver and that can be displayed, printed, or stored in a file. As we discussed in section 6.1.2, the message printOn: appends a string describing the receiver to the argument stream. This typically consists of its class name and instance variable values in some readable format. The default implementation for

---

[3] The messages inspect and browse are in the "user interface" protocol category in VisualWorks.

[4] The fact that a class has indexed instance variables is indicated by a bit in a variable format, one of whose fields gives the number of named instance variables.

printOn: in Object returns 'a' or 'an' followed by the receiver's class name, since Object does not know the meaning of the class's instance variables.

```
"instance method for class Object"
printOn: aStream
    "Append a sequence of characters that describes the receiver to aStream."

aStream nextPutAll:
    ((self class name at: 1) isVowel ifTrue: ['an '] ifFalse: ['a ']).
self class printOn: aStream
```

The class designer should re-implement printOn: with class-specific display behavior, as we did for the class Queue in section 6.1.2.

For convenience, Object also defines the message printString, which returns the string that describes the receiver. For example, you can send printString to a number to convert it to a string. Its method creates a stream, sends the receiver printOn: to append the descriptive string to the stream, then converts the stream to a string and returns it.

```
"instance method for class Object"
printString
    "Answer a string whose characters are a description of the receiver."

| aStream |
aStream := WriteStream on: (String new: 16).
self printOn: aStream.
^aStream contents
```

A class need only define printOn: and its instances can then respond to printString as well. Both the workspace print it command and the inspector text view use the message printString, so defining printOn: also obtains the correct behavior for these operations.

The protocol of Object distinguishes between messages that "print" an object for presentation to a human, and those that "store" a series of expressions that can be evaluated to reconstruct the object. The message storeOn: appends a string consisting of such a representation to its argument stream. For example,

```
"printing and storing messages"
| aSet |
aSet := Set with: 1 with: 2 with: 3.     "creates a set with the given elements"
aSet printString.                        "returns 'Set(1 2 3)'"
aSet storeString                         "returns '((Set new) add: 1; add: 2; yourself)'"
```

Usually, the expression storeOn: returns is evaluated to create an object by sending the class message readFrom: aStream. The storeOn: method in Object returns an expression that sends basicNew to the receiver's class object (or basicNew: if it contains indexed instance variables), followed by a series of system primitive messages that create and store each instance variable value directly in the object's representation. Like printOn:, a class should re-implement storeOn: if it requires different behavior or if it defines an instantiation message that storeOn: should use. The message storeString returns a string consisting of a sequence of expressions to be evaluated to recreate the receiver. Its method sends storeOn: to the receiver, similar to the definition of printString given in terms of printOn:.

The printing message isLiteral returns whether the receiver has a literal representation known to the parser. Its method returns false in Object, but returns true in the classes Character, String, Symbol, Boolean (actually, as we will see, in True and False), Array, ByteArray, UndefinedObject, Float, and the integer classes. Each of these classes overrides printOn: and storeOn: to use its literal format.

Dependency protocols

The protocol of Object includes four message categories that support dependency relationships among objects, so that the designer can coordinate the interactions among the objects that make up an application. These messages allow us to associate a number of *dependent* objects with a *sponsor* object, and notify them automatically if the state of the sponsor changes. The sponsor object informs itself of an event with a "changing" message, and that method signals the sponsor's dependent objects with an "updating" message, as illustrated in Figure 7.1. The argument aSymbol in Figure 7.1 indicates what kind of change occurred. As we saw in section 6.1.1, these dependencies are essential to the model-view-controller paradigm because they provide a mechanism that notifies view objects when the corresponding model object is updated (possibly through the controller for a different view). The dependency protocols are defined in Object because any object can be a model (unlike a view or controller). They are also useful in creating simulations that mirror dependencies in the problem domain.

The *dependents access* protocol of Object includes three messages. The messages addDependent: and removeDependent: add the argument to or remove the argument from the receiver's collection of dependents, and the message dependents returns an ordered collection of the receiver's dependents. For example in Visual-Works, the method for model: in the class ScheduledWindow sets the receiver's

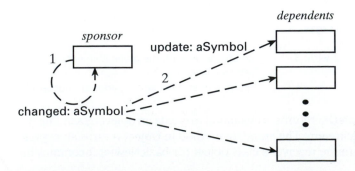

Figure 7.1 A sponsor sends itself changed:, and it dependents receive update: messages.

model to the argument, and also adds the receiver window as a dependent of that object. Object's *initialize-release* protocol contains the message release, which removes all the receiver's dependents. The dependency relationships are stored in a class variable of Object called Dependents, which is an identity dictionary. Each key in the dictionary is an object with dependents, and the associated value is an ordered collection of that object's dependents. The methods for these messages access and manipulate Dependents.

Messages in Object's *changing* protocol indicate that the receiver has changed, and an object sends one of these messages to self to inform its dependents of a change in state. For example, a model object sends itself a changing message to notify its views that they must be updated. This protocol defines the messages changed and changed:, whose argument is a symbol indicating the nature of the change. The message changed:with: allows the sponsor to pass an object to its dependents as the second argument. The messages changeRequest and changeRequest: indicate that the receiver wants to change, but must check with all dependents to make sure that it is valid to do so. The changing message broadcast: sends the argument symbol as a unary message to all of the receiver's dependents. broadcast:with: sends a keyword message with its first argument as the keyword and its second as the argument. The Object methods for the changing messages do not need to be overridden.

The methods for the changing messages notify the receiver's dependents by sending each a message in Object's updating protocol, which consists of the messages update:, update:with:, updateRequest, updateRequest:, performUpdate:, and performUpdate:with:. Figure 7.2 illustrates the correspondence between changing and updating messages. The arguments of an updating message are the arguments of the corresponding changing message. The default methods in Object for update: and update:with: do nothing (i.e., ^self). The default behavior defined in Object for updateRequest and updateRequest: is to grant the request (i.e., ^true). The messages performUpdate: and performUpdate:with: are implemented using the messages described in the next subsection.

To complete the dependency relationship, a dependent's class must implement the updating messages with the response to a change in the receiver's sponsor. For example, a class ListView might define a method for update: that changes the list the receiver displays if the argument is #list, or changes which item is selected if the

changing message from sponsor to itself	updating message sent to dependents
changed	update: nil
changed: aSymbol	update: aSymbol
changed: aSymbol with: anObject	update: aSymbol with: anObject
changeRequest	updateRequest
changeRequest: aSymbol	updateRequest: aSymbol
broadcast: aSymbol	performUpdate: aSymbol
broadcast: aSymbol with: anObject	performUpdate: aSymbol with: anObject

Figure 7.2   The correspondence between changing and updating messages.

argument is #listIndex. To trigger the first action, a model would send self changed: #list, and the method for changed: in Object would send update: #list to the model's dependents. Note that a dependent object does not know which objects its current sponsors are, but it does know how to respond to any changes in a sponsor, as defined by its class's updating methods.

Message handling protocol

Sometimes it is necessary to determine the selector for a particular message send at execution time. For example, a class ActionButtonView can define the behavior of its instances in response to its controller, but each pushbutton needs to send a different message to its model when the user activates it. An instance can maintain its message selector in an instance variable, say theMessage, but its method cannot just send the message model theMessage, because this sends the message with selector theMessage to model.

For such indirect invocations, Object defines *message handling* protocol. The message perform: takes a symbol argument that identifies a unary message, and its method sends that message to the receiver. The messages perform:with:, perform:with:with:, perform:with:with:with:, and perform:withArguments: allow the sender to pass arguments for an indirect invocation of a keyword message. For example, the method in Object for performUpdate:with: is defined as follows:

```
"instance method for class Object"
performUpdate: aSymbol with: anObject
    "Send the argument symbol as a keyword message with anObject as the receiver."

    self perform: aSymbol with: anObject
```

We will see another example of the use of perform:with: in section 7.4.6. The message handling messages are implemented by primitive methods.

System primitives protocol

Because the Smalltalk compiler, interpreter, execution environment, and programming tools are written in Smalltalk, the class Object includes *system primitives* protocol that supports direct access to an object's representation. These messages are implemented as primitive methods. Use of these messages by applications is strongly discouraged and violates the encapsulation of the system.

The messages instVarAt: and instVarAt:put: access the receiver's named instance variables by their position in the object's storage structure. (Instance variables are stored in the order given in the class definition message.) The message nextInstance returns the next instance after the receiver in the list of instances of its class. The message nextObject returns the next object after the receiver in the list of non-unique objects in the system. The messages basicAt:, basicAt:put:, and basic-

Size described previously in this section and the messages basicNew and basicNew: discussed in the next section have similar semantics. These messages provide direct access to the indexed instance variables of any object that has them.

Instances of variable-size classes that maintain their elements in instance variables, such as Set and OrderedCollection, might need to "grow" upon insertion of an element. This growth could be implemented by instantiating a new larger instance and copying the current elements to it, leaving the old instance to be deallocated. However, an instance referred to by more than one object may need to change size while preserving these references, and an assignment to self is not allowed. The system primitives message become: causes all references to the receiver to refer to the argument and vice versa, by swapping the "object pointers" through which all references to the objects are centralized. Their lists of dependents are also swapped. When a collection must grow in size and preserve references to itself, its method constructs a new larger object and sends self become: with the new object as the argument. The method for become: calls a primitive method to swap the object pointers of the receiver and argument, then swaps their collections of dependents.

7.1.3 Class Protocol

Purpose

All classes are descendants of Object, so all class objects respond to the class protocol of Object. In section 6.1.3, we saw that the protocol of class objects includes instance creation messages, the subclass creation message, type information messages, and accessors and initialization for class-specific information. (The class protocol of Object defines the first three kinds of class messages). We also mentioned in section 6.1.3 that the class object maintains type information needed by the translator and execution environment, such as the method dictionary and class hierarchy relationships. Recall also that type information messages are rarely used in applications, but are supported for the language implementation and programming tools, and to provide a query language for examining classes.

As we discussed in section 6.3.2, the classes Behavior, ClassDescription, and Class are ancestors of Object class, the metaclass of Object. These three classes define most of Object's type information class protocol and the corresponding instance variables. Note that the protocol of these three classes is listed as instance protocol, but those messages will be sent to class objects because the classes are ancestors of the root of the metaclass hierarchy (recall Figure 6.7).

The class Behavior

The system class Behavior is an abstract class that defines the basic state and behavior for class objects. Its protocol supports messages for creating instances, using type information, and compiling code. Behavior is a direct subclass of Object, and is defined as follows:

```
"definition of the class Behavior"
Object subclass: #Behavior
   instanceVariableNames: 'superclass subclasses methodDict format'
   classVariableNames: ''
   poolDictionaries: ''
   category: 'Kernel-Classes'
```

The instance variables defined in Behavior maintain the class's superclass, a list of its subclasses, its method dictionary, and a format code that indicates the number of named instance variables and whether the class has indexed instance variables. A MethodDictionary is a subclass of IdentityDictionary that uses the selector symbols as keys and instances of CompiledMethod as values (as discussed in section 6.1.1). Additional state information for class objects is defined in ClassDescription and Class.

The *instance creation* protocol of Behavior defines the basic instantiation messages new and new: for classes without and with indexed instance variables, respectively. A class for which there is a default initialization can refine new so that all instances have a valid value, as we did for the class PriorityQueue in section 6.2.2. Similarly, a class can disallow the message new if instances should only be created via a class-specific instantiation message that includes initialization arguments. The instance creation protocol also includes the system messages basicNew and basic-New:, which classes should not override (like basicAt: and so on in the previous section). All four messages are implemented by methods that call primitive methods, and send error messages if the receiver is not a class or is the wrong kind of class, or if the argument to new: or basicNew: is not an integer. For example, Behavior implements new as follows:

```
"instance method for class Behavior"
new
   "Answer a new instance of the receiver.  If the receiver is a class with indexed
   instance variables, allocate zero variables."

   <primitive: 70>
   self isVariable ifTrue: [^self new: 0].
   self primitiveFailed
```

The *copying* protocol of Behavior overrides shallowCopy and deepCopy to return the receiver, in order to prevent copying class objects.

The protocol of Behavior includes messages for manipulating and testing the type information in a class object. We will list several representative messages, organized by browser categories. Behavior's *testing* protocol returns information about the structure of the receiver, and includes the following messages:

```
"messages in the 'testing' protocol of Behavior"
instSize
   "Answer the number of named instance variables of the receiver."
```

isBehavior
  "Answer whether the receiver is a class object."
isMeta
  "Answer whether the receiver is a metaclass."
isVariable
  "Answer whether the receiver has indexed instance variables."
isFixed
  "Answer whether the receiver does not have indexed instance variables."
isPointers
  "Answer whether the receiver only contains pointers (i.e., is not unique or a byte array)."
isBits
  "Answer whether the receiver only contains bits (not pointers)."

In Behavior, isBehavior returns true, isMeta returns false, and the other testing methods check fields in the receiver's format.

Behavior defines extensive protocols for manipulating the subclasses and superclasses of a class object. The following are examples of messages in its *accessing class hierarchy, creating class hierarchy, testing class hierarchy*, and *enumerating class hierarchy* protocols:

    "messages in the 'creating class hierarchy', 'accessing class hierarchy', 'testing class
    hierarchy', and 'enumerating class hierarchy' protocols of Behavior"
    superclass
       "Answer the receiver's superclass."
    subclasses
       "Answer the receiver's subclasses."
    allSuperclasses
       "Answer an ordered collection of the receiver's superclass and ancestors."
    allSubclasses
       "Answer an ordered collection of the receiver's subclasses and descendants."
    withAllSuperclasses
       "Answer an ordered collection of the receiver, its superclass, and its ancestors."
    withAllSubclasses
       "Answer an ordered collection of the receiver, its subclasses, and its descendants."
    superclass: aClass
       "Change the receiver's superclass to be aClass."
    addSubclass: aClass
       "Add aClass as a subclass of the receiver."
    removeSubclass: aClass
       "Remove aClass from the receiver's subclasses."
    inheritsFrom: aClass
       "Answer whether aClass is an ancestor of the receiver."
    allSubclassesDo: aBlock
       "Evaluate aBlock for each of the receiver's subclasses."

Note the distinction between the message superclass, which accesses the receiver's superclass, and the message allSuperclasses, which returns all the receiver's ancestors (and similarly for subclass and allSubclasses). The methods for the class hierarchy messages access the instance variables superclass and subclasses. Behavior does not define a message for creating a new subclass. (Messages in the *creating class hierarchy* category, such as addSubclass:, create class hierarchy references.)

Behavior includes *accessing method dictionary, creating method dictionary*, and *testing method dictionary* protocols, such as the following messages:

```
"messages in the 'creating method dictionary', 'accessing method dictionary', and 'testing
method dictionary' protocols of Behavior"
selectors
    "Answer a set of the selectors in the receiver's method dictionary."
allSelectors
    "Answer a set of all the selectors that instances of the receiver can understand."
sourceCodeAt: selector
    "Answer the string giving the source code for selector."
compiledMethodAt: selector
    "Answer the compiled method associated with selector in the receiver's method
    dictionary.  If selector is not in the dictionary, create an error notification."
printMethod: selector on: aStream
    "Print the source code for the method associated with selector on aStream."
addSelector: selector withMethod: compiledMethod
    "Add the message selector with compiledMethod to the receiver's method dictionary."
methodDictionary: aDictionary
    "Store aDictionary as the method dictionary of the receiver."
removeSelector: selector
    "Remove selector from the receiver's method dictionary.  If selector is not in the
    dictionary, create an error notification."
hasMethods
    "Answer whether the receiver has any methods in its method dictionary."
includesSelector: aSymbol
    "Answer whether the receiver's method dictionary includes the selector aSymbol."
canUnderstand: selector
    "Answer whether the receiver can respond to the message selector, whether selector
    is in the method dictionary of the receiver or one of its ancestors."
whichClassIncludesSelector: aSymbol
    "Answer the ancestor of the receiver in which aSymbol will be found."
whichSelectorsAccess: instVarName
    "Answer a set of selectors whose methods access instVarName."
```

Again, note the distinction between the messages selectors and includesSelector:, which are specific to the receiver's method dictionary, and allSelectors and canUnderstand:, which also include inherited messages. The method dictionary messages are primarily used by the system browser, but the programmer can also use them to query type information. For example, the message whichSelectorsAccess: is useful if it is necessary to change the storage structure of a class or the name of one of its instance variables. The methods for these messages manipulate the instance variable methodDict, and some such as allSelectors and canUnderstand: access the receiver's superclass. The method for sourceCodeAt: uses the message decompile: described in the next paragraph.

Behavior defines *compiling* and *recompiling* protocols, including the following messages:

```
"messages in the 'compiling' and 'recompiling' protocols of Behavior"
compile: code notifying: requester
    "Compile code (a string or a stream of characters) as source code in the context of the
    receiver, but do not save the source code.  Notify requester if an error occurs."
decompile: selector
    "Decompile the compiled code associated with selector in the receiver's method
    dictionary, and answer the resulting source code as a string.  Signal an error if selector
    is not in the receiver's method dictionary."
recompile: selector
    "Recompile the method associated with selector in the receiver's method dictionary."
rebindAllMethods
    "Regenerate all the methods in the receiver's method dictionary."
rebindSelector: selector
    "Regenerate the method associated with selector."
```

The methods for these messages access the receiver's method dictionary, then create an instance of Compiler or Decompiler and send it messages with the source or compiled code as an argument. All but decompile: update the receiver's method dictionary.

The *accessing instances* and *enumerating instances* protocols of Behavior consist of the following messages:

```
"the 'accessing instances' and 'enumerating instances' protocols of Behavior"
instanceCount
    "Answer the number of instances of the receiver that currently exist."
allInstances
    "Answer a collection of all instances of this class."
allInstancesDo: aBlock
    "Evaluate aBlock for each current instance of the receiver."
allSubInstancesDo: aBlock
    "Evaluate aBlock for each current instance of the receiver's subclasses."
```

The method for allInstances invokes a primitive method, and the other accessing and enumerating instances methods call allInstances.

The class ClassDescription

The class ClassDescription is an abstract subclass of Behavior. It adds instance variables that maintain the class's instance variable names and its browser information. It provides protocol for manipulating this information, and for storing class descriptions on streams and filing classes in and out. ClassDescription is defined as follows:

```
"definition of the class ClassDescription"
Behavior subclass: #ClassDescription
   instanceVariableNames: 'instanceVariables organization'
   classVariableNames: ''
   poolDictionaries: ''
   category: 'Kernel-Classes'
```

The instance variable instanceVariables is an array of strings giving the class's instance variable names. The instance variable organization is an instance of the class ClassOrganizer that maintains a class's comment and the organization of its class and instance messages into categories. ClassOrganizer provides messages for accessing, manipulating, and printing this information, which are used in several ClassDescription methods. The categorization of classes is stored in a class organizer associated with Smalltalk, the system dictionary of global names.

The following are examples of messages in the *accessing, instance variables, method dictionary*, and *organization* protocols of ClassDescription:

```
"messages in the 'accessing', 'instance variables', 'method dictionary', and 'organization'
protocols of ClassDescription"
comment
    "Answer the receiver's class comment."
comment: aString
    "Set the receiver's class comment to aString."
instVarNames
    "Answer an array of the receiver's instance variable names."
allInstVarNames
    "Answer an array of all the receiver's instance variable names, including those
inherited
    from ancestors."
addInstVarName: aString
    "Add aString as an instance variable name of the receiver."
removeInstVarName: aString
    "Remove aString from the receiver's instance variable names."
addSelector: selector withMethod: compiledMethod category: category
    "Add the message selector with method compiledMethod to the receiver's method
    dictionary in category."
removeCategory: category
    "Remove each message in category, and remove the category."
category
    "Answer the system organization category for the receiver."
category: category
    "Categorize the receiver in category, and remove it from any previous category."
organization
    "Answer the class organizer that maintains the organization of the receiver's messages."
whichCategoryIncludesSelector: selector
    "Answer the category of selector in the organization of the receiver."
```

The methods for addInstVarName: and removeInstVarName: are deferred to the subclass Class.

ClassDescription also defines *printing* and *fileIn/Out* protocols, including the following messages:

```
"messages in the 'printing' and 'fileIn/Out' protocols of ClassDescription"
instanceVariablesString
    "Answer a string of the receiver's instance variable names separated by spaces."
classVariablesString
    "Answer a string of the receiver's class variable names separated by spaces."
sharedPoolsString
    "Answer a string of the receiver's shared pool names separated by spaces."
definition
    "Answer a string consisting of the class definition message that defines the receiver."
printOn: aStream
    "Append the class name to aStream."
storeOn: aStream
    "Append the class name to aStream."
printOutOn: aStream
    "Append the class definition, class comment, and methods by category on aStream."
printOutCategory: category on: aStream
    "Append a description of the methods in category on aStream."
fileOutSourceOn: aSourceFileManager
    "File out the receiver on aSourceFileManager."
fileOutMethodsOn: aSourceFileManager
    "File out the receiver's methods on aSourceFileManager."
```

ClassDescription defines the messages printOn: and storeOn:, even though its subclass Class defines the instance variable containing the class name (the methods obtain the name with self name). An instance of the class SourceFileManager maintains the files containing the source code in the system. This instance is stored as a class variable of SourceFileManager (rather than in Smalltalk), and is available via the class message default.

The class Class

The class Class is a subclass of ClassDescription that adds instance variables for the class name, the classPool of class variables, and the sharedPools of pool variables. It supports accessing protocol for this information and the class definition messages used to create subclasses. Class is defined as follows:

```
"definition of the class Class"
ClassDescription subclass: #Class
    instanceVariableNames: 'name classPool sharedPools'
    classVariableNames: ' '
    poolDictionaries: ' '
    category: 'Kernel-Classes'
```

As discussed in section 6.1.3, classPool is a dictionary in which the class variable names are keys and their referents are the associated values. sharedPools is a set of references to the pool dictionaries to which the class has access.

The following are examples of messages in the *accessing, class name, class variables*, and *pool variables* protocols of Class:

```
"messages in the 'accessing', 'class name', 'class variables', and 'pool variables' protocols
of Class"
classPool
    "Answer the receiver's dictionary of class variables."
name
    "Answer the receiver's name."
setName: aSymbol
    "Set the receiver's name to aSymbol."
renameAndFixSourceTo: newName
    "Set the receiver's name to newName, and then change all references in the system
    from the old name to newName."
classVarNames
    "Answer a set of the names of the receiver's class variables."
allClassVarNames
    "Answer a set of the names of the receiver's class variables, including those in its
    ancestors."
addClassVarName: aString
    "Add aString as a class variable name of the receiver."
removeClassVarName: aString
    "Remove aString from the receiver's class variable names."
sharedPools
    "Answer a set of the pool dictionaries shared by the receiver."
allSharedPools
    "Answer a set of the pool dictionaries the receiver shares, including those defined in
    its ancestors."
addSharedPool: aDictionary
    "Add aDictionary as a pool dictionary of the receiver."
removeSharedPool: aDictionary
    "Remove aDictionary from the receiver's pool dictionaries."
```

The *subclass creation* protocol of Class defines the class definition messages used in the browser.

```
"the 'subclass creation' protocol of Class"
subclass: newClass instanceVariableNames: instVars classVariableNames: classVars
poolDictionaries: poolDicts category: cat
    "This is the standard message for creating a new class as a subclass of the receiver."
variableSubclass: newClass instanceVariableNames: instVars
classVariableNames: classVars poolDictionaries: poolDicts category: cat
    "This is the standard message for creating a new class with indexable pointer variables
    as a subclass of the receiver."
```

variableByteSubclass: newClass instanceVariableNames: instVars
classVariableNames: classVars poolDictionaries: poolDicts category: cat
   "This is the standard message for creating a new class with indexable byte-sized
   nonpointer variables as a subclass of the receiver."

The methods for these messages create an instance of the system class ClassBuilder, pass it messages to set the various elements of a class definition, then send it the message reviseSystem. If the class is a new class, the class builder creates a metaclass and a class object; otherwise it modifies the existing class object.

Object **class protocol**

In addition to the protocol inherited from Behavior, ClassDescription, and Class, the class Object defines a *class initialization* message initialize, which creates the Dependents dictionary, and the *instance creation* messages readFromString: and readFrom:, which create an instance of the class from the contents of a string or stream, respectively. readFromString: is implemented in terms of read-From:, so descendants only need to override the latter method. The argument is expected to be a message expression whose evaluation creates and initializes a new object, and is usually the result of a storeOn: message, as described in the previous section. The readFrom: method passes the stream argument to a compiler for evaluation.

7.2 CLASSES FOR UNIQUE OBJECTS

7.2.1 The Class UndefinedObject

Purpose and definition

The unique object bound to the pseudo-variable nil is the sole instance of the class UndefinedObject. This object is the value of all uninitialized local, instance, or shared variables. It is also used as the null pointer in linked structures, and as the value "empty position" in hashed storage structures. The class UndefinedObject is a subclass of Object that defines no instance or class variables, and is in the class category Kernel-Objects.

The Smalltalk class library defines a separate class for the object nil, even though that class does not define any additional protocol, because nil must have its own behavior for certain messages, such as isNil, printOn:, and shallowCopy. In addition, this design facilitates debugging. When an object receives the message doesNotUnderstand:, the resulting notifier gives its class name and the selector. A common programming error is to omit initialization of a variable, in which case any message sent to its referent is sent to nil. With nil defined in its own class, the cause of an error due to using an uninitialized variable is obvious.

Implementation

UndefinedObject inherits Object's methods for ==, ~~, =, and ~=. Because there can be only one instance of nil in the system, the *instance creation* class message new is overridden to produce an error message, and the *copying* message shallowCopy returns self. As we discussed in section 7.1.2, the *testing* messages isNil and notNil are implemented in UndefinedObject as ∧true and ∧false, respectively, so that no conditional test is required in their methods in Object. The methods for the *printing* messages printOn: and storeOn: append the string 'nil' to the stream argument, and isLiteral returns true. The *dependents access* message addDependent: is disallowed for nil. The *class creation* protocol of UndefinedObject includes the class definition message subclass: ..., which is used only to define the class Object.

7.2.2 The Class Boolean

Purpose, definition and protocol

The class Boolean is a subclass of Object that represents logical values. As we saw in section 5.5.2, comparing and testing messages return boolean objects, and logical messages are defined in the protocol of Boolean. We saw in section 5.5.4 that conditional execution is a boolean message, and that a boolean-valued block is the receiver of a conditional iteration message. Boolean has exactly two instances, true and false, which are unique objects (recall section 5.4.2). The class Boolean defines no instance or class variables, and is in the class category Kernel-Objects.

Like UndefinedObject, the class Boolean inherits Object's methods for ==, ~~, =, and ~=, overrides the *instance creation* class message new to produce an error message, and returns self for the *copying* message shallowCopy. The *logical operations* protocol of Boolean was described in section 5.5.2 (see Figure 5.12), and consists of the messages &, |, not, eqv:, and xor:. Recall that the methods for & and | always evaluate their argument, unlike and: and or:. In section 5.5.4, we discussed the *controlling* protocol of Boolean, which consists of the messages ifTrue:, ifFalse:, ifTrue:ifFalse:, ifFalse:ifTrue:, and:, and or:. As we mentioned in that section, these methods are usually not invoked because conditional evaluation expressions are compiled inline for literal block arguments. The *printing* protocol of Boolean implements the message storeOn: aStream as self printOn: aStream. Methods for printOn: are defined in the classes True and False described in the next subsection.

The classes True and False

For efficiency, the class Boolean is an abstract class that has two concrete subclasses True and False, which define no instance or class variables and are in the class category Kernel-Objects. Each of these classes has a single instance and defines the methods for its value, except for eqv: and xor:, which are defined in Boolean in terms of ==. This design simplifies coding methods for booleans as there is no need for each method to include a test that determines which boolean object is the receiver. True and False each has its own method dictionary referenced by its instance, so the message resolution process selects the code to be executed directly. (Note the similarity with the implementation of testing messages such as isNil and isBehavior.) The classes True and False do not define any additional protocol.

&, |, not, and the controlling messages are implemented in Boolean as self subclassResponsibility, and are then defined in True and False. For example, the following are some example methods for the class True:

```
"instance methods for class True"

& aBoolean
    "Evaluating conjunction.  Since the receiver is true, answer aBoolean."

    ^aBoolean

ifFalse: alternativeBlock
    "Since the receiver is true, answer nil."

    ^nil

and: alternativeBlock
    "Non-evaluating conjunction.  Since the receiver is true, answer the result of evaluating
    alternativeBlock."

    ^alternativeBlock value

printOn: aStream
    "Since the receiver is true, append 'true' to aStream."

    aStream nextPutAll: 'true'
```

The methods for logical operations in Boolean, True, and False do not check whether the argument of the message is a boolean object. For example, if the message & is sent to false, it returns itself, but if that message is sent to true, it returns the argument, whatever object it is. The printing message isLiteral returns true in both True and False.

7.3 CLASSES FOR LINEARLY ORDERED OBJECTS

7.3.1 The Class Magnitude

The abstract class Magnitude is a subclass of Object whose protocol includes comparing messages relevant for linearly ordered objects such as numbers, characters, and dates. It is an abstract class because each concrete subclass has its own repre-

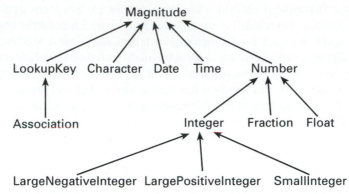

Figure 7.3   The descendants of the system class Magnitude (in Smalltalk-80).

sentation and method for determining the order of any two instances. The class Magnitude defines no instance or class variables, and is in the class category Magnitude-General.

The instance protocol of Magnitude includes one category, *comparing* protocol, which consists of the messages =, hash, <, >, <=, >=, between:and:, min:, and max:. The messages =, <, >, <=, >=, and between:and: return boolean objects, and min: and max: return either the receiver or the argument, depending on which is "greater". As we discussed in section 6.2.3, the messages <, = and hash are defined as ^self subclassResponsibility, and the other messages are implemented in terms of < and =. If a class supports ordering behavior, the designer defines it as a subclass of Magnitude and codes methods for <, =, and hash, and inherits the other comparing methods. Magnitude inherits Object's methods for ==, ~~, ~=, shallowCopy, testing messages, printing messages, and so on. It defines no class protocol.

Because Smalltalk is dynamically typed, the receiver and argument of a comparing message might not be instances of the same class. If this occurs, the error appears when the receiver's method for < sends the argument a message it cannot respond to. For example, consider the message aDate >= 3.0. Magnitude's method for >= sends the receiver <, and the < method for Date compares the receiver's and argument's year number and then day number. The error occurs when the Date method for < sends year to the argument 3.0.

Magnitude has five system subclasses: Date, Time, Character, Number, and LookupKey, a key for a dictionary access. The class LookupKey and its subclass Association are used in implementing the class Dictionary, and are discussed in section 8.2.3. The subhierarchy rooted at Magnitude is illustrated in Figure 7.3.

7.3.2 **The Class** Character

Purpose and definition

The class Character is a subclass of Magnitude that represents letters and special characters, and its instances are primarily used as elements of strings. It has 256 instances, and the values 0 through 127 represent characters according to the ASCII standard character set. We saw in section 5.4.2 that characters are unique immutable objects, so all instances with the same value are identical (according to ==). Conceptually, system initialization creates the instances, and using a literal or an instance creation message obtains an existing character object. As we discussed in section 5.4.2, a character object is actually represented by a flag and a value encoded within the variable's object identifier. Recall from section 5.2.2 that the literal notation for a printable character is $ followed by the character.

Character is defined as a subclass of Magnitude with no instance variables in the class category Magnitude-General. In Smalltalk-80, the class shares a pool dictionary CharacterConstants that includes the nonprintable characters and bit masks for testing whether a character is alphabetic, a digit, uppercase, etc. In VisualWorks, these masks are defined as class variables of Character.

Class protocol

The *instance creation* protocol of Character includes the messages value: and digitValue:, both of which take an integer argument. value: returns the character whose ASCII value is equal to the argument, and is implemented by a primitive method. digitValue: is provided for parsing representations of numbers in non-decimal bases, and answers $0 for 0, …, $9 for 9, $A for 10, …, and $Z for 35. The inherited instance creation messages new and basicNew are defined as self error: 'Use Character value: to create characters'. We can also access a character by sending the conversion message asCharacter to an integer.

The *accessing untypeable characters* protocol of Character provides mnemonic messages that return nonprintable characters. Examples include space, cr, esc, newPage, backspace, and tab. This protocol also defines the message maxValue, which returns the largest possible character value.

Instance protocol

The *comparing* protocol of Character defines the deferred methods of Magnitude, and inherits its other methods. The message = is implemented by a primitive method, and < converts the receiver and argument to small integers and compares the results with < (which allows comparing characters and integers for ordering). The methods for hash and identityHash return the integer value of the receiver.

The *testing* protocol of Character includes isAlphabetic, isAlphaNumeric, isDigit, isLetter, isLowercase, isUppercase, isSeparator (i.e., whether the receiver a whitespace character), and isVowel. The *converting* protocol of Character consists of asInteger (a primitive method returns the ASCII code), asLowercase, asUppercase, and asSymbol. If the receiver is not a letter, asLowercase and asUppercase return the receiver. Arithmetic is not supported directly for characters, but can be performed after conversion with asInteger. Characters also respond to the *accessing* message digitValue, which is the inverse of digitValue:. Character overrides the *printing* messages printOn: and storeOn: inherited from Object to append the receiver's literal notation to the argument stream, and overrides isLiteral to return true. The *copying* protocol overrides shallowCopy as ^self because characters are unique.

7.3.3 The Class Date

Purpose and definition

An instance of the system class Date represents a date in the Julian calendar. Date objects are treated as immutable objects that represent a particular date, rather than as containers for a date value, and the class defines no nonprivate methods that modify the state of an instance. Unlike booleans and characters, date objects are not unique. The class Date is a subclass of Magnitude that specifies two instance variables and four class variables, and is defined as follows:

```
"definition of the class Date"
Magnitude subclass: #Date
   instanceVariableNames: 'day year'
   classVariableNames: 'DaysInMonth MonthNames WeekDayNames FirstDayOfMonth'
   poolDictionaries: ''
   category: 'Magnitude-General'
```

The instance variable year is the receiver's year, and day is the day number within that year (i.e., from 1 to 366). The class variables store information about dates in general (we used them to illustrate class variables in sections 1.1.5 and 6.1.3).

- DaysInMonth is an array containing the number of days in each month.
- MonthNames is an array of symbols for the names of the months.
- WeekDayNames is an array of symbols for the names of the seven days of the week.
- FirstDayOfMonth is an array giving the day in the year of the first day of each month. FirstDayOfMonth is primarily used within Date methods.

Class protocol

The *instance creation* protocol of Date includes several descriptive messages for creating date objects.

```
"the 'instance creation' class protocol of Date"
newDay: day month: monthName year: year
   "Answer the date that is the day'th day of the month named monthName in the year year.
   year is relative to 1900 if it is less than 100."
newDay: dayCount year: year
   "Answer the date that is dayCount days after the beginning of the year year.
   year is relative to 0."
today
   "Answer the date representing the day and year right now."
```

fromDays: dayCount
   "Answer the date that is dayCount days since January 1, 1901."
readFrom: aStream
   "Answer a date read from aStream in any of the formats:
   1 April 1982, 1-APR-82, April 1, 1982, 1/5/82"

Note the difference in interpretation between the third argument of newDay:month:year: and the second argument of newDay:year:.[5] The second argument of newDay:month:year: can be either a symbol or a string. The methods for newDay:month:year: and newDay:year: use the private instance initialization message day:year:. The message readFromString: is inherited from the class protocol of Object, and can be used with all the formats for readFrom: to create date objects. Date does not disallow the inherited message new so we can create an uninitialized date object with this message, although an error will occur when we use that object.

    The class Date embodies general knowledge about the category of entities it represents. The *class initialization* message initialize initializes the class variables. The *general inquiries* protocol provides messages that access this information.

"the 'general inquiries' class protocol of Date"
daysInMonth: monthName forYear: year
   "Answer the number of days in the month named monthName in the year year."
daysInYear: year
   "Answer the number of days in the year year."
leapYear: year
   "Answer 1 if the year year is a leap year, or 0 if it is not. "
nameOfMonth: monthIndex
   "Answer a symbol representing the name of the month indexed by monthIndex, 1 - 12."
indexOfMonth: aSymbol
   "Answer the index, 1 - 12, of the month named aSymbol. Three letters, full month
names,
   and upper or lower case are accepted. Provide an error notification if no such month
   name exists."
nameOfDay: dayIndex
   "Answer a symbol representing the name of the day indexed by dayIndex, 1 - 7."
dayOfWeek: aSymbol
   "Answer the index in a week, 1 - 7, of the day named aSymbol. Provide an error
   notification if no such day name exists."
dateAndTimeNow
   "Answer an array with first element Date today and second element Time now."

The argument of an indexOfMonth: or dayOfWeek: message must be a symbol, not a string. Although indexOfMonth: permits some latitude in specifying its argument, the system method for dayOfWeek: requires its argument to be spelled out and capitalized (e.g., #Monday). The class message dateAndTimeNow may be sent to either

---

[5] Unfortunately, the system method for newDay:month:year: also computes negative year arguments relative to 1900.

Date or Time. Unfortunately, it returns an array containing a time object and a date because the system classes do not provide an encapsulation for both a time and a date with descriptive selectors. There is no public accessor for the class variable FirstDayOfMonth because that information is maintained for the use of Date methods such as newDay:month:year:.

Instance protocol

Instances of Date respond to several message that supply information about the receiver. The *accessing* protocol consists of the messages day, year, monthName, monthIndex, weekday (the name of the day of the week of the receiver), and leap (whether the receiver's year is a leap year). The *inquires* protocol returns information about the receiver and includes dayOfMonth, daysInMonth, daysInYear, daysLeftInYear, firstDayOfMonth, and previous: aSymbol (the first date before the receiver with day name aSymbol).

Date defines the *comparing* messages =, <, and hash, so the protocol of Magnitude is available for its instances. It also implements the *printing* messages printOn: and storeOn:. The latter appends an instance creation message to the stream argument, as follows:

```
"instance method in class Date"
storeOn: aStream
   "Append an expression to aStream that can be evaluated to construct a date equal to
   the receiver."

   aStream nextPutAll: '(', self class name, 'readFromString:'.
   self printOn: aStream.
   aStream nextPut: $)
```

Many systems also provide a message print:format:, which allows the client to specify a print format. Date supplies the *converting* messages asDays and asSeconds, which return the number of days or seconds since January 1, 1901 (not since January 1, 1900 or January 1, 0). The converting messages return negative values for dates before January 1, 1901.

The class Date also supports *arithmetic* protocol, which consists of the following messages:

```
"the 'arithmetic' instance protocol of Date"
addDays: dayCount
   "Answer a new date that is dayCount more days than the receiver."
subtractDays: dayCount
   "Answer a new date that is dayCount days before the receiver."
subtractDate: aDate
   "Answer the number of days between the receiver and aDate."
```

Note that addDays: and subtractDays: create a new date, rather than modifying the receiver. Having this behavior encapsulated within the system class relieves the programmer from having to handle the details of these calculations in an application.

7.3.4 The Class Time

Purpose and definition

An instance of the system class Time represents a particular time of day. To represent a specific time and date, we must use an instance of each class. Like date objects, time objects are treated as immutable objects, rather than as containers for a time value. Time is a subclass of Magnitude with three instance variables, and is defined as follows:

```
"definition of the class Time"
Magnitude subclass: #Time
    instanceVariableNames: 'hours minutes seconds'
    classVariableNames: ''
    poolDictionaries: ''
    category: 'Magnitude-General'
```

The instance variables represent the hours, minutes, and seconds of the receiver.

Class protocol

The *instance creation* protocol of Time consists of the following messages:

```
"the 'instance creation' class protocol of Time"
fromSeconds: secondCount
    "Answer a time that is secondCount seconds since midnight."
now
    "Answer a time representing the time right now (using a 24 hour clock)."
readFrom: aStream
    "Answer a Time as read from the argument aStream that is in the form:
    <hour>:<min>:<sec> <am/pm> (<min>, <sec> or <am/pm> may be omitted.)
```

The method for fromSeconds: calculates the hours, minutes, and seconds, then sends the new object the private initialization message hours:minutes:seconds:. Unfortunately, the method for fromSeconds: on many systems does no range checking, so an instance with a negative hours value or an hours value greater than 24 can be created. The methods for both Date today and Time now send Time dateAndTimeNow, which invokes a primitive method that returns the number of seconds since January 1, 1901. As with Date, we can use the message readFromString: to create an object representing a particular time.

Like Date, Time includes a *general inquiries* protocol.

"the 'general inquiries' class protocol of Time"
totalSeconds
  "Answer the total seconds since 1901 began."
millisecondClockValue
  "Answer the number of milliseconds since the millisecond clock was last reset or rolled over."
millisecondsToRun: timedBlock
  "Answer the number of milliseconds timedBlock takes to return its value."
dateAndTimeNow
  "Answer an array with first element Date today and second element Time now."

Instance protocol

The instance protocol of Time includes the *accessing* messages hours, minutes, and seconds. Like Date, Time implements the *comparing* messages =, <, and hash inherited from Magnitude, the *printing* messages printOn: and storeOn: inherited from Object, and the *converting* message asSeconds, which returns the total number of seconds since midnight represented by the receiver.

Instances of Time respond to the *arithmetic* messages addTime: and subtract-Time: with an argument that is either a time or a date by returning a new time object. The methods for addTime: and subtractTime: send the receiver and argument the message asSeconds before performing the arithmetic and creating the resulting time object with fromSeconds:. Therefore, a date argument to these messages is converted to the number of seconds between midnight January 1, 1901, and midnight of that date.

7.4 NUMERIC CLASSES

7.4.1 Numeric Objects

In traditional languages, numbers and arithmetic operations are provided by built-in types and operations. Hybrid object-oriented languages use the built-in types of the base language for arithmetic. For example, Simula uses the included subset of ALGOL, and C++ uses C's built-in types. In Smalltalk, numbers are objects (which have identity if they are not small integers), and mathematical operations are messages to these numeric objects. Recasting arithmetic operations in the message passing paradigm often seems rather strange and has encountered resistance, especially with respect to efficiency. Smalltalk does so to achieve the benefits of consistency and uniformity, as we have discussed several times. However, single polymorphism complicates implementing mixed-type arithmetic in which the method executed depends on the types of both the receiver and the argument. We will discuss two strategies for handling this problem in section 7.4.6.

The Smalltalk class library supports integers of any size, rational numbers, and floating point numbers. Numeric objects are immutable objects rather than containers for a value, and numeric operations always return a new object rather than modifying the receiver (like character, date, and time objects). Note also that, due to dynamic typing, the Smalltalk programmer does not have to choose which type of number the referent of a numeric variable is. Because all numeric classes are descendants of the abstract class Number, he or she can send messages in Number's protocol to the referent of a numeric variable without being concerned with whether the value is an integer or a floating-point number. In fact, the actual type of the referent may change (e.g., if the referent is an integer, and is then set to the product of that value and a floating-point number).

7.4.2 The Class Number

Purpose and definition

The class Number is an abstract ancestor for all the numeric classes. It specifies protocol available for all numbers and defines numerous methods that are inherited by the concrete numeric classes, but does not include a representation for a value. Number is a subclass of Magnitude that defines no instance or class variables, and is in the class category Magnitude-Numbers, like all the numeric classes.

Number has three subclasses Float, Fraction, and Integer, and Integer is also an abstract class, which has the concrete subclasses SmallInteger, LargeNegativeInteger, and LargePositiveInteger (see Figure 7.3). Instances of SmallInteger are unique objects, while instances of the other numeric classes are created and destroyed as needed.

Class protocol

Number defines very little class protocol and no class variables. Numeric objects are typically created by a compiler reading a literal, or as the result of a numeric operation. The *instance creation* protocol of Number defines a method for readFrom: that reads a numeric literal from its stream argument, and overrides new and new: as self shouldNotImplement. We can use the inherited message readFromString: to convert a string consisting of a literal to the corresponding numeric object.

Instance protocol

The *arithmetic* protocol of Number includes the binary messages +, -, *, / (which returns a fraction if the arguments are fractions or integers), //, and \\ (integer quotient and remainder respectively, rounded toward negative infinity). Recall that there is no precedence among binary selectors. The arithmetic protocol also contains the messages quo: and rem: (integer quotient and remainder rounded toward zero), abs, negated, and reciprocal. The methods for the binary selectors are deferred to concrete subclasses, and the other arithmetic messages are defined in terms of them.

The *mathematical functions* protocol of Number consists of the messages

- exp, ln, log, log: (the argument gives the base), and floorLog: (the floor of the log of the receiver in the base given by the argument)
- raisedTo:, raisedToInteger: (for efficiency), squared, and sqrt
- cos (with the receiver in radians), sin, tan, arcCos (with the result in radians), arcSin, and arcTan

As we discussed in section 6.2.3, many Number methods pass the receiver a message converting it to an instance of the numeric class that implements that message, then pass that result the original message. This provides the default behavior used in the classes that do not implement the message. For example, messages such as sin, exp, and sqrt are implemented in class Float by primitive methods, and the methods in Number are ^self asFloat sin, and so on.

Number's *testing* protocol consists of the messages isZero, negative, positive, strictlyPositive, sign (which returns 1, 0, or -1), even, and odd. The methods for negative, positive, strictlyPositive, and sign are defined as comparisons with 0, and isZero is deferred to concrete subclasses. The methods for even and odd test the result of self \\ 2.

The *converting* protocol of Number includes the messages degreesToRadians, radiansToDegrees, asInteger, and asFloat. Like sin and exp, Number implements the first two messages by converting the receiver to a float and then sending the message to that object. The method for asInteger is ^self truncated, and asFloat is deferred to concrete subclasses. The converting protocol also contains the binary selector @, which creates a new point with the receiver as the x coordinate and the argument as the y coordinate.

Messages in the *truncation* protocol of Number result in an integer. This protocol includes ceiling, floor, truncated, rounded, roundTo: (the multiple of the argument nearest to the receiver), and truncateTo: (the multiple of the argument nearest to the receiver in the direction toward 0). For example, 89 roundTo: 5 returns 90, and 89 truncateTo: 5 returns 85. The Number method for truncated is ^self quo: 1, and the other messages are implemented in terms of truncated.

The *printing* protocol of Number defines storeOn: in terms of printOn:, which is then defined in each concrete class to append a literal representation of the receiver, or (numerator / denominator) in class Fraction, to the argument stream. The messages printString and storeString return that literal, and supply conversions from numbers to strings.

The *intervals* protocol of Number consists of the messages to: and to:by:, which create instances of Interval, and to:do: and to:by:do:, which successively pass the elements of the specified interval to the block argument, as described in section 5.5.5. For example, the expression 1 to: 8 by: 2 creates an interval consisting of the elements 1, 3, 5, and 7.

Number also defines messages that implement mixed-class arithmetic, which we cover in section 7.4.6.

7.4.3 The Integer Classes

Representation of integers

The class Integer is an abstract class that has three concrete subclasses, SmallInteger, LargeNegativeInteger, and LargePositiveInteger. SmallInteger provides an efficient representation that is slightly smaller than an object reference. Instances of LargeNegativeInteger and LargePositiveInteger may be of any magnitude so there is no overflow for integers, but operations involving these objects can be time-consuming. Numeric methods return instances of SmallInteger automatically whenever possible. Conversions among the integer classes are transparent to the programmer.

The class Integer

The class Integer is a subclass of Number that defines no instance or class variables, and is in the class category Magnitude-Numbers. Like Number, Integer is an abstract class that does not define a representation.

The protocol of Integer includes that of its ancestors Number and Magnitude. The *arithmetic* and *comparing* protocols (except for equality tests) are implemented using the techniques described in section 7.4.6. Integer's *factorization* protocol consists of the messages factorial, gcd: (greatest common divisor), and lcm: (least common multiple). Integers can perform the *enumerating* message timesRepeat: discussed in section 5.5.5, as well as the interval enumeration messages to:do: and to:by:do: inherited from Number.

Integer defines the *converting* messages asCharacter, asInteger, asFloat, and asFraction. The method for asCharacter returns Character value: self. asInteger and asFraction return the receiver for efficiency (rather than using general methods inherited from Number). Integer defines a method for asFloat that is used by large integers.

The inherited *printing* message printOn: is defined using the Integer message printOn:base:, which prints the receiver on the argument stream in the radix given by the second argument. (The printOn: method uses base 10.) The messages printStringRadix: and storeStringRadix: return the print string or store string of the receiver in the radix given by the argument. For example, 69 printStringRadix: 8 returns the string '105', while 69 storeStringRadix: 8 returns the string '8r105'. Similarly, Integer redefines the *instance creation* class message readFrom: in terms of the Integer class message readFrom:radix:.

The class Integer also includes *bit manipulation* protocol, which interprets the value of an instance as a sequence of bits in the two's complement representation. For this purpose, positive numbers are regarded as having an infinite number of 0's preceding the first significant 1, and negative numbers begin with an infinite sequence of 1's. The bits in an integer are numbered with 1 (not 0) as the rightmost bit. The bit manipulation protocol consists of messages that perform bitwise logical operations, bit access, bit shifts, and masking:[6]

the 'bit manipulation' instance protocol of Integer
bitAnd: aNumber
   "Answer the bitwise and of the two's-complement representations of the receiver and the argument."
bitOr: aNumber
   "Answer the bitwise or of the two's-complement representations of the receiver and the argument."
bitXor: aNumber
   "Answer the bitwise exclusive-or of the two's-complement representations of the receiver and the argument."
bitInvert
   "Answer an integer whose bits are the complement of the receiver's bits."
bitAt: index
   "Answer the bit at the index'th position. The rightmost bit is bit number 1 (not 0)."
highBit
   "Answer the index of the high order 1 bit of the two's-complement representation of
   the receiver. Provide an error notification if the receiver is negative."
bitShift: anInteger
   "Answer the result of a bitwise shift of the two's-complement representation of the receiver. Shift left if the argument is positive, right if the argument is negative. Zeros are
   shifted in from the right for left shifts, and the sign bit is extended for right shifts."
allMask: mask
   "Answer whether all of the bits that are 1 in the argument are 1 in the receiver."
anyMask: mask
   "Answer whether any of the bits that are 1 in the argument are 1 in the receiver."
noMask: mask
   "Answer whether none of the bits that are 1 in the argument are 1 in the receiver."
maskClear: mask
   "Answer a copy of the receiver with the bits corresponding to bits in mask turned off."
maskSet: mask
   "Answer a copy of the receiver with the bits corresponding to bits in mask turned on."

Integer overrides three inherited *testing* methods: isInteger returns true, and even and odd use bit test operations for efficiency. The *truncation* messages ceiling, floor, rounded, and truncated are redefined as ^self for efficiency. The *accessing* protocol of Integer overrides numerator and denominator as ^self and ^1, respectively, for compatibility with Fraction methods.

Integer also defines a *private* message compressed, which is deferred. Its methods in LargePositiveInteger and LargeNegativeInteger return a small integer

---

[6] IBM Smalltalk also includes the binary selectors &, |, <<, and >>, which have the same meaning as bitAnd:, bitOr:, bitShift: with a positive argument, and bitShift: with a negative argument, respectively, as in C.

equal to the receiver (if possible), or the receiver. Its method in SmallInteger returns the receiver. Methods that create and return an integer must send that object compressed and return the result so that integers are converted to small integers whenever possible.

The class SmallInteger

SmallInteger is a subclass of Integer that defines no instance variables, and is in the class category Magnitude-Numbers. On some systems, SmallInteger defines class variables giving the minimum and maximum value for small integers. If so, its class protocol includes messages to initialize and access those values. As we have stated several times, instances of SmallInteger are unique, immutable objects.

SmallInteger does not add any messages to the protocol of Integer. The methods for the *arithmetic* protocol inherited from Number and the *comparing* protocol inherited from Magnitude invoke primitive methods, except for hash and identityHash, which return the receiver.[7] The bitwise logical operations and the *converting* message asFloat also are implemented by primitive methods. As in UndefinedObject, Boolean, and Character, the *copying* message shallowCopy returns self because small integers are unique.

The classes LargePositiveInteger and LargeNegativeInteger

An instance of LargePositiveInteger or LargeNegativeInteger maintains its absolute value as a sequence of bytes in indexed instance variables, so these classes are defined using the class definition message variableByteSubclass:.... For example, LargePositiveInteger is defined as follows:

```
"definition of the class LargePositiveInteger"
Integer variableByteSubclass: #LargeInteger
    instanceVariableNames: "
    classVariableNames: "
    poolDictionaries: "
    category: 'Magnitude-Numbers'
```

There is no internal representation of the sign of a large integer: Whether an object is positive or negative is represented by its class identity.

LargePositiveInteger and LargeNegativeInteger define no additional public protocol, but implement a number of methods. In fact, their abstract superclass Integer provides most of the implementation of these classes' methods. The *accessing* messages digitAt:, digitAt:put:, and digitLength are deferred in Integer (at:, at:put:, and size are disallowed), but Integer defines several methods that are the same for both large integer classes in terms of these messages. Examples include hash,

---

[7] For efficiency, SmallInteger defines all six equality and ordering comparisons as calls to primitive methods.

asFloat, printOn:base:, and several private messages such as digitAdd:, digitCompare:, and growBy:, used in methods for arithmetic, comparison, and bitwise operations. Both large integer classes define the accessing messages, and the *private* message compressed (which is also deferred in Integer).

The large integer methods for the *arithmetic* message negated change the class identity of the receiver. The *comparing* message = is defined to check the signs, sizes, and bytes of the receiver and argument.[8] The *testing* messages positive and negative return true and false in LargePositiveInteger, and vice versa in LargeNegativeInteger. The *bit manipulation* message highBit is implemented in LargePositiveInteger, and signals an error in LargeNegativeInteger.

7.4.4 The Class Fraction

Purpose and definition

The class Fraction is a subclass of Number, and is defined as follows:

```
"definition of the class Fraction"
Number subclass: #Fraction
    instanceVariableNames: 'numerator denominator'
    classVariableNames: ''
    poolDictionaries: ''
    category: 'Magnitude-Numbers'
```

The referents of numerator and denominator are large integers if necessary, so the class provides an exact representation for rational values. Like all numeric objects, we cannot modify a fraction once it has been initialized, and the class does not define messages to set the numerator or denominator independently (unlike the class Point, for example). The result of an arithmetic operation is a fraction if one operand is a fraction and the other is not a float, unless it can be expressed as an integer.

Class protocol

Fraction defines the *instance creation* class message numerator:denominator:, which calls the *private* initialization message setNumerator:denominator:. This method does not reduce the fraction given by the arguments before storing it. More frequently, we create instances by sending the binary selector / to an integer or fraction (if the result is not integral), or by an arithmetic operation. The methods for / and all Fraction arithmetic operations send the *private* message reduced to the result so that it is normalized.

---

[8] In VisualWorks, large integers use the method in their ancestor ArithmeticValue, which subtracts the argument from the receiver, and sends the result isZero. LargePositiveInteger and LargeNegativeInteger implement this message.

Instance protocol

Instances of Fraction respond to the protocol of its superclasses Magnitude and Number, as well as to the *accessing* messages numerator and denominator. The class implements several messages in terms of its instance variables. For example,

```
"instance methods in class Fraction"
negated
    "Answer a fraction that is the negation of the receiver."

    ^Fraction numerator: numerator negated denominator: denominator

hash
    "Answer a small integer unique to the receiver."

    ^numerator hash bitXor: denominator hash

truncated
    "Answer an integer nearest the receiver toward zero."

    ^numerator quo: denominator

asFloat
    "Answer a new float that represents the same value as the receiver."

    ^numerator asFloat / denominator asFloat

printOn: aStream
    "Append the receiver's numerator and denominator separated by / and enclosed in
    parentheses to aStream."

    aStream nextPut: $(.
    numerator printOn: aStream.
    aStream nextPut: $/.
    denominator printOn: aStream.
    aStream nextPut: $)
```

7.4.5 The Class Float

Purpose and definition

Instances of Float represent real numbers, and are stored in the native floating-point format of the platform. The representation of an instance's value is stored in a byte array of indexed instance variables, usually of size 4 (e.g., evaluate 3.0 inspect on your Smalltalk system). The class Float is a subclass of Number, defined as follows:

```
"definition of the class Float"
Number variableByteSubclass: #Float
```

```
instanceVariableNames: ''
classVariableNames: 'Pi RadiansPerDegree'
poolDictionaries: ''
category: 'Magnitude-Numbers'
```

The class variables store the values of the constant π and the number of radians per degree.

Class protocol

Float's class protocol consists of the *class initialization* message initialize, which initializes the class variables, and the *constants access* messages pi and radiansPerDegree. It does not include instance creation messages because we create instances with a literal constant (e.g., 3.5 or 6.02e23), an arithmetic operation with a float receiver or argument, or a message such as sqrt or asFloat that returns a float (most of which are primitive methods).

Instance protocol

Float inherits the instance protocol of its ancestors Magnitude and Number, and implements the *arithmetic*, *comparing*, and *mathematical functions* messages as primitive methods. Float defines the *converting* messages asFraction, degreesToRadians, and radiansToDegrees, and adds the *truncation* messages fractionPart and integerPart. The methods for rounded, truncated, and fractionPart invoke primitive methods, and integerPart is implemented as self − self fractionPart. printOn: appends a literal describing the receiver to the argument stream, usually with six decimal digits in the fraction part.

7.4.6 Mixed-Class Arithmetic in Smalltalk

Purpose

As we would expect, the sum of two integer objects is an integer, and similarly for fraction and float objects. If the magnitude of the result of an arithmetic operation involving two small integers is too large to be stored in that format, the method returns a large integer, and vice versa for a small result of an operation on large integers.

In an arithmetic or comparison operation in which the receiver is of a different class than the argument, one of them must be converted to the class of the other so that a meaningful operation can be performed. We want the language to provide this behavior automatically so that the programmer does not need to code explicit conversions, especially as the programmer should not need to know the exact class of a numeric object. In doing so, the mechanism used should preserve as much information as possible about the operands (e.g., it should convert an integer to a float rather than vice versa). In addition, commutative operations must perform the same computation and produce the same result if the argument and the receiver reverse roles in the message expression.

The strategy that supports mixed-class arithmetic operations must be designed in terms of message passing. As we stated in section 2.4.2, multiple polymorphism occurs when the selection of a method depends dynamically on the types of more than one operand or argument, as it does for mixed-class arithmetic in a dynamically typed language. Essentially, the two techniques described in this section use single polymorphism to implement an interaction in which multiple polymorphism applies. You need not be aware of the mechanism involved to use the numeric classes. However, if you create a new numeric class, it must interact correctly with the other numeric objects in the system. In addition, factoring out multiple polymorphism is a technique that is occasionally needed in coding applications. We will discuss two approaches to handling mixed-class arithmetic: coercive generality and double dispatching.

Coercive generality

Smalltalk-80 implements mixed-class arithmetic using a technique called *coercive generality*. Each concrete descendant of Number is assigned a *generality index*. For example, all integers can be represented exactly as fractions but not vice versa, so fractions have a larger generality index than integers (i.e., they are more general). The generality index of Float is greater than that of Fraction, which is greater than that of LargePositiveInteger and LargeNegativeInteger, which is greater than that of SmallInteger. Two objects are compatible with respect to arithmetic and comparison operations if their classes have the same generality index. If the operands of an arithmetic operation do not have the same generality index, the lower generality operand is passed a conversion message asking it to return an equivalent instance of the higher generality operand's class, and the higher generality class's operation is then performed with that result.

The *coercing* protocol of Number includes three messages: retry:coercing:, coerce:, and generality. The Number method for retry:coercing: encodes the general strategy of coercing the lower generality operand and then performing the higher generality operation. coerce: and generality provide the class-specific behavior it uses, and are deferred to Number's concrete descendants. In each numeric class, coerce: returns the result of coercing the argument to the receiver's class (which will be of higher generality), and generality returns the generality index of the receiver's class. That is, the receiver and the result of the message coerce: are always instances of the same class. For example, these messages are implemented in Float as follows:

"instance methods for coercive generality in class Float"

generality
    "Answer the number representing the position of the receiver in the generality ordering."

∧ 80

coerce: aNumber
  "Convert aNumber to a float object."

  ∧ aNumber asFloat

The generality index of Fraction is 60, that of Integer is 40, and that of SmallInteger
is 20. The method for coerce: is coded in the same way in each numeric class. Each
concrete numeric class defines a conversion message to every class with a higher
generality index. For example, the class Integer defines methods for asFraction and
asFloat. These methods are invoked by coerce: when an integer is the argument to
coerce: with a fraction or float receiver.

The methods for the arithmetic and comparing protocol of numeric classes
test the generality index of the class of the argument, and if it is the same as that
of the receiver's class, that class's operation is performed. If not, the message
retry:coercing: is sent to the receiver with the selector and the argument as its
arguments. For example, the method for + for the class Fraction has the following form:

```
"instance method for coercive generality in class Fraction"
+ aNumber
  "Answer a fraction that is the sum of the receiver and aNumber."

  (aNumber isMemberOf: Fraction)
    ifTrue: [ " ... code for adding fractions ... " ]
    ifFalse: [∧self retry: #+ coercing: aNumber]
```

The code for the other arithmetic and comparison methods is similar in all the
numeric classes. Many of these messages are implemented by primitive methods,
which fail if the argument is not the correct type. As we saw in section 6.1.2, primitive methods only return to the caller if they fail, so the rest of the method specifies the code to execute in that case. For example, the method for + for the class
Float is coded as follows:

```
"instance method for coercive generality in class Float"
+ aNumber
  "Answer a float that is the sum of the receiver and aNumber."

  <primitive: 41>
  ∧self retry: #+ coercing: aNumber
```

retry:coercing: takes a symbol giving the operation as its first argument, and a
numeric object of a different class than the receiver as the second argument. Its
method sends coerce: to either the receiver or the second argument, depending on
which has lower generality, then executes the operation again. To use the same
algorithm for all numeric classes, the selector symbol is passed to retry:coercing:,

and it uses the message perform: discussed in section 7.1.2 to send the corresponding message. retry:coercing: is implemented in Number as follows:

```
"instance method for coercive generality in class Number"
retry: aSymbol coercing: aNumber
    "The receiver and aNumber do not have the same generality.  Coerce whichever
    has lower generality to the generality of the other, and try aSymbol again."

    (aSymbol == #= and: [(aNumber isKindOf: Number) == false])
        ifTrue: [^false].
    self generality < aNumber generality
        ifTrue: [^(aNumber coerce: self) perform: aSymbol with: aNumber].
    self generality > aNumber generality
        ifTrue: [^self perform: aSymbol with: (self coerce: aNumber)].
```

The receiver and argument of the second send of the arithmetic message (i.e., from retry:coercing:) are the same class so that class's operation is performed directly. To recapitulate, the following series of messages is sent to evaluate the expression 3.0 + 3:

```
"trace of the messages sent in evaluating 3.0 + 3 with coercive generality"
3.0 + 3
3.0 retry: #+ coercing: 3
#+ == #=
3.0 generality
3 generality
80 < 20                          "compare the generalities"
80 > 20
3.0 coerce: 3
3 asFloat
3.0 perform: #+ with: (3 asFloat)
3.0 + (3 asFloat)
<primitive: 41>                  "float addition"
```

Suppose we want to add a new numeric class, perhaps for double precision floating-point or complex numbers. The class must be a subclass of Number so that it can use retry:coercing:. We decide on a generality index for the class, and implement the messages generality and coerce:, which are deferred in Number. Each of the numeric classes with lower generality must implement a conversion message to the new class, and the new class must provide conversion messages to all classes with higher generality. The new class's arithmetic and comparison methods must check the class of the argument before performing their operations, and send retry:coercing: if it is not the same as that of the receiver. The number of new methods necessary is linear in terms of the number of classes involved.

Double dispatching

An alternate implementation of mixed-type arithmetic used in some Smalltalk systems is *double dispatching*. In this technique, the receiver of an arithmetic message responds with a message to the argument that encodes its own class in the selector (e.g., sumFromFloat:). In the methods for that message, the classes of both the receiver and the argument are known, so the appropriate conversions can be coded directly.

To illustrate double dispatching, suppose that the system has only two numeric classes, Fraction and Float. The following messages and methods would be defined in Fraction to implement addition:

```
"instance methods for double dispatching in class Fraction"
+ aNumber
   "Answer the sum of the receiver and aNumber."

   ^aNumber sumFromFraction: self

sumFromFraction: aFraction
   "Answer the sum of the receiver and aFraction."

   " ... code for adding fractions ..."

sumFromFloat: aNumber
   ^aNumber + self asFloat
```

Similarly, in the class Float, the method for + would send sumFromFloat: to the argument, sumFromFloat: would invoke the primitive method for floating-point addition, and sumFromFraction: would send its argument asFloat and then send + self to that object. The binary expression x + y causes either sumFromFloat: x or sumFromFraction: x to be sent to y, depending on the class of the object bound to x. If the referent of y is of the same type as that of x, the addition method for their class is invoked, otherwise the conversion takes place and + is sent again, this time with operands of the same type. This second send of + will also send sumFromFloat: or sumFromFraction: again. To reduce the number of messages sent, the methods for arithmetic and comparison operations in classes that implement them by primitive methods can just attempt the primitive first. For example,

```
"instance method for double dispatching in class SmallInteger"
+ aNumber
   "Answer the sum of the receiver and aNumber."

   <primitive: 1>
   ^ aNumber sumFromInteger: self
```

In this case, the following messages are sent to evaluate the expression 3.0 + 3:

```
"trace of the messages sent in evaluating 3.0 + 3 with double dispatching"
3.0 + 3
3 sumFromFloat: 3.0
3 asFloat
3.0 + (3 asFloat)
<primitive: 41>        "float addition"
```

The term "double dispatching" refers to the strategy of sending the message + twice when a conversion is necessary. The same scheme is repeated for each operation that requires implicit conversions, and for all classes involved in each operation. Note that the additional messages such as sumFromFloat: are not intended to be used outside the classes' arithmetic methods.

Double dispatching is a more general technique for implementing multiple polymorphism than coercive generality because it does not require a linear ordering of the classes involved, and the classes do not need to share a common ancestor. For example, consider printing different types of documents on different kinds of printers. Because a double dispatching scheme includes a method for each combination of document type and printer type, each method can contain the operations for that particular combination.

As we saw in considering the evaluation of 3.0 + 3, double dispatching also sends far fewer additional messages to implement implicit conversions. Unfortunately, it leads to a proliferation of methods in the classes involved, and the classes are more tightly coupled since all the classes are listed explicitly in each other's protocol. (With coercive generality, a class's protocol refers only to classes that it can be converted to, e.g., asFloat.) If we perform double dispatching for the five messages +, -, *, /, and < with the three classes Float, Fraction, and Integer, each class must implement 15 methods, for 45 methods total. The total number of methods is proportional to the product of the number of operators and the square of the number of classes. Now suppose we add one new class, say Double, to this scheme. Five new messages such as sumFromDouble: must be implemented in each of the three existing classes, as well as the 20 methods for Double (i.e., four double dispatching methods for each of the five operations). We have gone from 45 methods to 80. Many of these methods will be the same, which makes the code faster to enter (using cut and paste), but more difficult to manage. The same problem occurs when adding to the protocol supported by any double dispatching scheme.

7.4.7 VisualWorks Numeric Classes

Overview

The VisualWorks system includes a more elaborate subhierarchy for numeric classes than the original Smalltalk-80 class library. It defines classes for complex numbers, fixed-point numbers, and both single and double precision floating-point numbers, and includes two additional abstract classes, ArithmeticValue and LimitedPrecisionReal. This subhierarchy is illustrated in Figure 7.4.

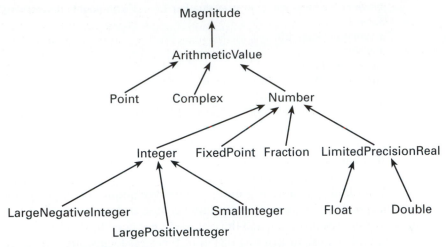

Figure 7.4   The VisualWorks numeric classes.

The class ArithmeticValue

The class ArithmeticValue is an abstract ancestor for all classes that participate in arithmetic operations. Because the binary selectors for the arithmetic and comparing messages are included in the protocol of the class Point (see the next section), Point is also defined as a subclass of ArithmeticValue in VisualWorks. The *arithmetic* protocol we described for Number in section 7.4.2 is defined in ArithmeticValue, and the methods for the selectors +, -, *, and / are deferred. ArithmeticValue's *testing* protocol consists of the messages isZero, negative, positive, strictlyPositive, and sign, and the messages even and odd are defined in Number. The Number converting message @ is not defined for ArithmeticValue because point coordinates should not be point or complex objects.

VisualWorks uses double dispatching for mixed-class arithmetic among double, floating-point, fraction, integer, and fixed-point numbers. The protocol of ArithmeticValue includes numerous *double dispatching* messages such as sumFromFloat:, productFromDouble:, and lessFromInteger: (for ordering comparisons). These messages are defined in each concrete numeric class, and we would expect them to be deferred in ArithmeticValue. However, to simplify adding new numeric classes, the ArithmeticValue methods for the double dispatching messages call retry:coercing:, and the *coercing* protocol of ArithmeticValue includes retry:coercing: and the deferred messages generality and coerce:. Because generality and coerce: are defined in Double, Float, Fraction, FixedPoint, and Integer, we can define a new numeric class and use it in mixed-class arithmetic expressions without defining new double dispatching methods for all the numeric classes and all the arithmetic and comparing selectors. Instead, we define the class's operations such that they call retry:coercing: if the argument is not of the receiver's class, and implement generality, coerce:, and the conversion messages discussed in the previous section. This combination of implementations of mixed-class arithmetic provides the speed of double dispatching for existing classes, and the convenience of coercive generality for defining new classes. The classes Point and Complex use coercive generality for mixed-class arithmetic.

The classes LimitedPrecisionReal **and** Double

Most computers now support both single and double precision floating-point operations, so VisualWorks includes a class Double. The class LimitedPrecisionReal is an abstract superclass for the classes Float (for single precision) and Double (for double precision). LimitedPrecisionReal defines the *truncation* and *conversion* messages we discussed for Float in section 7.4.5. Its *printing* message printString: takes an integer argument indicating the number of digits to be printed in the fraction part, and printOn: uses six digits.

Like Float, Double is defined as a variableByteSubclass:... of LimitedPrecisionReal that specifies two class variables Pi and RadiansPerDegrees. We write a double literal by using exponential notation with a d rather than an e (e.g., 6.02d23), or by appending the character d to a float literal (e.g., 3.3d). Like Float, Double implements the *arithmetic*, *comparing*, *mathematical functions*, and *truncation* messages as primitive methods. All the concrete numeric classes implement the *converting* message asDouble, which is used in Double's *double dispatching* methods, and in methods for messages such as sumFromDouble: in the other numeric classes.

The class Complex

The class Complex is a subclass of ArithmeticValue that defines two instance variables real and imaginary representing the real and imaginary part of a complex number. The instance variables may refer to float, double, fraction, or integer objects.

Complex defines the *instance creation* class message real:imaginary:, which calls the *private* initialization message setReal:setImaginary:. Number defines a converting message i that returns a complex number whose real part is zero and whose imaginary part is equal to the receiver. This message allows us to express a complex number in the usual fashion (e.g., as 3.0 + 3.0i). The Complex methods for printOn: and storeOn: also use this format.

The *arithmetic* protocol of Complex consists of the messages +, -, *, /, abs, and conjugated. The methods for the binary selectors check the class of the argument and send retry:coercing: if it is not a complex number. Complex also defines most of the messages in the *mathematical functions* protocol of Number. The method for the *comparing* message < signals an error because complex numbers are not regarded as ordered. The generality of Complex is higher than those of the other numeric classes, but lower than that of Point.

The class FixedPoint

The class FixedPoint provides an exact representation of non-integer numbers with a fixed number of decimal places after the decimal point. A common use for fixed-point numbers is currency values, which are rounded to the nearest hundredth in the United States. A fixed-point number could be represented as an integer and a scale factor, but if so, round-off errors can occur in calculations involving divisions. (For example, 1.000 / 3 would return .333, so 1.000 / 3 * 3 would be .999). Instead, FixedPoint is a subclass of Number that defines three instance variables numerator, denominator, and scale, so that the receiver's magnitude is maintained exactly as a fraction. The scale is used in printing the value, or if the object receives one of the *truncation* messages roundedToScale or truncatedToScale.

FixedPoint defines the *instance creation* class message numerator:denominator:scale:. We write a fixed-point literal as a real number followed either by s and an integer giving the scale, or by s alone, in which case the number of digits in the literal gives the scale. For example, 1.234s has a scale of 3, 1.234s5 has a scale of 5, and 1.234s2 signals an exception. The FixedPoint methods for printOn: and storeOn: also use this format.

FixedPoint includes the *accessing* message scale. The *arithmetic* and *comparing* selectors use double dispatching (e.g., the method for + sends sumFromFixedPoint: self to the argument). The scale of the result of an arithmetic operation on two fixed-point numbers is the maximum of their scales. In mixed-class arithmetic, an operation involving a fixed-point number and a limited precision real returns a real result, and an operation involving a fixed-point number and a fraction or integer returns a fixed point result. FixedPoint also defines the *converting* messages asFloat, asDouble, and asFixedPoint:, for which the argument is the scale of the result, and the *double dispatching* messages inherited from ArithmeticValue.

7.5 BASIC GRAPHICS CLASSES

7.5.1 The Class Point

Purpose and definition

An instance of the class Point represents a location in two-dimensional space, usually a point on a display canvas. Point objects also are used to encapsulate the *x* and *y* values for a translation factor, a scale factor, or the width and height of a rectangular extent (independent of its origin). We will see that points are treated like numbers in many ways, but point objects are not immutable. The class Point is a subclass of Object that defines two instance variables x and y for the point's coordinates, and is defined as follows:[9]

---

[9] In VisualWorks, Point is a subclass of ArithmeticValue because it understands messages such as + and <. It is not a subclass of Number because most mathematical functions are not applicable.

```
"definition of the class Point"
Object subclass: #Point
   instanceVariableNames: 'x y'
   classVariableNames: ''
   poolDictionaries: ''
   category: 'Graphics-Geometry'
```

The instance variable referents are usually either small integers or floats. Since Smalltalk uses a "left-handed" coordinate system with the origin at the upper left corner and x coordinates increasing to the right and y coordinates increasing downwards, so the coordinates of a point are non-negative unless it represents a translation.

Class protocol

We usually create point objects by sending the binary message @ to the x coordinate with the y coordinate as the argument, as we saw in section 5.3.2. That is, the selector @ provides a literal notation for creating points. The *instance creation* protocol of Point consists of the message x:y:, which takes initial values for the new object's coordinates. The Number method for @ calls this message. The method for x:y: does no type checking, but if a point is created with instance variables that are not numbers, an operation using the object will fail at some point. Some systems also provide a class message r:theta: so that the client can give the point's position in polar coordinates.

Instance protocol

The *accessing* protocol of class Point consists of the messages x, x:, y, and y:. Because the coordinates of an existing object can be modified, a point object can be used as a container for a two-dimensional value. The *polar coordinates* protocol of Point includes the accessor messages r and theta. (Angles are measured clockwise from the x axis.) The *printing* message printOn: prints the receiver using an infix @, and storeOn: stores a string that includes the instance creation message x:y:.

In many ways, points are treated as numeric objects. Point defines *arithmetic* protocol like that of Number, and the argument of the binary messages can be either a point or a number. For example, if the argument to + is a point, then the corresponding coordinates are summed to create a new point. If the argument is a number, the argument is added to both coordinates of the receiver to create a new point. For example, 2@3 + (3@5) returns 5@8, and 2@3 + 3 returns 5@6. The other arithmetic methods treat their argument similarly. The *arithmetic* protocol of Point consists of the following messages:

```
"the 'arithmetic' instance protocol of Point"
+ delta
   "Answer a new point that is the sum of the receiver and delta (which is either a
   point or a number)."
```

- delta
   "Answer a new point that is the difference of the receiver and delta."
* scale
   "Answer a new point that is the product of the receiver and scale."
/ scale
   "Answer a new point that is the quotient of the receiver and scale."
// scale
   "Answer a new point that is the quotient of the receiver and scale."
\\ scale
   "Answer a new point that is the modulo of the receiver and scale."
quo: scale
   "Answer a new point that is the quotient of the receiver and scale."
rem: scale
   "Answer a new point that is the remainder of the receiver and scale."
abs
   "Answer a new point whose x and y are the absolute values of the receiver's x and y."

To facilitate defining these methods, both the classes Point and Number define a *converting* message asPoint. Its method is ∧self in Point, and ∧self@self in Number. For example, the Point method for + is coded as follows:[10]

   "instance method in class Point"

   + delta
      "Answer a new point that is the sum of the receiver and delta."

      | deltaPoint |
      deltaPoint := delta asPoint.
      ∧x + deltaPoint x @ (y + deltaPoint y)

The other arithmetic methods for Point are coded similarly. We also want arithmetic expressions with a numeric receiver and a point object to return a point. For example, 3 + (2@3) should return 5@6. In systems that use coercive generality, the class Point implements generality and coerce:, and has a generality index higher than any numeric class. In VisualWorks, the message 3 + (2@3) invokes the primitive method for small integer addition, which fails so the message 2@3 sumFromInteger: 3 is sent. Point does not define this method, so the method of its superclass ArithmeticValue is executed, resulting in the message 3 retry: #+ coercing: 2@3. Because Point's generality is higher than that of small integers, the message 2@3 coerce: 3 is sent, resulting in the point 3@3, and point addition is performed.

---

[10] In VisualWorks, this method is coded as ∧delta sumFromPoint: self, and the sumFromPoint: method in ArithmeticValue sends retry:coercing:. The Point method for sumFromPoint: creates a new point whose coordinates are the sums of the corresponding coordinates of the receiver and argument, but this message is not implemented in the other numeric classes, so they use coercive generality.

Point's arithmetic messages facilitate coding graphic calculations. The selectors + and - translate a point further from or closer to the origin, and the selectors * and / scale a point further from or closer to the origin. For example, the following code fragment sets arrPoints to an array of numPoints equally spaced points along the line connecting startPoint and endPoint:

```
"set arrPoints to an array of numPoints equally-spaced points along the line
connecting startPoint and endPoint"
| incrementPoint |
incrementPoint := (endPoint - startPoint) / (numPoints - 1).
arrPoints := Array new: numPoints.
1 to: numPoints do: [ :index | arrPoints at: index put: startPoint + (index - 1) * incrementPoint]
```

Like Number, Point defines the *testing* message isZero, which returns true if both coordinates are zero, and *comparing* protocol like that of Magnitude. It overrides the message = to return true if the argument is a point whose coordinates are equal to those of the receiver.[11] A point is less than another point only if both of its coordinates are smaller than those of the other point (i.e., if it is above and to the left of the other point), and similarly for the other comparison operators. For example, (50@200) < (100@300) returns true, and (50@200) < (100@100) returns false. Note also that both (50@100) < (100@50) and (100@50) < (50@100) return false. The comparing protocol of Point includes the following messages:

```
"the 'comparing' instance protocol of Point"
< aPoint
    "Answer whether the receiver is 'above and to the left' of aPoint."
<= aPoint
    "Answer whether the receiver is 'neither below nor to the right' of aPoint."
> aPoint
    "Answer whether the receiver is 'below and to the right' of aPoint."
>= aPoint
    "Answer whether the receiver is 'neither above nor to the left' of aPoint."
hash
    "Answer a SmallInteger unique to the receiver."
max: aPoint
    "Answer the lower right corner of the rectangle defined by the receiver and aPoint."
min: aPoint
    "Answer the upper left corner of the rectangle defined by the receiver and aPoint."
between: minPoint and: maxPoint
    "Answer whether the receiver is within the rectangle defined by minPoint and maxPoint."
```

Note that the result of aPoint1 max: aPoint2 will be neither aPoint1 nor aPoint2 if neither aPoint1 <= aPoint2 nor aPoint2 <= aPoint1 is true. Like the arithmetic

---

[11] In VisualWorks, Point inherits the = method of its superclass ArithmeticValue, which sends isZero to the difference between the receiver and argument and returns that result.

methods, the Point methods for <, <=, >, and >= convert the argument with asPoint before comparing the *x* and *y* coordinates of the receiver and argument.

The *point functions* and *transforming* protocols of class Point perform graphic calculations, and consist of the following messages:

```
"the 'point functions' and 'transforming' instance protocols of Point"
dist: aPoint
    "Answer the distance between the receiver and aPoint."
dotProduct: aPoint
    "Answer the dot product of the receiver and aPoint."
grid: aPoint
    "Answer a new point that is the nearest rounded point to the receiver on the grid
    with spacing specified by aPoint."
truncatedGrid: aPoint
    "Answer a new point that is the nearest truncated point to the receiver on the grid
    with spacing specified by aPoint."
unitVector
    "Answer a new point that is the receiver scaled to unit length."
normal
    "Answer a new point representing the unit vector for the receiver rotated 90 degrees
    toward the y axis."
transpose
    "Answer a new point whose x is the receiver's y and whose y is the receiver's x."
nearestPointOnLineFrom: point1 to: point2
    "Answer the closest point to the receiver on the line determined by point1 and point2."
nearestIntegerPointOnLineFrom: point1 to: point2
    "Answer the closest integer point to the receiver on the line determined by
    point1 and point2."
scaledBy: factorPoint
    "Answer a new point scaled by factorPoint."
translatedBy: deltaPoint
    "Answer a new point translated by deltaPoint."
```

For example, 11@10 grid: 3@3 returns 12@9, while 11@10 truncatedGrid: 3@3 returns 9@9. Point provides both nearestPointOnLineFrom:to: and nearestIntegerPointOnLineFrom:to: because the latter's method is more efficient for points with integer coordinates, which are used much more often. The methods for these messages are simpler to code due to Point's arithmetic protocol. For example:

```
"instance methods in class Point"
dist: aPoint
    "Answer the distance between aPoint and the receiver."

    ^(aPoint - self) r
unitVector
    "Answer a new point that is the receiver scaled to unit length."

    ^self / self r
```

The *truncation* protocol of class Point consists of the messages rounded, truncated, and truncateTo:, which return a new point that results from sending that message to the receiver's coordinates. The argument of truncateTo: essentially specifies a grid, and can be either a number or a point. For example, 35@22 truncateTo: 3 returns 33@21, and 35@22 truncateTo: 2@5 returns 34@20.

In addition to asPoint, Point defines the *converting* messages corner: and extent:, which create a new rectangle with the receiver as the origin and the argument as the corner or extent.

7.5.2 The Class Rectangle

Purpose and definition

The class Rectangle represents a particular rectangle at a given offset from the origin of a canvas or view. Instances are used to specify the location and size of a window or view, the bounding box of an ellipse, and the clipping rectangle for a graphic operation. Like points, rectangles are not immutable objects. Rectangle is a subclass of Object that defines two instance variables origin and corner, and is defined as follows: [12]

```
"definition of the class Rectangle"
Object subclass: #Rectangle
    instanceVariableNames: 'origin corner'
    classVariableNames: ''
    poolDictionaries: ''
    category: 'Graphics-Geometry'
```

The referents of the instance variables origin and corner are points that represent the upper left and lower right corners of the receiver, respectively.

Class protocol

In practice, rectangles are usually created by sending one of the Point instance messages corner: or extent: to a point representing the origin of the new object. These messages provide a literal notation for rectangles (e.g., 20@30 corner: 100@150). Their methods invoke the Rectangle class messages origin:corner: and origin:extent:, respectively.

The *instance creation* protocol of Rectangle provides a number of messages that perform instantiation and initialization, including the following:

---

[12] In Visualworks, Rectangle is a subclass of Geometric, an abstract superclass for graphic objects that can be represented mathematically.

"the 'instance creation' class protocol of Rectangle"
origin: originPoint corner: cornerPoint
    "Answer an instance of the receiver whose top left and bottom right corners are
    the arguments."
origin: originPoint extent: extentPoint
    "Answer an instance of the receiver whose top left corner is originPoint, with width and
    height determined by extentPoint."
left: leftNumber right: rightNumber top: topNumber bottom: bottomNumber
    "Answer an instance of the receiver whose left, right, top, and bottom coordinates are
    the corresponding arguments."
vertex: vertexPoint1 vertex: vertexPoint2
    "Answer an instance of the receiver whose diagonally opposite vertices are specified
    by the arguments."
fromUser
    "Answer an instance of the receiver that is determined by having the user designate
    the top left and bottom right corners."
fromUser: gridPoint
    "Answer an instance of the receiver that is determined by having the user designate
    the top left and bottom right corners. The gridding for user selection is gridPoint."

The arguments of the first four messages provide an initial value for the new object. Like the Point x:y: class method, they do no type checking. In fact, the messages origin:corner:, origin:extent:, and left:right:top:bottom: do not normalize the result in the sense of ensuring that the new object's origin is less than its corner (although vertex:vertex: does). The message fromUser allows the user to select a particular rectangle relative to the display screen, and returns that rectangle. The method displays a "cross hairs" cursor, and when the user presses the selection mouse button, it displays a dashed outline of a rectangle with one corner anchored at the point of the button press. The user then drags the opposite corner of the dashed rectangle to the desired size and releases the mouse button.

Instance protocol

The class Rectangle defines an extensive *accessing* protocol for obtaining information about the receiver, and for modifying the receiver's origin and corner. This protocol includes

- origin, origin:, corner, corner:, extent, extent:, origin:corner:, and origin:extent:, which take or return points
- top, top:, bottom, bottom:, left, left:, right, right:, height, height:, width, and width:, which take or return numbers
- center, which returns the point at the center of the receiver, topCenter, which returns the center of the top side of the receiver, and topLeft, topRight, bottomLeft, bottomCenter, bottomRight, leftCenter and rightCenter, each of which returns the indicated point
- area, which returns the area of the receiver.

Rectangle refines the *comparing* messages = and hash, and overrides the *copying* message copy to copy the receiver's origin and corner. It defines the *printing* message printOn: to print the receiver using the Point instance message corner:. For example, a rectangle with origin (2, 3) and corner (7, 10) prints as '2@3 corner: 7@10'. The method for storeOn: stores a string consisting of the instance creation message origin:corner: with the receiver's instance variable values. Rectangle also defines the *truncating* messages rounded and truncated, whose methods create a new rectangle whose origin and corner are those of the receiver rounded or truncated.

Rectangle defines numerous messages for performing computations involving rectangles. Its *rectangle functions* protocol includes messages for intersecting, merging, and computing new rectangles.

```
"the 'rectangle functions' instance protocol of Rectangle"
intersect: aRectangle
    "Answer a rectangle that is the area in which the receiver overlaps with aRectangle. "
merge: aRectangle
    "Answer a rectangle that contains both the receiver and the argument aRectangle."
areasOutside: aRectangle
    "Answer an ordered collection of rectangles comprising the parts of the receiver that
    do not lie within aRectangle."
expandedBy: delta
    "Answer a rectangle that is outset from the receiver by delta, a rectangle, point or scalar."
insetBy: delta
    "Answer a rectangle that is inset from the receiver by delta, a rectangle, point or scalar."
insetOriginBy: originDeltaPoint cornerBy: cornerDeltaPoint
    "Answer a rectangle that is inset from the receiver by originDeltaPoint for the origin
    cornerDeltaPoint for the corner."
amountToTranslateWithin: aRectangle
    "Answer a point such that the receiver translated by that point is within aRectangle."
```

The following examples illustrate the use of this protocol:

```
"Example computations using the rectangle functions protocol of Rectangle"
"returns 1@5 corner: 7@15"
(3@5 corner: 7@12) merge: (1@6 corner: 4@15)
"returns 1@1 corner: 10@14"
(3@4 corner: 8@11) expandedBy: 2@3
"returns 5@7 corner: 6@8"
(3@4 corner: 8@11) insetBy: 2@3
"returns OrderedCollection (3@5 corner: 7@6 3@10 corner: 7@12 4@6 corner: 7@10 )"
(3@5 corner: 7@12) areasOutside: (1@6 corner: 4@10)
```

Rectangle's *transforming* protocol for translating, scaling, moving, and aligning rectangles consists of the following messages:

"the 'transforming' instance protocol of Rectangle"
translatedBy: factor
   "Answer a new rectangle that is the receiver translated by factor, a point or a scalar."
scaledBy: scale
   "Answer a new rectangle that is the receiver scaled by scale, a point or a scalar."
moveTo: aPoint
   "Change the receiver so that its origin is aPoint."
moveBy: factor
   "Change the receiver so that it is translated by factor, a point or a scalar."
align: aPoint1 with: aPoint2
   "Answer a new rectangle that is translated by aPoint2 - aPoint1."

Note that translatedBy: returns a new rectangle, but moveBy: modifies the receiver. Rectangle defines the following *testing* protocol for querying the receiver:

"the 'testing' instance protocol of Rectangle"
contains: aRectangle
   "Answer whether aRectangle is equal to or contained within the receiver."
containsPoint: aPoint
   "Answer whether aPoint is within the receiver."
intersects: aRectangle
   "Answer whether aRectangle intersects the receiver."

As is common in graphics programming, the bottom and right edges of a rectangle are not considered to be contained within the rectangle (e.g., by containsPoint: and intersects:). For example, painting the rectangles 2@3 corner: 4@7 and 2@7 corner: 4@10 does not paint the pixels on the line from 2@7 to 4@7 twice.

   The rectangle functions, transforming, and testing methods make extensive use of point arithmetic. For example,

"instance methods in class Rectangle"

intersect: aRectangle
   "Answer a rectangle that is the area in which the receiver overlaps with aRectangle."

   ^self class   "to allow subclass-specific refinement"
      origin: (origin max: aRectangle origin)
      corner: (corner min: aRectangle corner)

moveTo: aPoint
   "Change the receiver so that its origin is aPoint."

   corner := corner + aPoint - origin.
   origin := aPoint

contains: aRectangle
   "Answer whether aRectangle is equal to or contained within the receiver."

   ^origin <= aRectangle origin and: [aRectangle corner <= corner]

7.6 SUMMARY AND REVIEW

7.6.1 The Class Object

Definition

- The class Object is the only class that does not have a superclass, and is defined as a subclass of nil.
- Object defines no instance variables, so it is an abstract class.

Instance protocol

- Because all classes are descendants of Object, all objects respond to its protocol. Object defines methods that provide default behavior a class may inherit, replace, or refine.
- Object defines *copying* protocol, especially the message copy, whose method in Object does a shallow copy.
- The *comparing* protocol of Object includes identity tests, equality tests, and the messages hash and identityHash, all of which are implemented by primitive methods. Many classes override = and hash, but none should redefine == or identityHash.
- Object's *testing* protocol includes the messages isNil, notNil, isInteger, isString, isSymbol, and isBehavior, which return false in Object (except for notNil), and true in the appropriate class.
- The *class membership* protocol of Object consists of the messages class, isMemberOf:, isKindOf:, and respondsTo:.
- Object's *error handling* messages report errors via notifiers, and include the general message error: and the messages doesNotUnderstand:, shouldNotImplement, subclassResponsibility, nonIntegerIndexError:, subscriptBoundsError:, notFoundError, primitiveFailed, halt, halt:, and notify:. These messages are typically sent to self. The error handling protocol also includes inspect and browse.
- The *accessing* protocol of Object defines the messages for indexed instance variables at:, at:put:, and size, and the system messages basicAt:, basicAt:put:, and basicSize.
- The *printing* protocol of Object includes the messages printOn:, printString, storeOn:, storeString, and isLiteral. Printing an object returns a readable description of the object, and storing an object returns an expression that can be evaluated to recreate an equivalent object. The Object methods implement printString and storeString in terms of printOn: and storeOn:, so classes only need to define printOn: and storeOn:.
- The *dependents access* protocol of Object allows associating *dependent* objects with a *sponsor* object, and *changing* messages notify the dependents if the

sponsor's state changes. Object defines these methods, and classes for dependents must define the *updating* messages sent when the sponsor changes. In the Model-View-Controller paradigm, these messages are used to update the views of a model object when it changes. The Object class variable Dependents maintains the dictionary of dependencies.

- The *message handling* protocol of Object supports indirect messaging. The message perform: takes a symbol giving a unary message and sends that message to the receiver, and performWith: (and so on) allow passing an argument.

- The *system primitives* protocol of Object provides direct access to an object's representation for the compiler, execution environment, and programming tools. It also includes the message become:, which exchanges the receiver's identity with that of its argument.

Class protocol

- All class objects respond to the class protocol of Object, which includes instance creation messages, the subclass creation messages, and type information messages.

- The abstract classes Behavior, ClassDescription, and Class are ancestors of Object class, and define most of Object's class protocol and its variables for type information.

- The class Behavior is a subclass of Object. Its protocol includes messages for creating instances, using type information, and compiling code, and it defines instance variables for the class's superclass, a list of its subclasses, and its method dictionary.

- Behavior defines the *instance creation* messages new and new: as primitive methods, and some classes override these to provide default initialization. It overrides the *copying* messages shallowCopy and deepCopy to return the receiver.

- Behavior's *testing* protocol returns information about the structure of the receiver class, and its *class hierarchy* protocols access, create, test, and enumerate the receiver's ancestors and descendants. The *method dictionary* protocols manipulate the receiver's message selectors and methods. Behavior also defines *compiling*, *accessing instances*, and *enumerating instances* messages.

- The class ClassDescription is a subclass of Behavior that adds instance variables for the class's instance variable names and browser information. Its protocol defines messages for manipulating a class's instance variable names, comment, and message and class categories. ClassDescription also defines *printing* and *fileIn/Out* messages.

- The class Class is a subclass of ClassDescription that adds instance variables for the class's name, and for the dictionaries that contain its class variables and pool variables. Its protocol includes messages for manipulating this information, and the *subclass creation* messages.

- The class protocol of Object includes a *class initialization* message initialize that creates the Dependents dictionary, and the *instance creation* messages readFromString: and readFrom:. The argument is a message expression whose evaluation creates and initializes a new object, usually created by a storeOn: method. Descendants only need to override readFrom:.

7.6.2 Classes for Unique Objects

The class UndefinedObject

- The class UndefinedObject is a subclass of Object that defines no instance or class variables, and has one instance, the unique object nil. This object is the value of all uninitialized local, instance, or shared variables.
- Because its instance is unique, UndefinedObject inherits Object's methods for identity and equality tests, its new method produces an error notifier, and its shallowCopy method returns self.
- UndefinedObject implements the *testing* messages isNil and notNil, and its methods for the *printing* messages printOn: and storeOn: use its literal notation.

The class Boolean

- The class Boolean is a subclass of Object that represents logical values and defines conditional control messages.
- Because its instances are unique, Boolean inherits Object's methods for identity and equality tests, its new method displays an error notifier, and its shallowCopy method returns self.
- Boolean's *logical operations* protocol consists of the messages &, |, not, eqv:, and xor:.
- The *controlling* protocol of Boolean includes the messages ifTrue:, ifFalse:, ifTrue:ifFalse:, ifFalse:ifTrue:, and:, and or:.
- The classes True and False are subclasses of the abstract class Boolean, each of which has a single, unique instance. Each class defines the methods for its value without testing the receiver's value, and message resolution selects the code to be executed.

7.6.3 Classes for Linearly Ordered Objects

The class Magnitude

- The abstract class Magnitude is a subclass of Object that specifies protocol for comparing linearly ordered objects, but defines no instance or class variables.
- The *comparing* protocol of Magnitude includes the messages =, hash, <, >, <=, >=, between:and:, min:, and max:. The messages <, =, and hash are abstract, and the other messages are implemented in terms of these two. Each concrete

subclass defines its own representation and methods for <, =, and hash, and inherits the remaining comparing methods.

- Magnitude has five subclasses: Date, Time, Character, Number, and Lookup-Key.

The class Character

- The class Character is a subclass of Magnitude that represents letters and special characters, and its instances are used as elements of strings. It has 256 instances, and the values 0 through 127 represent the standard ASCII characters.
- Characters are unique, immutable objects, so new signals an error message, and shallowCopy returns the receiver.
- The *instance creation* class protocol of Character includes the message value:, which converts from an integer to the corresponding ASCII character.
- Character's *accessing untypeable characters* class protocol provides mnemonic messages such as space, cr, esc, and tab, which return nonprintable characters.
- The *comparing* protocol of Character defines the deferred methods of Magnitude.
- Character's *testing* protocol includes messages such as isAlphabetic, isDigit, isLowercase, and isSeparator.
- Character's *converting* protocol consists of asInteger, asLowercase, asUppercase, and asSymbol.
- Character's methods for the *printing* messages printOn: and storeOn: use its literal notation.

The class Date

- The class Date is a subclass of Magnitude whose instances are immutable objects representing a particular date, not containers for a date value.
- Date specifies two instance variables, year and day, and four class variables, DaysInMonth (the number of days in each month), MonthNames (the names of the months), WeekDayNames (the names of the seven days of the week), and FirstDayOfMonth (the day number of the first day of each month).
- The *instance creation* class protocol of Date consists of newDay:month:year:, newDay:year:, today, fromDays:, and readFrom:.
- Date's *general inquiries* class protocol provides messages that access the calendar information stored in the class variables (e.g., daysInMonth:forYear:, leapYear:, nameOfMonth:, and dayOfWeek:).
- The *accessing* protocol of Date consists of the messages day, year, monthName, monthIndex, weekday, and leap.
- Date's *inquires* protocol includes dayOfMonth, daysInMonth, daysInYear, daysLeftInYear, firstDayOfMonth, and previous:.

- Date implements the *comparing* messages =, <, and hash inherited from Magnitude, and the *printing* messages printOn: and storeOn: inherited from Object.
- The *arithmetic* protocol of Date relieves the programmer from coding date calculations, and consists of the messages addDays:, subtractDays:, and subtractDate:.
- Date supplies the *converting* messages asDays and asSeconds.

The class Time

- The class Time is a subclass of Magnitude, whose instances represent a particular time of day. An instance has three instance variables, hours, minutes, and seconds.
- The *instance creation* class protocol of Time consists of the messages fromSeconds:, now, and readFrom:.
- Time defines *general inquiries* class protocol consisting of totalSeconds, millisecondClockValue, millisecondsToRun:, and dateAndTimeNow.
- Time defines the *accessing* messages hours, minutes, and seconds, the *converting* message asSeconds, and the *arithmetic* messages addTime: and subtractTime:, which return a new time object.
- Time implements the *comparing* deferred methods of Magnitude and the *printing* messages printOn: and storeOn:.

7.6.4 Numeric Classes

Numeric objects

- In Smalltalk, numbers are objects, and mathematical operations are messages to numeric objects, rather than built-in types and operations defined by the language.
- Smalltalk supports integers of any size, rational numbers, and floating-point numbers, and numeric objects are immutable objects, rather than containers.
- We do not have to choose a type for a numeric variable, and can use the protocol of Number without being concerned with what kind of number the object is.

The class Number

- The class Number is an abstract subclass of Magnitude that specifies protocol for all numbers and defines many methods, but does not include a representation for a value.
- Number has three subclasses Float, Fraction, and the abstract class Integer, which has the concrete subclasses SmallInteger, LargeNegativeInteger, and LargePositiveInteger.
- Instances of SmallInteger are unique objects, while instances of the other numeric classes are created and destroyed as needed.

- The *instance creation* class protocol of Number implements readFrom:, and disallows new and new:. The inherited message readFromString: converts a literal string to the corresponding numeric object.
- The *arithmetic* protocol of Number includes the binary messages +, -, *, /, //, and \\, and the messages quo:, rem:, abs, negated, and reciprocal. The methods for the binary selectors are deferred, and the other messages are defined using those messages.
- Number's *mathematical functions* protocol defines numerous messages such as exp, log, raisedTo:, sqrt, and cos. Number implements many of these messages by methods that convert the receiver to a float and then send the message to that object.
- Number's *testing* protocol consists of the messages isZero, negative, positive, strictlyPositive, sign, even, and odd.
- The *converting* protocol of Number consists of the messages degreesToRadians, radiansToDegrees, asInteger, and asFloat.
- Number's *truncation* protocol includes ceiling, floor, truncated, rounded, roundedTo:, and truncated:, which all return an integer.
- The *printing* protocol of Number defines storeOn: in terms of printOn:, which each concrete class defines to use its literal representation.
- Number's *intervals* protocol contains the messages to: and to:by:, which create instances of Interval, and to:do: and to:by:do:, which enumerate the elements of the specified interval.

The integer classes

- The abstract class Integer is a subclass of Number that has three concrete subclasses, SmallInteger, LargeNegativeInteger, and LargePositiveInteger.
- A small integer is slightly smaller than an object reference, and large integers may be of any magnitude so integer operations do not overflow. Numeric methods return small integers whenever possible.
- The protocol of Integer includes that of its ancestors Number and Magnitude, and it implements *arithmetic* and *comparing* messages (except for equality tests) using either coercive generality or double dispatching.
- Integer's *factorization* protocol consists of the messages factorial, gcd:, and lcm:, and it defines the *enumerating* message timesRepeat:.
- Integer defines the *converting* messages asCharacter, asInteger, asFloat, and asFraction.
- The *printing* messages printStringRadix: and storeStringRadix: print or store the receiver in the radix given by the argument, and printOn: and storeOn: use base 10.
- Integer defines *bit manipulation* protocol that interprets the receiver as a sequence of bits, and includes messages that perform bitwise logical operations, bit access, bit shifts, and masking.

- The class SmallInteger is a subclass of Integer whose instances are unique, immutable objects. SmallInteger does not define any additional protocol, and many of its methods invoke primitive methods.

- The classes LargePositiveInteger and LargeNegativeInteger are subclasses of Integer whose instances maintain their absolute values as a sequence of bytes in indexed instance variables. The sign of a large integer is represented by its class identity.

- LargePositiveInteger and LargeNegativeInteger define little additional protocol, but they and their abstract superclass Integer implement a number of methods by *accessing* their bytes with the messages digitAt:, digitAt:put:, and digitLength.

The class Fraction

- The class Fraction is a subclass of Number that defines two instance variables numerator and denominator, which can be small or large integers. The result of an arithmetic operation is a fraction if one operand is a fraction and the other is not a float.

- We usually create fractions by sending the binary selector / to an integer or fraction, or by an arithmetic operation. Fraction also defines the *instance creation* class message numerator:denominator:.

- Fraction inherits the protocol of its superclasses Magnitude and Number, and defines the *accessing* messages numerator and denominator. The class defines numerous methods that are implemented in terms of its instance variables.

The class Float

- The class Float is a subclass of Number whose instances represent real numbers and store the platform's floating-point format in a byte array of indexed instance variables. Float maintains the constants Pi and RadiansPerDegree in class variables.

- Float's class protocol consists of the *class initialization* message initialize, which initializes the class variables, and the *constants access* messages pi and radiansPerDegree. Float objects are created by a float literal or a numeric message.

- Float inherits the instance protocol of its ancestors Magnitude and Number, and implements most of these messages as primitive methods.

- Float defines the *converting* messages asFraction, degreesToRadians, and radiansToDegrees, and the *truncation* messages fractionPart and integerPart.

Mixed-class arithmetic in Smalltalk

- If the receiver of an arithmetic or comparison operation is of a different class than the argument, one is converted to the other's class implicitly. The method invoked depends on the classes of both operands dynamically, and a Smalltalk system must implement this multiple polymorphism in terms of message passing.

- With *coercive generality*, each numeric class is assigned a *generality index*, and the generality index of Float is greater than that of Fraction, which is greater than that for large integers, which is greater than that of SmallInteger. If the operands of an arithmetic operation do not have the same generality index, the lower generality operand is converted to the higher generality operand's class, and the higher generality class's method is then performed.

- The Number *coercing* message retry:coercing: codes the general strategy of coercing the lower generality operand and then performing the higher generality operation. The deferred methods coerce: and generality provide the class-specific behavior it uses. The arithmetic and comparing methods in numeric classes send retry:coercing: if receiver and argument's classes do not have the same generality index.

- To add a numeric class with coercive generality, we define it as a subclass of Number, implement coerce: and generality, define a conversion message to the new class in each numeric class with a lower generality, and define conversion messages to all classes with higher generality in the new class.

- With *double dispatching*, the receiver responds with a message to the argument that encodes its own class in the selector. In the methods for that message, the classes of both the receiver and the argument are known, so the appropriate conversions can be coded directly. A message that requires a conversion is sent twice, once by the original client and then again with a receiver and argument of the same class.

- Double dispatching is more general than coercive generality and sends fewer messages to implement implicit conversions, but the number of methods required for each doubly-dispatched operation is the square of the number of classes involved.

VisualWorks numeric classes

- The VisualWorks system includes classes for complex numbers, fixed-point numbers, and both single and double precision floating-point numbers, and defines two additional abstract classes, ArithmeticValue and LimitedPrecisionReal.

- The class ArithmeticValue is an abstract class that specifies *arithmetic*, *double dispatching* (e.g., sumFromFloat:), and *coercing* protocol for its concrete descendants.

- The classes for doubles, floats, fractions, integers, and fixed-point numbers use double dispatching for mixed-class arithmetic.

- The double dispatching methods of ArithmeticValue call retry:coercing: so that new numeric classes can be defined using coercive generality. Complex numbers and points use coercive generality.

- The class Double represents double precision floating-point numbers. We write a double literal using exponential notation with a d rather than an e, or by appending a d to a float literal. The class LimitedPrecisionReal is an abstract superclass for Float and Double.

- The class Complex is a subclass of ArithmeticValue that defines two instance variables, real and imaginary, and represents complex numbers. Complex defines the *instance creation* class message real:imaginary:, and complex numbers can be written in the usual fashion using the Number converting message i (e.g., 3.0 + 3.0i). Complex defines *arithmetic* and *mathematical functions* protocol, but disallows *comparing* messages. The generality of Complex is higher than the other numeric classes, but lower than that of Point.

- The class FixedPoint represents numbers with a fixed number of decimal places after the decimal point. It is a subclass of Number with three instance variables numerator, denominator, and scale, so that the receiver's magnitude can be maintained exactly. A fixed-point literal is written as a real number followed by s, or by s and an integer giving the scale.

- FixedPoint defines the *instance creation* class message numerator: denominator:scale:, and the *accessing* message scale. Its *arithmetic* and *comparing* selectors use double dispatching. The scale of the result of a fixed-point arithmetic operation is the maximum of their scales. An arithmetic operation involving a fixed-point number and a real returns a real result, and an operation involving a fixed-point number and a fraction or integer returns a fixed-point result.

7.6.5 Basic Graphics Classes

The class Point

- The class Point is a subclass of Object that defines two instance variables x and y for the point's coordinates. Point objects also are used to encapsulate the *x* and *y* values for a translation factor, a scale factor, or the width and height of a rectangular extent.

- We usually create point objects by sending @ to the *x* coordinate with the *y* coordinate as the argument. The Point *instance creation* message x:y: takes initial values for the new object's coordinates.

- The *accessing* protocol of Point consists of the messages x, x:, y and y:, and its *polar coordinates* protocol includes the messages r and theta.

- Point defines *arithmetic* protocol like that of Number, and the argument can be a point or a number, which is added, multiplied, etc. into both coordinates. We use these messages to code graphic calculations since + and - perform translations and * and / perform scaling.

- Point defines the *testing* message isZero and *comparing* protocol similar to that of Magnitude. A point is less than another point only if both of its coordinates are smaller.

- The *point functions* and *transforming* protocols of Point perform graphic calculations and include messages such as dist:, grid:, unitVector, and nearestPointOnLineFrom:to:.

- Point defines the *truncation* messages rounded, truncated, and truncateTo:.

- The Point *converting* messages corner: and extent: create a new rectangle with the receiver as the origin and the argument as the corner or extent.

- Point's method for the *printing* message printOn: prints the receiver using @, and storeOn: uses the instance creation message x:y:.

The class Rectangle

- The class Rectangle is a subclass of Object that defines two instance variables origin and extent, which are points that represent the receiver's upper left and lower right corners.

- The *instance creation* class protocol of Rectangle includes the messages origin:corner:, origin:extent:, left:right:top:bottom:, vertex:vertex:, and fromUser. We can also create rectangles by sending the Point messages corner: or extent: to the origin of the new object.

- Rectangle defines numerous *accessing* messages such as origin, origin:, corner, corner:, extent, top, top:, bottom, left, right, center, topRight, bottomLeft, topCenter, height, and area.

- Rectangle's *rectangle functions* protocol consists of the messages intersect:, merge:, areasOutside:, expandedBy:, insetBy:, insetOriginBy:cornerBy:, and amountToTranslateWithin:. It defines the *transforming* messages translatedBy:, scaledBy:, moveTo:, moveBy:, and align:with:, and the *truncating* messages rounded and truncated. Its *testing* protocol consists of the messages contains:, containsPoint:, and intersects:. These methods make extensive use of point arithmetic.

- The method for the *printing* message printOn: for Rectangle prints the receiver using the point message corner:, and storeOn: uses the instance creation message origin:corner:.

7.7 EXERCISES

The best way to understand the system classes is to use the facilities of a Smalltalk system. Many of the exercises in this chapter ask questions that you should answer by using the browser, querying type information, or executing code fragments. The details of the answers to some exercises may vary among Smalltalk dialects.

   7.1 **(a)** Does the class Object define any deferred methods?
   (b) Which methods in the protocol of Object are typically overridden by a descendant class?
   (c) Which methods in the protocol of Object should not be overridden?

7.2 Why doesn't the Object method for the message isNil test whether the receiver is nil?

7.3 Which of Object's error handling messages are always sent to self, and which are not?

7.4 **(a)** Why are the messages at:, at:put:, and size defined in Object?

  (b) Why does Object define both at: and basicAt:?

  (c) Use your Smalltalk system to determine which classes override at:, and why each does so.

7.5 Describe the difference between the strings returned by the messages printString and storeString.

7.6 **(a)** Browse the senders of addDependent:. How would you characterize the classes whose methods send this message?

  (b) Browse the senders of changed: and changed:with:. How would you characterize the classes whose methods send these messages? Can you see why they use these messages?

  (c) Browse the implementors of update: and update:with:. How would you characterize the classes that define these methods?

7.7 Code the method for the Object instance message isKindOf:. Compare your answer to the method on your Smalltalk system.

7.8 Because primitive methods are not identified by selectors, it is not possible to browse the senders of a primitive method. Write an expression that returns a list of the selectors for class Object that invoke primitive methods. (Use the String message match:.)

7.9 Describe the purpose of each of the instance variables defined by the classes Behavior, ClassDescription, and Class.

7.10 Why is the message new defined as a class method in Boolean, but as an instance method in Behavior?

7.11 Recall the class PriorityQueue defined in section 6.2.2. What is the result of evaluating each of the following expressions?

  (a) PriorityQueue instSize

  (b) PriorityQueue isVariable

  (c) PriorityQueue allSelectors

7.12 Write an expression that returns each of the following:

  (a) the number of classes with indexed instance variables

  (b) the classes whose instances can respond to the message <

  (c) the subclasses of Magnitude that do not contain pointers

  (d) a dictionary whose keys are the names of the subclasses of Collection that define a method for addFirst:, and whose values are the corresponding source methods

7.13 Code the methods for the following Behavior instance messages. Compare your answers to the methods on your Smalltalk system.

  (a) allSuperclasses

  (b) inheritsFrom:

  (c) canUnderstand:

  (d) allInstancesDo:

7.14 Using your Smalltalk system, examine the protocol for the class ClassOrganizer. Write a method printProtocolOn: for the class ClassDescription that appends a string consisting of the receiver's protocol organized according to message categories to the argument stream. Use the protocol format we have used in this chapter. You may assume that the source code for a method consists of a line giving the message pattern, a comment enclosed in double quotes, and the method code.

7.15 **(a)** Define a method for exclusivelyBetween:and: for the class Magnitude.

(b) Give an advantage and a disadvantage of providing both this message and between:and:.

7.16 **(a)** Are there any classes in your Smalltalk system besides descendants of Magnitude that define a method for the selector <? For each, why does it define this method and why isn't it a subclass of Magnitude?

(b) Are there any classes in your Smalltalk system besides Magnitude that define a method for the selector >? If so, why do they?

7.17 What occurs when the expression Date new printString is evaluated on your system? Explain this behavior.

7.18 Write a method for the Date instance message addMonths: anInteger, which returns the date, which is anInteger, months after the receiver.

7.19 We want to define a Smalltalk method that returns a string consisting of a formatted calendar for a particular month and year.

(a) Should the message calendarForMonth:year: be a class message or an instance message?

(b) Code the method for message in part (a) (assume that you are using a fixed-width font).

(c) Code the method for an instance message calendar that prints the calendar for the receiver's month and year (you may use your answer to part) (b).

7.20 **(a)** What does the following message return on your Smalltalk system? (Time readFromString: '3:3:3') addTime: (Date readFromString: '3/3/95')

(b) Why do you think that addTime: and subtractTime: support date arguments, but not integer arguments? (Recall that the argument of the Date messages addDays: and subtractDays: are integers.)

7.21 We want to define a class TimeAndDate whose instances represent a particular time on a particular date.

(a) Which messages in the protocols of the classes Date and Time, should the class provide? Are there any additional messages necessary?

(b) Should the class be defined as a subclass of Date, Time, or Magnitude? Code whichever alternative you choose.

7.22 In the class Number, the methods for +, -, *, and / are implemented as ^self subclassResponsibility. Why are they included in Number at all?

7.23 Why are methods for mathematical functions such as sin and exp that require Float arguments implemented in class Number?

7.24 Most statically typed languages provide implicit coercions for numeric types, so that an integer can be passed to a function whose parameter type is floating-point.

(a) Why can't Smalltalk provide implicit coercions?

(b) Explain why the receiver of messages such as sqrt or sin can be an integer or a fraction.

(c) Compare implicit coercions and the Smalltalk technique discussed in part (b), especially with respect to defining new subprograms or messages.

7.25 Use your Smalltalk system to determine which selectors have methods in both Number and Integer. For each, explain why it is also defined in Integer.

7.26 Write a Smalltalk code fragment that determines the largest SmallInteger on your system.

7.27 **(a)** Why are there no Integer messages bitClear:, bitSet:, and bitInvert: (whose argument gives the number of the bit to be set, cleared, or inverted)?

(b) Suppose we want to define a class BitString that represents a fixed-size array of bits). What should its superclass be? Explain your answer.

(c) Define the class BitString that implements the bit manipulation protocol of Integer as well as bitClear:, bitSet:, and bitAt:put:. Instances are created with the message new:, whose argument gives the number of bits.

7.28 Give a trace of the messages sent to evaluate the expression 3 + 3.0 with coercive generality and with double dispatching. For each message, indicate which class defines the method executed. Compare them to traces of 3.0 + 3 in section 7.4.6.

7.29 **(a)** Discuss the advantages and disadvantages of coercive generality and double dispatching.

(b) How can you determine whether your system uses coercive generality or double dispatching?

(c) Explain why VisualWorks uses both coercive generality and double dispatching.

7.30 We want to code a class Vector that represents arrays whose elements are numbers. We want arithmetic operations on vectors to be performed on corresponding elements when the receiver and argument are both vectors, and we want an arithmetic operation to be mapped onto the elements of the receiver if the argument is a scalar, or vice versa. For example, both the expressions aVector * 2 and 2 * aVector should return a vector whose elements are the corresponding elements of aVector doubled. We also want the mathematical function of Number to be mapped onto elements (e.g., aVector sin should return a new vector such that each element is the sin of the corresponding element of aVector). Instances of Vector are created with new:, and must respond to at:, at:put:, and size. Do not worry about providing the rest of Array's protocol for Vector.

(a) Define the class Vector for a system that uses coercive generality. Suppose that aVector contains the element 3 and 3.0. Trace the messages sent to evaluate the expression aVector + (3 / 4).

(b) What would be involved in defining Vector on a system that uses double dispatching? Define the class Vector and any additional methods in other classes for such a system. Suppose that aVector contains the element 3 and 3.0. Trace the messages sent to evaluate the expression aVector + (3 / 4).

7.31 Code the methods for the following Point instance messages. Compare your answers to the methods on your Smalltalk system.

(a) //

(b) max:

(c) r

(d) nearestPointOnLineFrom:to:

(e) truncateTo:

(f) corner:

7.32 Write a Smalltalk code fragment that sets arrPoints to an array of numPoints equally-spaced points along the perimeter of a circle with center centerPoint and radius radius.

7.33 **(a)** Code a private Rectangle instance method normalize that ensures that the receiver is represented with its origin at its top left corner and its corner at its bottom right corner. (Hint: See the method for the class message vertex:vertex:.)

(b) Which Rectangle methods should send this message?

7.34 Code the methods for the following Rectangle messages. Compare your answers to the methods on your Smalltalk system.

(a) vertex:vertex:

(b) center

(c) areasOutside:

(d) intersects:

(e) printOn:

The Collection Classes

In this chapter, we will cover the Smalltalk classes that represent collections and streams, which allow us to access the elements of a collection or file in sequence. The chapter covers the following topics:

- an overview of the collection class subhierarchy (8.1.1)
- the class Collection, the abstract class that encapsulates the common protocol for collections (8.1.2 and 8.1.3)
- the classes Set (8.2.1) and Bag (8.2.2), which represent unordered collections
- the class Dictionary, which represents a set of values accessed via keys (8.2.3)
- the abstract class SequenceableCollection, the ancestor of the classes that represent ordered collections (8.3.1)
- the class OrderedCollection (8.3.2) and its subclass SortedCollection (8.3.3), which employ a sequential storage structure
- the class LinkedList, which uses a linked structure (8.3.4)
- the class Interval, which calculates its elements rather than storing them (8.3.5)
- the abstract class ArrayedCollection, which specifies protocol for fixed-size collections, and its concrete descendants Array, ByteArray, RunArray, String, Symbol, and Text (8.3.6)
- the abstract class Stream, which defines accessing protocol for all streams (8.4.1)

- the abstract class PositionableStream, which provides protocol for repositioning the stream's reference (8.4.2)
- the abstract class InternalStream and its concrete descendants ReadStream and WriteStream, which represent streams over collections (8.4.3)
- the abstract class ExternalStream and its subclasses, which support stream protocol for files and other external sources of information (8.4.4)
- the class Random, whose instances generate a stream of random numbers (8.4.5).

8.1 THE CLASS Collection

8.1.1 Overview of the Collection Class Subhierarchy

The class Collection is a subclass of Object, and is the root of a large subhierarchy of collection classes. Like Object, Collection is an abstract class that defines extensive protocol and numerous default methods for its descendants. This includes messages for

- adding and removing elements
- determining the number of elements in a collection, and testing whether a collection contains an element
- enumerating the elements of a collection
- printing and storing the elements of a collection
- converting among collection classes.

Like all abstract classes, Collection defines an interface we can use without having any concern about exactly what kind of collection an object is. We will discuss its protocol in detail in section 8.1.2, and its implementation in section 8.1.3.

Figure 8.1 is a diagram of the collection class subhierarchy, and is annotated with comments describing the characteristics of each subhierarchy or subclass. The Smalltalk collection classes includes the abstract classes SequenceableCollection and ArrayedCollection, and numerous concrete classes with various characteristics. Some collections are fixed-size while others can expand and contract; some collections are ordered and others are not; some collections permit access to elements via keys and others do not; and some collections have restrictions on the kinds of elements they can contain. You must be aware of these characteristics when choosing a collection class to represent a group of objects. Figure 8.2 gives the system browser class categories for the collection classes (and some supporting classes).

Instances of the classes Bag, Set, OrderedCollection, LinkedList, and their descendants are variable-size. Those collections increase in size (logically) when an element is added, and shrink when an element is removed. Instances of the class Interval and the descendants of ArrayedCollection are fixed-size.

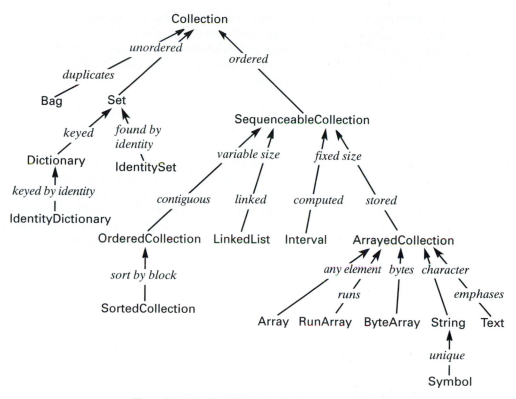

Figure 8.1   The Smalltalk-80 collection class subhierarchy.

class category	classes
Collections-Abstract	Collection, SequenceableCollection, ArrayedCollection
Collections-Unordered	Set, Bag, Dictionary, IdentitySet, IdentityDictionary
Collections-Sequenceable	OrderedCollection, SortedCollection, LinkedList, Interval
Collections-Arrayed	Array, ByteArray, RunArray
Collections-Text	String, Symbol, Text
Collections-Support	LookupKey, Association, Link

Figure 8.2   Browser categories for collection classes.

The unordered collections are Set, Bag, and Dictionary. Sets are unordered collections of objects without duplicate elements, and bags are unordered collections that permit duplicates. As we have discussed several times, a dictionary is a set of key–value pairs in which we usually access a value by its key with the messages at: and at:put:. Instances of the classes IdentitySet and IdentityDictionary use an identity test, rather than an equality test, to find an element or key. (There is no class IdentityBag.)

SequenceableCollection is the ancestor of the various concrete classes for ordered collections.[1] Usually, the client determines the order of the elements—for example, by the specific insertion and deletion messages used with an instance of OrderedCollection or LinkedList, or by giving the index value of an element, as with arrays and strings. For an instance of SortedCollection, the client supplies an instance-specific comparison block that determines the order of its elements. Because we can access an element in a sequenceable collection via at: and at:put: with its position in the collection as the key, we can regard sequenceable collections as being keyed. Dictionaries are keyed but not ordered.

Smalltalk is dynamically typed, so a collection can contain any type of object or objects of various types (including collections), and there is no need for generic collection types (as discussed in section 1.1.5). If a particular collection should only contain instances of a certain class, say Point, then inserting a date object does not cause an error. The error occurs later when that object is sent a message in the protocol of Point to which the date cannot respond. However, some collections can only contain certain types of objects by meaning or by design. For example,

- a string or a symbol contains characters
- an interval contains numbers
- a linked list contains instances of subclasses of Link
- a byte array contains integers between 0 and 255

Most collection classes store references to the elements in instance variables, but the elements of an interval are generated upon request.

The subhierarchy of collection classes illustrates a number of points about inheritance semantics. There are

- subclasses that are specializations with additional behavior, such as Dictionary
- abstract classes that implement some methods completely and implement others in terms of subclass-specific operations, such as SequenceableCollection
- subclasses that are restrictions of their superclass, such as Interval, SortedCollection, and Symbol

The system also includes a number of collection classes considered private to its implementation, which we will not discuss, such as SystemDictionary and DependentsCollection.[2]

---

[1] The class OrderedCollection represents a particular kind of ordered collection, namely one that is variable-size and allocated sequentially.

[2] For example, Collection allSubclasses size returns 85 in VisualWorks.

8.1.2 Protocol

Instance creation protocol

Collection inherits the *instance creation* class messages new, new:, and readFrom: from its superclass Object. new is refined in Bag, Set, and Ordered-Collection to initialize the new object's internal structure to an empty collection, and is disallowed in Interval. The message new: is used with fixed-size collections such as arrays, and the argument gives the number of elements. new: can also be used with some variable-size collections such as Set and OrderedCollection to give an initial value for the number of elements in the new object's storage structure. The class message readFrom: creates an instance from the contents of a stream, and uses the method in Object that sends the stream argument to a compiler.

We can create initialized instances of the classes String, Array, ByteArray, and Symbol with the literal notations described in section 5.2.1. Some collection classes also have mnemonic instance creation messages that take arguments specifying initialization, such as fromString: and string:emphasis: for Text, and sortBlock: for SortedCollection.

We can also create and initialize a collection with the instance creation messages with:, with:with:, with:with:with:, and with:with:with:with:, for which the arguments are the initial elements, and withAll:, which takes a collection as the argument. The new collection is the same type as the receiver because the methods for these messages use self new to create it. We can think of the first four messages as providing a literal notation for collection classes.

Adding and removing protocol

All collections respond to the *adding* messages add: and addAll:, and the *removing* messages remove:, remove:ifAbsent:, and removeAll:. For the messages addAll: and removeAll:, the argument is a collection, each of whose elements is inserted into or deleted from the receiver individually. remove: deletes one occurrence of its argument from the receiver, or signals notFoundError if the argument is not in that collection. We can specify special processing for this case by giving a block as the second argument of the message remove:ifAbsent:. For example:

```
"specifying error processing with the Collection message remove:ifAbsent:"
aSet                          "a set of numbers"
    remove: (Dialog request: 'Remove which element?') asNumber
    ifAbsent: [Dialog warn: 'It"s not there!']
```

If attempting to remove a nonexistent element from a particular collection is not an error, we use remove:ifAbsent: with an empty block as the second argument. The adding and removing messages return their argument, rather than the receiver. To return the receiver collection, cascade the message yourself with the adding or removing message.

Testing, accessing, and comparing protocol

The *testing* protocol of Collection consists of the following messages:

```
"The 'testing' instance protocol of Collection"
includes: anObject
    "Answer whether anObject is one of the receiver's elements."
isEmpty
    "Answer whether the receiver contains any elements."
occurrencesOf: anObject
    "Answer how many of the receiver's elements are equal to anObject."
```

Collection also defines the *accessing* message size, which returns the number of elements in the receiver.

Like all objects, we can compare collections with the binary selectors ==, ~~, =, and ~=. The unordered classes Bag, Set, and Dictionary use the default method for = in Object (i.e., an identity test). For the sequenceable collections, two instances are equal if they are the same type and size, and their corresponding elements are = (and the sort blocks must also be equal for instances of SortedCollection). This operation can be expensive, especially compared to an identity test.

Enumerating protocol

All collections respond to the *enumerating* messages do:, collect:, select:, and reject: (which we discussed in section 5.5.5), and Collection defines three additional enumerating messages. The message detect: evaluates its block argument for each element of the receiver, and returns the first element for which that result is true. detect:ifNone: allows the programmer to specify a block to be performed if no evaluation results in true as the second argument. The message inject:into: takes an initial value as its first argument, and a two-argument block as its second. For each evaluation of the argument block, the first block argument is the result of the previous evaluation of the block (or the first message argument for the first evaluation), and the second block argument is the next element of the collection. The final result returned by inject:into: is the value of the last evaluation of the block. The operation and use of this message is easier to understand if we consider an example:

```
"set numVowels to the number of vowels in word"
numVowels :=
  word inject: 0
    into: [ :count :char |
       count + (char isVowel ifTrue: [1] ifFalse: [0] ) ]
```

On the first evaluation of the block, count is 0 and char is the first character in word. On the second evaluation, count begins with its previous value (0 or 1, depending on the first character in word) and char is the second character, and so on. The result assigned to numVowels is the final value of count. Using this message rather than do: avoids defining and initializing a temporary variable outside the block that performs the computation.

The class SequenceableCollection defines additional enumerating messages for collections whose elements are ordered (see section 8.3.1).

Copying and converting protocol

We can also create new collection objects by sending copying or conversion messages to existing collections. The *copying* messages copyEmpty and copyEmpty: return a collection like the receiver with no elements. The latter is used with fixed-size collections, and the argument gives the size. Collection does not implement the message copy, so it defaults to shallowCopy and the elements of the new collection are identical to those of the receiver. We can send the message reverse to a sequenceable collection (except a linked list) to obtain a shallow copy in reverse order.

The *converting* protocol of Collection consists of asArray, asBag, asSet, asOrderedCollection, asSortedCollection, and asSortedCollection:. The argument for the last message is the "sort block" that determines the order of the elements in the new object (see section 8.3.3). The methods for these messages do not modify the receiver, but create and return a new collection with the same element references as the receiver (i.e., a shallow copy). When converting from an unordered collection to a sequenceable collection, the ordering of the elements in the result is arbitrary (actually, it depends on the storage structure of the unordered collection). There are no conversion messages to a linked list, interval, byte array, or string because the elements of the receiver may not be of the correct type.

Printing and storing protocol

The default behavior for printOn: defined in Collection prints the class name followed by a list of the elements' print behaviors enclosed in parentheses, as follows:

```
"the print format for instances of collection classes"
ClassName (element1 element2 ... )
```

Some collection classes have more specific behavior. Intervals print using the message to: or to:by:, and arrays, strings, symbols, and byte arrays print their literal notations. As with all classes, the message printString is also available.

Like all objects, collections respond to storeOn: by appending a string to the argument stream that can be evaluated to produce an equal instance. For collections, this string takes the following forms:

```
"the storage format for instances of variable-size collection classes"
((ClassName new) add: element1; add: element2; ... ; yourself)

"the storage format for instances of fixed-size collection classes"
((ClassName new: size) at: 1 put: element1; at: 2 put: element2; ... ; yourself)
```

Collection defines the general method for storeOn: and ArrayedCollection implements the method for fixed-size collections. Classes such as Symbol and Array that have literal representations use that format for storing, and intervals store using to: or to:by:.

The species of a collection

There are a number of messages in the enumerating and copying protocols of Collection that return a collection of the same kind as the receiver. For example, select: returns a subcollection of the receiver, and copyEmpty: returns an empty collection of the same type as the receiver. However, there are some special cases in which the result cannot be of the same class as the receiver. For example, the elements of an interval form an arithmetic progression defined by start, step, and stop values, and are computed upon request, rather than being stored individually. The following message cannot return an interval because its elements do not form an arithmetic progression, so it returns an array:

```
"an enumeration message that cannot return an instance of the same class as the receiver"
(Interval from: 1 to: 30 by: 3) reject: [:el | el \\ 5 = 0]     "returns #(1 4 7 13 16 19 22 28)"
```

Similarly, there cannot be multiple copies of the symbol corresponding to a particular string, so copying a symbol results in a string.

Collection defines the private message species, which it implements as ^self class. Instances of Interval respond with Array (i.e., the class object), and those of Symbol respond with String. Methods that create a new collection use self species rather than self class as the type of the new object.

8.1.3 Implementation

Collection is an abstract class because it does not define a storage structure that supports inserting, deleting, retrieving, and enumerating the elements in a collection. Each subclass defines a representation that is consistent with its semantics and efficient for its characteristics. Due to this lack of internal structure, Collection cannot implement some of its messages. The messages add:, remove:ifAbsent:, and do: are abstract, and all the messages we discussed in the previous section are implemented by methods that (ultimately) send these three messages to self. Each concrete subclass defines a storage structure, and only needs to define these three messages in terms of that structure to obtain the use of the entire Collection protocol.

The following are examples of methods in Collection that are defined in terms of its abstract messages:

"class method for class Collection"

with: firstObject with: secondObject
  "Answer a new instance of the receiver collection containing the two arguments."

  ^self new add: firstObject; add: secondObject; yourself

"instance methods for class Collection"

addAll: aCollection
  "Add each of the elements of aCollection to the receiver."

  aCollection do: [:element | self add: element].
  ^aCollection

includes: anObject
  "Answer whether anObject is one of the receiver's elements."

  self do: [:element | anObject = element ifTrue: [^true]].
  ^false

select: aBlock
  "Evaluate aBlock with each of the receiver's elements as the argument. Answer a new
  collection like the receiver containing the elements for which aBlock evaluates to true."

  | newCollection |
  newCollection := self species new.
  self do: [:element | (aBlock value: element) ifTrue: [newCollection add: element]].
  ^newCollection

asBag

  "Answer a new instance of Bag containing the same elements as the receiver."

  | newBag |
  newBag := Bag new.
  self do: [:element | newBag add: element].
  ^newBag

The other conversion methods are coded like asBag, except that asArray, asOr-deredCollection, and asSortedCollection send new: self size rather than new to the new class. The method for printOn: enumerates the elements using do: and sends printOn: to each. The message size is reimplemented to count the elements using do:, because its definition in Object returns the number of indexed instance variables. isEmpty is defined by the method ^self size = 0. Note that it is the ability to enumerate the elements of any collection transparently that permits defining so many methods in Collection.

Some subclasses refine particular messages due to differences in semantics (e.g., at:put: for Dictionary), or for efficiency (i.e., to make use of the characteristics of the storage structure). Some subclasses disallow messages—for example, Bag disallows at:put: because its instances are unordered, Interval disallows add:, and SequenceableCollection disallows remove:ifAbsent:.

8.2 UNORDERED COLLECTIONS

8.2.1 The Class Set

Purpose and protocol

The class Set is a direct subclass of Collection whose instances represent variable-size, unordered collections in which duplicates are not allowed, similar to sets in mathematics. Its methods use an equality test to find an element or determine whether a new element is a duplicate of an existing element. When an element is added that is equal to an element already in the set, no action is taken (i.e., it is not an error). The message size returns the number of elements, which is neither fixed nor bounded. For the enumerating protocol of Collection, the order in which the elements are supplied to the block is arbitrary, and depends on the internal representation. Because sets are unordered, Set disallows the messages at: and at:put:.

Set inherits the protocol of its ancestors Object and Collection, but defines no additional public messages. The class does not provide the mathematical set operations union:, intersection: and so on, mainly because its implementation is designed for efficient search rather than for efficient aggregate operations. Of course, we could define these operations by using new, do:, add:, and includes:.

Implementation

To avoid performing a sequential search to locate an element or check for a duplicate upon receiving add:, Set uses hashing with linear probing (also called open addressing). The table of elements is contained in indexed instance variables, and a named instance variable tally maintains the number of elements in the set. Storing the number of elements avoids accessing all the indexed instance variables and counting those that are not nil when responding to size or checking the load factor of the hash table. The class Set is defined as follows:

```
"definition of the class Set"
Collection variableSubclass: #Set
    instanceVariableNames: 'tally'
    classVariableNames: ''
```

```
poolDictionaries: ''
category: 'Collections-Unordered'
```

This implementation of sets does not require the elements to be orderable as would a binary search tree. However, it does require that elements respond to the message hash and that equal objects return the same hash value. The object nil marks empty positions in the hash table, so we cannot add nil to a set (and no action is taken if we attempt to do so).

The *instance creation* message new sends self new: 2, and new: is implemented as follows:

```
"class methods for class Set"
new: anInteger
    "Create an instance of Set with at least anInteger slots."

    anInteger >= 0 ifFalse: [self error: 'Inappropriate creation size'].
    ^(super new: (self goodSizeFrom: anInteger)) setTally
```

The *private* class message goodSizeFrom: returns the next prime greater than or equal to its argument, and the private instance message setTally sets the new object's tally to 0.

Set methods locate a position in the table for an object with the *private* instance method findElementOrNil:. This returns the index of its argument if it is present in the receiver, or if not, the index of an empty slot in the table at which that object can be inserted. It sends hash to the argument to determine its home address in the table, and begins a linear search of the table at that point. findElementOrNil: uses = to check for the argument, which is why objects that are = must have the same hash value. The methods for add:, remove:ifAbsent:, and includes: send self findElementOrNil: to locate the position of the argument. add: and remove:ifAbsent: then use basicAt: and basicAt:put: to manipulate the element references (since Set disallows at: and at:put:). For example,

```
"instance methods for class Set"
includes: anObject
    "Answer whether anObject is one of the receiver's elements."

    ^(self basicAt: (self findElementOrNil: anObject)) notNull

add: newObject
    'Include newObject as one of the receiver's elements.  Answer newObject."

    | index |
    newObject == nil ifTrue: [^newObject].
    index := self findElementOrNil: newObject.
    (self basicAt: index) == nil
        ifTrue: [
```

```
        self basicAt: index put: newObject.
        tally := tally + 1.
        self fullCheck].
    ∧newObject
```

The private message fullCheck calls the private message grow to increase the physical size of the table if it is 75 percent full upon an insertion. The grow method creates a larger set object, hashes the receiver's elements into it, and invokes the message become: described in section 7.1.2. The method for remove:ifAbsent: calls the private message fixCollisionsFrom: to adjust the table.[3] Recall that Smalltalk does not prevent clients from using these private messages.

Set implements the message do: to iterate through the elements using 1 to: self basicSize do:, so the elements are enumerated in an order determined by their hash values (and the order of insertion into the table). The method for do: accesses the elements with basicAt: and passes non-nil elements to the block argument. The size method returns tally (not the number of indexed instance variables). We can use the message new: (i.e., with an integer argument) with Set to give an initial table size. Set implements the messages at: and at:put: as ∧self notKeyedError because they are normally available for classes with indexed instance variables (which Set has, but does not make public).

The class IdentitySet

The class IdentitySet is a subclass of Set that uses an identity test rather than an equality test to find an element. IdentitySet inherits the protocol, storage structure, and methods of Set. In fact, findElementOrNil: is the only method defined in IdentitySet, and it is the same as the Set method, except that it uses identityHash to determine the home address of an element and an identity test to find an element.

8.2.2 The Class Bag

Purpose and protocol

The class Bag is a direct subclass of Collection, logically similar to Set except that its instances may contain duplicate elements. The protocol of Bag includes the protocols of Object and Collection, as well as the *adding* message add:withOccurences:. Like Set, Bag disallows the messages at: and at:put:.

Implementation

The implementation of Bag demonstrates an example of composition in the collection classes. A bag is represented internally by a single instance variable con-

---

[3] Recall from your data structures course that, in a hash table with linear probing, an element with the same home address as the deleted element may have been added after that element, in which case it will have been placed further from that home address. If so, either the hash table must mark that position as "deleted" (which is not possible for Set), or move elements back within the table.

tents, which is an instance of Dictionary. In each key–value pair, the key is the element and the value is the number of occurrences of that element in the bag. The method for new invokes a private instance message that creates the dictionary. Note that this means that when we remove an element from a bag, it may not be identical to the element we inserted.

The dictionary contents creates each association pair upon the first insertion of that element. Bag methods increment its value upon succeeding add: messages, decrement it upon remove:, and delete the association when the value reaches 0. The methods for add:, add:withOccurrences:, remove:ifAbsent:, includes:, occurrencesOf:, and do: pass the appropriate messages to the instance variable contents. For example,

```
"instance methods for class Bag"
includes: anObject
    "Answer whether anObject is one of the receiver's elements."

    ^contents includesKey: anObject

do: aBlock
    "Evaluate aBlock with each of the receiver's elements as the argument."

    contents associationsDo: [:assoc | assoc value timesRepeat: [aBlock value: assoc key]]
```

For efficiency, Bag re-implements size by summing the values in contents, and defines asSet as ^contents keys.

8.2.3 The Class Dictionary

Purpose and protocol

A dictionary is a keyed search table, that is, an index. It refines the *accessing* messages at: and at:put: to access values via the keys, rather than to refer to indexed instance variables. If the argument to at: is not a key in the receiver, it signals a keyNotFoundError. The message at:ifAbsent: allows the client to give processing to be performed in this case (like remove:ifAbsent: in Collection). Each key in a dictionary can only appear once, but there can be duplicates among the values in a dictionary. The keys in a dictionary are not ordered, so dictionaries are the only keyed, unordered collection. We may use any objects as the keys and values in a dictionary.

We usually view a dictionary as a set of values accessed via keys known to the client (i.e., the values are considered to be the elements of the collection). For example, includes: tests whether its argument is among the receiver's values and occurrencesOf: returns how often its argument occurs among the values, and neither method examines the receiver's keys. Dictionary refines the message inspect to open an instance of DictionaryInspector on the receiver. It lists the keys on the left (rather than instance variable names or indices), and prints the value associated with the selected key in the text view.

The message do: evaluates its argument block for each value in the dictionary, as do the other enumerating messages since they are implemented using do:. For the messages select: and reject:, the result is a dictionary that retains the keys associated with the values (even though only the values are passed to the condition block). However, collect: returns an ordered collection containing the results of applying the block to the values, not a dictionary including the corresponding keys. When a dictionary is converted to an instance of another collection class, the result contains only the values because the converting methods inherited from Collection use self do: to access the receiver's elements.

The classes LookupKey and Association

The class Association represents key–value pairs, and is a subclass of LookUp-Key, a subclass of Magnitude. LookupKey defines the instance variable key and the *accessing* protocols key and key:, and Association adds the instance variable value and the accessing messages value, value:, and key:value:. We can create instances of Association with the class method key:value:, or the binary selector -> (defined in Object), with the key as the receiver and the argument as the value. Associations print themselves as *key->value*. Associations are primarily used in the implementation of the system class Dictionary.

Representation

The class Dictionary is a subclass of Set, in which each element is an instance of Association, and each association contains a value and the key that accesses it. Figure 8.3 diagrams the storage structure for a dictionary. In the dictionary in the figure, the client has inserted two elements whose keys have the hash values 2 and 5.

Associations protocol

The adding messages inherited from Collection are allowed for dictionaries, but they apply to the associations because inserting a value without a key is not meaningful. The following two expressions have the same effect:

```
"add or modify the value associated with #entertainment in the dictionary budget"
budget at: #entertainment put: 100
budget add: (Association key: #entertainment value: 100)
```

If #entertainment is in the dictionary, the value associated with it is changed, and if it is not, an association is added. However, there is a subtle difference between using at:put: and add: when the key is new to the dictionary. The method for at:put: always creates a new association internally, while add: inserts the argument association, which preserves any references to it. Dictionary disallows the

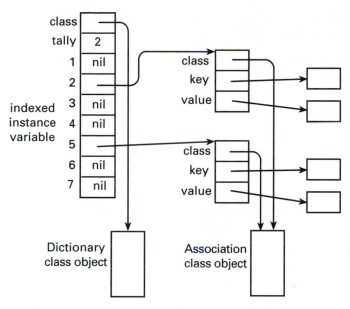

Figure 8.3   Storage diagram for an instance of Dictionary.

messages remove: and remove:ifAbsent: because a value can be associated with more than one key, so the client must specify a key when deleting a value. We use either removeKey: or removeAssociation: to remove an entry from a dictionary.

The protocol of Dictionary also includes several messages that are specific to its structure as a set of associations. The *accessing* protocol of Dictionary includes the following messages:

```
"the 'accessing' instance protocol of Dictionary"
keys
    "Answer a set containing the receiver's keys."
values
    "Answer an ordered collection containing the receiver's values."
associations
    "Answer an ordered collection containing the receiver's associations."
associationAt: key
    "Answer the association at key.  If key is not found, raise a signal."
associationAt: key ifAbsent: aBlock
    "Answer the association at key.  If key is not found, answer the result of
    evaluating aBlock."
keyAtValue: value
    "Answer the key whose value equals value.  If there is none, then provide an
    error notification."
keyAtValue: value ifAbsent: aBlock
    "Answer the key whose value equals value.  If there is none, answer the result of
    evaluating aBlock."
```

The *dictionary testing*, *dictionary removing*, and *dictionary enumerating* protocols consist of the following messages:

```
"the 'dictionary testing', 'dictionary removing', and 'dictionary enumerating'
instance protocols of Dictionary"
includesAssociation: anAssociation
    "Answer whether the receiver has an element that is equal to anAssociation."
includesKey: key
    "Answer whether the receiver has a key equal to key."
removeAssociation: anAssociation
    "Remove anAssociation, from the receiver.  If the key is not in the receiver,
    then provide an error notification."
removeAssociation: anAssociation ifAbsent: anExceptionBlock
    "Remove anAssociation, from the receiver.  If it is not found, answer the result of
    evaluating anExceptionBlock, otherwise answer anAssociation."
removeKey: key
    "Remove the association whose key is key from the receiver.  If key is not in the receiver,
    provide an error notification.  Otherwise, answer the value associated with key."
removeKey: key ifAbsent: aBlock
    "Remove the association whose key is key from the receiver.  If key is not in the receiver,
    answer the result of evaluating aBlock.  Otherwise, answer the value associated with key."
associationsDo: aBlock
    "Evaluate aBlock for each of the receiver's associations."
keysDo: aBlock
    "Evaluate aBlock for each of the receiver's keys."
keysAndValuesDo: aBlock
    "Evaluate aBlock with each of the receiver's key/value pairs as the arguments."
```

Method implementation

Like its superclass Set, Dictionary is implemented by hashing the associations into a table of indexed instance variables. The methods for at:ifAbsent:, associationAt:, at:put:, add:, includesKey:, and removeKey:ifAbsent: use the private message findKeyOrNil: to determine the home address of a key or association. These methods pass the key rather than the association to findKeyOrNil:, so the elements of a dictionary are located according to their keys.   The methods then access, modify, add, or test the association with basicAt: and basicAt:put:. As with sets, we cannot use nil as a key in a dictionary (or, therefore, insert nil into a bag).

As we stated, Dictionary redefines many Collection methods to access the values of the receiver's associations. Many of Collection's methods are coded in terms of do:, whose Dictionary method passes the values of the associations, rather than the associations themselves, to its block argument.

```
"instance method in class Dictionary"
do: aBlock
    "Evaluate aBlock with each of the receiver's elements as the argument."
```

```
tally == 0 ifTrue: [^self].
1 to: self basicSize do: [ :index | | assoc |
   (assoc := self basicAt: index) == nil
      ifFalse: [aBlock value: assoc value]]
```

The Dictionary methods for includes:, occurrencesOf:, values, and collect: are defined in terms of do: so they only examine the values. The inherited Collection methods for size, addAll:, and the converting messages such as asArray also use this method for do: when the receiver is a dictionary. Like the method for do:, keysAndValuesDo: and associationsDo: index through the receiver's table with basicAt: from 1 to self basicSize. The messages keyAtValue:ifAbsent: and keysDo: are defined in terms of keysAndValuesDo:, and the methods for associations, printOn:, storeOn:, and select: use associationsDo:.

The class IdentityDictionary

The class IdentityDictionary is a subclass of Dictionary that uses an identity test to match keys.

The storage structure of IdentityDictionary differs from that of Dictionary. It uses two parallel arrays of keys and values, the indexed instance variables and an instance variable valueArray, rather than a table of associations. IdentityDictionary overrides the inherited private initialization message setTally to create the referent of valueArray as well as to set tally to 0. It also overrides several Dictionary methods to use this storage structure. For example,

```
"instance method in class IdentityDictionary"

at: key put: value
   "Set the value at key to be value."

   | index |
   key == nil ifTrue: [^self subscriptBoundsError: key].
   index := self findKeyOrNil: key.
   (self basicAt: index) == nil
      ifTrue: [
         tally := tally + 1.
         self basicAt: index put: key].
   valueArray at: index put: value.
   self fullCheck.
   ^value

do: aBlock
   "Evaluate aBlock with each of the receiver's elements as the argument."

   1 to: self basicSize do: [ :index |
      (self basicAt: index) == nil
         ifFalse: [aBlock value: (valueArray at: index)]]
```

IdentityDictionary creates an association if requested (i.e., in response to associa-tionAt: or associationsDo:), so such an association will behave as a copy of infor-mation in the dictionary.   That is, obtaining an association reference from an instance of Dictionary allows a client to modify the dictionary itself, but obtaining an association does not for an instance of IdentityDictionary.

8.3 ORDERED COLLECTIONS

8.3.1 The Class SequenceableCollection

Purpose and subclasses

The abstract class SequenceableCollection is a subclass of Collection that encapsulates protocol for collections whose elements are ordered. For example, it defines messages that access the first element, obtain the index of a particular element, and copy and enumerate the elements in reverse order. An instance of one of the class's concrete descendants is ordered, so we can access or replace an element with the messages at: or at:put: by using the element's position in the ordering as the key (except for instances of SortedCollection, LinkedList, Interval, and Symbol, each of which disallows at:put:). Attempts to use an inte-ger key outside the range 1 through self size result in a subscriptBoundsError message.

SequenceableCollection has four subclasses: OrderedCollection, LinkedList, Interval, and ArrayedCollection. Instances of OrderedCollection and LinkedList are variable-size, and the order of their elements is determined by the messages the client used to insert and delete elements. The elements of an instance of Interval form an arithmetic progression defined by start, step, and stop values, which are fixed when the object is created. The abstract class ArrayedCollection is an ances-tor for fixed-size collections such as arrays and strings.

Protocol

SequenceableCollection inherits the *instance creation* messages of Object and Collection (with:, etc.), and defines no additional class protocol.

The *adding* and *removing* protocol inherited from Collection are relevant for some descendants of SequenceableCollection, but not for others. The messages add: and remove:ifAbsent: are available for OrderedCollection, SortedCollection, and LinkedList, but are disallowed in Interval because its elements are fixed, and in ArrayedCollection because the elements of a fixed-size collection can only be replaced, not added or removed.[4] When we add or remove an element, the

---

[4] Actually, the treatment of add: and remove:ifAbsent: for descendants of SequenceableCollection is somewhat inconsistent. add: is allowed in the superclass SequenceableCollection, but disallowed in Interval and ArrayCollection. On the other hand, remove:ifAbsent: is disallowed in SequenceableCollec-tion, but reimplemented in OrderedCollection and LinkedList.

indices of all succeeding elements in the collection are incremented or decremented.

SequenceableCollection includes numerous messages for accessing and replacing the elements of the receiver relative to their positions. It inherits the messages at: and at:put: from Object, and each subclass refines them to refer to an element's position in the ordering, rather than to indexed instance variables (which are not used in some subclasses). The *accessing* protocol of SequenceableCollection consists of the following messages:

```
"the 'accessing' instance protocol of SequenceableCollection"
first
    "Answer the first element of the receiver.  Provide an error notification if the receiver
    contains no elements."
last
    "Answer the last element of the receiver.  Provide an error notification if the receiver
    contains no elements."
indexOf: anElement
    "Answer the index of the first element in the receiver equal to anElement.  If the receiver
    does not contain anElement, answer 0."
indexOf: anElement ifAbsent: exceptionBlock
    "Answer the index of the first element in the receiver equal to anElement.  If the receiver
    does not contain anElement, answer the result of evaluating exceptionBlock."
identityIndexOf: anElement
    "Answer the index of the first element in the receiver identical to anElement.  If the
    receiver does not contain anElement, answer 0."
identityIndexOf: anElement ifAbsent: exceptionBlock
    "Answer the index of the first element in the receiver identical to anElement.  If the
    receiver does not contain anElement, answer the result of evaluating exceptionBlock."
lastIndexOf: anElement
    "Answer the index of the last occurrence of anElement in the receiver.  If the receiver
    does not contain anElement, answer 0."
lastIndexOf: anElement ifAbsent: exceptionBlock
    "Answer the index of the last occurrence of anElement in the receiver.  If the receiver
    does not contain anElement, answer the result of evaluating exceptionBlock."
nextIndexOf: anElement from: startIndex to: stopIndex
    "Answer the first index of anElement in the receiver between startIndex and stopIndex.
    If the receiver does not contain anElement, answer nil."
prevIndexOf: anElement from: startIndex to: stopIndex
    "Answer the last index of anElement in the receiver between startIndex and stopIndex.
    If the receiver does not contain anElement, answer nil."
indexOfSubCollection: aSubCollection startingAt: anIndex
    "Answer the index of the subcollection of the receiver equal to aSubCollection.  Begin
    the search at element anIndex of the receiver.  If no such match is found, answer 0."
indexOfSubCollection: aSubCollection startingAt: anIndex ifAbsent: exceptionBlock
    "Answer the index of the subcollection of the receiver equal to aSubCollection.  Begin
    the search at element anIndex of the receiver.  If no such match is found, answer the
    result of evaluating exceptionBlock."
atAllPut: anObject
    "Put anObject at every one of the receiver's indices."
```

atAll: aCollection put: anObject
  "Put anObject at every index specified by the integer elements of aCollection."
replaceAll: sourceElement with: destElement
  "Replace all occurrences of sourceElement in the receiver with destElement."
replaceAll: sourceElement with: destElement from: startIndex to: stopIndex
  "Replace all occurrences of sourceElement between startIndex and stopIndex in the
  receiver with destElement."
replaceFrom: startIndex to: stopIndex with: replacementCollection
  "Replace the elements between startIndex and stopIndex in the receiver with
  replacementCollection, which must be of size (stopIndex - startIndex + 1)."
replaceFrom: startIndex to: stopIndex with: replacementCollection startingAt: repStart
  "Replace the elements between startIndex and stopIndex in the receiver with elements
  from replacementCollection, starting at index repStart in replacementCollection. If there
  are not enough elements in replacementCollection, an error occurs."

To access each occurrence of an object in a sequenceable collection, we use indexOf:
to find the first occurrence, and nextIndexOf:from:to: to find successive occurrences.
The replacementCollection for the last two messages must be a sequenceable collection. There are a few inconsistencies among these messages. The messages indexOf:,
identityIndexOf:, lastIndexOf:, and indexOfSubCollection:startingAt: return 0 if the
element or subcollection is not in the receiver, while nextIndexOf:from:to: and prevIn-
dexOf:from:to: return nil if the element is not in the receiver. The argument corresponding to startingAt: for indexOfSubCollection:startingAt: gives a starting point in
the receiver, while for replaceFrom:to:with:startingAt: it gives a starting point in the
replacement collection.

    SequenceableCollection defines a number of copying messages, each of which
results in a shallow copy, rather than returning a deep copy or modifying the
receiver. The *copying* protocol of SequenceableCollection consists of the following
messages:

"the 'copying' instance protocol of SequenceableCollection"
, aSequenceableCollection "the binary selector ',' "
  "Answer a copy of the receiver concatenated with a SequencableCollection."
copyFrom: startIndex to: stopIndex
  "Answer a copy of the subcollection of the receiver's elements from startIndex to
  stopIndex."
copyWith: newElement
  "Answer a copy of the receiver with newElement as an additional final element."
copyWithout: oldElement
  "Answer a copy of the receiver with all occurrences of oldElement removed."
reverse
  "Answer a copy of the receiver with its elements in the opposite order."
copyReplaceAll: oldSubCollection with: newSubCollection
  "Answer a copy of the receiver in which all occurrences of oldSubCollection have been
  replaced by newSubCollection. If there are none, answer a copy of the receiver."
copyReplaceFrom: startIndex to: stopIndex with: replacementCollection
  "Answer a copy of the receiver such that:

1) If stopIndex is greater than startIndex, replace those elements from the receiver with replacementCollection (which may result in a different size collection than the receiver).
2) Otherwise, stopIndex should be exactly startIndex - 1, and replacementCollection is inserted into the copy before startIndex (or if startIndex = size + 1, replacementCollection is appended after the last element)."

The binary selector , returns a new collection that is the concatenation of the receiver and argument, rather than appending the argument to the receiver. The argument must be a sequenceable collection. The second meaning of copyReplaceFrom:to:with: should have been a separate message, say copyAddAll:beforeIndex:.

SequenceableCollection inherits the enumerating protocol of Collection, and an instance supplies its elements to the block argument in their order in the collection. SequenceableCollection also provides *enumerating* protocol that take the ordering into account, which consists of the following messages:

```
"the 'enumerating' instance protocol of SequenceableCollection"
findFirst: aBlock
   "Answer the index of the first element of the receiver for which aBlock evaluates as true."
findLast: aBlock
   "Answer the index of the last element of the receiver for which aBlock evaluates as true."
reverseDo: aBlock
   "Evaluate aBlock with each of the receiver's elements as the argument, in reverse order."
keysAndValuesDo: aBlock
   "Evaluate the two-argument block aBlock with each of the receiver's key/value pairs
   (indexes and elements) as the corresponding arguments."
with: aSequenceableCollection do: aBlock
   "Evaluate the two-argument block aBlock with each receiver elements and the
   corresponding element from aSequencableCollection.  The receiver and
   aSequenceableCollection must be the same size."
```

In addition to the converting messages inherited from Collection, SequenceableCollection defines the *converting* messages readStream and writeStream, which create a stream on the receiver (see section 8.4).

Implementation

Like all abstract classes, the implementation of SequenceableCollection is incomplete. It does not define a representation for storing elements, nor methods for add: and remove:ifAbsent:. However, it can still define many methods by accessing elements with at: and at:put:, and by enumerating the elements from index 1 through self size. The methods for at: and at:put: are inherited from Object and access indexed instance variables, so subclasses that use a different internal representation must override them.

SequenceableCollection refines the *comparing* messages = and hash inherited from Object such that two sequenceable collections are equal if they are the same type and contain equal elements in the same order, as follows:

```
"instance method for class SequenceableCollection"
= otherCollection
   "Answer whether the receiver and otherCollection are the same species,
    and contain equal elements in the same order."

   | size |
   self species == otherCollection species ifFalse: [^false].
   (size := self size) = otherCollection size ifFalse: [^false].
   1 to: size do: [:index |
      (self at: index) = (otherCollection at: index) ifFalse: [^false]].
   ^true
```

The method for hash computes a hash value for the collection from the hash values
of the receiver's elements by using bit shifts and bitwise exclusive-ors. SequenceableCollection also defines the *accessing* messages using at:, at:put:, size, and do:.
For example,

```
"instance methods for class SequenceableCollection"
last
   "Answer the last element of the receiver. Provide an error notification if the receiver has
   no elements."

   self emptyCheck.         "a private method in Collection"
   ^self at: self size

nextIndexOf: anElement from: startIndex to: stopIndex
   "Answer the first index of anElement in the receiver between startIndex and stopIndex.
    If the receiver does not contain anElement, answer nil."

   startIndex to: stopIndex do: [:index |
      (self at: index) = anElement ifTrue: [^index]].
   ^nil

atAll: aCollection put: anObject
   "Put anObject at every index specified by the integer elements of aCollection."

   aCollection do: [:index | self at: index put: anObject]
```

SequenceableCollection implements the *copying* messages by creating the result
with self species new: and the size of the new collection, and then adding or replacing elements with its accessing messages.

SequenceableCollection defines a method for the deferred message do: inherited from Collection that enumerates the elements from index 1 through self size
and accesses each with at:, as follows:

```
"instance method for SequenceableCollection"
do: aBlock
```

"Evaluate aBlock with each of the receiver's elements as the argument."

1 to: self size do: [:index | aBlock value: (self at: index)]

However, the method for size inherited from Collection uses do: to count the elements, and this method for do: invokes size. To avoid infinite mutual recursion between do: and size, SequenceableCollection defines size as ^self subclassResponsibility. This is necessary in any case because the method for determining the number of elements depends on the class's representation. Like do:, the methods for findFirst:, findLast:, and keysAndValuesDo: are defined using 1 to: self size do: [...]. The methods for collect: and select: create a write stream on the collection self species new: self size, index through the receiver from 1 to self size, add the appropriate elements, and then return the contents of that stream.

8.3.2 The Class OrderedCollection

Purpose and protocol

OrderedCollection is a concrete subclass of SequenceableCollection in which the sequence of insertion and deletion messages determines the order of the elements. That is, the client always indicates the position in the ordering at which an element is inserted or deleted. In addition to inheriting the protocols of Collection and SequenceableCollection, OrderedCollection defines adding, removing, and accessing messages that make use of the order of the receiver's elements. Smalltalk programmers usually use ordered collections rather than arrays for lists of objects so that they do not have to decide on a size for the collection.

OrderedCollection provides messages for inserting and deleting elements at the beginning or end of the collection, at a specified index, or before or after an existing element. The *adding* and *removing* protocols of OrderedCollection consist of the following messages:

```
"the 'adding' and 'removing' instance protocols of OrderedCollection"
addFirst: newObject
    "Add newObject at the beginning of the receiver. Answer newObject."
addLast: newObject
    "Add newObject at the end of the receiver. Answer newObject."
add: newObject after: oldObject
    "Add newObject at the position succeeding that of oldObject in the receiver.
    If oldObject is not in the receiver, provide an error notification. Answer newObject."
add: newObject before: oldObject
    "Add newObject at the position preceding that of oldObject in the receiver.
    If oldObject is not in the receiver, provide an error notification. Answer newObject."
add: anObject beforeIndex: anIndex
    "Add newObject at the position preceding anIndex in the receiver. Answer
    newObject."
addAllFirst: anOrderedCollection
    "Add each element of anOrderedCollection at the beginning of the receiver.
    Answer anOrderedCollection."
```

addAllLast: anOrderedCollection
"Add each element of anOrderedCollection at the end of the receiver.
Answer anOrderedCollection."
removeFirst
"Remove the first element of the receiver. If the receiver is empty, provide an
error notification."
removeLast
"Remove the last element of the receiver. If the receiver is empty, provide an
error notification."
removeAtIndex: anIndex
"Remove the element of the collection at position anIndex. Answer the object
removed."
removeFirst: numElements
"Remove the first numElements elements of the receiver, and answer an array of
them.
If the receiver has fewer than numElements elements, provide an error notification."
removeLast: numElements
"Remove the last numElements elements of the receiver, and answer an array of them.
If the receiver has fewer than numElements elements, provide an error notification."
removeAllSuchThat: aBlock
"Evaluate aBlock for each element of the receiver. Remove each element for which
aBlock evaluates to true."

Ordered collections are often used as stacks with the messages addLast: and removeLast. An ordered collection can also be used as a queue with addLast: and removeFirst, but this is much less efficient, as we will see in the next subsection. However, a client can also use the other OrderedCollection messages to access the object, which violates the stack or queue abstraction.

The OrderedCollection *accessing* messages before: and after: return the predecessor or successor of the first occurrence of the argument in the receiver. The accessing messages at: and at:put: are frequently used with ordered collections.

Implementation

An ordered collection stores a list of references to its elements contiguously in indexed instance variables. It also includes two named instance variables, firstIndex and lastIndex, that give the indices of the actual first and last elements within the allocated indexed instance variables. The class OrderedCollection is defined as follows:

```
"definition of the class OrderedCollection"
SequenceableCollection variableSubclass: #OrderedCollection
    instanceVariableNames: 'firstIndex lastIndex'
    classVariableNames: ''
    poolDictionaries: ''
    category: 'Collections-Sequenceable'
```

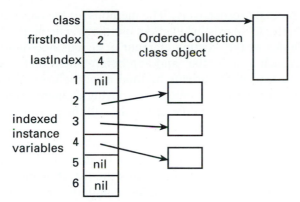

Figure 8.4 Storage diagram for an instance of OrderedCollection.

The storage structure for an ordered collection containing three elements is diagrammed in Figure 8.4.

We can give the initial physical size of an ordered collection as the argument to new:, but the new collection always begins empty. The argument to new: is not the number of elements, or even the maximum number of elements, but is the number of elements that can be stored before the physical size of the object is increased upon insertion. The OrderedCollection method for new: calls the *private* method setIndices, which sets firstIndex to 1 and lastIndex to firstIndex - 1 to indicate an empty collection.

OrderedCollection refines the *accessing* messages at:, at:put:, and size to use the receiver's logical indices and size, which are known to the client. For example,

```
"instance methods for OrderedCollection"
at: anInteger
    "Answer the element at index anInteger."

    anInteger isInteger ifFalse: [^self nonIntegerIndexError: anInteger].
    (anInteger < 1 or: [anInteger + firstIndex > lastIndex])
        ifTrue: [^self subscriptBoundsError: anInteger]
        ifFalse [^super at: anInteger + firstIndex - 1]

size
    "Answer the number of elements in the receiver."

    ^lastIndex - firstIndex + 1
```

The messages basicAt:, basicAt:put:, and basicSize are still available for use within OrderedCollection methods. For example, the message first is re-implemented as ^self basicAt: firstIndex for efficiency (and similarly for last). The *testing* message isEmpty is redefined as ^firstIndex > lastIndex for efficiency.

An insertion message increases the logical size of the receiver, and a deletion decreases its size. OrderedCollection implements the *adding* messages add: and addAll: as addLast and addAllLast:, respectively. The methods for messages such as add:after: and before: that refer to an existing element use the private method find:, which returns the actual index of the existing element or signals notFoundError. The methods for messages such as add:after: and add:beforeIndex: that insert an element in the middle of the list call the private method insert:before:, which creates an "opening" in the list for the new element by copying element references. Methods that remove an element in the middle of the list call the private message removeIndex:, which closes the "gap" in the list.

When an ordered collection receives the message addFirst: and its first indexed instance variable is occupied (i.e. firstIndex == 1), it sends itself the private message makeRoomAtFirst, whose method centers the list of element references within the receiver's indexed instance variables. Similarly, the method for addLast: calls makeRoomAtLast if lastIndex = self basicSize. If the method for makeRoomAtFirst or makeRoomAtLast finds that all the indexed instance variable are occupied, it sends the receiver the private message grow. This method creates an ordered collection with more indexed instance variables, copies the elements to it, and then uses the message become: described in section 7.1.2 to swap the identities of the receiver and the new object (as we discussed for Set in section 8.2.1).

OrderedCollection refines the *enumerating* message do: because using the do: method inherited from SequenceableCollection would involve range checking and recalculating a physical index for each pass through the enumeration. Its method for do: indexes through the elements from firstIndex to lastIndex.

```
"instance method for OrderedCollection"
do: aBlock
    "Evaluate aBlock with each of the receiver's elements as the argument."

    firstIndex to: lastIndex do: [:index | aBlock value: (self basicAt: index)]
```

Several other enumerating methods, such as detect:ifNone: and reverseDo:, are refined for the same reason. OrderedCollection refines collect: and select: to use add: rather than at:put: as in SequenceableCollection.

8.3.3 The Class SortedCollection

Purpose

SortedCollection is a subclass of OrderedCollection in which the order of the elements is determined by a boolean-valued *sort block* specific to that instance, not by the insertion messages sent by the client.[5]   Because the sort block determines

---

[5] To understand the distinction between "ordered" and "sorted", consider a linked list, which is always ordered but might not be sorted.

the position of an element, SortedCollection disallows the inherited adding messages that let us specify the position of the new element (such as addFirst: and add:after:). It also disallows the message at:put: for the same reason. In fact, add: and addAll: are the only adding messages for sorted collections. The removing messages of Collection and OrderedCollection are available since they preserve the receiver's order.

SortedCollection defines no additional protocol, except the messages described in this section that refer to the sort block. Sorted collections respond to the accessing, testing, copying, enumerating, and converting messages of Collection and SequenceableCollection.

The sort block

The sort function is represented by a two-argument block that returns true if the receiver precedes the argument in the receiver's order, and false otherwise (as we did for the class PriorityQueue in section 6.2.2). We can give the sort block with the *instance creation* class message sortBlock:, or by sending the *converting* message asSortedCollection: to a collection. For example,

```
"Create a sorted collection of shapes in order of decreasing area."
shapes := SortedCollection sortBlock: [:shape1 :shape2 | shape1 area > shape2 area]
```

The default sort block used when an instance is created with new, new:, or asSortedCollection is [:x :y | x <= y] (i.e., ascending order). The class stores this block as the value of the class variable DefaultSortBlock. We can access or change the sort block of an instance with the *accessing* messages sortBlock and sortBlock:. If it is changed, the elements are resorted by the private method reSort. If an element of the collection cannot respond to the messages in the sort block, a doesNotUnderstand: error will be signaled.

Implementation

SortedCollection inherits the storage structure of its superclass OrderedCollection, and adds the instance variable sortBlock and the class variable DefaultSortBlock.[6] The class SortedCollection is defined as follows:

```
"definition of the class SortedCollection"
OrderedCollection variableSubclass: #SortedCollection
    instanceVariableNames: 'sortBlock'
    classVariableNames: 'DefaultSortBlock'
    poolDictionaries: ''
    category: 'Collections-Sequenceable'
```

---

[6] In fact, SortedCollection is a subclass of OrderedCollection so that it can inherit its storage structure and many methods, a questionable use of inheritance. For this reason, SortedCollection must disallow many inherited messages.

In addition to sortBlock:, SortedCollection defines the *instance creation* class message withAll:sortBlock: whose first argument is a collection of initial elements. The method for new: sends super new: to allocate the object and set the inherited instance variables, then calls the instance method initialize to set the new object's sort block to the default sort block. (The argument of new: gives an initial physical size, as in the superclass.) The *class initialization* class message initialize initializes the class variable DefaultSortBlock.

SortedCollection re-implements the messages includes:, add:, and remove: to use a binary search to find or place the element. The methods for add: and remove: then invoke private superclass methods to position the new element and adjust firstIndex or lastIndex.

SortedCollection refines several inherited methods to take account of the sort block. The *comparing* method = checks the sort blocks of the receiver and the argument, and the *copying* message copyEmpty sets the new collection's sort block to that of the receiver. The method for the binary selector , adds each element of the argument to the result in its position in the ordering, rather than appending them to the copy of the receiver. The *enumerating* message collect: returns an ordered collection since the elements in the result may not be sortable by the receiver's sort block. The message reverse is also refined to return an ordered collection, as the sort block is no longer applicable.

8.3.4 The Class LinkedList

Purpose and protocol

LinkedList is a subclass of SequenceableCollection in which the client controls the order of the elements, and all elements are instances of descendants of the class Link. Like OrderedCollection, LinkedList defines the *adding* messages addFirst: and addLast: and the *removing* messages removeFirst and removeLast. The protocol of LinkedList does not include the other accessing, adding, and removing messages of OrderedCollection such as after:, add:beforeIndex:, and removeAllSuchThat:. The *accessing* message at: is available for linked lists, but at:put: is disallowed.

The class Link

The class Link is a subclass of Object that is not instantiated directly. An instance contains one instance variable, nextLink, a reference to the instance of a subclass of Link that is the object's successor in a linked list (like the class Linkable described in section 3.4.3). However, Link does not define an instance variable for the list element. The class designer who wishes to support linked lists of instances defines the class as a subclass of Link, which adds the instance variables that maintain the state of an instance. For example, we would define the class Node in section 6.1.2 as a subclass of Link that adds an instance variable element.

Link defines the *instance creation* class message nextLink:, which sets the new object's link to the argument. We can obtain or set the successor of a link with the *accessing* messages nextLink and nextLink:. If the argument to one of these messages is not an instance of a subclass of Link, an error will occur in traversing the list with the message nextLink.

Implementation

The class LinkedList defines two instance variables firstLink and lastLink that refer to the first and last elements in the list, like our Queue class in section 6.1.2. It refines the SequenceableCollection messages first and last to return these objects. The LinkedList methods perform the expected linked list processing using the instance variables and the Link accessing messages. For example, at: and size traverse the list, remove:ifAbsent: traverses the list to find its argument and then modifies the nextLink of its predecessor (unless it is the first link), and do: iterates until arriving at a nil link. The following are two example LinkedList methods:

```
"instance methods for class LinkedList"
addFirst: aLink
    "Add a link to the beginning of the receiver's list."

    self isEmpty ifTrue: [lastLink := aLink].
    aLink nextLink: firstLink.
    firstLink := aLink.
    ^aLink

do: aBlock
    "Evaluate aBlock with each of the receiver's elements as the argument."

    | aLink |
    aLink := firstLink.
    [aLink == nil] whileFalse: [
        aBlock value: aLink.
        aLink := aLink nextLink]
```

Like OrderedCollection, LinkedList implements add: as addLast:. It refines isEmpty as ^firstLink == nil.

8.3.5 The Class Interval

Purpose and protocol

Interval is a subclass of SequenceableCollection whose instances represent finite arithmetic progressions. An arithmetic progression is an ordered sequence of numbers determined by a start value, a limit value, and an increment used to calculate successive values. The elements of an interval may be instances of any of the numeric classes.

Interval defines the *instance creation* class messages from:to:, which uses an increment of 1, and from:to:by:, for which the increment may be positive or negative. (A negative increment creates a descending progression.) As we saw in section 7.4.2, the class Number supports the instance messages to: and to:by: that create intervals, which provides a literal notation for intervals. The following expressions produce equal intervals:

```
"two equal intervals, one from a Interval class message, the other from a Number
instance message"
Interval from: 50 to: 10 by: -0.5
50 to: 10 by: -0.5
```

Interval disallows the class message new because a start, limit, and increment must be given when creating an instance.

The elements of an interval are fixed when it is created and cannot be changed, so the class disallows the inherited adding and removing messages and the accessing message at:put:. Intervals respond to the accessing, testing, copying, enumerating, and converting messages of Collection and SequenceableCollection. Interval also defines the *accessing* message increment, which returns the receiver's increment. As we saw in section 5.5.5, Smalltalk programmers enumerate an interval to obtain the effect of a for loop in a traditional language.

Implementation

Intervals are represented internally by three instance variables start, stop, and step. These are initialized by the *private* method setFrom:to:by:, which the instance creation methods from:to: and from:to:by: send to the new object. However, the instance creation methods do no error checking. For example, the message 1 to: -33 creates an interval with start equal to 1, stop equal to -33, and step equal to 1. Sending size to that object returns 0, and first and last return 1 and -33. Sending at: results in a subscript range error, and do: does nothing.

Interval refines several inherited messages to use this storage structure. The *comparing* method = checks whether the argument has the same start, step, and stop as the receiver. However, because it cannot access the argument's instance variables directly, it uses the following method:

```
"instance method for Interval"
= anInterval
    "Answer true if the starts, steps and sizes of the receiver and anInterval are equal.
    If anInterval is not an interval, the superclass method will decide whether the
    receiver and anInterval are equal."

    (anInterval isKindOf: self class)
        ifTrue: [^start = anInterval first
            and: [step = anInterval increment
```

```
        and: [self size = anInterval size]]]
    ifFalse: [^super = anInterval]
```

The method for hash computes a hash value from those of the instance variables values. Accessing an individual element (e.g., in the methods for at:, first, last, and do:) involves computing its value, as does the method for size. For example,

```
"instance methods for Interval"
size
    "Answer how many elements the receiver contains."

    ^step < 0
        ifTrue: [start < stop ifTrue: [0] ifFalse: [stop - start // step + 1]]
        ifFalse: [stop < start ifTrue: [0] ifFalse: [stop - start // step + 1]]

last
    "Answer the last element of the arithmetic progression."

    ^stop - (stop - start \\ step)
```

The private message species is defined as ^Array, so the messages collect:, select:, and reject: and the copying messages return arrays. The method for the *printing* message printOn:: appends the string '(*start* to: *stop* by: *step*)' to the stream argument, and storeOn: calls printOn:.

8.3.6 Fixed-Size Collections

The class ArrayedCollection

ArrayedCollection is a subclass of SequenceableCollection that represents fixed-size collections. Unlike instances of OrderedCollection, which can grow and shrink (logically), an arrayed collection is of a fixed size determined when it is created, so its elements are replaced rather than inserted or deleted. It defines the message add: as self shouldNotImplement. remove:ifAbsent, which is disallowed in SequenceableCollection, remains unavailable. That is, ArrayedCollection is a restriction of its superclass. ArrayedCollection inherits the accessing, comparing, testing, copying, enumerating, converting, and printing protocols of its ancestors Collection and SequenceableCollection, but does not define any additional messages. ArrayedCollection is an abstract class because it does not define a storage structure.

ArrayedCollection has five subclasses, Array, ByteArray, String, Text, and RunArray. An array may contain references to any objects, the elements of a byte array must be integers between 0 and 255, and the elements of a string must be characters. Instances of Text represent a string and font and emphasis information. RunArray represents arrays that contain sequences of repeated elements.

The *instance creation* class message new: creates an instance whose size is given by the argument, with all its elements initialized to nil (excepts for byte arrays, whose elements are 0 initially). The message new:withAll: provides an initial value for all the elements as the second argument. The messages with:, with:with:, and so on are refined to create an instance of the correct size and then insert the arguments with at:put:.

ArrayedCollection defines the instance message size using the same primitive method as basicSize (i.e., it returns the number of indexed variables). Some subclasses override this method. The storeOn: method prints the format described in section 8.1.2 for fixed-size collections, and is overridden in descendants that have a literal notation.

The class Array

The concrete class Array is defined as a variableSubclass: ... of ArrayedCollection, and stores its element references in indexed instance variables. It inherits the protocol of Collection and SequenceableCollection, except for the messages disallowed by ArrayedCollection. The methods for the *accessing* messages at:, at:put:, and size are inherited from Object and use basicAt:, basicAt:put:, and basicSize (which all call primitive methods). As we saw in section 5.2.1, we can use Array's literal notation to create initialized instances. The *printing* message printOn: uses this notation, and storeOn: uses this notation if all of the elements of the array have literal notations.

The Smalltalk class hierarchy does not contain classes for multi-dimensional arrays.[7] We can obtain a similar effect by creating an array whose elements are arrays. Note that such an array need not be "rectangular" (i.e., each array element may be of a different size, like an array of strings in C).

The class String

The class String is a subclass of ArrayedCollection whose elements are instances of Character stored in indexed instance variables.[8] Instances can be created by a literal, or by the *instance creation* class messages fromString:, which creates a copy of the argument string, or readFrom:, which creates a string from the characters in the argument stream. The readFrom: method translates two successive single-quote characters in the stream to one single-quote in the result.

String inherits the protocols of its ancestors Collection and SequenceableCollection, which provide many of the familiar operations for strings. For example,

---

[7] Visualworks includes a class TwoDList with instance variables for the number of rows, the number of columns, and an array of elements. We access the elements with at: and at:put:, and the first argument is a point whose *x* coordinate gives the row number and whose *y* coordinate gives the column number.

[8] In VisualWorks, String is an abstract class with concrete subclasses ByteEncodedString and TwoByteString. The latter supports languages that have more than 256 characters. In addition, String and Text are subclasses of CharacterArray, which defines their common protocol.

- at: and at:put: access individual characters
- includes: tests whether a character is present
- indexOf: returns the first occurrence of a character
- , (comma) performs concatenation
- indexOfSubCollection:startingAt: searches for substrings
- replaceFrom:to:with: replaces substrings
- all the enumerating messages are supported.

Note that strings are fixed-size, so we cannot define methods that append a string to the receiver or remove characters from the receiver. Such methods must return a new string. When it is necessary to construct a string whose size is not known initially, we use a write stream of characters, as described in section 8.4.3.

String defines comparing protocol like that of Magnitude. Because Smalltalk does not support multiple inheritance, String cannot be defined as a subclass of both ArrayedCollection and Magnitude, so it defines a method for each comparing selector. The *comparing* protocol of String includes the binary selectors <, <=, >, and >=, and the message sameAs:. (String does not define min:, max:, and between:and:.) The collating sequence for these messages is ASCII order with case differences ignored. However, the String method for = does not ignore case differences, so the following expressions all return false: 'a' < 'A', 'a' > 'A', and 'a' = 'A'.

The comparing message match: regards the receiver as a pattern to be matched against the argument string, with # matching any single character, * matching any sequence of characters (including none), and case distinctions ignored. It returns a boolean that indicates whether the match was successful. The second argument of the message match:ignoreCase: is a boolean that specifies whether the matching process should ignore case differences (i.e., false indicates case sensitive matching). For example,

```
"the String messages match: and match:ignoreCase:"
'#tring' match: 'strinG'                              "returns true"
'#tring' match: 'strinG' ignoreCase: false           "returns false"
'#tring' match: 'tring'                               "returns false"
'st*g' match: 'string'                                "returns true"
'st*g' match: 'stg'                                   "returns true"
```

The class String defines *converting* protocol consisting of the messages asLowercase, asUppercase, asNumber, asSymbol, asText, and asFilename. The *printing* methods printOn: and storeOn: use the string literal notation.

The class Symbol

The class Symbol is a subclass of String, and symbols differ from strings in that they are unique and immutable. That is, there is never more than one instance of

Symbol corresponding to a particular sequence of characters. Because symbols are unique, the following comparison returns true:

```
"Symbols are unique objects."
('any' , ' string') asSymbol == 'any string' asSymbol          "returns true"
```

Symbols are used in identifying classes and message selectors, and as descriptive names of states or alternatives, like enumeration constants in a traditional language. For example, the Date class variables MonthNames and WeekDayNames are arrays of symbols. The class Symbol defines a class variable SymbolTable, a set that contains the symbols currently used in the image.

We can create symbols with the literal notation with a preceding #, by the Symbol class message readFrom:, or by the String instance message asSymbol. Symbol also defines the *instance creation* class messages intern:, whose argument is a string, and internCharacter:, whose argument is a character.

Because symbols are unique, the class implements = as == (and hash invokes a primitive method), and copy and shallowCopy as ^self. Symbols are also immutable, so Symbol disallows at:put: and replaceFrom:to:with: startingAt: (its ancestors disallow the adding and removing messages). The message species returns String, so copying messages, collect:, concatenation, asLowerCase, and so forth return strings. The *printing* methods printOn: and storeOn: use the symbol literal notation.

The class ByteArray

The class ByteArray is defined as a variableByteSubclass:... of ArrayedCollection, so its elements must be integers between 0 and 255. Byte arrays are usually only used in system programming. A byte array responds to the same messages as an array, and we can create instances with the literal notation described in section 5.2.1. The *accessing* messages at:, at:put:, size, basicAt:, basicAt:put:, and basicSize are redefined to invoke primitive methods that access the bytes in the receiver because the primitives invoked by the Object methods access object identifiers, not bytes. The *printing* methods printOn: and storeOn: use the byte array literal notation. ByteArray also defines *bit processing* messages for copying and replacing blocks of bits in the receiver, which invoke primitive methods.

The class RunArray

The class RunArray is a subclass of ArrayedCollection that provides a condensed representation for arrays consisting of sequences of repeated elements. It defines two instance variables runs and values, which are arrays. Each element of runs is an integer that indicates how many repetitions of the corresponding element in values appear in the run array. The *instance creation* class message runs:values: allows the client to give values for the instance variables of the new object. For example, the result of RunArray runs: #(2 3) values: #($$ $#) behaves as if it has 5 elements, $, $, #, #, and #. Run arrays are primarily used to give font and emphasis codes for an instance of Text.

The class Text

An instance of the class Text represents a string, together with a specification of fonts and typographic emphases such as bold or italic for each character. In addition to its inherited protocol, it defines *emphasis* messages such as allBold, emphasisAt:, for which the argument is a character index, and emphasizeFrom:to:with:, for which the third argument is an emphasis code.

Text defines two instance variables: string, which contains its characters, and runs, a run array that encodes its font and emphasis information. Each element of the run array gives the number of successive characters with the corresponding code from the values array. The codes in the values array are indices into an instance of TextAttributes, which describes the characteristics of characters with that code (e.g., their font, size, emphasis, color, etc.).

We can create a text object with the *instance creation* class message string:runs:, which gives initial values for those instance variables. The *accessing* methods of Text send the corresponding message to the string instance variable, and Text does not support the comparing protocol of String.

The class Text defines a class pool TextConstants, which gives the values of unprintable characters such as Tab and Ctrlc (control-C), and of commonly used emphasis codes such as BoldItalic and Subscripted.

8.4 THE STREAM CLASSES

8.4.1 The Class Stream

Purpose and definitions

A *stream* is an object that provides sequential access to a source or sink of information. In Smalltalk, a *read stream* supplies a series of objects one at a time via the message next. The objects obtained from a read stream can

- comprise the elements of a collection
- be read from an external source such as a file
- be generated by a computation.

We can test whether there are more elements in the read stream with the message atEnd. A *write stream* allows the client to add successive elements to a collection of objects or an external sink with the message nextPut:. The stream protocol is based on reading and writing sequential media such as tapes, terminal input/output, network connections, and printers.

If the source or sink of information is ordered and its objects can be accessed individually (e.g., a disk or main memory rather than a tape), then the stream can maintain a position at which objects are read or written (or can maintain separate read and write positions). Such a *positionable stream* supports protocol for manipulating the read/write position, and provides random access in addition to sequential access. In this section, we will see that the class Stream provides extensive protocol for sequentially accessing a stream of objects, and its subclass PositionableStream adds protocol for random access and for manipulating the read or write position in the stream.

The collection classes allow us to access, insert, and delete elements in various kinds of container objects, and provide protocol for enumerating those elements. However, we sometimes need to access an element, perform some processing, and then later access the next element, and so on. To supply this read stream protocol, we need a type of collection that maintains an internal position reference to keep track of which element to supply to the client next. The collection can also use the position reference to support write stream protocol and random access of collection elements.

The class designer can provide this "streaming" behavior for a collection class via either inheritance or composition. We illustrated using inheritance in section 3.1.2, where we defined PositionableList as a subclass of List, which adds the position reference instance variable and defines the additional behavior for sequential and random access. An instance of PositionableList responds to both streaming and list protocol. The Smalltalk class library uses composition. A stream contains instance variables that maintain the position reference and the collection, and its protocol defines the additional behavior. Streaming protocol is sent to the stream, and collection messages such as removing a particular element or converting to a different kind of collection are sent to the collection. We can keep more than one position reference in the same collection by creating several streams on that collection. However, if we send messages to a stream's collection that change its elements or their order, the stream may become invalid.

Descendants

The abstract class Stream is a subclass of Object, and is the ancestor of the stream classes. Note that Stream is not a subclass of Collection, and stream objects do not support collection protocol. Figure 8.5 is a diagram of the stream class subhierarchy.[9]

Stream has two subclasses, PositionableStream and Random. The abstract class PositionableStream is the ancestor of classes that stream over sequenceable collections and external sources such as files. An instance of the concrete class Random provides a stream of random floating-point numbers between 0.0 and 1.0. PositionableStream has two subclasses, InternalStream and ExternalStream, which are both

---

[9] As with collections, there are also stream classes such as ByteCodeStream, that are mainly used in the implementation of the system itself.

[10] The original Smalltalk-80 stream hierarchy presented in [Gol89] is somewhat simpler. There is no class InternalStream, and ReadStream and WriteStream are subclasses of PositionableStream. ExternalStream is a subclass of ReadWriteStream, and its only subclass is FileStream.

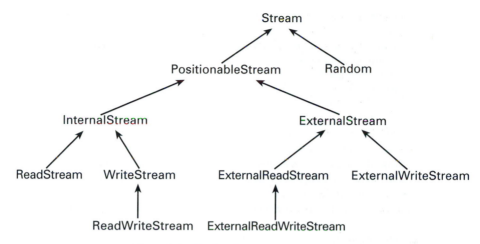

Figure 8.5   The Smalltalk stream subhierarchy.

abstract classes.[10] InternalStream represents stream over collections in memory, and has the concrete descendants ReadStream, WriteStream, and ReadWriteStream. ExternalStream represents streams that communicate with the outside world, and has the concrete descendants ExternalReadStream, ExternalWriteStream, and ExternalReadWrite-Stream. All the stream classes (except Random) are in the browser class category Collections-Streams.

Protocol for the class Stream

Stream disallows the *instance creation* class messages new and new: because the client must supply a source or sink of objects. We create a stream over a collection with the PositionableStream class message on: or the InternalStream class message with:, both of which take the collection as an argument. The method for on: positions the stream at the beginning of its collection, and that for with: sets the stream to the end of the collection. We can also obtain a stream by passing one of the messages readStream or writeStream to a sequenceable collection or an instance of Filename. We cannot create a stream on an unordered collection because stream methods access the collection using the messages at: and at:put:.

Stream defines numerous messages for reading from and writing to a stream sequentially. The subclass PositionableStream supplies additional protocol for random access of streams. The *accessing* protocol of Stream includes the following messages:

```
"the 'accessing' instance protocol of Stream"
contents
    "Answer a copy of the receiver's readable information."
next
```

"Answer the next element in the receiver."
next: anInteger
   "Answer the next anInteger elements of the receiver. An error occurs if there are
   not enough elements."
nextMatchFor: anObject
   "Read the next element and answer whether it is equal to anObject."
nextAvailable: anInteger
   "Answer the next anInteger elements of the receiver. If there are not enough elements
   available, answer a collection of as many as are available."
next: anInteger into: aSequenceableCollection startingAt: startIndex
   "Store the next anInteger elements of the receiver into aSequenceableCollection
   starting at startIndex in aSequenceableCollection. Answer aSequenceableCollection."
skipThrough: anObject
   "Skip forward to the occurrence of anObject, and leave the receiver positioned after
   anObject. If anObject is not found, position the stream at the end and return nil."
through: anObject
   "Answer a subcollection from the current position to the occurrence (if any, inclusive)
   of anObject. If anObject is not found, answer the remaining stream contents."
upTo: anObject
   "Answer a subcollection from position to the occurrence (if any, exclusive) of anObject.
   The stream is left positioned after anObject. If anObject is not found, answer the
   remaining stream contents."
upToEnd
   "Answer a subcollection from the current position to the end of stream."
nextPut: anObject
   "Put anObject at the next position in the receiver. Answer anObject."
nextPutAll: aCollection
   "Put each of the elements of aCollection starting at the current position of the receiver.
   Answer aCollection."
next: anInteger put: anObject
   "Replace the next anInteger elements of the receiver with anObject. Answer anObject."
next: anInteger putAll: aSequenceableCollection startingAt: startIndex
   "Store the anInteger elements of aSequenceableCollection starting at startIndex into the
   next anInteger elements of the receiver. Answer aSequenceableCollection"

The reading messages leave the position reference after the last object read, while the writing messages leave it after the last object written. Not all streams can respond to all of these messages. In particular, read streams cannot perform insertion messages such as nextPut:, and write streams cannot perform reading messages such as next and through:.

   The *testing* protocol of Stream consists of the message atEnd, which returns whether the position reference is off the end of the collection, and the deferred messages isReadable and isWritable. The *enumerating* message do: enumerates the elements of the collection beginning at the current position (i.e., it does not enumerate all the elements of the stream's collection), and leaves the position reference off the end. The other enumerating messages are not available for streams.

Stream also defines the *printing* messages print: and store:, which append the argument's print string or store string to the receiver. These messages are more convenient than printOn: and storeOn: when adding several objects to the same write stream because we can cascade messages with the stream as the receiver. The method for print: anObject is anObject printOn: self, and similarly for store:. As we saw in coding the Queue message printOn: in section 6.1.2, we use a write stream of characters to compose a string. To facilitate such processing, Stream defines *character writing* protocol consisting of the messages space, cr, tab, crtab, and crtab: (the argument for the last message is the number of tabs).

Implementation

Stream is an abstract class that does not define a representation, but describes the general protocol for its concrete descendants. It codes its methods in terms of the messages next, nextPut:, atEnd, and contents, and defines them as ^self subclassResponsibility. The following are some example Stream methods:

```
"instance methods for class Stream"

skipThrough: anObject
    "Skip forward to the occurrence of anObject, and leave the receiver positioned after
    anObject. If anObject is not found, position the stream at the end and return nil."

    [self atEnd ifTrue: [^nil].
    self next = anObject ifTrue: [^self]] repeat

through: anObject
    "Answer a subcollection from the current position to the occurrence (if any, inclusive)
    of anObject. If anObject is not found, answer the remaining stream contents."

    | newStream element |
    newStream := (self contentsSpecies new: 64) writeStream.
    [self atEnd] whileFalse: [
        element := self next.
        newStream nextPut: element.
        element = anObject ifTrue: [^newStream contents]].
    ^newStream contents

do: aBlock
    "Evaluate aBlock for each of the elements of the receiver."

    [self atEnd] whileFalse: [aBlock value: self next]
```

The *private* message contentsSpecies used in the method for through: returns the species of the stream's collection.

8.4.2 The Class PositionableStream

Purpose and definition

The class PositionableStream is a subclass of Stream that defines protocol for streams accessing sequenceable collections or files, and encapsulates protocol for manipulating the position reference. It is an abstract class because it does not implement the messages next and nextPut:. PositionableStream includes four instance variables, and is defined as follows:[11]

```
"definition of the class PositionableStream"
Stream subclass: #PositionableStream
    instanceVariableNames: 'collection position readLimit writeLimit'
    classVariableNames: ''
    poolDictionaries: ''
    category: 'Collections-Streams'
```

The instance variables are

- collection, a reference to the stream's collection
- position, an integer index into the collection
- readLimit, the size of the collection
- writeLimit, the farthest that has been written into the collection.

Protocol

We can create instances of concrete descendants of PositionableStream with the *instance creation* class messages on: (whose argument is the collection to access) and on:from:to: (which accesses a copy of the subcollection given by its arguments). Both messages call the private instance method on:, which sets collection to the argument, sets readLimit to the collection's size, and sets position to 0, that is, the beginning of the collection.

PositionableStream defines several *accessing* messages in addition to those it inherits from Stream, including the following:

```
"the 'accessing' instance protocol of PositionableStream"
peek
    "Answer the next element, without changing the position. If the receiver is at the end,
    answer nil."
peekFor: anObject
    "Answer true and increment the position if self next = anObject. Answer false and do not
```

---

[11] In VisualWorks, the functionality of this class is divided into two classes, PeekableStream and PositionableStream. PeekableStream is a subclass of Stream that allows the read position to back up one place in the collection, and defines methods for peek and peekFor:. PositionableStream is a subclass of PeekableStream that defines the remaining protocol and the four instance variables.

move the position if self next ~= anObject or if the receiver is at the end."
skipToAll: aCollection
"Skip forward to the next occurrence (if any) of aCollection. If found, leave the stream
positioned before the occurrence, and answer the receiver. If not found, answer nil,
and leave the stream positioned at the end."
throughAll: aCollection
" Answer a subcollection from the current position through the occurrence (if any,
inclusive) of aCollection, and leave the stream positioned after the occurrence.
If not found, answer the remaining stream contents, and leave the stream positioned
at the end."
upToAll: aCollection
" Answer a subcollection from the current position up to the occurrence (if any, not
inclusive) of aCollection, and leave the stream positioned before the occurrence.
If not found, answer the remaining stream contents, and leave the stream positioned
at the end."

The *positioning* protocol of PositionableStream provides random access to the
elements of the receiver's collection, and consists of the following messages:

"the 'positioning' instance protocol of PositionableStream"
position
"Answer the current position for accessing the stream."
position: anInteger
"Set the position to anInteger if anInteger is within the bounds of the receiver's contents.
If it is not, provide an error notification."
reset
"Set the receiver's position to 0."
setToEnd
"Set the receiver's position to the end of its stream of elements."
skip: anInteger
"Move the receiver's position by anInteger."
skipUpTo: anObject
"Skip forward to the occurrence (if any, not inclusive) of anObject. If anObject is not
found, answer nil. Leave the receiver positioned before anObject."

The *testing* protocol of PositionableStream includes the message isEmpty, which
returns true if the receiver's position is 0 (not if its collection is empty).

Implementation

Although it does not define next or nextPut:, PositionableStream defines
methods for its protocol, and for the Stream messages contents and atEnd. For
example,

"instance methods for class PositionableStream"

contents
"Answer with a copy of the receiver's collection from 1 to readLimit."

^collection copyFrom: 1 to: readLimit

peekFor: anObject
"Answer true and increment position if self next = anObject. Answer false and do not move the position if self next ~= anObject or if the receiver is at the end."

| nextObject |
self atEnd ifTrue: [^false].
nextObject := self next.
anObject = nextObject ifTrue: [^true].
self skip: -1.
^false

atEnd
"Answer whether the position is greater than or equal to the limit."

^position >= readLimit

position: anInteger
"Set position to anInteger if anInteger is within the bounds of the receiver's contents. If it is not, provide an error notification."

(anInteger >= 0 and: [anInteger <= readLimit])
    ifTrue: [position := anInteger]
    ifFalse: [^self positionOutOfBoundsError: anInteger]

8.4.3 Internal Streams

The class InternalStream

InternalStream is an abstract class for streams over collections in memory, and is a subclass of PositionableStream that adds no instance variables. It has three concrete descendants, ReadStream, WriteStream, and ReadWriteStream.

InternalStream defines the *instance creation* class messages with:, whose argument is the collection to stream over, and with:from:to:. Their methods call the *private* instance method with: to initialize the instance variables and set the position to the end of the collection. InternalStream also inherits the messages on: and on:from:to: from its superclass. InternalStream defines the *accessing* instance message size, which returns the number of elements in the receiver's collection.

The class ReadStream

The concrete class ReadStream is a subclass of InternalStream that provides read-only streaming over a collection. We usually create an instance with the class messages on: or on:from:to:, which positions the stream at the beginning of the collection. We can also obtain a read stream by passing readStream to a sequenceable collection or an instance of Filename. ReadStream inherits the protocols of its ancestors Stream, PositionableStream, and InternalStream, and defines no additional messages.

ReadStream disallows the message nextPut:, so writing messages such as nextPutAll: are also not available as their methods in Stream are defined in terms of nextPut:. ReadStream defines the following method for next:

```
"instance method for class ReadStream"
next
    "Answer the next object in the receiver."

    position >= readLimit
        ifTrue: [^self error: 'End of stream']
        ifFalse: [^collection at: (position := position + 1)]
```

ReadStream defines the *testing* messages isReadable and isWritable as ^true and ^false, respectively.

The class WriteStream

The concrete class WriteStream is a subclass of InternalStream that provides write-only streaming over a collection. We can create instances with the class messages with: or with:from:to:, which append the written objects to the collection. If we create an instance with on: or on:from:to:, it overwrites the existing elements of the collection. We can also obtain a write stream by passing writeStream to a sequenceable collection or an instance of Filename. Like ReadStream, WriteStream defines no additional protocol.

WriteStream disallows the message next, so messages such as next:, through:, and peekFor: whose methods use it are also not available. WriteStream defines the following method for nextPut::

```
"instance method for class WriteStream"
nextPut: anObject
    "Put anObject at the next position in the receiver.  Answer anObject."

    position >= writeLimit
        ifTrue: [self pastEndPut: anObject]
        ifFalse: [collection at: (position := position + 1) put: anObject].
    ^anObject
```

The *private* method pastEndPut: sends grow to the collection, sets writeLimit to the new size, increments position, and places anObject in the collection. That is, if the position reference is at the end of the collection, the new object is appended to the collection. Note that if the stream is not positioned at the end, nextPut: replaces the element at the position reference rather than adding the new object between existing elements, because its method uses at:put:. WriteStream defines the *testing* messages isReadable and isWritable as ^false and ^true, respectively.

Write streams are frequently used to construct strings because instances of the class String are fixed-size. To do this, we create a stream on: a string, append characters with nextPut:, append strings with nextPutAll:, and obtain the contents of the write stream. Recall that Stream also defines the messages space, tab, and cr to aid in such processing. For example, we saw in section 7.1.2 that Object's printString method creates a write stream with WriteStream on: (String new: 16), sends printOn: to the receiver with the stream as the argument, obtains the print string by sending contents to the stream, and returns it. As an example of the use of nextPut: and nextPutAll:, Collection defines the following method for printOn::

```
"instance method for class Collection"
printOn: aStream
    "Append a sequence of characters that identifies the collection to aStream."

    aStream nextPutAll: self class name , $(.
    self do: [:element | element printOn: aStream.  aStream space].
    aStream nextPut: $)
```

The class ReadWriteStream

The class ReadWriteStream is a subclass of WriteStream that supports both reading from and writing to the receiver's collection. It inherits the methods of WriteStream and defines the same methods for next and isReadable as ReadStream.

8.4.4 External Streams

The class ExternalStream **and its descendants**

The class ExternalStream is a subclass of PositionableStream that represents communication with input/output devices, the host file system, networks, and databases. It defines instance variables that maintain a buffer to mediate between client operations and slower block-oriented devices such as disks, and a connection with the host operating system. When a next message empties the buffer, data is read into the buffer from the external source. When a nextPut: fills the buffer, data is written to the external sink from the buffer. Some systems also define an instance variable that maintains the "line end character" (which varies among platforms) and protocol for accessing it.[12]

ExternalStream overrides the initialization instance message on: to create a

---

[12] In VisualWorks, the functionality of this class is divided into two classes, ExternalStream and BufferedExternalStream. ExternalStream is a subclass of PositionableStream that defines the nonhomogeneous accessing and positioning protocol. BufferedExternalStream is a subclass of ExternalStream that adds the buffer instance variable and the methods for emptying and refilling the buffer.

buffer and a connection to the operating system, and sets the collection instance variable to contents of the buffer. It also defines several private methods for handling the buffer and the connection to the operating system.

For an internal stream, any object can be an element of the collection accessed by the stream. In the case of secondary storage or input/output devices, the elements of a stream are typically accessed as individual bytes or arrays of bytes, rather than as objects. ExternalStream provides additional *nonhomogeneous accessing* protocol, including the following messages:

```
"the 'nonhomogeneous accessing' instance protocol of ExternalStream"
nextWord
    "Answer the next two bytes from the receiver as an integer."
nextWordPut: anInteger
    "Append anInteger to the receiver as the next two bytes."
nextNumber: numBytes
    "Answer the next numBytes bytes as a small or large positive integer."
nextNumber: numBytes put: anInteger
    "Append anInteger to the receiver as the next numBytes bytes.
    Pad with leading zeros if necessary."
nextString
    "Answer a new String read from the receiver. The first byte is the length of the string,
    unless it is greater than 192, in which case the first two bytes encode the length."
nextStringPut: aString
    "Append aString to the receiver."
```

The methods for these accessing messages access bytes with self **next** or self **nextPut:**. ExternalStream also defines *nonhomogeneous positioning* protocol that aligns the position reference with word boundaries.

```
"the 'nonhomogeneous positioning' instance protocol of ExternalStream"
padTo: bsize
    "Skip to next boundary of bsize characters, and answer how many characters
    were skipped."
padTo: bsize put: aCharacter
    "Pad using aCharacter to the next boundary of bsize characters, and answer how many
    characters were written."
padToNextWord
    "Set position on a word boundary (make it even), answering the padding character if any."
padToNextWordPut: aCharacter
    "Set position on word boundary, writing aCharacter if necessary. Answer nil if already on a
    word boundary."
skipWords: numWords
    "Set position after numWords number of words."
wordPosition
    "Answer the current position in words."
wordPosition: numWords
    "Set current position in words to be numWords."
```

The concrete classes ExternalReadStream, ExternalWriteStream, and External-ReadWriteStream are descendants of ExternalStream that provide streaming proto-col for external sources and sinks of bytes. ExternalReadStream defines a method for next that obtains the next character in the buffer or calls a private External-Stream method if the buffer is empty. ExternalWriteStream and ExternalRead-WriteStream define a method for nextPut: that places the argument character in the buffer or calls a private ExternalStream method if the buffer is full. External-WriteStream and ExternalReadWriteStream also define an *accessing* message flush that transfers any bytes in the stream's buffer to the external sink. You should always send this message before closing an external connection to ensure that all the output arrives at the sink.

Files

We can read and write binary data from files using the nonhomogeneous accessing protocol of ExternalStream. We can also read and write a string of char-acters that can be evaluated to create an object by using the stream as argument of the class message readFrom: and the instance message storeOn:, respectively. In Smalltalk-80, the programmer uses the class FileStream, a subclass of ExternalStream that provides access to files as streams of bytes or characters. He or she creates an instance with the class message fileNamed:, whose argument is a string giving a file name or a path in a hierarchical directory structure.

Newer Smalltalk systems use a somewhat different approach. In section 6.1.1, we briefly discussed the class Filename, which represents files and provides exten-sive class and instance protocol for manipulating files and directories. We create an instance of Filename with the class message named:, whose argument is a file name or path. The Filename instance messages readStream, writeStream, or read-WriteStream create an external stream on a file, and we can then send stream mes-sages to that object, rather than to the file name object. For example,

```
"storing the object 'budgetDict' to a file"
| filename extWriteStream |
filename := Dialog requestFileName: 'Enter a budget file name.'.
extWriteStream := (Filename named: filename) writeStream.
budgetDict storeOn: extWriteStream.
extWriteStream flush.    "make sure all the characters get to the file before closing it"

"loading the object 'budgetDict' from a file"
| filename |
filename := Dialog requestFileName: 'Enter a budget file name.'.
"requestFileName: returns an empty string if the file doesn't exist or can't be accessed."
filename = ''
ifTrue: [Dialog warn: 'There is no such file!']
ifFalse: [budgetDict := Dictionary readFrom: (Filename named: filename) readStream]
```

In this example, we stored the object budgetDict using the format defined by its class, rather than as a binary stream of data. We can also create a filename object from a string with the converting message asFilename.

8.4.5 The Class Random

Purpose and definition

In section 8.3.5, we discussed the collection Interval that generates its elements when necessary rather than storing them explicitly, and the same technique can be applied to streams. The class Random is a concrete subclass of Stream that generates the next element by performing a computation on the previous element. The current element is stored in an instance variable seed, and successive elements are computed by Lehmer's linear congruential method to produce a series of pseudo-random floating-point numbers uniformly distributed between 0.0 and 1.0. (See [Gol89] or your Smalltalk system for the details of the algorithm.) The class also defines a number of class and instance variables that maintain constants used in the algorithm. Unlike the other stream classes, Random is in the browser class category Magnitude-Numbers.

Protocol and implementation

The method for the *instance creation* class message new invokes a private instance method that initializes the seed from the system clock. In some cases, we need to reproduce the same stream of random numbers when testing a program. The instance creation message fromGenerator:seededWith: allows the programmer to set the initial parameters used by the generator algorithm. Its arguments are positive small integers.

An instance of Random computes and returns successive elements in response to the message next, and therefore next:, nextMatchFor:, and other reading messages are available. Because instances are read-only, Random disallows the Stream message nextPut:. Unlike an interval, an instance of Random has an infinite number of elements, so the class disallows contents and size, and atEnd always returns false. If the programmer uses do:, he or she must provide some way for the enumeration to terminate (e.g., returning from the method in the block argument). Like ReadStream, Random defines the *testing* messages isReadable and isWritable as ^true and ^false, respectively.

8.5 SUMMARY AND REVIEW

8.5.1 The Class Collection

Overview of the collection class subhierarchy

- The abstract class Collection is a subclass of Object, which is the root of a large subhierarchy of collection classes. It defines extensive protocol and default methods for its descendants.
- Bag, Set, Dictionary, OrderedCollection, SortedCollection, and LinkedList are variable-size, and Interval, Array, ByteArray, String, Symbol, and Text are fixed-size.

- The unordered collections are Set, Bag, Dictionary, IdentitySet, and Identity-Dictionary. The ordered collections are OrderedCollection, LinkedList, Interval, SortedCollection, Array, ByteArray, String, Symbol, and Text.

- A collection can contain any class of object, except for strings and symbols that contain characters, intervals that contain numbers, linked lists that contain instances of descendants of Link, and byte arrays that contain integers between 0 and 255.

- The collection subhierarchy includes subclasses that are specializations such as Dictionary, abstract classes such as SequenceableCollection, and subclasses that are restrictions of their superclass such as Interval, SortedCollection, and Symbol.

Protocol

- We can create collections with the *instance creation* class messages new (an empty collection), new: aSize, readFrom: aStream, and with: anObject, with: firstObject with: secondObject, etc. Strings, arrays, byte arrays, and symbols can be created with a literal.

- Collection defines the *adding* messages add: and addAll:, and the *removing* messages remove:, remove:ifAbsent:, and removeAll:.

- Collection defines the *testing* messages includes:, isEmpty, and occurrencesOf:, and the *accessing* message size.

- Equality tests for unordered collections use an identity test, and two sequenceable collections are equal if they are the same species and size, and their corresponding elements are equal.

- The *enumerating* protocol of Collection consists of do:, collect:, select:, reject:, detect:, detect:ifNone:, and inject:into:.

- Collection defines the *copying* messages copyEmpty and copyEmpty:, but not copy, which defaults to shallowCopy. Its *converting* protocol consists of asArray, asBag, asSet, asOrderedCollection, asSortedCollection, and asSortedCollection:, each of which returns a shallow copy of the receiver with the indicated type.

- The Collection method for the *printing* message printOn: prints the class name followed by a parenthesized list of the elements; the method for the message storeOn: stores an expression that creates an object with the receiver's class name and new or new:, then uses add: or at:put: to insert its elements.

- Some enumerating and copying messages return a collection of the same kind as the receiver, but for some classes, the result cannot be the same type. Collection defines the *private* message species, which it implements as ^self class. Instances of Interval respond with Array, and those of Symbol respond with String. Methods that create collections of the same kind as the receiver use self species rather than self class.

Implementation

- Collection is an abstract class and does not define a storage structure for maintaining elements.
- The messages add:, remove:ifAbsent:, and do: are deferred, and Collection methods send those three messages to self. Each concrete descendant defines a storage structure, and implements (at least) those three methods.

8.5.2 Unordered Collections

The class Set

- The class Set is a subclass of Collection that represents variable-size, unordered collections without duplicates.
- Set implements the protocol it inherits from Object and Collection, but defines no additional messages.
- Set is implemented by a hash table in indexed instance variables and an instance variable tally containing the number of elements in the set. This structure provides efficient search, and requires that two elements that are equal return the same value for hash.
- The class IdentitySet is a subclass of Set that uses an identity test rather than an equality test to locate an element.

The class Bag

- The class Bag is a subclass of Collection whose instances are unordered and may contain duplicate elements.
- Bag inherits the protocols of Object and Collection, and defines the *adding* message add:withOccurrences:.
- Bag defines one instance variable contents, a dictionary in which each key is an element and the value is the number of occurrences of that element in the bag. Bag refines new to call an initialization method that creates the dictionary, and implements the deferred methods of Collection by passing messages to the dictionary.

The class Dictionary

- The class Dictionary is a subclass of Set in which each element is an instance of Association, a key–value pair. The values are regarded as elements accessed via the keys.
- Dictionary refines the *accessing* messages at: and at:put: to access values via the keys, and refines Collection messages such as includes: and do: to consider the values as its elements. add: adds an association, and remove:ifAbsent: is disallowed.
- Dictionary also defines *accessing* messages such as keys, values, associations, and keyAtValue:, and *dictionary testing*, *dictionary removing*, and *dictionary*

enumerating messages such as includesKey:, removeAssociation:, and keysDo:. Associations are hashed according to their keys, so a dictionary cannot contain duplicate keys.

- The class IdentityDictionary is a subclass of Dictionary that uses an identity test to match keys.

8.5.3 Ordered Collections

The class SequenceableCollection

- The abstract class SequenceableCollection is a subclass of Collection that encapsulates protocol for ordered collections. We can access an element with at: and at:put: by using its index in the collection as the key.
- SequenceableCollection has four subclasses: OrderedCollection, LinkedList, Interval, and ArrayedCollection.
- The extensive *accessing* protocol of SequenceableCollection defines messages that access or replace elements relative to their positions in the receiver's order such as first, last, indexOf:, indexOfSubCollection:startingAt:, atAllPut:, replaceAll:with:, and replaceFrom:to:with:.
- The *copying* protocol of SequenceableCollection includes messages such as , (comma), copyFrom:to:, copyWith:, reverse, and copyReplaceFrom:to:with:.
- SequenceableCollection inherits the *enumerating* protocol of Collection, and defines the messages findFirst:, findLast:, reverseDo:, keysAndValuesDo:, and with:do:.
- SequenceableCollection defines the *converting* messages readStream and writeStream, which create a stream on the receiver.
- SequenceableCollection does not define a representation for storing elements. It defines many methods that access elements with at: and at:put: and enumerate them with do:.
- SequenceableCollection refines the *comparing* messages = and hash, and disallows the *removing* message remove:ifAbsent:.

The class OrderedCollection

- The class OrderedCollection is a concrete subclass of SequenceableCollection whose instances are ordered by the client's insertions and deletion messages. We use ordered collections rather than arrays for lists of objects so that we do not have to decide on a size.
- OrderedCollection defines *adding* protocol consisting of addFirst:, addLast:, add:after:, add:before:, add:beforeIndex:, addAllFirst:, and addAllLast:
- The *removing* protocol of OrderedCollection includes removeFirst, removeLast, removeAtIndex:, removeAll, and removeAllSuchThat:.

- OrderedCollection defines the *accessing* messages before: and after:.
- An ordered collection stores a list of references to its elements in indexed instance variables, and includes two named instance variables, firstIndex and lastIndex, that give the indices of the actual first and last elements.
- Insertions and deletions increase and decrease the logical size of an ordered collection, and its physical size is expanded if necessary. OrderedCollection refines the messages at:, at:put:, and size to use the logical indices and size.

The class SortedCollection

- The class SortedCollection is a subclass of OrderedCollection in which the order of the elements is determined by a boolean-valued *sort block*. The class disallows adding messages that allow the sender to specify the position of the new element.
- The *instance creation* class message sortBlock: and the Collection *converting* message asSortedCollection: give the sort block as an argument. The default sort block for the messages new, new:, and asSortedCollection is [:x :y | x <= y] (i.e., ascending order). An instance's sort block can be accessed or changed with sortBlock and sortBlock:.
- SortedCollection inherits the storage structure of its superclass OrderedCollection, and adds the instance variable sortBlock and the class variable DefaultSortBlock.

The class LinkedList

- The class LinkedList is a subclass of SequenceableCollection in which the order of the elements is controlled by the client, and all elements are instances of descendants of Link.
- To support linked lists of instances of a class, we define the class as a subclass of Link that adds the class's instance variables.
- LinkedList defines the *adding* messages addFirst: and addLast: and the *removing* messages removeFirst and removeLast.
- LinkedList defines two instance variables firstLink and lastLink, and its methods use the instance variables and the Link accessor messages nextLink and nextLink:.

The class Interval

- The class Interval is a subclass of SequenceableCollection that represents ordered sequences of numbers determined by a start value, a limit value, and an increment.
- Interval defines the *instance creation* class messages from:to: and from:to:by:, and Number provides the instance messages to: and to:by: that create intervals. Interval disallows new.

- The elements of an interval are fixed, so the class disallows adding and removing messages and at:put:.

- Interval defines three instance variables—start, stop, and step—fixed after initialization. Accessing and enumerating messages compute the requested elements.

- The species of Interval is Array.

- The *printing* messages printOn: and storeOn: print or store the string '(*start* to: *stop* by: *step*)'.

Fixed-size collections

- The abstract class ArrayedCollection is a subclass of SequenceableCollection that represents fixed-size collections. Elements are replaced rather than inserted or deleted, so the class disallows adding and removing messages. ArrayedCollection has five subclasses: Array, ByteArray, String, Text, and RunArray.

- The class Array is a concrete subclass of ArrayedCollection that stores element references in indexed instance variables. Array uses its literal notation for printing and storing if possible.

- The class String is a subclass of ArrayedCollection, whose elements are characters. Strings can be created by a literal, or by the *instance creation* class messages fromString: and readFrom:.

- String defines the *comparing* messages <, <=, >, >=, and sameAs:, which ignore case differences, and match: and match:ignoreCase: which matches the argument against the receiver. The String method for = does not ignore case differences. String's *converting* protocol consists of the messages asLowercase, asUppercase, asNumber, asSymbol, and asFilename.

- The class Symbol is a subclass of String whose instances are unique and immutable. We can create symbols with the literal notation with #, by the *instance creation* class messages intern:, internCharacter:, or readFrom:, or by the String instance message asSymbol. The species of Symbol is String.

- The class ByteArray is a concrete subclass of ArrayedCollection that stores integers between 0 and 255 in indexed instance variables, and is mainly used in system programming. Its literal notation is used for printing and storing.

- The class RunArray is a subclass of ArrayedCollection that provides an efficient representation for arrays consisting of sequences of repeated elements.

- The class Text is a subclass of ArrayedCollection whose instances represent a string of characters, together with a specification of typographic emphases.

8.5.4 The Stream Classes

The class Stream

- A *stream* provides sequential access to a source or sink of information such as a collection or a file. A *read stream* allows the client to access successive objects from its source with next, and test whether there are more elements with atEnd. A *write stream* allows the client to add successive elements to its sink with nextPut:. A *positionable stream* also provides random access of objects via a position reference in the source or sink of information.

- A stream over a collection maintains the collection and a position reference in the collection, and provides protocol for accessing elements and manipulating the position reference.

- The abstract class Stream has two subclasses: the abstract class PositionableStream and Random, a stream of random numbers. PositionableStream has two abstract classes: InternalStream, the ancestor of streams over collections, and ExternalStream, the ancestor of streams over external sources and sinks.

- Stream disallows the *instance creation* class messages new and new:. We create a stream over a collection with on: or with:, both of which take the collection as an argument. on: positions the stream at the beginning of its collection, and with: sets the stream to the end of the collection. We can also obtain a stream by passing readStream or writeStream to a sequenceable collection or an instance of Filename.

- Stream defines *accessing* protocol for sequential reading and writing, such as next, nextMatchFor:, through:, upTo:, nextPut:, and nextPutAll:.

- Stream defines the *testing* message atEnd, the *enumerating* message do:, the *printing* messages print: and store:, and *character writing* protocol consisting of the messages space, cr, tab, crtab, and crtab:.

- Stream is an abstract class that does not define a representation, and codes its methods in terms of the deferred messages next, nextPut:, atEnd, and contents.

The class PositionableStream

- The class PositionableStream is a subclass of Stream for streams that access sequenceable collections or files, and defines protocol for manipulating the position reference. It is an abstract class because it does not define methods for next and nextPut:.

- PositionableStream defines four instance variables: collection, position, readLimit, and writeLimit.

- PositionableStream defines the *instance creation* class messages on: and on:from:to: that set the position to the beginning of the collection.

- PositionableStream defines the *accessing* messages peek, peekFor:, skipToAll:, throughAll:, and upToAll:; the *positioning* messages position, position:, reset, setToEnd, skip:, and skipUpTo:; and the *testing* message isEmpty.

- PositionableStream defines methods for its messages and for the inherited messages contents and atEnd.

Internal streams

- InternalStream is an abstract subclass of PositionableStream whose concrete descendants ReadStream, WriteStream, and ReadWriteStream represent streams over collections in memory. It defines the *instance creation* class messages with: and with:from:to: that set the position to the end of the collection, and the *accessing* instance message size.

- The concrete class ReadStream is a subclass of InternalStream that provides read-only streaming over a collection. It defines next and disallows nextPut:.

- The concrete class WriteStream is a subclass of InternalStream that provides write-only streaming over a collection. It defines nextPut: and disallows next. If the position is not at the end of the collection, nextPut: replaces the element at the position reference, rather than inserting the new element after it (and incrementing the position).

- We use write streams to construct strings. We create a stream over a string, append characters with nextPut:, append strings with nextPutAll:, use the character writing messages of Stream, and then obtain the contents of the write stream.

- The class ReadWriteStream is a subclass of WriteStream that supports both reading of and writing to the stream's collection by defining next and inheriting nextPut:.

External streams

- The class ExternalStream is a subclass of PositionableStream that represents communication with files and other external sources and sinks of information. It defines instance variables that maintain a buffer and a connection with the host operating system.

- ExternalStream defines *nonhomogeneous accessing* protocol for character strings, machine words, and strings of bytes as large positive integers, and *nonhomogeneous positioning* protocol that aligns the position reference with word boundaries, such as padTo:, padToNextWord:, and skipWords:.

- The concrete classes ExternalReadStream, ExternalWriteStream, and ExternalReadWriteStream are descendants of ExternalStream that provide streaming protocol for external sources and sinks of bytes. ExternalWriteStream and ExternalReadWriteStream define an *accessing* message flush that transfers any bytes in the stream's buffer to the external sink.

- To read from or write to a file, create a file name object with Filename named: '*path*', and send it the message readStream, writeStream, or readWriteStream to create an external stream over the file.
- We can read and write binary data from files using the nonhomogeneous accessing protocol of ExternalStream, or can read and write objects with read-From: and storeOn:.

The class Random

- The class Random is a concrete subclass of Stream whose instances generate random floating-point numbers uniformly distributed between 0.0 and 1.0. It supports stream reading messages such as next, next:, and nextMatchFor:, but disallows nextPut:.
- An instance of Random has an infinite number of elements, so it disallows contents and size, and atEnd returns false.

8.6 EXERCISES

8.1 **(a)** Which collection classes are abstract?
  (b) Which concrete collection classes represent unordered collections?
  (c) Which concrete collection classes represent ordered collections?
  (d) Which concrete collection classes represent keyed collections?
  (e) Which concrete collection classes represent variable-size collections?
  (f) Which concrete collection classes represent fixed-size collections?
  (g) Which concrete collection classes have literal notations?
  (h) Which concrete collection classes have restrictions on the kinds of elements they can contain?

8.2 Define methods for the following additional Collection messages:
  (a) containsSuchThat: aBlock, which returns whether there is an element in the collection for which aBlock returns true
  (b) countSuchThat: aBlock, which returns the number of elements of the collection for which aBlock returns true
  (c) conformTo: aBlock, which returns true if aBlock returns true for every element of the collection, and false otherwise

8.3 Code the methods for the following Collection instance messages. Compare your answers to the methods on your Smalltalk system.
  (a) occurrencesOf:
  (b) detect:ifNone:
  (c) inject:into:
  (d) asArray
  (e) printOn:

8.4 Use your Smalltalk system to determine which Collection messages have methods in both Collection and one of its descendants. For each, explain why the descendant overrides the inherited method.

8.5 Define methods for the following additional Set messages:
  (a) hasSubset: aSet, which returns true if aSet is a subset of the receiver (either proper or equal), and false otherwise

(b) intersection: aSet, which returns a new set that is the intersection of aSet and the receiver

(c) union: aSet, which returns a new set that is the union of aSet and the receiver

(d) - aSet, which returns a new set containing the elements of the receiver that are not in aSet

(e) Would your methods work for instances of Bag, OrderedCollection or SortedCollection?

8.6 (a) Define a method for the binary selector = for the class Set that returns true if the argument is a set containing the same elements as the receiver, or false otherwise.

(b) What other method must we define for Set if we define = and why? Code a definition of this method. (Hint: See its definition in SequenceableCollection.)

8.7 Suppose we want to define a method for the message powerSet for the class Set that returns the set of all subsets of the receiver.

(a) Why will there be a problem with the current implementation of the system class Set?

(b) Code a method for powerSet, assuming that the problem in part (a) has been solved.

8.8 The class Set is implemented as a hash table in which "overflow" objects that hash to an occupied home address are also placed in the table according to linear probing. An alternative implementation of a hash table uses a linked list of objects at each home address. For example, the set in Figure 8.6 contains three objects, two of which hash to 1 and one of which hashes to 5.

With this storage structure, no adjustments need to be made when an element is deleted so the fixCollisionsFrom: method is no longer necessary. We can use the class

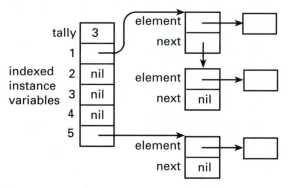

Figure 8.6 Storage diagram for an implementation of Set with chaining (class pointers and class objects not shown)

Node defined in section 6.1.2 to implement the linked lists. The table size is increased when the average length of the linked lists is 2.5 (rather than when the table is 75 percent full).

(a) Which existing Set methods can we use with this storage structure? (For example, the existing new: method is correct for this storage structure.)

(b) Define the necessary Set methods for this implementation of Set.

8.9 Trace the messages sent on your Smalltalk system when the expression Bag new is evaluated, and give the purpose and class of definition of each method executed.

8.10 What is the result of evaluating the expression Bag new add: 2; add: 2.0; yourself on your Smalltalk system? Explain this behavior.

8.11 Code the methods for the following Bag instance messages. Compare your answers to the methods on your Smalltalk system.
  (a) addWithOccurrences:
  (b) remove:ifAbsent:
  (c) size

8.12 As we discussed in section 8.2.3, the protocol of the class Dictionary provides two views of the receiver. What are they? Which Dictionary messages correspond to each view?

8.13 Why is there no Collection converting message asDictionary?

8.14 Code the methods for the following Dictionary instance messages. Compare your answers to the methods on your Smalltalk system.
  (a) at:ifAbsent:
  (b) at:put:
  (c) associations
  (d) select:
  (e) printOn:

8.15 Write a code fragment to determine whether the associations in the dictionary returned by passing select: to a dictionary are references to those in the receiver or to copies. Test your code on instances of Dictionary and IdentityDictionary.

8.16 Smalltalk does not provide a case control structure among the system classes. Suppose we decide to implement one by storing the case values and the associated blocks to be executed in a dictionary (i.e., with caseDictionary at: caseValue put: caseBlock). To execute a case, we would send the message case: caseDictionary default: aBlock to the object whose value is used for the selection. In which class's protocol should this message be added? Code this method.

8.17 Use your Smalltalk system to determine which SequenceableCollection messages have methods in both SequenceableCollection and one of its descendants. For each, explain why the descendant overrides the inherited method.

8.18 Code the methods for the following SequenceableCollection instance messages. Compare your answers to the methods on your Smalltalk system.
  (a) =
  (b) atAll:put:
  (c) replaceAll:with:from:to:
  (d) copy:from:to:
  (e) findLast:

8.19 Define methods for the following additional SequenceableCollection messages:
  (a) swap: anIndex with: anotherIndex, which swaps the positions of the elements with indices anIndex and anotherIndex
  (b) move: anObject by: anInteger, which moves anObject forward anInteger positions in the receiver, or backward in the receiver if anInteger is negative (or signals subscriptBoundsError: if the resulting position is out of range)
  (c) indicesOf: anObject, which returns an array of the positions at which anObject appears in the receiver
  (d) indexOfAny: aCollection from: startIndex to: stopIndex, which returns the index of the first occurrence of any element of aCollection in the receiver between startIndex and stopIndex
  (e) copyAddAll: aCollection beforeIndex: anInteger, which creates a copy of the receiver in which all the elements of aCollection are inserted before the object in the receiver with index anInteger

8.20 As we mentioned in section 8.3.1, add: is allowed in SequenceableCollection but disallowed in Interval and ArrayCollection, whereas remove:ifAbsent: is disallowed in SequenceableCollection, but reimplemented in OrderedCollection and LinkedList. Is there any difference between these two approaches to restriction?

8.21 The messages in the *adding*, *removing*, and *accessing* protocols of OrderedCollection are not in the protocol of SequenceableCollection.
(a) Do these messages fit with the semantics of SequenceableCollection?
(b) Which of them can be defined in SequenceableCollection? Define those methods.

8.22 Code the methods for the following OrderedCollection instance messages. Compare your answers to the methods on your Smalltalk system.
(a) after:
(b) add:before:
(c) removeLast:
(d) removeAllSuchThat:

8.23 (a) Why does SortedCollection's method for collect: return an ordered collection?
(b) Should the species of SortedCollection be OrderedCollection? (Hint: Browse senders of species.)

8.24 The *adding* and *removing* protocols of LinkedList have far fewer messages than those of OrderedCollection.
(a) Define methods for LinkedList for the additional adding and removing messages of OrderedCollection.
(b) What restriction are there on the arguments of the messages in part (b) for linked lists?
(c) Are the methods that LinkedList inherits from SequenceableCollection for its copying and enumerating messages appropriate for LinkedList? Refine each of SequenceableCollection's copying methods with an efficient version for LinkedList.

8.25 With the Smalltalk system class LinkedList, all the elements of a linked list must be instances of descendants of Link. However, we might need a linked list of objects whose classes cannot be derived from Link because they must have another superclass.
(a) Recall the classes Queue and Node that we defined in section 6.1.2. Define a class LinkedListOfAny that uses the same storage structure as Queue. Code the class as a subclass of SequenceableCollection that defines all the protocol of LinkedList.
(b) Define methods for LinkedListOfAny for the additional adding and removing messages of OrderedCollection. (Note that there are no restrictions on the arguments of these messages.)
(c) Define methods for each of SequenceableCollection's copying and enumerating messages for LinkedListOfAny.

8.26 (a) An interval is fixed-size, so should Interval have been defined as a subclass of ArrayedCollection? Would this make its definition simpler or more complex?
(b) Would this organization simplify any other classes? (Consider which classes in the subhierarchy rooted at SequenceableCollection define add: and remove:ifAbsent:.)

8.27 We want to define a class ComputedInterval for which each element is computed from the previous element by applying an instance-specific "step block", a one-argument block that takes and returns a number. For example, this class can be used to define an interval whose elements form a finite geometric progression. The class defines three instance variables: start, stop, and stepBlock.
(a) Which class should be the superclass of ComputedInterval? Why?

(b) Define the *instance creation* class message from:to:computedBy: that gives values for the new object's instance variables (and, of course, a *private* initialization method).

(c) Define the methods necessary so that ComputedInterval has the same instance protocol as Interval (except for the message increment), together with the *accessing* message stepBlock.

(d) Which ComputedInterval methods are less efficient than those in Interval?

8.28 Define methods for the following additional String messages:

(a) tokensDelimitedBy: delimiters, which returns an ordered collection of copies of the tokens in the receiver, where delimiters is a collection of token delimiters

(b) allSubstrings, which returns an ordered collection of all substrings of the receiver

(c) withoutSpaces, which returns a copy of the receiver with every space removed. (Hint: Use a write stream.)

8.29 Smalltalk-80 included a class MappedCollection, a subclass of Collection that represents an index into a keyed collection [Gol89]. An instance is represented by two instance variables: map, the index, and domain, the "data". Both components must be instances of collections with keys (i.e., either a dictionary or a sequenceable collection). The map has values that are keys in the domain, and the mapped collection associates the map values with the domain keys such that the values of the domain are accessed via the keys of the map. This pattern of access is illustrated in Figure 8.7.

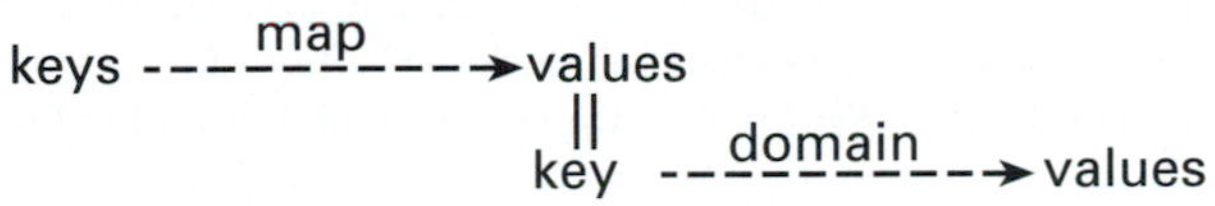

keys --- --- map --- --- →values
                          ‖
                       key -- -- domain -- -- → values

Figure 8.7   The map and the domain in the class MappedCollection.

In general, the map represents indirect access of a re-ordered subset of the values in the domain. We create instances of MappedCollection with the *instance creation* class message collection:map: in which the first argument is the domain, or by sending the *converting* message mappedBy: to an instance of a descendant of SequenceableCollection. The method for at: uses its argument as a key in the map, accesses the associated value, and returns the domain value whose key is that map value. at:put: replaces the value in the domain at the key that is the value associated with its first argument in the map. size returns the size of the map, which is also the size of the referenced subdomain. The *accessing* message contents results in a collection of the same species as the map in which each value is the domain value associated indirectly with that map key. The messages add: and remove:ifAbsent: are disallowed (but can still be sent to the map or the domain). do: is refined to access domain values via the map, so the elements produced are the subset of the domain values accessed by the map in the order defined by the map. The species of a mapped collection is the species of its domain. Define the class MappedCollection and its methods.

8.30 (a) Which Stream messages are available only for read streams? Which Stream messages are available only for write streams?

(b) Why do you think that both reading and writing protocol is defined in Stream, even though one portion or the other is not available for most concrete streams?

(c) Is there another way to organize the stream classes such that read streams do not have to disallow writing messages and write streams do not have disallow reading messages? (Remember that there are internal and external read and write streams.)

8.31 Streams inherit Object's method for = (i.e., an identity test). Write a stream method for = that tests whether the receiver and argument are streaming over equal collections and are set to the same position. In which class should this method be defined?

8.32 **(a)** Describe the difference between the stream class messages on: and with:.
(b) Can you think of better names for these messages?

8.33 Write a message expression that obtains the next line (i.e., from the current position to the first occurrence of the line delimiter) from a read stream.

8.34 Suppose we want to stream over an unordered collection such as a set. Clearly, the stream can maintain an index in the set's indexed instance variables as its position reference, and increment that value in its method for next, compare it to the set object's basic size for atEnd, and so on. However, this would require the stream to use the private protocol of Set (e.g., basicAt:), which is not prohibited in Smalltalk.
(a) Would all of the protocol of Stream be appropriate for a stream over a set? (In particular, does nextPut: make sense?)
(b) Because a set is unordered, some PositionableStream messages such as position and position: should not be available. Which PositionableStream messages are appropriate for a stream over a set?
(c) Define the class SetReadStream. Do not forget to disallow any inherited protocol that should be prohibited, or to implement any necessary messages that are not provided by the superclass you choose.
(d) Define the class BagReadStream. Again, disallow inappropriate inherited messages and implement messages that are not inherited.
(e) Will the class SetReadStream you designed in part (c) work for dictionaries?

8.35 Suppose we want to create a stream over an instance of LinkedList.
(a) Does the ReadStream method for next work if the receiver's collection is a LinkedList? Why would it be very inefficient for linked lists?
(b) Define a concrete class LinkedReadWriteStream that interprets its position as a reference to a link in a linked list. (Think about your choice of superclass.) Be sure to define any Stream and PositionableStream methods that must be re-implemented.

PART III

C++

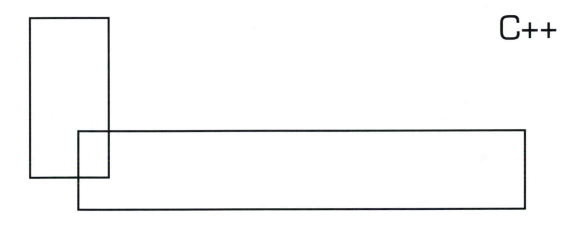

In Part III of the text, we will discuss the language C++ in detail. We choose to cover C++ because it illustrates a number of points about hybrid and statically typed object-oriented languages, such as the interaction between static typing and inheritance and the tradeoffs between efficient execution and the flexibility necessary for dynamic binding. Of course, C++ is also the most widely used object-oriented language, mostly due to its C heritage. In fact, a major advantage of C++ is that it is straightforward to use existing C libraries together with an application written in C++. In discussing C++, I will assume that you are somewhat familiar with C and its characteristics. If not, some examples were presented in Chapter 0, and there are numerous texts and references covering the language (e.g., [Ker88] and [Spu92]). Most C texts describe both ANSI and pre-ANSI C because both versions of the language are in widespread use.

For many years, the Annotated C++ Reference Manual [Ell90] was the source for a precise description of the syntax and semantics of the language. It also includes a discussion of design decisions, C compatibility issues, and techniques for implementing certain features. [Str94] presents a discussion of the more recent extensions to the language, and a more detailed description of the development of the language. The ANSI/ISO C++ Standards Committee has been meeting for several years, and has defined an updated standard for the language [ANS96]. The ANSI/ISO C++ Standard refines some details of the language and enhances the newer features of the language, such as templates and exceptions. Its biggest contribution is the ANSI/ISO C++ Standard Library, which defines functions, classes, and templates that support

- the language definition: properties of built-in types, memory management, type information, and exceptions
- some foundation classes: string, complex, and numeric arrays
- input/output: the iostream class library
- internationalization: parameterization for different character sets and locales
- some collections and iterators: bitset, deque, list, vector, set, and map.

The ANSI/ISO C++ Standard Library is not as complete as the class libraries with most object-oriented languages. There are no classes for times and dates, file system operations, graphics, user interaction, and so on. Because the standard is so new, few compilers are in total compliance and none supply the entire Standard Library. In discussing C++, we will discuss the recent changes in the standard version of the language separately, as your compiler may not support them all. We will also not go into complete detail about many features of the library because they are infrequently used or are still under development.

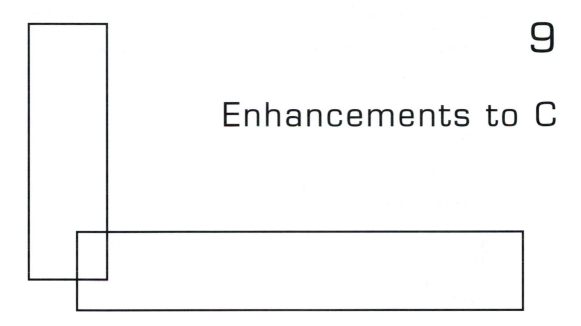

9

Enhancements to C

OVERVIEW

Many of the constructs added to C by C++ are not specifically object-oriented constructs, but are improvements to C resulting from research on programming languages since the introduction of C, and from experience using the language. For example, C++ includes features such as read-only variables, function overloading, and default parameter values that are present in Ada, but not in Pascal. In this chapter, we will cover the basic semantic features and procedural constructs of C++, describing them in detail only when they differ from those of C.[1] In the following four chapters, we will concentrate on the features that support the object paradigm, and will view the language from that perspective.

This chapter covers the following topics:

- the lexical structure, expression syntax, and control structures of C++ (9.1.1 and 9.1.2)
- declarations and definitions, file, function, and class scope, and the scope operator (9.1.3)

---

[1] We will occasionally need to distinguish between pre-ANSI C and ANSI C when discussing the features of C. When I simply refer to "C", I am discussing a feature that is the same in both versions of the language.

- object allocation policies, and the new and delete operators for dynamic allocation (9.1.4)
- built-in types, type constructors, the const specifier, the reference type, and type casts and conversions (9.1.5)
- function declarations and the function parameter list, which supports type checking, const parameters, pass and return by reference, and default parameter values (9.2.1 and 9.2.2)
- inline functions, and why they are better than macros (9.2.3)
- function overloading, and the rules for resolving ambiguous invocations of overloaded functions (9.2.4)
- function name encoding, which implements external linking of overloaded functions (9.2.5)
- pointers to functions (9.2.6)
- the basics of the iostream class library for input/output, and the use of the << and >> operators and stream manipulators (9.3)

9.1 BASIC LANGUAGE FEATURES

9.1.1 Lexical Structure

Comments

The delimiter // indicates that the remainder of the source code line in which it appears is a comment. For example,

```
// the C++ comment delimiter is useful for header or full-line comments
int num;                // and for trailing comments
```

This comment style avoids errors caused by a missing or mistyped closing delimiter and allows us to comment out a line of code that contains a trailing comment. In a multi-line comment such as the header comment describing a function, each line must begin with the // delimiter. With this delimiter, a comment cannot precede a language statement on a line or occur within a statement, but programmers rarely do these things. The C comment delimiters /* and */, which enclose a comment, are available for these uses, and are also helpful for commenting out a block of code containing // comments during debugging. The delimiter // is not significant when it occurs in a comment enclosed by /* and */, and vice versa.

Tokens, operators and expressions

An identifier is any sequence of letters, digits, and underscores (the _ character) beginning with a letter or underscore, and C++ sets no limit on the length of identifiers. Identifiers that begin with two underscores are reserved for the implementation and the standard library, so you should not use these. All C reserved words are used in C++ as they are in C, and C++ defines a number of additional reserved words such as new, class, operator, virtual, template, and throw for various purposes. The formats for numeric, character, and string literals are the same as those of C. The following are some examples:

```
// formats for C++ numeric literals
-1234                                    // int
0123                                     // octal int
0xFFFF                                   // hexadecimal int
-987654L                                 // long
9876U                                    // unsigned int
12.345                                   // double
12345E-3                                 // double
12345E-3L                                // long double
'c'  '%'  '\t'  '\0'  '\xFF'             // character literals
"hello"                                  // string literal
```

The rules for expression syntax are also the same as those of C. All 45 of the C operators are available, and the meaning, precedence, arity (number of operands), and associativity of each is the same as in C. C++ defines six additional operators, namely ::, new, delete, ::*, .*, and ->*, as we will see in various sections in this part of the text. Figure 9.1 lists the C++ operators, grouped by precedence.

level	operators	operations
17	:: ::*	scope operator, pointer to member declarator
16	-> . [] () ()	member selectors, subscription, function call, initialization
15	++ — + -	increment, decrement, unary plus, unary minus
	! ~	logical NOT, bitwise complement
	* &	pointer dereference, address-of
	(type) sizeof	type conversion or cast, size of a type or object in bytes
	new delete	dynamic allocation, dynamic deallocation
14	->* .*	pointer to member selectors
13	* / %	multiplication, division, modulus
12	+ -	addition, subtraction
11	<< >>	bitwise left shift, bitwise right shift
10	< <= > =>	relational operators
9	== !=	equality test, inequality test
8	^	bitwise XOR
6	|	bitwise XOR
5	&&	short-circuit logical AND
4	||	short,circuit logical OR
3	?:	conditional expression operator
2	= *= /= %=	
	+= -= <<= >>=	
	&= ^= |=	assignments
1	,	expression sequecing

Figure 9.1   C++ operators grouped by precedence.

Note that the unary operators have higher precedence than all the binary operators except component selection, subscription, function call, and initialization. (The use of parentheses for initialization is described in sections 9.1.4, 10.1.2, and 10.2.2.) All binary operators are left associative, except for the various assignment operators, which are right associative. As in C, the order of evaluation of the operands of an operator or of the arguments of a function call is undefined. As we will see in section 11.1, operators may be overloaded for class type operands.

9.1.2 Control Structures

C sequential control structures

Like C, C++ includes the conditional statements if-else and switch, and the conditional evaluation expression operators &&, ||, and ?:. As in C or Pascal, we use a compound statement consisting of a list of statements enclosed in braces to include a sequence of actions on a branch of a conditional, or as the body of a loop. For example,

```
// a C++ if statement
if ( num < 0 || num > 100 )
{
    cout << "Out of range, try again:" << flush;      // print a prompt
    cin >> num;                                        // read a value
}
else
    total += num;
```

The stream objects cout and cin and the << and >> operators provide date transfer, and are described in section 9.3.

Iteration is provided by the while, do-while, and for statements. We saw an example of the for statement in section 0.1.1, and the following example illustrates the while statement:

```
// a C++ while statement
while ( cin >> num )                 // read until end of file
{
    if ( num > 0 )
    {
        posTotal += num;
        posCount ++;
    }
}
```

The break statement exits the nearest enclosing iteration or switch statement, and the continue statement terminates the current iteration of a while, do-while, or for loop. The return statement exits a function and returns the value of the succeeding expression to its caller.

Like C, C++ originally did not define a Boolean type. An expression as the condition of one of the control structure statements or operators could return either an int or a pointer. The condition was treated as "false" if the resulting value was zero or a null pointer, and "true" otherwise. The comparison operators and the logical operators !, &&, and || returned 0 for false or 1 for true. The ANSI/ISO C++ Standard now defines a Boolean type bool, which we will discuss in section 9.1.5. Comparison and logical operators return bools rather than ints, and control structures support the bool type in conditions. However, control structures will continue to support ints and pointers in conditions for backward compatibility.

The main() function

Like C, C++ does not have a syntactic unit that represents the entire program. A C++ program is a collection of function, object, and type definitions, and execution begins in the function called main(). The language supports two argument signatures for the function main(), either with or without arguments.

```
// argument signatures for main()
// the return value indicates whether the program terminated successfully
int main();
// the arguments represent an array of strings passed to the program
// from the environment at run time
int main(int argc, char* argv[]);
```

We usually use the int return value of main() to pass a code to the program's environment indicating whether and how it failed. By convention, a value of zero indicates successful termination of the program. A return statement in main() calls the function exit() with the return value as the argument. If control reaches the end of main(), it is the same as executing return 0; (i.e., successful termination). The arguments for the argument signature (int, char*[]) are a count and an array of statically allocated strings that represents information passed to the program from the environment at the beginning of execution. For example, they are the command line arguments on a UNIX system. These argument signatures are guaranteed to be portable (but void main() is not).

In the rest of our C++ examples, we will enclose executable code in a main() function if no other function applies because executable code can only occur within a function. We will use the argument signature int main(), but will not code a return statement. Because declarations can appear at file scope, we will not use a main() function for examples that consist only of declarations.

Exceptions

C programmers use three techniques for signaling and handling errors. Many standard library functions return a value that indicates an error, which the caller can check and respond to. In ANSI C, the programmer can use the assert() macro to exit with an error message when a particular value is zero. To provide error propagation, the C standard library defines the functions setjmp() and longjmp() that we can use to transfer control to a previous function invocation.

Like many contemporary languages, C++ includes a facility for programmer-defined exception handling. These features provide a mechanism for explicitly separating error handling code from problem-solving code, which makes the program easier to read and maintain. Not all compilers support the exception facility because it has a major effect on implementation of the language and is a recent addition to the language. We will discuss defining, signaling, and handling exceptions in section 13.3.

9.1.3 Scope

Declarations and definitions

Declarations and definitions of objects and functions have the same syntax in C++ as in C. An object declaration introduces a name into a scope, and gives a type and possibly a storage class and linkage specification for its referent. The type name and other specifiers such as static, extern, or const precede a comma-separated list of identifiers.[2] Each identifier may also be preceded by an * (for a pointer) or an & (for a reference), and followed by [ ] (for an array) or an initializer for its type. The initial value can be preceded by an = as in C, or enclosed in parentheses.[3] As in C, an object declaration is also a definition that creates the object unless the extern specifier is used. For example,

```
// example C++ object definitions using built-in types
int num1 = 1;              // an int object initialized to 1
int num2(2);               // an int object initialized to 2
char *str1, *str2;         // two pointers to char (legal, but bad practice)
int arr[20];               // an array of 20 ints
double* arrPtr[10];        // an array of 10 pointers to double
```

We will discuss declarations of functions and pointers to functions in section 9.2.1 and 9.2.6. Type definitions are illustrated in sections 9.1.5 and 10.1.

Static scope

As in C, a "compound statement" is a series of statements enclosed by the symbols { and }, and compound statements may be nested. A compound statement that contains definitions of local variables is called a *block*, and defines a level of scope containing those identifiers. The body of a function definition is a block that

[2] Most coding standards recommend that only one identifier be introduced in each declaration.

[3] We will see in section 10.1.2 that the latter syntax is needed for class objects whose constructors take more than one argument.

introduces a new level of scope nested within the scope of the file in which the function is defined. The function name is declared within the file scope, while its parameters and local variables are declared within the local scope of the function. Blocks that include local variables can be nested within a function body (although C and C++ programmers rarely do so).

The usual static scope rules for disambiguating references within nested scopes apply in C++. An identifier declaration local to a block or function is not visible outside that block or function, and is visible anywhere within that scope unless it is redeclared within further enclosed scope. A local declaration hides declarations of that name in enclosing scopes. An identifier use refers to the declaration of that name in the scope in which the use appears, if any. Otherwise it refers to the declaration in the next enclosing scope that does declare that name. An identifier name cannot be used unless it lies within the scope of some declaration of that name.

C++ supports three kinds of scope, and each has its own characteristics. They are file scope, local scope (i.e., function or block scope), and class scope. The ANSI/ISO standard also includes "namespaces", which define a fourth kind of scope. Namespaces support name qualification and import declarations, like Ada packages or Modula-2 modules, and are discussed in section 13.4.

File scope

As in C, *file scope* consists of the portions of the program text in a translation unit that are not contained within any function or class definition. As we discussed with respect to C module scope in section 1.1.3, each source code file in a program defines a scope nested within the global scope of the entire program, so there are two levels of file scope (recall Figure 1.2). Both the global scope and the individual file scopes nested within it have the characteristics of file scope. The only statements allowed at file scope are declaration statements, which may also be definitions and include initializations. (In order words, executable statements can only appear in a local scope). A file scope identifier is visible from the point of its declaration throughout that file, except within contained scopes in which that name is redeclared. Every variable defined at file scope is statically allocated, whether it is global or local to a file.

All file scope declarations that are not specified as static are exported to the global scope of the entire application. For this reason, a non-static file scope identifier must refer to the same object, function, or type in each separately compiled file in a program. Two different non-static file scope definitions of the same name in different files in a program will cause a multiple definition error from the linker.

As in C, the extern specifier declares a file scope identifier without defining it, and allows a code file to access a global variable defined in another file. If the identifier is not defined in another file linked to the file, the linker signals an undefined symbol error. All function declarations (often called "function prototypes" in C) are extern by default, and the compiler enters them into the external symbol table used by the linker.

To declare a name in the scope of a code file rather than the global scope, we precede it with the reserved word static.[4] We can declare both variables and functions as static. The compiler does not enter a static file scope identifier into the file's external symbol table, so it is not visible in other files linked with the file containing it. If another file in the program uses that identifier at file scope, there is no name conflict, and each identifier refers to a different object or function. The following examples illustrate the different kinds of file scope object declarations:

```
// file scope declarations
// declares and defines num1 in the global scope enclosing this file's scope
int num1 = -1;
// declares num2 but does not define it, and num2 must be defined globally in another file
extern int num2;
// defines num3 in the scope of this file, but not in the global scope
static int num3;
```

Local function scope

A *local scope* is that portion of the program text within a function definition or a block. A local scope may contain both declarations and executable statements. Each function defines a distinct local scope enclosed within the file scope in which it is defined, and the parameters and local variables of the function are declared in this scope. If we specify a variable within a local scope as static, its value persists across invocations of the function, although its name is only visible within the scope in which it is defined.

In both C and C++, we cannot nest function definitions lexically as we can in Pascal. We code functions that are logically related in the same file, and declare those that are "auxiliary" functions not intended to be visible outside the module as static. Within a function, each block that includes declaration statements defines a local scope, and these local block scopes may be nested (although this is rarely done).

A common programming error is to use an identifier without first initializing it with a meaningful value. C requires all identifier declarations in a local scope to be placed at the beginning of a block or function. In C++, a local object definition can appear at any point in a function. A variable defined within a local scope is visible from the point of definition throughout the rest of that block or function, but not earlier. The chief reason for this feature is that many class objects require a significant amount of processing for initialization. Without the feature, if the information needed to initialize an object is not available at the beginning of the function, we would initialize the object in some default manner, and then re-initialize it later when that information becomes available. This feature avoids the first unnecessary initialization. Placing the declaration of an identifier closer to the point of first use also improves readability, and reduces the portion of the code in which an uninitialized variable exists.

---

[4] Note that this is not the same meaning as the use of static with a local function variable. A different reserved word, say intern, would have been less confusing.

A variable declaration can also occur in the body of a loop or a branch of a conditional. For example, the following statement defines a variable index within a for statement:

```
// index is defined within the for statement
static const int SIZE = 32;
void func()
{
    // ... other processing ...
    for ( int index = 0;  index < SIZE;  index++ )
    {
        // ... something useful ...
    }
    // ... other processing ...
}
```

In the original definition of the language, the identifier index is visible in the for statement and in the scope of func() following the for statement, because it is declared outside the scope of the compound statement within the for statement. (Of course, it is not visible before the for statement.) In the new ANSI/ISO C++ Standard, a variable declared within the condition of an if or while statement or in the header of a for statement is only visible in the associated compound statement (like a function parameter, which is declared outside the braces that delimites the function code but is still visible only within that block). If we need the value of a loop variable from the last iteration, we must assign it to a variable declared outside the loop before exiting the loop.[5] If a variable declared within a loop or conditional statement has an initializer, its value is initialized each time control passes through its declaration. If a declaration occurs within a block contained in a branch of a conditional (e.g., within the else part of an if statement), it is an error to use that identifier outside the block because control may not have entered that block during a particular execution.

Class scope

Each class defines its own *class scope*, and its data members and member functions are declared within that scope, like a C struct definition which defines a new level of scope for its members' names. The C programmer is not usually concerned with this level of scope, but we must be aware of it in C++ because function definitions can occur within a class scope. Those definitions include executable statements containing identifiers whose referents the compiler must determine according to static scope. Identifiers declared within a class scope hide declarations of the same name at file scope within the class. The local scopes of a class's "member functions" (i.e., its methods) are nested within the class's scope. Class scope in C++ is quite complex due to support for nested classes and multiple inheritance, and

---

[5] This is the same semantics for loop variables as in Ada and several other languages.

because of the distinction between visibility and accessibility for private superclass members. We will discuss class scope in detail in sections 10.3, 12.1.2, and 12.4.2.

The scope operator ::

C++ uses the *scope operator* :: for name qualification. Its left operand gives the name of the scope in which the right operand name is declared. We can use it to refer to a name either in global scope (with an empty left operand) or in a class scope. This feature provides us with the ability to refer to identifiers that are not visible according to the rules of static scope. We will see in section 10.3 that class scopes and the scope operator provide some of the characteristics of import/export scope for C++.

We can use the scope operator without a left operand (syntactically, as a unary prefix operator) to refer to a global variable hidden by a local declaration of the same name. For example,

```
// unary prefix use of the scope operator
int num = 3;            // file scope num
int func()
{
    int num = 5;        // num local to func()
    return ::num;       // refers to the file scope num
}
```

The primary use of the scope operator is with a class name as its left operand and an identifier declared within that class's scope as its right operand. This allows us to refer to a class member outside the scope of that class. For example, when we define the implementation of a method separately from the definition of the class's interface, we write the member function name as *Class::message*. Other uses of the scope operator include method refinement (section 12.1.2), class variable initialization (section 10.3.2), nested classes (section 10.3.4), disambiguation of name clashes with multiple inheritance (section 12.4.2), and namespaces (section 13.4). The scope operator cannot be used with a function name as its left argument, so it is not possible to refer to a local variable outside the scope in which it is visible.

The scope operator is unlike any other operator in the language. It does not have an argument signature indicating its parameter types in the usual sense. The left operand must be a class name (or, as we will see in section 13.4, a namespace name), not the name of an object or function. The right operand must be a name (of any type at all) that is declared in that class scope. In a unary usage, the operand must be a global identifier. The compiler uses the declaration of the qualified name in type checking the expression in which the use of the scope operator appears. If the identifier is an object name, the compiler interprets the name as denoting either an *l*-value or an *r*-value, depending on the context of its use. Essentially, the scope operator operates in the name space and its arguments are identifiers, not the associated objects. (Alternatively, since there are no other name space operators, the arguments of the scope operator cannot be expressions.)

9.1.4 Storage Allocation

Static allocation

All objects defined at file scope are statically allocated, whether the reserved word static appears or not. They are created when program execution begins and exist for the duration of that execution. If a file scope variable is specified as static, that identifier is not visible globally (i.e., in other files to which the file is linked), but it is visible for the rest of the file in which it is defined. As discussed in section 9.1.3, this usage of the reserved word static deals with the identifier's visibility rather than with the object's allocation.

As in C, a variable declared static within the local scope of a function maintains its value across function invocations, so it cannot be allocated in a stack frame. A static local variable is allocated in the static storage area for the duration of execution, and its value is initialized when control enters its definition for the first time. The identifier is only visible within the function scope in which it is defined.

If a file scope object contains an initializer, the language guarantees that the initialization will be performed before any function in that file is executed. The static objects in a file are initialized in their order in the file, but static objects in different code files can be initialized in any order. As in C, all static objects that do not have an explicit initialization are initialized to 0 or NULL (converted to the object's type).

Automatic allocation

Functions and blocks may define local variables, which are automatically allocated on the run-time stack for the lifetime of the function invocation or block execution.[6] Function arguments that are passed by value are also automatically allocated.

The compiler sometimes must allocate anonymous temporary objects that it needs to evaluate an expression. For example, in the following function, a temporary long double object whose value is that of arg is necessary:

```
// a temporary object "(long double) num" is necessary
void func(int arg)
{
    // ... other processing ...
    long double dbl = 3.0L + 3.5L / arg;
}
```

Temporary objects are also allocated in that function's stack frame (unless they can be kept in machine registers). The compiler knows the total amount of storage necessary for the temporaries necessary to execute a function. It can add this offset to

---

[6] This is referred to as the auto storage class in C and C++, and this specifier can be used in a local variable definition to indicate that the object is not static. However, no C++ programmers do so because it is the default.

the stack pointer after invocation and subtract the offset upon return, and assign
locations in that space for temporary objects.

Dynamic allocation

In C++, we allocate a dynamic object by applying the prefix new operator to
a type or class name. The operation creates an instance of that type on the heap,
and returns a pointer of the correct type that refers to the newly allocated object.
We can give an initial value for the newly created object in parentheses following
the type name. This *initializer* can be any expression that returns the given type (or
a type that can be converted to the given type).[7] For example, the following statement declares pDbl as a pointer to instances of double, allocates storage for the
pointer, invokes new to create a double value on the heap, initializes that object to
the value 3.3, and sets the pointer to refer to that object:

```
// defines a pointer and allocates and initializes a dynamic object
double* pDbl = new double(3.3);
```

Unlike the use of the C function malloc(), no sizeof or cast from void* are necessary
when using the new operator.

We allocate an array of objects dynamically by enclosing an expression giving
the number of objects in square brackets [ ] following the type name and new. For
example,

```
// allocates an array of chars on the heap
#include <string.h>
int main()
{
    char str[] = "hello";
    char* pStr = new char[strlen(str) + 1];
    strcpy(pStr, str);
}
```

Unfortunately, there is no syntax for initializing the elements of a dynamic array.
We allocate a dynamic array of pointers using the following syntax:

```
// allocating an array of pointers on the heap
const int STR_ARR_SIZE = 20;
// pArrStr is a pointer to a pointer to char
char** pArrStr = new char*[STR_ARR_SIZE];
```

Storage deallocation is controlled by the programmer in C++. The delete
operator deallocates the referent of its pointer operand, which must have been allocated by new. After the deallocation operation, the pointer's value is undefined, so

---

[7] We will see in section 10.2.2 that when creating an instance of a class dynamically, the initializer
must be the argument signature of one of the class's constructors.

you should not use it without assigning it a valid value. Applying delete to a pointer to an object that was not allocated dynamically is undefined, and is likely to cause a problem with management of the free store. However, applying delete to a NULL pointer is not an error, and does nothing. You also should not delete an object allocated with malloc(), or free() an object allocated with new. We use the delete [ ] operator to deallocate a dynamic array that was allocated with new [ ]. The following code fragment illustrates the use of the delete and delete [ ] operators (delete is an operator, rather than a function like free(), so we do not need to enclose the pointer name in parentheses):

```
// deallocation with the delete operator
const int STR_SIZE = 256;
int main()
{
    char* pChar = new char('c');
    char* pStr = new char[STR_SIZE];
    delete pChar;
    delete [ ] pStr;                    // deallocate the entire array, not just the first element
}
```

If we deallocated *pStr in the previous example with delete instead of delete [ ], only the first character would be deallocated, causing a memory leak. Like C, C++ does not distinguish between a pointer to an object and a pointer to an array of objects, so pChar and pStr in the preceding example are the same type. For this reason, it is the programmer's responsibility to use the correct deallocation operator.

As we will see in section 10.2.2, applying the new operator to a class name causes invocation of that class's "constructor", which provides programmer-controlled initialization of objects. new returns a type-correct pointer to a properly constructed object, a major advantage over malloc(), which returns a void* pointer that refers to a region of raw storage. Similarly, applying delete invokes a class instance's "destructor", which performs any "clean up" necessary when an object is destroyed. We will cover destructors in section 10.2.3.

When there is not enough free storage to satisfy an allocation request, the run-time system raises the exception bad_alloc. (We will discuss handling exceptions in section 14.3.4.) For compatibility with older language systems that do not support exception handling, the language provides a mechanism for registering an error handling function that is called when the free store is exhausted. The function set_new_handler(), which is defined in the standard header file new.h,[8] takes a pointer to function argument (see section 9.2.6), and registers it as the "new handler" to be called when an allocation fails. set_new_handler() returns the former new handler so that the programmer can restore it if necessary (like the C standard library function signal()). The new handler must make more memory available and return, or call exit() or abort() (or raise bad_alloc). If the programmer does not register an allocation error handler, new returns 0 when an allocation fails. For sys-

---

[8] The header file is named new (i.e., without the .h suffix) in the new ANSI/ISO Standard.

tems that support exceptions, the new handler is invoked upon an allocation failure, and if there is none, bad_alloc is raised.

9.1.5 Types

Primitive types

C++ supports all the built-in types of ANSI C, namely char, wchar_t (for "wide characters"), short int, int, long int, float, double, and long double. As in C, we may specify any of the integral types as signed or unsigned. The restrictions on the sizes of their instances and on their relative sizes are the same as in C. Instances of these types may be mixed freely in expressions and assignments, and the compiler can use the same implicit coercions defined for C.

As in C, the header files limits.h and float.h[9] define a number of constants that describe details of the implementation's representation of the built-in types, such as INT_MAX, LONG_MIN, DBL_EPSILON, and FTL_MANT_DIG. The new ANSI/ISO C++ Standard Library defines a class template numeric_limits<>[10] and specialized classes such as numeric_limits<unsigned int> and numeric_limits<float> for each built-in type. These classes include a number of messages for obtaining information about a type, such as min(), is_integer, and has_infinity. The class template numeric_limits<> is a new feature that is not supported by any current C++ systems.

The type void behaves syntactically like a built-in type, but there can be no instances of this type. Its primary use is as the return type of functions that do not return a value. In the following declaration, () does not return a value, and the compiler enforces this characteristic:

```
// func() does not return a value
void func(char*, int);
```

We can also use the type void to convert the result of an expression to void so that the expression may be used as a statement, for example, when the caller does not need the return value of a function call.[11]

The type void is also used to declare a pointer to an unknown type of object. A variable of type void*, sometimes referred to as a "generic" pointer, can be assigned the address of any object. This type is used when the exact type of an object is unknown or may vary. However, the compiler has no information on how to interpret the referenced memory, so the programmer cannot use the pointer without explicitly casting it to another pointer type. For example, a pointer to void cannot be dereferenced or assigned to an identifier declared as a pointer to a par-

[9] These header files are named climits and cfloat in the new ANSI/ISO Standard.

[10] Template classes are generic types, and are discussed in detail in section 13.2. We will using a trailing <> after a template name to remind us that it is a template, as C programmers use a trailing () after a function name. (The reason for the notation <> will be apparent in section 13.2.)

[11] An example of this usage appears in section 10.2.3.

ticular type. (This cast can be done implicitly in ANSI C.) By using an explicit cast, the programmer assumes the responsibility of ensuring that the operations to be performed on the pointer's referent are type-safe. The type void* is typically used for low-level routines that refer to "raw storage", such as the return type of the function malloc(). The types void and void* have been included in the ANSI C Standard.

C and C++ programmers who want to create a type for logical values often define a boolean type as an enumeration.

```
// a Boolean type for logical values
enum bool { false, true };
```

Others have used the preprocessor directive #define or ANSI C const int definitions to define the values false and true as 0 and 1, respectively. Programmers and class libraries have used the names bool, Bool, and Boolean for the type, and the identifiers false and true, F and T, FALSE and TRUE, and False and True for the values. To provide consistency (especially when using several class libraries), the ANSI/ISO C++ Standard includes a built-in type bool with the values false and true. The value false can be implicitly converted to the int 0 and vice versa. Nonzero int values can be implicitly converted to true, and true can be converted to the int 1. (These conversions are provided for compatibility with older C++ code and C code that uses ints for logical values.) Comparison and logical operators return bools, and control structures support the bool type in conditions.

Arrays

As in C, there is no array type constructor in C++. We define static and automatic array objects with the postfix [ ] operator, whose enclosed argument is a positive, constant-valued expression giving the number of elements. We create dynamic arrays in C++ using the new [ ] operator, as described in the previous section. An array can be created with any base type except void. Like C, C++ represents strings as null-terminated arrays of chars, and represents multidimensional arrays as arrays of pointers to arrays. We can initialize a static or automatic array upon definition by enclosing a list of literal values in braces, and can initialize character arrays with a string literal, as follows:

```
// array initialization syntax
int arrInt1[3] = { 1, 2, 3 };        // arrInt1[0] = 1, arrInt1[1] = 2, arrInt1[2] = 3
int arrInt2[] = { 10, 20, 30, 40 };  // the compiler determines the size of arrInt2[]
char str[] = "hello";                // a string literal initialization for an array of chars
```

Like C and Pascal, C++ uses the [ ] operator for subscription. As in C, array elements are numbered from 0 and no range checking is performed for array subscript references.

In C++, we can create an array type by defining an array class whose instances consist of a size member and an array or a pointer to a dynamically allocated array. The class can overload the [ ] operator so that we can use its instances in the same fashion as standard array objects (see section 11.1). The class can provide array assignment, equality tests, and other composite operations, and its methods can perform range checking for subscription if desired. To support arrays with various element types, we would define the class as a template (see section 14.2). In fact, the Standard Library defines a class template valarray<>, which is intended for arrays of numeric elements. It defines overloadings of the arithmetic operators that operate on the corresponding elements of their valarray<> operands, as well as a message that applies a function to each element, and aggregate messages such as min() and sum(). The library also defines classes and functions for defining slices of arrays and performing operations on them. We can also define classes for multidimensional arrays or matrices.

Pointers

Pointers and pointer operations in C++ are like those in C. We declare a pointer with a type name and the * operator, and the pointer can only refer to objects of that type. The prefix * operator dereferences a pointer and returns the *l*-value of the object it points to (recall the examples in section 0.3.5). The prefix "address of" operator & returns a type-correct pointer to its operand. As in C, it may be used even if the operand is statically or automatically allocated, or is an array or structure component. (There is less reason to use this operator in C++ as the language supports pass by reference.) C++ also supports pointers to functions, which we will discuss in section 9.2.6.

As in C, a pointer is treated as a machine address in a linearly addressed main store (as opposed to an individual object reference in Pascal). C++ supports pointer arithmetic, which indexes through memory locations as described in section 0.3.5, and performs these operations in units of the storage requirement of the pointer base type. An array name is considered to be a pointer to the first element of the array, and the programmer can access its elements by using arithmetic operations on a pointer initialized to refer to an array element. However, the language does not check for run-time range errors for pointers into arrays.

Enumerations

As in ANSI C, an enumerated type is treated as a list of constant integer values with the enumeration values implicitly initialized consecutively starting at 0. We can give a specific value for an enumeration value by following its name with the initializer =*intConstant*. The names of the enumeration type and values must be distinct from other identifiers in the scope in which the type is defined. Unlike C, C++ considers the tag name of an enumeration to be a type name, so the enum qualifier is not necessary in declaring an identifier or parameter of that type.[12] The following example defines an enumeration type and object:

```
// defines an enumeration: SUNDAY = 0, MONDAY = 1, and so on
enum Day  { SUNDAY, MONDAY, TUESDAY, WEDNESDAY,
                   THURSDAY, FRIDAY, SATURDAY };
// creates an instance of the type
Day payday = FRIDAY;              // "enum" is not necessary with Day
```

In C++, each enumeration is a separate type, and an enumeration value for one enumeration type cannot be assigned to a variable declared of another enumeration type. An enumeration value can be implicitly converted to an int, but an explicit cast is required to convert an int to an enumeration value.

```
// implicit conversions between enumerations and ints
int num = FRIDAY;               // promotion from Day to int
Day holiday = 6;                // error: no coercion from int to Day
Day holiday = (Day) 6;          // OK
```

Structures

The struct statement defines a structure type (and can also create instances, as in C). We access the members of a structure via component selection with the . (period) operator, or through a pointer with the -> operator. As we discussed in section 0.3.5, we can use the result of a component selection expression as an *l*-value or an *r*-value. Like an enumeration, the "tag name" of a struct is considered a type name. For this reason, the struct qualifier is not necessary when using the type name in identifier declarations or as an argument to sizeof(). No typedef is necessary (typically done when defining structures in C). C++ supports aggregate initialization of structures using the same syntax illustrated previously for arrays. The following example demonstrates defining a structure type and object, and accessing its members:

```
// defines the type Point, but does not create any instances
struct Point
{
    int x;
    int y;
};

int main()
{
    Point pt = { -1, -1 };          // "struct" is not necessary in an instance declaration
```

---

[12] Technically, the enum, struct, and union qualifiers are required for uses of the type name in C because there is a separate namespace for the names of each of these kinds of types. This is not true in C++.

```
    int num = pt.y;              // component access as an r-value
    pt.x = 1;                    // component access as an l-value
}
```

We can use a struct type as the type of a function parameter or return value, and the argument in an invocation must be of that type. Two structure types that have the same sequence of member types are regarded as different, incompatible types. Like C, C++ provides assignment of structures, but not equality tests. Like class definitions (and unlike C), structures in C++ may contain member function and access specifications. In fact, there is little need for the struct statement in C++ as it provides a subset of the capabilities of a class type definition. We will always use classes to define composite types.

Unions

As in C, we can use a union when we need an identifier that refers to different types of objects at different times, or do not know which of a set of types an object will be. The storage allocated to an instance of a union is the maximum of the storage requirements of its members. Within an instance, each member has the same address because the intention is that only one of the members can be stored in the object at a time. The members of a union can be of any types, so the same storage can be interpreted differently depending on the member name used to access it, which presents an opportunity for violating type safety. We access the members of a union object using the component selection operator, like those of a structure. The tag name of a union is a type specifier.

In C++ (but not in C), the tag name of a union is optional. We can define anonymous unions (i.e., unnamed unions of which no instances are defined), anywhere an identifier or member can be defined. In this case, the member names are declared in the enclosing scope, and must be distinct from other identifiers in that scope. When used as a member of a structure, the members of an anonymous union can be selected directly the same as the members of the structure. For example,

```
// defines a union as an anonymous member of a struct with a type tag
enum ValType { CHAR, INT, FLOAT };
struct Value
{
    ValType type;
    union
    {
        char chVal;
        int intVal;
        double dblVal;
    }
};

int main ()
{
```

```
    Value val;
    val.type = INT;
    val.intVal = 7;
    int num;
    if ( val.type == INT )
       num = val.intVal;
}
```

Because C++ does not support coherent assignment of all the members of a structure, the C++ union has the same lack of safety that we discussed for the Pascal variant record in section 0.3.5. Like structures, unions in C++ may contain member functions and access specifications. In fact, we rarely use unions in C++ because inheritance and dynamic binding provide much better support for safely using the same identifier to refer to instances of different types.

The const **specifier**

The C programmer uses the preprocessor command #define to associate a mnemonic name with a constant value once, then uses the name in a number of statements in the program. For example,

```
// using the preprocessor to name a constant
#define LINE_MAX 80
```

However, because the preprocessor merely performs text substitution at the point of use, there is no syntax or type checking, and unexpected problems can occur due to operator precedence when the substituted value is an expression.

As we discussed in section 0.3.1, the const keyword, which ANSI C also includes, indicates that the value of the associated identifier cannot be changed after it is initialized. It is a read-only object and cannot be modified (e.g., used as the left side of an assignment). Clearly, its definition must include initialization since a value cannot be assigned to the identifier.[13] We can also specify an instance of a programmer-defined structure or class as const, in which case none of its members may be modified. (This cannot be done with #define.) For example,

```
// the const type modifier
const int LINE_MAX = 80;
const Point origin = {0, 0};   // const struct object
```

Unlike a Pascal symbolic constant, a C++ const object is not a compile-time constant. For example, a local variable can be const, with its initial value supplied by an argument.

```
// a const whose value is not fixed at compile time
void func(int arg)
```

---

[13] We will see more examples of the distinction between initialization and assignment as we proceed.

```
    {
        const int initArg = arg;
    }
```

The use of const with pointers requires a special syntax because two objects are involved: the pointer itself and the object to which it refers. Consider the following definitions:

```
// const with pointers
const char* str = "hello";           // constant referent (pointer to const char)
char* const str = "hello";           // constant pointer (const pointer to char)
const char* const str = "hello";     // both the pointer and referent are constant
```

The first statement indicates that the value of the location pointed to by str cannot change—str is a pointer to a const object. This restriction holds even if str is reassigned to refer to a different object (i.e., it is safe for the pointer to refer to any read-only object of the correct type). The second declaration specifies that the pointer is const (i.e., the identifier str cannot appear on the left side of an assignment), but the referenced string can be changed (i.e., we can assign to *str). The third declares that both the pointer and the object are read-only.

We will see in section 9.2.2 that we can also declare a function parameter as const. This indicates that the function does not modify that argument, so a const object can be passed for that parameter.

The reference type

We can declare an identifier of type "reference to a given type" with the type name and the & operator. A reference definition gives an alias for an existing object, but does not create a new object. A reference definition must include an initialization giving an l-value of the correct type, and the reference name then becomes an alternate name for that object. Once initialized, all operations using the reference name operate on the object for which it is an alias. For example, the following definitions create an array of doubles and an alias lastElem for the last element of the array:

```
// operations are performed on the referent of the aliased identifier
const int ARR_SIZE = 100;
int main()
{
    double arrDbl[ARR_SIZE];
    double& lastElem = arrDbl[ARR_SIZE - 1];
    ++lastElem;                    // increments arrDbl[ARR_SIZE - 1]
    double* pDbl = &lastElem;      // pDbl points to arrDbl[ARR_SIZE - 1]
}
```

The last two statements use arrDbl[ARR_SIZE - 1] and, in fact, there is no lastElem object. Note that the "address of" operator & in the last statement is not the same operator as the reference type qualifier.[14]

There are no operations defined for the reference type itself: All operations applied to that name are actually applied to the referent of the aliased identifier. The language does not allow pointers or references to references, arrays of references, and the type void& (i.e., references are not first-class). The chief use of the reference type is to indicate pass or return by reference, as we will see in section 9.2.2. In fact, we rarely use reference variables (as opposed to reference parameters) because of the confusion caused for the reader when there are two names for the same object.

Newcomers to C++ are sometimes told to think of a reference as a "hidden pointer", presumably because reference parameters are usually implemented in this way. However, this approach will only confuse you further. Syntactically, a reference name behaves like an object, not like a pointer. For example, using the initializer &arrDbl[ARR_SIZE - 1] for lastElem in the previous code fragment would be incorrect. A pointer is a separate object from its referent, and each has a set of valid operations. There is no operator for dereferencing a reference analogous to the prefix * operator for pointers. In addition, there is no such thing as a "null reference" that does not refer to an object, and we cannot change the "value" of a reference after initializing it. (An assignment that uses a reference name on the left side would modify the object the reference refers to, not change what the reference refers to.) For these reasons, I encourage you to think of a reference as an alias, not an implicit pointer.

Type casts and conversions

C++ supports all the predefined C numeric conversions, even those that lose information such as from double to int. Unlike ANSI C, an int cannot be cast to an instance of an enumeration type implicitly. As in C, a pointer cast merely changes the type label on the pointer, but the result of any other conversion is a new temporary object that is an *r*-value. An *l*-value such as a variable name or structure member can be converted to a reference type. A reference conversion does not create a new object, and the result is an *l*-value. Unlike ANSI C, the compiler cannot cast a void* pointer to another pointer type implicitly. We will see in section 11.2 that we can define conversions between objects and built-in types, and between instances of various classes, and that the compiler can use these operations as coercions.

We code an explicit conversion by using the name of a built-in type or programmer-defined class as a function name, or by using the C "type cast" notation. If the operation is a cast, the programmer assumes the responsibility that operations on the result are type-safe. For example,

---

[14] If you find this confusing, you are not alone!

```
// explicit conversion and cast syntax
void func(void* pArg)
{
    int num1 = 39;
    int num2 = 7;
    double dbl = double(num1) / num2;      // function syntax with type name
    double dbl = (double) num1 / num2;     // C "type cast" syntax
    double* pDbl = (double*) pArg;         // pointer cast
}
```

The C type cast notation is supported because the C++ function syntax cannot be used for types that do not have single-identifier names, such as char*, long double, const char*, and int&.

Unfortunately, because of compatibility with C, pointer casts provide a loophole in C++'s type safety. The programmer can obtain a pointer to any object with the unary & operator, and can explicitly cast any pointer to a pointer of another type. In particular, casting a pointer to the type char* allows the program to access the referent's storage region as an array of bytes. But explicit pointer conversions are necessary for other reasons (e.g., to disambiguate overloaded function invocations or cast from the type void*), so they cannot be eliminated from the language. Type checking can prevent typographic and logical errors, but cannot stop intentional violations of type semantics.

Generally, the use of explicit casts is considered poor programming practice because it defeats the type system enforced by the compiler. There are two notorious problems with the C type cast syntax. It is difficult to search for casts (e.g., to determine whether a program uses casts), and the notation complicates parsing, both for the compiler and for programming tools. For these reasons, the ANSI/ISO C++ Standard introduces a new cast notation that uses reserved words. The static_cast<> operator denotes a cast or conversion that the compiler can perform.[15] We enclose the name of the target type in angle brackets (i.e., < and >)[16] following the reserved word static_cast and preceding the object being converted, which is enclosed in parentheses. We can use the static_cast<> operator for both value and reference conversions. C++ also introduces the reinterpret_cast<> operator for casts, such as from one pointer type to another or from an integral type to a pointer, that are potentially unsafe or implementation dependent. The following example illustrates this syntax:

```
// the new C++ static_cast<> explicit conversion syntax
void func(void* pArg)
{
    int num1 = 39;
    int num2 = 7;
```

[15] We will discuss the dynamic_cast<> operator, which requires run-time type checking, in section 12.2.5.

[16] We will see in sections 13.1 and 13.2 that angle brackets are also used to enclose the type parameters for a template.

```
   double dbl = static_cast<double>(num1) / num2;
   double* pDbl = reinterpret_cast<double*>(pArg);
}
```

The C++ programmer can also explicitly "cast away" the const attribute of a pointer. The result is a non-const pointer of the same type that refers to the original object. Removing the const attribute of a pointer can be done with either the function name or the C type cast syntax, and the language now also includes a const_cast<> operator for this purpose. A const cast differs from a static cast in that it does not change the type of the referent, but only changes whether it can be modified. The following example illustrates casting away const-ness:

```
// casting away the const-ness of a pointer
int main()
{
   int num = 3;
   const int* pConstInt;        // cannot modify the referent
   pConstInt = &num;            // OK, num cannot be modified through pConstInt
   // explicit cast from const int* to int* with the C "type cast" syntax
   int* pInt = (int*) pConstInt;
   // explicit cast from const int* to int* with the new const_cast<> operator
   pInt = const_cast<int*>(pConstInt);
   *pInt = 256;
}
```

The language definition states that casting away const-ness may cause an addressing exception, for example, if the compiler has placed the object in a read-only memory segment.

The typedef statement

As in C, we can use the typedef statement to give a mnemonic alias for a predefined, derived, or programmer-defined type. That identifier can then serve as a type specifier in declarations, parameter lists, and successive typedef statements. Note that the statement does not define a new type, but creates a synonym for an existing type. For example,

```
// the typedef statement introduces an alias for an existing type name
typedef unsigned char Age;       // there are no ages greater than 255
typedef char** StringArray;      // StringArray is a pointer to an array of char*'s
```

The typedef statement is used less frequently in C++ than in C because declarations of struct, enum, and union instances no longer need those reserved words. However, it is still useful for defining mnemonic type aliases or to simplify the use of pointers to function types. Identifier names declared with a typedef statement follow the usual static scope rules.

9.2 FUNCTIONS AND OVERLOADING

9.2.1 Function Declarations

C and C++ function declarations

Unlike Pascal but like C, a C++ function declaration is not introduced by a reserved word. We declare an identifier to be a function name with the unary postfix () operator, and use the same operator to denote a function invocation.[17] C and C++ programmers often refer to a function declaration to as a "function prototype".

In pre-ANSI C, a function declaration gave the return type but did not specify the parameter types. In fact, programmers did not even have to declare a function name before using it, and an undeclared function name was assumed to return an int. For this reason, the language did not guarantee type checking and implicit conversions of arguments. Most compilers did perform these checks within a file, but few did across code files. For example, it was possible for a function invocation in one file to push fewer arguments on the run-time stack than were used by the definition in another file, with unpredictable results. Similarly, if an int argument were passed to a function that had a double parameter but was not declared in that file, the compiler would not perform the conversion. The function code would interpret the argument's bytes (and probably succeeding bytes!) directly as a double value.

Like Pascal and Ada, C++ requires function declarations that give types for parameters and return values because parameter types are necessary to support type checking and overloading. A function must be declared before it is invoked. These requirements are now also part of the ANSI C Standard.[18] A function declaration need not give parameter names, although they are often helpful for the reader. If it gives parameter names, it is not necessary that they match those used in the function definition. As in C, a function declaration is extern by default, so each file scope function is declared in the global name space unless it is explicitly marked as static.

Type checking

The C++ compiler ensures that the number and types of arguments and the return type in a function invocation match those in its declaration, even if the definition and invocation are in different code files. The compiler will perform standard or programmer-defined coercions between the types of the arguments in an invocation and those of the parameters in the declaration if necessary. If the argument

---

[17] It is customary in C texts to include the postfix () operator with a function name to remind the reader that the identifier refers to a function. We will follow this convention, and will only include the argument signature within the parentheses when necessary.

[18] One difference between C++ and ANSI C is the interpretation of an empty argument list in a function declaration. ANSI C suppresses type checking to allow compatibility with pre-ANSI C. C++ interprets such a declaration as specifying that the function takes no parameters, and uses the ellipsis (...) for unchecked functions. ANSI C uses the parameter list (void) to indicate that there are no parameters.

types do not match the parameter types and no coercions are available, the compiler flags the invocation as an error. For example,

```
// type checking of function arguments in C++
double sqrt(double);
int main()
{
    double dbl = sqrt(7);        // double(7) applied implicitly
    dbl = sqrt("hello");         // error: no conversion from char* to double
}
```

9.2.2 The Function Parameter List

Argument passing

Function arguments are passed by value, except for reference parameters as described later in this section. Within the body of a function, parameters act like local variables in the function's stack frame initialized with the values of the argument expressions in the invocation. Function return values are also passed by value, that is, the caller receives a copy of the value of the expression in the function's return statement. Argument types are checked and implicit conversions are performed if necessary.

As in C, if we use an array as the type of a function parameter, the corresponding argument is converted to a pointer to its first element, which is passed by value. The compiler includes the pointer rather than the entire array in the stack frame to save stack space. Because the function receives a pointer to the original argument array, it can modify that array. The array's size must be passed as a separate parameter, except for arrays of char, which are terminated with the null character '\0' by convention.

As in C, the order of evaluation of the arguments of a function invocation is undefined, and in particular, it is not guaranteed to be left to right. For this reason, it is unsafe to perform a side effect in an argument expression that modifies the value of another argument expression.

```
// the order of evaluation of function arguments is not defined
int max(int, int);   // returns the maximum of the two int arguments
int main()
{
    int num = 3;
    int arrInt[6] = { 0, 1, 2, 3, 4, 5 };
    // the second argument to max() could be arrInt[3] or arrInt[4]
    int mx = max(++num, arrInt[num]);
}
```

const **parameters**

We can declare a function parameter as const, and the compiler uses this specification in type checking arguments. Because the compiler does not allow using a read-only object in a context in which it might be modified, it is an error to pass a const argument corresponding to a non-const formal parameter. The compiler also ensures that a const parameter is not modified within the function or passed as a non-const parameter to another function. Of course, constness is not an issue for value parameters because the function has a copy of the argument and cannot change the original. However, if the argument is a pointer or is passed by reference, const is meaningful. For example,

```
// the use of const function parameters
int strlen(const char*);
char* strcpy(char*, const char*);
int main()
{
    const char* pStr = "hello";
    int len = strlen(pStr);              // OK: const parameter
    strcpy(pStr, "hola");                // error: const argument for non-const parameter
}
```

Using the const specifier on a parameter is also helpful as a commentary for clients of the function. We can also declare a return value as const, which prevents the caller from modifying the value returned by the function. ANSI C also supports const parameters.

Reference parameters and return values

Unlike C, C++ supports pass by reference, which we indicate by declaring the function parameter with a reference type. In this case, the parameter name is an alias for the corresponding argument (like a var parameter in Pascal), and a use of that parameter within the function code refers to the argument as an *l*-value or as an *r*-value, depending on the context. As we discussed in section 0.1.2, we use pass by reference when the function must modify an object in the caller's environment, or to avoid the space and time overhead of copying a large argument into the function's stack frame (and, as we will see in section 10.2.5, to avoid invoking a copy constructor for class objects). To avoid copying the argument and also guarantee that it is not modified, we use a const reference parameter, which we will always use with parameters of class type.

When a C function must modify its argument, the caller passes a pointer to that object and the function dereferences the pointer argument within its code. The C++ programmer can pass the argument by reference, and uses of the parameter name on the left side of an assignment within the function will then modify the argument. For example, the following C++ function is called with arguments of type int, not int*:

```
// reference parameters are aliases for the actual arguments
void swapInts(int& int1, int& int2)
{
    int temp = int2;
```

```
      int2 = int1;
      int1 = temp;
   }

   main ()
   {
      int num1 = 1, num2 = 2;
      swapInts(num1, num2); // no prefix & operator is needed with the arguments
   }
```

The parameter names int1 and int2 are treated as aliases for the arguments num1 and num2 when the function body is executed. Although a reference parameter is typically implemented as a pointer in the stack frame, you will specify the argument type incorrectly if you think of a reference parameter as a "hidden pointer". The cast from a non-reference argument to the type of a reference parameter (i.e., from int to int& in this case) is performed implicitly by the compiler. We can also pass pointer parameters by reference, as follows:

```
   // pointer parameters passed by reference
   void swapPtrs(char*& pChar1, char*& pChar2)
   {
      char* pTemp = pChar2;
      pChar2 = pChar1;
      pChar1 = pTemp;
   }
```

Unlike Pascal var parameters, the actual argument corresponding to a reference parameter may be an expression in C++. However, if the function uses the parameter on the left side of an assignment, the object modified is the temporary object created by the compiler for expression evaluation.

A function can also return by reference by using a reference type as its return type. In this case, an invocation of the function is an alias for the object specified in its return statement. Returning a reference also allows using a function call as an *l*-value (e.g., on the left side of an assignment). In this case, the assignment modifies the object given in the function's return statement. For example,

```
   // return by reference
   int& lastElem(int arrInt[], int size)
   {
      return arrInt[size - 1];
   }

   int main()
   {
      int arr[ARR_SIZE];
      lastElem(arr, ARR_SIZE) = 10;   // assignment to arr[ARR_SIZE - 1]
   }
```

Return by reference is rarely used with built-in types, but it is useful with large objects of class type. Like pass by reference, returning a reference saves copying the returned object (and, as we will see in section 10.2.5, avoids the overhead of invoking a destructor and a copy constructor for class objects). As a general rule of thumb, you should only return a reference to an object that existed before the function invocation, that is, an argument or global (or the receiver for a "member function"). If the function returns a reference to an automatic variable, such storage is no longer valid when the function exits. If the function returns a reference to a new dynamically allocated object, the invoker of the function must deallocate that object so that there is no memory leak. Usually, this will not happen.

Default parameter values

For some functions, a particular parameter has the same argument value in most invocations, or some invocations must logically specify more arguments than others. In C++, we can specify default initial values for the trailing set of parameters to a function by giving initializers for those parameters in the parameter list. For example,

```
// the last argument is the space character if not specified
char* nextToken(char* string, char delim = ' ');
```

The default initial value must be a constant whose value is known at compile time. When a function with default values that has m parameters is invoked with $n < m$ arguments, the compiler maps the arguments onto the parameters from left to right (as always), and the $m - n$ trailing parameters assume their default values. If the $m - n$ trailing parameters do not all have default values or the types do not match for the first m arguments, the invocation is an error. For example,

```
// func() can be called with 1, 2 or 3 arguments
void func(int int1, char* str = "hello", int int3 = 0);
int main()
{
    func(3, "world");    // func(3, "world", 0) invoked
    func(3);             // func(3, "hello", 0) invoked
    func(3, 1);          // error: second argument must be char*
}
```

Use of default parameter values is similar to overloading because there is more than one argument signature for invocations of the function, but differs in the sense that the same code is executed in each case. We can give the default initial values either in the function definition or in any declaration of the function, but may only specify them once. Usually, we give the default parameter values in the function declaration (in a header file), so that the function's clients are aware of them.

Unspecified parameter types

We can define a function as having an unknown number and types of parameters by including an ellipsis (i.e., "...") at the end of its parameter list. This feature is provided to allow flexibility, especially for invoking C functions, but it suppresses type checking. For example, we declare the standard C function fprintf() as follows (the directive extern "C" is discussed in section 9.2.5):

```
// type checking is suppressed for third, fourth, etc. arguments
extern "C" int fprintf(FILE*, const char*, ...);
```

This declaration only specifies types for its first two arguments. There may or may not be succeeding arguments in an invocation. You should use this feature with caution as the compiler cannot check the number or types of arguments or perform argument conversions for such a function.

9.2.3 Inline **Functions**

Purpose

We sometimes need to use a very small function either to improve the readability of the code with a descriptive name for an operation (e.g., swapInts() in the previous section), or to hide the details of a storage structure. However, it is inefficient to use the invocation mechanism (i.e., saving and restoring the state of the computation, passing arguments, and so on) for a function consisting of just a few statements. Instead, we would like the compiler to substitute the function's code directly for a call when the invocation overhead is large compared with the processing performed by the function.

Preprocessor macros

When a C programmer wants to avoid the overhead of invocation for a function with a minimal body, he or she defines a preprocessor macro with #define. For example,

```
// a preprocessor macro: the right side code is substituted for an invocation
#define MIN(num1, num2)  (((num1) <= (num2)) ? (num1) : (num2))
```

The parentheses in the macro definition are necessary because the arguments in a "call" can be expressions, and operator precedence can cause unintended effects at the point of substitution. For example, without the parentheses, the call k * MIN(i, j) + 1 would be expanded to k*i <= j ? i : j+1, which is probably not what the programmer intended. A more serious problem with macros is a substitution whose arguments cause side effects, such as the following:

```
// a macro call with an argument that causes a side effect
main ()
```

```
{
    int int1 = 4, int2 = 2;
    // expands to (((int1) <= (++int2)) ? (int1) : (++int2)) so int2 is incremented twice
    int1 = MIN(int1, ++int2);
}
```

If a parameter appears more than once in the body of the macro, the corresponding argument will be evaluated more than once in the resulting text. In addition, if the macro contains a conditional expression, as in the above example, the number of executions of the side effect is not predictable. In this example, the number of times int2's value is incremented depends on the run-time values of int1 and int2, which is not likely to be the programmer's intention.

Macros have other difficulties because the preprocessor merely does text substitution prior to compilation. Syntax and type checking are not performed until after the text is replaced. Another less obvious problem with macros is that any identifiers in the substitution text that are not parameters are bound in the environment of the call. For example,

```
// dynamic scope is used in binding nonlocals in macros
const int incr = 2;
#define addIncr(num)  (incr + (num))
int main()
{
    int incr = 1;
    int num = addIncr(3);  // the local incr is used due to text substitution
}
```

The macro text with the argument substituted for num is inserted at the point at which the macro is called, so the declaration for incr is determined by that context, rather than by the environment in which the macro was defined.

The inline specifier

The inline reserved word indicates to the C++ compiler that it can substitute the function's code directly for a function call. [19] Doing so avoids the overhead of invocation at the expense of increased code size. If a function is inlined, the function code does not appear in the object module. Instead, the compiler stores the argument signature and the code in the symbol table, and substitutes the code for each invocation (with the appropriate handling of arguments passed by value or by reference). The resulting code can then be optimized together with code adjacent to the call (which can be very helpful with RISC architectures). Unlike macro substitution, the compiler performs type checking and conversions and uses static scope rules. We can code the MIN macro as an inline function, as follows:

---

[19] inline is a hint to the compiler that it can honor or not. For example, most compilers do not inline a function that contains a loop statement.

```
// an inline function definition
inline int min(int int1, int int2)
{
    return (int1 <= int2) ? int1 : int2;
}
```

Unfortunately, the fact that type checking is performed prevents us from using this function with double arguments (without conversions) and a double comparison, which we can do with the macro version. We would have to define separate overloading of the function with the declaration double min(double, double), as described in the next section. In section 13.1, we will discuss function templates for which a type parameter can be instantiated from the argument type, so that only one min() function need be coded.

Because the function code is needed in any code files that invoke the function, we must place the entire definition of an inline function in the header file included by clients. In addition, those clients must be recompiled if we modify the implementation of the function. A function should not be declared inline if the program will need a pointer to it (e.g., as an argument of a function invocation).

The inline construct is particularly useful for the class member access methods that are necessary for encapsulation, but often consist of a single statement that assigns or returns the hidden data member. In fact, with very short functions such as these, inlining may decrease the object code size.

9.2.4 Overloading

Purpose and use

In section 0.2.7, we discussed subprogram overloading, which Ada and other contemporary languages support. We can also overload function names in C++ (except main()). [20] Function overloading is particularly useful when the same logical operation is provided for different types of data, but the code is different in each case. We can use the same descriptive name for each function, with the compiler selecting the appropriate function definition for a particular invocation according to the argument types. For example, the functions that compute the average value of the elements of an array, a set, or a linked list can all be named average(). With function overloading, we can declare all of the following definitions within the same file scope:

```
// four overloadings of the min() function
int min(int, int);              // the minimum of two ints
double min(double, double);     // the minimum of two doubles
char* min(char*, char*);        // the minimum of two strings in ASCII order
int min(const int*, int);       // minimum of an array of ints, the second argument is the size
```

[20] Identifiers that do not denote functions—those that refer to objects or types—may not be overloaded.

Support for function overloading can also help eliminate name clashes when two different code libraries that use the same function name are linked. Both file scope functions and class member function names may be overloaded. As we will see in section 11.1, we can also overload operators for operands of class type.

We can declare several functions with the same name within the same scope, provided that each has a unique argument signature. The compiler uses the argument signature of the invocation to determine which function definition to execute, a process referred to as "argument matching". For example,

```
// resolving invocations of an overloaded function
int min(int, int);
int min(const int*, int);
int main()
{
    int num = 4;
    int arrInt[4] = { 3, 4, 5, 6 };
    int mn = min(num, 5);        // min(int, int) invoked
    mn = min(arrInt, num);       // min(const int*, int) invoked
    mn = min(num, arrInt);       // error: no matching argument signature
}
```

As described in section 9.2.2, a const argument only matches a const parameter. A function can be overloaded with two definitions that declare const and non-const parameters of the same type for a certain parameter, and the compiler will use the const-ness of the corresponding argument to determine which overloading to invoke.

Two argument signatures for an overloaded function name cannot differ in only the return types. The compiler could distinguish an invocation if the use of the return value is not ambiguous, but an invocation can be nested within an arbitrarily complex expression, and C++ includes many implicit conversions. Examining enough of the program to disambiguate a call would complicate parsing. In addition, two overloadings of the same function name cannot be distinguished by a parameter of type *Type* in one overloading and *Type&* in the other, because those types accept the same arguments. Similarly, there is no distinction between the parameter types *Type** and *Type[]*.

Resolving invocations with conversions

As described in section 9.2.1, the compiler will implicitly perform conversions between the type of an argument and the type of the corresponding parameter. However, coercions can be a source of ambiguity with overloading. For example,

```
// implicit conversions and overloading
void func(int);
void func(char*);
int main()
{
```

```
    func('c');                  // 'c' converted to an int and func(int) invoked
    void func(double);          // additional overloading visible from this point on
    func('c');                  // ambiguous?
    func(3L);                   // ambiguous?
}
```

The compiler can convert the argument in the last two invocations to either an int or a double, so these calls might be considered ambiguous. We will see that the second call func('c') is not ambiguous and is resolved to func(int), but that the invocation func(3L) is ambiguous.

The compiler can match an invocation with a function definition by an exact match of its argument signature, or by applying implicit conversions. In resolving an invocation of an overloaded function, C++ uses the following order of precedence among the categories of conversions:

1. an exact match or a *trivial conversion*: These are from *Type* to *Type&* or *Type&* to *Type*, from *Type*[] to *Type**, from *Type* to const *Type*, and from *Type** to const *Type**.

2. a *numeric promotion*: The promotions are char, short, bool, or enum to int, and float to double.

3. a *standard conversion*: All other C numeric conversions (e.g., int to long, double to int), and the argument 0 match any pointer type.

4. a *programmer-defined conversion*: Two mechanisms for defining conversions are discussed in section 11.2.

5. matching an ellipsis.

There is no preference among conversions in the same category. For example, the conversion from char to unsigned char is not preferred over the conversion from char to double. Each enum is considered a separate type, although any can be promoted to int.

To resolve an invocation of an overloaded function to a particular definition, the compiler first checks for an exact match with the argument signature of the call. If there is none, it checks for a definition that can be matched by a promotion, and so on for each category of conversion. If there is no match for the argument at some stage in the resolution process, then the next category of conversions is checked. If for any category there are multiple matches, the invocation is ambiguous, and the compiler flags the call as an error. If there is no match at all, the statement is also erroneous. If the process determines a single match at some stage, it does not encounter ambiguous matches at later stages. For example,

```
// disambiguation of overloading with conversions
void func(int);
void func(double);
void func(char*);
```

```
int main()
{
    func('c');        // func(int): promotion preferred over standard conversion
    func(0);          // func(int): exact match of 0 to int preferred over conversion to char*
    long lng = 3L;
    func(lng);        // error: both long to int and long to double are standard conversions
    func(double(lng));        // ambiguity resolved by explicit conversion
}
```

Ambiguous invocations of overloaded functions are detected at compile time. When this error occurs, you determine which function you intended to invoke, and code an explicit conversion to resolve the ambiguity. However, if the compiler selects an unintended overloading due to the preferences defined by the language, it might or might not be apparent from the subsequent behavior of the system.

For overloaded functions with more than one parameter, argument matching is more complex. After considerable discussion, the ANSI/ISO C++ Standard has adopted the "intersection rule" described in [Ell90], which uses the following procedure:

1. For each argument in the invocation, determine the set of function definitions that contain the best matches for that argument's type.
2. Take the intersection of these sets, and if the result is not a single definition, then the call is ambiguous.
3. The resulting definition must also match at least one argument better than every other definition.

Essentially, if a particular definition provides an equal or better match for every argument and also provides a strictly better match than all other overloadings for one or more arguments, then it is called. For example,

```
// argument matching with two parameters
func2(int, double);
func2(double, double);
int main()
{
    func2('c', 3);   // func2(int, double) invoked
}
```

In this example, the argument matching procedure selects func2(int, double) because it provides a better match for the first argument, and both definitions provide equally good matches for the second. That is, it is not just a matter of what the "worst" conversion necessary for each definition is. The numerous standard conversions present due to C compatibility can cause ambiguity for functions that are overloaded on the basis of more than one parameter. For example,

```
// conversions can result in ambiguous invocations of overloaded functions
int min(int, int);
```

```
double min(double, double);
int main()
{
    double dbl1 = 3.2, dbl2;
    int num = 3;
    // error: both double to int and int to double are standard conversions
    dbl2 = min(dbl1, num);
    dbl2 = min(dbl1, double(num));  // invoke double min(double, double)
    dbl2 = min(int(dbl1), num);        // invoke int min(int, int) and convert the result to double
}
```

You do not need to memorize all the rules of argument matching to use function overloading effectively because the rules intentionally err on the safe side. If the compiler finds an invocation to be ambiguous, you can use an explicit conversion to select the desired overloading.

9.2.5 Type-Safe Linkage

Header files

In C++, a program cannot call a function until it declares it, and there must be only one definition of a function name with a particular argument signature in any scope. C++ is a multi-paradigm language, and the programmer can use a function-oriented organization for an application. As discussed in section 1.1.3 for C, the programmer codes the interface of a module as a header file containing the declarations of its public file scope (non-member) functions. He or she includes the header file both in the code files that define its functions, and in client files that invoke them. In this way, all files that refer to a function have the same declaration, and if that declaration requires modification only one change must be made (although all the modules must be recompiled). By convention, we list default arguments in the declaration in the header file so that they are known to users of the function.

As stated in section 9.2.3, the entire definition of an inline function must be given in the header file so that the compiler can substitute that code when translating a file that invokes the function. Constants are also defined in header files so that the compiler has the value of the constant and can optimize the code for statements that use it. However, if more than one file in an application includes a header file containing definitions of constant objects and inline functions, a name conflict results at link time. For this reason, the default linkage for inline functions and const definitions is static, that is, internal to the file.[21] Each file can have its own constant object if necessary because there can be no modifications to the object that must be seen in the other files. Similarly, to avoid multiple definition errors from the linker, function and object definitions should not appear in a header file.

---

[21] This differs from ANSI C in which const definitions are declared at global scope by default.

Function name encoding

When a function name is overloaded, there is more than one definition of the same externally visible identifier. Unfortunately, most linkers resolve external references by name only, and cannot distinguish overloaded functions by their argument signatures. To deal with this situation, the C++ compiler identifies each function definition with a unique *encoded name* that includes argument signature information.[22] It places these encoded names in the external symbol tables used by the linker to resolve external references. For example, the linker might see the names __min_i_i and __min_d_d for the first two overloadings of min() in the previous section.

The compiler generates a different encoded name for each overloading of a function name, and maps each function call onto the appropriate encoded name. The correct definition is invoked, even when the call is not in the same code file as the corresponding function definition. Encoded names also ensure that the files that define and call a function use the same argument signature.

The exact name encoding scheme used depends on the compiler and linker. It may differ among implementations because there may be other translator dependencies, such as the order in which arguments are pushed on the stack or the layout of objects. Name encoding is also more complicated than what we have described here because it must accommodate type modifiers such as const and signed, class scope for member functions, operator overloadings, and constructors and destructors. In addition, abbreviations or hashing may be necessary due to limits on the length of identifiers distinguished by the linker. ([Ell90] presents a complete, compact scheme.) It would also be helpful for a programming environment to include a "name decoder" for use with linker errors and debuggers.

If we need to call a C function in a program compiled by a C++ compiler, we can disable function name encoding for that function with the linkage directive extern "C", as follows:

```
// disable name encoding for C linkage
extern "C" int fprintf(FILE*, const char*, ...);
```

Similarly, if a C++ program contains a file scope function that a C program must call, it uses the extern "C" directive with the function definition to disable name encoding. We can only use the extern "C" directive at file scope, and can only give it for one overloading of a function name. We can exempt a group of function declarations or an #include'd C header file from C++ name encoding by including them within braces after the extern "C" directive, as follows:

```
// disable name encoding for C linkage
extern "C"
{
```

---

[22] This process is sometimes referred to as "name mangling" and the resulting identifiers are called "mangled names".

```
    #include <math.h>
    void exit(int);
}
```

On most systems that support both C and C++, this will not be necessary for the C standard library header files such as math.h. Typically, the compiler defines a symbol indicating which language or version is being compiled (i.e., pre-ANSI C, ANSI C, or C++). An #ifdef preprocessor directive within the header file will test that symbol, and the preprocessor will include the appropriate version of the function declarations (i.e., with or without argument types or extern "C") in the source files in the program.

9.2.6 Pointers to Functions

Purpose and definition

The type *pointer to function* is available in C++ as in C, with the same rather confusing syntax. Like any type, we may use it as the type of a variable, a parameter, a return value, or a member. This type provides most of the characteristics of first-class status for function values in C and C++. However, unlike functional languages and Smalltalk, C++ provides no syntax for unnamed function objects.

As in ANSI C, the argument signature of the referent function is part of the pointer's type. For example, the following declaration declares pFunc to be a pointer that can refer only to functions with argument signature (char*, int) and return type int:

```
// defines a pointer to function pFunc
int (*pFunc) (char*, int);
```

A function with a different argument signature cannot be assigned to this pointer. The parentheses around the expression *pFunc are necessary because the postfix invocation operator () has higher precedence than the prefix dereference operator *. Without the parentheses the statement declares a function that returns a pointer to int rather than a pointer to a function.

```
// defines a function func that returns an int*
int* func(char*, int);
```

The syntax of a pointer to function declaration appears strange because the name being declared is enclosed within the parts of the declaration, but the same thing happens when declaring a function or array name. The type of pFunc is written as int(*)(char*, int), for example, when used as of a parameter type in a function declaration. An array of pointers to functions is defined as follows:

```
// defines an array of 10 pointers to functions
int (*arrPtrFunc [10]) (char*, int);
```

Using pointers to functions

The value of a pointer to function is the "address of" an actual function with the correct argument signature. We denote this value by applying the unary prefix & operator to a function name without the invocation operator () and its enclosed arguments. [23] That result (e.g., &func), can only be used in an initialization or assignment to a pointer to function variable or parameter. To invoke the function referred to by a pointer to function, we dereference the pointer with the prefix * operator, and then invoke the result with the postfix () operator and arguments. The following example illustrates these operations:

```
// assignment to a pointer to function and invocation of the referent of a pointer to function
int func1(char*, int);
int func2(int, char*);
main ()
{
    int (*pFunc) (char*, int);
    pFunc = &func1;                 // assignment of a value to a pointer to function
    pFunc = &func2;                 // error: type mismatch
    int num = (*pFunc) ("hello", 7);   // invoke the function which is pFunc's value
    num = pFunc("hello", 7);        // the same operation
}
```

Again, the parentheses around the expression *pFunc in the first invocation are necessary. The second invocation, though legal, is misleading because it appears as if there is a function named pFunc. As with function names, invocation is the only operation defined for a pointer to function.

We can declare a function parameter of type pointer to function to define a function that takes a function as an argument. For example, the following function returns the slope of the line connecting the points $(x_1, f(x_1))$ and $(x_2, f(x_2))$ for some function f. The first parameter is a pointer to a function that takes a double and returns a double, and the function argument to slope() is passed using & and the function name, as follows:

```
// use of a pointer to function parameter
double slope(double (*pFunc) (double), double x1, double x2)
{
    if ( x1 == x2 )
    {
        cerr << "Error: infinite slope" << endl;
        exit(1);
    }
    else
        return ((*pFunc)(x2) - (*pFunc)(x1)) / (x2 - x1);
}
```

---

[23] In fact, the & is not required as in C (i.e., there is an implicit conversion from a function type to a pointer to function type). However, its use makes the intent of the statement clearer.

```
// call the function slope()
double sqrt(double);
int main()
{
    double m = slope(&sqrt, 3.0, 5.0);
}
```

The declaration of the function slope() is double slope(double (*) (double), double, double); (i.e., the first line of the definition without the parameter names). If a function returns a pointer to function, we enclose the rest of that function's declaration within the pointer to function declaration. This is illustrated by the declaration of set_new_handler() in the next example.

Like C, C++ supports initialization, assignment, and equality comparisons for the pointer to function type, but not pointer arithmetic. There is a standard coercion from any pointer to function to void*, and a pointer of type void* can be explicitly cast to a pointer to function.

We can use the typedef statement to create an alias for a pointer to function type, to increase the readability of declarations that use the type. For example, the C++ built-in function set_new_handler() takes as its argument a function with no arguments and a void return type, and returns a value of the same type. It is declared as follows:

```
// set_new_handler() takes and returns pointers to functions
void (*set_new_handler(void (*) ()) ) ();
```

The following typedef makes the declaration considerably less obtuse:

```
// typedef makes declaration more readable
typedef void (*PtrVoidFunc) ();
PtrVoidFunc set_new_handler(PtrVoidFunc);
```

If we assign an overloaded function name to a pointer to function, only the definition whose argument signature is the same as that of the pointer is assigned to the pointer. For example:

```
// overloading with pointers to functions
int func(int);
void func();
int main()
{
    int (*pIntFunc)(int);
    void (*pVoidFunc)();
    double (*pDoubleFunc)(double);
    pIntFunc = &func;          // int func(int)
    pVoidFunc = &func;         // void func()
    pDoubleFunc = &func;       // error: there is no double func(double)
```

```
        int num = (*pIntFunc)(3);        // num = func(3)
        (*pIntFunc)();                   // error: void func() is not a referent of pIntFunc
    }
```

Note also that a pointer to function is an object, not a function, so its name cannot be overloaded.

9.3 BASIC INPUT/OUTPUT

9.3.1 C++ Input/Output Expressions

The iostream class library

We will discuss the basic format for C++ standard input/output in this section so that you can begin writing and testing C++ programs. We will cover the use of the iostream library classes and messages in detail in section 11.3.

Like C and unlike Pascal and FORTRAN, C++ does not include input/output statements as part of the language. Due to its C compatibility, the standard C input/output function library and the header file stdio.h that contains its declarations are available for use in C++ programs. However, most C++ language systems also provide a library based on the object-oriented *iostream* class library, which was originally designed and implemented at AT&T. The iostream library has been approved with some modifications as part of the ANSI/ISO C++ Standard Library. Most compilers and programming environments now use the AT&T iostream library, but newer releases will support the standard version of the library.

The iostream library defines an extensive hierarchy of classes and messages for terminal and file input/output. These include the class istream for input streams, the class ostream for output streams, and several other classes that we will discuss in section 11.3. The header file iostream.h[24] declares the interface for the stream library classes, and defines four stream objects for standard input and output. The objects cin, cout, and cerr provide terminal input/output and correspond to stdin, stdout, and stderr in C. clog is an ostream object associated with the standard error file that provides buffered output.

A stream has three components, as follows:

- a sequence of bytes
- a position reference at which bytes are inserted or extracted
- a descriptor that maintains its format and error state.

The stream object itself maintains formatting information, rather than it being specified for each item in an input or output function call, as we do with the C printf() and scanf() functions. Stream classes provide messages for testing and manipulating the state of the receiver.

---

[24] The new standard library will use the name iostream, that is, without the .h suffix.

Problems with printf() **and** scanf()

C programmers use the functions printf() and scanf() to output and input non-character values, and to control the format of input/output. The first argument is a string that gives the format for the string of characters read or written, and the succeeding arguments are the objects transferred. The format string can include codes beginning with the % character, which indicate the type of the object and the input/output format. Although these functions provide the ability to control the format of the input or output, the compiler cannot check for type agreement between the codes in the format string and the types of the succeeding arguments. For this reason, the use of these functions is notoriously error-prone.

With printf(), garbage is written if the format codes do not match or there are more codes than arguments. For example,

```c
// printf() prints garbage if the format codes don't match the argument types
#include <stdio.h>
int main()
{
    int num = 3;
    double dbl = 4.0;
    // (probably) prints the first byte of num as a char, followed by succeeding bytes of num
    // and some bytes of dbl, interpreted as a two's complement integer
    printf("%c\t%d\n", num , dbl);
}
```

scanf() presents several ways of violating type safety and the integrity of objects, and of causing errors that are difficult to trace. If we forget an argument with scanf(), it is not a compiler error, and some variable will not be updated as expected. If the type codes do not match the types of the succeeding arguments (or we omit an argument in the middle of the list), then invalid bit strings will be stored in those variables. If there are more format codes than arguments, then storage will be corrupted. For example,

```c
// scanf() corrupts memory if the format codes do not match the argument types or
// there are more codes than arguments
#include <stdio.h>
int main()
{
    int num;
    double dbl;
    scanf("%f%d", &num, &dbl);      // num and dbl receive invalid values
    scanf("%d%f%d", &num, &dbl);    // an integer is read into some location
}
```

In the first call in this example, scanf() writes a bit string representing a floating-point value into the storage for num and the first part of the storage for dbl, then writes a bit string representing a two's complement integer into the second part of the storage for dbl. In the second call, scanf() interprets the bytes following the address of dbl in its stack frame as an address, and reads an integer into that location. Clearly, the effect of this action can be almost anything, and it will be difficult to trace that effect back to its cause in the incorrect scanf() call. Another problem with scanf() is forgetting the & before an argument. Because the compiler cannot do type checking, it will not catch this error, again corrupting storage in an unpredictable way.

Besides being unsafe, scanf() and printf() are not extendible. We cannot create new format codes for our types so that their instances can be handled in the same way as instances of built-in types. As we will see, operator overloading provides a mechanism for uniform input/output of built-in types and programmer-defined classes.

The << and >> operators

Like functions, operators can be overloaded in C++. The iostream classes overload the << and >> operators for output and input, respectively. The left operand is the stream to which characters are written or from which characters are read, and the right operand is the object written or read. The library uses these operators because the operator symbols indicate the "direction" of data movement.

The << and >> operators are overloaded in iostream.h for all built-in types, and for the "stream manipulators" described later in this section that control the formatting of particular types of objects. As with argument matching for overloaded functions, the type of the operand to be written or read determines the actual operation performed. The printf()/scanf() format codes that indicate the type of the object are not necessary, and the type mismatch errors that can occur with printf() and scanf() are not an issue. (The iostream library also provides programmer-controlled formatting via manipulators and formatting messages that we discuss in sections 9.3.2, 9.3.3, and 11.3.4.) This technique is also faster at execution time because the correct operation has been selected by the compiler, rather than by the printf() or scanf() function interpreting the format codes.

The << and >> operator definitions return a reference to the stream—their return types are ostream& and istream&, respectively. This allows us to cascade a sequence of data transfer operations for the same stream, as in the examples in this section. (A sequence of << operators is evaluated from left to right.) That is, to transfer a series of objects, we use a sequence of applications of the corresponding operator, rather than specifying a sequence of operations as a list of arguments to printf() or scanf().

The << and >> operators provide extensible output and input because the class designer can overload them for class instances. This allows us to treat output and input of instances of built-in types and classes uniformly, and to view a file as a sequence of objects, possibly of various types.

The bit shift operators are still available in C++. When the left operand of << or >> is an integer rather than a stream, the bit shift overloading is invoked. The iostream operators have the same level of precedence as the bit shift operators.

9.3.2 Output

Stream insertion

The class ostream represents output streams, and we use its instance cout for terminal output. The class overloads the << operator, which is referred to as the *insertion* operator and can be read as "receives". The operator function converts the value of its right argument to a sequence of characters that represents it, and appends it to the receiver stream, which is its left operand. The << operator is over-loaded with definitions for each of the built-in types that provide the expected behavior, and the compiler uses argument matching to determine which operator definition to invoke, and, therefore, the characters that are appended to the stream. There are no format codes that must agree with the argument types. The following example illustrates the use of cout and the << operator:

```
// standard output with cout and the << operator
#include <iostream.h>
int main()
{
    double dbl = 3.0;
    char ch = 'Z';
    cout << "dbl = " << dbl << '\t' << "ch = " << ch << endl;
}
```

Because the first application of the << operator in this example has a char* as its right argument, that overloading is executed. It appends the string (without the null byte) to the stream cout, and returns a reference to the stream cout. The operator returns the stream, so the result of that operation can be used as the left operand of another application of the << operator. Next, the overloading of the << operator for a double appends a string representing the value of dbl and returns cout, then the overloading for a char (i.e., '\t') is performed, and so on. (We will discuss the stream manipulator endl in the next paragraph.) Note also that if the programmer changes the type of dbl to long during program development, he or she does not need to modify the output statement. The output stream classes also overload the << operator for pointer types, and write the address value in hexadecimal, except for char* pointers, for which they print the referenced string.

Stream manipulators

The *stream manipulator* endl (i.e., "end line") in the previous example inserts the newline character '\n' into the stream and flushes the buffer associated with the stream. Generally, stream manipulators deal with the format state of the stream, rather than with data transfer. For example, several manipulators control format-ting of numeric output such as the base for an int or the number of mantissa digits for a double. This mechanism allows us to use the same syntax for transferring bytes and for manipulating the stream format state, and to combine both operations in cascaded expressions.

We will present a few example manipulators in this section, and will cover many other formatting options and stream state member functions in section 11.3.4. (These correspond to print()/scanf() format codes, options, and flags.) The manipulator flush outputs any buffered characters immediately without appending a newline character, and is useful for displaying prompts. The manipulators dec, oct, and hex set the state of the stream such that succeeding integers are printed in decimal, octal, or hexadecimal, respectively (like the print()/scanf() format codes %d, %o and %x).[25] Once a stream is set to a particular integer format, it continues in that state until set to another format state (rather than specifying the format for each object). The setw() manipulator takes a parameter that gives a minimum field width for the next item transferred, and the print format of a numeric object is never truncated. (This corresponds to the %*num* print()/scanf() format code, where *num* is an integer.) The field width is reset to its default of 0 after each operation, which indicates that the next object should be printed without padding. You must include the header file iomanip.h when using manipulators such as setw() that take parameters. The following example illustrates the use of these format manipulators:

```
// output stream manipulators
#include <iostream.h>
#include <iomanip.h>    // for setw()
int main()
{
    int num = 100;
    // prints the string "  100  0x64\n" (right justification is the default)
    cout << setw(5) << dec << num << setw(6) << hex << num << endl;
    // cout is still in the "hex" state
}
```

We will discuss the implementation of manipulators in section 11.3.4.

9.3.3 Input

Stream extraction

The class istream represents input streams, and we use its instance cin for input from the terminal keyboard. The class overloads the >> operator, which is referred to as the *extraction* operator, for all built-in types in iostream.h. The operator removes a sequence of characters from its left operand stream, converts them to a value for the type of its right operand, and assigns the value to the right operand. Its right operand is passed by reference, so an & operator is not necessary with the argument identifier, as is done when calling scanf(). The implementations of the >> operator for built-in types consider whitespace char-

---

[25] As with the corresponding printf() format codes, the decimal format prints in sign and magnitude notation, while the octal and hexadecimal formats print the octal or hexadecimal version of the value's bit string. With the octal and hexadecimal formats, negative numbers appear as very large positive numbers due to the two's complement encoding.

acters to be delimiters between successive values, even if the right operand is of type char*. The operator overloading for a char* appends a null character to the string read into the referent of that pointer (like the print()/scanf() format code %s). Several manipulators such as hex may also be used with input streams. For example, the setw() manipulator sets the maximum number of characters the stream inserts into the referent of a char* argument, including the null character. The following example illustrates the use of cin, the >> operator, and the setw() manipulator:

```
// standard input with cin and the >> operator
#include <iostream.h>
#include <iomanip.h>          // for setw()
const int STRING_MAX = 256;
// We expect a string containing no whitespace, a whitespace character, and an integer.
// As in C, nothing reaches the program until the user types a carriage return.
int main()
{
    char label[STRING_MAX];
    int num;
    cin >> setw(STRING_MAX) >> label >> num;
}
```

The stream error state

A problem that we often must handle with input, especially interactive input from a user, is an input string that is not a valid encoding for a value of the type expected. We also need to be able to determine whether the end of the stream has been reached, or whether some other problem such as a device error has occurred. If an input stream detects an error or an incorrectly formatted string upon an extraction, it sets itself to a "fail state" in which further processing cannot proceed. For convenience in testing its state, we can use a stream in a conditional, and it returns true if it is usable or false if it is in the fail state.[26] (There are also stream messages that test the state of the receiver.) We will code an example that shows how to test the stream error state and recover from an invalid format error so that you can write programs that receive input from the keyboard and not worry about typos when you are testing the program.[27] The following example illustrates how to handle invalid input:

```
// handling invalid input with streams
#include <iostream.h>
const int LINE_SIZE = 80;
int main()
```

---

[26] We will discuss the mechanism that provides this behavior in section 11.3.3.

[27] The example uses the istream "member functions" istream::clear() and istream::ignore(). We will discuss C++ message passing syntax in section 10.1.2 and istream protocol in section 11.3.2.

```
{
    char prompt[] = "Enter an integer value followed by <enter>:";
    int num;
    cout << prompt << flush;
    for ( ; ; )
    {
        cin >> num;
        if ( cin )                          // was the format valid?
            break;                          // OK, process the value
        // The next two statements call "member functions" of the class istream.
        // clear the "bad format" flag in the stream state (see section 11.3.4)
        istr.clear(istr.rdstate() & ~ios::failbit);
        // flush characters up to and including a newline (see section 11.3.3)
        cin.ignore(LINE_SIZE, '\n');
        cout << prompt << flush;            // try again
    }
    // ... process num ...
}
```

An input stream sets itself to a "fail state" when it encounters an end of file upon an insertion. We can also use an application of the >> operator as a loop test condition to read strings from a stream until reaching the end of the file, since it returns a reference to the stream. The following example illustrates the general pattern:

```
// read strings until end of file or stream error
#include <iostream.h>
#include <iomanip.h>            // for setw()
const int STRING_MAX = 256;
int main()
{
    char buf[STRING_MAX];
    cin >> setw(STRING_MAX);
    while ( cin >> buf )
    {
        // ... process buf ...
        cin >> setw(STRING_MAX);
    }
}
```

9.4 SUMMARY AND REVIEW

9.4.1 Basic Language Features

Lexical structure

• The delimiter // marks the rest of the line on which it appears as a comment. C++ also supports the C comment delimiters /* and */.

- The lexical and syntactic rules for identifiers and expressions in C++ are the same as those for C. C++ defines five additional operators and several new reserved words.

Control structures

- The control structure statements and conditional evaluation expression operators in C++ are the same as those of C.
- Execution begins in the function called main(). Two argument signatures are supported, int main() and int main(int argc, char* argv[]), for which the arguments represent an array of strings passed to the program by its environment. The return value indicates whether the program terminated successfully, with nonzero values indicating errors.
- C++ supports exceptions, which we will cover in section 13.3.

Scope

- The rules for scope and identifier resolution and the syntax of declarations and definitions are the same in C++ as in C.
- As in C, file scope may only contain declarations, and all file scope variables are statically allocated. static file scope identifiers are local to a code file, and all other file scope identifiers are global. extern indicates that a declaration is not a definition.
- Function scope is like that in C, except that C++ allows a local variable declaration to appear at any point within the function. A local variable is visible from the point of declaration on, but not before.
- C++ also supports class scope, which we will cover in sections 10.3 and 12.1.2.
- C++ introduces the *scope operator* ::, which supports name qualification. We can use it as a prefix operator to refer to a file scope identifier, even if the identifier is hidden. As an infix operator, its left operand is a class name and its right operand is an identifier declared within that class.

Storage allocation

- C++ supports static, automatic, and dynamic storage allocation of objects, including instances of classes.
- Objects declared at file scope and static local variables are statically allocated, and are always initialized.
- Automatic allocation is used for nonstatic local variables, value parameters, and temporary objects.
- We apply the prefix new operator to a type or class name to allocate an object dynamically. The new operator returns a pointer of that type referring to the new object. An *initializer* for the object may follow the type name, enclosed in parentheses.

- To allocate a dynamic array of objects, the new operator and the type name are followed by the size of the array enclosed in square brackets.

- The new operator improves upon malloc() because it is type-safe and provides programmer-controlled initialization. Its returns a pointer to an object, rather than to a region of storage.

- The prefix delete operator deallocates the dynamic object referred to by its pointer argument. Unlike the C function free(), delete provides programmer-controlled type-correct finalization upon deallocation.

Types

- The built-in types of C++ are those of ANSI C, including the void type. C++ supports the same implicit and explicit conversions among built-in types as C.

- C++ supports a type bool for logical values with the values false and true.

- We define array instances and pointers as in C, and they have the same semantics.

- We define the composite types struct, enum, and union as in C, but the definition of an instance does not require the type reserved word as in C.

- Like ANSI C, C++ supports the const type modifier, which specifies that the object cannot be modified after it is initialized. You should use the const specifier rather than the preprocessor directive #define for a constant so that the compiler can perform syntax and type checking on its uses.

- C++ supports the *reference type*, which introduces an alias for an existing object and is indicated by a type name and &. A reference definition does not create an object, and there are no operations defined for the reference itself. All operations using the reference name are performed on the object for which it is an alias, and we cannot reassign a reference to alias another object. We use the reference type primarily for function parameters and return values.

- All C conversions are supported in C++. A pointer cast is a cast, but any other conversion creates a new object. We can code a conversion with the standard C cast syntax or by using a type name as a function name.

- To make casts easier to find, C++ defines the static_cast<> operator for standard conversions, the reinterpret_cast<> operator for pointer casts, and the const_cast<> operator for "casting away" const-ness. These operators are recent additions to the language that are not supported by all compilers.

- As in C, the typedef statement defines an alias for an existing type.

9.4.2 Functions

Function declarations

- A C++ function declaration must include the parameter types, and may include parameter names for readability.

- The type of each argument in a function invocation must either match or be coercible to the type of the corresponding parameter. If not, a compiler error results.

The function parameter list

- As in C, function arguments are passed by value except for arrays, for which a pointer to the first element is passed.

- If a function parameter is specified as const, then you can pass a const argument for that parameter. A const argument cannot be passed for a non-const parameter, so use const parameters wherever appropriate for safety.

- We indicate pass by reference by using a reference type for a function parameter. The parameter name is an alias for the argument. We use pass by reference to avoid the overhead of copying the argument, or to allow the function to modify the argument object.

- To pass a large object that should not be modified by the function, use a const reference parameter.

- A function can return by reference, in which case an invocation returns a reference to the object specified in the return statement. Return by reference avoids the overhead of copying the return value, but you should only use it for objects that existed before the function call.

- C++ allows us to specify default values for parameters by giving an initializer in either the function declaration or definition.

- An ellipsis in the parameter list indicates that the number and types of succeeding parameters are unspecified, and that the compiler cannot perform type checking.

inline **functions**

- C programmers use a preprocessor macro for a very small function for which the overhead of invocation is greater than the operations it performs. However, macros have a number of problems because they are implemented by text substitution prior to compilation.

- The inline reserved word informs the compiler that it can substitute the body of that function directly for an invocation, rather than using a function call.

- The complete definition of an inline function must be present in the header file that makes the function available to clients because the compiler needs the function code to substitute when translating the client code. For this reason, the default linkage for inline functions is static.

Overloading

- Like many contemporary languages, C++ supports function name overloading. Each overloading of a function must have a unique argument signature, and the compiler uses the argument signature of an invocation to select the definition to invoke.

- You can use the `const` specifier with a parameter type to distinguish over-loadings of a function name.

- Coercions complicate the process of resolving an invocation of an overloaded function to a single definition. If more than one coercion can be applied in an invocation, promotions take precedence over standard conversions, and standard conversions take precedence over programmer-defined conversions. If there is more than one match for the argument signature of the invocation at any stage in this process, a compile-time error results.

- With coercions for more than one argument of an overloaded function, if a particular definition is an equal or better match for every argument and is also a strictly better match for one or more arguments, then the argument matching process selects it.

Type-safe linkage

- In a function-oriented design as in C, the programmer declares file scope functions in header files. A header file is included in both the code file that defines its functions, and in code files that invoke them, so that all the files have the same declaration for each function.

- Shared `const` objects and `inline` functions must be defined in header files because the compiler needs them when translating client code. They have internal linkage by default so that multiple definition errors do not occur when that header file is included in more than one file in a program.

- Because C++ supports independent compilation of modules, the linker must resolve invocations of overloaded functions across code files. Because linkers resolve references by name only, the C++ compiler encodes the argument signature into the function names seen by the linker.

- You can disable name encoding when calling C functions with the `extern "C"` directive.

Pointers to functions

- C++ supports the pointer to function type, which can be used as the type of a variable, parameter, return value, or member. This construct provides almost first-class status for function values.

- A pointer to function pFunc is declared as *RetType* (*pFunc) (... *argument signature* ...);.

- The value of a pointer to function is the "address of" a function with the correct argument signature, for example, &*func*.

- To invoke the referent of a pointer to function, dereference the pointer and invoke the result, for example, (*pFunc) (... *arguments* ...);.

- If we assign an overloaded function name to a pointer to function, only the definition whose argument signature is the same as that of the pointer is assigned to the pointer.

9.4.3 Basic Input/Output

C++ input/output expressions

- C++ programs can use the C standard library functions declared in stdio.h, but the compiler cannot check for agreement between the format codes and argument types for printf() and scanf().

- Most C++ language systems supply the *iostream* class library, which defines a hierarchy of stream classes for terminal and file input/output.

- The header file iostream.h declares the interface of the iostream classes, and defines the objects cout, cin, and cerr, which correspond to stdout, stdin, and stderr in C.

- The iostream classes overload the << and >> operators for all built-in types to provide type-correct transfer between an object's storage structure and its representation as characters. The left operand is the stream and the right operand is the object.

- When we use the << and >> operators with a stream, the compiler determines which operator definition to invoke by the type of the right operand. We can also overload these operators for class objects.

- The definitions of the << and >> operators return a reference to the stream so that we can cascade applications of the operator.

Output

- The *insertion* operator << inserts a representation of its right operand into its left operand stream.

- The insertion operator is also overloaded for *stream manipulators* that provide operations such as setting the format state of the stream and flushing its buffer.

Input

- The *extraction* operator >> removes the characters that represent an instance of its right operand from its left operand stream, and assigns the corresponding value to the right operand.

- An additional consideration for input is the possibility of an invalid format. In this case, the stream sets itself to a fail state that we can test by using the stream as an if or while condition.

9.5 EXERCISES

9.1 Review the exercises covering expression syntax, control structures, built-in types, type constructors, and function definitions in your favorite ANSI C text.

9.2 **(a)** What are the advantages of the C++ // comment delimiter over the C comment delimiters /* and */?

(b) Are there capabilities provided by the C delimiters /* and */ that are not provided by the C++ delimiter //?

9.3 Which of the following declarations are definitions, and which are not? For those that are definitions, give the corresponding forward declaration. For those that are not definitions, give a corresponding definition.

(a) const int i = 1;

(b) static double square(double dbl) { return dbl * dbl; }

(c) char* str;

(d) struct Point;

(e) char* (*pFn) (int (*) (char*, int), char**);

9.4 Give three characteristics of file scope that are not true of local scope.

9.5 **(a)** What is the meaning of the extern specifier in C and C++? When is it used?

(b) What is the meaning of the static specifier in C and C++ when it appears at file scope? When is it used?

9.6 Give three advantages of the use of the new and new [ ] operators over the malloc() function for dynamic allocation.

9.7 In C, a two-dimensional array is represented as an array of pointers to one-dimensional arrays, each of which is a row in the two-dimensional array. Write a function that takes two int parameters giving the number of rows and columns, allocates such a structure on the heap using new, and returns a pointer to it. (What is the function's return type?)

9.8 In what way is the bool type in C++ less safe than the boolean type in Pascal?

9.9 The compiler will not allow a const object to be modified or assigned to an identifier through which it could be modified. Which of the following pointer initializations are invalid and why?

const int num = 5;
int* pInt1 = #
const int* pInt2 = #
int* const pInt3 = #
const int* const pInt4 = #

9.10 Suppose an int num has been defined.

(a) Explain why the following statement is erroneous:
int& rInt = #

(b) Carefully explain the difference in meaning between the following definitions:
int& rInt = num;
int* pInt = #

9.11 Why is it true that C++ is not completely type-safe?

9.12 Describe some difficulties that can occur with pre-ANSI C function declarations.

9.13 Is it necessary to declare every function parameter that is not modified by a function as const?

9.14 What is the purpose of a const reference parameter?

9.15 Will the following function operate correctly?
```
void swapInts(int& int1, int& int2)
{
    int& tmp = int2;
    int2 = int1;
    int1 = tmp;
}
```

9.16 Will the following functions operate correctly?

(a)
```
int& min(int& int1, int& int2)
{
    return (int1 <= int2) ? int1 : int2;
}
```

(b)
```
int& min(int int1, int int2)
{
    return (int1 <= int2) ? int1 : int2;
}
```

9.17 Why will the following macro give incorrect results in some cases:
```
#define cube(x) ((x) * (x) * (x))
```
How can this problem be avoided in C++?

9.18 Why must all callers of an inline function be recompiled if the function's implementation changes?

9.19 **(a)** Why would overloading be useful for a function that returns the absolute value of its numeric argument? (Consider the C standard library absolute value functions.)
(b) Why is overloading not useful for a function that returns the square root of its numeric argument, even though we want it to be able take different argument types?

9.20 Suppose we have the following three overloadings of a function func():
```
void func(int, double);
void func(long, double);
void func(int, char);
```
(a) For each of the following calls, indicate which overloading is invoked (if any). If the call is ambiguous, indicate which overloadings apply.
```
func('c', 3.0);
func(3L, 3);
func("three", 3.0);
func(3L, 'c');
func(true, 3);
```
(b) Write a program to test which overloading(s) would be selected by your C++ compiler for each call in part (a), and run it.

9.21 Why is it necessary for the C++ compiler to encode file scope function names? Why must this process be disabled when calling C functions?

9.22 Are the names of inline functions encoded? Why or why not?

9.23 We pointed out that all const definitions in C++ header files are static to avoid multiple definition errors. Will using the static specifier for this purpose work correctly for a non-constant object definition in a header file?

9.24 In what sense are function objects first-class in C++? In what ways are they not first class?

9.25 **(a)** Write a definition of a pointer to function that can point to the function slope() coded in section 9.2.6.

(b) Write a definition of a pointer to function that can point to the function set_new_handler() described in section 9.2.6.

9.26 Write a C++ function map() that takes three parameters and returns no value. The first parameter is a pointer to an array of doubles, the second is the size of the array (an int), and the third is a pointer to a function that takes a double parameter and returns a double value. The function map() replaces each element of the array by the result of applying the third argument function to that element.

9.27 Describe the action of the following expression: (*(pA1->vptr[2])) (). What is the type of vptr? (Hint: See section 12.3.6.)

9.28 Give two advantages of the use of the iostream operators >> and << over the C standard library functions scanf() and printf().

9.29 What does the following code do? (Try it.)
```
int int1 = 3, int2 = 5;
cout << int1 < int2 ? int1 : int2;
```

9.30 Write a program that prompts the user for a decimal integer, and then prints it in octal and hexadecimal. If the input is invalid, the program should prompt the user to reenter the value.

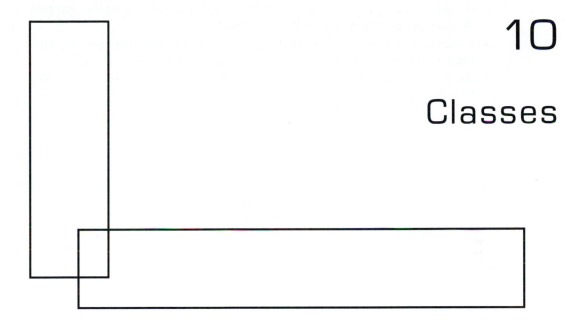

10

Classes

OVERVIEW

Chapter 9 covered the syntax and semantics of expressions, statements, and functions in C++. In this chapter, we discuss how the class designer defines classes and their components, specifies the accessibility of class components, defines initialization and finalization of class instances, and uses the class's scope as a unit of encapsulation.

This chapter covers the following topics:

- a class as an abstract data type and a scope, and the lack of class objects (10.1.1)
- the class definition that specifies both the *member functions* that provide the class's operations and the *data members* that implement its storage structure (10.1.2)
- the class header file that gives the class's interface and information for the compiler (10.1.3)
- access control specifiers and *friend functions* (10.1.3)
- the class code file that gives the class's implementation (the definition of its methods), and the this pointer (10.1.4)
- the creation of class instances statically, automatically, dynamically, and as value data members of another object (10.2.1)

- the difference in semantics between value and reference variables, and how the C++ programmer chooses between them (10.2.1)

- *constructor* member functions that provide automatic, designer-controlled initialization of instances of the class, and the *default constructor* (10.2.2)

- the *destructor* member function that provides automatic, designer-controlled finalization of instances of the class (10.2.3)

- the *constructor initialization list* that supports transparent initialization of data members of class type (10.2.4)

- the *copy constructor* that provides designer-controlled copying of class instances (10.2.5)

- a class as a scope in which the names of its members are declared and the scopes of its member functions are nested (10.3.1)

- *static data members* and *static member functions* that implement class variables and methods (10.3.2)

- use of the class scope as a namespace that can contain enumerations and auxiliary class definitions (10.3.3 and 10.3.4)

- *pointers to class members* (10.3.5)

10.1 THE C++ CLASS

10.1.1 Views of a Class

A class as an abstract data type

In Smalltalk, a class is an object in its own right that has behavior and state information independent of those of its instances. Like most statically typed hybrid languages, C++ supports the more traditional view that a class is an abstract data type with the additional properties of inheritance, class information, and dynamic binding. Like abstract data types, classes provide a construct for creating new classifications of objects with common attributes and operations, and for encapsulating a type's operations together with its storage structure and hiding the latter. Like types, we use classes to declare variables and parameters, allocate instances, and create composite types. Like a type, a class imposes syntactic constraints on expressions, specifies a storage mapping for values, and protects those bit patterns from unintended interpretation.

Class instances are first-class objects in C++. The language includes a number of mechanisms that allow the class designer to define a complete set of programming operations for the class so that clients can create and manipulate instances easily and transparently. These include automatic initialization and finalization, assignment, construction of anonymous instances, and operator overloading (including equality tests). However, there are some distinctions between the ways in which we can use classes and built-in types. For example, we cannot define member functions and subclasses for built-in types, overload an operator for built-in types alone, or obtain dynamic binding of functions on the basis of a built-in type. In a sense, classes are more first-class than built-in types.

A class as a scope

Like a C structure or a Pascal record, a C++ class also specifies a scope for the names of its members. For example,

```
// illustrates C structure scope
int x = 5;   // static object
struct Point
{
   int x;
   int y;
};

main()
{
   Point pt;
   pt.x = x;   // the first use of the name x is that in the scope of Point
}
```

Class scope is more complex than C structure scope because function scopes (i.e., methods) can be nested within a class scope. For this reason, a class scope can enclose executable code containing identifier uses that the compiler must resolve. The class scope is nested within the file scope in which it is declared (except for nested and derived classes, as described in sections 10.3.4 and 12.1.2). The data members and member functions of a class are defined within that class scope, and their names are only visible in that class scope and in scopes nested within it. The language uses static scope resolution, so file scope identifiers are visible within member function code if they are not hidden by a class member name.

Class scopes are named, and the programmer can refer to an identifier declared in a class scope outside that scope with a *qualified name* using the scope operator, as in the expression *Class::member*. We will see that we use qualified names to define member functions separately from the class definition, to refer to static class members, and to refine methods. Name qualification also allows the class designer to use class scope as a name space in which he or she can declare static objects and functions, enumerations, and auxiliary classes. We will discuss class scope in detail in sections 10.3, 12.1.2 and 12.4.1.

Absence of execution-time class objects

Classes themselves are not first-class objects in C++ in the sense that classes are not values that can be manipulated in programs, as in Smalltalk. A class object cannot be the value of a variable, nor can it be passed as an argument or return value of a function. C++ provides other language constructs that support the functionality of Smalltalk class objects, such as instantiation messages, class variables and messages, and type information.

Like most compiled languages, C++ does not maintain a run-time representation of type information or provide operations for obtaining information such as a class's ancestors or messages.[1] This characteristic is motivated by the language's design goals of efficiency, compatibility with C, and avoidance of imposing overhead for a feature on programs that do not use it. To support treating a class as an object, a statically typed language would have to provide a special "metatype" whose instances are type objects for classes or built-in types (like the Delphi Pascal class-reference type discussed in section 4.5.2). We would use this metatype as the type of a variable or parameter whose value is a type object, the type objects would exist at execution time, and the language would define protocol for using them. In addition, each object would have a pointer to its type object, like the Smalltalk class pointer. These constructs would allow querying the class of an object, performing class operations based on the class of an object, and providing class information.

The ANSI/ISO C++ Standard includes the *run-time type information* extension that provides some of these features [Str92]. It supports the dynamic_cast<> operator that we can use to determine whether an object is an instance of a given class. It also provides the type const type_info&, which represents object types, and the typeid operator, which returns an object's type. Instances of type_info can be compared for equality (i.e., to determine whether two objects are of the same type) or can return the name of the class. Because C++ is statically typed, the compiler (and the reader) can always determine the type of the referent of any identifier or expression whose type is a built-in type or a class that does not have subclasses. For this reason, run-time type information is only useful with inheritance, and we will discuss this feature in section 12.2.5.

The C++ template facility provides a limited way in which we can use a class or a built-in type as the value of a parameter. It supports generic functions and types in the same manner as the Ada generic abstract data types discussed in section 1.1.4. A *function template* describes a set of function definitions that have the same code, but differ in the types of their parameters (and perhaps local variables). The compiler creates a particular function definition when it encounters an invocation of that function name by substituting the actual argument types for the corresponding type parameters. Similarly, a *class template* describes a set of collection classes that only differ in the type of their elements. This template is realized by an actual class definition, which the compiler creates when an identifier declaration uses the collection class name with a particular element type. We will discuss the template facility in detail in sections 13.1 and 13.2.

---

[1] In fact, the compiler stores just enough information to perform dynamic binding for some messages, and to support the run-time type information extension.

10.1.2 Class Definition

The class definition

We create a class with a class definition, an expanded version of the C struct definition, encapsulating both operations and data.[2] A class definition begins with the reserved word class and the name of the new class. The body of the definition is enclosed in braces and terminated with a semicolon. Like the components of a C structure, we refer to the components of a class as *members*, but unlike C, they can be either data objects or functions. The *data members* of the class (or structure) correspond to Smalltalk instance variables, and the *member functions* correspond to methods. We will use the term "members" when referring to both kinds of class components.

The following is a simple class definition that we will use for illustration in this section (we will discuss the public and protected access specifiers in the next section, but their meaning should be apparent):

```
// a simplified definition of a class for points on a display screen
#include <math.h>              // for sqrt() in Point::distanceFrom()

class Point
{
public:
    // the "member functions" accessible to clients provide the class's interface
    Point()                    // the "constructors" Point::Point() provide initialization
    { x_ = y_ = 0; }
    Point(int initX, int initY)
    { x_ = initX;  y_ = initY; }
    int x() const              // get the x coordinate
    { return x_; }
    void x(int newX)           // set the x coordinate
    { x_ = newX; }
    int y() const              // get the y coordinate
    { return y_; }
    void y(int newY)           // set the y coordinate
    { y_ = newY; }
    // return the distance between the receiver and the argument
    double distanceFrom(const Point& argPt) const
    {
        int dx = x_ - argPt.x_;
        int dy = y_ - argPt.y_;
        return sqrt(dy*dy + dx*dx);
    }
    // ... other useful protocol for class Point ...
protected:
```

---

[2] In fact, the struct statement in C++ is a special case of the class definition in which the default access specification is public, and a struct definition may also contain member functions.

```
    // the inaccessible "data members" define the class's storage structure
    int x_;
    int y_;
};
```

Data members

Data member declarations follow the same format as all variable or structure member declarations, in which a type specifier is followed by the member name (see the declarations of x_ and y_ in the class Point). A data member cannot be declared of a class type unless the class's definition has been encountered so that the compiler can determine how much space to allocate for that member in instances of the class. Data members that are pointers or references to class objects can be declared if that class's name has been declared.

We can specify a data member as const. If so, each instance of the class can have a different value for that data member, but its value cannot be changed after the object has been initialized. The language does not allow explicit initialization of a data member within the class definition because the class definition does not create any objects. (If a data member should have the same value for all instances, you should use a static data member, as described in section 10.3.2.) We will see in section 10.2.4 that we initialize a const data member in the "initialization list" of the class's constructor.

Member functions

The member function declarations represent the messages that instances of the class can receive, and their definitions represent the corresponding methods. In the class Point, we have directly nested the member function code within the class definition to make the scope relationships explicit. (Note that no semicolon follows a member function definition given within a class definition.) We will see in the next two sections that a class's member functions are usually defined separately from the class definition.

The member functions of a class are declared within the scope of the class, rather than at file scope. A member function name does not conflict with a file scope function or member function of another class that has the same name and argument signature. When discussing a member function, we will use a qualified name such as Point::distanceFrom() to make explicit which function we are referring to. Like a nested procedure in Pascal, the member function name is declared in the class scope, and its parameters and local variables are declared within the local scope of the member function, which is nested within the class scope. For example, the name distanceFrom is declared within the scope Point, and the identifiers argPt, dx, and dy are declared within the scope of Point::distanceFrom().

Because a member function is within the class scope, it has full access privileges to both the public and protected members of instances of that class. The names of a class's members are visible throughout the class, so member function code can use them even if they are declared later in the class definition. Unlike Smalltalk, a data member and a member function cannot have the same name because both identifiers are declared within the same scope and object names cannot be overloaded. For this reason, we named the data members x_ and y_ in the class Point.

We can overload a member function name with more than one argument signature, as illustrated by Point::Point(), Point::x(), and Point::y(). A member function hides a file scope function with the same name within the class, rather than overloading it. Similarly, two member functions in different classes that have the same name are not overloadings from the point of view of the compiler because they are defined in different scopes.

C++ provides a special mechanism for automatic, programmer-defined initialization of the data members of an instance of a class. A *constructor* is defined as a member function that has the same name as the class (and no return type), as illustrated by the two overloadings of Point::Point(). A constructor is always invoked implicitly by the compiler whenever a class instance is created. The examples in the next subsection illustrate the syntax for passing arguments to the constructor. If a client creates an instance without giving an initializer, the compiler invokes the *default constructor* that takes no arguments so that the object is properly initialized and can respond to the class's messages. For the class Point, the default constructor sets both data members to 0 (i.e., we consider (0, 0) to be the default point). Constructors are discussed in detail in section 10.2.

We saw in section 9.2.2 that a function parameter can be declared const to indicate that the function does not modify that argument. We can also declare member functions const to specify that they do not modify the object receiving the message. As illustrated by Point::x(), Point::y(), and Point::distanceFrom(), we give the const keyword after the argument list in the function definition. This allows clients to pass those messages to a const receiver. We also give the const keyword in a declaration of the function, as it is an important part of the interface of the function. A member function can be overloaded with both const and non-const functions with the same argument signature, in which case the compiler uses the const attribute of the receiver to determine which function body to invoke.

The class type and instantiation

A class definition does not cause any objects to be created or storage to be allocated.[3] Once the class has been defined, we can use the class name as a type name for

- declaring identifiers, function parameters, and members
- defining new objects statically, automatically, or dynamically with new

---

[3] It is legal (but poor practice) to include an identifier definition list following a class definition, as you can with the struct statement in C. However, we will see in section 10.1.3 that a class definition is usually placed in a header file, and objects should not be defined in header files.

- creating arrays of objects of that class, and pointers and references to objects of that class.

Like the enum and struct definitions, the class keyword is not needed when using the class name as a type name. The following examples illustrate some uses of the class name and creation of instances:

```
// declarations using a class name as a type name
#include "Point.h"              // class header file as described in the next section
int main()
{
    Point pt(1, 5);             // the initializer provides the constructor arguments
    const Point origin;         // a constant class object set to (0, 0) by the default constructor
    Point* pPoint;              // a pointer to instances of class Point
    Point arrPoint[16];         // an array of Points, each set to (0, 0) by the default constructor
    Point& refPoint = pt;       // an alias for pt
    // dynamic instance creation, the initializer provides the constructor arguments
    pPoint = new Point(2, 3);
}
```

The initializer (1, 5) in the first definition is used to pass arguments to the class's constructor, and an initializer must be the argument signature of one of the class's constructors. For the class Point, the constructor simply sets the data members, but we will see in section 10.2 that a constructor can do much more. Because the definitions of origin and arrPoint give no initializers, they invoke the default constructor, with the result that the coordinates of the new objects are set to 0, rather than being "garbage" values.

Member access and message syntax

Like the members of a C structure, we refer to the public members of a class instance with the component selection operator . (period). The public members of the referent of a pointer to a class object may be accessed using the -> operator, in the same manner as the members of a C structure are referenced through a pointer. As we saw in sections 1.1.4 and 2.2.4, passing a message to an object appears like selection of that member function in the receiver. The following examples illustrate this syntax:

```
// message passing syntax in C++
#include "Point.h"              // class header file as described in the next section
int main()
{
    Point pt(1, 5);
    const Point origin;         // set to (0, 0) by the default constructor
    Point arrPoint[16];
    Point* pPoint = new Point(2, 3);
    int xVal = pt.x();          // get pt.x_
```

```
    pt.y(3);                    // set pt.y_ to 3
    arrPoint[0].y(pt.x());      // set arrPoint[0].y_ to pt.x_
    // pass the message Point::distanceFrom() to the referent of pPoint
    double radius = pPoint->distanceFrom(origin);
    // member functions with a const receivers
    int num = origin.y();       // OK: does not modify the receiver
    origin.x(-5);               // error: const receiver
}
```

Within the code for a member function, the receiver's data members can be accessed directly without component selection, as illustrated in the member functions of class Point. This usage refers to that data member in the receiver of the message, as it does in Smalltalk methods.

The class **declaration**

We can declare an identifier as the name of a class with the reserved word class. This declaration informs the compiler that the identifier is a type name, and allows us to use the name to define pointers to instances of that type. However, we cannot define a variable or value parameter of that type until the compiler has seen the definition of the class so that it can determine how much space to reserve for that instance. Similarly, messages cannot be sent to the referent of the pointer unless the compiler has encountered the class definition so that it can verify the validity of those messages. For example,

```
// use of a class declaration
class Point;
int dotProduct(const Point&);  // OK: no Point object created
int main()
{
    Point* pPoint;             // OK: no Point object created
    Point pt(-3, -3);          // error: compiler doesn't know the size yet
    pPoint = new Point;        // error: compiler doesn't know the size yet
}
```

10.1.3 The Class Interface and Access Control

Organization of source code

As we discussed in section 1.1.3, a C program is typically divided into code files on the basis of a function-oriented decomposition of the application. Each module specifies its own header file, which declares the nonstatic functions and global constants and objects in its interface, and other modules that invoke its functions or access its data include its header file. The main() function invokes the functions that implement the various subtasks of the application.

In C++, we can use an object-oriented design that decomposes the application according to the classes necessary to represent its model and user interface. We code the interface of a class (i.e., the information necessary for a client to use the class correctly) in a header file named *Class*.h. The methods (i.e., the bodies of the member functions) are defined in a code file named *Class*.cc, which includes the class header file. [4] A client program that creates and employs instances of the class includes the class header file, and is linked to the object file resulting from compiling the class code file. Other classes that use the class for composition or specialization also include its header file and are linked with its code file.

In a purely object-oriented design, there is a class that represents the application as a whole. The main() function simply creates an instance of this class, and sends it a message such as open() or run() that activates the instance's functionality. For example,

```
// the format of an application with an object-oriented design
#include "SpreadsheetApp.h"
int main(int argc, char* argv[])
{
    SpreadsheetApp theApp(argc, argv);
    theApp.open();  // or return a return value for main()
}
```

The class header file

The primary purpose of the class header file is to make the class definition available to clients so that they can create and manipulate instances. It also includes information that the compiler needs when compiling client code. The class header file may include any of the following items:

- the class definition that declares the class's members
- #include directives for the header files of classes used by the class, and for C standard libraries
- preprocessor directives for conditional expansion
- declarations of friend functions and other file scope functions associated with the class
- definitions of inline member functions or associated file scope functions
- definitions of const objects, enum types, and typedef's necessary for use of the class.

(We will discuss conditional expansion of header files and friend functions later in this section.)

Although they are not part of the interface of the class, the data members must appear in the header file so that the compiler can determine how much space to allocate for instances of the class in client code files. (Remember our discussion

---

[4] The exact suffixes for the header and code files depend on the compiler and system. Some systems use Class.hh for header files to distinguish them from C header files, and some systems use Class.cpp or Class.C for code files.

of the private section of an Ada package in section 1.1.4.) This means that clients of a class must be recompiled whenever a change is made to the class's storage structure. As we stated in section 9.2.3, the complete definition of an inline function must appear in the class header file so that the compiler has the function code to substitute in client code files. (Member functions defined within the body of a class definition are automatically handled as inline functions.) That is, the header file includes information that is not part of the class's interface, but is present for the use of the compiler.

A class header file must contain #include directives for the header files of the classes it uses as the types of data members, superclasses, or member function parameters. A class's header file can be included in more than one header file, and more than one of those can be included in another header or code file. This would result in a multiple definition error from the compiler (not the linker), even though the two definitions of the class are identical. For example, suppose we define a class Rectangle that defines two Point data members for the upper left and lower right corners of an instance. Rectangle.h includes the file Point.h to provide the type definition for those members, as follows:

```
// Rectangle.h: interface for a class representing rectangles
#include "Point.h"     // needed for data member declarations

class Rectangle
{
public:
   // ... member functions ...
protected:
   Point origin_;
   Point corner_;
};
```

A graphics application class GraphicEditor would have to include both of these header files, since it uses both points and rectangles. (In fact, it would probably include several other classes such as Circle and Polygon that include Point.h.) For example,

```
// GraphicEditor.h: interface for a graphic editor application
#include "Point.h"
#include "Rectangle.h"   // error: class Point defined more than once
// other necessary #include's, e.g. Circle.h, Canvas.h, etc.

class GraphicEditor
{
   // ... members ...
};
```

This causes a multiple definition error for the identifier Point when compiling GraphicEditor because Point is defined twice (after expansion of the #include directives).

To avoid this problem, we use conditional preprocessor expansion to prevent multiple inclusions of a header file. We enclose the header file for the class Point in a preprocessor directive, as follows:

```
// the preprocessor directive ensures that the class definition is included once in any file
// Point.h: interface for a class representing points
#ifndef POINT_H
#define POINT_H

class Point
{
    // ... as illustrated in section 10.1.2 ...
};

#endif  // Point.h
```

If Point.h has not yet been included in a particular file (e.g., when the compiler encounters #include "Point.h" in GraphicEditor.h), the symbol POINT_H will be undefined, so the text up to the #endif will be included in the code passed to the compiler. However, if the header file has already been included, that symbol will have been defined by the #define directive, and the class definition will not be included again (e.g., when #include "Rectangle.h" is expanded in GraphicEditor.h). We chose the symbol POINT_H because it is not likely to conflict with any other preprocessor symbols. It is common practice to use the capitalized class name followed by _H.

If a class C1 uses another class C2 only as the type of a pointer or reference parameter or data member, C1's header file may use a declaration of C2, rather than including C2's entire header file. Using a class declaration reduces the amount of included code and, therefore, the compilation time, and also avoids the compilation dependency between the header files. Instantiation and uses of the referent of that parameter or data member will appear in C1's class code file (described in the next section), which must include C2's header file.

Access control

C++ provides three levels of information hiding for the members of a class, which are indicated by the reserved words public, protected, and private. As we saw in the definition of the class Point, the access specifier is followed by a colon and then the members for which it applies. The default specification for a class definition is private, while that for a struct definition is public. We will list the public members of a class first so that the class's interface is given first and the access specifiers are explicit.

The *public* data members and member functions of a class are accessible wherever the class is visible, and make up the interface of the class. Outside the scope of the class, clients can access the public members of an instance with the component selection operator . (period), or with -> for a pointer. The *protected* members of a class are accessible only within the class and its subclasses, and are not accessible to clients of the class. The member functions and friend functions of a class can access the protected members of instances of the class via component selection. Access specifications are checked at compile time, and invalid accesses are flagged as errors.

```
// protected members are not accessible to clients
#include "Point.h"
int main()
{
    Point pt(1, 5);
    int num = pt.x_;    // error
}
```

A *private* member is accessible only within its class, and is not accessible to either the class's clients or its subclasses.

In C++, access to a member is granted by the designer of a class, not seized by a client. The class designer has complete control of the access specifications for each of the class's members. This contrasts with Smalltalk, in which all instance variables are protected and all messages are public, and it is not possible to hide a class component from the class's subclasses. In particular, the C++ class designer can specify auxiliary functions that aid in the implementation of other class methods as non-public (i.e., as protected or private) so that clients of the class cannot access them.

In addition, the class designer can specify data members as public in C++. However, the use of public data members is inconsistent with information hiding, and precludes representation independence for the class (recall section 1.1.4). During development, the designer may modify the class's implementation such that the information represented by that data member is computed rather than stored. If so, any client that accesses that information as a data member must be recoded using a member function invocation. For example, if we change the class Point to store instances in polar coordinates, we can still define both overloadings of Point::x() and Point::y() in terms of the data members r_ and theta_. Code that refers directly to the x_ member of a point would fail, but code that uses the member function Point::x() would only require recompiling. If a class provides inline accessor functions for nonpublic data members as does Point, there is no performance penalty for using a member function call rather than direct access of the data member.

friend **functions**

In some cases, a class's access specifications make implementing certain operations awkward. A common example occurs when overloading the stream input and output operators >> and << to handle class objects because the operator definition often needs access to the data members of the object. As we will see in section 11.1.1, the receiver of an overloaded operator is the left operand (as in Smalltalk), so we cannot define the operator as a member function of the object's class because the object is the right operand. We cannot add an overloading of the operator as a member function of the stream class because doing so would involve modifying the definition of the stream class in the system header file iostream.h. We will see in section 11.3.1 that we define the operator at file scope, thus it cannot access the non-public members of the object being transferred. If the operator function needs access to those members or can be coded more efficiently with that access, we declare it as a "friend" of the class.

The C++ *friend declaration* grants the specified function access to a class's non-public members, and we say that the function is a *friend* of the class. A class can declare a file scope function or a member function of another class as a friend. This feature is useful when a function needs access to the internal structure of more than one class, or must use a nonpublic member that has no accessor member function. In this way, the class does not require an accessor member function that should only be used by that function. A friend function typically describes an operation available for instances of the class, so its declaration is part of the interface of the class. Like access specifications, friendship is granted by the designer of a class, not seized by a client.

A friend declaration may only appear within a class definition, and consists of the reserved word friend followed by a function declaration. It specifies that the class grants that function access to its nonpublic members. If a friend function is a member function, the friend declaration uses a qualified name to indicate which function is being granted access. A friend declaration can appear in the private, protected, or public section of the class definition. We will place them at the beginning of the class so that they are conspicuous, as follows:

```
// example friend declarations
#include "Class2.h"

class Class1
{
friend void func(const Class1&);              // file scope function
friend int Class2::msg(char*, Class1&);       // member function of Class2
public:
   // ... member functions ...
protected:
   // ... data members ...
};
```

The friend function typically takes a parameter whose type is the class, and it can access any member of that argument using component selection. A friend function is not a member function: It is not invoked via an instance of the class, nor is its name within the scope of the class.

A separate declaration of a file scope friend before the class definition is not necessary because a friend declaration declares the named function in the same scope as that of the class name. If a friend function is a member function, its class must be declared before the friend declaration. A class definition must specify each argument signature of an overloaded function that it wishes to declare as a friend. This prevents a client from obtaining access to the nonpublic members by overloading a friend function.

A class may grant access to all the member functions of another class *Class* by using the declaration friend class *Class*;. This is useful for an auxiliary class used only in the implementation of the class granted access. All the members of the auxiliary class are declared as nonpublic, and the class that uses it is declared a friend. We will demonstrate this technique with the class Node in the next section. The friend relationship is neither transitive nor symmetric. That is, if the class C2 is declared a friend of the class C1, C2's friend functions do not have access to C1's members, nor does C1 have access to C2's members. Friend classes are also useful for "iterator" classes that enumerate the elements of a collection class (see section 13.2.3).

The friend construct is a departure from the norm in which the access specification for a component of an abstract data type is uniform for all clients. The friend mechanism gives the class designer control over the accessibility of the internal structure of a class's instances on a finer-grained, function-by-function basis. In a sense, a friend function is a violation of encapsulation because the function is tightly coupled with the class, but is not grouped within the class. Similarly, a friend function violates information hiding because it has access to the nonpublic components of the class, and it can be broken if the storage structure of the class is changed. An alternate view is that the friend function is part of the class conceptually, but is simply not defined within the class's scope, so it does not violate encapsulation and information hiding. (This perspective is only relevant for a file scope friend function, which is the most common usage.) Friend functions have other disadvantages as well. Unlike member functions, friend functions add to the global name space, are not inherited, and cannot be dynamically bound according to the class. For these reasons, the use of friend functions complicates understanding of a class and should be employed with care and restraint. You should implement a class operation as a member function rather than a friend function whenever possible.

An example class interface

Let us define a class representing a queue of elements that is implemented as a linked list. An instance has the data members front and back, which point to the first and last nodes in the queue. We define an auxiliary class Node for the nodes in the queue, each of which consists of an element elem and a pointer next to the next node in the storage structure of the queue. Figure 10.1 illustrates the structure of an instance of class Queue into which the elements 4, 2, 5, and 7 have been inserted.[5] We want to define the class such that the entire structure is treated as a single object. We also want clients of the class to be able to create and use instances

---

[5] As we will discuss further in section 12.2.2, C++ does not include a class pointer in objects whose classes do not define virtual functions.

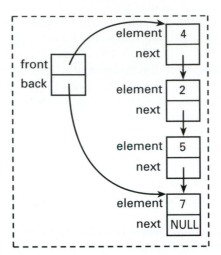

Figure 10.1   An instance of class Queue.

without being aware of the storage structure. In particular, a client should not have to deal with the details of allocation of the nodes, either when inserting or deleting elements, or upon destroying or copying a queue. We will see that C++ provides several features oriented toward these characteristics.

In a statically typed language such as C++, all the elements of a collection must be of the same type. A queue of ints is a different class than a queue of Strings and must have a different name, even though their implementations are identical except for the element type. In this example, we will define the queue as containing instances of the type ElemType, and then use a typedef statement to give the element type for a particular program. This use of a type alias allows us to use the same Queue class definition with different element types. However, the class definition cannot be used for queues of different element types in the same program without modifying the class names. We will discuss how inheritance allows creating heterogeneous collections in section 12.2, and how the template mechanism automatically generates a class definition for a given element type in section 13.2.

We define the class Queue and its auxiliary class Node as follows:[6]

```
// Queue.h: interface for a class for queues of elements (linked list implementation)
#ifndef QUEUE_H
#define QUEUE_H

// the type of elements inserted into and removed from the queue
typedef int ElemType;

// for class ostream and the cerr object used in the Queue::remove() method
#include <iostream.h>
```

---

[6] We do not use the const specifier on Queue parameters or member functions because a constant queue is pointless. The programmer should use an Array instance for a constant collection.

```
    class Node
    {
    friend class Queue;                    // all Queue member functions are friends of Node
    friend ostream& operator<<(ostream&, Queue&);
    protected:
        Node(const ElemType&);             // the constructor creates a node
        ElemType elem;
        Node* next;
    };

    // Node constructor (recoded for elements of class type in section 10.2.4)
    inline Node::Node(const ElemType& el)
    {
        elem = el;
        next = NULL;
    }

    class Queue
    {
    friend ostream& operator<<(ostream&, Queue&);
    public:
        Queue();                           // the constructor creates an empty queue
        ~Queue();                          // destructor (see section 10.2.3)
        Queue& insert(const ElemType&);    // insert an element into the receiver
        ElemType remove();                 // remove an element from the receiver
        bool isEmpty();                    // is the receiver empty?
    protected:
        Node* front;
        Node* back;
    };

    inline Queue::Queue()
    {
        front = back = NULL;
    }

    inline bool Queue::isEmpty()
    {
        return front == NULL ? true : false;
    }
        #endif                             // Queue.h
```

All of Node's members are protected and Queue is declared as a friend so that Queue's member functions can access the members of the nodes in the queue.[7] The

---

[7] We have coded Node as if it would only be used by the class Queue to illustrate this use of friends. Of course, this class could also be used by many other classes with linked storage structures, so either they can all be friends or Node can be coded with public accessor member functions.

function named operator<<() is the output operator for Queue. (We will discuss operator overloading in section 11.1, and will code operator<<() for queues in section 11.3.1.) We must declare it a friend of Node separately because it is not a member function of Queue. Because Node can only be used by its friend Queue, we did not define accessors for its data members.

The member functions Node::Node() and Queue::Queue() are the constructors for those classes. The constructor for Node takes an argument for the new object's elem member, and sets the next member to NULL. We pass its argument by reference for cases in which ElemType is a class whose instances are large or have constructors and destructors. (This parameter type would be inefficient when ElemType is typedef'd to char.) The constructor for Queue initializes the instance to be an empty queue. The destructor Queue::~Queue() deallocates any remaining nodes in the queue when a Queue instance is destroyed, and is invoked implicitly whenever a Queue instance is deallocated. We will discuss constructors and destructors in detail in section 10.2, and Queue::~Queue() is coded in that section.

The member functions Node::Node(), Queue::isEmpty(), and Queue::Queue() are declared inline. We could nest their definitions within the class definitions as we did for Point, but standard practice is to define them separately. In this way, clients can read the class definition more easily, and the class designer can move a member function definition to the code file easily if it is re-implemented such that it is not inline. When we define a member function outside its class definition, we must use a qualified name with the class name and the scope operator. For example, the name Queue::isEmpty() tells the compiler that we are defining that member function for the class Queue, rather than Set::isEmpty() or a file scope function called isEmpty(). We will code the definitions for Queue::insert() and Queue::remove() in the next section.

10.1.4 The Class Implementation

The class code file

The class designer defines non-inline methods for a class's member functions in the class "code file" (e.g., Queue.cc for the class Queue). File scope functions associated with the class—for example, an overloading of operator<<()—are also defined in the class code file. The code file includes the class header file and the header files of any classes used as parameter or variable types, and also includes C standard library header files if necessary. After compilation, the resulting object file is linked with client object files that use instances of the class and invoke its member functions.

Method definition

Within the code file for the class's member functions, we define the member functions lexically at file scope, and use a qualified name to indicate which function we are defining. C++ methods are written in the same manner as conventional C functions, using the expression syntax and control structures of the base language. As we saw in sections 2.2.4 and 10.1.2, we use component selection of the member function in the receiver to send a message. The left operand is the receiver of the message, and its class determines the scope of the member function invoked.

A member function definition is within the class scope, so if it has an argument of its class, its code may access the nonpublic members of that object. The expression argPt.x_ in Point::distanceFrom() in section 10.1.2 illustrates this use of nonpublic members. (Recall that this is not possible in Smalltalk.) Another difference between Smalltalk and C++ is that every Smalltalk message must be explicitly passed to some object. In particular, we must code a message to the receiver of the method self *message: arg.* In C++, we can invoke the member functions of the receiver directly within a member function (i.e., without component selection or name qualification) in the same manner as accessing the receiver's data members. The invocations of Queue::isEmpty() in the methods for Queue::insert() and Queue::remove() in this section illustrate this usage. In fact, such data member and member function uses are implicit references through the this pointer that refers to the receiver.

The this **pointer**

In C++, we can send a message to the receiver of the method without an explicit reference to the receiver. However, we need a name for the receiver when using it as an argument to a message, or as an operand of an operator within member function code.[8] The reserved word this is a pointer through which a member function can access the object receiving the message. It is like self in Smalltalk, except that self is a reference and this is a pointer. The declaration of this is *Class** const this;, so the -> operator is used to select members, and this matches a pointer type when used as an argument. The pointer is const so it cannot be changed to refer to another object (i.e., this may not appear on the left side of an assignment without dereferencing). Methods can modify the object to which it refers, that is, the receiver itself, to change its state. A method can overwrite the receiver with a copy of another object of its class by using *this on the left side of an assignment.

Explicit use of the this pointer allows a method to return the receiver so that message expressions can be cascaded. For example, a member function such as Queue::insert() that conceptually does not return a value can be defined with a return type of Queue& and return *this. (The dereference on this is necessary because the method returns a reference, not a pointer.) This allows clients to write expressions such as the following:[9]

---

[8] We will see in the next chapter that operators can be overloaded for class operands (and their operands must be given explicitly for the parser).

[9] As in C, successive applications of the component selection operation are parsed from left to right.

```
// cascading messages that return the receiver
#include "Queue.h"    // with typedef int ElemType;
int main()
{
   Queue intQu;
   int num1 = 0;
   int num2 = intQu.insert(1).insert(2).insert(num1).remove();
}
```

The member function Queue::insert() must return a reference, rather than a value, so that the receiver of the second message insert(2) is the same object that received the first message. If we used return by value, the receiver of the second message would be the temporary object created by the compiler rather than the original object intQu. In addition, returning by value would cause the entire queue to be copied to the temporary object (assuming that a copy constructor is written as described in section 10.2.5). An overloading of the assignment operator should also return a reference to the modified receiver because programmers expect to be able to use the expression *obj1 = obj2* within another expression. We will see in section 11.1.3 that we provide this behavior by returning *this in that method.

During execution, the member function code must be able to refer to the receiver denoted by the this pointer. Typically, the compiler translates each member function into a uniquely named function with one additional argument, the this pointer. It translates an unqualified data member reference within the member function code as an offset into the object accessed via that pointer, and adds the pointer as an argument in translating each invocation. The compiler also includes the class name in the encoded name visible to the linker; that is, the call *obj.message*(...) is translated as something similar to __*message_Class_*...(&obj, ...). This means that a C++ member function invocation can be statically bound, in which case it has exactly the same cost as calling a C function.

Example method definitions

Let us define the member functions Queue::insert() and Queue::remove() for the class presented in the previous section. The methods can refer to the members front and back and the function Queue::isEmpty() without component selection as they refer to members of the receiver. As described previously, Queue::insert() returns a reference to the resulting queue so that clients can cascade insertion messages. The Queue class code file appears as follows:

```
// Queue.cc: methods for class Queue
#include "Queue.h"
#include <stdlib.h>                              // for void exit(int);


// insert an element into the receiver
Queue& Queue::insert(const ElemType& el)
{
```

```
    Node* pNode = new Node(el);        // Node constructor invoked
    if ( isEmpty() )                   // i.e., this->isEmpty()
       front = back = pNode;
    else
    {
       back->next = pNode;             // must be a friend of Node
       back = pNode;
    }
    return *this;
}

// remove an element from the receiver
ElemType Queue::remove()
{
    if ( isEmpty() )
    {
       // throw an exception (see section 13.3) if implemented, otherwise:
       cerr << "attempted Queue::remove() on an empty queue" << endl;
       exit(1);
    }
    Node* pNode = front;
    front = front->next;               // must be a friend of Node
    ElemType retElem(pNode->elem);     // construct an ElemType object
    delete pNode;
    return retElem;
}
```

These member functions are quite small, and could have been defined as inline functions. To do so, we would code their definitions in the file Queue.h to make them
available to the compiler when translating a client source code file.

10.2 CREATION, INITIALIZATION, AND FINALIZATION OF OBJECTS

10.2.1 Object Creation and Identity

Allocation policies

Like a built-in type, a C++ class can be instantiated using any of the allocation
mechanisms available for objects in C. We can create a class instance

- by static allocation at file scope or as a static local function variable
- by automatic allocation of a local function variable, an argument passed by
  value, or a temporary object for expression evaluation
- by dynamic allocation using the new operator
- as a data member of another object (i.e., as a component object embedded in
  a composite object).

The following example illustrate these possibilities for the class Point:

```
// allocation of class objects
#include "Point.h"
const Point origin(0, 0);      // static definition and initialization of a class instance
int main()
{
   Point pt(1, 1);             // automatic definition and initialization of a class instance
   Point* pPt;                 // automatic allocation of a pointer to class objects
   pPt = new Point(3, 3);      // dynamic allocation and initialization of a class instance
   // rect contains two Point instances that are copies of the initializer arguments
   Rectangle rect(pt, *pPt);
}
```

In evaluating a nested expression, the compiler may need to create a temporary class instance. If a function or operator returns an object by value, and that result is used directly as an argument (rather than being assigned to a variable), that object must exist for the duration of execution of the expression. For example, suppose that class Point has a member function Point::midpoint(const Point&) that returns the midpoint of the line segment between the receiver and the argument. The result is returned by value since it is a new Point object. In the following example, the compiler creates (and then destroys) a temporary anonymous Point object, which is copied from the return value of the invocation of Point::midpoint(), and is the argument of Point::distanceFrom(): [10]

```
// creating a temporary Point object for expression evaluation
#include "Point.h"
int main()
{
   Point pt1(2,5), pt2(4,10), pt3(8, 2);
   double dbl = pt3.distanceFrom(pt1.midpoint(pt2));
}
```

The compiler also creates a temporary object for a cascaded expression in which the first message returns by value. However, if a function returns by reference as Queue::insert() does, the compiler does not create a temporary object because the function returns a reference to an existing object. For example,

```
// no temporary object is created with return by reference
#include "Point.h"
#include "Queue.h"              // with typedef int ElemType;
int main()
{
   Point pt1(2,5), pt2(4,10), pt3(8, 2);
```

[10] A well-designed compiler may not need to allocate a temporary object for a case like this in which there are no references to the temporary object and it has no destructor.

```
    // the temporary object pt1.midpoint(pt2) is the receiver of distanceFrom(pt3)
    double dbl = pt1.midpoint(pt2).distanceFrom(pt3);
    Queue intQu;
    // intQu is the receiver of insert(2)
    intQu.insert(1).insert(2);
}
```

You often must be aware of object lifetimes because C++ ensures that class objects are always initialized upon creation and finalized upon destruction. This initialization and finalization occurs whether the object is static, automatic (including temporary objects and arguments passed by value), dynamic, or embedded in another object as a data member. Initialization is performed by one of a class's constructors, and finalization is performed by its destructor. We will discuss the details of designing and coding these essential member functions in the next section.

Reference and value semantics for identifiers

As we discussed in section 5.4.1, C identifiers use a value representation. When we define a variable or structure member, the object it refers to is directly embedded in the function's stack frame or in a structure instance. A value representation considers a variable to be a container that stores an instance of a given type. In section 5.4.1, we saw that a dynamically typed language cannot support static or automatic object allocation or embedded instance variable values because the size of the referent of an identifier cannot be determined *a priori*. For this reason, all objects are allocated dynamically in Smalltalk and its identifiers have reference semantics. A variable refers to an object, rather than containing an object, and the storage for the variable contains a pointer (an object identifier in Smalltalk), not an object.

The situation is more complex for statically typed object-oriented languages such as C++. An identifier whose type is a built-in type or a class without subclasses can be represented by value because it is monomorphic. However, the compiler cannot determine the size of the referent of a superclass type identifier statically because the referent can be an instance of any of its subclasses. (We will discuss this issue further in section 12.2.) In most object-oriented languages, all identifiers of class type are references (usually implicitly), but built-in types are represented by value. Some, like C++, support both reference and value semantics for identifiers of class type.

In C++, we can declare a variable, parameter, or data member as a value, a pointer, or a reference, whether its type is a built-in type or a class. Pointers and references provide reference semantics. Support for value class objects allows you to use either reference or value semantics for each variable or data member, depending on which meaning is more appropriate for it, so you must understand the issues involved in making this decision. (An alternate perspective is that C++ forces you to make this decision for each class type identifier.)

Generally speaking, a value representation provides more efficient execution and a reference representation allows more flexibility and extendibility. To illustrate the trade-offs, consider the class Point. The reference and value representations of an instance of Point are illustrated in Figure 10.2.

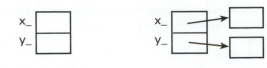

value representation   **reference representation**

Figure 10.2 Representations of an instance of class Point.

The C++ Point class defined in section 10.1.2 uses a value representation in which the instance variables for the x and y coordinates are ints embedded directly in each instance. The instance variables are immediately accessible and point objects use the minimum storage possible. In Smalltalk, the instance variables are references, which allows them to be either integers or floats, depending on the way in which the point instance is used. A reference (or pointer) is polymorphic, which allows dynamic binding of a message sent to that object and extendibility of the code using it. (We will see in section 12.2 that dynamic binding is not possible for value identifiers.) However, access to the referent is slower due to the indirection necessary. In addition, the referent of a reference instance variable must be allocated dynamically, which involves the overhead of execution of a storage management algorithm and extra storage in the object for heap bookkeeping information. The difference in access overhead is greater for composite objects whose instance variables are objects that have instance variables (and so on), such as instances of the class Rectangle. The reference and value representations of an instance of Rectangle are diagrammed in Figure 10.3. With the reference representation, accessing the x coordinate of the top edge of a rectangle requires following two pointers.

There are also differences in semantics between value and reference representations. For example, consider a class Employee that has an instance variable department. If that member only keeps track of an instance's department, we can code it as the value of an enumeration of department codes. Each employee object in a given department has its own copy of that value. On the other hand, if the application model contains a set of Department objects that maintain information about each department, then the department instance variable in an Employee object should be a pointer to the corresponding department object. In this case, all employee objects in a department have pointers to the same department object.

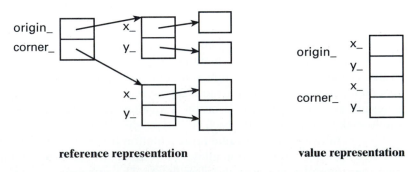

reference representation   **value representation**

Figure 10.3 Representations of an instances of class Rectangle.

That is, a value representation is appropriate when the instance variable is treated as an attribute, but a reference representation better captures the semantics of a relationship with another object that represents an abstraction whose unique identity must be maintained.

Assignments also have different semantics for value and reference variables. With an assignment to a value variable, the variable receives its own independent copy of the object. However, an assignment to a reference variable copies the reference, but not its referent, so both identifiers refer to the same object. With a reference instance variable (i.e., a pointer data member in C++), the class designer can (and must) decide whether the referents are copied by an assignment of the object. For example, when copying an employee object, the referent of the department instance variable should not be copied, so that its identity is preserved for both the source and target objects. In other cases such as the CharStack class defined in section 1.1.4, the referent of a pointer variable should be copied when the object is copied so that each stack object has a separate subobject.

The issue of value versus reference representations has implications for collection classes as well. In C++, the programmer can and must decide whether a collection should contain pointers to elements or element values. If the element objects have identities or if the element type is a class with subclasses (see section 12.2), then the collection should contain pointer elements. In this case, the same object may be an element of several collections. For example with the class Queue, if there are subcategories of the employee class in the model, we would define the element type for a queue of employee objects as typedef Employee* ElemType;. If the elements are treated as values (e.g., if they are instances of a built-in type), inserting an element copies it to a collection's storage structure, and the collection has no reference to the original object. With a value representation of elements, insertion invokes the element type's constructor because it creates a new object within the representation of the collection, and its destructor is called upon deletion because that object is deallocated. The collection's destructor must also invoke the element class's destructor for any remaining elements when the collection object is destroyed.

In coding a particular variable or data member, you should use values whenever possible, for efficiency. Operations involving that object will be faster because all the embedded information is directly available, and all messages to the object can be statically bound. However, when dynamic binding is necessary or the referent of the identifier is an object whose identity must be unique (rather than being copied into each object that refers to it), you should use a pointer or reference. Now, consider the disadvantage of choosing incorrectly for some variable or data member. Choosing a value representation can inhibit the extendibility of your code. If dynamic binding becomes necessary for the object that the identifier refers to, the code must be modified and compiled. If the object is a data member, all clients of the class must also be recompiled. However, using a reference representation unnecessarily results in less efficient execution.

Note also that if reference semantics are called for, the C++ programmer must choose between using a pointer and using a reference. In making this decision, keep in mind that a reference must be initialized and cannot be changed to alias a different object. In this sense, a Smalltalk variable is more like a C++ pointer variable than a C++ reference variable because we can assign it to refer to a different object, although in Smalltalk, dereferencing the variable is implicit and the object identifier is not directly accessible. Dynamic binding is possible for both pointers and references in C++.

10.2.2 Constructors

Purpose

In traditional programming languages, a special function must be invoked explicitly to properly initialize a complex data object before using it, as illustrated in section 1.1.4. Many programming errors are caused by using an object before it is initialized, forgetting to invoke an initialization function, or invoking it more than once. C++ includes a special feature to ensure that these problems do not occur for class objects. A *constructor* is a member function that initializes a new instance of the class. The constructor for a class is responsible for initializing the object's data members, obtaining any system resources the object needs, and performing any other side effects associated with creation of the object. In Smalltalk, instantiation is performed by a class method, while initialization is done by an instance method invoked by that class method. In C++, static or automatic allocation or the new operation perform instantiation, and the class constructor initializes the new object.

A constructor is executed whenever a class instance is created, whether by a static definition, an automatic definition, or through the use of the new operator.[11] Implicit invocation of constructors provides automatic guaranteed initialization of instances of the class, and removes the possibility of client initialization errors. The compiler also invokes a constructor for temporary objects and value data members of class type. Invocation of a constructor for the new class instance is the major advantage of the C++ new operator over the C malloc() function. Essentially, new returns a type-correct pointer to a valid object, while malloc() returns a void* pointer to a region of storage.

Dynamically allocated memory is the system resource most frequently needed by an object, for example, for a variable size object such as a set or a graph. However, a constructor can do much more than setting data members and allocating memory. For example, creation of a file stream object requires obtaining a file descriptor from the operating system and allocating buffers for blocking and unblocking data. A constructor can obtain or register the object with other system-managed resources such as network connections, interprocess communication mechanisms, threads, window handles, or fonts. The constructor for an object whose activity must be logged can initiate a database transaction. We might need

---

[11] We will see in section 11.1.3 that the constructor is not called when an identifier is assigned an object value.

to keep an index of the instances of a particular class, and its constructor can enter each new object into the index. In the next section, we will see that the class designer can define a destructor for the class in each of these cases so that these effects are undone automatically when the object is deallocated. Implicit invocation of constructors and destructors relieves the clients of a class from having to deal with the resources and side effects necessary to implement the class's functionality, and provides looser coupling between a class and its clients. This makes classes easier to use, and makes it easier for the class designer to control the resources used by a class's instances, and to re-implement the class if necessary.

Definition

We define a constructor as a member function whose name is the same as that of the class. Unlike other functions, a constructor does not specify a return type nor explicitly return a value. Let us review the constructors we saw in sections 10.1.2 and 10.1.3. Point::Point sets the x_ and y_ values of a new instance, Queue::Queue() initializes the front and back pointers of the new instance to NULL, and Node::Node() sets the elem member to its argument and sets the next member to NULL. Of course, it is the class designer's responsibility to ensure that every data member of the new object is given a meaningful value in each of the class's constructors. For many classes, the constructor is overloaded or provides default arguments to support a range of initialization options, as illustrated by the class String in the next paragraph.

Constructors for classes whose instances vary in size often allocate storage on the heap, which is referred to by a pointer data member. A number of special considerations are necessary for such classes. A common example is a String class with five overloadings of the constructor, as follows:

```
// String.h: interface for a class for variable-length character strings (#ifndef, etc. omitted)
// four public constructors are provided for clients
#include <string.h> // to use C standard library functions

class String
{
public:
    String();                   // initialize to an empty string
    String(char);               // initialize to a one-character string
    String(const char*);        // copy referent of the argument to a new subobject on the heap
    String(const String&);      // copy an existing String object (see section 10.2.5)
    ~String();                  // destructor, defined in the next section

    int length();               // return the number of characters in the receiver
    int indexOf(char);          // return the position of the argument in the receiver
    bool isSubstring(const String&);// is the argument a substring of the receiver?
    // return the concatenation of the argument and the receiver
    String concat(const String &);
    // ... other member functions ...
```

```
protected:
   String(int length);         // protected incomplete constructor for efficiency
   char* str_;
   int length_;
};

inline String::String(char ch)
{
   length_ = 1;
   str_ = new char[2];
   str_[0] = ch;
   str_[1] = '\0';              // null-terminated to use string.h functions in member functions
}

inline String::String(const char* argString)
{
   length_ = strlen(argString);
   // make a private copy of the argument string
   str_ = new char[length_ + 1];
   strcpy(str_, argString);
}
```

We make a copy of the argument string in String::String(const char*) because the client is responsible for allocation for the original character array, and because the new String instance is an independent object that should not be affected by changes to the client's object. These constructors (and the destructor defined in the next section) provide loose coupling between the class and clients that use the class for instantiation or composition because clients do not have to be concerned with storage allocation for the internal structure of string objects. This is the responsibility of the String class. We code these constructor definitions in the class header file so that the compiler can inline them. Because we can define constructors in the code file, a function name encoding scheme must also handle these functions.

As another example, we can implement a class Set as a dynamic array with data members for the number of elements, the actual size of the array, and a pointer to an array of elements allocated on the heap, like the class CharStack illustrated in Figure 1.4. We can place elements in the array as they arrive or position them by hashing. When the array is full upon an insertion, we allocate a larger array, copy the elements into the new array, and deallocate the old array (as in CharStack::grow() in section 1.1.4). The constructor allocates the initial array, sets the number of elements to 0, and sets the actual size of the array (like CharStack::initialize() in section 1.1.4).

Constructors may be defined with any access specification, but are typically public. A protected constructor may only be used by the member and friend functions of the class. For example, the class Node in section 10.1.3 has a protected constructor so that its friend class Queue is the only class that can create instances. We can also use a nonpublic constructor to perform partial initialization of a new object created in one of the class's methods, which is completed by that method before it returns the object to the client. For example, the class String includes the protected constructor String::String(int) for efficiency in methods that create a new string object, such as String::concat() and String::substring(). It sets the new object's length_ member and allocates a character array, but does not fill it. The member function code places the necessary characters in the array. String::String(int) and String::concat() are defined as follows:

```
// use of a nonpublic constructor
inline String::String(int size)
{
    length_ = size;
    str_ = new char[length_ + 1];
    // the member function must fill the character array
}

String::concat(const String& argString)
{
    String retString(length_ + argString.length_);
    strcpy(retString.str_, str_);
    strcat(retString.str_, argString.str_);
    return retString;
}
```

Without the partial constructor, the definition of the local object retString would have no initializer and the String default constructor would be invoked. Using this technique avoids creating a new empty string object, deallocating its dynamic array, and then allocating a new array of the correct size.

Invocation of constructors

When creating an object, the initializer gives the constructor arguments. The initializer is a parenthesized list of expressions that follows the identifier name for static and automatic definitions, or the class name with new. An object can only be created according to the initializations provided by the designer of the class. If the object's class does not define a constructor whose argument signature matches that of the initializer, the compiler signals an error (unless the class designer has not defined any constructor at all). With a static or automatic variable, a single constructor argument may follow an = symbol (i.e., the argument appears like an initial value in C), or a list of arguments may be given as = *Class*(...). The following examples illustrate the initialization syntax:

```
// constructor argument syntax for initialization
#include "Point.h"
#include "String.h"
int main()
{
```

```
    Point pt1(1, 1);                      // two-argument constructor invoked
    Point pt2 = Point(2, 2);              // alternate syntax for two-argument constructor
    Point pt3(3);                         // error: no constructor to match the initializer
    String str1('@');                     // one-argument constructor invoked
    String str2 = "hello";                // one-argument constructor, not an assignment
    Point* pPoint = new Point(3, 3);      // two-argument constructor, dynamic allocation
    String* pStr = new String("world");   // one-argument constructor, dynamic allocation
}
```

Strictly speaking, the second declaration in the previous example creates an unnamed temporary Point object and then copies it into pt2, although the compiler will recognize that the temporary is unnecessary in this case. Figure 10.4 illustrates the storage structure that results from these declarations (the dotted rectangles around the String objects indicate that both regions of storage are treated as a single object logically and that the use of dynamic memory for these objects is not known to the client main()).

Constructors provide coherent initialization of class objects. In C or Pascal, we would initialize a dynamic composite object such as the referent of pPoint in the previous example with a series of assignments to its components. The constructor

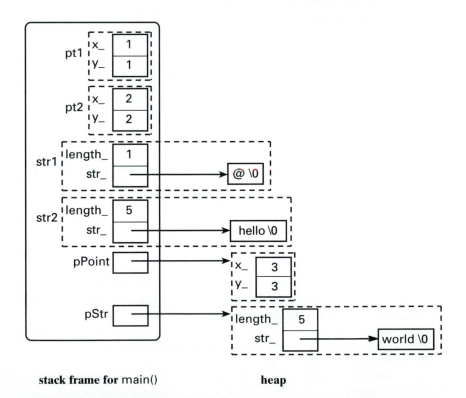

stack frame for main()   **heap**

Figure 10.4 Storage diagram for automatic and dynamic class instances.

for an object is executed immediately after it is allocated. With new, the constructor is not invoked if allocation fails.

    We can also invoke a constructor explicitly to create an object, perhaps as a
temporary object in an expression. This feature provides a literal notation for
anonymous class objects. For example,

```
// explicit invocation of a constructor to create an anonymous class instance
#include "Point.h"
int main()
{
    Point pt(1,1);
    double dbl = pt.distanceFrom(Point(5,5));
}
```

Explicit creation of an anonymous object is often used in the return statement of a
member function that returns a new object. For example, the following definition
implements the member function Point::midpoint() described in the previous section:

```
// the constructor is invoked to create the return value
inline Point Point::midpoint(const Point& argPoint)
{
    return Point( (x_ + argPoint.x_) / 2, (y_ + argPoint.y_) / 2);
}
```

Note that Point::midpoint() returns the new Point object by value so that it does not
return a reference to the temporary object that will be deallocated when it exits. If
you are concerned about efficiency (and who isn't?), you should know that the compiler can avoid creating anonymous objects that are immediately copied to another
object. For example, in the expression distanceFrom(Point(5,5)), the compiler can
create the object Point(5,5) directly on the stack where it will be passed to Point::dis-
tanceFrom(). It can do the same with the return object of Point::midpoint() for
expressions such as distanceFrom(pt1.midpoint(pt2)), especially since that member
function is inline.

    Because a constructor is invoked immediately after an object is created, the
constructors for static objects are executed before main() begins execution. (The
fact that a function can be called before main() seems strange at first.) A class
library or framework can use this fact to create an environment in which client programs execute. The library defines a static object (in a code file) whose constructor
performs the necessary setup. The object's destructor, which is invoked after main()
completes execution, finalizes the environment. For example, the iostream class
library uses this technique to ensure that the objects cout, cin, cerr, and clog are created before client code begins execution.

    Statically and automatically allocated arrays of class objects must also be ini-
tialized. The array declaration is followed by an = symbol and a list of initializers
enclosed in braces, as follows:

```
// initializing array elements of class type
#include "String.h"
String arrStr[3] = { String("hello"), "world", String('!') };
```

We will discuss initialization of dynamic arrays of objects in the next subsection.

The default constructor

A *default constructor* is a constructor with an empty parameter list, as defined in the classes Point, Queue, and String. It is a "default" in the sense that the compiler invokes it when the client does not give an initializer for a new object. Generally, the default constructor initializes the new object to a default state that is valid for that kind of object so that the new object can respond to the class's protocol correctly. For example, the default constructor for String initializes an object to the empty string:

```
// the default constructor initializes the new object to an empty string
inline String::String()
{
    length_ = 0;
    str_ = new char[1];        // [1] because the destructor uses delete [ ]
    str_[0] = '\0';
}
```

If a client needs to define a string object but does not know what its value is, he or she uses the default constructor so that the object has a valid state and can respond to String protocol. A constructor that has default values for all of its arguments also supplies a default constructor.

The default constructor is invoked when the programmer does not supply constructor arguments for an instantiation. You should not use parentheses in a static or automatic definition that invokes the default constructor. If parentheses follow the identifier name, the compiler will interpret the statement as a function declaration with an empty argument signature and a class return type.[12]

```
// parentheses are not used with initialization by the default constructor
#include "String.h"
String emptyStr;       // define a static object with a default constructor invoked
String emptyStr();     // function declaration (error together with the previous statement)
```

When creating a dynamic object, the parentheses are optional after the class name with new. If no initializer is given and the class does not define a default constructor, the instantiation results in a compile-time error because a constructor must be invoked whenever creating a class object. For example, the class Node does not define a default constructor, so the following would be an error:

---

[12] This syntactic inconsistency occurs because the ( ) operator is used for both initialization and function declaration, and because C and C++ do not identify function declarations with a reserved word.

```
                  // a default constructor is required if no initializer is given
                  Queue& Queue::insert(const ElemType& el)
                  {
                      Node node;          // error: there is no Node::Node() with no arguments
                      // ... function code ...
                  }
```

The compiler will create a default constructor for a class only if the class designer defines no constructors at all (which is poor practice because it defeats the language's support for automatic initialization). However, the compiler-generated default constructor does not initialize the class's data members, so the class behaves like a C structure.

The default constructor is necessary for a definition of a const object for which no initializer is given because a const identifier must be initialized (see the definition of origin in section 10.1.2). It is also required when creating an array of class instances dynamically with the new [] operator because there is no syntax for providing a series of initializers. For example,

```
// the default constructor is required for dynamic arrays
#include "String.h"
#include "Rectangle.h"                   // Rectangle does not define a default constructor
String* pArrStr = new String[20];       // all 20 objects are initialized to empty strings
Rectangle* pArrRect = new Rectangle[4]; // error
```

10.2.3 Destructors

Purpose

A *destructor* member function provides automatic finalization of objects. The destructor specifies any clean up of the environment necessary when an instance of that class is destroyed. For example, the member function CharStack::release() defined in section 1.1.4 should be defined as a destructor. Examples of destructor operations include

- deallocating the referent of a pointer member allocated by a constructor
- deallocating the nodes in a linked structure
- flushing a buffer and closing a file
- releasing system resources such as network connections or window handles
- erasing a graphic object from the display
- committing a database transaction
- removing the object from an index
- removing dependencies involving the object.

Essentially, the constructor initializes an object and obtains the system resources it needs, and the destructor releases those resources at the end of the object's lifetime. That is, the destructor finalizes the state and representation of the object. Usually, classes such as Point and Rectangle that only contain value data members do not require a destructor.

If an object's class defines a destructor, it is invoked implicitly when the object is deallocated. As we stated in the last section, automatic invocation of constructors and destructors relieves clients from having to deal with the resources necessary for a class's instances. For example, the class ofstream represents output file streams. It has a constructor that takes arguments for the file name and mode, and opens the file, sets up buffers, and so on. The destructor flushes buffers and closes the file. In C++, the user of this class need not be concerned with these details.

```cpp
// the client is not involved in resources allocation for the ofstream
#include <iostream.h>
#include <fstream.h>          // for file streams
#include "Database.h"
void createReport(Database& db)
{
    ofstream reportFile("report.txt", ios::out);      // ofstream constructor invoked
    if ( !reportFile )
    {
        cerr << "Opening report.txt failed" << endl;
        exit(1);
    }
    // ... reportFile << useful information ...
}                                                       // ofstream destructor invoked
```

Definition

We define a destructor as a member function whose name is the class name preceded by the tilde symbol ~ (i.e., it is the "complement" of the constructor). A destructor cannot take arguments or be overloaded, and does not give a return type or return a value. We code the destructor for the class String as follows:

```cpp
// the String destructor deallocates the subobject on the heap
inline String::~String()
{
    delete [ ] str_;
}
```

The destructor for the class Queue deallocates any nodes that remain when an instance is deallocated. It is coded as follows (we use the cast to void because Queue::remove() returns an ElemType):

```cpp
// the Queue destructor deallocates any remaining nodes
Queue::~Queue()
{
    while ( !isEmpty() )
        (void) remove();
}
```

These examples illustrate the most common use of destructors, that of deallocating the referents of pointer members to avoid a memory leak. This would not be necessary if C++ supported automatic storage deallocation, but destructors would still be useful to prevent other kinds of "resource leaks".

Invocation

The destructor for an object's class is invoked automatically just before deallocating the object, no matter what allocation policy was used to create the object. The destructor is executed when an object on the heap is deleted, when a scope containing an automatic object is exited, or immediately before program termination for static objects. For example,

```
// the destructor is invoked with delete
#include "String.h"
int func()
{
    String str("hello");
    String* pStr = new String("world");
    // String::~String is invoked to deallocate pStr->str_, and then *pStr is deallocated
    delete pStr;
}           //  String::~String is invoked to deallocate str.str_, and then func() exits
```

Figure 10.5 illustrates how deallocation is done for this example.

A destructor is not invoked when a pointer is deallocated or a reference goes out of scope because the object itself is not deallocated. You must use **delete** with a dynamic object such as *pStr in the previous example to ensure that its destructor is called.

An expression can create a temporary object whose class has a destructor, and that destructor must be invoked implicitly. For example,

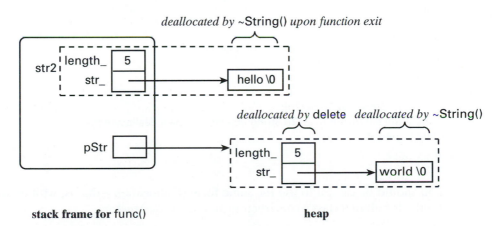

Figure 10.5   Storage diagram illustrating destructor invocation.

```
// temporary objects whose classes define destructors
#include "String.h"
int main()
{
    String str1("hello");
    String str2(", there");
    // an explicit temporary string object
    bool test = str1.isSubstring(String("ell"));
    // an implicit temporary string object
    cout << str1.concat(str2) << endl;
}
```

The ANSI/ISO C++ Standard committee had extensive discussions about when the destructor for a temporary object should be executed. The last possible time would be just before the function containing the expression returns, like an automatic object. However, several committee members felt that this policy would result in unnecessary overhead, so the standard states that the destructor is invoked just after the top-level expression or statement containing the temporary object.

If the class designer uses a class with a destructor as the type of a data member, he or she should not have to be concerned with the finalization necessary for that class's instances. For example, the designer of a class with a String data member should not deal with deallocation of referent of the str_ member of the data member value. C++ ensures that destructors for data members are invoked when such a composite object is deallocated, whether its class defines a destructor or not. If the composite class requires a destructor, that member function need not (and should not) include the code that finalizes class's components or invoke their destructors explicitly.

If we create a dynamically allocated array of objects, using delete with a pointer to the array only calls the destructor for the first element of the array. To invoke the destructor for each member of the array, we must use the delete [] operator.

```
// use of delete [ ] with dynamic arrays of objects
#include "String.h"
int main()
{
    String* pArrStr = new String[20];
    // apply the destructor to all 20 String objects and then deallocate the array
    delete [ ] pArrStr;
}
```

You should be careful to use the same form of allocation—that is, with or without the []—for all of a class's constructors and for its destructor.

10.2.4 The Constructor Initialization List

Composite classes

Many classes have data members whose types are programmer-defined classes. This occurs in composition relationships, and in situations in which a class is implemented using instances of another class in its internal structure. We refer to the containing class as a *composite class*. The storage structure of a composite class object has instances of the classes of its data members embedded within it. When an instance of the composite class is created, these objects must also be created and initialized according to their classes' constructors. Furthermore, the designer of the composite class should not need to know the details of the operation of those constructors. By providing a feature for invoking data member constructors in a class's constructor, C++ provides better support for transparent reuse of existing classes for composition.

As an example, let us define a composite class `Person` with four data members: two String members `name_` and `address_`, a Date member `birthday_` and a long member `ssn_`. The class `Person` is defined as follows:

```
// Person.h: a composite class with three data members of class type
#include "String.h"
#include "Date.h"

class Person
{
public:
    Person(const char* name, const char* address,
            const char* month, int day, int year, long ssn);
    Person(const char* name, const char* address, const Date& birthdate, long ssn);
    // ... other member functions ...
protected:
    String name_;
    String address_;
    const Date birthdate_;
    const long ssn_;
};
```

Figure 10.6 diagrams the storage structure for an instance of `Person` (we assume that an instance of `Date` is represented by two int data members giving the day in the year and the year).

To provide loose coupling and information hiding, the language needs a mechanism that enables the designer of the class `Person` to specify the initialization of `Person` objects without having to deal with the details of initializing the embedded `String` and `Date` objects.

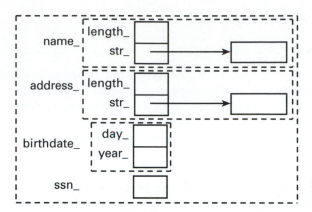

Figure 10.6 Storage diagram for a composite Person object.

Constructing class type data members

C++ includes a special syntactic construct for invoking data member's constructors in the composite class constructor, and for passing arguments to those constructors. The function header of a composite class constructor definition is followed by a colon and an *initialization list* that precedes the constructor body. Each entry in the initialization list gives a data member name followed by an initializer for that member, and each data member may only appear once in the list. The initializer for a member may be either a list of arguments to a constructor for its class, or an object of that class. Data members that are instances of built-in types or pointers may also appear in the initialization list, and are initialized with the value given. We give the initialization list in the constructor definition, rather than in its declaration, because it is part of defining the operation of the constructor. The constructors for the class Person are coded as follows:

```
// the constructor initialization list is specified in the constructor definition
// we assume that there is a constructor Date::Date(const char*, int, int)
inline Person::Person(const char* name, const char* address,
                      const char* month, int day, int year, long ssn)
    : name_(name), address_(address), birthdate_(month, day, year), ssn_(ssn)
{
    // ... any other setup for Person instances, e.g. adding the new object
    // to a ssn index stored as a Person class variable ...
}

inline Person::Person(const char* name, const char* address, const Date& bdate, long ssn)
    : name_(name), address_(address), birthdate_(bdate), ssn_(ssn)
{
    // ... any other setup for Person instances, e.g. adding the new object
    // to a ssn index stored as a Person class variable ...
}
```

Recall from the previous section that the class Person does not require a destructor if creation of an instance does not cause any side effects, because the compiler invokes the String destructor for the `name_` and `address_` data members automatically whenever a Person object is deallocated.

The initialization list provides looser coupling between classes because the designer of the class Person does not need to know the details of the representations of the classes String and Date. The designers of those classes are responsible for those storage structures and the manner in which they are initialized and finalized. If a class requires dynamic subobjects or any other resource allocation, that resource management should not be the responsibility of a client that uses the class for composition.

Let us reconsider the class Node we defined in section 10.1.3. Because the actual type typedef'd to ElemType can be a class, we should code the constructor for Node using the initialization list for the data member elem, as follows:[13]

```
// a constructor for class Node that supports a class as the ElemType
inline Node::Node(const ElemType& el)
    : elem(el), next(NULL)
{ }
```

Constructors such as this one that only perform initializations and have no code body are quite common. We will discuss the constructor that makes a copy of the argument el in the next section.

The identifiers in the data member initializers are usually arguments of the composite class's constructor, as in these examples. In general, an initializer argument can be an expression including literals or any names that are visible at the point of the composite constructor definition.

If a data member's class defines a default constructor, the class designer can omit that member from the initialization list, and the default constructor will be invoked to initialize it. All other class type data members must appear in the initialization list for each overloading of the constructor. If some class type data member is not listed and its class does not define a default constructor, a compiler error will result. For example, it would not be an error to write the first Person constructor as follows because String has a default constructor:

```
// inefficient version of Person::Person()
inline Person::Person(const char* name, const char* address,
                      const char* month, int day, int year, long ssn)
    : birthdate_(month, day, year), ssn_(ssn)
{
    // uses String::operator=(), which is covered in section 11.1.3
    name_ = name;
    address_ = address;
    // ... other setup ...
}
```

---

[13] Built-in type data members can be assigned values within the body of the constructor rather than using the initialization list. To be consistent, we will use the initialization list for all data member initializations.

However, this definition is very inefficient because it performs unnecessary dynamic allocation and deallocation. String's default constructor is invoked for the data members name_ and address_ as they are not included in the initialization list, so that subobjects are created for them. Then in the constructor body, the objects name and address are copied into the members name_ and address_ (i.e., assignments are performed). We will see in section 11.1.3 that the class String must define an assignment operator that deallocates the subobject of the target object and then creates a copy of the right-hand side operand's subobject for the target. Clearly, it is more efficient to construct the name_ and address_ data members directly. If String had no default constructor, this coding of Person::Person() would be invalid because it does not give any initialization for the name_ and address_ member objects.

Initializing const members

Because we cannot assign a value to a const object, we must use the initialization list to give values for const data members such as birthdate_ and ssn_. (We cannot initialize a const data member in the class definition because no object is created at that point and different instances can have different values.) The same requirement holds for data members that are references: They must be initialized via the initialization list, as they cannot be assigned.

The initialization list allows the class designer to specify an immutable data member. The data member is declared as a const protected member and initialized from a constructor argument via the initialization list, and the class defines no member functions that modify that member.

Order of constructor execution

Execution of a constructor consists of initialization of the data members according to the initialization list, followed by the start-up processing in the body of the constructor. That is, the data members' constructors are always executed before the body of the composite class constructor. If a data member that is a class instance also has class type data members the rule is applied recursively, so the "most embedded" objects are constructed first.

Normally, the order of execution of the class data member constructors is not important, but a constructor may cause a side effect that affects the operation of another constructor. The order of the initialization list does not determine a unique ordering because a data member that defines a default constructor might not appear on the list. Instead, the data member constructors are invoked in the order in which the member names appear in the class definition.

The order for calling the destructors for composite class objects is the reverse of the order of constructors. The destructor for the composite class is called first, those of its immediate data members are executed next, and so on.

10.2.5 The Copy Constructor

Implicit copying of objects by the compiler

There are three cases in which the compiler implicitly creates a copy of an existing object. When an object identifier is initialized with an instance of its type (e.g., int num1 = num2;), that object is copied into the new variable. The second case of implicit copying occurs when an object is passed by value to a function: The initial value of the corresponding local variable is copied from the argument. Similarly, when a function returns an object value, it is copied into a variable or temporary object in the caller. Pass and return by a reference do not result in an object initialization because the compiler does not create a copy of the argument or return value.

In C++, a constructor must be executed whenever a class instance is created. A class object can be initialized with an instance of its type, whether it is a static, automatic, or dynamic object, and a value data member can be initialized via an initialization list. For example,

```
// initialization by copying an existing object
#include "Point.h"
Point pt1(3, 3);
Point pt2(pt1);        // or, equivalently, Point pt2 = pt1;
// Rectangle::Rectangle(const Point&, const Point&) initializes its Point data members
// in its initialization list
Rectangle rect(pt1, Point(7, 7));
```

The second definition creates a new Point object referred to by pt2. In the third definition, the constructor arguments are copied into the storage for the object rect. A class object can also be passed or returned by value, and the result must be initialized by a constructor. In each of these three cases, the new object is initialized by an implicitly invoked *copy constructor*.

The default copy constructor

The compiler's *default copy constructor* performs a member-by-member initialization from the source object. It takes a const reference to an instance of the class, its initialization list initializes each data member of the receiver from the corresponding data member of the argument, and its body is empty. For example, the default copy constructor for the class Rectangle described in section 10.2.1 would be coded as follows:

```
// the default constructor for the class Rectangle
Rectangle::Rectangle(const Rectangle& argRect)
    : origin_(argRect.origin_), corner_(argRect.corner_)
{ }
```

If a data member of the object being created is a class instance, it is also initialized by memberwise initialization. For example, Rectangle::Rectangle(const Rectangle&) calls the default copy constructor Point::Point(const Point&) twice. We refer to this copy constructor as the "default" copy constructor because the compiler generates it when the class designer does not define a copy constructor.[14]

The copy constructor argument must be passed by reference because pass by value uses the copy constructor, so a value argument would cause an infinite recursion of copy constructor invocations. The parameter of the default copy constructor will be const as long as the copy constructors for all the data members can take a const parameter. The default copy constructor is always public, and cannot be generated if a data member's class only has nonpublic constructors.

The programmer-defined copy constructor

The default copy constructor is correct for a class such as Point whose data members are values directly embedded in the storage structure of an instance. However, it presents problems with a class such as String that contains a pointer member, allocates a dynamic subobject in the constructor, and deallocates the subobject in its destructor. Consider the following example:

```
// problems with default copy constructor with dynamic subobjects
#include "String.h"
void func()
{
    String str1("hello");
    String str2 = str1;        // both str1.str_ and str2.str_ refer to the same subobject
    // ... other processing ...
}                              // the destructors for both str1 and str2 are invoked
```

Upon initializing the automatic variable str2, the default copy constructor copies the pointer value str1.str_ to str2.str_, so both objects contain pointer members referring to the same region of memory, as illustrated in Figure 10.7.

In this case, str1 and str2 are not independent, self-contained objects. A mod-

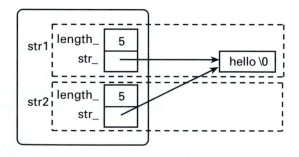

stack frame for func()   **heap**

Figure 10.7 Effect of the default copy constructor on instances of String.

---

[14] This terminology is a bit confusing because the default copy constructor is not a default constructor, nor is it written by the class designer, like the default constructor.

ification to str1 affects str2 (and vice versa), and can leave str2 in an inconsistent state (i.e., if it changes the length of str1). In addition, when func() exits, the destructor String::~String() is executed for both objects, deleting the char array on the heap twice. This typically corrupts the heap's data structure for keeping track of free space, eventually resulting in a run-time error whose cause is very difficult to determine. Consider also what would occur with the default copy constructor if the two string objects are not destroyed at the same time. When one object is destroyed, the dynamic subobject is deallocated by its destructor, but the other object's str_ member still points to that storage. Now the second object contains a reference to storage on the free list that might then be reallocated to another object, again causing effects that will be difficult to trace (or even reproduce).

The same problem occurs with the implicit copying performed when a function argument is passed by value.

```
// problems with the default copy constructor when an object with a dynamic subobject
// is passed by value
#include "String.h"
bool hasVowels(String argStr);
int main()
{
    String str("hello");
    // the str data members are copied to the local argStr object by the compiler
    // the destructor for argStr is invoked upon function exit
    bool wordTest = hasVowels(str);
    // str.str_ now points to a deleted subobject
}
```

Because the destructor is invoked for argStr upon exit from the function hasVowels(), str.str_ is left pointing to storage on the free list.

The solution is for the class designer to provide a copy constructor with the declaration *Class*(const *Class*&) that implements the correct behavior. That is, the class designer is responsible for providing semantically correct copying of instances. For a class such as String with a pointer member and a dynamic subobject, the copy constructor creates a new copy of the dynamic subobject for the target so that each object has its own subobject. In Smalltalk terms, copying requires a constructor that performs a "deep copy" of the object that copies the referents of pointer data members. The copy constructor initializes value data members from the corresponding members of the argument (there are no value instance variables in Smalltalk). If the class designer defines a copy constructor, the compiler invokes it for every initialization of an instance of the class from another.

We define the copy constructor for the class String as follows (recall that the protected str_ member of argStr is accessible within the String scope):[15]

---

[15] Note that we must use argStr.length_ + 1 rather than length_ + 1 as the size of the new char array because the str_ member is initialized first as it appears first in the class definition.

```
// the copy constructor for class String
#include <string.h>                          // for strcpy()
inline String::String(const String& argStr)
   : length_(argStr.length_), str_(new char[argStr.length_ + 1])
{
   strcpy(str_, argStr.str_);
}
```

With this copy constructor definition, the initialization of str2 in func() results in the storage layout in Figure 10.8 rather than that of Figure 10.7.

As another example, consider the class Queue defined in sections 10.1.3 and 10.1.4. If we initialize a variable of type Queue with an existing instance of that class, we want the new object to contain its own copy of the linked list. If the default copy constructor is used, only the pointers are copied, and a remove() operation on one queue will leave the front member of the other pointing to storage on the free list. We would define copy constructor Queue::Queue(const Queue&), which initializes the target object to an empty queue and then inserts each element of the source queue object.

In general, the class designer uses the copy constructor to deal with system resources or side effects necessary for creation of the new object. When an instance of a class requires a system resource that cannot be shared, the copy constructor allocates it for the new object. If a resource can be shared, the copy constructor registers the new object with that resource. A copy constructor is also necessary if an object contains history information that must be reset rather than copied to the new object. It is not always true that the copy constructor should copy the referent of a pointer data member. Whether this is necessary depends on the semantics of that member. For example, if the where data member in each Square object representing an object on a given Canvas points to the same instance of Canvas, then the Square copy constructor should not copy that object. In any case, the copy constructor feature allows the class designer to overload the initialization operation

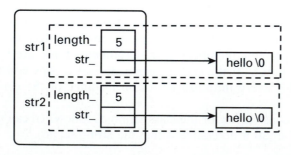

stack frame for func()   heap

Figure 10.8 Effect of the programmer-defined copy constructor on instances of String.

with the behavior required for the class. Most classes that have destructors require a copy constructor.

In some cases, it is semantically correct to prevent copying of a class's instances, for example, if each object must have a unique identity. The class designer can accomplish this by declaring a nonpublic copy constructor. In this case, a statement that specifies copying an instance results in a compile-time error. In fact, the class designer need not define that copy constructor as it can never be invoked.

Now that we have discussed what copying a complex object can involve, we can see the importance of using reference parameters and return types, especially const reference parameters. A String value parameter such as that in the function hasVowels() in the previous example could involve copying a large array of characters, even though creating the copy is not necessary for the function's task. Passing instances of variable-size classes, such as collections or classes, that require system resources by value also can cause a great deal of unnecessary overhead. Similarly, return by reference avoids invocation of a copy constructor for the return value and a destructor for the object local to the function. (Remember from our discussion of Point::midpoint() in section 10.2.2 that the compiler can also avoid invoking this copy constructor and destructor if a new object returned by value is an anonymous object created in the return statement.)

Copy constructors for composite classes

Suppose that a composite class does not define a copy constructor, but the class of one of its data members does. In this case, the composite class's default copy constructor uses the copy constructor of the data member's class to initialize that member. That is, we can think of the default copy constructor as having the correct initialization list (as indicated by the format given at the beginning of this section). For example, the compiler creates the following copy constructor for the class Person defined in the previous section:

```
// the default copy constructor for class Person
Person::Person(const Person& argPers)
  : name_(argPers.name_), address_(argPers.address_),
    birthdate_(argPers.birthdate_), ssn_(argPers.ssn_)
{ }
```

If there is no "other setup" in the constructor body for Person, then Person does not require a programmer-defined copy constructor because the compiler invokes those for String and Date for its members. Again, the designer of the composite class is not responsible for the resources needed by classes used for composition. However, if you define a copy constructor for a composite class, you must be sure to include the class type data members in that constructor's initialization list so that the members' copy constructors are invoked, rather than their default copy constructors.

10.3 CLASS SCOPE

10.3.1 Characteristics of Class Scope

Nesting and declarations

Each class maintains its own named scope, which is nested within the global scope of the program (except for nested and derived classes as described in sections 10.3.4 and 12.1.2). As with a function definition, the class name is declared in the global scope, and its member names are local to its scope. Member function definitions are nested within the scope of their class, and may contain executable statements. An object or function at file scope with the same name as a class member is hidden within the class, but may be accessed within class methods with the unary scope operator.

Like file scope, only declaration statements may appear in class scope. Unlike file or function scope variables, which are not visible until their declarations have occurred, the members of a class are visible throughout the class's scope, no matter where they are declared in the class definition.

Member function scope

Each member function name is defined at class scope, and each member function defines its own local scope for its parameters and local variables, which is nested within the scope of its class. Member function scopes have the same characteristics as all function scopes, for example, local object definitions can appear at any point. The usual identifier resolution procedure for static scope applies to statements in member function scopes. The compiler searches for the declaration corresponding to an identifier use beginning in the scope containing that use, and continuing through the series of enclosing scopes. An identifier use is resolved to a particular declaration by the identifier name, and only then are the accessibility and type compatibility checked. If a class member name is hidden within a member function of that class by a local variable, the method can use a qualified name to access it.

A file scope function or member function of another class that has the same name as a class's member function does not overload that member function. The functions are not defined within the same scope, that is, one function is visible in one scope and the other is visible in another. In a message expression *obj.msg*(...), the class of the receiver *obj* determines the scope examined in searching for a definition of the member function *msg*(). We cannot invoke a member function using the scope operator and class name (and no object) outside the class because there is no indication which instance of the class is the receiver. When such a qualified name is used within a member function of the class, the receiver is the receiver of that method.

Because each class defines a scope and all objects of that class share that scope, a method may refer to any member of an instance of its class, no matter what the access specification of that member is. In particular, if a member function argument is of the same class as the receiver, that function can access the argument's nonpublic members with component selection. Accessing nonpublic members is illustrated by the expression argPt.x_ in the definition of Point::distanceFrom() in section 10.1.2. That is, the unit of encapsulation in C++ is the class (in contrast to Smalltalk, for which it is the individual object).[16] For this reason, we often had to define private methods in Smalltalk for use by methods that must access the argument's instance variables (e.g., the = method for class Queue in section 6.1.2 and for PriorityQueue in section 6.2.2). This is not necessary in C++.

A class scope example

The following example illustrates class scope relationships (the statements are numbered so we can refer to them):[17]

```
// nesting of class and function scopes

int num;        // global scope
void func();

class Class      // the name Class is declared at file scope
{                // begin class scope Class::, which is nested within file scope
public:
  // this occurrence of the name func is declared in the class scope Class::
  void func(int arg)
  {
    // local function scope of Class::func()
    char ch;
    // num data member in the receiver (OK even though declared later)
    /* 1 */   num = arg;
    // num data member in the receiver
    /* 2 */   Class::num = arg;
    // global num
    /* 3 */   ::num = 1;
    // error: we cannot use the scope operator with a function name
    /* 4 */   func::num = 0;
    // local variable of Class::func()
    /* 5 */   ch = '3';
    // ch data member in the receiver (hidden by local ch)
    /* 6 */   Class::ch = 3;
    // error: func() with no arguments is hidden by Class::func(int)
    /* 7 */   func();
```

---

[16] Recall that Smalltalk has no syntax for referring to another object's instance variables, even those in an instance of the same class.

[17] Each of these name reuses is questionable practice with respect to code readability, and we do this here only to illustrate the characteristics of class scope.

```
                      // OK: invoke file scope func()
                      /* 8 */   ::func();
                  }
            protected:
                int num;
                int ch;
            };                    // end class scope Class::

            void func()   // this use of the name func() is declared at file scope
            {
                // local function scope of func()
                long num = 3;
                /* 9 */     int num1 = ::num;     // global num
                /* 10 */    Class::func(num);      // error: which receiver?
                Class cl;
                /* 11 */    cl.func(num);          // OK
            }
```

First, consider the statements in Class::func(). The member function Class::func() can use the data member name num in statement 1 even though its declaration occurs later in the class. A qualified name is not necessary as the function is within the class scope (although it could be used without error as in statement 2). Even though the global num is hidden by the data member num, Class::func() can access it as ::num as in statement 3. The local variable num within the file scope function func() cannot be accessed in this way in statement 4 because the scope operator cannot be used with function names.[18] When the unqualified name ch appears within Class::func() as in statement 5, it refers to the local variable of that member function. The hidden data member can be referred to with the qualified name Class::ch as in statement 6, and this refers to that data member in the receiver. Because the member function Class::func(int) hides rather than overloads the file scope function func() within the Class scope, an unqualified invocation of func() without an argument within Class as in statement 7 is an error. The file scope function can still be invoked within Class as ::func() as in statement 8. Now consider the statements in ::func(). The global num can be accessed as ::num in statement 9. The expression Class::func(num) in statement 10 is not valid because it does not indicate which object is the receiver. Invocation of a member function outside the class must send the message to a particular object, as does cl.func(num) in statement 11.

Encapsulation and information hiding

A class scope identifier does not conflict with a declaration of the same name in the global name space, and the class designer can use access control with class

---

[18] Using a function name with the scope operator would be meaningless because a non-static local variable does not exist outside the function unless an invocation is active, which cannot be determined at compile time.

scope identifiers. Because class scopes are named, we can refer to an identifier declared within a class scope outside that scope using a qualified name. (As we saw in section 1.1.3, C cannot support this capability because the compiler is not aware of the code file names.) These features provide some of the characteristics of module and import/export scope for names defined within classes. However, C++ does not provide a declaration that imports the names in a class scope so that the client can use them without qualification.

C++ provides the class designer with mechanisms to encapsulate other relevant behavior, information, and structure within a class scope in addition to its member functions and data members. Defining these items within the class increases cohesion by associating them with the class, and reduces the coupling between the class and program entities external to it. The class designer can define statically allocated objects as "static data members" of the class, and can encapsulate receiverless functions as "static member functions". Enumeration types and auxiliary classes can also be nested within the scope of a class. The class designer can specify these constructs as public, protected, or private.

The issue of name conflicts becomes more serious when using class libraries, especially when several class libraries are used in a project. The ability to create named scopes within the global scope is extremely helpful for managing class, function, and object names. The recent namespace extension supports defining named scopes and selectively importing names from these scopes, and is discussed in section 13.4. For example, class libraries for particular problem domains or platforms or libraries from particular vendors can each define their own namespace.

10.3.2 Static Class Members

Purpose

As we discussed in section 1.1.5, an application often needs to maintain some data such as a class constant or a set of instances that is relevant to the class as a whole, but is independent of any particular instance of the class. In section 6.1.3, we saw that Smalltalk represents this information as the class variables that comprise the state information of the class object. The class variables are accessible to the class object and to all instances of the class, but are not visible outside the class.

In C++, such a data object is declared as a *static data member* of the class. A static data member is similar to a global variable as it is statically allocated, but differs in that its name is only visible within that class's scope.[19] Its name does not conflict with uses of that name in other scopes, such as in global scope or other class or function scopes. There is only one instance of this member, no matter how many objects of the class exist (if any), and its value is not stored in instances of the class. The class designer can specify a static data member with any access specification, so it might or might not be accessible outside the class's scope. Like any object, a static member may be declared const.

---

[19] Note the similarity to a local variable declared static within a function in C.

A class can define member functions that access nonpublic static data members. However, the client would invoke the function by sending that message to a particular instance of the class, which is misleading because that object is not needed by the method. Instead, the class defines *static member functions* that perform these operations. The class designer also uses static member functions for class-related behavior that is not specific to an instance, such as Date::isLeapYear() or Employee::employeeWithID(). That is, static member functions are similar in meaning to class messages and methods in Smalltalk, and provide the same capability.

Static data members

A static data member is declared within the class definition in the same manner as any data member, together with the specifier static, which appears before the member's type. For example, suppose we want to keep track of the number of instances of the class Point that exist at any point during execution. In C or Pascal, this object would be declared as a global variable. In C++, we add a static data member to the class, as follows (we will discuss the static member function Point::numPoints() in the next subsection):

```
// the class Point with a static data member that maintains the number of instances
class Point
{
public:
   // ... other protocol as described in section 10.1.2 ...
   static int numPoints();   // "static member function" described in the next section
protected:
   int x_;
   int y_;
   static int numPoints_;
};
```

The class's constructors increment the static object numPoints_, and its destructor decrements it. (The class Point would now need a destructor as initializing a point object causes a side effect that must be undone.) Unlike a global variable, the class designer can declare a static data member as protected so that clients cannot access it directly, as we require for this piece of information. This allows us to provide the information represented by numPoints_ outside the class via the accessor function Point::numPoints(), without the possibility of a client modifying that variable. In addition, its name is declared with the scope Point:: and does not conflict with uses of that name in other scopes.

Specifying a static data member in the class definition does not define that object. If it did, including the class header file in several code files in a program would result in several copies of that object (and a multiple definition error from the linker). Unlike a static local variable in a function, we define and initialize a static data member outside the class definition. Because it must be defined and initialized exactly once, we do so in the class's code file rather than in its header file. If the static data member is of a class type, a constructor is invoked when it is initialized (i.e., before main() is executed). To refer to that variable at file scope in the class code file, we use a qualified name, as in the following example:[20]

```
// definition and initialization of Point::numPoints_ in the Point.cc file
int Point::numPoints_ = 0;
```

We can define and initialize a static data member outside the class in this way regardless of its access level because access specifications control read and write access, but not definition and initialization. (For example, we can also declare a protected member function in the class definition and define it in the class code file.)

Like any class member, a static member is directly accessible to all instances of that class because it is declared within the class's scope. This is true no matter which access specification is used. For example, we code the constructors and destructor of class Point as follows:

```
// a static data member is accessible within the class scope
inline Point::Point()
    : x_(0), y_(0)
{
    numPoints_++;
}

inline Point::Point(int initX, int initY)
    : x_(initX), y_(initY)
{
    numPoints_++;
}

inline Point::Point(const Point& argPt)
    : x_(argPt.x_), y_(argPt.y_)
{
    numPoints_++;
}

inline Point::~Point()
{
    numPoints_--;
}
```

Because a static data member is unique and is allocated for the duration of execution, it has different properties than a nonstatic data member. A static data member can appear in an initializer in the initialization list of a constructor (e.g., a class constant), or can be the default value for a member function argument. In

---

[20] Note that the static reserved word is not used in the definition in the code file.

addition, the type of a static data member can be its own class because the static data member is not stored in instances, so no infinite recursion of containment occurs. For example, the class designer can maintain a default instance of the class as a static data member.

Static member functions

Static member functions provide class-specific behavior. A static member function has no receiver—that is, it does not have an implicit this pointer—so it cannot access nonstatic data members of the class directly (without component selection).[21] It typically manipulates the static data members of the class and its arguments, and can access members of instances of the class with component selection and file scope names. For example, the static member function Point::numPoints() in the previous subsection provides controlled access to the static data member Point::numPoints_, and is defined as follows:[22]

```
// a static member function can access a static data member directly
inline int Point::numPoints()
{
    return numPoints_;
}
```

The Point::numPoints() method cannot access the data members x_ and y_ directly. In a sense, a static member function is like a file scope function whose name is encapsulated within the class scope.

As we will see in section 10.3.5, pointers to member functions require a special construct to account for the receiver in the argument signature. Because a static member function has no receiver, it can be assigned to a pointer to a function defined with its argument signature, just like a file scope function.

```
// a static member function has no receiver
#include "Point.h"   // with static members
int main()
{
    Point pt1(1,1), pt2(2,2);
    int (*pFunc) ();                    // a pointer to function, not a pointer to member function
    pFunc = &Point::numPoints(); // OK
    int num = (*pFunc)();           // OK
}
```

Static member function invocation

A class's methods can call a static member function without qualification because it is defined within that scope. Outside the class, clients can invoke a pub-

---

[21] Note the similarity with Smalltalk class methods, which cannot refer to the class's instance variables.

[22] Again, the reserved word static is not used in the function definition.

lic static member function either with a qualified name or by component selection through an instance of the class, as follows:

```
// invoking a static member function
#include "Point.h"
int main()
{
    Point pt(2, 2);
    Point* pPoint = new Point(3, 3);
    // preferred style for obtaining class information
    int currentNumPoints = Point::numPoints();   // OK, even if there are no point objects
    // misleading invocation through an instance of the class
    currentNumPoints = pt.numPoints();
    currentNumPoints = pPoint->numPoints();
}
```

Although all of these invocations are syntactically correct, the second and third are misleading because the responsibility for maintaining the number of points is assigned to the class Point, rather than to individual point objects. This information is about the class as a whole, rather than about a particular instance. Using an instance of the class to invoke a static member function specifies both a scope and a receiver, although the latter is not actually used. For example, the identifiers pt and pPoint in the previous examples appear to be supplying a receiver for the member function Point::numPoints(), but in fact they only specify a scope. Using a qualified name appears like a message to the class itself.

10.3.3 Enumerations in Class Scope

In many problem domain classes, a class has an instance variable whose value is one of a fixed set of states. For example, a traffic light can be in the state red, yellow, or green. Similarly, many object-oriented design methodologies use state diagrams to model a category of entities. We would like to give the state values descriptive names that are encapsulated within the class rather than being defined as global constants. A convenient way to represent this situation in C++ is to nest a definition of an enumeration of the states within the definition of the class. As with static members, this keeps the enumeration type name and value names from conflicting with names declared in the global scope. If the enumeration is defined within the public portion of the class, then those names are accessible to clients with the class name and the scope operator. For example, in a process scheduling simulation, we might have a class Process such as the following:

```
// an enumeration within a class scope (#ifndef, etc. omitted)
class Process
{
public:
    enum Status { running, ready, blocked, terminated, aborted };
```

```
        Status status() const
        { return status_; }
        void status(Status st)
        { status_ = st; }
        // ... other protocol ...
    protected:
        Status status_;
        // ... other state information ...
    };
```

A client can then refer to the process status type and its values using qualified names, as follows:

```
    // client use of a class scope enumeration
    #include "Process.h"
    int main()
    {
        Process proc1(...), proc2(...);
        Process::Status procSt = proc1.status();
        proc2.status(Process::aborted);
    }
```

In addition to removing the names Status, aborted, and so on from the global name space, the qualified names Process::Status and Process::aborted have more mnemonic value for the reader of the code. For example, consider the names TrafficLight::red and Color::red.

10.3.4 Nested Classes

Purpose

If a class is relevant only within a particular class, the class designer can nest its definition within the scope of that class. [23] In this case, the nested class's name is declared within the enclosing class's scope and does not conflict with uses of that name in other scopes. The most common use of a nested class is an auxiliary class used only in the implementation of another class, such as the class Node in section 10.1.3. In fact, several classes implemented by linked structures could each have a local Node class that has a different structure (e.g., with one link for a singly-linked list and two for a binary tree). These classes would be LinkedList::Node and BinaryTree::Node, and the scope in which the name Node appears would determine which class the name refers to. Another use of nested classes is a situation in which a class is only relevant in the context of another class. For example, the classes Vertex and Edge might be nested within a Graph class.

---

[23] A class can also be nested within a function, but the class can only be used in that function as the scope operator cannot be used with function names. For this reason, defining a class within a function is not very useful, and we will not discuss it further.

Definition, access control, and scope

Let us redefine the classes Node and Queue in section 10.1.3 with the auxiliary class Node nested within Queue. A class can be defined within the public, protected, or private section of another class. We define Node in the protected section of Queue so that Queue's clients cannot use it, and specify its members as public so that they are accessible within the scope Queue, as follows:

```
// an auxiliary class nested within the class that uses it (#ifndef, etc. omitted)
// Queue no longer needs to be a friend of Node

class Queue
{
friend ostream& operator<<(ostream&, Queue&);
public:
   // ... member function declarations as coded in section 10.1.3 ...
protected:
   class Node
   {
   friend ostream& operator<<(ostream&, Queue&);
   public:
      Node(const ElemType& el);
      ElemType elem;
      Node* next;
   };
   Node* front;
   Node* back;
};
```

The access specifications of the members of a nested class apply to the enclosing class and vice versa—that is, the nonpublic members of each class are not accessible to the other. If the Node members were protected, we would have to specify Queue as a friend of the nested class so that its methods could access Node members. The Node members are still not accessible outside the scope Queue because Node is in the protected section of Queue.

A nested class is not a subclass of the enclosing class. Its instances do not respond to the enclosing class's protocol, nor do they have values for the data members of the enclosing class (consider the classes Node and Queue). There is no enclosing class receiver "embedded" within the nested class object, so the member functions of the nested class cannot directly access the members of the enclosing class (even though they are visible by the rules of static scope).

Like the name and local variables of a nested procedure in Pascal, the name of a nested class is declared within the enclosing class scope, and its members are defined within the scope of the nested class. If the nested class is in the public section of the enclosing class, its name can be used outside the enclosing class if it is qualified with the name of the enclosing class (as we did with an enumeration in a class scope in the previous section). For example, the qualified name can be used as a type name to declare an instance of the nested class outside the enclosing class scope.

```
// a valid definition at file scope or in another class if Node were nested within
// the public section of Queue
#include "Queue.h"              // with typedef int ElemType;
Queue::Node node(3);
```

We defined the class name Node in the protected section of Queue to prevent this. Note that if Node were defined in Queue's public section, there would still be no name clashes with Node classes within other classes or at file scope.

If the class designer wants to code the member functions of a nested class outside the enclosing class, he or she can cascade applications of the scope operator to indicate the scope of the name, that is, *Outer*::*Inner*::*message*(). Such a qualified name is parsed from left to right, beginning with a scope name visible at file scope. For example, we can define the Node constructor in Queue.h as follows:[24]

```
// the cascaded scope operator is used when coding nested class member functions
// outside the enclosing class
inline Queue::Node::Node(const ElemType& el)
   : elem(el), next(NULL)
{ }
```

We can also use the cascaded scope operator to refer to a public static member of a nested class outside the enclosing class.

10.3.5 Pointers to Members

Pointers to member functions

A nonstatic member function is not the same type as a file scope function with the same argument signature due to the extra this argument. Unlike the file scope function, the member function code can refer to the receiver's members, and must be invoked with reference to a receiver. Therefore, a member function that returns an int and takes a char* argument cannot be assigned to a function pointer pFunc declared as int (*pFunc) (char*). The referent of pFunc would receive no argument corresponding to implicit or explicit uses of this because an invocation using pFunc cannot specify a receiver. Instead, a pointer to member functions must be declared using the syntax described in this section, which indicates the class of the receiver and the scope in which the function is defined, as well as the function's argument signature.

C++ supports the type *pointer to member function* to support parameterization of operations that are encapsulated within classes. For example, a quicksort function or a SortedList class constructor might take a parameter that gives the comparison function, and this function would be a member function in an object-oriented design. The language defines a special syntax for pointers to member functions that indicate the class scope. Such a pointer can only refer to member functions with the given ar-

---

[24] As we stated in discussing static data member initializations in section 10.3.2, a nonpublic access specifier does not prevent defining a protected identifier outside the class.

gument signature within the specified class. We will use the following example class
to illustrate pointers to members:

```
// an example class to illustrate pointers to members
class Example
{
public:
   Example(int, int);
   int msg1(char*, int);
   int msg2(char*, int);
   void msg3(int);
protected:
   int mem1;
   int mem2;
};
```

The following statement defines pMemFnEx as a pointer to member functions of
class Example that have an int return type and argument signature (char*, int): [25]

```
// defines pMemFnEx as a pointer to member functions of class Example
// with return type int and argument signature (char*, int)
int (Example::*pMemFnEx) (char*, int);
```

The type of a member function of class Example with int return type and argument
signature (char*, int) is written as int (Example::*) (char*, int), and this is the type of
the identifier pMemFnEx. The ::* operator is referred to as the "pointer to member
declarator". (Syntactically, ::* is a single operator, but it is easier to read if you think
of it as a combination of a scope specification and a pointer to function.) As with non-
member function pointers, using a typedef for a pointer to member function type
makes declarations considerably more readable.

```
// using a typedef for a pointer to member function
typedef int (Example::*PtrMemFnEx) (char*, int);
PtrMemFnEx pMemFnEx;
// two equivalent declarations of func(), which takes an instance of Example
// and a pointer to an Example member function
int func(Example&, int (Example::*) (char*, int));
int func(Example&, PtrMemFnEx);
```

   To obtain a value that can be assigned to such an identifier within the class,
we use the prefix & operator with the name of a member function of the class with
the correct argument signature. [26] Outside the class scope, the member function

---

[25] As with pointers to functions, the first set of parentheses in the identifier definition is necessary
because the precedence of the function definition operator () is higher than that of the dereference operator *.

[26] As with pointers to functions, the & operator in the assignment is optional but recommended.

name must be qualified with the class name. The same syntax is used to obtain an argument that can be passed to a function that takes a pointer to member function (e.g., func() in the previous example). We can also assign NULL to a pointer to member function to indicate that it does not currently refer to any member function. We send the message to which the pointer refers to an instance of the class with the dereferencing component selection operators .* or ->* (also called the "pointer to member operators"). The member function the pointer refers to must be accessible in the scope in which this application of the operator appears. These operations are illustrated by the following examples:[27]

```
// assigning to a pointer to member function and using it in an invocation
#include "Example.h"
int func(Example&, int (Example::*) (char*, int));
void func1(int arg)
{
    Example ex(arg, arg + 1);
    Example* pEx = new Example(arg - 1, arg);
    int (Example::*pMemFnEx) (char*, int);      // define a pointer to member function
    if ( arg < 0 )
        pMemFnEx = &Example::msg1;              // assign it a value
    else
        pMemFnEx = &Example::msg2;
    // both calls invoke the member function pMemFnEx refers to
    int num1 = (ex.*pMemFnEx) ("hello", 7);
    int num2 = (pEx->*pMemFnEx) ("hello", 7);
    // error: Example::msg3() has the wrong argument signature
    pMemFnEx = &Example::msg3;
    // passing a member function to another function
    func(ex, &Example::msg1);
}
```

Like ::*, the .* and ->* operators are single operators syntactically, but it is easier to read an expression that uses one if you think of the expression as dereferencing the pointer and then sending that message. The result of an application of either the .* or ->* operator—for example, the expression ex.*pMemFnEx—can only be used in an invocation of the member function that is the referent of the pointer. In particular, it cannot be stored as the value of a variable, passed to another function, etc.

Pointers to data members

The pointer to member declarator ::* can also be used to define a *pointer to data member* of a particular class. We can think of such a pointer as providing a type-correct offset into the representation of an instance of the class, rather than as

---

[27] Again, the first set of parentheses in the expression (ex.*pMemFnEx) ("hello", 7) is required because the precedence of the call operator () is higher than that of the dereferencing component selection operator.

a pointer to a data member within a particular object. Again, we obtain a value for such an identifier by using the & operator together with a data member name of the correct type, qualified with the class name if outside the class. That data member is accessed in an instance of the class using the .* or ->* operators, and the member must be accessible in the scope in which the expression occurs. The following member function illustrates these points:

```
// defining, assigning and using a pointer to data member
#include "Example.h"
void Example::msg3(int arg)
{
   Example ex(arg, arg - 1);
   int Example::*pMemEx;           // define a pointer to an int data member of class Example
   if ( arg < 0 )
     pMemEx = &Example::mem1;  // assign a value (an object offset) to the pointer
   else
     pMemEx = &Example::mem2;
   int num1 = ex.*pMemEx;          // access that data member in ex
   int num2 = this->*pMemEx;       // access that data member in the receiver
}
```

A fine point of syntax is that the & is required in the assignments within the if statement in this example (unlike assignments to pointers to functions or member functions in which it is optional). The name Example::mem1 (without the preceding &) refers to the data member itself when used in a scope in which it is accessible (e.g., within an Example member function). That is, the expression Example::mem1 is of type int, not of type int Example::*. Pointers to data members are rarely used.

10.4 SUMMARY AND REVIEW

10.4.1 The C++ Class

Views of a class

- A C++ class defines an abstract data type by specifying the operations and storage structure for its instances. The class can be used as the type of an object, a pointer, a reference, a function parameter, or a data member of another class.
- Classes are first-class types. The language includes constructs for assignment, automatic initialization, and finalization of instances, construction of anonymous instances, and operator overloading.
- A C++ class specifies a named scope in which its data member and member function names are declared. Because member functions definitions are enclosed within this scope, code containing identifier uses that must be resolved can appear in a class scope.

- Class scopes are named, and we can use a qualified name used to refer to an identifier declared in a class scope outside that scope. The class designer can use a class's scope as a name space to encapsulate static objects and functions, enumerations, and auxiliary classes.
- Unlike Smalltalk, C++ maintains a minimal representation of the class object at execution time, and classes cannot be manipulated in programs. The run-time type information facility allows the programmer to verify the class of an object, and check whether two objects are instances of the same class. The template facility supports type parameters for functions and classes, like those for generic abstract data types.

Class definition

- A class definition appears like a C structure definition that includes both data members and member functions, and specifies access control for the class's members.
- The *data members* of a class define the representation of an instance, that is, its instance variables. A data member can be const, in which case each instance has its own value, which cannot be changed after initialization.
- A class's *member function* declarations describe its messages, and their definitions give the class's methods. Member function names may be overloaded. We can specify a member function as const (after the parameter list) to indicate that it does not modify the receiver.
- A member function is declared in the scope of its class, and its name does not conflict with the names of file scope functions or member functions of another class. Because the scope of a member function is nested within the scope of the class, the members of a class are visible in member function code.
- We use the component selection operator to refer to the accessible members of an instance, for example, to pass a message to an object.

The class interface and access control

- In an object-oriented design, an application consists of a set of classes. Each class is divided into a header file containing the class definition and a code file that defines the class's methods. The class header file is included in the class's code file and in client code files, and the object files for the application's classes are linked to create the executable program.
- The class header file gives the class definition, definitions of inline functions, and include directives for other classes and C standard library header files, and is enclosed in a conditional expansion directive with #ifndef. It contains both the interface of the class for its clients, and information needed by the compiler when translating client code.
- To avoid multiple definition errors from the compiler when a header file is included more than once in a file, we enclose the class header file in a preprocessor conditional using #ifndef and a unique symbol.

- If one class uses another only as the type of pointers or references, it can declare that class, rather than including its header file.

- The C++ access specifiers control information hiding for the members of a class. Each member of a class can be *public*, *protected* (accessible to the class's subclasses but not its clients), or *private* to the class alone. Access specifications are checked at compile time.

- We can declare auxiliary member functions as protected or private in C++. To support representation independence for a class, do not specify its data members as public.

- The *friend declaration* permits the class designer to provide access to the non-public members of a class to a particular file scope or member function, called a *friend function*. It is used when a function needs access to the internal structure of more than one class, or cannot be defined as a member function for other reasons (e.g., a file scope operator overloading).

- Because friend functions increase coupling and are not inherited, you should use member functions rather than friends for the operations of a class whenever possible.

The class implementation

- We define member functions at file scope in the class's code file, and use a qualified name to specify the class scope. We code methods like C functions that can include C++ message expressions. A method may access the members of the receiver directly, and may access the nonpublic members of any instance of its class using component selection.

- Within a member function definition, the reserved word this is a constant pointer to the receiver. We can use it as an argument or a return value, but it is optional when sending a message to the receiver.

- The compiler translates a member function invocation as an encoded function call with an additional argument, namely the referent of this.

10.4.2 Creation, Initialization, and Finalization of Objects

Object creation and identity

- A class instance can be allocated statically, automatically, or dynamically, or as a data member of another object. The compiler can also create and destroy temporary class instances that are necessary for the translation of nested expressions.

- An identifier has *value semantics* if it behaves as a container for objects of its type. An identifier has *reference semantics* if it behaves as a name that can refer to objects of its type.

- Most object-oriented languages do not support static and automatic allocation of class objects because a value representation prevents the flexibility of allowing a polymorphic identifier to refer to objects of different classes (with different sizes). Built-in type identifiers use value semantics in statically typed object-oriented languages.
- C++ supports both value and reference semantics for class type identifiers. Pointer and reference variables, parameters, and data members provide reference semantics.
- In C++, you can (and must) decide whether each variable, parameter, or data member uses value or reference semantics. A value representation is more efficient, but a reference representation provides flexibility and extendibility because it permits polymorphism and dynamic binding of messages to the referent. Reference semantics also maintains the identity of each object.
- You should use value semantics when the identifier type is a built-in type or a class with no subclasses, and reference semantics if polymorphism or object identity are necessary.

Constructors

- A *constructor* is a member function that initializes a new instance of the class. The constructor is responsible for initializing the object's data members, obtaining the system resources it needs, and performing any side effects associated with creation of the object. Constructors relieve the class's clients from needing to know how an object is constructed or what system resources it uses.
- Every C++ object is initialized immediately after being allocated by one of its class's constructors, no matter what allocation policy is used for the object. Implicit initialization provides automatic guaranteed initialization of class instances, and prevents the common error of using an uninitialized object.
- We code a constructor as a member function whose name is the same as its class name. The constructor argument signature gives the arguments passed to initialize the new object, and the constructor can be overloaded. Constructors do not specify a return type or return a value. Constructors may be public, protected, or private.
- The initializer for a new object gives the constructor arguments, and follows the variable name for static and automatic variables, or the class name with the new operator. If the object's class has no constructor with that argument signature, the compiler signals an error.
- We can use a constructor invocation to create an anonymous instance of a class, which provides a literal notation for classes.
- The *default constructor* takes no arguments, and is invoked whenever an instance of the class is created without specifying an initializer.

Destructors

- The *destructor* finalizes an instance of the class by releasing any resources allocated to the object and undoing any side effects resulting from its initializa-

tion. Constructors and destructors relieve clients of the responsibility for dealing with the class's resource usage.

- We define the destructor as a member function whose name is the class name
  preceded by the tilde symbol ~. Destructors do not specify a return type or
  return a value.

- The destructor is invoked implicitly just before an instance of the class is deallocated, irrespective of what allocation policy is used for that object. In particular, destructors are invoked automatically for temporary objects and value
  data members.

- Classes that do not allocate resources or cause side effects do not require a
  destructor. A class does not require a destructor just because the class of a
  data member defines one.

The constructor initialization list

- A *composite class* contains data members of class type, in which case an
  instance has instances of those classes embedded within it. These embedded
  objects must be initialized by their respective constructors, and the designer
  of the composite class should not be concerned with the operation of those
  constructors.

- The definition of a constructor for a composite class specifies an *initialization
  list* that gives the name of each data member of class type and an initializer for
  that object. The list appears between the constructor header and body, preceded by a colon. This feature ensures that the embedded data member
  objects are properly initialized, and provides for passing arguments to those
  constructors.

- All data members of class type must appear on the initialization list, except
  those whose class defines a default constructor, in which case the default constructor is used to initialize that data member. Because constant and reference
  data members cannot be assigned values in the constructor body, they must
  also be included in the initialization list. Built-in type data members can also
  be given in the initialization list.

- The data member constructors are executed before the constructor body,
  and this rule is applied recursively so that an object is constructed from the
  inside out. Destructors are invoked in the reverse order before the object is
  deallocated.

The copy constructor

- The compiler creates a copy of an existing object when an identifier is initialized from an instance of its class, or when a function passes an argument or
  return value by value. For every class *Class*, the compiler generates a *default
  copy constructor* with the argument signature const *Class*& that initializes each
  data member of the new object from the corresponding data member of the
  copied object.

- The default copy constructor is inadequate for a class that allocates dynamic memory in its constructor because the corresponding pointer data members in the new and existing objects will both refer to the same storage. Changes to one object affect the other, and that storage is deallocated twice when both objects' destructors are executed.
- The designer of a class that uses system resources must define a *copy constructor*. For a class that allocates dynamic memory, the copy constructor gives each object its own subobject.
- A composite class does not require a programmer-defined copy constructor simply because a data member's class employs one, because the compiler's default copy constructor invokes the data member's copy constructor when creating an instance of the composite class.

10.4.3 Class Scope

Characteristics of class scope

- Each class definition specifies a named scope containing the declarations of its members. Member names hide global identifiers with the same name within the class, that is, within member function code. A member name is visible throughout the class, no matter where its declaration appears in the class definition.
- Member function names are defined at class scope, and each member function defines a local scope nested within the scope of its class. A member function with the same name as a file scope function does not overload that function because they are defined in different scopes.
- The unit of access control is the class, and a member function can access the nonpublic members of any instance of its class.
- The class designer can nest objects, functions, enumerations, and auxiliary classes within a class scope to encapsulate those items and reduce the number of identifiers in the global name space. These constructs may be specified as public, protected, or private, and if they are public, clients can access them using qualified names.

Static class members

- *Static data members* correspond to class variables, and are useful for information relevant to the class as a whole, or for constants needed in the class's storage structure.
- A static data member is represented by a single statically allocated object, rather than being stored in each instance of the class. It is declared in the class definition, and is defined and initialized in the class's code file using a qualified name. It is accessible in all the class's methods.
- *Static member functions* correspond to class messages and methods. A static member function has no receiver or this pointer, that is, it behaves like a file

scope function whose name is declared within the class scope. A static member function cannot refer to nonstatic member names directly.

- A client can invoke a public static member function either by using the scope operator and the class name or the component selection operator with an instance of the class. Using a qualified name is more appropriate because there is no receiver in an invocation of a static member function.

Enumerations in class scope

- The definition of a class-specific enumeration can be nested within the scope of the class, for example, to represent the values for an attribute or the state of an instance. The enumeration type and value names do not conflict with uses of those names at file scope or within other classes.
- If the enumeration is declared in the public part of the class, clients can use qualified names to refer to the type and value names.

Nested classes

- The class designer can nest a class within another class, for example, to encapsulate an auxiliary class or an associated class.
- We can define a nested class in the public or protected section of the enclosing class definition. The access specifications of the nested class apply to the enclosing class, and vice versa. If a nested class is public, its qualified name can be used as a type name outside the enclosing class.
- The member functions of a nested class can be defined at file scope by cascading applications of the scope operator.

Pointers to members

- A nonstatic member function is not the same type as a file scope function with the same argument signature because it has a receiver. C++ supports the type *pointer to member function* of a given class, and the class scope is specified as part of the type of these objects.
- A pointer to member function is declared with ::*, and a value for it is obtained by applying the & operator to a member function name of the correct type (qualified if necessary). The referent message is sent with the .* or ->* operator.
- C++ also supports *pointers to data members*, which are declared with ::*, and accessed with .* or ->*.

10.5 EXERCISES

10.1 Discuss the similarities and differences between the Smalltalk and C++ conceptions of a class.

10.2 (a) What is a const data member and what is its purpose?

(b) What is a const member function and what is its purpose?

10.3 **(a)** Why is a C++ class definition divided into a header and code file?

(b) List the contents of the class header and code files, and describe why each item is present.

(c) Explain how the class header and code files are used in creating an application that uses the class.

10.4 Why must all the clients of a C++ class be recompiled if the class's storage structure is changed?

10.5 Suppose that two classes both have data members that are pointers to instances of each other. (Why must they be pointers rather than value data members?) For example, an instance of an Employee class may have a pointer to the Manager object for that employee, and a Manager object may contain a list of pointers to the employees managed by that manager.

(a) Why can't the two class header files include each other?

(b) How can the class declarations and header file inclusions be organized for the header and code files of the two classes?

(c) Suppose that some member function of each class needs to invoke member functions of the other. What implications does this situation have for the organization of the class definitions?

10.6 Describe the mechanisms that provide the C++ class designer with explicit control over the accessibility of the class's components.

10.7 Give three examples of classes that would have a protected member function.

10.8 Why are class header files enclosed in an #ifndef preprocessor directive?

10.9 **(a)** How are self in Smalltalk and this in C++ similar? How do they differ?

(b) Give an example of an expression that would require using this (besides returning the receiver as Queue::insert() in section 10.1.4 does).

10.10 Define the following member functions for the class Point defined in section 10.1.2. Use const where appropriate in the declarations of the functions.

(a) Point::r() and Point::theta(), which return the receiver's coordinates in polar coordinates

(b) Point::translatedBy(), which returns the point resulting from translating the receiver by the argument point

(c) Point::scaledBy(), which returns the point resulting from scaling the receiver by the argument point

(d) Point::isAboveLeft(), which returns whether the receiver is above and to the left of the argument point (using the usual display screen coordinate system)

10.11 Define the following member functions for the class String defined in section 10.2.2. For each, first give the declaration using const where appropriate, and justify your use of a value or a reference for each parameter and return value. Then give the member function definition. You may use C standard library functions, and may ignore error conditions such as index range errors.

(a) String:: indexOf(), which returns the position of the first occurrence of its char argument in the receiver

(b) String::isSubstring(), which returns whether the string argument is a substring of the receiver

(c) String::substring(int start, int length), which returns a copy of the substring of the receiver beginning at the character with index start whose length is length

(d) String::removeSpaces(), which returns a copy of the receiver with whitespace characters removed

(e) String::asInteger(), which considers the receiver an int in the standard literal format and returns the corresponding int

(f) String::toLowerCase(), which changes any uppercase alphabetic characters in the receiver to lowercase

(g) String::append(), which appends the argument string to the receiver

(h) String::concat(), which creates a new string object that is the concatenation of the receiver and the argument string

(i) String::remove(), which removes occurrences of the argument character from the receiver

(j) String::remove(), which removes occurrences of all characters in the argument string from the receiver

10.12 **(a)** Write a program that creates an instance of the class String using each of the following allocation policies: static, automatic, temporary, and dynamic.

(b) Draw a storage diagram illustrating the string objects in your program in part (a).

(c) Describe when the destructor String::~String() is executed for each string object in your program in part (a).

10.13 **(a)** Discuss the differences in semantics and usage for value and pointer variables and data members.

(b) Discuss the differences in semantics and usage for value and pointer collection elements.

10.14 **(a)** What is the disadvantage of using a value data member, rather than a pointer?

(b) Suppose you have used a value data member and must change it to a pointer. What changes must be made in the definition of the class? What must be done to recreate the executable for a program that uses the class?

(c) What is the disadvantage of using a pointer data member, rather than a value?

(d) Suppose you have used a pointer data member and must change it to a value. What changes must be made in the definition of the class? What must be done to recreate the executable for a program that uses the class?

10.15 **(a)** What is the purpose of each of the following constructs?

  (i) the constructor
  (ii) the destructor
  (iii) the constructor initialization list
  (iv) the copy constructor

(b) How do each of these constructs increase information hiding and loose coupling for classes?

10.16 **(a)** Give three examples of classes that would have a default constructor (besides those discussed in the text).

(b) Give three examples of classes that would not have a default constructor (besides those discussed in the text).

10.17 How many times is the default constructor for String executed for the following definition?
String* arrStr[10];

10.18 **(a)** Give three examples of classes that would have a destructor (besides those discussed in the text).

(b) Give three examples of classes that would not have a destructor (besides those discussed in the text).

10.19 Why does it not make sense for a client to invoke a destructor explicitly?

10.20 Constructors and destructors can be useful to aid in debugging programs. Clearly, we can use them to indicate when the program creates and destroys instances of a class by writing a message to cout. We can also create a class, say Trace, that we can use to trace invocations and exits of functions. The constructor takes a char* or String argument that is the function name. Define this class and show how to use it.

10.21 **(a)** Like any functions, we can define constructors and destructors in one code file and invoke them in another. How can you determine what encoded names are used by your C++ compiler for these functions?

  (b) Do so with your compiler. Can you decipher the encoding scheme it uses?

10.22 **(a)** What is the constructor initialization list, and why is such a feature necessary?

  (b) What items must appear on this list?

10.23 Consider the following class definition:

```
class Rectangle
{
public:
    Rectangle(const Point& origin, const Point& corner);
    Rectangle(int x, int y, int width, int height);
    // ... other member functions ...
protected:
    Point origin_;
    Point corner_;
};
```

Code the constructors for the class Rectangle.

10.24 In constructing an instance of a composite class, the data member constructors are executed before the composite class constructor. Why is this so (consider the alternative)?

10.25 What is a copy constructor and what is its purpose? In what circumstances is it invoked implicitly?

10.26 In what way is the default copy constructor similar to Smalltalk's shallowCopy message? In what way is it different?

10.27 Why is the constructor *Class::Class(Class)* illegal in C++?

10.28 Suppose we define a class PersonName with three data members of type String for the first, middle, and last name of a person.

  (a) Code the constructor for this class that takes three String objects.

  (b) Is the compiler-generated copy constructor adequate for this class? Explain your answer.

  (c) Is it necessary to code a destructor for PersonName? Explain your answer.

10.29 **(a)** Draw a storage diagram illustrating what happens if the default copy constructor is used for the class Queue defined in sections 10.1.3 and 10.1.4, and there are subsequent insertions and deletions.

  (b) Write the copy constructor for the class Queue.

10.30 Give two ways in which class scope differs from local scope.

10.31 Explain whether the following statement is true or false: If a function's return value is of class type, a destructor and copy constructor are called for that value whenever the function is invoked.

10.32 Give three advantages of the use of a static data member rather than a global variable for class-related information.

10.33 How and where is a static data member initialized, and why?

10.34 Why is it illegal for a static member function to access nonstatic members of the class directly (i.e., without component selection)?

10.35 Suppose we are defining a class, say Employee, and we want to generate a unique identification number for each object and store it in a data member. Describe how we can do this using a static data member. Code the related portion of the class definition, and any member functions that access the static member.

10.36 We want to encapsulate an index of instances of the class Person described in section 10.2.4 together with the class. The index allows a client to obtain a pointer to a particular Person object given that person's name (the index stores references to instances of the class). You may assume that each person has a unique name, and that the following class has been defined:

```
typedef String KeyType;
typedef Person ValueType;
class Dictionary
{
public:
    Dictionary();          // an empty dictionary
    ~Dictionary();
    bool isElement(const KeyType&);
    Value& find(const KeyType&);
    insert(const KeyType&, const ValueType&);
    remove(const KeyType&);
// ... other members ...
};
```

(a) How is the dictionary object declared, defined, and initialized?

(b) How is the index accessed by clients?

(c) How is the index updated?

(d) Code the operations in parts a, b, and c. (Consider storage allocation carefully for the keys and values inserted into the index.)

10.37 Give three examples of problem domain classes for which an enumeration within class scope would be appropriate (besides those discussed in the text).

10.38 Why is it true that the member functions of a nested class cannot access the nonstatic members of the enclosing class directly (i.e., without component selection)?

10.39 **(a)** Define a pointer to member function of class Point that can refer to Point:: x(int) and Point::y(int). Write expressions that assign a value to the pointer and invoke its referent.

(b) Define a pointer to a data member of class Point. Write expressions that assign a value to the pointer. Where can such a pointer be used?

10.40 Define a class for arbitrary size sets of elements. The class copies elements into the storage structure of the receiver upon insertion. The class Set has the following interface:

```
typedef String ElemType;               // or whatever element type
class Set
{
public:
    Set();                              // create an empty set
    Set(const Set&);
    ~Set();
    bool isEmpty();
    int size() const;
    bool isElement(const ElemType&) const;
    Set& insert(const ElemType&);       // cascading is supported
```

```
    Set& insertAll(const Set&);
    Set& remove(const ElemType&);
    Set& removeAll();                       // empty the set
    // remove all elements of the receiver that satisfy the test function
    Set& removeAllSuchThat(bool (ElemType::*pTestFn) ());
    bool isSubset(const Set&) const;
    // create a list containing all elements of the receiver that satisfy the test function
    Set allSuchThat(bool (ElemType::*pTestFn) ());
    // operator=(), operator==(), operator!=(), operator+(), operator+=(),
    // operator-(), operator-=(), and operator<<() in exercises 11.8 and 11.32
};
```

Code the definition of the class Set and its member functions using each of the following storage structures. For each, define whatever nonpublic data members, static data
members, auxiliary functions, or auxiliary classes are necessary. In addition, describe
any behavior required for the ElemType class for each storage structure.

(a) a dynamic resizable array, as illustrated by the class CharStack in section 1.1.4 and
Figure 1.4 (or store the elements in the middle of the array and use two index data
members giving the first and last element as in the implementation of the Smalltalk
system class OrderedCollection)

(b) a sorted dynamic array

(c) a linked list similar to the class Queue in sections 10.1.3 and 10.1.4 (only one pointer
data member is necessary)

(d) a sorted linked list

(e) a binary search tree of elements

(f) a hash table in which each entry is a pointer to a linked list of elements that hash
to that home address

10.41 Define a class for arbitrary size lists of elements. The class copies elements into the storage structure of the receiver upon insertion. Two kinds of errors are possible for this
class: subscript range errors (e.g., in List::insertAt(), List::successor(), List::move(), and
List::sublist()), and reference to a non-existent element (e.g., in List::successor(),
List::insertAfter(), and List::remove()). When these occur, you may just print an error message and exit. (In general, client errors should throw an exception, as discussed in section 14.3.) The class List has the following interface:

```
typedef String ElemType;                     // or whatever element type
class List
{
public:
    List();                                  // create an empty list
    List(const List&);
    ~List();
    bool isEmpty();
    int size() const;
    bool isElement(const ElemType&) const;
    int indexOf(const ElemType&) const;      // returns 0 if not found
    ElemType predecessor(const ElemType&) const;
    ElemType successor(const ElemType&) const;
    List& insertFirst(const ElemType&);      // cascading is supported
    List& insertLast(const ElemType&);
    List& insertAt(int index);
    List& insertBefore(const ElemType& successor, const ElemType& newElem);
    List& insertAfter(const ElemType& predecessor, const ElemType& newElem);
    List& append(const List&);
    List& remove(const ElemType&);           // remove all occurrences of the argument
    List& removeAt(int index);
```

```
List& removeAll();                          // empty the list
List& removeAll(const List&);               // remove all elements of the argument
// remove all elements of the receiver that satisfy the test function
List& removeAllSuchThat(bool (ElemType::*pTestFn) ());
// move the indicated element "distance" in the list;  a negative distance indicates
// moving towards the beginning;
void move(int index, int distance);
// move the first occurrence
void move(const ElemType&, int distance);
bool isSublist(const List&) const;
// return a copy of the indicated sublist
List sublist(int startIndex, int length) const;
// return a list containing all elements of the receiver that satisfy the test function
List allSuchThat(bool (ElemType::*pTestFn) ());
void sort(bool (ElemType::*pCompareFn) (const ElemType&));
// operator=(), operator==(), operator!=(), operator[](), operator+(), operator+=(),
// operator-(), operator-=() and operator<<() in exercises 11.9 and 11.32
};
```

Code the definition of the class List and its member functions using each of the following storage structures. For each, define whatever nonpublic data members, static
data members, auxiliary functions, or auxiliary classes are necessary.

(a) a dynamic resizable array (two versions are described in exercise 10.40)

(b) a linked list

10.42 Define a class for sorted lists of elements for which there is no restriction on the number of elements in an instance. The class copies elements into the storage structure of
the receiver upon insertion, and sorts them using the < operator. (We will discuss operator overloading for class objects in the next chapter.) As in the previous exercise, you
may just print an error message and exit upon a subscript range error or a reference to
a non-existent element. The class SortedList has the following interface:

```
typedef String ElemType;                    // or whatever element type
class SortedList
(
public:
    SortedList();                           // create an empty list
    SortedList(const SortedList&);
    ~SortedList();
    bool isEmpty();
    int size() const;
    bool isElement(const ElemType&) const;
    int indexOf(const ElemType&) const;     // returns 0 if not found
    ElemType predecessor(const ElemType&) const;
    ElemType successor(const ElemType&) const;
    SortedList& insert(const ElemType&);    // cascading is supported
    SortedList& insertAll(const SortedList&);
    SortedList& remove(const ElemType&);    // remove all occurrences of the argument
    SortedList& removeAll();                // empty the list
    // remove all elements of the receiver that satisfy the test function
    SortedList& removeAllSuchThat(bool (ElemType::*pTestFn) ());
    bool isSublist(const SortedList&) const;
    // return a copy of the indicated sublist
    List sublist(int startIndex, int length) const;
    // return a list containing all elements of the receiver that satisfy the test function
    SortedList allSuchThat(bool (ElemType::*pTestFn) ());
    // operator=(), operator==(), operator!=(), operator[](), operator+(), operator+=(),
    // operator-(), operator-=() and operator<<() in exercises 11.10 and 11.32
};
```

Code the definition of the class SortedList and its member functions using each of the following storage structures. For each storage structure, define whatever nonpublic data members, static data members, auxiliary functions, or auxiliary classes are necessary.

(a) a sorted dynamic resizable array (two versions are described in exercise 10.40)

(b) a sorted linked list

(c) a binary search tree of element nodes

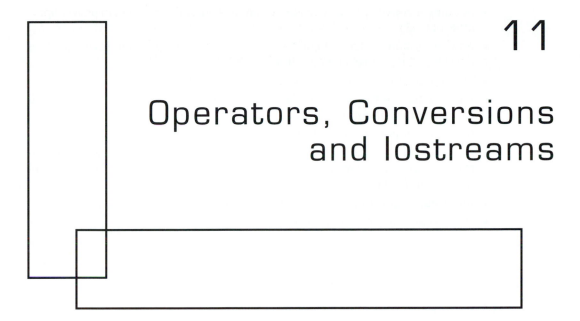

11

Operators, Conversions and Iostreams

OVERVIEW

In this chapter, we continue our discussion of classes in C++. We examine overloading operators so that clients can use the standard expression syntax with class instances, defining conversions among classes and between classes and built-in types, and object input/output and the iostream class library.

This chapter covers the following topics:

- overloading operators for class instances (11.1.1)

- determining whether to define an operator as a member function or a file scope function (11.1.2)

- overloading the assignment operator to provide the correct behavior for objects that allocate resources (11.1.3)

- overloading the new and delete operators to provide class-specific memory management (11.1.4)

- overloading the -> and prefix * operators to control access to instances of the class (11.1.5)

- reducing the number of overloadings necessary with implicit type conversions, and using conversions explicitly (11.2.1)

- defining a conversion as a single-argument constructor or a conversion operator (11.2.2)
- how programmer-defined conversions interact with resolving invocations of overloaded functions and operators (11.2.3)
- overloading the << and >> operators for classes (11.3.1)
- the structure of the iostream class library, and the new ANSI/ISO Standard Library for input/output (11.3.2)
- the input/output protocol of the iostream classes (11.3.3)
- the error and format state of a stream, the member functions and manipulators for accessing that information, and the techniques used to implement manipulators (11.3.4)
- file streams and stream positioning (11.3.5)
- streams of bytes in memory (11.3.6)

11.1 OPERATOR OVERLOADING

11.1.1 Programmer-Defined Operators

Purpose

The class designer can overload the standard predefined C++ operators so that clients can use class instances with the same familiar expression syntax as instances of built-in types. This feature is part of the language's support for providing first-class status for class instances. For example, the equality operator == is not predefined for class objects (as with structures in C). The C++ class designer can supply a definition for this operator and the != operator so that instances of the class can be compared using the usual syntax. The ordering comparisons <, <=, >, and >= can be defined in a manner appropriate for the class and then used in expressions, rather than using a named function such as lessThan(). Similarly, the designer of a numeric class such as Fraction or Complex can define functions for the various arithmetic operators so that clients can use arithmetic expression syntax with class instances.

The only predefined operators for a class are the assignment operator =, the component selection operator. (and therefore the -> operator for pointers to class objects), and the unary "address of" operator &. When creating the interface for a class, we may choose to define other operators as well. Examples include

- == and != for equality tests
- arithmetic operators for numeric classes, including vectors and matrices
- << and >> for output and input
- = for replacing an object's state with that of another
- <, >, <=, and >= for comparing objects for a linear ordering

- [ ] for accessing the nth element of an array, list, or string
- + for joining objects, such as string or list concatenation.

Each operator that we define should have a meaning and usage that correspond to those that it has for built-in data types so that the meaning of an expression in which it occurs is clear. Other semantics for any of these operators will certainly confuse both the reader and the programmer. Similarly, an application of + should result in a new object while += should modify the value of its left operand.

Given the opportunity to provide expression syntax for a class, programmers are often tempted to overuse this capability, especially programmers who prefer C's terseness. When the meaning of an operator for instances of a class is not obvious, it is better to use a named member function. For example, using the ++ and −− operators to convert strings to uppercase or lowercase, or using + or - to insert and remove elements of a collection may be confusing for the reader. Extending the semantics of an operator in an obvious way—for example, the use of + and += for string concatenation, or + and * (or perhaps & and |) for set intersection and union—is reasonable.

The language does not enforce the expected relationships among particular operators for operator overloadings, and the class designer must give a definition for each operator for it to be available with the class's instances. For example, it is up to the class designer to ensure that += performs the same operation as the binary +, and assigns that result to the left operand. Similarly, the relationships between == and !=, between ++ and —, among <, >, <=, and >=, and so on should be preserved in the definitions for those operators.[1]

Operator definition

We define an operator overloading in the same manner as any function by giving a function declaration and a function body. Essentially, an operator is a function that has a special invocation syntax the compiler is aware of. The function name used in the operator declaration or definition is the reserved word operator followed by the operator symbol(s). We can define an operator overloading either at file scope, or as a member function of the class of its operand for a unary operator, or of its left operand for a binary operator. That is, a binary operator defined as a member function is regarded as a message passed to its left operand with the right operand as the argument. Clearly, in a member function overloading of a unary operator, the operand is the receiver and there is no argument.

For example, we can overload the equality operator for the class Point as a member function, as follows:

```
// member function equality operator for class Point
inline bool Point::operator==(const Point& rhs) const
```

---

[1] The ANSI/ISO Standard Library includes a template function that defines the != operator in terms of the == operator, and three template functions that define the <=, >, and >= operators in terms of the < operator.

```
{
   if ( (x_ == rhs.x_) && (y_ == rhs.y_) )
      return true;
   else
      return false;
}
```

We must also define Point::operator!=() to use it with instances of the class. There can be any number of overloadings of an operator at file scope, within classes, or both, as long as each has a different argument signature. The compiler uses the same process for resolving overloaded operators as for disambiguating overloaded functions.

The [ ] operator should return an *l*-value (i.e., a reference) because clients expect to be able to use an application of the operator on the left side of an assignment or as an argument passed by reference. Returning a reference also avoids creating a temporary copy when the operator is used. In a declaration or definition of the [ ] or ( ) operator, the argument signature follows the function name as usual. The parser is aware that the argument is enclosed within the brackets or parentheses following the receiver in an invocation. For example, we can define the [ ] operator to access the nth character in a string object, as follows:

```
// index operator for class String
#include <iostream.h>        // for cerr and operator<<()
inline char& String::operator[](int index)
{
   if ( index < 0 || index > length_ - 1 )
   {
      // throw an exception (see section 13.3) if implemented, otherwise:
      cerr << "subscript range error on a string" << endl;
      exit(1);
   }
   return str_[index];
}
```

We can then write code such as the following:

```
// use of String::operator[]()
#include "String.h"
int main()
{
   String str1("foo"), str2("bar");
   char ch = str2[0];
   str1[0] = ch;
}
```

However, we cannot use this operator definition with a const string object because it is not a const member function. It is not const because the client can use the operator on the left side of an assignment to modify the receiver. We can define a const overloading as follows:

```
// index operator for const String objects
#include <iostream.h>        // for cerr and operator<<()
inline const char& String::operator[](int index) const
{
   if ( index < 0 || index > length_ - 1 )
   {
      // throw an exception (see section 13.3) if implemented, otherwise:
      cerr << "subscript range error on a string" << endl;
      exit(1);
   }
   return str_[index];
}
```

Because the result of this overloading of the operator is of type const char&, we cannot use the operator in a context in which the receiver would be modified (e.g., on the left side of an assignment or as a non-const char& parameter). The compiler will use the const attribute of the receiver to determine which overloading to invoke.

When overloading the ++ and — — operators to "increment" or "decrement" an object, the class designer usually needs to distinguish between overloadings of the prefix and postfix uses of these operators. For example, either a prefix or postfix use of the operator may be called for within the corresponding methods. Unfortunately, both the prefix and postfix uses of these operators have the same argument signature. To indicate which usage a definition overloads, the class designer defines a postfix member function overloading of operator++() or operator—() with an int parameter that is not used in the operator definition. The prefix usage is defined with a member function definition with no parameter.

Like functions, we can define operator overloadings in one code file and declare and invoke them in another. For this reason, the compiler's name encoding scheme must support operator functions using characters that are permitted in names visible to the linker.

Restrictions on operator overloading

An operator overloading must take at least one class argument. This restriction prevents a programmer from altering the behavior of an operator for built-in types. For example, we cannot overload the / operator so that it creates an instance of a class Fraction when we use it with two int operands. Only the existing C++ operators may be overloaded, so we cannot create new operators such as ** for exponentiation.[2] The predefined arity (number of operands) of an operator cannot

---

[2] We cannot use the ∧ operator for exponentiation because it has the wrong precedence and associativity.

be changed, and default arguments are not allowed for operator definitions. For example, the following declaration is invalid:

```
// invalid attempt to declare operator~() as a binary operator for class String
String String::operator~(const String&);
```

In addition, there is no mechanism for changing the associativity and precedence of an operator. Without these restrictions, the compiler's rules and tables for parsing expressions would have to be extensible, and the process of defining an operator overloading would be more complex. Understanding code that uses the new operators in expressions together with predefined operators would also be difficult because the reader would have to refer to the definitions of the new operators to determine the order of execution.

The operators ::, .*, ., sizeof, and ?: cannot be overloaded.

11.1.2 Member Versus File Scope Definition

Member and file scope definitions

When we define an operator overloading as a member function, it is encapsulated within the class of an operand and its code can access any member of the objects of that class directly. On the other hand, a non-member overloading can only access public members of its operands, unless it is declared a friend function of their class. The member function definition of an operator has one fewer parameter because of the implicit this pointer, and requires that its left operand be an object of its class. C++ requires the assignment =, subscript [ ], invocation ( ), and member selection -> operators to be defined as nonstatic member functions, rather than as file scope functions, so that the left operand will be a class object.

To illustrate member and file scope definitions of operators, let us define a class Complex with protected double data members real_ and imag_ representing the real and imaginary components of a complex number, as follows:[3]

```
// Complex.h: a class representing complex numbers (#ifndef, etc. omitted)
class Complex
{
public:
   Complex(double re = 0.0, double im = 0.0)
      : real_(re), imag_(im)
      { }
   double real() const
      { return real_; }
```

---

[3] The Standard Library defines a class complex for complex numbers. The class defines arithmetic operators and several mathematical functions such as real(), imag(), abs(), log(), exp(), pow(), sqrt(), sin(), and atan(). However, all these functions are defined as file scope functions rather than as messages, presumably because C programmers are used to calling those functions in that manner for the built-in numeric types.

```
double imag() const
        { return imag_; }
    // ... other member functions ...
protected:
    double real_;
    double imag_;
};
```

We will certainly want to overload the arithmetic operators for this class. As an example, consider overloading the + operator. This operator function should return a new Complex object rather than adding the right-hand side into the left-hand side object, because the latter operation would be operator+=(). The definition of the + operator for complex objects as a member function appears as follows:

```
// illustrates member function definition of operator overloading
inline Complex Complex::operator+(const Complex& rhs)
{
    return Complex(real() + rhs.real(), imag() + rhs.imag());
}
```

The operator function returns by value because it creates a new object. (Recall that the compiler can usually create that object directly in the caller.) A file scope non-member definition of the + operator for complex objects takes two arguments, and is coded as follows:[4]

```
// illustrates file scope nonmember definition of operator overloading
inline Complex operator+(const Complex& lhs, const Complex& rhs)
{
    return Complex(lhs.real() + rhs.real(), lhs.imag() + rhs.imag());
}
```

We can then use either definition in expressions. Operator functions can also be called using the function name syntax. The following examples illustrate these invocations:

```
// invoking an overloaded operator
#include "Complex.h"
int main()
{
    Complex cplx1(1.0, 1.0), cplx2(2.0, 2.0);
    Complex cplx3 = cplx1 + cplx2;              // for either definition
    Complex cplx4 = cplx1.operator+(cplx2);     // member function syntax explicit
    Complex cplx5 = operator+(cplx1, cplx2);    // file scope function syntax explicit
}
```

---

[4] It is common practice in C++ to use the identifiers lhs and rhs to refer to the "left-hand side" and "right-hand side" operands of an operator.

Conversion of the left operand with file scope definitions

In keeping with object-oriented design principles, we prefer an operator over-loading to be a member function so that it is encapsulated. However, we will see in this subsection that there is a particular circumstance in which we need to define an operator overloading for class objects at file scope.[5] This occurs when we want to allow conversion of the left operand of a binary operator or of the operand of a unary operator, because the compiler never applies a conversion to the receiver of a message.

In an expression that adds an int and a double, the compiler implicitly converts the int to a double and performs double addition. We would like to be able to add an instance of Complex and a double, with the double being converted to a complex object (i.e., with a zero imaginary part) and Complex addition being performed. For example,

```
// implicit conversions for arithmetic operations
#include "Complex.h"
int main()
{
    int num = 3;
    double dbl = 1.0;
    Complex cplx(2.0, 2.0);
    dbl = dbl + num;   // num converted to double
    cplx = cplx + dbl; // dbl converted to Complex
}
```

As we will see in section 11.2.2, the constructor Complex::Complex(double)[6] pro-vides the conversion from double to Complex, and the compiler can use that con-version implicitly if necessary in argument matching. Clearly, we want this conversion to be performed whether the double is the left or right operand of the + operator. However, double is a built-in type and cannot be the receiver of a mes-sage, and the compiler does not apply conversions to the receiver of a message. If we use the member definition Complex::operator+(), we would have to define a sep-arate file scope definition of operator+() that takes a double left operand and a Com-plex right operand.

For this reason, we define a single file scope overloading that takes two Com-plex arguments for each arithmetic operator. In this way, clients can use one oper-ator definition with either operand being converted from double to Complex, as in the following examples:

```
// conversion of either argument with file scope operator overloading
// the implicit conversion Complex::Complex(double) is discussed in section 11.2.2
```

---

[5] We will see in section 11.3.1 that input and output operator overloadings for class objects are also defined at file scope.

[6] This is Complex::Complex(double, double) with the default value used for the second argu-ment.

```
#include "Complex.h"
int main()
{
    double dbl = 3.0;
    Complex cplx1 = 1.0 + Complex(2.0, 2.0);     // left operand converted
    Complex cplx2 = cplx1 + dbl;                 // right operand converted
}
```

Therefore, to handle mixed-type operations involving class operands, the class designer uses a file scope operator overloading so that the compiler can apply an implicit conversion to either argument. The file scope overloading of the operator is declared in the class header file and defined in the class code file (unless it is inline), so that it is associated with the class and is included for use by clients of the class.

Similarly, the constructor String::String(const char*) provides a conversion from a (const or non-const) char* to an instance of String. We define operators for the class String such as operator==(), operator<() (for ASCII ordering), and operator+() (for concatenation) at file scope so that they can support both the argument signatures (String&, const char*) and (const char*, String&). Unlike the overloadings for Complex numbers, these operator definitions must be friends of the class String as they access the protected str_ members of both operands. For example, we define operator==() for strings as follows:

```
// the file scope friend definition for the operator allows either argument to be a char*
#include <string.h> // to use C standard library functions
bool operator==(const String& lhs, const String& rhs)
{
    if ( lhs.length_ != rhs.length_ )
        return false;
    if ( !strcmp(lhs.str_, rhs.str_) )
        return true;
    else
        return false;
}
```

Another case in which the class designer would use file scope definitions is arithmetic operators involving an instance of a Vector or Matrix class and an int or double (i.e., with the latter treated as a scalar).

On the other hand, an overloading for operator+=() for complex numbers requires a complex left operand because we want to be able to add a double value "into" a complex number, but not vice versa. We define this operator as a member function as follows (we discuss the necessity of returning the receiver in the next section):

```
// assignment operators are defined as member functions that return references
inline Complex& Complex::operator+=(const Complex& rhs)
{
```

```
        real_ += rhs.real_;
        imag_ += rhs.imag_;
        return *this;
    }
```

Note that this operator function does not create a new object.

11.1.3 The Assignment Operator

Returning a reference to the receiver

With built-in types, the assignment operators and the prefix ++ operator return the modified value so that the result of the operation can be used as an *r*-value in expressions. We should also support cascading of assignments for class objects, as in the following examples (right to left associativity is used for assignment operators, as in C):

```
// cascading of assignments with class objects
#include "String.h"
#include "Complex.h"
int main()
{
    String str1("foo"), str2("bar"), str3("quux");
    str1= str2 = str3;          // "quux" assigned to str2 and then str1
    Complex cplx1(1.0, 1.0), cplx2(2.0, 2.0), cplx3(3.0, 3.0);
    cplx1 += cplx2 += cplx3;  // cplx2 becomes 5.0+5.0i and cplx1 becomes 6.0+6.0i
}
```

To provide this behavior for the instances of a class, the class designer must implement these operators with methods that return *this. Because the object being modified by the assignment already exists, the method returns the receiver by reference to avoid copying and destroying a temporary object. For example, if the string assignment operator returned by value, the result of the assignment str2 = str3 in the previous example would be copied to a temporary object used as the right operand of the assignment to str1.

The default assignment operator

As we stated in section 1.1.4, assignment is a different operation than initialization for objects with dynamic subobjects, although both operations use the same symbol = in C++. The difference in semantics is that the target identifier of an assignment already refers to an existing object, whereas in an initialization, it merely refers to a region of storage.

As with structures in C, assignment is automatically supported for classes in C++. Like the default copy constructor provided for initializations and value arguments, the compiler provides a default function for assignment of one class object to another. This operator is supplied implicitly for each class when it is defined, and the programmer can use it to assign an object to an existing static, automatic, or dynamic object (i.e., an assignment to a dereferenced pointer). This *default assignment operator* is implemented by member-by-member assignment of the nonstatic data members of the argument to the data members of the receiver. That is, the compiler generates an operator definition of the following form:

```
// the format of the compiler-generated default assignment operator
Class& Class::operator=(const Class& rhs)
{
    mem1 = rhs.mem1;
    mem2 = rhs.mem2;
    // ... assignments for other members ...
    return *this;
}
```

However, objects with pointer members and dynamic subobjects have the same problems that we described for copy constructors in section 10.2.5. Consider the following example:

```
// problems with the default assignment operator for a class with dynamic subobjects
#include "String.h"
void func()
{
    String str1("hello");
    String str2("world");
    // both str1.str_ and str2.str_ refer to the same subobject,
    // and the old str2.str_ cannot be deallocated
    str2 = str1;
    // ... other processing ...
}                           // destructors for both str1 and str2 invoked
```

After the assignment, both str1.str_ and str2.str_ point to the same char array, as with the default copy constructor. With assignment, there is the additional concern that the region to which str2.str_ referred before the assignment can no longer be deallocated, causing a memory leak. This situation is diagrammed in Figure 11.1.

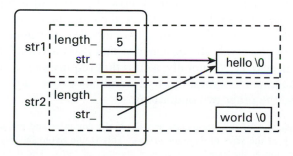

stack frame for func()   **heap**

Figure 11.1 Effect of the default assignment operator on instances of String.

The programmer-defined assignment operator

The solution is for the class designer to define an overloading of operator=() that performs the operations appropriate for that class. The assignment operator function takes a const *Class*& argument (like the copy constructor) and returns *Class*&. For the class String, the assignment operator method deallocates the receiver's subobject, and then sets its str_ member to a new copy of the argument string's subobject. Dealing with the target identifier's former value is what differentiates assignment from initialization. However, the code we just described will cause an error for an assignment from a variable to itself (e.g., str1 = str1), because the receiver's subobject is deallocated and then copied. The String assignment method deals with that case first. We code the assignment operator for class String as follows:

```
// assignment operator for class String
String& String::operator=(const String& rhs)
{
    if ( this == &rhs ) // comparing pointers, not operator==(String&, String&)
        return *this;
    length_ = rhs.length_;
    delete [ ] str_;
    str_ = new char[length_ + 1];
    strcpy(str_, rhs.str_);
    return *this;
}
```

As another example, the method for Queue& Queue::operator=(const Queue&) deallocates the receiver's linked list before copying the argument's linked list to the receiver. For a collection implemented as a dynamic array, such as the class CharStack in section 1.1.4, the assignment method checks whether the number of elements in the argument is less than the physical size of the receiver's array. If so, the method empties the receiver's array and then copies the argument's elements to it.[7] Otherwise it deallocates the receiver's array, allocates a new array large enough for the argument's elements, and copies those elements.

Generally, an assignment operator method performs assignments for value data members, and uses the code of a destructor followed by that of a copy constructor for a pointer member whose referent is allocated by the class's constructor. As we discussed with respect to copy constructors, the class designer assumes that if a value data member is of class type, the designer of that class has implemented an assignment operator if necessary. Generally, a class that requires a destructor, a copy constructor, or an assignment operator due to dynamic allocation or other class semantics, must also define the other two operations.

---

[7] We might consider doing this for the String class as well, as the compiler and memory management system must keep track of the sizes of dynamic arrays. This would avoid the overhead of dynamic allocation and deallocation at the expense of unused memory in *str_. The data member length_ would then reflect the number of characters in the instance rather than the size of the dyna array.

Assignment operators for composite classes

Suppose that a composite class does not define an assignment method, but the class of a data member does. In this case, the assignment in the body of the compiler-generated operator definition will invoke the assignment operator for the data member's class. For example, the compiler creates the following assignment method for the class Person introduced in section 10.2.4:[8]

```
// the default assignment operator for class Person
Person& String::operator=(const Person& rhs)
{
   if ( this == &rhs )
      return *this;
   name_ = rhs.name_;          // String::operator=() invoked
   address_ = rhs.address_;    // String::operator=() invoked
   birthdate_ = rhs.birthdate_;   // Date::operator=() invoked
   ssn_ = rhs.ssn_;
   return *this;
}
```

Because the default assignment operator invokes String::operator=() and Date::operator=(), the designer of Person need not define an overloading of the assignment operator. As discussed with respect to copy constructors, the designer of a composite class is not responsible for managing resources needed by the classes it uses for data members. However, if a composite class defines an assignment operator due to its resource usage, its method must include explicit assignments of data members so that they are copied correctly.

11.1.4 Class-Specific Memory Management

Purpose

new and delete are operators rather than reserved words, so the class designer can control dynamic allocation of the class's instances by overloading the new and delete operators. Doing so can increase the efficiency of a program that frequently creates and destroys many objects on the heap, because allocating and deallocating a number of objects of the same size is much more efficient than using a general-purpose storage management procedure. We can also overload these operators to customize memory management for particular memory architectures, such as for a given page size, or for objects in shared memory or an external database. As with the global versions of these operators, the class's constructor is invoked implicitly after the member new operator is executed, and its destructor is called before the member delete operator is executed. The operators new [ ] and delete [ ] can also be overloaded to control allocation of dynamic arrays of class instances.

---

[8] In fact, this assignment would not be allowed because the data members birthdate_ and ssn_ are const. We will ignore this detail for the purpose of this discussion.

The most common example of overloading the new and delete operators is a class for the nodes in a linked structure, such as the class Node in section 10.1.3. The class defines a static member that points to a linked list of regions for previously allocated nodes that will be reused when a new node is needed. When the client applies new, the class's new method removes an object from that list and returns it. When the client calls delete, that object's region is added to the list. If the list is empty when the client calls new (as it is initially), the class's new method invokes the global operator new [] for the type char to allocate a new block of storage, and that region is threaded into a linked list of regions.

Overloading the new and delete operators

An overloading of operator new() takes an argument of type size_t (this type is defined in the header file stddef.h), and has a return type of void*. The argument is the size of an instance of the type in bytes, and its value in an invocation is initialized by the compiler. The return type is void* because the operator returns a region of storage that has not yet been constructed into an object. An overloading of the delete operator declares a void* parameter and a size_t parameter, and returns no value. The type of the first parameter of the delete operator is void* because the object's destructor has already been executed. The new and delete operator member functions are automatically declared as static members functions.[9] They must be static because we cannot apply them to instances, and they cannot have a this pointer because the object is either not yet constructed or has already been finalized.

To implement this scheme for the class Node, the class defines a static data member that points to the linked list of free nodes, and a static constant data member for the number of nodes in a new region. Of course, clients cannot access these members, and the new and delete operators are only available to Queue methods. We code the modified Node class as follows (for simplicity, we do not nest it within Queue):

```
// Node.h: interface for a class that performs its own memory management
// (#ifndef, etc. omitted)
#include <stddef.h>          // for the definition of size_t

class Node
{
friend class Queue;
friend ostream& operator<<(ostream&, Queue&);
protected:
    Node(const ElemType& el);
    void* operator new(size_t);        // create a node
    void operator delete(void*, size_t);    // deallocate a node
    ElemType elem;
    Node* next;
```

[9] Again, note the similarity between C++ static member functions and Smalltalk class messages.

```
static Node* pFreeList;
static const int regionSize;
};
```

We define and initialize the static members and define the operators in the class code file, as follows:

```
// Node.cc: implementation of a class that performs its own memory management
#include "Node.h"

Node* Node::pFreeList = NULL;
const int Node::regionSize = 32;

void* Node::operator new(size_t size)
{
   Node* pList;
   if ( pFreeList == NULL ) // is freeList empty?
   {
      // use static_cast<Node*>() if available
      pFreeList = (Node*) new char[size * regionSize];
      // link the nodes in the new region
      for ( pList = pFreeList;  pList != &pFreeList[regionSize - 1];  pList++ )
         pList->next = pList + 1;
      pList->next = NULL;
   }
   // remove and return the first node on the free list
   pList = pFreeList;
   pFreeList = pFreeList->next;
   return pList;
}

void Node::operator delete(void* pNode, size_t size)
{
   // insert argument into the free list
   // use static_cast<Node*>() if available
   ( (Node*) pNode)->next = pFreeList;
   freeList = (Node*) pNode;
}
```

11.1.5 Smart Pointers

Purpose and overloading operator->()

In C++, the class designer can overload the -> operator to control access to the instances of a class, or to hide from clients the details of accessing a class's instances. A *smart pointer* is an object that provides access to another object. A smart pointer behaves like a pointer syntactically in the sense that clients use the -> operator to send a message to the object it handles. By overloading the -> operator, the designer of a smart pointer class can "intercept" accesses to instances of a class, and perform any special processing required to make an instance accessible or usable. Typically, a smart pointer class does not provide named member functions, so clients cannot use the . (period) operator with an instance (like a pointer).

Smart pointers are an abstraction that hides the details of making an object available or otherwise processing a use of the object for each access (as the constructor hides the details of initialization, and the destructor hides finalization). Example uses of smart pointer classes include

- providing a uniform access interface for local and remote objects in a distributed system
- providing an interface for persistent objects that are swapped in and out of storage transparently
- counting or logging each use of an instance of the handled class
- implementing reference counting for the handled class so that clients can ignore deallocation
- avoiding resource leaks that can occur with exceptions (see section 13.3.5).

When a client sends a message using -> through a smart pointer, its method for that operator does whatever is necessary to make the object available or process an access. We can also design a smart pointer class so that there are no undefined pointer values, as occur with dangling pointers.

Because clients may need to use the object handled by a smart pointer as a function argument (in addition to sending it messages), smart pointer classes usually overload the prefix * operator (i.e., the dereference operator) to return the handled object. Its method is similar to that of operator->(), except that, as we will see, it returns the handled object, not a pointer to it.[10] The designer of a smart pointer class can use its destructor to control finalization of the object it handles (e.g., to store it back to a database or deallocate it), and of the handle (e.g., to close a connection or release a lock). A smart pointer class can overload the copy constructor and assignment operator with the appropriate behavior, or can declare them as non-public to prevent their use. Pointer arithmetic and the [ ] operator are usually meaningless with smart pointers, but a class for smart pointers that access objects in a sequential file might provide them. It is a syntax error to apply delete to a smart pointer.

The concept of overloading -> to control the use of an object is fairly straightforward, but the details of implementing it in the language are somewhat peculiar. For most infix operators, say == or +, the two operands are expressions that have types, and the compiler uses the operand types to select the correct overloading. However, the right "operand" of -> is a member name, not a typed expression, and it doesn't make sense for it to be an argument of the operator function (e.g., the language has no variables or operators for member names). In fact, all we want to do

---

[10] Perhaps it would have been simpler if the language specified that pObj-> msg() calls operator*() and then selects the named member. In this way, a smart pointer class would just overload operator*().

is to perform some processing before that member is selected. For this reason, if the class of an object smPtr overloads operator->(), the language interprets the expression smPtr->msg(arg) as follows:

```
// the interpretation of smPtr->msg(arg) if ptr's class overloads operator->()
(smPtr.operator->()) -> msg(arg)
```

That is, the compiler invokes the left operand's operator->() function, dereferences the result, and sends the "right operand" message to that object. Therefore, an overloading of operator->() is considered a unary postfix operator, and it must return a pointer (or an object that responds to operator->(), i.e., a smart pointer). The smart pointer operator->() method performs the access processing and returns a pointer to the handled object.[11] An overloading of the -> operator must be defined as a member function, not as a file scope function.

Definition and use

To simplify our example, suppose we have an indexed file of instances of a class, accessed via a key. To illustrate processing each access to an object, suppose that the class maintains a cache of instances, and that the cache size is limited. We may need to write objects that the application might use later back to the disk when the cache is full and the application needs to load a new object. We will use smart pointers so that an object is reloaded into the cache if it is not present when a message is sent through a smart pointer, and is flushed from the cache by the smart pointer destructor.

For example, let us define a class for smart pointers to instances of the class Person described in section 10.2.4, for which the key is the social security number. The following example illustrates the definition and use of the class:[12]

```
// PersonPtr: a class for smart pointers to Persons

// declare the class used as the type of a constructor parameter and a pointer data member
class Person;          // described in section 10.2.4

// classes for static data members
#include "PersonFile.h"
#include "PersonCache.h"

class PersonPtr
{
```

---

[11] Even though an overloading of the -> operator is defined as a unary postfix operator, we cannot write expressions such as smPtr-> to access the pointer the method returns directly.

[12] Because the purpose and implementation of a smart pointer class depend on the object management scheme, not on the type of the object, we usually define smart pointer classes as class templates that are parameterized by the type of object handled. For example, the Standard Library defines a class template auto_ptr that we will discuss in section 13.3.5.

```
public:
    // get a handle to an person object via its social security number
    PersonPtr(long);
    // finalize (i.e., write the Person object back to the file if necessary)
    ~PersonPtr();
    //  send a message to the Person object handled by the receiver
    Person* operator->() const;
    //  obtain a reference to the Person object handled by the receiver
    Person& operator*() const;
protected:
    // the key used to access the object in the file if necessary
    long ssn;
    // the local copy of the persistent Person object used in this application
    // (NULL if the object is swapped out or has not been accessed)
    Person* pPerson;

    // we disallow these to simplify the class
    PersonPtr(const PersonPtr&);
    PersonPtr& operator=(const PersonPtr&);

    // the class PersonFile is implemented as an indexed or direct file 13
    static PersonFile personIndex("personIndexData");
    // the class PersonCache is implemented as a fixed size hash table
    static int CACHE_SIZE;
    static PersonCache cache(CACHE_SIZE);
};

// client use of PersonPtr
#include <Person.h>
#include <PersonPtr.h>
#include <iostream.h>

int main()
{
    long ssn;
    cin >> ssn;
    PersonPtr pPers(ssn);
    // access the person's name
    String str(pPers->name());
    // pass the object by reference to ostream& operator<<(ostream&, const Person&)
    cout << "The person with ssn " << ssn << " is " << *pPers << '.' << endl;
}                           // PersonPtr destructor called
```

The class **PersonPtr** has two data members, the access key (the social security number) and a pointer to a local **Person** object. The **PersonPtr** constructor stores the key, but doesn't load the object yet and sets the pointer data member to NULL.

---

[13] Like the smart pointer class, IndexedFile and Cache would actually be class templates parameterized for the key type and the record type.

A smart pointer's pointer data member is also set to NULL if its referent is flushed from the cache when a client accesses another object. The methods for Person-Ptr::operator->() and PersonPtr::operator*() check whether the hidden pointer is NULL, and reload the object if so. The smart pointer's destructor also checks the pointer and writes the object to the file and removes it from the cache if the pointer is not NULL. Whether the member pPers is null is not visible to the client. For example:

```
// smart pointer constructor and access operators
#include <PersonPtr.h>

inline PersonPtr::PersonPtr(long socSecNum)
   : ssn(socSecNum), pPerson(NULL)
{ }

inline Person* PersonPtr::operator->()
{
   if ( pPerson == NULL )
      // the cache finds space, and then loads the object;  the cache must keep a
      // reference to this->pPerson to set it to NULL if the object gets swapped out
      pPerson = cache.loadFromFile(ssn, personIndex, pPerson);
   return pPerson;
}

inline Person& PersonPtr::operator*()
{
   if ( pPerson == NULL )
      pPerson = cache.loadFromFile(ssn, personIndex, pPerson);
   return *pPerson;
}
```

Note that PersonPtr::operator->() returns a pointer and PersonPtr::operator*() returns the handled object (by reference so that it is not copied). Because the operator functions are inline, there is very little overhead for using a smart pointer instead of a regular pointer. In addition, PersonPtr does not need to be a friend of Person.

   We have disallowed the copy constructor and the assignment operator for PersonPtr to simplify the class and avoid deciding on their semantics. For example, if we wanted them to have the same meaning as copying and assigning regular pointers, these operations would result in more than one smart pointer handling an instance of Person. To implement this, we would need a count of the number of pointers that refer to a person object so that we only finalize the object when no more smart pointers refer to it. (Because the reference counts must be maintained with the handled objects, not with the smart pointers, we would also need an auxiliary class, e.g. CountedPerson.) In addition, the cache would require a list of the smart pointers for each object so that it could set their pointer members to NULL when the object is swapped out. Alternatively, we could specify that a copy or assignment transfers responsibility for the handled object to the target smart pointer.[14] This might be confusing for clients because it is not the same semantics as for regular pointers, and it would lead to the possibility of a "null" smart pointer, namely the source of the copy or assignment. We would certainly need an additional message PersonPtr::isNull() so that clients can check whether a smart pointer is currently handling an object.[15]

When we define a smart pointer class for accessing instances of a class, we don't want clients to use regular pointers to the handled objects because it defeats the purpose of defining the smart pointers. However, as the smart pointer operator*() method returns an instance of the class a client can get a regular pointer to an object with the expression &*pPers. This allows clients to bypass the access processing, and to invoke delete on that pointer. Clearly, either of these would be a problem with PersonPtr. We must assume that clients will not do this.

11.2 PROGRAMMER-DEFINED TYPE CONVERSIONS

11.2.1 Basic Concepts

Purpose

The purpose for implicit conversions is to reduce the number of overloadings necessary for functions and operators. For example, due to the predefined conversions among numeric types, we can define one sqrt() function and pass it an instance of any numeric type, rather than defining an overloading for each. Similarly, the compiler can implicitly promote a char or short to an int, and the language defines one operation taking int arguments for each of the arithmetic, comparison, and bitwise operators. Predefined standard conversions also allow the language to support mixed-type arithmetic operations. Implicit conversions can be used in initializations, assignments, and argument passing.

As we discussed in section 11.1.2, C++ also supports this capability for classes. The language provides two mechanisms for defining conversions for the instances of a class, namely

- a single-argument constructor for the class to which an object is converted (an "inward" conversion)
- a conversion operator member function for the class whose instance is being converted (an "outward" conversion).

---

[14] In this case, the parameters of the copy constructor and assignment operator would not be const because the method modifies the argument.

[15] The test pPers == NULL for a smart pointer pPers is a syntax error unless we overload PersonPtr::operator==(), or provide a conversion from the smart pointer to a regular pointer (as described in the next section). The latter would also allow passing a PersonPtr to a function that takes a Person*, but would give clients a way to bypass the access processing.

Invoking a conversion always creates a new object (except for a conversion to a reference type), rather than allowing the caller to treat the original object as an instance of the type to which it is converted. A programmer-defined conversion can create a class object from an instance of another class or a built-in type, or can create an instance of a built-in type from a class object. We cannot define additional conversions between instances of built-in types.

Once defined, these conversions may be used explicitly by the programmer to create an anonymous object, or invoked implicitly by the compiler to obtain an object of the correct type for initializations, assignments, function arguments, and operator operands. As we saw in discussing member and nonmember overloadings of operators, this feature supports mixed-type operations involving class instances. Programmer-defined conversions also play a role in argument matching and resolving function and operator overloadings. Care is necessary when defining and using conversions because implicit invocations can cause programs to behave in unanticipated ways, especially with overloaded functions.

Predefined conversions

The language supplies certain conversions for all types, and these apply to classes as well. These include

- the trivial conversions between a class and a reference to that class
- the trivial conversions between an array of class objects and a pointer to that class
- the trivial conversion from a class instance to a const class object
- the standard conversion from a pointer to a class object to the type void*.

The compiler can use these conversions implicitly in matching argument and parameter types. All other conversions involving class objects are defined by the designer of the class.

11.2.2 Definition

Constructors as conversions

Each constructor that takes a single argument defines a conversion operator from the type of the argument to that of the class. The argument can be either a built-in type or a class. This mechanism is the only way to define a conversion from a built-in type to a class object, as we cannot define a conversion operator member function for the type. We saw the explicit use of a constructor to create an anonymous object in sections 10.2.2 and 11.1.2, for example, Complex(3.0). The compiler can also use a single-argument constructor as a conversion implicitly.

For example, we can use the constructor for the class Complex defined in section 11.1.2 as a conversion operator because the default value for the second argument allows the constructor to be used with a single double argument. The implicit conversion allows us to use a double object or literal constant in an expression with a function or operator defined for Complex arguments.

```
// conversion using Complex ::Complex(double)
#include "Complex.h"          // defines Complex operator+(const Complex&, const Complex&)
int main()
{
    double dbl = 3.3;
    Complex cplx1(2.0, -3.0);
    // temporary double object converted to Complex
    Complex cplx2 = 1.7 * dbl + cplx1;
}
```

The Complex operation is performed transparently, so the class designer does not have to specify additional overloadings of each arithmetic operator for the argument signatures (double, const Complex&) and (const Complex&, double). As described in section 11.1.2, we define each Complex arithmetic operator as a file scope function so that clients can use a built-in type instance as either operand.

We can also use the constructor String::String(const char*) to convert a C string to an instance of the class String. Suppose we have a member function String::isSubstring(const String&) that returns whether the argument is a substring of the receiver. The compiler will implicitly convert a char* argument to a temporary String object using the single-argument constructor, to which the member function receives a reference.

```
// String::String(const char*) is used implicitly to convert the argument
#include "String.h"
int main()
{
    String str("hello");
    bool test = str.isSubstring("ell");
}
```

This avoids the inconvenience of providing both const String& and const char* overloadings for the numerous functions that take string parameters. However, there is execution-time overhead for this conversion in the case of a class such as String due to the allocation and deallocation of the dynamic subobject of the temporary String object built from a const char* argument. This overhead is not necessary for a function such as String::isSubstring(), which does not modify its argument (and may be frequently used). In this case, a library designer might also supply a separate definition with the signature String::isSubstring(const char*) for efficiency. For example, the Standard Library string class defines two argument signatures for member functions that take a string argument: one that takes a const String&, and another that take a const char*.

The compiler never applies a conversion to the receiver of a message. For example,

```
// the receiver is never converted
#include "String.h"
int main()
{
   String str1("hello");
   char cStr[] = "hello, world";
   bool test = cStr.isSubstring(str1);      // error: String::String(char*) not applied
}
```

Conversion operators

The class designer can also define a conversion operator as a member function of the class of the object being converted. (Conversion operators cannot be defined at file scope.) A conversion operator is the only way of supplying a conversion from a class to a built-in type as built-in types cannot have constructors. Its definition takes the following form:

```
// format for member conversion operator from Class to Type
Class::operator Type()
{... function code that returns Type ...}
```

Type gives the type to which the receiver is converted, and it can be any built-in type, derived type (e.g., a pointer type), or class. The declaration or definition of a conversion operator does not specify an argument list because the receiver is the object being converted. It does not give a return type, although a value of type *Type* must be returned in the function definition code. A conversion operator definition supplies an explicit conversion function the programmer can use with the function notation *Type(obj)*, the C-style cast notation (*Type*) *obj*, or the static cast operator. It also defines an implicit conversion from an instance of *Class* to an instance of *Type*. The compiler can use this conversion when initializing an identifier of *Type* from a *Class* object, or when passing a *Class* object to a function that takes a parameter of type *Type*.

For example, suppose we define a class Byte whose instances are integers in the range 0 to 255. The constructor uses the least significant byte of its argument (i.e., the argument is stored as an unsigned number modulo 256). The class can provide a conversion to int as follows:

```
// class Byte: illustrates definition of a conversion operator (#ifndef, etc. omitted)
class Byte
{
public:
   Byte(int val);          // "inward" int to Byte conversion
   operator int();         // "outward" Byte to int conversion
   // ... other member functions ...
protected:
   unsigned char value;
};
```

```
Byte::Byte(int val)
  : value(val & 0xFF)
{ }

Byte::operator int()
{
    return int(value);
}
```

The compiler can then use Byte::operator int() to convert a byte object to an int in expressions involving +, <, &, and so on. In this way, the class designer does not need to define overloadings of any of these operators for byte objects, nor for all possible argument signatures including bytes. Byte::operator int() can also be invoked implicitly when initializing an int variable from an instance of Byte, or when passing a byte object to a function that takes an int. For example,

```
// implicit use of Byte::operator int()
int gcd(int, int);       // the greatest common divisor of the arguments
#include "Byte.h"
int main()
{
    Byte bt = 0xAA;
    int num1 = bt;           // initializer converted to int
    num1 = num1 * bt;        // second operand converted to int
    int num2 = gcd(bt, 3);   // first argument of gcd() converted to int
    // second argument converted to int, int logical OR performed and
    // result converted to a Byte by Byte::Byte(int)
    Byte mask = 0x0F | bt;
}
```

11.2.3 Conversions and Overloading

Argument matching and resolving overloadings

The compiler disambiguates both operator and function overloadings by the argument matching process described in section 9.2.4. Now that we have discussed how to define conversions, let us review how classes and programmer-defined conversions fit into the argument matching process. The compiler checks for exact matches and trivial conversions, followed by numeric promotions, standard conversions, and finally programmer-defined conversions. In particular, the compiler tries standard conversions before programmer-defined conversions. If a definition of an overloaded function provides an equal or better match for every argument and supplies a strictly better match for one or more arguments, it is invoked.

As we have seen, a programmer-defined conversion can be either a one-argument constructor or a conversion operator. All such conversions are applied at the same stage in argument matching, namely after standard conversions (if no match has been found yet). For example,[16]

---

[16] We note that all of the following examples are presented to illustrate the details of disambiguation. Most would be poor programming practice due to the confusion they would cause for the reader.

```
// a standard conversion is preferred over a programmer-defined conversion
#include "Byte.h"
void func1(long);
void func1(Byte);
int main()
{
    func1(5);              // invokes func1(long)
    func1(Byte(5));        // invokes func1(Byte)
}
```

The first call in this example invokes the overloading func1(long) because the standard conversion from int to long is encountered at an earlier stage in the disambiguation process than the programmer-defined conversion from int to Byte. In the second statement, the programmer uses the Byte::Byte(int) constructor explicitly to ensure invocation of func1(Byte).

Implicit invocation of programmer-defined conversions can cause ambiguity that results in compile-time errors. For example,

```
// ambiguity due to multiple conversions
// defines Class1::operator int(), a conversion from Class1 to int
#include "Class1.h"
// defines Class2::Class2(const C1&), a conversion from Class1 to Class2
#include "Class2.h"
void func2(int);
void func2(const Class2&);
int main()
{
    Class1 c1(...);
    func2(c1);             // error: ambiguous
    func2(int(c1));        // invokes func2(int)
    func2(Class2(c1));     // invokes func2(const Class2&)
}
```

In this example, neither conversion takes precedence because both are programmer-defined. We resolve such an ambiguity with an explicit conversion, as in the last two invocations.

In attempting to match argument and parameter types, the compiler can also apply a standard conversion before or after a programmer-defined conversion. For example, this allows programmer-defined numeric classes to participate fully in arithmetic expressions and functions. However, the compiler will not apply more than one programmer-defined conversion implicitly to the same argument. The following example illustrates these points:

```
// both a standard conversion and a programmer-defined conversion can be applied implicitly
#include "Complex.h"
#include "Byte.h"
int main()
```

```
{
    Complex cplx(1.0, 1.0);
    Byte bt(4);
    // both the standard int to double conversion and Complex(double) are applied
    cplx = cplx + 1;
    // error: two programmer-defined conversions cannot be applied implicitly
    cplx = cplx +  bt;
    cplx = cplx + int(bt);   // OK
}
```

The compiler applies this combination of conversions at the last stage of the argument matching process, and it does not prefer a programmer-defined conversion alone over the combination. The fact that a programmer-defined conversion alone and a programmer-defined conversion with a standard conversion have the same precedence can also be a source of ambiguity.

```
// there is no distinction in precedence between the use of a programmer-defined conversion
// without or with a standard conversion
// defines Class3::Class3(int), a conversion from int to Class3
#include "Class3.h"
// defines Class4::Class4(long), a conversion from long to Class4
#include "Class4.h"
void func3(const Class3&);
void func3(const Class4&);
int main()
{
    func3(1);    // error: ambiguous
}
```

The invocation func3(1) in this example is ambiguous because both overloadings require a programmer-defined conversion, and the fact that func3(const Class4&) also requires a standard conversion does not mean it is less applicable. Again, the programmer can select the intended overloading with an explicit conversion of the argument.

Multiple conversions

The class designer should not define both a single-argument constructor and a conversion operator for the same class-to-class conversion due to the ambiguity that results. For example, suppose we have a class Polygon that represents an instance by storing a list of its corner points. We will need a conversion from a Rectangle, which only stores two points, to a Polygon in which a list of all four corners is stored, so that rectangle objects can be passed to functions that take an instance of Polygon or assigned to Polygon variables. We can define this conversion as a conversion operator in class Rectangle or as a Polygon constructor. However, if both definitions are present, the compiler flags every conversion from an instance of Rectangle to an instance of Polygon as ambiguous because it has two ways of performing the conversion.

```
// two definitions of a Rectangle to Polygon conversion
// defines Rectangle::operator Polygon()
#include "Rectangle.h"
// defines Polygon::Polygon(const Rectangle&), Polygon::intersection(const Polygon&),
// and Polygon::Polygon(const Point[], int)
#include "Polygon.h"

// Polygon::intersect() returns the intersection of the argument and the receiver
int main()
{
    Point arrPoints[] = { Point(1, 1), Point(2, 1), Point(3, 2), Point(3, 3) };
    Polygon poly1(arrPoints, 4);      // a four cornered polygon
    Rectangle rect(Point(2, 3), Point(3, 0));
    // error: ambiguous invocation since both conversions apply for the argument
    Polygon poly2 = poly1.intersection(rect);
}
```

Care is also necessary when defining both a conversion from one type to another, and from the other to the one. For example, a Byte can be converted to an int using Byte::operator int(), and an int can be converted to a Byte using the constructor Byte::Byte(int). This will not cause problems if the class designer does not define the same two-parameter operation for both byte objects and ints. However, suppose we define a conversion from String to char* so that a String object can be used as the argument to a function that takes a char* (e.g., a C library function). We define the conversion to const char* so that the user of the conversion cannot modify the str_ member of the receiver, as follows:

```
// conversion from String to const char*
inline String::operator const char*() const
{
    return str_;
}

// intended use of String::operator const char*()
#include "String.h"
#include <iostream.h>
#include <fstream.h>
int main()
{
    String filename;
    // istream& operator>>(istream&, const String&) is defined in section 11.3.1
    cin >> filename;
    // ofstream::ofstream(const char*, int) discussed in section 11.3.4
    ofstream reportFile(filename, ios::out);
}
```

The difficulty is that we define many binary operators for strings such as ==, !=, <, and so on at file scope to allow using a char* as either operand, with an implicit conversion via String::String(const char*). However, the language also defines these operators for any pointer type, including char*. With String::operator const char*(), an invocation including a char* operand and a String operand is ambiguous. For example,

```
// ambiguous use of operator!=() if the class String defines both String::String(char*)
// and String::operator const char*()
#include "String.h"
#include <iostream.h>
int main()
{
    String inStr;
    cin >> inStr;
    if ( inStr != "quit" )          // error: String or char* inequality test?
    {
        // ... process inStr ...
        cin >> inStr;
    }
}
```

In the expression in the if statement, the compiler cannot determine whether to convert the first argument via String::operator const char*() and compare String instances, or to convert the second argument via String::String(const char*) and compare pointer values. In general, the problem occurs when we have a conversion from class C1 to C2 and from C2 to C1, and there are functions that have both the argument signatures (C1, C1) and (C2, C2).

One solution is to always use an explicit conversion to select the desired overloading, for example, by using the expression inStr != String("quit") in this example. Alternatively, the designer of the class String can define the conversion as a named member function. In this way, clients can use the member function explicitly when necessary, but the compiler does not have a conversion that it can apply implicitly. For example, we can define and use a member function String::str() as follows:

```
// a String member function that converts a String to a const char*
inline const char* String::str() const
{
    return str_;
}
```

```
// intended use
#include "String.h"
#include <iostream.h>
#include <fstream.h>
int main()
{
    String filename;
```

```
    cin >> filename;
    ofstream reportFile(filename.str(), ios::out);
}
```

To help manage these kinds of problems, a new extension to the language allows the class designer to declare a constructor as explicit. This reserved word indicates that clients can use the constructor to create instances of the class, but the compiler cannot invoke it implicitly.

11.3 THE IOSTREAM CLASS LIBRARY

11.3.1 Object Input/Output Operators

Purpose and definition

As we saw in section 9.3.1, the << and >> operators are overloaded in iostream.h for all built-in types. One of the advantages of C++'s output and input operators over the C standard library functions printf() and scanf() is that the class designer can overload them to provide class-specific input/output. In this way, clients can use class objects in data transfer expressions in the same way as instances of built-in types. In addition, the class's input/output behavior is available in input/output operations for classes that use the class as a data member, element type, or superclass. To provide loose coupling among the input, display, and storage operations of related classes, objects should know how to read, print, or store themselves.

The class designer cannot define an overloading of the << or >> operator for the class's instances as a member function of the class because the object to be transferred is the right operand. It cannot be defined as a member of the stream class: That would involve modifying the definition of the stream class in iostream.h to include that member function declaration. (We probably do not have write access to this file, and other programmers are using it.) Instead, we define an overloading of the << or >> operator as a file scope function, but include it in the class's header and code files. In some cases, it may be necessary or more efficient for the operator function to be a friend of the class of the object being transferred. An overloading of the insertion or extraction operator must return a reference to the stream (the left operand) to allow cascaded input/output expressions.

Stream insertion

To print an instance of the class Complex in the standard format, we define the insertion operator as follows:

```
// in Complex.h: insertion operator for Complex objects
#include <iostream.h>
```

```
inline ostream& operator<<(ostream& ostr, const Complex& rhs)
{
    ostr << rhs.real() << '+' << rhs.imag() << 'i';
    return ostr;
}
```

This allows clients to use instances of Complex uniformly together with instances of built-in types, which is not possible with printf().

```
// uniform output of instances of built-in types and programmer-defined classes
#include <iostream.h>
#include "Complex.h"
int main ()
{
    double dbl1 = 1.0, dbl2 = -2.0;
    Complex cplx1 = dbl1 + Complex(dbl1, dbl2);
    cout << dbl1 << '\t' << dbl2 << '\t' << cplx1 << endl;
}
```

If the output operator method needs access to nonpublic members for which there are no accessor functions, it must be a friend of the class. For example, the following file scope function defines the << operator for use with instances of the class Queue defined in sections 10.1.3 and 10.1.4:

```
// defined in Queue.cc, and must be a friend of both the Node and Queue classes
#include "Queue.h"
#include <iostream.h>

ostream& operator<<(ostream& ostr, Queue& qu)
{
    ostr << "Queue ( ";
    Node* pNode;
    for ( pNode = qu.front;  pNode != NULL;  pNode = pNode->next )
        ostr << pNode->elem << ' ';
    ostr << ')' << endl;
    return ostr;
}
```

Note that an overloading of operator<<() for the type of the queue's elements must be present for this function to operate correctly. If not, a compile-time error results at the expression ostr << pNode->elem.

Stream extraction

An overloading of operator>>() must deal with some of the same considerations as an assignment operator method because its right operand already refers to an object. If the extraction operation succeeds, the function must deallocate this object's resources, and then construct a new object from the bytes it extracts from

the stream. An additional issue for input is the possibility of the extraction operation failing due to an invalid input format or a bad stream state. When this happens,
the operator>>() function must set the appropriate bits in the stream's error state so
that the client can test them.

   To illustrate these points, let us define an overloading of operator>>() for the
class String. To demonstrate the mechanism for signaling an invalid input format,
we use the format that a string is a series of characters enclosed in double quotes,
which allows a string to contain whitespace characters. (We will simplify the function code by ignoring the possibility of a double quote within a string.) Like the
extraction operators for built-in types, our function ignores leading whitespace
before the first double quote. To avoid choosing a maximum string length, we use
an ostrstream (a stream of bytes in memory) rather than a char array to hold characters while scanning for the terminal double quote (the class ostrstream is discussed in section 11.3.5). We code the operator>>() function for strings as follows:

```
// in String.cc
#include "String.h"
#include <iostream.h>
#include <strstream.h>      // for the ostrstream local variable

// extract a string (which can contain whitespace characters) enclosed by double quotes
// set failbit if the input format is invalid
istream& operator>>(istream& istr, String& rhs)
{
    if ( !istr )  // check for istr already bad
       return istr;
    char ch;
    istr >> ch;               // operator>>(istream&, char&) skips initial whitespace
    if ( ch != ' " ' )        // a double quote is expected, signal an error if not
    {
        istr.putback(ch);     // insert ch back into istr
        istr.clear(ios::failbit | istr.rdstate());        // set failbit (see section 11.3.3)
        return istr;
    }
    // read chars up to a double quote (istream::get(char&) extracts any character)
    // this code will read forever if no double quote is encountered and istr stays good
    ostrstream buf;
    while ( istr.get(ch) && (ch != ' " ') )
        buf.put(ch);
    if ( !istr )              // EOF or some other problem
       return istr;
    buf << ends;              // append '\0' and flush
    char* inStr = buf.str();  // ostrstream::str() returns a pointer to the buffer
    rhs = inStr;              // String(const char*) and String::operator=()
    delete [] inStr;          // client must deallocate buffer after calling ostrstream::str()
    return istr;
}
```

11.3.2 The Structure of the Iostream Class Library

Design goals

The iostream class library provides a hierarchy of classes for instantiation and inheritance. It defines concrete classes that support stream protocol for terminal input/output, files, and main memory that the programmer can instantiate in applications. The class designer can inherit from the abstract or concrete classes in the library to create problem domain or implementation-level stream classes, such as a stream for a specific file format. The class designer can also define a subclass of a stream class to provide the standard stream interface for other consumers and producers (e.g., to perform insertion into or extraction from an interprocess communication facility, network port, database, or graphic interface view). [Pla95] and [Tea93] discuss implementation of the iostream class library.

The iostream class library provides four advantages over the C standard input/output function library declared in stdio.h. These are

- data abstraction: Data transfer operations are encapsulated in stream classes, and their platform-specific implementations are hidden from clients.
- transparent object input/output: The class designer can overload data transfer operations for class objects (rather than all input/output being done in terms of numeric types and chars).
- type checking: Unlike calls of scanf() and printf(), the compiler can select the correct operation for the type of object.
- extendibility: A class designer can define a subclass of the classes in the stream hierarchy to create a new kind of stream, for example, for a network connection.

As we mentioned in section 9.3.1, most implementations of C++ provide the iostream class library, and the new ANSI/ISO C++ Standard defines a class library that will be required for implementations that conform to the standard. In this section, we discuss the stream and buffer classes that most current programming environments support (essentially, version 2.0 of the AT&T iostream library), and then describe the changes made in the design of the new standard input/output library. [17] In section 11.3.3, we cover messages for input/output, and section 11.3.4 discusses the stream error and format states, and their protocol and manipulators. We will examine file streams in section 11.3.5, and streams in memory in section 11.3.6.

The stream classes

Figure 11.2 illustrates the inheritance hierarchy relationships among the iostream classes. The abstract class ios is the root of the iostream class hierarchy,

---

[17] [Pla95] presents a somewhat out of date description of the Standard Library. The only current description of the Standard Library is the language standard itself [ANS96], which is still under discussion.

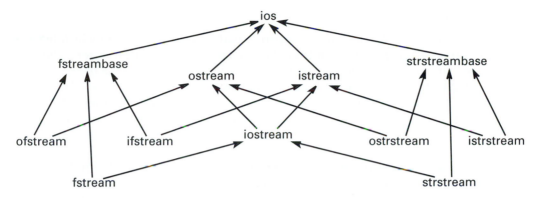

Figure 11.2   The iostream class hierarchy.

and it specifies behavior and state available for all stream classes. It includes the data members that maintain the error and format state of a stream, and the member functions and operators for accessing and manipulating that information. ios encapsulates four enumerations that specify codes for describing the error state, format state, file mode, and seek position, as well as static data members that aid in specifying a format state. It defines a nested class Init and a static data member of that type whose constructor creates the objects cout, cin, cerr, and clog. ios also defines a data member that points to the buffer associated with a stream.

The iostream library also defines

- the class istream for input streams, the class ostream for output streams, and the class iostream for input/output streams
- the classes ifstream, ofstream, and fstream for input and output to files
- the classes istrstream, ostrstream, and strstream, which support stream protocol for arrays of bytes in memory
- the abstract class fstreambase, which defines file protocol and data members that maintain the state of a file and a buffer for the file
- the abstract class strstreambase, which defines a storage structure for streams in memory
- the auxiliary classes streambuf, filebuf, and strstreambuf for the various kinds of stream buffers.

Because the classes ifstream, ofstream, and fstream are subclasses of istream, ostream, and iostream respectively, all the stream operations we discuss are available for file streams. They are also derived from fstreambase, which provides file behavior such as opening, attaching, and closing a file, and state information such as the file descriptor and mode. Programmers can create instances of the concrete file stream classes to transfer data to and from files, and class designers can define subclasses of the file stream classes to support domain or application specific file formats. The classes istrstream, ostrstream, and strstream can also be used for instantiation of and inheritance from streams of bytes in memory.

The buffer classes

The iostream class library supports buffered input/output in which bytes are not transferred directly to or from the ultimate consumer or producer. The buffer for a stream object such as cout or a file stream is an instance of a buffer class provided by the library, and is created automatically by the class's constructor.

The class streambuf is an abstract superclass for buffers that provide a source or sink of bytes for the associated stream, and obtain those bytes from the producer or transmit those bytes to the consumer. It defines protocol for allocating buffer space, inserting and extracting bytes, determining the number of bytes in the buffer, and manipulating the read and write position references in the buffer. It also declares the abstract messages streambuf::underflow() and streambuf::overflow(), which buffer class methods invoke when it is necessary to transfer bytes to the producer or consumer. That is, streambuf::underflow() is called when the stream attempts to read from an empty buffer, and streambuf::overflow() is called when the stream attempts to write to a full buffer.

The abstract class streambuf has two predefined subclasses. The subclass filebuf implements buffering for files, and is declared in fstream.h. It includes constructors, destructors, and member functions for associating a buffer with a file, and opening and closing the file, and defines protected data members that maintain the file descriptor, file mode, file position, and so on. It also implements the methods underflow() and overflow(), which transfer bytes between the buffer and the file. The class strstreambuf is a subclass of streambuf that implements methods for underflow() and overflow() for streams in memory, and is declared in strstream.h. Most programmers do not need to use the buffer classes directly.

To define a stream class that uses a different buffering strategy or a different device, the class designer must also define a subclass of the abstract class streambuf. The manual pages for streambuf (usually called sbuf.pub and sbuf.prot) describe the details of this mechanism, and the ANSI/ISO C++ Standard describes the operation of the methods in its stream buffer classes.

The ANSI/ISO C++ Standard Library input/output classes

The designers of the Standard Library made three major changes to the iostream library, which take advantage of newer C++ features not available when the original AT&T iostream library was developed. The Standard Library

- declares the stream and buffer classes in the standard namespace std
- supports internationalization by defining the stream and buffer classes as class templates that are parameterized for the character type, and by providing a class locale that encapsulates input/output conventions
- supports using exceptions to signal errors.

The Standard Library also makes a number of minor changes such as renaming and dropping some classes (e.g., istrstream is now called istringstream, and strstream no longer exists), and defining additional messages and format codes. (We will describe the minor differences between the Standard Library and the iostream library as we discuss the stream classes and messages throughout this section.) It defines input/output operations for the other Standard Library classes such as strings and collections as file scope operator functions in those class's header and code files, as we did in the previous section for the classes Complex, Queue, and String.

The programmer uses the directive #include <iostream>, rather than including iostream.h, to declare the interface of Standard Library input/output classes and objects. The new header file declares the stream classes in the standard namespace std, rather than at global scope.[18] (We will discuss namespaces in section 13.4.) The "header" iostream is also not necessarily a source file that client code files lexically include before compilation, but may be a file containing precompiled structures. Some other header files have been renamed (e.g., strstream.h is now called sstream) and reorganized (e.g., the header file fstream is now included in the header file iostream).

The ANSI/ISO C++ Standard defines two character types, char and wchar_t (the "wide character" type), the latter of which supports languages with more than 256 characters. The standard library defines the stream classes as templates that take a type parameter indicating which character type the stream contains. (We will discuss templates in sections 13.1 and 13.2.) The classes istream, ostream, streambuf, and so on are defined as specializations of the templates that use char elements. For example, the class istream is typedef'd as basic_istream<char>, the specialization of the basic_istream<> class template for chars. For use with wide characters, the standard also defines the classes wistream, wostream, wofstream, and so on, and the stream objects wout (analogous to cout), win, werr, and wlog. The abstract superclass basic_ios also defines a data member and accessors for an instance of the standard class locale, which defines a locale's character set, string collation sequence, numeric and date/time formats, and so on. Most programmers need not be concerned with these changes, because they can continue to use cout, ifstream, and so on, and the default locale (so we won't cover locales in detail). However, the templates allow a class designer to define new streams that contain new kinds of characters,[19] and locales for other countries.

Input/output operations that fail can raise an exception in addition to setting the stream error state. The programmer can select whether various stream errors raise an exception or not to provide compatibility with existing code, and because using exceptions is still somewhat controversial among C++ programmers. (We will

---

[18] We have mentioned the use of header file names without the .h suffix in the last two chapters. All of the functions, classes, and templates in the Standard Library are declared in the namespace std in the new header files.

[19] The class designer must also define a "traits" structure that gives characteristics such as the character set's null, newline, and end of file characters, and functions such as an ordering function and delimiter and whitespace tests.

discuss exception handling in section 14.3.) The abstract class ios_base defines a nested exception class ios_base::failure that is the type of exceptions the methods in the input/output library raise.

11.3.3 Input/Output Protocol

ostream **protocol**

As we saw in section 9.3.2, the << operator provides formatted insertion for built-in types (including bool in the Standard Library), void*, char*, and stream manipulators. The format state of the receiver (and the locale with the Standard Library) controls the details of the formatting, as we will see in the next section. The manipulators endl, flush, and ends are also defined for ostream objects. The actions of endl and flush were described in section 9.3.2, and ends inserts a null character and flushes the stream.[20] Output streams can also use the << operator with the format state manipulators discussed in the next section, and respond to the error and format state protocol discussed in the next section.

The protocol of ostream includes the member functions ostream::put() and ostream::write(), which perform unformatted insertion, and ostream:: flush(), which flushes the stream buffer. The following portion of the ostream class definition gives their declarations and comments describing their actions:[21]

```
// ostream member function declarations
// (the superclass specifications are described in chapter 12)
class ostream : virtual public ios
{
public:
    ostream(streambuf*);
    virtual ~ostream();
    // insert ch into the receiver
    ostream& put(char ch);
    // insert length chars into the receiver, beginning at buf
    ostream& write(const char* buf, int length);
    // transfer any bytes remaining in the buffer to the consumer
    ostream& flush();
    // ... operator<<() for built-in types and manipulators, and other members ...
};
```

The functions ostream::put() and ostream::write() insert individual characters and arrays of bytes, respectively. Like the insertion operator, these functions return

---

[20] In the Standard Library, the member function traits::eos() in the character traits object determines the null character.

[21] In addition to the member functions listed in this section for ostream and istream, the AT&T iostream library overloads each function that takes a char or char* parameter with an argument signature including a corresponding unsigned char or unsigned char* parameter. However, the Standard Library does not do so.

immediately if the receiver is in the fail state, or set its error state (and, possibly, raise an exception with the Standard Library) if the stream fails during an operation. These messages are typically used to write binary data. You should be careful about using them to write objects because of alignment issues. Clearly, we cannot use them directly with objects that contain pointer members or objects whose classes define virtual functions. These functions and ostream::flush() return a reference to the receiver to allow cascading output operations or testing the state of the stream. Programmers do not usually use the ostream constructor directly.

istream **protocol**

As we saw in section 9.3.3, the >> operator performs formatted extraction for built-in types (including bool in the Standard Library), void*, char*, and stream manipulators. The right operand is passed by reference so it should be an object rather than a pointer (except, of course, for void* and char*). As with output streams, the format state of the receiver controls the details of the formatting. The manipulator ws is defined for istream objects, and it extracts and discards any initial whitespace characters in the stream.[22] Input streams can also respond to error and format state protocol and use the >> operator with format state manipulators.

Like ostream, the class istream defines a number of member functions in addition to operator>>(). The following portion of the istream class definition gives their declarations and comments describing their actions:

```
// istream member function declarations
// (the superclass specifications are described in chapter 12)
class istream : virtual public ios
{
public:
  istream(streambuf*);
  virtual ~istream();
  // extract a char from the receiver and return the char or EOF 23
  int get();
  // extract a char from the receiver into ch
  istream& get(char& ch);
  // extract up to length - 1 chars from the receiver into str, but stop at delim and leave it
  // in the stream, and then append '\0' to str 24
  istream& get(char* str, int length, char delim = '\n');
```

---

[22] In the Standard Library, the member function traits::is_whitespace() determines whether a character is whitespace.

[23] In the Standard Library, the member function traits::is_eof() gives the end of file character.

[24] In the Standard Library, the default for delim is traits::newline(), traits::eof() gives the end of file character, and traits::eos() gives the null character.

[25] The Standard Library string class also defines a file scope function getline(istream&, string&, char delim = traits::newline()).

```
    // extract up to length - 1 chars from the receiver into str, but stop at delim and extract it
    // without storing it in str, and then append '\0' to str 25
    istream& getline(char* str, int length, char delim = '\n');
    // extract chars up to delim from the receiver into sb
    istream& get(streambuf& sb, char delim = '\n');
    // extract length chars from the receiver into buf
    istream& read(char* buf, int length);
    // return the number of chars extracted by the last unformatted input operation
    int gcount();
    // extract and discard up to length characters, or stop if delim or EOF is encountered
    istream& ignore(int length = 1, int delim = EOF);
    // return but do not extract the next character in the stream, or EOF if there is none
    int peek();
    // ... operator>>() for built-in types and other members ...
};
```

The member function istream::get() is overloaded with four argument signatures that perform unformatted extraction. The comments in the previous partial class definition describe the behavior of each. The message istream::getline() is useful for extracting lines from a stream containing newline-delimited text, and istream::read() is typically used for binary data. Unlike operator>>(), the unformatted extraction functions do not ignore leading whitespace or stop extracting at a whitespace character. Like the ostream functions, they set the receiver's error state if the extraction fails (or can raise an exception in the Standard Library), for example, if the istream::read() method encounters an end of file before reading length characters. If so, the argument they read into is not affected. The istream member functions also return a reference to the receiver to allow cascading output operations or testing the state of the stream. In particular, returning a reference allows us to use an extraction operation in the conditional of an input loop, so that the loop terminates at the end of the stream or when an error occurs. For example, we used while (cin >> buf) in the example in section 9.3.3, and will use while (istr.getline(line, LINEBUFSIZE)) in the next example. Programmers do not usually use the istream constructor directly.

Because the method for istream::operator>>(char*) stops extracting at a whitespace character and istream::getline() stops at a newline, we cannot use these messages to input a string that contain spaces and newlines (e.g., a memo or the contents of a scrolled text interface component). The same is true for the string class in most C++ libraries, and for the ANSI/ISO string class. (This is not a problem for ostream::operator<<(char*) because it inserts all characters from the string until it encounters a null character.) One simple work-around for programs that must store strings containing spaces and newlines in files and then retrieve them is to output the length of the string before the string itself. The input function can extract the string's length with istream::operator>>(int), and then extract the string with istream::get() or istream::read() with the length as an argument. (The function must also append a null character to the string if it uses istream::read().)

The following function illustrates the use of the messages istream::getline() and istream::gcount():

```
// using istream protocol
#include <iostream.h>

// Read a stream of lines, and list them on an 80 character wide screen.
// If a line is too long, replace the last character with a baskslash.
// Finally, print the number of characters and the number of lines.
void listLines(istream& istr)        // istr can be a file, a stream in memory, etc.
{
    const int LINEBUFSIZE = 81;      // 80 chars plus '\0'
    char line[LINEBUFSIZE];
    int charCount = 0;
    int longLineCount = 0;
    // extract a line, and stop at the end of the stream or a stream failure
    while( istr.getline(line, LINEBUFSIZE) )
    {
        charCount += istr.gcount();
        // istream::getline() sets failbit if it extracts length - 1 chars
        // without encountering delim 26
        if ( istr.fail() )
        {
            // partial long line
            line[LINEBUFSIZE - 2] = '\\';
            longLineCount++;
            // clear the fail bit in the stream state (see the next section)
            istr.clear(istr.rdstate() & ~ios::failbit);
        }
        else
            charCount—;    // don't count the newline
        cout << line << endl;
    }
    cout << "Number of characters displayed: " << charCount << endl;
    cout << "Number of lines clipped: " << longLineCount << endl;
}
```

iostream **protocol**

The class iostream inherits from both istream and ostream, so it supports all the protocol of both of those classes.[27]

---

[26] On some systems istream::getline() does not set ios::failbit when it extracts length -1 characters without encountering delim. In this case, we cannot distinguish between extracting a line of length length - 1 characters and encountering a line that exceeds the line length.

[27] The Standard Library does not define the class iostream, or any stream classes that support both insertion and extraction.

11.3.4 The Stream State

Iostream state descriptors

The superclass ios defines four enumerations nested within its scope:

- io_state lists names for flags in a stream's error state
- fmt_flags lists names for flags in a stream's format state
- open_mode lists names for file open mode flags
- seek_dir lists names for the reference points for stream positioning.

Defining these names within the class ios encapsulates that information and avoids declaring them in the global name space. The enumerations that define the symbolic names are public, but the data members that maintain a stream's state are protected, and we can only access them through member functions and manipulators described in this section. The following portion of the ios class definition defines these enumerations, and gives comments describing the purpose of each error and format flag:

```
// class ios: enums for error state, format state, file mode and seek starting point
class ios
{
public:
    // the error state of the stream
    enum io_state
    {
        goodbit = 0,            // the stream is in an operable state (no error are flags set)
        eofbit = 1,             // an extraction has reached the end of the stream
        failbit = 2,            // an extraction did not read the expected characters
        badbit = 4,             // the stream is in an unusable state, e.g. a device error
    };

    // the format state of the stream, a long int
    enum fmt_flags
    {
        skipws = 0x1,           // skip whitespace on input
        left = 0x2, right = 0x4,
            internal = 0x8,     // the padding location for the fill character
        dec = 0x10, oct = 0x20,
            hex = 0x40,         // the integer conversion base
        showbase = 0x80,        // show the leading "0x" for hex and leading "0" for octal
        showpoint = 0x100,      // show the trailing decimal point and zeros for floating point
        uppercase = 0x200,      // use uppercase "E" with floating point, and uppercase
                                // alphabetic digits and "X" (if any) with hex
        showpos = 0x400,        // show the leading "+" for positive numbers
        scientific = 0x800,
            fixed = 0x1000,     // mantissa/exponent or decimal floating point notation
```

```
    unitbuf = 0x2000,          // flush after each insertion ("unit buffering")
    stdio = 0x4000             // flush stdout and stderr after each insertion
};


// the open mode: described in section 11.3.5
enum open_mode
{ in = 1, out = 2, ate = 4, app = 8, trunc = 16, nocreate = 32, noreplace = 64 };


// the reference point for seek: described in section 11.3.5
enum seek_dir { beg = 0, cur = 1, end = 2 };


// constants for convenience in manipulating format states
static const long adjustfield;    // left | right | internal
static const long basefield;      // dec | oct | hex
static const long floatfield;     // scientific | fixed


// ... other data members and member functions described later in this section ...
};
```

We can see from the values for the error and format state flags that they are intended to be treated as bits in a "status word". To represent a combination of conditions, we OR the constant values together. For example, opening a file with the mode ios::out | ios::noreplace specifies both that it is an output file and that the operation should fail if the file already exists. To determine the value of a particular flag, we obtain the stream's error or format state, AND the value with that flag, and check the result. Note also that we cannot use the enum type as the type of a variable or parameter whose value is a set of flags, because then it could store only one flag value. Such a variable or parameter must be of type int (for an io_state or open_mode), or long (for a format state) to store an OR of flag values. For example, the message ios::rdstate() returns an int that gives the current stream error state, and the file stream constructors take an int argument that gives the file mode.

In this section, we will cover the meaning of the flags, the member functions and data members declared in ios that access, manipulate, and represent the error and format state, and the implementation of manipulators. We will discuss the open_mode and seek_dir flags in section 11.3.4 on file streams.

The ANSI/ISO C++ Standard Library makes a few changes and additions to the definition of ios and the stream state flags. Like its subclasses ostream and istream, the class ios is a specialization of the basic_ios<> template with char as the character type. The library also defines a specialization wios for streams of wide characters. In addition, the protocol and state of the class ios has been split into a superclass ios_base that defines the flag names and format state, and a subclass basic_ios<>, which is a class template that defines error state. Code that uses ios in qualified names (e.g., ios::out | ios::noreplace), is still correct because ios is a specialization of basic_ios<> and a subclass of ios_base.

The Standard Library defines an additional format flag boolalpha that controls the encoding of booleans. If that flag is not set, boolean values are read and printed as 0 and 1 (as in the original library). If the boolalpha flag is set, the strings that represent the values true and false are determined according to the character set and the locale of the stream.

The Standard Library defines the types ios_base::iostate, ios_base:: fmtflags, and ios_base::openmode (the library does not use the underscore in the type names) as "bitmask" types. A system can implement these types as enumerations, as we did in the previous partial ios class definition, or can generate them from the Standard Library class template bitset<>. A bitset is a fixed-length sequence of bits ("bit-string" would have been a better name since a bitset is fixed-size and ordered), and bitsets of different lengths are instances of different types.[28] The class defines constructors, destructors, assignment, equality tests, the bit manipulation operators, the [ ] operator, and several named member functions such as bitset<>::set(), bitset<>::count(), and bitset<>::any(). Values such as eofbit or dec are declared as static constants of bitset type, usually in the same scope as the bitset class. Variables, parameters, and return types that represent a group of flags are declared as bitsets, rather than as ints.

The error state

As stated in the previous partial ios class definition, the constant ios::good-bit means that the stream is usable, and the flag ios::eofbit is set when an extraction has reached the end of the stream. ios::failbit indicates that an extraction did not find characters in the stream that are a valid format for the type to be read, but the stream is still usable. The flag ios::badbit indicates that a problem has occurred with the producer or consumer of bytes. For example, the istream::operator>>() methods for the built-in types distinguish between ios::failbit and ios::badbit in this way. The methods for unformatted input/output such as istream::get() and ostream::write() can only set ios::badbit (and istream methods can set ios::eofbit).

The following partial ios class definition defines the member functions that access and manipulate of the stream error state:[29]

```
// class ios: protocol for accessing the error state
class ios
{
public:
   // ... the enum io_state was described previously in this section ...
   int rdstate() const              // return the receiver's error state
   { return state; }
```

[28] The class template uses an "expression parameter" for the size of the bitset (like the Stack_Size parameter to the Ada generic package Stack_Type in section 1.1.4), which we will discuss in section 13.2.3.

[29] In this section and the next, we will place methods within the class definitions, rather than defining them separately, because the methods are very short. These member functions are automatically inline.

```
    void clear(int st = goodbit);     // set the receiver's error state to the argument
    bool good() const                 // returns whether the receiver is usable
    { return state == 0; }
    bool eof() const                  // returns whether the receiver is positioned off the end
    { return state & eofbit; }
    bool fail() const                 // returns whether the receiver is unusable
    { return state & (failbit | badbit | hardfail); }
    bool bad() const                  // returns whether the receiver's badbit is set
    { return state & badbit; }
    operator bool()                   // allows use of a stream in a condition
    {
        if ( state & (failbit | badbit | hardfail) )
            return false;
        else
            return true;
    }
    bool operator!() const            // allows use of a stream in a condition
    { return fail(); }
    // ... other member functions ...
protected:
    int state;                        // the error state descriptor
    // ... other data members ...
};
```

The misnamed function ios::clear(int) clears the state only if the argument is the default of 0. For example, to set a stream's failbit without affecting the rest of its error state, we obtain the former state with ios::rdstate(), OR that value with the bit to be set, and use the result as the argument of ios::clear().

```
    // setting the failbit of a stream without affecting other error state flags
    #include <iostream.h>
    inline istream& setFail(istream& istr)
    {
        istr.clear(ios::failbit | istr.rdstate());
        return istr;
    }
```

For use with conditionals, the function ios::good() returns true if no flags are set in the receiver's error state, or false if some flag is set. Similarly ios::eof() and ios::bad() indicate whether the corresponding flags are set, and ios::fail() returns true if any error flag other than ios::eofbit is set.

As described in section 9.3.3, we can use a stream in a conditional expression or statement to test the state of a stream. To allow this usage, the class ios defines a conversion operator overloading that converts the stream to the type bool. The operator returns true if the receiver stream's state is valid, and false if it is in the fail state. Similarly, the unary operator!() is overloaded to return false if the stream is in a good state, and true if not. As most of the ostream and istream functions return the receiver, we can also use a stream message expression in a condition. We did this in the function listLines() in the previous section, and the following is another example:

```
// using stream instances in conditional tests
#include <iostream.h>
#include <stdlib.h> // for void exit(int);
int main()
{
    if ( !cin )                    // int ios::operator!() const;
        exit(1);
    char ch;
    while ( cin.get(ch) )          // ios::operator bool() is applied to the result of istream::get()
    {
        // ... process ch ...
    }
}
```

In the ANSI/ISO C++ Standard Library, the message basic_ios<>::rdstate() returns an instance of the bitset ios_base::iostate, rather than an int, and the parameter type of basic_ios<>::clear() is iostate. The class template also defines the message basic_ios<>::setstate(), which sets the flags in the receiver's state that are set in the argument, leaving the other flags unaffected. The major difference for the Standard Library with respect to the stream error state is support for exceptions. The class template basic_ios<> defines a data member of type ios_base::iostate that gives a set of "exception flags", each corresponding to an error state flag. If execution of basic_ios<>::clear() or basic_ios<>::setstate() sets an error flag that is set in the exceptions bitmask, then the method raises an exception of type ios_base::failure. The programmer can access the exception descriptor with the zero-parameter message basic_ios<>::exception(), or set it with the message basic_ios<>::exception(iostate). We will discuss exception handling in section 13.3.

The format state

The format state of the stream (together with the locale in the Standard Library) controls the details of the character string output by the insertion operator <<, or input by the extraction operator >> for built-in types. If the characters in the stream are not a valid encoding of the expected type, given the stream's format state, the operator>>() method sets ios::failbit. (An insertion cannot set ios::failbit, but it can set ios::badbit.)

The comments in the partial ios class definition at the beginning of this section describe the meaning of the format state flags ios::skipws, ios::showbase, ios::showpoint, ios::uppercase, and ios::showpos, and we discussed ios::dec, ios::oct, and ios::hex in section 9.3.2. For floating-point values, ios::fixed indicates decimal notation, and ios::scientific indicates normalized scientific notation (i.e., mantissa and exponent with one digit to the left of the decimal point in the mantissa). Recall from section 9.3.2 that we can set the "field width" of a stream with the setw() manipulator. When the field width is larger than the length of the output string for an instance of a built-in type, the stream pads the output string with a "fill character". The format flag values ios::left, ios::right, and ios::internal determine the position at which fill characters are inserted.

- ios::left specifies left justification of the output string within the field width, followed by padding if necessary
- ios::right specifies right justification of the output string
- ios::internal specifies that fill characters are inserted between the leading sign or base indication (e.g., 0x for hex) and the remainder of the output string.

In addition to the format flags, a stream also has three private data members that control various formatting details. The "field width" is an int that gives the minimum number of characters inserted. (It is the minimum, not the exact number of characters, because a numeric insertion never truncates the output string.) If the field width is zero, an output operation inserts exactly as many characters as necessary, and zero is the default value. The field width is reset to zero after each operation, so you must set the field width immediately before the operation it pertains to. Extractions ignore the field width, except for operator>>(char*), for which it gives the maximum number of characters read (i.e., if no whitespace is encountered). The "fill character" is the character used to pad an output string to the field width. The "precision" gives the number of digits after the decimal point when outputting a floating-point number, and its default value is 6.

Many stream format flags and data members represent the same information as the format codes used with the C functions printf() and scanf(). Figure 11.3 summarizes these.

C code	C++ stream format state
%d	dec is set (and hex and oct are clear)
%o	oct is set (and dec and hex are clear)
%x	hex is set (and dec and oct are clear)
%X	hex is set (and dec and oct are clear) and uppercase is set
%f	fixed is set (and scientific is not)
%e	scientific is set (and fixed is not)
%E	scientific is set (and fixed is not) and uppercase is set
%n1.n2	the field width is n1, and the precision is n2 (for floating point)
-	left is set (and right and internal are clear)
+	showpos is set
#	showbase is set

Figure 11.3 The correspondence between C stdio format codes and the C++ stream format state.

The following partial ios class definition lists the member functions that access and manipulate the stream format state (we will discuss manipulators that set the stream format state in the next subsection):

```
// class ios: protocol for accessing the format state
class ios
{
public:
    // ... the enum fmt_flags was described previously in this section ...
    // return the receiver's format state
    long flags() const
    { return x_flags; }
    // set the receiver's format state to the argument, and return its previous state
    long flags(long newFlags)
    {
        long retFlags = x_flags;
        x_flags = newFlags;
        return retFlags;
    }
    // set the flags in the receiver that are set in the argument, and return its previous state
    long setf(long mask);
    // set the flags in the receiver that are set in the second argument to their values in the
    // first argument, and return the receiver's previous state
    long setf(long values, long mask);
    // clear the flags in the receiver that are set in the argument, and return its previous state
    long unsetf(long mask);

    // return the receiver's width
    int width() const
    { return x_width; }
    // set the receiver's width to the argument, and return its previous value
    int width(int newWidth);                    // coded like long flags(long)
    // return the receiver's fill character
    char fill() const
    { return x_fill; }
    // set the receiver's fill character to the argument, and return its previous value
    char fill(char newFillChar);                // coded like long flags(long)
    // return the receiver's precision
    int precision() const
    { return x_precision; }
    // set the receiver's precision to the argument, and return its previous value
    int precision(int newPrecision);            // coded like long flags(long)
    // ... other member functions ...
protected:
    long x_flags;
    int x_width;
    char x_fill;
    int x_precision;
    // ... other data members ...
};
```

The messages ios::flags(long), ios::setf(), and ios::unsetf() return the receiver's previous format state so that the caller can restore it if necessary. The argument is typically either an OR of format flags or a previously stored stream state. The messages ios::width(int), ios::fill(char), and ios::precision(int) also return the receiver's former value, for the same purpose. Note that none of these member functions returns the receiver stream, so we cannot cascade them with other stream messages or manipulators, or use them as conditionals.

The following program illustrates the meaning of the ios format flags, and the use of ios::setf() and the constants defined in ios:

```
// ios stream format flags and ios::setf()
#include <iostream.h>
int main()
{
    int num = 166;
    cout.setf(ios::showpos);
    cout << "dec | showpos: " << num << endl;    // dec is the default
    cout.setf(ios::hex, ios::basefield);
    cout.setf(ios::uppercase);
    cout << "hex | uppercase: " << num << endl;
    cout.fill('*');
    cout.setf(ios::showbase);
    cout.setf(ios::internal, ios::adjustfield);
    cout << "hex | uppercase | showbase | internal: ";
    cout.width(8);
    cout << num << endl;

    double dbl = 20000.0 / 3.0;
    cout.precision(5);
    cout.setf(ios::fixed, ios::floatfield);
    cout << "fixed: " << dbl << endl;
    cout.setf(ios::scientific, ios::floatfield);
    cout << "scientific: " << dbl << endl;
    cout.setf(0, ios::showpos | ios::uppercase);
    cout << "showpos & uppercase off: " << dbl << endl;
}
```

The program produces the following output:

```
dec | showpos: +166
hex | uppercase: A6
hex | uppercase | showbase | internal: 0X****A6
fixed: +6666.66667
scientific: +6.66667E+03
showpos & uppercase off: 6.66667e+03
```

A stream prints in decimal by default, and the flag ios::showpos indicates that the sign should appear for positive numbers. The call cout.setf(ios::hex, ios::basefield) illustrates the use of the constant ios::basefield as the second argument of ios::setf(long, long). Because ios::basefield is dec | oct | hex, the call clears the dec or oct flag if either is set, as well as setting the hex flag. We use the constants ios::adjustfield and ios::floatfield in the same way. When the third line is printed, the flags ios::hex and ios::uppercase are still set, in addition to the flags ios::showbase and ios::internal. Note also that the invocation of ios::width() immediately precedes the corresponding insertion. The flags ios::showpos and ios::uppercase are still on when we print dbl, and are turned off for the last insertion. We will see in the next subsection that this program is much easier to read and write with manipulators.

In the ANSI/ISO C++ Standard Library, a stream also has a data member that maintains its locale. We can access this instance of the Standard Library class locale with the message ios_base::getloc() or set it with the message ios_base::imbue(), which also returns the previous locale. A stream's locale is set to locale::classic() by default, so programmers usually do not need to deal with the locale directly. The locale class provides functions that give the output strings for numeric values, times and dates, currency amounts, and booleans. In the Standard Library, the message ios_base::flags() returns an instance of the bitset ios_base::fmtflags, rather than a long, and the parameter type of ios_base::setf() and ios_base::unsetf() is ios_base::fmtflags.

Format state manipulators

The classes ios, ostream, and istream define a number of stream manipulators that allow us to write cascaded expressions intermingling data transfer operations and stream state manipulations in a uniform manner. Most manipulator functions modify the stream's state rather than performing an insertion or extraction. (The exceptions are the ostream manipulators endl, flush, and ends, and the istream manipulator ws.) The AT&T iostream library defines the following format state manipulators:

- dec, hex, and oct control the integer conversion base
- setioflags(long) sets the format flags that are set in the argument
- resetioflags(long) clears the flags that are set in the argument
- setw(int) sets the receiver's field width to its argument
- setfill(char) sets the receiver's fill character to its argument
- setprecision(int) sets the receiver's precision to its argument.

The manipulator dec clears ios::hex and ios::oct, and similarly for the manipulators hex, oct, left, right, and internal. Like ios::setf() and ios::unsetf(), the argument of setioflags() and resetioflags() is typically a logical OR of the flags the programmer wants to set or reset. The ANSI/ISO C++ Standard Library adds the following manipulators:

- left, right, and internal control the padding location
- fixed and scientific control the floating-point notation
- showbase and noshowbase control whether an octal or hexadecimal integer insertion prints the leading base indicator
- showpoint and noshowpoint control whether a floating-point insertion prints the trailing decimal point and zeros
- showpos and noshowpos control whether to print the leading + for positive numbers
- skipws and noskipws control whether an extraction skips leading whitespace
- uppercase and nouppercase control whether to print upper- or lowercase e with scientific floating-point, or x with hexadecimal integers
- boolalpha and noboolalpha control whether a bool is printed as 0 or 1, or as a locale-specific string.

The manipulator notation simplifies expression because of the cascading, and because the constants ios::basefield and the qualified names are not necessary. We can rewrite the program in the previous subsection more succinctly using manipulators, as follows:

```
// ios stream format flags with manipulators
#include <iostream.h>
int main()
{
    int num = 166;
    // showpos would be setioflags(ios::showpos) with the AT&T iostream library
    cout << showpos << "dec | showpos: " << num << endl;
    cout << hex << uppercase << "hex | uppercase: " << num << endl;
    cout << setfill('*') << showbase << internal;
    cout << "hex | uppercase | showbase | internal: " << setw(8) << num << endl;

    double dbl = 20000.0 / 3.0;
    cout << setprecision(5) << fixed << "fixed: " << dbl << endl;
    cout << scientific << "scientific: " << dbl << endl;
    cout << noshowpos << nouppercase << "showpos & uppercase off: " << dbl << endl;
}
```

In the Standard Library, the parameter type of setioflags() and resetioflags() is ios_base::fmtflags, rather than long. The Standard Library also defines a manipulator setbase(int) that sets the integer conversion base to dec, hex, or oct, depending on whether its argument is 10, 16, or 8.

Implementation of manipulators

First, let us discuss how the designers of the iostream library implement manipulators that do not take a parameter, such as endl and dec. A manipulator name is actually the name of a file scope function that takes a reference to a stream, performs some activity involving the stream, and then returns a reference to that stream. The stream classes define overloadings of the insertion and extraction operators that take a pointer to such a function as the right operand. When we write cout << endl, one of these overloadings is invoked because the "address of" operator & is optional when assigning or passing a function name to a pointer to function (i.e., the expression is actually cout << &endl). The following example illustrates the file scope function and insertion operator overloading that implement the endl manipulator:[30]

```
// implementation of manipulators that do not take arguments
// <iostream.h> specifies the following function and operator overloading

// endl() is a file scope function that inserts a newline character and calls ostream::flush()
inline ostream& endl(ostream& ostr)
{
    ostr << '\n';
    return ostr.flush();
}

// overloading of ostream::operator<<() for parameterless manipulators
inline ostream& ostream::operator<<(ostream& (*pManipFn)(ostream&))
{
    return (*pManipFn)(*this);
}

int main()
{
    // the right operand is actually &endl
    cout << endl;
}
```

Execution of the previous operator<<() overloading passes the receiver stream to the named file scope manipulator function, and returns the stream. The header file iostream.h declares the file scope functions used as manipulators. The format state manipulator functions take and return an ios&, ws() takes and returns an istream&, and endl(), flush(), and ends() take and return an ostream&. The classes ostream and istream also define the following operators for use with manipulators:

---

[30] In the Standard Library, the output and input manipulator functions are defined as templates so that they can be used both with ostream and istream, and with wostream and wistream.

```
// overloading of insertion and extraction operators for parameterless manipulators
istream& istream::operator>>(istream& (*pManipFn)(istream&));
ostream& ostream::operator<<(ios& (*pManipFn)(ios&));
istream& istream::operator>>(ios& (*pManipFn)(ios&));
```

The last two overloadings in this list are necessary because format manipulator functions take and return the type ios&, but a pointer to function of type ios& (*)(ios&) cannot be converted implicitly to the types ostream& (*)(ostream&) or istream& (*)(istream&).

We can also define additional stream manipulators by defining file scope functions that take and return a reference to a stream. For example, the following function defines a manipulator that makes the terminal beep when the expression cout << beep is executed:[31]

```
// file scope function to implement a beep manipulator
inline ostream& beep(ostream& ostr)
{
    return ostr << '\a' << flush;
}
```

The process of defining a manipulator such as setw() that takes parameters is more complex. In the expression cout << setw(5), the compiler interprets setw(5) as a function invocation because the function call operator () has higher precedence than the shift operator <<. The return value of the function call is the right operand of operator<<(). To achieve the desired behavior, the designers of the iostream library define an auxiliary class whose instances maintain the int argument and a pointer to a file scope function, in this case ostream& setWidth(ostream&, int), that manipulates the stream and returns it. The setw() function creates a temporary instance of the class, and passes the int and the pointer to function to the class's constructor. The auxiliary class has no public member functions besides its constructor, but has a friend overloading of operator<<() that is invoked when the programmer uses the setw() manipulator. We can define the auxiliary class and the friend extraction operator overloading used with ostream manipulators such as setw() that take a single int parameter as follows:

```
// an auxiliary class and friend function that implement output stream manipulators
// that take an int parameter
class OstrManipInt
{
friend ostream& operator<<(ostream&, const OstrManipInt&);
public:
    OstrManipInt(ostream& (*pFunc) (ostream&, int), int initArg)
       : pManipFn(pFunc), arg(initArg)
    { }
protected:
    ostream& (*pManipFn) (ostream&, int);
```

[31] ANSI C defines the code '\a' as the "alert" character '007'.

```
    int arg;
};

inline ostream& operator<<(ostream& ostr, const OstrManipInt& osManip)
{
    return (*osManip.pManipFn) (ostr, osManip.arg);
}
```

The operator<<() overloading accesses the OstrManipInt object's function and invokes it with the OstrManipInt object's int member as the argument. We define the function setw(int) as a file scope function that creates an OstrManipInt object containing a pointer to the file scope function setWidth() and the int argument. setWidth() sends ios::width() to its argument and returns the argument. We define the functions setw() and setWidth() as follows:

```
// setw() creates an instance of OstrManipInt to implement the setw manipulator
inline OstrManipInt setw(int newWidth)
{
    return OstrManipInt(&setWidth, newWidth);
}

// setWidth() sets the stream's width member and returns the stream
inline ostream& setWidth(ostream& ostr, int newWidth)
{
    ostr.width(newWidth);
    return ostr;
}
```

To recapitulate, the expression cout << setw(5) creates an OstrManipInt object containing &setWidth and 5. That object is the right argument of operator<<(), and the previous overloading of operator<<() invokes setWidth(5), which sets cout's field width. Note also that all the functions (including the OstrManipInt constructor) are inline.

In this example, the manipulator parameter is an int, but the technique is the same for any parameter type. To support manipulator parameters of any type, the iostream library actually uses a class template and a friend function template. To define a new manipulator (e.g., beep(int n) to beep the terminal n times) we must define both a function that returns an instance of the appropriate template class and a file scope function that performs the manipulation, analogous to setw() and setWidth() in the previous example. The manual pages for manip describe the class templates that facilitate defining additional stream manipulators. The header file iomanip.h gives the interface for the classes and functions that support parameterized manipulators, and for the manipulators defined by the library such as setw() and setiosflags(). Client code files that use parameterized manipulators or define manipulator functions must include that header file.

11.3.5 File Streams

The file stream classes

Unlike C, in which there is a single file type FILE*, input and output file streams are different classes in C++, and attempts to read from an ofstream or write to an ifstream are compile-time errors. The header file fstream.h declares the interface of the file stream classes ofstream, ifstream, and fstream and the auxiliary classes fstreambase and filebuf. Code files that use the file stream classes must include this header file.

Because ofstream is a subclass of ostream and ifstream is a subclass of istream, all the output and input operations described in section 11.3.3 apply to file streams as well. ofstream objects respond to the insertion messages ostream:: operator<<(), ostream::put(), and ostream::write(), and to ostream::flush(). We can extract bytes from an ifstream object using istream::operator>>(), istream::get(), istream::getline(), and istream::read(), and ifstream objects respond to the messages istream:: gcount(), istream::ignore(), istream::peek(), and istream::putback(). We can also use the same manipulators with the file stream classes that are defined for their superclasses. The class fstream is a subclass of iostream, so all the protocol we listed in 11.3.3 is available for its instances. Like all streams, a file stream has an error state and a format state that we can query and set using the ios functions and manipulators discussed in the previous section.

Like the classes ostream and istream, the ANSI/ISO C++ Standard Library defines the classes ofstream and ifstream as specializations of the templates basic_ofstream<> and basic_ofstream<> with char as the character type. The library also defines the specializations wofstream and wifstream for file streams of wide characters.[32] The Standard Library does not include the class fstream for input/output file streams or the abstract class fstreambase.

Open modes and file stream protocol

The comments in the following partial ios class definition describe the open mode values:

```
// class ios: meanings of open mode flags
class ios
{
public:
  enum open_mode
  {
    in,          // open for input (enables input for fstreams)
    out,         // open for output (enables output for fstreams)
```

---

[32] The Standard Library also defines the buffer classes filebuf and wfilebuf as specializations of the template basic_filebuf <>.

```
    ate,        / seek to the end of the file, does not imply ios::out ³³
    app,        // append to file (i.e., seek to the end of the file), implies ios::out
    trunc,      // with ios::out, truncate (discard) the file if it already exists
    nocreate,   // with ios::out, fail if the file does not already exist
    noreplace   // with ios::out, fail if the file already exists (opening must create the file)
};

    // ... other members ...
};
```

As with error and format states, we OR flags together to specify an open mode, and a variable or parameter that maintains an open mode must be of type int, not open_mode. For example, the file stream classes have constructors that take the name of the file and an int giving the open mode, which are used as follows:

```
    // ORing open_mode values when opening files with file streams
    #include <iostream.h>
    #include <fstream.h>
    // open an existing output file but do not create a new output file
    ofstream outFile("report.txt", ios::out | ios::nocreate);
    // open a file for both input and output
    fstream file("filename", ios::in | ios::out);
```

The ANSI/ISO Standard Library defines a bitset ios_base::openmode with the flags in, out, ate, app, and trunc, but not nocreate and noreplace. The Standard Library also defines an open mode flag binary, which specifies binary input/output mode, as opposed to text mode. Figure 11.4 gives the correspondence between the codes used with the C function fopen() and the Standard Library flags.

The file stream classes define constructors and destructors for file stream objects, and the member functions open() and close(). (Because open() and close() are usually the same for all file types, they are defined in the superclass

C code	C++ stream open state
"r"	in
"w"	out | trunc
"a"	out | app
"r+"	in | out
"w+"	in | out | trunc
a+"	in | out | app
with b	or with binary (Standard Library only)

Figure 11.4   The correspondence between C stdio open mode codes and the C++ open mode.

---

³³ ate reportedly stands for "at end".

fstreambase.) For example, the following is the interface for the class ofstream:[34]

```
// class ofstream: constructors, destructor and open and close member functions
class ofstream : public fstreambase, public ostream
{
public:
    // initialize a stream not attached to a file
    ofstream();
    // flush the file's buffer and close the file (if any), and deallocate the buffer
    ~ofstream();
    // initialize a stream attached to the file "filename", and open the file
    ofstream(const char* filename, int openMode = ios::out);
    // attach the receiver to the file "filename" and open the file
    void open(const char* filename, int openMode = ios::out);
    // flush the file's buffer and close the file
    void close();
};
```

A file stream object and a file are independent entities because we can use a particular file stream to access a series of files. The default constructor creates a file stream object that is not attached to a file by allocating a buffer and performing internal initialization of the stream. The member function ofstream::open() opens the named file and connects it to the receiver stream, and its arguments are the file name (or file system path) and the file mode. If the open() operation fails, then the method sets the file stream's ios::failbit. This occurs if the file stream is already attached to a file, if there is a permissions or file system error, or due to the meaning of the ios::nocreate or ios::noreplace flags. The constructor with arguments calls the default constructor and then open(). When we finish processing a file, we can send the message close() to the file stream object to flush its buffer, close the file, and disconnect the file from the stream. We can then reopen that file stream attached to another file. Each file stream class defines a destructor that flushes its buffer and closes the file if a file is attached, and then deallocates the buffer. These member functions are the same in the classes ifstream and fstream, except that their default values for the open mode in the constructor and open() are ios::in and ios::in | ios::out, respectively.

The following example illustrates using file stream protocol:

```
// opening and closing files with file streams
#include <iostream.h>
#include <fstream.h>
void exit(int);

int main()
```

---

[34] In many versions of the iostream library, the constructors and open() member functions take a third argument that gives the file permissions.

```
{
    ifstream infile("file1", ios::in);   // an input file stream attached to the file "file1"
    if ( !infile )
        fileError("Opening file1 failed.");
    // ... operations using file1 ...
    ofstream outfile;                     // an output file stream, not attached to any file yet
    outfile.open("file2", ios::out);      // an output file stream on the file "file2"
    if ( !outfile )
        fileError("Opening file2 failed.");
    // ... operations using file2 ...
    outfile.close();                      // outfile can be opened again on a different output file
    outfile.open("file3", ios::out);      // an output file stream attached to the file "file3"
    if ( !outfile )
        fileError("Opening file3 failed.");
    // ... operations using file3 ...
    outfile.close();
}                                         // destructors are called for both file stream objects

void fileError(const char* errorMessage)
{
    cerr << errorMessage << endl;
    exit(1);
}
```

To be safe, we should check the file stream state after each insertion or extraction operation (and even after closing a file). As we will see in section 13.3, exceptions simplify code such as this example considerably.

In the Standard Library, the type of the second parameter of the constructors and the open() message is the bitset ios_base::openmode, rather than int. The stream classes also define a member function is_open() that returns whether the receiver is attached to a file.

Stream positioning

An ostream has an insertion position that indicates the location in the streambuf at which bytes are inserted. The insertion position is often referred to as its "put pointer". Similarly, the class istream defines an extraction position (i.e., a "get pointer"). We can manipulate this position like the "file position" in a random access file with the following messages:[35]

```
// ostream positioning protocol
class ostream : virtual public ios
{
public:
    // adjust the receiver's insertion position to pos
    ostream& seekp(streampos pos);
```

---

[35] The p suffix in the ostream member function names refers to "put", and the g in the istream member function names refers to "get".

```
    // adjust the receiver's insertion position to off, relative to start
    ostream& seekp(streamoff off, ios::seek_dir start);
    // obtain the receiver's current insertion position
    streampos tellp();
    // ... other members ...
};


// istream positioning protocol
class istream : virtual public ios
{
public:
    // adjust the receiver's extraction position to pos
    istream& seekg(streampos pos);
    // adjust the receiver's extraction position to off, relative to start
    istream& seekg(streamoff off, ios::seek_dir start);
    // obtain the receiver's current extraction position
    streampos tellg();
    // back up the extraction position in the receiver's buffer by 1 character;
    // the argument must be the character before the get pointer
    istream& putback(char);
    // ... other members ...
};
```

We usually use these messages with file streams and streams in memory, and cannot use them with streams attached to standard input/output such as cout, cin, and so on. For a file stream, the stream position indicates the logical location in the associated file at which bytes will be inserted or extracted, respectively.[36] An fstream has a single position at which both input and output are performed, and the functions ostream::seekp(), istream::seekg(), ostream::tellp(), and istream::tellg() all refer to this position. The member function istream:: putback() backs up the extraction position in the receiver's buffer, which has the effect of putting its argument back in the stream.

The types streamoff and streampos indicate an offset and a position in the stream respectively, and are measured in bytes. These type names are typedef'd to long in iostream.h. The member functions ostream::tellp() and istream::tellg() return a streampos that gives the current stream position (or return streampos(-1) if the stream is in the fail state). The member functions ostream::seekp() and istream::seekg() have two argument signatures. One takes a streamoff and a seek_dir[37] that indicates whether the offset is relative to the beginning of the file (ios::beg), the end of the file (ios::end), or the current position (ios::cur). The other argument signature takes a single streampos argument that has been

---

[36] Because files are typically block-oriented, setting the position is mediated through the file buffer.

[37] The name seek_dir is misleading: The value gives a starting point relative to which the offset is taken, not a seek direction.

obtained using ostream:: tellp() or istream::tellg(), and positions the receiver at that point. For example,

```
// setting and querying the stream position
#include <iostream.h>
#include <fstream.h>
int main()
{
    fstream file("data", ios::in | ios::out);
    file.seekg(64, ios::beg);        // set the position 64 bytes after the beginning of the file
    // ... file i/o operations ...
    file.seekg(-16, ios::end);       // set the position 16 bytes before the end of the file
    // ... file i/o operations ...
    streampos pos = file.tellg();    // return the current file position
    file.seekg(16, ios::cur);        // move forward 16 bytes in the file
    // ... file i/o operations ...
    file.seekg(pos);                 // reset to the previously saved position
}
```

11.3.6 Streams in Memory

The classes istrstream, ostrstream, and strstream support stream protocol for arrays of characters or bytes in main memory. These "string stream" classes correspond to read and write streams over strings in Smalltalk (recall section 8.4.3). Like those classes, we use an input string stream to parse a string, and an output string stream to compose a string. The header file strstream.h defines the interface for these classes and the auxiliary classes strstreambase and strstreambuf, and must be included in code files that use these classes. Because ostrstream is a subclass of ostream, istrstream is a subclass of istream, and strstream is a subclass of iostream, the stream protocol we have discussed applies to these classes as well. This includes the input and output operations, the stream positioning messages, and the functions and manipulators that access and set the stream's error state and format state.

The string stream classes define constructors and destructors, and ostrstream and strstream provide an additional member function str() that returns the contents of the stream.

```
// protocol for string stream classes
class istrstream : public strstreambase, public istream
{
public:
    // create a stream that extracts chars from the null-terminated string str
    istrstream(char* str);
    // create a stream that extracts up to size chars from buf
    istrstream(char* buf, int size);
    ~istrstream();
};
```

```
// class strstream has the same protocol as class ostrstream
class ostrstream : public strstreambase, public istream
{
public:
    // create an unlimited size output string stream whose contents will be dynamically
    // allocated as necessary
    ostrstream();
    // create a stream that inserts chars into buf
    ostrstream(char* buf, int size, int mode = ios::out);
    ~ostrstream();
    // obtain the contents of the receiver
    // NOTE: the client must deallocate the array referred to by the pointer returned
    char* str();
};
```

For the constructor istream::istream(char*), the terminal null byte is not considered to be part of the stream. If an extraction from an istrstream reaches the end of the string that the stream accesses, the stream's ios::eofbit is set. Creating an ostrstream with the default constructor permits us to avoid declaring a maximum buffer size when reading in data (i.e., like using WriteStream on: String new in Smalltalk). When the string accessed by the stream is complete, we can use the member function ostrstream::str() to obtain a pointer to a dynamically allocated char array containing the stream's contents. (Recall that we used ostrstream::ostrstream() and ostrstream::str() in this way in the method for operator>>(istream&, String&) in section 11.3.1.) Once this member function has been called, further insertion into the stream is undefined, and deallocation of the string returned by the function is the client's responsibility. Whether ostrstream::str() is called or not, the class's destructor is responsible for deallocation of the stream's memory requirement. If the last argument of ostrstream::ostrstream(char*, int, int) includes ios::ate or ios::app, then the region is assumed to be null-terminated and insertion will begin at the position of the null character.

We can use an istrstream to scan numeric literals from a string into numeric variables, as is done with the C standard library function sscanf(). Similarly, an ostrstream can be used to convert numeric values to their literal representations, like the C standard library function sprintf(). For example, the following program reads a sequence of commands that manipulate an array of doubles (a command line consists of a letter giving the command, and a series of numeric arguments):

```
// using a string  stream to convert from literals to numeric objects
#include <iostream.h>
#include <strstream.h>
#include <stdlib.h> // for exit()
```

```
// a command consists of a letter giving the command, and a series of numeric arguments
int main()
{
    const int ARRSIZE = 100;
    double values [ARRSIZE];
    const int LINEBUFSIZE = 81;        // 80 chars plus '\0'
    char command[LINEBUFSIZE];
    char comChar;                      // the command character
    int index, count;                  // command arguments
    istrstream comStream(command, LINEBUFSIZE);
    char prompt[] = "Enter your command followed by <enter>:";
    cout << prompt << flush;
    while ( cin.getline(command, LINEBUFSIZE) )
    {
        comStream.seekg(0);            // reset the stream to the beginning of the command
        comStream >> comChar;          // extract a char
        switch ( comChar )
        {
        // insert: the first argument is the index (1 to ARRSIZE) and the second is the value
        case 'i':
            comStream >> index;        // extract an int
            if ( 0 < index && index <= ARRSIZE )
                comStream >> values[index - 1];   // extract a double
            else
                cout << "index out of range" << endl;
            break;
        // print: the argument is the number of elements to print (1 to ARRSIZE)
        case 'p':
            comStream >> count; // extract an int
            if ( 0 < count && count <= ARRSIZE )
            {
                for ( index = 0;  index < count - 1;  index++ )
                    cout << values[index] << ' ';
                cout << endl;
            }
            else
                cout << "count out of range" << endl;
            break;
        // quit
        case 'q':
            exit(0);
        // ... cases for other commands ...
        default:
            cout << "illegal command" << endl;
            break;
        }
        cout << prompt << flush;
    }
}
```

We simplified this example by not checking whether a command line contained the correct number and types of arguments. To do so, the program would check whether comStream is good after each extraction.

The insertion position and extraction position in a strstream are not tied together as they are in a fstream, so they can be queried and set independently. The member functions ostream::tellp() and ostream::seekp() access and manipulate the insertion position, and istream::tellg() and istream:: seekg() access and manipulate the extraction position.

The ANSI/ISO C++ Standard Library makes a number of changes to the string stream classes. It uses the names istringstream and ostringstream for istrstream and ostrstream, and does not include a class corresponding to strstream. The library's string stream header file is called sstream, not strstream.h. Like the file stream classes, the Standard Library defines the classes ostringstream and istringstream as specializations of the templates basic_ostringstream<> and basic_istringstream<> with char as the character type. The library also defines the specializations wostringstream and wistringstream for streams over wide character strings. Instead of string stream constructors that take a char* and an int giving the size, the constructors take a reference to the Standard Library string class. ostringstream::str() returns an instance of string by value, so the client is not responsible for deallocation of the return value. In addition, that member function has an overloading whose argument is a reference to a string, which sets that string to the contents of the receiver. The library also defines these messages for istringstream, and they return the remaining contents of the receiver.

11.4 SUMMARY AND REVIEW

11.4.1 Operator Overloading

Programmer-defined operators

- Classes can overload C++ operators so that clients can use their instances with the familiar expression syntax.

- Operators that are often overloaded include == and !=, =, << and >>, arithmetic operators, comparison operators, and [ ].

- An operator overloading should have the same semantics as that for built-in types, for example, == should perform an equality test and [ ] should return an *l*-value.

- We define or declare an operator overloading like any function, and the function name is the reserved word operator followed by the operator symbol(s). Operators overloadings may be defined as member functions or at file scope, and have encoded names for the linker.

- We cannot define new operators, and an operator overloading must take at least one parameter of class type. An operator overloading has the same number of operands, precedence, and associativity as the built-in definition of that operator. The operators ::, .*, ., sizeof, and ?: cannot be overloaded.

Member versus file scope definition

- In an object-oriented design, we define an operator overloading as a member function of the class of the operand (for a unary operator), or of the left operand (for a binary operator).

- We use a file scope definition for an operator overloading that must permit an implicit conversion of either the left or right operand, because conversions are never performed on the receiver of a message. Examples include the equality test, arithmetic, and comparison operators for Complex and String, which allow conversions from double and char*, respectively. We declare the function in the class's header file and define it in its code file.

- We use file scope definitions for overloading the insertion and extraction operators.

- The assignment = and subscription [ ] operators must be defined as nonstatic member functions.

The assignment operator

- Assignment is not the same operation as initialization because the target is already a constructed object.

- Like the default copy constructor, the compiler automatically supplies a default assignment operator for each class that performs member by member assignment of its data members.

- As with copy constructors, the default assignment operator is inadequate for a class that allocates dynamic memory or other resources, so the class designer defines an overloading of the assignment operator. For each value data member, it assigns that member of the receiver from the corresponding member of the argument object. For (most) pointer data members, it deallocates the receiver's subobject, allocates a new object, and copies the argument's subobject into it.

- An assignment operator overloading is a member function that takes a const reference to the class, and returns a reference to the receiver to allow cascading of assignments without the overhead of temporary objects.

- A composite class does not need an assignment operator overloading just because a data member has one. The overloading is necessary only if the composite class itself uses resources that it must deal with.

- Generally, a class that requires a destructor, copy constructor, or assignment operator also needs the other two member functions.

Class-specific memory management

- The operators new and delete control dynamic allocation, and the class designer can overload them to provide a class-specific allocation policy. For example, the class designer can use a more efficient fixed-size memory management algorithm, or can customize allocation for particular memory architectures, or for use with objects in shared memory.

- The compiler invokes class's constructor implicitly after the member new operator is invoked, and calls the destructor before the member delete operator is executed.

- operator new() takes an argument of type size_t that gives the object's size, and has a return type of void*. The delete operator takes a void* parameter that refers to the region to deallocate and a size_t parameter, and returns no value. The return type of new and the argument of delete are void* because either the constructor has not been executed (for new) or the destructor has been executed (for delete).

Smart pointers

- A *smart pointer* is an object that provides access to another object. It behaves like a pointer because we use the -> operator to send messages to the handled object and the prefix * operator to obtain the handled object.

- A smart pointer class overloads the -> operator to perform the processing required to make an object accessible, or any additional processing necessary when an object is used. Applications include distributed systems, databases, and logging or controlling access to objects.

- If smPtr's class overloads operator->(), then the compiler interprets smPtr->msg(arg) as (smPtr.operator->())->msg(arg). We code an overloading of operator->() as a unary postfix operator that returns a pointer, and must define it as a member function.

- A smart pointer class overloads the prefix * operator to return the handled object, and its destructor finalizes the handled object and the smart pointer. It can overload the copy constructor and assignment operator (although care is necessary in defining their semantics), or can declare them as nonpublic.

11.4.2 Programmer-Defined Conversions

Purpose and usage

- Implicit conversions reduce the number of overloadings necessary for a function or operator, and enable initializations and assignments from objects of compatible types. The class designer can define conversions between the class and other classes and built-in types to provide these capabilities for its instances.

- Programmer-defined conversions can be used implicitly by the compiler in argument matching, or explicitly by a client (e.g., to create a temporary object or to resolve an ambiguous invocation). A conversion is never applied implicitly to the receiver of a message.

- A conversion creates a new object (except for reference conversions).

- The conversions between *Class* and *Class*&, between *Class** and *Class*[], and from *Class* to const *Class* are predefined trivial conversions for all classes.

Definition

- A single-argument constructor defines a conversion from the type of the argument to that of the class (an "inward" conversion to the class).

- The class designer can define a conversion as an operator member function that converts the receiver to the built-in type (an "outward" conversion from the class). A conversion operator has no return type, even though its method returns a value.

- Because built-in types do not have constructors, we must define a conversion from a built-in type to a class object as a constructor, and a conversion from a class object to a built-in type as a conversion operator.

Conversions and overloading

- Due to implicit conversions, an invocation of an overloaded function or operator can match more than one of its argument signatures. The argument matching process prefers trivial conversions, promotions, and standard conversions over programmer-defined conversions.

- The compiler will apply a trivial conversion, promotion, or standard conversion together with a programmer-defined conversion if necessary in argument matching. However, it will not apply two programmer-defined conversions implicitly to the same argument.

- Do not define both a constructor and operator conversion from one class to another, because every invocation requiring that conversion will be ambiguous.

- If we have a conversion from class C1 to class C2 and from C2 to C1 and there are functions that have both the argument signatures (C1, C1) and (C2, C2), then invocations of those functions with the argument signatures (C1, C2) and (C2, C1) are ambiguous. We can resolve the problem by using an explicit cast, or by defining one conversion as a member function so that the compiler cannot invoke it implicitly.

- The reserved word explicit on a constructor indicates that it can be used to create instances of the class, but the compiler cannot invoke it implicitly. (This is a very new feature.)

11.4.3 The Iostream Classes

Object input/output

- The class designer can overload the << and >> operators for the class so that clients can use instances in input/output expressions in the same way as built-in types.

- We define an overloading of the << or >> operator at file scope because the class object is the right operand (and we usually cannot modify the stream definition in iostream.h). The operator definition returns a reference to the stream so that clients can cascade invocations, and is declared and defined in the class's header and code file.

- If an insertion or extraction operator method requires access to the nonpublic members of the object being transferred, we specify it as a friend of the class.

- The method for an extraction operator overloading modifies an existing object (much like an assignment), so it must deal with the object's resources. If the characters in the stream are not a valid format for the class being transferred, the method sets the stream to the fail state and does not modify the target object.

Structure of the iostream class library

- The iostream class library defines a hierarchy of classes that we can instantiate and subclass to perform data transfer in applications. The library provides data abstraction, object input/output, type checking, and extendibility.

- The abstract class ios defines the representation of the stream state, and the member functions and manipulators for accessing that information.

- The classes istream, ostream, and iostream define functionality for input, output, and input/output streams, respectively. The classes ifstream, ofstream, and fstream are subclasses of istream, ostream, and iostream respectively that supply streams whose bytes are produced or consumed by files. The classes istrstream, ostrstream, and strstream are subclasses of istream, ostream, and iostream that support stream protocol for arrays of bytes in memory.

- The iostream library also defines classes for the buffers that mediate between the stream and the associated producer or consumer of bytes. These include the abstract class streambuf and its subclasses filebuf and strstreambuf, which implement buffers for files and streams in memory, respectively.

- The class designer can define streams with other sources or sinks of bytes by defining a subclass of streambuf for the buffer and a subclass of istream, ostream, or iostream for the associated stream.

- The ANSI/ISO C++ Standard Library defines a set of classes for input/output that refine the iostream library. It declares the stream and buffer classes in the standard namespace, supports internationalization by defining those classes as templates parameterized for the character type, and uses exceptions to signal stream errors. Currently, no C++ language systems fully support the Standard Library, but all eventually will.

Input/output protocol

- In addition to the insertion operator, the class ostream defines the messages ostream::put() and ostream::write() for unformatted insertion, and ostream::flush() for flushing the buffer to the consumer. Their methods return immediately if the receiver is in the fail state, or set its error state if a stream operation fails. We can use the manipulators endl, ends, and flush with an ostream.

- The class istream defines the member functions istream::get(), istream::getline(), and istream::read() for unformatted extraction, and istream::peek(), istream::ignore(), and istream::putback() for interactions between the stream and the buffer.

The stream state

- The class ios defines four nested enumerations: io_state lists names for error state flags, fmt_flags lists names for format state flags, open_mode lists names for file open mode flags, and seek_dir lists names for stream positioning reference points.

- The enumeration values for the error and format state are initialized to powers of 2 so that we can represent a particular stream state as a logical OR of these values and use bitwise logical operations to manipulate stream state descriptors.

- The class ios defines data members that maintain the error state and format state of a stream, and member functions for accessing and manipulating that information.

- The error state indicates whether the stream is in a usable condition. The flag ios::eofbit indicates that an extraction has reached the end of the stream, ios::failbit indicates a failed formatted i/o operation, and ios::badbit indicates a problem with the producer or consumer.

- The member functions ios::rdstate() and ios::clear() access and set the error state, respectively. The messages ios::eof(), ios::fail(), ios::bad(), ios::operator bool*(), and ios::operator!() test the error state. The operators allow the programmer to use a stream object or an expression that returns a stream as the condition in an if, while, or for statement.

- The format state specifies flags that control the format of the string output by an insertion or input by an extraction, and are listed in section 11.3.4. The messages ios::flags(), ios::setf(), and ios::unsetf() access and set the format state.

- Three additional ios data members maintain the stream's field width, fill character, and floating-point precision. We can obtain or set this information with the messages ios::width(), ios::fill(), and ios::precision().

- The iostream library defines the manipulators dec, oct, hex, setioflags(), resetioflags(), setw(), setfill(), and setprecision(). For convenience, the Standard Library adds left, right, and internal, fixed and scientific, showbase and noshowbase, showpoint and noshowpoint, showpos and noshowpos, skipws and noskipws, uppercase and nouppercase, and boolalpha and noboolalpha.

- A parameterless manipulator is a file scope function that takes and returns a reference to a stream, and the stream classes define insertion and extraction operator overloadings that take a pointer to such a function as the right operand. We can create additional parameterless manipulators by defining such file scope functions.

- To create a parameterized manipulator, we define a manipulator function that creates an instance of an auxiliary class defined in iomanip.h, and a file scope function that performs the stream state manipulation.

File streams

- The file stream classes ofstream, ifstream, and fstream are defined in fstream.h. They are subclasses of ostream, istream, and iostream respectively, and each responds to the protocol of its superclass, including input/output operators, unformatted input/output messages, error and format state messages, and manipulators.

- The enumeration ios::open_mode defines flags that indicate whether the file is open for input, output, or both, and whether an output file should be appended to, overwritten, or created. Like the state flags, these values can be ORed to specify an open mode.

- Each file stream class provides constructors, a destructor, the message open(), which associates a file with a file stream object, and close(), which flushes the buffer and closes the file. The default constructor initializes a file stream object that is not connected to a file. The constructor and the member function open() take a file name and an int specifying an open mode, and open the file and connect the stream to it. The file stream destructors close the file associated with the stream, if any. If opening a file fails, the file stream method sets the error state of the receiver.

- The class ostream defines an insertion position at which bytes are inserted (a "put pointer"), and istream defines an extraction position (a "get pointer"). The messages ostream::tellp() and ostream::seekp() access and set the insertion position, and istream::tellg() and istream::seekg() access and set the extraction position.

- The values of the enumeration ios::seek_dir specify the point relative to which a stream offset is taken. We use it as the second argument of ostream::seekp() or istream::seekg().

- C++ supports random access files via stream positioning. An fstream has a single position for both insertion and extraction, and we can obtain that position with ostream::tellp() or istream::tellg() and set it with ostream::seekp() or istream::seekg().

Streams in memory

- The classes ostrstream, istrstream, and strstream provide stream protocol for arrays of bytes in memory. They are subclasses of ostream, istream, and iostream respectively, and are defined in strstream.h.

- The string stream classes define constructors and destructors, and the constructor for each class takes an initializer specifying the array.

- ostrstream and strstream define a default constructor that creates a dynamically resized region for the contents of the stream, and a member function str() that returns the contents of the stream as a dynamically allocated char array.

- An istrstream can scan numeric literals from a string into numeric variables (like C's sscanf()), and an ostrstream can convert numeric values to their literal representations (like sprintf()).

- The insertion and extraction positions in a strstream are not tied together as they are in an fstream, and can be accessed and set independently.

- The ANSI/ISO C++ Standard Library string stream classes are called istringstream and ostringstream, and are declared in the header file sstream.

11.5 EXERCISES

11.1   Each of the following operator overloadings has been used in a C++ text or class library. Evaluate the readability of each. (Hint: Code a statement that uses the operator.)

    (a) List::operator+(), which returns the concatenation of its two list operands, and List::operator-(), which returns a list containing the receiver's elements with any elements of the argument list removed (Consider also List::operator+=() and List::operator-=() with analogous meanings.)

    (b) String::operator++(), which changes lowercase characters in the receiver to uppercase, and String::operator--(), which changes uppercase characters to lowercase

    (c) Set::operator<(), which indicates whether the left operand is a subset of the right operand (Assume that <=, > and >= are also defined appropriately.)

    (d) List::operator<(), which indicates whether the left operand is a sublist (in the same order) of the right operand (Assume that <=, >, and >= are also defined appropriately.)

    (e) Date::operator+(), which takes an int parameter and returns the date that many days after the receiver, and Date::operator-() which takes an int parameter and returns the date that many days before the receiver

    (f) PositionableList::operator++() and PositionableList::operator--(), which move the position reference forward or backward one element in the list

(g) PositionableList::operator()(), which has two argument signatures: With no parameter, it returns the next element in the list and advances the position reference; with one parameter that is a reference to the element type, it sets the argument to the next element and advances the position reference. (Remember that this operator is predefined for both function invocation and initialization.)

(h) Point::operator<(), which returns true if both the receiver's data members are less than the corresponding data members of the argument (as in Smalltalk)

(i) Polynomial::operator<(), which indicates whether the left operand has a lower degree than the right operand (The class Polynomial is described in exercise 11.14.)

(j) operator,(), which represents concatenation of lists, arrays, or strings (as in Smalltalk)

11.2 Give three reasons why operator^() should not be defined to perform exponentiation.

11.3 (a) Define operator+() for the class String defined in section 10.2.2, which returns the concatenation of its argument strings. Clients should also be able to use the operator with a standard C string as an operand.

(b) Explain why you used a member function or file scope definition.

(c) Explain why you chose to pass arguments by value or by reference in coding the concatenation operator.

(d) Explain why you chose to use return by value or return by reference in coding the concatenation operator.

11.4 (a) Define operator+=() for the class String defined in section 10.2.2, which appends the argument to the receiver.

(b) Explain why you used a member function or file scope definition.

(c) Explain why you chose to pass arguments by value or by reference in coding the operator.

(d) Explain why you chose to use return by value or return by reference in coding the operator.

11.5 Define the operators -, -=, *, *=, /, and /= for the class Complex introduced in section 11.1.2.

11.6 Determine what encoded names are used by your compiler for a number of different operators. Try both file scope and member definitions.

11.7 (a) Why is the compiler-generated assignment operator inadequate for the class Queue defined in section 10.1.3?

(b) Define the method for the assignment operator for the class Queue.

11.8 Recall the class Set whose interface was given in exercise 10.40. Define the following operators for any of the implementations described in that problem:

(a) Set::operator==() and Set::operator!=()

(b) Set::operator=()

(c) Set::operator+() and Set::operator+=(), which perform set union

(d) Set::operator*() and Set::operator*=(), which perform set intersection.

11.9 Recall the class List whose interface was given in exercise 10.41. Define the following operators for any of the implementations described in that problem:

(a) List::operator==() and List::operator!=()

(b) List::operator[](), which can be used as an *r*-value or an *l*-value

(c) List::operator=()

(d) List::operator+(), which creates a new list by concatenating the List argument and the receiver, and List::operator+=(), which appends the argument to the receiver

(e) List::operator-(), which creates a new list containing the elements in the receiver

that are not in the List argument, and List::operator-=(), which removes the elements in the argument from the receiver

11.10 Recall the class SortedList whose interface was given in exercise 10.42. Define the following operators for any of the implementations described in that problem:

(a) SortedList::operator==() and SortedList::operator!=()

(b) SortedList::operator[](), which cannot be used as an *l*-value (why?)

(c) SortedList::operator=()

(d) SortedList::operator+(), which creates a new list by merging the SortedList argument
and the receiver, and SortedList::operator+=(), which merges the argument into the
receiver

(e) SortedList::operator-(), which creates a new list containing the elements in the receiver
that are not in the SortedList argument, and SortedList::operator-=(), which removes
the elements in the argument from the receiver

11.11 **(a)** Define a class Array for fixed-size collections of elements. The class has two data
members, an int giving the size of the instance and a pointer to a dynamically
allocated array. There are three constructors: one with an int argument giving
the size of an instance, another whose two arguments are a pointer to a C array
used to initialize the object and the array's size, and a copy constructor. The
class should also have a destructor, and the member functions size(), operator=(),
operator==(), and operator[](). Use a typedef for the element type as illustrated
in section 10.1.3.

(b) It is often useful to be able to "map" a function onto the elements of an array or
list. Write the definition of a member function Array::map() that takes an argument
which is a file scope function that takes and returns an ElemType. The member
function returns a new array whose elements are the results of applying the argument function to each element of the receiver.

(c) Code an overloading of the function Array::map() described in part b that takes a
pointer to an ElemType member function that returns an ElemType.

11.12 Define a class Dictionary for an index of key–value pairs in which the values are
accessed via the keys (like the Smalltalk class Dictionary). A minimal class definition
and the typedefs for the KeyType and ValueType types are given in exercise 10.36.
However, instead of using the named functions Dictionary::find(), and
Dictionary::insert(), we want to define Dictionary::operator[]() such that the argument
gives the key and the result gives the associated value. Unfortunately, this means that
the operator must perform different operations when it is used on the left or right side
of an assignment. On the right side, it returns the associated value. One the left side,
it replaces the associated value if the key is present in the dictionary, or creates a new
pair if it is not. Recall the use of an auxiliary class in the definition of parameterized
manipulators. We can use the same technique here. An application of
Dictionary::operator[]() creates an instance of the auxiliary class (and is the only way to
do so), say DictionaryRef, that has two public operations. A conversion from DictionaryRef to ValueType is defined for uses of Dictionary::operator[]() on the right side of
an assignment or as an argument. The member function DictionaryRef::operator=(const
ValueType&) is invoked when Dictionary::operator[]() is used on the left side of an
assignment. If the key is already in the dictionary, its method sets the value to the argument, and if not, it creates a new dictionary entry. You may use any of the storage
structures described in exercise 10.40 for sets (suitably modified to access values
through keys).

11.13 Define a class Fraction for rational numbers with two long data members numerator_ and denominator_ and the following functions. The constructor can take two longs or one long, and in the latter case the denominator is set to 1. The internal representation of an instance is always "reduced", and the sign of the denominator data member is always positive. The accessor member functions are Fraction::numerator() and Fraction::denominator(), and the member functions Fraction::integerPart() and Fraction::fractionPart() return the indicated values. In addition, define the operators ==, !=, +, -, *, /, +=, -=, *=, and /= for use with fractions.

11.14 Define the member functions for a class Polynomial whose instances maintain a symbolic representation of a polynomial in one variable. We represent a polynomial as a linked list in which each node encodes a term and has the members coefficient (a double), exponent (an int), and next (a pointer to the next term node in that polynomial). The member functions are easier to implement if you keep the list sorted by exponent. The class is defined as follows:

```
class Polynomial
{
public:
    Polynomial();
    Polynomial(double* arrCoef, int* arrExp, int size);
    Polynomial(const Polynomial&);
    ~Polynomial();
    Polynomial& operator=(const Polynomial&);
    int degree();
    double evaluate(double x);
    bool operator==(const Polynomial&);
    bool operator!=(const Polynomial&);
    Polynomial operator+(const Polynomial&);
    Polynomial operator-(const Polynomial&);
    Polynomial operator*(const Polynomial&);
    Polynomial& operator+=(const Polynomial&);
    Polynomial& operator-=(const Polynomial&);
    Polynomial& operator*=(const Polynomial&);
    Polynomial dx(const Polynomial&);    // differentiate
protected:
    class TermNode
    {
    public:
        TermNode(double coef, int exp, TermNode* nxt = NULL)
            : coefficient(coef), exponent(exp), next(nxt)
        { }
        double coefficient;
        int exponent;
        TermNode* next;
    };
    TermNode* poly;
};
```

11.15 Define a class Integer that represents unlimited size integers (e.g., to compute 100!). An instance is represented as a dynamic array of longs. (The maximum value of a long is given by the value LONG_MAX in the ANSI C header file limits.h, and is implementation dependent.) The constructor takes a long initial value with a default of 0, and the class needs a copy constructor and destructor. In addition, define the assignment operator, the equality and magnitude comparison operators, the arithmetic operators (including %), the increment and decrement operators, the bitwise and shift operators, and the corresponding arithmetic and bitwise assignment operators. Which of these operators should be defined at file scope, and why?

11.16 Define a class for 24-hour Clock objects, for example, for use in a simulation. We can initialize an instance with an unsigned int giving the starting time in seconds, or with three unsigned ints giving the starting time in hours, minutes, and seconds. The default constructor initializes the Clock object to start at 0:00:00. We also need a message Clock::reset() that takes an unsigned integer and sets the receiver's current time to that value, and the default value of its argument is 0. If the argument to Clock::reset() or to the single-argument constructor is greater than 24*60*60-1, the method should "wrap it around" into the correct range. In addition, define Clock::operator++(), which increments the clock when sent by other parts of the application (and the time 23:59:59 is followed by 0:00:00).

11.17 What is the argument signature of each of the following operators, and why?
(a) the assignment operator
(b) the new and delete operators
(c) the -> operator
(d) the insertion and extraction operators

11.18 Recall the binary search tree implementation of the class Set described in exercise 10.40e. Define Node::operator new() and Node::operator delete() for the auxiliary node class it requires.

11.19 In section 11.1.5, we discussed using a smart pointer class to control access to the instances of a class. An alternative is to define a nonpublic member function that performs the access processing, which is called at the beginning of every method in the class. What are the advantages of each technique?

11.20 Define a smart pointer class for pointers to instances of the class Person described in section 10.2.4 that counts the number of uses of a person object through that handle. Its destructor writes the count and the social security number to a log file called trace when the smart pointer is destroyed. (How do you ensure that the file is opened and closed?) The smart pointer class should provide both the -> and * operators.

11.21 **(a)** What is the purpose of implicit conversions?
(b) Give two cases in which a programmer would code an explicit conversion.

11.22 Describe the two ways of defining a conversion. Why are two constructs necessary?

11.23 Recall the class Fraction described in exercise 11.13.
(a) Define a conversion from an instance of Fraction to double.
(b) Explain what happens when the compiler encounters the third statement in the following code example:

```
#include "Fraction.h"
int main()
{
    Fraction frac1(5, 2);
    long num = 5;
    Fraction frac2 = frac1 * num;
}
```
            Check what your compiler does.

11.24 Recall the class Polynomial described in exercise 11.14. If we define a constructor Polynomial::Polynomial(double) that creates a constant polynomial, how would it affect the use of the class? How would it affect the rest of the class definition?

11.25 Recall the class Clock described in exercise 11.16. Give an advantage and a disadvantage of defining an int conversion operator that returns the current time in seconds.

11.26 Recall the classes Complex and Byte introduced in section 11.1.2 and 11.2.2. Suppose we have the following three overloadings of a function func():

```
void func(Byte, int);
void func(long, long);
void func(double, Complex);
```

For each of the following calls, indicate which overloading is invoked (if any). If the call is ambiguous, indicate which overloadings apply.

```
func(3, 3);
func(Byte(3), 3.0);
func(3L, 3.0);
func(3L, '3');
func(3, Byte(3));
```

(b) Write a program to test which overloading(s) would be selected by your C++ compiler for each call in part (a) and run it.

11.27 (a) Recall the class PersonPtr in section 11.1.5. Define a conversion operator from the class to the type Person*. (Why shouldn't it be to const Person*?)

(b) Are there operations that a client should not perform with the result of the conversion defined in part (a)? If so, what are they, and why is each a problem?

11.28 In section 11.2.3, we described two ways of providing a conversion from the class Rectangle to the class Polygon. Code each of them. (You may assume that a polygon is represented by a data member of type PointList, and that PointList has a constructor that takes the number of points, and overloads operator[]() to access and set its elements.)

11.29 (a) The member functions of the Standard Library string class that take a string argument are overloaded with both the parameter types const String& and const char*. Why is this so?

(b) Would using two overloadings of member functions be worthwhile in defining the class Complex, which has a conversion from double?

11.30 Why is the code for an extraction operator overloading more complex than the code for an insertion operator overloading?

11.31 Define operator<<() and operator>>() for each of the following classes. For each, indicate whether the operators must be friends of the class.

(a) the class Point introduced in section 10.1.2

(b) the class Fraction described in exercise 11.13

(c) the class Polynomial described in exercise 11.14 (because subscripts cannot be indicated for ostreams such as cout, use a format such as 32x7 + 12x4 - 2x3 + 23)

(d) the class Integer described in exercise 11.15

(e) the class Clock described in exercise 11.16 (use the standard "hours:minutes:seconds" format)

11.32 Define operator<<() for each the following classes using the output format used with the Smalltalk collection classes (like the definition for the class Queue in section 11.3.1). For each, indicate whether the operator must be a friend of the class.

(a) the class Array described in exercise 11.11

(b) any of the implementations of the class Set declared in exercise 10.40

(c) any of the implementations of the class List declared in exercise 10.41

(d) any of the implementations of the class SortedList declared in exercise 10.42

11.33 **(a)** Describe the purpose, protocol, and state information defined in the class ios.

(b) Why are the enumerations io_state, fmt_flags, open_mode, and seek_dir defined within the class ios?

11.34 Describe the differences between the AT&T iostream library and the ANSI/ISO C++ Standard Library input/output classes.

11.35 Suppose another programmer suggests that we can store an instance obj of class Class with the statement outfile.write((char*) &obj, sizeof(Class)).

(a) Name two classes for which this technique is adequate.

(b) Describe conditions under which this technique does not give the correct behavior.

(c) Even for the classes you gave in part (a), the technique is not portable. Why?

11.36 Write a member function ios::printState() that inserts the complete error state and format state (including the width, etc.) of the receiver in a readable format into its stream argument, for example, for debugging purposes.

11.37 Code each of the following functions that take a stream argument:

(a) a function call that clears ios::eofbit without affecting the other error state flags

(b) a function call that sets the padding location to left justified

(c) a single function call that turns off whitespace skipping, sets internal justification, sets decimal conversion, shows the + for positive values, and sets scientific notation for floating-point values

(d) a function call that sets the extraction position 10 bytes before the end of the stream.

11.38 Suppose we want to define a class TextStream that we can use to output text that includes an indications of the characters' style—bold, italic, underlined, superscript, etc. How would manipulators make the class easier to use?

11.39 **(a)** Implement the manipulator left that sets ios::left (it must also clear ios::right and ios::internal).

(b) Describe the evaluation of the expression cout << left.

11.40 **(a)** Using the class OstrManipInt defined in section 11.3.2, define the functions necessary to implement a manipulator beep(int n) that makes the terminal beep n times.

(b) Describe the evaluation of the expression cout << beep(3).

11.41 Explain why the second argument of ostream::open() is an int, but the second argument of ostream::seekp() is of type ios::seek_dir.

11.42 Write a program using file streams that prompts the user for the name of a file to copy and the new file name, and copies the file. If the file cannot be opened, notify the user. If the output file already exists, query the user as to whether to proceed.

11.43 Write a file scope function convert() that takes as arguments a char array, a double array, and an int giving the maximum size of the double array. The char array contains a series of double values that are encoded in scientific notation. The function convert() uses an istrstream to convert those values and store them in the array of doubles, and returns the number of values stored.

11.44 Suppose we wish to define a class IndexedFile that provides direct access to the objects in a file based on a primary key returned by the message key(). (Again, use typedef's to specify the KeyType and ValueType as illustrated in exercise 10.36.) The class uses the same protocol as described for the class Dictionary in exercise 11.12. That is, clients use operator[]() to access, insert, or modify objects in the file, and IndexedFile uses an auxiliary class as described in that exercise. Define the class IndexedFileStream with two data members of type fstream; the index file and the file of objects. You may use either hashing or a B-tree to implement the index file.

11.45 Suppose we have a sequential file of instances of a class, and that all the objects in the file are the same size. (For concreteness, imagine that the objects are rectangles and that each is stored as a series of four ints written using ostream::write(..., sizeof(int)). Use a typedef for the element type in your class.) We want to define a smart pointer class FilePtr for the objects in the file such that clients can treat the smart pointers as pointers into an array of objects. In particular, clients can use the ->, prefix *, [ ], =, ==, !=, ++, −−, +=, and -= operators in the same way as with regular pointers. The smart pointer constructor takes an int giving the index of the object in the file, with 0 indicating the first object. To implement lazy fetching of objects in the file, the smart pointer class defines a static array of pointers to objects that are initially NULL. When the object at a particular index is accessed (but not necessarily when a pointer to it is created), the object is allocated dynamically and copied from the file, and a pointer to the object is placed in that position in the array. For this exercise, assume that the class is only used with one file, and that the client must invoke the class message FilePtr::set-File(const char* filename) before attempting to use an instance. (We will describe how to avoid this issue in Chapter 13.) The class also defines a class message FilePtr::size() that returns the number of objects in the file. If a constructor argument or pointer arithmetic results in a pointer that is out of range, print an error message and exit if the client accesses the object it points to. You must also ensure that any objects that are modified by the program are written back to the file. (There are several ways of doing this. Try to do it without writing to the file unnecessarily.)

12

Inheritance and Dynamic Binding

In this chapter, we will cover C++ support for inheritance, which it refers to as *class derivation*. First, we discuss defining subclasses and subclass constructors, scope, and access control. Next, we discuss the complexities that arise due to the interaction between static typing and inheritance with respect to assignments, method binding, run-time type identity, object allocation, and conversions. Because C++ is statically typed, dynamic binding is only possible because of inheritance, so these two features are closely related. We discuss virtual member functions, refinement, virtual destructors, pure virtual functions, and implementing dynamic binding. Finally, we examine C++ support for multiple inheritance, and discuss features for dealing with inherited name conflicts and repeated inheritance.

This chapter covers the following topics:

- subclass definition, and requirements for classes used for derivation (12.1.1)
- why subclasses do not inherit constructors and assignment operators, and the subclass constructor initialization list and copy constructor (12.1.2)
- derived class scope and visibility of inherited members (12.1.3)
- access specifications, which provide separate interfaces for a class's clients and subclasses (12.1.4)
- language design issues with static typing and inheritance (12.2.1)

- object and identifier polymorphism, the static and dynamic class of an identifier, polymorphism and assignments, and static and dynamic method binding (12.2.2)
- storage allocation for base class value identifiers, and the difference in semantics between value and pointer object identifiers (12.2.3)
- type conversions among classes that are related hierarchically (12.2.4)
- the dynamic_cast<> operator and run-time type information (12.2.5)
- virtual member functions, and static invocation of virtual member functions (12.3.1)
- method refinement, why overridden method must be virtual, and related design issues (12.3.2)
- virtual destructors and copying (12.3.3)
- abstract classes and abstract messages, called *pure virtual functions* in C++ (12.3.4)
- the implementation of dynamic binding, and an object's vptr and a class's vtbl (12.3.5)
- multiple inheritance, and its effect on hierarchy and scope structure, conversions, and dynamic binding (12.4.1)
- resolving name conflicts among inherited members (12.4.2)
- repeated inheritance and *virtual base classes* (12.4.3).

12.1 CLASS DERIVATION

12.1.1 Subclass Definition

The derivation list and derived class members

In C++, we refer to a superclass as a *base class* from which its subclasses are *derived*. To specify inheritance in a class definition, we follow the class name with a colon and a *derivation list* of base classes from which the class inherits members. The compiler must have encountered the definitions of the base classes so that it knows the inherited protocol and the size and format of derived class objects.[1] Usually, the header file that defines the class contains #include's for the base class header files. A superclass is not required for a class definition, so the inheritance structure of a C++ application can be a forest or a directed acyclic graph with multiple inheritance. A root class that encapsulates behavior available for all objects, as in Smalltalk, is not necessary, and is often not present.

A derived class inherits all the data members and member functions (including operators) of each of its base classes, except for the constructors and assignment operator (as discussed in the next section). In defining the derived class, we only

---

[1] As we will see in section 12.3.5, the compiler must also know which ancestor member functions are virtual.

give the additional data members and member functions and the methods that override inherited methods. The class body and member function definitions of a derived class are written as we described in Chapter 10.

For example, let us define a class for priority queues like the one we coded in Smalltalk in section 6.2.2. When we insert an element into a priority queue, an ElemType comparison function specific to the priority queue object determines the new element's position in the queue. Upon a deletion, we remove the "least" element in the queue according to its comparison function. We derive the class PriorityQueue from the class Queue defined in sections 10.1.3 and 10.1.4. Its protocol is the same as that of its superclass, with two exceptions. It provides an additional member function first() which returns the first element in the queue (i.e., the one with the highest priority) without removing it. Its constructor takes a pointer to the new object's comparison function. We will code the class PriorityQueue with the comparison function as an ElemType member function, rather than as a file scope function,[2] and the constructor argument has a default value of &ElemType::operator<() (i.e., ascending order). The subclass inherits the storage structure of Queue[3] and the methods for Queue::remove() and Queue::isEmpty(). It adds a data member that is a pointer to the comparison function, and methods for the constructor and PriorityQueue::first(). The class PriorityQueue also refines Queue::insert() to use the comparison function when placing a new element in the queue (see section 12.1.3).

We code the header file containing the definition of the class PriorityQueue as follows:

```
// PriorityQueue.h: interface for priority queues of elements (linked list implementation)
// The function used for ordering comparisons is a member function of class ElemType
#ifndef PRI_QUEUE_H
#define PRI_QUEUE_H

// The type of a priority queue element and the auxiliary class Node are included
// from the header file for the superclass Queue.
// (PriorityQueue is added as a friend of Node.)
#include "Queue.h"

class PriorityQueue : public Queue
{
public:
    PriorityQueue(bool (ElemType::*)(const ElemType&) = &ElemType::operator<);
```

[2] For example, the class String defines its order comparison operators as file scope functions to permit conversion of the left operand from a char*. Unfortunately, we would have to code a different PriorityQueue class to use such a class as the type of the elements, with a different class name. Neith these classes would permit priority queues of built-in type instances because we cannot obtain a pointer to an built-in operator. For such priority queues, the comparisons in PriorityQueue::insert() would be hardcoded using the < operator. These complications do not occur in Smalltalk, in which every operation is a message to a receiver and all types are classes.

[3] Of course, this is not the most efficient storage structure for a priority queue.

```
    ElemType first();
    virtual PriorityQueue& insert(const ElemType&);
protected:
    bool (ElemType::*pCompareFn)(const ElemType&);
};

inline PriorityQueue::PriorityQueue(bool (ElemType::*cmp)(const ElemType&))
    : Queue(), pCompareFn(cmp)
{ }

inline ElemType PriorityQueue::first()
{
    if ( isEmpty() )
    {
        // throw an exception (see section 13.3) if implemented, otherwise:
        cerr << "attempted PriorityQueue::first() on an empty queue" << endl;
        exit(1);
    }
    return front->elem;
}


#endif
```

As you would expect, an instance of PriorityQueue responds to the messages
insert(), remove(), isEmpty(), and first(), and contains the data members front,
back, and pCompareFn. We will discuss the base class access specification (public, in this example), the constructor initialization list, the virtual reserved word
for PriorityQueue::insert(), and the definition of that method later in this chapter. The PriorityQueue::first() method can access the front member of the
receiver because that member is protected, and because the scope of a derived
class is nested within the scope of its base class (see section 12.1.3). It can also
access the elem member of its referent for reasons given in the next subsection.
Clients use an instance of PriorityQueue in the same fashion as an instance of
Queue, and can also use the message first() to determine the current first element in the queue.

Requirements for base classes

   Unlike classes that do not have descendants, classes that are used as base
classes raise the following three issues:

- all member functions that are overridden by any descendant must be declared
  virtual so that they are dynamically bound
- derived classes cannot access inherited private members
- derived classes are not automatically friends of a class that declares the base
  class as a friend, nor are friends of the base class automatically friends of the
  derived class.

We will cover the reasons for the first requirement in sections 12.3.2 and 12.3.5. If a class designates data members or auxiliary member functions as private, then they are not accessible in descendant methods. Friendship is not inherited, for reasons we will discuss in section 12.1.4.

To use Queue as a base class, we must make two modifications to the definition of the class Queue (i.e., to the file Queue.h). We must specify the member functions Queue::insert() and Queue::~Queue() as virtual so that they are dynamically bound (we discuss dynamic binding for destructors in section 12.3.3). If the auxiliary class Node is not nested within the class Queue, then Node must declare the class PriorityQueue as a friend, because PriorityQueue methods need to access the Node data members (e.g., the use of elem in the PriorityQueue::first() method). In addition, if we had defined Queue's data members as private, we would have to change that access specifier to protected. The revised Queue class appears as follows:

```
// changes to Queue.h necessary to derive PriorityQueue

// ... #ifndef, typedef, #include <iostream.h> as presented in section 10.1.3 ...

class Node
{
friend class Queue;
friend class PriorityQueue;          // PriorityQueue methods need access
// ... members as in section 10.1.3 ...
};

class Queue
{
friend ostream& operator<<(ostream&, Queue&);
public:
    virtual ~Queue();                              // dynamic binding is necessary
    virtual Queue& insert(const ElemType&);    // dynamic binding is necessary
    // ... other member functions as in section 10.1.3 ...
protected:                       // cannot be private: PriorityQueue methods need access
    // ... data members as in section 10.1.3 ...
};
```

12.1.2 Constructors, Destructor, and Assignment Operator

Constructors

A derived class does not inherit the constructors of its base classes because it may define additional data members that the base class constructors cannot initialize. That is, if the base class defines a constructor with a given argument signature, clients cannot use that argument signature to initialize a derived class object (unless,

of course, the derived class also defines a constructor with that signature). Therefore, every class must define its own constructor(s). [4]

Destructor

Destructors are inherited in the sense that the compiler always ensures that
the base class destructor is executed when the base class subobject in a derived class
object is destroyed. That is, if a base class or the class of a data member defines a
destructor and the derived class does not, the compiler generates a derived class
destructor that calls those of the base classes and data members. We did not define
a destructor for the class PriorityQueue because its destructor does not need to perform any processing other than that done by its superclass's destructor.

A derived class destructor is only responsible for resources or side effects that
result from initializing the data members the derived class defines itself, not those
for inherited members. Its method does not call the base class destructor (as in
refinement) because that processing is triggered automatically whenever a derived
class instance is destroyed.

The initialization list

As we saw in section 10.2.4, class objects embedded within a composite object
must be initialized according to their classes' constructors when the composite
object is initialized, and clients using a class for composition should not be responsible for knowing how this is done. These principles also apply to the base class
part of a derived class object. A base class constructor must be called in initializing an instance of a derived class, and we need a mechanism for passing arguments
to the base class constructor. We use the initialization list of the derived class constructor to invoke and pass arguments to base class constructors, as well as to those
for derived class data members. The constructor body performs any other start-up
processing necessary. To summarize, the initialization list is used to invoke constructors for

- the base class portions of the new object
- the derived-class-specific class-type member objects
- the derived class const and reference data members.

In the initialization list of a derived class constructor, each base class name
(not the names of the inherited data members) is followed by an initializer whose
signature matches a base class constructor. The initializer may also be an instance
of the base class or of a class derived from it, or of a class for which there is conversion to the base class (i.e., if a derived class constructor argument is one of these).
If the base class does not define a copy constructor, the compiler uses the default

---

[4] If a class defines no constructors at all, the compiler will generate a default constructor that calls
the default constructors of its base classes and data members, if any. However, this constructor does not
initialize data members or base class subobjects that do not define default constructors.

base class copy constructor to initialize the inherited data members. For example, let us define a class Employee as a subclass of the class Person defined in section 10.2.4. We code the class and its constructors as follows:

```
// using the initialization list to invoke base class constructors
#include "Person.h"              // class Person defined in section 10.2.4
class Employee : public Person
{
public:
    Employee(const char* name, const char* addr, const Date& birthdate, long ssn,
       long employeeID, const char* dept, int vacDays = Employee::defaultVacationDays);
    Employee(const Person& pers, long employeeID, const char* dept,
       int vacDays = Employee::defaultVacationDays);
    // ... other member functions ...
protected:
    long employeeID_;
    String department_;
    int vacationDays_;
    static int defaultVacationDays;
};

inline Employee::Employee(const char* name, const char* addr, const Date& birthdate,
                          long ssn, long empID, const char* dept, int vacDays)
    : Person(name, addr, birthdate, ssn),
      employeeID_(empID), department_(dept), vacationDays_(vacDays)
{
    // ... special processing for employees ...
}

inline Employee(const Person& pers, long empID, const char* dept, int vacDays)
    : Person(pers), employeeID_(empID), department_(dept), vacationDays_(vacDays)
{
    // ... special processing for employees ...
}
```

Note that, in the initialization list, the base class subobject uses the class name (i.e., Person), while the data member subobjects use the data member name (e.g., employeeID_). The constructor String::String(const char*) will be called to initialize the department_ member of the new employee object. Because the Employee constructor invokes the Person constructor, the body of the Employee constructor should not repeat any processing that the Person constructor performs.

You should not include inherited data members in the derived class initialization list, because the base class constructor invoked through the initialization list initializes them. For example, the constructor Person::Person() calls the constructor String::String(const char*) to initialize the name_ and address_ members of a new employee object, so its descendants' constructors do not. Similarly, data members inherited from ancestors further up the hierarchy are initialized when the constructor for the class that defines them is executed.

If a base class has a default constructor, that class may be omitted from the initialization list, and the default constructor will be invoked to initialize the base class subobject. For example, it was not actually necessary to include `Queue()` on the initialization list of PriorityQueue::PriorityQueue() in the previous section.

Order of initialization and finalization

As stated in section 10.2.4, the language defines the order of execution of constructors in initializing an object because one constructor could cause a side effect affecting the operation of another constructor involved. The constructors that are invoked upon execution of a derived class constructor are called in the following order. First, the base class constructors are invoked in the order of the class derivation list (not in the order of the initialization list), including default constructors for base classes not in the initialization list. This rule is applied recursively if a base class is also derived (since the base class's initialization list is invoked before its body). Therefore, the constructors for ancestors higher in the class hierarchy are executed first, and the object is constructed from the "inside out". Next, the constructors for class data members are called in the order in which the members appear in the class definition (again, including default constructors for members not in the initialization list). Like base class constructors, their initialization lists are executed before their bodies, so their inherited and class type data member constructors are called first. Finally, the constructor body for the derived class is invoked.

The corresponding destructors are invoked in the reverse order so the object is finalized from the "outside in". The derived class destructor is invoked, and then data member destructors are called in reverse order of member declaration in the class definition. Finally, base class destructors are invoked from right to left in the derivation list. Again, this process is done recursively for each class data member and base class.

Copy constructor

The default copy constructor for a derived class, which the compiler uses to create a copy upon initialization or pass by value, invokes the copy constructors of its base classes and class data members. It initializes each embedded base class subobject in the order of the derivation list, and then initializes each derived class member in the order of the class definition. The base class subobject is initialized by a programmer-defined copy constructor, or, if there is none, by memberwise initialization. As we discussed in section 10.2.5, we can think of the compiler-generated copy constructor for the derived class as having the correct initialization list, that is, having the following form:

```
// the format of the compiler-generated default copy constructor with inheritance
Derived::Derived(const Derived& argDer)
   : Base1(argDer), Base2(argDer), ..., mem1(argDer.mem1), mem2(argDer.mem2), ...
{ }
```

The base class initializers in the previous example are valid because there is a standard conversion from an instance of a derived class to an instance of a base class (see section 12.2.4). This conversion is well-defined because there is an instance of the base class embedded within the derived class instance.

If a derived class allocates system resources or contains instance-specific state information, the designer can provide a copy constructor for the class. Unlike destructors, copy constructors do not call non-default base class copy constructors automatically. The derived class copy constructor must include each base class on its initialization list (unless its default constructor is desired). For example, if new instances of Employee required some specific processing, we would code its copy constructor as follows:

```
// the copy constructor for a derived class must invoke the base class copy constructor
Employee::Employee(const Employee& empl)
   : Person(empl), employeeID_(empl.employeeID_),
     department_(empl.department_), vacationDays_(empl.vacationDays_)
{
   // ... special processing for Employee objects ...
}
```

Assignment operator

The left operand of a binary operator is the receiver of the message, so the type of the left operand of an object assignment determines the class whose method is invoked. As we saw in section 11.1.3, if the class of the target identifier does not overload the assignment operator, the compiler performs a member-by-member assignment. If the target's class is a derived class, this default assignment operator invokes the assignment method for each base class or class data member that defines one. Those that do not define the operator are copied by their compiler-generated defaults, which perform memberwise assignment. (Note that using a base class assignment method alone to copy a descendant object would not copy the descendant-specific data members, resulting in an inconsistent object.)

As we saw in section 11.1.3, classes that require a copy constructor also need an assignment operator overloading. If a derived class requires its own assignment definition, that method must deal with inherited data members and class type data members. It must include assignments in its body that will either trigger their operator definitions or use the compiler-generated defaults. With data members, the assignment method can use the member name to identify the type and target of the assignment, that is, this->*mem* = rhs.*mem*;. However, the inherited subobject is anonymous, and using *this on the left side of an assignment would be a recursive call. To assign to the base class subobject of the receiver, we can use a reference cast on the left side of an assignment, that is *(Base&)* *this = rhs;. (We use a reference cast because a value cast would create a new temporary object, which would be assigned and then deallocated.) Alternatively, we can use a qualified name with the scope operator to specify the base class operator function (as in method refinement). However, we must use the function name syntax rather than the infix syntax for the operator, that is, *Base*::operator=(rhs),. For example, we might code the assignment method for Employee as follows:[5]

```
// a derived class assignment operator method
Employee& Employee::operator=(const Employee& rhs)
{
    if ( this == &rhs ) return *this;
    // *this is the receiver, i.e. the left operand.  The Employee object rhs is cast
    // to a Person object, and then Person::operator=(const Person&) is invoked
    (Person&) *this = rhs;                  // or Person::operator=(rhs);
    employeeID_ = rhs.employeeID_;
    department_ = rhs.deptartment_;         // invokes String::operator=(const String&)
    vacationDays_ = rhs.vacationDays_;
    // ... special processing for Employee objects ...
    return *this;
}
```

12.1.3 Derived Class Scope

Nesting of derived class scope

The enclosing scope of a class with no superclasses is the file, class, or function scope in which it is defined. The scope of a derived class is enclosed within the scopes of its immediate base classes.[6] This scope relationship has two important results:

- the names of base class members are visible in derived class member functions
- clients can send base class messages to derived class objects.

That is, the search for the declaration of an inherited member name is a special case of the identifier resolution process. The name of the derived class is declared in the scope in which the class definition occurs (i.e., at file scope if it is not a nested class), not the base class scope. For example, although the scope of the class PriorityQueue is nested within the scope of the class Queue, the name PriorityQueue is declared at file scope, not within the scope of Queue. Therefore, when defining its methods at file scope, we do not use the cascaded scope operator, for example, Queue::PriorityQueue::first().

Derived class methods may use an inherited member name directly (i.e., without component selection), in the same manner as subclass-specific member names. Such a use refers to an inherited data member of the receiver or a message sent to

---

[5] Recall from section 11.1.3 that this assignment would not actually be allowed because the data members birthdate_ and ssn_ in class Person are const. Again, we ignore this detail for the purpose of this discussion.

[6] Note that, due to support for multiple inheritance, a derived class scope may be directly nested in more than one scope.

the receiver. For example, the data member front inherited from Queue and the member function Queue::isEmpty() are visible within the PriorityQueue:: first() method. Similarly, a derived class method can access the non-private inherited members of an instance of the derived class (e.g., a member function argument).

As we saw in section 10.3.1, the class of the receiver identifier in a message expression determines the scope searched for the member function name. If that class does not define that member function name and it has a base class (i.e., an enclosing scope), the base class scope is searched next, and so on (for non-virtual member functions). In the following example, Queue::isEmpty() is executed with pq as the receiver because PriorityQueue does not define this member function:

```
// a scope search is used to find the method corresponding to a message
#include "Date.h"              // defines bool Date::operator<(const Date&)
#include "PriorityQueue.h"     // with typedef Date ElemType; in Queue.h
int main
{
   PriorityQueue pq;
   // ... operations on pq ...
   while ( !pq.isEmpty() )      // invokes Queue::isEmpty()
      // ... process dates ...
}
```

Like the search for an inherited member name in a derived class method, static method binding is handled by the process of identifier resolution. The compiler performs the scope search and translates the invocation as an encoded function call. This search proceeds from the class of the identifier up the class hierarchy, that is, outward through enclosing scopes. The same search process occurs with respect to this (e.g., see the invocation of isEmpty() in the method for PriorityQueue::insert() later in this section).

The local scopes of the derived class's member functions are nested within its scope, and the member function names are declared within the class scope. A local variable of a derived class member function is declared within that scope, and hides an inherited or derived class member with the same name within that member function. We can refer to the hidden member within the derived class member function with a qualified name.

Although a nested class and a derived class both define class scopes nested within a class scope, they have different properties with respect to the enclosing class. An instance of the nested class cannot perform the protocol of the enclosing class, nor does it have an instance of the enclosing class embedded within it. For this reason, using an enclosing class member name without component selection in a nested class member function is not valid. In addition, the derived class name is visible at file scope while the nested class name is not, so we use the cascaded scope operator for lexically nested classes, but not for derived classes.

To illustrate these scope relationships, suppose that we nest the class Node within the class Queue as illustrated in section 10.3.4, and derive PriorityQueue from

Queue. Figure 12.1 diagrams the scope relationships for class Queue, its member functions and friend function, and the nested class Node and the derived class PriorityQueue and their members (as in Figure 0.2, we use lines to demarcate the scope boundaries).

Redefining inherited member names

Although nonprivate inherited members can be accessed in derived class methods and objects, their names belong to the scope of the base class. If a derived class defines a member with the same name as an inherited member, each of those identifiers is defined in a different scope. The base class identifier is hidden in the derived class scope, and unqualified references to that name within derived class member functions will be taken to refer to the derived class declaration. Derived class methods can still access the base class identifier with the scope operator and the base class name.

A derived class can override a base class member function, including operator and conversion definitions. To do so, it defines a method with the same name and argument signature as in the base class. Because the class of the left side of a component selection determines the member accessed, base class variables will use the base class method, and derived class variables will use the derived class method. However, a base class pointer can refer to a derived class object, and an overridden member function must be dynamically bound so that the method invoked is determined by the class of the receiver object, not by the class of the identifier. We must declare a member function virtual as we did with PriorityQueue::insert(), for it to be dynamically bound. Method binding is complicated in C++, and discussion continues throughout this chapter.

Suppose a derived class defines a member function with the same name as a base class member function, but with a different argument signature. Because the base class definition is hidden in the derived class scope, the compiler rejects an invocation of the function with the base class signature passed to a derived class identifier. That is, the new argument signature hides the inherited signature, rather than overloading it. Of course, an invocation with the derived class argument signature for a base class object is an error because the derived class member function is defined in a scope nested within that of the base class. In addition, if a base class pointer refers to a derived class object, the derived class signature cannot be used via that pointer. The following example illustrates these points:

```
// the semantics of defining a message name in a base class and a derived class
// with different argument signatures
#include "Base.h"        // defines void Base::msg(char*)
#include "Derived.h"     // a subclass of Base that defines void Derived::msg(int)
int main()
{
    Base bs(...);
    Derived der(...);
```

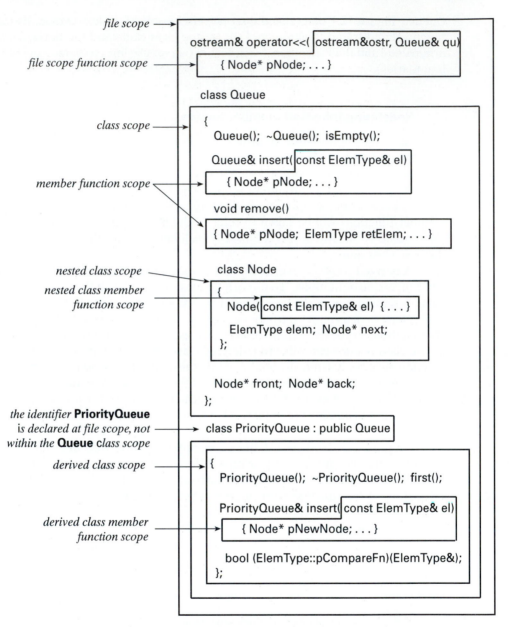

file scope

ostream& operator<<(ostream&ostr, Queue& qu)

file scope function scope

{ Node* pNode; ... }

class Queue

class scope

{
  Queue(); ~Queue(); isEmpty();

  Queue& insert(const ElemType& el)

member function scope

    { Node* pNode; ... }

  void remove()

    { Node* pNode; ElemType retElem; ... }

nested class scope

  class Node

nested class member function scope

  {
    Node(const ElemType& el) { ... }

    ElemType elem; Node* next;
  };

  Node* front; Node* back;
};

*the identifier **PriorityQueue** is declared at file scope, not within the **Queue** class scope*

class PriorityQueue : public Queue

derived class scope

{
  PriorityQueue(); ~PriorityQueue(); first();

  PriorityQueue& insert(const ElemType& el)

derived class member function scope

    { Node* pNewNode; ... }

  bool (ElemType::pCompareFn)(ElemType&);
};

Figure 12.1 Scope diagram for class Queue.

```
    Base* pBase = &der;  // OK, a Derived object is also a Base object
    // Derived::msg(int) hides Base::msg(char*) rather than overloading it
    der.msg("hello");    // error: no Derived::msg(char*)
    bs.msg(7);           // error: no Base::msg(int)
    pBase->msg(7);       // error even though the referent is Derived: no Base::msg(int)
}
```

The last invocation in the previous example must be an error to maintain type safety. The pointer pBase may, in fact, point to a Base object or an instance of another subclass of Base that does not define msg(int). Because it is rarely the class designer's intention to hide the base class argument signature in the derived class, most compilers issue a warning when this does occur.

Now, suppose we want to provide an additional argument signature for an inherited member function name. To do so, we must declare both signatures in the derived class scope. We define an additional overloading of the function name with the base class signature in the derived class, whose method invokes the base class member function using the scope operator. For example, in some applications of priority queues, the client needs to remove a specified element from the queue, no matter what its position is (e.g., a process scheduler must be able to remove a terminated process from semaphore or resource queues). To include the additional argument signature PriorityQueue::remove(const ElemType&) in the class PriorityQueue, we would code the class as follows:

```
// adding an argument signature for a member function name in the derived class
#include "Queue.h"                // defines Queue::remove()
class PriorityQueue : public Queue
{
public:
   void remove(const ElemType&);
   ElemType remove();
// ... other members as in section 12.1.1 ...
};

inline ElemType PriorityQueue::remove()
{
   return Queue::remove();
}
```

Because the methods for both Queue::remove() and PriorityQueue::remove() are exactly the same, this is one case in which static binding can be used for an overridden function. Note also that PriorityQueue::remove() is inline.

Suppose a data member name, say mem, is redeclared in the derived class. In this case, its instances have two data members with that name. However, each name is declared in a different scope: One member is Base::mem and the other is Derived::mem, and a derived class method must use a qualified name to refer to the base class member. (Clearly, such name reuse is questionable programming style.)

Refinement with name qualification

As we saw in section 3.2.4, an object-oriented language requires a feature that distinguishes method refinement from recursion because both the superclass and subclass methods have the same name and receiver. In section 6.2.2, we saw that the Smalltalk class designer uses the pseudo-variable super as the receiver to indicate that the method search begins in the superclass of the class defining the method. In C++, we use a qualified member function name to specify the base class whose method is invoked. The language must use a feature that includes the base class name because it supports multiple inheritance. That is, we must state the ancestor path in the class hierarchy along which the overridden member function is defined. A derived class method can invoke the method of any public ancestor in the class hierarchy in this way (including ancestor methods hidden by a definition in an intervening class in the hierarchy). We can also refine an operator definition by using the function name syntax for the operator, as in the expression Base::operator==(rhs).

For example, we define the member function PriorityQueue::insert() such that it invokes the superclass method if the queue is empty or if the element being inserted belongs at the back of the queue (as in section 6.2.2), as follows:

```
// refining the base class method Queue::insert()
PriorityQueue& PriorityQueue::insert(const ElemType& el)
{
    if ( isEmpty() || ((back->elem).*pCompareFn)(el) )
        Queue::insert(el);                 // use superclass method
    else                                   // subclass-specific processing
    {
        Node* pNewNode = new Node(el);
        if ( (el.*pCompareFn)(front->elem) )
        {
            pNewNode->next = front;
            front = pNewNode;
        }
        else
        {
            Node* pPred = front;
            // we have already checked for insertion at the back of the queue
            for ( Node* pCurr = front->next; ((pCurr->elem).*pCompareFn)(el);
                pCurr = pCurr->next )
                    pPred = pCurr;
            pPred->next = pNewNode;
            pNewNode->next = pCurr;
        }
    }
    return *this;
)
```

Without name qualification, the invocation of insert() in the if statement in the previous method would be a recursive call of the same method.

The expression Queue::insert(el) specifies invocation of the definition of insert() in effect in the scope Queue, whether it is defined there or in an enclosing (i.e., ancestor) scope. Like super in Smalltalk, name qualification specifies a starting point for a search up the class hierarchy, which is equivalent to a static scope search in C++. When overriding a base class member function, the derived class must use the same argument signature so that the functions are invoked uniformly. As we will discuss in section 12.3.2, the only difference permitted is that a base class reference or pointer return type can be a derived class reference or pointer in the derived class member function, as was done in the previous example.[7]

Because classes define named scopes, clients of a class can also use a qualified name when invoking a member function. This allows a client to explicitly select a particular ancestor method for use with a derived class receiver, as follows:

```
// clients can also use the scope operator (but should not)
#include "Date.h"           // defines bool Date::operator<(const Date&)
#include "Queue.h"          // with typedef Date ElemType;
#include "PriorityQueue.h"
int main()
{
    PriorityQueue pq;
    pq.insert(Date("1/1/90")).insert(Date("5/1/90"));
    pq.Queue::insert(Date("3/1/90"));              // legal but bad practice
}
```

However, clients should not do this because invoking a base class method directly for a derived class object can violate the consistency of that object, as occurs in this example.

Inherited static members

Because a derived class scope is nested within the scope of its base classes, the static members of the base classes are visible in the derived class scope (if they are not hidden by a derived class member name). They are accessible in derived class methods if they are not private. In addition, we can refer to a base class static member with the scope operator and the derived class name (if it is not hidden), for example, to invoke an inherited class message. Of course, the member must be accessible at that point, that is, it must be public for a client to use it.

There is exactly one object corresponding to each static data member—that is, the derived class does not have its own object with that name. If a base class and a derived class must each maintain its own value for some class information, then each defines its own static data member, and both classes define a static member function that accesses its member. The class name used by a client when calling the static function determines which function is called, and, therefore, which value is returned.

12.1.4 Access Control

Protected and private members

A protected member is accessible within the member and friend functions of the class and classes derived from the class, but is not accessible to clients. We have

---

[7] This special case is a recent addition to the language which many compilers do not yet support.

used protected access for data members and auxiliary member functions so that they are available to descendants, but not to clients. We can also use the protected section of a class to restrict access to constructs that are usually public. Declaring a class's constructors as protected restricts instantiation of a class to its descendants and friends. The class name and its public protocol are still accessible to the rest of the program. For example, a protected constructor can perform a partial initialization of the receiver that descendant constructors refine to complete (recall the constructor String::String(int) in section 10.2.2). As another example, suppose we want creating a stream over a collection to be the responsibility of the collection, and to force clients to obtain a stream over a collection from that collection. To do so, we define the stream constructor as protected and the collection as a friend of the stream class. A class or enumeration nested within the protected portion of a class is available to classes derived from the enclosing class, but is not accessible outside that subhierarchy. This is useful for an auxiliary class that is only necessary in that subhierarchy— the class Node in Figure 12.1 is accessible only to the class Queue and its subclasses.

With derivation, C++ supports an additional distinction in access control. Unlike Smalltalk, C++ supports separate interfaces for clients of a class (i.e., programmers creating instances) and for class designers creating subclasses. The private specifier hides a member from both groups. (That is, protected describes the access specification of instance variables in Smalltalk.) A *private* member is accessible only within the class's member and friend functions, and not within those of its descendants or clients. The designer of a class intended for reuse and derivation must choose between private and protected access for each member with care, especially if the source code will not be available to designers of descendants.

Generally, we specify the data members of a class as protected rather than private because they are needed when coding subclass methods, as in the Priority-Queue methods. However, sometimes the designer must hide the implementation of a class from designers of descendants. For example, when a class is still under development, its state information and representation might not yet be stable even though some descendants are already defined. Similarly, when a vendor markets a proprietary class library or a library that accesses proprietary functionality in other software systems, it may need to restrict access to that information. In these cases, the designer can provide a protected interface to the private information, just like supplying a public interface to protected information. The protected interface enables the designer to provide controlled access to the class's implementation to designers of descendants, without providing acess for clients.

Accessibility versus visibility

A semantic issue that you will find confusing at first is that access specifications control the accessibility of the referent object, but scope determines the visibility of the identifier name. In resolving an identifier use, the compiler finds the name by searching enclosing scopes, and then checks its access specification and type. In particular, if a class declares a private member, that declaration hides a global identifier with the same name from its descendants, even though that member is not accessible in the descendants. An unqualified use of that name in a descendant method is an error, not a reference to the global identifier. Friends of a descendant class have the same access as its member functions. The following example illustrates this distinction:

```
// access specifications do not control scope and visibility of names
int num;              // file scope definition

class Base
{
public:
   // ... member functions ...
private:
   int num;           // hides file scope definition of num in scopes nested within Base scope
};

class Derived : public Base
{
friend int func(Derived&);
public:
   int msg();
private:
   // ... data members ...
};

int Derived::msg()
{
   return num;        // syntax error: Base::num is visible here, but is private
   return ::num;      // OK: file scope num
}

int func(Derived& der)
{
   return der.num;    // error: num is private in derived (it is visible, but not accessible)
   return num;        // OK: file scope num is visible to the file scope function func()
}
```

Access specifications have this meaning so that changing an access specifier does not affect the meaning of descendant methods. For example, suppose that access specifiers controlled visibility so that Derived::msg() in the previous example could refer to the global num directly because Base::num is private and, therefore, is not visible. If we change Base::num's access to protected during development, the operation of Derived::msg() changes without warning, because its unqualified use of num now refers to Base::num. With the semantics defined by the language, if we use num in an expression without a scope specification in Derived::msg(), a compiler error results. We then recognize the problem, and use a qualified name to specify the intended global identifier (irrespective of the inherited member's access level).

Inheritance and access specifications

Each inherited member has the same access specification in the derived class as declared for it in the base class, with public derivation (see the next subsection). Inherited public members are available to the clients of the derived class, and inherited protected members are accessible to its descendants. Inherited private members are not accessible within the member functions of the subclass or its descendants, even though inherited private data members have values in instances of the derived class.

Although derived class member and friend functions can access inherited protected members in derived class instances, they have no special access to those members in instances of the base class. They are clients of the base class object, and as such only, they have access to its public members. For example,

```
// the derived class is a client of base class objects
class Base
{
   // ... other members ...
protected:
   int mem;
};

class Derived : public Base
{
public:
   void msg1(Base& bs)
   {
       mem++;        // valid: protected member of Derived receiver
       bs.mem++;     // error: Derived::msg1() has no access to non-public members of Base
   }
   void msg2(Derived& der)
   {
       der.mem++;    // valid: Derived::msg2() has access to non-public members of Derived
   }
   // ... other members ...
};
```

This restriction may seem peculiar, but note that the argument passed to Derived::msg1() might be an instance of any class derived from Base. If Derived had access to that object's protected members, then classes with a common ancestor could access the inherited portions of each others' internal structures.

Friendship is not inherited. That is, the friend functions of a base class are not friends of its derived classes, and vice versa. Only the functions that are explicitly listed as friends in a class's definition have access to its nonpublic members. The friend functions of a class have the same access as its member functions to inherited members in instances of the class: They can access protected members but not private members. A base class friend function also has access to base class members in instances of the derived class (i.e., it is a friend of the embedded base class subobject), which it can receive as the argument corresponding to a base class parameter.[8] For example, we can use the << operator to output instances of PriorityQueue because the Queue overloading of that operator can access the inherited members of the PriorityQueue object. However, a base class friend cannot access members unique to the derived class; they are defined in an enclosed scope, and are not visible in the scope of which it is a friend.

In addition, descendants of a friend class are not friends of the class. This is why we would have to declare PriorityQueue as a friend of Node if we defined that auxiliary class at file scope. This restriction can be inconvenient, but it prevents a programmer from seizing access to a class by deriving a class from a friend class.

Base class access control

A class definition can specify each base class in the class derivation list as public, protected, or private. A base class's access level affects the accessibility of the members inherited from that class within the derived class, its descendants, and its clients. The access level of each inherited member is the "more restricted" of its level in the ancestor definition and that of the derivation. Within derived class methods, an inherited member still has the access level declared in the ancestor, even if the derivation is private. The default access level for each base class is private, so we must specify each as public to reflect specialization.

The public, protected and private members of a public base class (whether inherited or defined in that class) remain public, protected, and private in the derived class, respectively. The public and protected members of a protected base class become protected members of the derived class. They are not accessible to clients in instances of the derived class and its descendants, but are accessible within the member functions of the derived class and its descendants. When the base class derivation is private, all inherited members are inaccessible to both clients and descendants of the derived class. Nonprivate inherited members are still accessible within the member functions of the derived class, but are not accessible within its descendants. The following example illustrates these rules:

```
// the effect of base class access specifications
class Base
{
public:
    void msg();
protected:
    int mem;
};

class ProtDerived : protected Base
{
public:
```

[8] As described in section 12.2.4, there is a standard conversion from a class to any of its ancestors.

```
      void protMsg()
      { mem++; }                // OK: mem is protected in ProtDerived
};

class PrivDerived : private Base
{
public:
   void privMsg()
   { mem++; }                // OK: mem behaves like a private member of PrivDerived
};

class PublPrivDerived : public PrivDerived
{
public:
   void publPrivMsg()
   {
      mem++;                 // error: mem is private in PrivDerived
      msg();                 // error: msg() is private in PrivDerived
   }
};

int main()
{
   ProtDerived protDer(...);
   PrivDerived privDer(...);
   PublPrivDerived publPrivDer(...);
   protDer.msg();            // error: msg() is protected in ProtDerived
   privDer.msg();            // error: msg() is private in PrivDerived
   publPrivDer.msg();        // error: msg() is private in PublPrivDerived
}
```

We prefer public derivation because it correctly reflects the specialization relationship in which the base class protocol is available for instances of the derived class and its descendants. In addition, with public derivation, each member always has the access specification declared for it in the ancestor that introduced it, which avoids the complexity illustrated in the preceding example. Unfortunately, because the default access level for derivation is private, we must remember to give the specifier public for each base class.

Private inheritance supports inheriting a class's state without inheriting its behavior, so a class designer can use it to represent composition or to use one class's implementation within that of another. This usage may be motivated by a C programmer's tendency to think of an object in terms of its storage format, rather than its functionality. If the proposed derived class is not intended to be a specialization of the base class, a better design would be to use a data member whose type is that of the class whose implementation it uses. In this way, the language feature used to design the class matches the intended semantics, so the program is easier to understand and maintain, as is the class hierarchy. However, private inheritance allows access to a class's nonpublic members (violating the intention of its access specifications), while using a class data member does not. This access can be useful, but it increases the coupling between the classes more than composition, which uses the class's public interface.

When the class designer uses non public derivation, he or she can exempt individual public member functions of the base class from the effect of the non-public derivation. This allows the derived class to inherit the base class's state and a portion of its protocol. To do so, the designer lists the qualified member function name only (i.e., with no return type or argument signature) in the public portion of the derived class, such as *Base::message;*.

We will see in section 12.2.4 that there is a standard conversion from a derived class to its base class, due to the semantics of inheritance. However, with nonpublic derivation, the derived class cannot respond to the public protocol of the base class, so the language does not support an implicit conversion in this case. If such a conversion is necessary, the programmer must use an explicit conversion.

12.2 INHERITANCE AND STATIC TYPING

12.2.1 Language Design Issues

A programming language with strong static typing provides compile-time type and access checking based on the types of object and subprogram identifiers. Static typing allows compile-time code binding for many message expressions and value representations for identifiers, and does not require a run-time representation of type information to prevent invalid operations. Because more errors are caught and more decisions are resolved at compile time, programs in the language are safer and program execution requires less run-time support from the language system. Static typing also provides information on identifier usage, which is helpful in reading programs.

In a sense, static typing with inheritance is an intermediate stage between monomorphic static typing and dynamic typing, in which there is no constraint on the type of the referent of an identifier. It provides the flexibility and polymorphism of dynamic typing, together with a mechanism for restricting the set of types whose instances can be bound to a particular identifier. This inheritance mechanism is defined by the programmer and reflects his or her semantic intent. A class type identifier can be bound to an instance of any class in the subhierarchy rooted at that class, but not to objects of other classes. This is safer than dynamic typing because the compiler can verify that all messages passed to the referent of an identifier are in the protocol of its class. However, it is less flexible because the compiler rejects an invocation of a descendant-specific message (as opposed to performing the check at run time), even though it may be valid in a particular case. In addition, a message cannot be dynamically bound between two classes unless they share an ancestor in the class hierarchy that defines that message so that the programmer can define an identifier that can be bound to instances of both classes.

Unfortunately, the interaction between inheritance and static typing in object-oriented languages complicates the semantics of many language features. This reflects a common tradeoff in language design between safety and flexibility. As we discuss these effects in the context of C++ in this section, keep in mind that the way C++ resolves these issues is affected by the language's design goals of run-time efficiency, and of not incurring a cost for a feature for programs that do not use it. We will see that

- the class of an ancestor identifier can differ from the class of its referent, and the compiler might not know the exact class of the referent
- some potentially valid assignments are disallowed to avoid run-time type checking
- method binding can be either static or dynamic
- C++ supports value identifiers of class type, but there is an important distinction between the semantics of a base class value and a base class pointer or reference
- built-in types and classes without subclasses do not participate in dynamic binding
- implicit conversions from descendant classes to ancestor classes are valid
- the run-time type information facility provides some type information accessible to the programmer.

When using a dynamically typed language such as Smalltalk or CLOS, we do not need to deal with this complexity. In those languages, all assignments are valid, all variables are references, no assignments or message expressions are disallowed by the compiler, all method binding is dynamic, and explicit type identity and run-time type objects are always available. Implicit conversions are not necessary because all overloaded message sends are dynamically bound (including those to the arguments of messages). However, the gains in safety and efficiency present in C++ are not available in these languages.

12.2.2 Identifier Polymorphism

Object polymorphism

With inheritance, both objects and identifiers can be polymorphic due to the semantics of specialization. A subclass instance is polymorphic because it is an instance of the class instantiated when it was created, and is also an instance of each of that class's ancestors. It can respond to all the protocol of those classes, and has an anonymous instance of each ancestor embedded within its storage structure. As we would expect, we can use an object in any context that requires an instance of an ancestor of its class.[9] However, we will see in section 12.2.3 that some unexpected effects can occur due to C++'s storage allocation policy for value

---

[9] This is only true in C++ if each derivation in the path in the hierarchy between the object's class and the ancestor class is public.

identifiers. Instances of built-in types or classes that do not have superclasses are not polymorphic.

The static and dynamic class

With inheritance, identifiers can also be polymorphic because the object bound to an identifier can be an instance of any of the descendants of its class. Again, this is valid because the descendant class object contains an instance of the identifier's class and can respond to messages defined for the class of the identifier. A typical example is an initialization or assignment of a base class identifier from a derived class object (we use a base class pointer for reasons described in section 12.2.3):

```
// identifier polymorphism in C++
#include "Queue.h"
#include "PriorityQueue.h"
#include "Person.h"
#include "Employee.h"
int main()
{
    // OK: PriorityQueue is publicly derived from Queue
    Queue* pQueue = new PriorityQueue;
    // OK: Employee is publicly derived from Person
    Person* pPers = new Employee(...);
}
```

When the class of an identifier does not match the class of the object it is bound to (i.e., the latter is a descendant of the former), we refer to the class of the identifier as the *static class* (Person or Queue in these examples), and the actual class of the referent object as the *dynamic class* (Employee or PriorityQueue in these examples). The dynamic class is always either equal to or a descendant of the static class. The effects we will describe in this section occur because the static class and the dynamic class can differ, and, in general, the compiler cannot determine the actual class of the referent of a polymorphic identifier because it may depend on run-time conditions (e.g., a user selection). The programmer can only determine the dynamic class via the run-time type information facility.

C++ built-in types cannot participate in this polymorphism or the dynamic binding it enables because they cannot be base classes or derived classes. Similarly, if a class has no subclasses, then the static and dynamic class of an identifier of that type are always the same.

Validity of initializations and assignments

In statically typed languages, the identifier polymorphism that results from inheritance complicates the validity of initializations and assignments. For example, suppose a class Derived is derived from class Base, and we define variables bs of class Base and der of class Derived. Now consider the assignments bs = der and der = bs. (Assume for the moment that the identifiers have reference semantics, as in every object-oriented language but C++.) The first statement, which assigns a derived class instance to an identifier of base class type, is always safe because the derived object can respond to any protocol that the compiler permits for that identifier. In considering the second assignment, we note that an instance of Base is not an instance of Derived because it cannot respond to subclass-specific protocol. However, bs could also refer to a Derived class object, in which case the assignment would be valid. That is, the validity of the assignment der = bs can only be determined at execution time. In fact, these considerations hold for any two classes that are hierarchically related.

Many statically typed object-oriented languages do not allow assignments from an ancestor class identifier to a descendant class identifier, even though they may be meaningful in particular cases.[10] This policy avoids maintaining type hierarchy information at execution time and including code to check these relationships. In C++, the type of the right-side expression of an assignment must be the class of the left-side identifier, one of its descendant classes, or a class or type for which a conversion to one of those classes is defined. An object of a particular class can be assigned to an identifier declared of that class or of any of its ancestor classes. Thus, the assignment der = bs is not allowed in C++. These rules are true for initialization, parameter passing, and conversions as well.

Method binding

Conceptually, method resolution proceeds up the class hierarchy from the class of the receiver of the message, searching for a member function whose name and argument signature match that of the invocation.[11] With static typing and inheritance, the static and dynamic class of the identifier may differ, so the language must specify which to use as the starting point of the method search. C++ supports both static and dynamic binding. Because efficiency and C compatibility are design goals of C++, the language uses static binding wherever possible. We discussed static and dynamic binding in general terms in section 2.4.2. In this section and section 12.3.2, we will review those concepts with respect to C++.

With *static binding*, the method search begins in the class of the identifier, and the compiler performs method resolution via a scope search (e.g., when isEmpty() or remove() is sent to a priority queue). The compiler can translate a statically bound message as a function call using name encoding, so there is no execution-time overhead and the message send has the same cost as a C function invocation. Static binding can always be used for monomorphic identifiers and built-in type operations, and we will see that C++ also uses static binding for file scope function invocations, messages to value identifiers, and method refinements.

---

[10] The Modula-3 compiler allows such assignments, but the language system checks the type of the object at execution time.

[11] We will see in section 12.3.5 that C++ avoids this run-time search of the hierarchy due to additional information that the programmer provides the compiler.

With *dynamic binding*, the method search starts in the class of the referent object, which is equal to or a descendant of the class of the identifier. To maintain type safety, the message must also be in the protocol of the static class. Dynamic binding requires reference semantics, execution-time method dispatching, and class identity information in objects. Statically typed languages cannot support dynamic binding among classes that do not have a common ancestor. We will discuss dynamic binding in C++ in detail in section 12.3.

Because static binding is more efficient, it is the default in C++. The class designer must indicate when to use dynamic binding for a member function by specifying it as virtual (see section 12.3.1). As we discussed in section 2.4.2, static binding inhibits extendibility because it requires modifying and recompiling existing code when adding subclasses to make messages dynamically bound and identifiers polymorphic. (Therefore, it also requires the source code.) Because C++ is designed to be usable in a simple environment (like C), the language does not require the language system to manage these dependencies, nor does it expect the language system to deduce which message expressions can be statically bound. (Recall that the latter requires knowledge of all the classes and messages used by the application.) Most commercial C++ programming environments have a project manager that automatically handles these compilation dependencies (but not the code modifications). We will discuss the design ramifications of these features in section 12.3.2.

Type identity

When we assign a descendant class object to an ancestor identifier, it loses its class identity in the sense that the compiler only knows that it is an ancestor object. We cannot pass it messages that are defined in the descendant class but not in the ancestor, nor can we assign it to a descendant identifier. (Dynamically bound messages will still use the method in the receiver's class.) The same effect occurs when initializing an ancestor identifier with a descendant class object, or when passing a descendant class instance for an ancestor parameter. In addition, when we insert an object into a collection whose element type is an ancestor of its class, it loses its class identity when accessed through the collection. For example (we assume that the class QueueList provides insert and overloads the [ ] operator),[12]

```
// loss of subclass type identity with assignment to a superclass identifier
#include "Date.h"            // defines bool Date::operator>(const Date&)
#include "Queue.h"           // with typedef Date ElemType;
#include "PriorityQueue.h"
#include "QueueList.h"       // List<Queue*> with templates (see chapter 13)

int main
{
    PriorityQueue pq(Date::operator>);
```

[12] Again, the base class identifier must be a pointer or reference for reasons presented in the next section.

```
    Queue* pQueue = &pq;
    // OK: PriorityQueue::insert() invoked since it is virtual and insert() is in Queue's protocol
    pQueue->insert(Date("1/1/90"));          // copies temporary Date object
    // error: no Queue::first()
    Date firstDate(pQueue->first());
    // error: compiler may not know the referent is a PriorityQueue
    PriorityQueue pq1(*pQueue);
    QueueList quList;
    quList.insert(new Queue).insert(pQueue);
    // OK: PriorityQueue::insert() invoked since it is virtual and insert() is in Queue's protocol
    quList[2].insert(Date::today());
    // error: no Queue::first()
    Date firstDate = quList[2]->first();
}
```

If the programmer is certain that the referent of a polymorphic identifier such as pQueue in the previous example is an instance of a particular descendant, he or she can use a dynamic cast to permit using descendant protocol, as described in sections 12.2.4 and 12.2.5.

In dynamically typed languages, the representation of an object must contain an indication of its class to implement dynamic binding, and this information is usually available to the programmer as well. Statically typed languages do not require this information for all class instances, and might not make it available at runtime. Most object-oriented languages support querying the class of an object, but C++ did not until recently. C++ originally did not provide run-time type information for efficiency and C compatibility [Ell90]. In addition, the language designers did not want to encourage writing code with explicit type dependencies. Recently, the ISO/ANSI C++ Standard committee [Str92] approved the run-time type information extension, which we will cover in section 12.2.5. However, the language only provides type information for classes that require dynamic binding (i.e., classes that have virtual member functions). Clearly, the compiler (and the reader) can always determine the type of the referent of a monomorphic identifier, that is, one whose type is a built-in type or a class without subclasses.

12.2.3 Storage Allocation for Value Identifiers

Type compatibility among different-sized objects

As we saw in sections 2.2.3 and 5.4.1, with dynamic typing an object of arbitrary size can be bound to an identifier, so static and automatic allocation and value instance variables are not feasible. The same problem occurs with static typing and inheritance. When a subclass adds instance variables to its superclass, the storage requirement of its instances is larger than that of superclass objects, and the various descendants of a class may have different sizes. However, we can assign an instance of any of the descendants to an identifier of ancestor type. The problem is that there are objects of different sizes that are type compatible, and static and automatic allocation must reserve a fixed amount of storage for an identifier.

As stated in section 2.2.3, in other statically typed object-oriented languages such as Simula, Objective-C, Java, Modula-3, and Object Pascal, all class type identifiers are references and all class objects are allocated dynamically. As in Smalltalk, the programmer does not use a dereference operator when accessing the referent of an object identifier, each object has a unique identity, and assignments and comparisons of object identifiers use reference semantics. The programmer can assign an instance of any descendant of an identifier's type to the identifier, and the operation is implemented by copying a pointer. In this way, the loss of subclass-specific information that we discuss in this section does not occur. However, built-in types and record identifiers are allocated by value and use copying of values upon assignment, so built-in type and class type identifiers do not have the same semantics. (Recall our discussion of value and reference semantics in section 10.2.1.)

Allocation policies for value identifiers

Because efficiency and C compatibility are design goals of C++, the language supports static and automatic variables, value parameters, and value data members of class type. When a method defines an automatic variable or value parameter whose type is a class that has descendants, the compiler must allocate space for that object in the method's activation record. Similarly, the representation of a value data member is directly embedded in the composite object. An object-oriented language with this capability must specify whether the compiler allocates the maximum possible storage requirement (i.e., that of the largest descendant of the identifier type) or the minimum storage requirement (i.e., that of the static class of the identifier).

Allocating the maximum requirement is essentially the technique used for unions in C and variant records in Pascal. This policy allows storing an instance of any descendant of the identifier's class in the region bound to that identifier. However, C++ does not use this policy for automatic allocation or value data members because the compiler must scan the entire program, that is, all modules, to determine the size necessary for each type (unlike a variant record type, which is defined in one place). Even more serious, whenever a programmer defines a descendant class with additional data members, he or she must recompile all modules that define an automatic variable or object with a value data member whose type is any of the ancestors of the new class, so that assignments from instances of the new class are correct.

For these reasons, C++ uses the minimum allocation policy for static and automatic variables, value parameters, and value data members, namely the storage requirement of the identifier type (i.e., the static class). If the object is an instance of a class that has virtual member functions, it will contain a class pointer (termed the vptr in C++). If not, it has the same size and layout as a C structure instance with the same member types.

Loss of descendant class information

The minimum allocation policy for value identifiers can result in the loss of information upon executing a legal initialization or assignment. When we assign an instance of a descendant class to a value ancestor identifier, the data members of the ancestor target are assigned from the corresponding members in the descendant object. The values of the data members specific to the descendant class are lost because there is no storage for them in the target object.[13] The type identity of the descendant object is also lost because the type of the result is the ancestor. (We will see in the next section that such an assignment is actually a value conversion from the descendant class to the ancestor class.)

Conversely, if we assigned an instance of an ancestor class to a descendant value identifier, there would be undefined data members in the resulting object, namely the descendant class specific members. The object would be in an inconsistent state with new ancestor information and invalid or old descendant information. It is also not clear whether the result has the class identity of the source or the target of the assignment. For these reasons, C++ does not allow these assignments.

When we assign a descendant class pointer to an ancestor pointer, both pointers refer to the same object and information loss does not occur. Similarly, when we initialize an ancestor reference parameter or variable with a descendant object, the reference refers to the complete object. The following example illustrates the difference between value and pointer initialization from a descendant object:

```
// The subclass Employee defines additional data members
#include "Person.h"
#include "Employee.h"
int main()
{
    Employee empl(...);
    Person pers1(...);
    // values for the additional Employee data members are lost upon initialization
    Person pers2 = empl;
    // values for the additional Employee data members are lost upon assignment
    pers1 = empl;
    // error: the Employee object is not completely specified
    empl = pers2;
    // the implicit pointer cast from Employee* to Person* is valid, and empl is not affected
    Person* pPers = &empl;
}
```

As only the operations for the static class Person are syntactically correct for the identifiers pers1 and pers2, this information loss is not as inappropriate as it seems at first. The object pers1 in this example has a class pointer to Person, and the fact that it was assigned from an employee object is lost. The referent of pPers has a

---

[13] C++ programmers sometimes refer to this as "slicing".

class pointer to Employee, even though the compiler only permits Person protocol through pPers.

Pointer versus value assignment semantics

In C++, you must be aware that assignments to ancestor identifiers behave differently, depending on whether the identifier represents an instance of the class or a pointer to an instance of the class. Invoking a virtual function through a value identifier uses the method in the static class because only that class's state information is present (even if the object had been assigned from a descendant class instance). With a pointer or reference, an assignment from a pointer to a descendant class instance preserves the entire object and its class identity, so the dynamic class method can be executed. That is, C++ only uses dynamic binding through pointers and references. For example,

```
// differing behavior for base class value identifiers and base class pointer referents
#include "Date.h"         // defines bool Date::operator<(const Date&)
#include "Queue.h"        // with typedef Date ElemType;
#include "PriorityQueue.h"
int main
{
   PriorityQueue pq;
   pq.insert(Date("1/1/90")).insert(Date("5/1/90"));
   // initializing an automatic base class identifier from a derived class object
   // the implicit conversion uses the Queue copy constructor (see the next section)
   Queue qu = pq;
   // pQueue points to a complete PriorityQueue object
   Queue* pQueue = &pq;
   // must invoke Queue::insert() because there is no pCompareFn in qu
   qu.insert(Date("3/1/90"));
   // invokes PriorityQueue::insert() because Queue::insert() is virtual
   pQueue->insert(Date("3/1/90"));
}
```

In this example, the initialization of the variable qu from pq uses the Queue copy constructor, which copies all the nodes in the list (but keeps the Queue class pointer). This same information loss occurs upon initialization of parameters passed by value.

```
// subclass-specific data members are lost by pass-by-value copying

#include <iostream.h>
#include "Person.h"        // defines virtual void Person::print(ostream&)
#include "Employee.h"     // defines virtual void Employee::print(ostream&)

// parameter passed by value (a local copy of the argument)
void invite(Person pers)
{
```

```
    // print on mailing list
    pers.print(cout);
}

int main()
{
    Employee empl(...);
    invite(empl);          // Person::print() invoked in invite() due to information loss
}
```

To avoid this information loss upon initialization or assignment, and to permit dynamic binding, you should always define variables, data members, parameters, and collection elements of ancestor type as pointers or references. This is similar to the semantics of identifiers in Smalltalk and other object-oriented languages, except that we use an explicit dereference operation when referring to the object through a pointer. Using reference semantics also provides extendibility without recompiling when descendants are added. Because a reference must be initialized and cannot be changed to alias a different object, C++ programmers usually use pointers for variables of ancestor type. However, we define parameters as references because a parameter is an alias for an object.

Collections of ancestor class elements

Loss of descendant class information also affects the semantics of collections. As we discussed in section 10.2.1 and this section, if the type of a collection's elements is an ancestor class, the collection class must use pointers or references for its elements. In this way, inserting an element does not lose descendant-specific data members, and messages to collection elements can be dynamically bound. For example, suppose we need a queue of instances of the class Person and its descendant classes. Using typedef Person ElemType; in Queue.h would not suffice because the elem member of Node is a value data member. If we insert an Employee or Customer object into the queue, descendant-specific information is lost when elem is initialized.

For the class Queue, we can use typedef Person* ElemType; in Queue.h. We would insert and remove pointers to objects, and the objects themselves would not be copied to the elem data member. The destructor Queue::~Queue() deletes any remaining instances of Node in a queue when it is deallocated, but it does not deallocate the corresponding elements. However, we will see in section 13.2.6 that some collection classes require different implementations, depending on whether the elements are values or pointers, so we must define two different classes (class templates, actually).

12.2.4 Class Hierarchy Type Conversions

The standard class to ancestor class conversion

An object can respond to all the protocol of its class's ancestors, and contains a instance of each of those classes embedded within it. Therefore, the conversion from a class to any ancestor class is type-safe because it is semantically consistent, and the resulting object can be defined unambiguously. Languages with static typing and inheritance support both explicit and implicit conversion of an object to an instance of any of its class's ancestors. An implicit conversion may occur in initialization, assignment, expression evaluation, or argument passing. None of the conversions described in this section are available with nonpublic derivation.

In C ++, an object can appear in any context that requires an instance of one of its ancestors without an explicit conversion. We can use an object to initialize an identifier whose type is any of its class's public ancestors, or can pass it to a function whose (value) parameter is of ancestor type. The resulting ancestor object is initialized from the inherited data members of the descendant object. [14] This predefined standard conversion uses the ancestor copy constructor to create the new object, whether programmer-defined or compiler-generated. If the descendant class has more data members than the ancestor, those members are lost by this value conversion, as described in the previous section. For example,

```
// implicit derived class to base class value conversion
#include "Person.h"
#include "Employee.h"
void invite(Person);    // argument passed by value
int main()
{
    Employee empl(...);
    Person pers(...);
    invite(empl);        // empl converted to a Person object, which is passed to invite()
    pers = empl;         // conversion to Person and Person::operator=()
}
```

We can also define a value conversion as an ancestor constructor or as a descendant class conversion operator if some special initialization is necessary, like a copy constructor.

The compiler will also perform an implicit conversion from a descendant pointer or reference to an ancestor pointer or reference, as we have done several times in this chapter. With a pointer or reference conversion, the referent object is the original object, and that object receives messages sent through the identifier and is affected by the methods executed. We also use this conversion (together with the trivial conversion from an object to a reference) when passing a descendant object for an ancestor reference parameter. That parameter is an alias for the ancestor subobject in the argument. For example,

```
// implicit derived to base reference and pointer conversions
#include "Person.h"
#include "Employee.h"
void invite(const Person&); // argument passed by reference
```

---

[14] Recall that a value conversion creates a new object rather than allowing the derived class object itself to be treated as a base class object.

```
int main()
{
    Employee empl(...);
    // OK: implicit conversion from Employee* to Person*
    Person* pPers = &empl;
    // OK: invite() receives a reference to the Person part of empl
    invite(*pPers);            // the same as invite(empl)
}
```

The result of a conversion to an ancestor pointer may be a different address value than the original value. This occurs when the compiler does not store that ancestor subobject at the beginning of the descendant object. (In fact, this will be true for some ancestor with multiple inheritance.) This does not affect programming, but you may notice it when examining pointer values with a debugger. This adjustment is also made in implementing references.

Resolving overloadings

The existence of implicit conversions from a class to any of its ancestors affects the argument matching process. The conversion from a descendant object, pointer or reference to an ancestor object, pointer, or reference is a standard conversion, not an exact match. If an exact match does not exist, this standard conversion is attempted before considering any programmer-defined conversions. For example,

```
// the conversion to an ancestor class is a standard conversion
#include "Base.h"
#include "Derived.h"          // defines Derived::operator const char*()
void func(const char*);
void func(const Base&);
main
{
    Derived der(...);
    // invokes func(const Base&)
    func(der);
    // applies Derived::operator const char*() and then invokes func(const char*)
    func((const char*) der);
}
```

In the first invocation in the previous example, the standard conversion from Derived to Base is preferred over the programmer-defined conversion Derived::operator const char*(). The second invocation explicitly invokes the programmer-defined conversion.

Among the conversions to ancestors, the compiler prefers a conversion to an ancestor closer to the descendant class along the same path in the inheritance hierarchy graph. Recall also that the compiler will use a standard conversion together with a programmer-defined conversion if necessary to achieve a match. As described in section 11.2.2, if you want to invoke a different conversion than the one the language selects, code an explicit conversion.

Inheritance of conversions

Like all member functions, conversion operators are inherited. Clients can apply ancestor conversion operators (i.e., from that class to another class or built-in type) to instances of descendant classes implicitly or explicitly. This outward conversion is valid because the descendant class instance specifies an ancestor object that the operator method uses. (The inherited method can only access the inherited members of the descendant object.) As we saw in section 11.2.2, a constructor for some class that takes an ancestor parameter defines a conversion to that class from the ancestor. This constructor also provides a conversion from a descendant object to that class, because the compiler will apply both the standard conversion to ancestor and the programmer-defined constructor conversion implicitly. Therefore, both kinds of conversions from an ancestor class are valid for descendant class objects.

Constructors are not inherited, so an ancestor single-argument constructor from a type does not provide a conversion from that type to one of its descendants. That is, we cannot initialize a descendant class instance using that type, nor can we use an instance of that type in a context that requires a descendant class object. This conversion is not valid because the ancestor constructor provides no initialization for the descendant-specific data members. If the descendant class requires a conversion from the type, the class designer must define a method for that single-argument constructor in the descendant class as well.

Ancestor to descendant value conversion

A conversion from an ancestor to a descendant class is not supplied automatically because the descendant class may define additional protocol that an ancestor object cannot perform. In addition, descendant-specific data members in the result will be undefined if the object bound to the ancestor type identifier does not contain those data members. (Recall our discussion of ancestor to descendant assignments in section 12.2.2.)

The class designer can define a conversion from an ancestor to a descendant class if appropriate, either as a one-argument constructor for the descendant or as a conversion operator for the ancestor. If the descendant class defines additional data members, the conversion method must determine values for those members so that the resulting object is completely initialized. For example, we can define a conversion from the class Queue to its subclass PriorityQueue that uses the default argument for the comparison function data member and creates a sorted copy of the linked list in the Queue object. If we define this conversion as a PriorityQueue constructor, then it must be a friend of the class Queue so that it can access the storage structure of the queue argument. We define this constructor as follows:

```
// a programmer-defined base to derived conversion
// must be a friend of Queue to access qu.front
PriorityQueue::PriorityQueue(const Queue& qu)
  : Queue(), pCompareFn(&ElemType::operator<)
{
```

```
   // PriorityQueue::insert() is used because insert() is virtual and the receiver is a PriorityQueue
   for ( Node* pNode = qu.front;  pNode != NULL;  pNode = pNode->next )
      (void) insert(pNode->elem);
}
```

Note that this constructor is a programmer-defined conversion, not a standard conversion.

Explicit ancestor to descendant pointer conversion

Sometimes, the compiler has lost the specific class identity of an object, but the programmer knows its type. That is, the programmer knows that a pointer identifier whose type is an ancestor class actually refers to an instance of a particular descendant. There are two common ways this can happen:

- A collection of ancestor pointers contains only pointers to instances of a certain descendant.
- The programmer is using a library method whose parameter and return type is a library class from which he or she has derived a class used in this invocation.

To use descendant-specific protocol with the collection element or the pointer returned by the method, the programmer must explicitly convert the ancestor class pointer to a descendant class pointer. This is often referred to as a "downcast" because of the direction of the conversion in the class hierarchy. If the programmer is wrong and the object is an instance of the ancestor class, when the descendant method refers to descendant-specific data members, it accesses storage that does not belong to the object, causing a bug that will be difficult to find. Similarly, if the object is an instance of a different descendant class, invalid results will be obtained or its storage structure may be corrupted.

For example, suppose we have a list of display objects and DisplayObject has subclasses Square, Spiral, etc., so the list's elements are of type DisplayObject*. If a particular display object list only contains squares, the programmer still must code a conversion to use Square protocol with an element obtained from the list. Before the introduction of the run-time type information extension, this conversion was coded like a pointer cast, as follows:

```
   // a "downcast" from a base class pointer to a derived class pointer
   #include "DisplayObject.h"       // does not define DisplayObject::diagonal()
   #include "Square.h"              // defines Square::diagonal()
   #include "DisplayObjectList.h"   // List<DisplayObject*> with templates (see chapter 13)

   int main()
   {
      DisplayObjectList picture;
      picture.insert(new Square(...)).insert(new Square(...)).insert(new Square(...));
      // The programmer knows that all the elements in this picture are Squares.
      DisplayObject* pDisObj = picture[2];
```

```
    // error: no implicit ancestor to descendant conversion
    Square* pSquare = pDisObj;
    // OK: the compiler believes the programmer
    Square* pSquare = (Square*) pDisObj;
    // invokes Square::diagonal()
    double diag = ((Square*) pDisObj)->diagonal();
}
```

The outer parentheses in the last statement are necessary because the cast operator ((Square*) in this case) has lower precedence than the -> operator. We do not need to explicitly define this conversion operator because a pointer conversion only results in a logical conversion for the sake of the compiler.[15] We will see in the next section that the dynamic cast operator provides a safer downcast.

The conversion from an ancestor pointer to member

Although it seems reversed at first, the conversion from a pointer to ancestor member to a pointer to descendant member of the same type is safe. That is, we can assign the "address of" an ancestor member to a pointer to descendant member if their types are the same. This conversion is valid for either a pointer to member function or a pointer to data member. The member function conversion is safe because the descendant inherits the member functions with the argument signature given by the pointer declaration. The data member conversion is valid because a descendant instance contains any data members that the ancestor pointer could refer to. The value of the pointer to data member is the inherited member in the descendant instance.[16] The reverse conversions are not safe because the referent of a pointer to a descendant member may not be present in an ancestor instance.

12.2.5 The Run-Time Type Information Facility

Purpose

As stated in section 12.2.2, C++ did not originally provide run-time type information because of the overhead involved, and because the designers of the language felt that it should not encourage coding a switch on type identity. An indication of an object's class was only available if the class designer provided it, for example, as an enumeration data member. In this case, clients could test that information and explicitly cast the ancestor pointer to a descendant pointer to use descendant protocol. For example, suppose that the class DisplayObject defines a nested enumeration giving the types of display objects and a data member that maintains an object's type. We can check the type code to determine whether we can send an element messages in the protocol of one of the descendants, as follows:

---

[15] Again, an offset may be involved, depending on the storage layouts of the classes.

[16] Like a pointer to an ancestor subobject, the offset that represents the pointer to data member may differ if the ancestor subobject is not stored at the beginning of descendant objects.

```
// type identification provided by the class designer
#include "DisplayObject.h"
#include "Square.h"                    // defines Square::diagonal()
#include "Spiral.h"                    // defines int Spiral::spacing()
#include "DisplayObjectList.h"         // List<DisplayObject*> with templates (see chapter 13)

int main()
{
    DisplayObjectList picture;
    picture.insert(new Square(...).insert(new Spiral(...). ...;
    DisplayObject* pDisObj = picture[2];
    double num;
    if ( pDisObj->type() == DisplayObject::square )
        num = ( (Square*) pDisObj )->diagonal();
    if ( pDisObj->type() == DisplayObject::spiral )
        num = ( (Spiral*) pDisObj )->spacing();
}
```

Clearly, this kind of code is a serious problem for maintenance (recall our discussion of loose coupling and extendibility in section 2.4.3), and a similar use of run-time type information would have the same drawbacks. Whenever semantically possible, you should define an operation performed on the basis of an object's class as a virtual member function, with methods defined in each class. In this way, the transparent extendible dynamic binding provided automatically by the language performs the selection.

Unfortunately, there are times when the source code for an ancestor class is not available to the class designer—for example, if it is in a proprietary class library. When we override a member function in an ancestor that had not previously been overridden, we must modify the source code of that ancestor and recompile it to provide dynamic binding for that function (as we will discuss in section 12.3). For example, suppose we are extending a class in a vendor-supplied library. The classes in the library will always use pointers or references of types the library defines, not our descendants of them. When we receive such a pointer or reference, we might need to know whether the referent is, in fact, an instance of a descendant we defined so that we can perform particular operations. Similarly, when a program obtains an object from a collection of ancestor elements, it may need to verify that it can send a particular message to the object. C++ supplies the run-time type information facility to implement programmer-defined dispatching for such situations.

As mentioned in section 10.1.1, the ANSI/ISO C++ Standard includes the *run-time type information* extension, which supports determining the dynamic class of a polymorphic identifier and defines a class for type information. The type information class only supplies the name and identity of a class, but a language system can extend it with more complete information. The designers of C++ considered this extension necessary because several class libraries (e.g., the NIH class library [Gor90], Interviews [Lin89], and the Microsoft Foundation Classes [Mic96]) chose to provide some run-time class information, and make it available to the programmer via a "class description" class (similar to a metaclass). However, the facilities provided by the various class libraries are not uniform or compatible, which makes it difficult to use more than one such library on a project. In addition, they usually provide this information with preprocessor macros that complicate the process of defining a class. A standard language-supported feature would not have these drawbacks.

The run-time type information extension adds the following three features to the language:

- the dynamic_cast<> operator for a pointer or reference conversion to a descendant with a run-time check
- the class type_info, which represents information about classes
- the typeid operator, which returns a reference to the type_info object that represents its operand's class.

The dynamic cast operator

To support safe down-casting, the run-time type information extension provides the *dynamic cast* operator. This operator converts its pointer operand to a pointer of the indicated class only if the referent of the pointer is an instance of that class or one of its descendants. If the conversion is not valid, the pointer operand is set to NULL. To use the operator, we enclose the desired pointer type in angle brackets after the reserved word dynamic_cast (like the syntax of the static cast operator discussed in section 9.1.5). [17] For example,

```
// type identity provided by the run-time type information extension
#include "Square.h"          // defines Square::diagonal()
#include "Spiral.h"          // defines int Spiral::spacing()
#include "DisplayObjectList.h"   // List<DisplayObject*> with templates (see chapter 13)
int main()
{
    DisplayObjectList picture;
    picture.insert(new Square(...).insert(new Spiral(...). ...;
    DisplayObject* pDisObj = picture[2];
    Square* pSquare = dynamic_cast<Square*>(pDisObj);
    Spiral* pSpiral = dynamic_cast<Spiral*>(pDisObj);
    double num;
    if ( pSquare )
        num = pSquare->diagonal();
    if ( pSpiral )
        num = pSpiral->spacing();
}
```

Clearly, the dynamic cast operator is safer than an explicit conversion—i.e., a cast with no run-time type check—because the explicit conversion results in an

---

[17] Like the static_cast<> operator and template definitions (see Chapter 13), angle brackets enclose a type parameter.

invalid operation if the dynamic class is not correct. However, for the language system to implement the dynamic cast operator, it must maintain run-time type information for classes and a type information pointer in class instances. As we will see in section 12.3.5, this information must be present for classes that define virtual functions to implement dynamic binding. So that no cost is incurred for classes that do not employ dynamic binding, the dynamic cast operator is only valid for classes that define virtual functions. Again, the usage in the previous example is a problem for maintenance, and you should use virtual functions whenever possible to hide the method dispatching and provide extendibility.

We can also use the dynamic cast operator with reference types, for example, to apply dynamic_cast<Square&> to a DisplayObject reference. However, there is no "null reference" value that the program can test for. For this reason, an invalid dynamic cast of a reference throws a bad_cast exception, and a program can only test for an invalid conversion by handling this exception, as described in section 13.3.4.

The type_info **class and the** typeid **operator**

Instances of the class type_info represent type information for classes, and the class is defined in the standard header file typeinfo.h as follows:

```
// type info.h: a standard header file for run-time type information
class type_info
{
public:
    virtual ~type_info();   // virtual destructors are described in section 12.3.4
    bool operator==(const type_info&);
    bool operator!=(const type_info&);
    const char* name() const;
private:
    type_info(const type_info&);
    type_info& operator=(const type_info&);
    // ... implementation-dependent representation ...
};
```

The comparison operators allow equality comparisons for instances of type_info, to determine whether two objects are the same type. The member function type_info::name() returns the name of the type represented by the receiver type_info object. The class declares its copy constructor and assignment operator as private so that clients cannot copy instances. (In fact, the language system might not implement this information using distinct objects for each type.)

Applying the typeid operator to an expression returns a const type_info& that represents the actual class of the expressions value. We can also use a type name as the operand to obtain a reference to the corresponding type information object. For example,

```
// using the typeid operator
// (the statements are numbered so we can refer to them in the following text)
#include <type_info.h>
#include <iostream.h>
#include "Person.h"
#include "Employee.h"

int main()
{
    Person* pPers = new Employee(...);
    Person& rPers = *pPers;
    bool test;

    // pPers is of type Person*
    /* 1 */    test = ( typeid(pPers) == typeid(Person*) );        // test = true
    /* 2 */    test = ( typeid(pPers) == typeid(Person) );         // test = false
    /* 3 */    test = ( typeid(pPers) == typeid(Employee*) );      // test = false
    /* 4 */    test = ( typeid(pPers) == typeid(Employee) );       // test = false

    // the referent of pPers is of type Employee
    /* 5 */    test = ( typeid(*pPers) == typeid(Employee) );      // test = true
    /* 6 */    test = ( typeid(*pPers) == typeid(Person) );        // test = false
    /* 7 */    test = ( typeid(*pPers) == typeid(Employee*) );     // test = false
    /* 8 */    cout << typeid(*pPers).name() << endl;              // prints "Employee"

    // rPers is an alias for *pPers, an instance of class Employee
    /* 9 */    test = ( typeid(rPers) == typeid(Employee) );       // test = true
    /* 10 */   test = ( typeid(rPers) == typeid(Person) );         // test = false

    // &rPers is the address of an Employee object
    /* 11 */   test = ( typeid(&rPers) == typeid(Employee*) );     // test = true
    /* 12 */   test = ( typeid(&rPers) == typeid(Person*) );       // test = false
}
```

The identifier pPers is of pointer type and so is monomorphic, as the results of the comparisons in statements 1 through 4 illustrate. Statement 2 shows that Person* and Person are different types. The comparisons in statements 5 through 7 show that the typeid operator returns the dynamic type of an expression (and, again, that a class and a pointer to that class are not the same type). Statement 6 demonstrates that the typeid operator returns the exact class of the object, unlike the dynamic_cast<> operator, which is valid for any ancestor of the object's class. Statement 8 illustrates the use of the message type_info::name(). The comparisons in statements 9 through 12 show that the typeid operator returns the dynamic class with references, and that the typeid operator does not distinguish between a class and a reference to that class. We can also use the typeid operator with monomorphic classes and built-in types, although this is not particularly useful because the resulting type can be determined by inspection.

To minimize the overhead involved for this feature, the class name is the only information the ANSI/ISO C++ Standard requires for type_info objects. A particular language system can extend the type information it provides by deriving a subclass from type_info. For example, to support a programming environment, the system can define a derived class that supplies on-line class documentation, tables of member function names and source code references, lists of the ancestors, descendants, or instances of a class, object storage layouts, and other information that the programmer and tools can query.

A type_info reference does not provide an object that we can use in the same fashion as a class name, that is, as a type. In particular, the run-time type information extension does not provide execution-time selection of the class of an object to be created. In Smalltalk, we can create an instance of whatever class of object is bound to the identifier obj with the message expression obj class new. Similarly, given a string, we obtain the class object with that name from the global dictionary Smalltalk and send it new. In C++, the programmer must give the class of a new object explicitly in the source code, whether the object is a static or automatic variable or is created dynamically with new, and cannot give it using a type_info reference.

A common example in which dynamically selecting the class of a new object would be useful is reading a file of objects of various classes. The method does not know type of the next object in the file until it has read some tag information, so it must select the type to instantiate according to the class tag. The method can either code a switch or a series of else ifs, or can create a dictionary of class tags and pointers to object extraction functions to invoke. However, the type of the identifier the object is assigned to must be an ancestor of all of the classes possible, and the new object's class identity is not available to the compiler. In addition, adding new classes to the scheme involves modifying the source code, either the conditional or the table.

12.3 DYNAMIC BINDING

12.3.1 Virtual Member Functions

The virtual specifier

To provide loose coupling and extendibility, C++ supports dynamic binding via *virtual member functions*. The reserved word virtual in a class definition identifies member functions that require dynamic method resolution among classes derived from the class.[18] Operators and conversions defined as member functions may also be designated as virtual. The definition of a descendant class that overrides that function does not need to use the virtual specifier for that function name, but it is conventional to include it as a reminder to the reader (as we did in the definition of PriorityQueue in section 12.1.1). When coding a member function definition separately from the class definition, we do not give the virtual reserved word. Classes that contain virtual member functions are fundamentally different from other classes in C++ because they permit dynamic binding, and are often referred

---

[18] The reserved word virtual originally appeared in Simula 67.

to as *polymorphic classes*. Their instances must include a class pointer to implement dynamic binding (which is called the vptr in C++).

The first class that defines a member function as virtual is the root of the sub-hierarchy that uses dynamic binding for that function name and argument signature. The class that first declares a virtual function must also supply a definition for that function. It may be either a function definition that provides a default method for derived classes that do not override the message, or a specification that the function is a *pure virtual function* (i.e., an abstract message) as described in section 12.3.4. This restriction prevents the possibility of calling an undefined function. In a statically bound member function call, the compiler and linker can ensure that the function invoked is defined for the receiver's class. A virtual function call can invoke an ancestor method through an identifier of descendant class type, and the method invoked can only be determined at execution time. Therefore, a virtual function must have a definition.

A descendant of a polymorphic class can introduce further virtual functions for itself and its descendants. These functions are available for dynamic binding through a pointer or reference of descendant type, but are not in the protocol of the ancestor class.

Dynamic method binding

When we invoke a virtual function through a public ancestor pointer or reference, the method executed is determined by the class of the object referenced, not by the class of the identifier (recall the examples in section 12.2.2). For example, we specified Queue::insert() as virtual so that invoking the insert() method through a Queue* or Queue& identifier executes the method in the dynamic class. Virtual functions provide some respite from the class identity problem. When a descendant class object is accessed via a pointer of polymorphic ancestor class type, invocations of a virtual function through that pointer are resolved to the definition in the dynamic class, without the compiler or the programmer having to be aware of the exact class of the object. Virtual member functions are also dynamically bound when they are invoked through a pointer to member function. We have seen that inheritance can result in invocation of methods defined above the static type in the class hierarchy. A virtual function call can invoke a method defined below the type of the identifier in the hierarchy.

C++ only performs dynamic binding on the basis of the receiver of a message. We cannot declare static member functions and file scope functions as virtual because there is no receiver in an invocation. However, invocations of virtual member functions for reference or pointer parameters or local variables within a function are dynamically bound. For example, suppose we want to provide dynamic binding of output operations for a hierarchy of classes. We must define an overloading of the insertion operator as a file scope function, so its invocations cannot be dynamically bound. To provide the desired behavior, we define a virtual function within the hierarchy involved, which the file scope function invokes for a parameter whose type is a reference to the root class. For example, we can define a virtual member function print() in the classes Person and Employee, and a definition of operator<<() with a Person& parameter that calls that function, as follows:

```
// dynamic binding of output operations for classes derived from Person

class Person
{
public:
   virtual void print(ostream&) const;
   // ... other member functions ...
protected:
   // ... data members defined in section 10.2.4 ...
};

inline void Person::print(ostream& ostr) const
{
   ostr << name_ << '\t' << address_ << '\t' << birthdate_ << '\t' << ssn_;
}

// defined in Person.h;  need not be a friend of Person if Person::print() is public
inline ostream& operator<<(ostream& ostr, const Person& pers)
{
   pers.print(ostr);
   return ostr;
}

class Employee : public Person
{
public:
   virtual void print(ostream&) const;
   // ... other member functions ...
protected:
   // ... data members defined in section 12.1.2 ...
};

inline void Employee::print(ostream& ostr) const
{
   Person::print(ostr);
   ostr << '\t' << employeeId_ << '\t' << department_ << '\t' << vacationDays_;
}
```

Because the second parameter of operator<<() is passed by reference, there is no information loss when the argument is an Employee object, and that entire object is available within the operator definition. Therefore, the print() method invoked will be that of the argument object's class for an instance of any descendant of Person.

   We also note that the member functions Person::print() and Employee:: print() are inline, but the compiler cannot translate them inline when using dynamic binding. As described in the next paragraph, there are circumstances in which virtual function invocations are statically bound, and in these cases, the compiler translates an invocation of print() inline.

Static invocation of virtual functions

There are three situations in which the compiler can safely translate a virtual function invocation statically as an encoded function call, as follows:

- when the receiver of the message is a value variable, data member, or parameter (rather than a pointer or reference)
- when the invocation uses a qualified function name
- when a virtual function is invoked within a constructor or destructor.

As we saw in section 12.2.3, the compiler can use static binding with value identifiers because only the ancestor data members are present in that object, even if it was assigned from a descendant class object. This is also true of a value function parameter of ancestor type for which the corresponding argument is a descendant object. For example, if the second argument pers in the overloading of operator<<() in the previous example were of type Person rather than Person&, the print() message in the operator definition could not be dynamically bound because only the Person data members would be present in the receiver.

When a virtual function invocation uses a qualified name, the programmer has indicated to the compiler which method to invoke, even if a scope search is necessary to find it. This occurs with method refinement, for example, the invocation of Person::print() in Employee::print() in the previous example. However, if the ancestor method calls other virtual functions for the receiver, those calls are resolved dynamically.

Static binding must be used for a virtual function invocation within a constructor or destructor. We might expect dynamic binding to take place when the receiver is an instance of a descendant class, that is, when an ancestor constructor is called from a descendant constructor initialization list. However, the compiler must use static binding because the descendant class object is either not completely built yet (within the constructor), or has been partially destroyed (within the destructor). For example, suppose we define a copy constructor for the class Queue whose method uses the virtual function Queue::insert(). We might attempt to use that constructor in the conversion constructor PriorityQueue::PriorityQueue(const Queue&) discussed in section 12.2.4 as insert() is virtual, as follows:

```
// copy constructor for Queue using the virtual member function insert()
Queue::Queue(const Queue& qu)
    : front(NULL), back(NULL)
{
    for ( Node* pNode = qu.front;  pNode != NULL;  pNode = pNode->next )
        (void) insert(pNode->elem);
}
```

```
// incorrect base to derived conversion: PriorityQueue::insert() cannot be used in
// Queue::Queue(const Queue&) because the receiver's pCompareFn is not installed yet
PriorityQueue::PriorityQueue(const Queue& qu)
    : Queue(qu), pCompareFn(&ElemType::operator<)
{ }
```

When the PriorityQueue conversion constructor calls the Queue copy constructor via its initialization list, the PriorityQueue::insert() method cannot be invoked
in the Queue::Queue() method because the PriorityQueue receiver is not initialized yet. In particular, the pCompareFn data member has not yet been set, so
using the PriorityQueue::insert() method would be invalid. Unfortunately, we
must use the default Queue constructor and duplicate the Queue::Queue(const
Queue&) method code in the definition of PriorityQueue::PriorityQueue(const
Queue&), as we did in section 12.2.4.

12.3.2 Method Overriding

Refinement

For each inherited member function, a class may either inherit the ancestor
method, or override it with a class-specific definition that matches the name and
argument signature of the ancestor definition. If the class refines the ancestor
function, then its method invokes the ancestor method using a qualified name, as
we did in the definitions of Employee::print() in the previous section and PriorityQueue::insert() in section 12.1.3. This invocation is statically bound, and refers
to the method in effect in the named scope, which may be inherited from an
ancestor.

The problem with nonvirtual overriding

As discussed in section 12.2.2, C++ supports both static and dynamic method
binding, and static binding is the default mechanism because it is more efficient.
Whenever a member function is not virtual, the compiler translates an invocation as
a call of the definition in effect for the static class, so there is no method binding
overhead. In this way, C++ imposes no cost for dynamic binding on classes that do
not require it. However, the result of this policy is that the class designer must
decide whether dynamic binding is necessary for each member function in the class.
We will see in section 12.3.5 that the compiler can use a particularly efficient implementation of execution-time method dispatching if it knows which messages require
dynamic binding. However, for the language system to deduce which messages can
be statically bound, it must have knowledge of the entire application (i.e., of all the
classes it uses) so it can determine which methods are overridden. Like C, C++ has
no knowledge of which code files make up the application. This information is only
available at link time. Because C++ is intended to be usable in simple environments,

it is the class designer's responsibility to inform the compiler of which messages require dynamic binding.

We must always declare a member function whose method is overridden in any descendant as virtual. Suppose the static class and the dynamic class differ, for example, a base class pointer refers to a derived class instance. When passing a statically-bound (nonvirtual) message through that pointer, the base class function will be invoked, even if the derived class overrides that function name with another method with the same argument signature. However, if the same message is sent to the same object through a derived class pointer, the derived class function is executed. For example, consider what would happen if Queue::insert() were not virtual.

```
// suppose that both Queue and PriorityQueue define insert(), but it is not virtual
#include "Queue.h"           // with typedef int ElemType;
#include "PriorityQueue.h"
int main()
{
    PriorityQueue* pPriQu = new PriorityQueue;
    Queue* pQueue = pPriQu;
    pPriQu->insert(3);        // invokes PriorityQueue::insert()
    pQueue->insert(1);        // invokes Queue::insert()
}
```

Clearly, we do not want the operation an object performs to depend on the type of the identifier that refers to it. To ensure consistent operation, we must always specify an overridden member function as virtual in the highest ancestor in the class hierarchy that defines it. In this way, the method invoked is that of the class of the object, no matter what class of pointer or reference the message expression uses.

The fact that both virtual and nonvirtual method replacement are legal can be the source of subtle errors. In particular, if the class designer forgets the virtual specifier in an ancestor and a descendant overrides that message, a message sent to a descendant instance through an ancestor pointer is not erroneous, but its operation is not what the programmer intended. All expressions that send the message are statically bound and use the definition in the class of the identifier, which may leave the receiver in an inconsistent state (like the invocation of Queue:: insert() for a priority queue in the previous example). For this reason, it would be helpful for the compiler to issue a warning when the programmer overrides a nonvirtual member function.

Design ramifications

We must always declare a member function as virtual if the class is used for derivation and the implementation of that message depends on the class of the receiver. This requirement allows efficient execution and efficient implementation of dynamic binding, but inhibits flexibility in subclassing. In particular, suppose we define a new subclass that must redefine a message that had not been overridden previously, and, therefore, is not virtual. We must add the virtual reserved word for that member function in the ancestor class definition, and then recompile the ancestor, all its descendants, and all clients that create instances of any of those classes. We will see in section 12.3.5 that this is necessary because the vtbls (i.e., the method dictionaries) for the ancestor and all its descendants will be different. Clearly, this also requires having the source code for the ancestor and all its descendants and clients.

As we saw in section 12.2.3 and the previous section, the class designer must declare all variables, parameters, and data members of polymorphic class type as pointers or references so that messages sent to those identifiers are dynamically bound. Suppose we were to use a value representation for instances of a class because it has no subclasses. If we then defined a subclass that overrides methods or adds data members, each use of that class as a type name for a variable, parameter, or data member would have to be changed to a pointer or reference. In addition, the referents of those identifiers would need to be dynamically allocated, and if a pointer were used, we would have to change all expressions that used the identifier to dereference it. We would also have to add statements that deallocated those objects at the appropriate time. Finally, all the affected code files would need to be recompiled.

These policies have a major impact on the design of class libraries, especially commercial libraries that do not supply the source code. The vendor must specify all member functions that a client descendant might possibly override as virtual (which may require a psychic friend). The efficiency of static binding is not available for those messages, even when a particular client does not need to override them. The vendor must also declare all variables whose class might be used as a base class as pointers or references. The efficiency of a value representation is not available for those objects, even when a particular client does not define subclasses. As we discussed with respect to private and protected members, the designer of a C++ class intended for reuse and derivation must exercise care in deciding whether to make each member function virtual, and whether to use values or references for variables and data members. If the designer errs on the side of efficiency in making these decisions, clients will be seriously inconvenienced if they need extendibility. Clients can use the dynamic cast operator to implement method dispatching, but have no recourse for cases in which the library uses value semantics.

Argument signatures

As we discussed in section 12.1.3, if the argument signature of a particular member function does not match that of an inherited member function with the same name, then the class's function hides the inherited function within the scopes of the class and its descendants. If the function is invoked through an ancestor pointer that refers to an instance of the class using the ancestor argument signature, the ancestor method is executed. If the class's argument signature is used with this ancestor pointer, an error occurs. These considerations are true for a virtual member function as well, so dynamic binding through an ancestor pointer cannot occur when the argument signatures of the member functions do not match.

As we mentioned in section 12.1.3, there is one exception to this rule. A recent extension to the language allows a base class virtual function whose return type is *Base** or *Base&* to be overridden in a derived class with a method that returns a *Derived** or *Derived&*, respectively, and invocations of that function are still dynamically bound. For example, recall that the return type of the function PriorityQueue::insert() differs from that of Queue::insert() in this way. We want this to be true so that the compiler will allow the result of an expression involving PriorityQueue::insert() to receive PriorityQueue-specific protocol, or to be assigned to a PriorityQueue identifier or parameter, without a cast. For example,

```
// we want PriorityQueue::insert() to return PriorityQueue&
#include "Date.h"                    // defines bool Date::operator<(const Date&)
#include "PriorityQueue.h"           // with typedef Date ElemType; in Queue.h
int main()
{
    PriorityQueue pq;
    // expressions that would fail if PriorityQueue::insert() returns a Queue&
    Date firstDate = pq.insert(Date("1/1/90")).first();
    PriorityQueue pq1 = pq.insert(Date("1/1/90"));
    // code that we must use if PriorityQueue::insert() returns a Queue&
    // (as it must with older compilers)
    Date firstDate = ((PriorityQueue&) pq.insert(Date("1/1/90"))).first();
    PriorityQueue pq1 = (PriorityQueue&) pq.insert(Date("1/1/90"));
}
```

Returning a derived class reference or pointer is safe in this case because any context in which the function is called requires a base class reference or pointer, and the derived class reference or pointer can appear there without violating that requirement. This is a recent extension that not all current compilers support.

However, the language cannot allow the same substitution for the parameter types of dynamically bound member functions.[19] For example, suppose that both Queue and PriorityQueue define operator==() as a virtual member function, with the class of the definition as the parameter type, as follows:

```
// operator==() is declared virtual in class Queue
bool Queue::operator==(const Queue& rhs)
{
    Node* pThis = front;
    Node* pArg = rhs.front;
    while ( pThis != NULL && pArg != NULL && pThis->elem == pArg->elem )
    {
        pThis = pThis->next;
        pArg = pArg->next;
```

---

[19] This is an example of the principle of *contravariance* [Har91]. A more specific function can return a more specific value (which is referred to as *covariance)*, but the reverse relationship holds for parameters: a more general parameter results in a more specific function.

```
        }
        if ( pThis == NULL && pArg == NULL )
            return true;
        else
            return false;
    }

    bool PriorityQueue::operator==(const PriorityQueue& rhs)
    {
        if ( Queue::operator==(rhs) && pCompareFn == rhs.pCompareFn )
            return true;
        else
            return false;
    }
```

Clients would expect to be able to use the operator with all four possible argument signatures. However, if the calls are dynamically bound, the function invoked is that of the receiver, the left operand.

```
// not valid: attempting to allow dynamic binding with a Base& parameter in the base class
// and a Derived& parameter in the derived class

#include "Queue.h"            // defines Queue::operator==()
#include "PriorityQueue.h"    // defines PriorityQueue::operator==()
int main()
{
    Queue qu;
    PriorityQueue pq1, pq2;
    bool test;
    // ... operations on qu, pq1 and pq2 ...
    // invokes PriorityQueue::operator==()
    test = ( pq1 == pq2 );
    // invokes Queue::operator==() with conversion of the right operand
    test = ( qu == pq1 );
    // error: allowing this call would cause an error in the PriorityQueue::operator==() method
    // since qu has no rhs.pCompareFn
    // (actually, the argument involves an invalid down-cast)
    test = ( pq1 == qu );
}
```

The third comparison is invalid because the argument (the right operand) does not have the pCompareFn data member that the PriorityQueue::operator==() method uses. Consequently, when the parameter types differ, the base class function is hidden in the derived class. If we want to allow the third comparison in this example and omit testing the pCompareFn member when the argument to PriorityQueue::operator==() is an instance of Queue, we code the derived class operator function with a base class reference parameter. Its method uses a dynamic cast to determine whether to perform the pCompareFn comparison, as follows:[20]

```
// allows comparison of priority queues and FIFO queues on the basis of elements only
// dynamic binding can be used
bool PriorityQueue::operator==(const Queue& rhs)
{
   // check the elements in order
   if ( !Queue::operator==(rhs) )
      return false;
   PriorityQueue* pPriQu = dynamic_cast<PriorityQueue*>(&rhs);
   // check the comparison functions if the argument is a priority queue
   if ( pPriQu != NULL )
      return pCompareFn == pPriQu->pCompareFn;  // rhs.pCompareFn would be invalid
   else
      return true;
}
```

Like all explicit type dependencies, this technique becomes a problem if there is further derivation from Queue later.

Access specifications

Each class that contributes a method for a virtual member function may define the function as public, protected, or private, and the function may be defined with a different access specification in different classes. Because the compiler enforces access control, whether it allows a member function invocation is determined by the function's access specification in the static class of the identifier through which it is invoked.

For example, suppose that a virtual function is public in a base class and protected or private in a derived class. The compiler permits invocations of that function through a base class pointer, whereas access through a derived class pointer is not allowed. If a client invokes the function through a base class pointer referring to a derived class object, the nonpublic member function of the derived class is executed, due to dynamic binding. However, that same method is not available through a derived class pointer. The inverse situation occurs if the virtual function is non-public in the base class and public in the derived class.

Because accessibility for a message should be uniform no matter how it is invoked, defining a virtual function with different access specifications in different classes in the corresponding subhierarchy is questionable practice.

---

[20] We might consider overloading PriorityQueue::operator==() with both a Queue& and a PriorityQueue& parameter. However, the method executed would be determined by the class of the identifier, not the class of the object.

12.3.3 Virtual Destructors and Copying

Virtual destructors

We specify overridden member functions as virtual so that the correct class-specific method is executed for a descendant object, irrespective of the type of the pointer used to send the message. Note also that an instance of a descendant class that defines or requires its own destructor may be deleted through an ancestor pointer. For example,

```
// the need for dynamically bound destructors
#include "Person.h"
#include "Employee.h"
int main()
{
    Person* pPerson = new Employee(...);
    // should use Employee::~Employee() to invoke String::~String() for the
    // department_ data member
    delete pPerson;
}
```

When we apply delete in the second statement, the compiler invokes the destructor Person::~Person() due to the type of the pointer pPerson. Similarly, a collection that contains instances of the various classes in a subhierarchy refers to its elements through a pointer to the common ancestor. If a client needs to destroy the elements in a collection, he or she will obtain the successive elements via a pointer of ancestor type, and the ancestor destructor will be executed when calling delete through that pointer.

To deal with these cases properly (and to avoid coding a switch on the class within the ancestor destructor), the language must provide a mechanism for dynamic binding of destructors. We can declare a destructor as virtual, for example, by specifying the Person destructor as virtual ~Person() in the class definition. If this is done, the destructors for all classes descended from this class are dynamically bound. If an ancestor pointer refers to a descendant class object, when delete is applied to that pointer the descendant class destructor is invoked, followed by the destructors for its member objects and base classes. This situation is unlike other virtual functions because the destructors for the various classes each have different names, although they are invoked uniformly just before an object is deallocated.

It might seem that the destructor for a class used for derivation should be virtual by default, as we can always delete a descendant object through an ancestor pointer. We will see in section 12.3.5 that the presence of virtual member functions causes each instance of the class to have an additional class pointer in its storage structure through which methods are selected. If destructors were virtual by default, all instances of classes with destructors would need this pointer, and all those classes would require method dispatch tables because the compiler does not know at the time of definition whether a class will be used for derivation. However, this would cause unnecessary overhead for classes that define destructors but do not have sub-classes. In addition, an object with a class pointer is not compatible with a C object with the same data members.

For these reasons, it is the class designer's responsibility to choose whether the destructor for a class is virtual. Clearly a class's destructor should be virtual if any of its descendants define destructors, or if a descendant adds a data member whose class defines a destructor. Unfortunately, the designer of a class may not know whether this will happen. The general rule of thumb is to declare a class's destructor virtual whenever it defines virtual member functions, because class pointers and a method dispatch table are necessary for dynamic binding for that class anyway.

Dynamically bound copying

There is no virtual constructor analogous to the virtual destructor because the type of the new object must be given explicitly in the source code whenever an object is created. However, class-specific copying is sometimes needed. For example, if we have a collection whose element type is a pointer to a polymorphic class and we need to make a copy of the collection and its elements, each element must be copied according to its own class. To deal with this situation, we can define a virtual member function, say copy(), which can be invoked to make a copy of a descendant object through an ancestor pointer. For example, we can define the following implementation of dynamically bound copying for the classes Person and Employee:

```
// dynamic binding of object copying for classes derived from Person
class Person
{
public:
    // the client must delete the result! (there is a hidden "new")
    virtual Person* copy() const;
    // ... other member functions ...
protected:
    // ... data members defined in section 10.2.4 ...
};

inline Person* Person::copy() const
{
    return new Person(*this);        // copy constructor defined in section 10.2.4
}

class Employee : public Person
{
public:
    virtual Employee* copy() const;   // use Person* return type for older compilers
    // ... other member functions ...
protected:
    // ... data members defined in section 12.1.2 ...
};
```

```
inline Employee* Employee::copy() const
{
   return new Employee(*this);            // copy constructor defined in section 12.1.2
}

int main()
{
   Person* pPers1 = new Employee(...);
   Person* pPers2 = pPers1->copy();       // Employee::copy() invoked
   // don't forget to delete pPers2!
}
```

There is an asymmetry here because the client did not call new explicitly for pPers2, but must call delete to deallocate its referent. We might consider defining the copy constructor for class Person such that it calls the virtual function copy() to create a copy of whatever object is passed as the argument.

```
// invalid attempt to obtain dynamic copying in a copy constructor
Person::Person(const Person& pers)
{
   // *this = *copy(pers) would lose subclass-specific data members
   this = copy(pers);
}

int main()
{
   Person* pPers1 = new Employee(...);
   // we want pPers2 to refer to a new Employee object
   Person* pPers2 = new Person(*pPers1);
}
```

However, this technique will not work because operator new() allocates space for a Person object for the expression new Person(*pPers1), and we cannot assign to this because it is const.[21]

At the beginning of this subsection, we discussed using such a dynamic copy() method to implement a deep copy operation for a collection of polymorphic type elements. The collection class may define the operation as a copy constructor or as a named member function, and the collection documentation must state the requirement that the element type must provide the message copy to permit the collection copying operation.

---

[21] We could also overload Person::operator new() to allocate the correct amount of space for the actual class of the argument, but this would involve a switch on the class identity of the argument. (The sizeof operator is always implemented by the compiler and returns the size of the static class, although the language definition does not actually specify this behavior.) The problem with this being const would still remain.

12.3.4 Abstract Classes

Pure virtual functions

As we described in section 3.4, the protocol for an abstract class includes abstract messages whose methods are deferred to concrete descendants. These messages provide a common interface for those descendants, and each concrete descendant must override them with class-specific methods. A language construct that specifies that such messages are included within the protocol of an abstract class is particularly important for statically typed languages. An abstract class provides a type for the static class of an identifier through which invocation of dynamic binding occurs, and the compiler must be informed of the validity of these messages. As we have seen, this identifier will be a pointer or reference of abstract class type in C++.

In C++, an abstract message is referred to as a *pure virtual function*, and is indicated syntactically by initializing the declaration of the virtual function to 0 in the class definition. For example,[22]

```
// a class that defines a pure virtual function is an abstract class
class Display Object
{
public:
    virtual void draw(Canvas&) =0;   // a pure virtual function (an abstract message)
// ... other members ...
};
```

Note that using the =0 initializer is not the same as defining a function with an empty body. It is an error to create an instance of a class containing pure virtual functions, whether by static, automatic, or dynamic allocation, or by a value conversion. Similarly, we cannot define value data members or value parameters of that type. Any of these definitions results in a compile-time error. These restrictions are not enforced for a class containing a function definition with an empty body. The type of a variable, data member, or function parameter can be an abstract class pointer or reference. This identifier may then refer to instances of its concrete descendant classes, and provides dynamic binding for the virtual functions in that subhierarchy.

A class containing pure virtual functions can only be used for derivation. If a derived class does not override a pure virtual function, then it is also an abstract class subject to these same restrictions. An abstract class may define a constructor even though the class cannot be instantiated. For example, the constructor can initialize common data members defined in the abstract class, and can be invoked through the initialization list of a derived class. This constructor would be listed in

---

[22] A reserved word, such as abstract, would have been more perspicuous, but Stroustrup found that many programmers strongly resisted attempts to introduce new reserved words into the language [Str94].

the non public section of the abstract class definition. An abstract class can also provide a method for a pure virtual function, for example, to supply a basis for refinement. The result of calling a pure virtual function that is not defined (e.g., by using a qualified name) is undefined, and results in a run-time error.

Examples

Let us define an abstract class for queues of objects that use a linked representation. The protocol of such collections includes insertion and deletion of elements, and upon deletion, some characteristic of the queue determines which element is removed. The client can also test whether an instance is empty, in which case an attempt to remove an element is an error. The size of an instance, the actual elements in an instance, and their ordering for removal are not visible externally. The abstract class AbstractQueue defines the protected nested class Node, a default constructor, a virtual destructor, the messages AbstractQueue:: isEmpty() and AbstractQueue::remove(), and an output operator. It also defines the pure virtual function AbstractQueue::insert(). Some example derived classes are FIFOQueue (the Queue class defined in sections 10.1.3 and 10.1.4), PriorityQueue (defined in sections 12.1.1 and 12.1.3), and LIFOQueue (i.e., a stack). Each of these defines its own insert() method, which positions the new element in the correct order in the instance's internal linked list. We define the abstract class AbstractQueue and the subclass FIFOQueue as follows:

```cpp
// AbstractQueue.h: an abstract class for queues (linked list implementation)
// some subclasses might be FIFOQueue, PriorityQueue, LIFOQueue, etc.

// the type of elements inserted into and removed from the queue
typedef int ElemType;

// for the class ostream and the cerr object used in the method for AbstractQueue::remove()
#include <iostream.h>

class AbstractQueue
{
friend ostream& operator<<(ostream&, AbstractQueue&);
public:
   virtual AbstractQueue& insert(const ElemType&) =0;   // abstract message
   ElemType remove();              // coded like Queue::remove() in section 10.1.4
   bool isEmpty();
protected:
   class Node
   {
   public:
     Node(const ElemType&, Node*);
     ElemType elem;
     Node* next;
   };
```

```
    AbstractQueue();
    virtual ~AbstractQueue();              // coded like Queue::~Queue() in section 10.2.3
    Node* front;                           // back not needed for LIFOQueue
};

inline AbstractQueue::Node::Node(const ElemType& el, Node* pSucc = NULL)
    : elem(el), next(pSucc)
{ }

inline bool AbstractQueue::isEmpty()
{
    return front == NULL ? true : false;
}

inline AbstractQueue::AbstractQueue()
    : front(NULL)
{ }

// FIFOQueue.h: a first-in first-out queue
class FIFOQueue : public AbstractQueue
{
public:
    FIFOQueue();
    // coded like Queue::insert() in section 10.1.3
    virtual FIFOQueue& insert(const ElemType&);
protected:
    Node* back;
};

FIFOQueue::FIFOQueue()
    : AbstractQueue(), back(NULL)
{ }
```

As we discussed in section 3.3.3, an abstract class can define methods that provide higher-level algorithms, which invoke subclass-specific operations via dynamic binding, often of deferred methods defined in its concrete descendants. A descendant can then define the pure virtual functions and inherit the implementations of these methods. The member functions that encode the higher-level algorithms (e.g., DisplayObject::moveTo() need not be virtual because the method is the same for all descendants, and messages passed to the receiver within the method will use dynamic binding. For example, we can define an abstract class Orderable, which is analogous to the class Magnitude in the Smalltalk system classes, as follows:

```
// Orderable.h: an abstract class defining protocol for linearly orderable objects
// concrete subclasses must define operator==() and operator<()

class Orderable
```

```
    {
public:
    virtual bool operator==(const Orderable&) const =0;
    virtual bool operator<(const Orderable&) const =0;
    bool operator!=(const Orderable& rhs) const
    { return !(*this == rhs); }
    bool operator<=(const Orderable& rhs) const
    { return *this < rhs || *this == rhs; }
    bool operator>(const Orderable& rhs) const
    { return *this != rhs && !(*this < rhs); }
    bool operator>=(const Orderable& rhs) const
    { return !(*this < rhs); }
    Orderable& min(const Orderable& rhs) const
    { return *this <= rhs ? *this : rhs; }
    Orderable& max(const Orderable& rhs) const
    { return *this >= rhs ? *this : rhs; }
    bool between(const Orderable& low, const Orderable& high) const
    { return low <= *this && *this <= high; }
};
```

The compiler can expand all of the defined member functions inline.

Static typing complicates using a class like Orderable. First, the return type of Orderable::min() and Orderable::max() is an Orderable reference, which requires a downcast to use as a subclass instance, as we saw in section 12.3.2. To avoid this, we could specify these functions as virtual in Orderable, and then override them in a descendant with a definition that returns a reference to the descendant class. The body of the functions would simply invoke the Orderable function and then cast the result. However, if they are virtual functions, an invocation is not inlined.

A similar problem occurs with the parameter types. Recall from section 12.3.2 that a descendant must redefine virtual functions with the same argument signature, in this case with a parameter of type const Orderable&, rather than of the descendant type. Unfortunately, this allows the argument to be an instance of any descendant of Orderable, and the compiler cannot ensure that the argument is the same type as the receiver. The ordering comparison methods must prevent comparison of objects of unrelated classes because the result would be meaningless. To deal with this problem, the equality test method can use a dynamic cast to determine whether the argument is the same type as the receiver, and return false if it is not. For example, suppose we order instances of the class Person based on the value of the ssn_ data member, and derive the class from Orderable to obtain use of the abstract class's protocol. We define the deferred methods as follows:

```
// overloading of pure virtual functions inherited from class Orderable
#include <iostream.h>    // for the cerr object in Person::operator<()
#include <stdlib.h>      // for void exit(int)
```

```
class Person : public Orderable
{
public:
    virtual bool operator==(const Orderable&) const;
    virtual bool operator<(const Orderable&) const;
    // ... other member functions ...
protected:
    // ... data members defined in section 10.2.4 ...
};

inline bool Person::operator==(const Orderable& rhs) const
{
    Person* pPers = dynamic_cast< Person*>(&rhs);
    // pPers is not NULL if rhs is an instance of any descendant of class Person
    if ( pPers == NULL )
        return false;
    // rhs.ssn_ is not valid because rhs can refer to any orderable object
    return ssn_ == pPers->ssn_;
}

inline bool Person::operator<(const Orderable& rhs) const
{
    Person* pPers = dynamic_cast< Person*>(&rhs);
    if ( pPers == NULL )
    {
        // throw an exception instead if available
        cerr << "Attempt to compare unrelated types of objects for ordering" << endl;
        exit(1);
    }
    return ssn_ < pPers->ssn_;
}
```

We might consider defining the type checking as methods for the pure virtual functions in Orderable, and then coding the concrete descendant methods as refinements of these methods. However, the dynamic cast operator and the declaration of the pointer used as its return value require the descendant class name.

Providing this type checking explicitly is not necessary in a dynamically typed language that performs type checking at execution time. For example, subclasses of the Smalltalk system class Magnitude do not have to implement type checking. If the classes of the receiver and the argument are unrelated, an error will be signaled when the receiver's < method is executed because the argument will not be able to respond to the messages sent by that method.

12.3.5 Implementation

The vptr **and the** vtbl

In this section, we will describe the implementation of dynamic binding for virtual member functions with single inheritance. (We will discuss the additional information necessary with multiple inheritance in section 12.4.1.) This will help us to appreciate how little execution-time overhead is involved in C++, and to understand why we must indicate which functions require dynamic binding. Recall that the compiler handles all cases involving static binding of function invocations using encoded names.

When creating an instance of a class that defines or inherits virtual functions, the compiler includes an additional pointer in that object's storage structure, which is termed its vptr. This pointer is analogous to the class pointer in a Smalltalk object, but the "class object" that it refers to is much less extensive. This pointer is not present in instances of a class that does not define virtual functions. In this way, there is no overhead for such a class, and its instances are compatible with instances of a C structure type with the same members and member types.

In C++, the compiler knows the names of all member functions that require dynamic binding for each class because the class designer has declared (or included) them. For each class that contains virtual member functions, the compiler sets up a table of pointers to the class's methods for those functions, which is referred to as the class's vtbl. This table is used to select the correct method when an instance of the class receives a message that requires dynamic binding. The vptr in each instance of a class with virtual functions points to that class's vtbl. For example, Figure 12.2 illustrates the vtbl for the class Square, which has three virtual functions, draw(), resize(), and rotate(), and the vptr in an instance of the class.

The vtbl for each descendant of a class has the same number of entries (if it does not define further virtual functions), and the order of the method pointers for the corresponding member function names is the same. For example, the vtbl for the other subclasses of DisplayObject have the same layout as in Figure 12.2. If a subclass overrides a member function, then its vtbl has a pointer to its own method in that position in the table. If it does not override an inherited virtual function, then its vtbl entry for that function points to the same function as the corresponding entry in its superclass's vtbl. That is, when a class's vtbl is built, its entries point to the same methods as those in its superclass's vtbl for functions it does not define, rather than containing a superclass pointer to follow during method resolution as in Smalltalk. If a descendant defines further virtual functions, it will have additional entries below these in its table, as will classes derived from it. No vtbls are allocated for classes that do not define virtual functions.

The compiler must build a vtbl for an abstract class even though no vptr will refer to it, because the class may include virtual function definitions. The vtbls of

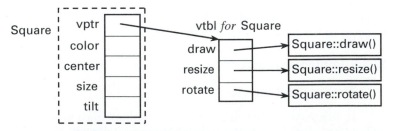

Figure 12.2   The vptr and vtbl for the class Square.

its descendants have entries pointing to these methods if they do not override them. A pure virtual function indicates to the compiler that it should create a vtbl entry, even though that class does not define a method for that function. [23]

An important property of this implementation is that we can code and compile a new class independently, and add it to the system without recompiling any existing code. For example, if we create a new subclass of DisplayObject, its vtbl will have the same layout as that in Figure 12.2, and will interact correctly with clients of that subhierarchy. When a client sends a message to an instance of the new class through a DisplayObject pointer, the code that the compiler had generated to select and invoke a method will operate correctly. The new class's vtbl will have the correct method pointers in the correct positions in the table because the compiler had the ancestor class definitions available as included header files while compiling the new class.

The vptr of an instance of a class that contains virtual functions is installed by its constructor. This is another reason why virtual function invocations in constructors cannot be dynamically bound. The compiler cannot use a derived class method when the base class constructor is called from the derived class constructor initialization list because the derived class object's vptr is not installed yet.

To support run-time type information, the vtbl for a class can also contain type information or a pointer to a type_info object or table entry. This information is also used at execution time to verify a use of the dynamic_cast<>() operator on a pointer that refers to an instance of the class, and to adjust the pointer value if necessary. (Recall that a dynamic cast to any of the object's ancestors is valid.)

One remaining issue is where to allocate the vtbls and how to set vptrs in client objects. A simple implementation is to allocate a vtbl for a class with virtual functions in every code module that includes the definition of that class. However, this approach can waste a considerable amount of space in a large program with many code files and many instances of polymorphic classes. To avoid duplicating vtbls, the compiler can create the vtbl for a class in the object module that results from compiling the class's code file. (To be more precise, it can create the vtbl in the code file that defines the first virtual member function in the definition of a polymorphic class.) In addition, the vtbl must have an external name encoded with the class name and known to the linker so that it can set vptrs in client code files to refer to the vtbl. Some entries in the vtbl, namely those that point to methods defined in a different code file, such as inherited methods, will be installed by the linker.

Method dispatching

To translate a virtual function call, the compiler inserts code that selects and invokes the correct function code at run time. This code consists of

---

[23] Presumably, it is this pointer which is initialized to NULL by the =0 pure virtual function specifier.

1. dereferencing the receiver's vptr to obtain its vtbl
2. adding the offset corresponding to the virtual function
3. dereferencing that entry
4. invoking the resulting function.

This simple implementation is possible because each class that responds to a particular virtual function has a pointer to its method for that function at the same position in its vtbl. No search of the class's method dictionary is required, and when invoking a virtual function for an instance of a class that inherits that function's method, no search of the hierarchy is necessary. The total time overhead necessary for dynamic binding is an extra indexed access through the receiver object's vptr to obtain a pointer to the correct method, and one more access to follow that pointer. In a sense, the vtbl implements the switch in the sender, which is not needed due to the dynamic binding supplied by the language.

Let us consider an example that illustrates the use of these data structures for a hierarchy of classes. Suppose we have an abstract class A with subclasses B1 and B2, and class B1 has an abstract subclass C1 that has a concrete subclass D1, as illustrated in Figure 12.3. Each class defines a number of virtual member functions, and we will create three instances of the concrete classes and pass them messages to illustrate how the correct method is selected. The example class definitions, member function declarations, object allocations, pointer initializations, and member function invocations are as follows (the actual definitions of the methods are irrelevant for our purpose):

```
// example classes, objects and message expressions to illustrate
// the implementation of dynamic binding
class A
{
public:
    virtual void msg0();
    virtual void msg1() =0;
```

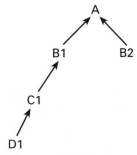

Figure 12.3 An example class hierarchy to illustrate the implementation of dynamic binding.

```
      virtual void msg2(int);
      // ... other members ...
  };

  class B1 : public A
  {
  public:
      virtual void msg1();
      virtual void msg2(int);
      // ... other members ...
  };

  class B2 : public A
  {
  public:
      virtual void msg0();
      virtual void msg1();
      // ... other members ...
  };

  class C1 : public B1
  {
  public:
      virtual void msg1();
      virtual void msg3() =0;
      // ... other members ...
  };

  class D1 : public C1
  {
  public:
      virtual void msg0();
      virtual void msg3();
      // ... other members ...
  };

  int main()
  {
      A* pA1 = new B1(...);
      A* pA2 = new B2(...);
      A* pA3 = new D1(...);
      pA1->msg0();              // invokes A::msg0()
      pA1->msg1();              // invokes B1::msg1()
      pA2->msg1();              // invokes B2::msg1()
      pA2->msg2(3);             // invokes A::msg2()
      pA3->msg0();              // invokes D1::msg0()
      pA3->msg1();              // invokes C1::msg1()
      pA3->msg2(3);             // invokes B1::msg2()
  }
```

Figure 12.4 illustrates the pointer identifiers, the referent objects and their vptrs, the vtbls associated with the various classes, the code for the member functions, and their interrelationships.

As we can see in Figure 12.4, each class has a table that contains pointers to its methods, and no interclass relationships are represented. For example, class B1's vtbl entry for msg0() points directly to the code for A::msg0(). The message send pA1->msg2(3) is translated as code equivalent to (*(pA1->vptr[2])) (pA1, 3) (we include a pointer to the receiver as the first argument to the function). That is, the code fetches the pointer located at pA1->vptr, adds twice the size of a pointer, dereferences that result, and then invokes that function. This procedure is correct for an invocation of msg2() for an instance of any descendant of class A.

12.4 MULTIPLE INHERITANCE

12.4.1 Basic Concepts

Class definition

As we discussed in section 3.4.1, problem domain analysis or system design sometimes indicates that a class is a specialization of more than one class, or should inherit behavior from more than one class. In C++, the class designer can represent this situation directly by specifying a *derivation list* of base classes in the class definition. The order of the base classes in the list is not significant, other than determining the order of execution of their constructors when the derived class is instantiated. In particular, the order is not used in disambiguating name conflicts among inherited members (as it is in CLOS). The default access specification for each base class is private, so we must specify each base class as public if we intend the class to be a specialization of that base class.

A class inherits all of the member functions of each of its base classes, so its protocol is the union of the protocols of those classes. It also inherits the data members of each of its base classes, so its storage structure contains an embedded instance of each base class and its ancestors. Of course, the class can also define additional protocol and data members, and can override inherited methods. For these reasons, an instance of the derived class can be referred to by a pointer or reference whose type is any of its public ancestors.

As with single inheritance, a class does not inherit the constructors of its base classes. The class designer must specify each base class on the constructor initialization list, unless invocation of its default constructor is desired. If the derived class defines a copy constructor and assignment operator, those methods must invoke the corresponding functions for each base class.

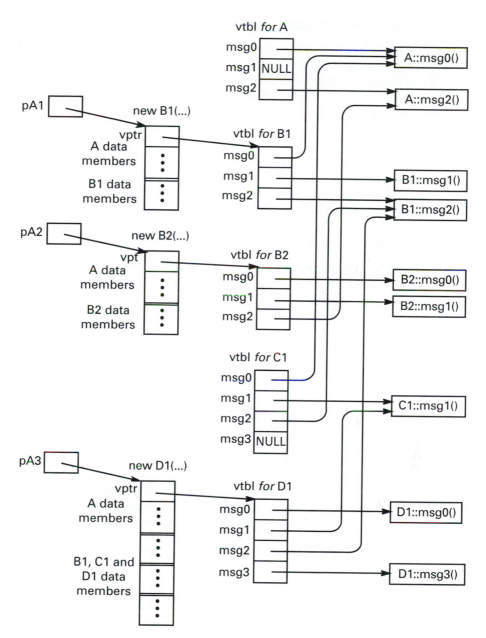

Figure 12.4 Data structures for implementing dynamic binding with single inheritance.

Hierarchy and scope structure

When a class has more than one superclass, the class hierarchy structure is a directed acyclic graph rather than a forest. As an example, recall Figure 11.2, which illustrates the iostream class hierarchy. The graph may or may not have a single root class like ios, depending on whether there is some functionality that the designer of the application or class library requires for all objects in the system.

A derived class scope is nested within the scope of its base class, so the scope of a class with more than one base class is directly nested in more than one scope. As stated in section 3.4.1, a class can inherit the same member name along different ancestor paths in the inheritance hierarchy, or one class may be an ancestor of another class along more than one path in the hierarchy. We will discuss the features for handling these situations in the next two sections.

Conversions to ancestors

Value, pointer, and reference conversions from a class to any of its public ancestors are valid standard conversions, and can be performed implicitly by the compiler or explicitly by the programmer. As stated in section 12.2.4, the value conversion uses the ancestor copy constructor from the ancestor subobject of the object converted.

As mentioned in section 12.2.4, a pointer conversion can result in changing the address value of the pointer. For example, suppose we derive a class Derived from Base1 and Base2, and Base1 has the base class Ancestor1. Figure 12.5 illustrates the class hierarchy and the storage structure for an instance of the class Derived. With this storage layout, conversion of a Derived* identifier to a Base2* value is valid, but involves adding the size of a Base1 object to the pointer value so that the Base2* pointer refers to the Base2 subobject. In general, it is implementation-dependent whether the embedded instance of Base1 or Base2 occurs first in the Derived storage structure (although most compilers do allocate the base class parts in the order of the class derivation list), and does not affect programming.

Multiple inheritance can cause additional ambiguity in the argument matching process because there is no preference among conversions to ancestors along dif-

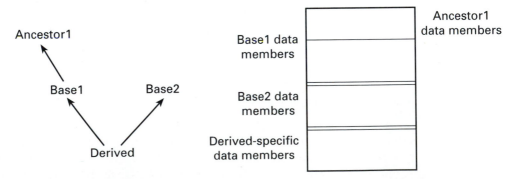

Figure 12.5 Class hierarchy and storage structure with multiple inheritance.

ferent paths in the inheritance hierarchy. For example, the following call using the classes illustrated in Figure 12.5 is ambiguous:

```
// ambiguous call due to more than one conversion to ancestor with multiple inheritance
class Ancestor1 { . . . };
class Base1 : public Ancestor1 { . . . };
class Base2 { . . . };
class Derived : public Base1, public Base2 { . . . };
void func(const Ancestor1 &);
void func(const Base2 &);
int main()
{
    Derived der(...);
    // error: both func(const Ancestor1 &) and func(const Base2 &) are applicable via
    // standard conversions
    func(der);
}
```

Recall from section 12.2.4 that the argument matching process prefers a conversion to an ancestor fewer steps removed along the same path in the inheritance hierarchy graph. With the classes in the previous example, the compiler prefers a conversion from Derived to Base1 over a conversion from Derived to Ancestor1 if both apply.

Dynamic binding

If both Ancestor1 and Base2 in Figure 12.5 define virtual member functions, then each of the corresponding subobjects in an instance of Derived contains a vptr. In addition, the class Derived has two vtbls, one for its method pointers for the virtual functions inherited from each base class. For an invocation of an inherited virtual function, the compiler uses the vptr in the base class subobject from which Derived inherits that message. If a class inherits a virtual member function with the same name and argument signature from more than one base class, there is a name conflict that must be resolved, as discussed in the next section.

Suppose that the class Base2 in Figure 12.5 defines virtual functions that Derived does not override. When those methods are invoked with an instance of Derived as the receiver, the this pointer must be adjusted to refer to the Base2 part of the Derived object before executing the method. Therefore, the Derived vtbl for Base2 virtual functions must also store an offset with each method pointer, and this offset is the size of the Base1 subobject for inherited methods and 0 for methods defined in Derived. That is, to correctly implement dynamic binding with multiple inheritance, a class's vtbl also includes an offset associated with each method pointer. This offset is zero for methods defined in the class or in ancestors whose subobject is stored at the beginning of its instances. For methods inherited from other ancestors, the compiler can compute the offset because it knows the storage layout of the class's instances and the ancestor from which the class inherits the method.

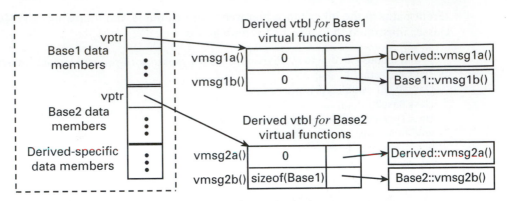

Figure 12.6 The implementation of dynamic binding with multiple inheritance.

For example, suppose that Derived inherits the virtual functions vmsg1a() and vmsg1b() from Base1, and the virtual functions vmsg2a() and vmsg2b() from Base2, and defines its own methods for the virtual functions vmsg1a() and vmsg2a(). This results in the storage structure illustrated in Figure 12.6.

The additional run-time overhead necessary to support multiple inheritance consists of the offsets in the vtbls and the addition to adjust the this pointer.

12.4.2 Name Conflicts

With the usual scope structure found in block-structured languages, two scopes are either nested one within the other or are disjoint, and there are no overlapping scopes. In sections 0.2.3 and 12.1.3, we used figures with rectangles (or sometimes polygons) marking the scope boundaries to illustrate scope nesting relationships. An identifier use in an expression is always resolved to one declaration by a search of enclosing scopes, or is undeclared in that context. For example, a use of an identifier defined both in a base class and in an ancestor of that base class is resolved to the definition in the base class.

With multiple inheritance, a class scope can be nested directly within more than one scope (i.e. those of its base classes), so the base class scopes overlap. Now suppose that two enclosing scopes declare the same name, for example, two base classes include the same data member name. Whether that name is defined in the base class or is inherited from an ancestor, an unqualified use of that name within a derived class method is ambiguous, and results in a compiler error. This ambiguity reflects the storage structure of a derived class instance, which contains two data members with that name, one in each embedded base class object. The name conflict occurs even if the members' types differ or if one of the ancestors specifies the data member as private, because names are found first and then types and access specifications are checked.

The situation is different for inherited member function names because function names can be overloaded. If member functions inherited from different base

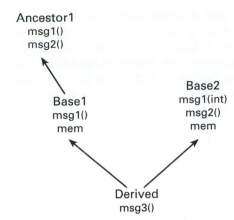

Figure 12.7 Example classes and members illustrating name conflicts.

```
// examples illustrating name clashes with multiple inheritance (see figure 12.7)
#include "Ancestor1.h"
#include "Base1.h"
#include "Base2.h"
#include "Derived.h"
int main()
{
   Derived der(...);
   // msg1() is overloaded in class Derived
   der.msg1();              // invokes Base1::msg1()
   der.msg1(5);             // invokes Base2::msg1(int)
   // msg2() is ambiguous in class Derived
   der.msg2();              // error: both Ancestor1::msg2() and Base2::msg2() are visible
   Base1* pBase1 = &der;
   pBase1->msg2();          // Ancestor1::msg2() applied to der

   // the scope operator can be used to resolve ambiguity or select a hidden method
   der.Base1::msg2();       // OK: Ancestor1::msg2()
   der.Base2::msg2();       // OK
}
```

The member function msg1() is overloaded in class Derived with one argument signature contributed by each base class, and Ancestor1::msg1() is hidden. msg2() is ambiguous in Derived because Ancestor1::msg2() and Base2::msg2() have the same argument signature. This would be true even if msg2() were not public in Ancestor1 or Base2. However, if the Derived object is sent a message through a pointer or reference of ancestor type (pBase1 in this example), that class's method is selected via a scope search. (Recall that the pointer refers to the embedded ancestor object.) As the last three invocations illustrate, we can resolve hidden or ambiguous names by using qualified names. The same ambiguity occurs within the member functions of the derived class for inherited protected members.

classes have the same name and argument signature, then a name conflict occurs in the derived class. This is true even though the receivers of those functions are different embedded subobjects. If inherited member functions with the same name have different argument signatures, then that member function name is regarded as being overloaded with those signatures within the derived class scope. The argument signature of the message expression determines which method is executed.

If a name conflict among inherited members occurs, the programmer must qualify that name with the desired base class name to specify which member is intended. A class definition that includes a potential name ambiguity does not cause a compiler error because the error only occurs when an ambiguous statement is encountered. To illustrate these points, consider the following class definitions:

```
// example classes and members that illustrate name conflicts with multiple inheritance
// figure 12.7 illustrates the hierarchy and member names
class Ancestor1
{
public:
    virtual void msg1();
    void msg2();
};

class Base1 : public Ancestor1
{
public:
    virtual void msg1();
protected:
    int mem;
};

class Base2
{
public:
    void msg1(int);
    void msg2();
protected:
    int mem;
};

class Derived : public Base1, public Base2
{
public:
    void msg3();
};
```

Figure 12.7 illustrates the corresponding inheritance and scope structure (Figure 12.5 diagrams the storage structure of an instance of Derived). Now consider the following examples:

```
// name ambiguity within a derived class member function
void Derived::msg3()
{
   mem++;              // error: Base1::mem or Base2::mem?
   Base1::mem++;       // OK: explicit reference
}
```

Such name conflicts are also present in further derivations from the derived class. In addition, the ambiguity extends to users of the class if both inherited members are public, as occurs with msg2() in this example. When a public member function name is ambiguous, the class designer must decide what the class's interface will be for that message name, since we prefer that clients do not use qualified message names. If the derived class method is a refinement of the inherited methods, we code the method using qualified names to indicate which inherited method to execute, as follows:[24]

```
// the derived class method invokes both inherited methods
inline void Derived::msg2()
{
   Base1::msg2();
   Base2::msg2();
   // ... Derived-specific processing ...
}
```

For this method to be executed via a pointer of either base type using dynamic binding, the member function name must be declared as virtual in both base classes. If separate messages for both inherited methods are necessary in the derived class, they should have different names for clients. This can be handled by a technique similar to the Eiffel renaming feature. We create a new member function name in the derived class, whose method merely invokes the desired inherited function using a qualified name, as follows:

```
// resolving name conflicts by renaming the affected member functions
inline void Derived::Base1msg2()
{
   Base1::msg2();
}
inline void Derived::Base2msg2()
{
   Base2::msg2();
}
```

This may seem trivial, but it has the advantage that the member functions Base1msg2() and Base2msg2() are explicitly listed in the protocol of class Derived, which is known

[24] In our code examples, we refer to the member function Ancestor1::msg2() as Base1::msg2() in keeping with the principle that the class designer should need to know as little as possible about the classes used for derivation.

to its clients. The client does not need to be aware of the name conflict or of the ancestors of Derived. However, this technique has the disadvantage that a virtual function is not dynamically bound when using the scope operator.

12.4.3 Repeated Inheritance and Virtual Base Classes

Semantics of multiple derivations from an ancestor

With multiple inheritance a class may be derived from two base classes that share a common ancestor. For example, the class iostream inherits from istream and ostream, which both are derived from ios, and the class ifstream inherits from both istream and fstreambase, which also are subclasses of ios.

As we discussed in section 3.4.3, in some cases it is semantically correct to have multiple instances of an ancestor class object within a derived class object, one within each base class object. In that section, we illustrated this meaning with the example of deriving the classes Customer and Employee from an abstract class Linkable so that an application can maintain lists of each kind of object (like the Smalltalk system class Link described in section 8.3.4). An instance of the descendant class CustomerEmployee would need to include both types of links because it can be on both kinds of lists. In other cases, there should only be one embedded ancestor object, which is the receiver of all ancestor class messages. This meaning is correct for the concrete descendants of ios because a stream object should have exactly one state descriptor. In section 3.4.3, we illustrated this meaning with the example of deriving the classes Customer and Employee from the class Person. Clearly, an instance of the descendant class CustomerEmployee should only have one embedded Person subobject.

Multiple embedded ancestor objects

Recall the class CustomerEmployee that we discussed in section 3.4.3 and illustrated by Figures 3.5 and 3.6, which we repeat as Figure 12.8:

The classes Linkable, Customer, Employee, and CustomerEmployee might be defined as follows in C++:[25]

```
// a repeated ancestor
class Linkable
{
public:
    Linkable* next() const
    { return next_; }
```

---

[25] This simple definition of Linkable as an abstract class for derivation has the disadvantage that it is not type-safe. An instance of any descendant class can be linked to an instance of any other descendant, unless all member functions are virtual, and are overridden to return the descendant class type (in which case the class is pointless). This is similar to the attempt to use inheritance for the type of an element in section 13.2.2, and the same solution of defining Linkable as a class template would be safer and more convenient. We ignore this issue for the purpose of this example.

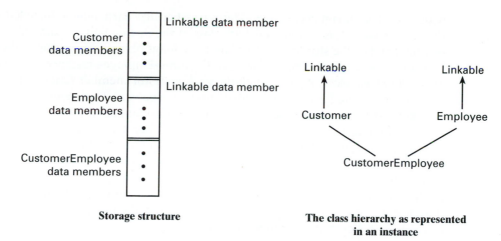

Figure 12.8 Multiple embedded ancestor objects.

```
   void next(Linkable* nxt)
   { next_ = nxt; }
protected:
   Linkable(Linkable* nxt = NULL)
      : next_(nxt)
   { }
   Linkable* next_;
};


class Customer: public Linkable
{
   // ... members described in section 3.2.1 ...
};


class Employee: public Linkable
{
   // ... members defined in section 12.1.2 ...
};


class CustomerEmployee : public Customer, public Employee
{
public:
   Linkable* nextCustomer()
   { return Customer::next(); }
   Linkable* nextEmployee()
   { return Employee::next(); }
   // ... other members ...
};
```

When a class appears as an ancestor of another along two or more paths in the inheritance graph, all of the ancestor's member names are lexically ambiguous

within the descendant class scope. This is true because each name is included within
the name space of more than one base class of the descendant. Again, this characteristic matches the storage structure of descendant objects, for example, there are
two copies of the data member next_ in CustomerEmployee instances, one in each
embedded base class object. Similarly, each ancestor member function is, in fact,
two messages, one for each embedded ancestor receiver. These ambiguities would
be inherited by any classes derived from the descendant as well.

An unqualified reference to a nonstatic member name declared in a repeated
ancestor is ambiguous because the compiler does not know which embedded ancestor object the use refers to. We can resolve this ambiguity by using the scope operator with the name of an "intermediate" class, as in the reference to Employee::
next() in the Employee::nextEmployee() method in the previous example. Note that
if we use the scope operator with the ancestor name, the use is still ambiguous. For
example, for clients of CustomerEmployee,

```
// name ambiguity for clients with a repeated ancestor
#include "Linkable.h"
#include "CustomerEmployee.h"
int main()
{
    CustomerEmployee* pCustEmpl = new CustomerEmployee(...);
    Linkable* pNext;
    // error: Customer::next() or Employee::next()? (i.e., which embedded receiver?)
    pNext = pCustEmpl->next();
    // error: Customer::next() or Employee::next()?
    pNext = pCustEmpl->Linkable::next();
    // OK: Customer::next()
    pNext = pCustEmpl->Customer::next();
    // OK: same function as the previous statement, but with a different receiver
    pNext = pCustEmpl->Employee::next();
}
```

The same name ambiguity occurs within the scope of derived class methods for protected members.

```
// name ambiguity within descendant class methods with a repeated ancestor
void CustomerEmployee::msg()
{

    Linkable* pNext;
    // error: Linkable::next_ in the Customer or Employee subobject?
    pNext = next_;
    // error: which Linkable::next_?
    pNext = Linkable::next_;
    // OK: Linkable::next_ in the Employee subobject
    pNext = Employee::next_;
}
```

A conversion from the descendant class to the repeated ancestor is also ambiguous because there are two such subobjects to which the result can refer.

```
// ambiguity of descendant to ancestor conversion with a repeated ancestor
#include "Linkable.h"
#include "Employee.h"
#include "CustomerEmployee.h"
int main()
{
    CustomerEmployee* pCustEmpl = new CustomerEmployee(...);
    Linkable* pLink;
    // error: Link object in the Customer or Employee subobject?
    pLink = pCustEmpl;
    // OK: Link object in the Employee subobject
    pLink = (Employee*) pCustEmpl;
}
```

Explicit conversions to the repeated ancestor are also ambiguous unless there is an intermediate base class conversion that specifies the subobject intended, for example, ((Linkable*) (Employee*) pCustEmpl.

This ambiguity does not occur for a static data member defined by a repeated ancestor because there is exactly one object with that name. Similarly, because static member functions do not have a receiver, an invocation of a static member function inherited from a repeated ancestor also does not require an intermediate base class name to resolve the ambiguity. The derived class can use static ancestor member names without qualification, and clients can use them with the scope operator and the name of the repeated ancestor (if they are public). In addition, if an enumeration is nested within the repeated ancestor, the enumeration value names do not need to be qualified by an intermediate base class name (recall our use of ios::eofbit, ios::out, and so on in section 11.3).

Virtual base classes

The *virtual base class* feature is a mechanism for specifying that an instance of a class that has a repeated ancestor should contain only one copy of the ancestor data members. That is, all base class subobjects in the descendant object share the same ancestor subobject, which is the receiver for all ancestor class messages. To indicate this meaning, we declare the ancestor whose instance is to be shared as a virtual base class of the intermediate base classes of the descendant class. For example, recall from section 11.3.2 that the classes istream and ostream specify ios as a virtual base class so that instances of class iostream have a single stream state descriptor. The ancestor and descendant class definitions are unaffected—there is no indication of the virtual derivation in the definitions of iostream and ios. Although the issue arises when the descendant class is created, the solution involves changes in the definition of the intermediate base classes.

For example, suppose that we derive the classes Customer and Employee from the class Person, and that we derive the class CustomerEmployee from Customer and Employee. In this case, we want the meaning represented by Figure 3.7, in which there is a single class Person, which is an ancestor of CustomerEmployee in the hierarchy. To do this, the classes Customer and Employee specify Person as a virtual base class, as follows:

```
// using virtual base classes to specify a single ancestor subobject
class Person
{
public:
    String name() const
    { return name_; }
    // ... members defined in section 10.2.4 ...
};

class Customer: virtual public Person
{
    // ... members described in section 3.2.1 ...
};

class Employee: virtual public Person
{
    // ... members defined in section 12.1.2 ...
};

class CustomerEmployee : public Customer, public Employee
{
    // ... other members ...
};
```

The virtual specifier indicates that the base class objects embedded in the derived class object each have a pointer to a single region containing the virtual ancestor members, rather than there being an ancestor subobject directly embedded in each. Figure 12.9 diagrams the storage structure for an instance of class CustomerEmployee. This diagram illustrates why we must specify the intermediate classes as using virtual derivation. The storage structures of instances of those classes include a level of indirection in accessing the inherited data members, even when they are not embedded within a descendant object. This indirection allows sharing the ancestor object when the base class object is embedded in an instance of a derived class with a repeated ancestor. Syntactically, derived class methods access virtual base class data members in the same manner as any other member (i.e., the compiler provides the indirection). The diagram also shows why nonvirtual derivation is the default: Virtual derivation provides less efficient access to the inherited data members. If the same ancestor is inherited by a descendant via both virtual and nonvirtual derivation, then descendant instances contain one subobject shared by all base classes that specify the ancestor as a virtual base class, and one

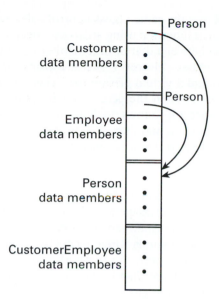

Figure 12.9 Storage structure with a single embedded ancestor object.

embedded ancestor object in each base class that specifies it as a nonvirtual base class.

Clearly, whether to use virtual derivation is an important issue for the designer of a class library. He or she must be able to anticipate whether descendant classes that blend functionality from more than one class will be needed by clients of the library, especially if the library does not provide source code. As we discussed with respect to virtual functions, a library designer may have to declare some derivations as virtual because of this possibility, which results in some additional overhead for clients that might not be necessary in some cases.

Because the derivation is virtual, unqualified uses of the data member names inherited from Person within CustomerEmployee methods are not ambiguous. In addition, an invocation of a Person member function with a CustomerEmployee receiver is not ambiguous. For example,

```
// repeated ancestor member names are not ambiguous with virtual derivation
#include "CustomerEmployee.h"
#include "String.h"
#include "Customer.h"
int main()
{
    CustomerEmployee* pCustEmpl = new CustomerEmployee(...);
    String aName;
    aName = pCustEmpl->name();                  // OK: Person::name()
    aName = pCustEmpl->Customer::name();        // OK: Person::name()
}
```

Virtual derivation follows the same access control rules as nonvirtual derivation. If the virtual base class is inherited using an access specifier other than public, the more strict specification between that of the member and that of the base class holds for each inherited member. However, the ancestor may be a virtual public base class of one base class and a virtual private base class of another, but there is only one ancestor subobject. When the access specifiers differ in this way, the derivation of the repeated ancestor follows the least strict access level, that is, public in this case. The virtual keyword may appear before or after the base class access specifier (usually, we give it first so that it is conspicuous).

Dominance

With virtual derivation, there is an additional issue if one of the intermediate base classes overrides an ancestor message and the other does not. For example, suppose that Employee redefines Person::name()—say, to perform some additional processing such as checking permissions when accessing an employee name—but Customer does not. In this case, both the methods Employee::name() and Person::name() (through Customer) are visible within the scope of the class CustomerEmployee, as illustrated in Figure 12.10. However, there is only one embedded name_ data member in CustomerEmployee's instances. Because a CustomerEmployee object is an instance of Employee, it would be proper to use the Employee method. We say that Employee::name() *dominates* Person::name().[26]

The dominant method is invoked when that message is passed to an instance of the descendant, for example, in an expression such as custEmpl.name(). (If the derivation were not virtual, then this invocation would be ambiguous.) In addition, the dominant method must be invoked for a descendant class object, no matter what type of pointer the message expression uses.

```
// the dominant method must be invoked for a descendant object
#include "Person.h"        // Person::name() is virtual for this example
#include "Customer.h"      // inherits Person::name()
#include "Employee.h"      // Employee::name() dominates Person::name() for this example
```

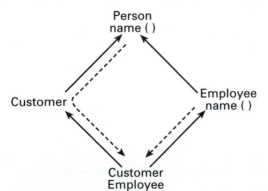

Figure 12.10 Employee::name() dominates Person::name().

[26] If both Customer and Employee defined the member function name(), then there would be a name conflict, as described in the previous section.

```
#include "CustomerEmployee.h"
#include "String.h"
int main()
{
    CustomerEmployee* pCustEmpl = new CustomerEmployee(...);
    Person* pPers = pCustEmpl;
    Customer* pCust = pCustEmpl;
    Employee* pEmpl = pCustEmpl;          // not the same value as pCust
    String theName;
    theName = pCustEmpl->name();          // OK: Employee::name() dominates
    theName = pPers->name();              // OK: Employee::name()
    theName = pEmpl->name();              // OK: Employee::name()
    theName = pCust->name();              // OK: Employee::name()!!
}
```

Note that the message expression pCust->name() invokes a method defined in a sibling of the static class (the method is defined in an ancestor of the dynamic class, though). Without the dominance rule, the invocation pCust->name() would invoke Person::name() since the pointer refers to the Customer subobject.

In general, Base::mem dominates Ancestor::mem within the descendants of Base if Base is derived from Ancestor. That is, the "most derived" method for an overridden member function name dominates, and is the method executed for descendant class instances. In fact, the dominance rule applies to any member name. If an intermediate base class and the virtual ancestor define the same data member name (which would be questionable practice), an unqualified use of that name in a descendant class method refers to the data member defined in the base class, rather than being ambiguous.

Initialization with virtual derivation

Having a single embedded ancestor object also affects how descendant class objects are initialized. Because a descendant object includes only one repeated ancestor subobject, the language must ensure that the ancestor constructor is called once in creating the descendant object, even though that constructor is on the initialization lists of both intermediate base classes. For example, if the Person constructor adds the new object to an index of its instances, that operation should only be done once for a CustomerEmployee object.

Normally, the order of execution of multiple base class constructors is given by the order of the classes in the class derivation list (and their derivations). For example, without virtual derivation, the constructors for a CustomerEmployee object would be executed in the order Person(), Customer(), Person(), Employee(), CustomerEmployee(). In addition, we only list the constructors for immediate base classes in the initialization list. The use of virtual derivation is an exception to both these rules. A virtual ancestor constructor is executed once before all other constructors when a descendant class object is created. With virtual derivation (i.e., in the intermediate base classes), the descendant class constructor must include the ancestor constructor in its initialization list, even though it is not a direct base class.

For example, the following illustrates the initialization list for the CustomerEmployee constructor:

```
// with virtual derivation, a descendant constructor initializes the ancestor subobject directly
// the calls of Person::Person() from the Customer and Employee initialization lists
// are not performed
CustomerEmployee::CustomerEmployee(...)
    : Person(...), Customer(...), Employee(...), ...
{ ... }
```

The constructors for the classes Customer and Employee also provide initializers
for class Person. However, those initializations are suppressed when initializing
an instance of CustomerEmployee. If Person does not appear on the initialization
list for CustomerEmployee, its default constructor is used (and the initializations
of Person specified by the Customer and Employee constructors are still not
done). With virtual derivation, the designer of a class must be aware of details of
the class hierarchy possibly distantly removed to write a correct class definition.
If there is more than one virtual ancestor, the constructors for those that are
"closer" to the descendant class in the hierarchy are invoked first in the order of
the class derivation list.

Suppose a method in the virtual ancestor is refined in both intermediate base
classes, that is, both methods invoke the ancestor method. If a method refinement
in the descendant class invokes the methods in both base classes, then the ancestor
method will be called twice (unlike the virtual ancestor constructor). The language
does not include a feature for avoiding such multiple invocations when they conflict
with the intended semantics, as it does for constructors. We can deal with this situation by defining protected methods in each base class that performs its class-specific operations only. Each base class method for the message invokes the ancestor
method and its own protected method. The descendant class method invokes the
ancestor method once and the protected methods for each immediate base class,
rather than using the public base class methods available to clients.

12.5 SUMMARY AND REVIEW

12.5.1 Class Derivation

Subclass definition

- A C++ superclass is called a *base class*, and a subclass is called a *derived class*.
- A class definition may specify a *derivation list* of base classes, and a derived
  class may add members and override inherited member functions. A derived
  class inherits all the member functions and data members of its base classes,
  except for their constructors.

- When we use a class as a base class, we must specify members needed in derived class methods as protected rather than private, and must specify member functions that are overridden as virtual.

Constructor, destructor, and assignment operator

- Base class constructors are not inherited because the derived class may add data members that the base class method cannot initialize.
- The compiler invokes the base class destructor to finalize the base class subobject whenever a derived class instance is destroyed. A derived class destructor does not invoke its base class's destructor.
- We invoke base class constructors from the initialization list of the derived class constructor using the base class name and a valid base class initializer. The derived class initialization list should not include inherited members.
- An object is built from the inside out: Ancestor constructors are called first, beginning with the most embedded ancestor objects. Next, constructors for class data member are invoked, again beginning with the most embedded objects. Finally, the class's constructor body is executed. Destructors for ancestors and class data members are invoked in the reverse order when an object is finalized.
- The default copy constructor and assignment operator for a derived class invoke the copy constructor and assignment operator of its base class.
- If a derived class needs to define a copy constructor and assignment operator, those methods must invoke the base class methods. We can invoke the base class assignment operator with either a reference cast or a qualified name.

Derived class scope

- The scope of a derived class scope is nested within that of its base class, and the derived class name is declared within the scope in which it is defined. Base class member names are visible in the derived class scope (if they are not hidden by derived class members).
- Clients can send public base class messages to derived class objects, and derived class methods can use nonprivate inherited members of the receiver directly.
- The scopes of derived class member functions are nested within the derived class scope.
- Both derived and nested classes define scopes nested within a class scope, but derived class objects include the members of the base class.
- If a derived class defines a member with the same name as a base class member, the base class member name is hidden in the derived class. If a derived class member function has a different argument signature than a base class function with the same name, it hides the base class function in the derived class scope. If the derived class needs both argument signatures, its definition must specify both signatures.

- If both the base and derived classes define a member function with the same name and argument signature, the member function must be declared virtual so that invocations are dynamically bound.
- To refine a base class method, we use a qualified member function name.
- A derived class has access to the static members of its base class because they are declared in an enclosing scope. It does not have its own copy of base class static data members.

Access control

- C++ supports three levels of access control for the members of a class, so the class designer can provide separate interfaces for the clients of a class and for its subclasses. Protected members are accessible to designers of subclasses but not to clients, whereas private members are not accessible to either group.
- If necessary, the class designer can hide the implementation of a class from designers of subclasses by declaring it private, and providing a protected protocol for their use.
- A private base class member is not accessible in a derived class, but it is visible in the derived class scope in the sense that it hides declarations of that name in scopes that enclose the base class scope.
- Friends of a base class are not friends of its derived classes, and vice versa.
- A derived class definition gives an access specification for each base class. Within the derived class, inherited members have the more restricted of the access specifications of the member definition and the derivation.
- You should use public derivation because it correctly reflects the specialization relationship, although it is not the default.

12.5.2 Inheritance and Static Typing

Language design issues

- Inheritance enables polymorphism and dynamic method binding for a statically typed language. Static typing with inheritance is an intermediate stage between monomorphic static typing and the unrestricted polymorphism of dynamic typing. However, there is an inherent tension between the safety and run-time efficiency of static typing, and the polymorphism necessary for object-oriented programming.
- With static typing, the compiler can perform type checking, restrict the objects bound to an identifier according to the semantics specified by the programmer, and translate messages sent to instances of non-polymorphic classes as statically bound function calls. However, a statically typed language provides less flexibility, especially in exploratory programming, because the programmer must choose a type for each identifier, and cannot send messages to the referent of the identifier that are not in the protocol of the identifier type.

Identifier polymorphism

- An instance of a derived class is polymorphic because it is an instance of each of its class's ancestors, and inherits the member functions and data members of each ancestor. A derived class object can function correctly in any context that requires a base class object.

- An identifier whose type is a class with subclasses is polymorphic because it can refer to an instance of any descendant of its type, due to the semantics of inheritance. The type of the referent, the *dynamic class*, may differ from the type of the identifier, the *static class*. The compiler might not know the exact type of the referent of an ancestor identifier because it can depend on run-time conditions.

- Instances of built-in types or classes without superclasses are not polymorphic. Identifiers whose type is a built-in type or a class without subclasses cannot be polymorphic.

- To avoid the overhead of run-time type checking, the type of the right side of an assignment must be the class of the target identifier or a descendant of that class.

- C++ supports both static binding, in which the method search begins in the class of the identifier, and dynamic binding according to the class of its referent (for virtual member functions only).

- Static binding is the default because it is more efficient, and a statically bound message send has the same cost as a function invocation. However, static binding inhibits extendibility because it requires modifying code when adding subclasses.

- Because the compiler does not know the exact type of the referent of a polymorphic identifier, it only permits messages in the class of the identifier and assignments from the identifier to identifiers of its class.

Storage allocation for value identifiers

- When a derived class adds data members, its instances are larger than those of its base class, and there are different-sized objects that are type compatible.

- In other statically typed object-oriented languages, all identifiers of class type are references, and all class instances are created dynamically. C++ supports value representation of class type identifiers because it provides more efficient allocation and access of an object's components.

- The storage allocated for a static or automatic identifier or for a value parameter or data member is the requirement of the class of the identifier.

- An assignment to a value identifier from a descendant instance is allowed, but it loses descendant-specific data members because there is no storage for them in the target object. This information loss does not occur for pointer or reference assignments, so initialization, assignment, parameter passing, and polymorphic operations have different semantics for value and pointer identifiers.

- Because identifier polymorphism is only possible for pointers and references, you should always define variables, data members, parameters, and collection elements of ancestor class type as pointers or references.

Class hierarchy type conversions

- A class inherits the data members of each of its ancestors, so we can convert an object to an instance of any of its public ancestors. The resulting object is created by applying the ancestor copy constructor to the object's inherited members.

- The conversion to an ancestor type is also valid for pointer and reference identifiers, and does not affect the referent object.

- When performed implicitly by the compiler, the conversion to an ancestor is a standard conversion, preferred over programmer-defined conversions in argument matching.

- Outward conversions are inherited by descendants, including ancestor conversion operators and constructors for classes that take an ancestor parameter. Like constructors, inward conversions are not inherited because the resulting descendant object may not be completely defined. The class designer can supply a conversion from ancestor to descendant, if necessary.

- Occasionally, the programmer needs to cast an ancestor pointer to a descendant type when he or she knows that the referent is a descendant object and wants to send it descendant messages. You should use the dynamic cast operator for this if your compiler supports it.

- Although it seems reversed, the conversion from a pointer-to-ancestor member to a pointer-to-descendant member is valid.

The run-time type information facility

- The run-time type information facility supports class identity for referents of polymorphic identifiers and type information for polymorphic classes.

- Generally, you should avoid type dependencies in your code because they inhibit extendibility. However, there are situations such as derivations from classes for which the source is not available in which you may need to verify the class identity of the referent of a polymorphic pointer. The C++ run-time type information facility provides the dynamic cast operator for this purpose.

- The dynamic cast operator converts its operand to the indicated class if the referent of the pointer is an instance of that class, or to NULL if it is not.

- The type_info class supports a limited but extendible representation of type information for classes. Applying the typeid operator to an object or a type name returns a reference to the type_info object that represents its class. We cannot use a type_info object as a class name.

12.5.3 Dynamic Binding

Virtual member functions

- Static binding is the default because it is more efficient, so we must indicate when dynamic binding is necessary for a member function by declaring it as virtual.
- Invocations of a *virtual member function* are dynamically bound for instances of the class and its descendants. The class that first introduces a virtual member function must either define it or specify it as an abstract message.
- The language only provides dynamic binding through the receiver of a message, so file scope functions and static member functions cannot be declared virtual. However, the compiler does use dynamic binding for virtual function invocations through polymorphic pointers or references within those functions.
- The compiler translates a virtual member function call statically for invocations through value identifiers, invocations that use a qualified name, and invocations within a constructor or destructor.

Method overriding

- If a member function is overridden, the class designer must specify it as virtual in the highest ancestor in the class hierarchy that defines it. In this way, the method executed is determined by the object's class, rather than by the class of the pointer or reference the message expression uses.
- You must specify as virtual every member function that might require a class-specific implementation in some descendant.
- An overriding of a virtual function must have the same argument signature as that in the ancestor that defined it to allow dynamic binding. The only exception is that a virtual function that returns a pointer or reference to the ancestor can return a pointer or reference to the descendant in the descendant definition.
- Because the compiler enforces access control on the basis of the identifier type, you should use the same access specification for each definition of a virtual member function.

Virtual destructors and copying

- An object can be deallocated through a pointer of ancestor type, so the class designer can specify a destructor as virtual. In this way, an object is finalized correctly, irrespective of the type of the pointer used in the deallocation operation.
- There is no analogous virtual constructor, although we can supply dynamically bound copying via a virtual member function.

Abstract classes and pure virtual functions

- In C++, an abstract message is referred to as a *pure virtual function*, and is specified by following a virtual member function declaration with =0 in the class definition.

- If a class defines or inherits pure virtual functions, it is an abstract class and instantiation of the class is an error. Pointers and references of that type can be defined, and these can refer to instances of any of the class's concrete descendants.
- A descendant class that defines methods for all inherited pure virtual functions is a concrete class that can be instantiated.
- Abstract classes often define methods that provide higher-level algorithms, which invoke descendant-specific operations via dynamic binding, and these member functions need not be virtual in C++.

Implementation of dynamic binding

- To provide dynamic binding, the compiler builds a table of pointers to the methods for dynamically bound member function for each polymorphic class, termed the class's vtbl. Each instance of a polymorphic class contains a pointer to its class's vtbl, which is called its vptr. These correspond to the class object and the class pointer in Smalltalk, respectively.
- Classes without virtual functions and built-in types do not have vtbls, and their instances do not have vptrs.
- Because the compiler has the definitions of a class's ancestors and knows every function that requires dynamic binding, it can install every entry in a class's vtbl when the class is defined. Method pointers are identified by indices and vtbls do not require a "superclass" pointer, so no search of the vtbl or of ancestor vtbls is necessary for dynamic binding.
- The compiler translates a virtual function invocation with code that dereferences the receiver's vptr, indexes into its class's vtbl, dereferences the result, and invokes that function. This procedure will select the correct method for any object, even for instances of classes that are added to the application later.
- We must specify an overridden member function as virtual in the root class of the subhierarchy that defines it so that the vtbl of each class in that subhierarchy includes an entry for that member function.

12.5.4 Multiple Inheritance

Basic concepts

- To represent multiple specialization relationships, we can specify a list of base classes from which the class inherits members. The inherited protocol of the class is the union of the protocols of its base classes, and its instances contain an embedded instance of each base class (and of each ancestor). The class may also define additional data members and member functions and override inherited methods.
- With multiple inheritance, the inheritance and scope structure of the application or class library is a directed acyclic graph.

- The language provides standard conversions from a class to any of its public ancestors. A pointer conversion may change the value of the pointer to refer to the correct subobject.
- If more than one base class defines virtual functions, instances of the class contain more than one vptr, one in each embedded base class object.
- To implement dynamic binding with multiple inheritance, a class's vtbl also includes an offset associated with each method pointer to adjust the this pointer so that it refers to the subobject corresponding to the ancestor whose method the class uses.

Name conflicts

- With multiple inheritance, a class can inherit a member with the same name from more than one base class. If the multiply-inherited member is a data member or a member function for which both argument signatures are the same, a name conflict occurs (even if one of the members is private).
- If inherited member names conflict, the class's methods must use the scope operator and a base class name to indicate which member is intended. If the member is public, clients of the class must also use a qualified name.
- If a multiply-inherited name is a member function and the argument signatures in the base classes differ, then that name is overloaded in the derived class scope. The argument signature of a message expression selects the inherited member function to invoke.

Repeated inheritance and virtual base classes

- When a class is an ancestor of another along more than one path in the inheritance graph, instances of the descendant contain more than one embedded instance of that ancestor. Nonstatic member names inherited from the repeated ancestor are ambiguous in the descendant. A data member name is ambiguous because it could refer to that member in any embedded subobject, and a member function name is ambiguous because any embedded subobject could be the receiver of the message.
- With nonvirtual repeated inheritance, both descendant methods and client code must qualify ancestor member names with the name of a direct base class (not with the name of the ancestor). Direct conversions from the descendant to the ancestor are also ambiguous. Unqualified references to ancestor static members are not ambiguous.
- To specify that a class's instances should include only one instance of a repeated ancestor, use virtual derivation in the base classes derived from the ancestor. For example, the classes ostream, istream, fstreambase and strstreambase specify ios as a virtual base class so that all stream objects have exactly one state descriptor.
- When a base class is virtual, derived class methods access its data members indirectly (although this is not reflected in the method code). In this way, two

classes that have the same virtual base class that are both base classes of a descendant share the same ancestor subobject in instances of the descendant.

- With virtual derivation, unqualified references to nonstatic members of the repeated ancestor in descendant methods or client code are not ambiguous.
- If a virtual member function in the repeated ancestor is overridden in an ancestor lower in the hierarchy above the descendant, the definition in the lower ancestor *dominates* in the descendant class. That method is invoked for descendant class instances, no matter what pointer type is used in the message expression.
- With virtual derivation, the descendant constructor initialization list provides an initializer for the repeated ancestor. When a descendant object is created, the embedded ancestor object is initialized once, and the ancestor initializations in the base class constructors are not performed.

12.6 EXERCISES

12.1 Recall the class IndexedFile described in exercise 11.44. Why didn't we derive the class from fstream?

12.2 Recall the class PriorityQueue defined in section 12.1.1.
  (a) Redefine the class such that the comparison function is defined as a file scope function, for example, for a String element type.
  (b) Under what conditions would it be possible to use both the class you defined in part (a) and the PriorityQueue class defined in section 12.1.1 in the same program?

12.3 Suppose we decide to allow a client to change the comparison function for an existing instance of the class PriorityQueue defined in section 12.1.1 (i.e., as we can change the sort block for an instance of the Smalltalk system class SortedCollection). Define member functions for the class PriorityQueue that query and set the comparison function.

12.4 Many caching applications maintain a list of accessed items and choose the least recently used item for replacement. To keep track of the items, we need a collection into which a client can insert elements. Upon removing an element, the collection returns the least recently used element. We can use a queue of elements for which the front element is removed as usual, and an element is inserted at the rear if it is not already in the queue. If the element to be inserted is already in the queue, it is now the most recently entered so it is pushed to the rear (and not inserted again). Code the class LRUQueue ("least recently used" queue) as a subclass of the class Queue described in sections 10.1.3 and 10.1.4.

12.5 **(a)** Recall the class List defined in exercise 10.41. Define a derived class for a PositionableList that provides the protocol described in section 3.2.2. Recall from section 3.2.4 that List::remove() must be refined, as must List::move(). Define the class for both implementations of List described in exercise 10.41.
  (b) Are any changes to the class List necessary to define PositionableList as a subclass? If so, what are they?
  (c) The class PositionableList could also be defined using a List* data member (like the Smalltalk stream classes). Compare the characteristics of this definition with the definition of PositionableList as a derived class.

12.6 Recall the class Clock defined in exercice 11.16. We want to derive a class AlarmClock that also maintains a list of alarms. Each alarm is represented by a Clock object that indicates the time at which it should occur, and a pointer to a file scope function with no parameters or return value, which is invoked when the receiver is set to the associated time. There can be more than one alarm at a given time. The methods for AlarmClock::operator++() and AlarmClock::reset() must invoke any alarm functions when the associated time occurs. We will also need the member functions addAlarm(const Clock&, void (*) ()) and deleteAlarm(const Clock&). The latter removes all alarms at that time, and an alarm remains active until it is deleted. An AlarmClock object is initialized in the same manner as a Clock object, or may be initialized with a Clock object. In any case, the alarm list is initially empty.

To implement the alarms, we use a nested class AlarmClock::Alarm that maintains the alarm time and the associated function. To implement the alarm list, we can use a PriorityQueue data member; an alarm is only invoked when the clock has been incremented to that value, so we use typedef AlarmClock::Alarm ElemType; in Queue.h. You will have to add the function PriorityQueue:: remove-(const ElemType&) as described in section 12.1.3. Unfortunately, we notice that there is a problem due to the "wrap-around" of elapsed seconds. We deal with this by using two priority queue data members, one for alarms for "today" (i.e., with times between the current time and 24*60*60-1), and the other for alarms for "tomorrow" (i.e., with times between 0 and the current time). We must also make the tomorrow queue today's and vice versa when the elapsed time turns over upon incrementing the clock, which can be done more efficiently if we use pointer data members and allocate the priority queues on the heap.

(a) What changes must be made to the definition of the class Clock, and why?

(b) What member functions must AlarmClock::Alarm define to be used with the modified PriorityQueue class? Define these functions.

(c) Code the class AlarmClock with the required constructors and destructor, and the member functions AlarmClock::addAlarm() and AlarmClock::delete-Alarm(), AlarmClock::operator++(), and AlarmClock::reset().

12.7 Why is it invalid for a class to appear twice on another class's derivation list?

12.8 **(a)** Explain why a class does not inherit its base class's constructors.

(b) Is it accurate to say that a class inherits its base class's destructor? Explain your answer.

12.9 Why is it incorrect to specify initialization for inherited data members on the initialization list of a derived class?

12.10 Suppose that we have a class Rectangle with two data members origin_ and corner_ of type Point. Consider the following class definition:

```
class FilledRectangle : public Rectangle
{
public:
    FilledRectangle(const Rectangle& rect, const Color& color);
    FilledRectangle(const Point& origin, const Point& corner,
        const Color& color);
    FilledRectangle(int x, int y, int width, int height, const Color& color);
    // ... other member functions ...
protected:
    Color color_;
};
```

Code the constructors for the class FilledRectangle.

12.11 Suppose that a class has base classes and class type data members, and that its base classes have base classes and class type data members. Describe the order in which those classes' constructors are invoked in initializing an instance of the class.

12.12 Is it necessary to code a copy constructor and assignment operator for the class PriorityQueue defined in section 12.1.1? Explain your answer.

12.13 Recall the class PositionableList defined in exercise 12.5. Suppose we wish to set the position reference to "invalid" (i.e. "off the end") in a new instance of PositionableList created by copying an existing instance. Code the copy constructor and assignment operator for the class PositionableList such that they have this behavior. Define the member functions for both implementations of List described in exercise 10.41.

12.14 Code the copy constructor and the assignment operator for the class AlarmClock defined in exercise 12.6.

12.15 Why is the scope of a derived class regarded as nested within the scope of its base class?

12.16 Suppose that a derived class wants to define an additional argument signature for an inherited member function. How does it do so?

12.17 Both derived class and nested class scopes are nested within another class scope. In what ways are derived classes and nested classes similar? In what ways are derived class and nested classes different?

12.18 Discuss the issues involved in deciding whether to define the auxiliary methods and storage structure of a class as protected or private.

12.19 Suppose a class Derived is intended to be a restriction of a class Base in the sense that the class designer does not want to include the public message Base::msg() in the protocol of Derived. Is it sufficient to redefine that message in Derived with a nonpublic method that does nothing to prevent its use with Derived objects?

12.20 Why can't derived class methods access protected members in base class objects?

12.21 Why do you think that C++ supports protected and private inheritance (no other object-oriented languages do)?

12.22 Discuss the advantages and disadvantages of employing static typing and inheritance rather than dynamic typing in an object-oriented language.

12.23 Recall the class LRUQueue defined in exercise 12.4. Explain why the last assignment in the following code is invalid. (Give a specific explanation that deals with the classes involved, not a general explanation.)

```
#include "Queue.h"
#include "LRUQueue.h"
int main()
{
    LRUQueue* pLRUQueue = new LRUQueue;
    Queue qu = *pLRUQueue;
    // ... operations using *pLRUQueue and qu ...
    *pLRUQueue = qu;     // error: why?
}
```

12.24 How do identifier semantics and object allocation policies differ in C++ from other statically typed object-oriented languages?

12.25 **(a)** In Java, all identifiers of class type are implicitly references, as in Smalltalk. Give an advantage and a disadvantage of this design decision.
(b) A Java class can be designated as final, which specifies that it cannot have subclasses. Describe optimizations that the translator can perform for final classes.

12.26 Give three reasons why parameters of class type should never be passed by value.

12.27 (a) Why must a collection class whose element type is a polymorphic class use a pointer as the type of the elements?

(b) Discuss whether a collection of polymorphic elements should copy an element upon insertion or just keep a pointer to the existing object. (Consider copying and destroying the collection, object identity, and insertion of static and automatic objects.)

(c) For each of the alternatives in part (b), write the documentation for the collection class that informs clients of the class's semantics.

12.28 Is the following statement true or false? "A derived class pointer can be implicitly converted to a base class pointer but it cannot refer to a base class object."

12.29 Why is the conversion from Derived** to Base** invalid in C++ even though the conversion from Derived* to Base* is a predefined standard conversion?

12.30 Suppose we have the following declarations of the file scope function invite(). Which function is invoked for the two calls in the following code? Why?

```
#include "Person.h"
#include "Employee.h"
void invite(const Person&);
void invite(const Employee&);
int main()
{
    Employee* pEmpl = new Employee(...);
    Person* pPers = pEmpl;
    invite(*pEmpl);
    invite(*pPers);
}
```

12.31 Which conversions are inherited and which are not? Explain your answer.

12.32 Explain why conversion of a pointer to member to a pointer to ancestor member is not safe. Consider both pointers to member functions and pointers to data members.

12.33 Describe the purpose and meaning of each of the features provided by the run-time type information facility.

12.34 (a) Why does C++ support both static and dynamic binding?

(b) Why must a C++ programmer indicate when a function requires dynamic binding (as opposed to other object-oriented languages in which it is not necessary)?

(c) Why must a virtual member function be defined in the class that introduces it?

12.35 Suppose that two classes define the same member function with the same argument signature. What is required so that invocations of that member function with instances of the classes can be dynamically bound?

12.36 Describe the circumstances in which a virtual function invocation is statically bound.

12.37 (a) Why must all overridden member functions be declared as virtual?

(b) Why must an overriding of a virtual function have the same argument signature as that in the ancestor that defined the function?

(c) Why should all overridings of a member function have the same access specification?

12.38 Name three aspects of the definition of a C++ class that the class designer must be concerned with if the class is to be used for derivation, but would not be issues for a class used only as an abstract data type. Describe the issues involved for each.

12.39 In exercise 12.5, we derived a class PositionableList from the class List defined in exercise 10.41. As we stated, the method for List::remove() must be refined to set the position reference to its successor if the current element is removed. In this exercise, we will consider what must be done if List::remove() is not virtual and the source code for List is not available. A List* pointer pList can refer to either an instance of List or PositionableList, but List::remove() will always be called for the expression pList->remove(obj) because it is not virtual. We must assume that we have determined whether List uses a linked list or a dynamic array.

    (a) If each list member function is defined in a different code file, we can recode and recompile List::remove() such that it uses a dynamic cast to determine the class of the receiver, and then performs the appropriate processing. Code this member function.

    (b) If it is not possible to recompile List::remove(), each time the message remove() is sent through a List*, the client must check whether the referent is an instance of List or PositionableList, and then perform the appropriate processing. Can you think of a technique that encapsulates the test and the required processing so that it can be defined once?

    (c) What other changes may be necessary in the library code if the derived class PositionableList is added?

    (d) Will you ever buy a C++ class library without source code?

12.40 Are there base classes whose destructors do not have to be virtual? Explain your answer.

12.41 Recall the classes Set described in exercises 10.40 and 11.8, List described in exercises 10.41 and 11.9, and SortedList described in exercises 10.42 and 11.10. Assume that the collection class is defined such that the element type is a pointer so that instances of polymorphic classes can be stored in the collection.

    (a) Code a deepCopy() method for any implementation of each collection class that assumes that the referent of the element type implements a dynamic copy() message as illustrated in section 12.3.3.

    (b) Should the copy constructor for these classes perform a shallow copy or a deep copy?

12.42 **(a)** Code the class PriorityQueue defined in section 12.1.1 as a subclass of the class AbstractQueue described in section 12.3.4.

    (b) Code the class LRUQueue described in exercise 12.4 as a subclass of the class AbstractQueue described in section 12.3.4.

    (c) Can we define a copy constructor and assignment operator in AbstractQueue for the use of its descendants?

12.43 Recall the classes Set described in exercises 10.40 and 11.8, List described in exercises 10.41 and 11.9, and SortedList described in exercises 10.42 and 11.10. Give the definition of an abstract class Collection that encapsulates the common protocol of those classes. You may include the message Collection::insert() which will be defined as insertFirst() in List. You may also include the message Collection::isSubcollection() rather than using SortedList::isSublist(), List::isSublist(), and Set::isSubset(). Messages that take parameters of the type of the receiver can take parameters of type Collection.

12.44 Again, consider the concrete classes Set, List, SortedList, and the abstract superclass Collection described in the previous exercise. Suppose that we have decided to implement all three concrete subclasses using a linked list with front and back pointers and a data member giving the number of elements. We will also define a nested class Collection::Node like that described in section 10.3.4.

    (a) Give the definition of the abstract class Collection that encapsulates the common protocol and storage structure of those classes.

(b) We would like to define as many methods in Collection as possible. Which member functions can we define in Collection and which Collection member functions must be pure virtual functions? Define the methods for the former. You may also define any protected member functions that aid in the implementation of the member functions, for example Node* Collection::findPredecessor(const ElemType&). (Read parts (c), (d), (e), and (f) of this problem before you begin.)

(c) In coding part (b), we notice that there are methods that are the same for two of the three concrete subclasses, for example, we can use the same method for insert() for List and Set, but not for SortedList. There are two different ways of handling this situation, one using a virtual member function in Collection, and the other using a pure virtual member function. Describe and code both techniques for insert() for the abstract class and the three concrete subclasses.

(d) Two collections are equal if they are the same type and contain the same elements, which must be in the same order for List or SortedList. That is, the definitions of operator==() and operator!=() must use run-time type information facilities to check the types of the receiver and argument. Consider the discussion in part (c) and code both implementations of these operators.

(e) For Collection::isSubcollection(), a sorted list or list is a subcollection of a sorted list or list if the elements are present in the same order. A sorted list or list is a subcollection of a set if all its elements are in the set. A set cannot be a subcollection of a list or a sorted list because it is not ordered. Recall the discussion in part (c) and code both implementations of these operators.

(f) In coding part (b), we also notice that there are member functions such as Collection::operator+() and Collection::allSuchThat() that return a new collection. We cannot create an instance of the class Collection, so these methods should return an instance of the receiver's class. There are two solutions to this problem. We can code methods in each subclass that create an instance of that subclass and insert elements. Alternatively, we can use run-time type information facilities to select the class to be instantiated, and code the methods once in the superclass Collection using the pure virtual function insert(). Code both alternatives. Can a switch be avoided when coding the methods in the superclass? Which alternative do you prefer? (In deciding, consider what is necessary if we add a new subclass of Collection, e.g., Array.)

(g) Define the concrete subclasses of Collection and their methods.

12.45 Redo exercise 12.44 using the same storage structure as the Smalltalk classes OrderedCollection and SortedCollection—a dynamic array with data members indicating the firstIndex and lastIndex.

12.46 Would exercises 12.44 and 12.45 be simplified if we defined an abstract subclass SequencedCollection of Collection that has the subclasses SortedList and List (e.g., consider 12.44(d) and 12.44(e))? Recode the subhierarchy in this way.

12.47 Again, consider the concrete classes SortedList, List, Set, and the abstract superclass Collection described in the previous three exercises. We discussed a number of storage structures for each of the concrete classes. Suppose that we want to define the abstract superclass Collection without specifying any storage structure, for example, so that Set can be implemented using a binary search tree or a hash table. We would still like to define some of the methods in the superclass.

(a) If we define a protected pure virtual function in Collection that can be used to enumerate the elements in a collection, which member functions in Collection can we define by methods that call this function and other pure virtual functions? Define those methods.

(b) Choose an implementation for each concrete subclass of Collection and define the classes and their methods for your definition of Collection in part (a).

12.48 In exercise 10.40, we presented six storage structures for a class Set, each with its own access, insertion, and deletion characteristics. Discuss whether we should define an abstract class AbstractSet with each of the implementations defined as a concrete subclass. (A simpler version of this exercise is to consider a class AbstractList with subclasses LinkedList and SequentialList.)

12.49 Explain why it is necessary to use the dynamic cast operator in concrete subclasses of the class Orderable defined in section 12.3.4.

12.50 Give two ways in which method binding is more efficient in C++ than in Smalltalk. Explain why these techniques can be used.

12.51 Describe how dynamic binding of virtual functions is implemented in C++ for single inheritance.

12.52 **(a)** Describe an implementation for the typeid operator and type_info references. Recall that the operator can be applied to either a type name or an expression, and that equality and inequality comparisons and class names are the only messages provided. (Hint: Use the vtbls.)

(b) Can the structures you designed in part (a) be used to implement the dynamic cast operator as well? If not, what else is necessary?

(c) Is it possible to omit the information described in part (a) for programs that do not use those facilities? If so, when can this decision be made?

(d) Suppose that we want to overload operator<() for the class type_info to return true if its left operand represents a class that is an ancestor of the class represented by its right operand. Sketch an implementation of this capability.

12.53 Describe the issues that arise with multiple inheritance that do not occur with single inheritance. How is each handled in C++?

12.54 Consider the following class hierarchy and conversions and declarations for the overloaded function func(). Which definition of func() is called for each of the invocations in main()? If a call is ambiguous, indicate which declarations match. A call may also be in error because none match.

```
class D { /* ... members ... */ };
class A { /* ... members ... */ };
class B : public A
{
public:
    B(const A&);
    //... other members ...
};
class C : public A, public D
{
public:
    C(const B&);
    //... other members ...
};
void func(const A&, const B&);
void func(const A&, const D&);
void func(const B&, const D&);
```

```
void func(const D&, const D&);
void func(const B&, const C&);
int main()
{
    A a(...);
    B b(...);
    C c(...);
    D d(...);
    // which definition of func() is invoked for each?
    func(b, b);
    func(c, d);
    func(d, b);
    func(a, a);
    func(b, d);
    func(a, c);
}
```

12.55 **(a)** What is the meaning of the virtual base class specification?

   (b) Suppose you are designing the class Derived, which inherits from Base. How do you decide whether to use virtual derivation for Base?

12.56 Suppose that we have defined a class hierarchy that does not use virtual derivation, and have written some portion of an application that uses that library. We then discover that we must create a class that has a repeated ancestor, but we want its instances to contain one copy of the repeated ancestor. Describe what must be done and why it must be done.

13

Templates, Exceptions, and Namespaces

In this chapter, we will discuss three major extensions to C++ that were introduced after the language had been in use for some time.[1] Each of these features is provided specifically to aid in handling situations that occur in large-scale development projects. The template extension supports type parameterization for function and class definitions, which enables reuse of code in a way that is safer and more convenient than using preprocessor macros or inheritance and casting. The exception facility supports signaling, defining, and handling exceptions. It implements safe error propagation, provides for transferring information from the signaler to the handler, and performs finalization of environments that are exited while locating the correct handler. Namespaces provide a construct for reducing name conflicts in the global name space, especially of the names of classes supplied by different libraries used in a project.

This chapter covers the following topics:

- the motivation for templates, and type parameters (13.1.1)
- definition of function templates (13.1.2)
- instantiation of function templates and invoking template functions (13.1.3)
- scope with function templates (13.1.4).

---

[1] In fact, templates and exceptions were part of Stroustrup's original conception of the language, but were not supported until later due to the complexity of implementing them [Str94].

- implementation of templates and how support for templates affects compiling and linking (13.1.5)
- issues for the type of a collection element (13.2.1)
- creation of type-independent collection classes without templates (13.2.2)
- definition of class templates and member function templates (13.2.3)
- instantiation and use of class templates (13.2.4)
- scope with class templates (13.2.5)
- inheritance and templates (13.2.6)
- error handling and error propagation in C, and the motivation for exceptions (13.3.1)
- signaling exceptions (13.3.2)
- definition of exception classes (13.3.3)
- handling exceptions (13.3.4)
- propagation of exceptions and environment finalization (13.3.5)
- the motivation for namespaces (13.4.1)
- definition of namespaces (13.4.2)
- access and importing the identifiers declared in a namespace (13.4.3)

13.1 FUNCTION TEMPLATES

13.1.1 Introduction

Motivation

Many common algorithms, such as sorting an array or searching a particular data structure, are the same irrespective of the types of the elements of those structures. However, in a statically typed language, the function that sorts an array of integers must be a different function from the function that sorts an array of dates, even though each definition has the same body. In a language that supports overloading, those functions may have the same name, but each must still be defined separately. In C, we can use preprocessor macros to obtain the effect of having several such functions that only differ in their parameter types without giving a separate definition for every possible type. However, as we saw in section 9.2.3, macros do not provide type checking for arguments or correct name resolution for nonlocal identifiers, and problems can occur with argument expressions that cause side effects.

We would like a language construct that allows us to define the code for such a function once without having to specify the types of its parameters beforehand. When we invoke the function, we specify the parameter types or the compiler deduces them by matching the argument signature of the call. The compiler then generates and compiles a function definition with those parameter types. For example, in section 9.2.3, we defined a function min() that returns the minimum of its two arguments. We would like the compiler to do the following:

```
// suppose that Type& min(const Type&, const Type&) is defined for any Type
// (this construct is described in the next section)
int main()
{
    double dbl = 5.0;
    String str1("hello");
    String str2("world");
    // double& min(const double&, const double&) created for this call
    double mn = min(dbl, -4.0);
    // String& min(const String&, const String&) created for this call
    str1 = min(str1, str2);
}
```

Function templates provide this capability.

Type parameters

As we have discussed in sections 10.1.1 and 12.2.5, types are not first-class objects in C++, the language supports very few operations on types,[2] and there is no metatype that allows a class object to be a variable value or function argument as in Smalltalk. However, the language does provide function and class "templates", which allow us to write code that is parameterized for the type of a function parameter or collection element. A *type parameter* is an identifier whose "value" is an actual type when we use the template that defines the type parameter.[3] That is, that identifier stands for a type in the same manner that a function parameter stands for an object, namely as the argument passed in an invocation. The type bound to a type parameter when we use its template can be either a class or a built-in type.

The C++ template constructs that include type parameters are fundamentally different from other language components because they do not define a class, function, or object. In fact, translating a template definition does not generate any object code. Instead, the construct defines a "template" that the compiler can use to generate a function or class definition when the programmer uses that name. The compiler creates this definition by substituting an actual type for occurrences of the type parameter in the template definition, and then compiling this result into object code. The type parameter list of a template definition is enclosed in angle brackets (i.e., < and >) rather than parentheses to highlight this difference.

Development of the template facility

As stated in the introduction to Part III of the text, the first precise language standard for C++ was the Annotated C++ Reference Manual [Ell90], commonly called the "ARM". It defined a somewhat restricted template facility because the

---

[2] sizeof is supported for types as in C, and the run-time type information facility provides safe downcasts, the typeid operator, and type_info messages for polymorphic classes.

[3] The concept of type parameters is the same as that for generic packages in Ada.

language designers did not yet have a great deal of experience implementing and using templates (nor did designers of other languages). They did not want to include features that would turn out to be difficult or inefficient to implement, or that would complicate using and implementing other language features. (It is much easier to add constructs to a language than to remove them.) As the ANSI/ISO standardization process progressed, several features were proposed and implemented that provided new capabilities or additional convenience in using the facility, and other features were refined. Unfortunately, language systems vary considerably with respect to their support for these features. In discussing templates, we will indicate which capabilities are newer features that your compiler may not provide. You should check the documentation for your language system to clarify this issue.

13.1.2 Definition

A *function template* is a construct that allows us to define a function body, and to parameterize the types of any subset of a function's argument signature (including the return type). A function template specifies, but does not define, an unlimited set of overloaded functions referred to as *template functions*. Each of these functions has the same definition, except for the actual types that are substituted for the type parameters in the function template. The functions that will be generated from a function template for an application (or even the number of such functions) is not known at the point at which the template is defined. In this section, we will discuss function templates for file scope functions. As we will see in section 13.2, we can also define class templates and member function templates.

A function template can only be defined at file scope. A function template definition is introduced by the reserved word **template** and a non-empty type parameter list enclosed in angle brackets. In that list, each type parameter name must be unique and each preceded by the keyword **class**. The type parameter list is followed by a function definition that uses the type parameters as type names. The general format of a function template definition appears as follows:

```
// format for a function template definition
template <class Type1, class Type2, ...>
RetType function( ..., Type1 arg1, ..., Type2 arg2, ... )
{ ... function code ... }
```

The identifiers *Type1*, *Type2*, etc. are type parameters, and may be used in any context within the function body in which a type name can appear. Those identifiers are local to the function template definition, and they hide file scope definitions of those names within the template. Type parameter names cannot be redeclared within the template definition. Although the syntax uses the reserved word **class**, a type parameter may be bound to a built-in type, a programmer-defined class, or a derived type such as a pointer or const type.[4] If the function template definition requires the reserved words inline or static, they appear before the function declaration, rather than before the template reserved word or the type parameter list.

In the version of the template facility described in the ARM, each type parameter name must appear as a type in the argument signature of the function, and a type parameter used as the function's return type must also appear as the type of a function parameter. The compiler determines binding for each type parameter in a particular invocation of that function name by the type of the corresponding argument. As we will see in the next section, a recent extension to the template facility allows the programmer to explicitly provide bindings for function template type parameters in an invocation. The restrictions stated in the ARM does not hold for compilers that support this capability.

The following is an example function template definition:

```
// a function template for functions that return the minimum of their two arguments
template <class Type>
inline Type& min(const Type& arg1, const Type& arg2)
{
    return arg1 < arg2 ? arg1 : arg2;
}
```

If we also defined operator<=(), operator>(), max(), between(), and so on as function templates that invoke operator<() and operator==(), the abstract class Orderable described in section 12.3.4 would not be necessary. The template alternative allows using file scope and member function overloadings of operator<() and built-in type comparisons. It also enforces the compile-time constraint that both operands must be instances of the same class, although we must use the file scope invocation syntax with the functions min(), max(), and between(). In fact, the new C++ Standard Library includes a function template that defines the != operator in terms of ==, and templates that define the >, <=, and >= operators in terms of <. For example,

```
// a function template from the C++ Standard Library
template <class Type>
inline bool operator>(const Type& lhs, const Type& rhs)
{
    return rhs < lhs;
}
```

These templates are defined in the header <utility>.

A function template declaration includes the template reserved word, the type parameter list, and the function declaration, as follows:

---

[4] A reserved word is necessary to identify type parameters in the template's parameter list because a template can also specify nontype parameters (see section 13.2.4). The language uses the identifier class so that it does not require an additional reserved word for this purpose, such as type.

```
// a function template declaration
template <class Type>
Type& min(const Type&, const Type&);
```

A function template name can be overloaded with other function templates (and also non-template functions) if the compiler can distinguish the argument signature of each definition by the number or types of type parameters. For example, we can define an overloading of the min() function template in which the first function parameter is an array, name and the second gives the size of the array, as follows:

```
// a function template for functions that return the minimum of a C array
template <class ElemType>
ElemType min(const ElemType array[], int size)
{
    ElemType minElem(array[0]);
    for ( int index = 1;  index < size;  ++index )
        if ( array[index] < minElem )
        minElem = array[index];
    return minElem;
}
```

Note the use of the type parameter as the type of a local variable. As with function overloading, we cannot define two overloadings of a function template whose argument signatures differ only in their return types.

A function template name can also be overloaded with template functions that specialize the template for a particular set of actual parameter types. For example, if we use the min() function template with C strings (i.e., with objects of type char*) as arguments, it uses the pointer meaning of the < operator. To handle this special case correctly, we can define the following overloading of min():[5]

```
// a function template specialization that returns the minimum of two C strings
#include <string.h>
const char* min<const char*>(const char* str1, const char* str2)
{
    return strcmp(str1, str2) < 0 ? str1 : str2;
}
```

As we will see in the next section, classes can be parameterized for types as well. For example, we can define a class template List<Type> for lists of elements of type Type. A type parameter of a function template can be bound by the type parameter of a template class used as an argument to the function. For example, suppose that the List<Type> class template defines the member functions List<Type>::size() and List<Type>::operator[](). We can define a function tem-

---

[5] The explicit specification of the type parameter bindings (i.e., min<const char*>) is a recent extension to the language. With earlier compilers, we would define this overloading as a nontemplate function named min.

plate for file scope functions that find the minimum of the elements of a list as follows:

```
// binding a function template type parameter by the type parameter of a
// template class argument
#include "List.h"
template <class ElemType>
ElemType min(const List<ElemType>& list)
{
    ElemType minElem(list[1]);
    for ( int index = 2;  index <= list.size();  ++index )
        if ( list[index] < minElem )
            minElem = list[index];
    return minElem;
}
```

The actual type bound to the parameter ElemType when this function is called will be the element type of the list object that is the argument in the invocation.

Recall that none of this complexity is necessary with dynamically typed languages such as Smalltalk.

13.1.3 Template Function Invocation

Instantiation

You must be clear on exactly what a function template definition represents. It does not define a function, but rather serves as a pattern that the compiler can use to create a function definition with a given set of actual types substituted for the type parameters. This process is referred to as *instantiation* of the template, and it is performed when the compiler encounters an invocation using the function template name.[6] The function template itself has no run-time representation other than the object code resulting from translation of the functions that the compiler generates from it. For example, the compiler creates four instantiations of various function templates when it translates the following code:

```
// instantiating function templates
template <class Type> Type& min(const Type&, const Type&);
template <class ElemType> ElemType min(const ElemType[], int);
#include "List.h"              // defines the class template List<>
template <class Type> Type min(const List<Type>&);
int main()
{
    int int1 = 1, int2 = 2;
    // the compiler creates the function int& min(const int&, const int&) { ... }
    // from the first min() template
```

---

[6] As we will discuss in section 13.1.5, exactly where and when the compiler generates the template function object code is complicated by linkage and efficiency issues.

```
    int1 = min(int1, int2);
    Date date1("1/1/90"), date2("5/1/90");
    // the compiler creates the function Date& min(const Date&, const Date&) { ... }
    // from the first min() template
    date1 = min(date1, date2);
    const char str[] = "hello";
    // the compiler creates the function char min(const char[], int) { ... }
    // from the second min() template
    char ch = min(str, 5);
    // the compiler creates the class List<double> from the class template in List.h
    List<double> listDbl;
    listDbl.insert(1.0).insert(2.0).insert(3.0);
    // the compiler creates the function double min(const List<double>&) { ... }
    // from the third min() template
    double least = min(listDbl);
}
```

To determine bindings for a template's type parameters, the compiler compares the type of each parameter in the function declaration with the type of the corresponding argument in the invocation. If a function parameter type is given by a type parameter, then that type parameter is bound to the type of the corresponding argument. In the previous example, the type parameter Type is bound to int in the first invocation, and to Date in the second. If a function parameter type is a derived type based on a type parameter, then equivalent type modifiers are removed from the function parameter type and the corresponding argument type to determine a match for the type parameter. For example, for the third invocation in the previous example, the const and [ ] type modifiers are removed from the type of the first function parameter and the corresponding argument type to bind ElemType to char. Once a type parameter is bound to an actual type from an argument in the invocation, arguments corresponding to any further occurrences of that type parameter name in the function's argument signature must match that same actual type (exactly, in the ARM definition of templates). The compiler then creates a function definition with the parameter types determined by this process, if one does not yet exist.

Specifying type parameter bindings

In the definition of the template facility in the ARM, the compiler must be able to deduce type parameter bindings from the argument types in the invocation. If it cannot, the call is an error. In addition, no conversions are performed for template function arguments. These characteristics simplified compiling and coding template function invocations, but forced programmers to use explicit conversions in many cases that were not inherently ambiguous. The language now includes a feature that allows us to explicitly specify the bindings for type parameters in a template function call. To do so, we give a list of actual types enclosed in angle brackets following the function name and preceding the argument list in an invocation.

For example, with this capability, we can code a template function invocation that requires conversions for argument types, as follows:

```
// the recent extension for specifying bindings for function template type parameters
template <class Type> Type& min(const Type&, const Type&);
int main()
{
    int num = 4;
    // OK: double& min(const double&, const double&) with conversion of num
    double mn = min<double>(3.3, num);
}
```

Without this feature, we would have had to code an explicit conversion of the second argument, that is, double(num).

Compilers that support giving type parameter bindings in an invocation also permit the programmer to define a function template with type parameters that do not appear in the function argument signature. An invocation must explicitly give bindings for those type parameters since the compiler cannot deduce them from a call. For example, an invocation can specify the return type of the instantiated template function. (In general, the compiler cannot deduce the return type from the expression that uses the conversion.) In fact, this syntax is identical to the use of dynamic_cast<Type*> in which the actual type Type* specifies the return type of the conversion. A template function invocation can also give fewer actual types than there are type parameters in the template if the compiler can determine bindings for the trailing type parameters from the argument types, like giving fewer arguments when calling a function with default parameter values.

The ANSI/ISO C++ Standard also permits giving default bindings for template type parameters, using the same syntax as for default function parameter values. The type parameter is followed by an = symbol and the name of the actual type that gives its default binding. For example,

```
// a function template with a default binding for the type parameter
template <class Type = double>
inline Type& min(const Type& arg1, const Type& arg2)
{
    return arg1 < arg2 ? arg1 : arg2;
}
```

Current compilers support these features to varying degrees.

Conversions and resolving overloadings

The rules for performing conversions and resolving an invocation of an overloaded function name with templates have also changed recently. The rules described in the ARM [Ell90] do not perform conversions in matching the type parameters of a function template. If a type parameter appears more than once in the function parameter list, each corresponding argument must be exactly the same type. Any nonparameterized types in the function parameter list, such as the second parameter of the array overloading of min(), must also match the argument type exactly. For example, the following call is an error with these rules:

```
// in the ARM language definition, no conversions are performed when matching
// template type parameters
template <class Type> Type& min(const Type&, const Type&);
int main()
{
    char ch = '3';
    // error: no promotions are allowed in the ARM language definition
    int mn = min(3, ch);
}
```

In the ARM Standard, trivial conversions are not applied either, although most language systems perform them. Without them, we would have to code two versions of the first min() template, one with value parameters and return type, and the other with reference parameters and return type. The value overloading would be used for any object accessed through a value parameter and would cause copying of the object. In fact, we would also need versions of each of these definitions with and without const. The array min() template would need overloadings with both Elem-Type[] and ElemType* (and with and without const!) for the first function parameter. The new language standards permit type conversions in matching function template invocations.

Many language systems still use the process described in the ARM for resolving an invocation of an overloaded function name with templates, which proceeds as follows. If there is a nontemplate function definition that matches the argument signature exactly, then that function is called. If there is no exact match or match involving a trivial conversion, function templates are examined (often with trivial conversions allowed). If no function template matches without conversions and the invocation has not been determined to be ambiguous, then nontemplate functions are checked with promotions and conversions as described in sections 9.2.4 and 11.2.3. We can summarize the conversion preferences for the ARM overloading resolution rules as follows:

1. an exact match or a match using a trivial conversion with a nontemplate function
2. an exact match with a function template (or possibly a trivial conversion)
3. a numeric promotion
4. a standard conversion
5. a programmer-defined conversion
6. matching an ellipsis.

The designers of the language recognized that these rules were too restrictive, especially as the standard derived to base conversion is not performed when matching template type parameters. For example, suppose that a class Base defines operator<() and has a subclass Derived. If bs is an instance of Base and der is an instance of Derived, the invocation min(bs, der) is an error. The ANSI/ISO C++ Standard states that the compiler should determine the set of function definitions including any template instantiations that could apply in an invocation, and then follow the overloading resolution rules given in section 9.2.4 among these (i.e., using the categories of preferences and the intersection rule). You should check the documentation for your compiler or programming environment to clarify what overloading resolution procedure it uses.

Errors upon template instantiation

Whenever a program uses a type name or an instance of the type, that context specifies certain operations that must be present for the type or its instances. This is true for type parameters in function template definitions as well. Suppose a template function definition sends messages to a type parameter instance or uses such an object as a function argument. If that message or function is not defined for the actual type bound to the type parameter, a syntax error results in the instantiated template function. Of course, such an error cannot be detected at the point at which the function template is defined.

For example, whatever class or type instantiates the type parameter Type in the first min() function template in the previous section must define operator<().[7] In the array overloading of the min() function template, the function code creates a copy of an instance of the type bound to the type parameter as a local variable and assigns objects to that variable. If the type bound to ElemType is a class that defines a nonpublic copy constructor or assignment operator, that instantiation fails. Similarly, if a type parameter is used with the scope operator or with multi-argument constructor syntax within a template, it cannot be bound to a built-in type or a pointer type.[8] Exactly how such an error is reported to the programmer depends on the language system, because the error occurs in a statement generated by the compiler.

There is no mechanism in C++ for enforcing such requirements for the type bound to a type parameter, other than compile-time type and syntax checks of the statements resulting from the template instantiation.[9] Any way of specifying that particular operation must be present, for a type can complicate the template syntax even more. The language Eiffel, which also supports type parameters, includes a feature for indicating that the types in an instantiation are restricted to a particular subhierarchy. For example, the programmer can specify that the type bound to the type parameter of min() must be a subclass of Orderable. This technique has not

---

[7] Recall that the function created from the template will work correctly whether operator<() for the actual type bound to Type is a file scope function, a member function, or a built-in type comparison.

[8] For this reason, initializations of built-in type instances may also use the C++ initializer syntax, for example, int num(1);.

[9] As discussed in section 13.1.5, these checks may not actually occur until link time if the template is defined in a different code file than the invocation.

been adopted for C++ because it might encourage programmers to use inheritance specifically to represent such constraints (which may not represent a specialization relationship), and because built-in types do not participate in the inheritance hierarchy in C++ [Str94].

13.1.4 Scope

A function template definition defines a scope nested within the file scope in which it is defined. Its type parameter names and the parameters and local variables of the associated function definition are local to this scope.

As discussed in section 9.2.3, nonlocal identifiers in macros are resolved according to dynamic scope because the macro is expanded at the point of invocation and the resulting code is compiled at that point. To ensure consistency and minimize confusion and surprises, nonlocal names in a template definition should be bound statically in the environment of the definition, rather than dynamically in the environment of the invocation. For example, if a function template uses a file scope variable, it should refer to the variable with that name in the file in which it is defined, not a variable with that name in the file in which it is called (as a macro would).

However, there are some nonlocal identifiers in a template definition whose bindings must depend on the actual type bound to a type parameter to provide the correct semantics. These include the names of messages passed to an instance of that type, and of any functions that include parameters of that type or of types to which it can be converted (e.g., its ancestors). For example, the definition of operator<() which is invoked in an instantiation of one of the min() function templates defined in section 13.1.2 must be the definition for the actual type bound to Type or ElemType. Therefore, the binding for that name must be determined according to the environment of the invocation. Only function names can depend on a type parameter, so the names of all nonlocal objects and types are bound at the point of the template definition.

The nonlocal identifiers in a template are divided into two categories, namely those that do not depend on a type parameter binding and those that do.[10] The former are bound at the point at which the template is defined, and the latter are bound according to the type parameter binding. When there is no declaration in the environment of the invocation for an identifier that depends on a type parameter name, then that template instantiation results in a syntax error, as described in the previous section.

13.1.5 Linkage and Templates

Creating an application's template functions

In order for the compiler to instantiate a function template, it must have the complete definition of the template, not just its declaration, because it needs the

---

[10] See [Str94] for a complete discussion of precisely which names depend on a type parameter.

function code. One possibility would be to #include the function template definition in every file that invokes that function—that is, to place the entire template definition in the header file. However, if an invocation of min() with Date arguments occurs in more than one code file in a program, then the compiler will create more than one Date& min(const Date&, const Date&) function, and the linkage step will fail due to the multiple definitions of that function. A simple solution would be for each function template instantiation to be static, as is done with inline functions and const static objects defined in header files. In this case, each definition would be local to a compilation unit, and the multiple definition error would not occur. Unfortunately, this would result in duplicating the function code in each object module that invokes that argument signature, which could increase the size of the executable considerably if the application uses numerous templates.[11]

We would like the executable for a program to contain one instantiation of a function template for each set of type parameter bindings the program uses. However, if two code files in a program are compiled at different times and both invoke min() with Date arguments, instantiation of the function template would have to be delayed until link time to prevent generating the function code twice. That is, the set of template instantiations required for a program can only be determined after the entire program has been compiled. Linking previously compiled code files could cause further compiling to be necessary, namely of template instantiations (and this compilation could result in syntax errors, as we discussed in section 13.1.3). After the template instantiations are generated and compiled, the object files are linked, possibly resulting in more compilation and so on. Note also that the compiler must be able to determine which source code files contain the necessary template definitions.

The difficulty here stems from the fact that templates are not like any other C or C++ construct. A function template definition is not source code to be translated into object code, so it is not like the function definitions that are usually contained in code files. Neither is a template definition a function or class interface that should be contained in a header file to be included and compiled in client code. The process of instantiation described in the previous paragraph is not possible with the simple C-style linkage model in which each code file is compiled independently and all interactions among the compilation units in a program are defined in terms of external symbols. In fact, it was the difficulty of efficiently implementing compilation and linkage with function templates that delayed incorporation of this feature into the language.

The responsibility for ensuring that there is only one instantiation of a template for a particular set of type parameter bindings can be handled either by the programmer or by the programming environment. To permit the former, the language must provide a feature that allows the programmer to specify that a template function definition with a given set of type parameter bindings should be created and compiled in a particular code file. It would then be the programmer's respon-

---

[11] This duplication of the code generated is also a drawback of the use of preprocessor macros.

sibility to decide which object file should contain each template instantiation necessary to avoid multiple instantiations and linker errors. Alternatively, the language system can maintain a database of template definitions and invocations so it can generate and link one copy of each template function needed by the application.

Explicit instantiation

A recent extension to the language allows the programmer to explicitly specify instantiation of a function template, as follows: [12]

```
// a programmer-specified function template instantiation
template String& min<String>(const String&, const String&);
```

The specified template function is then created and compiled in that code file. The file must contain the entire template definition (e.g., by including a header file) so that the compiler can create the instantiation. Note the syntactic difference between this "instantiation specification" and a function template declaration in which a type parameter list follows the keyword template. The language does not require the programmer to code an explicit instantiation, and it is not necessarily an error to specify the same template instantiation more than once in a program. [13] This feature is provided primarily to permit the efficient use of templates with simpler programming environments that do not automatically handle function template instantiations. It also allows us to create files of template instantiations that we would link into applications that use them.

Programming environments

If the programming environment controls the compiling and linking necessary with templates, then it maintains a *repository* file for each application. This file is a database containing an index of the template definitions and instantiations in the application's code files. When a code file declares and invokes a function template, the compiler enters this fact together with the type parameter bindings and the file name into the repository, rather than creating the template function at that point. When a template definition occurs in a code file, the compiler checks the repository to verify that it has not already been defined, and then enters it into the repository together with the file name. Some compilation steps such as parsing may also be performed on the template definition at that point. When the program is linked, the repository is used to generate, compile, and link the necessary template instantiations. The repository can also be used to maintain compilation dependencies and trigger recompilations as the program is developed.

---

[12] Programmers had previously created instantiations by mentioning the desired argument signature in a typedef statement.

[13] That is, an implementation might or might not treat duplicate instantiations in different code files as a multiple definition linkage error.

13.2 CLASS TEMPLATES

13.2.1 The Type of a Collection Element

The primary purpose for supporting class templates is to permit definition of the interface and implementation of a collection class independently from the type of the collection elements. A collection class for a particular element type is then generated when necessary. First, let us review the issues that have to do with the type of a collection element in statically typed languages.

In a statically typed language, all the elements of a collection must be of the same type, and the compiler can ensure that an object of the wrong type is not added to the collection. The use of templates for defining collection classes with a type parameter for the element type does not avoid this requirement. With dynamic typing, heterogeneous collections can be created, but checking the type of an object when it is inserted into the collection is either performed explicitly by the programmer or occurs indirectly when that element receives a message sent via the collection.

With inheritance and static typing, the elements of a particular collection are restricted to instances of a set of classes, namely those that are descendants of the class of an element. If an application needs a collection containing various types of elements, inheritance allows the class designer to derive the classes for the element types from an ancestor class, and use a collection of ancestor elements. As discussed in section 12.2.3, we use a pointer or reference of ancestor type as the element type in C++ so that loss of descendant-specific data members does not occur and dynamic binding is supported for messages to elements. The designer of the collection must also decide whether the elements are copied upon being inserted into the collection. It is not possible to mix built-in type values with class objects in a collection (without conversions), because built-in types cannot be subclasses.[14]

When using an ancestor class as the element type for a collection, the class identity of the elements is lost to the compiler, and the programmer may only use ancestor protocol with objects accessed through the collection. To provide descendant-specific behavior through dynamic binding, common member functions must be specified as virtual in the ancestor. To send a descendant class message to an element, we must code an explicit conversion using a dynamic cast.

13.2.2 Creating New Collection Classes Without Templates

Using text substitution

We want to define the protocol and the mechanics of insertion, deletion, and so forth for a particular kind of collection once, and then reuse that specification for collections of different types of objects. For example, a class for a linked list of

---

[14] If this is necessary, the programmer can use a "wrapper class" that contains a data member of that type, or a union with a type indicator member.

strings is identical to a class for a linked list of dates, except for the element type. Suppose that we have defined an implementation for a set of integers, and want to create a collection class for a set of strings. We might copy the integer set code, replace every occurrence of the identifier int that refers to an element (but not others!) with String, and then give each of the set classes a different name (e.g., IntSet and StringSet). Each occurrence of the class name in the header and code files, for example, as a member function parameter type or in the qualified member function names in the code file, must also be changed. However, this process is tedious and error-prone, and becomes an administrative problem as the number of collection classes and element types increases. It is especially difficult to manage if modifications must be made to the collection interface or implementation after creating several classes.

In our collection classes in the previous three chapters, we have used the identifier ElemType as the collection's element type, and then used a typedef statement to declare that identifier as an alias for the desired element type. For example, this technique permitted us to use one definition of the class Queue for queues of Strings, queues of Dates, etc., without modifying any code. Unfortunately, we can only use this definition of the class Queue for one element type in each program because a queue of Strings is a different class than a queue of Dates and must have a different name. When using a collection class with more than one element type, we can duplicate the header and code files, and then change the typedef, the class name, and the header and code file names in the copy. Although this technique avoids some of the search and replace editing described in the previous paragraph, it still has the same drawbacks for large-scale use, and for classes under development.

The preprocessor can be used to automate the process of substituting an actual type for an element type in a generic module definition. The collection type and its operations are defined as a macro with a parameter used as the element type in the module code. The client then calls the macro with an actual type name as the argument, and it generates the code that defines a collection type with a specific element type by giving the actual type name as the macro argument. This process is unsafe because the preprocessor just does text substitution and has no knowledge of type checking or scope. In addition, the macro must generate a different name for each actual collection type, and the facilities for doing so are system-dependent (e.g., see [Lip91] for details).

Using inheritance

For language systems that do not support templates, class library designers have used inheritance to provide collection classes with each having a single definition and permitting various element types. In languages such as Object Pascal and Java that do not support generics, these techniques are the only way to provide type-independent collection classes. For example, the NIH C++ class library [Gor90] provides a hierarchy of collection classes inspired by the Smalltalk collection classes, and the elements of each collection are of type Object*. If a programmer wants to create a collection of elements that are instances of descendants of DisplayObject, he or she defines DisplayObject as a subclass of Object, and defines some additional methods such as DisplayObject::compare() and DisplayObject::hash() that are used in the implementation of the collections. The abstract class Object defines these member functions as pure virtual functions.

To create a list of display objects, the programmer instantiates the class OrderedCltn and only adds display objects to it. The compiler cannot enforce this constraint, although the library provides the programmer with run-time type information via a class ClassDescription. However, when accessing an element of the collection, the programmer must cast it down to the type Display-Object* so that he or she can send DisplayObject-specific messages to it. For example, [15]

```
// using inheritance to reuse a collection class definition for different element types
#include "OrderedCltn.h"
#include "Point.h"
#include "Circle.h"
#include "DisplayObject.h"
int main()
{
    OrderedCltn picture;   // only instances of subclasses of DisplayObject are inserted
    Point pt1(50, 50);
    picture.insert(new Circle(pt1, 10));        // Circle(Point center, int radius)
    // the cast is necessary because draw() is not in the protocol of Object
    ((DisplayObject*)picture.first())->draw();
}
```

Of course, this technique will not work directly for collections of built-in type elements because those types cannot be made subclasses of Object. The programmer must create a "wrapper class"—for example, a class Character with a char data member—that defines the pure virtual functions in Object so that those methods are invoked dynamically by the collection's methods. A similar technique is to use void* as the type of the elements of a collection.

An alternative for linked storage structures follows the pattern of the Smalltalk system classes Link and LinkedList. For example, we can define a GenericQueue class that implements the insertion and removal operations in terms of instances of GenericNode. To create a class for queues of objects of some particular type, we derive a node class from GenericNode that adds an elem field of that type, and derive a queue class from GenericQueue that refines the GenericQueue member functions. For example, we can define the interface of the generic classes as follows:

---

[15] We use unsafe C casts in this example because run-time type information is a more recent extension than templates. Any language system that provides run-time type information will support templates, and templates are a better solution than inheritance for parameterizing the element type.

```
// GenericQueue: the interface for a linked implementation of queues
```

```
// an elem data member of the desired type is added by the subclass
class GenericNode
{
friend class GenericQueue;
protected:
  GenericNode();
  GenericNode* next;
};
```

```
// GenericQueue must implement its insert() and remove() functions in terms of GenericNodes
// it cannot allocate the nodes since it does not know their type
class GenericQueue
{
public:
  bool isEmpty();
protected:
  GenericQueue():
  ~GenericQueue();
  GenericQueue& insert(GenericNode*);
  GenericNode* remove();
  GenericNode* front;
  GenericNode* back;
};
```

All of GenericQueue's members are protected except GenericQueue::isEmpty(), including its constructor, so that functions other than derived class methods cannot create or use instances of that class. The methods for the GenericNode and GenericQueue inline member functions are like those of the corresponding methods of the classes Node and Queue in section 10.1.3. The methods for GenericQueue::insert() and GenericQueue::remove() add nodes to the linked list and remove nodes from the linked list as illustrated in section 10.1.4. However, the subclass insert() member function must create a node because GenericQueue::insert() does not have the actual type of the node, which must be given in the new operation. Similarly, the subclass remove() function is responsible for destroying nodes. For this reason, insertion takes a pointer to the new GenericNode and removal returns a pointer to the detached GenericNode. We create a class for a linked queue of ints by defining two subclasses, as follows:

```
// IntQueue.h: interface for a linked queue of ints derived from a generic queue that
// defines the implementation but not the element type
```

```
class IntNode : public GenericNode
{
friend class IntQueue;
protected:
  IntNode(int);
  int elem;
};
```

```
inline IntNode::IntNode(int el)
  : GenericNode(), elem(el)
{ }


class IntQueue : public GenericQueue
{
public:
  IntQueue();
  IntQueue& insert(int);
  int remove();
};

inline IntQueue::IntQueue()
  : GenericQueue()
{ }

// create an IntNode, use the generic insert() and cast down the return value
// the new nodes are deallocated by GenericQueue::remove() or by
// GenericQueue::~GenericQueue() which calls it
inline IntQueue& IntQueue::insert(int el)
{
  return (IntQueue&) GenericQueue::insert(new IntNode(el));
}

inline int IntQueue::remove()
{
  IntNode* pNode = (IntNode*) GenericQueue::remove();
  int retElem(pNode->elem);
  delete pNode;
  return retElem;
}
```

The reference cast in the return statement in IntQueue::insert() is valid because *this in the return statement in GenericQueue::insert() refers to the original receiver, an instance of IntQueue. This approach has the advantage that the downcasts are hidden within the member functions of the IntQueue class, so clients do not need to code them. IntQueue need not be a friend of GenericNode because the manipulations of the next member are only performed by the member functions of GenericQueue. We might consider using private derivation in this case as the derivation is not motivated by specialization. Because clients of the subclasses must be able to use the message GenericQueue::isEmpty(), it would be exempted from the private derivation by declaring it in the public section of IntQueue. Unfortunately, the programmer must still code a class definition each time a collection is used for a new element type.

13.2.3 Class Template Definition

Purpose

It would be much more convenient if we could create and use a collection for a particular element type without editing source code, using casts, or coding a subclass. The C++ template facility allows the class designer to define a collection class and its operations generically, together with a parameter that represents the type of the elements. A client can specify the collection type and the element type when creating a collection object, with the compiler generating the definition of the collection class for the given element type automatically. That is, once we have defined a class template, the compiler instantiates the template whenever we use the class template name as a type specifier. Class templates do not avoid the limitation inherent in statically typed languages that prevents us from creating heterogeneous collections.

In contrast to function templates for which the compiler can deduce the bindings for the type parameters from the argument signature of the invocation, the actual types must be given explicitly when instantiating a class template. For example,

```
// suppose that Set<Type> represents a set of elements of type Type for any Type
// (the next section covers defining the construct)
#include "Point.h"
#include "String.h"
int main()
{
    Set<Point> ptSet;       // create the class Set<Point> and allocate an instance
    Set<String> strSet;     // a set of strings
    Set<int> intSet;        // a set of ints
    intSet.insert(3).insert(5);  // use the object, i.e. send it Set<int> messages
    ptSet.insert(Point(3, 3)).insert(Point(5, 5));
    strSet.insert(4);            // error: no conversion from int to String
}
```

Note that Set<int> and Set<String> are different classes, that is, their instances are not type compatible and their member functions have different argument signatures.

Class template declaration

A declaration of a class template consists of the reserved word **template**, a type parameter list, the reserved word **class**, and the class template name, as follows:

```
// class template declarations
template <class ElemType> class List;
template <class KeyType, class ValueType> class Dictionary;
template <class IndexType, class ElemType> class Array;
```

An example class template definition

We can only declare or define a class template at file scope. A class template definition consists of the reserved word **template**, a type parameter list enclosed in angle brackets, and a standard class definition in which the type parameters may be used as type names. Like a function template, a class template provides a description that the compiler can use to generate an unlimited set of template classes with the same protocol (except for occurrences of the type parameter in the argument signatures of the messages).

The following is a definition for a class template for queues of elements implemented by a linked list:[16]

```
// the class templates Queue<> and Node<> for queues of elements
// (linked list implementation)
#include <iostream.h>    // for class ostream

template <class ElemType>
class Node
{
friend class Queue<ElemType>;
friend ostream& operator<<(ostream&, Queue<ElemType>&);
protected:
   Node(const ElemType&);
   ElemType elem;
   Node<ElemType>* next;
};

template <class ElemType>
class Queue
{
friend ostream& operator<<(ostream&, Queue<ElemType>&);
public:
   Queue();
   virtual ~Queue();        // derivation is possible
   virtual Queue<ElemType>& insert(const ElemType&);
   ElemType remove();
   bool isEmpty();
protected:
   Node<ElemType>* front;
   Node<ElemType>* back;
};
```

---

[16] We will not divide our class templates (and the associated member function templates) into header and code files because language systems differ on whether and how this is done. Classes are divided on the basis of what information is necessary to compile client code files, but the compiler needs all the class and member function codes to generate the template class and its member functions.

As in function templates, we can use a type parameter such as ElemType as a type name within the body of the class definition, for example, as a data member type or a member function parameter type. An actual type will be bound to that type parameter when a template class is created. Like its constructor, the data members of an instance of Node<ElemType> are only accessible to its friend function and its friend class Queue<ElemType>, where both ElemTypes are bound to the same type. That is, Queue<int> is a friend of Node<int>, but is not a friend of Node<String>. We will discuss the use of the specification <ElemType> in the types of the data members and member function parameters in the next paragraph.

Class template and template class names

A class template name alone, such as Queue or Node, is not a class name, and cannot be used as a type specifier. To use a class template name as a class name, we must give bindings for all its type parameters enclosed in angle brackets following the template name. These bindings may be actual type names that specify instantiation of a *template class* as illustrated at the beginning of this section, or the type parameters of an enclosing template definition, as in the definition of the Queue class template. In either case, the resulting name (e.g., Set<Point> in a program or Queue<ElemType> within a template definition) specifies a class name that can be used as a type or scope name. Because class templates are not classes (and because we are now using class template names that we used as class names earlier), we will use a trailing <> with class template names (e.g., Queue<>), like the trailing () we use with function names.

When we use a class template name with its type parameter bindings given by the type parameters of an enclosing template definition (e.g., the types of the member function parameters and data members in the class templates Node<> and Queue<>), the class template is not instantiated. Instantiation will occur when the function or class template being defined is instantiated. For example, Node <String> is created whenever Queue<String> is generated as a result of a programmer defining a variable of that type.

Class template member and friend functions

The member functions of a class template also must be parameterized for the element type, so we define them as templates. Like a class template definition, a member function template definition does not create any member function definitions, but provides a template for generating them when necessary. A friend function that has a parameter whose type is the class template must also be a function template. For example, the file scope overloading of operator<<() for the Queue<> class template is a function template so that the insertion operator can handle every possible type of queue template class.

A template can use one of its type parameters as a type name or as a type parameter binding for a class template name within its definition. For example,

the member function templates that implement the Queue<> class template methods declare ElemType as a type parameter, so they can use Queue<ElemType> and
Node<ElemType> as type names. That type parameter will be bound to an actual
type when the compiler instantiates the class template and its member function
templates.

Like all member functions defined at file scope, a member function template
definition must use a qualified name to indicate the class template scope. We can
use Queue<ElemType> as a scope specifier in the member function template definitions because the template type parameter list gives a binding for the identifier
ElemType. Again, the type parameter will be bound when the class template is
instantiated.

We define the member and friend function templates for the class templates
Node<> and Queue<> as follows:

```
// member and friend function templates for the class templates Queue<> and Node<>

template <class ElemType>
inline Node<ElemType>::Node(const ElemType& el)
   : elem(el), next(NULL)
{ }

template <class ElemType>
inline Queue<ElemType>::Queue()
   : front(NULL), back(NULL)
{ }

template <class ElemType>
inline bool Queue<ElemType>::isEmpty()
{
    return front == NULL ? true : false;
}

template <class ElemType>
inline Queue<ElemType>::~Queue()
{
    while ( !isEmpty() )
       (void) remove();
}

template <class ElemType>
Queue<ElemType>& Queue<ElemType>::insert(const ElemType& el)
{
    Node<ElemType>* pNode = new Node<ElemType>(el);
    if (isEmpty())
       front = back = pNode;
    else
    {
       back->next = pNode;
```

```
        back = pNode;
     }
     return *this;
}


template <class ElemType>
ElemType Queue<ElemType>::remove()
{
     if (isEmpty())
        // signal an exception (see section 13.3)
        throw EmptyError;
     Node<ElemType>* pNode = front;
     front = front->next;
     ElemType retElem(pNode->elem);
     delete pNode;
     return retElem;
}


template <class ElemType>
ostream& operator<<(ostream& ostr, Queue<ElemType>& qu)
{
     ostr << "Queue ( ";
     Node<ElemType>* pNode;
     for ( pNode = qu.front;  pNode;  pNode = pNode->next )
        ostr << pNode->elem << " ";
     ostr << " )" << endl;
     return ostr;
}
```

Note that the type parameter for Queue<ElemType>::remove() does not appear in the argument signature of the function, so an invocation does not give an argument whose type determines the type parameter binding. This is valid for member functions because the compiler can use the type of the receiver to determine a binding for the type parameter when that message is sent.

As we discussed in section 13.1.3, a template definition requires that the actual type bound to its type parameter include the operations that the template uses for its instances. In the case of Queue<> and Node<>, that type must have a public copy constructor so that an instance can be copied to the elem data member of a node and then copied to the local variable and return value of Queue<ElemType>:: remove(). If a type does not define the operations used in the template, a compiler error occurs upon instantiation because the template class and all its member functions are generated at that point. However, the overloading of operator<<() for Queue<> is not a member function, so it is not instantiated until a client outputs an instance of a queue template class. That is, clients can instantiate a queue template class of any type, but if the queue attempts to print itself and the class bound to ElemType does not define an overloading of operator<<(), a compile-time type violation occurs at the operator invocation ostr << pNode->elem;.

Parameterizing a class template for a component type

A class template is useful whenever a class is parameterized for a type. This primarily occurs for the type of a collection element, but we can also use a class template to specify a set of classes that have the same protocol and structure, yet differ in the type of the information they maintain. For example, we can define a class template Point<> whose type parameter specifies the type (and therefore the range and precision) of the coordinates of a template class's instances, as follows:

```
// a class template Point whose instantiations have different coordinate types

template <class CoordType>
class Point
{
public:
    // the default constructor requires a meaning for 0 or a conversion from 0 in CoordType
    Point();
    Point(const CoordType& initX, const CoordType& initY);
    CoordType x() const;
    void x(const CoordType&);
    CoordType y() const;
    void y(const CoordType&);
    bool operator==(const Point<CoordType>&) const;
    // ... other member functions ...
protected:
    CoordType x_;
    CoordType y_;
};
```

In this way, we define the protocol and implementation once, and clients can create the classes Point<int>, Point<long double>, Point<Rational>, and so on by instantiating the template. Numeric arguments to the class's constructor and other messages will be converted to the coordinate type of the instance.

Access control and friends

The access specifiers public, protected, and private have the same meaning for class templates as for classes. Two template classes generated from the same class template are not related in any way, and do not have access to each other's non-public members. For example, the classes Queue<String> and Queue<Date> are two different classes, and can only interact through their public protocols.

If a class template declares a nontemplate function as a friend, that function is a friend of all classes generated from the class template. If a class template declares a function template as a friend and each type parameter of the friend is bound to a type parameter of the class template definition, then each template function is a friend of the corresponding template class. This relationship is illustrated by the friend operator<<() declaration in the Node<> and Queue<> class templates, and the friend class Queue<ElemType> declaration in the Node<> class template. For example,

Queue<int> and operator<<(ostream&, Queue<int>&) are friends of Node<int>, but are not friends of Node<String>.

   If the designer of a class template wants each function or class generated from another template to be a friend of all classes generated from the class template, the friend declaration specifies a complete template, with the template keyword and a type parameter list. The reserved word friend follows the template heading and precedes the function or class declaration, and the type parameter names are different from those of the class template of which it is a friend. For example,

```
// each instantiation of the func() template and the member functions of each
// instantiation of the FriendClass class template are friends of all instantiations
// of the ClassTemplate template
template <class Type1, class Type2>
class ClassTemplate
{
template <class Type3> friend void func(const ClassTemplate<Type3>&);
template <class Type4> friend class FriendClass;
// ... members ...
};
```

Declaring a friend template in this way is a newer feature that is not in the ARM and might not be supported by your compiler.

Iterators

   A common use of friends with template classes for collections is to define an *iterator* over a collection, which accesses the collection's elements, like a stream over a collection in Smalltalk. Suppose that a client of a collection template class wants to apply some processing to each element of the collection. The class template can provide messages like the Smalltalk enumerating messages that take a pointer to a function, which performs some operations on instances of the element type. For example, a class template Set<> could include messages such as the following:

```
// a class template Set<> that provides enumerating protocol
template <class ElemType>
class Set
{
public:
  Set();
  // replace each element with the result of evaluating the argument function on it
  void do(ElemType (ElemType::*pReplaceFn)());
  // return the set of elements for which evaluation of the argument function returns true
  Set allSuchThat(bool (ElemType::*pTestFn) ());
  // ... other members ...
};
```

However, there are some problems with this approach. Because C++ does not support function literals (like blocks in Smalltalk or the λ-expressions we discussed in section 1.2.3), a client must define a named function each time he or she wants to process a collection's elements. The class should also provide overloadings for the enumerating messages for both ElemType member functions and file scope functions that take ElemType arguments. Instead, we would like to allow clients to write the code that processes the elements in the same fashion as a for loop over a C array. Clients of a List<> class template that overloads operator[ ]() can write such a loop, but it is inefficient to do so. If the list is implemented as a linked list, each access traverses the list from the beginning to the indexed element, and if the list is implemented as a dynamic array (like the Smalltalk class OrderedCollection), an offset is computed for each access. In addition, some collections such as Set<> do not provide indexed access to elements.

For example, if Set<> is implemented as a hash table, the iterator contains a data member which is an index that begins at the first element in the table and skips over empty positions in the table when it is advanced. We can define a class template for iterators over instances of Set<> template classes as follows:

```
// an iterator class template that enumerates the elements of a set
// must be declared as a friend of Set<ElemType>
template <class ElemType>
class SetIterator
{
public:
    SetIterator(const Set<ElemType>&);
    void reset();            // set the iterator to the "first" element
    void advance();          // advance the iterator to the "next" element
    bool atEnd();            // is the iterator "off the end" of the set?
    ElemType& current();     // obtain the current element
    ElemType& next();        // obtain the current element and advance the iterator
protected:
    Set<ElemType>& set;      // an instance always iterates over the same set
    int currentIndex;        // an index into the hash table, or -1 if the iterator is "off the end"
};
```

The class template Set<> must define the class template SetIterator<> as a friend (with the same type parameter bindings) because it accesses the storage structure of a set. Clients can then use the iterator class to process elements, as follows:

```
// using an iterator class
#include "Set.h"             // template version
#include "SetIterator.h"     // template version
int main()
{
    Set<String> names;
    // ... add elements to names, etc. ...
    SetIterator<String> namesIter(names);
    for ( namesIter.reset();  namesIter.atEnd();  namesIter.advance() )
```

```
        {
            // ... process names.current() ...
        }
    }
```

An iterator over an ordered collection such as List<> could also provide positioning protocol such as ListIterator<>::skip(int offset), like the Smalltalk class Position-ableStream discussed in section 8.4.2.

Expression parameters

A class template may also declare *expression parameters*, which provide non-type (i.e., object) parameters for the template. These parameters are declared in the type parameter list in the same way as in function parameters lists, and the parameter's type can be an integer type (including enumerations) or a pointer type. When creating an instantiation of such a template, the client must give values for the expression parameters as well as types for the type parameters. For example, suppose that we decide that two arrays with different index ranges have different types (as in Pascal). We can define an Array<> class template with a type parameter that gives the type of the elements and expression parameters that give the lower and upper index bounds for the array, as follows:

```
    // a class template for arrays with expression parameters
template <class ElemType, int low, int high>
class Array
{
public:
    Array();                                    // ElemType must have a default constructor
    Array(const ElemType& initValue);           // set all elements to initValue
    Array(const Array<ElemType>, low, high>&);
    Array<ElemType, low, high>& operator=(const Array<ElemType>, low, high>&);
    int size() const;
    ElemType& operator[](int index);
    bool operator==(const Array<ElemType>, low, high>&) const;
    // ... other member functions ...
protected:
    int low_;
    int high_;
    ElemType elems[high - low + 1];
};
```

If two array objects have different index ranges, they are not type compatible because they are instances of different classes. If a client attempts to assign or compare such objects, a compiler error will result, so the methods for those operations do not need to check the range of the argument. We can still write functions that operate on arrays with various ranges by coding a function template with expression parameters (unlike the original Pascal array type described in section 0.3.5).

Having the size of the array available in the class definition allows the elems array to be a value data member, which avoids the overhead and indirection necessary when allocating that array on the heap. However, this technique increases compilation time because each array with different bounds causes generation of a new class definition.

The member function templates also use expression parameters, as follows:

```
// member function templates for a class template with expression parameters
template <class ElemType, int low, int high>
ElemType Array<ElemType, low, high>::operator[](int index) const
{
    return elems[index - low];
}

template <class ElemType, int low, int high>
bool Array<ElemType, low, high>::operator==(const Array<ElemType, low, high>& rhs) const
{
    for ( int index = 0; index < size(); index++ )
        if ( elems[index] != rhs.elems[index] )
            return false;
    return true;
}
```

The value of an expression parameter cannot be modified by the class template's methods.

The value given in a template class name for an expression parameter must be a constant whose value the compiler can determine.

```
// expression parameter values must be constants
#include "Array.h"
#include "Point.h"
int main()
{
    const int low = 1;
    int high = 20;
    // ... other operations ...
    Array<String, low, 20> strArr;      // OK
    Array<String, 1, high> strArr;      // error: high is not known at compile time
}
```

No conversions of any kind are performed when initializing an expression parameter, so the programmer must supply an explicit conversion if necessary. A template can also give default values for expression parameters, but only for the trailing parameters. For example, if we want to give the default value 1 for the expression parameter low in the Array<> template, it must follow the parameter high in the parameter list.

Specialization

If particular bindings for the type parameters of a class template require special handling, the programmer can define a specialized template class and its member functions. These definitions cannot be given until the compiler has encountered the definition of the corresponding class template. For example, once the Node<> and Queue<> class templates have been defined, we can define the following template class for elements that are C strings:

```
// defining a specialized template class
#include "Queue.h"              // template version
#include <string.h>
class Node<char*>
{
friend class Queue<char*>;
friend ostream& operator<<(ostream&, Queue<char*>&);
protected:
   Node(const char* str);
   ~Node();
   char* elem;
   Node<char*>* next;
};

inline Node<char*>::Node(const char* str)
   : elem(new char[strlen(str) + 1]), next(NULL)
{
   strcpy(elem, str);
}

inline Node<char*>::~Node()
{
   delete [ ] elem;
}
```

Note the use of the template class name Node<char*> as a scope specifier in defining its member functions. The compiler will use the specialized template class or member function for an instantiation using that type parameter binding. A template specialization for a particular type parameter binding cannot be defined after the template has been instantiated for that type because the compiler has already generated a template class with that name. For example, we cannot define the previous specialization if we have created a variable of type Queue<char*>.

Member templates

Occasionally, we would like to define a template that can be used to generate new member functions for a class. That is, we want to define a template for member functions within the class (e.g., with a type parameter that appears in the member function's parameter list) that the compiler uses to generate an overloading of that member function with the argument type given in an invocation (as it does for function templates). The ARM does not define a mechanism for doing so because it was not clear what the implications of such a feature might be at the time. The ANSI/ISO C++ Standard includes a new feature for defining a *member template* for generating member functions. With this extension, we can define templates within class scope, including within class templates.

For example, suppose we want to define a conversion from instances of the template class Point<int> to instances of Point<double>. We could define a function template that performs the conversion with two type parameters, one for the type parameter binding of the source object and one for that of the target, as follows:

```
// a conversion from Point<CoordType1> to Point<CoordType2>
template <class CoordType1, class CoordType2>
Point<CoordType2> convert(Point<CoordType1>& argPt)
{
    // valid if there is a conversion from CoordType1 to CoordType2
    return Point<CoordType2>(argPt.x(), argPt.y());
}
```

However, it would be more convenient if we could define this operation as a constructor or conversion operator for Point<> so that the compiler could perform the conversion implicitly. To do so, we need to define a constructor for Point<> whose parameter type is another point template class, with that definition parameterized for any point template class argument. The compiler would generate a new constructor for a given argument type when a program uses an instance of one point template class in a context that requires another. A member template begins with the reserved word template and a type parameter list (like the declaration of a friend function template). When a member template appears in a class template, it uses a different type parameter from that of the class template, as illustrated by the following example:

```
// a class template with a member template
template <class CoordType>
class Point
{
public:
    // the template is used to generate constructors with a point template class argument
    template <class CoordType1> Point(Point<CoordType1>&);
    // ... other members ...
};
```

If a programmer initializes a Point<double> variable with an instance of Point<int>, the compiler generates the constructor Point<double>::Point (Point<int>) from this member template. That is, it uses the member template to create additional member functions for the template class Point<double> when necessary. Nontemplate classes can also define member templates.

The syntax for defining the member template separately from the class is unusual because it involves nesting the member template definition within another template that gives bindings for the type parameters of the enclosing class. For example, the following is the definition of the Point<> template member used to generate constructors:

```
// defining a member template outside the enclosing class template
template <class CoordType>
   template <class CoordType1>
   Point<CoordType>::Point(Point<CoordType1>& argPt)
      : Point<CoordType>(argPt.x(), argPt.y())
   { }
```

There is one important restriction on member templates: They cannot be virtual. If virtual member templates were allowed, instantiating the new member would involve changing the layout of the class's vtbl to accommodate the new member function.

13.2.4 Instantiation

As discussed in the previous section, a class template name together with a set of actual types enclosed in angle brackets constitutes the name of a template class. For example, List<String> is the name of a class generated from the List<> class template that has instances of String as its elements. The compiler must have encountered the definitions of the actual types bound to the template's type parameters so that it can generate the template class definition. Like any class name, we can use a template class name as a type specifier for object and pointer declarations, function parameters, data member declarations, class derivations, and type parameter bindings. Clearly, the bindings given for the template's type parameters must be type names.

When we use a template class name, the compiler automatically generates a type-specific instantiation of the corresponding class template and its member function templates. It creates the new class and member function definitions by substituting the actual type name given in the template class name for each occurrence of the corresponding type parameter in those templates. The compiler then translates this definition and creates a symbol table entry giving the template class name and the type object for the class. If the template class is the type of a variable, that object is allocated and initialized, and we use it in exactly the same fashion as any other class instance.

The following example presents some uses of template class names:

```
// instantiation of class templates
#include "Queue.h"          // template version
#include "Date.h"
#include "Array.h"          // template version
#include "String.h"
```

```
#include "Point.h"                 // template version
int main()
{
    // instantiates the template classes Queue<char> and Node<char>
    Queue<char> charQu;
    // instantiates the template classes Queue<Date> and Node<Date>
    Queue<Date>* pDateQu;
    pDateQu = new Queue<Date>;        // Queue<Date> and Node<Date> already exist
    // instantiates the template class Array<String, 1, 20>
    Array<String, 1, 20> strArr;
    // instantiates the template class Point<int>
    Point<int> intPt(3, -3.2);

    // invokes Queue<char>& Queue<char>::insert(const char&)
    charQu.insert('a').insert('b').insert('c').insert('d');
    // invokes ostream& operator<<(ostream&, Queue<char>&)
    cout << charQu;
    // invokes String& Array<String, 1, 20>::operator[](const int) and String(const char*)
    strArr[5] = "fifth";
    // invokes Queue<Date>& Queue<Date>::insert(const Date&) and Date(const char*)
    pDateQu->insert("1/1/90");
    // invokes Point<int>::y(int)
    intPt.y(2);
}
```

In the first declaration, the compiler generates and compiles definitions of the
template classes Queue<char> and Node<char> if they have not yet been defined,
and then calls the Queue<char> constructor. In the second example, both
Queue<Date> and Node<Date> are instantiated, even though the statement does
not create objects of either type.[17] When the compiler encounters the third statement, it uses the existing definitions of Queue<Date> and Node<Date>. The next
definition instantiates the template class Array<String, 1, 20> and creates an
instance. The String default constructor is used to initialize each entry in the
strArr.elems array. The fifth definition instantiates the template class Point-<int>
and invokes the Point<int> constructor to initialize the new object. The second
argument is converted via the standard double to int conversion. The next few
statements demonstrate that we use instances of template classes in exactly the
same way that we use any object, and the comments remind us of the member
functions invoked.

We can use a template class name in any context in which a class name can
appear, not just in variable declarations. A template class can be the type of a function parameter or data member, or the binding for a type parameter, as in the following examples:

---

[17] In the ARM, all the class template's member function definitions are instantiated when the template class is generated, whether they are invoked or not. In the ANSI/ISO Standard, the language system can delay defining the member functions of a template class until they are used, if at all.

```
// a template class name as the type of a function parameter
#include "Person.h"
#include "List.h" 18                    // template version
void invite(const List<Person>&);


// a template class name as the type of a data member
#include "DisplayObject.h"
class Picture : public DisplayObject
{
public:
    // ... protocol ...
protected:
    List<DisplayObject*> elements;
};


// a template class name as a type parameter binding
#include "Point.h"              // template version
// instantiates Point<double> and List<Point <double> >
List<Point <double> > corners;
```

Again, the compiler generates the template class if necessary. When using a template class as a type parameter binding, a space must appear between the closing angle brackets in a template class name such as List<Point<double> > so that the lexical analyzer does not interpret the last two characters as the right shift or extraction operator.

Like any class name, a template class name (i.e., with actual type names in the parameter list) can be used as a scope specifier. For example, we use it when defining the member functions of a specialized template class at file scope (e.g., the definition of Node<char*>::Node() in the previous section), or when accessing a static member of a template class.

If you find a class name such as Array<Point<double>, 1, 10> unwieldy, you can use a typedef statement to define an alias. This technique is also useful for creating a domain- or application-specific name for a template class. For example,

```
// using typedef's with template class names
typedef Array<Point<double>, 1, 10> ArrayOf10DblPoints;
typedef Dictionary<Date, String> Datebook;
```

As with function templates, the programmer can explicitly specify instantiation of a class template in a particular code file, as follows:

```
// a programmer-defined class template instantiation
template Queue<String>;
```

---

[18] As we will see in section 13.2.6, the list class template for a list of pointers (i.e., for the data member Picture::elements) may be different than the one for a list of values.

13.2.5 Scope

Name resolution

The rules for resolving local identifier uses in a class template definition are the same as those for class definitions. Member names are visible throughout the class template scope (no matter where they are declared), and the scope of a member function template is nested within the scope of its class template.

The process of resolving nonlocal names in a class template or member function template definition is the same as that described in section 13.1.4 for function templates. Names that depend on the binding of a type parameter are bound according to the actual type substituted in an instantiation. (This is why the compiler must have encountered the actual type's definition.) Identifiers that do not depend on type parameters are resolved according to the lexical environment of the class template definition.

Static members

Class templates can also define static members. If a class template defines a static data member, each template class generated from the template has its own static object with that name. To initialize or access a static member of a template class, we use the class template name with type parameter bindings as a scope specifier. For example in section 10.2.2, we recoded the class Point with a static data member that keeps track of the number of instances of that class, and a static member function that provides access to that information. We can provide the same class information for the classes generated from the class template Point<>. The definition and initialization of the static data member at file scope (not within the class template definition) is also expressed as a template (an "object template"?), and is declared within the class template scope. We define the class template Point<> and the static data member template as follows:

```
// the point<> template with a static data member that maintains the number of instances
// each template class has its own static member
template <class CoordType>
class Point
{
public:
    // all three constructors increment numPoints_
    Point();
    Point(const CoordType& initX, const CoordType& initY);
    Point(const Point<CoordType>&);
    // the destructor decrements numPoints_
    ~Point();
    static int numPoints();
    // ... other member functions ...
protected:
    CoordType x_;
```

```
   CoordType y_;
   static int numPoints_;
};


// the template definition and initialization allocates an object and initializes it
// when the corresponding template class is generated
template <class CoordType>
int Point<CoordType>::numPoints_ = 0;
```

To invoke a static member function of a template class, we use the scope operator with the template class name.

```
   // invocation of template class static member functions
   #include "Point.h"
   #include <iostream.h>
   main()
   {
      Point<long> longPt1(1L, 1L)
      Point<long> longPt2(2L, 2L);
      Point<double>* pDblPt = new Point<double>(3.0, 3.0);
      cout << "Number of long point instances: " << Point<long>::numPoints() << endl;
      cout << "Number of double point instances: " << Point<double>::numPoints() << endl;
      delete pDblPt;
   }
```

The template classes Point<long> and Point<double> each have their own static data member, and each is accessed by its own static member function.

In section 11.1.4, we discussed modifying the class Node so that it performs its own storage management by overloading new and delete and declaring a static member that points to the free storage list. If we did this for the class template Node<>, then each template class would have its own free list pointer and free list.

Nested classes

We can also define the auxiliary class Node as a class nested within the class template Queue<>. However, it cannot be a class template because class template definitions may only occur at file scope. For this example, this is not a problem because there is a one-to-one correspondence between template classes generated from Queue<> and uses of Node. We can define Node as a nontemplate class nested within the Queue<> class template, and there will be a Node class embedded within each template class definition generated. For example, a program that uses queues of both integers and strings would instantiate both the Queue<int>::Node and Queue<String>::Node classes from the Queue<> class template. The type parameter of the Queue<> class template is available within the definition of the nested class Node (e.g., for the elem member) because Node is defined within that scope. The compiler will substitute the actual type for those uses of the type parameter when the class template is instantiated, so Queue<int>::Node and Queue<String>::Node will have different elem data member types. We define the Queue<> class template with the nested class Node as follows:

```
// a class template with an auxiliary nested class
template <class ElemType>
class Queue
{
friend ostream& operator<<(ostream&, Queue<ElemType>&);
public:
    // ... member function declarations as coded in section 13.2.3 ...
protected:
    class Node
    {
    friend ostream& operator<<(ostream&, Queue<ElemType>&);
    public:
        Node(const ElemType&);
        ElemType elem;
        Node* next;
    };
    Node* front;   // not Node<ElemType>* front
    Node* back;
};
```

As with nested classes, we use cascaded applications of the scope operator when defining the member functions of the nested class separated from its definition.

Similarly, if an enumeration is nested within a class template, each template class generated from the template includes its own nested enumeration.

13.2.6 Inheritance

Templates and derivation

A template class is a class like any other, and can be used as the base class of a nontemplate class. The template class will be generated if necessary when the derived class is defined. For example,

```
// a template class can be the base class of a nontemplate class
// Pixel inherits the protocol and data members of Point<short>
#include "Point.h"
#include "Color.h"
class Pixel : public Point<short>
{
public:
    Pixel(short initX, short initY, Color col = Color::black);
    Pixel(const Point& initPt, Color col = Color::black);
    // ... other protocol ...
```

```
   protected:
      Color color_;
   };
```

A class template can also have a nontemplate class or an instantiated template class as a base class. In this case, each class generated from the template has the same base class. For example, in the ANSI/ISO C++ Standard Library, the abstract class ios_base is the superclass of the class template basic_ios<>, which has instantiations for the two types of characters char and wchar_t, as in the following declarations:

```
   // a nontemplate class can be the base class of a class template
   // an excerpt from the ANSI/ISO C++ Standard Library
   class ios_base
   {
      // ... bitsets for iostate, fmtflags, opernmode;  other members ...
   };

   template <class CharType, class TraitsType = ios_traits<CharType> >
   class basic_ios : public ios_base
   {
      // ... stream state, locale, etc., and accessors ...
   };

   // both ios and wios are subclasses of ios_base
   typedef basic_ios<char> ios;
   typedef basic_ios<wchar_t> wios;
```

This example also illustrates the use of the new feature of default argument bindings for type parameters. The typedef for ios only gives a binding for the first type parameter, so the second takes its default value, the class ios_traits-<char>. (ios_traits<> defines characteristics of the character type such as the newline character, a whitespace test function, and so on.)

In addition, we can derive a class template from another class template. The type parameter of the base class template must appear in the type parameter list of the derived class template so that it has a valid binding when the derived class is used. Usually, the derived class template uses the same type parameter binding as the base class template. The compiler generates an instance of the base class template (if necessary) whenever it instantiates the derived class template. For example, we can define the class PriorityQueue introduced in section 12.1.1 as a class template derived from the Queue<> class template defined in section 13.2.3. We code the PriorityQueue<> class template definition and the inline member function templates as follows:

```
   // a class template for priority queues (linked list implementation)
   // the comparison function is a member function of the class ElemType
   #include "Queue.h"              // template version defined in section 13.2.3
```

```
template <class ElemType>
class PriorityQueue : public Queue<ElemType>
{
public:
  PriorityQueue(bool (ElemType::*)(const ElemType&) = &ElemType::operator<);
  ElemType first();
  virtual PriorityQueue<ElemType>& insert(const ElemType&);
protected:
  bool (ElemType::*pCompareFn)(const ElemType&);
};

template <class ElemType>
inline PriorityQueue<ElemType>::PriorityQueue(bool (ElemType::*cmp)(const ElemType&))
  : Queue<ElemType>(), pCompareFn(cmp)
{ }

template <class ElemType>
inline ElemType PriorityQueue<ElemType>::first()
{
  if ( isEmpty() )
    // signal an exception (see section 13.3)
    throw EmptyError;
  return front->elem;
}
```

Whenever a programmer uses a template class such as PriorityQueue<Date>, the corresponding Queue<Date> and Node<Date> template classes are instantiated. Each template class generated from the Queue<> template or the PriorityQueue<> template has its own virtual function definitions and vtbl.

In this section, we have derived a nontemplate class from a template class, a class template from a nontemplate class, and a class template from a class template. However, if we use a class template as a base class, the derived class must also be a class template (not just a standard class) because a use of the derived class must give a type parameter binding for generating an actual base class. That is, if a base class is a template parameterized for a type, its derived classes must be as well.

Inheritance among type parameter bindings

Recall that there is no relationship between two template classes generated from the same class template—for example, between List<Point> and List<String>. In particular, if one template class's type parameter binding is derived from that of another class generated from the same template, it is not a subclass of the other template class, nor is there a standard conversion to the other template class. For example, consider the classes Queue<DisplayObject*> and Queue<Square*>. A value assignment (i.e., a conversion that creates a new object) from a queue of squares to a queue of display objects is valid (although the language does not provide it) because all the elements of the source of the assignment are valid elements of the target. However, we cannot treat a queue of squares as if it were a queue of display objects (i.e., a pointer conversion is not valid). Consider the following example:

```
// there is no standard conversion to ancestor in matching type parameter bindings
#include "Queue.h"              // template version
#include "DisplayObject.h"
#include "Square.h"             // a subclass of DisplayObject
#include "Line.h"               // a subclass of DisplayObject
void func(Queue<DisplayObject*>& disObjQu, const DisplayObject* pDisObj)
{
    disObjQu.insert(pDisObj);
}


int main()
{
    Queue<Square*> sqrQu;
    Square* pSquare = new Square(Point(3, 3), 3);
    sqrQu.insert(pSquare);
    Line* pLine = new Line(Point(2,2), Point(4,4));
    // error: there is no conversion from Queue<Square*> to Queue<DisplayObject*>
    func(sqrQu, pLine);
}
```

If the initialization of the first parameter of func() from sqrQu were allowed, it would permit inserting a pointer to an instance of any descendant of DisplayObject into sqrQu. The elements of sqrQu can respond correctly to messages that the elements of a queue of display objects can receive, but the queue of squares itself cannot permit some operations that are valid for a queue of display objects, namely adding instances of other descendants of DisplayObject. Therefore, it is incorrect to consider Queue<Square*> a subclass of Queue<DisplayObject*>. Because the conversion to ancestor for a type parameter binding is not valid for pointers or references, the language does not support this conversion. The designer of the class template (Queue<>, in this example) can provide the value conversion as a constructor member template, as illustrated in section 13.2.3 (if that feature is supported).

Value and reference type parameter bindings

As we discussed in sections 10.2.1 and 12.2.3, the designer of a collection class must consider whether a client requires value or reference semantics for the elements of the collection. Value elements provide more efficient access, and are appropriate for small objects that are treated as attributes, such as instances of built-in types or classes like Point and String. Reference or pointer elements are necessary for polymorphic classes to prevent loss of descendant-specific data members and permit dynamic binding. Reference semantics is also required for objects whose unique identity must be maintained.

In some cases, clients can use the same collection class for both value and reference elements. For example,

```
// using both value and reference element semantics with the same collection class template
#include "Queue.h"
#include "Person.h"
#include "Employee.h"
int main()
{
    // int values are directly embedded in nodes
    Queue<int> intQu;
    intQue.insert(3);
    // the elem member of the nodes are of type Person* and are polymorphic
    Queue<Person*> persQu;
    // the queue contains a pointer, not a copy of the employee object
    persQu.insert(new Employee(...));
}
```

This strategy is sufficient for a class template such as Queue<> that simply copies and then returns its elements. However, if the collection class performs other operations on its elements, value elements and pointer elements use different syntax. For example, the method for PriorityQueue<>::insert() compares the new object to each of the elements of the queue so that it can place the new node correctly in the linked list. The comparison expression results in a type error if pointers are passed as the receiver and argument to the function bound to pCompareFn. (Even if the PriorityQueue<>::insert() method used the < operator for comparisons, the operation would be incorrect because the expression would perform a pointer value comparison.) If the elements of a priority queue are pointers, the comparison expression in PriorityQueue<>::insert() must dereference the element identifiers. Another example that must dereference pointer elements is the equality comparison in the method for List<>::isElement(). Similarly, if the collection class template sends a named message to an element, it must use . (period) for objects and -> for pointers.

If a class template's methods cannot operate correctly on both values and pointers, there are two ways of supporting polymorphic elements. The designer can define one template for both value and reference elements (because message passing syntax is the same for values and references). However, we will see that some templates cannot use reference elements so the designer must define two class templates, one for value elements and one for pointer elements. In addition, because a C++ reference variable cannot be modified to refer to a different object, most programmers use pointer variables for polymorphic identifiers (rather than references), so a collection of pointers is more intuitive than a collection of references.

Consider whether we need to modify the Queue<> class template to permit a template class such as Queue<Person&> for polymorphic elements. The elem data member of Node<> would be a reference, which is valid because it is initialized from the Node<> constructor initialization list and is never modified. The return type and local variable of Queue<>::remove() can also be references. However, the parameter types of Queue<>::insert() and the Node<> constructor would be invalid because they would be references of a reference. If we defined those parameters as values (i.e., as const ElemType rather than const ElemType&), the template works for a reference type parameter binding. Unfortunately, template classes that use a nonreference type parameter binding do extra copying when an element is inserted because it is passed by value. We would not be able to use the PriorityQueue<> class template as written with a reference type parameter binding because the type parameter is used as the scope name for the pointer to member function parameter and data member. If we used a file scope comparison function or hard-coded the < operator in the PriorityQueue<>::insert() method, the template could be recoded to work with a reference type parameter binding.

    If a collection class uses an array of elements as its internal representation, it cannot use references to elements because the language does not support arrays of references. In addition, a reference cannot be changed to alias a different object, which some collection classes must do with element fields (e.g., when moving elements in a hash table). In these cases, the class designer must define two collection classes, one for use with value elements and one for use with pointer elements, for example ListOfObjects<> and ListOfPointers<>. The two classes have different semantics because the collection of values makes its own copies of the elements inserted, and destroys those copies when elements are removed or the collection is deallocated. Their methods also differ because the methods for the collection of pointers dereference the element identifiers. The class designer must inform the client of the semantics of the collection classes, and a client must choose the correct collection class for his or her purpose.

    For example, we can define two array class templates as follows:[19]

```
// defining two class templates for a collection

// for use with built-in types or classes without subclasses: elements are copied to the array
template <class ElemType, int low, int high>
class ArrayOfObjects
{
    // ... like the class template Array<> defined in section 13.2.3 ...
};

// for use with polymorphic classes: pointers to elements are copied to the array
template <class ElemPtrType, int low, int high>
class ArrayOfPointers
{
public:
    // ... member functions ...
protected:
    int low_;
```

----

[19] We have written the class template ArrayOfPointers<> such that a client would use the template class name ArrayOfPointers<Person*> rather than ArrayOfPointers<Person>.

```
   int high_;
   ElemPtrType elems[high - low + 1];


};
```

The ArrayOfObjects<> class template is defined like the Array<> class template in section 13.2.3. In ArrayOfPointers<>, each occurrence of ElemType or ElemType& in the ArrayOfObjects<> class template definition is replaced by ElemPtrType. The difference between the two class templates occurs in their methods. If the collection class template sends any messages to an element or uses an element as an argument of a message, the ElemPtrType object must be dereferenced when it is passed to that function. For example, if the ArrayOfPointers<> class template uses operator<() to find its minimum, we would code the member function ArrayOfPointers<>::min() as follows:

```
   // dereferencing pointers to elements within a member function template
   template <class ElemPtrType, int low, int high>
   ElemPtrType ArrayOfPointers<ElemPtrType, low, high>::min()
   {
      ElemPtrType pMinElem(elems[0]);
      for ( int index = 1;  index < size();  index++ )
          if ( *(elems[index]) < *pMinElem )
             pMinElem = array[index];
      return pMinElem;
   }
```

The dereference operators in the if condition do not appear in the method for ArrayOfObjects<>::min(). If the ArrayOfPointers<> class template is instantiated with a nonpointer type bound to ElemPtrType, then a syntax error occurs when the compiler generates a template member function whose method performs a dereference.

13.3 EXCEPTIONS

13.3.1 Purpose and Background

Review

As we discussed in section 0.1.3, run-time errors include hardware-detected errors, system errors that occur in the use of operating system facilities, logical errors resulting from a client violating constraints on the use of a class, and application-specific errors that violate problem domain semantics. Often a method in a class can detect a system error or a logical error, but the designer of that method does not know how a particular application is using the class. When this happens, the error must be propagated through a sequence of invocations to a method that can handle it.

Error handling in C

C programmers typically use three techniques for error handling (not counting blind faith): return values that give error codes, the assert() macro, and the setjmp() and longjmp() library functions. Many standard library functions such as fopen() and malloc() return a NULL or special value when an error occurs. The programmer must explicitly test the return value of each operation and handle its errors separately.

```c
/* using return values as error indications in C */
#include <stdio.h>
#include <stdlib.h>
const int BUF_SIZE = 256;
int main()
{
    FILE* inFile;
    char buf[BUF_SIZE];
    int numRead;
    if ( (inFile = fopen("dataFile", "r")) == NULL )
    {
        fprintf(stderr, "Error opening data file\n");
        exit(1);
    }
    if ( (numRead = fread(buf, 1, BUF_SIZE, inFile)) == 0 )
    {
        fprintf(stderr, "Error reading data file\n");
        exit(2);
    }
    else
    {
        // ... process buf ...
    }
}
```

Most of the code in this example is concerned with error handling rather than with the normal operation of the program. This situation is particularly annoying in an application that performs many operating system calls. The additional code obscures the logic of the program, and the tedium of coding an error response for each operation often causes programmers to omit error handling. In addition, if a function must return a value, its return value cannot be used to signal an error unless there is some invalid value that can be designated as an error indication. For example, there is no obvious value that can be used to signal integer overflow for a function such as pow().

ANSI C provides the assert() macro, which is defined in the standard header file assert.h. The value of its argument is checked at execution time and if it is zero (i.e., false), a diagnostic message including the line number in the source code is printed on stderr and then the program exits. The caller cannot specify any error handling code and execution cannot continue if the argument is zero. The run-time checks can be turned on or off with a compiler option. As with error return codes, each operation must be checked explicitly, but there is no error handling code interspersed with application code.

Error propagation in C

Suppose an error can occur in one function and the program must propagate that event to another function that can handle the problem. If the program uses return values as error codes, then each function in a sequence of invocations must explicitly check for the error, and if the error occurs, return the error value rather than proceeding. Unfortunately, the code for each of these functions must deal with an error that is not intrinsic to the purpose of that function, and they cannot use their return values to return information to their callers. Using an additional parameter for the error code would solve the latter problem, but not the former, which is more serious.

The ANSI C standard header file setjmp.h defines the structure jmp_buf and declares the functions setjmp() and longjmp(), which provide goto-like transfer of control between functions. A function calls setjmp() to save the information necessary for restoring its environment (i.e., its register contents and the contents and location of its activation record at that point) in an instance of the jmp_buf structure. That object is usually defined globally to avoid passing it through each function in a sequence of invocations. When a function it calls (possibly indirectly) detects an error, that function calls longjmp() to perform a direct return to the environment stored in the jmp_buf object. setjmp() returns zero from the call that establishes a jmp_buf, and returns the second argument of the longjmp() call when control reaches that point via a longjmp() invocation. To use this mechanism for error propagation, the function that can handle the error calls setjmp(), and checks its return value to determine whether to perform normal processing or error handling.

```
/* using setjmp() and longjmp() for error propagation in C */
#include <setjmp.h>
struct jmp_buf handler;
void func()
{
    int errorCode;
    if ( (errorCode = setjmp(handler)) == 0 )
    {
        /* any function called from this block (possibly indirectly) can transfer control
           directly to the error handling code by calling longjmp(handler, num), where
           num gives the error code */
        /* ... normal processing ... */
    }
    else
    {
        /* ... error handling ... */
    }
}
```

This facility has the advantages of not cluttering intervening functions in a sequence of invocations with error propagation, and of allowing the programmer to specify error handling for several operations in one place. However, there is no guarantee that the stack frame saved in a jmp_buf by a call of setjmp() is still active when longjmp() is called, there is no clean-up of the intervening activation records, the signaler and handler are tightly coupled because they must use the same jmp_buf object and the technique is difficult to use with multiple types of errors. As we will see in this section, the C++ exception facility is an improvement over the use of the setjmp() and longjmp() functions for error propagation in a number of ways.

- The handler's stack frame is guaranteed to exist.
- Local variables in stack frames that are exited are finalized.
- The signaler and handler communicate through an exception object, and no global jmp_buf object is needed.
- Multiple types of errors are supported transparently.
- Information can be passed from the signaler to the handler.

The C++ exception facility

As discussed in section 0.1.3, error handling is an essential part of programming and is an important issue in the design of reusable components, so many newer languages such as ML, CLU, Ada, and C++ support the features necessary for programmer-defined exception handling. The programmer does not have to check each operation separately and specify error handling code for that operation. Instead, he or she can define exception handlers for a function or block that apply to all the operations within that unit, so that error handling code can be defined separately from application logic (perhaps later during program development). The programmer can specify different handlers for the different types of exceptions that can occur in a function or block. In addition, the exception facility does not allow a program to ignore a run-time error and continue in an invalid state. If no handler is defined for an exception that occurs, the program terminates. In C++, exceptions are defined as class objects that are passed to the handler, and related exceptions can be defined and handled using class derivation.

An exception mechanism is particularly useful for an object-oriented language because vendor-supplied class libraries must have a way of signaling errors to clients. The designer of a class can recognize that an error has occurred within a method, but cannot know how the executing application should handle it. On the other hand, the user of the class library knows what his or her program must do upon encountering various types of errors, but cannot detect the occurrence of an error intrinsic to the classes in the library. Exceptions are an important part of the interface of a class and provide looser coupling between a class and its clients.

Exceptions solve another problem that occurs in the design of C++ classes. Constructors and conversion operators do not have a return type, so it is not possible to use return values to signal errors due to invalid arguments or unavailable resources.[20] Destructors also have no way to signal an error if there is a problem in releasing an object's resources. Exceptions provide this capability.

The C++ exception facility is a somewhat recent addition to the language, which is not supported by all current language systems. Implementing exceptions is different from providing support for all other language features (except templates) because the processing necessary cannot be directly translated to similar C code. Support for exceptions changes the model for control flow among function activations, and can impact function calls and returns even in programs that do not use exceptions. It is also not straightforward to support exceptions in a manner that allows calling C functions from C++ code.

Generally, an implementation of the exception facility assumes that exceptions occur much less frequently than standard function calls. The implementation can then be designed so that there is no additional time overhead for a function call, although there is some space overhead for bookkeeping information in all programs (see [Str94]). However, a considerable amount of overhead is incurred when an exception is signaled, so you should not regard exceptions as an alternate control structure to be employed for transferring control from one function to within another. This view is also not appropriate because of the difficulty of understanding features whose semantics depend on the dynamic behavior of the program, as do exceptions.

13.3.2 Signaling an Exception

The throw **expression**

When a method or function detects an error condition that it cannot deal with itself, it can signal an exception with a *throw expression*.[21] We can think of the throw expression as a nonlocal goto statement that transfers control to an exception handler defined at a previous point in the execution of the program (if any). Signaling an exception is unlike a function call because control does not return back to the function that signaled the exception. It is unlike a return statement because control is not necessarily transferred to the function's caller. However, signaling an exception is similar to a function call or return in the sense that an object is transmitted to the handler in which control resumes. We will see in section 13.3.4 that this transfer of control is safe because the process returns to an existing environment and calls the destructors for automatic objects in all intervening environments.

A throw expression consists of the reserved word throw and an expression whose result is passed to the exception handler. That object's type determines which of the client's handlers is executed when the exception occurs. Usually

---

[20] In fact, a constructor could use a reference argument to pass an error code but it would still have to be tested explicitly by the client and propagated if necessary.

[21] The keyword throw was chosen because "raise" and "signal" are already the names of functions in the C standard library.

the operand of a throw expression is an explicit constructor invocation, as follows:

```
// format for messages that throw exceptions
RetType Class::message(... parameter list ...)
{
   // ... other processing ...
   if ( ... error condition ... )
      throw Error(... initializer ...);
   // ... other processing ...
}
```

In this example, *Error* is the class of the object passed to the exception handler, and exception classes are defined like any class. When the throw expression is evaluated, an instance of the exception class is created and initialized. In fact, a throw expression can pass any object to the handler, including built-in type values, such as a char* that gives a string describing the error. However, it is better practice to design a class specifically for this purpose. Clearly, the compiler must have encountered the definition of the class whose instance is thrown.

For example, suppose that we define the exception EmptyError, which is signaled by methods in collection classes such as Queue when a client attempts to remove an element from an empty collection. (We will discuss defining exception classes in the next section.) The methods for Queue<>::remove() in section 13.2.3 and PriorityQueue<>::first() in section 13.2.6 signal an exception with a throw expression that creates an instance of EmptyError using its default constructor.

As another example, we will define an exception class SubscriptError in the next section, which indicates that a subscript value is out of bounds for fixed-size classes such as Array and String. The constructor arguments for the class are the invalid index and the size of the collection. The String::operator[ ]() method signals this exception when the index supplied by the caller is invalid, as follows:

```
// index operator for class String that throws the exception SubscriptError
#include "SubscriptError.h"
char& String::operator[](int index)
{
   if ( index < 0 || index > length_ - 1 )
      throw SubscriptError(index, length_);
   return str_[index];
}
```

Exception specifications

The errors that a function can signal are part of its interface. A function declaration may inform clients of the exceptions it can raise by including an *exception specification* (also called a "throw list") in its declaration. This specification follows the parameter list, and consists of the reserved word throw followed by a parenthesized list of the types of exceptions that the function can signal. For example,

```
// an exception specification declares which exceptions a function can signal
template <class ElemType>
ElemType Queue<ElemType>::remove() throw (EmptyError);


char& String::operator[](int index) throw (SubscriptError);
```

A function may also throw instances of any descendants of the exception classes listed in its exception specification. A function that gives an empty exception specification declares that it does not raise any exceptions. For compatibility with code written before exceptions were supported, functions are not required to give an exception specification, and a function that does not include one may signal any exception. To determine the exceptions that such a function may raise, a client programmer must examine the function's code (if available), and the code of any functions it calls directly or indirectly. The exception specification is not part of the function's type, that is, it is not used in argument matching or in determining whether an assignment to a pointer to function is valid.

If a function does declare an exception specification, it may not raise exceptions that are not on that list, directly or indirectly. The exception specification must include exceptions that may be propagated through the function from functions that it calls (i.e., if it does not handle them). If a function with an exception specification signals an exception that is not in its list (i.e., because it calls a function without an exception specification that can signal an exception), then the predefined function unexpected() is invoked immediately, which terminates execution. In effect, unexpected() handles the exception, and it can no longer be handled by the function's caller (and so on). The programmer must then add the exception to the function's exception specification so that it correctly gives the function's interface, and recompiles the function. Checking for undeclared exceptions cannot be done at compile time, but occurs when a function signals such an exception.

The default implementation of unexpected() calls the predefined function terminate(), whose default implementation calls abort() (see section 13.3.4). The programmer can provide a definition for unexpected() by passing a pointer to his or her function to the function set_unexpected().[22] set_unexpected() takes and returns a pointer to a function with no parameter or return value (like the function set_new_handler() described in section 9.2.6), and returns a pointer to the previous unexpected() function so that it can be restored if desired. A programmer-defined implementation of unexpected() cannot return to its caller. It must re-throw the exception, signal another exception, or terminate execution by calling terminate(), exit(), or abort().

---

[22] set_unexpected() was originally declared in a header file called except.h, and is declared in the header file <exception> in the ANSI/ISO C++ Standard Library.

13.3.3 Exception Classes

Predefined exceptions

Many languages that support exception handling define particular exceptions. For example, Ada defines a number of exceptions that can be raised by operations on built-in types such as NUMERIC_ERROR, or on programmer-defined types such as CONSTRAINT_ERROR (e.g., due to an invalid array index). C++ does not specify any predefined exceptions for errors that can occur in operations on built-in types such as arithmetic overflow.[23] The new operator signals the exception bad_alloc (formerly xalloc) when there is not enough free storage available to allocate an object. As stated in section 12.2.5, the run-time type information extension specifies that an invalid attempt to perform a dynamic reference cast signals a bad_cast exception.

The ANSI/ISO C++ Standard Library defines exceptions that are used to signal various errors detected by the methods of library classes. As we discussed in section 11.3.4, the iostream classes can be set to signal the exception ios_base::failure when a stream error occurs. The Standard also defines a hierarchy of exceptions, which has been reorganized several times during the standardization process. Figure 13.1 illustrates this exception hierarchy. The class exception (formerly xmsg) is the root of this hierarchy, and defines a virtual member function exception::what() that returns a const char* describing the error. Its subclasses are logic_error (formerly xlogic), which represents exceptions due to programming errors such as violating preconditions on methods, and runtime_error (formerly xruntime), which represents exceptions due to errors that can only be detected at execution time. The meanings of the exceptions domain_error, invalid_argument, out_of_range, range_error, and overflow_error should be obvious from their names. An instance of length_error is signaled when a method attempts to create an object that is larger than its maximum allowable size. Each descendant of exception defines a constructor that takes a const char* which is returned by the message exception::what(). These classes are declared in

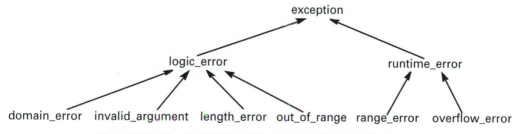

Figure 13.1 The ANSI/ISO C++ Standard Library exception class hierarchy.

---

[23] As in C, many language systems raise the signal SIGFPE upon detecting many floating-point arithmetic errors. A handler for this signal can be registered by using the function signal(), which is declared in the header file signal.h. However, only one handler can be specified for the entire program for a signal and signal handling is not portable because not all language systems support this feature.

the standard header <stdexcept> (not <exception>). For example, index errors in the array and string classes in the library signal out_of_range. If your language system supports these classes, use the appropriate class for signaling errors in your methods or define your exception classes as subclasses of the appropriate class. For example, we would derive the class SubscriptError discussed in this section from out_of_range.

The standard header <exception> defines an exception class bad_exception which is signaled by the language system when a function signals an exception that is not in its exception specification. It also declares the function set_unexpected() discussed in the previous section, and the function set_terminate(), which we discuss in section 13.3.5.

Defining exception classes

The class designer can define an exception that simply identifies the type of error as follows:

```
// definition of the exception class EmptyError in Queue.h
class EmptyError { };          // the compiler-generated default construct does nothing
```

Like an exception in Ada, this exception class allows clients to handle that type of exception separately from other exception types, but does not provide any information about the error that occurred. The class designer can define an exception class used to identify errors detected by the methods of a particular class or subhierarchy as nested within the class or the root of the subhierarchy (e.g., Queue<>::EmptyError). This encapsulates the exception class and reduces the possibility of name conflicts in the global scope.

The class designer can use the exception object for type-safe transfer of information from the signaler to the handler of the exception. The function that signals the exception uses its constructor arguments to place information in the object, and its protocol provides access to that information for the client's handler. For example, let us define the exception class SubscriptError, which indicates that a subscript value is out of bounds for classes such as Array and String. (We saw an example of signaling this exception in the previous section.) The constructor arguments for the class are the invalid index and the size of the collection so that this information is available to the code that handles the exception. We define the class as follows:

```
// an exception class for index range errors
// the accessor messages can be used by client exception handlers
class SubscriptError
{
public:
    SubscriptError(int indx, int sz);
    String message() const;
```

```
    int index() const;
    int size() const;
protected:
    int index_;
    int size_;
};

inline SubscriptError::SubscriptError(int indx, int sz)
    : index_(indx), size_(sz)
{ }

inline String SubscriptError::message() const
{ return "subscript error"; }

inline int SubscriptError::index() const
{ return index_; }

inline int SubscriptError::size() const
{ return size_; }
```

The class designer may also include a data member in the exception object that refers to the receiver of the method that raised the exception, and a message for accessing this information. In this case, *this would appear in the initializer for the exception object in throw expressions in the class's methods. This information would allow the client handler to identify the receiver of the message that caused the error.

Constructors and destructors can also throw exceptions to signal errors in acquiring or releasing system resources. This allows clients to use exception handling to detect errors in creating an object, rather than checking an isValid() message after each object creation operation (like checking ios error flags). For example, we might define a class File (like the Smalltalk class Filename discussed in section 6.1.1) whose methods signal exceptions that identify error conditions, as follows:

```
// using exceptions with the class File
class File
{
public:
    File(const String& path)
        throw (FileDeviceError, FileNotFoundError, FilePermissionsError);
    File(const Directory& where, const String& name)
        throw (FileDeviceError, FileNotFoundError, FilePermissionsError);
    ~File()
        throw (FileDeviceError);
    bool isExecutable() const;
    int size() const;
    void remove()
        throw (FileDeviceError, FilePermissionsError);
```

```
    // ... other protocol ...
};
```

Exception hierarchies

The class designer can also define hierarchies of exceptions by using derivation among exception classes. For example, we might define an abstract exception
base class MathError with subclasses such as UnderflowError, OverflowError, Divide-
ByZeroError, and so on for numeric messages. We can imagine a fairly large hierarchy rooted at IOError which includes errors upon data transfer to and from displays,
files, and networks, such as those in the previous example.

Derivation among exception classes allows a client of the classes that signal
those exceptions to use one handler to deal with a category of exceptions by specifying a handler for an exception base class. The designer of the exception classes
can provide class-specific behavior for such handlers by defining virtual functions
for those classes (e.g., for error messages). Like all class hierarchies, this organization provides extendibility because the designer can derive new exception classes
and existing handlers can deal with them.

13.3.4 Handling Exceptions

The try block

The caller of a function that can signal an exception (or its caller and so
on) can specify the operations to be performed when an exception occurs. To
respond to exceptions, the programmer encloses the code that calls functions
that can signal exceptions in a *try block* associated with a set of *exception handlers*. Each exception handler is defined as a block introduced by the reserved
word catch, and gives a single parameter type that specifies the exception class
that handler deals with. An ellipsis (...) as the parameter type of a handler
indicates that it handles all exceptions. When an exception is signaled, the type
of the object created by that throw expression is matched against the catch handler parameters to determine which handler to invoke (if any). The exception
object is then available to the handler like a function argument (except within a
catch(...) handler), so the handler may use any protocol defined by that object's
class.

For example, a program that uses queues and strings can specify exception
handlers as follows:

```
// format for the C++ try/catch statement used for exception handling
#include "String.h"          // includes the definition of class SubscriptError
#include "Queue.h"           // includes the definition of class EmptyError
int main()
{
    try
    {
        Queue<String> strQu;
```

```
        // ... other useful operations ...
      }
      catch (SubscriptError subErr)
      {
        // ... SubscriptError handler code using subErr ...
      }
      catch (EmptyError empErr)
      {
        // ... EmptyError handler code using empErr ...
      }
      catch (...)
      {
        // ... handler for any other exceptions ...
      }
      // execution continues here if no exception occurs,
      // or after execution of any handler that does not exit
  }
```

Because each handler is a block, it can define local variables. The exception handlers are not lexically nested within the associated try block, so they do not have access to identifiers declared in that scope. Identifiers in the scopes enclosing the try block are visible in the handlers.

Selecting an exception handler

Suppose a method invoked in a try block signals an exception. If more than one exception handler is associated with the try block, the type of the object created by the throw expression is matched against the parameter type of each handler in sequence. When a match is found, that handler is executed and subsequent handlers for the try block (and for previous try blocks in the sequence of invocations) are ignored. The exception resolution process can apply trivial conversions, the standard conversion to an ancestor type, or the standard conversion from a pointer to void* in matching the thrown object with a handler parameter. It does not apply numeric conversions or programmer-defined conversions. After execution of the selected handler, flow of control continues at the statement after the entire try/catch construct. If no handler matches the type of the exception object, then the previous invocation in the sequence of invocations is searched for a matching handler.

Because the compiler can apply the standard conversion to ancestor to the thrown object, an exception handler can deal with a subhierarchy of exception classes by specifying a reference to the root class as its parameter type. The handler parameters are matched in order, so a client can also provide special handling for a particular class in the hierarchy by placing a handler for that class before the handler for the root class. For example, suppose that we have the class File described previously and FilePermissionsError is derived from FileError. A client can provide a handler for FilePermissionsError and another handler for all other descendants of FileError as follows:

```
// a handler for an exception base class uses a reference parameter
// handlers are matched in the order given
#include "File.h"              // defines FileError and its descendants
int main()
{
   try
   {
      File("info/dataFile");
      // ... other operations ...
   }
   catch (FilePermissionsError filePermErr)
   {
      // ... FilePermissionsError handler code ...
   }
   catch (FileError& fileErr)
   {
      // ... handler code for all other file errors ...
   }
}
```

A base class handler parameter must use a reference to avoid losing descendant-specific information, and to allow dynamic binding of exception class messages. Of course, the handler does not know the class identity of the object caught, unless it uses the dynamic cast operator.

Unlike the argument matching procedure used for overloaded functions, the order of the exception handlers is significant in choosing a handler. Placing a handler for a descendant exception class after a handler for an ancestor is invalid because the descendant handler can never be selected. Similarly, a handler with an ellipsis as the parameter type must be the last handler, and the programmer cannot specify two handlers with the same parameter type for the same try block. The compiler issues an error in these cases as the programmer most likely did not intend to code a handler that could not be selected.

13.3.5 Control Flow and Finalization

Locating a handler

As discussed in section 0.1.3, when a method or function signals an exception, it triggers a process of searching back through the sequence of invocations leading up to that function activation, looking for a handler for that type of exception. If the signaling function was called from a try block with a handler whose parameter matches the exception type, that handler is executed. If the function's caller does not define a matching handler, its caller's caller is examined for a matching handler (i.e., the function does not have to pass the exception on to its caller explicitly). The process continues until encountering an invocation from a try block with a matching handler. That is, the handler executed is the one with a matching parameter whose try block was most recently entered by the flow of control. Once a handler is

selected, the resolution process regards the exception as being handled, and does not consider any other matching handlers further back in the sequence of invocations. If a function handles a particular exception, its callers will never receive that exception (unless its handler "re-throws" the exception as described later in this section).

When the matching handler is found, the remainder of that try block is skipped and control is transferred to the handler. If the handler does not terminate execution of the program, then execution continues at the point following the associated try block. That is, execution does not continue at the statement following the function call in that try block that triggered the exception, nor at the point following the statement including the throw expression.

If no handler whose parameter matches the type of the thrown object is found in the sequence of active invocations, then the predefined function terminate() is invoked, rather than continuing execution with unpredictable results. terminate() is also called if the stack appears to be corrupted, or if a destructor signals an exception during the process of searching for a handler (as described in the next subsection). The default implementation of terminate() calls the C standard library function abort(), which terminates execution immediately (without calling any destructors, even those for static objects). As with unexpected(), the programmer can provide a definition for this function by passing a pointer to his or her function to set_terminate(). Like set_unexpected(), it takes and returns a pointer to a function with no parameter or return value, and returns a pointer to the previous terminate() function. A programmer-defined implementation of terminate() cannot return to its caller, but must call exit() or abort() after performing any clean-up necessary before the application exits.

Some languages include a feature for retrying the operation that originally raised the exception after performing the exception handler, which is termed the *resumption model* of exception handling. For example, this capability is useful for handling user errors such as an invalid input or inserting the wrong floppy disk. However, to implement this feature, it is necessary to re-establish each activation record in the sequence of invocations leading up to the operation that failed. Therefore, C++ supports the *termination model*, in which popping a stack frame terminates that function invocation. If the program can perform some clean-up (e.g., re-prompting the user) and try the operation again, it encloses the try block and handler in a loop that exits when the function call is successful. The handler performs whatever operations are necessary before retrying the operation. For example,

```
// retrying an operation that causes an exception with the termination model
#include <iostream.h>
#include "String.h"
#include "File.h"

int main()
{
    String filename;
    bool obtainedFilename = false;
```

```
    while ( !obtainedFilename )
    {
      try
      {
        cout << "Enter the file name" << flush;
        cin >> filename;
        File infile(filename);
        obtainedFilename = true;          // the constructor didn't signal an exception
      }
      catch (FileError& fileError)
      {
        cout << "File not there or can't be opened!" << endl;
      }
      // after handling the error (or completing the try block), execution continues here
    }
    // ... process the file ...
}
```

Signaling exceptions in handlers

An exception handler can catch an exception, perform some processing, and then determine that it actually cannot deal with that error. If so, it can "re-throw" the exception by executing a throw expression with no operand. (If a throw expression without an operand appears anywhere besides a handler, terminate() is invoked.) In this case, the search for a handler that matches the original exception continues back through the sequence of calls on the run-time stack (not with the succeeding handlers for the same try block). The exception object thrown is the original object (even if it is a descendant class object caught by a handler for ancestor objects with a value parameter). That is, the exception resolution process must maintain the current exception object until the selected handler completes execution.

Suppose a handler signals an exception (i.e., rather than re-throwing the exception it caught). Because control exits the handler, the exception process considers the original exception as having been dealt with. That is, only one exception is active at a time, and there is no stack of exceptions (as is often implemented for hardware interrupts). The new exception can only be dealt with by the caller of the function in which the handler's try block appears, not by subsequent handlers of that try block. For example, if an exception handler throws the same exception type that it handles, it does not cause an infinite loop. A new exception is signaled and the search begins in the caller of the function containing the handler's try block.

Environment finalization

As the search for a matching handler proceeds, the activation record for each function that does not define a matching handler is popped from the run-time stack, beginning with the function that signaled the exception. An important aspect of the C++ exception resolution process is that it invokes the destructors for all the objects in each activation record that it releases. The destructors for the local variables of the function that signaled the exception are executed, followed by destructors for the local variables of each function in the sequence of invocations, back to the function called in the try block whose handler was selected. However, the resolution process cannot call destructors for objects that were created dynamically by any of those functions. The receiver of a message is not destroyed when the activation record for its method is popped because that stack frame contains a pointer to the receiver (i.e., this), not an embedded copy of that object.

As the exception resolution process unwinds the stack, it only calls destructors for automatic objects or subobjects that have been completely constructed. For example, suppose we have a class IndexedFile that has two fstream data members, indexFile and dataFile. Recall that the fstream constructor opens the associated file and that its destructor closes the file. Now suppose that during execution of the IndexedFile constructor, indexFile is constructed successfully, but an exception occurs during construction of dataFile that the IndexedFile constructor does not handle. When the stack frame for the IndexedFile constructor is released, the destructor for indexFile is executed but the destructor for dataFile is not. If the caller of the IndexedFile constructor does not handle the exception and its stack frame is popped, the destructor for its IndexedFile object is not invoked because that object's constructor did not execute to completion. Similarly, if a stack frame contains an array of class instances and an exception is raised in constructing one of those objects, only the destructors for the array elements that were completely constructed are executed if the function does not handle that exception.

As stated in the previous subsection, only one exception is active at any time. Suppose that in the process of unwinding the stack while searching for a handler, a destructor for an automatic object in a stack frame being released signals an exception. Because the original exception can no longer be handled, terminate() is executed in this case. If at all possible, a destructor should handle any errors that its execution can trigger rather than raising or propagating an exception.

Dynamic allocation and exception resolution

Consider a class whose constructor allocates dynamic memory and then performs some other initialization, with its destructor deallocating that storage. If an exception occurs during that initialization and the stack frame containing the object is released, a memory leak occurs because the constructor did not complete execution. The constructor should catch any exceptions generated by the initialization functions with a handler that deallocates the storage and then re-throws the exception. Unfortunately, this duplicates code from the class's destructor, and it becomes complicated if the constructor performs several dynamic allocations.

The problem of an exception propagated through a function causing a resource leak for a dynamically allocated object is not unique to constructors. To prevent this, we can encapsulate the dynamic allocation and deallocation using a separate class that allocates the storage in its constructor and deallocates it in the destructor. This is essentially what our String class in section 10.2.2 does: Rather than using a char* variable and dynamic allocation and deallocation of a char array, a function uses an automatic variable of type String. If the exception resolution process causes that function's stack frame to be exited, the String destructor is called automatically.

To provide automatic finalization in the presence of exceptions for all classes, the ANSI/ISO C++ Standard Library includes the class template auto_ptr<> as a smart pointer class (recall section 11.1.5) whose destructor deallocates the referent of the pointer it owns. This template is defined in the header <memory> as follows:

```
// the ANSI/ISO C++ Standard Library class template auto_ptr<>
template <class Type>
class auto_ptr
{
public:
    explicit auto_ptr(Type* argPtr = NULL) : ptr(argPtr) { }
    ~auto_ptr() { delete ptr; }
    Type* operator->() const { return ptr; }
    Type& operator*() const { return *ptr; }
    // ... other protocol ...
private:
    Type* ptr;
};
```

With this class template, the client must create the dynamic object because the template cannot be parameterized for that object's initializer (recall that expression parameter values must be compile-time constants). For example,

```
// using the class template auto_ptr<>
void func()
{
    List<String>* pNames = new List<String>;
    auto_ptr<List<String> > pNameList(pNames);
    // ... other processing using pNameList as a pointer ...
}
```

The function func() in this example need not deallocate the referent of pNames because the destructor for the object pNameList will do so, even if the function's activation record is released by the exception resolution process because an exception was signaled by a function func() calls and not handled. A class whose constructor may trigger exceptions can use auto pointer members rather than pointer members so that their referents are deallocated if an exception occurs that the constructor does not handle. The destructor for the class no longer needs to deallocate that storage.

In section 11.1.5, we briefly discussed the semantics of copying for smart pointers. The C++ Standard Library auto_ptr<> template class permits copying a pointer, and its copy constructor and assignment operator transfer ownership of the referent object to the target of the initialization or assignment. Some implementations of auto_ptr<> also provide equality tests and a member template that permits conversions among auto pointers if the underlying types are convertible.

Allocation of the exception object

Signaling an exception creates the object specified in the throw expression. The exception object cannot be allocated in the activation record of the function that throws the exception, because it will be lost when that stack frame is released during the process of locating a handler. If the exception handler parameter is passed by value, the compiler can allocate the exception object on the heap, copy it to the handler's stack frame, and then deallocate it. To handle heap overflow exceptions, the language system can pre-allocate static storage for this purpose, rather than using the heap.

When an exception handler uses a reference parameter so that it can handle a set of exception classes, copying the exception object to the handler's stack frame is insufficient because descendant-specific data members would be lost. In this case, the actual object can be allocated on the heap or in pre-allocated storage, with the argument implemented by a pointer to it, as usual for pass by reference. The compiler must arrange to finalize and deallocate the exception object when the exception handler terminates.

13.4 NAMESPACES

13.4.1 Purpose

Handling global name conflicts

In C++, there is one global name space for all identifiers that are not defined within a class scope, a function scope, or a code file scope (i.e., as a static file scope object or function). In addition, type names cannot be specified static file scope identifiers, so the names of all non-nested classes are declared in the global name space. This "pollution" of the global name space is a problem for large applications, especially for programs that use several class libraries. For example, most class libraries define foundation classes such as strings, dates, and rectangles, whose names will cause conflicts when the program is linked.[24]

Class designers have used two techniques to deal with this problem. One approach is to prepend a distinguishing prefix to all the identifiers in a library or framework. For example, the Free Software Foundation class library might define classes with names such as FSFString, FSFPushButton, and so on. If a project uses both the Free Software Foundation library and another library that defines the class

---

[24] The fact that each library needs these classes is a motivation for development of a standard class library for C++.

MITString, a name conflict does not occur. However, this technique is inconvenient for clients because it lengthens names without adding useful information (other than free advertising for the vendor).

An alternative is to use an enclosing class as a name space only. The designer nests a set of classes, functions, and objects within that class, with the functions and objects declared as static members. Clients must qualify each use of those class, function, and object names with the enclosing class name and the scope operator (e.g., FSF::String, FSF::PushButton, etc.). However, this approach misuses the class construct. The enclosing class FSF does not represent a category of entities or components, and is not intended to define a type for instantiation. In fact, it has no non-static members. Like using a prefix, the names are unnecessarily verbose, and the code is not perspicuous and can be confusing for clients. Another problem is that there are already numerous C++ class libraries available, so there will eventually be conflicts among the prefixes or enclosing class names unless they are long, which increases the inconvenience for clients.

The namespace extension

The C++ namespace extension allows a class designer or library vendor to define a *namespace* in which a set of identifiers is declared. A namespace definition creates a named scope, but does not define a type like a class definition. Like the import/export scope supported by Modula-2 modules and Ada packages (recall sections 0.2.5 and 1.1.3), the namespace extension provides us with explicit control over the names that are present in a scope. We can select among conflicting names, import names and use them without qualification when possible, and use qualified names if necessary. Unlike modules, namespaces do not support a feature for declaring that an identifier is local to a namespace and is not exported, except if it is a non-public member of a class in the namespace. We can use namespaces with large systems to encapsulate the set of classes that make up each subsystem. Library vendors can also use namespaces to manage successive releases of class libraries.

The namespace extension provides three ways to use identifiers declared within a namespace in other scopes:

- explicitly qualifying the identifier with the namespace name
- importing an identifier with a using declaration
- making an entire library available with a using namespace directive.

In the ANSI/ISO C++ Standard, the C standard function library and the C++ standard class library are defined within the namespace std, and programs cannot add to that namespace. The namespace facility is the most recent extension to the language (in fact, it is not mentioned in the ARM), and few language systems support it at this time.

13.4.2 Namespace Definition

Definition and code organization

A namespace definition begins with the reserved word namespace and the namespace name, which are followed by a list of declarations enclosed in braces. Namespace scope has the same properties as file scope: Only declaration statements may appear, and an identifier is visible from the point of its declaration forward. Each type or object name in a namespace must be unique, and function names may be overloaded. (A namespace can contain extern "C" declarations, but these function names cannot be overloaded.) A namespace can also include template definitions. Namespaces can only be defined at file scope or within other namespaces—that is, namespaces can be nested. Language systems that support namespaces regard global scope as an unnamed namespace.

We define namespaces in header files that define classes and templates and declare functions and objects, which are included in client code files. The namespace's methods, functions, and objects are defined in code files. Like class header files, namespace header files must use the #ifndef preprocessor directive to avoid multiple definition errors from the compiler for the enclosed classes and templates. The namespace name for a function or object must be encoded into the name seen by the linker (like the class scope of a member function).

The following example illustrates defining a namespace (note that, unlike a class definition, there is no terminating semicolon):

```
// an example namespace defined in "examples.h"
namespace examples
{
  class String
  {
      // ... as defined in chapter 11 and 12 ...
  };
  inline bool operator==(const String&, const String&);
  // ... other String operator definitions that had been defined at file scope ...

  template <class ElemType>
  class Queue
  {
  protected:
    class Node
    {
        // ... as defined in section 10.2.4 ...
    }
    // ... as defined in section 13.2.3 ...
  };

  void func1(const String&);    // defined in the namespace code file
  void func2(int);              // defined in the namespace code file
```

```
        int num1;                    // defined and initialized in the namespace code file
        int num2;                    // defined and initialized in the namespace code file
    }                  // end namespace examples
```

Namespaces for class libraries can be quite large, so the language allows the designer to split a namespace into several header files. When the compiler encounters more than one global definition of the same namespace name, it regards them as contributing their enclosed declarations to the same namespace. For example, we can split the previous namespace definition into as many header files as desired. This feature allows the library designer to use separate header files for each class in the library, with all the classes defined within the same namespace. It also reduces compile time for clients, as they only need to include the header files for the classes or functions they use in their code.

Unnamed namespaces

Each code file in a program may define a local unnamed namespace nested within the global unnamed namespace. We can declare identifiers within this namespace by enclosing them in a namespace definition without a namespace name.

```
// each code file contains a local unnamed namespace
namespace
{
    // ... declarations visible only in this code file ...
}
```

The identifiers in the unnamed namespace are visible throughout that code unit without qualification or with the unary scope operator. This feature is intended to replace the use of the reserved word static at file scope to declare an identifier as being visible in the file, but not in the global scope of the program. An expression in another code file cannot access these identifiers because using the unary scope operator in that file refers to its own unnamed scope. Unlike static file scope, types and classes can be defined within the unnamed namespace.

Namespace aliases

All namespace names are visible globally (except those defined within another namespace), so each identifier that names a distinct namespace must be unique. (Recall that if two namespace definitions use the same namespace name, the definitions both contribute identifiers to the same namespace, rather than there being a multiple definition error.) To provide for enough different namespace names, the namespace extension allows the programmer to define a local alias for a namespace name. In this way, the namespace designer can use a longer name such as FreeSoftwareFoundation, and a client can define a shorter alias such as FSF for use within his or her code. The shorter alias is only visible within that code file, and that identifier must be unique within that scope. The definition of a namespace alias appears like an initialization, as follows:[25]

```
// a programmer can provide a shorter alias for a namespace name
namespace ex = examples;
```

This feature also allows us to change libraries or versions of a library easily. We use the alias rather than the library name within the code, and when switching libraries, we only need to modify the namespace alias definition.

13.4.3 Using Identifiers Declared in a Namespace

Explicit qualification

We can refer to an identifier declared in a namespace by using the namespace name and the scope operator. For example,

```
// explicit qualification with a namespace name by a client in another scope
#include "examples.h"
int main()
{
    examples::String str("hello");
    examples::func1(str);
    examples::func2(examples::num2);
}
```

Using a qualified name does not import the identifier into the scope in which that expression occurs. For example, the identifiers String, func1, func2, and num2 in the previous example can also be declared in the scope of main() with a different meaning. This format is verbose, but it avoids conflicts with other names in that scope, and can be a useful documentation of which library's identifier is used. Because global scope is the unnamed namespace, the unary prefix use of the scope operator (e.g., ::name) always refers to a global definition of that identifier.

We can define methods, functions, and objects declared in a namespace header file in the namespace code file using qualified names, like the definitions of class's member functions and static data members in the class code file. The methods of classes defined in the namespace are defined using cascaded applications of the scope operator. For example,

```
// examples.cc: using qualified names in a namespace code file
#include "examples.h"

int examples::num1 = 1;
int examples::num2 = 2;
```

---

[25] Perhaps the alias definition should have used the & symbol since it does not create a new namespace, but supplies a reference to an existing namespace.

```
void examples::func1(const examples::String& str)
{
    // ... function definition ...
}


template <class ElemType>
ElemType examples::Queue<ElemType>::remove() throw (examples::EmptyError)
{
    // ... as defined in section 13.2.3 ...
}


// ... other definitions ...
```

Within the definitions of methods and functions in a namespace, identifiers in that namespace need not be qualified with the namespace name because the qualified name in the function's definition specifies the namespace scope. For example, if the code for examples::func1() calls examples::func2(), that invocation does not require name qualification. This is exactly like defining member function definitions separately from the class definition, in which qualification of member names with the class name is not necessary.

We also use a cascaded application of the scope operator to refer to a static member of a class declared within a namespace. For example, if the class Point with static members as defined in section 10.2.2 were declared in the namespace examples, we would use the expression examples::Point::numPoints() to invoke its class method. Cascaded applications of the scope operator are also used to refer to identifiers declared in nested namespaces.

The class designer can also use qualified names to declare a class within a namespace and define the class separately from the namespace definition.

```
// examples.h: using qualified names to define classes and inline member functions
// separately from the namespace definition
namespace examples
{
    class String;
    // ... other declarations ...
}


class examples::String
{
    // ... as defined in chapter 11 and 12 ...
};


inline examples::String& examples::String::operator=(const examples::String& argStr)
{
    // ... as defined in section 11.1.3 ...
}
```

The using declaration

We import a particular identifier in a namespace into a scope with a *using declaration*, which consists of the reserved word using followed by the qualified name to be imported. A using declaration allows the programmer to use that identifier without qualification in the scope in which it appears. Essentially, it adds a local alias for that identifier to the scope, which has the characteristics declared for the identifier in its namespace (i.e., whether it is a type, function, or object, what its type is, and so on). If the imported name is a function name that is overloaded in the namespace, the using declaration imports all its definitions. Only one name can be imported in each using declaration. A using declaration can appear at file scope, or within a class, function, or namespace.

Because a using declaration adds an identifier to the scope in which it is given, it is invalid if that declaration causes an illegal name conflict. That is, a using declaration is an error if that identifier is already declared in the scope in which it occurs and the imported identifier is not a new overloading of an existing function name. This error is detected at the point at which the redeclaration of the name occurs. In addition, a using declaration hides a declaration of the same name in an enclosing scope.

The following examples illustrate the semantics of the using declaration with the example namespace defined in the previous section:

```
// the using declaration imports a name into a scope
#include "examples.h"
int num1 = 0;
void func1(long);
void func2();
using examples::func1;          // OK: func1 is overloaded at file scope

int main()
{
    using examples::String;     // "String" cannot already be declared in this scope
    String str("hello");        // no qualification is necessary (i.e., examples::String)
    using examples::num1;       // import num1 into the scope of main()
    num1++;                     // examples::num1
    ::num1++;                   // the global num1
    using examples::func2;      // hides ::func2() within main()
    func2();                    // error: only func2(int) is declared in this scope
    ::func2();                  // OK: explicit qualification
    func2(num1);                // OK: examples::func2(int)
    int num2 = 2;               // a local declaration
    using examples::num2;       // error: multiple declaration
}
```

Note that a using declaration does not give the identifier's type, so we must examine its declaration in the namespace for this information. The declaration using examples::func1; adds that function name (with the argument signature given in examples) to the file scope. Even though a declaration of that identifier already exists, it is not an error because function names can be overloaded. The declaration using examples::String; adds a local alias for examples::String so that qualification is not necessary. The declaration using examples::num1; adds that object's name to the scope of main(), but the global num1 is still visible via a qualified name. The declaration using examples::func2; hides the global func2() within main(), rather than adding an overloading. The declaration using examples::num2; is an error because num2 is already defined within main() (unlike num1, which is defined in an enclosing scope).

The using directive

We often need a way to use an entire library without qualifying names or listing each class, function, and object name the program uses. The *using directive* makes all the identifiers in a namespace available in the scope in which it appears, but does not declare those identifiers in that scope. The directive consists of the reserved words using namespace and the namespace name. It allows using identifiers within the specified namespace in that scope without qualification, if there is no existing local declaration of that name. If an identifier in the namespace matches an existing local name (or a name imported by a using declaration), the directive is not an error. An unqualified reference to that identifier in that scope refers to the local name. The identifier in the namespace can still be accessed by qualifying it with the namespace name. The using directive also makes identifiers in any using declarations or using directives in the specified namespace available.

The using directive allows a client to use all the names in a library easily, but makes an unknown set of names available, with the chance that this set of names may change during the life of the program. The using directive does not declare all the namespace's identifiers in the new scope because doing so could cause numerous and unexpected conflicts. Generally, you should use the using declaration rather than the using directive because it is more explicit and more selective, and, therefore, is safer.

Because the using directive makes a set of names available without declaring them in the scope in which it occurs, it has the effect of adding an enclosing scope that contains the identifiers in the given namespace. This scope is added at the level of the outermost scope enclosing the scope in which the directive occurs. The result is similar to the scope structure that occurs with multiple inheritance in the sense that there are two enclosing scopes at the same level, the namespace of the directive and file scope. If a name occurs in both those enclosing scopes, the directive is not an error. As with multiple inheritance, an error occurs at the point of use if the programmer uses that identifier without qualification. Like the scope rules for multiple inheritance, if the multiply-defined identifier is a function name with different argument signatures in each scope, qualification is not necessary and the argument signature of the call is used to select the function definition invoked.

The following examples illustrate the semantics of the using directive with the examples namespace defined in the previous section:

```
// the using directive makes all the identifiers in the namespace available,
// but does not declare them in that scope
#include "examples.h"
int num1 = 0;
void func1(long);

int main()
{
    int num2 = 2;                    // local definition
    // the directive makes all the names in the namespace examples available
    using namespace examples;
    String str("hello");             // no qualification is necessary
    func1(str);                      // OK: examples::func1(const String&)
    func1(3L);                       // OK: ::func1(long)
    num2++;                          // the local num2
    examples::num2++;                // OK: explicit qualification
    num1++;                          // error: global ::num1 or examples::num1?
    ::num1 += examples::num1;        // OK: explicit qualification of each
}
```

The using directive makes all the names in the namespace examples available in main(), so names that are not hidden by local declarations can be used without qualification. func1() is now overloaded with the argument signature declared at global scope and the argument signature declared in the namespace. A using directive does not actually add the identifiers in the namespace to that scope, so the directive does not multiply define num2. Both the local object num2 and the object declared in the namespace are visible, the latter with a qualified name. num1 is essentially declared in two scopes that both enclose main(), so an unqualified use of that identifier is ambiguous.

Suppose a scope contains using directives for two different namespaces, for example, for two different libraries. In this case, all the identifiers in both namespaces that are not hidden by a local declaration are available without qualification. If an identifier is declared in both namespaces, the second directive is not an error. Within the scope in which the directives appear, a qualified name must be used to indicate which declaration of that identifier is intended. Again, if the multiply-defined identifier is a function name with different argument signatures in each namespace, the argument signature of the call selects the function that is invoked.

The using directive is convenient for the designer of a namespace as well as for his or her clients. For example, we can use it in a namespace code file to reduce the amount of name qualification necessary.

```
// namespace.cc: using the using directive in a namespace code file
#include "examples.h"
// the directive makes all the names in the namespace examples visible without qualification
using namespace examples;

int num1 = 1;
```

```
int num2 = 2;

void func1(const String& str)
{
    // ... function definition ...
}

template <class ElemType>
ElemType Queue<ElemType>::remove() throw (EmptyError)
{
    // ... as defined in section 13.3.2 ...
}

// ... other definitions ...
```

When namespaces are first introduced, the standard C and C++ header files can include a using directive for backward compatibility. For example, the header file math.h can contain using namespace std; so that existing code can continue to use those function names without qualification. The new ANSI/ISO header <cmath> that declares those functions in the namespace std would be used with new code.[26] When vendors use namespaces to manage releases of class libraries, clients can migrate from one version of the library to another either incrementally (i.e., with using declarations for particular classes or functions), or all at once (i.e., by changing a using directive or a namespace alias).

13.5 SUMMARY AND REVIEW

13.5.1 Function Templates

Introduction

- We sometimes need two or more functions that contain the same code, but differ in the types of their parameters. With static typing, each of these must be defined as separate functions (and with overloading, they can have the same name).

- A *function template* allows us to write a function definition without specifying types for its parameters. A function template includes *type parameters* that are bound to actual types when a function definition with that argument signature is needed.

- Templates are inherently different from other language constructs because a template definition is not source code that is translated to object code. Instead, a function template is a description that the compiler can use to generate a function definition with a given set of parameter types when it encounters an invocation using arguments of those types.

[26] The ANSI/ISO C++ Standard Library uses this naming convention for all the C standard headers.

Definition

- A function template describes an unlimited set of *template functions* with the same name that have the same definition except for their parameter types.
- A function template definition consists of the reserved word template, a list of type parameters enclosed in angle brackets, and a function definition that uses the type parameters as type names (e.g., as the type of a parameter, local variable, or dynamic object).
- We can overload a function template name with other function templates, and with nontemplate functions.

Template function invocation

- When we use a function template name in an invocation, the type of each argument provides a binding for the corresponding type parameter. The compiler then *instantiates* the template to generate a function definition using those actual types, and compiles that definition (if it has not already done so).
- The ANSI/ISO C++ Standard allows a template function invocation to specify bindings for the template's type parameters by including a list of actual types enclosed in angle brackets after the function name. This feature allows us to define a function template with type parameters that do not appear as parameter types in the associated function definition, because the caller can give bindings for those type parameters explicitly.
- The ANSI/ISO C++ Standard also permits giving default bindings for template type parameters by following the type parameter with an = symbol and the name of an actual type.
- In the ARM, the process of resolving an overloaded function invocation prefers an exact match or a trivial conversion with a nontemplate function over instantiating a function template, and prefers an exact match with a template instantiation over a nontemplate function that involves a promotion or conversion. No conversions are performed in matching type parameters.
- The ANSI/ISO C++ Standard states that, to resolve an overloaded function call, the compiler determines the set of function definitions including template instantiations that could apply via any conversion, and then uses the categories of preferences given in section 9.2.4 and the intersection rule among these.
- If an instance of the actual type bound to a type parameter cannot be used in the way that the function definition uses an instance of that type parameter, a syntax error occurs in the resulting template function. Language systems vary on how this error is reported.

Scope

- The scope of a function template definition is nested within the file scope in which it is defined, and includes its type parameter names and the parameters and local variables of the associated function definition.

- If a nonlocal identifier in a function template definition is the name of a message passed to a type parameter instance or a function applied to a type parameter instance, it is resolved to the definition of that name for the actual type bound to the type parameter. Any other nonlocal identifier is resolved according to its definition in the enclosing file scope.

Linkage and templates

- The compiler must have the entire template definition available to generate a template function when it encounters an invocation.
- If the compiler generates and translates a template function with a particular set of type parameter bindings in each file that invokes that argument signature, the executable for the application might include the same object code several times.
- To avoid duplication of the code for a template function in a program's executable, generating template functions must be delayed until link time when all the argument signatures the program uses are known.
- To ensure that each template function is created once, a recent extension to the language allows the programmer to specify creation of a function template with a given set of type parameter bindings in a particular code file by giving the template function declaration preceded by the reserved word template. This technique is sufficient for small programs and simple programming environments.
- An integrated programming environment can maintain a *repository* file of template information for each program, which the system's compiler and linker use to generate the necessary template functions when building the executable.

13.5.2 Class Templates

The type of a collection element

- In a statically typed language, all the elements of a collection must be of the same type, and the compiler can ensure that the program does not add an object of the wrong type to the collection. With dynamic typing, we can create heterogeneous collections, but type checking for elements occurs indirectly at execution time.
- With inheritance and static typing, the elements of a collection are restricted to instances of the descendants of the element's class.

Creating new collection classes without templates

- The protocol, storage structure, and methods for a particular collection class are independent of the type of its elements, so we would like to define that information once and reuse it for different element types.
- Without support for class templates, we can generate a collection class for a particular element type using either text substitution or inheritance.

- Using text substitution to generate collection classes is tedious and error-prone, and managing large-scale use of this technique is complicated, especially if we must make changes to the definition of the collection class.
- To use inheritance to allow writing collection classes once, the designer can define all collection classes with the same element type, say Object*, and then derive all classes for "collectable" objects from that type. The type specifies the messages needed in the collection methods as pure virtual functions that an element class must implement.
- With collections of Object* elements, the compiler cannot restrict the elements of a collection to instances of a particular class and loses their type identity, so the programmer must downcast objects accessed through a collection.
- To use inheritance to generate collection classes, we can create an abstract collection class that gives the protocol, storage structure, and methods. We then define a collection with a specific element type as a subclass, with the casting hidden within its methods. However, we must explicitly code a definition for each collection of each element type needed.

Class template definition

- A *class template* allows us to parameterize the definition of a collection class for the type of the element.
- A class template definition consists of the reserved word **template**, a type parameter list, and a class definition that can use the type parameters as type names, for example, as the type of a data member or member function parameter.
- A class template name alone is not a class name. A *template class* name gives bindings for all the template's type parameters enclosed in angle brackets following the template name, and names a type and a scope.
- The member functions and friend functions of a class template also must be parameterized for the element type, and are defined as function templates. Member function template definitions are declared within the class template scope.
- Class templates are also useful when we need to parameterize other aspects of a class, such as a component type.
- Access specifiers have the same meaning for class templates as for classes.
- If a nontemplate function is a friend of a class template, it is a friend of all classes generated from the template. If a function template is a friend of a class template and its type parameters are bound to type parameters of the class template, then each template function is a friend of the corresponding template class.
- A class template can declare a function template as a friend so that each function generated from that template is a friend of all classes generated from the class template.
- A class template may declare nontype parameters, which are referred to as *expression parameters*. The parameter's type can be an integer type (including enumerations) or a pointer type.

- Once a class template is defined, the designer can define a specialized template class if particular type parameter bindings require special handling.
- The ANSI/ISO C++ Standard supports defining a *member template* for generating member functions within a class or class template. To define the member template separately from the enclosing class template, we nest its template definition within a template that binds the type parameters of the enclosing class. Member templates cannot be virtual.

Instantiation

- A class template name alone without type parameter bindings is not a class name. To name a template class, we specify the actual types enclosed in angle brackets following the template name, for example, Queue<String>. The compiler then generates and translates an instantiation of the class template and member function templates with the specified type parameter bindings (if not yet done).
- We can use a template class as the type of a variable, a pointer, a parameter, a data member, a type parameter binding, or a base class. The syntax for using an identifier whose type is a template class is the same as if its type is a class or a built-in type.
- When using a template class as a type parameter, a space must appear between successive closing angle brackets in a class name such as List<Point-<double> >.
- A template class name also specifies a scope, for example, for accessing a static member or defining specialized member functions.

Scope

- Identifiers local to a class template definition are resolved in the same manner as the local identifiers in a class definition.
- As in function templates, nonlocal identifiers that depend on a type parameter are bound according to the actual type associated with that parameter, and other nonlocal names are resolved statically.
- If a class template defines static members or nested enumerations or classes, each template class instantiated from the template contains its own members or nested types, because each defines a separate scope.

Inheritance

- We can use a template class as the base class of a nontemplate class or a class template. That class will be instantiated when the derived class is defined or the derived class template is instantiated.
- We can derive a class template from a nontemplate class, in which case all classes generated from the template have the same base class.

- We can derive a class template from another class template with the same type parameters bindings. When the compiler instantiates the derived template, it generates the corresponding template base class, if necessary.

- If a class template defines virtual functions, then each template class has its own vtbl and methods.

- The class List<*Derived**> is not a subclass of List<*Base**>. A value conversion from the former to the latter is valid (but is not provided by the language), but a pointer conversion is not valid because we cannot use an instance of the former in a context declared for an instance of the latter. The value conversion can be defined as a List<> constructor member template.

- The client of a collection class may require either value or reference elements, depending on the semantics of the element type. If pointer elements are required to provide reference semantics due to characteristics of the collection implementation, the class designer often must provide different class templates for value and pointer elements.

13.5.3 Exceptions

Purpose

- Many C standard library functions return a value that indicates whether an error was detected during an invocation. To handle errors, each call must explicitly test for an error and specify the code to be executed if the error occurs. This error handling increases the code size and clutters the application with code not relevant to its normal operation.

- Cluttering the application code with error handling code becomes worse when an error condition must be propagated through a sequence of invocations. The programmer can use the C standard library functions setjmp() and longjmp() to propagate an error from a function invocation to an earlier invocation that can handle it. However, the target of the transfer of control is not guaranteed to still be active, and there is no clean-up of the intervening environments that are exited.

- The C++ exception facility provides constructs for defining, signaling, and handling errors. We can separate normal processing from error handling and specify the response for each class of errors once. The reliability of programs is increased because exceptions cannot be ignored.

- Exceptions are important for reusable components and loose coupling because a class designer can detect the errors that can occur in the class's methods, but cannot specify how those errors should be handled since he or she does not know how the receiver is being used in an application.

- An implementation of this facility provides error propagation and safe transfer of control, handler selection on the basis of the exception type, transfer of information from the signaler to the handler, and finalization of the local variables in stack frames that are exited.

- Exceptions are generally implemented such that signaling an exception is much more expensive than calling a function, so you should only use this control mechanism for error handling.

Signaling an exception

- To signal an exception, a method or function uses a *throw expression* consisting of the reserved word throw and an operand which is passed to the exception handler. The type of that object determines which of the client's handlers is executed when the exception occurs.

- A function declaration may indicate the exceptions it can raise by including an *exception specification* consisting of the reserved word throw followed by a parenthesized list of exception types.

- A function is not required to give an exception specification, but if it does, it cannot signal exceptions that are not listed. If it does so, the predefined function unexpected() is invoked immediately, and execution terminates. The programmer can provide a definition for unexpected() by passing a pointer to that function to set_unexpected(). That function must re-throw the exception, signal another exception, or terminate execution.

Exception classes

- C++ does not specify exceptions for operations on built-in types. The new operator signals the exception bad_alloc when there is not enough free storage available, and an invalid dynamic reference cast signals a bad_cast exception. Instances of iostream classes can be set to signal the exception ios_base::failure when a stream error occurs.

- The ANSI/ISO C++ Standard Library defines a hierarchy of exception classes declared in the standard header <stdexcept>. The class exception is the root of this hierarchy and defines a virtual function exception::what() that returns a const char* describing the error. Its subclasses are logic_error and runtime_error. The subclasses of logic_error are domain_error, invalid_argument, length_error, and out_of_range, and the subclasses of runtime_error are range_error and overflow_error. If they are available, you should use these classes or derive your exception classes from them.

- In C++, the exception is an object, and we can use this object to transfer information from the signaler to the handler. The exception object is initialized by the signaling function, and its protocol provides access to that information for the handler.

- We define exception classes like any other class, and can define hierarchies of exception classes to specify related exceptions. This allows the client to specify a handler for a category of exceptions by defining a handler for an exception base class.

Handling exceptions

- A client of a function can respond to the exceptions that the function can signal by enclosing an invocation in a *try block* and defining exception handlers for the try block. An *exception handler* consists of the reserved word catch, an exception parameter type, and a block of code to execute if that exception is signaled from within the associated try block.

- If an invocation in a try block raises an exception, the exception object type is matched against the parameter types of the associated handlers in the order in which they appear to determine which handler to execute. The matching process can perform trivial conversions, the standard conversion to ancestor, and the standard pointer to void* conversion. The exception object is available in the handler code, like a function argument.

- A client can handle a hierarchy of exceptions by using a reference parameter whose type is the root of that hierarchy.

Control flow and finalization

- When an exception is signaled, the exception resolution process searches back through the sequence of invocations on the run-time stack for a try block with a matching handler. If a matching handler is found, it is executed, and then control continues after the associated try block if the handler does not terminate the program.

- If no matching handler for an exception is encountered among the active invocations, then the function terminate() is invoked. The programmer can provide a definition for terminate() by passing a pointer to that function to set_terminate(), and that function must terminate execution rather than returning.

- C++ does not provide a feature for retrying the operation that caused the exception to occur after performing the handler. If the program can perform some clean-up and try the operation again, it encloses the try block and handler in a loop that exits when the function call is successful.

- A handler can re-throw the exception it caught by executing a throw expression with no operand, or it can signal another exception. In either case, the exception resolution process continues with the caller of the function containing that handler's try block, and does not consider succeeding handlers for that try block.

- As the exception resolution process proceeds, the activation records for functions that do not define matching handlers are popped from the run-time stack. When each stack frame is deallocated, the destructors for all completely constructed automatic objects and subobjects are executed.

- When the exception resolution process releases an activation record, it does not deallocate dynamic objects created in that method or function. To deal with this, we can encapsulate the dynamic allocation with a class that allocates the storage in its constructor and deallocates it in the destructor.

- The ANSI/ISO C++ Standard Library defines the class template auto_ptr<>
  as a smart pointer class whose destructor deallocates the referent of the
  pointer it owns.

13.5.4 Namespaces

Purpose

- A C++ program contains one global name space for the names of all non-nested classes, file scope functions, and global variables.

- Global name conflicts are a problem for applications that use several class libraries because most libraries define foundation classes such as String and Point. Some class libraries use a distinguishing prefix for all class names and file scope identifiers, which lengthens these names without adding any information. Other designers nest a set of classes, functions, and objects within a class, with the functions and objects as static members. This technique misuses the class construct because the class does not represent a category of entities or define a type, and the client must always qualify those names.

- The C++ namespace extension allows a class designer or library vendor to enclose a set of identifiers in a *namespace*, which defines a named scope. It also provides features for importing names from a namespace into another scope, so that the programmer can control which identifiers are declared in a scope and which are accessed using qualified names.

Namespace definition

- A namespace definition consists of the reserved word namespace, the namespace name, and a list of declarations enclosed in braces. We can define namespaces at file scope or within other namespaces, and only declaration statements are allowed in a namespace.

- Namespaces are usually defined in header files that define classes and templates and declare functions and objects, and are included in client code files. The methods, functions, and objects are defined in a namespace code file.

- For the convenience of designers and users of large libraries, a namespace definition can be divided into several header files. All namespace definitions with the same namespace name contribute their declarations to the same namespace (rather than being a multiple definition error).

- Each code file may contain a local unnamed namespace nested within the global unnamed namespace. This feature replaces the use of static file scope identifiers.

- A client can define a local alias for a namespace name. This feature allows the designer of a class library to use a long name to avoid conflicts among namespace names without inconveniencing clients.

Using identifiers declared in a namespace

- We can use an identifier declared in a namespace in another scope by quali-fying it with the namespace name. This does not import the identifier into the scope, so it does not cause a name conflict with an identifier local to that scope. We can use cascaded applications of the scope operator to refer to members of a class declared within a namespace.

- A *using declaration* consists of the reserved word using and a qualified name, and declares a local alias for an identifier from a namespace so that it can be used without qualification. It is invalid if that name is already declared in the scope in which it appears (unless it overloads a function name), and it hides declarations of that name in enclosing scopes.

- A *using directive* consists of the reserved words using namespace and a name-space name, and makes all the names in that namespace available, as if they were declared in an enclosing scope. If a name in the namespace is already declared in the scope in which the directive occurs, it is not an error and unqualified uses of that name are resolved to the local declaration. The name-space identifier can be accessed with a qualified name.

13.6 EXERCISES

13.1 (a) How are template type parameters similar to function parameters?
(b) How are template type parameters different from function parameters?

13.2 Why are templates unnecessary in a dynamically typed language such as Smalltalk?

13.3 (a) Write a function template for the set of functions called swap() that interchange the values of their two arguments.
(b) What requirements must be satisfied for classes that instantiate the type parame-ter in the template in part (a)?

13.4 (a) Define a function template qsort() with a type parameter ElemType whose template functions take three parameters. The first is a C array of ElemType objects, the sec-ond is the array's size, and the third is a pointer to a file scope function used to order instances of ElemType. Such a function takes two const ElemType references and returns a bool. The default value of the third function parameter is &opera-tor<(). The function body sorts the array using the quicksort algorithm with the comparison function.
(b) Define a function template qsort() which is like that in part (a), except that the third function parameter is a pointer to a member function of ElemType used to order instances.
(c) Can both of these templates be used in the same program?

13.5 (a) Define operator<=(), operator>=(), max(), and between() as function templates that invoke operator<() and operator==().
(b) Discuss the advantages and disadvantages of using these templates rather than the class Orderable defined in section 12.3.4 .

13.6 (a) Define a function template convert() for functions that convert an instance of one type to an instance of another. Show how to use the function.

(b) Why can't we define the function template in part (a) with the version of the template facility described in the ARM?

13.7 As we discussed in section 13.1.3, the compiler does not perform the standard conversion to ancestor type in matching type parameters of templates according to the ARM (and most current language systems). For this reason, it rejects some template function invocations that are semantically correct.

(a) Give an example of such an invocation for the function template min() defined in section 13.1.2 that returns the minimum of its two arguments.

(b) Can this problem occur with a single-parameter file scope function template?

(c) Does this problem affect using the member functions of a collection class template?

(d) If the compiler rejects an invocation, how does it report this error? How can the programmer solve the problem?

13.8 Suggest a syntax for specifying the operations that a template requires for its parameter bindings.

13.9 (a) Why is resolution of nonlocal names more complicated for template definitions than for class and function definitions? How does it differ?

(b) How does resolution of nonlocal names in templates relate to errors that can occur when instantiating a template?

13.10 What does it mean to compile a template definition?

13.11 (a) Discuss why efficient support for templates conflicts with the C++ model for external linkage.

(b) Describe the two solutions to this problem.

13.12 Explain why support for class templates in C++ facilitates development of homogenous collection classes, but does not provide heterogeneous collections.

13.13 Recall the class GenericQueue in section 13.2.2. If its destructor is virtual, then we could code the complete method for remove() in the superclass GenericQueue. What is the disadvantage of this design?

13.14 Why do we regard Queue<int> and Queue<Point> as different classes?

13.15 Redefine each of the following classes as class templates. You may use any of the implementations described in the original exercises in Chapters 10 and 11.

(a) the class Set described in exercises 10.40, 11.8, and 11.32

(b) the class List described in exercises 10.41, 11.9, and 11.32

(c) the class SortedList described in exercises 10.42, 11.10, and 11.32

(d) the class Dictionary described in exercise 11.12

13.16 In section 11.3.4, we discussed implementing parameterized manipulators such as setw() with an auxiliary class and friend file scope function. In that section, we defined OstrManipInt and operator<<() for use with an int manipulator parameter and suggested that they should actually be defined as templates to support a manipulator parameter of any type.

(a) Define the class template OstrManip<> and function template necessary to provide this capability.

(b) Define the functions necessary to implement the manipulator setfill() described in section 11.3.4.

(c) Examine the header file iomanip.h for your system to determine how it implements this functionality.

13.17 (a) Is there any reason to separate the definition of a class template and its member functions into a header file and a code file?

(b) If so, which file should contain the definitions of inline member function templates?

13.18 The C and C++ standards specify a type wchar_t for "wide characters", which provides support for alphabets such as Japanese that have more than 256 characters. Redefine the class String described in sections 10.3.2, 10.3.5, and 11.1.3, and exercises 10.11, 11.3 and 11.4 as a template so that it can be used with either char or wchar_t characters. (The ANSI/ISO C++ Standard Library includes this class template as basic_string<>.)

13.19 **(a)** Redefine the class Complex described in section 11.1.2 and exercise 11.5 as a template to allow different component types. Define all the necessary operators. (The ANSI/ISO C++ Standard Library includes this class template complex<>.)

(b) Redefine the class Polynomial described in exercise 11.14 as a template to allow different coefficient types.

13.20 Recall our discussion of iterators for collection template classes in section 13.2.3.

(a) Define iterators for the class templates Set<>, List<>, and SortedList<> described in exercise 13.15 for each of the implementations described in the original exercises in Chapters 10 and 11.

(b) Discuss the advantages and disadvantages of defining a common superclass for the class templates in part (a).

(c) Suppose we want to define an iterator for the class template Dictionary<> described in exercise 13.15(d). Should accessing an element return a key–value pair or a value? If you choose the latter, should we also provide an iterator for the dictionary's keys? Define whichever version you choose.

13.21 **(a)** Recall the class template Array<> discussed in section 13.2.3. Complete the definition of the class template with the messages described in exercise 11.11, including the two overloadings of map(). Define all the member function templates. (You will discover something peculiar in the constructor definitions.)

(b) In many cases, arrays contain numeric values so we want to provide protocol for coherent operations, that is, for vector arithmetic. Define Array<> member function templates for the +, -, *, and / operators, which create a new array whose elements are the results of applying that operator to the corresponding elements of the array operands. Define methods for the +=, -=, *=, and /= operators, and for the messages min() and max() which return the minimum and maximum value in the receiver, respectively. Define the member function sort(), which sorts the array. Can you think of any other numeric protocol that might be useful?

(c) Would you consider it advisable to define the following member function, which creates a new array that is the result of adding the second operand to each element of the first?

```
template <class ElemType, int low, int high>
Array<ElemType, low, high>
Array<ElemType, low, high>::
    operator+(const Array<ElemType, low, high>&, const ElemType&);
```

13.22 **(a)** Redefine the Array<> template in exercise 13.21 with an additional type parameter for the index type (like the array type constructor in Pascal).

(b) What types can be used as the index type? Why can't other types be used?

13.23 Expression parameters are useful whenever we have a type such that objects with different sizes should be regarded as having different types. A typical example is a class for bit strings. Define a class template Bitstring<> that is parameterized for the length of an instance. (Note that this template has no type parameter!) What initializers should the class provide? Define all the appropriate operators and messages for accessing, testing, clearing, setting, and inverting individual bits in an instance (e.g., examine the bit manipulation protocol of the Smalltalk class Integer discussed in section 7.4.3).   (The ANSI/ISO C++ Standard Library includes this class template as bitset<>.)

13.24 **(a)** Why is initialization of a List<Complex> identifier from a List<double> object invalid?

     (b) How can we define this conversion? Do so.

13.25 Suppose we wish to define an object keywordIndex that maintains the occurrences of a collection of keywords in a collection of files, together with the line numbers on which a keyword occurs in each file. That is, it is an index of information accessed by the keywords, and the information for each keyword is also an index that gives a set of line numbers for each file name. Given the class templates Dictionary and Set described in exercise 13.15 and the class String discussed in Chapters 11 and 12, how do we declare the type of the variable keywordIndex?

13.26 In the definition of the template facility in the ARM, instantiating a template generates all its member functions. However, in the ANSI/ISO C++ Standard, a template member function is only generated if that member function is invoked. Discuss how this affects whether we should define the additional protocol for the class template Array<> described in exercise 13.21(b).

13.27 Describe how to initialize a static data member of a class template.

13.28 Define the new and delete operators for the Node<> class template defined in section 13.2.3 such that each node template class maintains its own free list as described in section 11.1.4.

13.29 In section 13.2.5, we redefined the Queue<> class template defined in section 13.2.3 with the class Node as a nested class.

     (a) Why isn't it necessary to specify a type parameter binding for the data members of the Queue<> class template in this case?

     (b) Define the constructor for the nested class Node separately from the Queue<> class template definition.

13.30 Why must a subclass of a class template also be a template?

13.31 Can we define the class template PriorityQueue<> defined in section 13.2.6 with a parameter for the comparison function such that we can use the same class template with either a file scope or a member comparison function?

13.32 **(a)** Give a convincing argument that initialization of a List<Person*> from a List<Employee*> should be allowed.

     (b) Why doesn't C++ support this conversion?

13.33 **(a)** Redefine the abstract class AbstractQueue described in section 12.3.4 as a class template. Code the member function templates as well.

     (b) Define the class templates Queue<> defined in section 13.2.3 and PriorityQueue<> defined in section 13.2.6 as subclasses of the class template AbstractQueue<> in part (a). Code the member function templates as well.

13.34 In exercise 13.20, we defined iterators for the class templates Set<>, List<>, and SortedList<> described in exercise 13.15. Because instances of template classes generated from List<> and SortedList<> are ordered, we can define "positionable iterators" for them. Derive the class template PositionableListIterator<> from the class template ListIterator<> defined in exercise 13.15(b), which adds the member functions skip(int) whose argument can be positive or negative, skipUpto(const ElemType&), and operator==().

13.35 Recall the classes Set described in exercises 10.40 and 11.8, List described in exercises 10.41 and 11.9, and SortedList described in exercises 10.42 and 11.10, which were redefined as class templates in exercise 13.15.

(a) For each, discuss whether we can use each implementation of the class's interface directly with elements of polymorphic class type. That is, determine whether each method will operate correctly with a pointer type as the type parameter binding.

(b) For the implementations that do not, define a class template that expects a pointer type as the type parameter binding, and the class template's methods.

13.36 Describe four ways in which the C++ exception facility improves on the use of setjmp() and longjmp() for error propagation.

13.37 In this exercise, we will explore what would be involved if we used setjmp() and longjmp() to implement code like the try block at the beginning of section 13.3.4. Consider the following program:

```
#include "String.h"
#include "Queue.h"
#include <iostream.h>
#include <stdlib.h>   // for exit()
int main()
{
    try
    {
        Queue<String> strQu;
        String str1, str2;
        cin >> str1;
        cin >> str2;
        strQu.insert(str1).insert(str2);
        String str2 = strQu.remove();
        cout << strQu.remove();
        cout << str2[5];
        cout << strQu.remove();
    }
    catch (SubscriptError subErr)
    {
        cerr << subErr.message() << ", index: " << subErr.index()
            << ", size: " << subErr.size() << endl;
        exit(1);
    }
    catch (EmptyError)
    {
        cerr << "Queue<ElemType>::remove() on an empty queue" << endl;
        exit(1);
    }
}
```

(a) Recode this program using setjmp() rather than a try block, and recode String::operator[]() and Queue<ElemType>::remove() to use longjmp() rather than throw expressions. The second argument of longjmp() is the return value of the setjmp() when an error is raised, so it can be used to indicate the type of the error.

(b) Discuss whether the methods can be coded to signal errors to arbitrary clients using longjmp().

(c) Suppose we add another class to the program whose methods can signal errors at some later time, and we want to handle those errors. Describe what is necessary for the version that uses exceptions. Describe what is necessary for the version that uses setjmp() and longjmp() to handle these new errors.

13.38 In Ada, the construct pragma SUPPRESS(... *exception list* ...) can be used to disable exception handling for the listed exceptions. Give arguments for and against including such a feature in the language.

13.39 **(a)** What is the purpose for exception specifications?
(b) Can the compiler verify that a function's exception specification is correct?
(c) Why are exception specifications optional?

13.40 **(a)** Which operations on built-in types can result in invalid values? Give a set of exceptions for these errors and list the operations that can signal each.
(b) Ada built-in type operations signal an exception when an error occurs, while those in C++ do not (and do not in the ANSI/ISO C++ Standard). Give two reasons why C++ built-in type operations do not signal exceptions. (Consider C++'s design goals.)

13.41 In Ada, an exception is identified by a name alone, whereas in C++, an exception is an object. Describe two capabilities that are provided by C++ that are not possible in Ada.

13.42 **(a)** The current version of the iostream class library maintains information indicating whether a stream is usable or not within that instance, and the client must explicitly query the stream to determine if it is in a usable state. Describe the advantages and disadvantages of this approach versus signaling an exception whenever an operation causes an error.
(b) As we discussed in section 11.3.4, a stream can be set to raise an exception of type ios_base::failure when particular error states occur. Why do you think the designers of the library took this approach? Why don't the stream member functions give exception specifications?
(c) Why might we decide to define different exceptions for different types of stream errors? What exception classes would you define, and how would you organize that subhierarchy? Give the member function declarations with exception specifications for all stream messages that could signal these exceptions.

13.43 Suppose we want to redefine the exception class SubscriptError such that its instances also contain a pointer to the object in which the subscription error occurred and a message for accessing that object, as suggested in section 13.3.3.
(a) If we wish to use this exception for the class String and the class templates List<>, SortedList<>, and Array<>, what effect does including this information have on the class hierarchy?
(b) Define the exception class SubscriptError with this additional data member and member function, given the inheritance structure discussed in part (a).
(c) Recode String::operator[]() to use this new definition of SubscriptError.
(d) Recode the constructors of the class template Array<> discussed in section 13.2.3 and exercise 13.21 such that they throw a SubscriptError exception if the low index value is greater than the high index value.
(e) Recall the class List described in exercises 10.41 and 11.9, which is recoded as a class template in exercise 13.15. Which messages can raise a SubscriptError exception? Redefine those methods to signal the exception.

13.44 Recall the class template Dictionary<> described in exercises 11.12 and 13.15. Suppose we want to recode this class template so that the exception KeyNotFoundError is raised when a client attempts to access the value associated with a key that is not present in the receiver's table.
(a) What information should a KeyNotFoundError object contain?

(b) Define KeyNotFoundError<> as an exception class template parameterized for the key type.

(c) Define the class KeyNotFoundError as an exception class nested within the class template Dictionary<>.

(d) For each of the definitions of KeyNotFoundError in parts (b) and (c), write a program that uses a dictionary and specifies a handler for this exception.

13.45 **(a)** Define a class Integer with a single int data member that overloads the arithmetic operations to signal OverflowError exceptions when appropriate. The class has a constructor that takes an int, with a default value of 0, and conversion operator from Integer to int.

(b) Can we arrange to have the Integer constructor signal an exception when a client attempts to initialize an instance with a long or double value that is too large? If so, how do we do this?

(c) Write a program using the class Integer that sums the square of a series of integers from an fstream until reaching an end-of-file, then prints the result. If an overflow occurs in calculating the sum, the program prints an error message, the sum thus far, and the number of inputs read, and then exits.

13.46 Rewrite the following function so that it explicitly calls unexpected() when it receives any exceptions that are not listed in its exception specification:

```
void func() throw(Error1, Error2)
{
    // ... function body ...
}
```

13.47 Name two ways in which matching an exception object against handler parameters differs from matching an argument against the corresponding parameter in resolving an invocation of an overloaded function.

13.48 In section 0.2.5, we stated that dynamic scope has a negative effect on readability because the programmer (and programming tools) cannot determine the meaning of a nonlocal identifier without understanding the dynamic behavior of the program.

(a) Discuss whether this is also a problem for exception handling.

(b) Exception handlers are bound statically in CLU, that is, according to the nesting of scopes in the program, rather than according to the sequence of invocations. Discuss whether dynamic or static binding of handlers more correctly reflects the desired semantics.

13.49 Describe in detail the flow of control in each of the following cases:

(a) A function signals an exception that is eventually caught by a handler that does not exit the program.

(b) A function signals an exception that is caught by a handler that re-throws the exception.

(c) A function signals an exception that is caught by a handler that throws a different exception.

13.50 Some language designers feel that an exception should only be propagated one level, that is, to the caller of the function that signaled the exception.

(a) Suppose that C++ uses one-level propagation semantics for exceptions. Show how the programmer can implement multi-level propagation using existing language features.

(b) Why do you think the designers of C++ chose not to use one-level propagation since the programmer can implement multi-level propagation?

13.51 Why is it inadvisable to throw a dynamically allocated exception object?

13.52 Describe the similarities and differences between namespace scope and class scope.

13.53 Would access control be useful in namespaces?

13.54 Give an advantage and a disadvantage of each of the three ways of accessing an identifier declared in a namespace.

13.55 Is there any reason why a programmer would use a using declaration for an identifier in a namespace that has already been made available via a using directive?

13.56 Suppose two using directives appear in the same scope. How is this situation similar to the scope structure that occurs with multiple inheritance?

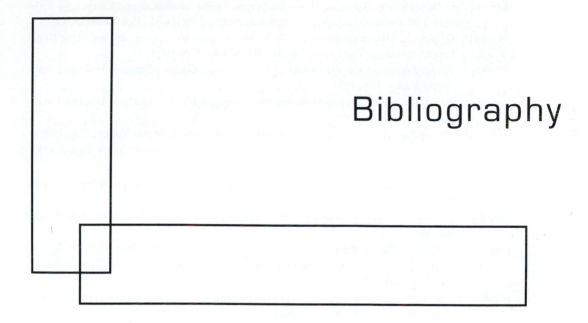

Bibliography

[Abb83]   R. Abbott, "Program Design by Informal English Descriptions," *Communications of the ACM*, Vol. 26, No. 11, 1983.

[Agh86]   G. Agha, *Actors: a Model of Concurrent Computation in Distributed Systems*. MIT Press, Cambridge, MA, 1986.

[Ans97]   Accredited Standards Committee (X3J16/95-0087), *International Standard for Information Systems—Programming Language C++*. American National Standards Institute, 1997.

[Arn96]   K. Arnold and J. Gosling, *The JavaProgramming Language*. Addison-Wesley, Reading, MA, 1996.

[Atk91]   C. Atkinson, *Object-Oriented Reuse, Concurrency and Distribution: an Ada-Based Approach*. Addison-Wesley, Reading, MA, 1991.

[Bec89]   Kent Beck and Ward Cunningham, "A laboratory for teaching object-oriented thinking," *OOPSLA 1989 Conference Proceedings*. Addison-Wesley, Reading, MA, 1989.

[Ben92]   A. Benson and G. Aiken, *OI Programmer's Guide*. Prentice-Hall, Englewood Cliffs, NJ, 1992.

[Ber93]   E. Berard, *Essays on Object-Oriented Software Engineering*. Prentice-Hall, Englewood Cliffs, NJ, 1993.

[Bir85]   N. Birrel and M. Ould, *A Practical Handbook for Software Development*. Cambridge University Press, Cambridge, England, 1985.

[Boe86]   B. Boehm, "A Spiral Model of Development and Enhancement," *Software Engineering Notes*, Vol. 11, No. 4, 1986.

[Boh66]   C. Bohm and G. Jacopini, "Flow Diagrams, Turing Machines, and Languages with only Two Formation Rules," *Communications of the ACM*, Vol. 9, No. 5, 1996.

[Boo94]   G. Booch, *Object-Oriented Analysis And Design With Applications*. The Benjamin/Cummings Publishing Co., Redwood City, CA, 1994.

[Bor91]   *Turbo Pascal 6.0 Object-Oriented Programming Guide*. Borland International, Scotts Valley, CA, 1991.

[Bor96a]   *Borland C++ 5.0 Object-Oriented Programming Guide*. Borland International, Scotts Valley, CA, 1996.

[Bor96b]   *Object Pascal Language Guide*. Borland International, Scotts Valley, CA, 1996.

[Bor96c]   *ObjectWindows Programmer's Guide*. Borland International, Scotts Valley, CA, 1996.

[Bra85]   R. J. Brachman and H. J. Levesque, eds., *Readings in Knowledge Representation*. Morgan Kaufmann, Los Altos, CA, 1985.

[Bra90]   I. Bratko, *Prolog Programming for Artificial Intelligence*. Addison-Wesley, Reading, MA, 1990.

[Bro75]   F. Brooks, *The Mythical Man-Month*. Addison-Wesley, Reading, MA, 1975.

[Bud91]   T. Budd, *An Introduction to Object-Oriented Programming*. Addison-Wesley, Reading, MA, 1991.

[Car85]   L. Cardelli and P. Wegner, "On Understanding Types, Data Abstraction and Polymorphism," *ACM Computing Surveys*, Vol. 17, No. 4, 1985.

[Cen93]   *ObjectCenter User's Guide*. Centerline Software, Inc., Cambridge, MA, 1993.

[Chu41]   A. Church, *The Calculi of Lambda Conversion*. Princeton University Press, Princeton, NJ, 1941.

[Clo81]   W. Clocksin and C. Mellish, *Programming in Prolog*. Springer-Verlag, New York, NY, 1981.

[Coa91]   P. Coad and E. Yourdon, *Object-Oriented Analysis*. Prentice-Hall, Englewood Cliffs, NJ, 1991.

[Coa92]   P. Coad and E. Yourdon, *Object-Oriented Design*. Yourdon Press, Englewood Cliffs, NJ, 1992.

[Coa92]   P. Coad and J. Nicola, *Object-Oriented Programming*. Yourdon Press, Englewood Cliffs, NJ, 1993.

[Con79]   L. Constantine and E. Yourdan, *Structured Design*. Prentice-Hall, Englewood Cliffs, NJ, 1979.

[Coo89]   W. Cook and J. Palsberg, "A Denotational Semantics of Inheritance and its Correctness," *OOPSLA 1989 Conference Proceedings*. Addison-Wesley, Reading, MA, 1989.

[Cox86]   B. Cox, *Object Oriented Programming: An Evolutionary Approach*. Addison-Wesley, Reading, MA, 1986.

[Dah67]   O. J. Dahl, B. Myhrhaug, and K. Nygaard, *SIMULA 67: Common Base Language*. NCC Publication S22, Norwegian Computer Centre, Oslo, Norway, 1967.

[Dan88]   S. Danforth and C. Tomlinson, "Type Theories and object-oriented programming," *ACM Computing Surveys*, Vol. 20, No. 1, 1988.

[Deu89]   L. P. Deutsch, "Design, Reuse and Frameworks in the Smalltalk-80 System," in *Software Reusability, Vol. II*, T. Biggerstaff and A. J. Perlis, eds. ACM Press, New York, NY, 1989.

[Dij68]   E. W. Dijkstra, "Go To Statement Considered Harmful," *Communications of the ACM*, Vol. 11, No. 3, 1968.

[Ell90]   M. Ellis and B. Stroustrup, *The Annotated C++ Reference Manual*. Addison-Wesley, Reading, MA, 1990.

[Fis93]   A. Fischer and F. Grodzinsky, *The Anatomy of Programming Languages*. Prentice-Hall, Englewood Cliffs, NJ, 1993.

[Fol94]   J. Foley, A. van Dam, S. Feiner, J. Hughes, and R. Phillips, *Introduction to Computer Graphics*. Addison-Wesley, Reading, MA, 1994.

[Gea97]   D. Geary and A. McClellan, *Graphic Java*. Prentice-Hall, Englewood Cliffs, NJ, 1997.

[Gib90]   S. Gibbs, D. Tsichritzis, E. Casais, O. Nierstrasz, and X. Pintado, "Class Management for Software Communities," *Communications of the ACM*, Vol. 33, No. 9, 1990.

[Gol84]   A. Goldberg, *Smalltalk-80: The Interactive Programming Environment*. Addison-Wesley, Reading, MA, 1984.

[Gol89]   A. Goldberg and D. Robson, *Smalltalk-80: The Language*. Addison-Wesley, Reading, MA, reprinted 1989.

[Gor90]   K. Gorlen, S. Orlow, and P. Plexico, *Data Abstraction and Object-Oriented Programming in C++*. John Wiley & Sons, New York, NY, 1990.

[Gos89]   J. Gosling, D. Rosenthal, and M. Arden, *The NeWS book: Introduction to Network/Extensible Window System*. Springer-Verlag, New York, NY, 1989.

[Gra94a]   I. Graham, *Migrating to Object Technology*. Addison-Wesley, Reading, MA, 1994.

[Gra94b]   I. Graham, *Object-Oriented Methods*. Addison-Wesley, Reading, MA, 1994.

[Har92]   S. Harbison, *Modula-3*. Prentice-Hall, Englewood Cliffs, NJ, 1992.

[Har91]   W. Harris, "Contravariance for the Rest of Us," *Journal of Object-Oriented Programming*, Nov./Dec., 1991.

[Hat87]   D. Hatley and I. Pirbhai, *Strategies for Real-Time System Specification*. Dorset House, New York, NY. 1987.

[Hen90]   B. Henderson-Sellers and J. Edwards, "The Object-Oriented Systems Life Cycle," *Communications of the ACM*, Vol. 33, No. 9, 1990.

[Hen94]   B. Henderson-Sellers and J. Edwards, *BOOKTWO of Object-Oriented Knowledge: The Working Object*. Prentice-Hall, Sydney, Australia, 1994.

[Ing81]   D. H. Ingalls, "Design Principles Behind Smalltalk," *BYTE*, Vol. 6, No. 8, 1981.

[Jac92]   I. Jacobson *et al.*, *Object-Oriented Software Engineering: A Use Case Driven Approach*. Addison-Wesley, Reading MA, 1992.

[Kra88]   G. Krasner and S. Pope, "A Cookbook for Using the Model-View-Controller User Interface Paradigm in Smalltalk-80," *Journal of Object-Oriented Programming*, Vol. 1, No. 3, 1988.

[Kee89]   S. Keene, *Object-Oriented Programming in COMMON LISP*. Addison-Wesley, Reading MA, 1989.

[Ker88]   B. Kernighan and D. Ritchie, *The C Programming Language*. Prentice-Hall, Englewood Cliffs, NJ, 1988.

[Kir89]   B. Kirkerud, *Object-Oriented Programming With SIMULA*. Addison-Wesley, Reading MA, 1989.

[Kuh62]   T. Kuhn, *The Structure of Scientific Revolutions*. University of Chicago Press, Chicago, IL, 1962.

[LaL90]   W. LaLonde and J. Pugh, *Inside Smalltalk, Volume I.* Prentice-Hall, Englewood Cliffs, NJ, 1990.

[Lie89]   K. Lieberherr and Arthur Riel, "Contributions to Teaching Object-oriented Design and Programming," *OOPSLA 1989 Conference Proceedings.* Addison-Wesley, Reading, MA, 1989.

[Lin89]   M. Linton, J. Vlissides, and P. Calder, "Composing User Interfaces with Inter-Views," *Computer*, Vol. 22, No. 2, 1989.

[Lis77]   B. Liskov, A. Snyder, R. Atkinson, and C. Schaffert, "Abstraction Mechanisms in CLU", *Communications of the ACM*, Vol. 20, No. 8, 1977.

[Mac82]   B. MacLennan, "Values and Objects in Programming Languages", *ACM SIG-PLAN Notices*, Vol 17, No. 12, 1982.

[Man94]   S. Mann, *The Smalltalk Resource Guide.* Creative Digital Systems, San Francisco, CA, 1994.

[Mar95]   J. Martin and J. Odell, *Object Analysis and Design: The Fundamentals.* Prentice-Hall, Englewood Cliffs, NJ, 1995.

[Mar96]   J. Martin and J. Odell, *Object Analysis and Design: The Pragmatics.* Prentice-Hall, Englewood Cliffs, NJ, 1996.

[McI68]   M. McIlroy, "'Mass Produced' Software Components," in *Software Engineering: A Report On a Conference Sponsored by the NATO Science Committee*, P. Naur and B. Randell, eds., Gamisch, Germany, 1968.

[Met96]   Metrowerks, *CodeWarrior PowerPlant Book.* Metrowerks, Austin,TX, 1996.

[Mey88]   B. Meyer, *Object-oriented Software Construction.* Prentice-Hall, London, UK, 1988.

[Mey92]   B. Meyer, *Eiffel, the Language.* Prentice-Hall, Englewood Cliffs, NJ, 1992.

[Mic96]   The Microsoft Foundation Classes. Microsoft Corp., Redmond, CA 1996.

[Min75]   M. Minsky, "A Framework for Representing Knowledge" in [Bra85].

[Moo86]   D. Moon, "Object oriented programming with Flavors," *OOPSLA 1986 Conference Proceedings.* Addison-Wesley, Reading, MA, 1986.

[Pap80]   S. Papert, *Mindstorms.* Basic Books, New York, NY, 1980.

[Par72]   D. Parnas, "On the Criteria to Be Used in Decomposing Systems into Modules, " *Communications of the ACM*, Vol. 15, No. 12, 1972.

[Pla95]   P. Plauger, *The Draft Standard C++ Library.* Prentice-Hall, Englewood Cliffs, NJ, 1995.

[Pol75]   R. Polivka and S. Pakin, *APL: The Language and its Usage.* Prentice-Hall, Englewood Cliffs, NJ, 1975.

[Pra96]   T. Pratt and M. Zelkowitz, *Programming Languages, Design and Implementation.* Prentice-Hall, Englewood Cliffs, NJ, 1996.

[Pre92]   R. Pressman, *Software Engineering, a Practitioner's Approach.* McGraw-Hill, Inc., New York, NY, 1992.

[Qui67]   M. R. Quillian, "Word Concepts: a Theory and Simulation of Some Basic Semantic Capabilities," in [Bra85].

[Rum90]   J. Rumbaugh *et al., Object-Oriented Modeling and Design.* Prentice-Hall, Englewood Cliffs, NJ, 1990.

[Sch92]   R. Scheifler and J. Gettys, *X Window System.* Digital Press, Burlington, MA, 1992.

[Seb93]   R. Sebesta, *Concepts of Programming Languages.* The Benjamin/Cummings Publishing Co., Redwood City, CA, 1993.

[Shl88]   S. Shlaer and S. Mellor, *Object-Oriented System Analysis: Modeling the World in States*. Yourdan Press, Englewood Cliffs, NJ, 1988.

[Shl92]   S. Shlaer and S. Mellor, *Object-Oriented System Analysis: Modeling the World in Data*. Yourdan Press, Englewood Cliffs, NJ, 1992.

[Som96]   I. Somerville, *Software Engineering*. Addison-Wesley, Reading, MA, 1996.

[Smi95]   D. Smith, *IBM Smalltalk: The Language*. The Benjamin/Cummings Publishing Co., Redwood City, CA, 1995.

[Spr89]   G. Springer and D. Friedman, *Scheme and the Art of Programming*. MIT Press, Cambridge, MA, 1989.

[Spu92]   D. Spuler, *Comprehensive C*. Prentice-Hall, Englewood Cliffs, NJ, 1993.

[Sta92]   R. Stansifer, *ML Primer*. Prentice-Hall, Englewood Cliffs, NJ, 1992.

[Ste86]   M. Stefik and D. G. Bobrow, "Object oriented programming: themes and variations," *The AI Magazine*, Vol. 6, No. 4, 1986.

[Ste90]   G. Steele, *COMMON LISP The Language*. Digitalk Press, Burlington, MA, 1990.

[Str67]   C. Strachey, *Fundamental Concepts of Programming Languages*. Oxford University Programming Research Group, Oxford, England, 1967.

[Str91]   B. Stroustrup, *The C++ Programming Language*. Addison-Wesley, Reading, MA, 1991.

[Str92]   B. Stroustrup and D. Lenkov, "Run-time type identification for C++ (revised)," *Proceedings of the USENIX C++ Conference*, Aug. 1992.

[Str94]   B. Stroustrup, *The Design and Evolution of C++*. Addison-Wesley, Reading, MA, 1994.

[Sym90]   *THINK Pascal Object-Oriented Programming Manual*. Symantec Corp., Cupertino CA, 1990.

[Tea93]   S. Teale, *C++ IOStreams Handbook*. Prentice-Hall, Englewood Cliffs, NJ, 1993.

[Tes85]   L. Tesler, "Object Pascal Report," Apple Computer, Santa Clara, CA, 1985.

[Tho89]   T. Thompson, "The NeXTStep," *BYTE*, March 1989.

[Tur86]   D. Turner, "An Overview of Miranda," *ACM SIGPLAN Notices*, December 1986.

[Vis95]   *VisualWorks User Guide*. ParcPlace Systems, Sunnyvale, CA, 1995.

[War85]   P. Ward and S. Mellor, *Structured Development for Real-Time Systems*. Yourdon Press, Englewood Cliffs, NJ, 1985.

[Was90]   A. Wasserman, P. Pircher, and R. Muller, "The Object-Oriented Structured Design Notation for Software Design Representation," *Computer*, Vol. 23, No. 3, 1990.

[Who56]   B. Whorf, *Language, Thought and Reality*. MIT Press, Cambridge, MA, 1956.

[Wil90]   D. Wilson, L. Rosenstein, and D. Shafer, *C++ Programming with MacApp*. Addison-Wesley, Reading, MA, 1990.

[Wir90a]   R. Wirfs-Brock, B. Wilkerson, and L. Weiner, *Designing Object-Oriented Software*. Prentice-Hall, Englewood Cliffs, NJ, 1990.

[Wir90b]   R. Wirfs-Brock and R. Johnson, "Surveying Current Research in Object-Oriented Design," *Communications of the ACM*, Vol. 33, No. 9, 1990.

[Yon86a] A. Yonezawa and M. Tokoro, eds., *Object-Oriented Concurrent Programming.* MIT Press, Cambridge, MA, 1986.

[Yon86b] A. Yonezawa, E. Shibayama, T. Takada, and Y. Honda, "Modeling and Programming in the Object-Oriented Concurrent Language ABCL/1," in [Yon86a].

[Yok86] Y. Yokote and M. Tokoro, "Concurrent Programming in Concurrent Smalltalk," in [Yon86a].

[You94] D. Young, *The X Window System, Programming and Applications withXt (OSF/MOTIF Edition).* Prentice-Hall, Englewood Cliffs, NJ, 1994.

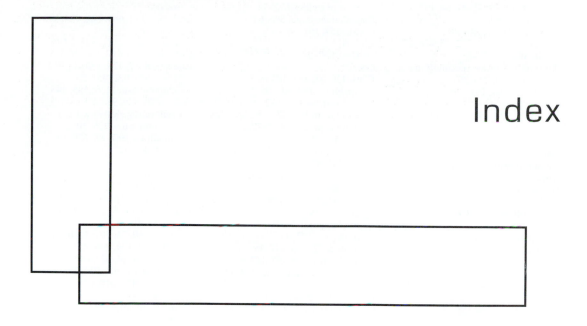

Index

#define directive, 44, 635, 645 46
#ifndef directive, 682
#include directive, 651, 680–82, 819

A

Abstract class, 235, 249–56
  C++, 871–75
  kinds of methods, 255
  Smalltalk, 472–74
Abstract data type, 77, 114–30,
  288, 672
Abstract message, 250–56
  C++, 871
  Smalltalk, 472
Abstraction, 98–101, 104, 106, 117,
  130
Access control, 194–95
  accessibility versus visibility,
    C++, 834–35
  base class, 837–39
  C++, 195, 264, 682, 725,
    833–39, 867, 936–37
  Smalltalk, 441, 444
Accessor, 183, 193
Activation record, 14–15, 21, 34,
  49, 141–44

Ada
  abstract data type, 122–24
  constraint feature, 68
  derived type, 63
  enumerated type, 67
  exception handling, 22
  generic package, 128–30
  overview, 289
  package, 110, 122–24
  parameter modes, 18
  range and precision
    specification, 56
  record initialization, 73
  scope, 106
  string type, 57
  subtype, 63
  type attribute, 62
  type safety, 80
  unconstrained array type, 71
  variant record, 76
Ada95, 315–18
Algol, 68, 58, 75
Alias declaration, 30
Allocation, 45, 47–52, 199–200
  automatic, 48, 627
  C++, 627–30, 691, 844–48
  dynamic, 49–52, 64, 212, 628

  Smalltalk, 366–67
  static, 47, 48, 106, 627
Analysis, 151–53, 157–64, 183, 237,
  281
Ancestor, 235
Annotated C++ Reference
  Manual (*See* ARM)
ANSI/ISO C++ Standard, 615,
  854, 920, 942
  Library, 616, 916, 949, 961,
    970, 972
Application class, 165, 201
  Smalltalk, 398–99
Applicative paradigm (*See*
  Functional paradigm)
Argument, 13, 48
Argument matching, 648 (*See also*
  Overloading, resolving with
  conversions)
Argument signature, 29, 41, 217
  C++, 648, 829–31, 864–67, 874
ARM, 914, 916, 919, 920–21, 942
Array, 68–72
  byte, 353, 588
  C++, 631–32
  Smalltalk, 353, 360, 586
Assertion, 194, 296

Assignment, 29, 46–47, 64, 137, 139, 144, 695
  C++, 841–42, 846–48
  operator, C++, 752–55, 826–27
  Smalltalk, 371–73
Automatic storage reclamation, 51–52, 200, 276, 367
Auxiliary class, 197, 448

B

Base class, 819, 821–22
Basic, 58
Binary message, 361–62
Binding, 25–26
Block, 31, 33–34
  C++, 622
  Smalltalk, 377, 378–82, 385, 389, 581
Block-structured language, 31
  implementation, 34–37
Boolean, 56
  C++, 621, 631
  Smalltalk, 356, 377–78, 508–9
Browser
  class hierarchy, 283–84
  file, 405–6
  method, 405
  Smalltalk, 284, 400–3, 438–40
Built-in type, 54
  C++, 630–31
  Smalltalk, 426
Bytecode, 276, 298
  Smalltalk, 364, 398

C

ANSI function declaration, 28, 640
  array, 71–72
  built-in types, 54
  casts and conversions, 80
  definition of types and objects, 54
  enumerated type, 67
  error handling, 955
  error propagation, 956–57
  module, 111–14, 120
  pointer, 65
  scope, 106, 111, 113
  string, 58
  union, 76
  view of a type, 136
C++
  abstract data type, 124–28
  background, 318
  features missing in Java, 299
  overview, 318–20

view of a class, 672–74
Cascaded message, 363–64
CASE, 154, 161, 281–82
Cast, 80
  C++, 637–39
cin, 656, 775
Class, 130–31, 157, 183–203
  attribute, 189–90, 196
  declaration, 679, 682
  definition, 192–97
  definition, C++, 675–77, 819–22, 880
  definition, Smalltalk, 438–40, 461–62
  determining components, 187–92
  documentation, 194
  generic, 185
  implementation, 196–97
  interface, 192–95
  nested, 724–26, 947–48
  semantics, 130, 157, 183–87
Class definition message, 439, 441, 454, 506
Class flattener, 263, 285
Class hierarchy, 134, 235–37, 257, 262
Class identity, 135, 218, 244
  C++, 843–44, 853–58
  Smalltalk, 454, 493
Class library, 164–66, 279
Class message, 133, 193, 198, 200, 202
  C++, 722–23
  Smalltalk, 454, 456, 462
Class method, 133, 197
  C++, 722–23
  Smalltalk, 457, 475
Class object, 198, 200, 218, 244
  C++, 673–74, 876
  Smalltalk, 453–61, 469, 474–79, 493
Class pointer, 218, 244
  C++, 876
  Smalltalk, 368–69
Class variable, 132, 196, 197, 200, 243
  C++, 719–22
  Smalltalk, 455–56, 462, 475
Classification, 98
Client, 101, 107
CLOS, 203, 216, 219, 248, 256, 257, 275, 277, 324–29
Closure, 141–44
  Smalltalk, 381–82
Cluster (*See* Subsystem)
Cobol
  lack of types, 58

record, 72
Code file, 112, 688, 721, 924, 973
Coercion, 81
Coercive generality, 525–27
Cohesion, 108, 118, 156, 187, 202
Collection, 12, 128, 185–86, 212
  C++, 695, 931, 951–54
  element type, 130, 185, 446, 686, 926, 951–54
  generating classes without templates, 926–30
  Smalltalk, 387–88, 556–58
Color, 434
Comment
  C++, 618
  Smalltalk, 351
Compilation dependency, 110, 113
Compiled language, 4, 29, 397
Compiler, 18, 31, 34–35, 41, 44–45, 47–49, 60, 73, 79–81, 103–5, 110, 122, 129, 209, 217
  C++, 623–24, 627, 646, 652, 680–81, 701, 711, 763, 841, 845, 876, 918, 923–25, 941, 943–44
Component selection, 73, 201, 263, 441
Composition, 97–98, 100, 163, 190, 232–34, 258, 707, 838
Computer-aided software engineering (*See* CASE)
Concrete class, 250, 251
Concurrency, 23–24, 214–15
  Smalltalk, 389–92
Conditional control structure, 8
  C++, 620
  Smalltalk, 383–84
const specifier, 635–36, 641–42, 676, 677
Constant, 44
  C++, 635
Constructor, 200, 677, 696–703, 763–64, 822, 851, 861, 869, 877, 957
  copy, 711–15, 753, 825–26
  default, 702–3
  initialization list, 707–10, 823–25, 895–96
  order of execution, 710, 825
const_cast operator, 639
Control structure, 7
  C++, 620
  Smalltalk, 377
Conversion, 41, 80
  C++, 637–38, 648–51, 750–52, 762–71, 848–53, 855–56, 882–83, 922, 942, 965
  class hierarchy, 848–53

Conversion (*cont.*)
   programmer-defined, 762–71
Conversion operator, 765–66, 851
Copying, 64, 127
   C++, 711–15, 754–55, 825–27,
     869–70
   Smalltalk, 375–76, 450, 469–71,
     492, 561, 574
Coupling, 108, 118, 156, 187, 202,
   264
cout, 656, 775

D

Dangling pointer, 51, 65
Data abstraction (*See* Abstract
   data type)
Data flow diagram, 152–53,
   158–59
Data member, 125, 676, 819
Data structure, 16, 49, 59
Data type (*See* Type)
Deallocation, 45, 50–52, 276
   automatic (*See also* Automatic
     storage reclamation)
   C++, 628
   programmer-controlled, 50–51,
     64, 200, 210
   Smalltalk, 367
Debugger, 408–11
Declaration, 26, 32, 37
   C++, 622
Declarative programming, 145
Decomposition, 97–98, 100
Deferred method (*See* Abstract
   message)
Definition, 27
   C++, 622
delete operator, 628, 629, 755–57,
   868
Delphi Pascal, 313–15
   class-reference type, 313
Dependent, 432, 496–98
Derivation list, 819, 880
Derived class, 819
Descendant, 235
Design, 151, 153, 156–64, 192, 237
Destructor, 200, 703–6, 823, 861,
   958
   virtual, 868–69
Disallowed message, 235
Domain, 78
Dominance, 894–95
Double dispatching, 528
Downcast, 852
Dynamic binding, 29 (*See also*
   Method binding, dynamic)
Dynamic class, 841, 859, 863

Dynamic link, 15, 35, 37
Dynamic subobject, 124
Dynamically typed language, 29,
   42, 79, 185, 199, 212, 218, 275,
   839–40
dynamic_cast operator, 855–56

E

Eiffel, 194, 195, 199, 256, 259, 261,
   295–98
Encapsulation, 100, 167, 201, 249,
   263
Encoded name, 652
Enumerated type, 66
   C++, 632–33, 723–24
Enumerating message, 387–88,
   560, 575
Equality test, 41, 59, 65, 124
   C++, 865–67
   Smalltalk, 373–75, 450, 470,
     492
Error propagation, 19
Exception, 19, 193
   class, 961–64
   specification, 959–60
Exception handling, 20–22
   C++, 957–71
   control flow, 21, 966–68
   environment finalization,
     968–71
   resumption model, 21, 967
   Smalltalk, 392–95
   termination model, 21, 967
Expert system, 148
Export, 40, 105
Expression, 5, 139
Extendibility, 166–68, 217, 221–22,
   262
extern "C" directive, 652
extern declaration, 28, 111, 623
External symbol table, 104, 113

F

Field, 72, 196
Finalization, 127
   C++, 703–6
Finite state machine, 137, 184
First-class, 59, 62, 69, 74, 78, 115,
   139, 140
   C++, 672, 914
   Smalltalk, 438, 454, 459
Floating-point, 55
Fortran
   array, 69
   built-in types, 54
   lack of types, 58

   parameter passing, 18
   weak typing, 79
Forward declaration, 27, 193
Foundation class, 184
Fragmentation, 50
Framework, 164–66
   application, 165–66, 187
   application, Smalltalk, 430–33
   domain, 165, 183
Free store, 50
Friend function, 195, 683–85,
   836–37, 936–37
Function object, 140–42
   Smalltalk, 378–82
Functional decomposition, 28, 31,
   102, 107, 153, 156, 159, 222
Functional language, 6, 8, 47,
   139–45
   function versus procedure, 138
Functional paradigm, 138, 144–45

G

Garbage collection, 51, 277
Generic function, 219, 327–29
Generic subprogram, 61
Generic type, 61, 128–30
Global, 31, 39
Global variable
   Smalltalk, 355–56
goto statement, 6
Graphic notation, 152, 161, 190,
   191, 281
Graphics classes, 433–37
Graphics context, 436–37

H

hash, 565, 570
Header file, 112–13, 651, 680–82,
   924, 973–74
Heap, 50
Hidden, 32
Hybrid object-oriented language,
   131, 201, 274–75, 278, 304

I

Identifier, 25, 30, 39
   C++, 618
   Smalltalk, 353
   use, 32, 37
Identifier resolution, 32, 37
Identifier semantics, 198–99
Image, 396
Imperative paradigm, 137–38, 151
Implementation, 40, 101, 105, 107,
   115, 151, 163

Implicit iteration, 12
  Smalltalk, 387–88
Import, 40, 105
Incremental compilation, 276
  Smalltalk, 398
Incremental development, 167
Information hiding, 27, 101, 116,
  167, 264
Inherit, 231
Inheritance, 133–35, 163–64,
  230–65, 287
  advantages, 261–62
  C++, 818–96
  disadvantages, 262–65
  overhead, 262–63
  Semantics, 133, 231–35
  Smalltalk, 461–74, 558
Initialization, 46, 116, 124, 127,
  200
  C++, 624, 699–702, 707–15,
    823–26, 841–42, 895–96
  Smalltalk, 457–60
  versus assignment, 127, 753–54
Initializer, 628, 699
Inline function, 645–47, 651
Inspector, 407
Instance, 43, 53, 130, 198
Instance message, 193
  C++, 676
  Smalltalk, 462
Instance method, 196–97
  C++, 688–90
  Smalltalk, 442–45, 462
Instance variable, 131, 190, 191,
  196, 242
  C++, 676
  indexed, 441, 494
  named, 441
  Smalltalk, 441–42, 461
Instantiation, 45, 124, 163,
  199–200
  C++, 691
  Smalltalk, 457–60
Interface, 40, 101, 104, 107, 115,
  163
Interface builder, 285, 433
Interpreted language, 5, 29, 276,
  342–43
Iostream
  ANSI/ISO C++ Standard
    Library, 776–78, 783–84,
    786, 790, 791, 795, 796
  class library, 656, 774–78
  error state, 661–62, 784–86
  extraction operator, 658,
    660–61, 772–73
  file stream, 795–98
  format state, 786–94
  insertion operator, 658, 659,
    771–72

manipulator, 659–60, 790–94
memory stream, 800–3
state descriptor, 782–84
stream positioning, 798–800
Iteration, 10–12
  C++, 620
  Smalltalk, 384–88
Iterator, 937–39

J

Java, 195, 203, 215, 217, 264,
  298–304
  class library, 300–2
  interface, 277

K

Keyword message, 359–61

L

l-value, 43, 46
Lambda calculus, 140, 144
Law of Demeter, 187
Lazy evaluation, 6
Linker, 28, 103–4, 108, 110, 113,
  652, 924–25
  dynamic linking, 104
  static linking, 104
Lisp, 6, 29–30, 51, 145, 212, 324
  Common Lisp, 38, 145
Literal
  C++, 619
  notation, 59
  Smalltalk, 351–53
Local, 31, 32
Local variable, 14, 48
Locality, 187, 263
Logic paradigm, 145–48
Logo, 145, 436
Loose coupling, 132, 213, 216

M

main() function, 621
Maintenance, 151, 155, 159, 166
Make utility, 113
Member function, 125, 676–77,
  716, 748, 819
Memory leak, 51, 65, 210
Memory management, 47, 50
  C++, 755–57
Message, 131, 188, 214 (*See also*
  Class message; Instance
  message)
Message expression, 201–2
  C++, 678
  Smalltalk, 357–64
Message pattern, 440

Metaclass, 474–79
Method, 131, 243 (*See also* Class
  method; Instance method)
Method binding, 134, 216–23,
  244–46
  C++, 842–43
  dynamic, 135, 163–64, 167, 198,
    218, 219–23, 843
  dynamic, C++, 858–80, 883–84
  implementation, C++, 875–80
  Smalltalk, 365–66
  static, 217, 222, 842
Method dictionary, 440, 502
Mixin, 257
Model-View-Controller, 186–87,
  430–33, 496
Modula-2
  module, 108–10, 120
  scope, 106, 113
  support for subprogram
    variables, 144
Modula-3, 193, 203, 215, 307–10
Module, 28, 40, 102–14, 202
  data abstraction, 118–22
  scope, 105–6
Monomorphic, 211, 220–22
Multiple inheritance, 256–61, 277
  C++, 880–96
  mimicking, 258

N

Name ambiguity, 258–59
Name conflict, 30, 105, 971–72
  multiple inheritance, C++,
    884–88
Name encoding, 652
Name qualification, 105 (*See also*
  Qualified name)
Namespace, 972–80
  alias, 974–75
  definition, 973–74
new operator, 628, 755–57
NIH C++ class library, 927–28
nil, 63
  Smalltalk, 354, 356, 371, 441,
    443, 507
Nonlocal, 32, 35
Notifier, 408, 411
Numeric type, 55
  C++, 630
  Smalltalk, 352, 516–17

O

Oberon, 310–12
Object, 42–43, 130, 157, 198
  identity, 370–71, 694–95
  lifetime, 45
  relationships, 190–92

Object identifier, 368, 371
Object Pascal, 193, 195, 200, 203, 305–7
Object-based decomposition, 117
Object-based language, 288
Object-oriented decomposition, 156
Object-oriented methodology, 161–62
Object-oriented paradigm, 148–50, 154–58
Object-oriented pseudocode, 203
Objective-C, 198, 322–24
Operator, 5, 40–41, 54–55
    C++, 619–20
    Smalltalk, 361–62
Overloading, 40–42, 132, 213
    function, C++, 647, 651, 917
    message, Smalltalk, 365
    operator, 41
    operator, C++, 744–62, 771–73, 785–86, 792
    resolving with conversions, 648–51, 766–71, 850, 921–22
Overriding, 133, 243, 244, 328
    C++, 829, 862–67
    Smalltalk, 462, 471

P

Paradigm, 136
Parameter, 13
    C++, 641–45
    default value, 14, 644
    Smalltalk, 443
Parameter mode, 13
Parnas's rule, 107, 118
Pascal
    array type, 70
    built-in types, 54
    definition of types and objects, 53
    enumerated type, 66
    error handling, 19
    parameter passing, 18
    string, 57
    subprogram parameter, 77, 143
    subrange type, 67
    symbolic constant, 44
    type constructor, 60
    variant record, 75, 80, 220, 243
    view of a type, 136
Pass by constant reference, 18
    C++, 642
Pass by name, 17
Pass by reference, 17
    C++, 642–43, 849, 860
    Smalltalk, 373
Pass by value, 17
    C++, 641

Pass by value-result, 18
Pixel, 433
Pixmap, 433
Pointer, 49, 63–65, 199
    C++, 632
    smart, 757–62
    to data member, 728–29
    to function, 78, 144, 653–56
    to member function, 726–28
Polymorphism, 29, 131, 163, 199, 211–14, 238–39
    ad hoc, 213
    identifier, 212–13, 218, 222, 238, 694, 841–44
    inclusion, 214, 238
    message, 213–14, 222
    multiple, 218–19, 327
    object, 212, 238, 840
    parametric, 214
    universal, 213
Pool dictionary, 356
Pool variable, 356
Popup menu, 396
Postcondition, 144, 194, 296
Precedence, 5
    C++, 619
    Smalltalk, 362–63
Precondition, 144, 194, 296
Preprocessor macro (*See* #define directive)
Primitive method, 444
Primitive type (*See* built-in type)
Private identifier, 122
Private member, 683, 834, 836
Private method, 197
    C++, 683
    Smalltalk, 444, 459
Private variable, 354
Problem domain, 42, 52, 96, 134, 149, 156–59, 165, 183–84, 231, 256, 261, 451
Procedural language, 47, 138
Procedural paradigm (*See* Imperative paradigm)
Process, 23, 215
    Smalltalk, 389–92
Programming environment, 280, 282–83
Programming language semantics, 3–4
Programming paradigm, 136
Prolog, 146–48
Protected member, 683, 833–34, 836
Protocol, 131, 188–89
    Smalltalk, 440
Pseudo-variable, 356, 443
Public member, 682
Pure object-oriented language, 131, 201, 274–75

Q

Qualified name, 32
    C++, 688, 721, 725, 832–33, 885–87, 890, 934, 975–76
    Modula-2, 109

R

r-value, 43
Rapid prototyping, 168
Read-only variable, 45
Receiver, 131, 197, 201, 209, 215, 216, 219
    C++, 678–79, 683, 689–90, 828, 859
    Smalltalk, 345, 356, 357–58, 368–69, 441, 445–46, 464–67
Record, 72–74
Recursion, 16, 140, 446
Reference counting, 51
Reference semantics, 196, 199, 212, 368
    C++, 693–95
    Smalltalk, 371–75
Reference type, 30
    C++, 636–37
Referent, 25
Referential transparency, 144
Refinement, 246–49
    C++, 831–33, 862
    Smalltalk, 465–67
reinterpret_cast operator, 638
Repeated inheritance, 259–61
    C++, 888–96
Representation independence, 116, 131
Requirements specification, 151
Reserved words, 25
Restriction, 234–35
    Smalltalk, 471–72
Return by reference, 210
    C++, 643–44
    Smalltalk, 373
Return by value, 210
Return expression, 443
Reuse, 162–64, 167, 189, 222, 261–62
Run-time stack, 15, 21, 142, 408
Run-time type information, 674, 854 (*See also* Type information, C++)
    C++, 858

S

Scope, 30–40, 105, 106
    C++, 622–26, 673, 716–29, 827–33, 884–88, 890–91, 923, 946–48, 973–80

Scope (*cont.*)
  class, 625, 673, 716–29, 827–33, 884–88, 890–91
  declaration, 31
  dynamic, 33, 37–38
  file, 111, 623–24
  import/export, 38–40, 106, 109
  lexical, 33–37
  nested, 31–39
  Smalltalk, 380, 443
  static, 33–37
Scope operator, 125, 202, 626, 726, 975–76 (*See also* Qualified name, C++)
Selector, 357, 360
self, 197, 209–11, 246, 264
  Smalltalk, 445–46, 464–65
Semaphore, 23
  Smalltalk, 391
Sequence control structure, 7
  Smalltalk, 376
Shared variable, 355
Side effect, 5, 38
Simula67, 286–88
Simulation, 149, 158
Smalltalk
  background, 290
  class library, 293–94, 426–37, 490–601
  programming environment, 291–92, 342–48, 395–411
  uniformity of concept, 290–91
  user interface, 395–96, 428–29
Snobol, 58
Software engineering, 150–52, 296
Software life cycle, 151, 160–61
Specialization, 231–34
species, 562
Stack frame (*See* Activation record)
Statement, 6, 137, 139
Static class, 841, 843, 863
Static data member, 719–22, 833
Static declaration, 111, 624
Static distance, 35, 144
Static link, 35, 49, 141, 143–44, 381
Static local variable, 48, 624, 627
Static member function, 722–23, 833
Static typing and inheritance, 199, 212, 218, 221, 251, 264, 693, 839–58
Statically typed language, 13, 29, 37, 79, 128, 185, 193, 196, 216, 220, 275, 839–40
Statically typed object-oriented language (*See* Static typing and inheritance)
static_cast operator, 638
Stream, 589–90
  C++ (*See* Iostream)
  Smalltalk, 589–601

String, 57, 204–6
  C++, 631
  Smalltalk, 352, 374, 586–87
Strongly typed language, 13, 79–80, 216
  C++, 640–41
  Smalltalk, 368–70
struct type, 633–34
Structure chart, 153, 159
Structured methods, 150–54, 160, 162, 166, 222
Subclass, 133, 231, 236, 239
  C++, 819–21
  implementation, 242–44, 249
  interface, 240–42
  Smalltalk, 461–62
Subprogram, 12–19, 33, 37, 38, 101
Subprogram type, 77
Subrange, 67
Subscription, 69
  C++, 632
  Smalltalk, 360
Subsystem, 156–57, 202
super, 247, 264, 465–67
Superclass, 133, 231, 236, 249
  C++, 819
  Smalltalk, 439, 461–62
Symbol, 352, 371, 374, 587–88
Symbol table, 28, 31, 343
Syntax error
  Smalltalk, 364–65

T

Template, 674, 913–54
  class template, 931–43
  errors upon instantiation, 922–23, 935
  expression parameter, 939–40
  friend function, 936–37
  function template, 915–18
  inheritance, 948–54
  instantiation, 918–23, 924–25, 943–45
  member function template, 933–35
  member template, 941–43
  repository, 925
  scope, 923, 946, 948
  specialization, 941
  static member, 946–47
  template class, 933, 943–45
  template function, 915, 918–20
  translation, 923–25
Temporary object, 627, 692, 701, 706
terminate() function, 967
Text window, 344–48, 399–400
this pointer, 689–90, 722
Thread, 23
throw expression, 958–59, 968

Throw list, 959
Transcript, 400
try statement, 964–66
Turbo Pascal, 313
Type, 52–53, 58–62, 136, 197
  declaration, 61
  definition, 60–61
  type constructor, 59
Type alias, 62
Type checking, 29, 79–80 (*See also* Strongly typed language)
Type identity, 29 (*See also* Class identity)
Type information, 60–62
  C++, 856–58
  Smalltalk, 460–61, 500–4
Type object, 60–62, 64, 66, 68, 69, 72, 75, 198 (*See also* Class object)
Type operation, 61–62, 198
Type parameter, 128, 914–16, 919–20, 931–36, 942, 943, 950–54
typedef statement, 62, 639, 655, 686, 945
typeid operator, 856–57

U

Unary message, 358–59
unexpected() function, 960
Union, 75–76
  C++, 634–35
Unique object, 371
using declaration, 977–78
using directive, 978–80

V

Value semantics, 199, 368
  C++, 693–95, 845–48
Variable, 43
View, 396
Virtual base class, 888, 891
Virtual function, 843, 847, 858–80
  pure, 871–75
  static invocation, 861–62
Virtual machine, 276, 298, 364
Visible, 26
VisualWorks, 393–95, 433, 436–37, 455, 529
vptr, 876–80
vtbl, 876–80, 883–84

W

Waterfall model, 152, 160
Weakly typed language, 79
Whorf's hypothesis, 135
Workspace, 399

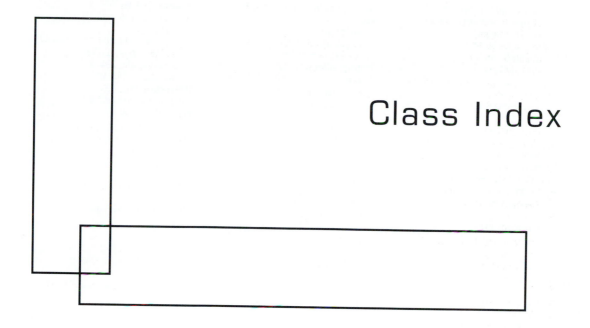

Class Index

AbstractQueue, 872–73
ArithmeticValue, 530
Array, 586
ArrayedCollection, 585–86
Association, 568
auto_ptr, 971

bad_alloc, 629
Bag, 566–67
Behavior, 478, 499–503
BlockClosure, 378–82
Boolean, 377–78, 508–9
ByteArray, 588

Character, 510–12
CharStack, 125–27
Class, 478, 505–7
ClassDescription, 478, 503–5
Collection, 559–64
Complex
    C++, 748–51, 772
    Smalltalk, 531

Date, 512–15
DeductibleHistory, 462–64,
    476–77
Dictionary, 567–71

DisplayObject, 253–56
Double, 531

Employee, 824
exception, 961
ExternalStream, 598–600

Filename, 428, 600
FinancialHistory, 451–53, 462
FixedPoint, 532
Float, 523–24
Fraction, 522–23
fstream, 797

IdentityDictionary, 571
IdentitySet, 566
ifstream, 797
Integer, 519–21
InternalStream, 596
Interval, 583–85
ios, 774–75, 782–96
iostream, 781
istream, 779–81, 799
istrstream, 800–2

LargeNegativeInteger, 521–22
LargePositiveInteger, 521–22

LimitedPrecisionReal, 531
Link, 582
LinkedList, 582–83
List, 240–41
LookupKey, 568

Magnitude, 473, 509–10
Metaclass, 478–79

Node
    C++, 687, 711, 725, 756–57,
        932, 934, 941
    Smalltalk, 446–48
Number, 473, 517–18

Object, 426–27, 457, 460, 491–99,
    507
ofstream, 797
Orderable, 252–53
OrderedCollection, 577–80
ostream, 778–79, 798–99
ostrstream, 801

Person, 707–8, 759–61
Point
    C++, 675–76, 745–46
    Smalltalk, 433–34, 532–37

PositionableList, 241, 247
PositionableStream, 594–96
PriorityQueue
    C++, 820–21, 952
    Smalltalk, 467–71
Process, 390–91

Queue
    C++, 685–88, 690–91, 704, 725, 772, 932, 934–35
    Smalltalk, 446–51

Random, 601
ReadStream, 596–97
ReadWriteStream, 598
Rectangle, 434, 537–40
RunArray, 588

Semaphore, 391

SequenceableCollection, 572–77
Set
pseudocode, 234
    Smalltalk, 564–66
    SmallInteger, 521
SortedCollection, 580–82
Square
Ada95, 316–18
    C++, 320–21
    CLOS, 329
    Delphi Pascal, 314–15
    Eiffel, 297
    Java, 302–3
    Modula-3, 308–9
    Oberon, 311–12
    Object Pascal, 306–7
    Objective-C, 323–24
    pseudocode, 207–11, 273–74
    Smalltalk, 294

Stream, 589–93
streambuf, 776
String
    C++, 697–99, 704, 714, 746–47, 751, 769–70, 773
    pseudocode, 204–5
    Smalltalk, 586–87
strstream, 801, 803
SubscriptError, 962–63
Symbol, 587–88

Text, 589
Time, 515–16
type_info, 856

UndefinedObject, 507–8

WriteStream, 597–98